My aim has been to make the Globe a cheerful, attractive and useful newspaper that would enter the homes as a kindly, helpful friend of the family. My temperament has always led me to dwell on the virtues of men and institutions rather than upon their faults and limitations. My disposition has always been to build up rather than to join in tearing down. My ideal for the Globe has always been that it should help men, women and children to get some of the sunshine of life, to be better and happier because of the Globe.

February 20, 1962
Glenn Orbits Earth 71

August 15, 1962
$2M Mail Robbery in Plymouth 72

October 23, 1962
JFK Orders Cuba Blockade 73

November 22, 1963 (Evening Globe)
President Kennedy Slain in Dallas 74

November 25, 1963
Oswald Shot Dead in Dallas Jail 75

July 3, 1964
LBJ Signs Civil Rights Bill 76

February 8, 1965
US Jets Bomb North Vietnam 77

March 10, 1965
A March in Selma; Ministers Beaten 78

November 10, 1965
Power Outage Leaves Northeast in Dark 79

October 2, 1967
Red Sox Win Pennant 80

April 5, 1968
Martin Luther King Shot Dead 81

June 5, 1968 (Evening Globe)
Robert Kennedy Assassinated 82

August 29, 1968
Humphrey Wins Democratic Nomination 83

October 18, 1968 (Evening Globe)
Jacqueline Kennedy to Marry Onassis 84

July 21, 1969
Man Walks on Moon 85

October 16, 1969
Peace Rally on Boston Common 86

May 5, 1970
4 Students Killed at Kent State 87

May 11, 1970
Orr's Goal Wins Stanley Cup 88

November 3, 1970
Cardinal Cushing Dies 89

June 22, 1971
Globe Publishes Pentagon Papers 90

July 16, 1971
Nixon to Visit China 91

March 5, 1972
Globe Is 100 Years Old 92

June 18, 1972
Hotel Vendome Fire 93

September 6, 1972
Terror Hits Munich Olympics 94

August 1, 1973
Jet Crashes at Logan Airport 95

October 21, 1973
Nixon's Saturday Night Massacre 96

August 9, 1974
Nixon Resigns 97

December 11, 1974 (Evening Globe)
Desegregation Strife at South Boston High 98

April 30, 1975
Saigon Falls 99

October 22,1975
Fisk Homer Wins Game 6 for Red Sox 100

July 5, 1976
Bicentennial Celebration 101

September 10, 1976
Mao Tse-tung Dies 102

August 17, 1977
Elvis Presley Is Dead 103

William O. Taylor, Publisher 1978 - 1997 104

February 8, 1978
Blizzard Paralyzes Region 105

September 18, 1978
Camp David Accords 106

September 20, 1978
King Wins; Gov. Dukakis Out 107

November 21, 1978
Mass Suicide at Jonestown 108

February 2, 1979
Last Edition of the Boston Evening Globe 109

March 31, 1979
Danger at Three Mile Island 110

October 2, 1979
Pope John Paul II Visits Boston 111

November 5, 1979
Iranians Seize US Embassy 112

December 16, 1979
Spotlight Report on the MTA 113

February 25, 1980
US Hockey Team Wins Gold at Lake Placid 114

May 19,1980
Mount St. Helens Erupts 115

December 9, 1980
John Lennon Shot Dead on Street 116

January 21, 1981
Reagan Inaugurated; Hostages Freed 117

March 31, 1981
Reagan Wounded in D.C. Shooting 118

May 14, 1981
Assassin's Shots Hit Pope 119

October 7, 1981
Anwar Sadat Assassinated 120

October 24,1983
Marine Barracks Car-Bombed in Lebanon 121

November 16, 1983
Flynn Is Mayor, Beats Mel King 122

March 30, 1984
Spring Gives a Winter Wallop 123

November 17, 1984
Famine Devastates Ethiopia 124

November 24, 1984
Flutie Beats Miami With Last-Gasp Pass 125

January 27, 1986
Bears Clobber Patriots in Super Bowl 126

January 28, 1986
Space Shuttle Challenger Explodes 127

April 29, 1986
Disaster at Chernobyl 128

June 9, 1986
Celtics Win Another NBA Title 129

October 26, 1986
Buckner Bobble Costs Red Sox Game 6 130

October 20, 1987
Stock Market in Big Dive 131

November 9, 1988
Bush Easily Beats Dukakis 132

December 22, 1988
Jet Blown to Pieces Over Lockerbie 133

January 5, 1990
Charles Stuart in Apparent Suicide 134

March 19, 1990
Art Theft at the Gardner Museum 135

June 24, 1990
Nelson Mandela Visits Boston 136

October 3, 1990
Berlin Wall Falls 137

November 7, 1990
Weld Tops Silber in Governor's Race 138

January 17, 1991
Gulf War Begins 139

December 26, 1991
Soviet Union Disbanded 140

April 30, 1992
Rodney King Verdict Sparks Riots 141

January 25, 1993
Thurgood Marshall Dies 142

April 20, 1993
Inferno in Waco 143

June 11, 1993
New York Times Company to Purchase Globe 144

July 28, 1993
Reggie Lewis Fatally Stricken 145

September 14, 1993
Handshake for Peace in Mideast 146

January 6, 1994
Tip O'Neill Is Dead 147

January 18, 1994
Earthquake Devastates Los Angeles 148

May 20, 1994
Jacqueline Bouvier Kennedy Onassis Is Dead 149

June 18, 1994
O.J. Simpson Bronco Chase 150

November 9, 1994
GOP Captures Congress 151

December 31,1994
Fatal Killings at Preterm Clinic 152

April 20, 1995
Federal Building Bombed in Oklahoma City 153

October 4, 1995
O.J. Simpson Not Guilty 154

November 5, 1995
Rabin Assassinated 155

April 16, 1996
100th Running of the Boston Marathon 156

July 18, 1996
TWA Flight 800 Blows Up 157

November 6, 1996
Clinton Wins Second Term; Kerry Beats Weld 158

January 27,1997
Patriots Lose Super Bowl XXXI 159

March 4, 1997
125th Anniversary Edition 160

When The Boston Globe published its first edition on March 4, 1872, echoes of Civil War battles were still ringing in the air. It was an exciting and exacting time for the city the Puritans had built, and the new-born Globe was itching to tell the stories of the age and beyond. And tell those stories we have: The terrible fire in November of 1872 in the heart of Boston; 1,000 businesses destroyed, damage put at $250 million. The advent of the telephone (in Boston, yet), the automobile, the airplane, the computer. Revolution and assassinations and wars, declared and undeclared. Elections aplenty, from Grant against Greeley to Clinton against Dole, and all the way down the electoral line to the tiniest town hall in New England's frosty hill country.

The Globe has chronicled, in daily chapters, the evolution of Boston and surrounding regions from a place where shrewd Yankee businessmen financed the growth of the vast land to the west to a large community taken over politically by scrappy and colorful Irish-Americans named Curley and Fitzgerald and Lomasney and McCormack and O'Neill and Kennedy to a multi-ethnic modern metropolis that is a world capital of academia, medicine and high technology.

While the changes in news-gathering and printing have come a long way since our first edition a century and a quarter ago, our purpose has remained the same: to chronicle the news and events of the day in a professional manner, serving the interests of our readers and the communities where they live. It has been the privilege of the Taylor family to manage The Boston Globe enterprise since 1873, when Gen. Charles H. Taylor and Boston businessman Eben D. Jordan set a course for the newspaper that we continue to follow today.

Wm. O. Taylor
Chairman of the Board

Ben Taylor
Publisher & President

W.O. Taylor (left) walking with his father, Gen. Taylor, on Beacon Street in front of the State House in the 1890s.

Publishers of The Boston Globe from 1873 - 1997

Charles H. Taylor

William O. Taylor

William Davis Taylor

William O. Taylor

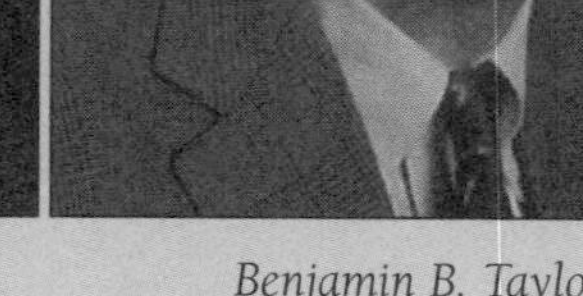

Benjamin B. Taylor

Maturin Ballou
Editor
1872 - 1873

The Boston Globe, New England's pre-eminent newspaper and one of the most prestigious daily journals in the country, almost didn't make it past its second birthday. The paper was launched in February of 1872 by six Boston businessmen, led by Eben D. Jordan, the founder of the Jordan Marsh department store and New England's most successful retailer. Dissatisfied with the ten existing Boston newspapers, they set their sights on a more effective and dynamic advertising vehicle to sell their goods. They jointly invested $100,000 to underwrite the project, and the Globe produced its first issue on March 4, 1872.

Years of Ordeal: 1872-1878

The new Globe paper was considered a quality publication, but it failed to appeal to a broad spectrum of readers. By August 1873, most of the investors were gone. For Jordan, then 51, developing the vast Jordan Marsh empire was his paramount focus. For the Globe to survive, someone had to be found who could turn around the business and create an exciting editorial product.

Jordan recruited Charles H. Taylor, at 27 a Civil War veteran, politician, and a highly-respected newspaperman, to help out as the Globe's temporary business manager. "Temporary" turned out to be 50 years as the energetic Taylor soon emerged as the driving force behind a newly aggressive Globe. He was the first of five Taylors to become publisher of the newspaper and to a remarkable degree, the character and business sense of the Taylors have shaped and guided the Globe over the last century and a quarter.

Born in Charlestown on July 14, 1846, he became a "printer's devil" by age 15, then joined the Boston Traveller a year later just before enlisting in the 38th Regiment of the Massachusetts Volunteers. Eighteen months later, he was seriously wounded in battle and spent three months in a Federal army hospital in New Orleans before being discharged.

On his return to Boston, he rejoined the Traveller as a journeyman printer, then worked his way into a reporting job while he mastered stenography. At the age of 20, he married Georgiana Davis and with the new need for additional income, he became the Boston correspondent of The New York Tribune, an assignment that introduced the young Taylor to the prominent men in the state.

Eben D. Jordan, founder of Jordan Marsh in Boston and one of the original six investors in The Boston Globe.

Three years later, he became military secretary to Massachusetts Governor William Claflin, a position that entitled him to be called Colonel Taylor. He used that title for the next 20 years until another Bay State governor, William E. Russell, named him commissionary general, with the rank of brigadier general. He was General Taylor from then until his death three decades later.

Edwin M. Bacon
Editor
1873 - 1878

Edwin C. Bailey
Editor
1878 - 1880

On leaving Claflin's office, he ran for a seat in the state House of Representatives and served in that chamber in 1872 and 1873, serving Somerville, where he had purchased a home after his first child's birth. While in the Legislature, he published a successful magazine called American Home, with a unique format targeting the entire household: women, men, boys and girls. But The Great Boston Fire of November 1872, which destroyed 65 acres in the heart of the city's business district, wiped out American Home's operation. Taylor moved quickly to keep himself and his family afloat financially, getting himself elected as Clerk of the Massachusetts House, a position that paid $2,500 per year.

Although the historic fire had spared the Globe's building, the paper itself was floundering, and when Globe editor Maturin Ballou quit in June 1873, Eben Jordan contacted Taylor, who turned down the offer. Jordan asked again in August, and Taylor agreed to come on board "for a few weeks" to help. He never left.

And so The Boston Globe became Charles H. Taylor's life mission. As Scribner's Dictionary of American Biography described things, "For grim determination and enormous industry, Taylor's first four years can hardly be surpassed in American journalism. He often said he never was more than one jump ahead of the sheriff. His workday covered 16 hours. His assets were such intangibles as intelligence, energy and integrity. . . A sense of humor and his unfailing optimism sustained him. He mastered every phase of newspaper work, 'Upstairs' and 'Downstairs' in both newsroom and counting room."

Taylor told it this way: "When I took charge of The Boston Globe in 1873, it had sunk $300,000 and was losing $60,000 a year. . . . These dollars were buried in the Globe between 1872 and 1878. Eben Jordan alone believed that I could win, and stood by me even when the battle seemed almost hopeless. No amount of debt and trouble could shake his confidence." The Globe's circulation and advertising grew steadily despite a severe economic depression. Revenue went into wages, newsprint and, above all, servicing the debt from the paper's first 18 months. Taylor mortgaged his own house to pay newsprint bills.

In 1877, convinced of the Globe's potential, he realized what had to be done to position the paper for success, not just survival. While on Martha's Vineyard selling resort advertising, Colonel Taylor heard of a financing plan that saved the Martha's Vineyard Railroad from bankruptcy. He proposed that Jordan recapitalize The Globe Publishing Company and create a new corporation. Jordan put up the money, and on February 5, 1878, the Globe Newspaper Company was born, erasing $100,000 in debt.

Five Globe correspondents on Newspaper Row, Washington Street, Boston in 1890.

Building the New Globe: 1878-1900

Even after the reorganization, it was a struggle just to meet each week's payroll and newsprint bill, but at long last Taylor could begin to implement his personal vision of what Boston wanted and needed in a newspaper. In his 1972

Charles H. Taylor
Editor
1880 - 1921

book, "Newspaper Story: One Hundred Years of The Boston Globe," Louis Lyons made this observation of what Charles Taylor had done in those early days: "In 1878, at age 31 and with five children and a mortgage on his home, he was about to make a radical breakthrough in newspaper methods. He turned a losing morning paper into an all-day newspaper while making it a Democratic journal and he inaugurated a new policy [for that era] to deal impartially with news . . . and to add a broad family dimension to his newspaper's appeal." The Globe's new readers were the Irish and the working classes, and the paper championed their issues and concerns. Taylor started a five-cent, eight-page Boston Sunday Globe on October 14, 1877. In 1878, he dropped the price of the daily from three cents to two cents. "He began doing all these things at once and in less than three years the Globe circulation went from 8,000 to 30,000. By 1886, the Globe was selling 100,000 daily and Sunday. Within ten years it became the dominant paper of the region. Its publisher was hailed as "the wizard of journalism," and his Globe as one of the most exciting papers in the country," wrote Lyons.

Gen. Taylor's wife, Georgiana Davis Taylor (left) with daughters, Elizabeth (center) and Grace (right).

As a result of his loyalty and remarkable success, Taylor, who was already president, soon became publisher as well. His innovations and techniques were copied nationwide. By the mid-1890s, circulation was at 300,000 daily.

The Globe's ultimate success exceeded Jordan's fondest hopes as the newspaper had become a tremendous advertising vehicle for Jordan Marsh. When Taylor launched the Sunday Globe, Jordan and other retailers were delighted to find that Mondays – once the slowest selling day of the week – had become one of the best. That Globe-created market change alone probably returned Jordan's initial investment many times over.

Mr. Rogan covers a late 19th century whippet race for the Globe.

Jordan took almost paternal pride in Taylor's hard-won accomplishments and ingenuity. If the Globe is ultimately a monument to Charles H. Taylor's character and vision, Eben Jordan's timely financial backing and unwavering faith in Taylor's abilities were essential to the Globe's survival. Their 22-year partnership was one of mutual trust and affection. After Jordan's death in 1895, his son Eben became a Globe director, and he was succeeded, in turn, by his son Robert in 1917.

Just as he had built Jordan Marsh, Eben Jordan understood that Charles Taylor had built the Globe. He never interferred. He gave shrewd advice when advice was sought, although General Taylor once chuckled, "he could never understand why I should pay our reporters more than he paid his ribbon clerks."

Charles H. Taylor's three sons: from left, C.H. Jr., W.O., and John I., pictured at the turn of the century.

"At one point," says William O. Taylor II, a Taylor great-grandson, "Eben Jordan offered to sell the entire paper to the general, but with all the support that he'd received in those hard years, he just asked to buy up to 50 percent. He felt that both families should benefit from the good times as well." That pattern of Taylor management and Taylor-Jordan equal ownership continued for four generations and a remarkable 116 years.

Transition: 1900-1921

The general and his wife had five children: three sons, Charles H. Jr., William O., and John I., and two daughters, Elizabeth (later, Pillsbury) and Grace (later, Armstrong). The three sons, who had grown up at the paper, joined the Globe full time during the 1890s after leaving Harvard. By January 1890, Charles, the oldest, was assistant managing editor, and four months later, assistant business manager. The second son, William O., completed Harvard in 1893 and joined the business office. The youngest son, John I., joined the city room and eventually moved to help-wanted advertising, a classification the Globe was developing vigorously. By 1900 the Globe had become the largest newspaper in New England. Editorially, it steered a moderate, middle course, continuing to emphasize news of interest to women as well as men, with a strong concentration on sports, and adding columns and new departments. Strong coverage in these areas has been a hallmark of the Globe's success ever since.

In 1904, General Taylor purchased the American League professional baseball team (then known as the Pilgrims and soon renamed the Red Sox) and appointed his son John the club's president. While it was fun to own a franchise that was both popular and successful regionally and nationally, the Taylors soon decided that they would be better off covering what the team did on the field than running it off the field, so they determined to sell it when the time was right.

At the time, the ballclub was a tenant at the Huntington Avenue Grounds, and the family felt the team would fetch a much higher price if it came with its own ballpark. Over several years, the family had quietly assembled a large tract of land near Kenmore Square on which John I. and his father built Fenway Park, then and now one of the game's most charming and classic baseball venues. Just as planned, the team and the ballpark then were sold.

"General Taylor, with his editorial department in confident hands and his sons sharing the business work, relaxed," Louis Lyons wrote. "He was much in demand outside the office as an after-dinner speaker or toastmaster. The elite Algonquin

James Morgan, editorial eminence at the Globe for 60 years, and his friend Will Rogers.

W. O. Taylor
Editor
1921 - 1955

Club was 'a monument to his sagacity and enthusiasm and above all to his infinite capacity for friendship,' said the club's resolution on his retirement from 20 years of its presidency."

The General's two older sons stayed with the newspaper. Charles (C.H.) and W.O. shared an office with back-to-back rolltop desks until Charles retired in 1937. It was the General's philosophy that a family working in such close quarters minimized potential conflict, while all aspects of the business were conducted within earshot. Both were men of character and complementing abilities.

C.H., a lively, dynamic man of many talents and interests, established the industry's first in-house photoengraving department at the Globe. A skilled negotiator, he handled the Globe's labor relations and was a founder of the New England Arbitration Association. He was impatient, with a quick temper and a ready laugh. He patrolled the paper for accuracy, spelling, and editorial "free puffs" for businesses. "Let them buy an ad" was his philosophy. His vivid memos to editorial and the composing room were legendary.

In contrast, W.O. was a shy, quiet man, totally absorbed in the nuts and bolts of the newspaper industry. He was a businessman of steady temperament, probity and utter reliability. According to Lyons, he was a behind-the-scenes manager during the Globe's most difficult years and a classic introvert who was never known to give a speech at a Globe or industry function. C.H. served as the Globe's primary spokesperson until his retirement, when William Davis Taylor, W.O.'s youngest son, who joined the Globe in the early 1930s, took over those public chores.

W. O. Taylor: 1921-1955

When General Taylor died in 1921, William O. took over as publisher, concentrating on the business side but retaining the title of editor. The second publisher's great challenge came with the Depression years, when a collapsed economy, a cautious journalistic approach, and competition from Boston's nine other daily newspapers resulted in the Globe slipping in popularity.

The paper received a needed burst of energy in 1937 when Laurence L. Winship became managing editor. Winship had joined the Globe as a reporter shortly before World War I and was named Sunday editor in 1918. Under his leadership, the Sunday Globe became an exciting, vital newspaper. Now his talents were to extend to all editions of the newspaper.

By World War II, the Globe was again competitive but not dominant in Boston. During the war years, however, Davis Taylor advised his father to follow an unusual business strategy that set the stage for the paper's ultimate success. With wartime newsprint rationing in effect, all newspa-

Marjory Adams, Globe movie reporter and critic for a half century, chats with the actress Leatrice Joy.

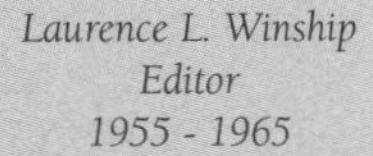

Laurence L. Winship
Editor
1955 - 1965

pers had to cut back on advertisements along with news space. W. O., alone among Boston publishers, defied conventional wisdom and chose not to limit classified ads. The thousands of people who placed and depended upon classified ads to find jobs, rent apartments, buy cars, used and read the Globe during the war years. These readers developed an allegiance to the Globe that made the paper the classified market leader, a position it holds to this day.

After World War II, television, population shifts to the suburbs, and the growth of suburban dailies, among other things, combined to radically change Boston newspapers. The Globe got the message early: It was time to re-think operations and adjust. One such move came in 1953, when the two companies that had provided wagon and truck distribution for the Globe going back to the horse and buggy days, the Hotel and Railroad News and the Wilson Tisdale Company, merged. The Globe promptly purchased Wilson Tisdale as a subsidiary, to better control and expand its own delivery system.

John I. Taylor, grandson of Gen. Taylor

William Davis Taylor: 1955-1977

When William O. Taylor died in 1955, his son William Davis Taylor (known to most as Davis) became publisher. Lyons quotes Globe advertising executive Jack Reid Sr. as observing that "W.O. held the Globe together, and Davis took the lid off." The paper was faced with changes and challenges on many fronts. Under Davis Taylor's skillful leadership, the Globe navigated a major generation shift and the start of a dynamic new era. His first cousin, John Ingalls Taylor (John I.'s son), had joined the Globe in the 1930s and worked as a reporter and editor and later served as promotion manager. Upon becoming publisher, Davis moved John into the publisher's office as treasurer, then a few years later as president. As had W. O. and C. H., Davis and John shared an office for years. Another cousin, Charles H. Taylor III, the son of C.H. Jr., was a sturdy member of the Globe team for 50 years. Before his retirement in 1970, he had worked in many departments before becoming clerk of the corporation and assistant treasurer.

There has always been room at the Globe for eager journalists from the extended Taylor family. By the late 1990s, C.H. Jr.'s great-grandson, Stephen E. was an executive vice president; Alexander B. Hawes Jr., a grandson of General Taylor's daughter Grace, was assistant to the president, after serving in the newsroom as a reporter and editor; Henry Riemer, a great-grandson of William O., was the anchor statistician on the night sports desk; and, Matthew Taylor, a great-grandson and grandson, respectively, of the John I. Taylors, was a reporter in the newsroom.

There was no question that by the mid-1950s the Globe needed a new printing facility. In May 1958, after 87 years on Washington Street's "Newspaper Row," the Globe moved to a new facility on Morrissey Boulevard in Boston's Dorchester section. Davis Taylor's 26-year-old son, William O. Taylor II, oversaw every aspect of the new building's construction.

During the 1940s and 1950s, several Boston newspapers, notably The Transcript and the Post, closed or merged, evidence of an industry shake-

Dwight D. Eisenhower rides in motorcade down Washington Street in front of the Globe building in the mid-1950s.

Grace Taylor Armstrong, Gen. Taylor's daughter, starts the presses at the opening of the new Morrissey Boulevard plant.

Thomas Winship
Editor
1965 - 1984

out that reflected dramatic shifts in readership and advertiser patterns. Unlike other Boston newspapers, the Globe adapted to its new environment and followed post-war readers from urban areas into the suburbs, building and expanding its home delivery and distribution system.

Davis Taylor wanted a vigorous new editorial direction. When he succeeded his father, he named Laurence L. Winship as editor, the title the two previous Taylor publishers had kept for themselves. And in 1958, he brought the Globe's Washington correspondent, Thomas Winship, a son of Laurence, back to Boston as the paper's first metropolitan editor. As in the Globe's earliest days, the paper began to take a more aggressive position on civic affairs and public issues and reporters were encouraged to tackle tough and sensitive issues.

In 1965, Thomas Winship succeeded his father as editor. By the time he retired 20 years later, he had led the Globe into the front ranks of American newspapers. Under his tutelage, the Globe won its first Pulitzer Prize in 1966 for exposing the lack of credentials of a federal judgeship candidate nominated by the Kennedys. Since that time, the Globe has garnered 14 more Pulitzer citations for distinguished journalism across the spectrum of newsroom endeavors.

Winship, a whirlwind in and out of the newsroom, soon prodded the Taylors into taking additional measures to enhance the presence and authority of the Globe: The paper resumed taking strong editorial positions on pressing issues of the day; it endorsed candidates for public office for the first time since the latter years of the 19th century; and advertisements disappeared from the front page.

In October 1969, the Globe became the first US newspaper to editorially call for the unilateral withdrawal of American troops from Vietnam. In June 1971, the Globe published portions of the Pentagon Papers, the Defense Department's classified internal history of the Vietnam conflict. The paper also took a strong editorial stand in favor of the integration of Boston's public schools in the 1970s. Its coverage of this continuing story won the Pulitzer Prize for Meritorious Public Service.

Charles H. Taylor III, grandson of Gen. Taylor

The Globe wins its first Pulitzer Prize - 1966. Part of the team, from left: Joseph Harvey, Robert Healy, Martin Nolan, Thomas Winship, Anson Smith, Richard Connolly, Charles Whipple.

Michael C. Janeway
Editor
1985 - 1986

John S. Driscoll
Editor
1986 - 1993

Dexter Eure, (center) Community Relations Director at the Globe from 1960 to 1987, receives a Black Achievers Award in 1979.

William O. Taylor: 1978-1997

Davis Taylor retired as 1977 came to a close, and his son, William O., took over as publisher. He also became chairman of the board and chief executive officer of Affiliated Publications, a parent company founded in 1973 when the Globe went public. Harvard-educated, William O. Taylor came to the Globe in 1956, after two years in the US Army. His leadership as publisher and his business acumen were instrumental in the Globe's sure-footed and steady rise to journalistic eminence regionally and across the country in the spirit his father had evoked.

The fourth publisher diligently maintained a distinction between the business and news sides of the Globe house, but he was always at the ready with a willingness to put the company's strength and resources behind legal issues he and his editors deemed critical to every newspaper's First Amendment rights.

After 20 years of acquisitions in radio, television, magazines, books, and even cellular telephone technology, William O. Taylor returned Affiliated Publications to its newspaper roots, selling all other media properties. Under his guidance, the newspaper computerized many of its newsroom and production processes, and added color to its news and advertising pages. He supervised the building of a satellite printing plant in Billerica, greatly enhancing the Globe's production capacity; oversaw a major Sunday zoned news-and-advertising editions project; and acquired a site in Westwood for use as a state-of-the-art preprint distribution facility.

Stephen E. Taylor great-great-grandson of Gen. Taylor

Alexander B. Hawes Jr. great-grandson of Gen. Taylor

Matthew V. Storin
Editor
1993-

His strong sense of community is reflected in his belief that the company and the newspaper should be part of the fabric of the community – and part of the solution to its problems. This commitment is demonstrated not only in the pages of the newspaper but also in the community activities and programs sponsored by the Globe, led by The Boston Globe Foundation, which he established in 1982.

In October 1993, a new era began for the Globe when it merged with and became a wholly-owned subsidiary of The New York Times Company. The move was prompted by the impending dissolution in 1996 of two family trusts that owned the majority of Affiliated Publications stock – The Taylor Trust and The Jordan Trust. The Boston Globe-Times Company merger, put at a price of $1.1 billion, was the largest single newspaper merger in US history.

This historic combination marked the end of more than 120 years of local family ownership of the Globe. But it also marked the beginning of an alliance of two great newspapers and two great newspaper families – the Sulzbergers of the Times and the Taylors of the Globe.

And while ownership is new, the Taylor tradition at the Globe continues to this day. On April 1, 1997, Benjamin B. Taylor, son of John I., second cousin to William O., and great-grandson of the general, moved into the publisher's office, becoming the fifth member of his family to assume responsibility for the direction of The Boston Globe, still on the move at age 125.

The Globe joins the New York Times Company. William O. Taylor (left) and Arthur Ochs Sulzberger make the announcement in 1993.

The Boston Globe's Pulitzer Prizes

Paul Szep

Ellen Goodman

William Henry III

Stan Grossfeld

David M. Shribman

Robert Campbell

Eileen McNamara

1966

Meritorious Public Service , The Boston Globe

For a campaign to prevent the confirmation of Francis X. Morrissey as a Federal District Judge In Massachusetts

Thomas Winship, Editor; Robert Healy, Assistant Executive Editor and Political Editor; Charles L. Whipple, Editor of the Editorial Pages; Joseph M. Harvey, Court Reporter; Joseph Keblinsky, City Hall Reporter; Martin F. Nolan, Globe Washington Bureau; James S. Doyle, Globe Washington Bureau; Jeremiah V. Murphy, General Assignment Reporter; Richard J. Connolly, General Assignment Reporter; Anson H. Smith Jr., General Assignment Reporter.

1972

Local Reporting , The Boston Globe Spotlight Team

For a report on widespread municipal corruption in the city of Somerville, Massachusetts.

Timothy Leland, Editor; Staff Reporters Gerard O'Neill and Stephen Kurkjian; Researcher Ann Desantis.

1974

Editorial Cartooning

Paul Szep

1975

Meritorious Public Service, The Boston Globe

For coverage of the desegregation of the Boston Public Schools.

Thomas Winship, Editor.

1977

Editorial Cartooning

Paul Szep

1980

Distinguished Commentary

Ellen Goodman

1980

Distinguished Criticism, Television

William Henry III

1980

Special Local Reporting, The Boston Globe Spotlight Team

For a report on waste and mismanagement inside the Massachusetts Bay Transportation Authority.

Stephen Kurkjian, Editor; Staff Reporters Nils Bruzelius, Alexander B. Hawes Jr., and Joan Vennochi; Globe Correspondent Robert Porterfield.

1983

National Reporting, The Boston Globe Magazine

For a special supplement entitled "War and Peace in the Nuclear Age," published October 17, 1982.

Michael C. Janeway, Sunday Managing Editor; Harry E. King, Assistant Living Arts Editor; William Beecher, Diplomatic Correspondent; Randolph Ryan, Editorial Writer; Christina Robb, Magazine Writer; John Powers, Feature Writer; and Fred Kaplan, Pentagon Correspondent; Ronn Campisi, Design Director; Lucy Bartholomay, Assistant Designer.

1984

Local Reporting, The Boston Globe

For a series entitled "Boston: The Race Factor," a six-part series on blacks in the workplace and a four-part series on comparing Boston with six other major U.S. cities.

John S. Driscoll, Executive Editor; Norman Lockman, State House Bureau Chief; Ron Hutson, Assistant Metro Editor; Kirk Scharfenberg, Deputy Editor, Editorial Page; Reporters Gary McMillan, Jonathan Kaufman, David Wessel, Ross Gelbspan, Kenneth J. Cooper and Joan FitzGerald.

1984

Spot News Photography

For photos of the effects of war in Lebanon

Stan Grossfeld

1985

Feature Photography

For photos of hunger in Ethiopia

Stan Grossfeld

1995

Distinguished Beat Reporting

For national political reporting as chief of the Globe's Washington D.C. Bureau

David M. Shribman

1996

Distinguished Criticism, Architecture

Robert Campbell

1997

Distinguished Commentary

Eileen McNamara

The Boston Daily Globe.

VOL. I.....NO. 1. BOSTON, MONDAY MORNING, MARCH 4, 1872. PRICE FOUR CENTS.

AMUSEMENTS.

BOSTON MUSEUM.
Acting Manager..........Mr. R. M. FIELD.

EXTRA ATTRACTION.

A New Play! And Engagement of the distinguished Actress,

MISS KATE REIGNOLDS,

This Evening at 7½, and Wednesday and Saturday afternoons at 2½. First time of the famous play (from the French of Sardou) after elaborate preparation and full rehearsal, entitled

A SCRAP OF PAPER.

Suzanne..........Miss Kate Reignolds, and a most brilliant cast. Also the screaming Farce of

MY TURN NEXT.

Taraxicum Twitters..........Mr. W. Warren.

FRIDAY—Benefit of Miss Kate Reignolds—A very attractive bill, and first appearance of Miss Annie Clarke since her late serious accident.

SATURDAY NIGHT—An Extraordinary Bill.
mar 4—3t

BOSTON THEATRE.
MR. J. B. BOOTH..........LESSEE AND MANAGER.

The Event of the Season!

MR. BOOTH respectfully announces that he has arranged with Messrs. Jarrett & Palmer, of Niblo's Garden, N. Y., for the production here on

THIS MONDAY EVENING, March 4,

the Grand Spectacular Drama of the

BLACK CROOK,

(By Chas. M. Barras, Esq.,) universally admitted to be THE MOST BRILLIANT SPECTACLE OF MODERN TIMES.

WITH

Miss Kate Santley,
Those Wonderful Majiltons,
Corps de Ballett of Sixty Artists,
Under the direction of Sig. COSTA,
M'lle Petrina Sassi,
Cora Adrienne, Bedon Felicita,
Bonni Bambina, Clotilda Marcheal,
The Egyptian Jugglers,
Infant Ballet Troupe,
Prof. Smith and Children,
Samwell's Trained Animals,
The Canine Clown Grimaldi.

CHARMING MUSIC, MAGNIFICENT SCENERY, WONDERFUL PRISMATIC LIGHTS, ELEGANT COSTUMES, HANDSOME PROPERTIES, AND ELABORATE MECHANISM.

The Entire Dramatic Company in the Cast. For characters, and full catalogue of Attractions, see Street Bills.

The Drama terminates with the

DAZZLING TRANSFORMATION SCENE

By the Brothers BREW, of London, Revealing a series of the most beautiful stage pictures ever shown the Boston public.

EVERY EVENING at 7.30; SATURDAY AFTERNOON at 2.

Seats now ready. Doors open at 1.30 and 7. Begins at 2 and 7.45.
mar 4—1t

HOWARD ATHENÆUM.
RICH & STETSON..........Proprietors.

EVERY EVENING AT 7½—WEDNESDAY AND SATURDAY AFTERNOONS at 2½.

Reconstruction of the Spectacular Sensation

BLACK ROOK.

Additional Novelties! New Artists! Funny Things! First appearance of the charming and beautiful European Danseuse,

ADELE PAGLIERI.

Also, will be introduced the original and celebrated French Grotesques, THE ZIG ZAGS! M. Brassaux, Varie, Robert and Rojade, in their laughable specialty, THE ESCAPED LUNATICS! HARRY CODONA in his Comic Stilt Performance. THE COMIC ELEPHANT! Exhibited by his trainer in feats that have never been attempted before by any Elephant. The most beautiful and accomplished BALLET in the world. The great Ethiopian Comedian HUGHEY DOUGHERTY. The Acrobatic Wonders, WALHALLA BROTHERS, in their remarkable feats. SIGNORA CODONA, the Spanish Tight Rope Artist. First appearance of JAMES COLLINS, Comedian.

All the Stock Company in New Acts. tf—mar 4

BOSTON ATHENÆUM.
Beacon Street.

Exhibition of Paintings, Statuary, and Chromo-Lithographs after Italian, German and Flemish frescoes. Open from 9 A. M. till sunset. Admission 25 cents. Season tickets 75 cents.
mar 4—tf

WALKER'S PRIVATE DANCING ACADEMY, 121 Pleasant street
Lessons in Plain and Fancy Dancing at all hours.
mar 4—1m

RICE, LIVERMORE & CO.,

SOLICITORS OF

American and Foreign

PATENTS,

AND NEGOTIATORS OF

PATENT RIGHTS,

9 Pemberton Square,

BOSTON.

NEW YORK—102 Wall Street.

WASHINGTON—517 Seventh Street.
mar4—1t

GET THE BEST

WEBSTER'S

Unabridged Dictionary.

10,000 WORDS AND MEANINGS NOT IN OTHER DICTIONARIES.

3000 Engravings; 1840 Pages Quarto. Price $12.

Whenever I wish to obtain exact definitions, I consult it. [Schuyler Colfax.

Every Scholar knows its value. [W. H. Prescott, the Historian.

Been one of my daily companions. [John L. Motley, the Historian, &c.

So far as I know, best defining Dictionary. [Horace Mann.

The best guide of students of our Language. [John G. Whittier.

Excels all others in defining scientific terms. [President Hitchcock.

Remarkable compendium of human knowledge. [W. S. Clark, Pres. Agri. College.

A necessity for every intelligent family, student, teacher and professional man. What Library is complete without the best English Dictionary.

ALSO,

WEBSTERS NATIONAL PICTORIAL DICTIONARY.

1040 Pages Octavo. 600 Engravings. Price $5.

The work is really a GEM of a Dictionary—just the thing for the million.—*American Educational Monthly.*

Published by G. & C. MERRIAM, Springfield, Mass. Sold by all Booksellers. Mit—mar 4

LOOKING GLASS

WAREHOUSE,

85 Hanover Street.

FACTORY, 516 HARRISON Av.

PARTICULAR ATTENTION TO MAKING

MIRRORS

and

CORNICES

TO FIT SPACES AND TO MATCH.

SOULE & WARD.
mar 4—tf

WM. BUTTERFIELD & WOODMAN,

45 High Street, Boston.

ORIGINAL SHOE MACHINERY DEPOT.

The largest and best assortment of BOOT and SHOE MACHINERY and WAX THREAD SEWING MACHINES. Send for our new Illustrated Catalogue, or call and see machines moving by hand and power.
mar 4—1t W. B. & W.

NEWSPAPERS.

THE BEST PAPER

—ON THE—

FACE OF THE GLOBE

—IS THE—

Commercial Bulletin!

WHICH CONTAINS

FORTY LONG COLUMNS

—OF—

BUSINESS AND LITERATURE.

THE ONLY PAPER

—ON—

THE FACE OF THE GLOBE

THAT PUBLISHES

THE BUSINESS CHANGES

OF THE UNITED STATES

—IS THE—

BOSTON BULLETIN.

Every reader of the English language,

IN ANY PART OF THE GLOBE,

Is referred to the

Commercial Bulletin,

Which is the only paper on the Globe which gives

The Manufacturing News of the United States,

By its Own Special Reporters.

THE GREAT POPULAR WEEKLY IS

THE BOSTON BULLETIN.

—AND—

The Only Paper in Boston

That enlarged its size January 1, 1872, was the

COMMERCIAL BULLETIN,

Which gives the most reliable and

THE BEST

Market Reports—Editorials—Money Articles—Stock Sales and Stock Manipulations—Gossip of Trade—Financial News—Original Sketches by Best Authors—Dramatic and Musical by Skilled Critics—The Spice of Life by the Most Noted Wits—Correspondence by Skilled Writers, Etc.

OBSERVE, ALSO THIS

TRUE, IF NOT MODEST STATEMENT.

The Editorial and Literary Staff employed on the Boston Commercial Bulletin is not excelled by that of any paper, Daily or Weekly, in Boston.

Terms of the Bulletin, $4 Per Year.

TO ADVERTISERS.

THE BOSTON BULLETIN

—IS—

NOT A QUARTO,

or four sheet paper, but a great

FORTY COLUMN, SINGLE SHEET,

Easy of access to readers, and

ADVERTISEMENTS ARE EQUALLY

Conspicuous on Every Page.

SPECIMENS FREE.

CURTIS, GUILD & CO.,

PROPRIETORS,

BULLETIN BUILDING,

No. 129 Washington Street..........Boston.
mar 4—1t

"THE COMMONWEALTH"

HONORS

"THE GLOBE"

In its larger extent and scope, but, like its namesake, the Pilgrim community

GATHERS UP THE CHOICEST THINGS

Of New England, that The Globe, with its attendant satellites of daily revolution, will present. In other words,

"The Commonwealth"

IS A SATURDAY JOURNAL OF

POLITICS, LITERATURE, ART & NEWS,

Bright, Fresh and Readable, in every issue, full to brim, and constantly abreast of the times.

SUBSCRIPTIONS—$2 50 to mail patrons in the country; $3 to city patrons by carrier, or boy.

ADVERTISEMENTS—Have intelligent and freely buying readers in

THE COMMONWEALTH.

ADDRESS

CHARLES W. SLACK & SON,

Publishers.

m4 1t 25 BROMFIELD STREET, BOSTON.

FINE ART ROOMS.

ESTABLISHED 1810.

WILLIAMS & EVERETT

have just received several rare and beautiful pictures, from some of the most prominent artists of Europe.

They are Sole Agents, for the sale of Braun's Carbons, Rogers' Groups and various art publications of interest and beauty.

SPECIAL ATTENTION GIVEN TO STYLE AND QUALITY OF FRAMING.

ROOMS, 219 WASHINGTON,

Opposite Franklin,

And 10 Bromfield Street.

mar 4—tf

DAMASKS.

TABLE CLOTHS. NAPKINS.
DOYLIES.
TOWELLING LINENS. PILLOW LINENS
LINEN SHEETINGS.
HUCK TOWELS. DAMASK TOWELS
HUCKABACKS.
BLANKETS. LACE CURTAINS
QUILTS.

New Goods of every quality, of the best manufacture at VERY LOW PRICES.

PALMER, JACOBS & CO.,

230 WASHINGTON STREET,

Importers, and dealers exclusively in Housekeeping Dry Goods.
mar 4—3t

WANTED

$30,000, $25,000, $15,000, $10,000, $8,000 $6,000, $5,000.

On desirable Mortgages in Boston and vicinity.
MERRILL & SMITH,
mar 4—3t 14 and 15 Traveller Building.

NEW PUBLICATIONS.

James R. Osgood & Co. have issued in two octodecimo volumes, "Passages from the French and Italian Note Books of Nathaniel Hawthorne." These note books cover a period from January, 1858, to May, 1860, and are, essentially,

"The harvest of a quiet eye,
That broods and sleeps on his own heart."

But the eye, in this case, is as piercing as it is quiet. Hawthorne's peculiar genius appears in the slightest jottings set down in his journals. The most familiar objects, passed through his magical though somewhat morbid imagination, assume an air of strangeness. Original perceptions, thoughts and judgments, start unexpectedly out of regions sacred to commonplace, the moment his meditative and moody but sharp-seeing mind touches them. His impressions of the masterpieces of painting and sculpture are given with a frankness which is a continual surprise to the reader. Even when his decisions are wrong we feel their truth in relation to his own moods. The Venus di Medici seems to have made the strongest mark on his mind and heart. To her he repeatedly returns in loving adoration, and once goes to the extreme of wishing all other statues of women destroyed in order that this may be left as the one and perfect representation of womanhood. The notes of conversation with eminent personages, such as Powers, Story, Gibson, the Brownings, are very charming. The style has the ease, grace, lucidity, and simplicity characteristic of this master in prose composition.

"Poor Miss Finch," the latest of Wilkie Collins's novels has been published by the Harpers, in a thin octavo volume. It is one of the most ingenious and original of his romances, though perhaps the reader is not so puzzled by the complications of the plot, and does not have the leading incidents come upon him with such a shock of unexpectedness as in "The Moonstone and "Armadale." Miss Finch herself is the author's most delicate and interesting feminine creation, and there are touches of pathos in the delineation which are above Collins's usual manner. Oscar, the hero, is as characterless, though not quite so *colorless* as the writer's other heroes—a being made not to act but to be acted upon. The Rev. Mr. Finch, a solemn clerical coxcomb, with a little body enclosing a big bass voice, uttering inanities in resounding tones; Madame Pratolungo, the imagined narrator of the story; and Dr. Grosse, the oculist, with his delightful broken English, are, after Lucilla, the most striking characters. The plot is intricate enough to rank among mechanical inventions, and to entitle the author to consideration at the office of the most exacting Commissioner of Patents.

J. B. Lippincott & Co., of Philadelphia, have published the first volume of "A Commentary, Critical, Experimental and Practical, on the Old and New Testaments." The present volume, which is a clearly printed octavo of seven hundred pages, is by the Rev. Robert Jamieson, D. D. It begins with Genesis, extending to Deuteronomy, which it includes. The Commentary, which is exhaustive, is at the foot of each page. The volume seems to contain everything necessary to interpret the text to the devout believer, and is evidently the result of much thought and investigation, directed to the establishment or confirmation of "orthodox" views of the Old Testament.

"The Leaders of Public Opinion in Ireland," by W. E. H. Lecky has been published by D. Appleton & Co., of New York. It contains critical biographies of Swift, Flood, Grattan and O'Connell, whose characters are estimated with discrimination, fairness, and a commendable absence of partisan heat. The paper on O'Connell is perhaps the most judicious ever written on that formidable combination of demagogue, patriot, statesman and reformer. The extracts from the speeches of Flood, Grattan and O'Connell, with their fiery Irish vehemence of expression, contrast curiously with the staid decorum, the even elegance, the philosophic serenity of Mr. Lecky's style. It seems at first a little odd that the historian of "Rationalism" and of "European Morals" should have selected such topics; but then, Mr. Lecky is an Irishman as well as philosopher.

J. R. Osgood & Co., of Boston, have published, in an imperial octavo of over a thousand pages, a "Dictionary of American Biography, including Men of the Time," by Francis S. Drake. It contains nearly ten thousand notices "of persons of both sexes, of native or foreign birth, who have been remarkable, or prominently connected with the arts, sciences, literature, politics or history of the American continent." This big book, condensed in its facts to the smallest possible space, represents an amount of industry which cannot be too highly praised. It is essentially a work of reference. It supersedes all previous compilations for it includes them, while it adds much that cannot be found anywhere else in a printed form. Mr. Gradgrind himself could find little in it to criticise. It is a labor-saving machine to everybody who wishes for facts and dates relating to the lives of prominent Americans, whether in the flesh or out of it. That we have nearly ten thousand Americans worthy of appearing in such a biographical dictionary is not the least of the claims of the volume on our attention.

A good biography of the founder of a great religious sect is a boon both to its champions and its adversaries. And by a good biography we mean one which is exhaustive in its facts, and at the same time brings us close to the soul of the m[an]. Of those who have attempted to write the life of Wesley, Southey is the only writer whose work belongs to literature as well as to theology; but it seems that Southey's biography, as judged by the Methodists, is "defective in details and is incorrect and misleading;" is unintentionally "full of errors, and, for want of dates and chronological exactitude, extremely confusing." The Rev. L. Tyerman has therefore devoted many years to the task of writing "The Life and Times of the Rev. John Wesley, M. A., Founder of the Methodists," the first volume of which has been issued by the Harpers, of New York. Mr. Tyerman considers Wesley as the man, "who, under God, was the means of bringing about the greatest reformation of modern times," thus reducing all other religious reformers, whether Roman Catholic or Protestant, to a secondary rank. His point of view is therefore partizan; but he is the first biographer who has collected all documents, printed or existing only in manuscripts, which illustrate Wesley's internal life and external career, and fused them into a biographical one. His own style is tart, crisp, rapid, dogmatic, epigrammatic; indeed, in reading him, we occasionally feel as if we were reading the life of Jacob Boehm as undertaken by Macaulay. But his matter is invaluable. His criticism of the "Times" of Wesley is altogether too exclusive, too passionately and brilliantly inexact; but his representation of the "Life" is, as far as we can judge from the first volume, singularly complete. We look forward to the appearance of the second and third volumes with great interest.

Mrs. A. L. Wister has shown not only an exceptional felicity in translating German into real English, but an exceptional sagacity in selecting books for translation. Her latest work is a translation of "The Little Moorland Princess," from the German of E. Marlitt, the author of "The Old Mam'selle's Secret." The novel is pleasing, without being specially powerful, and piques the curiosity of the reader by detailing the steps by which an ingenuous girl of seventeen falls in love with an elderly man of business, against whom she was at first violently prejudiced. One of the most romantic of stories is this made to culminate in an event seemingly unromantic. Mrs. Wister, in her translation, gives the spirit, the flavor, the peculiar sentiment of the German original. The book is not merely translated, but transfused into English.

D. Appleton & Co. of New York, have published a small volume entitled Christian Theology and Modern Skepticism, by the Duke of Somerset, K. G. In this book the proudest of English aristocrats breaks with the religion of his country, whether established or dissenting. He adopts the criticism of German scholars, and repudiates the mildest theological views of his most compromising countrymen. His decisions have somewhat the imperativeness of his rank. As Duke of Somerset, he decides that educated people, or "educated society," have reduced christianity to a myth. It has no real force except on its moral side. Its doctrines are erroneous, and its historical basis unsound.

The "popular" theology is indeed threatened, when a duke of at least twelve descents, comes out as a confirmed sceptic. To stand by the English church was once at least a political duty with all lords of the land. These lords are now absolved from their allegiance to her by the Duke of Somerset, K. G.

The Websters of the United States have attained considerable European celebrity, but they are somewhat confused in the English mind. Thus, at the time of the Parkman trial, we all remember the anecdote of the intelligent Londoner, who wondered that a man who, while he was a prominent statesman of the Republic, had not only undertaken the vast labor of a dictionary of the English language, but *had found time* to commit *such* a murder. In looking at every new edition of *Webster's Unabridged* we are more and more impressed with the sinewy power of work of the Noah who first constructed this linguistic ark, and of the industry and sagacity of his successive editors. The new edition contains 10,000 additional words.

BOOKS RECEIVED.

Leaders of public opinion in Ireland: Swift—Flood—Grattan—O'Connell. By William Edward Hartpole Lecky, M. A. New York: D. Appleton & Co. 1 vol. 12mo, pp. 320.

The Little Moorland Princess. Translated from the German of E. Marlitt, Author of "The Old Mam'selle's Secret," "Gold Elsie," "Countess Gisela," &c. By Mrs. A. L. Wister. Philadelphia: J. B. Lippincott & Co. 1 vol. 12mo, pp. 408. (For sale by Lee & Shepard.)

Physiology of the Soul and Instinct, as Distinguished from Materialism. With Supplementary Demonstrations of the Divine Communication of the Narratives of Creation and of the Flood. By Martyn Payne, A. M., M. D., LL.D., Professor in the Medical Department in the University of New York. Author of the "Institutes of Medicine," &c. New York: Harper Brothers. 1 vol. 8vo. pp. 707. (For sale by A. Williams & Co.)

THE SUNDAY PULPIT.

Owing to the agreeable change in the weather yesterday the attendance at the various city churches was unusually large. Most of the congregations were represented by their own pastors, though in one or two instances the services were conducted by clergymen from abroad. By request, Rev. John Weiss repeated his discourse upon "The Law of Marriage" before the 28th Congregational Society, at Fraternity Hall. The morning services at the School street church were conducted by the junior pastor, Rev. H. I. Cushman. After the conclusion of the sermon Mr. Cushman introduced the Rev. George Moses, a native Delaware Indian, now laboring among the remnants of his tribe in Canada West, who related the circumstances of his conversion to Universalism and gave some account of the progress of that belief among his people. The Rev. Warren H. Cudworth preached before the Music Hall Society, in the morning, upon "The Gradual Development of the Human Race." At the Shawmut Avenue Baptist church the Rev. George C. Lorimer spoke upon "The Importance of a Correct Belief," in the morning, and in the evening upon "Our Protestant Birthright." At the Church of the Disciples Rev. James Freeman Clarke preached upon "Love to God in its Relation to Human Life." At the Central Church the services were conducted by the pastor, Rev. John De Witt. At the Beach street Presbyterian the pastor, Rev. J. B. Dunn, preached his farewell sermon, previous to his departure for Europe. Communion services were held at Grace Church, on Temple street, in the morning, with preaching in the afternoon. At the Berkeley street Church the pulpit was filled by the pastor, Rev. William B. Wright, the communion service following the morning sermon. At the Third Presbyterian Church the Rev. Dr. Mc Corkle preached in the morning, communion being held at 3 o'clock. At the Park street Church Mr. Murray was listened to as usual by a large congregation. At Trinity Church communion services were held in the morning, Rev. Phillips Brooks preaching in the evening. At the Lynde street Church Dr. Bartol preached as usual, taking for his subject "The Christian Stand." At the Church of the New Jerusalem, on Bowdoin street, the Rev. James Reed spoke upon, "The Divinity of Christ." Rev. George H. Vibbert, pastor of the Central Square Universalist Church, East Boston, took for his subject yesterday morning, "Magdalenism, or the Social Evil."

In the evening the Rev. James Freeman Clarke D.D., delivered the fourth lecture of the Young People's Course at Music Hall, announcing his subject as "Led by the Spirit." Vesper worship was held at the Church of the Unity, conducted by Rev. C. W. Wendte, of Chicago. Rev. Henry Morgan lectured in Morgan Chapel upon "My Experience in the Brick Business." Rev. T. M. Post, of St. Louis, Mo., delivered the eighth lecture in the "Boston Course" at the Old South Chapel, his subject being "God Manifest in the Flesh."

TWENTY-EIGHTH CONGREGATIONAL SOCIETY.

The Rev. John Weiss lectured, yesterday morning, before the Twenty-eighth Congregational Society, his subject being "The Laws of Marriage." After the usual preliminary services by the society, he spoke substantially as follows:

It is well to accept the discussions which are springing up, a fruitful crop of mingled witch-grass and clover, upon the field of that great social problem of marriage. I call it still a problem, though so many people are inclined to think that if anything might be left to take care of itself in this age which "peeps and botanizes" upon its grave, it is this relation of two married persons, which extols and regulates. But the married persons are the first to appear with the suspicion that there is a mistake somewhere, since the reasonable expectations have not been generously fulfilled. If Nature means anything more than merely to get her man and woman paired, if she cherishes the secret hope of delighting them by surprises of Divine companionship, after they have hurried into her baited trap, she has in so many cases overrated her ability, to please high-minded souls, that the cry of the captives escapes from the gilded bars, and is a piteous suit before society. What is the matter? Who is in fault? Can the fault be remedied? If not, can the parties be released from its bitter influence? Mr. Weiss now referred to the difference of the feeling before marriage and the subsequent feeling when the act of living together subjects two persons to a knowledge of each other. Hereditary folly and infirmities are unmasked more quickly in marriage than in any other human relation. The recriminating criticisms of either party on the weaknesses of the other were contrasted by him with the thoughts of each concerning the other before marriage.

The imperfect tendencies on either side after marriage are equally annoying;—coarseness is repulsive, so is triviality; a sensual impulse destroys peace, but so does a bad temper. The worldliness of the street is no worse than that of the parlor. His anxiety for advancement goes farther towards rent and taxes than the desire of the wife in many cases to equal her neighbor in appearances, and the angel of before marriage becomes so expensive that the man recalculates the whole cost of her society. In how many ways the dissonant moments creep into the house it is useless to enumerate them, and if we did, the only advantage we should derive would be that of seeing more clearly than before that mutual infirmity is an inevitable element of the plea to develop maturity out of youthfulness, and the spiritual out of the natural. He thought that this mutual ignorance would be modified by a mixed education of the sexes, and introduced a strong plea in favor of this theory and of this system of education, answering the many objections which are commonly expressed, and refuting the arguments against its adoption. In this connection he showed that the advocates of early marriage should favor this plan, as essential to the salutary working of their theory. A picture of the homes of ill-mated couples was now graphically sketched, and the effect upon the children portrayed. They would either become the very elements in society which would be discountenanced by the virtuous, or enemies which would destroy a happy marriage and home where the well married couple stoop to blow the firelight, and the children's eyes answer, flickering like hearths where refuse and rubbish are consumed. Would you discover where the watershed of this country stretches to, drain soft[...] brawl and turbidness into the Atlantic and Pacific seas? Behold this range of roofs which the fire of marriages have upheaved. Mr. Weiss now noticed the causes which would procure a legal divorce, and thought he would add to them chronic ill temper, and defined it by picturing its results in the marriage relation.

He would have a special court of divorce, on whose bench noble matrons should sit by the side of accomplished men, to throw the instinct of wifehood and the subtle judgement of the woman into their grave balancing. He hoped women would demand this when the right of suffrage was accorded them, and planned a method of procedure when cases should be presented to such a tribunal. The erruptions of new affinities were alluded to, and the writings of the yellow covered literature referred to; but the speaker thought that these wonderful dispositions which were therein made of unnecessary persons, could not be depended on in real life. In opposition to this, he proposed the doctrine that marriage protects two people, till their tender romance hardens into the firmness of a spiritual affinity. The natural affinity of sex is born, but spiritual affinities are made. In conclusion, he offered two propositions of a practical nature, which contain suggestions for a reform of some matrimonial faults and follies. Let people defer to the laws of health, of sanity, of hereditary soundness, and respect the limits which have been set up by the commonsense of God. Let simplicity characterize the manner of living, and not the love of appearances. Reduce to the lowest point the disturbances which arise from ignorance or vanity, or artificial learning, and marriage is liberated for a more effective discharge of its spiritual purpose. He would have this taught to the children; he would have them warned against the affectations which undermine respect. We need not be afraid of teaching them too much, youth cannot be converted into premature maturity. Teach them these truths, and they will better be prepared to discover that marriage withholds felicity, until it has been earned.

CHURCH OF THE NEW JERUSALEM.

At the Swedenborgian Church on Bowdoin street the services were conducted by the pastor, Rev. James Reed, who took for the text on which to have his discourse the 17th and 18th verses of the 28th chapter of Mathew: "And when they saw him they worshipped him; but, some doubted. And Jesus came and spake unto him saying, all power is given unto me in heaven and in earth."

The object of the speaker was to prove from the text the divinity of Christ, and to meet the doubts and cavilings so freely indulged in by the sceptics and materialists of the present day. Should they worship the risen Christ or not, was the question which agitated the minds of the disciples. Their hopes had been based on an earthly Messiah. They had clung to him—all but one—until they had seen him upon the cross. Then even Peter denied him, for he, too, doubted. But when they saw him risen, when they marked the prints of the nails in his hands and the hole in his side, they felt assured of his divinity, and worshipped him. But Jesus, seeing that some still doubted, said in the words of the text: "All power is given unto me in heaven and in earth." The meaning of these words should be thoughtfully considered. If their truth was accepted, absolutely all power was given to the Lord Jesus Christ.

The question asked by the doubters among the disciples was still asked by many who classed themselves as Christians. Some believed he was but one of three divine persons; others, that he was the Godhead himself; and still others, that he was simply a man, the son of a carpenter. Under the growing light of the present day, the doctrine of three Gods in one seemed irrational and absurd, while that of the human alone was yet more so. There never was a time when the divinity of Christ was so frequently and thoroughly discussed as the present, and there never was more need of that vital point of doctrine being understood. Never were sceptics and infidels so loud or argumentative as at the present day. The old dispensation of Christianity was passing away, and the new one was beginning. Modern rationalism was in a great measure the reaction from the creeds of the old church. Men were losing their hold of old things without grasping the new. The new Church was in the possession of doctrines based upon the Scriptures, which shed a new light upon points which had heretofore been stumbling blocks.

CENTRAL CHURCH.

The pastor of the Central Church, on Berkeley street, Rev. John De Witt, preached yesterday forenoon from the text of Mark xv: 23: "And they gave him to drink wine mingled with myrrh, but he received it not."

The sermon had immediate reference to the c[...] munion service which took place in the aftern[...] and presented many of those reflections natu[...] arising upon a review of the circumstances of [...] Saviour's crucifixion. The record of the few la[...] hours of his life was more connected and deta[...] than that of any period of similar length durin[...] career, yet much relating to his personal feelings [...] the considerations governing his conduct in [...] trying experience was necessarily subject only to [...]ference. We could not pretend to be [...] above what is written, and the full significanc[...] all his acts we could not know. The humiliat[...] and privations which Christ was compelled to un[...]go after his betrayal were portrayed by the prea[...] and the condition of physical exhaustion in whic[...] reached the mount of Calvary was especially [...] marked upon. Under these circumstances a sol[...] prompted by kindliness of heart, offered him [...] mingled with myrrh, a potion which would hav[...] tendency to relieve his sufferings. That he sh[...] refuse it seems inexplicable upon ordinary con[...]erations. Conscious of the agony of the ter[...] death which was before him, why should he dis[...] the draft which might mitigate that prolonged ph[...]cal suffering?

The hypothesis was presented, that the full mea[...] and intensity of these sufferings were indispensab[...] the fulfilment of that mission which Christ had ta[...] upon himself, and were consistent only with the [...]pointed ordinance of a loving God. In this wa[...] was faithful to the last to that cause for which [...] came into the world. If, as has been said, Ch[...] were a mere man, who lived for himself and died [...] himself, and wrought his own salvation merely, i[...] that could be said of his death was that he fell an [...]nocent victim of Jewish malice, the refusal which [...] text implies seemed not susceptible of reasonable [...]planation.

Even were the miraculous elements of the go[...] record eliminated there were many other thing[...] which the expression of the text was an exam[...] which were not to be explained upon rational grounds. The act of Christ in refusing the temp[...] draught, was, in the view of it taken by the prea[...] proof of his utter unselfishness, a sacrifice more [...] human of personal comfort in the fulfillment of [...] mission as the Saviour of men. No trait of ordi[...] human nature is more familiar than that the tim[...] danger and suffering awakens in mankind all t[...] latent selfishness. In a crowd of men overcome [...] sudden peril the sentiment, if not the utteranc[...] each is that every one must care for himself, and i[...] struggle the strong crush and trample down the w[...] The claim that Christ was more than human, ma[...] rested upon the one fact of his perfect unselfish[...] Christ's conduct as evinced by the text shoul[...] taken also as a hint for the guidance of his disci[...] when called upon to decide upon a course of con[...] under various and perplexing circumstances. [...] act referred to in the text was governed by the controlling purpose of his life, and questions of doubtful solution respecting conduct should ever be subjected to this Christian test.

PARK STREET CHURCH.

Rev. Mr. Murray preached, yesterday morning from Romans xii., 9: "Abhor that which is evil." Paul intended to indicate in this text what should be the feeling of the Christian toward sin. Have we felt as Paul did, an abhorrence of sin, a detestation of it, a shrinking from it as a woman shrinks from a snake in her path? Not to have this feeling was a proof that our spiritual and moral condition was not good. We knew how Christ felt in regard to sin, and one proof of the existence of Christ in us, was, abhorrence of sin. Had we this at all times? Were we troubled by the tricks of trade? Did we vote as we pray? Were we as religious at the polls as at the altar?

For centuries the foremost question had been: What do you believe? The perceptive faculties had dominated over the motives of men. He granted the value of intellect, but the perceptive faculties were not supreme. Faith was not the fulfilment of the law. It was the heart and not the mind that was regenerated by the Holy Ghost. The object of Christianity was not to improve man's philosophy, but his practices. It was not Christ in the head that was needed so much as Christ ruling over the heart. Have you that piety of the heart, which says to the hand, "You are my servant, not my master?"

The text also taught us to abhor *that* which was evil,—not the person, but the evil in him. If Christianity taught us to abhor the wrong-doer, it would be a religion of hate, not one of love. God hated sin, not the sinner. The father does not cease to love his disobedient son. True, the crime must be punished through the criminal, but the object of abhorrence was the deed, not the doer. The record was that notwithstanding the sin which was in it, "God so loved the world that he gave his only begotten Son, that whosoever believeth in Him should not perish, but have everlasting life."

This abhorrence of evil was a triumph of grace and not of nature. The impulse of even the highest form of manhood was not that of love. Christianity was not an improvement upon old religions and philosophies, but a new religion. Some of its principles had been enunciated centuries before, but the Spirit which clothed the dry bones with flesh was born on Calvary, and there alone. If we were in Christ we should take sin by the throat and the sinner by the hand. It was not natural to hate sin. Men err easily. Thieves, and burglars, and murderers did not become martyrs. As a race men were not amiable. Orthodoxy taught the sinfulness of men, not because Calvin and Edwards asserted it, but because everything about us proved it. If people wished further proof of the doctrine let them look into their own hearts and answer whether it is easy to be virtuous. The agony came when one tried to project himself into God-likeness. Hail, then to the words: "By grace are ye saved." It was not for the heaven He has to give, but for the heaven already given, that the speaker thanked God. He knew not what the future might have for him, but he knew that he was now redeemed, emancipated, free in Christ Jesus. No longer as a beggar, but as one redeemed from poverty, did he seek God in prayer. Let men kill first the sin which is killing them fastest, the one which begets others. Whatever it may be which leads to sin, let it be destroyed; that man may enter into life a redeemed soul.

"CHRISTIANITY AND SKEPTICISM."

The ninth lecture in the course, upon "Christianity and Skepticism," was delivered in the Old South church, last evening, by Rev. Dr. Post of St. Louis, the subject being: "God manifest in the flesh." To evolve and apply the moral forces needed to bring the creature into sympathy with the Creator is the work of God, and He must do it by a revelation of Himself, either in the fixed order of nature, or by the interruption of those laws in attestation of a verbal revelation, or in a person. The consciousness of man supplementing the first develops natural religion, supplementing the second, the Jewish, and supplementing the last, Christianity.

The incarnation of Christ is the distinctive feature of Christianity. The incarnations of Brahma and Buddha were entirely different. The unity of Father and Son are spoken of many times, in language which can teach nothing else but that He was the revelation of God, not of all His attributes, but of His moral nature, which, when beheld, will change us from glory to glory.

In order to salvation, man must, in his nature, be conformed to God. This conformity can only be produced by sympathy with Him. This sympathy can only result from the revelation of God in a human person. No happiness is possible to one not in harmony with God. The power which will secure this harmony exists only in God. The god we worship forms us to its likeness. The power to re-create is the power which first created. Salvation comes through faith in a person. Christianity is not a system of graces and virtues, but is embodied in a Person who wears them all. Abstraction cannot save. The God revealed by and in the laws of nature does not possess the qualities necessary to the salvation of the world, for He has no sympathy, no feeling, no love. He has power, and that alone.

The power of a Person exhibiting His doctrines in His life may be perpetuated by the agency of the Holy Spirit, and will adapt itself to the different natures of those it affects. The mission of Christianity is to draw men into assimilative sympathy with God. By the sympathy of soul with soul God binds man to Himself. In order to effect this the Incarnate must be a person of love; one with feelings and sympathies; one who can convince us that God loves, pities, forgives. We love Him because He first loved us.

God must be revealed in a human person, also. If unlike us we cannot sympathize with Him. Philosophy may postulate an impassive God; but the Being to draw men must have emotions; He must be capable of sacrifice. The Captain of our salvation must be made perfect through suffering. If he has no feeling He cannot have our sympathies.

Faith applies this force to the soul, and binds the creature to the Creator. Christ reveals God the Father to us, as a brother, suffering and thus winning our sympathy. The impassible is revealed in the passible and this revelation has shown itself superior to all others in its power to save the world. Natural religion has failed and the Hebrew religion could not save the chosen race from corruption, but Christianity has wrought more mightily than all others powers and still works. Can this be other than the revelation of God? If it is aught else history and philosophy are dumb.

This lecture will be repeated in Freeman Place Chapel this afternoon at three o'clock.

YOUNG MEN'S CHRISTIAN UNION.

The usual Sunday evening service, under the auspices of the Young Men's Christian Union, was held at Music Hall, last evening, a large audience being in attendance. Rev. James Freeman Clarke conducted the service, and preached from the text of Romans 8:14—"As many as are led by the Spirit of God, they are the Sons of God."

Almost everything in the world, he said, has a body and a soul. The body is that which we perceive by the senses, but the soul is the inward and invisible part. Things seen are fleeting and temporal, things unseen are permanent and eternal. There is a philosophy indeed that pretends to teach that we know only that which is material, that we know single facts as phenomena, grouped facts as laws. This philosophy the preacher deemed utterly fallacious. As an example of the spirit of things he adduced the remains of that pilgrim ship which were thrown up a few years since by a storm from that ocean bed, to which the vessel sunk two centuries before. The wreck was exhibited on Boston Common, and was visited by thousands of the descendants of the Pilgrims, who saw in it more than the decayed timbers of which it consisted. These did not differ from the wreck of any other vessel in their outward aspects, but those who beheld these relic felt that there was a spirit per-

The first two historic front pages of this book, March 4, 1872 and November 11, 1872 were printed in the years before Charles H. Taylor became the publisher of The Boston Globe.

yesterday to hear his lecture entitled, "The Life and Character of Buddha," felt that they could, without fear of disappointment, expect to hear something deeply interesting as well as instructive; nor were they disappointed. Beginning with a few remarks on the doubt which existed as to the comparative nobility of the two types of character, that which steps downward from wealth, or that which overcomes the drawbacks of an humble position, and stating whence he derived his authority for the statements which he was about to make, the lecturer went on to present the life of Siddartha the Buddha, or Sakyamuni, in a series of vivid word-paintings, mingled with expositions of the doctrines of the great teacher. First, he drew the portrait of the young prince, surrounded by the fond care of his father with every luxury which could tend to render him thoughtless, stricken with horror at the first sight of age, sickness and death, leaving his palace, his wife, leaving the boy that day born to him, whose face he had never seen, donning the yellow robe, and assuming the hatchet, needle and filter of the mendicant monk, and going forth into a strange city to beg from door to door the coarse food eaten by his order. Then he painted the enthusiastic seeker after truth going to Brahman after Brahman seeking spiritual truth and never finding it, joining a band of ardent religious enthusiasts, practising their austerities for six years, leaving them so suddenly as to be deemed an apostate by them, and, after passing through an experience symbolized under the form of a contest with demons who shook the mountains but not him, and whose weapons turned to garlands of flowers when they touched him, while the whole universe rejoiced at his victory, at last resolving to teach the doctrine which had been revealed to him, although half-fearful that men would not strive to understand it. The third picture had for central its figure the aged teacher, after forty-five years devoted to preaching self-denial and forbearance among all classes, dying in the arms of his followers, bidding them not to be concerned about his remains after his body should have entered Nirvana, but rather to be solicitous to practice the virtues which lead men to perfection.

Various particulars of Buddhist doctrine tending to more clearly show the character of the founder of the sect were stated at some length, by Colonel Higginson. The four principal points of the Buddhist doctrine, those which constitute "The Wheel of the Law" as it is called, are the existence of pain, the source of pain in unregulated desires, the destruction of pain by destroying these desires, and the means of effecting this work. Upon these four points, around this wheel, revolves the whole system of Buddhism. When first beginning to teach, Sakya-Muni found that not only spiritual but moral forces were arrayed against him; the doctrine of caste was deeply rooted in all life. Public execution, or the direst torture was a trifling penalty compared to that which he incurred who violated caste, for he condemned himself to eternal degradation, from which no form of transmigration could raise him. This the Buddha destroyed, not by saying anything against it, but simply crushing it by the force of his example, and to-day in all the East, Hindustan is the only country where caste remains in force. Buddhism, wherever it goes, elevates the condition of women; its founder hesitated at first about admitting them to the priesthood, lest they should impair the stability of those institutions which have, after all, endured for two thousand two hundred years.

In conclusion, Col. Higginson said that it had been remarked by one of the foremost thinkers of the country, that all prophets had one central word around which their systems revolved; that of Buddha was renunciation, that of Jesus, love, but he should prefer to say that Buddha taught renunciation and love, and Jesus love and renunciation. When humanity should make up its criticism on these two religions, it would say that both too much ignored the Greek ideals of beauty and truth, and would occasionally turn from their solemn temples to the sunny life of Socrates, and to his death, refusing to distrust the author of the universe, or believe that anything could be otherwise than well. All three doctrines were needed; no one channel was wide enough for the religion of the world; we needed India and Judea as well as Greece and Rome, and should not quarrel with one because it was not the other. It had been said that when, in the reign of King Asoka, the door of the Buddha's tomb was opened, it was found that after two hundred and eighteen years the lamps were still burning, the flowers still fresh, the perfumes more fragrant than ever, "and so," said the lecturer, "after more than two thousand years we open that tomb again, and find that the lights still burn, the perfumes are still fresh, and the perfume of that noble life still remains immortal."

LYNDE STREET CHURCH.

Rev. C. A. Bartol preached, yesterday forenoon, his 35th anniversary sermon, at the West Church, Lynde street. His subject was "The Christian Stand." Dr. Bartol explained the word "Stand" by saying that we receive knowledge not only from the material world, through the five doors to the brain, but also from an inner sense of right and duty, implanted by God himself. On this higher nature he would base the Christian Stand, and on this he urged all to take *their* stand, as being higher than all others.

He would not reject all material knowledge as having no bearing whatever, but rather combine the two as forming the grand whole. Neither would he condemn all other sects as being wrong; but would rather think of them as building upon the same foundation, a structure differing in some minor points.

He said this higher stand is for happiness as well as for life, that it is like some structure on the shore, used both as a dwelling and a fort, combining the comforts of the one with the strength of the other. When one has attained to this high stand, and, looking back, sees some one below him, he should invite him to the higher stand; but it would be useless to hold out as inducement the scenery that he beholds from the summit, for it is invisible to one who is still in the valley below; yet he should do all that can be done to lift him up to his own level.

He said that the Christianity of Jesus had been one of the great agencies in raising the condition of man, not, as some claimed, the only agency. He was willing to take other Bibles and compare them with our Bible, to compare other teachers with Jesus.

CURRENT NOTES.

Colorado is knocking at the door.

Gold in this world covers up as many sins as charity does in the next.

Good Baldwin apples are selling in England *to-day* for a penny apiece, here they are five cents, and from that upwards.

North Adams, in this State, is soon to have a first-class flouring mill.

Minister Washburne has sustained a remarkable popularity among natives and foreigners in Paris, through good and evil report, and at last commands the respect of all.

And now the New Yorkers are betting largely on the acquittal of Stokes.

Theodore Woodhull and Victoria Tilton are nominated for president and vice-president.

The woman question,—question of age.

Syracuse, N. Y., is said to have salt on the brain, and well she may have, after producing nine million bushels last year.

The railroad freight lines from the west terminating in this city, are now worked to the very extent of their capacity.

New York contains one quarter, at least, of all the Jews in the country.

The New York savings banks have not yet recovered from the late panic.

The fortune of Mr. A. T. Stewart, of New York, is estimated at between fifty and sixty millions.

Brooklyn, N. Y., shows a mortality more than double that of this city.

Ceremonies, like flags, are best waived.

Russia sends to this country for large amounts of machinery, and hundreds of locomotives are built for her railways in Philadelphia.

Small-pox is increasing at Baltimore.

The year 1872 is not likely to close, we fear, without some wild work in Europe.

They have "fire bugs" in Rome, Italy, as well as in other unfortunate localities.

O. W. Holmes says that humility is the first of the virtues—for other people.

It is singular that when apples are scarce and dear, cider should be so cheap and plenty. Political economists having given up, the chemists are solving this riddle.

San Francisco merchants sent 180 tons of teas eastward upon one train lately.

The citizens of Troy, N. Y., propose to establish a college for women in that city.

Richmond, Va. aspires to a hotel on the European plan. Good for the landlord.

Barefooted Irishmen wear Cork soles.

Wilmington University, Delaware, has at present sixty-one female students.

Brazil no longer rests under the stigma of slavery, and already shows other hopeful signs of advancing civilization. The schoolmaster will be abroad next.

Revolvers are now sold by the *barrel* in Boston and, of course, *go off* briskly.

There's a policeman in every man's conscience though not always on duty.

Western lately *walked* two days *running*, and was *weak* for a *fortnight* afterwards.

The French have a very significant saying: "What a woman wills, God wills also."

Our friend Quiz says he has two vehicles, one in the barn, and his wife's a little sulky.

Divorce is as facile as ever in Indiana.

The lamb-like Apaches, of the western plains, have again been gathering a few scalps.

It seems that a man was "severely frozen to death," according to a Canadian jury lately.

The fine Inman Steamer the "City of Brussels," is the fastest ocean steamship afloat.

The tide of travel sets from Europe to this side of the Atlantic at the present time.

The state of Alabama has six large and profitable cotton factories running at present.

Washington, D. C., has been particularly deficient in public amusement this winter.

Philadelphia has over one hundred and fifty citizens who are counted millionaires.

Henry Wilson says, to be an American citizen, is as good as a title of nobility in Europe.

[illegible] think it anything to have 10,000,000 [illegible] at Chicago.

[illegible] comes impregnated with [illegible]

The press— [illegible]

The District of Columbia, [illegible] sections, owes the sum of $3,000,000.

In the early history of Harvard College, corporal punishment was of daily occurrence.

One crime is everything, two nothing, says the unscrupulous but clever Madame Deluzy.

Hay is very scarce and very dear, all through New England, where it can be got to market.

France—a vale of Thiers.

According to Agassiz man existed upon this earth one hundred and fifty thousand years ago!

It costs the city of New York, as a corporation, a million of dollars a year for illuminating gas.

Leading article,—a locomotive.

It is said that after Lot's wife was turned to salt, he got a *fresh* one.

The Japanese are now brewing lager beer of excellent quality at Yokohama.

The French Assembly has in its organization forty physicians. Probably with a view to operate on its Constitution.

A colored gemman's sign in Mercer street, New York, reads, "Boots blacked inside."

A mouse in a New Jersey bank sadly complicated the cashier's accounts by making a nest of three or four thousand one dollar bills.

According to the papers, over one hundred ladies are studying law in this country.

The first street car lately commenced running in Denver, Colorado.

Some one calls poker a *grate* game.

Small-pox, rowdyism and reform are on the increase in New York.

There are twenty-eight orphan asylums in the State of New York, sheltering 9000 children.

The Indian meaning of Missouri—Muddy.

The season just closed has been the gayest one in the fashionable society of Philadelphia for more than ten years.

There are fifteen cities in Massachusetts.

Fifteen new passenger cars have lately been added to the rolling stock of the Eastern Railroad, and more are building.

Hartford is following the good example of Boston in the establishment of Holly Tree coffee houses.

The Michigan Central Railroad will next season begin another track from Detroit to Chicago. It will be of steel.

Autumn hues—cutting fire wood.

The first Presbyterian Church of Elizabeth, N. J., has not missed a service for two hundred and seven consecutive years.

A New Bedford whale ship took a fish lately in the North Pacific that yielded one hundred and forty-one barrels of sperm oil.

A Parisian barber, "crossed in love," shot himself the other day, before the false one's door. Probably with a *hair-trigger.*

Carlyle says, that every battle is a bloody conjugation: "I kill, thou killest, he kills; we kill, you kill they kill." Killing idea.

No franking privilege exists in England.

A New York paper estimates that there are three hundred thousand smokers in that city, averaging two cigars each per day.

The Hartford Courant is, we believe, the oldest newspaper in America, having been issued consecutively for more than a century.

The Northern Pacific Railroad has the small subsidy of 50,000,000 acres of valuable land, composed of fertile plains and rich valleys.

We are indebted to that able and indefatigable press correspondent, Major BEN: PERLEY POORE, for valuable public documents.

A Cincinnati inventor has a machine which will accurately weigh gas in place of the ordinary style of measurement, thus registering quality as well as quantity.

Voice of nature,—the mountain's peak.

There is considerable excitement, in private circles, about a late misalliance in New York, but such things have happened ever since King Cophetua loved the beggar maid.

It has been announced, several times, that the average consumption of water in Boston amounts to seventy gallons daily for every inhabitant within the city; a great waste, certainly.

Punch calls a sneeze, a head wind.

German emigrants have been specially directing their steps, for a year or more, towards Texas. They are a thrifty class of people, and generally arrive in this country with pecuniary means.

It looks very much as though the Black and Caspian Seas would be united by a broad and serviceable canal. It is shown that it can be done for about fifty million of dollars, and Russia seems in earnest.

Movement in real estate,—earthquakes.

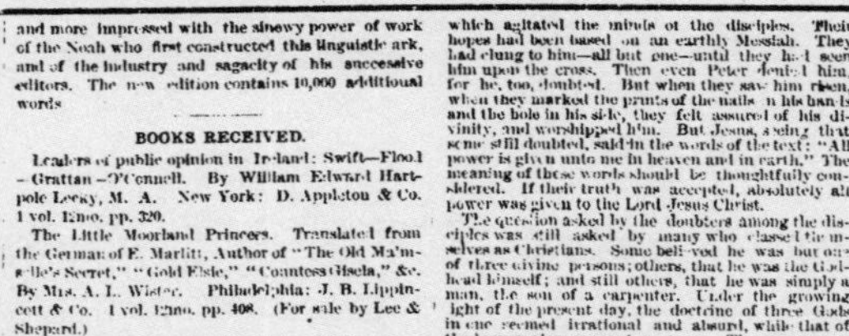

The Boston Daily Globe.

VOL. II......NO. 114. BOSTON, MONDAY MORNING, NOVEMBER 11, 1872. PRICE FOUR CENTS.

AMUSEMENTS.

BOSTON MUSEUM.

THE GLOBE.

A MOST ATTRACTIVE PROGRAMME!

LOUIS XI.

SPECTRE BRIDEGROOM!

BOSTON THEATRE.

MISS CHARLOTTE CUSHMAN, As "MEG MERRILIES," in GUY MANNERING.

THE GLOBE. - - SPECIAL CARD.

MR. DION BOUCICAULT

ARRAH-NA-POGUE; Or, THE WICKLOW WEDDING.

HOWARD ATHENÆUM.

THE TICKET-OF-LEAVE MAN.

MAN, KNOW THYSELF!

CLOG DANCING.

BANJOS!

ACADEMY OF MUSIC, CHELSEA. EDWIN BOOTH. HAMLET AND RICHELIEU.

LECTURES, &c.

TREMONT TEMPLE. Prof. J. H. PEPPER, F. C. S.

THE ILLUSION OF THE GHOST.

PARKER FRATERNITY LECTURES. 5 CHOICE LECTURES FOR $1. ANNA E. DICKINSON

BOSTON UNIVERSITY LECTURES.

BOSTON LYCEUM. Wednesday Evening, November 13, BRET HARTE.

THE EIGHTH ANNUAL LECTURE OF REV. J. D. FULTON, D. D., WILL BE DELIVERED IN TREMONT TEMPLE, NOVEMBER 13, 1872.

NOTICES.

HIGHLAND STREET RAILWAY COMPANY.

DEDICATION OF THE NEW ENGLAND HOSPITAL FOR WOMEN AND CHILDREN.

NOTICE. ALL FRIENDS OF THE Consumptives' Home, ... FAIR TO BE HELD IN JANUARY, 1873. ... WESLEYAN HALL, 36 Bromfield Street, on Monday, November 11th, at 11 o'clock A. M.

TO INVALIDS. GETTYSBURG KATALYSINE WATER!

WHITNEY BROS., General Agents, 227 South Front Street, Philadelphia.

WEEKS & POTTER, CARTER & WILEY, and GEO. C. GOODWIN & CO., Boston, and Druggists generally.

WHELPLEY & STORER'S Crushers and Pulverizers, 311 BROADWAY NEW YORK.

PULVERIZED FUEL PROCESS.

TRAVELLERS' LETTERS OF CREDIT. COMMERCIAL CREDITS, AND BILLS OF EXCHANGE.

F. A. HAWLEY & CO., Bankers, 1 Devonshire, Cor. State Street.

JOHN C. FENNELLY,

FAIRBANKS STANDARD SCALES. FAIRBANKS SCALE WAREHOUSE, 118 MILK STREET, BOSTON.

IN BANKRUPTCY—DISTRICT OF MASSACHUSETTS.

CORNS, Bunions, Bad Nails, Sore Insteps.

GOODALL'S PLAYING CARDS

LADIES' GOODS.

GRAND OPENING. GRAND OPENING OF PARIS NOVELTIES. MRS. JOHN G. FORD, 51 TEMPLE PLACE.

STITCHED AND WOVEN CORSETS, LADIES' FURNISHING GOODS.

INFANTS' WARDROBES.

SPECIAL NOTICE. A LARGE JOB LOT OF BLACK BRILLIANTINES, JUST PURCHASED. Will be Ready for Sale This Day AT THE NEW STORE, 19 SUMMER STREET. James J. Smith & Co.

CARPETINGS. CARPETINGS. CARPETINGS. Goldthwait, Snow & Knight, FOREIGN AND DOMESTIC CARPETINGS, OIL CLOTHS, Etc., GOLDTHWAIT, SNOW & KNIGHT, 43 and 45 Washington Street, BOSTON.

FURNISHING GOODS. GLOVES. THE LONDON STREET GLOVE. HEWINS & HOLLIS, 47 Temple Place. MEN'S FURNISHINGS. FINE SHIRTS MADE TO ORDER. 47 TEMPLE PLACE, (Near Washington Street.)

FOR ALL CATARRHAL AFFECTIONS, Influenza, or Stuffed Colds in the Head, ... Dr. Wilton's Catarrh Cure. SOLD BY ALL DRUGGISTS.

TRIPLE WASHER. THE BEST FIVE-DOLLAR WASHING MACHINE MADE.

LINEN AND COTTON HOSE. N. E. LINEN HOSE MANUFACTURING CO., 170 WASHINGTON STREET.

Boston Daily Globe.

MONDAY MORNING, NOVEMBER 11.

CONTENTS.

FIRST PAGE.—The Great Fire: Full Particulars.

SECOND PAGE.—Correspondence ...

THIRD PAGE.—Foreign Matters ...

FOURTH PAGE.—News in Brief—Editorials ...

FIFTH PAGE.—All the latest news by Special Despatches, etc.

SIXTH PAGE.—New England News ...

SEVENTH PAGE.—Financial Matters in Boston and New York—Commercial News—Naval Gazette—Arrival and Closing of Mails—Marine Records, etc.

EIGHTH PAGE.—The Great Fire (continued).

DEVASTATION!

A Terrible Conflagration in Boston.

$250,000,000 LOSS!

CHICAGO REPEATED.

LOSS OF HUMAN LIFE.

RICH MEN BEGGARED IN A DAY.

TRIUMPH OF THE FIRE-FIEND.

GENERAL NOTES.

There is nothing more remarkable in the dreadful calamity that has befallen our city than the awful rapidity that marked the progress of the flames. There is something appalling, too, in the contemplation of the success with which they persistently defied every means that were taken to conquer them. Whole blocks were literally mowed down by the flames like wheat before the reaper's scythe. Granite was of no more avail against them than so much card-board. No sooner did the heat touch it, than it began to crumble away piecemeal, and, gathering force and volume on its way, fell, crunching and thundering to the ground in huge masses, with the roar and resistless fury of an avalanche, blocking up the roads and blotting every trace of a street from view. The scene had more of the terrible than the grand in it. The sky was lighted up for miles around, and was disfigured by great patches of dun smoke, across whose disc burning fragments darted like angry meteors. Now it would be light as midday, and presently an ominous darkness spread like a pall across the heavens, and was only relieved by the lurid forks of flame that writhed tortuously through it, and disappeared in its depths.

The air was filled with burning cinders that were hurled wildly above, where they hovered confusedly for a moment and then descended like a shower of gold to the earth, where they hissed, sputtered and crackled as though in malicious glee at the ruin of which they were a part. Every now and then a broad wave of light would suddenly show distant spires, sharp and clear against the dark sky, from which the next instant they would fade like spectres, as the thick curling masses of smoke swelled upward and spread ghastly smears of black across the heavens. At one moment a faint scintillation was to be seen on the cornice of a roof, where it fluttered, star-like, for a moment, and then changed into a thin snaky fork of flame that ran rapidly along the edge of the parapet, until it hung there a trembling fringe of fire. In another moment, dense volumes of black smoke rose sluggishly, and rolled over and over, turning their dun folds outward and swelling in size until they turned into ragged white clouds through which fiery tongues darted in all directions.

Bare walls started forth from solid masses of granite stores with appaling quickness, and stood like ghostly monitors of ruin in the midst of a sea of fire. Without the slightest warning a dart of fire would leap up through the darkness, and, in a flash, another large building was in flames, and presently went down as though it was so much tinder. Now one or two windows of some huge warehouse would reflect a faint light from within, then the whole pile would brighten up the darkness from its myriads of panes, and, before there was time for surprise, flames belched [illegible]

[illegible]

wagons, carriages, hacks and even wheelbarrows. The sidewalks of the streets adjacent to the fire were heaped up with bedding, desks, furniture, boxes and goods of every description. The "birds of prey," who fatten on the calamities of their fellows, hovered about, eager to pilfer upon any opportunity that offered. They skulked in the shadows of the houses, watching with greedy eyes for a chance to gratify their rapacity. Well-dressed gentlemen were hustled by them with a view to watches and pocket-books. They crouched in dark niches, ready to dart forth and pounce upon any neglected trifle. They leered horribly in the faces of timid women, and uttered coarse jests in their hearing. [illegible] The firemen seemed composed. They worked incessantly and with the most touching earnestness, but they were baffled completely, and were driven back step by step by the fire they sought to conquer. At length it was proposed to try the effect of powder in staying the progress of the flames. A train was laid; the crowd was urged backward by the police to a position of safety. [illegible] The air is obscured by a thick cloud and tainted by a sickening odor. There is a momentary hope that the flames are stayed, but they break forth again in all their fury, apparently stimulated to fresh rage by the efforts made to thwart them. And these scenes are enacted over and over again with but little variation through the weary night, [illegible] and a thick, blood-red cloud hovering over the city and filling the hearts of all with an ominous and indefinable mixture of terror and sadness.

Origin of the Fire and Its Course.

The origin of this fearful calamity that has fallen thus heavily upon us was of so apparently trifling a nature that it is hardly possible even now, with a full knowledge of the fact strong within us, to fully realize that results so awful in their magnitude could have arisen from so simple a beginning. The fire broke out in the large granite block on the southeast corner of Summer and Kingston streets, and was first discovered about a quarter-past seven o'clock on Saturday evening. It began in the lower story, and probably caught from the engine. When the firemen arrived the flames had crept up to the fourth story, and the building being surmounted by a Mansard roof, the fire soon sped upward and enveloped the woodwork. [illegible]

Summer street, beginning at Broad and extending towards Washington, presents a desolate appearance. [illegible]

Franklin Street.

Of Franklin street little can be said, except that of the magnificent buildings, by which, forty-eight hours ago, it was bordered, nothing now remains but huge piles of cracked and powdered stone and brick which cumber the street, making passage through extremely difficult, if not actually impossible. [illegible]

Milk Street.

On the northerly corner of Milk and Washington streets still stands the Old South Church, [illegible]

Hawley Street.

Hawley street, like many others, is in such a condition as to be unrecognizable, every house, without exception, being down.

Washington Street.

All the injury done on Washington street was between Summer and Milk, and almost entirely on the east side. [illegible]

Arch Street.

Arch street, which runs from Summer to Franklin, being situated where the flames were fiercest, retains to-day not a single structure having the faintest resemblance to a house.

Winthrop Square and Its Vicinity.

Winthrop square and its vicinity, including Otis street, cannot be described except by stating that every thing within that area is consumed.

Broad Street.

The burnt district on Broad street extends from the foot of Summer street, beginning with the Boston, Hartford and Erie Railroad depot, and reaching on both sides of the street as far as Prescott and Chapin's coal wharf, which is entirely destroyed. The wharf immediately north of this used for the same purpose by Batchelder Brothers, was kept uninjured, mainly through the good service performed by tug boat Lewis Osborn, which lay off in the water and prevented the flames from extending in a northeasterly direction. Yesterday, all along on the water side of Broad street huge mounds of coal were burning, producing a dense, black smoke, which completely filled the street. The tracks of the Union Freight railway were torn and bulged up, caused no doubt by the intense heat. Everything connected with the depot of the Boston, Hartford and Erie railroad was destroyed, even the freight cars standing on the tracks, so that not a wall or timber arose above the ground more than half a dozen inches.

Oliver Street.

Oliver street, on the east side, was but slightly injured, but on the west, from Sturgis to Broad, was entirely destroyed. On the west side were piled up immense quantities of wool in bales, cases of boots and shoes, bales of leather, and various other kinds of merchandise.

Hamilton and Sturgis Streets.

Hamilton street seems to have escaped entirely, and such was also the case with Sturgis from Broad to Oliver, but from the latter point to Pearl street, everything was destroyed.

Purchase Street.

From Broad to Oliver, Purchase street was uninjured, but beyond that, reaching to Pearl, no vestige was left but piles of misshapen stone and brick. The Sailors' Home, corner of Oliver and Purchase streets, remained safely perched on its lofty eminence. Yesterday afternoon, large quantities of household furniture were deposited on the vacant land opposite the Sailors' Home, but the greater part of it was removed before evening.

High Street.

The same must be said of High street as of many others, every building being burned to the ground.

South Street.

South street escaped injury further than the destruction of three houses near the corner of Summer street.

Lincoln Street.

At the head of Lincoln street two houses on each side were consumed.

Bedford Street.

Bedford street from Lincoln to Columbia is in ruins, but beyond the latter there has been no injury done.

Kingston Street.

In Kingston street, two houses on the east side are entirely ruined, also one in the same condition on the west side, in addition to another partially destroyed.

Chauncy Street.

In Chauncy street, the building of Forbes, Richards & Co., on the west side, is partly consumed, and a block on the east side entirely.

Pearl Street.

All the magnificent stone buildings on Pearl street, throughout its entire length from Milk to Broad streets, are now but unsightly, misshapen heaps of ruins.

Water Street.

The fire came no further up Water street than the new post-office building on one side and the building of the Boston Post newspaper on the other. These two structures remain intact. The post-office building may be likened to a rocky promontory projecting into the sea of flame, beyond which the billows of fire raged triumphant, but against which they lashed in vain. Even the wooden staging upon the unfinished Mansard roof of the lofty structure stands almost unscathed. Here and there a flickering tongue of flame caught upon it, but was promptly extinguished by a slight dash of water. The building of the Post newspaper was so completely exempt that composition and press-work was carried on as usual there last evening. Below these two conspicuous buildings, Water street as far as Liberty square is a complete ruin on both sides. Nothing is visible but material which is absolutely incombustible. The front walls of the stores have generally fallen outward, and passage down the street can only be effected by careful footsteps, over blocks of granite and heaps of bricks lying in all positions except that most favorable for the sole of the pedestrian. The office of the Post is No. 30, and the next thing on that side of Water street which has anything of a perpendicular aspect, is the rear wall of No. 50. On both sides of this the rear walls, as well as the front ones, are down, leaving substantially an open space from No. 30 to Liberty square and extending back to the rear of Cochran's wine store, which fronts on Congress square, to the side wall of E. J. Andrews' wine store, which fronts on Congress street to the new granite building called Congress building, and to the front walls of buildings on Lindall street. Of this area, fronting southwardly on Water street and eastwardly on Kilby, the facade walls are all down, except those of the Revere Copper Company's store, No. 47.

The right-hand side of Water street, going down, is also a heap of fallen ruins, clear back to Milk street and as far down as Kilby street. On Kilby street, between Liberty square and Milk street, no front wall is standing on either side of Kilby, but on the corner of Water and Kilby a unique monument is left rising, in perpendicular melancholy, to the height of the eaves, and measuring in breadth about six feet on Kilby and six on Water street. The corner post bears the lettering, "J. Porter & Co., Burbank's varnishes," and the column seems to indicate that the business remains of that firm there repose, and, it may doubtless be added, in the full hope of an early resurrection.

Liberty Square.

Standing in Liberty square, and looking southeast, things retain their former general aspect. The buildings fronting north on Liberty square and east on Batterymarch street, present their facades to the eye as heretofore, while their interior toward Milk and Kilby streets is clean gone. This wall, fronting as above named, then marks the extreme limit of the conflagration at this point. The Liberty square front may be more definitely fixed in mind by some if it be added that the prominent signs on the front are "Glenden Iron Company," "W. B. Lang," "Automatic Gas Company." The old building with a steep sloping roof and red brick front walls, bearing the signs of Small, Wetherell & Co., Boston Drug Mills, and others, is untouched, and good as new, and the same is true of the lofty granite building extending from the above-named on the east side of Batterymarch street to Milk street. Any other view of Liberty square than that thus indicated gapes with ruin. The flames got across the square and struck the buildings on the lower part of Water street, but extended no further on Water than No. 104, occupied by D. Curry, oil dealer. This building escaped fire, though considerably damaged by water and the manipulations of the axemen. The block with a carved frontage, occupied by George Upton, glue manufacturer, and others, is burnt out, and the front walls have fallen into the street. From No. 36, a printing office, to Central street, the front walls are intact, and the building at the corner of Kilby and Central street is standing in tolerable preservation, and may be repaired. This block, occupied by Upton and others, is the only building on the seaward side of Liberty square which was destroyed by fire, and this marks the extreme northeasterly point which the conflagration reached.

Kilby Street.

The condition of this street has been indicated in part in connection with what is above written. From a Liberty square point of view, looking west, nothing is left but the front walls of No. 36, printers, and No. 47, Revere Copper Company. The express office building at the corner of Kilby and Water is flat, Dodge, Gilbert & Co.'s building is ditto, and both corners of Kilby and Lindall streets have nothing to show but piles of brick and stone. Indeed the northerly corner, occupied by W. V. Hutchins and W. H. Vincent, insurance agents, in the lower story, and by other parties in the upper stories, has hardly this to show upon its site, for it was here that one of the successful powder explosions was made, which flung the entire walls of the building into the street. Huge blocks of granite lie across Kilby street at this point, and down Central as far as Nos. 13 and 14 every pane of glass in every window was shivered into fragments by the force of the explosion. Next to the insurance agency building the walls are still standing, and the partly burned and dislocated timbers show that energy and persistency of the firemen here proved more than a match for the destroyer, and here again his "proud waves were stayed." No. 25, on the same side, is badly damaged by water, and the rear of the roof somewhat burned. No. 23, the next building toward State street, occupied by G. White Williams, saddlery hardware dealer, is somewhat drenched by water, but his goods were well covered by rubber cloths, so that he opens business in this line this morning with but little competition, nearly all stores doing business in that line having been destroyed. The chief indication of damage in this store is a large aperture in the roof of the rear part, caused by a stone, weighing about a hundred pounds, which was thrown up in the explosion of the insurance agency. Above this point on Kilby street the buildings present their usual appearance on both sides, except here and there a pane of glass minus.

State Street.

Soon after midnight it became evident to the sagacious ones that the real objective point of the fire fiend was the bank vaults of State street. To revel there among the greenbacks and bullion were for him delight indeed. The fire department, jagged and weary as they were, took up the gauntlet with the spirit of Leonidas, and the result is that not a front on State street is scorched, and the only building on that street which the fire got at in the rear was the post-office, the back entrance of which was from Lindall street. The latter street, as already indicated in referring to Water and Kilby streets, was pretty thoroughly demolished on the southeasterly side. The other side fared about the same. The post-office building was burned into nearly half way from the rear, but the front was successfully defended, and not even the glass of the letter boxes nearest State street was fractured. The whole Merchants' Exchange building was flooded with water, which poured like a cataract down the broad stairway into State street. Every hydrant in the vicinity was made available to defend this "key of the situation," and lines of hose were carried to the same point through buildings on Kilby street and others on Congress street. The Congress street entrance remains as it was, except some panes of glass disappeared during the operations of the firemen. It was in furtherance of the determination that the fire should not reach State street, that several buildings on Congress and Water streets, besides that mentioned on Kilby street, were demolished by gunpowder.

Congress Street.

That part of Congress street nearest State street remains intact. The first building on the left going from State street, seriously injured, is J. Cottle's grocery store. Here the timber work is in good part left, showing the efficient labor of the firemen. Next to this comes the new marble-front building called Congress block. The facade of this stands, except a portion of the coving nearest Lindall street, which has fallen. The interior is burned out. The next building beyond was blown up with powder, as was Learned's eating-house building on Congress street, opposite. Beyond the site of these two to Water street is a mass of fallen ruins. On the right hand side of Congress, the first building burned out is No. 25, occupied by E. J. Andrews, wine merchant. No. 21, next door north, [illegible] injured, and may [illegible]. This marks the northern limit of the fire on the west of Congress street. In Congress square everything is secure, except the Learned & Co. building, S. Q. Cochrane's wine store being the final limit of the fire, and this being successfully defended.

Federal Street.

Federal street is entirely destroyed on both sides, from the Boston, Hartford and Erie depot to Milk street.

Devonshire Street.

The burnt portion of Devonshire extends from Summer street, including both sides, to Milk street.

BUILDINGS BURNED.

Owners, Occupants and Values.

Below is an accurate record of the buildings burned with their values, as estimated by the city assessors on the first of October. In all cases the names of the parties owning the buildings are stated first:

Summer Street.

[illegible]

Continued on Eighth Page.

Manager/Publisher

1873 - 1921

CHARLES H. TAYLOR (1847-1921) He joined the year-old Boston Daily Globe, one of 12 newspapers publishing in Boston, in August of 1873 as business manager. During the next 48 years, General Taylor (he was given the title in 1890, when Massachusetts Governor William E. Russell made him an honorary member of his military staff) was the publisher and chief editor of the newspaper that came to dominate its field in Boston and New England.

The Boston Daily Globe.

VOL XLIII—NO 172. BOSTON, WEDNESDAY MORNING, JUNE 21, 1893.—TWELVE PAGES. PRICE TWO CENTS.

LAST SCENE IN THE GREAT BORDEN TRIAL.

Clerk—Mr Foreman, look upon the prisoner; prisoner, look upon the jury. What say you, Mr Foreman—
Foreman (interrupting)—Not guilty!

CONTENTS OF TODAY'S GLOBE.

Page 1.
Lizzie A. Borden acquitted, returns to Fall River; Howard pictures extraordinary scene as verdict was announced; argument of Dist Atty Knowlton and charge of Judge Dewey; opinions of bench, bar and press.

Page 3.
...lander wins the great suburban race.
...officials accused of smuggling Chinese and opium.

Page 5.
Smugglers at Gloucester.

Page 6.
... killed and many injured by derailment of a race train in New York.
Tuesday at the World's fair.
Cornell freshmen beat the Columbia ... crew at New London.
Town of Gibson, N B, nearly wiped out by ...

Page 7.
Dist Atty Knowlton's summing up for the government.
Plans for unveiling of Farragut statue.
Bayne, the pitcher of the U. of P. team, ... suddenly from effects of a surgical operation.

Page 8.
New organization of railroad employes ...
Trotting at Worcester.

Page 9.
Brooklyn easily defeats Boston; result of the games in national league.
The ... orders

Page 12.
William C. Todd's offer of $2000 annually to newspapers accepted by public library trustees.
... in Boston alleys.
Commencement at Wellesley and other institutions of learning.
Marriage of James H. Walsh and Miss Mary E. Franey.

LOCAL FORECAST.

For New England Wednesday.

Fair weather, continued warm over the interior, cooler during the day near the coast; variable winds, becoming easterly on the coast; probably showers Wednesday night or Thursday morning.

The Temperature Yesterday

Indicated by the thermometer at Thompson's: 3 a m, 69°; 6 a m, 72°; 9 a m, 87°; 12 m, 93°; 3 p m, 93°; 6 p m, 91°; 9 p m, 82°; 12, mid, 79°. Average temperature yesterday, 85 11-21°.

NOT GUILTY.

Lizzie A. Borden is Acquitted.

Decision Reached on First Ballot.

Judge's Charge a Plea for the Innocent.

Ingeniously Knocked Down Government Props.

Knowlton Hurt Case by a Comparison.

Howard Pictures the Scene in Court.

Extraordinary Spectacle When Verdict Was Announced.

Warmly Welcomed Home by Her Loyal Friends.

Bench, Bar, Press, Everybody Express Opinions.

NEW BEDFORD, June 20—"I want to go home; take me straight home tonight."

"Tonight?"

"Yes, tonight. I want to see the old place and settle down at once."

That Lizzie Borden should throw her hands upon the rail, her face upon her hands, and indulge in hearty sobs after the ordeal of facing, her hand uplifted above her head, the foreman of the jury as he pronounced the words, "Not guilty," was to have been expected.

Nothing else?

Well, yes. If she were an ordinary woman she would have cried and cried, perhaps fainted, then smiled, and in effective pose reasserted the habitudes of her sex.

The difficulty is she is not an ordinary woman; she is a puzzle psychologic.

Presumed by the law to be innocent, and as it now appears, judged by the law of the land so to be, she has lived in the broad glare of red-hot publicity nearly a year.

Every great newspaper in the land has had its reporters, its staff correspondents, its artists, and its pests, male and female, watching, searching, studying, analyzing, photographing, sketching, picturing, and if possible interviewing her.

They found texts for columns in her looks, her bearing, her method of speech, her personal habits, her ability to sleep, her fattening process, her approaching trial and everything connected with her.

The great Beecher used to say that a public man could not blow his nose on his own doorsteps without its report being echoed throughout the entire city, and so it has been with Lizzie Borden, whether she washed her face, wiped her eyes, blew her nose, puckered her mouth or raised her hand, whatever she did, wherever she [illegible] mitigated assault by the gossips of the time.

During all this period, to use a vulgarism, she has not given herself away once, by which means she has done nothing of which might reasonably have been expected from an ordinary woman in her trying and embarrassing circumstances.

The police have watched her like lynxes, the state detectives felt at liberty to examine her correspondence to inform themselves at every point and not only the power but the money of the commonwealth has been poured out like water, not for the purpose of probing the mystery of the Borden murders, but that Lizzie Borden might be proved an assassin of women and a parricide.

She is an abnormality, but she does not look it nor would one have the right to so [illegible] judge her, were nothing known of her beyond the simple

Christian Life She Led

down to the moment of her arrest.

In works of good repute she passed her time. A member of the band of Christian Endeavor she visited those in prison and comforted her kind in trouble. A manager of the Fall River hospital she visited the sick, and gave not only words of cheer and cups of cold water, but her presence and individual interest to her brothers and sisters of low degree.

The Bible class, the Sunday school and the prayer meeting were about the most exciting of her pleasures and she grew to woman's estate the favorite of a hard natured, close fisted, money saving, but daughter loving New England miser.

Womanly traits and christian qualities were the only developments of Miss Lizzie Borden's character, save such petulances and outbursts of temper as are natural enough in every household in the land and might well be looked for in a home where a father of the Borden type had taken to himself a second wife, thereby furnishing to his daughters a stepmother of the Mrs Borden type.

Who says all this? Not the police, not the state detectives, not madam rumor or dame gossip.

But who does tell it?

First the jury, her sister and her uncle. Next the pastor of her church and the city missionary, to whom she often went with contributions of money and that which sometimes costs us more than money, personal presence and individual interest. Then come the neighbors and the church folk.

Just here a point. It would have done you women who read this story, heart good to have seen the women of Fall River on the stand for the first time in their lives testifying to their love and confidence for and admiration of this young christian woman, flesh of their flesh in the church, bone of their bone in the good works which as one good old lady naively expressed it, "naturally interest our young people."

No one could have studied, as I did, the contrast afforded by the witnesses for the prosecution, and the men and women called by the defence, leaving out of consideration, obviously the experts whose testimony was negative, if not almost entirely substantiating the claims of the defence.

Police marshals, police captains who had been promoted from patrolmen through the year, police medical examiners, and policemen of every possible grade furnished the contradictory evidence for the prosecution, handicapping the climax with the matron of the station house.

In all my experience, which includes attendance upon the chief criminal trials since the famous Burdell murder, somewhere in the later 50's, I have never seen

A Prosecution so Handicapped,

first by the crime, abnormal and extraordinary in its character; second, by the absolute barrenness of direct proof; third, by the contradictions of its own witnesses, and fourth, by the utter impassiveness and stolid self-reliance of the accused party herself.

The opening of Dist Atty Moody was not only ingenious, but clean-cut, admirable in delivery and effective, while the closing plea of Dist Atty Hosea M. Knowlton entitles him to rank with the ablest advocates of the day.

It is fair to remember that it is much easier to assault than to defend and in forming an estimate of ex Gov Robinson's interesting and convincing plea for the defense, it must be remembered that after he had reexposed the police officers in their great act of tumbling one over the other, of riddling the matron because of her unnecessary and ridiculous story, there really was little left for him to do beyond those glittering generalities of which Rufus Choate, the master of pyrotechnic oratory, was so fond.

During all this, a period of intensest heat, leading up to the beastly temperature of today, which in fervid caloricity discounts its most humid predecessor, the defendant has broken down but once, and because that was an isolated case I took the pains to inform myself about it, that I might correctly diagnose it.

Sitting far out upon the beach on a projecting rock, the wild waves literally dashing saline refreshment upon his revered individuality, sat Mr Justice Dewey, panting with the heat, which surcharged his portly person and made great streams of sweat roll from his thickest hair across the well-developed forehead and down his bearded cheeks.

This was the night before Lizzie's breakdown.

Where was she?

She was in jail.

Her frail physique was superheated too, the sweat rolled from beneath her thickest hair and over her troubled brow, as she sat panting by the grated window of her cell, for although it was larger than some, it was a cell for all that.

She saw no clouds in the sky, no sea gulls skimming the air and no salt water waves broke near her shapely feet.

It was late. Her light had been extinguished by order. She could no longer read, so she threw herself upon her bed, and like a top turned from side to side until the early pencilling of a red hot dawn ushered in a blistering, sizzling dog day in June.

Unrefreshed, her sleepless night passed, she rose, attempted a modest breakfast, was driven to the court house, where she suffered the agonies of an unbearable heat, the same heat that upset every masculine organization in the court room before the noon recess was reached.

Sleepy, tired, weary beyond measure, by the dry perfunctoriness of the learned brothers, she

Leaned Her Head Upon the Rail

immediately back of her and fell asleep.

A few moments later, waking suddenly and possibly not realizing where she was, she saw upon a table, not four feet from her, an ordinary handbag wide open, in which were the ghastly skulls, bleached, whitened, with their ample sockets for eyes and nose revealed, of her own dead father, and of the woman also of whose murder she stood accused.

And then she fainted.

[illegible]

You wouldn't have fainted, would you, madam, mother, wife, sister, daughter?

You would have looked straight into those evidences of assassination, reminders of your good old father and of your caretaking, if not well-loved stepmother.

Yet, tremendous as the surprise must have been, outrageous as the exposure seemed then and seems now to me, had she been prepared as we who were awake were prepared, for the introduction of those awful evidences of some one's crime, I believe she would either have nerved herself not alone for the sight, but for the terrible scrutiny of old dame rumor and madam gossip and all New Bedford's best and worst, or else, as she has frequently done on similar occasions since, have hid her face behind her protecting fan.

Now and then during the somewhat unnecessary details indulged in by her own counsel Lizzie Borden shed a furtive tear, and when Chief Justice Mason, to whom she looked almost hoping against hope for exclusion of the inquest testimony sustained the position taken by ex Gov Robinson, overcome by joy and recognizing the full horizoned significance of the aid her case had received, she broke down, and for two or three minutes indulged in the luxury of a first-class cry.

With these exceptions the defendant has sat as motionless, as expressionless and apparently as uninterested as a wooden Indian.

Therefore I say she is, as counsel on both sides have characterized, a woman of extraordinary mentality and unusual self-control.

In view of her life, as pictured by the solid men and women of the city of her residence, all this seems strange. Yet the fact is she was always peculiar in her ways, as was shown by her selection of old Mrs Russell, for instance, as an intimate, and the further fact that she never cared at all for the society of men, old or young.

Yesterday was a corker. Today knocks sun spots out of it.

I never suffered so much from literal heat as I did in the court room today, although appropriately clad and provided with all the creature comforts that a freely spent fortune could procure.

The chief justice, buttoned to the neck, was as dignified as ever and much more uncomfortable. The learned brothers, the associate judges, Dewey, who was to deliver the charge, and Blodgett, who is regarded as one of the brainiest men on the bench in Massachusetts, sought the seductive refreshment which the water pitcher grants.

This has been an extraordinary day, aside from the heat, which, as I have intimated, was the worst of the season, a regular old-time scorcher, without the suggestion of a breeze.

There is no need to tell you of the crowds outside, or the sweltering masses inside, save that I was confidentially informed by a gentleman who apparently knew all about it, that "the very best people of New Bedford and Fall River and Brockton are here today," and they looked it.

They were a better dressed and more intelligent band of curiosity mongers than their sisters of other days, but they were just as curious and just as regardless of the feelings of the prisoner at the bar as the women who have been here on other occasions, presumably not of our best people.

Hon W. W. Crapo, Rev Edward Everett Hale, several judges and counsellors of local repute were inside the rail, forming an admirable setting for a colored brother learned in the law who succumbed to the furnace-like condition of the apartment and the day and nearly snapped his head from his backbone, as during his sleep he snored, ultimately arousing even himself.

The jury were on their mettle. They had listened courteously to ex Gov Robinson and to Dist Atty Knowlton the day before, but by the exercise of a God-given intuition they felt in their bones that this day was their last, and bore themselves in their best bibs and tuckers like men and brethren conscious of the heavy responsibility resting upon them.

Lizzie was Very Pale,

but self-contained, as usual, and having riveted her eyes upon Dist Atty Knowlton accepted every blow without a flinch and endured to the very end like a woman of pluck and grit and tremendous self-reliance.

Mr Knowlton has had a tough time in various ways the past month. He has had [illegible] has held the laboring oar in this great case.

He has seen, little by little, how unstable and unsatisfactory were the men and women upon whom he depended.

He felt, right or wrong, that the dress handed to him from the Borden house was not the gown he wanted, and he knew that a great wave of popular disgust with a verdict obtained by circumstantial evidence in New York in the cases of Carlyle Harris and Dr Buchanan had swept so thoroughly over the entire country as to affect very seriously the chances for conviction.

I never in my life was so impressed with the outrageous point to which modern habit has brought the state's attorney in his desire for conviction as in this admirably managed trial.

In other days, when accused persons were not defended by paid counsel of their own choosing they were safe in the hands of the lawyers of the commonwealth, and his sole idea was to ascertain truth, and nothing but the truth.

The modern practice which enables wealthy people to hire lawyers for their defense and leave courts to assign lawyers to defend people too poor to hire them for themselves, is responsible for the feeling which district attorneys now invariably have, that a verdict against the prisoner is a victory for them, while a resultant not guilty is a defeat for the county or the commonwealth.

This was noticeably shown in the present instance, and with the same pride of bearing, the same earnestness of purpose, the same tremendous potentiality which we find displayed in the engine No. 999 on its 20-hour trip from New York to Chicago was superbly developed in that magnificent specimen of God's handiwork, Hosea M. Knowlton, today.

As the verdict has been rendered and Lizzie Borden is now flitting from room to room in the old homestead in Fall River, as the dignified and courteous judges are now taking their last good night meal in the adjoining dining room together, as the Fall River police have returned to their dens disappointed, disgruntled and growling, as the lawyers for the prosecution and the counsel for the defense are now hobnobbing in the pleasant quarters of ex Gov Robinson, just beyond my own, and as the jurors have but in the moment filed past my door, wiping the satisfied lip, refreshed by

The Cup of Enjoyment,

there is no need to weary the eye or sting the heart or burden the wires with the splendid periods uttered by the counsel of the commonwealth during his plea of the morning, nor to rehearse, as he did, the day's story in the Borden house, of Mr Borden himself, of the unfortunate wife and stepmother, of Lizzie or of Bridget.

The point in his argument, after the killing of the stepmother, was to show a motive for the assassination of Mr Borden. He argued that it was the one crime intended, but after that came the consequences that had not been thought of.

At this time Lizzie was a study.

Innocent, how could she bear the accusations, the epithets, the sneers, the finger-shakings, the pointings and the denunciations without breaking down?

Ordinary men like you and me can understand how nerve pure and unadulterated could enable a guilty man or even woman to bear up with defiance against any accusation.

Here, however, was a young woman, short and, although stouter than she was a year ago, fragile and delicate, who never [illegible] and her assailant straight in his flashing eyes.

Mr Knowlton ridiculed the story of the barn and her being in the hay loft on a brutal day in August, and made unquestionably a good point when he asked:

"Where is the bit of iron with which to fix the door; where is the sinker with which to go a-fishing?"

I was not pleased with Mr Knowlton's frequent iterations of his desire to remember at all times that the defendant was a woman, his desire to be truthful and his appeal to heaven to do something dreadful to his arm and seriously embarrass his tongue if he were to be in any sense unfair or prejudiced in the conduct of this case. In other words, he protested too much, a fault most grievous when viewed in the light of his otherwise magnificent work.

He appeared chagrined and mortified to find that he had been fooled by the defense or misled by the police about the dress that Miss Lizzie wore on the fatal day.

He was evidently convinced that she wore the bedford cord and subsequently burned it, and in accounting for the fact that the police did not find the dress at the time of their thorough search, he said they were not especially careful, because they believed they had the dress they wanted in their possession.

He thought no one would hesitate a moment as between Lizzie Borden and Alice Russell, insisting with great show of earnestness that Miss Russell was a woman with a conscience, and when with great impressiveness he said, turning to the jury, "You saw her," a smile ran through the court room and one irreverent member of the bald-headed club remarked, "We did."

Mr. Knowlton hurt his case seriously by drawing very unnecessarily a contrast between Lizzie Borden and Bridget Sullivan, the rich and the poor, the mistress and the maid, the educated and the uninformed.

It was unnecessary, because Lizzie Borden has no better friend than Bridget Sullivan, and no witness on the stand did so much as Bridget to help the cause of the defense, who sought to persuade the jury that the house was not the home of hate and malice, when she testified that in all her term of service she heard no quarrels and witnessed no disagreement.

During the recess a large pile of letters were handed to Lizzie by sheriff Wright, some of which she read, smelling bottle and fan in hand.

It was uphill work for the able district attorney, and sweltering spectators regarded him with curious interest, such as is manifested when a strong man bursts chains that are bound about the muscles of his arm or a thousand-pound weight is lifted by the teeth by the woman of the iron jaw.

His contention that the story told by the matron was told in Lizzie's interest was so manifestly grotesque as to make even the police officers smile. Mrs Reagan did not care a rap for Lizzie or anybody else; what she was thinking of was her own bread and butter.

The ax and hatchet theory was then exploited, and he took them up one by one, literally, as he subsequently did the skulls metaphorically, protesting with a weakness of voice that it disturbed his sensitive nature to be compelled by the strict mandate of sternest duty to talk of such horrid things in the presence of a real born lady.

He made a strong analysis of the story of the note, its non-confirmation and importance to the case, and closed with an eloquent peroration praising the evidence produced by the prosecution as an array of impregnable facts.

The argument was rather long and the jury were tired when at 12.05 they took recess until 1.45. At this everybody stood up, while Lizzie held quite a reception.

At 1.45 the mercury having mounted to the very tip top of the thermometer, everybody fagged, worn out, impatient and cross, Judge Dewey standing, the jury standing, the court room perfectly quiet, the charge began.

An extraordinary picture was then presented, a picture I hope for the credit of the old commonwealth will be preserved in permanent form.

After talking a few moments, reading from his manuscript, Judge Dewey courteously suggested that the jury sit. From that moment, at an angle of 45°, every profile in the box was turned straight toward the speaking justice and during the entire delivery, occupying one hour and one-half, not a position changed, not a head moved.

It was an extraordinary spectacle.

That Lizzie Borden sat on the edge of her

Continued on the Second Page.

DAILY GLOBE 185,394 AUGUST AVERAGE.

The Boston Daily Globe.

SUNDAY GLOBE 250,196 AUGUST AVERAGE.

VOL LII—NO 63. BOSTON, WEDNESDAY MORNING, SEPTEMBER 1, 1897—TWELVE PAGES. PRICE TWO CENTS.

CONTENTS OF TODAY'S GLOBE.

Page 1.

Boston and Chicago play 11 innings, and the score is 8-8, when the umpire calls the game on account of darkness; Baltimore wins and New York twice beats Cincinnati.

Judge Whitehouse in the Roberts-Patten case at Bath, Me, decides that criminal intimacy never existed between Mrs Roberts and Hon John O. Patten; case closed except the final decision; believed children will go to the mother.

Subway opened for traffic; one-third of underground system put in use this morning; remainder to be completed by next spring.

Resignation of Pres Andrews of Brown to be accepted today for an entirely new reason.

Page 2.

Hoodlum again beats the Cock Robin, and settles the question of the two boats in moderate airs.

Alcidalia captures the rich Nutmeg purse at Charter Oak. Passing Belle and American Belle the other winners.

Lottie Lorine at Dover cuts the New Hampshire record to 2.07¾; three other miles made inside the previous mark.

Old Stoughton musical society holds its annual "sing" at Highland park.

Program of today's parade and playout of veteran firemen at Springfield.

Syndicate owning hotel La Touraine negotiating for Winthrop schoolhouse property on Tremont st.

Cases of raided Nantasket cottages come up in Hingham court.

Handsome young woman commits suicide in a Chicago hotel, leaving no clew as to her identity.

Addie and Thordis win first and second class races of Wellfleet Y. C.; third class did not finish.

Page 3.

All Paris turned out to greet Pres Felix Faure, in honor of his return from Russia with the alliance in his pocket; bomb exploded at the church of the Madeleine just after he had passed.

Ethel Day, 18 years, attempts suicide at Waterville because of lovers' quarrel.

Past Department Commander Innis back from Buffalo; speaks in praise of new commander-in-chief.

Engineer and fireman killed in a boiler explosion at Fredericksburg, O.

Chicago lawyer a stowaway on steamer Michigan.

Page 4.

Newport beats Taunton, New Bedford beats Fall River and Brockton beats Pawtucket in N. E. league.

Providence beats Buffalo in a 12-inning game; Eastern league games.

Pursuit race between men, representing the east and west will be held at Charles River track about Sept 25; news for wheelmen.

Sewer trench at Arlington caves in burying two men, only one of whom is rescued alive.

Carlisle Indians will have a strong football team in the field this season.

National circuit bicycle races at Worcester.

Page 5.

Annual sports and illuminations of Houghs neck.

Citizens' union will today formally announce that Hon Seth Low will be its candidate for mayor of greater New York.

Entries for the N. E. A. R. A. regatta promise some good sport on Labor day.

New Hampshire veterans and distinguished guests gather at The Weirs for annual reunion.

Burglars ransacked apartments of Winthrop L. Marvin at 1073 Boylston st during absence of family from city.

Herbert Harriman and Quincy A. Shaw Jr make the best scores in the opening round of the Newport annual golf tournament.

Page 6.

Catholic Young Men's national union convention opens; addresses made by Pres Galvin, Pres McGuid, Mgr Conaty and others; reception in evening by Catholic union.

Insurance department to again examine the Bay State beneficiary association; Maj Merrill replies to his critics.

Conference on exceptions in O'Neil murder case to be held here Sept 10.

Page 7.

George W. Rumble, a returned Alaskan miner, tells of the riches of the wonderful country.

People of Skaguay request Seattle chamber of commerce to notify people intending to leave for Klondike that the trail from Skaguay is impassable, and that there will be much misery there this winter.

Warden Bridges promulgates the rule that hereafter no callers will be admitted to see prisoners on holidays.

Death of Mrs John Drew, the actress, at Larchmont, N.Y.

Man giving his name as Dr Edward N. Bates of Boston assaults the conductor of Nantasket band for alleged insult to a woman.

Collision of sections of broken freight train near West Winsted, Conn; 20 cars damaged.

Page 8.

Mrs Bert Sawtelle and George Lorver of Fairfield, Me, alleged to have eloped.

Executive committee of Institute of Technology to meet Tuesday to elect a president.

Page 9.

Straine and Larson of the United Telegram company held in $10,000 each for Sept 24, both furnishing sureties.

Failure of Cuthbert & Co of New York.

Ferry boat Revere crashed into and nearly demolished pier at East Boston; captain and engineer disagree as to signals.

Page 10.

Reunion of descendants of John Bean held at Haverhill.

Page 11.

Important auction sales of horses and carriages.

Page 12.

Pennsylvania democrats in convention at Reading nominate Walter E. Ritter and M. E. Brown for auditor general and state treasurer respectively; the convention, by a vote of 290 to 131, ratified the committee plank placing James M. Guffey in the place of William F. Harrity, which friends of the latter fought against.

Senator Lindsay of Kentucky says the action of the Pennsylvania democrats in ousting William F. Harrity from the national committee was unwise, as it will probably end all efforts of the gold men to bring about harmony with their old friends, the silver men.

Labor delegates in St Louis receive and act on a platform that strongly condemns injunctions; possible settlement of miners' strike by arbitration.

Watchman Bialk in the Luetgert trial in Chicago tells of the night of May 1, how two barrels of caustic potash were emptied into a vat and liquefied; steam was on all night, with the receptacle covered once while the contents boiled; the vat was then cleaned, after which the police found therein bones and finger rings.

Trustees of Marcella st home perplexed by the educational problem which confronts them.

CARS NOW RUNNING IN THE SUBWAY.

SUBWAY ROUTE—HEAVY LINE INDICATES SECTIONS OPENED TODAY.

NOW FOR SPEED

Subway Opened Without Any Formality.

First Car to Enter at Gradient at 6.

Timed to Go Through in 4 Minutes.

Veteran Employes the Ones Honored.

"March 28, 1895—Sept 1, 1897," Historic Dates.

One-Third of the System Now Equipped.

Whole Will Be Completed For Use in the Spring.

The Boston subway is open for public travel; underground transit is no longer a dream in the hub.

Before the readers of The Globe, or at least the majority of them open their morning paper today, the hum of the electrics will have turned the underground railroad into a scene of human activity wholly new to the busy life of Boston.

Two and a half years of patient waiting on the part of the public will have been partially rewarded, and blockades on Tremont st will probably have been made a thing of the past.

Before 9 some thousands of people will undoubtedly have entered the underground system in the public garden, be whirled along at a rate of speed which they have never experienced in the same locality before, and projected out of the earth at the Park st exit of the subway.

The work which was begun on March 28, 1895, will have brought forth fruit so far as one-third of the subway enterprise is concerned.

Chairman Crocker of the transit commission, who turned the first sod of earth for the subway, is still in active work on the great project.

Jones & Meehan, who built the first section, from the entrance at the public garden to Tremont st, and for a distance of several hundred feet on Tremont st, are still alive.

But Gov Greenhalge, whose interest in the subway project was deep and abiding, is no longer alive to witness the first fruits of the great work to which he gave his approval.

Allston Car First.

The first car was timed to reach the entrance to the subway a few seconds before 6 this morning, from Allston. It is due at Park st daily at 6.01, coming in by way of Pearl st, Cambridge, and the Harvard bridge.

The distinction of having charge of the first car thus fell, by accident, or right of early rising, to James Reed, motorman 9032, and George Trufant, conductor

Continued on the Seventh Page.

HEATED MEETING.

Brown Corporation Will Assemble Today.

Rumor That Pres Andrews Will be Dismissed.

Entirely New Reason May be Alleged.

Committee Report Couched in No Uncertain Words.

President, Too, May "Cry Aloud and Spare Not."

PROVIDENCE, Aug 31—Tomorrow, according to those who are most familiar with the subject, the corporation of Brown university will accept the resignation of Dr E. Benjamin Andrews, the president, who feels that the corporation has unduly interfered with his reasonable liberty of utterance.

One of the professors in the university, presumably Prof Appleton, will be designated as acting president until the corporation can find another president more in touch with the views of the board of fellows and the trustees of the university.

The Globe correspondent understands from the best of authority that the method of procedure and the result of tomorrow's deliberations may be stated as follows. The corporation will be called to order at 10 a m by Pres Andrews.

Petitions of various classes of alumni, of many hundreds of graduates who signed the big alumni petition recently circulated, of the alumnæ and the leaders of thought throughout the country will be presented, praying that Dr Andrews' resignation be not accepted, or that he be asked to withdraw it.

The special committee appointed by the corporation at its last meeting to wait on Dr Andrews will then make a red-hot report. This committee consists of Hon Francis Wayland, LL D; Hon Thomas Durfee, LL D, and Chancellor William Goddard, who is now in Europe.

The committee members will relate at length the details of its meeting with Dr Andrews, the arguments they advanced and which he answered, and will utterly refute the contention that it proposed to Dr Andrews the curtailment of his "reasonable liberty of utterance." It is said that this report will throw a flashlight on the situation, and put an entirely new face on Dr Andrews' resignation and the cause of it.

Then the corporation will name a committee to consider and report upon the resignation, and to make recommendations, and while this committee is deliberating the corporation will take a recess of several hours. It is not probable that the entire body will assemble until late in the afternoon, when the special committee will report.

It is believed that this report has already been prepared. It will recommend that Dr Andrews' resignation be accepted, but not on the ground that a "reasonable liberty of utterance" has been denied him. It will declare, it is said, that the best interests of the university require a severance of the ties existing between it and its president, and give in firm language the reasons for it.

It is calculated that this report will set the corporation and the university right before all sensible people, and disabuse their minds of the idea that Dr Andrews has been persecuted or denied any rights to which he could justly lay claim. This report, it is certain, will have the support of nine-tenths of the corporation, and will be adopted by their votes.

"The corporation cannot retreat," the writer's informant said. "It will not accept Dr Andrews' resignation on the grounds he alleges, it will not permit him to withdraw the resignation, but it will dismiss him in a way he does not expect and which the civilized world will approve." How much truth there is in this statement tomorrow's meeting will reveal.

Today the advisory executive committee was called together by Pres Andrews and his resignation was discussed. The committee consists of Pres E. Benjamin Andrews, Hon Thomas Durfee, Hon Rowland G. Hazard, Rev Thomas D. Anderson, Hon Arnold B. Chace, Hon Oscar Lapham and Hon John Carter Brown Woods, Robert I. Gammell,

Continued on the Sixth Page.

What Custom-House Statistics Show.

The custom-house statistics show that for the fiscal year ending July 1st about one-half of all the fine CARPETINGS and ORIENTAL RUGS brought into the port of Boston was imported by JOHN H. PRAY, SONS & CO. That is to say, Messrs. JOHN H. PRAY, SONS & CO.'S importations were equal in value and quantity to that of all the other dealers in this class of goods in Boston combined.

THE WEATHER.

WASHINGTON, Aug 31—Forecast for Wednesday: For New England, generally fair, southwesterly winds. For eastern New York, fair, westerly winds.

Local forecast—Fair weather, westerly winds.

The temperature yesterday, as indicated by the thermometer at Thompson's spa: 3 a m 68°, 6 a m 66°, 9 a m 70°, 12 m 75°, 3 p m 77°, 6 p m 74°, 9 p m 70°, 12 m 68°; average temperature yesterday 70 3-21°.

FINE

The weather Thursday—Fair and generally clear weather will continue through Thursday and probably fair Friday, though with more cloudiness. The temperature will probably change but little during the next two or three days.

FIRST GAME A TIE.

Eleven Innings at South End Grounds And the Score 8--8.

ANSON VERY MUCH IN THE GAME.

YESTERDAY'S LEAGUE GAMES.

	Attendance
Boston 8, Chicago 8, 11 innings, darkness	5,300
Baltimore 12, St Louis 5	1,960
New York 7, Cincinnati 6, first game	11,000
New York 9, Cincinnati 1, second game	
Brooklyn 9, Cleveland 1	1,391
Washington 8, Pittsburg 4	2,300
Philadelphia 5, Louisville 4	1,912

National League Standing.

	Won	Lost	Pc won
Baltimore	72	32	.692
Boston	74	34	.685
New York	66	38	.635
Cincinnati	62	42	.598
Cleveland	54	50	.519
Chicago	50	58	.463
Philadelphia	48	61	.440
Louisville	48	61	.440
Pittsburg	46	59	.428
Brooklyn	46	61	.430
Washington	45	60	.429
St Louis	26	81	.243

National League Games Today.

Chicago at Boston.
St Louis at Baltimore.
Cincinnati at New York.
Cleveland at Brooklyn.
Louisville at Philadelphia.
Pittsburg at Washington.

ROOTERS IN SUSPENSE.

After 11 Innings the Call on Account of Darkness Comes as Relief.

Capt Anson and his Chicago team were the attraction at the South end grounds yesterday. After playing 2¾ hours and 11 innings darkness cast a mantle over the field with the score tied at 8.

From a spectacular standpoint the game was a success, but from the standard of good clever ball playing there was much to find fault with. The Boston men were too anxious in many instances and lacked ginger just when the move called for business.

The visitors played an offhand brilliant game that caught the fancy of the crowd, and the three home runs off Klobedanz gave the home team more than it could take care of. The three home runs were responsible for five of the eight runs made by the colts, and forced the Boston men to play an uphill game.

The boys made a game stand, however, after the sixth, when every time up they found the visitors one or two runs to the good. It looked like one more of Boston's famous finishes in the ninth, when Stahl, Duffy and Lowe came with telling hits, but Bergen and Kloby were not equal to the emergency.

Herman Long was in the game for seven innings, and then gave way to Allen. It is doubtful if Long is seen for some time in harness again, as he has no control of his left hand and was forced to bat with one hand.

The features of the game were the fielding and hitting of Bobby Lowe, the hitting of Stahl and Hamilton and Tenney for the home team. For the colts

Continued on the Fourth Page.

BAD BURDEN LIFTED.

Judge Whitehouse Gravely Attests Mrs Roberts' Chastity.

THE ROBERTS TWINS, MARJORIE AND NATHALIE.
Five Years Old, for Custody of Whom Father and Mother Are Contending at Bath, Me.

BATH, Me, Aug 31—Of the many and dramatic situations that have marked from time to time the proceedings in the sensational Roberts-Patten case, the greatest of all was perhaps that of today.

The evidence for the defense, when near the noon hour, was announced as all in, and the court asked if there was to be any evidence in rebuttal.

"Yes, your honor," said attorney Whitehouse. "We intend to offer evidence strictly admissable, of a very private nature, and may it please the court, and if agreeable to the counsel on the other side, we ask that the testimony be in private, and that the court room be cleared."

Judge Whitehouse said the suggestion was a wise one and had he been informed in advance of the nature of yesterday's proceedings he would have had the court room cleared of spectators while the evidence was being taken.

The court room today held at the opening of the forenoon session the largest number of spectators seen there since the trial began and, as has been the rule, women were largely in the majority.

Following the remarks of the court the counsel in the case were called to the bench and asked by the court to join him in the ante room where there was a consultation bearing upon the new evidence that it had been proposed to offer as a part of this remarkable case.

The court returned in about 30 minutes and commanded the sheriff to clear the court room of every one present as a spectator. With apparent reluctance the large crowd vacated the room and the sheriff closed the doors.

Another conference of the court and counsel was held in the judge's private chamber.

The "private testimony" was not put in, and then it was whispered in the court room that Mr Patten and Mrs Roberts-Patten would be vindicated of the charge of criminal intimacy by a finding of the court to be given later.

The witnesses of the rebuttal were Mrs Roberts-Patten and her husband, Hon John O. Patten. The former took the stand. She said she heard the story

Continued on the Third Page.

WILL MOVE TO COLORADO.

Edward Bellamy's Health Requires a Higher Altitude Than the East.

CHICOPEE, Aug 31—Edward Bellamy, the noted author, with his family, will soon move from this city to Denver, Colo.

Mr Bellamy's health has been poor for some time.

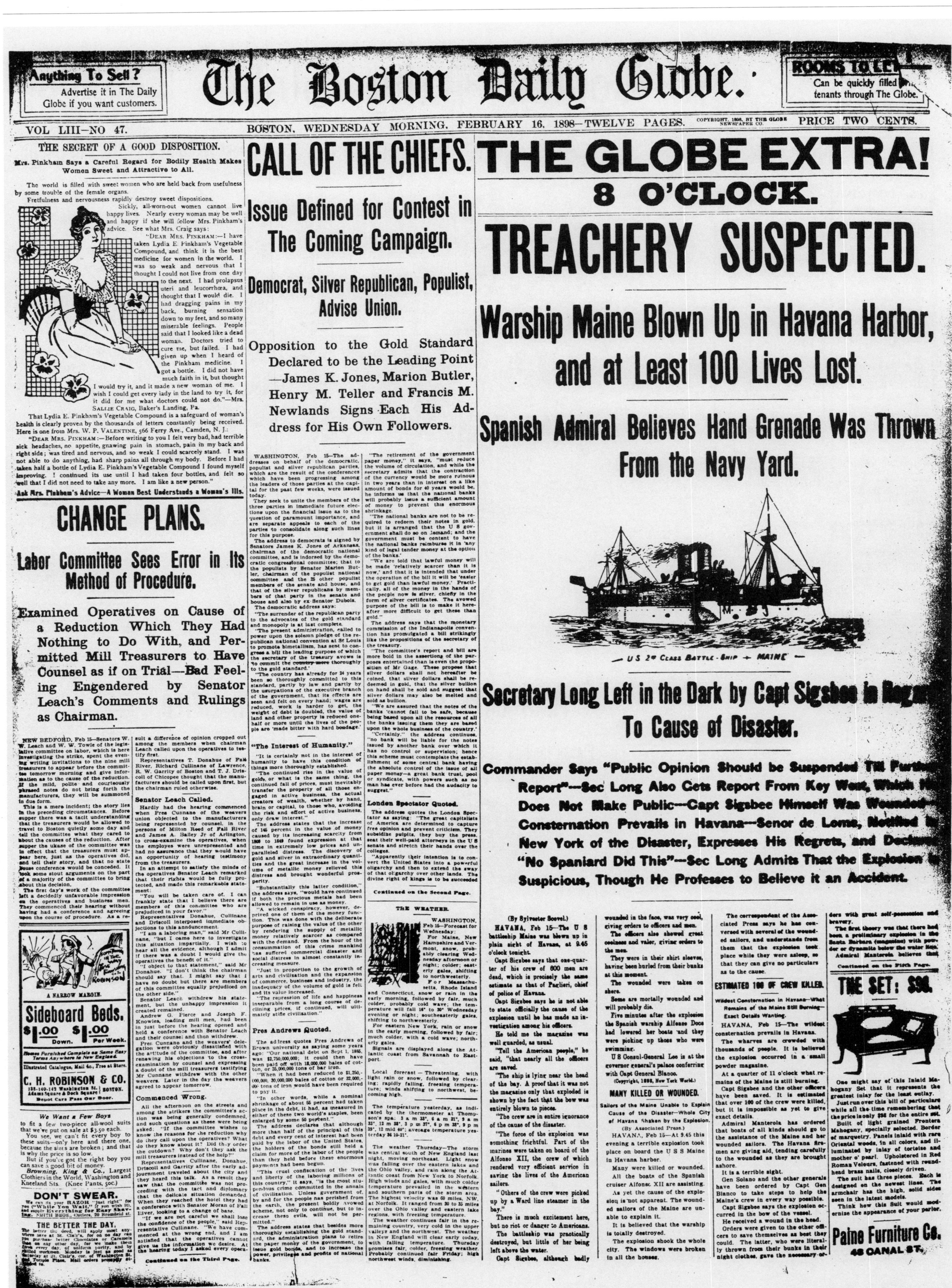

The Boston Daily Globe.

VOL LIII—NO 47. BOSTON, WEDNESDAY MORNING, FEBRUARY 16, 1898—TWELVE PAGES. COPYRIGHT, 1898, BY THE GLOBE NEWSPAPER CO. PRICE TWO CENTS.

CHANGE PLANS.

Labor Committee Sees Error in Its Method of Procedure.

Examined Operatives on Cause of a Reduction Which They Had Nothing to Do With, and Permitted Mill Treasurers to Have Counsel as if on Trial—Bad Feeling Engendered by Senator Leach's Comments and Rulings as Chairman.

NEW BEDFORD, Feb 15—Senators W. W. Leach and W. W. Towle of the legislative committee on labor, which is here investigating the strike, spent the evening writing invitations to the nine mill treasurers to appear before the committee tomorrow morning and give information as to the cause of the reduction. If the mild, polite and courteously phrased notes do not bring forth the manufacturers, they will be summoned in due form.

This is a mere incident; the story lies in the preceding circumstances. Before supper there was a tacit understanding that the treasurers would be allowed to travel to Boston quietly some day and tell the committee what they cared to about the causes of the reduction. After supper the ukase of the committee was in effect that the treasurers must appear here, just as the operatives did, and tell their story, and that no state house conference would be conceded. It took some stout arguments on the part of a majority of the committee to bring about this decision.

The first day's work of the committee left a decidedly unfavorable impression on the operatives and business men. They commenced their hearing without having had a conference and agreeing upon the course of procedure. As a result a difference of opinion cropped out among the members when chairman Leach called upon the operatives to testify first.

Representatives T. Donahue of Fall River, Richard Cullinane of Lawrence, R. W. Garrity of Boston and T. J. Driscoll of Chicopee thought that the manufacturers should be called upon first, but the chairman ruled otherwise.

Senator Leach Called.

Hardly had the hearing commenced when Pres Cunnane of the weavers union objected to the manufacturers being represented by counsel, in the persons of Milton Reed of Fall River and James A. Bailey Jr of Arlington, to cross-examine the operatives, when the operatives were unrepresented and had no assurance that they would have an opportunity of hearing testimony from the treasurers.

In an attempt to satisfy the minds of the operatives Senator Leach remarked that their rights would be fully protected, and made this remarkable statement:

"You will be taken care of. I can frankly state that I believe there are members of this committee who are prejudiced in your favor."

Representatives Donahue, Cullinane and Driscoll interposed immediate objections to this announcement.

"I am a laboring man," said Mr Cullinane, "but I came here to investigate this situation impartially. I wish to hear all the evidence, although I admit if there was a doubt I would give the operatives the benefit of it."

"I object to that statement," said Mr Donahue. "I don't think the chairman should say that. I might say that I have no doubt but there are members of this committee equally prejudiced on the other side."

Senator Leach withdrew his statement, but the unhappy impression it created remained.

Andrew G. Pierce and Joseph F. Knowles, leading mill men, had been in just before the hearing opened and held a conference with Senator Leach and their counsel and then withdrew.

Pres Cunnane and the weavers' delegation were obviously dissatisfied with the attitude of the committee, and after renewing his objections to the cross-examination by counsel and expressing a doubt of the mill treasurers testifying Mr Cunnane withdrew with the other weavers. Later in the day the weavers agreed to appear tomorrow.

Commenced Wrong.

All the afternoon on the streets and among the strikers the committee's action was being generally condemned, and such questions as these were being asked: "If the committee wishes to know the reasons for the reduction why do they call upon the operatives? What do they know about it? Did they order the cutdown? Why don't they ask the mill treasurers instead of the help?"

Representatives Cullinane, Donahue, Driscoll and Garrity after the early adjournment traveled about the city and they heard this talk. As a result they saw that the committee was not proceeding with the tact and diplomacy that the delicate situation demanded. When they reached the hotel they had a conference with Senator Moran of Fall River, looking to a change of base.

"If we are not careful we shall lose the confidence of the people," said Representative Cullinane. "We have commenced at the wrong end, and I am satisfied that the operatives cannot give us the information we desire. At the hearing today I asked every opera-

Continued on the Third Page.

CALL OF THE CHIEFS.

Issue Defined for Contest in The Coming Campaign.

Democrat, Silver Republican, Populist, Advise Union.

Opposition to the Gold Standard Declared to be the Leading Point—James K. Jones, Marion Butler, Henry M. Teller and Francis M. Newlands Signs Each His Address for His Own Followers.

WASHINGTON, Feb 15—The addresses on behalf of the democratic, populist and silver republican parties, which are the result of the conferences which have been progressing among the leaders of those parties at the capital for the past few weeks, were issued today.

They seek to unite the members of the three parties in immediate future elections upon the financial issue as to the question of paramount importance, and are separate appeals to each of the parties to consolidate along such lines for this purpose.

The address to democrats is signed by Senators James K. Jones of Arkansas, chairman of the democratic national committee, and is indorsed by the democratic congressional committee; that to the populists by Senator Marion Butler, chairman of the populist national committee and the 25 other populist members of the senate and house, and that of the silver republicans by members of that party in the senate and house and also by ex-Senator Dubois.

The democratic address says:

"The surrender of the republican party to the advocates of the gold standard and monopoly is at last complete.

"The present administration, called to power upon the solemn pledge of the republican national convention at St Louis to promote bimetallism, has sent to congress a bill the leading purpose of which the secretary of the treasury avows is 'to commit the country more thoroughly to the gold standard.'

"The country has already for 24 years been so thoroughly committed to this standard, partly by law and partly by the usurpations of the executive branch of the government, that its effects are seen and felt on every hand; wages are reduced, work is harder to get, the weight of debt is doubled, the value of land and other property is reduced one-half or more until the lives of the people are 'made bitter with hard bondage.'

"The Interest of Humanity."

"It is certainly not in the interest of humanity to have this condition of things more thoroughly established.

"The continued rise in the value of gold, or what is the same thing, the continued fall of prices, must inevitably transfer the property of all those engaged in active business, the actual creators of wealth, whether by hand, brain or capital, to those who, avoiding the risk and effort of active business, only draw interest."

The address states that the increase of 145 percent in the value of money caused by its increasing scarcity from 1808 to 1849 found expression at that time in extremely low prices and unparalleled distress. The discovery of gold and silver in extraordinary quantities and the great increase in the volume of metallic money relieved this distress and brought wonderful prosperity.

"Substantially this latter condition," the address says, "would have continued if both the precious metals had been allowed to remain in use as money.

"A wicked conspiracy, however, deprived one of them of the money function. This was done with the deliberate purpose of raising the value of the other by rendering the supply of metallic money relatively scarcer as compared with the demand. From the hour of the consummation of this crime mankind has suffered commercial disaster and social distress in almost constantly increasing measure.

"Just in proportion to the growth of arts and civilization and the expansion of commerce, business and industry, the inadequacy of the volume of gold is felt and its value increased.

"The repression of life and happiness inseparable from a long course of declining prices, if continued, will ultimately stifle civilization."

Pres Andrews Quoted.

The address quotes Pres Andrews of Brown university as saying some years ago: "Our national debt on Sept 1, 1865, was $2,750,000,000; it could then have been paid off with 18,000,000 bales of cotton, or 25,000,000 tons of bar iron.

"When it had been reduced to $1,250,000,000, 30,000,000 bales of cotton or 32,000,000 tons of iron would have been required to pay it.

"In other words, while a nominal shrinkage of about 55 percent had taken place in the debt, it had, as measured in either of these two world's staples, been enlarged by some 60 percent."

The address declares that although more than half of the principal of this debt and every cent of interest had been paid by the labor of the United States, the holders of the bonds still held a claim for more of the labor of the people than they held before these enormous payments had been begun.

"This cruel confiscation of the lives and liberty of the laboring millions of this country," it says, "is the most stupendous crime committed in the annals of civilization. Unless government of, by and for the people has perished from the earth, the present boldly avowed scheme, not only to continue, but to increase these evils, will not be permitted."

The address states that besides more thoroughly establishing the gold standard, the administration plans to retire the paper money of the government, to issue gold bonds, and to increase the power, privileges and profits of national banks.

"The retirement of the government paper money," it says, "must reduce the volume of circulation, and while the secretary admits that the contraction of the currency would be more ruinous in two years than in interest on a like amount of bonds for 40 years would be, he informs us that the national banks will probably issue a sufficient amount of money to prevent this enormous shrinkage.

"The national banks are not to be required to redeem their notes in gold, but it is arranged that the U S government shall do so on demand; and the government must be content to have the national banks reimburse it in 'any kind of legal tender money at the option of the banks.'

"We are told that lawful money will be made 'relatively scarcer than it is now,' and that it is intended that under the operation of the bill it will be 'easier to get gold than lawful money.' Practically, all of the money in the hands of the people now is silver, chiefly in the form of silver certificates. The avowed purpose of the bill is to make it hereafter more difficult to get these than gold."

The address says that the monetary commission of the Indianapolis convention has promulgated a bill strikingly like the propositions of the secretary of the treasury.

"The committee's report and bill are more bold in the assertions of the purposes entertained than is even the proposition of Mr Gage. These propose that silver dollars shall not hereafter be coined, that silver dollars shall be redeemed in gold, that the silver bullion on hand shall be sold and suggest that silver dollars may also be melted and sold as bullion.

"We are assured that the notes of the banks 'cannot fail to be safe, because being based upon all the resources of all the banks issuing them they are based upon the whole business of the country.'

"Certainly," the address continues, "no bank will be liable for the notes issued by another bank over which it has no control or supervision; hence this scheme must contemplate the establishment of some central bank having the absolute control of the issue of all paper money—a great bank trust, pool or syndicate, with powers such as no man has ever before had the audacity to suggest."

London Spectator Quoted.

The address quotes the London Spectator as saying: "The great capitalists of America are determined to capture free opinion and prevent criticism. They subsidize pulpits, they buy the press, seat their well-paid attorneys in the U S senate and stretch their hands over the colleges.

"Apparently their intention is to convert the United States into a powerful oligarchy and then to extend the sway of that oligarchy over other lands. The divine right of kings is to be succeeded

Continued on the Second Page.

THE WEATHER.

WASHINGTON, Feb 15—Forecast for Wednesday:

For Maine, New Hampshire and Vermont, snow, probably clearing Wednesday afternoon or night; colder; easterly gales, shifting to northwesterly.

For Massachusetts, Rhode Island and Connecticut, snow or rain in the early morning, followed by fair, much colder, probably cold wave; the temperature will fall 16° to 20° Wednesday evening or night; southeasterly gales, shifting to northwesterly.

For eastern New York, rain or snow in the early morning, followed by fair; much colder, with a cold wave; northerly gales.

Signals are displayed along the Atlantic coast from Savannah to Eastport.

Local forecast — Threatening, with light rain or snow, followed by clearing; rapidly falling, freezing temperature; winds shifting to northwest, becoming high.

The temperature yesterday, as indicated by the thermometer at Thompson's spa: 3 a m 33°, 6 a m 31°, 9 a m 33°, 12 m 38°, 3 p m 37°, 6 p m 38°, 9 p m 39°, 12 mid 40°; average temperature yesterday 36 10-21°.

The weather Thursday—The storm was central south of New England last night, moving northeast. Light snow was falling over the eastern lakes and the Ohio valley, and rain along the Atlantic coast from New York to Norfolk. High winds and gales, with much colder temperature prevailed in the western and southern parts of the storm area. The highest velocity was 60 miles, NW, at Norfolk. It ranged from 20 to 35 miles over the Ohio valley and eastern lake regions, with freezing temperature.

The weather continues fair in the remaining country, very cold in the upper valleys and the northwest. The weather in New England will clear early today, with falling temperature. Thursday promises fair, colder, freezing weather. Probably continued fair Friday; high northwest winds, diminishing.

THE GLOBE EXTRA!

8 O'CLOCK.

TREACHERY SUSPECTED.

Warship Maine Blown Up in Havana Harbor, and at Least 100 Lives Lost.

Spanish Admiral Believes Hand Grenade Was Thrown From the Navy Yard.

US 2ND CLASS BATTLE-SHIP MAINE

Secretary Long Left in the Dark by Capt Sigsbee in Regard To Cause of Disaster.

Commander Says "Public Opinion Should be Suspended Till Further Report"—Sec Long Also Gets Report From Key West, Which He Does Not Make Public—Capt Sigsbee Himself Was Wounded—Consternation Prevails in Havana—Senor de Lome, Notified in New York of the Disaster, Expresses His Regrets, and Declares "No Spaniard Did This"—Sec Long Admits That the Explosion is Suspicious, Though He Professes to Believe it an Accident.

(By Sylvester Scovel.)

HAVANA, Feb 15—The U S battleship Maine was blown up in plain sight of Havana, at 9.45 o'clock tonight.

Capt Sigsbee says that one-quarter of his crew of 600 men are dead, which is precisely the same estimate as that of Paglieri, chief of police of Havana.

Capt Sigsbee says he is not able to state officially the cause of the explosion until he has made an investigation among his officers.

He told me the magazine was well guarded, as usual.

"Tell the American people," he said, "that nearly all the officers are saved.

"The ship is lying near the head of the bay. A proof that it was not the magazine only that exploded is shown by the fact that the bow was entirely blown to pieces.

"The crew are in entire ignorance of the cause of the disaster.

"The force of the explosion was something frightful. Part of the marines were taken on board of the Alfonso XII, the crew of which rendered very efficient service in saving the lives of the American sailors.

"Others of the crew were picked up by a Ward line steamer in the bay."

There is much excitement here, but no riot or danger to Americans.

The battleship was practically destroyed, but little of her being left above the water.

Capt Sigsbee, although badly wounded in the face, was very cool, giving orders to officers and men.

The officers also showed great coolness and valor, giving orders to the men.

They were in their shirt sleeves, having been hurled from their bunks at this moment.

The wounded were taken on shore.

Some are mortally wounded and will probably die.

Five minutes after the explosion the Spanish warship Alfonso Doce had lowered her boats and they were picking up those who were swimming.

U S Consul-General Lee is at the governor general's palace conferring with Capt General Blanco.

(Copyright, 1898, New York World.)

MANY KILLED OR WOUNDED.

Sailors of the Maine Unable to Explain Cause of the Disaster—Whole City of Havana Shaken by the Explosion.

(By Associated Press.)

HAVANA, Feb 15—At 9.45 this evening a terrible explosion took place on board the U S S Maine in Havana harbor.

Many were killed or wounded.

All the boats of the Spanish cruiser Alfonso XII are assisting.

As yet the cause of the explosion is not apparent. The wounded sailors of the Maine are unable to explain it.

It is believed that the warship is totally destroyed.

The explosion shook the whole city. The windows were broken in all the houses.

The correspondent of the Associated Press says he has conversed with several of the wounded sailors, and understands from them that the explosion took place while they were asleep, so that they can give no particulars as to the cause.

ESTIMATED 100 OF CREW KILLED.

Wildest Consternation in Havana—What Remains of the Maine Still Burning—Exact Details Wanting.

HAVANA, Feb 15—The wildest consternation prevails in Havana.

The wharves are crowded with thousands of people. It is believed the explosion occurred in a small powder magazine.

At a quarter of 11 o'clock what remains of the Maine is still burning.

Capt Sigsbee and the other officers have been saved. It is estimated that over 100 of the crew were killed, but it is impossible as yet to give exact details.

Admiral Manterola has ordered that boats of all kinds should go to the assistance of the Maine and her wounded sailors. The Havana firemen are giving aid, tending carefully to the wounded as they are brought ashore.

It is a terrible sight.

Gen Solano and the other generals have been ordered by Capt Gen Blanco to take steps to help the Maine's crew in every way possible.

Capt Sigsbee says the explosion occurred in the bow of the vessel.

He received a wound in the head.

Orders were given to the other officers to save themselves as best they could. The latter, who were literally thrown from their bunks in their night clothes, gave the necessary orders with great self-possession and bravery.

The first theory was that there had been a preliminary explosion in the Santa Barbara (magazine) with powder or dynamite below the water line.

Admiral Manterola believes that

Continued on the Fifth Page.

The Boston Daily Globe.

VOL. LIX NO. 22. BOSTON, TUESDAY EVENING, JANUARY 22, 1901—TWELVE PAGES. COPYRIGHT 1900, BY THE GLOBE NEWSPAPER CO. PRICE TWO CENTS.

THE GLOBE LATEST—7.30 P. M

QUEEN VICTORIA IS DEAD.

LATEST PICTURE OF VICTORIA

End Came Quietly at 1.45 p m, Boston Time, Children at Bedside.

LONDON, Jan 22—7:02 P M—A telegram from the prince of Wales to the lord mayor, timed at Osborne 6:45 p m (Boston time 1:45 p m) says:

OSBORNE, 6:45 P M—My beloved mother has just passed away, surrounded by her children and grandchildren.

Albert Edward.

COWES, Jan 22—The news from Osborne house at noon confirmed the belief of every one that the death of her majesty was imminent.

The weather is cold and rainy. Beyond the newspaper correspondents few persons were about the gate of the royal residence.

Mounted messengers from Osborne rode through Cowes at intervals, at breakneck speed, sending off the latest tidings to officials and foreign courts.

The rector of Whippingham church remained at Osborne throughout the morning.

None of the royal personages went driving or walking.

LONDON, Jan 22—A bulletin posted at the Mansion house at 4:35 p m read as follows:

"Osborne, 4 p m—My painful duty obliges me to inform you that the life of our beloved queen is in the greatest danger.

"Albert Edward."

COWES, Isle of Wight, Jan 22—4 p m—The end is very near. The prince of Wales has not left the vicinity of the queen's bedroom since 9 a m. Emperor William and all the royal family are near her majesty's bedside.

With the members of the royal family gathered at the queen's bedside, the bishop of Winchester and the rector of Whippingham read prayers for those in extremis. Happily the queen was able to recognize those around her.

They came to her bedside, but the physicians had warned them against attempts to speak to her. Naturally the family, while recognizing the claim for public information, insist that the details of the events round the deathbed shall be sacred for the present, and imposed the strictest secrecy on the whole household.

The arrival of Lord Clarendon (the lord chamberlain), is considered ominous, because the arrangements for the succession to the throne will be in his hands.

QUEEN'S END WAS PAINLESS.

She Passed From Life as One Sinking Into Sleep—Great Solemnity and Gloom Fell Over London.

LONDON, Jan 22—6:55 p m (1:55 p m Boston time)—Queen Victoria is dead.

She died at the royal residence, Osborne house, Cowes, Isle of Wight, at 6:45 today.

Members of the royal family and household were at her bedside.

Death came to the aged sovereign in its gentlest form. She passed from life as one sinking to sleep [illegible]

Continued on [illegible]

GALE-SWEPT.

Three Days of Blizzards in Vineyard Sound.

Wreck-Strewn Shores and Frostbitten Seamen.

No Human Beings Lost, Owing to Bravery of Life-Savers—Sailors of Schooner George F. Davenport Have Fearful Experience.

WOODS HOLE, Jan 22—Wreck-strewn shores and frostbitten sailors tell the tale of the blizzards which swept the shores of Vineyard sound during the past three days.

No lives were sacrificed during the recent gale, owing to the great bravery of the life savers along the coast, but nearly every vessel that arrives in port brings additional evidence of the fury of the wind. All along the coast of cape Cod, from Highland light to the shores of Cuttyhunk, the life savers were called upon to render assistance to imperiled craft, and scattered along the shore, from Chatham to Nashawena, lie the bones of once stanch ships.

On Nashawena the big three-masted schooner George F. Davenport, lies among the rocks, with the seas breaking over her and grinding her to pieces.

On Kilpond bar, near Chatham, the schooner T. W. Allen is held fast in the grasp of the shoals that stretch out under the sea there, while further along on Harding's beach is the big three-masted schooner Eleeta Bailey, which was driven ashore during the blow of Sunday last.

There is practically no hope of saving the Bailey, as she is an old vessel. A considerable quantity of ice was sweeping down toward her this forenoon and it was expected she would be knocked to pieces. The crew is still at Chatham life-saving station. The two who were badly frostbitten Sunday night, Liperton and Scott, were attended by a physician today. Their faces and hands are in bad condition and they probably will be obliged to stay here several days.

The owner of the schooner is expected to arrive today to see if it is possible to save the vessel.

The Davenport is ashore near the spot where the steamer Admiral Dewey and the big Clyde line steamer Cherokee narrowly escaped annihilation. The weather conditions according to the statement of the captain of the Davenport were almost identical to those which existed at the time the Dewey struck there. The shores were snow-clad and a thick mist hung over the water, rendering it almost impossible to see a ship's length ahead.

A strong current sets in in the sound at the entrance between Gay Head on one side and Cuttyhunk on the other, and the Davenport was swept to her destruction. There is absolutely no hope of saving her, the decks being already washed out. The sea along the sound shore this morning is still running riot and the wreckage from the ill-fated craft is being scattered all along the coast between here and Cuttyhunk, a distance of nearly a dozen miles.

The crew of the Davenport reached here today by boat from Vineyard Haven, where they were taken yesterday on the tug Storm King. They are on their way to Boston.

They speak in the highest terms of the kindly treatment of the life-savers and residents of Cuttyhunk, and also of those at the Vineyard.

The sailors bear evidence of the fearful experiences through which they passed during the time they were aboard the ship after she struck, and while they lost many of their personal effects, they are all thankful that they escaped with their lives.

"It was a fearful time for us all," said one of the sailors, "as we were being driven before the gale to what we know meant certain destruction for the ship, and what seemed sure death for us all.

"If we had struck without seeing the land the shock would not have been half as terrible as the suspense that we endured while the ship was plowing her way at a lightning rate through the breakers and on to the rocks. It was too late to work the ship off shore when we learned our position. The only thing that we could do was to stand by and take what was coming.

"The sea ran mountains high in the sound and several times on the trip ashore the boat was filled and came near swamping. Still the brave fellows kept to their oars, not seeming to mind it in the least. The life-savers confess that the task of taking us ashore was most difficult and attended with greater risk then has ever before been their experience."

The schooner Silver Spray was another vessel that narrowly escaped going down on the shoals. Capt Eldredge and his crew put out to the imperiled craft, as she was being driven on to the rips on Bearses shoal, and assisted the benumbed crew to make repairs and to get the vessel underway. The schooner was badly iced up, her sails torn, and her men suffering great agony from frostbites. The schooner when last seen was proceeding to an anchorage at the Vineyard. The Silver Spray has a cargo of granite from Blue Hills, Me, and is on her way to Brooklyn, N Y.

The schooner Lizzie Cochrane also came dangerously near being driven on to the shoals, and, were it not for the timely assistance of Capt Eldredge and his crew, it is likely that she would have never weathered the gale.

The schooner, after being assisted, got underway and with shortened sail also proceeded on her way.

Continued on the Twelfth Page.

STARTED FOR UTRECHT.

Mr Kruger Says He is in Very Good Health.

THE HAGUE, Jan 22—Mr Kruger has started for Utrecht, where he will pass some weeks. He was greeted by a crowd at the railroad [illegible] very well on coming out for the first time since his recent illness.

No Choice of Senator in Utah.

SALT LAKE, Utah, Jan 22—The republican senatorial caucus met last night and took 19 ballots without making a nomination.

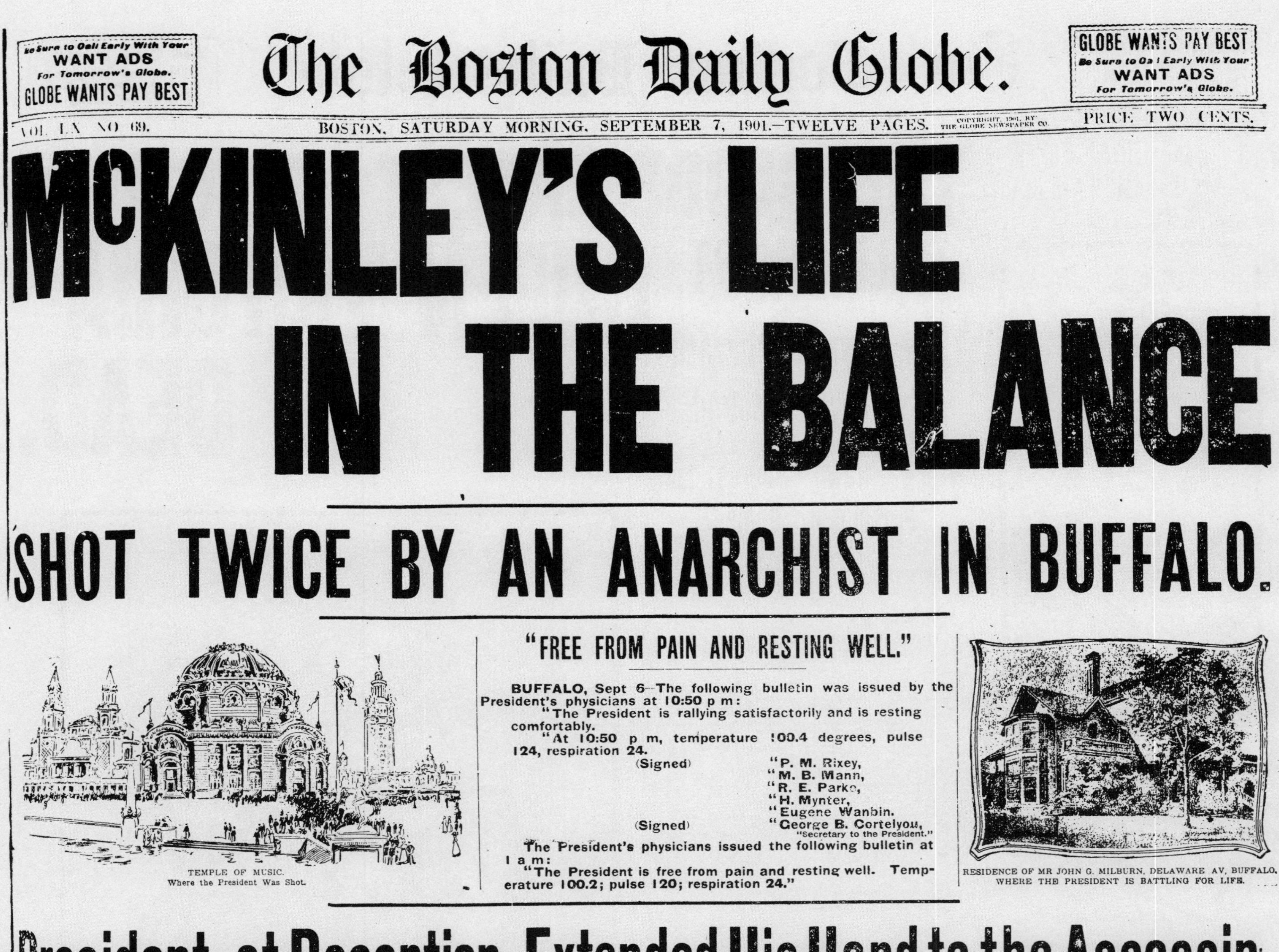

The Boston Daily Globe.

VOL LX NO 69. BOSTON, SATURDAY MORNING, SEPTEMBER 7, 1901.—TWELVE PAGES. COPYRIGHT, 1901, BY THE GLOBE NEWSPAPER CO. PRICE TWO CENTS.

McKINLEY'S LIFE IN THE BALANCE

SHOT TWICE BY AN ANARCHIST IN BUFFALO.

TEMPLE OF MUSIC.
Where the President Was Shot.

"FREE FROM PAIN AND RESTING WELL."

BUFFALO, Sept 6—The following bulletin was issued by the President's physicians at 10:50 p m:

"The President is rallying satisfactorily and is resting comfortably.

"At 10:50 p m, temperature 100.4 degrees, pulse 124, respiration 24.

(Signed) "P. M. Rixey,
"M. B. Mann,
"R. E. Parke,
"H. Mynter,
"Eugene Wanbin.

(Signed) "George B. Cortelyou,
"Secretary to the President."

The President's physicians issued the following bulletin at 1 a m:

"The President is free from pain and resting well. Temperature 100.2; pulse 120; respiration 24."

RESIDENCE OF MR JOHN G. MILBURN, DELAWARE AV, BUFFALO, WHERE THE PRESIDENT IS BATTLING FOR LIFE.

President, at Reception, Extended His Hand to the Assassin, Who Fired Handkerchief-Covered Revolver.

BUFFALO, Sept 6—President McKinley was shot at 4:12 o'clock this afternoon while holding a reception in the Temple of Music at the Pan-American Exposition.

He was approached by Leon Czolgosso, a Pole, an anarchist from Cleveland, O, his hand swathed in a handkerchief hiding from view the 32-caliber revolver he carried.

The President reached out to shake hands and was shot twice. One bullet struck the breastbone and glanced off. The other pierced the stomach, going through into the back. Efforts to remove this bullet were unsuccessful. The President was removed to the home of Pres Milburn of the Pan-American association.

The assailant was overpowered, disarmed and locked up. Mrs McKinley received the news with great courage.

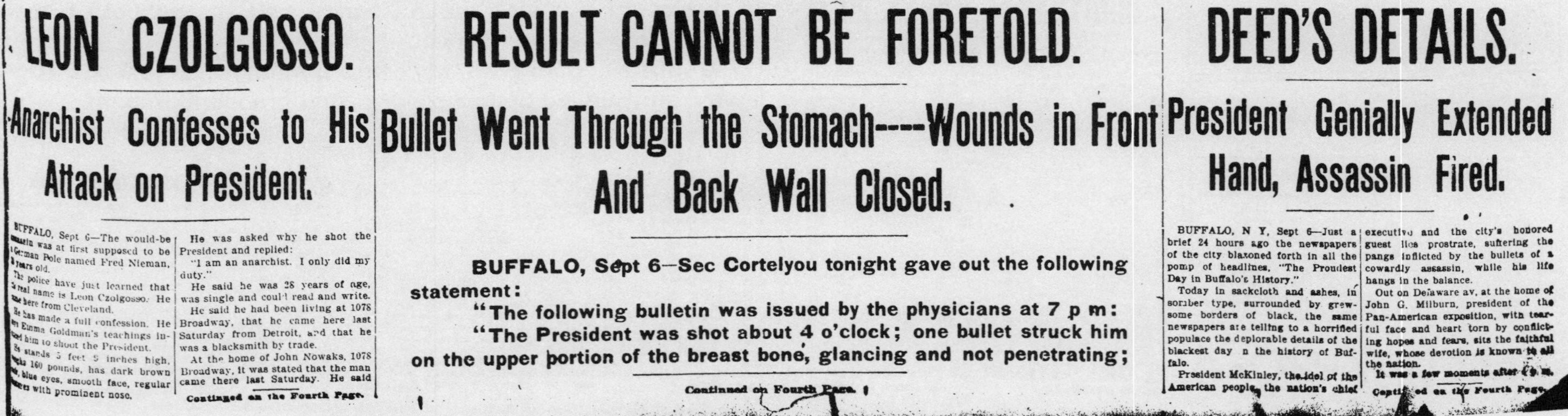

LEON CZOLGOSSO.

Anarchist Confesses to His Attack on President.

BUFFALO, Sept 6—The would-be assassin was at first supposed to be a German Pole named Fred Nieman, 28 years old.

The police have just learned that his real name is Leon Czolgosso. He came here from Cleveland.

He has made a full confession. He says Emma Goldman's teachings inspired him to shoot the President.

He stands 5 feet 9 inches high, weighs 160 pounds, has dark brown hair, blue eyes, smooth face, regular features with prominent nose.

He was asked why he shot the President and replied:

"I am an anarchist. I only did my duty."

He said he was 28 years of age, was single and could read and write.

He said he had been living at 1078 Broadway, that he came here last Saturday from Detroit, and that he was a blacksmith by trade.

At the home of John Nowaks, 1078 Broadway, it was stated that the man came there last Saturday. He said

Continued on the Fourth Page.

RESULT CANNOT BE FORETOLD.

Bullet Went Through the Stomach---Wounds in Front And Back Wall Closed.

BUFFALO, Sept 6—Sec Cortelyou tonight gave out the following statement:

"The following bulletin was issued by the physicians at 7 p m:

"The President was shot about 4 o'clock; one bullet struck him on the upper portion of the breast bone, glancing and not penetrating;

Continued on Fourth Page.

DEED'S DETAILS.

President Genially Extended Hand, Assassin Fired.

BUFFALO, N Y, Sept 6—Just a brief 24 hours ago the newspapers of the city blazoned forth in all the pomp of headlines, "The Proudest Day in Buffalo's History."

Today in sackcloth and ashes, in somber type, surrounded by grewsome borders of black, the same newspapers are telling to a horrified populace the deplorable details of the blackest day in the history of Buffalo.

President McKinley, the idol of the American people, the nation's chief executive and the city's honored guest lies prostrate, suffering the pangs inflicted by the bullets of a cowardly assassin, while his life hangs in the balance.

Out on Delaware av, at the home of John G. Milburn, president of the Pan-American exposition, with tearful face and heart torn by conflicting hopes and fears, sits the faithful wife, whose devotion is known to all the nation.

It was a few moments after 4 p m.

Continued on the Fourth Page.

More Help Wanted?
Apartments For Rent?

The Boston Daily Globe.

Real Estate For Sale?
Business For Sale?
Advertise in the Globe.
Globe Ads Pay Best.

VOL LXIX NO 108. BOSTON. WEDNESDAY EVENING. APRIL 18. 1906—SIXTEEN PAGES. COPYRIGHT 1906 BY THE GLOBE NEWSPAPER CO. PRICE TWO CENTS.

GLOBE LATEST—7:30 P M

GREAT FIRE AFTER EARTHQUAKE

Shock Did Vast Damage and Killed Hundreds in Cheaper Hotels of San Francisco.

LOOKING UP CALIFORNIA ST, SAN FRANCISCO.
The Cable Line Extending Up "Nob Hill," to the Residences of the Wealthier Classes.

Few Lives Were Lost in Residence Part.

Valencia Hotel and Kingsley Worst.

About 75 Persons Killed in Each of Them.

Conflagration Sweeping Through Market St and Water Front.

Only Way of Stopping Flames is By Dynamiting, Water Mains Having Been Broken.

SAN FRANCISCO, April 18, 8 a m—In the confusion which reigns everywhere it is almost impossible to learn details of the disaster caused by the earthquake this morning. It may be said that the district lying between Market and Howard sts from the bay, as far west as the City hall, has been badly wrecked.

The hotels in the vicinity of 3d and Market sts were badly shaken up, but there seems to have been no loss of life.

The Call and Examiner buildings as well as the Western Union building have been badly wrecked. The large department stores in this neighborhood were also ruined, but the earthquake occurred at an hour when they were empty and no loss of life is reported.

Farther east on Market st, toward the ferry slips is a section occupied by cheap lodging houses and hotels, and here the loss of life is reported to be very great, though the extent of it could not be ascertained at this hour.

Fires are burning in a number of places along Market st and the water mains having burst, the authorities have resorted to dynamite to check the progress of the flames.

The residence section of the city, while badly shaken, reports no loss of life or serious damage.

8.30 A M—As reports come in the magnitude of the disaster grows. Fires are raging in all directions and people moving out of the downtown section. The loss of life may reach into the hundreds. Millions of dollars' worth of property has been destroyed.

The Valencia hotel, between 17th and 18th sts, on Valencia st, a five-story frame building, toppled into the street, burying 75 people, only the top story remaining intact.

A house on 14th st was wrecked, killing two people.

Many of the fire houses are damaged so badly that it is impossible to get the fire apparatus out. A lodging house on 7th st, known as the Kingsley, entirely collapsed. It is on fire, and 75 to 80 people are believed to be buried in the flaming ruins.

At 22d and Mission sts, the dry goods store of Lipman, is on fire, threatening the destruction of the entire block. At 18th and Valencia sts there is a crevice in the street six feet wide, and entire sidewalks are torn up. The street car tracks are badly twisted.

In the southern section of the city traffic is at a standstill.

At the Southern Pacific hotel water is being carried into the building for the use of the patients. Many injured persons are making their way to the hospitals.

The Episcopal church, on 11th st, is badly damaged, and at the Studebaker carriage factory, on 10th and Market sts, the top story caved in, badly wrecking the entire building.

At 8:15 a m there had just been another shock with intensified panic. People started to rush into the streets, but the shock was of short duration and alarm subsided.

Palace Hotel is Vacated by Guests.

The fire, which has been raging in the vicinity of 4th and Stevenson sts, has got beyond control and the flames have leaped to the Winchester rooming house on 3d st. Unless the flames can be checked here the Palace hotel, one block distant, will be endangered.

The water supply is inadequate and powder is being used to check the flames.

The rooms in the Palace hotel were vacated early in the morning, and guests are gathering up their effects. All sorts of vehicles are being used to carry out of the danger zone everything of value.

The loss of life seems to have been confined to the poorer districts and manufacturing territory. For the benefit of eastern people who have friends visiting here, it is safe to say that they have not been injured.

Every few minutes explosions are heard as buildings are blown up to stop the progress of the flames. The fires are spreading, and if the wind comes up San Francisco will experience the greatest conflagration of modern times. On lower Market st, the main thoroughfare of the city, many blocks of substantial buildings have been destroyed.

A big fire is raging on the corner of Sansome and Pine sts, one block from the Associated Press office.

The wildest rumors as to loss of life are coming to the newspapers, but it is impossible to confirm them.

No reports have been received outside of San Francisco, but the damage about the bay must be enormous. Oakland is said to have suffered severely.

Fires Raging on Whole Water Front.

A fire, which broke out in the building of the Mack wholesale drug company, in Fremont st threatened at 8:30 a m, to destroy the entire block. Practically the entire water front is on fire. From Pine and Dupont sts fires can be seen raging in all down-town districts. A brisk westerly wind is coming up and the destruction of the entire business district is threatened.

The hall of justice is momentarilly expected to fall.

The city hall is almost an entire wreck. The damage here is estimated at $500,000.

The Mechanics pavilion has been converted into an emergency hospital. The Grand Opera house has been much damaged.

At 9:15 the fire in the vicinity of the Palace and Grand hotels was rapidly approaching the buildings, and from present indications they will fall a prey to the flames within half an hour. The Examiner and Call buildings are also in imminent danger.

The Santa Fe roundhouse and machine shops, at Point Richmond, across the bay, have collapsed.

Fire Advancing Down Market St.

The fire at 9:30 a m was coming down Market st, and was less than one block from the Postal telegraph building, No. 534. The Palace and Grand hotels were in great danger from fire.

The Postal telegraph company and Commercial cable company will open a temporary office at Oakland as soon as a boat can be procured to carry the operators across the bay.

At 10:15 a m, coast time, the fire extended from Ferry st to Front st on one side, and pretty near all south of Market st and out to about 7th st, with sporadic fires in the park section and the western division. There is no way of estimating the number of the dead.

The Postal telegraph operators, who are at their posts, are taking their lives in their hands, as the building is collapsing, and the fire within half a block. The Call and Examiner buildings are liable to go at any moment.

Flames Threaten Entire City.

The fires are spreading rapidly, and unless the wind comes up from the west and blows the flames toward the bay, nothing can stop the destruction of the city.

The whole north end of the city is wrecked, and the flames are spreading in all directions. In the absence of water the fire department has resorted to the use of dynamite, and buildings are being demolished in the hope of staying the conflagration.

The block bounded by Sansome, California, Pine and Battery sts, is

Continued on the Second Page.

SCENE ON MARKET ST, SAN FRANCISCO,
One of the Borders of the Area Most Badly Damaged by the Earthquake—The Fountain in the Foreground is the Gift of Lotta, the Boston Actress. The Postal Telegraph Office is Opposite the Farther End of the Palace Hotel.

THE WEATHER.

U S weather bureau forecasts:

For Boston and its vicinity: Fair weather tonight and Thursday; light, variable wind.

For New England: Fair tonight and Thursday, fresh, variable wind, shifting to southerly.

Eastern New York: Fair tonight, warmer in the interior; Thursday fair; wind becoming south and fresh.

Fair and generally clear weather continues to prevail over the Rocky mountains and eastern portion of the country, with little change in the general conditions since yesterday morning.

The temperature is generally higher. At 8 a m, in New England, it ranged between 40 and 50. At New York it was 54, Washington 56, Atlanta 56, Jacksonville 60, New Orleans 62, St Louis 52, Chicago 52, St Paul 56, Bismarck 50, Omaha 56, Denver 44.

Observations in Boston at 8 a m: Barometer 30.26, temperature 52, maximum temperature 58, minimum temperature 46, humidity 47 percent, clear; wind north, eight miles an hour.

The Temperature Today.

The thermometer at Thompson's spa records the temperature up to 3 p m as follows:

	1905	[illegible]
3 a m	35	[illegible]
6 a m	35	48
9 a m	41	54
12 m	48	60
1 p m	49	57
2 p m	49	58
3 p m	50	58

Cobb, Bates & Yerxa Co

Good Things at the Right Prices

CORN

	Can.	Doz.
ELITE brand, country gentleman variety; very small kernel, packed in N. Y. State by the Oneida Community	13c	1.50
HONEY DROP, long known as the finest corn packed in Maine	12c	1.40
FAMILY PRIDE, a very fine, tender corn, packed in Maine	10c	1.15
TIP TOP, fancy Indiana packed	9c	1.00
GARNET, a good Indiana	7c	80c
Western or Southern standard quality	6c	70c

Price List Mailed upon Application

Cobb, Bates & Yerxa Co
55 Summer St.
And at All Our Branches.

Made in New York

AQUAPROOF rain coats have the sanction of the best dressed men of New York.

Always designed and made in strictly the latest London and New York Fashion. They are the Raincoats of Quality.

Made exclusively by Alfred Benjamin & Co. in their tailor shops, a block from Broadway, a minute's walk from Fifth Avenue, from cloths proofed and shrunk by their own process, in striped effects, mixtures and solid plain colors.

Alfred Benjamin & Co MAKERS NEW YORK

Correct Clothes for Men

Exclusive Representatives Here

THE Wm. H. RICHARDSON Co.

388 Washington St. Near Franklin — We Occupy Entire Building—4 Floors.

Each Morsel a Surprise

Smooth, rich cream, refreshing fruits, fine selected nuts, velvety caramels, luxurious oriental nougat, and many other surprises hide beneath the thick, rich chocolate coat of

Trade Mark Necco Sweets New England Confectionery Co Boston

Lenox Chocolates

The realization of the ideal chocolate. The Seal of Necco Sweets is on each box of Lenox Chocolates and also on 499 other kinds of candies. This seal is your guide in buying confectionery—look for it and you will be sure of getting the best. You will find it on simple Tablets and Wafers—Chocolates and Bon Bons.

THE NEW ENGLAND CONFECTIONERY CO.,
Summer and Melcher Streets, Boston, Mass.

ELECTRICITY

Certainty of pressure, and therefore regularity of speed, are among the advantages gained by users of Electric Power who receive Electricity from the supply wires of this Company.

Have you learned to be power-wise?

Comparative costs are in favor of Electric Power, as shown by cases (selected at random) where it costs from $7 to $69 per horse-power per year. Our Contract Agent will show you if you'll write him, or call, or telephone Oxford 1150.

The Edison Electric Illuminating Company of Boston,
3 Head Place.

He Gained 16 Pounds.

"I gained 16 pounds in six weeks while taking Fr John's Medicine."—James B. Rice, Fairmount, W Va. Guaranteed.

Don't Neglect a Spring Cold. It's the germ from which Pneumonia Develops. Dr Hilton's Specific No. 3 kills a cold, absolutely PREVENTS pneumonia.

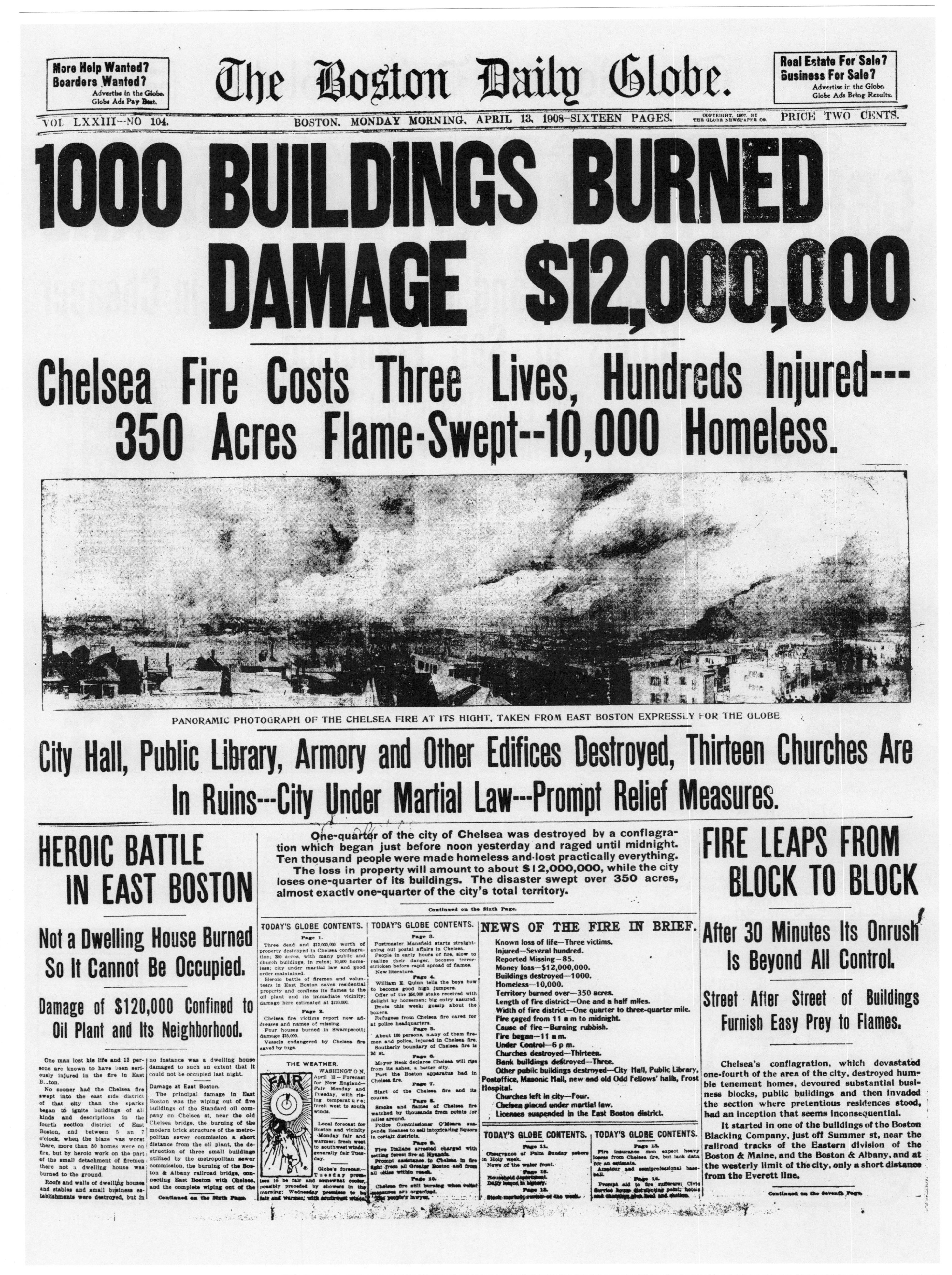

The Boston Daily Globe.

VOL LXXIII—NO 104. BOSTON, MONDAY MORNING, APRIL 13, 1908—SIXTEEN PAGES. COPYRIGHT, 1907, BY THE GLOBE NEWSPAPER CO. PRICE TWO CENTS.

1000 BUILDINGS BURNED DAMAGE $12,000,000

Chelsea Fire Costs Three Lives, Hundreds Injured---350 Acres Flame-Swept--10,000 Homeless.

PANORAMIC PHOTOGRAPH OF THE CHELSEA FIRE AT ITS HIGHT, TAKEN FROM EAST BOSTON EXPRESSLY FOR THE GLOBE.

City Hall, Public Library, Armory and Other Edifices Destroyed, Thirteen Churches Are In Ruins---City Under Martial Law---Prompt Relief Measures.

One-quarter of the city of Chelsea was destroyed by a conflagration which began just before noon yesterday and raged until midnight. Ten thousand people were made homeless and lost practically everything.

The loss in property will amount to about $12,000,000, while the city loses one-quarter of its buildings. The disaster swept over 350 acres, almost exactly one-quarter of the city's total territory.

Continued on the Sixth Page.

HEROIC BATTLE IN EAST BOSTON

Not a Dwelling House Burned So It Cannot Be Occupied.

Damage of $120,000 Confined to Oil Plant and Its Neighborhood.

One man lost his life and 13 persons are known to have been seriously injured in the fire in East Boston.

No sooner had the Chelsea fire swept into the east side district of that city than the sparks began to ignite buildings of all kinds and descriptions in the fourth section district of East Boston, and between 5 an 7 o'clock, when the blaze was worst there, more than 50 homes were on fire, but by heroic work on the part of the small detachment of firemen there not a dwelling house was burned to the ground.

Roofs and walls of dwelling houses and stables and small business establishments were destroyed, but in no instance was a dwelling house damaged to such an extent that it could not be occupied last night.

Damage at East Boston.

The principal damage in East Boston was the wiping out of five buildings of the Standard oil company on Chelsea st, near the old Chelsea bridge, the burning of the modern brick structure of the metropolitan sewer commission a short distance from the oil plant, the destruction of three small buildings utilized by the metropolitan sewer commission, the burning of the Boston & Albany railroad bridge, connecting East Boston with Chelsea, and the complete wiping out of the

Continued on the Sixth Page.

TODAY'S GLOBE CONTENTS.

Page 1.

Three dead and $12,000,000 worth of property destroyed in Chelsea conflagration; 350 acres, with many public and church buildings, in ruins; 10,000 homeless; city under martial law and good order maintained.

Heroic battle of firemen and volunteers in East Boston saves residential property and confines its flames to the oil plant and its immediate vicinity; damage here estimated at $120,000.

Page 2.

Chelsea fire victims report new addresses and names of missing.

Four houses burned in Swampscott; damage $15,000.

Vessels endangered by Chelsea fire saved by tugs.

THE WEATHER.

WASHINGTON, April 12—Forecast for New England—Fair Monday and Tuesday, with rising temperature; fresh west to south winds.

Local forecast for Boston and vicinity Monday fair and warmer; fresh west to southwest winds; generally fair Tuesday.

Globe's forecast—Tuesday promises to be fair and somewhat cooler, possibly preceded by showers in the morning; Wednesday promises to be fair and warmer, with southwest winds.

TODAY'S GLOBE CONTENTS.

Page 3.

Postmaster Mansfield starts straightening out postal affairs in Chelsea.

People in early hours of fire, slow to realize their danger, become terror-stricken before rapid spread of flames.

New literature.

Page 4.

William E. Quinn tells the boys how to become good high jumpers.

Offer of the $50,000 stake received with delight by horsemen; big entry assured.

Bouts this week; gossip about the boxers.

Refugees from Chelsea fire cared for at police headquarters.

Page 5.

About 100 persons, many of them firemen and police, injured in Chelsea fire.

Southerly boundary of Chelsea fire is 2d st.

Page 6.

Mayor Beck declares Chelsea will rise from its ashes, a better city.

Part the Boston apparatus had in Chelsea fire.

Page 7.

Start of the Chelsea fire and its course.

Page 8.

Smoke and flames of Chelsea fire watched by thousands from points for miles around.

Police Commissioner O'Meara suspends licenses to sell intoxicating liquors in certain districts.

Page 9.

Five Italians arrested charged with setting forest fire at Hyannis.

Prompt assistance to Chelsea in fire fight from all Greater Boston and from all cities within reach.

Page 10.

Chelsea fire still burning when relief measures are organized.

The people's lawyer.

NEWS OF THE FIRE IN BRIEF.

Known loss of life—Three victims.
Injured—Several hundred.
Reported Missing—85.
Money loss—$12,000,000.
Buildings destroyed—1000.
Homeless—10,000.
Territory burned over—350 acres.
Length of fire district—One and a half miles.
Width of fire district—One quarter to three-quarter mile.
Fire raged from 11 a m to midnight.
Cause of fire—Burning rubbish.
Fire began—11 a m.
Under Control—6 p m.
Churches destroyed—Thirteen.
Bank buildings destroyed—Three.
Other public buildings destroyed—City Hall, Public Library, Postoffice, Masonic Hall, new and old Odd Fellows' halls, Frost Hospital.
Churches left in city—Four.
Chelsea placed under martial law.
Licenses suspended in the East Boston district.

TODAY'S GLOBE CONTENTS.

Page 11.

Observance of Palm Sunday ushers in Holy week.

News of the water front.

Page 12.

Household department.

Daily lesson in history.

Page 13.

Stock market review of the week.

TODAY'S GLOBE CONTENTS.

Page 13.

Fire insurance men expect heavy losses from Chelsea fire, but lack data for an estimate.

Amateur and semiprofessional baseball.

Page 14.

Prompt aid to fire sufferers; Civic Service house distributing point; hotels and churches give food and shelter.

FIRE LEAPS FROM BLOCK TO BLOCK

After 30 Minutes Its Onrush Is Beyond All Control.

Street After Street of Buildings Furnish Easy Prey to Flames.

Chelsea's conflagration, which devastated one-fourth of the area of the city, destroyed humble tenement homes, devoured substantial business blocks, public buildings and then invaded the section where pretentious residences stood, had an inception that seems inconsequential.

It started in one of the buildings of the Boston Blacking Company, just off Summer st, near the railroad tracks of the Eastern division of the Boston & Maine, and the Boston & Albany, and at the westerly limit of the city, only a short distance from the Everett line.

Continued on the Seventh Page.

The Boston Daily Globe.

VOL LXXXI—NO 106. BOSTON. MONDAY MORNING. APRIL 15. 1912—SIXTEEN PAGES. COPYRIGHT, 1912, BY THE GLOBE NEWSPAPER CO. PRICE TWO CENTS.

GLOBE EXTRA!

TITANIC SINKING AT SEA AFTER CRASH WITH BERG

Steamers Racing for the Scene in Answer to "C.Q.D." by Wireless.

GIANT STEAMSHIP OLYMPIC, Sister Ship of the Titanic.

Women Take To Boats.

Carries 1300 Passengers.

Mr and Mrs John Jacob Astor, Maj Archie Butt, William T. Stead, Henry B. Harris, C. H. Hays Among Passengers.

CAPE RACE, N F, April 15—At 10:25 last night the steamship Titanic called "C. Q. D," and reported having struck an iceberg. The steamer said that immediate assistance was required.

Half an hour afterward another message came reporting that they were sinking by the head and that women were being put off in the life boats.

The weather was calm and clear, the Titanic's wireless operator reported, and gave the position of the vessel 41.46 North latitude and 50.14 West longitude.

The Marconi station at Cape Race notified the Allan liner Virginian, the captain of which immediately advised that he was proceeding for the scene of the disaster.

The Virginian at midnight was about 170 miles distant from the Titanic and expected to reach that vessel about 1 a m Monday.

The Olympic at an early hour Monday morning was in latitude 40.32 North and longtitude 61.18 West. She was in direct communication with the Titanic and is now making all haste toward her.

The steamship Baltic also reported herself as about 200 miles east of the Titanic and was making all possible speed toward her.

The last signals from the Titanic were heard by the Virginian at 12:27 a m. The wireless operator on the Virginian says these signals were blurred and ended abruptly.

NEWS BY WIRELESS.

Word Received in Montreal of the Mishap to the Titanic—Help on the Way to Her.

MONTREAL, April 14—The White Star Liner Titanic is reported in advices received here late tonight to have struck an iceberg.

The news was received at the Allan Line offices here in a wireless message from the captain of the steamer Virginian of that line.

It was stated that the Virginian had been in wireless communication with the Titanic, she had reported being in collision with an iceberg and asked for assistance.

The Virginian reported that she was on her way to the Titanic.

The Virginian sailed from Halifax this morning and at the time the wireless was sent she is reckoned to have been about abeam of Cape Race. She has 900 passengers on board, but can

Continued on the Fifth Page.

MAN FROM STOCKTON NOW WIDELY SOUGHT

Lynn Police Identify the Runabout Repeatedly Seen in Ireson Av.

PORTION OF IRESON AV, LYNN, Showing at Extreme Left Home of Dr Charles W. Bergengren, Who Saw the Mysterious Auto Standing on Several Occasions at Part Marked With a Cross. The Arrow Indicates Home of George E. Marsh.

California End of Marsh Family History May Have to Do With Murder Mystery.

LYNN, April 14—The Globe today came upon an entirely new set of facts which may have a bearing upon the murder of George E. Marsh, the wealthy soap manufacturer whose body was found on the marsh on Friday morning.

These facts were discovered while seeking more information about the mysterious man from Stockton, Calif, with whom the police wish to talk before making an arrest.

The Stockton man has disappeared and the police do not know his whereabouts. Three of the four inspectors who are working on the murder mystery have left Lynn to search for him, after covering the city itself and the surrounding towns very thoroughly.

They also wish to talk with the man who hung about the corner of Ireson av and Chatham st, according to Dr Charles W. Bergengren, at intervals for a week before Mr Marsh's death, and who has not been seen since Thursday. He is the man who had the runabout motor car. It is supposed that he was also the man who managed to persuade Mr Marsh to go with him in the car instead of going to his home on Thursday night.

Can Identify Car.

The police say that they know the number of the car, and know its history, having found the dealer who sold it. They do not, however, know its present whereabouts. Either it still carries its mysterious and unknown driver or he has disposed of it elsewhere.

He is said to be a man of about 35

Continued on the Fifth Page.

ROOSEVELT LEAD MORE

Pleased With Prospects.

Off on Tour of West Today.

Not Ready to Claim Nomination.

Will Have 65 if Not 67 Votes from Pennsylvania.

Penrose Organization is Badly Shattered.

PHILADELPHIA, April 14—Col Roosevelt's sweeping victory in Pennsylvania at Saturday's primary election kept growing today as the returns continued to come in.

Incomplete returns from every district give the ex-President 65 of the State's 76 delegates in the Republican National convention. The Roosevelt supporters are claiming 67 and later returns may carry the figures to that total.

Col Roosevelt won 53 of the 64 district National delegates and his followers elected enough delegates to the State convention to give them control of that body. The State convention will name 12 delegates-at-large.

Gov Woodrow Wilson of New Jersey, who had no organized opposition, will have 74 of the 76 delegates from Pennsylvania in the Democratic National Convention.

In the 28th Congressional District the two Democratic National delegates elected are favorable to Champ Clark.

Politicians look upon the triumph of Col Roosevelt with astonishment. The supporters of the ex-President were without a State organization and without an organization in many of the 32 Congressional districts.

Blow to Organization.

The regular Republican organization, headed by United States Senator Boies Penrose, which has weathered many a political storm, suffered a crushing defeat in the loss of control of the State convention. It is the first time in the present generation that it has lost control of that body.

Besides naming the 12 delegates at large to Chicago, the convention will select 38 Presidential electors, four candidates for Congressman at large and candidates for State Treasurer and Auditor General, all to be voted for at the November election.

The significance of the Roosevelt victory can be realized when it is remembered that the delegates in control of the State convention have the power to select the State chairman and under the party rules the delegation to the National convention elects the National

Continued on the Fourth Page.

BABY INNOCENT VICTIM.

Killed by Stone Hurled by a New York Boy During an Altercation With Foreigners.

NEW YORK, April 14—Frank C. Baker, a Queens Borough youth, during an altercation with a dozen foreigners near his home today, hurled a stone toward the group.

The stone struck the head of a baby, whose mother, with the boy in her arms, was passing. The baby's skull was fractured and it died within an hour.

Baker, after being rescued from an infuriated mob, which was beating him badly, was arrested and held on a charge of homicide.

READ THE ADVERTISEMENTS IN TODAY'S GLOBE.

T. JEFFERSON COOLIDGE JR DIES

End Comes in House at Manchester.

Well-Known Financier Had Been Ill Several Years.

Prominent in Business at Early Age.

MANCHESTER, Mass, April 14—T. Jefferson Coolidge Jr, the well-known banker and financier of Boston, died at his home here this morning after an illness of several years. For the past months he has had been gradually forced to give up the cares of business.

T. Jefferson Coolidge Jr was born in Boston, March 16, 1863, the son of T. Jefferson Coolidge, the manufacturer and former minister to France, and Hetty Sullivan (Appleton) Coolidge.

After a preparatory education at Noble's School he entered Harvard College, from which he was graduated in 1884. While a member of the freshman class in 1881 he won the intercollegiate half-mile championship. He was also president of his freshman class, secretary and vice president of the Hasty Pudding Club, and at one time manager of the Varsity ball nine.

After graduation he went abroad for a year and then spent a year each in the Harvard Graduate School and the Harvard Law School. In 1887 he went to work with the Bay State Trust Company and there found that in banking was his natural calling.

Started Old Colony Trust.

Three years later, when only 27 years old, he organized the Old Colony Trust Company and was made its first president. He continued to hold this office until 1903, when he resigned to become the chairman of the board of directors. Again, after the company's consolidation with the City Trust Company, he was made chairman of the executive committee.

By 1890 he had become a director of the Bay State Trust Company, and in 1904 he was made president of this company also. Since 1890, likewise, he had been vice president and director of the National Bank of Commerce, and he was a trustee of the Suffolk Savings Bank for Seamen and Others.

Continued on the Fifth Page.

WHITMAN TO WED MISS CROCKER

Ex-Tennis Champion the Groom-to-Be.

Bride Expectant Is Mistress of $10,000,000 Fortune.

She Is Famed as Athlete in Varied Sports.

NEW YORK, April 14—Miss Jennie Crocker, mistress of a fortune estimated at $10,000,000, will be married to Malcolm Douglas Whitman, former lawn tennis champion of America. The announcement was made today.

Miss Crocker's father was Col Frederick Crocker, a California pioneer, who came out of the days of '49 with great wealth. Miss Crocker was one of three children and received a third of her father's millions on her 18th anniversary, February, 1906.

Mr Whitman is a son of Mr and Mrs William Whitman of Brookline, Mass. He married Miss Janet McCook, a daughter of John J. McCook, in April, 1907, and Miss Crocker was a bridesmaid. Mrs Whitman died Dec 17, 1909, in her home, 115 East 60th st, a few days after the birth of a son.

Miss Crocker, whose elder sister, Mary, is Mrs Burton Harrison, is as well known in Newport, New York and the American colonies abroad as in San Francisco. Her prowess as an athlete and her beauty and vivacity are qualifications which have brought her into friendly rivalry with Miss Eleonora Sears.

Continued on the Fifth Page.

THE WEATHER.

RAIN

WASHINGTON, April 14—Forecast for New England: Showers Monday; warmer in interior Tuesday. Tuesday showers, brisk east to south winds.

For Eastern New York—Showers and warmer Monday; Tuesday showers, cooler by night; moderate to brisk east to south winds.

Local forecast for Boston and vicinity—Monday occasional showers; Tuesday continued unsettled, warmer, probably with showers; moderate and brisk east to south winds.

The Globe's forecast—Tuesday probably showers, warmer; Wednesday fair; brisk south to west winds.

TODAY'S GLOBE CONTENTS.

Page 1.
Lynn police turn attention to "man from Stockton" clew in the Marsh murder mystery.
Roosevelt will have at least 65 of the 76 delegates from Pennsylvania.
Liner Titanic, largest steamer afloat, runs into an iceberg on her maiden voyage and sends wireless call for help.
T. Jefferson Coolidge Jr dead.
Former tennis champion Whitman to marry Miss Jennie Crocker, a San Francisco heiress.
Page 2.
Dr Louis Nelson dies as result of bacteriological experiments.
Greater Boston telephone operators to demand wage increase.
Page 3.
Plans for the Episcopal Diocesan convention April 24.

Page 4.
School track athletics.
Amateur and semiprofessional ball teams arranging their schedules.
Congressman Gardner challenges Col Roosevelt to joint debate.
Chairman McKinley of Taft bureau, in statement on Pennsylvania primaries, says Roosevelt is conducting campaign of vilification and assault on President Taft.
Page 5.
Express train kills Miss Jessie Fowler.
Page 6.
Rockingham entry list a promise of more good sport this season; news for horsemen.
Schoolboy baseball games scheduled.
Clash in local boxing dates.
Page 7.
Red Sox in good trim to keep up the pace; Cicotte may be sent in against the Athletics today.
Detroit shuts out Cleveland and St Louis beats Chicago in the American League.
Live tips and topics.
News of the oarsmen.
Page 8.
American Academy of Arts and Sciences to open fine new building on Newbury st on May 1.
Page 9.
Man beaten and robbed on entrance steps of East Boston Tunnel.
Page 10.
"The War Day by Day 50 Years Ago."

Page 11.
Textile skies now generally fair, the only big cloud now being over Clinton.
Henri Brisson, president of French Chamber of Deputies, is dead.
Stories of the stage and chats with players.
"Wrong Use of Energy," by Ruth Cameron.
Page 12.
Household Department.
Daily Lesson in History.
Page 13.
Stock Market; review of the past week.
News from the Lake Superior copper mines.
Statistics of the Real Estate Trust stocks.
Page 14.
Standings in the bowling leagues.
News of the water front.
The mystic orders.
Page 16.
Mexican government and the rebels warned by the United States to protect Americans and other foreigners.

TWO BODIES IDENTIFIED.

The body of the man who was fatally injured last Thursday night by an electric car on Charlestown bridge was identified yesterday at the North Grove st morgue as that of Mark Carroll, aged 23, unmarried, of 29 Charles st, this city.

At the morgue yesterday morning the body of the young woman floating in the Charles River Basin Friday morning was identified as Mary Kupesenko, aged 18, of 640 Somerville av, Somerville. A brother of the girl said she had been in poor health for some time.

The Boston Daily Globe.

VOL LXXXV—NO 14. BOSTON, WEDNESDAY MORNING, JANUARY 14, 1914—EIGHTEEN PAGES. COPYRIGHT, 1913, BY THE GLOBE NEWSPAPER CO. PRICE TWO CENTS.

CURLEY WINS BY 5720 MAJORITY

Carries 16 Wards, Kenny 10--McDonald, Coleman And Woods Council Winners, Scannell and Corcoran For School Committee.

MAYOR-ELECT JAMES M. CURLEY AT HIS DESK.

MAYOR-ELECT CURLEY THANKS VOTERS AND SAYS HE WILL SERVE ENTIRE PEOPLE

Congressman James M. Curley gave out this statement last night:

"The result of the election is most gratifying and the responsibility attaching to the office tremendous. I am grateful to the electorate for the splendid tribute accorded, and shall do my utmost to merit the confidence reposed in me.

"My public platform I consider a binding, positive, concrete contract to so adminster the affairs of the municipality as to promote industry and add to the prosperity of the community.

"It is my purpose as Mayor to serve honorably, honestly and efficiently the entire people, and in this work I solicit the aid of every Bostonian"

Leaders With Kenny Fail To Hold Their Districts.

Total Vote 12,000 Less Than That Cast Four Years Ago.

Three Referendums Adopted--Big Majority For License.

VOTE FOR MAYOR.

James M. Curley	43,262
Thomas J. Kenny	37,542
Curley's Majority	5,720

With the temperature below zero 81,804 Boston voters went to the polls yesterday and by a majority of 5720 elected James M. Curley Mayor over Thomas J. Kenny, who was backed by the Citizens' Municipal League, the Good Government Association and the Republican City Committee.

There was a falling off of 12,000 from the vote of four years ago, when the contest for Mayor was between John F. Fitzgerald and James J. Storrow. Storrow had the support of the same organizations as Kenny. Fitzgerald had the backing of most of the Democratic ward chairmen four years ago.

Curley's Lone Fight.

Curley made practically a lone fight, with most of the 26 Democratic ward chairmen against him. He was supported by most of the Progressives, whose local leaders were bitterly opposed to the reform forces.

Curley had little, if any, newspaper support; but he made one of the most remarkable campaigns ever waged in this city, equal to if not surpassing the one made by Mayor Fitzgerald four years ago.

While Mayor Fitzgerald did not come out in the open, he was charged by Curley with secretly helping Kenny.

Curley Carries 16 Wards.

In percentage of total registration yesterday's vote was the smallest in many years. Four years ago 85 percent of the total was cast; in 1907 it was 80 percent; in 1905 it was 81 percent; in the Collins-Swallow campaign of 1903 it was 69.91 percent. Yesterday it was 72 percent.

The big vote of four years ago in the Storrow-Fitzgerald fight, the largest vote ever cast in a political campaign in this city, exceeding 93,000 for the two leading candidates, shrunk 14 percent. Yesterday Curley received almost 92 percent of the Fitzgerald vote of four years ago and Kenny got about 81 percent of the Storrow vote.

Curley carried every ward except 10, 11, 12, 15, 20, 21, 23, 24, 25 and 26, which went to Kenny. Kenny's own ward, 15, gave him a niggardly majority of 146, but Curley's ward, 17, rolled up a majority of more than 2000 for him.

VOTE ON LICENSE.

Yes	48,341
No	26,908
Majority,	21,433

VOTE FOR COUNCILORS

*McDonald	49,110
*Coleman	36,877
*Woods	34,306
Hagan	34,040
Kearns	30,707
Kneeland	27,946

*ELECTED.

VOTE FOR SCHOOL COMMITTEE

*Scannell	50,831
*Corcoran	44,855
Bogan	29,991
Keyes	21,961

*ELECTED.

Leaders Couldn't Deliver.

The Democratic leaders who were lined up with Kenny couldn't deliver their wards. City Clerk James Donovan worked hard to carry Ward 9 for Kenny, but failed by nearly 300 votes.

Mayor Fitzgerald's old home, Ward 6, flopped to Curley, and Senator Timilty's Ward 18 went over to the Curley column 400 strong. Ward 8 was in line for Curley.

Ward 26, Hyde Park, recently annexed to Boston, cast its first Mayoralty vote for the reform candidate by a decisive majority.

Kenny's main strength came from the Back Bay, Roxbury, Dorchester, West Roxbury and Brighton. Curley carried two of the three South Boston wards, Charlestown, East Boston

Continued on the Fifth Page.

FEAR LOSS OF 120 LIVES

Cobequid, Filling, Sends Last Cry For Help.

CROSS MARKS THE SPOT WHERE THE COBEQUID WAS REPORTED AGROUND.

Record Cold Brings Suffering In Boston and Vicinity.

Four Deaths, Many Accidents, 137 Cases in Hospitals Here.

ON THE LEDGES OF GRAND MANAN

HALIFAX, N S, Jan 13—A wireless cry for help from the Royal Mail steamer Cobequid, fast on the dreaded ledges of Grand Manan, just before dawn today, followed five hours later by a final flicker of her radio saying that the ship was filling, has caused grave concern for the 120 persons on board.

The Cobequid was bound for St John, N B, from the British West Indies, in command of Capt Hawson. She had a crew of 102 men, a number of second class passengers and the following in the first class cabin: L. S. Navarro, L. Botta, W. C. Zoller, Mrs Zoller and child.

The Cobequid was completing her

Continued on the Third Page.

BOSTON HIT BY SEVERE COLD

DEATH TOLL FROM THE SEVERE COLD

MRS MARY CARROLL, aged 40, died at City Hospital from burns received in South Boston, caused in attempting to thaw frozen water pipes.

CHARLES E. MILLS, aged 62, of Melrose Highlands, died at Relief Hospital, after being overcome by the cold on Summer st.

ISRAEL MENDELBERG, dropped dead from the cold, while thawing out water pipes in Somerville.

JOHN REDMOND, aged 39, 79 Union st, Salem, found dead at Phillips Beach under a piazza.

YESTERDAY'S TEMPERATURES

1 a m	4	1 p m	—2
2 a m	3	2 p m	1
3 a m	2	3 p m	—2
4 a m	0	4 p m	—3
5 a m	—2	5 p m	—3
6 a m	—4	6 p m	—4
7 a m	—6	7 p m	—6
8 a m	—4	8 p m	—7
9 a m	—4	9 p m	—8
10 a m	—3	10 p m	—8
11 a m	—3	11 p m	—8
Noon	—2	Midnight	—8

Widespread suffering came simultaneously with a marked drop in temperature and a northwest gale which swept Boston and all New England yesterday, the coldest day in a dozen years according to official figures.

Except for a brief time around 2 o'clock yesterday afternoon, when the mercury crept up to 1 above, the temperature remained at zero or below for 20 consecutive hours and was still below zero early this morning.

The deaths of three persons, one woman and two men, were due to the cold snap. They were:

Mrs Mary Carroll, aged 40, who died in City Hospital from burns received in a fire in South Boston, caused by an attempt to thaw out frozen pipes.

Charles E. Mills, aged 62, of Melrose Highlands, a Boston insurance man, who died in the Relief Hospital after being overcome by the cold in Summer st.

Israel Mendelberg, who dropped dead while thawing out water pipes in Somerville last night.

In many parts of the city and suburbs men and women were injured by the exploding of the waterfronts of ranges that had frozen over night, when fires were started in them yesterday morning.

Homeless Given Shelter.

Slowly rising temperature today and tomorrow were late last night forecasted by the Weather Bureau. Today will continue fair, with moderate westerly to southerly winds; tomorrow may be unsettled.

The lowest official reading up to the time the Weather Bureau shut up shop last night was 7 below, recorded at 8 p m, but at that hour the temperature

Continued on the Fourth Page.

ONE DEAD, THREE HURT

Firemen Hit as Wall Falls.

Bacon Store Burned, Big Area Menaced.

Five Alarms Bring Out Strong Fighting Force.

Loss Estimated by the Owner at $150,000.

With the thermometer registering some eight degrees below the zero mark, fire, that was discovered shortly after midnight this morning, raced through the department store of W. & A. Bacon, 2175 to 2193 Washington st, Roxbury, resulting in the death of one fireman, the serious injuring of three others and a monetary loss estimated to be at least $150,000.

Not for years have the Boston firemen been forced to work under greater difficulties. The cold was so intense that it was practically impossible for them to render a good account of themselves, but they stuck by their posts.

Men were cased in ice so thick that, even though the emergency arose, they would have been almost powerless to save themselves. They stood high in the air on ice-coated fire escapes, up which they dragged heavy lines of ice-covered hose, and they mounted ladders made dangerous by ice to direct streams into the fire.

Wall Falls on Firemen.

An unidentified fireman was killed half an hour after the fire was discovered. He died while directing a deck gun from the wagon of Engine Company 23 when, without warning, the upper portion of the wall on the Ruggles-st side of the building fell, crushing him amid the ruins and the vehicle on which he stood.

Joseph A. Hackett, chauffeur for Deputy Chief Peter McDonough, is missing and it is possible that it was his body that was taken from the ruin.

Hoseman P. L. Farren of Engine Company 37 was nearby when the wall fell, but he managed to escape death, although caught by a flying portion of the wall that hurled him to the ground.

He was extricated with difficulty and carried into a house on Ruggles st, where he was attended by Dr Raymond E. Bennison of 60 Kenilworth st, Roxbury. He found that Farren had been injured about the right forearm and right hip. Later he was sent to the City Hospital.

Two Hurt by Fall From Ladder.

When the wall came crashing down there was a scurrying on the part of

Continued on the Second Page.

THE WEATHER.

WASHINGTON, Jan 13—Forecast for Southern New England: Fair, continued cold Wednesday; Thursday, fair, warmer, northwest winds, diminishing and becoming variable.

For Northern New England: Fair, continued cold Wednesday; Thursday, not so cold, north winds, diminishing and becoming variable.

For Eastern New York: Fair, continued cold Wednesday; Thursday, fair, warmer, moderate north winds, shifting to southeast by Wednesday night.

Local Forecast for Boston and Vicinity—Fair Wednesday and Thursday, slowly rising temperature Wednesday night and Thursday; moderate westerly winds, becoming variable.

Total precipitation 24 hours proceding 8 p m yesterday, 0.

The Temperature at 8 Last Night—Albany, —10; Atlantic City, 19; Bismarck, 26; Buffalo, —6; Charleston, 44; Chicago, 26; Denver, 40; Des Moines, 36; Eastport, —12; Galveston, 53; Hatteras, 36; Helena, 36; Jacksonville, 46; Kansas City, 42; Montreal, —22; Nantucket, 0; New Orleans, 50; New York, —2; Philadelphia, 8; Pittsburg, 10; Portland, Me, —8; Portland, Or, 46; San Francisco, 56; San Diego, 58; St Louis, 34; St Paul, 20; Washington, 16.

The temperature yesterday at Thompson's Spa: 3 a m, 1; 6 a m, —3; 9 a m, —5; 12 m, —2; 3 p m, —3; 6 p m, —4; 9 p m, —7; 12 mid, —8. Average temperature yesterday, —3½; average one year ago, 20 11-12.

The Globe's Forecast—Thursday, fair; Friday, unsettled, probably fair, warmer, moderate westerly to southerly winds.

TODAY'S GLOBE CONTENTS.

Page 1.

James M. Curley elected Mayor by 5720 majority over Kenny; McDonald, Coleman and Woods win for Council and Dr Scannell and Corcoran for School Board; three referendums are adopted and city goes license.

Grave fears for the Royal Mail Steamer Cobequid, fast aground on the dreaded ledges of Grand Manan and reported filling, with 120 persons on board.

One fireman killed and three seriously injured when store of W. & A. Bacon is burned early this morning in Roxbury.

Boston has the coldest Jan 13 in the history of the local Weather Bureau and suffers severely.

Page 2.

Fires in many parts of Boston, due indirectly to the cold, keep firemen on the jump.

Gannon factory fire in Salem causes total losses of $15,000.

of a fishing schooner.

Simultaneous fires tax Beverly department.

Page 3.

Coskata lifesavers rescue three men from a barge stranded on Nantucket Bar.

Many commuters held up in waits for trains here as a result of the cold snap.

Herbert M. Sears elected commodore of the Eastern Yacht Club.

Page 4.

Remarkable speed made in election returns enabled Globe to announce Curley's election as early as 5 o'clock.

More than 1800 crowd Faneuil Hall and give Mayor-Elect Curley an extraordinary reception.

Page 5.

Boston votes in intense cold.

Page 6.

Winthrop High beats Quincy in league basket-ball game.

Porky Flynn beaten by Battling Levinsky in New York bout.

Page 6.

Many awards made on opening day of Boston Poultry Show.

Irish-American A. A. beats Pilgrims, 6 to 4, in hockey game.

Bowling results.

Page 7.

Harvard track team to take part in eight meets this Winter.

Salem, N H, will probably decline dates assigned in Grand Circuit and Cleveland will open the racing.

Page 8.

Financial news.

Boston & Maine plan to exchange its Maine Central stock for bonds declared off, and another method of meeting obligations of Feb 3 must be found.

Page 9.

Commercial news.

Judge Putnam says it is not the amount of business done by United Shoe Machinery Company, but manner in which it was done, that is in question.

News of the water front.

Price of woolen goods reduced at wholesale, but ultimate consumer may not benefit.

Page 10.

National Shoe Retailers' Association told to keep advertising in the newspapers, and Louis A. Coolidge explains the relation of the United Shoe Machinery Company to the small manufacturer.

Diplomats attend White House reception.

Nine income tax appointments in Massachusetts.

Page 11.

Famine threatens Japan in the north; eruptions and earthquakes in the south.

John Chancellor Crafts of Brighton leaves use of his home and $1200 annuity to housekeeper to care for his dog.

Williams nominated to be controller of the currency.

Page 11.

Proclamation of general strike in South Africa met by retaliation by martial law.

Chelsea men plan organization of Chamber of Commerce at meeting in State Armory.

Page 12.

One thousand women attend luncheon of Massachusetts Antisuffrage Association.

"The War Day by Day 50 Years Ago." Daily Lesson in History.

Page 13.

Flood of Legislative proposals offered at the State House.

Miss Annie Barker of Lynn found dead after six days' absence.

Bills referred to committees in the House and Senate of the Legislature.

All records broken at Boston hospitals in cases of frostbite treated.

H. W. Huguley Company employes have concert and dance at Catholic Union Hall.

Page 14.

Household Department.

Page 15.

Personal sketches of the careers of Mayor-Elect Curley and other successful candidates yesterday.

At Jerome's request, further hearing on bail for Thaw likely to go over to

Page 16.

Real estate transactions.

News of the courts.

Page 18.

Huerta Government announces it will default interest payment on bonds; Washington accepts move as result of United States' policy.

Underwood promises an industrial awakening that will put "panic preachers to shame."

President Wilson reads trust message to Cabinet.

Gen Wood makes important recommendations for improving the Army.

The Boston Daily Globe EXTRA

VOL LXXXVI—NO. 106. BOSTON, WEDNESDAY MORNING, OCTOBER 14, 1914—EIGHTEEN PAGES. COPYRIGHT, 1914, BY THE GLOBE NEWSPAPER CO. PRICE TWO CENTS.

GREAT BATTLE NEAR OSTEND

Fighting Between Dixmude Ypres and Dunkirk.

Belgian Government Moved to Havre, Warsaw in Danger.

WAR NEWS IN BRIEF

Severe battle is proceeding between Ypres, Dixmude and Dunkirk.

Germans advance on Bruges and Ostend; latter city in panic.

Belgian Government removes from Ostend to Havre, in France.

British consul at Ostend turns affairs over to American.

Germans recapture Lille.

French attack at Hazebrouck and Bethune and make "notable progress" between Arras and Albert, also at Berry-au-Bac.

German headquarters reports heavy fighting in Argonnes Hills, where Kaiser's troops bring forward siege guns.

Germany notifies Holland that neutrality of the Scheldt River will be respected.

Boer commander in South Africa revolts.

Capture of Warsaw by Germans imminent.

Russians claim they are still besieging Przemysl.

CLAIM TWO GERMAN SUBMARINES LOST

LONDON, Oct 14, 3:10 A M—The Petrograd correspondent of the Exchange Telegraph Company says it is officially announced by the commander of the Russian Naval forces in the Baltic that two German submarines were destroyed during the attack on the Russian cruiser Pallada.

LONDON, Oct 13, 3:03 A M—"A fierce battle is proceeding in the triangle of Dixmude, Ypres and Dunkirk," says the Times Ostend correspondent, telegraphing Monday.

"Gen von Kluck's right is making a determined effort to cut through the Allies' lines, but thus far it has been frustrated."

A dispatch to the Daily News from Ostend, dated Monday, midnight, says:

"The Germans are approaching Ostend by three roads, from Ypres by way of Dixmude, from Coutral through Thourout and from Eecloo through Bruges."

A Daily Mail correspondent in Belgium says:

"Immediately south of Ghent there was stiff fighting yesterday and today, with the south-going German column heavy losers. It is reported that the famous Death's Head Hussars have suddenly appeared in this region."

GERMANS ADVANCING PAST GHENT AND BRUGES

AMSTERDAM, via London, Oct 13—The Germans are now marching in the direction of Ostend, and German bicyclists already have been seen in the vicinity of Eecloo, 11 miles northwest of Ghent, according to dispatches appearing in the Telegraaf today.

German cavalrymen are quite near Bruges. The inhabitants of the country west of Ghent are fleeing in the direction of Ardenburg, and the Germans are throwing a pontoon bridge over the river at Selzaete, 10 miles to the north of Ghent.

Ghent, which is about 35 miles to the east of Ostend, was occupied by the Germans on Monday, after two days of fighting near Quatrecht and Melle. Cavalrymen appeared at first, but did not stay. Later infantry advanced from all sides, occupied the City Hall and camped in the streets.

BIG GERMAN FORCE DRIVES ALLIES BACK

LONDON, Oct 14, 1:55 A M—An Ostend dispatch to the Daily Tele-

Continued on the Fourth Page.

WRECKING BY BOMBS

Two Exploded in New York.

Catholic Cathedral Suffers Damage.

Also Rectory of Church Idle Army Visited.

Several Injured by the Flying Fragments.

NEW YORK, Oct 13—Bombs were exploded on two church properties in this city today—the first in famous St Patrick's Cathedral, 5th av, late this afternoon, when two persons were injured and part of the interior of the edifice was wrecked, and the second, set off tonight, seven hours later, when the concussion from a bomb that had been placed in an areaway close to the rectory of St Alphonsus' Roman Catholic Church on West Broadway, broke every window in the rectory. Falling glass cut the hand of a priest in that building.

The police are mystified by the explosions. They indicated that they were without clews to connect the two incidents, but the circumstances were so similar that the police theories were inclined to point toward an association of the explosions one with the other.

There was no apparent motive for what occurred in St Patrick's, the priests of the 5th Avenue Church suggesting that the work of placing a bomb was done by a demented person with a fancied grievance against the church or its clergy.

In investigating the second explosion the police recalled that it was this church that Frank Tannenbaum and his Industrial Workers of the World followers entered during their demonstrations of unemployment last Winter. They were ousted and Tannen-

Continued on the Fifth Page.

WORLD'S CHAMPIONSHIP COMES BACK TO BOSTON

Four Straight for Braves, No Team Ever Being Beaten So Quickly As Were Athletics.

THIS YEAR'S WORLD'S SERIES WAS SHORTEST EVER PLAYED

Year	G	Year	G	Year	G
1914	4	1910	5	1906	6
1913	5	1909	7	1905	5
1912	8	1908	5	1904	*
1911	6	1907	5	1903	8

*No series played.

EACH BRAVE GETS $2708.91 AND EACH MACKMAN $1950.42

	*4th Game	*3d Game	†2d Game	†1st Game	Totals
Paid Attendance	34,365	35,520	20,562	20,562	111,009
Receipts	$62,653.00	$63,808.00	$49,639.00	$49,639.00	$225,739.00
National Commission	6,265.30	6,380.80	4,963.90	4,963.90	22,573.90
Players	33,832.62	34,456.32	26,806.00	26,806.00	121,900.94
Clubs	22,555.08	22,970.88	17,870.10	17,870.10	81,266.16
Each Club's Share	11,277.54	11,485.44	8,935.05	8,935.05	40,632.58

The Braves receive 60 percent of the players' receipts, or a total of $73,140.56, and this sum is divided among 26 players and Manager Stallings, making each share worth $2708.91.

The Athletics receive 40 percent of the players' receipts, or a total of $48,760.38, to be divided among 24 players and Manager Mack, making each share worth $1950.42.

*At Fenway Park. †At Philadelphia.

TODAY'S GLOBE CONTENTS.

Page 1.

Von Kluck attacks Allies in the Dixmude-Ypres-Dunkirk region; Belgian Government moved to Havre, France, while Germans approach Ostend.

Boston Braves win 1914 World's Series, taking fourth straight game from Philadelphia Athletics by 3 to 1.

Mack calls the Braves "the best team that has ever played baseball."

Explosion of two bombs in New York damages St Patrick's Cathedral and rectory of the Church of St Alphonsus.

Page 2.

First treaty to prevent sudden war now in effect with Guatemala.

Page 3.

Southern Senators to propose Government bond issue to buy cotton.

Page 4.

Capture of Warsaw by Germans likely, American consul cables.

Boer command in Northwest Cape Province revolts against England.

Belgian Government transferred to Havre by permission of France.

Page 5.

Four straight victories by the Braves prove honesty of baseball, John I. Taylor says.

Logan and Rollins rejoin the Harvard Varsity football squad and both will be in shape to play by the end of the week.

Gilbert Gallant defeats Leach Cross in a 12-round bout at the Atlas A. A.

Page 6.

J. C. O'Leary tells how George Stallings built World's Champions out of tailenders.

Braves believe young pitchers of the Athletics will display excellent form, George Stallings Jr says.

TODAY'S GLOBE CONTENTS.

Page 7.

Germany said to have new guns of 21.45 caliber that will shoot 25 miles.

Harry Cain sails from Boston to join brothers and sisters on battlefield.

Tsingtau to be cleared of neutrals and combatants before final attack.

Unitarian Club hears addresses on the war by Samuel J. Elder and Dr Charles W. Eliot.

Bullets from across Mexican border hit American trooper.

Page 8.

Demonstration at Fenway Park.

Royal Rooters have a big final demonstration; paraders march through streets to cheers of thousands.

Maranville discusses the fourth game of the World's Series.

Page 9.

Batting and fielding averages of Braves and Athletics in the World's Series.

Manager Stallings of the World's Champions tells how the Braves became a great team.

New York Nationals win series from New York Americans.

Page 10.

Gardner to ask Congress to investigate Nation's preparedness for war.

Cardinal Gasparri chosen Papal Secretary of State.

Right of Public Service Commission to interfere questioned at hearing on mileage rates.

Real estate news.

Page 11.

Gov Walsh suspends the open season on upland game on account of forest fires.

No sign of a real rainstorm in New England.

George R. Freeman, aged 7, knocked down by delivery auto at Hyde Park, dies at hospital.

President Wilson on record as opposed to single term plank.

Women's locker building at Carson-st bathhouse burned.

Page 12.

Many independent candidates file nomination papers for State election.

"War Will Help Motor Industry," discussed by Uncle Dudley.

The War Day by Day 50 Years Ago.

Page 13.

Financial and commercial news.

Effect of European war on American trade discussed by Holland.

TODAY'S GLOBE CONTENTS.

Page 14.

Household Department.

Little Stories for Bedtime by Thornton W. Burgess.

"Better Be Wrong Than Positive," by Ruth Cameron.

Page 15.

What's to Become of Peggy, by Ethel Lloyd Patterson.

Dinner of Boston Credit Men's Association.

Page 16.

News of the water front.

Page 18.

Samuel W. McCall assails method by which the Boston Port Board was organized at rally in New Bedford.

Angry because husband had been discharged by court, Mrs John H. Lewis of 76 Ruggles st attempts suicide.

North Atlantic Conference declared not to be illegal combination; "fighting ships" enjoined.

Cincinnati Palestinian meeting called off on advice of Brandeis.

Ex-Gov Forbes made receiver of Brazil Railroad in suit at Portland, Me.

THE WEATHER.

FAIR

WASHINGTON, Oct 13—Forecast for New England and Eastern New York: Generally fair Wednesday and Thursday, warmer.

For Boston and Vicinity: Generally fair Wednesday and Thursday, moderate northeast to east winds.

Globe's Forecast: Thursday promises to be fair with variable winds; Friday fair with winds becoming southwest with higher temperature.

The Temperature Yesterday at Thompson's Spa—3 a m, 54; 6 a m, 50; 9 a m, 51; 12 m, 52; 3 p m, 53; 6 p m, 53; 9 p m, 51; 12 mid, 47. Average temperature yesterday, 51 19-24; average one year ago, 54.

Temperatures at 8 Last Night—San Francisco, 60; Bismarck, 36; St Louis, 52; Chicago, 56; Nantucket, 48; Portland, 44; Eastport, 42; New York, 54; Washington 62;

CALLS BRAVES BEST TEAM YET

Mack's Comment as He Leaves the City.

Few Persons Are at Station to See Athletics Depart.

Two Managers Exchange No Final Courtesies.

With only a few of their intimate personal friends present to commiserate with them on the double misfortune of having lost four straight games and the World's Championship the tribe of Cornelius McGillicuddy departed for Philadelphia on a special train at 9 o'clock last night from the Back Bay station.

Just before that hour the manager and his players with their wives and those who had come to Boston with them gathered in the lobby of the Copley Square Hotel and said their farewells. A number of the team went by auto to the Back Bay station, while others preferred to walk the short distance.

Just before leaving the hotel Connie Mack said: "The Boston Braves are the best team that has ever played baseball. We lost fair and square and in saying that the Braves are the best team that has ever played the game, nothing more remains to be said."

With his usual reticence Mr McGillicuddy then closed the interview and left the hotel accompanied by his wife. A number of the players had preceded the manager to the Back Bay Station, while a few followed him on his departure from the hotel.

The only member of the Braves who personally greeted Mack at the hotel before his departure was "Hank" Gowdy, the famous catcher of the Braves. Before his arrival, however, Johnny Evers and Fred Mitchell called at the hotel and met a number of the players but did not exchange courtesies with the famous manager.

In speaking with a Globe reporter Johnny Evers stated that he was not present to call on Mr McGillicuddy. He said: "Courtesy requires Mr Connie Mack to call on the Braves, not the Braves to call on Mr Mack. We are the victors, and if you remember in 1910 when I was a member of the club Mack did not call on us when his team won the championship from Chicago."

Neither Mack nor George Stallings exchanged any courtesies after the game and each showed feeling because of the telephone conversation they had last Thursday. Mack stated that it was not "up to him" to call on Mr Stallings after what happened last week, and Mr Stallings was just as vehement in declaring that as the Braves had won it was not his place to speak to Mack about it.

Despite the fact that for the first time in the World's Series they were the first to be beaten four straight games, the Athletics showed splendid spirit as they started for the Back Bay Station.

Just as the train pulled in they gripped the hands of the few friends present to say goodby to them, and it seemed as if the train barely stopped before they were swinging aboard and waving goodby.

THE OFFICIAL SCORE.

BOSTON	AB	R	BH	TB	PO	A	E
Moran rf	4	1	1	2	0	0	0
Evers 2b	3	1	1	1	3	6	0
Connolly lf	2	0	0	0	0	1	0
Mann lf	2	0	0	0	1	0	0
Whitted cf	3	0	2	2	1	0	0
Schmidt 1b	4	0	1	1	12	0	0
Gowdy c	2	0	0	0	8	2	0
Maranville ss	3	0	0	0	1	3	0
Deal 3b	3	0	0	0	1	4	0
Rudolph p	2	1	1	1	0	0	0
Totals	28	3	6	7	27	16	0
PHILADELPHIA							
Murphy rf	4	0	0	0	0	0	0
Oldring lf	4	0	1	1	3	0	0
Collins 2b	4	0	1	1	1	4	0
Baker 3b	4	0	1	1	1	4	0
McInnis 1b	4	0	1	1	15	1	0
Walsh cf	2	0	1	2	1	0	0
Barry ss	3	1	1	1	0	5	0
Schang c	3	0	0	0	3	0	0
Shawkey p	2	0	1	2	0	3	0
Pennock p	1	0	0	0	0	1	0
Totals	31	1	7	9	24	18	0

Innings	1	2	3	4	5	6	7	8	9	
Boston	0	0	0	1	2	0	0	0		—3
Philadelphia	0	0	0	0	1	0	0	0	0	—1

Two-base hits, Walsh, Shawkey, Moran. Hits, off Shawkey, 4 in 5 innings; off Pennock, 2 in 3 innings. Stolen base, Whitted. Double play, Gowdy and Evers. Left on bases, Philadelphia 4, Boston 5. Bases on balls, by Shawkey 2, by Pennock 2, by Rudolph. Struck out, by Pennock 3, by Rudolph 7. Passed ball, Schang. Wild pitch, Rudolph. Time, 1h 49m. Umpires, plate, Byron; bases, Hildebrand; left field, Klem; right field, Dineen.

Rudolph's Pitching and Evers' Hitting Win Final Game, 3 to 1.

By T. H. MURNANE.

Good morning, Braves.

Champion baseball team of the world, and never was title more honestly obtained.

Defeating the Athletics yesterday afternoon at Fenway Park by 3 to 1, ending the World's Series with four straight victories (a wonderful performance and unprecedented in baseball), the Boston National League Champions once more come into their own as the undisputed champion ball team, and as such entitled to 60 percent of the players' share of the gate receipts.

Cleanest Cut of All Victories.

It was by all odds the cleanest cut victory ever attained on the ball field, for the Braves went against a wonderful combination, with nine-tenths of the best critics claiming that the Boston team had very little show to carry off the honors.

The Boston Braves' winning streak started in the middle of last July; it seemed to increase in vigor and smoothness as the season went on, to reach a climax at Fenway Park yesterday afternoon before an immense crowd of baseball enthusiasts.

Stallings Takes No Chances.

The Boston men were victorious as the result of holding their nerve, and fighting from the first to last with their heads up, while their celebrated opponents from Philadelphia displayed very little fight either as a combination or as individuals. This was plain to a most distressing degree to those in sympathy with the Mackmen.

As the men squared away for what might be the last game of the series it was seen that George Stallings was taking no chance on a youngster in the box. Instead he sent Rudolph to the mound. Rudolph is one of the most efficient pitchers in the game today, and although hit quite freely in the first part of the game, he usually

Continued on the Sixth Page.

Sunday Globe Advts—Order Them Today. Autos For Sale? Summer Boarders Wanted? Cottages To Let? Advertise in the Globe.

Boston Evening Globe

Evening Edition 1c

VOL. LXXXVII NO. 127 — BOSTON, FRIDAY EVENING, MAY 7, 1915–SIXTEEN PAGES — COPYRIGHT, 1914, BY THE GLOBE NEWSPAPER CO — PRICE ONE CENT

EVENING EDITION—7:30 O'CLOCK—LATEST

LUSITANIA SUNK

Not Known How Many Passengers Saved

TORPEDOED BY GERMANS, REMAINED AFLOAT 12 HOURS

CUNARD STEAMSHIP LUSITANIA, TORPEDOED OFF THE HEAD OF KINSALE, IRE.

TORPEDOED OFF THE IRISH COAST

Left New York Last Saturday With 1253 Passengers.

WASHINGTON, May 7—Ambassador Page at London has cabled:

"Lusitania torpedoed and sunk within 30 minutes. No news of passengers yet."

LONDON, May 7—The Cunard Line steamer Lusitania, from New York May 1 for Liverpool with 1253 passengers on board, was torpedoed at about 2 o'clock this afternoon at a point about 10 miles off Old Head, Kinsale, Ireland, and later went down.

It is believed that her passengers are safe. No details of how they may have been rescued, however, are at hand. One message received here says:

"It is not known how many of the Lusitania's passengers were saved."

QUEENSTOWN, 4:59 P M—Wire begins "About 20 boats of all sorts belonging to our line are in vicinity where Lusitania sunk. About 15 other boats are making for ship to render assistance."

The third cablegram was dated Liverpool and reads as follows:

"Following received by Almiralty: Galley Head, 4:25 p m. Several boats, apparently survivors, southeast nine miles. Greek steamer proceeding to assist."

Continued on the Eighth Page.

ULTIMATUM TO CHINA

Japan's Cabinet Issues an Official Statement.

TOKIO, May 7—In presenting its ultimatum to China, Japan omitted from the present negotiations all items in Group 5 of the amended Japanese ultimatum.

The principal provisions of Group 5 have to do with the appointment of Japanese military and political advisers for China and for Japanese supervision over the manufacture or purchase by China of munitions of war.

The Japanese Government has instructed Eki Hioki, Japanese Minister at Pekin, to advise China to give due regard to Japan's wishes and to the conciliatory spirit of the Tokio Government, in view of which Japan believes China should give a satisfactory response.

In response to inquiries by the Associated Press, Japanese officials said they had heard nothing of any action on the part of the United States looking to mediation by that country between Japan and China. It was explained that Japan, having committed herself, must stand by her ultimatum, i' the situation should reach further discussion.

"If the situation should reach a stage in which mediation might be resorted to," these officials said, they believed the United States, if it took action, would first consult China. The question would then arise whether Japan would give its consent.

Group V includes the stipulations against which China raised the most vigorous objections. The decision of Japan to defer these matters is made known in an official communication of 3500 words, which was issued here

Continued on the Second Page.

UNITED STATES MAKES INQUIRY

Wants to Learn Japan Allies' Attitude.

Consults Great Britain, France and Russia on Status.

Japanese - Chinese Crisis Not Indifferent to It.

WASHINGTON, May 7—The United States, within the last 24 hours, through its ambassadors abroad, has consulted Great Britain, France and Russia, as the allies of Japan, to learn their attitude toward the present status of the Japanese-Chinese negotiations.

"SEVERAL BOATS NINE MILES OFF QUEENSTOWN"

As fast as the New York office of the Cunard Line receives news, it is forwarded by telephone to the Boston office. The latest wire received before 3 p m read:

"Galley Head, 4:25. Several boats, apparently survivors, southeast, nine miles off Queenstown. Greek steamer proceeding to assistance."

Galley Head is 23 miles southeast of Kinsale and 45 from Cork Harbor.

THE WEATHER.

RAIN

United States Weather Bureau forecasts:

For Boston and its vicinity and for Southern New England: Local rains tonight; Saturday rain; fresh southwest wind.

For Northern New England: Unsettled tonight and Saturday, probably rain. Variable wind, becoming southeast and moderate.

For Eastern New York: Rain tonight; Saturday unsettled, probably local rain in south and central portions; cooler west portion; fresh, probably strong, south and southwest wind.

There have been general copious showers except in the Middle and North Atlantic States. Temperatures last night, Denver 28, Northfield, Vt, 36. At 8 a m, Northfield 50, Boston 64, New York 60, Washington 62, Chicago 56, St Paul 38, Denver 30.

The Temperature Today.

The thermometer at Thompson's Spa records the temperature up to 3 p m as follows:

	1914	1915
3 a m	53	56
6 a m	52	54
9 a m	58	64
12 m	63	67
1 p m	66	65
2 p m	69	64
3 p m	70	66

New River & Ohio Coal Co Bankrupt.

CHARLESTON, W. Va, May 7—A petition in involuntary bankruptcy was filed here today for the New River & Ohio Coal Company. The company's liabilities are estimated at $286,000, with assets approximating $115,000.

WASHINGTON HIT LIKE A BOMB.

WASHINGTON, May 7—News of the torpedoing of the Lusitania struck official Washington like a bomb. While disposed to await full details before expressing opinions, all administration officials realized that the incident was probably the most serious Washington has faced since the beginning of the war.

ARROW INDICATES WHERE LUSITANIA WAS TORPEDOED.

ELBERT HUBBARD "NOW ABLE TO DO KAISER JUSTICE"

Elbert Hubbard, publisher of the Philistine, said when he boarded the Lusitania at New York, that "if he was on board the liner when she was torpedoed, he would be able to do the Kaiser justice in his magazine."

The Boston Daily Globe EXTRA

VOL XC—NO. 133 BOSTON, FRIDAY MORNING, NOVEMBER 10, 1916—TWENTY PAGES COPYRIGHT, 1916, BY THE GLOBE NEWSPAPER CO PRICE TWO CENTS

REELECTION OF PRES WILSON SHOWN ON FACE OF RETURNS

Republican Chairman Concedes California—North Dakota and New Mexico Democratic by Small Pluralities—New Hampshire For Wilson by 74 Votes, According to Globe's Count—Hughes Holds Lead in Minnesota and West Virginia—Democrats Have Lead of Four Seats in House With Five Districts to Be Heard From—Senate Democratic by 12 Majority—First Woman Congressman Believed Elected in Montana

HOW BILLY SUNDAY PUTS BUSINESS INTO RELIGION

Morgan Calls Him Captain of Religious Industry With 20th Century Efficiency

George Sunday Outlines Campaign Plan of Field Marshal of Militant Christianity

This is one of a series of articles in which Mr Morgan, after a personal investigation, is interpreting for Globe readers a widely debated man and movement, Billy Sunday and his extraordinary religious campaign, which has swept the country from the Rocky Mountains to the Atlantic, where he will begin his campaigning in Boston next Sunday morning. The man, his unique organization and methods, his staff, his great meetings, his humor, his slang, his theology, and his power over men will be sketched.

In the Globe tomorrow: "At Supper With Billy Sunday and His Unique Staff."

By JAMES MORGAN

As I came away from my call on Billy Sunday, in the spacious mansion seated in a park which covers an entire square on an avenue of millionaires in Detroit, I found myself puzzled to match up those luxurious surroundings with the man I had seen in the bath robe.

I wondered at the choice of such a palatial dwelling by this evangel of the Son of Man who had not where to lay his head. Why not live on locusts and wild honey? Why not go afoot with scrip and staff, rather than by special trains and high-powered automobiles? The question troubled me a bit, because it was my business to get an interpretation of the man from his own point of view. That is the more useful way to interpret any one.

A Religious Machine

By keeping my mouth shut and my eyes open the problem was solved for me on my second visit. Billy Sunday himself was living almost like a hermit in that great, ornate house, living as simply as an athlete in his training quarters. But the big establishment was serving him and his staff as a campaign headquarters, and no busier scene could be presented by the headquarters of a political committee when the campaign is in its last stretch to the polls.

Again the evangelist was in bed, going over his sermon for the evening, while down stairs, his workers, local committeemen, visiting clergymen, delegations and reporters were

Continued on the Second Page.

THE ELECTORAL TABLE

Based on the Latest Returns to the Globe

Total Electors 531
Necessary to choice 266
Wilson, reported 276
Hughes, reported 255

State	Electoral College	Wilson	Hughes
Alabama	12	12	..
Arizona	3	3	..
Arkansas	9	9	..
California	13	13	..
Colorado	6	6	..
Connecticut	7	..	7
Delaware	3	..	3
Florida	6	6	..
Georgia	14	14	..
Idaho	4	4	..
Illinois	29	..	29
Indiana	15	..	15
Iowa	13	..	13
Kansas	10	10	..
Kentucky	13	13	..
Louisiana	10	10	..
Maine	6	..	6
Maryland	8	8	..
Massachusetts	18	..	18
Michigan	15	..	15
Minnesota	12	..	12
Mississippi	10	10	..
Missouri	18	18	..
Montana	4	4	..
Nebraska	8	8	..
Nevada	3	3	..
New Hampshire	4	4	..
New Jersey	14	..	14
New Mexico	3	3	..
New York	45	..	45
North Carolina	12	12	..
North Dakota	5	..	5
Ohio	24	24	..
Oklahoma	10	10	..
Oregon	5	..	5
Pennsylvania	38	..	38
Rhode Island	5	..	5
South Carolina	9	9	..
South Dakota	5	..	5
Tennessee	12	12	..
Texas	20	20	..
Utah	4	4	..
Vermont	4	..	4
Virginia	12	12	..
Washington	7	7	..
West Virginia	8	..	8
Wisconsin	13	..	13
Wyoming	3	3	..
Total	531	276	255

THE WEATHER

Forecast for Boston and Vicinity: Friday fair, with falling temperature; Saturday fair, continued cool; strong westerly winds, diminishing.

Washington Forecast for New England and Eastern New York: Partly cloudy, colder Friday; Saturday overcast.

The Globe Forecast: Fair Saturday and Sunday; not much change in the temperature; moderate westerly winds.

The Temperature Yesterday at Thompson's Spa—3 a m, 52; 6 a m, 50; 9 a m, 54; 12 m, 64; 3 p m, 68; 6 p m, 65; 9 p m, 63; 12 mid, 64. Average temperature yesterday, 59 7-12; average one year ago, 53 1-6.

Temperatures at 8 Last Night: San Francisco, 66; Bismarck, 38; St Louis 54; Chicago, 50; Nantucket, 56; Portland, 54; Eastport, 50; New York, 62; Washington, 68.

WOODROW WILSON
© UNDERWOOD & UNDERWOOD

GLOBE TOTAL ON NEW HAMPSHIRE

Figures Show Wilson in Lead by 74 Votes

Missing Districts' Ballots Secured by Newspaper's Efforts

In order to have a tabulation of the total vote of New Hampshire, the Globe yesterday afternoon succeeded in gathering the complete vote of the State for President, and the result of the Globe's

Continued on the Eleventh Page.

GLOBE SEARCHLIGHT ENDED THE SUSPENSE

Flash From Customhouse Said, "Wilson Reelected"

Waiting Thousands Pay Tribute to This Newspaper's Reliability

Exactly as the illuminated hands of the huge clock on the Customhouse tower pointed to five minutes of eleven last night, the Globe's fateful pencil of light moved across the sky.

Would two more flashes follow im-

Continued on the Eleventh Page.

PLAN RECOUNT IN CALIFORNIA

Electoral Vote of State May Be Divided

Both Parties Prepare to Watch Official Tabulation

SAN FRANCISCO, Nov 9—Except in the event of some exceptional happening, President Wilson has carried California, it was conceded by Republican Chairman Rowell at 8:25 tonight.

Continued on the Eleventh Page.

TODAY'S GLOBE CONTENTS

Page 1.
President Wilson reelected on the face of the returns.
Morgan tells how Sunday put business into religion.
Plan recount in California.
Globe's own return from missing New Hampshire districts gives Wilson plurality of 74 votes.
Thousands satisfied on result of election by Globe's flash from Customhouse.

Page 2.
Sunday's barrel of sermons arrives in Boston in care of Mrs Rose Foutts.
Nashua, N H, man who shaved head in premature payment of election bet hoping friend must follow suit.

Page 3.
Search for more bodies in the harbor unsuccessful.

Page 4.
Constitutional provisions and legal precedents in cases of contested electoral delegations from States.

Page 5.
Germany, after the war, will be too busy and too much handicapped at home to flood American markets with manufactures, leading industrialists tell Herbert Bayard Swope.

Page 6.
Lowell police captain and officer wounded in shooting duel with an alleged intoxicated man in Tewksbury.
First Squadron Cavalry reach home.
One private held, another sought, after attack on Lieut Ingalls of Co I 8th Regiment, at Lynn.
Firemen to vote on affiliation with the Federation.

Page 7.
Rumanians and Russians recapture Hirsova and swiftly approach Tchernavoda; Germans advance northwest of Bucharest.
German Chancellor announces that Germany is ready to cooperate in a league for peace if Entente Allies give up plans for conquest.
Asquith declares England wants peace only on one condition—that the war shall not have been in vain; no question of separate peace.

Page 8.
Harvard practically finishes preparation for Princeton game tomorrow.
Bob Bingham, Yale halfback, sent to his home in Methuen with kidney trouble.
Brady beats Tellier in golf match, 8 and 7.
Faux Pas, winner of many prizes in French Bulldog Club show, may lose them all through protest.

Page 9.
Mel Coogan, fouled by Harry Carlson, awarded decision in Lawrence bout.
Ten teams remain tied in the six-day bicycle race.
Russians in new ballets at Boston Opera House.

Page 10.
President Wilson on his way to Williamstown; will return from there to Washington, ending vacation.
Republicans admit that plans are being made for recounts in close States.
Democrats' plurality in the lower House of Congress, with five districts undecided, only four votes over Republicans.

Page 11.
New Hampshire's turnover to Democratic column leads to immediate move for securing recount.
Sec Tumulty notifies President Wilson of his reelection.

Page 12.
Ralph Adams Cram explains to real estate men plan for beautiful civic center of Boston.
Two scholarships named for Ex-Gov Guild announced at "Melting Pot" dance in aid of Boston College.
Hickey boy killed by auto in Brookline while rolling a hoop.
Hermann Soehne make Capt Koenig of Deutschland an honorary member.

Page 13.
Death sentence of Adam Tarsein commuted.
Eight more candidates take out papers for Boston City Council.

Page 14.
"Election Upsets Due to Voters' Independence," by Uncle Dudley.
State clinics for after-care of paralysis cases to be established.

Page 15.
Household Department.

Page 16.
Financial news.

Page 17.
Commercial news.

Page 18.
Deacon Elnathan F. Duren, oldest man in Maine, dead in 103d year.

Page 20.
Sante Fe Railroad attacks constitutionality of the Adamson act.

Indicated Line-Up Will Give Wilson 276 Electoral Votes; Hughes 255

Recounts Probable in All the States Where Margin of Victory Was Small

LATEST RETURNS FROM THE VERY CLOSE STATES

CALIFORNIA
With 36 Precincts missing out of the 5870 the vote stands:
WILSON 465,669 HUGHES 462,538
Wilson's Lead 3131

MINNESOTA
With 83 Precincts missing out of the 3034 the vote stands:
WILSON 175,511 HUGHES 176,545
Hughes' Lead 1034

NEW HAMPSHIRE
Complete vote of State, tabulated by the Globe:
WILSON 43,775 HUGHES 43,701
Wilson's Plurality 74

NEW MEXICO
With 111 Precincts missing out of the 638 the vote stands:
WILSON 33,015 HUGHES 31,054
Wilson's Lead 1961

NORTH DAKOTA
With 26 Precincts missing out of the 1859 the vote stands:
WILSON 54,449 HUGHES 52,831
Wilson's Lead 1618

WEST VIRGINIA
With 99 Precincts missing out of 1713 the vote stands:
WILSON 132,176 HUGHES 135,266
Hughes' Lead 3090

On the face of the returns from every State in the Union, Woodrow Wilson has been reelected President.

It appears that he will receive 276 votes in the Electoral College, and Mr Hughes will have 255.

The latest returns from the States which have been doubtful give California, New Hampshire, New Mexico and North Dakota to President Wilson.

Minnesota and West Virginia are the only ones of the very close States which remain in the Hughes column.

Complete figures have not been received from all the States. In California, for example, 45 of the 5870 voting precincts have not been heard from at the hour of going to press, but President Wilson's lead of about 2900 votes on those which had been sent in was large enough to make Chairman Rowell of the Republican State Committee admit that nothing but some surprising development in the missing precincts could give the State to Mr Hughes.

Wilson Carries New Hampshire by 74 Votes

President Wilson has a lead of 74 votes in New Hampshire. Every voting precinct in that State has been heard from.

In New Mexico, 111 of the 638 voting districts have not sent in their returns, but President Wilson has a lead of 1960 votes, and men who are familiar with that State say that a change to Mr Hughes is practically out of the question.

Only 26 voting districts are missing in North Dakota; President's Wilson's plurality on the precincts already heard from is more than 1660—apparently a safe one.

So much for the States which have apparently gone for President Wilson.

In Minnesota 84 of the 3024 voting precincts are missing; Mr Hughes' plurality is a little more than 1000.

He has a lead of more than 3000 in West Virginia; 99 of the 1713 voting districts in that State have not yet been heard from.

Continued on the Eleventh Page.

ORDER YOUR SUNDAY GLOBE ADVTS TODAY
Used cars for sale? Real Estate For Sale? Advertise in the Globe.

Boston Evening Globe

FINAL EVENING EDITION 1c

VOL. XCI—NO. 96 BOSTON, FRIDAY EVENING, APRIL 6, 1917—SIXTEEN PAGES COPYRIGHT, 1917, BY THE GLOBE NEWSPAPER CO PRICE ONE CENT

EVENING EDITION—7:30 O'CLOCK—LATEST

IT IS WAR

Proclamation by President Wilson

GERMAN SHIPS ARE SEIZED

CREWS BUNDLED OUT OF BEDS

By LAWRENCE J. SWEENEY.

[illegible]'s participation in the German-American war occurred at daybreak this morning, less than two hours after Congress had passed the resolution which plunged the United States into the bitter struggle, when five of the six German steamers, which have found a haven of refuge in Boston Harbor since the outbreak of the European war, were seized upon order of Collector of the Port Edmund Billings.

While the seizure of the five ships—they were the Amerika, Cincinnati, Koln, Wittekind and Ochenfels—was effected by the representatives of the United States Treasury Department, and, therefore, was a civil process, the collector and the customs guards were assisted by the United States Navy Department, the Department of Commerce as representd by the immigration inspectors and by approximately 80 patrolmen and sergeants of the Boston Police Department, under the personal supervision of Supt Michael H. Crowley.

Immigration Commissioner Henry J. Skeffington, who had reached the

Continued on the Second Page.

[illegible] the Sunday Globe regularly from your newsdealer or newsboy. Read the Sunday Globe Magazine.

D. H. SPECKERMANN ARRESTED AS A PLOTTER

Government officials made an important arrest today in the person of D. H. G. Speckermann, 25. He is tall, with military bearing, and well dressed. He was captured by Deputy United States Marshals McGrath and [illegible]agley, and is alleged to have conspired with other persons, unknown to the complainant, to obstruct and destroy the property of a common carrier used in connection with the transportation of mail matter in the United States, on Feb. 1.

The defendant, it is also charged, received a telegram from Galveston, Tex, of such serious import that the Government officials are loth to discuss the details. The charge is said to be a serious one. The defendant, when arraigned before United States Commissioner Hayes, pleaded not guilty and was held in $5000 for a hearing on the 11th. He is locked up, in default of bail, in the Marshal's cage in the Federal Building.

In the pocket of the man was a notebook which contained three quotations. Two of the quotations were "The Service of Love" and "The Precious Anointment."

Here are the phrases in one of the quotations: "Friends of Jesus, service of love, precious ointment, example of love, divine anointing the great commandment."

While these may be, as they purport to be, religious sentiments, it is pointed out that they may be key words to be used as part of a secret cipher code in telegrams and letters.

SCORE OF GERMAN SUBMARINES

Are Reported Waiting at Mexican Bases

Advices to Government From European Neutral So Asesrt

WASHINGTON, April 6—Persistent but hitherto unconfirmed reports of German submarines waiting in the Gulf of Mexico for the opening of hostilities with the United States were further supported today by advices to the Government from Europe.

The full nature of the Government's information is not disclosed but it was received from one of the neutrals contiguous to Germany which has served as a clearing house for German information since the severance of diplomatic relations.

It was reported at the source of origin of the Government's information that more than a score of German submarines are already in Mexican waters. Persons here who have been giving attention to the subject think the estimate of numbers is high, but feel no doubt that German submarines are somewhere on this side of the Atlantic, most probably in Mexican waters, and that some of them have been there since early in February.

There is no doubt here that if the U-boats are in the Gulf they are being supplied from Mexican shore bases.

Continued on the Sixth Page.

THE WEATHER

RAIN

United States Weather Bureau forecasts:

For Boston and its vicinity and for Southern New England: Rain, followed by clearing tonight; Saturday fair, with somewhat lower temperature; southeast, shifting to northwest, gale.

For Northern New England and Eastern New York: Probably rain tonight and Saturday morning, followed by clearing and colder during Saturday. East gale, shifting to west Saturday.

Temperatures at 8 a m: Concord, N H, 32; New York, 44; Washington, 42; Chicago, 36.

Shippers' Forecast: Prepare shipments north during the next 36 hours for temperatures of 20 to 30; west, 25 to 30; south, 25 to 30; Boston and its vicinity, 25 to 30.

Boston observations, 8 a m—Barometer 29.50 inches; temperature 38; highest yesterday 47; lowest last night 35; humidity 98 percent; wind east, 22 miles, raining; precipitation .41 inches.

The Temperature Today

The thermometer at Thompson's Spa records the temperature up to 3 p m as follows:

	1916	1917
3 a m	43	39
6 a m	42	39
9 a m	46	40
12 m	48	43
1 p m	48	44
2 p m	48	45
3 p m	48	45

Superficial Elegance

"Don't you admire the hand of iron in a glove of velvet?"

"Yes," replied Miss Cayenne; "but what you more frequently observe is the rough neck under a fur collar."—Baltimore Star.

SECURE 30 NEW BLUEJACKETS

Advance Over Previous Day's Recruiting

Men Flocking to Enlist in Marine Corps and the Army

TOO PROUD TO SHIRK APRIL 5

NAVY—146 Tremont St.

Louis Watson, Wilbraham.
Samuel C. Holt, 691 State st, Sprigfield.
Charles G. O'Connell, 30 Holyoke st, Northampton.
Henry S. Fleming, Bellows Falls, Vt.
Louis W. Kendall, 42 Beaconsfield road, Worcester.
John J. Mullin, 75 Chestnut st, Spencer.
Roy L. Keizer, Carter st, Berlin.
Patrick J. Healey, 167 Oak st, Providence.
Gerald D. Dickie, 16 Highland av, Lonsdale, R I.
George D. Murphy, 27 Liberty st, Lowell.
George W. Nathan, 120 Amesbury st, Lawrence.
Edward B. Keating, 114 Granite st, Malden.
John T. Wilson, 21 Acorn st, Cambridge.
Otis W. Godfrey, 14 Ditson st, Dorchester.
James R. Smith, 95 Thorndike st, Cambridge.
Walter R. Prentiss, 38 Summer st, Ipswich.

Continued on the Fifth Page.

MISS RANKIN SOBS AS SHE WHISPERS "NO"

WASHINGTON, April 6—Miss Jeannette Rankin, the new woman member of the House from Montana, voted negatively. After failing to answer to the calling of her name twice on the first rollcall, Miss Rankin rose on the second roll call, trembling, obviously badly frightened, and with a sob in her voice declared:

"I want to stand by my country, but I cannot vote for war."

Still she did not formally announce her vote and half a dozen of her colleagues, wearied by the protracted debate, demanded, "Vote! Vote!" in raucous voices. Sinking into her seat, Miss Rankin whispered "No." Jerry South, chief clerk, went to her seat to corroborate her vote.

ONLY 12 COAST PATROL BOATS

New England Defense Needs 500 U-Boat Chasers

Has as Many Miles of Coastline—"Great Many" Men Lack Vessels

With war against Germany now a cold, hard fact, the news comes from the Charlestown Navy Yard today that the New England coast, from Eastport, Me, to Chatham, is defended against attack by submarines by only 12 boats.

This condition is due largely to the failure of power boat owners to "come across" with their craft and turn them over to the Navy, to be converted into coast patrol boats.

Washington has set a mark of 500 coast patrol boats to be mobilized for the defense of New England.

Every power boat and other small craft owned in this district should, of course, be submitted to Government inspectors, and if found acceptable for service in this vitally important work

Continued on the Sixth Page.

SIGNING OF THE WAR RESOLUTION

WASHINGTON, April 6—President Wilson at 1:11 today signed the resolution of Congress declaring a state of war between the United States and Germany.

The resolution was signed at 12:14 p m today by Vice President Marshall.

Speaker Clark had signed it early this morning, after it was passed by the House.

Proclamation Also Signed

The President also signed a proclamation formally declaring a state of war between the United States and Germany. In the proclamation he called upon American citizens to give support to all measures of the Government.

By the signing of the resolution, the war which Germany actually has been making on the United States for many months is recognized in official form, and the United States thus announces to the world its determination to take up what President Wilson characterized in his address to Congress as Germany's "challenge to

Continued on the Eleventh Page.

The Boston Daily Globe EXTRA

VOL XCIV—NO. 74 BOSTON, THURSDAY MORNING, SEPTEMBER 12, 1918—FOURTEEN PAGES COPYRIGHT 1918, BY THE GLOBE NEWSPAPER CO. PRICE TWO CENTS

MAN POWER OF NATION POURS OUT TODAY

GERMANS PREPARE FOR BIG RETREAT

St Quentin, Cambrai, Douai and The Aisne to Be Given Up, Berlin Is Now Told

Already Evacuating Main Base At Douai—Allies Advance Steadily by Attacks

Under cover of an increased show of resistance near the Hindenburg line and the hights around Laon, the Germans are hastening preparations for another stage of their retreat.

Official advices to the Government at Washington describe their systematic evacuation of war material from the town of Douai, one of the important forward bases of the present German line in France—a movement that has been in progress 10 days.

From his advanced position, only 14 miles distant, where he broke the Hindenburg second line, Gen Horne stands in position to carry Douai by storm and turn in behind Cambrai.

The German rulers are already preparing the people to hear of complete abandonment of the Hindenburg line, including Cambrai and St Quentin, and all territory up to the Chemin-des-Dames. The cable brings the substance of a significant article by Capt von Salzmann, military critic of the Vossische Zeitung of Berlin, in which he predicts that a heavy British attack will soon be made on Cambrai.

He declares the German lines before Cambrai cannot be regarded as final lines of resistance.

To Fall Back on Laon

Von Salzmann deprecates the importance of the St Quentin Canal and says the main defense lines lie further east.

He adds that the Germans can, without running any risk, voluntarily abandon all the territory south of the Aisne and retire to the Chemin-des-Dames.

Marshal Foch and the Allied staffs, with the vast armies of three great Allied Nations, are prepared to break up the enemy's plan by forcing another great battle—perhaps the greatest of the war—along the Hindenburg line, or strike the enemy in his retreat toward the Belgian frontier.

There has been little doubt that Douai could be held only at great cost if the British are sent forward to take it, since Sir Douglas Haig's men crushed through the Descourt

Continued on the Seventh Page.

McCORMICK WINS ON LOYALTY ISSUE

Defeats Chicago's Mayor in Senate Primary

Choice of President Nominated in Georgia Race

CHICAGO, Sept 11—In the face of the early returns from today's Statewide primary, Medill McCormick has defeated Mayor William Hale Thompson for the Republican nomination for United States Senator.

With half of the returns from Chicago at 9 o'clock, Thompson was leading McCormick in the city by 9475. At that hour, returns from 492 out of 2973 precincts in the State outside of Cook County gave McCormick 21,105 and Thompson 9635.

If the present ratio of voting continues, it was estimated that Thompson will carry Chicago by approximately 20,000, while McCormick will come to the Cook County line with a plurality of approximately 71,000. Congressman George E. Foss was running third.

The Democratic nomination has been won by Senator James Hamilton Lewis. The principal issue between McCormick and Thompson was one of loyalty.

Continued on the Third Page.

RED SOX WIN SIXTH GAME AND THE TITLE

Beat Cubs 2-1, Tyler's Wildness and Flack's Muff Accounting For Victory

THE OFFICIAL SCORE

BOSTON	AB	R	BH	TB	PO	A	E
Hooper rf	[illegible]						
Shean 2b	[illegible]						
Strunk cf	[illegible]						
Whiteman lf	[illegible]						
McInnis 1b	[illegible]						
Scott ss	[illegible]						
Thomas 3b	[illegible]						
Schang c	[illegible]						
Mays p	[illegible]						
Totals	[illegible]						

CHICAGO	AB	R	BH	TB	PO	A	E
Flack rf	[illegible]						
Hollocher ss	[illegible]						
Mann lf	[illegible]						
Paskert cf	[illegible]						
Merkle 1b	[illegible]						
Pick 2b	[illegible]						
Deal 3b	[illegible]						
Zeider 3b	[illegible]						
Killifer c	[illegible]						
O'Farrell c	[illegible]						
Tyler p	[illegible]						
Hendrix p	[illegible]						
*Barber	[illegible]						
†McCabe	[illegible]						
Totals	[illegible]						

*Batted for Deal in 8th inning.
†Batted for Tyler in 8th inning.

Innings	1	2	3	4	5	6	7	8	9	
Boston	0	0	2	0	0	0	0	0	—	2
Chicago	0	0	0	1	0	0	0	0	0	1

Earned run, Chicago. First base on errors, Boston 1. Left on bases, Boston 5, Chicago 2. Hits, off Tyler 5 in 7 innings; off Hendrix, none in one inning. Sacrifice hits, Hooper, Thomas. Stolen base, Flack. Struck out, by Tyler, by Mays. Base on balls, by Tyler 5, by Mays 2. Hit by pitched ball, by Mays (Mann). Time, 1h 46m. Umpires, Hildebrand at plate, Klem at first base, Owens at second base, O'Day at third base. Losing pitcher, Tyler.

By EDWARD F. MARTIN

Boston is again the capital of the baseball world, history repeating itself yesterday when the Red Sox, who have never faltered in this great classic, defeated the Cubs, 2 to 1.

Flack's muff of a liner from Whiteman in the third inning, with two out and Sox runners on third and second, made possible the Red Sox victory that carried with it the world's title.

Only 15,238 saw the farewell battle. Of course the weather was far from ideal, but the disagreement between the National Commission and the contesting players, which held up the starting of Tuesday's game, was the thing that kept the public away yesterday.

Money Differences Forgotten

With many minds wandering in serious channels, it can plainly be seen that it was a fatal mistake for baseball men to argue over dollars,

Continued on the Eighth Page.

AMERICAN TROOPS LAND AT ARCHANGEL

Petrograd Reported Afire—Effort to Slay Hun Envoy

WASHINGTON, Sept 11—American troops have landed at Archangel to assist the other Allied forces there in their campaign to the reestablishment of order in Northern Russia. This announcement was authorized tonight by Gen March, chief of staff.

For military reasons the number of soldiers landing was not revealed, nor was it made clear from whence they had embarked. It was assumed, however, that the soldiers had been sent from English camps, where Americans are training.

The troops are the first from the United States to be sent into Northern Russia. The American forces previously landed on the shores of the White Sea were marines from warships.

A dispatch from the American legation at Christiania today said reliable information had reached there that Petrograd was burning in 12 different places and that there was indiscriminate massacre of people in the streets.

Sec Lansing, in announcing receipt of the message, said it did not indicate whether the massacre was organized or merely was a result of a general state of anarchy.

U. S. TROOPS SPEAK RUSSIAN

ARCHANGEL, Wednesday, Sept 4 (By A. P.)—American troops have arrived safely at Archangel. Many of them speak the Russian language fluently.

Most of these troops are from States where the Winters are like those in Russia. Their voyage was quick and tranquil. The men suffered few discomforts, except there was a heavy list of seasick.

TRIED TO KILL HELFFERICH

STOCKHOLM, Tuesday, Sept 10 (By A. P.)—July and August were months of horror which never will be forgotten by persons who watched Russia's two

Continued on the Sixth Page.

THE WEATHER

RAIN

Forecast for Boston and Vicinity: Rain Thursday and Thursday night, slightly warmer; Friday probably fair; moderate south and southwest winds.

Washington Forecast for Southern New England: Rain Thursday in the west; Thursday and Thursday night in the eastern portion, slightly warmer; Friday probably fair. For Northern New England—Rain Thursday or Thursday night and probably Friday; warmer Thursday.

Globe's Forecast—Fair weather, with slowly rising temperature, Friday and Saturday; moderate west and southwest winds.

The Temperature Yesterday at Thompson's Spa: 3 a m, 50; 6 a m, 48; 9 a m, 51; 12m, 54; 3 p m, 57; 6 p m, 56; 9 p m, 54; 12 mid, 53. Average temperature yesterday, 53¾; average one year ago, 52 5-24.

Temperatures at 8 Last Night—San Francisco, 76; Williston, 78; St Louis, 80; Chicago, 66; Nantucket, 48; Portland, 48; Eastport, 46; New York, 58; Washington, 66.

German Women Aviators Fighting the Americans

WITH THE AMERICAN ARMY IN FRANCE, Sept 11 (By A. P.)—That the Germans are using women as military aviators is indicated in a report that in a machine recently brought down by the Americans the pilot, who was killed, was a woman.

JUDGE BRALEY FINDS FOR MRS C. S. EATON

Allows Widow to Sue to Break Will—Holds Husband Did Not Keep Agreement Fairly

Finding that Charles S. Eaton, founder and late proprietor of Thompson's Spa, had purposely manipulated his property so as to diminish the share that would go to his widow, Mrs Ella F. Eaton, upon his death, under the terms of an ante-nuptial agreement, Judge Braley in the Supreme Court, yesterday, dismissed a bill in equity filed by Ezra S. Eaton et al, executors of Mr Eaton's will, against Mrs Eaton seeking to have her restrained from contesting the will or asking for a widow's allowance.

Judge Braley spent weeks in hearing the evidence and has had the case under consideration all Summer.

The relief sought by the executors was grounded on the ante-nuptial agreement made July 2, 1908, the day before the couple were married. At that time Mr Eaton was 52 and Mrs Eaton, who was formerly Mrs Bartlett, was 33. They had met in a Winter resort at Pasadena, Calif. They were married there. Mrs Eaton had lived in Los Angeles.

Under the terms of the contract she was to get one-quarter of the estate of Mr Eaton at his death in lieu of her dower rights. She was to share equally with the three sons of Mr Eaton by his previous marriage, Ezra, Malcolm and Charles.

The executors contended that Mrs Eaton was barred from making a contest over the will of Mr Eaton by the ante-nuptial agreement, but she maintained that she was not bound by it, since Mr Eaton had violated it, having diminished the estate by manipulation of it, and correspondingly having reduced her share in the estate and increased the shares of his sons.

Fairness Essential

Referring to the ante-nuptial agreement, Judge Braley says, in part: "The conception of having such an agreement was the testator's.

"It is unnecessary to cite authorities to the effect that such an agreement, not only in its inception and execution, but in its subsequent performance, recognizes the relation between the contracting parties to be one of full trust, where absolute fairness is an essential and continuous element.

"It is to be observed that no power of revocation is reserved to the testator, but having chosen to restrict himself in the manner described he is bound by the restriction.

"The defendant was to share alike with the sons, as if she were the testator's child.

The Pasadena House

"For some years before his marriage the testator spent his Winters in Pasa-

Continued on the Second Page.

THREATENS TO TIE UP SHEET METAL TRADES

Union Demands Immediate Adjustment of Wages

WASHINGTON, Sept 11—A strike of all workers in the sheet metal trades affiliated with the Amalgamated Association of Iron, Steel and Tin Workers will be called Monday in the territory west of the Mississippi River, unless certain demands of the men regarding the sliding wage scale are adjusted immediately, the War Labor Board was informed today.

Such a strike, officials said, would tie up a large proportion of the steel industry and probably result in the closing of munitions plants in the entire affected area.

The Labor Board indicated tonight that it would hold an immediate hearing on the men's grievances in an effort to avert a strike. A delegation of workers in the iron, steel and tin trades, headed by M. F. Tighe and D. J. Davis of Chicago, arrived in Washington today to appear before the board.

MUNITIONS STRIKERS DEFY UNION ORDER

BRIDGEPORT, Conn, Sept 11—Five thousand striking union machinists from Bridgewater munitions plants, at a meeting late today, listened to the reading of a message from William H. Johnston, president of the International Association of Machinists, calling on the men to return to work within 48 hours, and then voted unanimously to continue the strike.

Pres Johnson telegraphed S. Laditt, head of the Bridgeport union, from Washington that while the War Labor Board umpire's decision in their case was unsatifactory, the integrity and honor of the association were at stake, and that for patriotic reasons, if for no other, the men should go back to work and make an appeal if they failed to work out a solution of their problem.

If the Nation were not at war, the telegram stated, the association would give unlimited support to the enforcement of the strikers' demands, but the workers were called upon to remember that the forces at the front need the munitions manufactured at Bridgeport.

The strikers adopted a resolution outlining their position, which was wired to Mr Johnston. The resolution said:

"We, the machinists on strike, knowing as we do that we are out for a just cause, will continue on strike until we hear from President Wilson as to the justice of our contention in remaining on strike until the manufacturers grant our demands.

"We will stick; we will stick to the end."

Although Samuel Lavit, business agent of the local Machinists' Union, had said a strike call would be sent to workers in six other cities if a satisfactory settlement was not made by 2 p m today, no call was sent out. Labor leaders claimed tonight, however, that they were assured of support in other cities.

The strike committee announced tonight that 1400 machinists have left the city since the strike began. Boy Scouts were employed by some of the local plants today putting up placard advertising for women munitions workers to replace the men on strike.

Army of Volunteers Ready to Enroll 13,000,000 Between 18 to 45 Years, Inclusive

Flags to Fly and Bands Play—Naval Reservists Told by Department to Register

Today's Registration Duties in a Nutshell

WHEN—7 a m to 9 p m. If possible, registrants should avoid the congestion which will come between 7 a m and 10 a m, at noon and after 7 p m. The best hours in which to register will be between 9:30 and 12 a m, and between 1:30 and 6:30 p m.

WHERE—In Boston and other large cities, in each registrant's regular voting precinct; in other communities, in central registration booths, a list of which will be found posted in some prominent place.

WHO—Every male who today has reached his 18th birthday and has not reached his 46th birthday, unless he has already registered, or is in active service in the Army or Navy. This includes Spanish War veterans, discharged soldiers and sailors, absentees and invalids. Invalids should send a representative to the registration booth early in the day.

NAVAL RESERVISTS NOT ON ACTIVE DUTY MUST REGISTER

Uncle Sam's sons between 18 and 45 years, inclusive, not already registered—13,000,000 of them—are to register today under the provisions of the Man Power act, recently passed by Congress and signed by President Wilson, who fixed this day as the time for the second general call to enroll sounded since the United States entered the war against the Central Powers of Europe.

From 7 a m to 9 p m names will be enrolled in every city and town from the tip of Cape Cod to the Pacific slope, and within several days questionnaires will be circulated among registrants. Inside of a month, according to the latest news

Continued on the Fourth Page.

2800 SOLDIERS SAVED FROM LINER

U-Boat Sunk Following Persic Attack

Officials Say Efficiency of Convoy System Is Proven

WASHINGTON, Sept 11—News of the torpedoing of the British liner Persic with 2800 American troops on board in the war zone on Sept 6 was given to the American people today first through the British Admiralty and then later through the Navy Department. All the soldiers were rescued by accompanying destroyers, the steamer itself was beached and the enemy submarine is believed to have been accounted for.

Officials here viewed the result of the attack more as an Allied success than a disaster. The fact that the steamer was torpedoed while endeavoring to overtake the convoyed fleet of transports, after overcoming engine trouble which had forced her to lag, convinced officials that submarine commanders still are fearful of attacking troop ships in convoy.

The immediate and successful assistance rendered by the destroyers was taken as additional evidence that the convoying system now in vogue is practically perfect.

First word of the attack on the Persic, it was learned officially, reached the

Continued on the Second Page.

AUTOS BADLY NEEDED TO AID DRAFT WORK

Less than one-third of the automobiles needed by Boston draft officials for the transportation of volunteer clerks to various points in the city today have been volunteered.

At least 100, probably more, are needed. Have you a machine that you are patriot enough to spare for this most essential part of the Registration Day work?

If so, get in touch with Division 8 headquarters, 1 Beacon st, as early as possible today. The telephone number is Haymarket 1373. Provisions have been made for the parking of cars on Somerset st and in Pemberton sq.

EX-CZARINA AND FOUR DAUGHTERS REPORTED KILLED BY BOLSHEVIKI

LONDON, Sept 12—The Daily Express claims to have unquestionable information that the former Empress of Russia and her four daughters have been murdered by Bolsheviki.

The Express adds that "the whole immediate family of the late Czar has thus been exterminated. It is further understood that the Dowager Empress, who with her daughter and son-in-law, the Duke of Oldenburg, has been staying at Yalta, was recently attacked by Red Guards, who sought to kill all three. Sailors of the Black Sea fleet intervened and fought the Red Guards. It is now understood that the Dowager Empress is safe."

The four daughters of the former Emperor and Empress of Russia are: Grand Duchess Olga, born in 1895; Grand Duchess Tatiana, born in 1897; Grand Duchess Marie, born in 1899, and Grand Duchess Anastasie, born in 1901. The former Empress Alexandre was born Princess Alix of Hesse, in 1872.

YANKEE RAIDS TAKE CAPTIVES IN LORRAINE

Army Ordered to Kill All Who Urge Surrender

WASHINGTON, Sept 11—The carrying out of successful raids by American troops in Lorraine was reported in Gen Pershing's statement for today, received tonight at the War Department. The Americans entered the enemy trenches, inflicting losses and capturing prisoners.

The statement follows:

"Headquarters, American Expeditionary Force, Sept 11, 1918.

"Section A: In the course of successful raids in Lorraine, our detachments penetrated the enemy's trenches, inflicting losses and capturing prisoners. There is nothing else of importance to report."

The Americans today maneuvered cautiously along the Vesle front over the rain-soaked battlefield where the Germans Tuesday night and sent hundreds of gas shells. The infantrymen improved their positions at a few places.

Owing to the wet ground the gas remained longer than usual. The rain hindered operations more than the shells. The Germans Tuesday night and at intervals Wednesday shelled the hills just south of the Vesle, but the French and American artillerymen returned two projectiles for every one the Germans fired.

The Americans and French continued today to pound the La Petite Montagne tableland and the German machine gun positions along the hills northeast of Revillon, but more rain in the afternoon slowed down the operations.

"The Town Blouse," from The Blouse [illegible], Fifth Avenue, New York, is now shown by Wm. Filene's Sons Company.

TODAY'S GLOBE CONTENTS

THURSDAY, SEPTEMBER 12, 1918

Page 1.

Thirteen million register today under new man power law.

Germans are evacuating their base at Douai, while Berlin is prepared to hear the Hindenburg line down to St Quentin and the Aisne River are to be given up.

American troops, presumably from camps in England, have landed at Archangel, Russia.

American raids in Lorraine bring back prisoners; our troops press forward on the Aisne River.

Washington Naval officials elated over successful methods used to neutralize submarine effectiveness, as shown by recent attack on troopship.

Judge Braley rules in favor of Mrs Charles S. Eaton in suit over estate of her husband.

Red Sox beat the Cubs in sixth game of World's Series, 2 to 1, winning the championship and making the count four to two in favor of Boston.

Bridgeport strikers defy union's demand that they return.

Sheet metal workers threaten to strike Monday.

Medill McCormick wins Illinois Senate nomination over W. H. Thompson, Mayor of Chicago.

Miss Wanda Kreutingzer, telegrapher, arrested under the Spy act.

Page 2.

Albert O. Petersen arrested on charge of stealing $9000 from firm by which he was employed as cashier.

New England Red Cross asked to furnish four tons of second-hand clothing for the Belgians.

Page 3.

Sec Tumulty questions Republican Chairman Hays about Labor Day talk.

Page 4.

America faces huge gasoline shortage unless conservation steps are taken, Dr Garfield tells the Senate.

Page 6.

"Roll Call," by Uncle Dudley.

American Consul General in Moscow arrested, Globe correspondent cables.

Indications that fresh German divisions are manning the Hindenburg positions.

War Industries Board orders inquiry into waste of paper by Government agencies.

Germans are mining all towns and churches in their immediate rear in France, for wholesale destruction as they retreat.

Page 7.

Financial and commercial news.

French threaten rear of St Gobain Forest.

Sharp criticism of German Army by Ludendorff captured.

Page 8.

A. J. Furbush of Brighton amateur world's record for team trotting to wagon at the Syracuse Grand Circuit meeting.

Live Tips and Topics.

Page 9.

New England casualties number 87.

Page 10.

Household Department.

"Bedtime Stories," by Thornton W. Burgess.

Page 10.

Changes proposed at Army camps will cost $30,000,000.

Page 11.

Use of Military in slacker round-ups called unlawful.

Page 14.

Delegates to Massachusetts A. F. of L. convention are urged by D. A. Tobin not to strike, but allow Government to settle disputes.

National House plans to rush the proposed Bond Exemption bill.

First review of 12th Division will be conducted at Camp Devens Saturday morning.

Eugene V. Debs admits Government's case and pleads in own behalf at espionage trial in Cleveland.

ADMITS SCORING OF SCHWAB

JERSEY CITY, N J, Sept 11—Richard Rowe, lawyer and contractor, of Washington, who claimed as his friends several high Government officials, was arrested here today and held in $2500 on a charge of making seditious remarks.

He is alleged to have made remarks derogatory to the management of the shipbuilding program to a soldier and a sailor, and said that the officials in charge were using vessels "stolen" from Germany and other countries to send troops abroad. In court he said he was loyal to America, but admitted criticising Charles M. Schwab.

Strike Will Be Investigated

HAVERHILL, Sept 11—Herbert Williams, agent of the Allied Shoe Workers, about 250 of whom are still on strike, has received word from the National War Labor Board that a representative will come to this city to investigate the strike.

MISS KREUTINGZER HELD UNDER SPY ACT

Telegrapher Accused of Helping the Kaiser

NEW YORK, Sept 11—Information has been obtained that Miss Wanda Kreutingzer, a Postal Telegraph operator taken into custody here today, has transmitted directly to the German Government important information regarding munition ships, obtained from cablegrams and telegrams which passed through her hands, announced Federal officials tonight.

These transmissions, the statement said, were made in 1914 and 1915. But within the last six weeks, it is asserted, Miss Kreutingzer has furnished similar information "to persons she believed to represent the Imperial German Government." She has been under surveillance for some time.

Miss Kreutingzer, who is a registered enemy alien, told her examiners she was born in Posen, Germany, 43 years ago. She has been employed by the Postal company for 18 years and has been in this country 30 years. The statement says Miss Kreutingzer received no money for her service, doing the work because of her "love of the homeland."

A Presidential warrant for her internment as a dangerous enemy alien has been requested, it was announced.

S. S. Berwind Sinks, Crew Safe

BRIDGETOWN, Barbados, Sept 11—The steamship Berwind, from New York, has sunk in the harbor. All the crew was saved.

Help your newsdealer to regulate his Globe order. On Friday, November 15th, the price of the Evening Globe will be two cents per copy. To make sure of your copy of the paper, arrange to have it regularly.

The Boston Daily Globe

EXTRA 6 A.M.

VOL. XCIV—NO. 134 BOSTON, MONDAY MORNING, NOVEMBER 11, 1918—TWELVE PAGES COPYRIGHT, 1918, BY THE GLOBE NEWSPAPER CO. PRICE TWO CENTS

ARMISTICE SIGNED

FIGHTING IN BERLIN NEW POWER SUPREME

Great Overturn Is Accomplished With Little Violence

Red Flag Floats From Royal Palace—Crowds Sing the "Marseillaise"

LONDON, Nov 10 (By A. P.)—According to dispatches from Amsterdam and Copenhagen the revolution in Germany is extending rapidly, but in most places the desired effect is being achieved without violence or serious disorders.

Berlin is reported to have been occupied Saturday by forces of the Soldiers and Workmen's Council. A Berlin dispatch says a people's government has been instituted and that the garrison has gone over to this government.

In some places—notably in Anhalt, Hesse Darmstadt and Mecklenburg-Schwerin—the princely houses are

Continued on the Fifth Page.

FOCH'S ARMIES DRIVE AHEAD ON LONG FRONT

Foe Abandons Supplies in Precipitate Retreat

All along the battle line from Belgium to Lorraine, the Germans continue to give ground under heavy blows of Foch's victorious Allied armies.

Marshal Haig's forces have driven forward across the Belgian frontier

Continued on the Fourth Page.

SPEEDY PEACE NEW CHANCELLOR'S AIM

Must Prevent Famine and Civil War, Says Ebert

Liberty Gained by People Must Be Guarded, His View

WASHINGTON, Nov 10—Friederich Ebert, upon assuming office yesterday as Chancellor, issued a proclamation announcing that the new Government at Berlin has taken charge of business to prevent civil war and famine.

In a manifesto addressed to the "citizens" of Germany, the Chancellor said he was going to form a people's Government to bring about peace "as quickly as possible" and to confirm the liberty which the Government has gained.

The text of the proclamation and the manifesto were sent out by the German wireless station at Nauen, and picked up today by Naval radio stations in America.

In making them public the State Department said it would not vouch for the accuracy of the facts presented.

Text of Proclamation

The proclamation said:

"A new Government has taken

Continued on the Seventh Page.

KAISER ABDICATES, HEADS FOR HOLLAND

Officers and Crown Prince Accompany Ex-Ruler

Hindenburg May Be in Party—"On Way to Paris?" Cry Belgians

LONDON, Nov 10—Emperor William signed a letter of abdication Saturday morning at the German Grand Headquarters in the presence of Crown Prince Frederick William and Field Marshal von Hindenburg, according to a dispatch from Am-

Continued on the Seventh Page.

THE WEATHER

FAIR

Forecast for Boston and Vicinity: Fair Monday and Tuesday; moderate variable winds.

Washington Forecast for New England and Eastern New York: Fair Monday and Tuesday; not much change in temperature.

Globe's Forecast: Tuesday will be fair with seasonable temperature, and light variable winds. Wednesday fair and warmer, with winds becoming southwest.

The Temperature Yesterday at Thompson's Spa—3 a. m. 54; 6 a. m. 55; 9 a. m. 58; 12 m. 59; 3 p. m. 56; 6 p. m. 51; 9 p. m. 48; 12 mid. 42. Average temperature yesterday, 53½; average one year ago, 47⅝.

Temperatures at 8 Last Night—San Francisco, 58; St Paul, 32; St Louis, 46; Chicago, 42; Nantucket, 48; Portland, 44; Eastport, 44; New York, 46; Washington, 46. Precipitation in Boston, 24 hours, to 8 p. m. 06.

EBERT AT HEAD OF GOVERNMENT

Revolutionists in Control of Big German Cities

People's Councils in Control—Three More Kings Abdicate

With revolt sweeping like wildfire through the German Empire, with Berlin in the hands of the revolutionists and with the victorious Allied forces rapidly smashing through the shattered ranks of his once mighty legions, William Hohenzollern, ex-War Lord, ex-Emperor of Germany and ex-King of Prussia, is reported to have crossed the frontier into Holland and will seek refuge in Middachten Castle, in the town of Desteeg.

The Kaiser's party reached the Dutch frontier at 7:30 yesterday morning, according to London Daily Mail advices. It is said he was accompanied by the whole German General Staff and that Field Marshal von Hindenburg was in the party.

According to London dispatches the Kaiser signed

Continued on the Seventh Page.

War Ends at 6 A. M. Today, Boston Time, Says Washington

Announcement Made at 2:45 A M by State Department

WASHINGTON, Nov 11—By A.P.—Armistice terms have been signed by Germany, the State Department announced at 2:45 o'clock this morning.

The war will end this morning at 6 o'clock, Washington time, 11 o'clock Paris time.

The announcement was made verbally by an official of the State Department in this form:

"The armistice has been signed. It was signed

Continued on the Fourth Page.

Peace Brings Dangers That Your Money Will Prevent

A soldier in battle has plenty to do to keep his mind occupied. It is during the long, dull months when he is just waiting for something to happen—waiting to come home—that he especially needs the recreation and companionship which are given to him by the

Young Men's Christian Association
Young Women's Christian Association
National Catholic War Council—K. of C.
Jewish Welfare Board
American Library Association
War Camp Community Service
Salvation Army

It will take a year and more to get our army home. During that time, the boys will have very little **interesting** work to do. That is why demobilization is always **dangerous.**

The seven War Work Organizations are going to do everything possible to **prevent** this danger. They are going to stay with those boys until the last one of them is returned to his native soil and the **good** influences of home and friends.

This is a big undertaking and an expensive one. But isn't it worth every cent of the $250,000,000 which **must** be raised by the United War Work Campaign to accomplish their purpose?

Those soldiers went away to fight for you. You should give—and give to your utmost—to help bring them back—**clean** and **wholesome** and **manly.**

Mail contributions to Alfred L. Aiken, Treasurer, care of National Shawmut Bank, Boston

Exhibition of War Relics—Bacons' Store—Admission Free

GIVE

TODAY'S GLOBE CONTENTS

Page 1.

Chancellor Ebert issues proclamation announcing new Government and declaring first aim to be peace.

Germany may be allowed extension of time for replying to armistice terms.

Upheaval in Germany accomplished with little violence.

Allied armies drive Germans all along the battlefront from Belgium to Lorraine.

Kaiser signed letter of abdication at Army headquarters Saturday.

Page 2.

Bay State Street Railway Company will cease on Dec 1 to operate cars on 125 miles of track.

Ex-Lieut Gov Everett J. Lake of Connecticut lauds 101st Infantry at United War Work rally in Quincy.

Lieut Edouard V. Isaacs, U. S. N., who escaped from German camp, arrives home.

Boston planning for a celebration when official word of signing of armistice comes.

Memorial tablet dedicated in front of Winchester Town Hall.

Peace prospects give Revenue bill framers some new problems.

Page 3.

Campaign for $25,000,000 for United War Work Fund opens in New England.

Victory Boys and Girls' membership campaign, part of United War Work drive, opens in Faneuil Hall.

Score of mass meetings held in Catholic diocese in interest of United War Work campaign.

Page 4.

First and Second American Armies advance on front of 71 miles, capture Stenay, Grimaucourt and many fortified positions in Lorraine.

Republic proclaimed in Poland.

Dispersal sales interesting the harness horsemen seeking candidates for the futurities.

School football games this week likely to give a good line on the title chances.

Andover's chances considered good this year to break Exeter's winning streak.

Boxing bouts in many cities this week in aid of the War Work fund.

Father John's Medicine

Builds strength to fight off grip, colds and pneumonia. Builds up.—Advt.

TODAY'S GLOBE CONTENTS

Page 4.

Boston Base and U. S. S. New Jersey play 0-0 tie and Little Building defeats Hingham N. T. S. in Navy football games at Braves Field.

Stanley B. Bold and Charles M. Parker, Boston business partners, believed drowned in Florida.

Page 5.

Casualties for the country reported yesterday number 559.

Count von Reventlow flees to Denmark.

Germany unlikely to follow in Russia's footsteps, belief of Dousch-Fleurot.

Crews of German dreadnoughts join in revolt.

Page 6.

"Der Tag" by Uncle Dudley.

Cardinal O'Connell arranges for services of thanksgiving throughout the diocese when the armistice with Germany shall be signed.

The People's Lawyer.

Chaplain De Valles popular at front as "Father John."

Italians in Boston have big victory celebration.

Great enthusiasm for United War Work shown at Symphony Hall rally.

Page 7.

Gov McCall issues "Victory Day" proclamation.

German idea of Government goes down in ruin.

Krupp gun works in hands of rebels, Bertha Krupp arrested.

Deputy Ebert, new German Chancellor, long leader in Socialist party.

Attempt made to kill Prince Henry of Prussia.

Page 8.

Household Department.

Page 9.

Local organized labor optimistic over return of peace.

Albert Ballin, head of Hamburg-American Steamship Company, dies suddenly in Germany.

Evelyn Nordahl, 12, Randolph, killed by auto.

Page 12.

Bootleggers sell liquor two-thirds other to Devens men.

Bay State people called on to save 1,400,000,000 pounds of food for the Allies next year.

Finance Commission urges abolition of city Statistics Department.

Use the Globe's want and classified columns to get the best results. Business for sale? Autos for sale? Help wanted? Advertise in tomorrow's and Wednesday's Globe.

WINSLOW, ME, ALREADY 50 PERCENT OVER ITS QUOTA

PORTLAND, Me, Nov 10—Although soliciting for the War Work Campaign in Maine does not begin until Monday morning the town of Winslow in Kennebunk County reported to State headquarters today that it had already exceeded its quota by 50 percent, having raised nearly $5000 against an allotment of $3146. The canvass in Portland starts with an advance subscription of $83,000, nearly half the city's quota.

AMERICAN AIRMAN DROWNED

LONDON, Friday, Nov 8—Lieut George Nolonsbe, an airman of California, crashed into the sea Wednesday night and was drowned.

Evening Globe 2 Cents

Beginning Friday, Nov. 15th

Sunday Globe 6c and 7c

Beginning Sunday, Nov. 17th

Because of the increased cost of everything which enters into the production of a newspaper and in compliance with the expressed wishes of the War Industries Board, the price of the Evening Globe will advance on November 15 to 2 cents per copy. The Morning Globe will remain at 2 cents; the Sunday Globe price will be advanced to 6 cents in Boston and vicinity and sell for 7 cents elsewhere.

The white paper situation has become so acute that papers, which during the past year have gone to 2 cents, are already announcing a retail price of 3 to 5 cents per copy, finding the additional revenue did not begin to cover the increased expenses of the past few years.

Globe readers, to be sure of their copy of the Evening and Sunday Globe, should order the paper regularly, as newsdealers will have to adjust their orders to the actual demand.

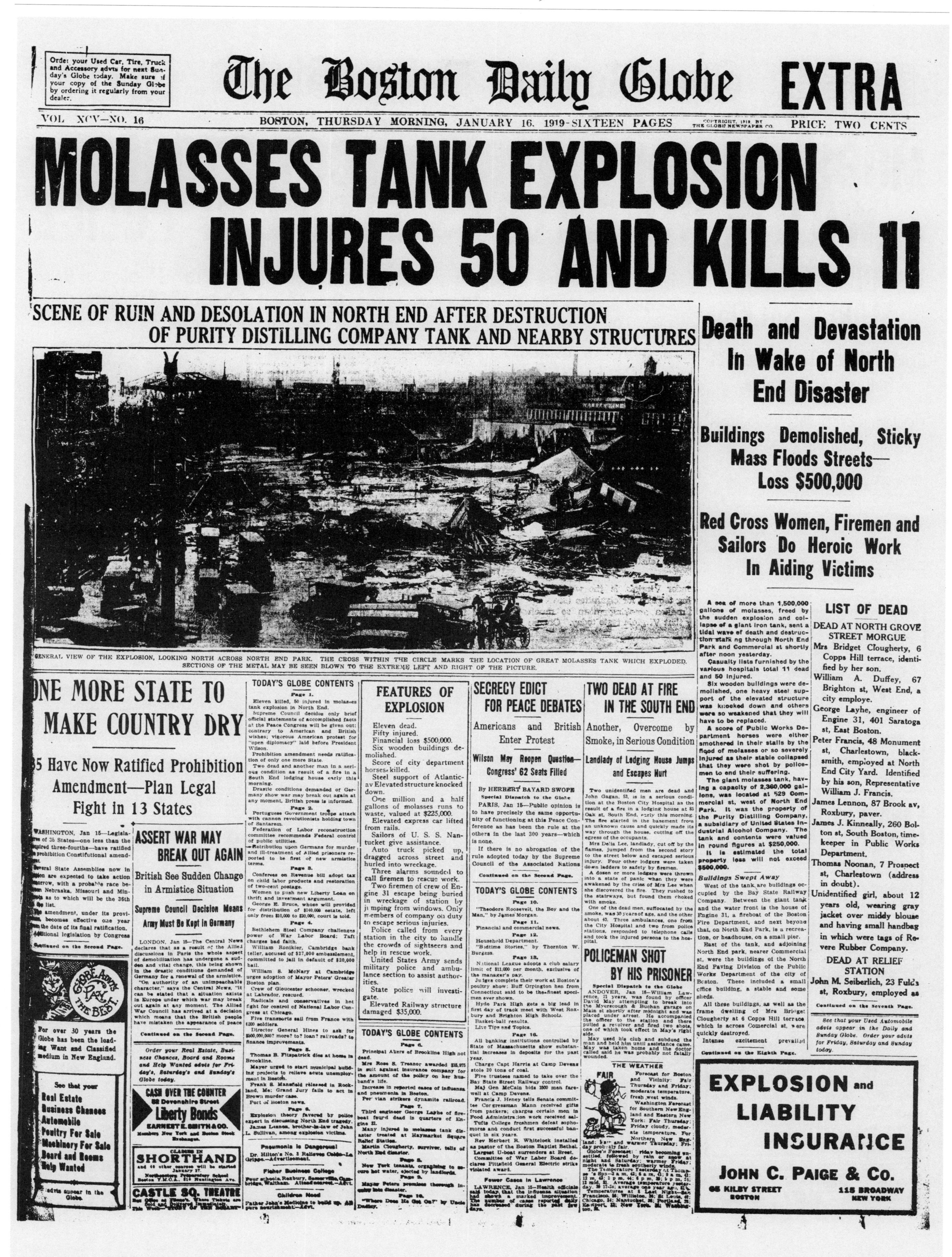

The Boston Daily Globe EXTRA

VOL XCV—NO. 16 BOSTON, THURSDAY MORNING, JANUARY 16, 1919—SIXTEEN PAGES COPYRIGHT, 1919, BY THE GLOBE NEWSPAPER CO. PRICE TWO CENTS

MOLASSES TANK EXPLOSION INJURES 50 AND KILLS 11

SCENE OF RUIN AND DESOLATION IN NORTH END AFTER DESTRUCTION OF PURITY DISTILLING COMPANY TANK AND NEARBY STRUCTURES

GENERAL VIEW OF THE EXPLOSION, LOOKING NORTH ACROSS NORTH END PARK. THE CROSS WITHIN THE CIRCLE MARKS THE LOCATION OF GREAT MOLASSES TANK WHICH EXPLODED. SECTIONS OF THE METAL MAY BE SEEN BLOWN TO THE EXTREME LEFT AND RIGHT OF THE PICTURE.

Death and Devastation In Wake of North End Disaster

Buildings Demolished, Sticky Mass Floods Streets—Loss $500,000

Red Cross Women, Firemen and Sailors Do Heroic Work In Aiding Victims

A sea of more than 1,500,000 gallons of molasses, freed by the sudden explosion and collapse of a giant iron tank, sent a tidal wave of death and destruction stalking through North End Park and Commercial st shortly after noon yesterday.

Casualty lists furnished by the various hospitals total 11 dead and 50 injured.

Six wooden buildings were demolished, one heavy steel support of the elevated structure was knocked down and others were so weakened that they will have to be replaced.

A score of Public Works Department horses were either smothered in their stalls by the flood of molasses or so severely injured as their stable collapsed that they were shot by policemen to end their suffering.

The giant molasses tank, having a capacity of 2,360,000 gallons, was located at 529 Commercial st, west of North End Park. It was the property of the Purity Distilling Company, a subsidiary of United States Industrial Alcohol Company. The tank and contents were valued in round figures at $250,000.

It is estimated the total property loss will not exceed $500,000.

Buildings Swept Away

West of the tank are buildings occupied by the Bay State Railway Company. Between the giant tank and the water front is the house of Engine 31, a fireboat of the Boston Fire Department, and next beyond that, on North End Park, is a recreation, or headhouse, on a small pier.

East of the tank, and adjoining North End park, nearer Commercial st, were the buildings of the North End Paving Division of the Public Works Department of the city of Boston. These included a small office building, a stable and some sheds.

All these buildings, as well as the frame dwelling of Mrs Bridget Clougherty at 6 Copps Hill terrace which is across Comercial st, were quickly destroyed.

Intense excitement prevailed

Continued on the Eighth Page.

LIST OF DEAD

DEAD AT NORTH GROVE STREET MORGUE

Mrs Bridget Clougherty, 6 Copps Hill terrace, identified by her son.

William A. Duffey, 67 Brighton st, West End, a city employe.

George Layhe, engineer of Engine 31, 401 Saratoga st, East Boston.

Peter Francis, 48 Monument st, Charlestown, blacksmith, employed at North End City Yard. Identified by his son, Representative William J. Francis.

James Lennon, 87 Brook av, Roxbury, paver.

James J. Kinneally, 260 Bolton st, South Boston, timekeeper in Public Works Department.

Thomas Noonan, 7 Prospect st, Charlestown (address in doubt).

Unidentified girl, about 12 years old, wearing gray jacket over middy blouse and having small handbag in which were tags of Revere Rubber Company.

DEAD AT RELIEF STATION

John M. Seiberlich, 23 Fulda st, Roxbury, employed as

Continued on the Seventh Page.

ONE MORE STATE TO MAKE COUNTRY DRY

35 Have Now Ratified Prohibition Amendment—Plan Legal Fight in 13 States

WASHINGTON, Jan 15—Legislatures of 35 States—one less than the required three-fourths—have ratified the prohibition Constitutional amendment.

Several State Assemblies now in session are expected to take action tomorrow, with a probable race between Nebraska, Missouri and Minnesota as to which will be the 36th on the list.

The amendment, under its provisions, becomes effective one year from the date of its final ratification.

Additional legislation by Congress

Continued on the Second Page.

ASSERT WAR MAY BREAK OUT AGAIN

British See Sudden Change in Armistice Situation

Supreme Council Decision Means Army Must Be Kept in Germany

LONDON, Jan 15—The Central News declares that as a result of the Allied discussions in Paris the whole aspect of demobilization has undergone a sudden and vital change, this being shown in the drastic conditions demanded of Germany for a renewal of the armistice.

"On authority of an unimpeachable character," says the Central News, "it can be stated that a situation exists in Europe under which war may break out again at any moment. The Allied War Council has arrived at a decision which means that the British people have mistaken the appearance of peace

Continued on the Second Page.

TODAY'S GLOBE CONTENTS

Page 1.

Eleven killed, 50 injured in molasses tank explosion in North End.

Supreme Council decides only brief official statements of accomplished facts at the Peace Congress will be given out; contrary to American and British wishes; vigorous American protest for "open diplomacy" laid before President Wilson.

Prohibition amendment needs ratification of only one more State.

Two dead and another man in a serious condition as result of a fire in a South End lodging house early this morning.

Drastic conditions demanded of Germany show war may break out again at any moment, British press is informed.

Page 2.

Portuguese Government troops attack with cannon revolutionists holding town of Santarem.

Federation of Labor reconstruction committee recommends Federal control of public utilities.

Retribution upon Germans for murder and ill-treatment of Allied prisoners reported to be first of new armistice terms.

Page 3.

Conferees on Revenue bill adopt tax on child labor products and restoration of two-cent postage.

Women to push new Liberty Loan on thrift and investment argument.

George E. Bruce, whose will provided for distribution of $140,000 estate, left only from $10,000 to $20,000, court is told.

Page 4.

Bethlehem Steel Company challenges power of War Labor Board; Taft charges bad faith.

William Ronikier, Cambridge bank teller, accused of $27,000 embezzlement, committed to jail in default of $20,000 bail.

William S. McNary at Cambridge urges adoption of Mayor Peters' Greater Boston plan.

Crew of Gloucester schooner, wrecked at Labrador, rescued.

Radicals and conservatives in hot fight for control of National Labor Congress at Chicago.

Five transports sail from France with 1200 soldiers.

Director General Hines to ask for $500,000,000? more? to? loan? railroads? to finance improvements.

Page 5.

Thomas B. Fitzpatrick dies at home in Brookline.

Mayor urged to start municipal building projects to relieve acute unemployment in Boston.

Frank S. Mansfield released in Rockland, Me; Grand Jury fails to act in Brown murder case.

Port of Boston news.

Page 6.

Explosion theory favored by police expert in discussing North End tragedy.

James Lennon, brother-in-law of John L. Sullivan, among explosion victims.

FEATURES OF EXPLOSION

Eleven dead.

Fifty injured.

Financial loss $500,000.

Six wooden buildings demolished.

Score of city department horses killed.

Steel support of Atlantic-av Elevated structure knocked down.

One million and a half gallons of molasses runs to waste, valued at $225,000.

Elevated express car lifted from rails.

Sailors of U. S. S. Nantucket give assistance.

Auto truck picked up, dragged across street and hurled into wreckage.

Three alarms sounded to call firemen to rescue work.

Two firemen of crew of Engine 31 escape being buried in wreckage of station by jumping from windows. Only members of company on duty to escape serious injuries.

Police called from every station in the city to handle the crowds of sightseers and help in rescue work.

United States Army sends military police and ambulance section to assist authorities.

State police will investigate.

Elevated Railway structure damaged $35,000.

TODAY'S GLOBE CONTENTS

Page 6.

Principal Akers of Brookline High not dead.

Mrs Rose S. Treanor awarded $15,975 in suit against insurance company for the amount of the policy on her husband's life.

Increase in reported cases of influenza and pneumonia in Boston.

Peruvian strikers dynamite railroad.

Page 7.

Third engineer George Layhe of fireboat found dead in quarters of Engine 31.

Many injured in molasses tank disaster treated at Haymarket Square Relief Station.

Martin Clougherty, survivor, tells of North End disaster.

Page 8.

New York tenants, organizing to secure hot water, ejected by landlords.

Page 9.

Mayor Peters promises thorough inquiry into disaster.

Page 10.

"Where Does He Get On?" by Uncle Dudley.

SECRECY EDICT FOR PEACE DEBATES

Americans and British Enter Protest

Wilson May Reopen Question—Congress' 62 Seats Filled

By HERBERT BAYARD SWOPE

Special Dispatch to the Globe

PARIS, Jan 15—Public opinion is to have precisely the same opportunity of functioning at this Peace Conference as has been the rule at the others in the last 300 years—which is none.

If there is no abrogation of the rule adopted today by the Supreme Council of the Associated Nations

Continued on the Second Page.

TODAY'S GLOBE CONTENTS

Page 10.

"Theodore Roosevelt, the Boy and the Man," by James Morgan.

Page 11.

Financial and commercial news.

Page 12.

Household Department.

"Bedtime Stories," by Thornton W. Burgess.

Page 13.

National League adopts a club salary limit of $11,000 per month, exclusive of the manager's pay.

Judges complete their work at Boston's poultry show; Buff Orpington hen from Connecticut said to be the finest specimen ever shown.

Hyde Park High gets a big lead in first day of track meet with West Roxbury and Brighton High Schools.

Basket-ball results.

Live Tips and Topics.

Page 16.

All banking institutions controlled by State of Massachusetts show substantial increases in deposits for the past year.

Charge Capt Harris at Camp Devens stole 20 tons of coal.

Five trustees named to take over the Bay State Street Railway control.

Maj Gen McCain bids 1500 men farewell at Camp Devens.

Francis J. Heney tells Senate committee Congressman Mann received gifts from packers; charges certain men in Food Administration work received salaries.

Tufts College freshmen defeat sophomores and conduct first successful banquet in six years.

Rev Herbert R. Whitelock installed as pastor of the Boston Baptist Bethel.

Largest U-boat surrenders at Brest.

Committee of War Labor Board declares Pittsfield General Electric strike violated award.

Fewer Cases in Lawrence

LAWRENCE, Jan 15—Health officials said today that the influenza situation had shown a marked improvement. The number of cases reported daily has decreased during the past few days.

TWO DEAD AT FIRE IN THE SOUTH END

Another, Overcome by Smoke, in Serious Condition

Landlady of Lodging House Jumps and Escapes Hurt

Two unidentified men are dead and John Gagan, 53, is in a serious condition at the Boston City Hospital as the result of a fire in a lodging house at 85 Oak st, South End, early this morning. The fire started in the basement from an unknown cause and quickly made its way through the house, cutting off the egress of the occupants.

Mrs Delia Lee, landlady, cut off by the flames, jumped from the second story to the street below and escaped serious injury. Four other lodgers were taken down ladders to safety by firemen.

A dozen or more lodgers were thrown into a state of panic when they were awakened by the cries of Mrs Lee when she discovered the fire. They rushed to the stairways, but found them choked with smoke.

One of the dead men, suffocated by the smoke, was 30 years of age, and the other about 40. Three ambulances, one from the City Hospital and two from police stations, responded to telephone calls and took the injured persons to the hospital.

POLICEMAN SHOT BY HIS PRISONER

Special Dispatch to the Globe

ANDOVER, Jan 16—William Lawrence, 21 years, was found by officer David May attempting to break into the Myerscough & Buchan garage on Main st shortly after midnight and was placed under arrest. He accompanied the officer to the station and there pulled a revolver and fired two shots, one of which took effect in May's right side.

May used his club and subdued the man and held him until assistance came. May was taken home and the doctor called said he was probably not fatally wounded.

THE WEATHER

FAIR

Forecast for Boston and Vicinity: Fair Thursday and Friday; moderate temperature, fresh west winds.

Washington Forecast for Southern New England and Eastern New York: Fair Thursday; Friday cloudy, moderate temperature. For Northern New England: Fair and warmer Thursday; Friday probably fair.

Globe's Forecast: Friday becoming unsettled, followed by rain or snow at night and Saturday; warmer Friday; moderate to fresh southerly winds.

The Temperature Yesterday at Thompson's Spa—3 a m, 42; 6 a m, 41; 9 a m, 41; 12 m, 43; 3 p m, 44; 6 p m, 39; 9 p m, 31; 12 mid, 31. Average temperature yesterday, [illegible]; average one year ago, [illegible].

Temperatures at 8 Last Night—San Francisco, 56; Williston, 28; St Louis, 42; Chicago, 34; Nantucket, 38; Portland, [illegible]; Eastport, [illegible]; New York, [illegible]; Washington, [illegible].

The Boston Daily Globe EXTRA

VOL. XCVI NO. 72 — BOSTON, WEDNESDAY MORNING, SEPTEMBER 10, 1919—EIGHTEEN PAGES — PRICE TWO CENTS

MOBS SMASH WINDOWS, LOOT STORES
WILD NIGHT FOLLOWS STRIKE OF POLICE

Lawless Throngs Surge Through Unprotected City, Demolishing Property—Members of Union Quit Stations at 5:45 in Afternoon, Leaving Only 30 Out of Usual 420 Patrolmen On Duty—Metropolitan Police Rushed to Quell Trouble in South Boston

WASHINGTON ST STORES SACKED

Goods Worth Thousands of Dollars Are Stolen

Plundering Everywhere, Hoodlums Roam South Boston Streets

A crowd of fully 200, in which there was a sprinkling of young women, a few sailors and soldiers, swept up Washington st just before midnight, starting at Milk st, breaking in the windows of numerous stores and stealing the contents of the windows. It is estimated that hundreds of dollars worth of goods were stolen.

The window of Adams, the Tailor, 357 Washington st, was the first attacked. The crowd gathered, and someone either kicked in the window or hurled some hard substance against it. There was a crash and the window was quickly cleaned of its goods.

In order the same treatment was meted out at Aronson's shoe store, 355 Washington st, Peter, the Rabbi, a hat store, 367 Washington st, United Cigar Stores Company, 369 Washington st, the Boston Tailoring Company, 371 Washington st, and Feener's, at Avery and Washington sts.

Near Winter st a lone policeman appealed to the crowd to disperse, but

Continued on the Fifth Page.

Street Lights Burn All Night

Shortly after 1 o'clock this morning Supt Crowley requested the Edison Electric Illuminating Company to keep all street lights burning until daylight, and assurance was given that the request would be complied with.

Use the Globe's Help Wanted columns to get good help. If out of town, mail your advts for next Sunday's Globe today.

STRIKING POLICEMEN MEET AT FAY HALL

Officers From Other Greater Boston Cities Attend

Union Officers Report 1400 Patrolmen Are Out

Members of the Metropolitan Park Police and policemen from Greater Boston cities attended the meeting of the Boston Policemen's Union at Fay Hall, Washington and Dover sts, last night. They came, it was stated, to discuss the situation.

While the identity of the men from outside of this city was carefully guarded, not even the cities from which they came being given out for publication, it was stated that these officers came to discuss the possibility of an attempt to bring them to this city. None of these men, it was said, have been approached directly on this question.

It was stated last night that when the order was given for a large number of Metropolitan Park policemen to prepare to come to Boston from Revere Beach, Nahant, Swampscott and Middlesex Fells

Continued on the Fifth Page.

Now is the time to rent rooms, apartments and houses for the Fall and Winter months. If out of town, kindly mail your advts for next Sunday's Globe today.

FIFTY STUDENTS AT HARVARD ENROLLED

Will Help Protect Life and Property in Boston

Action Urged by Pres Lowell and Emergency Committee

About 50 Harvard students had signed for the Boston Police emergency force at the Harvard enrolling office at 2 University Hall at midnight.

Coach Robert T. Fisher of the football team denied a statement that he had called off gridiron practice for the duration of the strike. The enrolling committee records showed the name of no Crimson gridiron star, and the emergency committee at Cambridge insisted that the students will be used only as a reserve force in case of extreme need, and not as a corps to patrol the streets immediately.

The Harvard students who signed will report to Supt Pierce this morning at

Continued on the Fifth Page.

THE WEATHER

RAIN

Forecast for Boston and Vicinity: Wednesday unsettled, occasional showers; Thursday generally fair; moderate northwest winds.

Washington Forecast for Northern New England: Cloudy Wednesday and Thursday; continued cool.

For Eastern New York—Cloudy Wednesday, rain in extreme south; Thursday cloudy.

For Southern New England—Cloudy Wednesday; rain in east and south; Thursday cloudy.

Globe Forecast—Unsettled, generally fair Thursday and Friday; temperatures near normal; light shifting winds.

The Temperature Yesterday at Thompson's Spa—3 a m, 58; 6 a m, 57; 9 a m, 57; 12 m, 57; 3 p m, 62; 6 p m, 63; 9 p m, 60; 12 mid, 50. Average temperature yesterday, 58 11-12; average one year ago, 58 5-12.

Temperatures at 8 Last Night—San Francisco, 64; Williston, 76; St Louis, 92; Chicago, 68; Nantucket, 58; Portland, 52; Eastport, 54; New York, 62; Washington, 76. Precipitation in Boston, 24 hours, to 8 p m, .62.

SUMMARY OF THE STRIKE SITUATION

Strike began at 5:45 yesterday afternoon. Only 30 of the 420 first-half men reported for duty.

Mayor Peters issued appeal to citizens to maintain order.

Volunteer force to be called out at 8:00 this morning.

Stores looted all over the city; in South Boston, all along Washington st, in Andrew sq, and down Hanover st.

Highway robbery on Washington st in the presence of a crowd of 500 people.

Metropolitan Park Police rushed to Bowdoin sq and to South Boston to disperse rioters.

South Boston streets a mess of looted and wasted provisions.

Mayor Peters and Police Commissioner Curtis conferred at 3 o'clock with Gov Coolidge at State House.

Gov Coolidge wrote Mayor Peters that improvements named by Pres McInnes of Policemen's Union should initiate with Mayor and City Council.

Mayor Peters denied he refused salary increase and declared he gave policemen and firemen, as well, all they asked.

Pres Lowell issued call for all Harvard students to prepare themselves to be ready to assist in preserving order.

Harvard Emergency Committee organized and issued call for volunteers. Says Harvard men will not be "strikebreakers."

Tremendous volume of strike and riot insurance placed by Boston business houses and many insurance offices open last night handling unusual volume of business.

Large number of false alarms sent in from boxes in outlying districts.

Extra armed guards on duty in the banking district.

Peters Calls on Citizens to Aid Officials of the City in Preserving Order

Volunteers to Begin Duties at 8 This Morning—Coolidge Won't Oust Curtis

Following a quiet and orderly strike of the police patrolmen of Boston last night, hoodlums took possession of the downtown streets, and by midnight had done a great deal of damage all over the city.

Except for a few minor injuries from flying glass, nobody was hurt. But store fronts were smashed and goods of all sorts were stolen by the roughs absolutely at will. For the first time in the memory of man, Boston was given over to lawlessness.

The volunteer policemen were not called to duty, and will not be called until 8 this morning. The Metropolitan Park police were sent into the city and distributed in squads where the trouble seemed thickest. Thirty went over to South Boston, where a crowd was pulling trolleys off the wires and smashing car windows and robbing stores.

Ten others were sent in haste at midnight to Court st. Here a big crowd was having its own way with the shop windows. It had been roving about for two hours, had smashed in several stores and stolen everything in the windows. It was moving up Court st when Sergt Flaherty faced it with his pistol in his hand.

Several reports like pistol shots were heard in the crowd; they

Continued on the Fourth Page.

BURNS HOLDS CROWD BACK WITH REVOLVER

Saves Employer's Goods as 5000 Threaten

With a 38-caliber revolver in his hand, James J. Burns, aged 70, held at bay a crowd of 5000 men and boys who were having things all their own way in the Scollay sq and Haymarket sq section late last night, while oranges from the smashed windows of the Wholesale Provision Company rolled around his feet.

The crowd had just smashed the windows of the Lewis shoe store, had raided the Dock-sq Fruit Company's stand and was jamming down Union st.

Continued on the Fourth Page.

SCORES VOLUNTEER FOR POLICE DUTY

Harvard Athletes Among Those Ready to Serve

While scores of volunteers offered their services at the Chamber of Commerce in the event of a police strike, Supt William H. Pierce yesterday issued the summons which, it is believed, may place many civilians on duty today as policemen on the streets of Boston.

This statement is made on the authority of Prof Edwin H. Hall of Harvard, who was the first man to volunteer for the emergency force, and not

Continued on the Fifth Page.

BYSTANDERS MUST ASSIST OFFICERS

In the event that a police officer, sheriff, deputy sheriff, constable or watchman needs assistance in making an arrest, they have the right, under the law, to call upon any bystander for assistance and should the latter refuse to give such assistance, he subjects himself to arrest and may be punished by imprisonment for not more than one month or by a fine of not more than $50.

Boston police officials, in coaching the volunteer policemen for possible strike duty, are believed to have laid emphasis upon this provision of the statutes.

TODAY'S GLOBE CONTENTS

Page 1.

Police strike begins; night of disorder and lawlessness follows.

Stores in business districts looted by crowds.

Scores volunteer for police duty.

Man with revolver saves employer's goods from crowd of 5000.

About 50 Harvard students enroll for emergency police force.

Page 2.

John A. Realer thinks Boston Elevated would be a good purchase for the State.

Sharp clash among counsel at Christian Science litigation hearing.

Striking policemen meet at Fay Hall; patrolmen from other cities there.

Postal employes urge salary raises before Congressional joint commission at New York.

Lower prices on clothing coming soon.

Bergen, Norway, wireless station hears mysterious voice from America.

Page 3.

Cardinal Mercier arrives in New York, receiving the welcome of a hero.

Middle West stock raisers defend the packers before the Senate Agriculture Committee.

Bay State carmen's leaders may call strike today to start Friday morning.

Prices for women's clothing were never so high in Paris as at present.

Paris actors' strike compromised.

Page 4.

Bernard J. Rothwell and 47 other volunteers for police duty issue public appeal for citizens to aid.

Governor, Mayor and Police Commissioner confer at State House.

Page 5.

Uniformed policemen missing from streets on first night of strike

Page 6.

"Do Not Get Out the Magnifying Glasses," by Uncle Dudley.

Page 7.

Walter Cox, the New England reinsman, wins $10,000 Empire State stake at Syracuse, driving McGregor the Great.

National League—Pittsburg 6, Boston 3 (first game); Pittsburg 6, Boston 1 (second game), Philadelphia 2, Cincinnati 0. Chicago 4, New York 1 (first game); New York 7, Chicago 1 (second game). St Louis 4, Brooklyn 2.

American League—Chicago 1, Washington games postponed, rain.

Red Sox and Browns to play two games this afternoon.

TODAY'S GLOBE CONTENTS

Page 7.

Harvard football squad increased to an even 100; Coach Fisher denies any plan to call off practice to enlist men for police work.

Garland, Yale, beat Helm, Harvard, in singles in the intercollegiate tennis tourney.

Jesse P. Guilford wins the Massachusetts open golf championship.

Suspicion of fake in Parker-Donovan bout in Mechanic's Building; two crowds rush doors and gain entrance free.

Page 8.

Financial news.

Page 9.

Financial and commercial news.

Autone Soares, Taunton, killed as train hits auto in that city.

Page 10.

First Division to follow Gen Pershing down New York's 5th av today.

John Mitchell, labor leader, dies in New York following operation.

Massachusetts branch, A. F. of L., at Greenfield, demands removal of Police Commissioner Curtis and votes for recognition of Irish republic, Eamonn De Va'era giving address.

John F. Hardy appointed supervisor of the Federal census in Suffolk County.

Page 11.

Alleged slayer of Somerville man caught after running revolver fight with the police.

Policemen and firemen of Brookline are given salary increase.

Dr Samuel G. Inman admits before Senate sub-committee his inability to prove some of statements as to Mexican affairs.

Miners at convention at Cleveland insistent on demands for more pay and shorter hours.

Fishing smack founders off Tom Moore's Rocks, Marblehead.

G. A. R. veterans to parade in Columbus, O, today.

Marriage intentions.

Page 12.

Household Department.

Page 13.

Brave skipper saved crew of fishermen off Eastern Point.

Penal Institutions Commissioner Bates charges inaccuracies in Finance Commission report, urging the abandoning of Deer Island.

Hundreds attend funeral of John F. Dever.

Port of Boston news.

Page 18.

President Wilson in Minnesota declares reduction of cost of living depends on peace treaty's ratification as preliminary to labor adjustments and increased production.

British Trades Union Congress pledges cooperation for immediate revision of "harsh provisions" of the German peace treaty.

German peace treaty to be reported to Senate today.

VOLUNTEERS REPORT AS CITIZENS, SAYS LOWELL

At a late hour last night Pres Lowell of Harvard University gave out the following statement:

"The university has received a message from Gov Coolidge, through the Governor's secretary by telephone, asking that students at Harvard willing to volunteer for police duty be requested to report to Supt Pierce in the morning.

"The fact should be emphasized that these volunteers are reporting simply as citizens of the Commonwealth in response to a call from the Governor."

Students in the Summer School who volunteer for police duty will be excused from classes should they be on duty as emergency police officers, and will be allowed to take make-up final examinations.

TODAY'S GLOBE CONTENTS

Rumania announces she will refuse to sign the Austrian treaty without reservations, which Allies will reject, signatures by Serbia and Greece in doubt.

AFTERNOON	EVENING
10th Salem	Haverhill
11th Medford	Cambridge
12th Framingham	Marlboro
13th Wakefield	Lynn
14th Sunday	Morning—Waltham
Malden	Westboro
16th Lowell	Quincy
17th Attleboro	Taunton
18th Fall River	New Bedford
19th Fitchburg	Worcester
20th Greenfield	Holyoke
21st Sunday	Morning—Pittsfield
Westfield	Northampton
22nd Melrose	Chelsea
23rd Gloucester	Newburyport

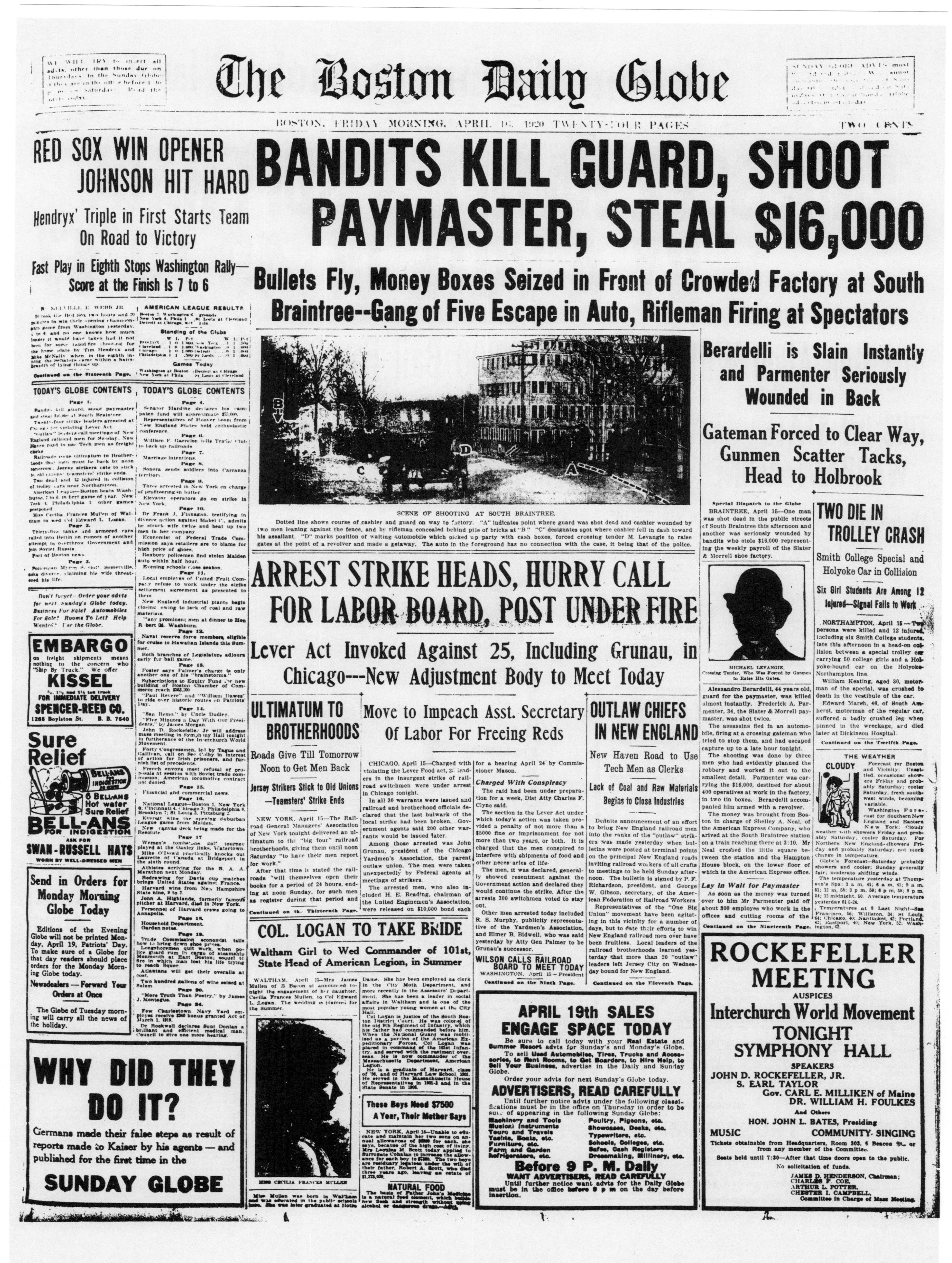

The Boston Daily Globe

BOSTON, FRIDAY MORNING, APRIL 16, 1920 TWENTY-FOUR PAGES — TWO CENTS

BANDITS KILL GUARD, SHOOT PAYMASTER, STEAL $16,000

Bullets Fly, Money Boxes Seized in Front of Crowded Factory at South Braintree--Gang of Five Escape in Auto, Rifleman Firing at Spectators

SCENE OF SHOOTING AT SOUTH BRAINTREE.

Dotted line shows course of cashier and guard on way to factory. "A" indicates point where guard was shot dead and cashier wounded by two men leaning against the fence, and by rifleman concealed behind pile of bricks at "B." "C" designates spot where cashier fell in dash toward his assailant. "D" marks position of waiting automobile which picked up party with cash boxes, forced crossing tender M. Levangie to raise gates at the point of a revolver and made a getaway. The auto in the foreground has no connection with the case, it being that of the police.

Berardelli is Slain Instantly and Parmenter Seriously Wounded in Back

Gateman Forced to Clear Way, Gunmen Scatter Tacks, Head to Holbrook

Special Dispatch to the Globe

BRAINTREE, April 15—One man was shot dead in the public streets of South Braintree this afternoon and another was seriously wounded by bandits who stole $16,000 representing the weekly payroll of the Slater & Morrell shoe factory.

MICHAEL LEVANGIE, Crossing Tender, Who Was Forced by Gunmen to Raise His Gates.

Alessandro Berardelli, 44 years old, guard for the paymaster, was killed almost instantly. Frederick A. Parmenter, 34, the Slater & Morrell paymaster, was shot twice.

The assassins fled in an automobile, firing at a crossing gateman who tried to stop them, and had escaped capture up to a late hour tonight.

The shooting was done by three men who had evidently planned the robbery and worked it out to the smallest detail. Parmenter was carrying the $16,000, destined for about 400 operatives at work in the factory, in two tin boxes. Berardelli accompanied him armed with a revolver.

The money was brought from Boston in charge of Shelley A. Neal, of the American Express Company, who arived at the South Braintree station on a train reaching there at 3:10. Mr Neal crossed the little square between the station and the Hampton House block, on the lower floor of which is the American Express office.

Lay in Wait for Paymaster

As soon as the money was turned over to him Mr Parmenter paid off about 300 employes who work in the offices and cutting rooms of the

Continued on the Nineteenth Page.

RED SOX WIN OPENER JOHNSON HIT HARD

Hendryx' Triple in First Starts Team On Road to Victory

Fast Play in Eighth Stops Washington Rally—Score at the Finish Is 7 to 6

By MELVILLE E. WEBB JR

It took the Red Sox two hours and 20 minutes to win their opening championship game from Washington yesterday, 7 to 6, and no one knows how much longer it would have taken had it not been for some rapid fire shooting for the home plate by Tim Hendryx and Mike McNally when, in the eighth inning, the Senators came within a hairsbreadth of tying things up.

Continued on the Sixteenth Page.

AMERICAN LEAGUE RESULTS

Boston 7, Washington 6. New York 4, Phila 1. St Louis at Cleveland grounds. Detroit at Chicago, wet grounds.

Standing of the Clubs

	W	L	Pct		W	L	Pct
Boston	1	0	1.000	New York	1	1	.500
Cleveland	1	0	1.000	Washington	0	1	.000
Chicago	1	0	1.000	Detroit	0	1	.000
Philadelphia	1	1	.500	St Louis	0	1	.000

Games Today

Washington at Boston; Detroit at Chicago; New York at Phila; St Louis at Cleveland

TODAY'S GLOBE CONTENTS

Page 1.

Bandits kill guard, shoot paymaster and steal $16,000 at South Braintree.

Twenty-four strike leaders arrested at Chicago for violating Lever Act.

"outlaw" leaders call meetings of New England railroad men for Sunday. New Haven road to use Tech men as freight clerks.

Railroads issue ultimatum to Brotherhoods that men must be back by noon tomorrow. Jersey strikers vote to stick to old unions; teamsters' strike ends.

Two dead and 12 injured in collision of trolley cars near Northampton.

American League—Boston beats Washington, 7 to 6, in first game of year. New York 4, Philadelphia 1; other games postponed.

Miss Cecilia Frances Mullen of Waltham to wed Col Edward L. Logan.

Page 2.

Thirty-five tanks and armored cars called into Berlin on rumors of another attempt to overthrow Government and join Soviet Russia.

Port of Boston news.

Page 3.

Policeman Myron S. Goff, Somerville, asks divorce, claiming his wife threatened his life.

Page 4.

Senator Harding declares his campaign fund will approximate $75,000.

Representatives of Hoover boom from New England States hold enthusiastic conference.

Page 6.

William F. Garcelon tells Traffic Club to back up railroads.

Page 7.

Marriage intentions.

Page 8.

Sonora sends soldiers into Carranza territory.

Page 9.

Three arrested in New York on charge of profiteering in butter.

Elevator operators go on strike in New York.

Page 10.

Dr Frank J. Flanagan, testifying in divorce action against Mabel C., admits he struck wife twice and beat up two men in her company.

Economist of Federal Trade Commission says retailers are to blame for high price of shoes.

Roxbury policemen find stolen Malden auto within half hour.

Evening schools close season.

Page 11.

Local employes of United Fruit Company refuse to work under the strike settlement agreement as presented to them.

New England industrial plants begin closing owing to lack of coal and raw materials.

Many prominent men at dinner to Hon Robert M. Washburn.

Page 12.

Naval reserve force members eligible for cruise to Hawaiian Islands this Summer.

Both branches of Legislature adjourn early for ball game.

Page 13.

Foster says Palmer's charge is only another one of his "brainstorms."

Subscriptions to Equity Fund for new building of Boston Chamber of Commerce reach $563,300.

"Paul Revere" and "William Dawes" to ride over historic routes on Patriots' Day.

Page 14.

"San Remo," by Uncle Dudley.

"Five Minutes a Day With Our Presidents," by James Morgan.

John D. Rockefeller Jr will address mass meeting in Symphony Hall tonight in furtherance of the Interchurch World Movement.

Forty Congressmen, led by Tague and Gallivan, call on Sec Colby in interest of action for Irish prisoners, and further list of precedents.

French envoys meet refusal of proposals at session with Soviet trade commission; American locomotive contract not denied.

Page 15.

Financial and commercial news.

Page 16.

National League—Boston 1, New York 0; Cincinnati 6, Chicago 3; Philadelphia 8, Brooklyn 7; St Louis 3, Pittsburg 2.

Everett wins the opening Suburban League game from Malden.

New canvas deck being made for the Resolute.

Page 17.

Women's tombstone golf tourney played at the Oakley links, Watertown.

Mike O'Dowd practically knocks out Laurent of Canada at Bridgeport in the sixth round.

Athletes arriving for the B. A. A. Marathon next Monday.

Redrawing for Davis cup matches brings United States against France.

Harvard wins from New Hampshire State nine, 9 to 2.

John A. Highlands, formerly famous pitcher at Harvard, died in New York.

Personnel of Harvard crews going to Annapolis.

Page 18.

Household Department.

Garden notes.

Page 19.

Trade Commission economist tells how to bring down shoe prices.

Longshoremen quit work when police guard run to cargo of steamship Monmouth at East Boston; sequel to fire in which man lost his life trying to reach liquor.

Atlantans will get their overalls at cost.

Two hundred gallons of wine seized at Salem.

"More Truth Than Poetry," by James J. Montague.

Page 20.

Few Charlestown Navy Yard employes receive $240 bonus granted Act of March 1, 1919.

Dr Rockwell declares Supt Donlan a brilliant and efficient medical man. Council to give one more hearing.

Send in Orders for Monday Morning Globe Today

Editions of the Evening Globe will not be printed Monday, April 19, Patriots' Day. To make sure of a Globe for that day readers should place orders for the Monday Morning Globe today.

Newsdealers — Forward Your Orders at Once

The Globe of Tuesday morning will carry all the news of the holiday.

ARREST STRIKE HEADS, HURRY CALL FOR LABOR BOARD, POST UNDER FIRE

Lever Act Invoked Against 25, Including Grunau, in Chicago---New Adjustment Body to Meet Today

ULTIMATUM TO BROTHERHOODS

Roads Give Till Tomorrow Noon to Get Men Back

Jersey Strikers Stick to Old Unions —Teamsters' Strike Ends

NEW YORK, April 15—The Railroad General Managers' Association of New York tonight delivered an ultimatum to the "big four" railroad brotherhoods, giving them until noon Saturday "to have their men report for work."

After that time it stated the railroads "will themselves open their books for a period of 24 hours, ending at noon Sunday, for such men as register during that period and

Continued on the Thirteenth Page.

Move to Impeach Asst. Secretary Of Labor For Freeing Reds

CHICAGO, April 15—Charged with violating the Lever Food act, 25 leaders in the insurgent strike of railroad switchmen were under arrest in Chicago tonight.

In all 30 warrants were issued and railroad and brotherhood officials declared that the last bulwark of the local strike had been broken. Government agents said 200 other warrants would be issued later.

Among those arrested was John Grunau, president of the Chicago Yardmen's Association, the parent outlaw union. The men were taken unexpectedly by Federal agents at meetings of strikers.

The arrested men, who also included H. E. Reading, chairman of the United Enginemen's Association, were released on $10,000 bond each for a hearing April 24 by Commissioner Mason.

Charged With Conspiracy

The raid had been under preparation for a week, Dist Atty Charles F. Clyne said.

The section in the Lever Act under which today's action was taken provided a penalty of not more than a $5000 fine or imprisonment for not more than two years, or both. It is charged that the men conspired to interfere with shipments of food and other necessaries of life.

The men, it was declared, generally showed resentment against the Government action and declared they would continue the strike. After the arrests 300 switchmen voted to stay out.

Other men arrested today included R. S. Murphy, publicity representative of the Yardmen's Association, and Elmer B. Bidwell, who was said yesterday by Atty Gen Palmer to be Grunau's successor.

WILSON CALLS RAILROAD BOARD TO MEET TODAY

WASHINGTON, April 15 – President

Continued on the Ninth Page.

OUTLAW CHIEFS IN NEW ENGLAND

New Haven Road to Use Tech Men as Clerks

Lack of Coal and Raw Materials Begins to Close Industries

Definite announcement of an effort to bring New England railroad men into the ranks of the "outlaw" strikers was made yesterday when bulletins were posted at terminal points on the principal New England roads inviting railroad workers of all crafts to meetings to be held Sunday afternoon. The bulletin is signed by P. F. Richardson, president, and George W. Gibson, secretary, of the American Federation of Railroad Workers.

Representatives of the "One Big Union" movement have been agitating in this vicinity for a number of days, but to date their efforts to win New England railroad men over have been fruitless. Local leaders of the railroad brotherhoods learned yesterday that more than 20 "outlaw" leaders left Jersey City on Wednesday bound for New England.

Continued on the Eleventh Page.

COL. LOGAN TO TAKE BRIDE

Waltham Girl to Wed Commander of 101st, State Head of American Legion, in Summer

WALTHAM, April 15—Mrs James Mullen of 25 Bacon st announced tonight the engagement of her daughter, Cecilia Frances Mullen, to Col Edward L. Logan. The wedding is planned for the Summer.

Miss Mullen was born in Waltham and was educated in the public schools here. She was later graduated at Notre Dame. She has been employed as clerk in the City Moth Department, and more recently in the Assessors' Department. She has been a leader in social affairs in Waltham and is one of the most popular young women at the City Hall.

Col Logan is justice of the South Boston District Court. He was colonel of the old 9th Regiment of Infantry, which his father had commanded before him. When the National Guard was mobilized as a portion of the American Expeditionary Forces, Col Logan was placed in command of the 101st Infantry, and served with the regiment overseas. He is now commander of the Massachusetts Department, American Legion.

He is a graduate of Harvard, class of '98, and of Harvard Law School, 1901. He served in the Massachusetts House of Representatives in 1903-3 and in the State Senate in 1906.

MISS CECILIA FRANCES MULLEN

These Boys Need $7500 A Year, Their Mother Says

NEW YORK, April 15—Unable to educate and maintain her two sons on an annual allowance of $6000 for each, she says, because of the high cost of living, Mrs Loraine M. Scott today applied to Surrogate Cohalan to increase the allowance for each boy to $7500. The two boys are residuary legatees under the will of their father, Robert A. Scott, who died three years ago, leaving an estate of $1,370,000.

TWO DIE IN TROLLEY CRASH

Smith College Special and Holyoke Car in Collision

Six Girl Students Are Among 12 Injured—Signal Fails to Work

NORTHAMPTON, April 15—Two persons were killed and 12 injured, including six Smith College students, late this afternoon in a head-on collision between a special trolley car carrying 50 college girls and a Holyoke-bound car on the Holyoke-Northampton line.

William Keating, aged 30, motorman of the special, was crushed to death in the vestibule of the car.

Edward Marsh, 46, of South Amherst, motorman of the regular car, suffered a badly crushed leg when pinned in the wreckage, and died later at Dickinson Hospital.

Continued on the Twelfth Page.

THE WEATHER

CLOUDY

Forecast for Boston and Vicinity: Unsettled, occasional showers Friday and probably Saturday; cooler Saturday, fresh southwest winds, becoming variable.

Washington Forecast for Southern New England and Eastern New York: Cloudy weather with showers Friday and probably Saturday; cooler Saturday. For Northern New England—Showers Friday and probably Saturday; not much change in temperature.

Globe's Forecast—Saturday probably showers and cooler; Sunday generally fair; moderate shifting winds.

The temperature yesterday at Thompson's Spa: 3 a m, 41; 6 a m, 41; 9 a m, 51; 12 m, 58; 3 p m, 59; 6 p m, 59; 9 p m, 54; 12 midnight, 50. Average temperature yesterday 51 5-24.

Temperatures at 8 Last Night—San Francisco, 56; Williston, 34; St Louis, 64; Chicago, 40; Nantucket, 42; Portland, 42; Eastport, 40; New York, 52; Washington, 62.

Boston Evening Globe

Latest Evening Edition

BOSTON, WEDNESDAY EVENING, AUGUST 18, 1920—14 PAGES—TWO CENTS

7:30 FINAL—CLOSING STOCKS

TENNESSEE RATIFIES SUFFRAGE BY A VOTE OF 49 TO 47

Atty-Gen Allen Will Demand $100,000 Bail For Ponzi

THIS ON STATE WARRANT ALONE

Alleged Ponzi Agent, Neilsen, Is Held in $5000

Atty Gen J. Weston Allen stated this afternoon that at the present time his office will insist on $100,000 bail for Ponzi. This bail would be merely on the State's warrant against Ponzi. Any bail claimed by the Federal authorities or other claimants would be additional.

"After receivers are appointed matters might be altered," said Mr Allen.

Two Italians from Passaic, N J, came to the office this morning bringing $85,000 in Ponzi notes. They said they had been delegated by a large group of Ponzi investors in that town to bring the notes to Boston and record their claims with the Attorney General. Both of the men held large notes of their own.

Ponzi agents were apparently busier in New Jersey than in any other State outside of New England. It is the only State outside of New England from which claims have been recorded with the Attorney General, it is understood.

Ponzi Likely to Stay in Jail

Ponzi will be likely now to remain

Continued on the Fourteenth Page

AMBASSADOR DAVIS ON HIS WAY HOME

He Is Accompanied From London by Family

LONDON, Aug 18—John W. Davis, American Ambassador to Great Britain, left for America this morning. He was accompanied by his family.

ONE MAN LOSES LIFE, EIGHT INJURED

Side of Plant Blown Out at Muskegon, Mich

MUSKEGON, Mich, Aug 18—An explosion in the tire department of the Brunswick-Balke-Collender plant here this morning caused the death of one man and serious injuries to eight others.

One side of the building was blown out. The cause of the blast has not been determined.

GROWTH OF CHARLESTON, S C, AND GREELEY, COLO

WASHINGTON, Aug 18—The Census Bureau announced these population figures today:

Greeley, Colo, 10,883, increase 2704, or 33.1 percent.

Charleston, S C, 67,957, increase 9124, or 15.5 percent.

Lewiston, Me (revised), 31,791. Previously announced as, 31,307.

Thomson Won Hurdle Race in Record Time

HE WON 110-METER HURDLES FOR CANADA IN WORLD RECORD TIME

EARL J. THOMSON OF DARTMOUTH

CONNOLLY GETS IN 1500-METER FINAL

Best U. S. Could Do in Shot-put Was Take Third

OLYMPIC STADIUM, Antwerp, Aug 18 (by A. P.)—The six best hurdlers of the Olympic meet got away to a perfect start in the final heat of the 110-meter hurdlers today. For the first 50 yards Earl Thomson of Dartmouth College, running for Canada; H. E. Barron of the Meadowbrook Club, Philadelphia, and Fred S. Murray of the New York A. C. were taking the hurdles abreast.

At this point Thomson began to draw away with a perfect gliding stride. He gained a lead of 10 feet and it was seen he would be an easy winner unless he should fall over a hurdle. Thomson continued gaining to the tape, which he broke in 14-5s, smashing the world's record of 15s flat made by the American, F. C. Smithson, in the London Olympics of 1908.

Thomson was 2½ yards ahead of Barron at the end of the race, with Murray third by an inch. The New Zealander, Wilson, just nosed out Walker Smith of the Chicago A. A. for fourth place. Carl Christiernssen of Sweden was outclassed, finishing a poor last.

Just before the start of the final it was announced that Orfidan, the French hurdler, credited with a place in the final, was not Orfidan at all, but the New Zealander, Wilson. The error was due to faulty announcement and confusion in numbers.

At the finish of the race it was discovered the Belgian committee had not provided a Canadian flag to raise over the entrance tower, so it was necessary to hoist the British flag.

Sweden Won Broad Jump

Peterson of Sweden won the final of the broad jump with 7.15 meters. C. E. Johnson, University of Michigan, was

Continued on the Fifth Page.

THIS COMPLETES ACTION FOR NATION

Reconsideration Is Possible Within Next Two Days

NASHVILLE, Tenn, Aug 18—Ratification of the Federal suffrage amendment was completed today by favorable action by the Tennessee House, which voted 49 to 47 in favor of the resolution for ratification. This followed favorable action by the Senate last week, the vote there being 25 to 4.

House Speaker Walker, opposed to suffrage, in an attempt to have the action reconsidered, changed his vote to aye and moved that such action be taken.

Walker's change of his vote gave ratification a majority of 50 to 46, for the time being.

Mr Walker is privileged to call up the resolution for reconsideration at any time within the next two days.

Adjournment was taken until 10 a m tomorrow.

The first vote today was taken on a motion to table the Federal suffrage ratification resolution. It resulted in a tie vote of 48 to 48, according to the clerk's record, but various leaders who kept tallies said the vote was 49 to 47. The rollcall was ordered taken a second time, again resulting in a tie, so that the motion to table the resolution was lost.

The vote on the resolution to ratify followed, being announced as 49 to 47.

Intensive Drive Ends

Ratification by the Tennessee Legislature was the culmination of an intensive drive made by suffrage proponents to have the amendment made effective in time for the women of the country to vote in the Presidential election in November. The drive was started when West Virginia became the 34th State to ratify, early this year.

Washington was the 35th State to ratify, and on the same day it acted—March 22—Gov Townsend of Delaware called a special session of the Legislature of that State to act on the amendment. The Delaware Assembly met early in May and the Senate quickly ratified, but action by the House was delayed, despite pressure brought to bear by the leaders of both great political parties and by President Wilson. Finally, on June 2, the Legislature adjourned with the ratification resolution still in the House Committee on the Whole.

Louisiana Wouldn't Ratify

Meantime, the Louisiana Legislature met and efforts were made to have it act favorably. President Wilson appealed to Gov Parker to recommend ratification, but the Governor declined to do so. The ratification resolution was taken up late in May and was debated at intervals

Continued on the Fourth Page.

To get good help use the Globe's Help Wanted columns. During the seven months ending July 31, the Globe printed 132,530 Help Wanted advts.

DANZIG CORRIDOR TO SEA CLEARED OF RUSSIANS

Polish Forces Are Still Driving Eastward, Says French Mission in Warsaw

PARIS, Aug 18—The Polish counter-offensive with Thorn as its base has successfully cleared the Danzig corridor of Russian troops, according to a report received from the French mission in Poland today.

The Polish forces are still driving eastward, the report says.

SOVIET PEACE TERMS ARE READ TO POLISH DELEGATES

MOSCOW, Aug 17 (by A. P.)—The Russian Soviet peace terms were read to the Polish delegates at their first meeting with the Soviet representatives in Minsk today. The Polish answer will be returned tomorrow.

An official statement with regard to the meeting of the delegates says:

"The Minsk conference opened today at 7 p m with a speech by Chairman Danishevsky, after which credentials were exchanged. Danishevsky emphasized Russia's respect for Poland's independence, sovereign rights and right to determine her own form of government, and said Russia accorded Poland more territory than the Entente.

"Danishevsky said Russia must demand from the landlords of Poland such guarantees against renewed attacks as would not be necessary from the workers and peasants of Poland. The Polish delegates proposed to hold the next sitting Aug 19, but the Russians insisted it be

Continued on the Fifth Page.

THE WEATHER

FAIR

United States Weather Bureau forecasts:

For Boston and its vicinity, for Southern New England and Eastern New York: Generally fair tonight and Thursday; cooler in the interior tonight; fresh northeast wind.

For Northern New England: Fair tonight and Thursday; moderate temperature, moderate north and northeast wind.

Lowest temperature in New England last night: Greenville, Me. 54. Temperatures at 8 a m: New York, 74; Washington, 72; Chicago, 70; Portland, Or, 18.

Highland Light, 8 a m: Wind east, light breeze, fog and rain; temperature 62 degrees; sea smooth.

Boston observations, 8 a m: Barometer, 30.24 inches; temperature, 66 degrees; highest yesterday, 80; lowest last night, 64; humidity 85 percent; wind north, 14 miles, cloudy; precipitation last 24 hours, .10 inch.

The Temperature Today

The thermometer at Thompson's Spa records the temperature up to 12 m today as follows:

	1919	1920		1919	1920
3 a m	62	60	1 p m	63	67
6 a m	62	70	2 p m	62	67
9 a m	64	67	3 p m	63	67
12 m	65	68			

BAN ON SOME BANKS AS STATE DEPOSITORIES

Governor Says He Will Not OK Those Advertising Through State Treas Burrell

"What they've got to do is to discontinue that practice while I have any power," said Gov Coolidge this morning, in discussing the depositing of State funds in banks and trust companies which place advertising through the advertising agency conducted by State Treas Fred J. Burrell.

"I don't think it is a practice likely to inspire public confidence, although I am not criticising the Treasurer or the banks, I do not wish to be responsible for that way of doing State business. It might be perfectly all right, but I don't wish to be a party to it."

Thus Gov Coolidge makes it clear that he will not approve as depositories for State funds banks and trust companies which have advertising contracts with

Continued on the Fourth Page.

GLOBE WANTS
GLOBE DISPLAY ADVTS
READ THEM TODAY

If Out of Town

MAIL YOUR ADVTS FOR NEXT SUNDAY'S GLOBE TODAY

The earlier in the week you order your Sunday Globe advts the better service we can give you.

Owing to the great volume of the Globe's advertising business, advertisers will please observe the rules printed below.

1. We cannot guarantee the insertion of Sunday Globe advts ordered on Saturdays. We will try to insert all advts except those listed below if they are in the office before 1:30 p. m. on Saturday.

2. Until further notice advts under the following classifications must be in the office on Thursday in order to be sure of appearing in the following Sunday's Globe:

Machinery and Tools
Musical Instruments
Tours and Travel
Yachts, Boats, etc.
Furniture, etc.
Farm and Garden
Refrigerators, etc.
Poultry, Pigeons, etc.
Showcases, Desks, etc.
Typewriters, etc.
Schools, Colleges, etc.
Safes, Cash Registers
Dressmaking, Millinery, etc.

3. Advts for the Daily Globe must be in the office before 9 p. m. of the day preceding publication.

Publisher

1921 - 1955

WILLIAM O. TAYLOR (1872-1955) General Taylor's second son succeeded to the publisher's chair in June 1921. Using his acute eye for business, William O. managed the family's newspaper through the Roaring '20s, the Great Depression, the surprises of the New Deal, the lows and highs of World War II and the beginnings of the Cold War. Often short of cash, but long on ways to use wisely what he had, William O. Taylor handed over to his son a publishing enterprise with potential.

Boston Evening Globe

Latest Evening Edition

BOSTON, FRIDAY EVENING, AUGUST 3, 1923—24 PAGES—TWO CENTS

7:30 FINAL EDITION

PRESIDENT COOLIDGE GIVEN OATH BY FATHER

Old-Fashioned Oil Lamp Lit Scene in the Living Room of Vermont Farmhouse

PRESIDENT CALVIN COOLIDGE

WARREN G. HARDING

© UNDERWOOD & UNDERWOOD WASHINGTON

NOW ON WAY TO WASHINGTON

(Special Dispatch to the Globe)

PLYMOUTH, Vt, Aug 3—In the old-fashioned living room of his father's farmhouse in the village of his birth, by the light of an oil lamp, Calvin Coolidge, the fourth Massachusetts man to achieve the Nation's highest political honor, became the 30th President of the United States at 2:47 this morning, Eastern Standard time.

For the first time in the history of the country the oath of office was administered by the father of an incoming President.

Over a special telephone wire, hurriedly installed by telephone workers to connect the little Vermont farmhouse with Washington, the Vice President received the exact form of oath required by the Constitution, and it was administered to him by his father, John C. Coolidge.

New President Added "So Help Me God"

A little group of friends and Federal officials looked solemnly on while Calvin Coolidge, a pale, frail figure in

Continued on the Seventh Page.

MRS HARDING SHOWS HEROISM

SAN FRANCISCO, Aug 3 (by A. P.)—Mrs Harding, although greatly shocked by the death of her husband, arose early ths morning after a short sleep, directing all affairs and looking after the welfare o fthe patry.

Mrs Harding retired at 1 o'clock this morning and lsept fitfully, it was said by members of the official party, who added that she this morning, as always, was considering others before herself. One member of the aprty said she was facing the fact of the President's death with "heroism."

DEATH CAME WITHOUT WARNING

SAN FRANCISCO, Aug 3 (by A. P.)—A Nation today mourns the passing of its leader.

The American people from coast to coast and from lakes to gulf and in the territories beyond the seas bow their heads in grief, for their President is dead. In the early hours of last evening, after a day which had brought renewed hope of recovery, death came suddenly and struck down Warren G. Harding with a stroke of cerebral apoplexy.

The end came instantaneously and without a single warning, at 7:30 o'clock (11:30 p m Boston time). There was no time to summon additional physicians, no time to call the members of his official family, and no time for medical skill to exercise its knowledge. It was all over in the twinkling of an eye, and it left a Nation and the world shocked and in grief.

Wife Faithful to the End

Mrs Harding, the constant companion of her distinguished husband, was faithful to the end. She was reading to him a few minutes before 7:30, when she noticed a shudder run through the frame of the man she had loved, encouraged in adversity and praised in success. Before she could arise from her chair, Mr Harding collapsed in his bed, and she rushed to the door, calling for the physicians to come quickly.

Brig Gen Sawyer, chief of the staff of physicians who had been attending the Chief Executive, who

Continued on the Eleventh Page.

"READ SOME MORE," PRESIDENT'S LAST WORDS, TO MRS HARDING

SAN FRANCISCO, Aug 3 (By A. P.)—"That's good. Go on, read some more."

These were the last words uttered by President Harding to Mrs Harding.

Mrs Harding was at his bedside reading aloud when she paused and looked at the President, according to Alfred Holman, San Francisco publisher and close peronal friend of the President, who visited the sick room a few moments before the end came.

Mr Holman told interviewers that the President's hand raised as he asked Mrs Harding to continue reading. Instantly his expression changed. He was dead.

Mrs Harding was reading an article entitled, "A Calm Review of a Calm Man," in which the President was the man reviewed.

HARDING'S BODY TO BE TAKEN TO TRAIN AT 6

SAN FRANCISCO, Aug 3 (by A. P.)—The body of President Harding will be taken at 6 this evening from the hotel here, where he died, and will be borne direct to the train at the 3d and Townsend-st Station. The train will leave as soon thereafter as possible.

The route of the funeral train from Chicago to Washington had not been decided upon up to 10 this morning, such detailed plans being held up pending the arrival of Secretary Christian from Los Angeles.

COOLIDGE GOES TO NEW DUTIES

Left Rutland, Vt, at 9:40 A M in a Private Car

By ARTHUR GRANGER

RUTLAND, Aug 3—President and Mrs Calvin Coolidge left here at 9:40 a m, Standard time, this morning in a special car for Washington.

The President arrived in Rutland just before the train left. On the way over from Plymouth he stopped at a cemetery by the side of the road where his mother is buried, and paused at her grave.

At the station a large crowd had gathered to greet him, headed by Gov Proctor, Ex-Gov Clement and National Committeeman Kinsley of Rutland. He posed for photographers at the station and then boarded the special car. He wore a blue suit, and Mrs Coolidge wore a dark brown dress.

After he boarded the train he proceeded to the rear platform where he stood until the train pulled out.

Continued on the Seventh Page.

The Boston Sunday Globe

Reg. U. S. Pat. Off.
VOL CXI NO. 142 — Entered as second class mail matter at Boston, Mass. under the act of March 3, 1879—242 Washington St.
THE BOSTON SUNDAY GLOBE—MAY 22, 1927—110 PAGES
READ THE SUNDAY GLOBE MAGAZINE AND EDITORIAL SECTION
COPYRIGHT, 1927, BY THE GLOBE NEWSPAPER CO.
(5) PRICE 10 CENTS

CAPT LINDBERGH LANDS PLANE SAFELY AT PARIS AFTER CROSSING ATLANTIC ALONE IN 33 1-2 HOURS

25,000 Madly Cheering Frenchmen Take Tired Young American To Their Hearts—America Goes Wild at News, Raising Deafening Din From One Coast to the Other

SIRENS AND GONGS SPREAD GLAD NEWS

"Let 'er Go!" Comes in Second as Word of Landing Is Flashed to Fire Department by Globe

Through the cooperation of the Boston Fire Department and the Boston Globe, news of the arrival of Lindbergh in Paris was relayed throughout all sections of the city yesterday afternoon within a minute of the time the first official report was received by the Globe.

The official news reached the Globe at 5:31 and at 5:32 fire bells, sirens and whistles were shrieking madly the length and breadth of the city, as well as in the harbor.

Arrangements had been made early in the afternoon for the Fire Department to give all possible aid in spreading the news should the history-making flight be completed. Fire stations were notified throughout the city and

Continued on the Twelfth Page.

HARVARD VICTOR IN THREE RACES

Wins Varsity, Junior and the Freshman

Coach Brown's Crews Make Fine Showing on the Charles

Eli Class Eight Wins, Penn Takes the "150"

HOW THE CREWS FINISHED

Harvard was triumphant in the three most important races of the Harvard-Pennsylvania-M. I. T. races on the Charles River yesterday, the Crimson

Continued on the Twentieth Page

THE WEATHER

CLOUDY

Forecast for Boston and Vicinity: Mostly cloudy and warmer Sunday and Monday; moderate southerly winds.

Washington Forecast for Southern New England: Mostly cloudy and warmer Sunday and Monday.

Northern New England: Mostly cloudy and warmer in the interior Sunday and Monday, with probable light showers in New Hampshire and Vermont.

NATION'S HEAD SENDS PRAISE

President Speaks for American People

Cable to Lindbergh Tells of His Joy at Successful Flight

Governor Fuller Sends Congratulations

WASHINGTON, May 21 (A. P.)—President Coolidge, in a congratulatory cablegram to be delivered to Charles A. Lindbergh in Paris, told the trans-atlantic flyer that the "American people rejoice with me at the brilliant termination of your heroic flight."

The message of the President, sent to the American Embassy in Paris for transmission to Lindbergh immediately on his arrival, follows:

"The American people rejoice with me at the brilliant termination of your heroic flight. The first nonstop flight of a lone aviator across the Atlantic crowns the record of American aviation, and in bringing the greetings of the American people to France you likewise carry the assurance of our

Continued on the Eighteenth Page

CAPT CHARLES A. LINDBERGH

"Well, Here We Are," Is Only Speech of Flyer—Mother In Detroit, Sobs Happily

Youth, Asleep on Feet, Thinks Until Last of Ship—Feat Marks Epoch of Air

LINDBERGH'S TIMETABLE

FRIDAY

*7:51 A. M.—Took off from Roosevelt Field, Long Island, vanishing a moment later over Westbury, bound for Paris, 3640 miles away.
9:40 A. M.—Sighted at Halifax, Mass.
12:25 P. M.—First observed over Nova Scotia, at Cape St Mary, 10 miles from Meteghan, Digby County.
3:30 P. M.—Sighted over St Pierre, Miquelon.
7:15 P. M.—Passed St John's, N F, and headed over the Atlantic.

SATURDAY

8:10 A. M.—Sighted by Dutch freighter Hilversum, 500 miles from the Irish coast.
1:30 P. M.—Sighted over Dingle Harbor, Kerry County, in Southwestern Ireland.
3:30 P. M.—Reached Cherbourg, France.
5:21 P. M.—Landed at Le Bourget Field, at Paris.

*All times, Eastern daylight.

CHAMBERLIN FLIGHT PUT OFF INDEFINITELY

Friends Persuade Pilot Not to Make Paris Attempt

Bellanca Breaks With Levine—Fire Threatens the Columbia

ROOSEVELT FIELD, N Y, May 21 (A. P.)—The Paris flight of Clarence Chamberlin was "indefinitely postponed" tonight, when friends persuaded him not to make an immediate attempt. He had announced late today that he planned to take off for France at 8 o'clock tonight if he could make necessary arrangements.

Chamberlin had said that the hop-off would be made if he could locate Carl Schory, secretary of the contest committee of the National Aeronautical Association, to seal the barograph of the Bellanca monoplane Columbia. He would not say whom he expected to

Continued on the Sixth Page.

LINDBERGH'S MOTHER TOO HAPPY FOR WORDS

"I Felt He Would Win," She Said Later—Bravely Taught Classes, And Endured Long Vigil

Special Dispatch to the Globe

DETROIT, May 21—"I am grateful. There is no use attempting to find words to express my happiness."

These were the first words of Mrs Evangeline Lodge Lindbergh, mother of the intrepid flyer, as she received word that her famous son had safely landed his plane in Paris.

The mother awaited the word of her son's victory or death in a modest home at 178 Ashland av. It is a frame dwelling set far back from the street. Through the back yard runs Fox Creek, up which motorboats constantly sped while the mother awaited the word which she has been hoping for since early Friday morning.

Continued on the Seventh Page.

FLYER'S SPEECH TO CROWD IS, "WELL, HERE WE ARE"

LE BOURGET FLYING FIELD, Paris, May 21 (A. P.)—When Capt Charles Lindbergh arrived this evening after his great flight from New York he was seized by the crowd and carried on their shoulders for 20 minutes while the throng of 25,000 cheered.

Finally their voices gave out and those near Lindbergh pressed forward to catch the hero's first words.

Lindbergh cleared his throat.

"Well," he said, "here we are."

Somehow that didn't seem quite enough. So he tried again.

"I am very happy," he added.

And that was the tired flyer's only public comment.

PARIS, May 21 (A. P.)—Capt Charles A. Lindbergh, the young American aviator who hopped off from New York yesterday morning all alone in his monoplane arrived in Paris tonight, safe and sound.

The sandy-haired son of the Middle West dropped down out of the darkness at Le Bourget Flying Field, a few miles from Paris, at 10:21 oclock tonight (5:21 p m Boston time), only 33½ hours after leaving Long Island—the first man in history to go from New York to Paris without changing his seat.

Hailed as Greatest Air Hero

To the young American it was seemingly merely the achievement of an ambition. To Paris, to France, to America and to the world, his landing tonight made him the greatest of heroes mankind has produced since the air became a means of travel. A crowd of at least 25,000 surrounded his plane, the Spirit of St Louis, when it came to earth after its epochal voyage from the new world to the old.

The airman was lifted from the seat, where for two days and a night he sat fixed, guiding his plane over land and sea. For 40 minutes he was hardly able to talk or do anything else, except let himself be

Continued on the Fourteenth Page.

TODAY'S GLOBE CONTENTS

Page 1.
Lindbergh arrives safely in Paris after 33½ hours' flight from New York.
President cables congratulations of American people to "Flying Fool"; Gov Fuller also sends congratulations.
Lindburgh's mother cannot find words to tell her happiness over son's safety and success; taught while he was flying, slept part of night, feeling he would win.
News of landing spread all over Boston by Globe and Fire Department in a few seconds.
Chamberlin's proposed flight for Paris in the Bellanca plane Columbia indefinitely postponed.
Harvard wins three chief races, battling Penn and Tech on the Charles.
Page 4.
Ten injured when trolley car crashes into train at Harvard-sq subway station in Cambridge.
Veterans of Foreign Wars give banquet and purse of gold to National Commander Stitt.
Capt Lindbergh's former commanding officer praises him as flyer and officer.
Americans beaten in doubles at St Cloud.
Page 6.
Explosion, killing power company superintendent, mars flight celebration at Groton, Conn.
Page 7.
Lindbergh likely to try next to conquer Pacific.
Page 8.
Registrar Goodwin says brake testing shows the cars in Greater Boston are better equipped in this respect than formerly.
Gov Fuller studying Sacco-Vanzetti case over week-end.
Exceptions overruled on conviction of Jerry Gedzium of murder.
Page 9.
University of Maine wins New England intercollegiate, Bowdoin second, Tech third.
Page 11.
Children's outing sponsored by automobile dealers of Boston will be held June 8.
Page 12.
Greatest public interest felt in years shown over Lindbergh's Paris flight; 1000 telephone calls an hour pour into the Globe office and great crowds hear bulletins of his victory by Globe radio, wire and street announcements.
Four injured in Dorchester auto crash.
De Pinedo, Italian flyer, in Newfoundland, delayed his start across the Atlantic for the Azores, on report of heavy storm there, but planned to get away about midnight.
Lindbergh's backers opposed his going it alone.
Page 13.
Dinner to Alexander Brin, editor of Jewish Advocate, who is to be married in June.
Page 14.
Lindbergh's route shortest possible distance.
St Louis indulges in wild celebration of its favorite son's epic aviation feat.
Round $1,000,000 within Lindbergh's grasp.
Page 15.
Louisiana flood cuts path 150 miles long and 50 miles wide.
David H. Walton dead.
Deckhand of city steamer rescues man, 70, from harbor at Long Island.
Port of Boston news.
Page 16.
Henry Ford, at Sudbury with family, sees filming of scenes for "Mary's Little Lamb."
Actors in "The Night Hawk" at the New Park Theatre strike at end of first act, telling audience they weren't paid; patrons get their money back.
Mrs Thomas Bailey Aldrich, widow of author, dead in Maine.
Page 17.
Nearly 400 honors awarded at Dorchester Girl Scout rally.
Disabled veterans elect State officers at Worcester.
Page 18.
Traits of his father found in Lindbergh.
Audience at Pops honors Lindbergh.
Page 19.
Collie bites two children, two dogs, in Cambridge.
About 400 boys and girls of New England take part in music festival here.

TODAY'S GLOBE CONTENTS

Page 20.
Yale first varsity crew defeated by Tiger in rowing upset at Princeton.
Malden High defeats Haverhill High in 12 innings, 1 to 0.
Boston English defeats Dorchester High, 4 to 2, on diamond.
Page 21.
National League Results—St Louis 5, Boston 3 (first game); St Louis 6, Boston 2 (second game); Pittsburg 6, New York 3; Cincinnati 5, Philadelphia 2 (first game); Cincinnati 6, Philadelphia 5 (second game); Chicago 6, Brooklyn 4 (first game); Chicago 11, Brooklyn 6 (second game).
American League Results: St Louis 7, Boston 4; Chicago 7, Philadelphia 5; Washington 6, Detroit 5; Cleveland 5, New York 4 (12 innings).
Page 22.
Yale defeats Harvard in track meet at New Haven, 71½ to 63½.
Harvard nine ties graduates, 3 to 3, defeats Waseda, 3 to 2.
Moses Brown defeats Tabor Academy baseball team, 8 tot 7
St John's Prep defeats Holy Cross with Nekola pitching.
Georgetti defeats Keenan in feature race at Revere track.
Rickard plans to send Sharkey against Dempsey next.
Jack Sharkey given great welcome on return home from New York.
Page 23.
Largest field ever for annual championship of Women's Golf Association of Boston tomorrow at Woodland G. C.
Cambridge Latin clinches Suburban baseball title by defeating Rindge Technical, 9 to 5.
Whittalls Carpet wins State Cup final by 1—0.
Results of weekly golf tournaments in Greater Boston.
Page 24.
Albia Todd makes fastest time at matinee races on the Charles River Speedway.
Page 33.
Vivid picture of Nicaraguan Revolution by Naval officer who was there when first Marines landed there.
Page 40.
Edward N. Hurley, ex-chairman of Shipping Board, tells in new book how he helped start Woodrow Wilson towards political office.
Page 41.
Evidence that prehistoric man lived in Kentucky, says Prof Burroughs.
Page 49.
Reproduction of interesting ancient deed to Connecticut land.
Page 55.
Radio broadcasts.
Page 56.
Danger that Mississippi flood will destroy modern "Land of Evangeline."
Page 57.
How Mrs Richard Boardman has succeeded in solving the mooted servant problem by arbitration.
Pages 58 and 59.
Stock market and financial news.
Page 60.
How Paris victimizes the gullible American woman shopper. College boys act as shopping guides.
Boston newsboys have their own court and trial board, administering self discipline.
Pages 61, 62 and 63.
Table Gossip.
Page 62.
St Anselm's College at Manchester, N H, honors Frank French, artist.
Page 64.
Local Lines.

EDITORIAL AND NEWS FEATURE SECTION

Page 1
Bellanca, aviator extraordinary, was born high up in the air; as a child he flew kites over the Italian mountains; now builds transatlantic planes.
Page 2
Providence to have $250,000 community theatre.
Ship's log tells stirring tale of hazardous voyage.
Page 3
Pola Negri now has a Prince of her own; was in love with Rudy, also, Hollywood gossip has it.
Page 4.
The modern world is moving toward a larger unity, says Uncle Dudley.
European Nations lining up again in old groups.

TODAY'S GLOBE CONTENTS

Page 4.
Bruce Barton discusses seriousness and cheerfulness in business.
Page 5
Milk Island is newest bird sanctuary.
Page 6
Irvin Cobb discusses a sense of humor.
Cambridge wages safety campaign for children.

TODAY'S GLOBE CONTENTS

Page 6.
Frank Sullivan looks amusedly at life.
Page 7
Abe Martin talks about "Livin' with husbands."
Amesbury Hospital needs to be filled.
Page 8
Parthenon, fairest temple of Hellas, is being restored. L. P. presents another of his prose pictures.

TODAY'S GLOBE CONTENTS

Page 9
John Hays Hammond, engineer magnificient, scented gold a mile beneath the African veldt and changed the course of an empire.
Drummers' Day at Wellfleet, a homely institution that has passed.
Page 10
Drama—Music—Pictures.
Page 12
Music and musicians.
Lancaster school gives girls a new start in life.
Page 13
Coach Brown of the Harvard crew won his AB 20 years after leaving college; John D. Merrill gives an appreciation of this unique figure in sports.
Huggins hopes the "aged" Wilcy Moore will save the pennant for the Yankees.
Page 14
Will Rogers tells Globe readers of his visit with Gov Fuller and the latter's views of the Sacco-Vanzetti case.
Page 15
Capt Harrison P. Snow, veteran mariner of the Seven Seas, is Hull's grand old man at 90.
Mary Lyon's first school still stands; founder of Mt Holyoke began teaching in Buckland Center.
Pages 16, 17 and 18
Household department.

INDEX TO CLASSIFIED ADVERTISEMENTS

CLASSIFICATION	PAGE	CLASSIFICATION	PAGE	CLASSIFICATION	PAGE
Agents, Salesmen Wanted	54	Furniture, etc.	24, 51	Real Estate Mortgages	58
Amusements	Page 11 of Editorial-Feature Section	Heating and Cooking	24, 42	Refrigerators	24
Antiques, Stamps, Coins	24	Horses, Carriages, etc.	24	Safes	47
Apartments and Tenements	24, 39, 42	Hotels	58, 52, 54	Schools, Colleges, etc.	43
Auction Sales	24, 51	Houses to Let and Wanted	39	Sewing Machines	50
		Information Wanted	24	Showcases, Desks, etc.	24
		Legal Notices	24	Situations Wanted, Female	24, 46
		Live Stock	24		

TODAY'S GLOBE CONTENTS

Page 19
Gen Lee Christmas started many wars and won most of them; America's most picturesque soldier of fortune as seen by his bodyguard.
Page 20
Bobby Jones discusses the Southern Open and tournament play in general.
Page 22
Automobile news.
Page 25
Nova Scotia and the liquor question.
Page 27
Dr Morris Fishbein, editor of the Journal of the American Medical Journal, discusses psycho-analysis.

TODAY'S GLOBE CONTENTS

Page 28
Pres Glenn Frank and Prof Alexander Meikeljohn of the University of Wisconsin, experiment with a college within a college.

CROSS-WORDPUZZLE
PAGE 7
of Magazine Section
RADIO PROGRAMS
PAGE 55

The Boston Daily Globe

BOSTON, TUESDAY MORNING, AUGUST 23, 1927—TWENTY-FOUR PAGES (3) TWO CENTS

MADEIROS, SACCO, VANZETTI DIED IN CHAIR THIS MORNING

Electrocuted in That Order Soon After Midnight—All Reject Religious Consolation to the Last—Two Make Statements

POLICE TAKE 156 OF "DEATH WATCH"

Sacco and Vanzetti Demonstration in Front Of State House Is Broken Up Several Times—Some Rearrested

With the taking into custody of 23 adults and three juveniles shortly after 5 o'clock police brought the total number of arrests of State House pickets yesterday to 156, there having been 130 persons arrested previously.

Some of those arrested early returned to the State House after being bailed and were arrested again. Thousands of persons gathered on the Common and Beacon st to watch the pickets and the activity of the police.

All the prisoners were bailed out at police stations and released by Commissioners Joseph Fahey and William Brophy, with the exception of Helen Crowe, who refused bail but later accepted it when she was taken to the City Prison.

Men Locked in Cells

The men were locked in cells, while the women were detained in the guard

Continued on the Ninth Page.

TODAY'S GLOBE CONTENTS

Page 1.
Sacco, Vanzetti and Madeiros die in electric chair at Charlestown prison.
Legal battle to save Sacco and Vanzetti continues to within two hours of time set for execution.
W. G. Thompson, formerly chief counsel for Sacco and Vanzetti on farewell call to men in death house, says they reiterated their innocence.
Total of 156 Sacco-Vanzetti sympathizers arrested yesterday in front of State House.
Gov Fuller refuses to interfere in behalf of Sacco and Vanzetti.
Veritable army of police on guard in State Prison area.
Will Rogers' dispatch.
Page 2.
Bertaud and Hill hope to start flight to Rome today, but French send warning of hurricanes.
Grand Lodge of Massachusetts, Sons of Italy, elects officers.
Coal mine officials in Belmont County, O. attacked by union sympathizers.
Twenty-five New York prohibition agents dismissed.
Page 3
Former substitute clerk in Boston postoffice given three years in jail for theft of letters.
A. O. H. and its auxiliary open annual State convention at Hotel Statler.
Bay City, Mich. girls seek correspondence with members of Marine Corps flyers.
Prof Mather describes Jewish world of Joshua as one of magic.
Senator Bingham says he believes his plea to Chang in Peking saved Mme Borodin from execution.
Page 4.
Thirty excursionists drop into mud when Oak Bluffs pier collapses.
Mine inspector charges Lawrence Ashley's "Nick-a-Jack" cave disappearance a publicity stunt.
Page 5.
Naval and Federal officials forecast ban on stunt flights as search for missing Pacific flyers is extended to Thursday.
Radio telephone used to talk with air mail pilot 150 miles away.
Port of Boston news.
Page 6.
French troops surround American Embassy at Paris in fear of retaliation for execution of Sacco and Vanzetti.
Mayor Bateman of Peabody presides at Sacco protest meeting in that city.

TODAY'S GLOBE CONTENTS

Page 6.
Head of American Federation of Labor wires Gov Fuller urging commutation of sentence for Sacco and Vanzetti.
Supporters of Sacco and Vanzetti, at Headquarters, receive news of executions silently.
Page 7.
Pennsylvania State trooper shot to death while dispersing Sacco protest meeting at Ambridge.
Orderly crowd waits for Globe bulletins in Newspaper row.
Extraordinary press arrangements made at prison to get story of executions to newspapers of the world.
Worcester County Courthouse under heavy guard as Judge Thayer presides at criminal session.
Mrs Ella Bloor, 65, arrested for inciting to riot in addressing Sacco crowd of 3000.
Page 8.
State officers of American Legion assure Gov Fuller the Legion stands behind him.
Chronological story of the Sacco-Vanzetti case.
Little disorder in New York as police break up Sacco meeting.
Outline of Celestino Madeiros' case in courts.
Orderly crowd on Common and smaller group on sidewalk watch developments at State House.
Two men digging hole near Boston & Maine roundhouse at Reading Highlands flee in auto when challenged by watchman.
Mrs Jessica Henderson and woman companion call on Mrs Fuller at Summer home.
Bodies of executed men removed to Northern Mortuary, under guard.
Page 9.
Acting United States Atty Gen Farnum says the Department of Justice has no file on Sacco-Vanzetti case.
Page 10.
National League Results—Boston 5, Chicago 3; St Louis 1, Philadelphia 0.
American League Results—Cleveland 9, New York 4; Detroit 4, Washington 3 (first game); Detroit 7, Washington 3 (second game); Chicago 6, Philadelphia 2.
New England League Results—Lynn 8, Salem 3; Lewiston 4, Nashua 0 (first game); Nashua 4, Lewiston 1 (second game); Portland 2, Lawrence 1.
Page 11.
Mrs Corbiere defeats Mrs Wightman in women's tennis championship; Mrs Godfree withdraws, other top-ranking players win.
Japanese Davis' Cup players practice at Chestnut Hill.
Youthful players shine in opening rounds of Newport tennis tournament.
Plain Mary upsets favorite to win 2:20 trot at Goshen.
Sleep Barbara wins Kings Cup.
Webb and Stevenson certain of places on American polo team in matches against British.
George Owen Jr to play Tilden in Newport tennis tournament today.
Page 12.
Two women aviators plan transatlantic flight.
Two children killed by automobiles.
Lita Grey is granted interlocutory divorce from Charles S. Chaplin, film comedian.
Florence Rogers Cooke objects to former husband's efforts to make her give up 12-room suite.
Murder charge against 19-year-old girl to be changed to lesser offense.
Auto in which child is asleep is stolen, then abandoned, in Cambridge.
Page 13.
Attractions at the theatres.
Katharine Wilson and Richard Barthelmess to wed.

PRISON IS GUARDED BY VERITABLE ARMY

Six Establishments of Police on Duty

Riot Squads and Machine-Gun Groups at Stragetic Points

Mobilized silently and quickly, with the precision of a well-trained army, police of six different establishments representing the Boston and Cambridge departments, the Metropolitan District Commission, State Police Patrol, Boston & Maine Railroad detectives and the prison force united last night to guard the State Prison at Charlestown and its vicinity during the straining hours preceding and following the execution of Sacco, Vanzetti and Madeiros.

Allowing no one not properly accredited within 150 yards of the prison walls, the police, numbering close to 800 armed men, established a cordon of steel about the area, ready to handle any disorder.

Floodlights set up on the prison walls virtually turned night into day, riot and machine guns were carried by capable looking officers, high-presure fire hose was in the hands of picked firemen at strategic points, and the greatest concentra-

Continued on the Seventh Page.

TODAY'S GLOBE CONTENTS

Page 15.
Eugene Homans and Phillips Finlay, schoolboy stars lead field in national amateur golf championship at end of 18 holes.
Ogg's 67 sets new course record at Franklin Country Club.
Bobby Jones declares medal play a better test in championships than match play.
Sandust wins run to Kittery Point.
Twilight League results: Fore River 3, Malden 0; Reading 7, Lynn G. E. 3.
Page 16.
Household Department.
Dorothy Dix' letter box.
Page 17.
Household Department.
"The Snob," by Vida Hurst.
"Teepee Tales," by El Comancho.
"Harvey Garrard's Crime," by E. Phillips Oppenheim.
Page 18.
Trend of prices on New York market is to higher level.
Page 19.
Commercial and financial news.
Johnny Risko will give Jack Gagnon a stiff test in Braves Field ring tonight.
South End Playground wins the championship of Woburn.
League of Nations Palace stormed during Sacco riot; bystander killed.
Page 20.
Comic Stripe.
The Globe's cross-word puzzle.
Page 21.
"The Once Over," by H. I. Phillips.
Comparative strength of radio waves over land and water to be tested at South Dartmouth.
Disabled veterans intending to visit France with the American Legion urged to take physical examination, necessary for proper treatment if taken ill in that country.
Page 24.
President and party begin Yellowstone tour with visit to Tower Fall; Coolidge cracks jokes in unusual jovial mood.
Westport mother drowns trying to save son in pond; child saved.
Young Cambridge elopers to be remarried.
W. F. Bartlett, Medford business man, falls dead in home.

WINTHROP JOKER SETS OFF FIRECRACKERS AS A SCARE

WINTHROP, Aug 23—Shortly after midnight, when the executions were in progress, two loud reports were heard at Cottage Cove and Hern Bar av. The sound was heard over Winthrop. People rushed to the scene; the explosion was but 200 feet away from the huge standpipe, containing 1,000,000 gallons of water, which supplies the town. There had been threats, according to the police, that the standpipe would be blown up.

Arriving at the scene police found that the reports came from two giant firecrackers, tossed in the road by some practical joker with a distorted sense of humor.

RADIO PROGRAMS PAGE 21

CELESTINO MADEIROS — NICOLA SACCO — BARTOLOMEO VANZETTI

LAST-MINUTE PLEAS BOMBARD GOVERNOR

Wife and Sister of Men Beg Mercy And Lawyers Ask More Time In Long Day at Office

Although continuously besieged for nearly 14 hours to grant a respite or otherwise exercise executive clemency, Gov Alvan T. Fuller left the State House at 12:12 this morning without taking any action toward intervention in the execution of Sacco and Vanzetti. When he left he made no statement. As he passed through the group of waiting newspaper men he said, "Good night."

There was not a moment from his arrival at 10:40 yesterday morning when he was not engrossed in the details of the case. He remained in his office all the time and twice had lunches brought to him.

His day was given over to listening to appeals in behalf of the condemned men. Not the least trying was an interview, late yesterday evening, with Mrs Rosa Sacco, wife of Nicola Sacco, and Miss Luigia Vanzetti, sister of Bartolomeo Vanzetti.

Kane Last to Appear

The last person who saw the Governor in behalf of the men was Francis Fisher Kane of Philadelphia, an attorney retained by one committee of Sacco-Vanzetti sympathizers. Mr Kane left the State House at 11:57, after a few minutes' talk with the Governor.

William G. Thompson, formerly counsel for Sacco and Vanzetti, was with the Governor for some time, leaving at 11:45. Mr Thompson said when he left the Governor's office, "I was trying to do my full duty by my former clients whom I believe to be innocent and who have not had a fair trial. If I had not believed it I would not have been here tonight."

At 9 o'clock last evening Mrs Sacco and Miss Vanzetti had a long audience with the Governor when they went to the State House. With them were Gardner Jackson, chairman of the Sacco-Vanzetti Defense Committee, his sister, Miss Edith B. Jackson, Aldrico Felicanni, treasurer of the committee, and Michael A. Musmanno, who has been associated with Arthur D. Hill in the recent handling of the case for the accused men.

Three Go Into Office

Of these, only Mrs Sacco, Miss Vanzetti and Mr Musmanno, who acted as interpreter, went into the Governor's office, where, besides Gov Fuller, were Lieut Gov Frank G. Allen, Joseph Wiggin, the Governor's personal counsel, and Herman A. MacDonald, the Governor's private secretary. Atty Gen Arthur K. Reading was at times in the room.

The conference lasted for an hour and a half. Both women spoke through Mr Musmanno. Mrs Sacco urged the Governor to be merciful. She said her husband had been convicted largely through the evidence of a witness who said she saw Sacco lying under an automobile soon after the murder, trying to make repairs on the car. Mrs Sacco declared that her husband had

Continued on the Sixth Page.

PARADERS DISPERSED AT CHARLESTOWN

Police Feared March on Prison Imminent

Eight Arrested and Others Break Their Formation

The much-feared march of Sacco-Vanzetti sympathizers to the Charlestown Prison, which accounted for the extraordinary guard of nearly 800 police about its walls all last night, seemed imminent just before midnight, when a formation of 50 Sacco-Vanzetti sympathizers started through the streets of Charlestown in the direction of the prison.

Quick work by the handful of police left in the Charlestown Police Station at City Square prevented what might have been a serious disturbance, although the paraders were in no position to threaten the armed guards.

The police made eight arrests, each on the technical charge of violation of the City Ordinance relative to the carrying of placards, and dissolved the parade without untoward incident.

Passed Police Station

The arrested persons include those who gave their names as Isadore Lovett, Helen Peabody of Cambridge, Frederick Beade of Lawrence, Frank Zito, John Horn, John Gorman, Dora Dolavitch and Amellia F. Borris.

The procession marched over the new Charlestown Bridge from the direction of Boston proper and circled City sq.

It seemed that the paraders purposely passed the City-sq Police Station, and it was this fact that proved their undoing. They were carrying placards making known their sympathies and a cheer here and there aroused the police.

Six Others Arrested

Sergt Kuhlman and special officer William J. Bonner rushed outside and attempted to stop the parade, and succeeded in placing two men, who seemed like leaders, under arrest.

They thought then that the parade was broken up, but the others formed into line of fours again, raised their placards and headed toward the prison. At Union and Washington sts, near the prison, another detail of police stepped in and arrested the other six and completely routed the marchers.

There was never any danger at any time and the police were satisfied that the parade was simply a demonstration rather than any effort to march on the prison.

MEN REITERATED THEIR INNOCENCE

Atty Thompson Quotes Sacco and Vanzetti

Ex-Chief Counsel Denies He Had Access to Federal Files

After a surprise visit to the death house early in the evening, William G. Thompson, for four years chief counsel for Sacco and Vanzetti, gave out a statement to the newspapermen, quoting both men in reiteration of "their absolute innocence" and declaring that Vanzetti stated:

"No lawyer who has ever been concerned in my defense has any right to say or hint that I, in any form of words whatever, said anything which could possibly be interpreted as an admission of any guilt whatever."

Mr Thompson branded as "absolutely untrue" statements that he has had access to the files of the Department of Justice.

Opinion Not Altered

Regarding the action of Gov Fuller, Mr Thompson said: "I cannot with due regard for professional propriety engage in any public discussion or

Continued on the Fourth Page.

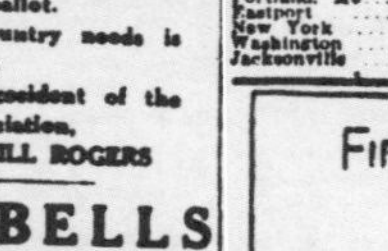

Will Rogers' Dispatch

(Special to Boston Globe—Copyright, 1927)

TOPEKA, Kan, Aug 22—This is Topeka, the home of both Kansas Senators. Capper's life has been dedicated to the farmers and Curtis' to the helping of the Indians. Both denominations, the farmers and the Indians, are now destitute.

Tonight in Kansas City I am to be made president of a large body of men, the ex-Mayors' Association, an earnest bunch of men trying to come back, all placed where they are by the honesty of the ballot.

What this country needs is more ex-Mayors.

Yours, the President of the ex-Mayors' Association,

WILL ROGERS

DUMB-BELLS

Madeiros in Stupor—Other Two Face Death Calmly

Judges Holmes, Anderson And Lowell Refuse Final Appeals

VANZETTI FORGIVES, SACCO SAYS GOODBY

Nicola Sacco and Bartolomeo Vanzetti are dead.

Between midnight and 12:30 this morning, at the Charlestown State Prison, they paid with their lives for a crime of which they had been convicted by a jury of their peers.

Sacco marched to his death at 12:11:12, with defiance on his lips for the social order which executed him, and a farewell for his family and friends. He was dead seven minutes and 50 seconds later. Vanzetti's last words were a cry of innocence and forgiveness. He was brought into the death chamber at 12:20:38, and was dead at 12:26:55.

Woodenly, without word or sign, Celestino Madeiros had been executed a few minutes before. His life was the penalty for a murder and robbery, a penalty which would have been paid long before except for the

Continued on the Eighth Page.

SEVEN-YEAR BATTLE IN COURTS FAILURE

The seven-year legal battle to save Sacco and Vanzetti continued with unabated vigor last night until within two hours of the expiration of the respite when defense counsel had exhausted every legal recourse.

In the last few hours before midnight the battery of defense counsel appealed for a second time to Justice Oliver Wendell Holmes of the United States Supreme Court, to Judge James A. Lowell and to Judge George W. Anderson, both of the United States District Court. All of these last minute efforts, however, were unavailing.

These appeals supplemented those of the past few days during which three justices of the United States Supreme Court were appealed to, also the full bench of the Massachusetts Supreme Court and several judges of the Supreme Court. The United States Supreme Court Justices who were visited with an

Continued on the Ninth Page.

THE WEATHER

SHOWERS

Forecast for Boston and Vicinity: Tuesday partly cloudy, probably light local showers. Wednesday partly cloudy and cooler. Moderate southeast and south winds. Washington Forecast for New England and Eastern New York: Tuesday cloudy, probably showers. Wednesday partly cloudy and cooler.

The Temperature Yesterday at Thompson's Spa: 3 a m, 64; 6 a m, 67; 12 m, 74; 3 p m, 72; 6 p m, 78; 9 p m, 71; 12 mid, 69. Average temperature yesterday, 69 1-4.

THE WEATHER ELSEWHERE

Boston Evening Globe

Reg. U. S. Pat. Off.

VOL. CXVI NO. 120 — Entered as second class mail matter at Boston, Mass. under the act of March 3, 1879—243 Washington St.

BOSTON, MONDAY EVENING, OCTOBER 28, 1929—28 PAGES—2 CENTS

COPYRIGHT, 1929, BY THE GLOBE NEWSPAPER CO.

LATEST NEW YORK CLOSING BOSTON PRICES
N. Y. Ticker About 2½ Hours Late —Closing Prices Delayed
7:30 FINAL NEWS

BANKING SUPPORT FAILS TO RALLY STOCKS IN NEW YORK

SOUTH END FIRE DRIVES OUT 200

Smoke Affects Many Firemen —Three Alarms Rung

Smoke from a fire which early this morning wrecked the three-story wooden addition in the rear of the unoccupied New Glenwood Hotel, 1164-1168 Washington st, South End, drove out from 200 to 250 occupants of nearby tenements and nearly overcame a score of firemen who fought the blaze. Dense and acrid clouds spread into Fay st, Harrison av, Laconia st and other nearby thoroughfares due to an odd movement of wind, which held the smoke close to the ground, and scores were awakened as the choking fumes entered their windows.

Four horses in the stable of Isaac Blair & Co, contractors, at 433 Harrison av, in the rear of the fire, were led out of their stalls by members of Ladder 13.

Three alarms were sounded for the fire, which for the first 15 minutes threatened the crowded tenement district. Engine 3 and Ladder 3, whose firehouse is just across the street at Harrison av and Bristol st, responded on a still alarm, but the blaze had made such progress that three box alarms followed quickly. Only the prompt response of the nearby apparatus kept the flames

Continued on the Seventeenth Page

Censure of Bingham by Fellow Senators Indicated

News Summary

FLYERS

DETROIT—Soviet plane, whose crew will be Ford guests, arrives from Chicago.

GENOA, Italy—Two bodies recovered by searchers for air liner City of Rome which was lost in storm.

MIAMI—Seaplane Buenos Aires returns here on way to Pensacola for repairs.

LOCAL

State troopers halt 6790 cars over week-end; 331 drivers to appear in court.

Early morning fire in South End drives 200 from their homes.

Thirty-seven acres of "made land" added to Boston by B. & M. development project.

Why the American Navy is different from others; a lesson for visitors to Navy Yard today.

Alabias slain in East Boston for revenge, police believe.

State may close woodlands to all within a few days unless there is rain. Firemen kept busy in many places fighting forest and brush fires.

Policeman almost nabs Traffic Commissioner Fisher as latter directs traffic in direction contrary to signs.

Tea Party Chapter, D. A. R., places bronze marker on site of birthplace of Benjamin Franklin, on Milk st.

Roxbury man, in stolen auto, faces three charges.

Public Utilities Commission orders that electricity be furnished to Dorchester man upon payment of $20 deposit.

STATE

CAMBRIDGE—Exhibition of paintings and sculptures by Harvard Society for Contemporary Art.

LYNNFIELD—Malden woman badly hurt in collision of Lynn deputy chief's auto and another on Turnpike.

NEWTON—Halloween Party held for inmates of the New England Peabody Home for Crippled Children.

FITCHBURG—Police arrest bride-to-be on charge of having escaped from State Home at Wrentham.

MALDEN—S. A. Brown, 19, of Everett held in $10,000, charged with assault on two women.

WEYMOUTH—Firemen recalled to Summer st after all-night fight with woods fire.

NATICK—Mrs L. J. Landers burned trying to save canary.

NEW ENGLAND

ISLAND FALLS, Me—Quincy, Mass boy, asleep in auto, killed when father tries to cover him and loses control of car.

PROVIDENCE—Carl G. Hockett of Uxbridge, Mass, is given 15-year sentence for Slatersville, R I, bank hold-up.

NATIONAL

WASHINGTON—Count and Countess Karolyi granted visas to enter the United States.

NEW YORK—Stock prices again crash; bank executives confer.

CHICAGO—Dr Alton S. Pope, Chicago Health Department epidemiologist, accepts appointment as an instructor in Massachusetts School of Public Health.

NEVADA, Mo—Patent leads to finding long lost daughter.

EUREKA, Utah—Fugitive, respected for 10 years, shoots self, fearing discovery.

MUNCIE, Ind—Student slain by garage man who set trap.

MIAMI, Fla—Girl born in airplane 1200 feet above city.

NEW YORK—Heavy selling of stocks resumed as exchanges opened; first half-hour total $16,600 shares.

WASHINGTON—Senator Bingham strikes back at his accusers, particularly Senators Caraway and Blaine.

SPORTS

WASHINGTON—Heads of West Point and Annapolis academies to meet this week to discuss football differences.

BOSTON AND N Y CLEARINGS

Boston clearings	$89,000,000
Boston balance	30,000,000
New York clearings	000,000,000
New York balance	210,000,000

WASHINGTON, Oct 28 (A. P.)—Treasury receipts Oct 25 were $4,604,781; expenditures, $10,651,817; balance, $219,058,367.

POLICEMAN ALMOST NABS TRAFFIC CHIEF

Commissioner Fisher Directing Autos To Go Contrary to Signs

A man in civilian clothes directing traffic to enter Pemberton sq from Somerset st, contrary to the rules as displayed on one-way street signs, was about to be escorted from the highway this morning until he introduced himself.

Patrolman William Murphy, assigned to Pemberton sq, saw the man directing traffic into the square from the customary exit route and stepped up to inquire the reason for the apparent voluntary assistance from a civilian.

"My name is Fisher," the civilian explained, "the Traffic Commissioner."

"Pardon me," said officer Murphy.

"Don't apologize, you're right on your job, and as soon as I can get a uniformed officer he'll be stationed here to right this tangle."

Traffic was in somewhat of a tangle during the morning hours, and will remain that way for three more days. A number of temporary traffic regulations affecting Tremont, Boylston and nearby streets went into effect this morning while a new surface is being laid on Tremont st, between Park and Beacon sts.

Making Pemberton sq a one-way street from Somerset st to Scollay sq during the emergency was not among the changes in normal direction announced by the commission, and his change caused considerable confusion to motorists who were going by the map and rules issued Sunday by the Traffic Commission.

The principal change in traffic today and for the next few days was the making of Tremont st a one-way street from Scollay sq to Temple pl and from Boylston st to Stuart st. Boylston st is temporarily made one way from Tremont to Washington, with no parking on either side, and parking is also forbidden on Avery st.

A new left turn for motorists going south on Tremont st is also in effect, allowing these drivers to turn from Tremont into Boylston and go to Washington. The left turn from Boylston into Tremont is permitted between 10 a m to 3 p m. The left turn from Washington into Winter st is banned. The left turn from Boylston into Tremont, between 10 and 3, is at the suggestion of the Retail Trade Board.

While traffic was slowed up considerably by the changes they will be only temporary and the normal flow will be resumed by Thursday, it is expected.

WILLIAM FISHER
Traffic Commissioner

MAY CLOSE WOODLANDS TO ALL WITHIN FEW DAYS

Fire Menace Most Serious Massachusetts Has Faced In Long Time

The freedom of the woodlands of Massachusetts will be denied to the public within a few days, unless there is a considerable downfall of rain before that time.

Not only will hunters be denied the privilege of going forth to seek their furry and feathered prey, but even plain, unarmed nature lovers, hikers and horseback riders will be barred from the forests of the State until such time as a downpour of rain provides a relief from the present serious fire menace which members of the State Department of Conservation believe is the most dangerous which this State has faced for some years.

Commissioner of Conservation William A. L. Bazeley stated today that, unless a heavy rainfall occurs within the next two days, he will request Gov Allen and the Executive Council to order the woods closed, so that no one will be permitted to go into any woodland not his own property.

Legislation enacted several years ago empowers the Governor and Council to act in cases of emergency and it is expected that the cooperation of the Chief Executive and the Council will be accorded the Department of Conservation in the present extremity.

Giving the hunters of the State a surprisingly clean bill of health, State Fire Warden Maxwell C. Hutchins told the Globe this morning that more than 75 forest and brush fires took place yesterday, a day when hunters were not in the woods at all. Mr Hutchins believes that the blame for many of the fires lies with outing and petting parties who are careless with cigarette stubs and matches. In some instances, he avers, those responsible for the fires do not even know that they have caused them, for cigarette butts often smoulder for a long time before bursting into flame.

Hunters Exonerated

During last week, he states, there were about 25 forest and brush fires, although the woodlands were crowded with hunters. This figure, he states, is not remarkable, for a certain number of fires are expected at this time of year. The record of Sunday brush and wood fires is another matter, says Warden Hutchins. Expressing sympathy for the lovers of nature who would be denied access to the woods, he asserted that the only possible way to preserve the beauty of the forests of the State is to take the steps contemplated by the department on Wednesday, in requesting that the Governor and Council order the woods closed.

Warden Hutchins feels that the persons from city sections who ride out into the country Sundays, Saturday afternoons and holidays to gather Au-

Continued on the Seventeenth Page

Radio Programs PAGE 25

Other Features

	Page
Uncle Dudley	16
Dorothy Dix	26
Will Rogers' Dispatch	16
Comics	24
Cross-Word Puzzle	26
Financial and Commercial	17, 18, 19
Health Talk	21
Household Department	20, 21
Milady Beautiful	21
Movie Facts and Fancies	14
"Short Skirts"	21
Short Story	25
Sports	12, 13
Teepee Tales	26
The Once Over	16
Theatres and Pictures	22
"Treasure House of Martin Hews"	21

NORRIS INTENDS TO ASK IT

Bitter Clashes Between Bingham and Others

WASHINGTON, Oct 28 (A. P.)—Presentation of a resolution of censure of Senator Bingham, Republican, Connecticut, was forecast in the Senate today, at the close of two hours of savage personal exchanges between the Connecticut Senator and members of the Lobby Committee, who condemned his relations with the Connecticut Manufacturers' Association.

Chairman Norris of the Judiciary Committee, who appointed the Lobby Committee, announced he intended to offer a resolution shortly.

Later he explained that in view of the attack made by Bingham upon the committee and in view of the committee's condemnation of Bingham, he felt the Senate should place itself on record.

"I don't know what kind of resolution I shall offer," Norris asserted, "but I will offer one later today or tomorrow, as soon as I have read the charges made by the Connecticut Senator. I think the Senate should go on record."

Defends Using Eyanson

Fighting back at the lobby committee, Bingham, in an hour's address, defended his use of Charles L. Eyanson, a salaried representative of the Connecticut Manufacturers' Association, to help him in the tariff bill. He accused the lobby investigating committee of deliberately seeking to injure him and "befoul" him with "political slime and corrupt innuendoes."

When Bingham had concluded, Chairman Caraway and three others of the five members of the lobby committee replied. The entire exchange was filled with some of the most bitter personal language heard in the Senate in many years.

Senator Robinson, Republican, of Indiana, concluded the counter attack by the lobby committee, declaring he didn't approve, "the Republican party doesn't approve, and

Continued on the Seventeenth Page

THE WEATHER

COLDER

United States Weather Bureau forecasts:

For Boston and Its Vicinity: Fair and slightly colder tonight; Tuesday increasing cloudiness; moderate northerly wind.

For Southern New England and Eastern New York. Partly cloudy, slightly cooler tonight; Tuesday increasing cloudiness; fresh north wind.

For Northern New England: Partly cloudy, slightly cooler tonight; Tuesday partly cloudy; fresh northwest and north wind.

This morning there was a marked barometric depression centered over Colorado, Denver reading being 29.72. To the northwest, over Wyoming and parts of Utah, Idaho and Montana, snow was falling this morning. To the east and southeast the weather was rainy as far as St Louis, Nashville, Tenn, and Montgomery, Ala. New Orleans reported over four inches fall.

Morning temperatures: New York, 46; Washington, 46; Chicago, 40; White River, Ont, 4; Highland Light, 32; wind northwest, 20 miles.

Boston observations at 8 a m: Barometer at sea level, 30.02; temperature, 41; highest yesterday, 74; lowest last night, 40; humidity, 57 percent; sky clear; wind northwest, 16 miles per hour.

The Temperature Today

The thermometer at Thompson's Spa records the temperature up to 3 p m today as follows:

	1928	1929		1928	1929
3 a m	46	40	1 p m	56	54
6 a m	46	46	2 p m	56	54
9 a m	49	46	3 p m	56	54
12 m	54	52			

PRICES SLUMP TO NEW LOW LEVELS

CLOSING PRICES OF SEVERAL STOCKS

Hudson Motors, 60, off 3.
United States Steel, 186, off 17½.
Studebaker, 43, off 6.
Pan Pet B, 58, off 6⅝.
United Aircraft, 60⅛, off 14⅛.
Sinclair, 27⅝, off 3⅝.
Briggs, 15⅝, off 2⅜.
Cons Gas, 97⅛, off 30.
Barnsdall A, 22⅛, off 5⅛.
Andes Cop, 40¼, off 4⅛.
Am Can, 136, off 17⅛.
Balt & Ohio, 115¼, off 13⅝.
S O of N J, 64¾, off 8.
Sears Roe, 11¼, off 16.
Warner Bros, 44, off 6¼.
Gen Foods, 48⅛, off 6⅛.
Para Famous, 49¼, off 10⅝.
Col Graph, 26¾, off 8½.
United Corp, 33½, off 8¾.
N Y Central, 186, off 22⅝.
Westinghouse, 145, off 34¼.
Atlantic Refining, 40⅝, off 9⅛.
Commonwealth & So, 15, off 3⅛.
Anaconda, 93½, off 9.
Gen Motors, 47½, off 6¾.
Erie, 55, off 11⅛.
Chrysler, 40, off 5.
Tex Corp, 55, off 3¾.
Gen Elec, 250, off 47½.
Packard Motors, 18¼, off 3⅛.
Cerre de Pasco, 77½, off 5.
Am Smelt, 90, off 7¾.
Tex Gulf, 55⅝, off 7¾.
Kennecott, 70⅝, off 6⅝.
Johns Manv, 132, off 27½.
Union Pacific, 240, off 16.
Bethlehem Steel, 94⅛, off 9⅝.
National Cash Register, 75, off 19.
Radio Corporation, 40¼, off 18⅝.
Woolworth, 80, off 7.
National Dairy, 50½, off 9¼.
Union Carbide, 84, off 20.
Montgomery Ward, 59½, off 15⅝.
Can Pacific, 203, off 9.
Gold Dust, 40, off 12.
Am Telephone, 232, off 34.
Am & Foreign Power, 77½, of 21⅝.
Col Gas, 70¾, off 22.
Vanadium, 61½, of 10½.
Mo, Kansas & Tex, 35, off 16.

NEW YORK, Oct 28 (A. P.)—Banking support rushed to the aid of the Stock Market early this afternoon proved ineffective and prices broke sharply to new low levels as heavy liquidation was renewed in the late afternoon. Total sales crossed the 6,000,000 share mark before 2 o'clock, the ticker running nearly 1½ hours behind the market.

Renewal of selling pressure against United States Steel common, which broke to a new low on the current decline at $188.50, off 15, after having rallied to $198 on reports that J. P. Morgan & Co brokers were buying the stock, sent the market into another nose dive in the last hour of trading.

Radio, which had touched $51 on the rebound, dropped back to $46.50. American and Foreign Power fell from $78.50 to $74, or nearly $25 below last Saturday's close. Westinghouse Electric sold down to $145.25, off $34. Dozens of other high-priced issues sold $10 to nearly $45 a share below the final sales of last week.

Sharp declines also took place in many of the bank stock traded in "over the counter." First National dropped $300 a share, being quoted at $6900 bid and $7100 offered.

The market tended to rally for a time in the afternoon, when United States Steel improved moderately under buying attributed to J. P. Morgan interests. But in the last hour the market broke wide open. United States Steel dropped 15 points to a new low for the movement at 188½. High priced stocks recorded enormous losses. General Electric broke more than 44 points, Standard Gas 34, and such shares as Western Union, Westinghous Electric and New York Central about 30 points.

The close was weak.

Total sales approximated 3,500,000 shares.

Heavy liquidation from the opening of the market indicated that last week's casualties in the market had been much more severe than generally believed, and that it was aapparently necessary to close out hundreds of weakened speculative accounts which had been previously overlooked.

Wall Street looked for a strong opening market today on the theory that organized banking support would be forthcoming, as a result of the many optimistic statements on business issued last week when the market was in the midst of its nose-dive. Instead, prices began to slide off from the opening and this brought about heavy liquidation by panic-stricken speculators, many of whom had held on through last week's decline by the narrowest of margins.

"Bear" traders, sensing the market's weakness, began to hammer away at the high priced issues which dropped $1 to $5 a share between salues as bids were hastily withdrawn.

Shortly after 1 p m, Richard Whitney, generally recognized as the "J. P. Morgan broker," began to place buying orders for United States Steel common, and other market leaders. This led to a hasty covering movement, but the rallies generally averaged only a few dollars a share, and the rebound invariably attracted fresh offerings.

United States Steel common rallied from 193 to 198, then broke to $190.50, off $13, a new low for this movement.

Johns-Manville rallied from 137½, Radio from 47¾ to 52¾, Westinghouse Electric from 152½ to 159, and General Electric from 254 to 261.

T. B. MacAulay, president of the Sun Life Assurance Company of Canada, one of the largest individual

Continued on the Eighteenth Page

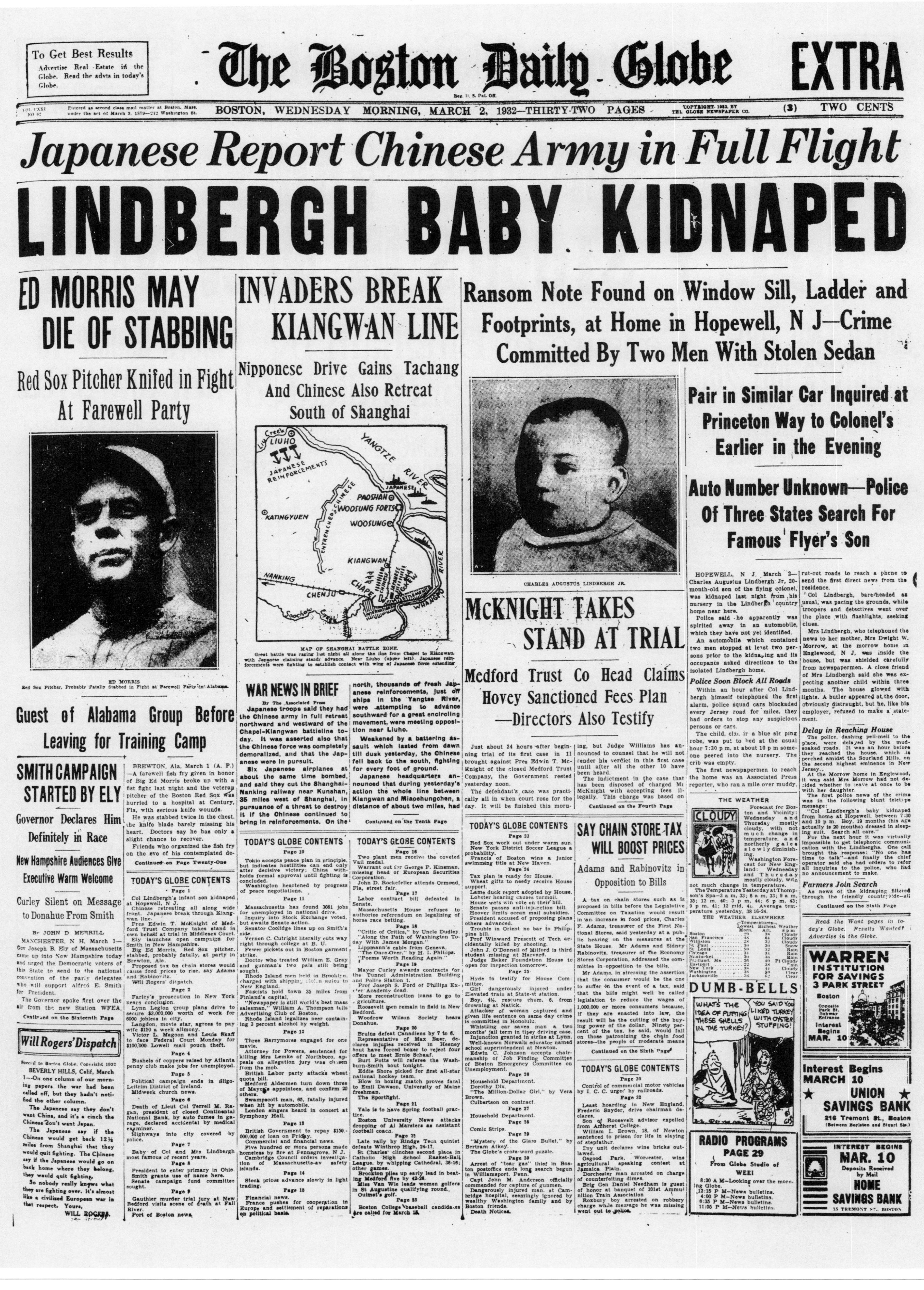

To Get Best Results
Advertise Real Estate in the Globe. Read the advts in today's Globe.

The Boston Daily Globe — EXTRA

Reg. U. S. Pat. Off.
VOL CXXI NO 62 — Entered as second class mail matter at Boston, Mass, under the act of March 3, 1879—212 Washington St.
BOSTON, WEDNESDAY MORNING, MARCH 2, 1932—THIRTY-TWO PAGES — (3) TWO CENTS

Japanese Report Chinese Army in Full Flight

LINDBERGH BABY KIDNAPED

Ransom Note Found on Window Sill, Ladder and Footprints, at Home in Hopewell, N J—Crime Committed By Two Men With Stolen Sedan

CHARLES AUGUSTUS LINDBERGH JR.

Pair in Similar Car Inquired at Princeton Way to Colonel's Earlier in the Evening

Auto Number Unknown—Police Of Three States Search For Famous Flyer's Son

HOPEWELL, N J, March 2—Charles Augustus Lindbergh Jr, 20-month-old son of the flying colonel, was kidnaped last night from his nursery in the Lindbergh country home near here.

Police said he apparently was spirited away in an automobile, which they have not yet identified.

An automobile which contained two men stopped at least two persons prior to the kidnaping and its occupants asked directions to the isolated Lindbergh home.

Police Soon Block All Roads

Within an hour after Col Lindbergh himself telephoned the first alarm, police squad cars blockaded every Jersey road for miles. they had orders to stop any suspicious persons or cars.

The child, clad in a blue sleeping robe, was put to bed at the usual hour 7:30 p m, at about 10 p m someone peered into the nursery. The crib was empty.

The first newspapermen to reach the home was an Associated Press reporter, who ran a mile over muddy, rut-cut roads to reach a phone to send the first direct news from the residence.

Col Lindbergh, bare-headed as usual, was pacing the grounds, while troopers and detectives went over the place with flashlights, seeking clues.

Mrs Lindbergh, who telephoned the news to her mother, Mrs Dwight W. Morrow, at the morrow home in Englewood, N J, was inside the house, but was shielded carefully from newspapermen. A close friend of Mrs Lindbergh said she was expecting another child within three months. The house glowed with lights. A butler appeared at the door, obviously distraught, but he, like his employer, refused to make a statement.

Delay in Reaching House

The police, dashing pell-mell to the place, were delayed by the mud-soaked roads. It was an hour before they reached the house. which is perched amidst the Sourland Hills, on the second highest eminence in New Jersey.

At the Morrow home in Englewood, it was said Mrs Morrow had not decided whether to leave at once to be with her daughter.

The first police news of the crime was in the following blunt teletype message:

"Col Lindbergh's baby kidnaped from home at Hopewell, between 7:30 and 10 p m. Boy, 19 months (his age actually is 20 months) dressed in sleeping suit. Search all cars."

For the next hour it was virtually impossible to get telephonic communication with the Lindberghs. One call brought the response: "No one has time to talk"—and finally the chief operator said she had orders to refer all inquiries to the police, who had no announcement to make.

Farmers Join Search

As news of the kidnaping filtered through the friendly countryside—all

Continued on the Sixth Page

ED MORRIS MAY DIE OF STABBING

Red Sox Pitcher Knifed in Fight At Farewell Party

ED MORRIS
Red Sox Pitcher, Probably Fatally Stabbed in Fight at Farewell Party in Alabama

Guest of Alabama Group Before Leaving for Training Camp

BREWTON, Ala, March 1 (A. P.)—A farewell fish fry given in honor of Big Ed Morris broke up with a fist fight last night and the veteran pitcher of the Boston Red Sox was hurried to a hospital at Century, Fla, with serious knife wounds.

He was stabbed twice in the chest, the knife blade barely missing his heart. Doctors say he has only a slight chance to recover.

Friends who organized the fish fry on the eve of his contemplated de-

Continued on Page Twenty-One

INVADERS BREAK KIANGWAN LINE

Nipponese Drive Gains Tachang And Chinese Also Retreat South of Shanghai

MAP OF SHANGHAI BATTLE ZONE.
Great battle was raging last night all along the line from Chapei to Kiangwan, with Japanese claiming steady advance. Near Liuho (upper left), Japanese reinforcements were fighting to establish contact with wing of Japanese force extending

WAR NEWS IN BRIEF

By The Associated Press

Japanese troops said they had the Chinese army in full retreat northward and westward of the Chapei-Kiangwan battleline today. It was asserted also that the Chinese force was completely demoralized, and that the Japanese were in pursuit.

Six Japanese airplanes at about the same time bombed, and said they cut the Shanghai-Nanking railway near Kunshan, 35 miles west of Shanghai, in pursuance of a threat to destroy it if the Chinese continued to bring in reinforcements. On the north, thousands of fresh Japanese reinforcements, just off ships in the Yangtse River, were attempting to advance southward for a great encircling movement, were meeting opposition near Liuho.

Weakened by a battering assault which lasted from dawn till dusk yesterday, the Chinese fell back to the south, fighting for every foot of ground.

Japanese headquarters announced that during yesterday's action the whole line between Kiangwan and Miaochungchen, a distance of about two miles, had

Continued on the Tenth Page

McKNIGHT TAKES STAND AT TRIAL

Medford Trust Co Head Claims Hovey Sanctioned Fees Plan —Directors Also Testify

Just about 24 hours after beginning trial of its first case in 11 brought against Pres Edwin T. McKnight of the closed Medford Trust Company, the Government rested yesterday noon.

The defendant's case was practically all in when court rose for the day. It will be finished this morning, but Judge Williams has announced to counsel that he will not render his verdict in this first case until after all the other 10 have been heard.

The indictment in the case that has been disposed of charged Mr McKnight with accepting fees illegally. This charge was based on

Continued on the Fourth Page

SMITH CAMPAIGN STARTED BY ELY

Governor Declares Him Definitely in Race

New Hampshire Audiences Give Executive Warm Welcome

Curley Silent on Message to Donahue From Smith

By JOHN D MERRILL

MANCHESTER, N H, March 1—Gov Joseph B. Ely of Massachusetts came up into New Hampshire today and urged the Democratic voters of this State to send to the national convention of the party delegates who will support Alfred E. Smith for President.

The Governor spoke first over the air from the new Station WFEA,

Continued on the Sixteenth Page

Will Rogers' Dispatch

Special to Boston Globe, Copyright 1932

BEVERLY HILLS, Calif, March 1—On one column of our morning papers the war had been called off, but they hadn't notified the other column.

The Japanese say they don't want China, and it's a cinch the Chinese don't want Japan.

The Japanese say if the Chinese would get back 12½ miles from Shanghai that they would quit fighting. The Chinese say if the Japanese would go on back home where they belong, they would quit fighting.

So nobody really knows what they are fighting over. It's almost like a civilized European war in that respect. Yours,

WILL ROGERS.

TODAY'S GLOBE CONTENTS

Page 1
Col Lindbergh's infant son kidnaped at Hopewell, N J.
Chinese retreating all along wide front. Japanese break through Kiangwan line.
Pres Edwin T. McKnight of Medford Trust Company takes stand in own behalf at trial in Middlesex Court.
Ely launches open campaign for Smith in New Hampshire.
Big Ed Morris, Red Sox pitcher, stabbed, probably fatally, at party in Brewton, Ala.
Proposed tax on chain stores would cause food prices to rise, say Adams and Rabinovitz.
Will Rogers' dispatch.
Page 2
Farley's prosecution in New York nears conclusion.
Lynn Legion group plans drive to secure $3,000,000 worth of work for 6000 jobless in city.
Langdon, movie star, agrees to pay wife $150 a week alimony.
Victor L. Magoon and Louis Skaff to face Federal Court Monday for $100,000 Lowell mail pouch theft.
Page 4
Bushels of coppers raised by Atlanta penny club make jobs for unemployed.
Page 5
Political campaign ends in Sligo-Leitrim District of Ireland.
Midweek church news.
Page 6
Death of Lieut Col Terrell M. Ragan, president of closed Continental National Bank, by auto fumes in garage, declared accidental by medical examiner.
Highways into city covered by police.
Page 7
Baby of Col and Mrs Lindbergh most famous of recent years.
Page 8
President to enter primary in Ohio.
Smith grants use of name here.
Senate campaign fund committee sought.
Page 9
Gauthier murder trial jury at New Bedford visits scene of death at Fall River.
Port of Boston news.

TODAY'S GLOBE CONTENTS

Page 10
Tokio accepts peace plan in principle, but indicates hostilities can end only after decisive victory; China withholds formal approval until fighting is concluded.
Washington heartened by progress of peace negotiations.
Page 11
Massachusetts has found 3081 jobs for unemployed in national drive.
Inquiry into Stock Exchange voted, but awaits Senate action.
Senator Coolidge lines up on Smith's side.
Vernon C. Cutright literally cuts way right through college at B. U.
Fewer pickets out in Boston garment strike.
Doctor who treated William E. Gray and gunman's two pals still being sought.
Rhode Island men held in Brooklyn, charged with shipping stolen autos to New England.
Fascists hold town 35 miles from Finland's capital.
"Newspaper is still world's best mass salesman," William A. Thompson tells Advertising Club of Boston.
Rhode Island legalizes beer containing 3 percent alcohol by weight.
Page 12
Three Barrymores engaged for one movie.
Attorney for Powers, sentenced for killing Mrs Lemke of Northboro, appeals on allegation jury was chosen from the mob.
British Labor party attacks wheat quota bill.
Medford Aldermen turn down three of Mayor's appointees, and confirm 20 others.
Swampscott man, 65, fatally injured when hit by automobile.
London singers heard in concert at Symphony Hall.
Page 13
British Government to repay $150,000,000 of loan on Friday.
Commercial and financial news.
Five hundred or more persons made homeless by fire at Pennsgrove, N J.
Cambridge Council orders investigation of Massachusetts-av safety islands.
Page 14
Stock prices advance slowly in light trading.
Page 15
Financial news.
France pushes for cooperation in Europe and settlement of reparations on political basis.

TODAY'S GLOBE CONTENTS

Page 16
Two plant men receive the coveted Vail medal.
Warrant out for George P. Kinsman, missing head of European Securities Corporation.
John D. Rockefeller attends Ormond, Fla, street fair.
Page 17
Labor contract bill defeated in Senate.
Massachusetts House refuses to authorize referendum on legalizing of horse race betting.
Page 18
"Critic of Critics," by Uncle Dudley.
"Along the Path of Washington Today With James Morgan."
Lippmann's cable from Geneva.
"The Once-Over," by H. I. Phillips.
"Poems Worth Reading Again."
Page 19
Mayor Curley awards contracts for the Tunnel Administration Building and Police Station 1.
Prof Joseph S. Ford of Phillips Exeter Academy dead.
More reconstruction loans to go to agriculture.
Roosevelt men remain in field in New Bedford.
Woodrow Wilson Society hears Donahue.
Page 20
Bruins defeat Canadiens by 7 to 6.
Representative of Max Baer, declares injuries received in Heeney bout have forced boxer to reject four offers to meet Ernie Schaaf.
Burt Potts will referee the Washburn-Smith bout tonight.
Eddie Shore picked for first all-star national hockey team.
Blow in boxing match proves fatal to Emil Dawson, University of Maine freshman.
The Sportlight.
Page 21
Yale is to have Spring football practice.
Boston University News attacks dropping of Al Marsters as assistant football coach.
Page 22
Late rally by Rindge Tech quintet defeats Winthrop High, 24-17.
St Charles' clinches second place in Catholic High School Basket-Ball League, by whipping Cathedral, 36-16; other games.
Brockton piles up early lead in beating Medford five by 42-26.
Miss Van Wie leads women golfers in St Augustine qualifying round.
Ouimet's golf.
Page 23
Boston College baseball candidates are called for March 15.

TODAY'S GLOBE CONTENTS

Page 23
Red Sox work out under warm sun.
New York District Soccer League a probability.
Francis of Boston wins a junior swimming title at New Haven.
Page 24
Tax plan is ready for House.
Wheat gifts to needy receive House support.
Lame duck report adopted by House.
Lobster hearing causes turmoil.
House wets win vote on their bill.
Senate passes anti-injunction bill.
Hoover limits ocean mail subsidies.
President accused of proposing plans others advanced.
Trouble in Orient no bar to Philippine bill.
Prof Winward Prescott of Tech accidentally killed by shooting.
John J. O'Donnell of Milford is third student missing at Harvard.
Judge Baker Foundation House to open for inspection tomorrow.
Page 25
Hyde to testify for House Committee.
Girl dangerously injured under Elevated train at State-st station.
Boy, 4½, rescues chum, 6, from drowning at Natick.
Attacker of woman captured and given life sentence on same day crime is committed in Honolulu.
Whistling ear saves man a two months' jail term in tipsy driving case.
Injunction granted in strike at Lynn.
Well-known Norwalk educator named school superintendent at Newton.
Edwin C. Johnson accepts chairmanship of Job Finding Committee of Boston Emergency Committee on Unemployment.
Page 26
Household Department.
Dorothy Dix.
"The Million-Dollar Girl," by Vera Brown.
Culbertson on contract.
Page 27
Household Department.
Page 28
Comic Strips.
Page 29
"Mystery of the Glass Bullet," by Bertram Atkey.
The Globe's cross-word puzzle.
Page 30
Arrest of "tear gas" thief in Boston postoffice ends long search begun in Williamsport, Penn.
Capt John M. Anderson officially commended for capture of gunmen.
Dangerously injured man, at Cambridge hospital, seemingly ignored by wealthy Washington family and by Boston friends.
Death Notices.

SAY CHAIN STORE TAX WILL BOOST PRICES

Adams and Rabinovitz in Opposition to Bills

A tax on chain stores such as is proposed in bills before the Legislative Committee on Taxation would result in an increase in food prices, Charles F. Adams, treasurer of the First National Stores, said yesterday at a public hearing on the measures at the State House. Mr Adams and Sidney Rabinovitz, treasurer of the Economy Stores Corporation, addressed the committee in opposition to the bills.

Mr Adams, in stressing the assertion that the consumer would be the one to suffer in the event of a tax, said that the bills might well be called legislation to reduce the wages of 1,000,000 or more consumers because, if they are enacted into law, the result will be the cutting of the buying power of the dollar. Ninety percent of the tax, he said, would fall on those patronizing the chain food stores—the people of moderate means

Continued on the Sixth Page

TODAY'S GLOBE CONTENTS

Page 30
Control of commercial motor vehicles by I. C. C. urged by railroads.
Page 32
Least hoarding in New England, Frederic Snyder, drive chairman declares.
Son of Roosevelt advisor expelled from Amherst College.
William I. Brown, 18, of Newton sentenced to prison for life in slaying of stepfather.
Dry unit declares wine bricks outlawed.
Osgood Park, Worcester, wins agricultural speaking contest at Jamaica Plain.
Dorchester man arrested on charge of counterfeiting dimes.
Brig Gen Daniel Needham is guest of honor at banquet of 101st Ammunition Train Association
Roxbury boy arrested on robbery charge while message he was missing went out to police.

THE WEATHER

Forecast for Boston and Vicinity: Wednesday and Thursday mostly cloudy, with not much change in temperature, and northerly gales slowly diminishing.

Washington Forecast for New England: Wednesday and Thursday mostly cloudy, with not much change in temperature.

The Temperature Yesterday at Thompson's Spa—3 a m, 33; 6 a m, 33; 9 a m, 35; 12 m, 40; 3 p m, 44; 6 p m, 43; 9 p m, 41; 12 mid, 41. Average temperature yesterday, 38 16-24.

THE WEATHER ELSEWHERE

	Temperatures— Lowest Morn.	Highest Aft.	Weather 8 p m
Boston	29	38	Cloudy
San Francisco	48	64	Cloudy
Williston	28	32	Cloudy
St Paul	30	30	Snow
St Louis	50	52	Rain
Chicago	34	34	Rain
Nantucket	30	36	Rain
Portland, Me	26	40	Pt Cloudy
Eastport	22	38	Rain
New York	38	44	Cloudy
Washington	38	50	Clear
Jacksonville	56	82	Clear

DUMB-BELLS

Boston Evening Globe

Reg. U. S. Pat Off.

VOL CXXI NO 142 — Entered as second class mail matter at Boston, Mass, under the act of March 3, 1879—347 Washington St

BOSTON, SATURDAY EVENING, MAY 21, 1932—16 PAGES—2 CENTS

FINAL CLOSING
NEW YORK AND
BOSTON STOCKS
7:30 FINAL COMPLETE

AMELIA LANDS IN IRELAND

First Woman to Fly the Atlantic Alone

SEEK RUM RUNNER IN LINDBERGH CASE

Police Hunt Man Who Said Baby Was Dead and Near Home

BALTIMORE, May 21 (A. P.)—A man long identified with New Jersey liquor running activities was disclosed today as the "mysterious gangster in Maryland," sought for questioning in the Lindbergh kidnaping case.

The man who remained unnamed, informed Arthur Mills, identification expert at the Maryland House of Correction, that the body of the kidnaped child would be found within five miles of the Lindbergh estate, two days before it actually was discovered.

Mills, formerly a member of the Maryland State Police, said the rum runner further informed him that the baby had been killed by blows on the head, and that the body had been hidden near the flyer's home.

Ignored It at Time

"I didn't pay any attention to it at the time," Mills said, "but later, when I read that the body had been found, I communicated my information to Col H. Norman Schwarzkopf of the New Jersey police. Two officers came here yesterday to investigate it."

Mills said he had first known the man at Ocean City, Md, in December, 1929, when more than a score of men were arrested while attempting to land a cargo of liquor on the beach.

He said he saw the rum-runner two days before the body of the Lindbergh baby was found, and that he complained of the police activity which hampered his liquor activities.

"If somebody doesn't do something about the case soon, I will," Mills quoted the man as having said. He also told him he knew several people connected with the case and that three or four persons were involved, Mills said.

Mills declined to give the name of the man, but said he had sent it to the New Jersey police officials investigating the kidnaping.

Reference to "Jafsie"

That part of the morning bulletin dealing with matters other than the search for the rum-runner follows:

"Dr Condon (the "Jafsie" who paid a futile $50,000 ransom for return of the murdered baby) was taken to New Rochelle (yesterday) by our investigators to look over the criminal rogues' gallery in an effort to identify the man known as John, but failed to make any identification.

"Joseph Perrone (the taxi driver who took a note from the supposed kidnapers to Dr Condon instructing him about ransom payment) had formerly looked over the criminal rogues' gallery in New York city and failed to identify anyone and yesterday he went over the gallery at the central bureau of identification at the State Police Headquarters in Trenton, but failed to make any identification. He will be taken to another Police Department today.

"The King kidnaping case (a mysterious case thought to have possible connection with the Lindbergh case mentioned for the first time by Schwarzkopf yesterday) was gone into by our investigators yesterday, but no information of value could be ascertained."

Doubt Curtis' Motive

The possibility that John Hughes Curtis' story of his astonishing lie may in itself have been false in part, received police attention today.

A portion of the Norfolk shipbuilder's confession that his intermediation in the Lindbergh baby case was a hoax already was considered disproved.

Continued on the Third Page

WARNER BROTHERS' PROFIT $9,251,000

Sale and Purchase of Their Company's Stock Described by Gray

WASHINGTON, May 21 (A. P.)—Indication that the three Warner Brothers profited $9,251,000 in 1930 by purchase and sale of Warner Brothers Pictures, Inc, stock was continued in the story of operations traced today in the Senate's stock market investigation.

As Harry M. Warner took the stand, William A. Gray, counsel for the inquiry, said he would establish "that this man through undercover channels and by covering up his transactions sold his stock while certain journals were boosting the value before the public." He said the buying was when the newspapers began to depress the price.

The president of the moving picture production concern said his trades were for himself and his two brothers, Albert and J. L. Warner, jointly. The business was done through several different brokers and through accounts under the names of Moe Rosenberg and Edward Charns.

Mr Warner called Samuel Schneider, his counsel, to sit by him as the examination progressed. The lawyer said the deals were under other names because it had been found that trading in the Warner name influenced others.

William A. Gray, committee counsel, had previously announced that he wanted to question Mr Warner about dealings in the stock of his own company.

Mr Warner was dressed in a brown suit without a vest. His face was tanned and he wore glasses.

Before Mr Warner was called, Senator Brookhart, Rep, Iowa, asked Mr Gray to have Richard Whitney, president of the Exchange, present to the committee a pool operation which he considered honest. "I want to know whether there is anything honest in this institution," Mr Brookhart said.

Gray Has Data On 50 Pools

Mr Gray replied that when Mr Whitney was on the stand he professed ignorance of the existence of any pools on the exchange.

At Mr Brookhart's request, the committee agreed to have Mr Gray communicate with Whitney to ask him to name some syndicate whose operations he believes to be entirely honest.

Mr Gray said he would then go into the activities of the syndicate or take whatever action the committee might desire. The counsel remarked that he himself had data on "50 to 69 pools."

Mr Warner was photographed as he was being sworn.

"Do you want his finger prints, too?" Senator Glass, Dem, Virginia, asked.

Mr Warner said he has been in the moving picture business 28 years and previously was in the shoe business.

"Have you made money?" Senator Couzens, Rep, Michigan, asked.

"We have."

"More than in the manipulation of stocks?"

"Everything we made we made out of the development of pictures," Mr Warner said. He testified that he had bought stocks, however.

Mr Couzens said he wanted to know whether they were more interested in the manipulation of stocks than in development of the company.

Brothers Had 303,484 Shares

Warner Brothers' Pictures, Inc, was organized in 1923 with 550,000 shares of common stock. When the Stanley Company, a theatre-owning corporation, was acquired about four years

Continued on the Third Page

TAILOR SLAIN IN ROCKPORT

Attacked While at Work in His Shop

ROCKPORT, May 21—Andrew Oker, 60, a tailor, was found in his shop at 77 Main at this noon badly beaten about the head, and, in the opinion of Dr E. E. Cleaves and the Rockport police, he was a victim of foul play. He died in a police ambulance on the way to the Addison Gilbert Hospital in Gloucester.

The police base their opinion that the man was the victim of foul play on the evidence found of the severe beating about the head and also on the fact that at the time he was found he clutched a needle in his hand. He had evidently been sewing when attacked.

The discovery of the man was made by his son, who became alarmed when his father did not come home to lunch.

His only survivor is hisson.

'JAFSIE' ON WAY TO PAWTUCKET

Also Going to New Bedford in Hunt for "Scoundrel"

DANBURY, Conn, May 21 (A. P.)—Dr John F. Condon, "Jafsie" of the Lindbergh kidnaping case, arrived at a roadhouse on the outskirts of Danbury shortly before noon today, after driving here at a high rate of speed from New York.

Shortly after his arrival at Danbury, Dr Condon said his next stop would be Pawtucket, R I, and that he also wanted to go to New Bedford, Mass.

"I have received a communication," he said, "and expect to receive other communications along the way."

He did not say what the communications were.

Somebody asked him if he was heading for Block Island, off the Rhode Island coast, for a vacation.

"I want to take a vacation there sometime," he replied, "but I'm not taking any vacation now. I want to bring those scoundrels to justice."

Two New York detectives, trailing him in another car, said they did not kno wthemselves where he and they were going.

"We haven't the slightest idea," one of them said.

Condon announced he was going to have lunch at the roadhouse, but did not say where he was going from there.

He ran into some acquaintances in the cafe and, pointing to the reporters and the detectives with a smile, said:

"I just can't seem to get away for a quiet little jaunt by myself."

Two New Jersey State policemen called at his home in the Bronx before he left. It had been announced he would examine rogues' gallery pictures in Newark today.

SAYS FIRST MASS AT MOTHER'S BEDSIDE

CLINTON, May 21 (A. P.)—Although she was probably unaware, a son carried out the wishes of his mother today when Rev James Gerald Joyce said his first mass at the bedside of his mother, Mrs Hannah H. Joyce. His mother, critically sick, was in a coma throughout the services.

Rev Fr Joyce was ordained in the Dominican Order yesterday at Washington, and arrived here at midnight, after a hurried trip.

Will Rogers' Dispatch

Special to Boston Globe. Copyright 1932

BEVERLY HILLS, Calif, May 20—Congress is human for the first time in years. They are broke, just like everybody else, and are running around in a circle trying to pay what they owe.

They got an eighteen billion dollar first plaster on the country, and now they are pop-eyed trying to get a second mortgage. They will eventually find out they are just like other folks, they will have to cut down.

No taxpayer is going to make 'em a loan if they are going to keep as much help as they always have. Yours,

WILL ROGERS.

TREASURY BALANCE

WASHINGTON, May 21 (A. P.)—Treasury receipts for May 19 were $5,672,348; expenditures, $14,517,295; balance, $481,256,806. Customs duties for the 19 days of May were $11,196,116.

MOTHER AND SISTER DELIGHTED AT NEWS

W Medford Family Had Not Worried About Mrs Putnam's Flight

WIDE WORLD PHOTO

MRS AMY OTIS EARHART, MOTHER OF MRS AMELIA EARHART PUTMAN, AND MRS MURIEL EARHART MORRISON, SISTER OF AMELIA

"We're delighted to know she made dry land safely," said Mrs Muriel Earhart Morrissey, sister of Amelia Earhart Putnam, when she was informed by the Globe this morning of the safe conclusion of the transatlantic flight. "Any landing is good under the circumstances. We are sorry, of course, she did not get to Paris."

Mrs Amy O. Earhart, mother of Mrs Putnam, said she was very confident of her daughter's ability. She added that she had flown with her daughter a number of times, and had enjoyed it very much.

Asked to pose for a picture, Mrs Earhart said, "We simply don't go in for that sort of thing."

The family had not been sitting up all night or worrying, Mrs Morrissey said. The latter, this morning, was busy taking care of her two children, David, 3, and Amy, 9 months. She had just put Amy to bed for her morning nap.

The family lives at 180 Traincroft road, West Medford.

Edwin E. Earhart, father of Mrs Amelia Earhart Putnam, took up residance in California about four years ago and died there in 1930.

U. S. WOMEN GOLFERS BEAT BRITISH TEAM

Won All Three Foursomes and Two Singles, Halving Another

WENTWORTH, Surrey, Eng, May 21 (A. P.)—A United States team of women golfers today defeated an English side led by Joyce Wethered in a series of nine matches.

In the morning the Americans won all three foursomes, but in the afternoon singles they only managed to win two matches and halve another.

Mrs Vare, Helen Hicks and Maurein Orcott, three leading players of the United States group, were beaten. Virginia van Wie and Mrs Leona Cheney won their matches.

Mrs Cheney won her match with Elsie Corlett, 4 and 3. Maureen Orcutt fell before Diana Fishwick and Mrs Opal Hill halved her match with Molly Gourlay to make the final score: United States, five matches; Great Britain, three matches; one halved.

Sweep in Foursomes

The United States team swept the three foursome matches to take a commanding lead. The foursomes were played on the Scotch plan, the players taking alternate strokes.

Mrs Glenna Collett Vare and Mrs Opal Hill defeated Joyce Wethered and Wanda Morgan by one hole, Helen Hicks and Virginia van Wie won from Enid Wilson and Mrs J. B. Watson, 2 and 1, and Maureen Orcutt and Mrs Leona Cheney defeated Molly Gourlay and Doris Park by one hole.

Best Golf in This Match

The Misses Hicks and van Wie had the easiest sailing and played the best golf of the three matches. They were never behind in their match with the British champion and her partner, and had a medal score of 64 for the 17 holes they had to play.

The cards:

Hicks-van Wie:
Out ....4 4 4 3 5 4 4 4 4—36
In 2 5 3 4 4 3 4 3

Wilson-Watson:
Out ....5 5 3 4 4 4 3 4 4—36
In 3 5 2 4 4 4 4 4

Miss Wethered again missed a short putt on the 16th, which the Americans won, and her third shot on the last hole was bunkered after Miss Morgan had missed her second, giving the Americans the hole with a loose 6 and

Continued on the Third Page

DO-X HOPS OFF FOR THE AZORES

Starts Atlantic Flight at Holyrood, N F

HARBOR GRACE, N F, May 21 (A. P.)—The German Airliner Do-X took off from Holyrood for a transatlantic flight to the Azores at 3 a m, Eastern standard time, today.

The wind was southwest, blowing moderately, and the weather was clear as the big ship hopped.

She had been lying at Holyrood, refueling, after a 40-mile hop from Dildo, where she landed Thursday, after running short of gasoline.

The sun was just rising when the great flying boat and its crew of 14 sprang into activity. One by one the 12 big engines were started, and mechanics listened for any sign of irregularity.

On shore and on small craft about the harbor, early morning watchers turned out to bid farewell to the flying boat, tugging at its moorings.

The clear sky, and steady, moderate southwest wind gave promise of almost ideal flying weather conditions as the last preparations for the take-off were completed.

Capt Frederick Christiansen gave the order to cast off the moorings, and the huge flying machine slipped away from its supply base, taxied out of the narrow confines of Holyrood Harbor, and into the broad expanse of Conception Bay.

Once out in the bay, the big craft shot forward, steadily gathering momentum. Slowly it arose from the water and then began to climb steadily. Still gaining altitude, the big ship headed away to the eastward and soon was a speak on the horizon.

DO-X 500 MILES SOUTH-EAST OF CAPE RACE, N F

NEW YORK, May 21 (A. P.)—The Radio Marine Corporation announced the receipt at 9:30 a m, Eastern Standard time, today, of this message from the German airliner DO-X:

"Position 14° Greenwich mean time (9 a m Eastern standard time), 44° north 41° 15' west. Winds west southwest. Speed 90 knots All clear."

The position given by the DO-X is approximately 500 miles east southeast of Cape Race, N F.

Radio-Marine attaches interpreted the phrase, "all clear," to mean that the flight was proceeding smoothly.

RADIO PROGRAMS
PAGE 8
From Globe Studio of WEEI

4:00 P. M—News bulletins.
6:35 P M—News bulletins.
11:05 P M—News bulletins.

Other Globe Features

	Page
Uncle Dudley	10
Dorothy Dix	12
Will Rogers' Dispatch	1
Anagram	15
Aviation	9
Church News	13
Comics	14
Confidential Chat	12
Cross-Word Puzzle	9
Culbertson on Contract	9
"Dancing Feet"	12
Emily Post	12
Financial and Commercial	4
Fish and Game Chat	6
"Girl and the Game"	10
Household Department	12, 13
Latest Books	15
Milady Beautiful	12
Movie Facts and Fancies	8
Movie Timetable	8
"Mystery of Mary Grier"	9
Poems Worth Reading Again	15
Short Story	12
Sports	6, 7
The Once Over	10
Thornton Burgess	14
Walter Lippmann	10

THE WEATHER

United States Weather Bureau forecasts:

For Boston and its vicinity: Partly cloudy and cooler, possibly with light showers tonight; Sunday fair and cooler; moderate southwest wind, shifting to northwest.

For Southern New England and Eastern New York: Mostly cloudy and cooler, probably showers tonight; Sunday generally fair and cooler.

For Maine: Showers this afternoon and probably tonight; cooler tonight; Sunday fair and cooler.

For New Hampshire and Vermont: Mostly cloudy and cooler, probably showers over the southern portion tonight; Sunday fair and cooler.

Boston observations, 7:40 a m, standard time: Barometer at sea level, 29.95; temperature, 64; highest yesterday, 83; lowest last night, 55; humidity, 56 percent; clear; wind west, six miles per hour; no rainfall in last 24 hours.

The Temperature Today

The thermometer at Thompson's Spa records the temperature up to 3 p m today as follows:

	1931	1932		1931	1932
3 a m	64	67	1 p m	72	70
6 a m	66	69	2 p m	73	70
9 a m	69	70	3 p m	74	70
12 m	70	72			

BRINGS HER PLANE DOWN IN CULMORE

Engine Trouble Forces Her to Cut Flight Short

A.P.

AMELIA EARHART PUTNAM

CULMORE, Ulster, Ire, May 21 (A. P.)—Amelia Earhart Putnam brought down her red and gold monoplane in a field on the Donegal side of Lough Foyle this afternoon, and thereby became the first woman ever to fly the Atlantic alone.

She landed on this side of the ocean five years to the day after Col Charles A. Lindbergh arrived at Le Bourget, France, successfully completing the first solo flight across the Atlantic by a man.

The flyer brought her plane down at 2:30 p m (9:30 a m, Boston daylight time). This meant she was in the air 15 hours and 39 minutes She left Harbor Grace at 4:51 p m Friday, Eastern standard time.

"I've Done It"

"I've done it!" Mrs Putnam exclaimed when she got out of her ship.

She had intended to go to Paris, but it was necessary to cut the flight short because her exhaust manifold had burned out and the gasoline gage was broken, causing a little leakage.

The lithe, blonde flyer, who took off from Harbor Grace, N F, at 4:51 p m, E. S. T., yesterday, got a lift by motor to Londonderry, five miles away, where the first thing she did was to get on the telephone to report her success to London, in order that her husband, George Palmer Putnam, New York publisher, and her friends back home might know that she was safe.

Her plane was not damaged in the landing and she was unhurt.

Much Fog and Rain

"For a lot of the way," Mrs Putnam said, "I was flying through storms—mist, rain and a little fog.

"To my friends in New York I want to send this message: I am very glad to have come across successfully, but I am sorry indeed I did not make France.

"I am going to speak to my husband as soon as I can by the Atlantic phone."

It was the flyer's second airplane trip across the Atlantic. Back in June, 1928, before her marriage to Mr Putnam, she made the crossing, that time as a passenger.

Leaves Londonderry

"There is no comparison," she said in reply to a question about which trip she liked better. "On this go I was flying low the whole time and had to rely on myself.

"I am afraid I am a bit deaf after the terrible roar of the engine in my ears all the time, but at any rate I have done it."

All Britain and France had been waiting eagerly for news of her, special interest centering on the fact that today was the fifth anniversary of the flight of Col Lindbergh, to whom attention had been directed anew by the tragic death of his child. child.

When Mrs Putnam had reported that she was safe, she got into an automobile and left Londonderry for an unannounced destination.

Continued on the Third Page

FLIGHT IN FIGURES
By A. P.

Distance—2026.5 miles.

Time—15 hours, 39 minutes.

Average Speed—129.5 miles per hour.

Left Harbor Grace, N F, 4:51 p m, Eastern standard time, Friday.

Arrived Culmore, Northern Ireland, 8:30 a m, Eastern standard time, Saturday.

NO GLOBE SUBSCRIPTION SOLICITORS

The Globe does not employ subscription solicitors, and any so representing themselves should be turned over to the police

The Boston Daily Globe EXTRA

Reg. U. S. Pat. Off.

VOL. CXXII NO 132 — Entered as second class mail matter at Boston, Mass. under the act of March 3, 1879—242 Washington St.

BOSTON, WEDNESDAY MORNING, NOVEMBER 9, 1932—TWENTY-EIGHT PAGES

(5) TWO CENTS

TIDAL WAVE FOR ROOSEVELT DEMOCRATS SWEEP COUNTRY

Massachusetts Carried Along With Rest, but Senators Watson, Moses, Smoot and Bingham Go Down With Chief As Victors Capture Control of Congress in Greatest Gain They Have Made in 80 Years

ELY LEADS ROOSEVELT IN BAY STATE SWEEP

Massachusetts Governor's Plurality 117,000 And National Ticket Wins by 59,000—Hoover Runs Ahead of Youngman

By JOHN D. MERRILL

Massachusetts gave Gov Joseph B Ely a plurality of perhaps 117,000 in yesterday's election, while Gov Franklin D. Roosevelt, the Democratic candidate for President, apparently carried the State by about 59,000.

These figures are subject to revision, as the returns are far from complete, but there is no doubt that the State has given a very large majority to the heads of the national and State tickets.

The Democratic victory was overwhelming. The towns, on the whole, did well for the Republican candidates, but Boston and the other cities rolled up enormous votes for the Democratic candidates.

The result was hardly in doubt after the first returns. New Bedford, which closed its polls at 2 o'clock, gave Roosevelt and Ely a plurality of more than 7000. There was at first some doubt whether this might not be due to local pride in a member of the Delano family, which is well known in that community, but as other returns came in it became clear that New Bedford was characteristic of the other large centers of population. Cambridge, unusually early in reporting, gave Roosevelt a plurality of more than 18,000.

Only Two Cities for Hoover

Brockton and Gloucester are the only cities in the State which are known to have gone for Hoover, but others may be reported later.

The story was the same everywhere except, as has been said, in the towns; most of them held to their Republican moorings, but they were outweighed by Boston, which went for Roosevelt by 99,700 and for Gov Ely by more than 106,000, which is more than that given to Alfred E. Smith four years ago.

The figures thus far received place Gov Ely considerably ahead of the Democratic candidate for President.

Mr Hoover, however, ran ahead of Lieut Gov Youngman, the Republican candidate for Governor.

The Democratic sweep, which came across the Alleghenies and the Hudson River, was almost, if not quite, as far-reaching here as elsewhere. There is doubt at this minute whether Roosevelt and Ely car-

Continued on the Fourteenth Page

DEMOCRATS WIN NEW YORK STATE

Record Tammany Vote Cast for Ticket

Lehman, Wagner and Bray All Carried Into Office

NEW YORK, Nov 8 (A. P.)—Riding the crest of a precedent-shattering triumph, Franklin D. Roosevelt won the 47 electoral votes of his home State in today's Presidential election by overwhelming Herbert Hoover in the metropolitan area with a plurality exceeding 862,000.

This huge figure wiped out a 200,000 advantage for the Republican candidate in the up-State areas and gave the Democratic standard-bearer a margin in New York as a whole of more than 660,000.

It was the first time since 1912 that New York had gone Democratic in a Presidential election.

Record Vote in City

As the Tammany-controlled Democratic organization of New York city buried its Republican opponents beneath a virtual three-to-one avalanche, a total vote of more than 2,000,000 was polled in the city for the first time in history.

The Democratic sweep in the city also carried to victory the State ticket headed by Senator Robert F. Wagner and Lieut Gov Herbert H. Lehman, candidate to succeed Gov Roosevelt.

A midnight tabulation of returns from 7794 of the 8837 districts in the State gave Roosevelt 2,408,574; Hoover, 1,748,532.

The complete totals for the 3794 New York city districts gave: Roosevelt, 1,437,231; Hoover, 575,031.

Although Hoover four years ago piled up a lead of half a million up-State, which wiped out Alfred E. Smith's New York city plurality and gave him the State, his plurality north of the city line was far too slim this year to bring him victory.

Lehman 875,000 Ahead

Lehman, in whose interest Roosevelt and Smith met for the first time since their convention fight to urge his nomination, was running more than 875,000 ahead of his Republican rival, William J. Donovan, in returns from seven-eighths of the State's dis-

Continued on the Fourteenth Page

VOTE OF STATE

(ESTIMATED)

FOR PRESIDENT

Roosevelt	798,162
Hoover	738,456
Roosevelt's Plurality	59,706

VOTE IN 1928

Smith	792,758
Hoover	775,566
Smith's plurality	17,192

FOR GOVERNOR

(ESTIMATED)

Ely	821,735
Youngman	704,567
Ely's Plurality	117,168

VOTE IN 1930

Ely	606,902
Allen	590,238
Ely's plurality	[illegible]

ROOSEVELT, ELY SWEEP BOSTON

Governor Carries City by 106,068 Margin

President-Elect's Plurality Just Under 100,000

The same sentiment that swept the nation for the Democratic party was reflected in the vote of Boston citizens yesterday when Gov Franklin D. Roosevelt and Gov Joseph B. Ely rolled up tremendous pluralities.

Outstanding was the remarkable indorsement given Gov Ely, who carried Boston by 106,068, which was more than 31,000 above his figures of two years ago and even in excess of the record vote given his friend, Ex-Gov Alfred E. Smith four years ago.

Gov Ely led Gov Roosevelt in the Boston vote by more than 6000, the President-elect's plurality being just under the 100,000 mark.

The complete Boston figures for the presidential and gubernatorial contests, tabulated early this morning were as follows: Gov Roosevelt, 178,662; President Hoover, 78,956; Gov Ely, 181,735; Lieut Gov Youngman, 75,667.

Little "Cutting" of Ticket

The figures for the minor offices, though not complete this morning, indicated that Democrats voted the straight ticket and there was little or none of the "cutting" that rumors said would feature the voting in Boston.

On the basis of estimates at 5 o'clock this morning, all Democratic candidates on the State ticket had great pluralities in Boston over their Republican opponents. None, of course, approached the margins of Gov Roosevelt or Gov Ely, but estimates indicated that John E. Swift of Milford, candidate for Lieutenant Governor, would run in the vicinity of 85,000 ahead of his

Continued on the Fourteenth Page

TRUSTIES HELP FIGHT FIRE AT DEER ISLAND

328 in Outlying Wings Unaware of Blaze

With the aid of 10 trusties, 15 guards and two officers of the Suffolk County House of Correction on Deer Island in Boston Harbor desperately fought and extinguished a fire on the fourth floor of Hill Prison last night while 328 prisoners slept in their cells in the two fireproof wings of the prison building, unaware that the main section of their building was on fire. The damage was estimated at several thousand dollars.

Although the sirens and steam whistle were sounded after the discovery of the fire, the prisoners assumed that it was for an escape or for a water leak and went back to sleep. Guards quietly closed the fireproof doors that cut the wings off from the main section and, leaving a skeleton force on guard, went to man the fire hose.

Ten prisoners only were told of the fire, and these 10 trusties braved dense clouds of suffocating smoke in order to maneuver the single line of hose on

Continued on the Second Page

THE WEATHER

RAIN

Forecast for Boston and Vicinity: Wednesday rain, probably ending on Thursday morning, with colder Thursday, and fresh northeast winds.

Washington Forecast for Southern New England: Wednesday rain, probably ending Thursday morning, with colder Thursday.

New Hampshire and Vermont: Wednesday rain; Thursday rain, possibly changing to snow flurries, and colder.

Maine: Wednesday and probably Thursday rain in the southwest and rain or snow in the east and north portion, with not much change in temperature.

The Temperature Yesterday at Thompson's Spa—8 a m, 49; 6 a m, 49; 9 a m, 50; 12 m, 51; 3 p m, 50; 6 p m, 47; 9 p m, 46; 12 mid, 46. Average temperature yesterday, 48 11-24.

THE WEATHER ELSEWHERE

[illegible]

Precipitation in Boston, 12 hours to 8 p m, .04.

HERALD-TRIBUNE GIVES ELECTION TO ROOSEVELT

NEW YORK, Nov 8 (A. P.)—The Herald-Tribune, Republican, at 9:30 p m conceded the election of Gov Franklin D. Roosevelt.

In its first edition tonight it carried the headline, "Roosevelt Sweeps Country."

The newspaper also conceded the election of Lieut Gov Herbert H. Lehman, Democrat, for the Governorship over Col William J. Donovan, Republican.

RADIO PROGRAMS PAGE 10

From Globe Studio of WEEI

8:30 A M—Looking over the morning Globe.
12:15 P M—News bulletins.
4:00 P M—News bulletins.
6:30 P M—News bulletins.
11:00 P M—News bulletins.

President-Elect

GOV FRANKLIN D. ROOSEVELT

ELECTORAL COLLEGE

(Based on Latest Returns to the Globe)

TOTAL ELECTORS	531
NECESSARY TO CHOICE	266
HOOVER, reported	59
ROOSEVELT, reported	464
NOT REPORTED	8

State	Electoral Vote	Hoover	Roosevelt
Alabama	11	..	11
Arizona	3	..	3
Arkansas	9	..	9
California	22	..	22
Colorado	6	..	6
Connecticut	8	8	..
Delaware	3	3	..
Florida	7	..	7
Georgia	12	..	12
Idaho	4	..	..
Illinois	29	..	29
Indiana	14	..	14
Iowa	11	..	11
Kansas	9	..	9
Kentucky	11	..	11
Louisiana	10	..	10
Maine	5	5	..
Maryland	8	..	8
Massachusetts	17	..	17
Michigan	19	..	19
Minnesota	11	..	11
Mississippi	9	..	9
Missouri	15	..	15
Montana	4	..	4
Nebraska	7	..	7
Nevada	3	..	3
New Hampshire	4	4	..
New Jersey	16	..	16
New Mexico	3	..	3
New York	47	..	47
North Carolina	13	..	13
North Dakota	4	..	4
Ohio	26	..	26
Oklahoma	11	..	11
Oregon	5	..	5
Pennsylvania	36	36	..
Rhode Island	4	..	4
South Carolina	8	..	8
South Dakota	4	..	4
Tennessee	11	..	11
Texas	23	..	23
Utah	4	..	4
Vermont	3	3	..
Virginia	11	..	11
Washington	8	..	8
West Virginia	8	..	8
Wisconsin	12	..	12
Wyoming	3	..	3

HOOVER WON 28 FEWER VOTES THAN SMITH IN 1928

Ex-Gov Smith, in 1928, received 87 votes in the Electoral College, carrying eight States. President Hoover carried six States, giving him 59 votes, against Smith's 87.

VOTE OF BOSTON

(Complete)

FOR PRESIDENT

Roosevelt	178,662
Hoover	78,956
Roosevelt's plurality	99,706

VOTE IN 1928

Smith	186,280
Hoover	87,445
Smith's plurality	98,835

FOR GOVERNOR

Ely	181,735
Youngman	75,667
Ely's plurality	106,068

VOTE IN 1930

Ely	137,944
Allen	63,004
Ely's plurality	74,940

REFERENDUM

796 Voting Precincts out of 1707 in the State give the following vote on the Preprimary Convention question:

Yes	219,924
No	103,617

MINOR STATE OFFICES

966 Scattered Voting Precincts Give

LIEUT GOVERNOR

Bacon, R	397,929
Swift, D	369,835

SECRETARY

Cook, R	390,902
J F Buckley, D	361,954

TREASURER

C F Hurley, D	382,813
Prescott, R	363,498

AUDITOR

F X Hurley, D	387,909
Cook, R	354,366

ATTORNEY GENERAL

Warner, R	400,106
J P Buckley, D	350,670

For Contents Today's Globe See Page 2

Record Tammany Vote Helps Roosevelt and Lehman Win Decisively in That State

Returns at 6 A M Give Hoover Only Six States With Total Electoral Vote of 59

By JAMES MORGAN

A Roosevelt tidal wave has swept the country, and the Democrats have won their greatest victory in 80 years.

Massachusetts wung into the Roosevelt column, with an impressive plurality for him, and she reelected [illegible]

New York city heaped up an unprecedented Democratic vote, which fell not far short of the pre-election estimate of the party organization. Meanwhile, Hoover was coming down the State with only a fraction of the normal Republican margin. Lehman was carried into the Governorship, Wagner back to the Senate and O'Brien to the Mayoralty.

Ohio Among the First

Ohio, Indiana and Wisconsin were the first among the great States of the Middle West to give signs of having gone for Roosevelt. South Dakota was the earliest to send in a report of his success in the farther West. The South came up solidly for him and the border States were also in line.

All signs in the returns from the start pointed to a Senate and House of the same political complexion as the President-elect. As the Democratic figures came like an avalanche, it was impossible to set limits to the victory.

Maine Withstands Crash

Strangely, Maine, which started it in her September State election, returned to her accustomed Republican allegiance in the test of a Presidential contest. Vermont also withstood the crash of the political elements, but New Hampshire may not have escaped, as she remains in doubt at this hour. But Rhode Island and Connecticut consistently showed a Democratic trend.

Pennsylvania apparently is in her usual place on the Republican side. But neighboring West Virginia swung over to the Democrats. Illinois disclosed an early tendency toward the Democrats, from the top of the ticket down. Kansas and Nebraska both headed, at the outset, in the direction of Roosevelt.

Illinois Sweep for Party

All returns from Illinois indicated a tremendous plurality for Roosevelt. Chicago gave him a lead of 185,000 and down-State was adding to it. Len Small has lost the Governorship contest to Henry Horner and Senator Glenn is defeated for reelection.

Roosevelt held a lead from the first in the returns from Minnesota,

Continued on the Fourteenth Page

NO GLOBE SUBSCRIPTION SOLICITORS

The Globe does not employ subscription solicitors, and any so representing themselves should be turned over to the police.

Will Rogers' Dispatch

Special to Boston Globe. Copyright 1932

BEVERLY HILLS, Calif, Nov 8—If your side lost don't take it too much to heart, remember, there is always this difference between us and Italy. In Italy Mussolini runs the country, but here the country runs the President.

As I dispatch this little message along late in the evening it looks like the only thing can beat the Democrats is honest counting.

Certainly brought out a big vote, there was actually women went to the polls that didnt have a new hat; humiliation couldn't even stop 'em.

Yours, WILL ROGERS.

DUMB-BELLS

The Boston Daily Globe

Reg. U. S. Pat. Off.
NRA — WE DO OUR PART
Entered as second class mail matter at Boston, Mass. under the act of March 3, 1879—242 Washington St.
BOSTON, THURSDAY MORNING, DECEMBER 7, 1933—THIRTY-SIX PAGES
COPYRIGHT, 1933, BY THE GLOBE NEWSPAPER CO. (3) TWO CENTS

LIQUOR LICENSE AND SUPPLY PROBLEMS IN CITY
THIN CROWDS SEEKING LEGAL DRINKING PLACES

"FINE CONDITIONS" LINDY'S SPEECH

Couple Too Tired to Take Part in Brazilian Festivities After 16-Hour Hop From Africa

NATAL, Brazil, Dec 6 (A. P.)—Col Charles A. Lindbergh and his wireless-operating wife, the former Anne Morrow, alighted on the harbor today at 3:10 p m Brazilian time (1:10 p m E. S. T.) after flying from Bathurst, Gambia, Africa, 1875 miles away, in 16 hours, 10 minutes.

It was their first view of America since July 22, when they took off from Cartwright, Labrador, for Greenland on a survey flight across the North Atlantic.

The whole population of Natal, its stores and offices closed for the fiesta of welcome, its streets decorated, packed the waterfront.

First Woman to Cross

At 2:50 p m a keen-eyed watcher caught the first glimpse of the great red monoplane as it headed in from the Atlantic. Launch whistles blared and from the crowd arose a mighty roar of "viva!"

Straight in toward the harbor the plane flew, and passed above the cheering throng. Lindbergh banked it

Continued on the Twelfth Page

MAYOR SEEKS JOBS FOR 4000

Curley and Mansfield Meet at State House

Would Drop Huntington-Av Subway for New Program

Presentation before the State Emergency Finance Board of a $6,000,000 public works program for the city of Boston brought Mayor Curley and Mayor-Elect Mansfield together for the first time since the election at the State House yesterday afternoon. Mayor Curley promised Chairman Bartlett of the Finance Board "the Huntington-av subway project is 'out the window' if you approve this program."

Continued on Page Twenty-Three

PRESIDENT SHIFTS CODES AFTER PROTEST BY PEEK

Report Farm Chief Threatened to Resign If "Brain Trust" Stayed—Hewes May Quit Treasury

WASHINGTON, Dec 6 (A. P.)—The White House announced tonight that all codes under the Industrial Recovery act, including those under negotiations by the Agricultural Adjustment Administration, will be turned over to Hugh S. Johnson, N. R. A. administrator.

This announcement was made after President Roosevelt had conferred with George N. Peek, Farm Administrator, who has had charge of formulating codes under the Farm act and was reported today to have told Secretary Wallace that he would resign unless "radical members of the 'brain trust'" in the Agriculture Department were asked to leave.

While talking with Peek at the White House, the President also was in communication with Johnson and Wallace by telephone.

Peek is known to have had differences with Rexford G. Tugwell, assistant Secretary of Agriculture and Jerome Frank, Farm Administration counsel, over the drafting and administration of codes and marketing agreements.

All to Johnson but Processing

A statement issued by Stephen T. Early, one of the President's secretaries, said:

"Following a conference tonight with Secretary Wallace, George Peek and Gen Johnson, the President authorized the statement that, for the purpose of coordination, all codes under the N. I. R. A. including those under negotiation by the A. A. A. will be turned over to the Administrator of the N. R. A.

"The only exception to this is codes pertaining to the manufacturers engaged in the first processing of agricultural products and handlers previous to the first processing. This work will be continued under the A. A. A."

Peek was asked by reporters after his talk with the President if he had told the Chief Executive that he intended to resign.

"Nothing was said about that," Peek replied.

The White House statement was regarded as indicating that the President had determined to place the codes under N. R. A. administration as a means of removing any differences that exist in the Agriculture Department.

Clash With Young Liberals

Earlier this week rumors were current that resignations were imminent because of differences between the "young liberal" element in the Agricultural Adjustment Administration, headed by Tugwell and Frank, and the "conservative" group headed by Peek. All of the supposed dissenters, however, denied any major dissension in the agricultural organization and Tugwell and Frank specifically denied any intention of resigning.

Tugwell inferred that the situation had been magnified beyond justification and Frank said that he "had a

Continued on Page Twenty-Three

RADIO PROGRAMS PAGE 21

From Globe Studio of WEEI
8:05 A M—Looking over the morning Globe.
12:15 P M—News bulletins.
4:00 P M—News bulletins.
6:30 P M—News bulletins.
11:05 P M—News bulletins.

Little Evidence of Over-Indulgence Is Observed on Streets of Boston Though Most of 214 "on Premises" License-Holders Serve Throngs Until the Closing Hour of One O'Clock

CITY COLLECTOR WILLIAM H. McMORROW RETURNS THE SMILES OF THE HAPPY GROUP WAITING IN LINE TO PAY FOR LIQUOR LICENSES

AUTO PLUNGES THROUGH DRAW

Pair Escapes With Minor Hurts at Warren Bridge

False Tale That [illegible] Four Starts Useless Hunt

After a miraculous escape from death when an automobile plunged 12 feet into an open drawbridge on the Warren bridge last night, Jack Lyons of Dorchester, one of two men who escaped with only minor injuries, kept police and firemen busy for two hours because of his erroneous belief that two other men were in the car and had been drowned.

Lyons, who had been drinking, was treated for minor bruises, immersion, and alcoholism, at Haymarket Relief

Continued on the Fourteenth Page

ROOSEVELT REBUKES ROLPH ON LYNCHING

President Declares Commandment Violated—Says New Deal's Aim Is Like That of Churches

WASHINGTON, Dec 6 (A. P.)—President Roosevelt, in an address tonight, called lynching "a vile form of collective murder."

The President also indirectly rebuked Gov James Rolph of California who recently expressed approval of mob action in San Jose, Calif, which resulted in the death of two men.

"We do not excuse those in high places or in low who condone lynch law," Mr Roosevelt said.

He did not, however, in his speech before the Federal Council of Churches of Christ of America, directly refer to the California lynching or to similar incidents recently in Missouri and Maryland.

Faith in "New Generation"

Mr Roosevelt expressed faith in the "new generation" as a preliminary to his strong condemnation of mob violence.

"This new generation, for example," he said, "is not content with preaching against that vile form of col-

Continued on the Eighteenth Page

SEEKS BILLION AT 2¼ PERCENT

Treasury Certificates to Run for Year

Nation Will Save $6,000,000 Interest by Securities Swap

WASHINGTON, Dec 6 (A. P.)—To meet notes falling due and pay interest on other obligations, the Government tonight sought to borrow nearly $1,000,000,000 for one year at 2¼ percent.

With payments of $842,000,000 to be made on Dec 15, the Treasury offered to the investing public $950,000,000 "or thereabouts" in certificates of indebted-

Continued on Page Twenty-Two

"L" WOULD BAN CHISELING TAXIS

Asks Law to Balk City's New "Jitney" System

Wants Ban on Standees Lifted, Horse-Car Era's Rules Ended

The public trustees of the Boston Elevated Railway Company have asked the General Court for legislation which will permit the State Department of Public Utilities:

To license the company to run busses on routes operated in more than one city or town when licenses for the operation of such bus lines have been granted by one of the municipalities on the said route.

To permit the company to carry a reasonable number of standing passengers in busses. Boston and Cambridge, by municipal ordinance, now forbid the carrying of any standing passengers in busses, but other cities and towns served by the company allow some standing passengers to be carried.

To do away with irregular and illegal taxicab operation which, the trustees allege, has become as serious as it was in the days of the jitneys and takes away large amount of business from the Elevated and from legitimate taxicab operators.

Repair Rule Protested

To relieve the company from the obligation to keep in repair the

Continued on the Eighteenth Page

Some Persons Slake Their Thirst On Stronger Beer Available Since Prohibition Repeal

Need For Expert Bartenders Obvious in Some Resorts Catering to Drinkers

Repeal went into its second day in Boston without the headaches generally associated with a night of hilarity and without the over-indulgence which was supposed to have been part and parcel of the first few days of open drinking.

As early as noon yesterday intoxicated persons were seen on the streets, but they were few and far between. Licensed places were crowded from noon to closing hour at 1 this morning, but in very few places were there signs of drunkenness.

The license problem was still one of concern to operators of restaurants, package stores and hotels, and the bit of paper which legalizes the sale of hard liquor was hard to obtain.

In Newspaper Row one restaurant did not get its first delivery of liquor until 8 o'clock last night, 24 hours after repeal. A mirror bar was waiting. Signs were in the back room to inform customers of the arrival of the "hard stuff." But there was no rush to sample it.

Stronger Beer Popular

In many places it appeared that beer had made a greater impression since April than the thought of hard liquor. Customers were seeking the brew, of a higher alcoholic content than 3.2 and where it could be found, so that where the six and seven per-

Continued on the Sixteenth Page

LOWER LIQUOR PRICES SOUGHT

Federal Board Will Allow Imports

Distribution Difficulties Seen as Contributing Factor

WASHINGTON, Dec 6 (A. P.)—Quietly, but somewhat awkwardly, Americans went about revamping their drinking habits today while Federal officials sought to straighten out distribution tangles to make legal liquor available to them at reasonable prices.

The first full day of repeal brought few reports of untoward incidents, compared with the riotous last hours of pre-prohibition. Citizens went about their business in the score of wet States somewhat curious about where and when a drink might be purchased at reasonable prices.

High prices quoted in various cities were said by Government officials and distillers' representatives to be due to the lack of distribution facilities more than to scarcity.

Will Allow Imports

Expectant of a chaotic condition for several days, the Federal Alcohol Control Administration indicated it would be lenient during the immediate period. Officials said, however, they

Continued on the Sixteenth Page

THE WEATHER

COLDER

Forecast for Boston and Vicinity: Thursday partly cloudy and slightly colder, with moderate to fresh northwest winds diminishing; Friday partly cloudy.

Washington Forecast for Southern New England: Thursday partly cloudy, with slightly colder in the east portion of Massachusetts and in Rhode Island and Connecticut; Friday partly cloudy.

New Hampshire and Maine: Thursday fair and slightly colder, followed by rain or snow at night or on Friday.

Vermont: Thursday fair, with not much change in temperature, followed by rain or snow at night or on Friday.

The Temperature Yesterday at Thompson's Spa—3 a m, 43; 6 a m, 44; 9 a m, 50; 12 m, 55; 3 p m, 56; 6 p m, 51; 9 p m, 46; 12 mid, 43. Average temperature yesterday, 48 3-24.

THE WEATHER ELSEWHERE

	Temperatures— Lowest Morn.	Highest Aft.	Weather 8 p m
Boston	35	50	Clear
San Francisco	46	58	Cloudy
Williston	28	48	Snow
St Paul	16	40	Pt Cloudy
St Louis	30	42	Clear
Chicago	24	32	Clear
Nantucket	38	50	Cloudy
Portland, Me	32	42	Clear
Eastport	32	44	Rain
New York	42	50	Cloudy
Washington	44	52	Cloudy
Jacksonville	54	70	Clear
Miami	66	80	Clear

Precipitation in Boston, 12 hours to 8 p m, .09

DUMB-BELLS

WHEN WE GET MARRIED I WANT TO HAVE A BRIDESMAID!
OF COURSE DEAR—I DON'T EXPECT YOU TO DO ALL THE HOUSEWORK YOURSELF!
BY CAR

Will Rogers' Dispatch

Special to Boston Globe. Copyright, 1933

BEVERLY HILLS, Calif, Dec 6—Well, sir, from what I can read and hear today, folks stood the shock of getting a drink (without giving their name) in mighty good shape.

Course the ones that are clear "out" we won't hear of for days. But it looked like everything went off better than expected. You see the whole problem is getting people from bad drinks back onto good drinks. You take a good bucking horserider, he would rather ride a bad horse than a nice gentle one. So it's going to take time to get 'em to having a sociable drink without watching the door.

Yours, WILL ROGERS.

TODAY'S GLOBE CONTENTS

Page 1
Few intoxicated persons seen second day of repeal in Boston; license problem persists.
Lindberghs fly from Africa to Brazil in 16 hours.
Treasury to borrow $950,000,000 for year at 2¼ percent.
Roosevelt rebukes Rolph in address to churchmen.
Federal Government speeds liquor distribution to bring down prices.
Elevated asks State to end taxicab chiseling, standee rules.
Agricultural codes given to Johnson by President after "brain trust" protest from Peek.
Two men escape with minor injuries when auto goes through open draw of Warren bridge.
Mayor Curley submits works plans for $6,000,000, to employ 4000 after C. W. A. ends.
Will Rogers' dispatch.
Page 2
North Dakota Governor bars shipment of beef cattle out of State.
Page 4
Cousins claim Mrs Morton was eccentric at funerals.
Government seeks means of spurring construction of new homes.
Ellsworth vessel nearing pack ice.
Page 5
Worcester Probate Court allows will of Samuel Slater.
Port of Boston news.
Page 7
Salt Lake City reporter claims he hoaxed Utah repeal delegates into hastening action.
Louisiana woman declared elected to Congress offers to run race over again.
Page 8
Some Bay State cities and towns have liquor, others still dry.
First N. R. A. bulletin goes out to schools today.
Lomasney estate valued at $244,722.14.
Page 11
McClelland Barclay and his ex-wife settle alimony row.
Judge refuses to restrain Rudy Vallee from getting divorce outside New York.
Page 12
Lindberghs' log shows Anne busy most of trip.
Page 14
Dedham society against horse thieves still active.
Dawes pleads for support of the President.
Five dead in Pacific Northwest storms.
Alexander Legge left nearly $1,000,000 toward formation of a "Farm Foundation," it is announced after his funeral.
Page 15
Teller sticks to identification of trio [illegible]

TODAY'S GLOBE CONTENTS

Page 15
British Government rejects proposal in House of Lords to break off relations with Irish Free State.
President opposes changes that would weaken the Securities act.
Chicago packers boost wages almost 10 percent.
Prof Kirtley Mather of Harvard assails Gov Rolph.
Page 16
N. R. A. cites two coal mine operators for prosecution.
Ex-dry chief here expects bootleggers to continue struggle.
Silk Code Authority asks right to reduce production 25 percent by shutdown.
Union secretary expects 2000 bartenders will be employed in Boston soon.
Photoelectric eye surpasses world's largest telescope in exploring mysteries of skies.
Page 17
War declared on speakeasies by New York police head.
National Labor board takes up Springfield truck strike issue.
White House reception procedure revolutionized.
Page 18
Eight jurors picked in Solomon case.
Son of Waxey Gordon killed by train.
Page 19
Emergency Council created to keep country informed on Recovery policies.
Psychologist tells what ails Al Smith.
Page 20
Editorial Page.
Walsh and McCormack propose law to make permanent the judgeship vacated by Lowell's death.
Page 21
Mrs Emma F. Cudworth dies suddenly at Marshfield Hills.
Dr Roscoe W. Thatcher, former president of Massachusetts State College, is dead.

TODAY'S GLOBE CONTENTS

Page 21
Presentation party for Miss Alice Moseley Clark and Miss Sally Pillsbury.
Page 22
Federal hearing on amendments to code for Boston milk area.
Aldrich renews attack on Wiggin's methods.
Dr Henry F. Munro adresses Canadian Club of Boston.
Page 23
Oklahoman argues sound money with Gov Ely.
Livelier dollar in 1934 means business spurt.
Filene's Cooperative Association Ball.
Row marks victory of last auction pair title by Cleveland man at bridge tournament.
Page 24
Richard Crooks sings at Statler musicale.
Editor publishes own account of his arrest for being drunk.
Page 25
Callahan-Dundee title bout here Friday night causes cancellation of Lawrence political rallies.
Pat Fraley throws Bull Martin in Arena wrestling final.
Papers Chandler Hovey and others plan to refit Yankee to race in America Cup trials.
Dr Newell will be oldest Mayor Gloucester ever had.
Boston man arrested at Rensselaer, N Y, on charge of holding up bus.
Page 26
Tufts players gain four positions on all-Massachusetts small college eleven.
College football attendance increased 13 percent in 1933.
Lawrence-Malden game Saturday may be played in Boston Garden, if outdoor playing conditions are unsuitable.
New York Americans and Ottawa may merge.
Bird & Son to meet Lynn Riversides in National Cup second-round game.
[illegible]

TODAY'S GLOBE CONTENTS

Page 27
Hubbell leads National League pitchers in effectiveness.
Boston College awards letters to 31 football players.
Harvard basket-ball squad cut to 14 men; shooting emphasized in practice.
Harvard Spring track schedule announced.
U. S. G. A. is not likely to follow British ruling body's revised amateur code.
The Sportlight.
Page 28
Williamstown and places in Rhode Island and Connecticut given Federal allotments.
The Globe's cross-word puzzle.
Witness in case lands in dock.
Page 29
Thirty more tax changes, including bar on taking losses by family sales, proposed by subcommittee.
Lykes, steamship man, worked for promotion of Jenkins in Fleet Corporation, says Black.
Page 30
Stock leaders are well supported under profit-taking.
Page 32
Household Department.
Dorothy Dix' letter box.
"Sandra," by Vida Hurst.
Culbertson on contract.
Page 33
Household Department.
"Murder in a Library," by Charles J. Dutton.
Page 34
Comic Strips.
Page 35
Death Notices.
Page 36
Ely pardoned 44 in year, summary shows.
Widening of Newburyport turnpike recommended to State.
Planning Board lists 10 projects.

TODAY "Twelve Days That Wrecked a World" By COL. FREDERICK PALMER Starts Today On the Editorial Page TODAY

The Boston Daily Globe

Reg. U. S. Pat. Off.

EXTRA

VOL. CXXVI NO 23 — Entered as second class mail matter at Boston, Mass. under the act of March 3, 1879—242 Washington St.

BOSTON, MONDAY MORNING, JULY 23, 1934—TWENTY PAGES

COPYRIGHT, 1934, BY THE GLOBE NEWSPAPER CO. (3) TWO CENTS

FEDERAL AGENTS KILL OUTLAW DILLINGER AS HE LEAVES MOVIE THEATRE IN CHICAGO

Notorious Desperado Draws Pistol But Is Shot As He Walks Into Trap--U. S. Operatives Fire When He Attempts to "Shoot Way Out"

THE LATE JOHN DILLINGER

Scores Watch Dramatic Ending To Drama Like That Seen By Quarry in Playhouse

Chief Agent Purvis Reveals Undercover "Tip" Brought End to Long Man-Hunt

CHICAGO, July 22 (A. P.)—John Dillinger, arch-criminal of the age, was shot dead tonight by a group of Department of Justice operatives as he walked out of a Chicigo movie theatre.

He whipped an automatic pistol out of his pocket and had it half-raised, when the operatives loosed a withering blast of pistol fire that dropped him mortally wounded. He died a few minutes later.

Fifteen operatives had surrounded the theatre, after information had reached Melvin H. Purvis, Chicago agent for the Department of Justice, that Dillinger would attend the theatre. Not a word was spoken as the outlaw ran into the cordon of officers.

Dillinger knew what was coming. He gave a hunted look, reached quickly into his pocket, and the agents' guns cracked.

Got Undercover "Tip"

The end of the greatest man-hunt in contemporary criminal annals came in the swift tempo in which the notorious outlaw had lived.

The Federal men watched the desperado buy his ticket, and then for more than two hours "the longest two hours I ever spent," Purvis said, kept the theatre surrounded.

"It was late yesterday when I received undercover information that Dillinger would attend the movie, 'Manhattan Melodrama,' at the Biograph Theatre," Purvis said. "I hurriedly made arrangements to surround the theatre with picked men from among my investigators. They were armed only with pistols. No shotguns or machine guns were issued, for I

Dillinger

Continued on Page 10

12 DIE, 26 HURT IN FLAMING BUS

"Gas" Tank Explodes as Vehicle Goes Over Embankment

Group on Way to Prison Game at Ossining, Lumber Plant Destroyed

OSSINING, N Y, July 22 (A. P.)—Twelve Brooklyn men and women were burned to death and 26 were injured today, when a bus carrying them to a Sing Sing Prison baseball game plunged down a 25-foot embankment and trapped them in a sheath of flame.

Screaming passengers, their clothing ablaze, fought their way out of broken windows after the gas tank exploded, igniting the bus and a large lumber yard into which it had toppled.

Some were frantically hauled to safety by onlookers, but the flames engulfed the bus so rapidly that rescuers were forced back.

Eleven bodies, all seared, were taken to morgues as soon as the wreckage cooled. Another woman died of burns in Ossining Hospital.

The identified dead: Mrs Tose Thompson, 40, and Mrs William Hayes.

Songs Change to Screams

The bus, last in a procession of seven carrying a gay party of Young Democratic League members and their friends, picked the wrong road as it entered Ossining.

Bus Accident

Continued on Page 5

ONE KILLED, 15 HURT IN CRASH

Four Automobiles Figure in Worcester Accident

Machines Collide, Two Others Crash Into Wreckage

Special Dispatch to the Globe

WORCESTER, July 22—One man was killed and 15 persons were injured when two automobiles collided head-on on the Southwest Cutoff at the Worcester-Auburn line about 6:30 tonight. Two other machines plowed into the wreckage, but neither driver was hurt.

The dead man is William Stamps, 40, of High st, Rockville, Conn. He died at St Vincent's Hospital shortly after the accident. All the other victims will recover.

Auto Accidents

Continued on Page 3

SECOND-TO-NONE AIR CORPS URGED

KARL T. COMPTON
President of M. I. T., member of committee

NEWTON D. BAKER
Aviation Committee head

Baker Committee Recommends Five Major Factors—Calls For 1000 Planes Quickly

WASHINGTON, July 22 (A. P.)—Warning that the first clashes of "the next great war" will take place in the air, the War Department's special aviation committee today recommended the building of an Army Air Corps second-to-none.

The committee of 11 prominent civilians and generals, headed by Newton D. Baker, Secretary of War during the World War, capped an exhausting three-months inquiry into Air Corps conditions with a call for "more financial support" for military aviation.

Laying down five major recommendations, along with dozens of

Air Corps

Continued on Page 2

Today's Globe Contents

Page 1

Dillinger killed by United States agents as he walks into trap at Chicago and draws pistol.
Twelve die, 26 injured, when bus plunges down bank and "gas" tank explodes.
Harvard-Dartmouth Expedition pair scale Mt Crillon, Alaska.
Army Air Corps second-to-none recommended by Baker Committee.
Three dead in automobile accidents.
Five lose lives by drowning in N. E. waters.
Charge E. R. A. labor and material illegally diverted.
Wrentham man collapses while hunting for missing bride.
Gov Ely to close forests today.

Page 2

Worcester teacher left fortune for jobless Scots.
Truck drivers' meeting turbulent.
Malden girl elopes.
Boston University Catholic group sails for cruise on steamer Steel Pier.
Madame Curie praised at King's Chapel service.

Page 3

Heat and drouth cause 256 deaths.
N. R. A. expects business spurt.

Page 4

Refrigeration boosts South African gold production.

Page 5

Framingham man among claimants to estate of $17,500,000.
Port of Boston.

Page 6

Wright-McPhail win Jaques Cup.
Davis Cup doubles today.
Boston Twi games.

Page 7

Cape baseball games.

GUIDE TO FEATURES

Burgess	11	Financial	4
Comics	18	Household	16, 17
Cross-Word	19	Movies	11
Culbertson	19	Radio	15
Death Notices	19	Seeing N. E.	13
Dr Wiggam	15	Short Story	12
Editorials	14	Sports	6, 7, 8, 9

SERIAL STORIES

"Lead Law" 17
"Slander" 16

Page 7

National League Results—St Louis 5, Boston 4 (first game); St Louis 4, Boston 2 (second game); Brooklyn 3, Pittsburg 2 (first game); Brooklyn 15, Pittsburg 10 (second game); New York 2, Cincinnati 1 (11 innings); Philadelphia 6, Chicago 5 (12 innings).
American League Results—Cleveland 4, Boston 2 (first game); Cleveland 6, Boston 5 (second game); Philadelphia 1, Detroit 0 (first game); Detroit 17, Philadelphia 8 (second game); New York 8, Chicago 2 (first game); New York 15, Chicago 2 (second game); Washington 6, St Louis 4.

Page 8

Rockingham Grand Circuit meet starts soon.
Rockingham enters final week.
Johnson's $50,000 purse lost.

Page 9

Big fleet in Marblehead races.
Endeavour starts for U. S. today.
U. S. athletes win in Germany.
Junior yachting eliminations held at Annisquam.
Golf addicts play without caddies as result of walkout.
Three killers escape from Texas prison, one confederate killed.

CHARGE E. R. A. WORK DIVERTED

Private Homes Benefit, Say Discharged Folk

Charges that thousands of dollars' worth of material and labor had been illegally diverted by E. R. A. executives for use on unauthorized projects are being investigated by the office of Maj Roswell G. Hall, E. R. A. administrator in Boston, it was learned last night.

The charges were made in affidavits by William S. Henessey Jr of 25 Pay-

E. R. A.

Continued on Page 5

SEVEN DROWNED IN N. E. WATERS

B.C. Track Star Succumbs in Collapse at Milton

MILTON, July 22—Arthur Glavin, 23-year-old Boston College track star, of 12 Manley st, Dorchester, was drowned early this morning in Houghton's Pond, at the foot of Blue Hill, when he sustained a heart attack while in swimming.

The young runner was spending the week-end with three companions at a camp near the pond. This morning

Drownings

Continued on Page 5

TODAY'S GLOBE CONTENTS

Page 10

Throng views body of Bishop Daniel F. Feehan.
To hunt down Dillinger's pals, Hoover promises.
Eyewitness' story of slaying.

Page 11

Longshoremen voting on arbitration at 'Frisco.
Telephone service between Boston and State of Maine is restored.
Aviation club for aged formed in Chicago.
All Hawaii prepares to give Roosevelt royal reception.
Roosevelt within 650 miles of Hawaii.

Page 12

Brin sees Democracy as lamp that lights the world.
Autos kill 15 in State week of July 12-20.
Bankers back United States housing program.

TODAY'S GLOBE CONTENTS

Page 12

301st Infantry Veterans at Devens.
Film producers have broken faith, Cardinal's spokesman declares.
Ingenuity helps man solve drouth problem at North Saugus.

Page 15

Funeral of George R. Alley.
Taxi man held up.

Page 20

Pickpockets pluck three victims at Jamaica Plain carnival.
Mr and Mrs Jaques of Lynn mark Golden Wedding.
Drawhouse on Chelsea Bridge tilts as piles sink.
Labanese festival featured by wedding in traditional manner.
"Wild Kid" dies of Revere motorcycle crash injuries.
"Hands Across Sea" service at Cathedral Church of St Paul.

MT CRILLON SCALED BY COLLEGE PARTY

Washburn and Carter, Advance Of Harvard-Dartmouth Expedition, Reach Top

The Harvard-Dartmouth Expedition has attained its objective in scaling Mt Crillon, towering peak of the Alaskan coastal range. This is one of a series of dispatches describing the hardships endured by the mountain-climbers and the Expedition's scientific work.

By BRADFORD WASHBURN
Leader, Harvard-Dartmouth Mt Crillon Expedition.

(Copyright, 1934, by N. A. N. A., Inc.)

CRILLON LAKE, Alaska, July 22—(By Radio)—Adams Carter and the writer, forming the advance climbing party of the Harvard-Dartmouth Expedition, have successfully reached the summit of Mt Crillon, the highest unscaled peak of the Fairweather Range in Alaska.

Two previous attempts by a Harvard group, in 1932, failed, and last year's climbing party also failed, after reaching an altitude only a scant 300 feet below the peak.

Our successful climb was the result of months of careful planning, fast climbing and excellent weather conditions.

The Great Barrier, a cliff between the altitudes of 7000 and 8000 feet, which thwarted the 1932 party and was a dangerous obstacle last year, was scaled by means of ropes.

Six Start Ascent

Henry Woods, Howard Kellogg, Edward Streeter, Waldo Holcombe, Carter and I were in the group that started the ascent of the mountain. We reached the great ice plateau, 4000 feet below the summit of Mt Crillon, at 7 o'clock in the morning.

Our route up the cliff was altogether different from that taken last

Mt Crillon

Continued on Page 5

COLLAPSES IN HUNT FOR MISSING BRIDE

Wrentham Man in Hospital Bares Suicide Note

Broken-hearted over the disappearance of his bride of a year, Paul Janson, 24, of Wrentham, collapsed yesterday on Belvidere st, Back Bay, exhausted with three days of sleepless search for his wife, who five days before had left a suicide note.

Janson, from his cot at City Hospital, told police that his wife left home last Wednesday. On Friday he found her note, which he said she had left in a bureau drawer at their home. Grief-stricken, Janson came to Boston and started his search.

Chief Perley Dexter of Wrentham started dragging the waters of Lake Pearl and Lake Archer, yesterday, when he heard Janson's story from Boston police. Mrs Janson had not

Bride

Continued on Page 5

DUMB-BELLS

THEY DON'T THINK MUCH OF MY COOKING - I NOTICED THEM PRAYING BEFORE THEY STARTED TO EAT!
7-23 ©BY THE PUBLIC LEDGER INC

ELY TO CLOSE FORESTS TODAY

Necessary to Protect Woodlands, He Says

WESTFIELD, July 22 (A. P.)—Gov Joseph B. Ely stated here tonight that he would issue a formal proclamation closing the woods of the State tomorrow unless rain should fall. He announced that while he regretted to do this the drouth conditions had become so serious that it seemed necessary to take the step for the protection of the woodlands. Gov Ely was requested to do this last week by Conservation Commissioner Samuel A. York.

Will Rogers' Dispatch

Special to Boston Globe. Copyright, 1934

SS MALOLO, SAN FRANCISCO, Calif, July 22—Just steaming out of beautiful San Francisco Bay. Putting a bridge across it. They will bridge to Honolulu if the Government don't run out of credit.

Could wire later in the afternoon, but better get this off while I am able. As a sailor I am as big a success as a "Red" trying to run a strike.

Drove to San Francisco and stayed all night. You have seen towns full of many things, but did you ever see one full of "alibis"? Everybody on both sides of the strike had nothing to do with starting it and every one of 'em was responsible for stopping it.

Everybody has a sore back from taking bows. Nobody seems to be responsible for starting this strike. I just know it was that darn Dillinger again.

Ship ahoy.
Yours, WILL ROGERS.

THE WEATHER

FAIR

Forecast for Boston and Vicinity: Monday and Tuesday continued fair and moderately cool, with gentle to moderate north and northwest winds.

Washington Forecast for Massachusetts, Rhode Island and Northern New England: Monday and Tuesday fair with little change in temperature.

Temperature Yesterday at Thompson's Spa—3 a m, 74; 6 a m, 75; 9 a m, 75; 12 m, 76; 3 p m, 76; 6 p m, 74; 9 p m, 72; 12 mid, 70. Average temperature yesterday, 74 6-24.

THE WEATHER ELSEWHERE

	Temperatures Lowest Morn.	Temperatures Highest Aft.	Weather 8 p m
Boston	69	78	Clear
San Francisco	54	34	Clear
Williston	68	84	Clear
St Louis	84	102	Pt Cloudy
Chicago	82	102	Pt Cloudy
Nantucket	66	76	Clear
Portland, Me	64	76	Clear
Eastport	56	70	Clear
New York	72	88	Pt Cloudy
Washington	74	94	Cloudy
Jacksonville	72	90	Rain
Miami	74	90	Cloudy

SEE PAGE 14 —for— "Twelve Days That Wrecked a World" —by— Col Frederick Palmer

A Complete Family Newspaper
Order your Sunday Globe today. Advertisements for next Sunday's Globe—order them today.

The Boston Daily Globe

Reg. U. S. Pat. Off.

A Baby Is the Berries
"Hotel Stenographer" On the Comic Page
TODAY

VOL. CXXVI NO. 34 — Entered as second class mail matter at Boston Mass. under the act of March 3, 1879—242 Washington St.

BOSTON, FRIDAY MORNING, AUGUST 3, 1934—TWENTY-EIGHT PAGES

(3) TWO CENTS

HITLER ABSOLUTE DICTATOR

Abolishes Presidential Title, Becomes Untrammeled Ruler of Germany, Exacts Oath Of Personal Allegiance as Hindenburg Dies—Europe Watches With Forebodings

WOULD RETIRE 13 POLICE OFFICERS

CAPT JOSEPH J. DONAHUE of Cambridge Police Department

CAPT EDWARD J. WELCH of Cambridge Police Department

Cambridge Mayor Acts on Test Reports—Two Captains Are Included in List

Acting on the findings of the recent physical tests of members of the Police Department, Mayor Richard M. Russell last night asked the Cambridge City Council to retire 13 members on pensions, on the ground they are unfit for further useful service. Capts Joseph J. Donahue and Edward J Welch are included in the group

Mayor Russell forwarded communications from City Physician M. L. Dressler and Police Chief John J. McBride Each of the 13 officers has served at least 20 years in the department

The Mayor said "due recognition must be made of their years of faithful service to the city, but also it must be recognized that the public safety must be served, and public safety under modern conditions demands a force fully competent for active police duty. Also, I believe,

Retirements

Continued on Page 10

TRIO FACE DEATH IN VAIN FOR MISS

Brookline Maid Succumbs to Shock at Bar Harbor

BAR HARBOR, Me Aug 2 (A. P.)—Miss Emily McDougall, 33 of 22 High st Brookline Mass, died tonight of shock after being rescued from drowning in the ocean at Thunderhole, about five miles from this village.

Three others were in a hospital, one in serious condition, as a result of heroic efforts to save the young

Rescue Tragedy

Continued on Page 4

DIVORCEE KILLED AS CAR CRASHES

Broker Lies Near Death After Back Bay Mishap

Mrs Loughman Is Victim—Auto Hits Bridge on Beacon St

A woman, Mrs Edith Loughman, 24, mother of two children, was instantly killed and her escort, Warren Wood, 31, of 52 Hammondswood road, Newton, was so seriously injured that he may die, when a coupe in which they were riding struck an upright of the railroad bridge on Beacon st, above Kenmore sq, early this morning

Identification of the dead woman was made by her divorced husband, who told police that she lived at 70 Chiswick road, Brighton. Wood is listed in the city directory as president and director of a Federal-st brokerage house Loughman told police that he and the victim of the accident had been divorced for four years.

The car was traveling from Kenmore sq towards the Brookline line when it struck an upright of the railroad bridge squarely in the center.

The small car buckled with the

Crash

Continued on Page 8

MRS VAUGHAN PLANS TO BATTLE FOR BODY

Retains Counsel for Fight Over Husband's Burial

Claiming—despite her divorce—she is the legal widow of Dr Walter W. Vaughan of Newton, Mrs Margaret R. Vaughan yesterday retained attorney Francis Juggins of Boston to begin legal proceedings for the exhumation and removal of her hus-

Vaughan

Continued on Page 6

A. P. Photo

ADOLF HITLER, GERMANY'S SOLE RULER

Surprise Move Crushes Any Rivalry—Orders Plebiscite Aug 19

Chancellor Will Give Address At Funeral of Soldier and Statesman Tuesday

Adolf Hitler rules as absolute dictator over Germany.

His sudden seizure of the Presidential power instead of awaiting election has aroused apprehension in other European Nations, which will scan his speech at Hindenburg's funeral for signs of peaceful or war-like attitude

President von Hindenburg, who died yesterday morning at Neudeck, East Prussia, will be entombed in the tower of the monument raised for his famous victory at Tannenberg.

Immediately upon the death of the President, the Chancellor assumed the powers of the Presidency, merging them with those of Chancellor and thus practically abolishing the President's office.

In another surprise move the Chancellor ordered the army and navy to take oath of personal allegiance to him, which they swore without demur He also ordered a plebiscite on Aug 19 for indorsement of his new control.

Removal of the restraining influence of Hindenburg is regretted in all quarters, especially in England and France, who feel less confidence in German intentions.

Praise of the veteran soldier and statesman is universal, for his loyalty and resistance to radical influences.

BERLIN, Aug 2—Adolf Hitler in a series of lightning-like moves made himself absolute dictator of Germany today.

He concentrated in his own hands the functions of President and of Chancellor as soon as the aged President and patriot, Paul von Hindenburg, died at Neudeck.

Then he called for and received an oath of personal allegiance from officers and men of the entire Army and Navy.

After these moves, amounting to a virtual coup d'etat, the former lance corporal who succeeded a Field Marshal called for a plebiscite on Aug 19.

Although desiring the functions of the Presidency, Hitler declined tonight to accept the title, holding that the "greatness of the deceased has given to the title of Reichspresident unique and non-recurring significance."

In a letter to Wilhelm Frick, Minister of the Interior, Hitler outlined his plans to assume the office without title, saying he desired henceforth to be known as before as "Fuehrer and Reichschancellor."

He directed that a "free secret election" be held at which the centralization of power in his hands and such other matters as may be necessary be held.

Hitler's Order Taking Power

"The necessity for regulating the question of the Chief of State, caused by the national misfortune that has

Hitler

Continued on Page 23

ANXIETY OVER HITLER POWER

British Cool, King Ignores Him in Regrets

French Ask If It Portends War or Means Peace

LONDON, Aug 2 (A. P.)—Great Britain's apprehension over Germany's future, now that von Hindenburg is dead and Adolf Hitler has become the sole arbiter of that Nation's affairs, is sharpened by a noticeable "cooling off" in Anglo-

Europe's Reaction

Continued on Page 23

WESTERN CATTLE FOR BAY STATE

First Herd of 53 Already in Westport Pasture

Outlines of a tentative plan to transport thousands of cattle from drouth-stricken Western grazing lands, to fatten on Massachusetts pastures until they are ready either to be milked or eaten, were revealed at State E. R. A. headquarters last night by A. D. Cobb, special Government representative. He came to superintend arrival of the first 53 Western animals in Westport.

The 53 dairy cows now eating and drinking to their hearts content in a Westport pasture are the vanguard of thousands of beef and dairy cattle soon to know the comparative luxury of Massachusetts pastures, it was indicated by Mr Cobb, although he made it plain that the plans are still in a formative stage so far as Massachusetts is concerned.

Reports Due Soon

Bernard F. McElligott, assistant to State E. R. A. Administrator Joseph P. Carney said his research into the cattle situation is nearly ended and he will have complete reports by the first of the week as to how many thousand head of cattle will be brought to this State for distribution as meat to the poor, also how many dairy cattle might be utilized here as a means of partial support in rural areas.

He said most of the dairy cows are being taken South but indicated

E. R. A.

Continued on Page 23

HINDENBURG TO REST IN TANNENBERG TOWER

Monument to His Victory Will Be Scene of Pomp

NEUDECK, Ger, Aug 2—Paul von Hindenburg, aristocrat, soldier and statesman, was honored tonight by his Fatherland in death as he had been in life.

The body of the Reichspresident lay in state in his country home, where he died at 9 a m today (3 a m, Eastern standard time), and a detachment of his beloved Reichswehr stood proudly on guard.

Next Tuesday a great national funeral will be held for the man who in nearly 87 years served his country in three wars and for nine years stood at the head of the Nation through troubled times.

Death came peacefully and without pain after weeks of suffering.

Hindenburg

Continued on Page 23

CONSERVATOR MUST PAY ESTATE $70,791

Held Responsible for Mrs Wood's Losses in Stocks

Inasmuch as the estate depreciated in value because he failed to sell certain securities when he should have done so, and because he purchased other stocks that were not good investments, William B. Stearns of Boston, must pay $70,291 to the estate of Mrs Elizabeth H. S. Wood of Boston for whom he has been acting as conservator. The amount represents the losses incurred through investments.

The shrinkage in the estate occurred between October, 1929, and October, 1932. Accounts filed by Stearns during that period were objected to by Mrs Elizabeth S. W. Horton and Mrs Caroline S. McClure of New York city, sisters of Mrs Wood, with the result that

Conservator

Continued on Page 6

Today's Globe Contents

Page 1
Hitler absolute dictator of Germany.
Army guards Hindenburg's body, to be buried in monument.
European Powers anxiously await Hitler's first move as absolute ruler.
Cambridge Mayor asks retirement of 13 police officers.
Divorcee killed in automobile crash broker may die.
Cattle from West to be sent to Massachusetts.
Court orders conservator to pay Wood estate $70,291 for losses.
Mrs Vaughan wants doctor's body moved.
Man stung by hornets collapses.

Page 2
Peace move in Minneapolis strike.
Autoist who plowed through Rehoboth house puts repairs up to kin.

Page 4
Trio brave death in vain to save Brookline miss.
Dr V J Giradi of North Adams drowns after heart attack.
State Milk Board fixes production and marketing areas.
Taunton boy killed, another injured as automobile hits bicycle.

Page 5
Mayor cleared of charges.
Gov Ely home in Westfield after Western trip.
Bentz taken to Michigan to face bank robbery charge.
Port of Boston news.

GUIDE TO FEATURES

Burgess	17	Financial	12, 13
Comics	18	Household	24, 25
Commercial	13	Movies	18
Cross-Word	14	Radio	26
Culbertson	24	Seeing N. E.	11
Death Notices	26	Short Story	25
Dr Wiggam	18	Sports,	
Editorials	16		20, 21, 22, 26, 27

SERIAL STORIES
"Man of Dangerous Secrets" ... 17
"Slander" ... 24

Page 6
English Deep Sea Scouts here.
Swedish training ship to arrive at Boston tomorrow.
Order stops excavation of forgotten Effingham cemetery.

Page 7
Bay State about to spend last of $8,000,000 road fund.
State Board gives Waltham woman a liquor license.
Lehman plea ignored by Assembly.

Page 8
President Roosevelt to land at Portland, Or, today.
Gen Johnson attacks his newspaper critics.
Marie Dressler left small fortune to Negro servants.

Page 9
Prices in the retail markets.

Page 10
Quakes occur almost daily.

Page 14
Ex-wife denies Willys gave her $7,650,000.
Station at Audubon refused.
Poderjay indicted for perjury.
Half Dillinger's brain dissolved in chemicals.

Page 15
Court orders Huey Long to demobilize troops.
First wife of George Bancroft amends her suit.
Morgenthau bars any political activity by Treasury employes.

Page 17
Joseph Harriman, sportsman, dies of pneumonia.
Kirby finds cinema situation here much improved.

Page 19
Son of famous author in cast of revue.

Page 20
Hughes scores tripe at 'Gansett.
Paine's craft wins at Duxbury.

Page 21
Tidemark wins at Rockingham.

Page 22
National League Results—Boston 8, New York 0; Chicago 6, St Louis 2; Brooklyn 8, Philadelphia 7; Pittsburg 13, Cincinnati 3.
American League Results — New York 12, Boston 4; Detroit 3, Cleveland 0; St Louis 9, Chicago 8; Washington-Philadelphia, wet grounds.

Page 23
Hindenburg's death regretted throughout Europe.
Hindenburg's career as war chief and President.
Dr Schurman says Hindenburg restrained attack on Jews.
President Roosevelt sends regrets to Hitler on Hindenburg death.
Maynard denies use of his office for political purposes.

Page 26
Clare wins N. E. Amateur golf title.

Page 27
Three cup stars to play at Longwood.

Page 28
Funeral of murdered Fitchburg man.
Governor's Day at Fort Devens.

PUFFS! POWDER!! PFT!!! THREE GO TO HOSPITAL

OKMULGEE, Okla, Aug 2 (A. P.)—W. H. Brecht, an oil-well driller, lit his pipe while driving his car today and the Brecht family went to the hospital.

A small quantity of powder in the back of the car was ignited by sparks from the pipe.

Brecht, his wife and baby daughter suffered severe burns.

DRIVER STUNG BY HORNETS COLLAPSES AT TRUCK WHEEL

Alfred Martini, 26, of 2 Magoun av, Medford, was so severely stung by hornets yesterday afternoon in a wooded area in Dedham that he was taken to Boston City Hospital after he had collapsed in front of the West Roxbury Police Station.

Martini, who is employed by the American Chain Link Company of Medford, was delivering a fence at an estate in Dedham. As he was making his way through a section of heavy brush he aroused the hornets.

He was stung badly about the face, head and arms as he hurriedly retreated to the street. He boarded his truck, reached the West Roxbury Station and collapsed.

At the hospital his condition was considered serious, but physicians said he will recover.

DUMB-BELLS

THE WEATHER

SHOWERS

Forecast for Boston and Vicinity: Friday showers with moderate to fresh southwest winds; Saturday fair and not much change in temperature.

Washington Forecast for New England and Eastern New York: Friday showers; Saturday fair with not much change in temperature.

Temperature Yesterday at Thompson's Spa—3 a m, 70; 6 a m, 68; 9 a m, 75; 12 m, 79; 3 p m, 87; 6 p m, 83; 9 p m, 78; 12 mid, 77. Average temperature yesterday, 77 5-24.

THE WEATHER ELSEWHERE

	Temperatures Lowest Morn.	Temperatures Highest Aft.	Weather 8 p m
Boston	64	84	Cloudy
San Francisco	54	66	Clear
Williston	64	86	Clear
St Louis	82	102	Pt Cloudy
Chicago	74	98	Cloudy
Nantucket	68	82	Cloudy
Portland, Me	58	78	Cloudy
Eastport	54	72	Clear
New York	70	78	Rain
Washington	74	86	Cloudy
Jacksonville	78	92	Pt Cloudy
Miami	74	86	Cloudy

Will Rogers' Dispatch

Special to Boston Globe. Copyright, 1934

HONOLULU, Aug 2—With Dollfuss, the conservative, gone, and that fine level headed old patriot Von Hindenberg gone, it looks like it takes a radical to live. England saying that her borders reached to the Rhine was good news to these islands for that means that ours at least reach our own possessions.

The army and navy ought to be flying this route all the time. It's like carrying the mail, we ask 'em to do something right now and then blame 'em because they have had no practice. If we ever had to fly here we would have to ask 'em to postpone the emergency till we learned it, so don't blame the boys. They will have to wait now till commercial lines do it first.

Yours,
WILL ROGERS.

KING EDWARD'S MESSAGE OF ABDICATION

LONDON, Dec 10 (A P)—King Edward's words, in renouncing the British Throne, were:

"I have determined to renounce the Throne.

"After long and anxious consideration I have determined to renounce the Throne to which I succeeded on the death of my father and I am now communicating this, my final and irrevocable decision.

"Realizing as I do the gravity of this step, I can only hope that I shall have the understanding of my peoples in the decision I have taken and the reasons which have led me to take it.

"I will not enter now into my private feeling, but I would beg that it should be remembered that the burden which constantly rests upon the shoulders of a sovereign is so heavy that it can only be borne in circumstances different from those in which I now find myself.

"I conceive that I am not overlooking the duty that rests on me to place in the forefront public interest when I declare that I am conscious that I can no longer discharge this heavy task with satisfaction to myself.

"I have accordingly this morning executed an instrument of abdication in the terms following:

"I, Edward VIII, of Great Britain, Ireland and the British Dominions beyond

Message

Continued on Page 19

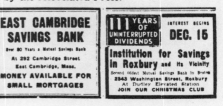

EDWARD VIII

RED STREAK FINAL

CLOSING PRICES

7:30 FINAL COMPLETE

The Rotogravure Section
Read it in Sunday's Globe. Order your Sunday Globe today.

VOL CXXX — NO. 163 . . . Entered as second class mail matter at Boston, Mass. under the act of March 3, 1879—242 Washington St.

BOSTON, THURSDAY EVENING, DECEMBER 10, 1936—40 PAGES—2 CENTS

EDWARD ABDICATES YORK BECOMES KING

BALDWIN EXPLAINS ACTS TO COMMONS

House Tense as He Describes His Parting With Edward

LONDON, Dec 10 (A P)—Premier Baldwin in the House of Commons today gave the following account of his activities up to the abdication of King Edward.

"I have to move that His Majesty's most gracious message be now considered.

"No more grave message has ever been received by Parliament and no more difficult and I might say more repugnant task has been imposed upon the Prime Minister.

"I will ask the House, which I know will not be without sympathy for me now, to remember that in the last week I have had little time in which to compose a speech for delivery today.

"And so I must tell what I have to tell, truthfully, sincerely and plainly with no attempt to dress up or to adorn, and I shall have little or nothing to say in the way of comment or criticism, of praise or blame.

"I think my best course today and one that the House would desire is to tell them so far as I can what has passed between His Majesty and myself and what has led up to the present situation.

"I would like to say at the start that His Majesty as Prince of Wales has honored me for many years with a friendship which I value and I know that he would agree with me in saying to you that it was not only a friendship between man and man but a friendship of perfection.'

Tells of First Interview

"I would like to tell the House when I begin that when I said 'goodby' on Tuesday night at Fort Belvedere we both knew and felt

Baldwin

Continued on Page 19

HER NAME WAS

WALLIS WARFIELD

The Life Story of Mrs Ernest Simpson

By Edwina H. Wilson

CHAPTER V

The headlines were alarming—inch-high, in black type: "RUSSIANS ATTACK BRESLAU FORTS WHILE FRENCHMEN AIM AT FRIEBURG"; "ALLIES BEGIN A FORWARD MOVEMENT—BIG GUNS FIRING ALONG WHOLE FRONT"; "GERMANS ON NEW BATTLE LINE IN POLAND—REINFORCEMENTS FROM WEST—A NEW GERMAN ARMY MOVES ON PIOLRKOW—"

There was talk of "preparedness" by those who thought that national defenses were inadequate and those who thought

Life Story

Continued on Page 15

POPE PIUS HAS HAD A RELAPSE

Physician, Hastily Called, Gives Stimulants

VATICAN CITY, Dec 10 (A P)—It was reliably reported at the Vatican that Pope Pius XI suffered a relapse today from paralysis.

The Holy Father, who was first stricken last Saturday, had been reported as recovering.

An oral bulletin issued by the Pope's physicians in the morning had said that while the 79-year-old Pontiff was remaining in bed, his condition was the same.

The Pope's physician, Dr Amanti Milani, after a second morning visit, said he was quite satisfied with his patient's condition. He said the Holy Father probably would be con-

Pope

Continued on Page 15

DR MACKEY IS FINED $175

Dr Charles E. Mackey of Broadway, South Boston, now a member of the Boston School committee and its former chairman, was fined a total of $175 in Suffolk Superior Court this noon by Judge Ernest Hobson, after the finding of guilty

Mackey

Continued on Page 15

The Markets Today

NEW YORK STOCKS—Market responded to the news from London by showing strength at the opening and then continued advancing into the late trading. Steels and rails were features with more than a score of stocks making highs for the year or longer. Superior, Republic and Truscon Steels made highs. Atlantic Coast Line made a high in the rails, as did Southern Railway preferred. American Telephone had better than a point gain.

BONDS—Generally firmer price range, though some irregularity in late trading. BOSTON STOCKS—Irregular. New England Telephone up, Edison off a point.

Globe Features

Uncle Dudley .22
Lippmann 22
Dorothy Dix ..34
Anagrams 37
Beauty Talk ..34
Burgess 36
Calling All Dogs! 36
Case Records .36
Comics ... 37, 38
Confidential ..34
Cross-Word ..36
Culbertson 37
Deaths 19, 38
Emily Post 35
Financial ..26, 27
"Hollywood Is Asking" 36
Household .34, 35
Marjorie Hillis .36
Movies-Stage 24, 25
Myrtle Eldred 34
Once Over ...22
Radio 38
Short Story ...36
Society 11
Sports ..29, 30, 31
Wiggam 35

SERIAL STORIES
"The Vampire" 33
"Woman in Love" 34

TREASURY BALANCE

WASHINGTON, Dec 10 (A P)—Treasury receipts for Dec 8 were $14,940,826; expenditures, $15,405,804; balance, $1,408,965,311. Customs receipts for the month were $11,427,404.

The Temperature Today

The thermometer at Thompson's Spa records the temperature up to 3 p m today as follows:

	1935	1936		1935	1936
3 a m....	42	39	1 p m....	49	47
6 a m....	42	39	2 p m....	48	47
9 a m....	45	45	3 p m....	47	47
12 m	47	46			

Britain's New King and Queen

THE DUKE AND DUCHESS OF YORK

Wide World

Race Results

CHARLES TOWN
DAILY DOUBLE

Stickemup and Cautious Bo paid $173.80.

FIRST RACE—$300, claiming, 2-year-olds, 4½ furlongs.
Crushed Ice, 109, Macado 3.80 3.00 2.40
Tweety, 109, Booker 8.80 3.80
Betty Tour, 107, Coff'an 3.60
Time, 0:52. Welsh Lad, Hasty Wave, Monologue, Dunpris, Turn Up also ran.

SECOND RACE—$400, claiming, 3-year-olds and up, Charles Town course, 6 furlongs 40 yards.
Stickemup, 114, Machado 23.40 8.40 5.00
Grandma's Boy, 110, Sh'ks 4.60 3.20
Goggles, 114, Palumbo 2.60
Time, 1:21. Anjor, Sable Isle, Peggy Can, Lady Buck, Royal Veil also ran.

Continued on Page 31

THE WEATHER

RAIN

United States Weather Bureau forecasts:

For Boston and its vicinity: Occasional rain is probable, with slight temperature change tonight and Friday; lowest tonight, near 40 degrees; moderate to fresh northeast to east wind, strong off the coast, with some fog. Central and northern New Hampshire and Maine it will be 25 degrees to 30 degrees, elsewhere above freezing next 36 hours.

For southern New England: Rain is probable tonight and Friday; not much change in temperature.

ONLY 13 SHOPPING DAYS BEFORE XMAS

12-10

WEDDING PLANS REMAIN SECRET

Report He Will Leave Britain Tomorrow Night

(By the Associated Press)

LONDON, Dec 10—Edward the Eighth, for 324 days King of England, abdicated today rather than reign alone on the world's mightiest throne without the American-born woman he loves.

He surrendered sovereignty over nearly half a billion people around the whole globe to his tall brother, Albert Frederick Arthur George, Duke of York, sober, steady, Prince of Windsor.

Within two days the new King, probably choosing the name of George VI, will formally ascend with his Queen, Elizabeth, radiant Scottish peeress.

By that time, Edward likely will be out of England—perhaps never to return. He may be at the side of Wallis Warfield Simpson, the woman he is so firmly determined to wed, in France or elsewhere. She will be free to marry next April 27, if not sooner. She now holds an incomplete divorce decree nisi from Ernest Aldrich Simpson, all-but-forgotten ships' broker, who once served in the King's Coldstream Guard.

The King's decision to abdicate was conveyed to Commons in one of the most moving sessions of any legislative body. Then, Prime Minister Stanley Baldwin, his voice broken and low, gave Parliament and the world an amazing, frank and friendly exposition of the whole, tremendous Constitutional crisis.

He told every detail of the

King

Continued on Page 18

CORONATION TO BE HELD MAY 12, AS SCHEDULED

Plans for holding the British Coronation ceremonies next May 12 will not be changed because of the abdication of Edward. George VI, who as Duke of York has been busy making arrangements for the ceremonies, will be crowned on the date set for his elder brother's coronation, according to information obtained by the Associated Press.

The Boston Daily Globe — EXTRA

Reg. U. S. Pat. Off.
VOL. CXXXI NO. 127 — Entered as second class mail matter at Boston, Mass., under the act of March 3, 1879—242 Washington St.
BOSTON, FRIDAY MORNING, MAY 7, 1937—FORTY-EIGHT PAGES — COPYRIGHT, 1937, BY THE GLOBE NEWSPAPER CO. — (3) — TWO CENTS

34 DEAD ON HINDENBURG

Sudden Explosion Tears Ship Apart and Sets It Afire as It Descends at Lakehurst; 50 or More, Many Horribly Burned, Leap or Are Thrown Free, Escaping Death

(Wide World Wired Photo to Globe from New York)
THE FLAMING WRECKAGE OF THE HINDENBURG SINKS TO THE GROUND
A dramatic photograph of the crash of the airship, with men running from the flying debris of the big ship as it falls at Lakehurst.

Both Skippers of Craft Survive, Capt Lehmann Is Given Last Rites

Hydrogen Gas Believed Cause Of Sudden Blast—Landing Crew Runs For Lives

LAKEHURST, N J, May 6 (A P)—Germany's great silver Hindenburg, the world's largest dirigible, was ripped apart by an explosion tonight that sent her crumpling to the naval landing field a flaming wreck with horrible death to about a third of those aboard her.

Exactly how many died was still in dispute as the flames licked clean the twisted, telescoped skeleton of the airship that put out from Germany 76 hours before on its opening trip of the 1937 passenger season.

The American Zeppelin Company, through its press representative, Harry Bruno, placed the death toll at 34 of the 97 aboard. The company listed 20 of the 36 passengers and 44 of the 61-man crew as the disaster's survivors. One man died of injuries in a hospital.

These figures were at slight variance with unofficial estimates of the number of dead.

Many May Not Survive

In the crowded hospitals in the communities neighboring this hamlet in the pine-covered New Jersey coastal plain, many of the survivors were in critical condition, a number suffering from excruciating burns. Some were so gravely injured, among them Capt Ernest Lehmann, that the last rites of the Roman Catholic Church were administered to them. Lehmann, skipper of the ship's 1936 flights, made the ill-fated flight as an observer. Capt Max Pruss, the commander, was listed among the injured survivors.

Storms and buffeting headwinds had delayed the slim, graceful ship far behind her schedule for the maiden trip, and she nosed down in the early evening to keep the unexpected rendezvous with disaster.

She had been due to tie up at the snub mooring mast at 5 A. M. (E. S. T.) but radioed last night that the bad weather had retarded her speed so much that she would land around sunset.

Ship Cruises Over New York

After cruising down over New York's crowded streets in the afternoon, she hove into sight at the air station here at 3:12 p m, but landing conditions were not favorable and she circled around idly in full view of the small crowd of spectators who had assembled for what was to be a routine hurry-up arrival and de-

Hindenburg
Continued on Page 31

FEUD DARK NOTE AT MT HOLYOKE

President-Elect Ignored in Centennial Program

Dr Woolley's Wishes Granted in Interest of Harmony

Celebration Opens Today With Festive Pageantry

By LOUIS M. LYONS

SOUTH HADLEY, May 6—Clearing weather after rain is predicted tonight for Mt Holyoke's centennial festival that begins at dawn. But the prospect is clouded for many members of the official family of this pioneer women's college by the realization that the program of the anniversary itself presents evidence of the stubbornly smouldering bitterness over the election of the first man to the presidency of a college that observes 100 years of women's leadership.

Pres-elect Roswell Ham is not attending the most significant anniversary in the life of the college he has been chosen to lead into its second century. The chairman of the college trustees has felt so keenly that Mr Ham is being slighted in the centennial, that he also declined to attend, but has reconsidered and is coming with other trustees in time for the role expected of them.

They will present to the educational world, represented by 350 delegates, the appearance of harmony at Mt Holyoke.

But it is a patched up picture. Leading trustees and influential alumnae have urged that a part be given Mr Ham in the elaborate proceedings that will present dozens of speakers in the two-day program. The partisans of the president-elect have just one explanation of his omission. Pres Mary Woolley wouldn't have him.

Has Solved Problem Himself

"Deplorable" is the word one used of the situation. "Implacable" is a trustee's description of Pres Woolley's attitude toward her male successor.

Pres Woolley's close associates insist that Mr Ham solved the problem himself by sending word well in advance that he felt it would be appropriate if he remained away.

Nobody from the college ever made any attempt to persuade him that his participation would be ap-

Mt Holyoke
Continued on Page 4

State Inspector Declares Explosion "Very Strange"

Never Saw Anything Like It, Says Chief of New Jersey Aviation Unit

LAKEHURST, N J, May 6 (A P)—Gill Robb Wilson, New Jersey aviation director, describing the wrecking of the German dirigible Hindenburg, said there was "a hydrogen explosion in No. 2 cell from the rear."

"There was something very strange about the explosion," he said. "The Hindenburg had stopped completely and was preparing to hitch when flames broke out from the rear.

"The only persons possibly saved were those who were in the engine gondolas.

"Those in the belly of the ship absolutely had no chance.

"In all my 21 years of flying experience I have seen crackups, explosions, flaming airplanes but nothing measures up to the explosion of the Hindenburg.

Explosion
Continued on Page 28

OCEAN AIR LINE WILL NOT STOP

Germany to Continue Service Over Atlantic

BERLIN, May 7—(Friday)—(A P)—Stunned by the Hindenburg disaster, official Germany's first utterance early today nevertheless was a defiant announcement the Zeppelin service will continue.

A Government communique recorded Germany's and the world's distress over the tragedy but pointed out an airship already is under construction "to carry the German flag as ambassador from continent to continent."

"With deep distress, the German people and the whole world will receive the news of the destruction of the proud airship Hindenburg," the communique said.

"German airship navigation, which heretofore achieved incomparable and unique successes in opening airways over the South and North Atlantic, now unfortunately also is not spared from disaster such as afflicted airship navigation in other countries in recent decades."

No Mishap Till Now

"For years service was maintained with South America without the slightest mishap.

Germany
Continued on Page 25

Sudden Blast Fires Airship As Passengers Wave Gaily

Spectators on Ground See Flames Sweep Great Hindenburg, Then Rush to Rescue

LAKEHURST, N J, May 6 (A P)—The Queen of the skies—German dirigible Hindenburg—sailed serenely into Lakehurst tonight, its silver bag gleaming despite the sullen atmosphere.

Passengers stood at the windows, waving gaily.

There were few spectators on the broad sandy field to wave a return greeting, for the comings and goings of the Queen of the skies, which 10 times before had dropped to earth here, were considered now of little more significance that the docking of an ocean liner.

The ship's motors droned loudly. Two noselines were dropped. In a few minutes, the ship would be fast, the passengers departing.

Blast Heard 15 Miles

It was 6:23 p m (E. S. T.).

An explosion rent the air—so loud one person said he heard it at Point Pleasant, 15 miles away.

The stern broke into flames.

Bystanders, unable to comprehend it, unable to believe it, gasped.

The happy shouts of arriving passengers turned to shrieks of dying men and women. Smiling faces of spectators became tear-splotched.

More explosions followed—intermittently they continued for hours.

There was confusion, but the ground crew made the best of the situation.

After a first shout, "Run for your lives," they ran to the ship as fast as they had retreated—doing rescue work instead of mooring.

Navy Men Turn Rescuers

"The navy boys dove into the flames like dogs after rabbits," was the way Gill Robb Wilson, state aviation commissioner, described it.

Passengers and crew—those who were elsewhere then in the blazing stern—jumped.

"I landed on my stomach, and crawled 30 or 40 yards to escape the flames," Philip Mongone of New York told his two daughters at Paul Kimball Hospital, Lakewood.

Two stewards and a little cabin boy jumped from a window—saved.

Murray Becker, an Associated Press photographer, said that in the twinkling of an eye, "There was nothing left but the skeleton.

"There wasn't much smoke," he said.

One witness said the ship buckled as the flames spread.

"I saw the ship just sink down and the flames go through it," he said. "The fabric burned away in a few seconds. I turned back with others to go as close to the ship as possible to pick up the survivors."

For Dr Carl A. Gesswern of Matawan, it was the first catastrophe he had witnessed and he said he never wanted to see another.

Scene
Continued on Page 28

THE WEATHER

FAIR

Forecast for Boston and Vicinity: Friday generally fair and slightly cooler, with gentle moderate west or northwest winds; Saturday fair.

Washington Forecast for Southern New England: Friday generally fair and slightly cooler; Saturday fair.

The Temperature Yesterday at Thompson's Spa—3 a m, 60; 6 a m, 58; 9 a m, 63; 12 m, 65; 3 p m, 67; 6 p m, 72; 9 p m, 66; 12 mid, 64. Average temperature yesterday, 64.

THE WEATHER ELSEWHERE

	Temperatures Lowest Morn.	Temperatures Highest Aft.	Weather 8 p m
Boston	52	68	Clear
San Francisco	42	56	Cloudy
Williston	54	74	Clear
St Louis	48	[illegible]	Clear
Chicago	44	[illegible]	Pt Cloudy
Nantucket	48	58	Cloudy
Portland, Me	52	56	Cloudy
Eastport	46	58	Rain
New York	54	70	Rain
Washington	56	74	Clear
Jacksonville	66	82	Pt Cloudy
Miami	70	80	Cloudy
Montreal	48	58	Cloudy

Total precipitation for month to date 0.00
Departure from normal 0.38

FOR TODAY'S GLOBE CONTENTS SEE PAGE 2

Train Kills Woman and Man Walking on Track at Hyde Park

Ignorance of the fact that freight trains are sometimes run on the opposite track, to allow faster trains to pass them on the customary track, cost the lives of a mother of eight children and a man when they were killed by a southbound train running on a northbound track on the Midland Division, New Haven Railroad, about 100 feet north of Fairmount Station, Hyde Park, at 9:15 last night.

The victims were Mrs Nancy Bonito, 41, of 13 Winter st, and Luigi Gaetano, 41, a laborer, of 11 Winter st, Hyde Park.

Taking Short Cut

The pair were taking a short cut on their way home, from a foot

Train
Continued on Page 4

AMERICAN LEAGUERS WIN ALL-STAR GAME, 8 TO 3

Globe RED STREAK SPORT EXTRA

CLOSING PRICES

7:30 FINAL COMPLETE

Boston Evening Globe
Reg. U. S. Pat. Off.

VOL CXXXII NO. 7 • • • Entered as second class mail matter at Boston, Mass, under the act of March 3, 1879—242 Washington St.

BOSTON, WEDNESDAY EVENING, JULY 7, 1937—28 PAGES—2 CENTS

NO TRACE OF LOST PLANE

ALL-STAR BOX SCORE

AMERICAN	AB	R	BH	TB	PO	A	E
Rolfe 3b	4	2	2	4	0	2	2
Gehringer 2b	5	1	3	3	2	5	0
DiMaggio rf	4	1	1	1	1	1	0
Gehrig 1b	4	1	2	6	11	1	0
Averill cf	3	0	1	1	2	0	0
Cronin ss	4	1	1	2	3	4	0
Dickey c	3	1	2	3	2	0	0
West lf	4	1	1	1	5	0	0
Gomez p	1	0	0	0	0	0	0
Bridges p	1	0	0	0	0	1	0
dFoxx	1	0	0	0	0	0	0
Harder p	1	0	0	0	0	1	0
Totals	35	8	13	21	27	15	2

NATIONAL	AB	R	BH	TB	PO	A	E
Waner rf	5	0	0	0	0	0	0
Herman 2b	5	1	2	2	1	4	0
Vaughan 3b	5	0	2	2	3	0	0
Medwick lf	5	1	4	6	1	0	0
Demaree cf	5	0	1	1	3	1	0
Mize 1b	4	0	0	0	7	0	0
Hartnett c	3	1	1	1	6	0	0
bWhitehead	0	0	0	0	0	0	0
Mancuso c	1	0	0	0	1	0	0
Bartell ss	4	0	1	1	2	3	0
Dean p	1	0	0	0	0	0	0
Hubbell p	0	0	0	0	0	0	0
Blanton p	0	0	0	0	0	0	0
aOtt	1	0	1	2	0	0	0
Grissom p	0	0	0	0	0	0	0
cCollins	1	0	1	1	0	0	0
Mungo p	0	0	0	0	0	1	0
dJ Moore	1	0	0	0	0	0	0
Walters p	0	0	0	0	0	0	0
Totals	41	3	13	16	24	10	0

aBatted for Blanton in fifth inning.
bRan for Hartnett in sixth inning.
cBatted for Grissom in sixth inning.
dBatted for Bridges in sixth inning.
eBatted for Mungo in eighth inning.

Innings	1	2	3	4	5	6	7	8	9
American	0	0	2	3	1	2	0	0	x—8
National	0	0	0	1	1	1	0	0	0—3

Two-Base Hits—Medwick (2), Ott, Cronin, Dickey, Gehrig.
Three-Base Hit—Rolfe.
Home Run—Gehrig.
Double Play—Bartell to Mize.
Struck Out—By Dean, Gehrig, Gomez; by Hubbell, Bridges; by Blanton, DiMaggio; by Grissom, Gehrig, Averill; by Mungo, DiMaggio.
Base on Balls—By Dean, DiMaggio; by Hubbell, Dickey; by Mungo, Rolfe, Averill.
Umpires—McGowan (A. L.), plate; Pinelli (N. L.), first base; Quinn (A. L.), second base; Barr (N. L.), third base. The umpires shifted places going into the last of the fifth, Barr replacing McGowan behind the plate, while Pinelli exchanged places with Quinn.
Attendance—34,000.

GRIFFITH STADIUM, Washington, July 7—The American League All Stars beat the National Leaguers, 8 to 3, this afternoon before a crowd of 34,000 and the record for the annual contests now is four wins for the Americans and one for the Nationals. The President was in the capacity throng.

The American Leaguers broke the ice in the last half of the third inning. After two were out, Joe DiMaggio, Yankees' star outfielder and "goat" of this game a year ago, worked Dean for a pass. Lou Gehrig then stepped up to the plate for the 13th time in these games. Working the count to three and two, Gehrig poled the "cripple" into the distant right field stands for a home run, scoring his teammate DiMaggio, ahead of him. It was Gehrig's third home run in the All-Star series.

The Nationals got one of these

All-Star Game

Continued on Page 23

BISHOP, HEATH, TIED AT 149

Both Score 75 in State Amateur Golf Today

By TOM FITZGERALD

WINCHESTER COUNTRY CLUB, July 7—Milan Heath, veteran Brae Burn shot-maker and Ted Bishop, elongated entry from Woodland, were tied at 149 for the leadership in the qualifying round of the state amateur golf championship as the field struggled through a second scorching day's play this afternoon.

Both of the pace [illegible]tters added 75s to their previous totals of 74, with Bishop yielding his chances for lone leadership by a spotty performance on the inward nine. Heath, playing more steadily than brilliantly approximately maintained the pace which he hit yesterday, and held up well under the tiring influence of

State Golf

Continued on Page 23

TWO CONVICTED ON GIRL'S STORY

Long Prison Sentences for Kelley and Fleming

Found guilty by a jury in Suffolk Superior Court today of criminal assault on a young woman, James F. Kelley, 27, of West 7th st, South Boston, was sentenced by Judge John E. Swift to serve eight to 10 years in State Prison, and Edmund Fleming, 28, of Silver st, South Boston, was given 10 to 15 years.

The jury, out one hour, found that the two men took Miss Alva Blaquiere, 21, of Minto, N B, from the home of her sister in South Boston, where she was vacationing, to Glen Echo in Stoughton. This was on June 18 of this year. At Glen Echo, testified Miss Blaquiere, Fleming knocked her down a number of times, and both men attacked her.

Before the jury went out, Kelley addressed it in his own behalf. He said that he was married just two months to the day before the date of the alleged assault.

MERCURY RISES NEAR 90 MARK

Death of Lynn Man Laid to Heat

TEMPERATURE READINGS

The temperature readings of today:

a m			
1	73	11	88
2	71	Noon	91
3	71	p m	
4	70	1	92
5	70	2	92
6	71	3	92
7	76	4	
8	78	5	
9	81		
10	85		

In the second day of the three-day hot wave predicted by the Weather Bureau one death from heat prostration was reported from Lynn, and thousands sweltered in offices and streets.

The top temperature of 92 was official from the calibrated instruments at the East Boston Airport, but on top of the 16-story Federal building in the United States Weather Bureau observatory the temperature was recorded as only 88.

The populace, which lives and works on the ground, was all for accepting the airport figure of 92 as a conservative estimate. Beaches were thronged and city and state departments operated with skeleton forces.

The state annual amateur golf championship got off to a warm start at the Winchester Country Club with players and galleries suffering despite their enthusiasm.

TREASURY BALANCE

WASHINGTON, July 7 (A P) — Treasury receipts for July 3 were $29,546,498; expenditures, $31,028,784; balance, $2,543,041,995. Customs receipts for the month were $4,225,068.

Starred at Bat in Today's Game

LOU GEHRIG
Hit homer and double

JOE MEDWICK
Made four hits

PRETTY TEACHER GETS AID FROM CITIZENS

Cocktail Party Rumor Has No Basis Says Saugus Supt of Schools After Investigation

SAUGUS, July 7—More than 1000 residents of this town have signed a petition to reinstate pretty, blonde Isabelle Hallin, 26, as a teacher of English at Saugus High School.

Daniel J. Canning, Miss Hallin's attorney, told of the petition and said, "There is a strong feeling in the town about it."

Miss Hallin, meanwhile, has insisted on a public hearing and has labeled as "nonsense" the rumor that she was supposed to have entertained High School pupils at her home with cocktails and cigarettes.

Talented Actress

Supt of Schools Vernon L. Evans said that her work was satisfactory and recommended her for reappointment, but Miss Maria Smith, Waldo B. Russell and Harry F. Wentworth of the School committee said, "No," and voted against a public hearing, too. Miss Hallen was graduated from Jackson College four years ago and has taught two years at Saugus High. Summers she is a member of the Garrick Players at Kennebunkport, Me, and is considered a talented actress. Hollywood has scouted her screen tests but she prefers to teach English.

Basis of the School committee's action is said to be rumors around the town that while acting as coach for High School dramatics, Miss Hallin entertained a High School group of amateur actors with cocktails and cigarettes at her home. Miss Hallin denies this and Supt Evans reported to the committee that he had investigated the rumor and found no evidence to support it.

WHITE FUND SPENDING SURPRISE TO TRUSTEES

John I. Fitzgerald Says "We Never Dreamed Expenditures Would Run to $50,000"

Trustees of the George Robert White Fund had an expectation that repairs on property under the management of Maj Roswell G. Hall in 1935 would be about the same as the $80 spent in the previous year by the manager, Gen Logan, but "We never dreamed in our wildest moments that expenditures would run to $50,000 in one year," City Councilor John I. Fitzgerald was quoted as saying to the Finance Commission investigator today.

The statement was read into evidence by special counsel George R. Farnum investigating dealings between the White Fund and the Codman Hill Construction Company as a part of his private examination of John I. Fitzgerald, to refute testimony of Maj Hall as to his assumption of the knowledge trustees had of what he was doing.

Hall was called to the witness stand shortly before noon after the F[illegible] Com. had heard [illegible]idence that Codman Hill had charged hundreds of dollars to the fund for repairs never made and after City Auditor C[illegible]es J. Fox, an ex-officio trust[illegible], had admitted that while he knew the Fin. Com. had re[illegible]tedly named Codman Hill as a favored contractor and opposed the manner in which Hall did business with the firm, he had made no inquiry as to Codman Hill's character, personnel and responsibility when Hall began to give them all the White Fund work, amounting in the aggregate to $137,000.

According to the evidence summed up by special counsel Farnum as Fox left the stand after two weeks as the sole witness in the inquiry, Codman Hill Construction Company was the object of inquiry by the Finance Commission on other jobs, including repairs to Quincy Market and Deer Island. In those investigations Farnum read reports which Fox admitted had come to him in which Codman Hill was named as a "favored contractor," and in which

White Fund

Continued on Page 2

NORTH POLE WEATHER

SOVIET POLAR CAMP (by radio to Moscow) July 7 (A P)—Low hanging clouds and fog cut the visibility today to a scant 100 yards. The temperature was just freezing, **32 degrees above zero Fahrenheit.**

Eddie Welch Picks Four in a Row

Eddie Welch, Globe's picker of horses and official leading handicapper of New England, is setting a killing pace at Rockingham. Today Welch picked the first four winners in a row, including the daily double, which paid $43.60.

Starogan won the first race, Gay Balko copped the second, Handsome Hal the third and Pharatime the fourth, just as Eddie had them in his chart.

JUDGE NAMED BY GOVERNOR

Edward Morley Appointed to Gloucester Court

Replacement of five trustees of Lowell Textile Institute, a new judge for the Gloucester District Court and a new sheriff for Nantucket County were among the principal nominations submitted today by Gov Hurley at the regular meeting of the Executive Council.

The five new trustees of the Lowell Textile Institute are Albert

Judge

Continued on Page 23

POLICE GUARD WOOL TRANSFER

With police protection and more than 75 strikers looking on, wool was transferred this morning from a D-st warehouse to freight cars as wool dealers continued their effort to break the three weeks' wool handlers' walkout.

Wool

Continued on Page 2

DI STASIO'S SON TO DIE IN CHAIR

After defense counsel had made a heated argument, referring to President Roosevelt's attempt to change the United States Supreme Court and asserting that "it would be a blessed thing here in Massachusetts if changes might be made in our Supreme Court," Anthony Di Stasio, 25, of Reservoir av, Revere, convicted as an accessory before the fact to the so-called Hudson "torch murder," was sentenced in Middlesex Criminal Court this morning to die in the electric chair during the week beginning Sept 12.

On June 14 the defendant's father, Frank Di Stasio, 54, Revere candymaker, was sentenced to die during

Di Stasio

Continued on Page 23

THE WEATHER

FAIR

United States Weather Bureau forecasts.

For Boston and its vicinity: Generally fair and continued warm tonight and Thursday; gentle to moderate southwest to west wind.

For eastern New York: Generally fair tonight and Thursday except possibly local thunderstorms Thursday afternoon in extreme north portion. Slightly warmer tonight, continued warm Thursday.

Globe Features

Uncle Dudley	16	Dr Crane's Cases	13
Dorothy Dix	18	Emily Post	18
Anagrams	22	Financial	20, 21
Beauty Talk	18	Hollywood	17
Boake Carter	17	Household	18, 19
Bob Burns	22	Marjorie Hillis	14
Burgess	22	Movies-Stage	13
Calling All Dogs!	27	Myrtle Eldred	18
Comics	22, 26	Once Over	16
Confidential	18	Radio	17
Cross-Word	17	Short Story	19
Culbertson	15	Society	15
Deaths	17	Sports	23, 24, 25
		Wiggam	17

SERIAL STORIES
"Death Party" ... 14
"Reckless Lady" ... 18

CONTEST ... Page 26

104,000 MILES OF SEA COVERED

Search for Amelia Yields No Clew; Ocean Is Calm

SAN FRANCISCO, July 7 (A P)—A tentative reservation on the Philippine Clipper plane leaving at 3 p m, P. S. T., today for Honolulu was made by George Palmer Putnam, husband of the missing flyer, Amelia Earhart. Pan American officials informed Putnam that a seat in the big plane was available.

By the Associated Press

HONOLULU, July 7—Navy ships and planes, coordinating efforts in the vast hunt for Amelia Earhart, aimed today at a new region in the South Pacific regions where growing belief and some facts indicated the missing aviatrix may be marooned.

The Coast Guard at San Francisco said it had been checking with the cutter Itasca throughout the day, but had no news of the missing flyer and her navigator.

Walter McMenamy and Carl Pierson, Los Angeles, amateur operators, who have eight receiving sets operating, said they had heard nothing on the Earhart wavelength throughout the night.

Five discouraging days of scanning the immense area north northeast of bleak Howland Island, which the aviatrix missed last Friday, turned the search to the corresponding area centered south southeast of Howland, where 280 miles away center the Phoenix Islands.

The Coast Guard cutter Itasca and navy mine sweeper Swan have searched more than 104,000 square miles north of Howland without a trace of the missing world-girdling plane.

The Itasca methodically scanned an area 300 nautical miles in each direction while the Swan covered a strip 15 miles wide by 240 miles long.

The battleship Colorado, speeding toward an early morning meeting with the Coast Guard cutter Itasca, planned to release its three deck planes late today for the first aerial search of the area which holds the fate of Miss Earhart and her navigator, Frederick [illegible] Noonan.

The two vessels were to me[illegible] dawn (about 12:30 p m, E. S. [illegible]

Amelia

Continued on Page 2

RECITE MARRIAGE VOWS, TAKE POISON

Mansfield Boy, Dighton Girl Found Unconscious in Gloucester

GLOUCESTER, July 7—Confronted with the problem of a youthful love for each other, a Mansfield youth and a North Dighton girl tried suicide here, early today, after reciting wedding vows to each other. Both are in Addison Gilbert Hospital in serious condition.

The couple is Edward A. Friedland, 18, of 14 Bliss st, Mansfield, and Miss Thelma E. Simmons, 19, of 61 Prospect st, North Dighton. Police said three notes in the automobile in which they were found near the John Hays Hammond estate, explained how they tried to marry themselves by repeating vows to each other.

Police refused to give out the contents of the notes. Two of them were addressed to members of their families and the third one was not addressed. At the hospital, it was said the couple took a sleeping potion which is poisonous in an overdose.

Find Wedding Ring

William E. Campbell, night watchman at the Hammond estate, found the young couple early today. He notified police who rushed both to the hospital. In the car police said they found a small pine box in which were a wedding ring and notes, which included instructions for their burial as well as an explanation of their act.

The family of the Simmons girl told police that she and young Friedland had left Wareham Monday morning together. Both had been working near there for the Summer. Late Monday night, neither had returned, so a brother of the girl began a search for them. He went to Mansfield and talked to police there.

Miss Simmons is the daughter of Mr and Mrs Leon Simmons. Her father has been a foreman in a finishing mill there and the girl has been employed in the mill. She has been working at Wareham where her father moved for the Summer.

Friedland left Mansfield for Wareham in order to be near the girl, police said they learned. Both left Wareham Monday in the girl's automobile. They bought the wedding ring and made a trip to Revere Beach. They then drove down here and stopped near the Hammond estate.

The condition of the two young people was reported at 9:30 a m as "critical."

That the girl evidently regretted the deed, according to the police, was a statement that she made in a moment of semiconsciousness that the cause of her illness was from fried clams eaten several hours before at a roadside restaurant. However, two tell-tale vials in the bottom of the car served to bear out the text of the note.

Parents of both came here this morning.

Racing Results

DAILY DOUBLE
Starogan and Gay Balko Paid $43.60

Zembla Wins Rockingham Sixth

SIXTH RACE—$800, claiming, 3-year-olds and up, 1 1-16 miles.

Zembla, 103, McCombs	8.70	4.80	2.60
Irksome, 108, Tucker		4.70	2.60
Notice Me, 112, Jaekle			2.20

Time, 1:46 3-5. Our Bud, Hasty Hanna also ran.

Rockingham Races
Earlier Race Charts on Page 23

STORM EXTRA! - LIST OF VICTIMS ON PAGE 11

Don't Neglect Business Start Fall Advertising
Order your Sunday Globe advts today.

Boston Evening Globe

LATEST NEWS and SPORTS
CLOSING PRICES
7:30 FINAL COMPLETE

BOSTON, THURSDAY EVENING, SEPTEMBER 22, 1938—28 PAGES—2 CENTS

HURRICANE DEAD 275

VIEW OF RUINS OF FIRST UNITARIAN CHURCH ON MAIN ST., WORCESTER

Will the Hurricane Return?

There is no reason to anticipate that the New England hurricane will make a return visit, G. Harold Noyes, chief of the United States Weather Bureau here, said this afternoon. Yesterday's big wind has petered out, he said, somewhere in the wilds of Quebec. All is serene on the weather map and sunny skies are in prospect.

SUMMARY OF HAVOC

10,000 evacuated from homes in Springfield as flood crest is awaited at 10 o'clock tonight.

New Haven train rolled over at Stonington, Conn.

Western Express, Chicago to Boston on B. and A. marooned since 9 yesterday morning at West Brookfield.

Tidal wave at Buzzard's Bay.

CAMBRIDGE—Man killed by falling debris. Many hurt. Trees down. Church cupola blown off. Cambridge Post, A. L., does storm duty.

SOMERVILLE—Part of church roof collapses. All Police, Fire and Highway Department employees called out.

BROOKLINE—Damage at least $750,000.

DEDHAM—Headstones flattened in cemetery. All call firemen, off-platoon men and police reserves called.

BEVERLY—Yachts ashore. Heavy damage. A. L. Post helps clear trees from streets and local Boy Scouts give their aid.

EVERETT—Man fatally injured when struck by piazza roof torn off by wind. National Guard called out.

CONCORD—Part of 30-foot Concord Reformatory wall blown down; prison officials not alarmed. Roofs crushed by falling trees in several sections. Falling chimneys hurt several.

HINGHAM—More than 20 boats sunk in the harbor. Many more ashore.

LEXINGTON—Tree crashes

Summary
Continued on Page 10

Tidal Wave, Fire, Flood Follow Gale--Many Areas Still Isolated

By JOHN BARRY

Death and devastation in the wake of the hurricane which veered from its seaward course to lash Boston and all New England last night left great areas of the East virtually paralyzed today.

In the work of reconstruction, clearing the debris of thousands of trees, wrecked homes, fallen wires, poles, washed-out roadbeds and tracks, thousands were engaged today. The W. P. A. in Massachusetts suspended all projects on orders of Administrator John J. McDonough to throw 80,000 workers into the breach and speed the clean up.

Transportation and communication facilities were at a standstill. Bridges are gone, rivers have climbed their banks to create inland flood conditions as menacing as the great flood of 1936. And along the sea, where a tidal wave of typhoon proportions smashed its way 1000 feet inland with a frightful toll of lives and property, the shores were strewn with dead bodies this morning.

Fear Death List Will Exceed 275

The mounting roster of the dead is expected to exceed the horrifying total of 275. Late today there were 243 known dead as a result of the tornado-like gale. Of that number 209 were in New England. New York, also hard hit, had 32 dead and in Jersey and Canada two were killed.

The toll of the hurricane in Massachusetts was 77 dead. In Rhode Island there were 87 bodies recovered from the sea and the floods. Connecticut had 31 known dead. In New Hampshire 13 died. In Vermont one person was dead.

Today the threat of disease hung over many New England cities. Water supplies had become polluted. Chlorinators were being put into use and anti-typhus serums were flown by the National Guard to threatened areas.

Twenty-three different communities saw National Guardsmen patrolling their streets where the hurricane in its mad fury had left the thoroughfares as desolate as the shelled cities

Storm
Continued on Page 12

Find Five Bodies in Somerset and Swansea

Four bodies were recovered from the waters at Brayton Point Beach in Somerset. They are Joseph Mancin, 57; Williamson, 70, and David Cornell, no age, all of Whitley road in Somerset. All are at an undertaking parlor in Fall River.

A wooden bridge on Old Fall River road in North Swansea was demolished. At Ocean Grove, Swansea, a man's body was recovered and taken to an undertaker's parlor in Fall River. Forty cottages along this section have been demolished.

TREASURY BALANCE

WASHINGTON, Sept. 22 (A. P.)—Treasury receipts for Sept. 20 were $46,672,676; expenditures $18,027,659; net balance $3,112,525,142, including $2,513,005,536 working balance. Customs receipts for the month were $18,646,875.

The Temperature Today

The thermometer at Thompson's Spa records the temperature up to 3 p. m. today as follows:

	1937	1938		1937	1938
3 a m....	54	61	1 p m....	65	74
6 a m....	53	58	2 p m....	65	73
9 a m....	57	61	3 p m....	65	73
12 m	63	66			

THE WEATHER

FAIR

Forecast for Boston and Vicinity: Thursday fair and cooler; Friday fair and warmer. Diminishing southwest or west wind.

Weather Reports, Tides and Almanac on Page Fourteen

Boston Schools Will Be Open Tomorrow

In a statement issued this afternoon Arthur L. Gould, superintendent of Boston schools, said:

"A survey of school buildings in all parts of the city was made today by the Department of School Buildings, the engineer and the custodian of the School committee.

"Whatever damage has occurred is being taken care of by a large force of workers and I am assured that all school buildings will be ready for occupancy tomorrow."

HURLEY GOES TO CAPE

Gov. Hurley, accompanied by Maj. William H. Harrison, left this afternoon for a tour of inspection of the Cape, with stops at Wareham, Bourne, Fairhaven, Marion and Falmouth, which towns were reported to be especially hard hit by the hurricane.

-EXTRA!-

Boston Evening Globe
Reg. U. S. Pat. Off.
Copyright, 1939, by the Globe Newspaper Co.

Entered as second class mail matter at Boston Mass., under the act of March 3, 1879—242 Washington St.

BOSTON, TUESDAY EVENING, MAY 23, 1939—22 PAGES—2 CENTS

RED STREAK FINAL
LATEST NEWS AND SPORTS

63 TRAPPED IN SUB

Ships Rush to Rescue Men Imprisoned 240 Ft. Below Surface Off Rye Beach

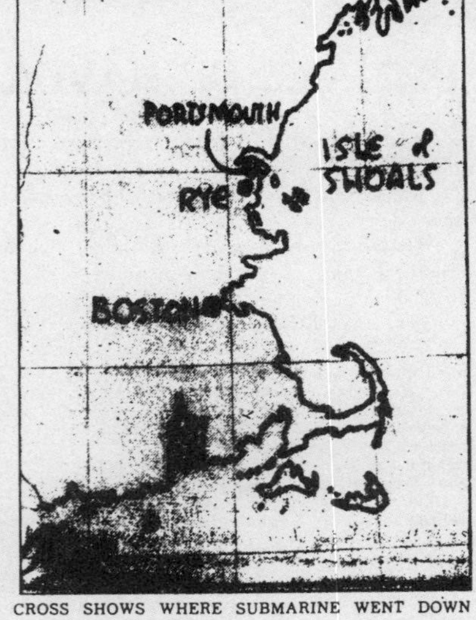

CROSS SHOWS WHERE SUBMARINE WENT DOWN

PORTSMOUTH, N. H., May 23—Sixty-three officers, enlisted men and civilians were locked in deadly peril this afternoon aboard the water-logged submarine Squalus, 240 feet below the ocean surface off the Isles of Shoals, awaitiny the arrival by air of the divers who may rescue them.

The tug Wandank, from the deck of which divers can operate, was due to arrive at the scene of the accident this afternoon. Eight divers from the Navy Yard at Washington, D. C., were on their way by airplane.

It was believed that diving operations would begin before dark tonight. The sea was smooth, and it was thought that the divers could work right through the night. The trouble was in an induction valve, which can be fixed from the outside.

Divers Trying to Beat Failing Air Supply

The problem seemed likely to develop into a race against time, the divers against the failing air supply within the sub.

Lieut. Oliver F. Naquin, commander of the submerged sub, was in radio telephone communication with the Sculpin, sister vessel, which was at the scene.

This was the first serious accident of this kind at the Portsmouth Navy Yard. News of the accident, which occurred at 8:40 this morning, was not made public until the middle of the afternoon.

Officers at the Portsmouth Navy Yard expressed optimism. They said that if the divers could fix the valve in time the Squalus, a new vessel, could raise herself. But alongshore and throughout the country ran a shudder of apprehension, as people recalled the awful disasters which have overtaken submarines off the New England shore at Block Island and Provincetown.

The crew's quarters were flooded and the after engine room. But watertight doors were holding the water out of the rest of the sub. The people aboard still had lights late this afternoon and no injuries were reported.

The officers on the submarine are Lieut. O. F. Naquin, commanding; Lieut. William Boyle Jr., Lieut. R. N. Robinson, Lieut. J. C. Nichols and Ensign J. H. Patterson. Ensign Patterson is the son-in-law of Capt. H. R. Greenlee, master of the yard at Portsmouth.

The submarine was launched Sept. 12 at the Portsmouth Navy Yard. It is 299 feet long and 26 feet wide. It has a displacement of 1450 tons.

Smoke Bomb Marks Place

The Squalus submerged for a

Submarine
Continued on Page 9

LIST OF MEN ON SUBMARINE

Members of the crew of the ill-fated submarine Squalus follow:

James A. Aitken.
John J. Batick.
Judson T. Blanchard.
William D. Boulton.
Allen C. Bryson.
Joshua Casey.
John A. Chestnut.
Gavin J. Coyne.
Eugene D. Cravens.
Elvin L. Deal.
Felichano Alvina.
William J. Fitzpatrick.
Lionel H. Fletcher.
Lawrence J. Gainor.
Kenneth R. Garrison.
John P. Hathaway.
Eugene A. Hoffman.
William Isaacs.
Theodore Jacobs.
Alexander B Keegan.
Charles F. Kuney.
Lloyd Z. Maness.
John P. Marino.
Robert P. Thompson.
Huie K. McAfee.
Gerald C. McLees.
Francis Murphy Jr.
Carol N. Pierce.
Carleton B. Powell.

Men Aboard
Continued on Page 9

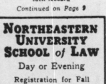

QUEEN MARY IN AUTO CRASH

LONDON, May 23 (A. P.)—Queen Mother Mary was officially announced to be "suffering from considerable bruising" from effects of an automobile accident this afternoon and to have been ordered "some days complete rest."

The Queen's automobile was overturned in a collision with a two-ton truck at Putney, London suburb.

Bulletin Issued from Queen's Home

The following bulletin was issued from her home at Marlborough House at 7:30 p. m. (1:30 p. m., E. S. T.).

"Her Majesty Queen Mary is suffering from bruising and shock as the result of an accident this afternoon in which Her Majesty's car was overturned.

"Though the bruising is considerable and will need some days' complete rest, Her Majesty's general condition is this evening satisfactory.

"Signed, Stanley Hewett and Dawson of Penn."

Kingn and Queen Told of Accident

At Jackfiesh, Ont., news of the accident was given to King George and Queen Elizabeth as their train pulled out of the tiny coaling station on the north shore of Lake Superior.

Queen Mary, who will be 72 Friday, was attended by Sir Stanley Hewett and Lord Dawson of Penn, who attended King George V and is probably England's most noted physician.

The royal car collided with a two-ton truck carrying steel tubes and was badly damaged.

After the Queen—who will be 72 next Friday—had been driven to her Marlborough House residence it was learned that she complained of slight pains in her back, which were believed to be due to bruising. She was authoritatively reported "bruised and badly shaken" but otherwwise unhurt.

The front of the truck crashed into the rear wheel of the Queen's car, but only the radiator of the truck was damaged.

Queen Mary, mother of King George VI, was helped from the damaged car to a nearby house which proved to have been the home of a physician who died last week, Dr. H. S. Revell.

Queen Mary
Continued on Page 9

BISHOP SPELLMAN INSTALLED, 40 PRELATES AT CEREMONIES

Archbishop Francis J. Spellman, second from left, arrives at St. Patrick's Cathedral, New York, this morning for installation ceremonies. In the rear may be seen Ex-Gov. Alfred E. Smith, a Papal chamberlain.

By JOSEPH F. DINNEEN

NEW YORK, N. Y., May 23—Bishop Amleto G. Cicognani (pronounced Chickenarney), Papal delegate to the United States, a small man with a round head, wearing a great purple cloak with a long train, a cape and hood of purple silk, his physical stature magnified by his vestments, walked up three steps on the left hand side of the vaulted stone altar to a throne, a very large high-backed chair of square lines and sharp angles that appeared to be made of dark walnut elaborately carved.

He placed upon the head of Most Rev. Francis J. Spellman a tall white and gold headdress very similar to the one in which the bishop frequently has been pictured during confirmation ceremonies in Greater Boston, and the former auxiliary bishop of the archdiocese of Boston became Archbishop of the richest archdiocese in the largest city in the western world at exactly 11:06 this morning.

Between 6000 and 7000 spectators were in magnificent St. Patrick's Cathedral to witness this ceremony; 1500 priests, members of religious orders and church dignitaries participated in it, and outside a crowd of 50,000 stood in roped off streets to listen to the same radio broadcast of the ceremony that New Englanders heard on their own radios.

In a front row pew was Mrs. Maurice Tobin, wife of Boston's Mayor, smart and chic in street attire. Not far from her was Ex-Gov. James Michael Curley, Mrs. Curley and Mr. and Mrs. Donnelly. A few feet away were United States Senators Walsh and Lodge and within easy whispering distance of all of these was Atty. Gen. Paul Dever. In the front row, center, were Archbishop Spellman's father, his two sisters and his two brothers and their families.

A little farther away was Police Commissioner Joseph P. Timilty, a model, as usual, of sartorial excellence in striped trousers and tails, and alsewhere in the congregation were Judge Francis J. W. Ford, F. C. Dumaine, former Fire Commissioner Edward McLaughlin and probably 300 to 500 Bostonians who came to New York for the installation.

Two Long Pauses

There are some things about the ceremony that the radio could never convey. Only a picture, perhaps, can do justice to the appearance of that remarkable prelate, Msgr. Michael J. Lavelle, a tonic to the eyes of any man over 65 who thinks, perhaps, that he is getting old. He stood in the stone pulpit of the cathedral, strong, firm, rugged and healthy at 83, read the Papal bulls preliminary to the installation, without eyeglasses, and, if you listened on the radio and wondered what happened when he stopped for long pauses twice:

The first time he choked up and

Spellman
Continued on Page 6

SOX-TIGERS

At Boston	1	2	3	4	5	6
Tigers	1	0	0	2		
Red Sox	0	1	0			

Batteries—Rich and Peacock, Newsom and Tibbetts.

Story of Game on Page 11

House Votes 138 to 49 for $3500 Salary

The Massachusetts House of Representatives this afternoon voted that salaries of members of the General Court be $2000 for this year and $1500 for next. Under the law the salary would be $2000 for the entire biennial session but agitation for extra compensation resulted in the additional $1500. The vote was 138 to 49 by a standing vote. A roll call which would have recorded the names was refused.

Republic Steel Sues C. I. O. for $7,500,000

CLEVELAND, May 23 (A. P.)—Republic Steel Corporation, principal target of the Congress of Industrial Organization in its 1937 strike against "Little Steel," struck back today with a $7,500,000 damage suit.

Republic, the nation's third largest steel producer, in a Federal Court action named John L. Lewis, C. I. O. chieftain; Philip Murray, C. I. O. vice president, and other officers of the C. I. O. and its constituent Steelworkers' Organizing Committee and Amalgamated Association of Iron, Steel and Tinworkers of North America. These organization also were named defendants, as were approximately 700 Ohioans whom Republic identified, in a statement to the press, as "individual strikers and union officers."

Conspiracy Charged

The steel company, headed by Tom Girdler, charged the defendants conspired in 1937 to force complete or partial closing of its plants in Ohio, Pennsylvania, Maryland, Illinois, New York and elsewhere, and then "knowingly, maliciously, recklessly, wantonly and wilfully committed, among others," the following alleged acts:

Caused plants to be blockaded and surrounded, threw missiles at workers, formed pickets into "armed mobs . . . which mobs provoked commotion and riots . . . and

C. I. O.
Continued on Page 9

Report Britain, Soviet Ready to Sign Pact

PARIS, May 23 (A. P.)—An accord "in principle" between representatives of Britain and Soviet Russia to bring the latter into the British-French common front was understood in authoritative French circles tonight to have been reached at Geneva.

It was understood to provide for a pact between Britain and Russia similar to France's mutual assistance treaty with Moscow.

TREASURY BALANCE

WASHINGTON, May 23 (A. P.)—Treasury receipts for May 20 were $8,216,867; expenditures, $18,087,202; net balance, $2,996,917,437, including $2,329,307,754 working balance; customs receipts for the month were $17,653,482.

3000 Club Women Hear German on Nazi Activity

By DOROTHY G. WAYMAN

SWAMPSCOTT, May 23 — More than 3000 women, on the second day of the meeting of the Massachusetts State Federation of Women's Clubs, jammed every seat in the large auditorium of the New Ocean House here this forenoon and burst into spontaneous applause when a German, Dr. Gerhardt Seger, declared that he never wished to see America by armed intervention follow the paths taken in 1917. Later the doctor stated that because of the racial sympathies of the Germans and the Russians, Hitler and Stalin, as opportunist leaders, either have now a secret or would have shortly an open alliance.

He said that the German-Americans in this country hope that not by armed force but by making democracy work would preserve human civilization which is at stake today.

Concentration Camps

Explaining his own history in Germany, he said that he was a former member of the Reich, and that he was arrested in 1933 because he was opposed to Hitler. He declared that he is an Aryan. He said that he spent three months in prison and six months more in a concentration camp before escaping to America.

Club Women
Continued on Page 6

Commons Backs Chamberlain's Palestine Policy

LONDON, May 23 (A. P.)—The House of Commons by a vote of 268 to 179 today approved the Government's new Palestine policy after two days' debate. Opposition in the House of Lords had been withdrawn earlier.

Col. Lawrence Ashamed of Role in Arab Revolt

LONDON, May 23 (A. P.)—A hitherto suppressed chapter of the late Col. T. E. Lawrence's "Seven Pillars of Wisdom," published today, says Lawrence was "continually and bitterly ashamed" of his part in the Arab revolt against Turkey in the World War.

Lawrence wrote that the Arabs were deceived by a British conspiracy with promises of self-government.

"I had to join the conspiracy and for what my word was worth assured the Arabs of their reward. In our two years' partnership under fire they grew accustomed to believing me and to think my Government like myself sincere.

"Instead of being proud of what we did together it was continually and bitterly ashamed.

"It was evident from the beginning that if we won the war these promises would be a dead paper and had I been an honest adviser of the Arabs I would have advised them to go home and not risk lives fighting for such stuff."

For this reason, Lawrence wrote, he refused all honors and later joined the Royal Air Force as a private. He was killed in 1935 in a motorcycle accident.

"Yankee Clipper" Lands

SOUTHAMPTON, England, May 23 (A. P.)—The flying boat Yankee Clipper, inaugurating transatlantic air service, landed at Southampton at 12:45 a. m. (6:45 a. m., E. S. T.) today from Marseille, where she had taken off at 7:50 a. m. (1:50 a. m., E. S. T.). The Clipper left New York Saturday.

Racing Results

AT SUFFOLK DOWNS
DAILY DOUBLE
Sculptress and Wakita paid $80.20.

FIRST RACE—$1000, maiden 2-year-olds, 4½ furlongs.
aSculptress, 113, Robart 7.60 5.40 4.00
aHigh Arch, 113, Leblanc 5.40 4.00
Kantaka, 113, Polk 5.80
Time .56 1-5. Polina, True Knightess, Ian's Folly, Close Quarters, Sun Kit also ran.
aMrs. W. C. Stroube and Stroube and Collins entry.

SECOND RACE—$1000, claiming, 3-year-olds, 1 mile 70 yards.
Wakita, 101, Krovitz 18.20 9.60 5.20
Post Office, 104, Merritt 5.80 3.20
Proud King, 110, Leblanc 3.20
Time 1:47. aAbbot's Lark, Big Bully, Charming, aDrosera, Butterman, Trans-Fer, Scoria also ran.
aH. P. Metcalf and R. S. Clark entry.

THIRD RACE—$1000, claiming, fillies and mares, 4-year-olds and up, 1⅛ miles.
Tobacco, 115, Robart 3.40 2.80 2.40
Country Lass, 112, LeBlc 3.60 2.60
Hallie's Play, 114, Krovitz 3.60
Time 1 .83. Summer Hall, Mobcap, Bright Gem also ran.

AT BELMONT
FIRST RACE—$1000, claiming, maiden 2-year-olds, 5 furlongs (on Widener course).
Fortissimo, 108, Wagner 40-1 15-1 8-1
Hunting Song, 115, Peters 2-5 1-5
Atom Re, 118, Hardy 8-1
Time, 0.59 3-5. Okapilida, Millchic, Preferred Time, Buffoon, Sun Ivy, Running Cedar, Yellow Dust also ran.

SECOND RACE—$1200, steeplechase, claiming maiden 4-year-olds and up, about 2 miles.
He Goes, 146, B Ansteatt 9-2 8-5 7-10
Greek Idol, 137, Mogavero 5-2 7-5
Atophan, 140, H Murdock 4-5
Time, 3:48 4-5. Calculate, Broom Topper, Tom's Boy, John Broom, Adilber, Slieve Reigh also ran.

THIRD RACE—$1000, allowances, 2-year-old fillies, 5 furlongs on Widener Course.
Rosetown, 111, H. Richards 9-5 3-5 1-5
Scurry, 116, Haab 4-1 8-5
Up, 116, Longden 1-4
Time, 0.58 1-5. Not Down, Paradise Girl, Piquet, Bow Low, also ran.

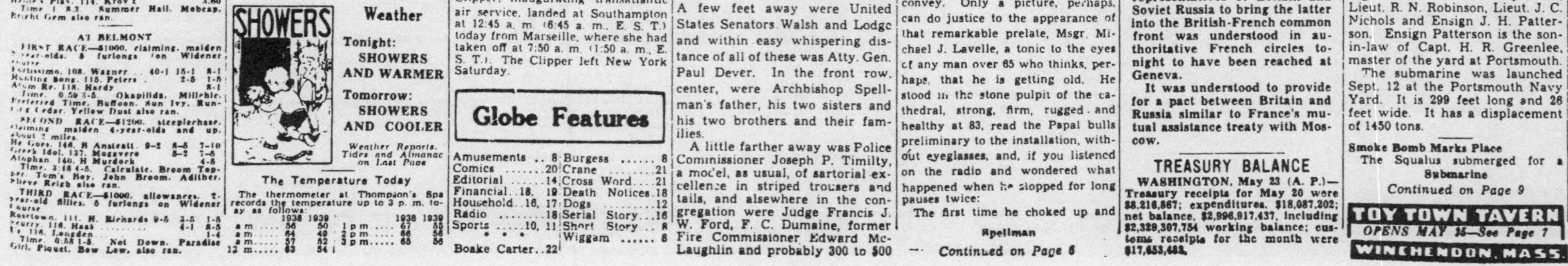

Weather

Tonight:
SHOWERS AND WARMER

Tomorrow:
SHOWERS AND COOLER

Weather Reports, Tides and Almanac on Last Page

The Temperature Today

The thermometer at Thompson's Spa records the temperature up to 3 p. m. today as follows:

	1938	1939		1938	1939
a m	56	50	1 p m	67	55
a m	64	49	2 p m	66	56
a m	57	52	3 p m	65	56
12 m	63	54			

Globe Features

Amusements	8	Burgess	8
Comics	20	Crane	21
Editorial	14	Cross Word	21
Financial	18, 19	Death Notices	18
Household	16, 17	Dogs	12
Radio	18	Serial Story	16
Sports	10, 11	Short Story	8
		Wiggam	8

Boake Carter..22

Boston Evening Globe

Reg. U. S. Pat. Off.
Copyright, 1939, by the Globe Newspaper Co.
VOL. CXXXVI ● ● ● ● ● NO. 63
Entered as second class mail matter at Boston, Mass., under the act of March 3, 1879—242 Washington St.
BOSTON, FRIDAY, EVENING, SEPTEMBER 1, 1939—28 PAGES—2 CENTS

RED STREAK FINAL
LATEST NEWS AND SPORTS

WAR BEGINS

Poland Invaded; Cities Bombed

Italy to Keep Out of Conflict

Ultimatums by French, British

PARIS, Sept. 1 (A. P.)—The French Government tonight announced that an ultimatum demanding that Germany "immediately stop all aggressive actions and withdraw troops from Poland" would be handed the German Government at once.

LONDON, Sept. 1 (A. P.) (Passed through British Censorship)—Prime Minister Chamberlain told an emergency session of Parliament today that Great Britain and France had given Germany her final warning.

Complete Mobilization Of Military Forces

Earlier today King George VI signed an order for complete British Army, Navy and Air Force mobilization after the Polish Ambasador had called on Britain to help Poland against Germany.

If Germany does not cease aggressive action and withdraw her forces from Polish territory, Britain and France unhesitatingly will fulfill their obligations to Poland, the Prime Minister said.

The British and French Ambassadors in Berlin have been instructed to ask for their passports unless Germany's reply is favorable, Chamberlain declared.

And, he added, "I do not suggest it is likely to be otherwise" than unfavorable.

The House approved a resolution offered by Sir John Simon, Chancellor of the Exchequer, to provide £500,000,000 ($2,110,000,000) to pay expenses that may be insurred in defense, maintenance of public order and prosecution of the war.

The Ministry of Transport took over British railroads.

Britain

Continued on Page 12

No Military Action by Italy Is Cabinet Announcement

ROME, Sept. 1 (A. P.)—The Italian Cabinet announced today that Italy would refrain from starting any military operations.

The Ministers had met with Mussolini at 3:50 p. m. (10:50 a. m., Boston time) to decide Italy's course of action as an ally of Germany.

They met knowing of French mobilization and that Hitler had declared Italy's aid would not be solicited in the German hostilities with Poland for the present.

Before the Cabinet met at Viminale Palace, where Il Duce has an office as Minister of Interior, British Ambassador Sir Percy Loraine had sought an interview with Italian Foreign Minister Count Galeazzo Ciano to learn Italy's intentions.

The Cabinet session lasted less than an hour. It was announced officially that the Cabinet approved the precautionary military measures already taken together with "the necessary economic and social measures" which accompanied them.

However, it was asserted that Italy would "not take any initiative of military operations" as a result of the war between Germany and Poland.

The official announcement said the Cabinet had examined the situation which had arisen in Poland as the result of the German-Polish conflict, "the origin of which goes back to the Versailles Treaty."

The Cabinet, said the statement,

Italy

Continued on Page 13

Air Attack on Berlin Feared; Sirens Sound

BERLIN, Sept. 1 (6:57 P. M., 12:57 P. M., (E. S. T.) (A. P.)—Warning air raid sirens howled through Berlin tonight, announcing the advance of enemy war planes. The populace immediately rushed to cellars and other protective shelters.

BULLETINS

HELSINKI, Finland, Sept. 1 (A. P.) (Passed through British censorship)—Unconfirmed reports were received here today that the German fleet had bombarded Gdynia, Poland's port on the Baltic Sea.

* * *

LONDON, Sept. 1 (A. P.)—(Passed through the British censorship)—The German Embassy today began burning some files, apparently as a precaution in preparation for possible withdrawal from London.

* * *

BERLIN, Sept. 1 (A. P.)—A report by D.N.B. German News Agency, said that Polish airplanes attempted to raid the outskirts of Beuthen, in German Silesia at 4 a. m (11 p. m. Boston time) Thursday and dropped six bombs in the homestead settlement on Hohenlinde Strasse. The report said there were no casualties and little damage.

D. N. B. also reported that Polish artillery had shelled the Beuthen railroad station at 11:30 a. m. (6:30 a. m. Boston time), firing five shells of 7.5 centimeter caliber, which hit the rail embankment and caused no damage.

* * *

BERLIN, Sept. 1 (A. P.)—The Army High Command issued a communique at 5:45 p. m. (12:45 p. m. Boston time) which said the German Army which advanced on Poland from

Continued on Page 10

FAIR

Weather
Tonight: FAIR
Tomorrow: FAIR
Weather Reports Tides and Almanac on Last Page

Globe Features

Amusements	23	Burgess	27
Comics	26	Crane	10
Editorial	16	Cross-Word	17
Financial	18, 19	Death Notices	19
Household	24, 25	Dogs	26
Radio	19	Serial Story	24
Sports	20, 21, 22	Short Story	27

TREASURY BALANCE

WASHINGTON, Sept. 1 (A. P.)—Treasury receipts for Aug. 30 were $10,335,677; expenditures, $16,305,360; net balance, $2,306,491,901, including $1,614,918,511 working balance; customs receipts for the month were $26,037,995.

The Temperature Today

The thermometer at Thompson's Spa reports the temperature up to 3 p. m. today as follows:

	1938	1939		1938	1939
3 a m	72	62	1 p m	80	71
6 a m	72	60	2 p m	82	71
9 a m	72	64	3 p m	83	71
12 m	78	71			

By the Associated Press

The German Army today invaded Poland in undeclared warfare.

Poland appealed to Great Britain and France for aid.

British Prime Minister Chamberlain told an extraordinary session of Parliament Britain unhesitatingly would fulfill her obligations to Poland unless Germany ceased her aggressive action and withdrew her forces from Polish soil.

Heart of Warsaw Bombed by Germans

As he spoke, German air raiders were bombing the heart of Warsaw. Three German Armies were driving across Poland, preceded by war planes bombing Polish cities.

Britain already had started setting her war machine in gear.

King George VI signed an order in council completing mobilization of the British Army, Navy and Air Force.

France had ordered general mobilization.

President Roosevelt appealed to Britain, France, Germany, Italy and Poland for pledges they would not bombard civilian populations.

White House sources said there would be no immediate action for invoking the Neutrality act or calling Congress into special session.

The Canadian Parliament was called for an emergency meeting Sept. 7.

Premier Mussolini called the Italian Cabinet to meet at 3 p. m. (10 a. m., Boston time).

Bomb explosions were heard in Warsaw, but no deaths or casualties were reported there up to 11:30 a. m. (6:30 a. m., Boston time).

Official Polish sources, however, were without information at that time of the extent of damages or casualties in air raids elsewhere in the country.

Polish cities bombed, the Foreign Office said, included Krakow, Katowice, Czestochowa, Tczew and Grudziaz.

It confirmed that fighting had started in Danzig.

The reported point of heavy German troop massing in East Prussia is opposite a Polish frontier only 80 miles from Warsaw.

German troops also crossed the Polish border between the Vistula River and Deutsch-Eylau. German planes attacked Tczew and the bridge over the Vistula, it was learned in Budapest.

German tanks were directed against Poland's Mukolowo region, Zakopani, a section of Kraszta and Praepice.

An infantry battalion moved

Europe

Continued on Page 13

German Planes Drop Bombs on Warsaw, Polish Capital

By LLOYD LEHBAS

WARSAW, Sept. 1, 5:35 p. m. (12:35 p. m. Boston time) (A. P.)—German warplanes swooped over Warsaw this afternoon in an air attack in advance of three German armies invading this country.

I am telephoning this dispatch to Budapest with the phone in one hand and a gas mask in the other.

From where I am I can hear the wail of power-diving fighting ships and can see 14 German bombers slowly, steadily following the course of the Vistula River, Poland's outlet to the sea.

Apparently Trying to Destroy Bridges

Apparently they are attempting to destroy all bridges.

The raid began at about 4:30 p. m. (11:30 a. m., Boston time) and is still continuing more than an hour later.

The German air raiders now—5:35 p. m. (12:35 p. m., Boston time)—are coming back after making a wide circle.

Poland

Continued on Page 13

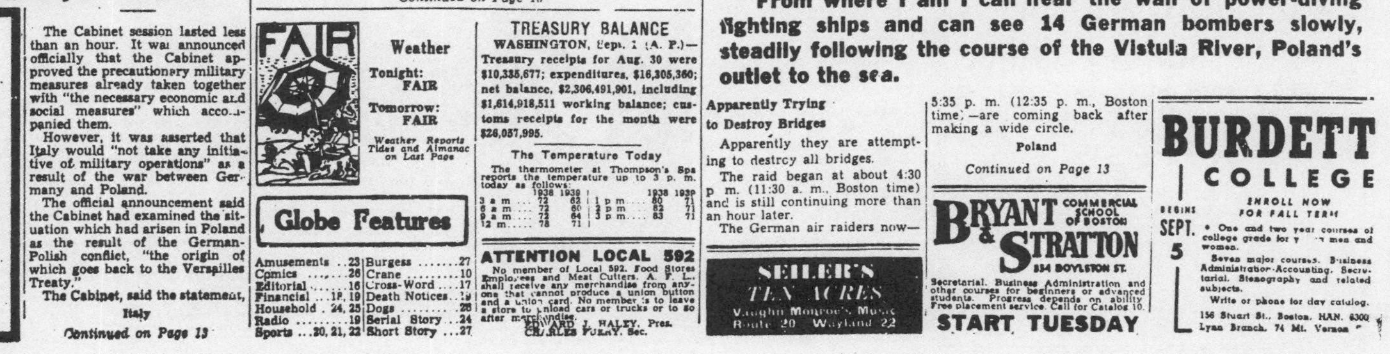

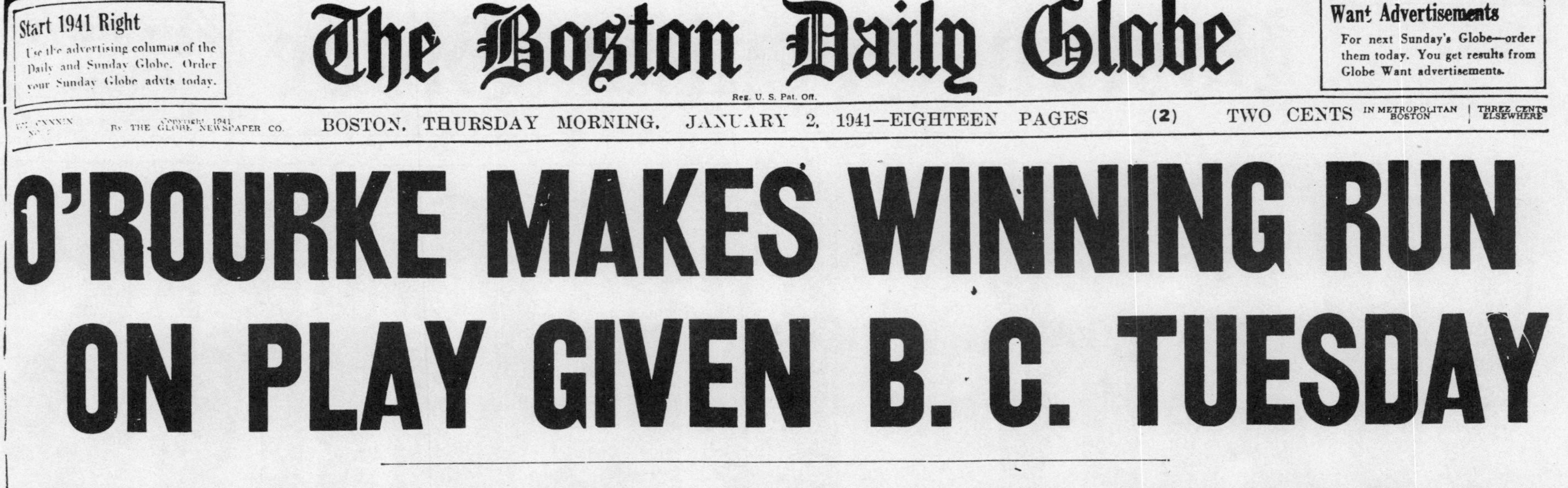

The Boston Daily Globe

Reg. U. S. Pat. Off.

VOL. CXXXIX NO. 2 — Copyright 1941 By THE GLOBE NEWSPAPER CO. — BOSTON, THURSDAY MORNING, JANUARY 2, 1941—EIGHTEEN PAGES (2) TWO CENTS IN METROPOLITAN BOSTON | THREE CENTS ELSEWHERE

O'ROURKE MAKES WINNING RUN ON PLAY GIVEN B. C. TUESDAY

Federal Reserve Offers Program to Block Inflation

THE HAPPY PAIR—Arthur Farnsworth and Bette Davis at lunch.

Actress Bette Davis Bride of Arthur Farnsworth

Star Weds Boston Flyer in West After N. E. Home Hunting Romance

A romance which began in Sugar Hill, N. H., two Summers ago when she wanted to buy a house and he had a house to sell, culminated New Year's Eve in the marriage of film star Bette Davis and Arthur Farnsworth of Rutland, Vt., Sugar Hill and Boston.

The marriage, which took place Tuesday night at Rimrock, Ari., was announced yesterday by Warner Bros. studio. The ceremony was performed at the ranch home of Mr. and Mrs. Justin Dart —Mrs. Dart is the former Jane Bryan of motion pictures—by Dr. Price, Methodist minister of Parkdale, Ari.

Among the witnesses were Mrs. Ruth Davis, the screen star's mother, and her brother-in-law and sister, Mr. and Mrs. Robert Pelgrem.

Bette Davis Weds

Continued on Page 10

Fire Captain Swims to Pull Man From Auto

Special Dispatch to the Globe

SWAMPSCOTT, Jan. 1—With a [illegible] Swampscott [illegible] waded and swam [illegible] a partially submerged car [illegible] Lynn Shore drive [illegible] a motor[illegible] with a fractured [illegible]

[illegible], 28, of 12 Boynton [illegible] the car, but [illegible] emerge Burns' [illegible]

[illegible] District Commis[illegible] Burns to the Lynn [illegible] for treatment of his [illegible]

Asks Removal of F. D.'s Power Over Dollar

Also Urges Bank Loan Curb; Seeks Balanced Budget

WASHINGTON, Jan. 1 (AP)—In an unprecedented move to forestall any possible inflation of the nation's money, the Federal Reserve System today proposed removal of the President's power to devalue the dollar, repeal of "greenback" legislation, an eventual balanced budget, and restrictions on bank lending.

System officials said it was not presented as an Administration proposal, and neither the White House nor other official quarters would express an opinion on the plan, which would require Congressional action to make it effective.

First reaction among the few members of Congress in town was generally favorable. For example, Senator King, Dem., of Utah, said the plan was "by and large very wise" and that the President's monetary powers constituted a "sword of Damocles hanging over the financial system."

Reserve Offers Plan

Continued on Page 3

Five Auto Deaths Mar New Year's Start in N. E.

The Bay State wound up one of its most profitable, most boisterous New Year's Days on record last night in hailing the advent of 365 days which couldn't be much worse than the 366 preceding ones. But it departed from a national trend when five persons—one more than the year previous—were killed in automobile accidents.

Except for the automobile death toll, the year's beginning was auspicious. Crime was relatively non-existent as hotel and restaurant owners counted up record receipts for the holiday celebrations.

Five Auto Deaths

Continued on Page 2

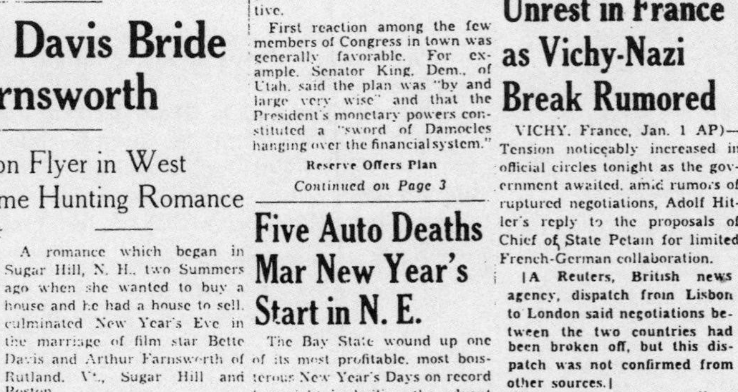

O'ROURKE CLINCHES VICTORY—Eagles' triple threat in 24-yard touchdown run that beat Tennessee. George Kerr (47) and Joe Manzo (17) are ready to block for him.. No. 16 is Lloyd Broome of the Volunteers.

Unrest in France as Vichy-Nazi Break Rumored

VICHY, France, Jan. 1 (AP)—Tension noticeably increased in official circles tonight as the government awaited, amid rumors of ruptured negotiations, Adolf Hitler's reply to the proposals of Chief of State Petain for limited French-German collaboration.

[A Reuters, British news agency, dispatch from Lisbon to London said negotiations between the two countries had been broken off, but this dispatch was not confirmed from other sources.]

The government met all reports with silence, and at Marshal Petain's new year's reception of foreign diplomats there was no indication of new friction in the negotiations. But Petain did tell those assembled:

"I am certain my country will resume its place among nations."

Negotiations between Petain's government and Germany have been at a standstill since Naval Minister Jean Darlan took the old marshal's latest proposals to Hitler somewhere in occupied France on Christmas Day.

Vichy Breaks With Nazis

Continued on Page 2

Mother Falls Into Newton Burglar Trap

NEWTON, Jan. 1—Captured in a trap set by the occupants of a house she is alleged to have broken into four times in the past month, a young mother of two children was arrested today and held in $1000 bail.

Mrs. Antonette Murray, 29, of Boylston st. was turned over to Newton police after she allegedly climbed through the window of the home of a neighbor, Mrs. Daniel Antonelli of 374 Boylston

Newton Woman

Continued on Page 18

Red Lanterns Placed by Quincy Assailant Near Woman Victim

QUINCY, Jan. 1—Three red lanterns placed near the unconcious form of a young Weymouth wife by the assailant who brutally beat her early today brought police to the assistance of the critically injured woman.

The victim, Mrs. Blanche Hall, 23, of Front st., Weymouth, was found in a field off Washington st. by patrolman Joseph Pangraze, who saw the lanterns. She was suffering a fractured jaw, lacerations of the chin and head injuries.

B. C. Grads Start Home After 'Painting City Red'

NEW ORLEANS, La., Jan. 1—A record crowd of 73,181 sat in on this seventh, and attested by all as easily the most thrilling Sugar Bowl contest, and 73,181 stayed to see the joyful Boston rooters get a decision over the police force in the battle for the multi-colored goal posts.

The police, stationed hurriedly at the north end of the field at the game's end greeted the onrushing hordes of bald eagles from the stands with their clubs, defending the crossbars. They held the fort for only a few moments. The entire stadium throng cheering the B. C.'ers rose en masse as the posts finally toppled and the happy invaders started on a parade down through the city.

Alumni Celebrate

With good reason the B. C. alumni fairly burned up the city tonight, taking over the lobbies of the big hotels, and gathering on the principal corners of the main stem to let the folks know (if they didn't already) that a great B. C. team came from behind twice today to gain the top honors in collegiate football.

The three alumni specials will leave at 2 a. m. tomorrow morning, heading home across Florida for a stopover tomorrow night at Jacksonville. Friday the party will stop at Southern Pines, N. C., for three hours, and follow through to Washington, arriving at the Capital at 8 p. m. The specials are due to arrive early Saturday morning at the South Station.

Bowl Results

Sugar—Boston College 19—Tenn. 13.
Rose—Stanford 21—Nebraska 13.
Cotton—Texas A. & M. 13—Fordham 12.
Orange—Miss. State 14—Georgetown 7.
Sun—W. Reserve 26—Arizona State 13.
Pineapple—Fresno State 3—Hawaii 0.
Charity Game at San Francisco—West 20—East 14.

Mayor Maurice J. Tobin, who sat among the 3000 Bostonians on the 55-yard section of the massive east side of the stadium, was literally walking on air tonight when interviewed by the Globe in his suite at the Hotel Roosevelt. "It came out pretty near the way we predicted," he said, with a grand smile lighting up his face. "Charley O'Rourke can have a key to Boston any time he chooses. I have been watching B. C. football games for two decades but never saw anything like that Alger run today. I am certainly proud to be the Mayor of a city that is the toast of the nation tonight."

The Mayor's car will be hitched to the train that will carry the champion Eagles home tomorrow, leaving here at 9 a. m., and getting into Boston Saturday afternoon.

Three Greater Boston rooters, who figured in the goal-post melee with the police after the game and were carted to the Charity Hospital, were all released soon after being treated.

Howard Murray of Lynn had two stitches taken in his head. Bill Godfrey and John Mahoney sustained shoulder injuries. All joined in the downtown post celebration. They make them tough down Boston way. Ray Finnegan.

O'Rourke

Fake Pass Practiced Only Once

Clinches Victory for Eagles, 19-13, in Closing Minutes

By VICTOR O. JONES

NEW ORLEANS, Jan. 1—The story behind the story of Boston College's epochal 19-13 win over Tennessee in the Sugar Bowl today is that the fake pass play on which Charley O'Rourke scored the winning touchdown was concocted only yesterday. When Charley broke loose three minutes before the final whistle, and raced 24 yards to pay dirt, he was retracing steps he had paced out only a few times before, during the Eagles' final, secret practice session at the Bay St. Louis Mission High School gym.

Extraordinary secrecy surrounded this practice. For the first time in history, the two team surgeons and even the team's trainer were barred as the coaches and players held their final workout in sneakers. Coach Frank Leahy had given the team two new plays earlier in their stay down South and had thought up this particular one on one of the several days he spent in bed nursing a bad cold.

Until this play was unveiled, B. C. had no apparent pass plays developing into runs. Sometimes Eagle passers have run the ball when they found all eligible men covered. But this play was called in the huddle as a run and the blocking assignments were taken care of accordingly. Tennessee was completely fooled, because the play started like the pass plays immediately preceding it.

O'Rourke Made Difference

The difference, once again, was Charley O'Rourke, the spindle-shanked 155-pounder with the Buster Keaton dead pan. Battered and bruised in the first half of today's great Sugar Bowl classic, he came back in the final quarter and led a magnificent Boston College team in an irresistible last ditch charge which carried the ball 80 yards in nine plays for the touchdown which dissolved a 13-to-13 tie and just about gave Boston College the mythical football championship of the nation.

The little Malden towhead himself carried the winning touchdown over on a 24-yard cut-back through Tennessee's famous line after first faking a pass. In those nine plays

Boston College

Continued on Page 9

Today's Globe Contents

GUIDE TO FEATURES

Alsop-Kintner	13	Movies, Stage	6
Burgess	16	Obituaries	13
Boake Carter	13	Port of Boston	15
Cross-Word	15	Radio	4
Culbertson	16	Serial Story	15
Death Notices	17	Short Story	15
Dr Wiggam	15	Society	13
Editorials	12	Sports	7-9
Financial	4	Women	14-15

Page 2
Italy given smashing air blows by British in Mediterranean area.
Italian defense line at Klisura penetrated by Greeks.

Page 3
Taxes and aid to Britain loom as top issues when Congress convenes Friday.

Page 4
Harvard professors differ with manufacturers on education system.

Page 5
U. S. may build 400 warplanes for China this Spring.
Foreign Policy Association warns "drastic steps" necessary to save Britain.
Maritime Commission to order two 35,000-ton liners capable of conversion into aircraft carriers.

Page 6
Dr. Koussevitzky chides critics for frigid reception to young Russian composer's symphony.

Page 10
Forty families lose furniture as flames ravage warehouse in Brockton.
Imports and exports through port of Boston for 1940 show substantial increase.
Many familiar numbers missing from radio programs as most of nation's broadcasting stations do without music controlled by ASCAP.

Page 11
More than million Catholics attend holdy day services in Boston.
Doggoned foxhounds and web-spinning flies among oddities in monkeyshine marathon.
Scientists find human eye most sensitive thing in nature.

Page 13
W. L. White inspects ruined city of London.

Legislature Organizes, Inducts Saltonstall Today

By JOHN J. HARRIS

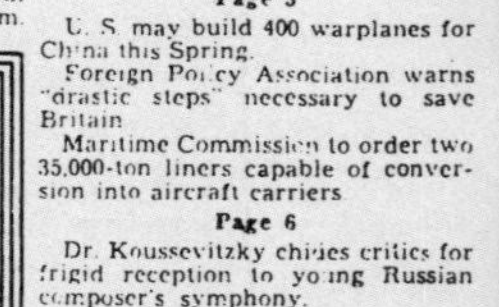

IMPORTANT PREPARATION for Legislative session. Miss Catherine E. Falvey wields powder puff before meeting of House.

With both branches of the Legislature organized in traditional fashion at ceremonies yesterday at the State House, Gov. Saltonstall, Lieut. Gov. Cahill and members of the newly elected Executive Council will appear before them at noon today to be given their oaths of office.

Unusual in the proceedings will be the fact that consuls of all of the invaded countries of Europe will be absent. Italy, one of the Axis powers, will be represented by Marquis Carlo deConstantin, but Germany's consul, although sent an invitation, up to a late hour last night had not sent his acceptance.

Goodwin Senate President

As far as could be learned last night at the State House, today's inaugural will be the first in many years not attended by the accredited representative of Germany—unless an acceptance appears today or the German consul himself joins the score of consuls, including those of Ireland, England and Finland, who have signified they will be in the procession of dignitaries.

State Legislature

Continued on Page 18

25-Minute Talk Prevents Suicidal Jump at Waltham

WALTHAM, Jan. 1—Vita Blekaitis, captain of the Waltham High School football team in 1932, prevented a man from committing suicide this noon by talking with him for 25 minutes—while the man stood poised on the outside of the railing of the Beaver Brook overpass—until police came.

The man was taken to the Boston Psychopathic Hospital for observation.

Blekaitis, on his way to a New Year's Day party, spotted the man as he apparently was just about to hurl himself 35 feet to the railroad tracks below.

Jumping out of his car, Blekaitis ran toward the man, shouting, "What are you going to do?"

That was the first opening in a long conversation—during which the man refused Blekaitis' invitation to come down from his perch to listen to the Boston College-Tennessee game, as well as to come with him to the dinner party—which ended when a passing messenger boy, sensing the situation, called the police.

Mystery Plane Drops Bombs Near Dublin

DUBLIN, Ireland, Jan. 1 (AP)—An airplane of unidentified nationality dropped bombs in County Meath, near Drogheda, 30 miles north of Dublin, tonight. First reports indicated no damage.

Boston Marine One of Five Held 17 Hours by Japanese

PEIPING, China, Jan. 1—Col. Allen H. Turnage, commander of United States Marines here, was understood today to be preparing to demand a formal apology from the Japanese for asserted maltreatment of five Marines after a cabaret fracas.

One of them was Corp. Francis A. Barber, 25, of 19 Carmen st., Dorchester, Mass.

United States officials declared that all five were held 17 hours and that four of them were injured by Japanese gendarmes.

The American version was this:

The five were arrested in the cabaret shortly before midnight Monday by gendarmes who threatened all Marines present with pistols and swords and refused admission to the cabaret to Marine military police who arrived during the incident.

They were released only after three demands by Col. Turnage.

The five Marines declared they were insulted and threatened in the cabaret by armed and drunken Japanese civilians. One of the Marines was said by American sources to have been floored and kicked in the face by the gendarmes.

Five U. S. Marines

Continued on Page 2

THE WEATHER

Forecast for Boston and Vicinity: Thursday mostly cloudy, light rain in the afternoon, warmer at night. Friday warmer followed by rain. Gentle easterly winds Thursday.

Weather Reports, Tides and Almanac on Back Page

WARMER | **WEATHER** MONDAY — Cloudy and warmer. TUESDAY — Light rain and snow; colder. Full Report, Page 12.

The Boston Daily Globe EXTRA

Reg. U. S. Pat. Off.

VOL. CXL. NO. 161 — Copyright, 1941 by The Globe Newspaper Co. — BOSTON, MONDAY MORNING, DECEMBER 8, 1941—TWENTY-FOUR PAGES (4) TWO CENTS IN METROPOLITAN BOSTON | THREE CENTS ELSEWHERE

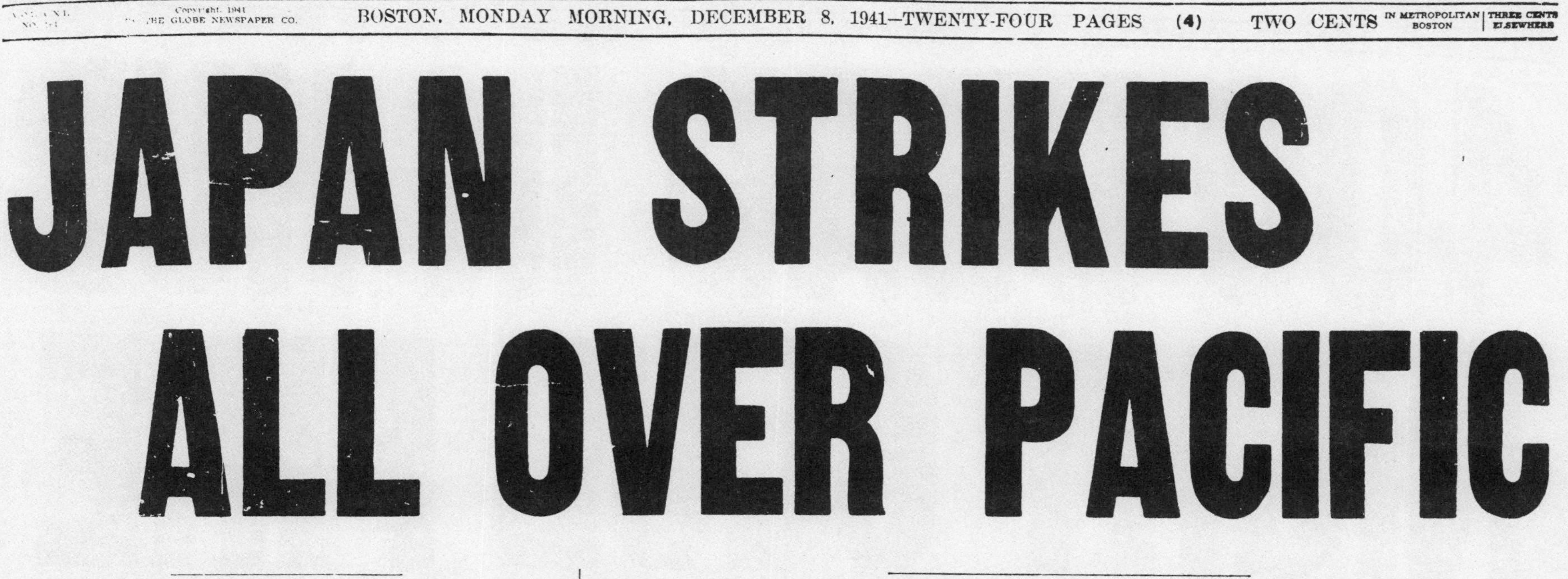

JAPAN STRIKES ALL OVER PACIFIC

THE OLD AXIS STRATEGY . . . By Barker

JAPAN WOULD LIKE HONORABLE DISCUSSIONS CONTINUE
DIPLOMAT
WAR LORDS
Barker

Bombs Hawaii, Guam, Philippines Takes Heavy Toll—Sea Battle On F. D. Will Address Congress Today

(By the Associated Press)

Japan assaulted every main United States and British possession in the central and western Pacific and invaded Thailand today (Monday) in a hasty but evidently shrewdly-planned prosecution of a war she began Sunday without warning.

Her formal declaration of war against both the United States and Britain came two hours and 55 minutes after Japanese planes spread death and terrific destruction in Honolulu and Pearl Harbor at 7:35 a. m., Hawaiian Time (1:05 p. m., E. S. T.) Sunday.

The claimed successes for this fell swoop included sinking of the United Statees battleship Weest Virginia and setting afire of the battleship Oklahoma.

The German radio reported that a sea battle betweeen the Japanese Navy on one side side and the British and the United States on the other was in progress in the Western Pacific, with a third United States warship hit in addition to the West Virginia and Oklahoma.

As compiled from official and unofficial accounts from all affected countries, the record ran like this:

Honolulu bombed a second time:

Lumber-laden United States Army transport torpedoed 1300 miles west of San Francisco and another transport in distress:

Shanghai's International Settlement seized: United States gunboat Wake captured there and British gunboat Peterel destroyed:

Capture of the United States island of Wake;

Bombing of the United States island of Guam;

Bombing of many points throughout the Philippine Islands;

Invasion of northern Malaya and bombing of Singapore;

Invasion of Thailand (Siam) and bombing of Bankok.

The first United States casualty report list-

Japanese Bomb U. S. Outposts

Continued on Page 10

War Bulletins

Japanese Land in North Malaya; British Troops Engage Invaders

SINGAPORE, Dec. 8 (Monday) (AP)—The Japanese have landed in North Malaya, it was announced officially today. The invaders are being engaged, the announcement said.

Aircraft Carrier Used in Attack on Pearl Harbor Reported Sunk

NEW YORK, Dec. 7 (AP)—Roundabout, unconfirmed reports from Panama and London said tonight that a Japanese airplane carrier from which planes operated to attack Pearl Harbor had been sunk by United States Navy ships.

OTTAWA, Dec. 7 (AP)—Canada declared war on Japan tonight.

War Bulletins

Continued on Page 9

New England Moves Quickly, Yards Guarded

Defense Machinery in Six States Leaps Into Action as Long Planned

By LOUIS M. LYONS

"America attacked!" Crackling air waves penetrated the Sunday fireside circle in New England homes to set the quiet Sabbath atingle, 5000 miles from America's island outpost in mid-Pacific.

Instant was the response as realization swept through the community that war had come to America without warning in a swift stroke intended to surprise her at the vital center of her Pacific defense.

Neighbors carried the news across the street and sat a while for solemn discussion of what it surely meant.

As the details came of the bombings made without any announcement of a state of war, indignation rose in a grim reaction of anger and determination.

New England was surprised. But New England was also prepared. In Boston and through New England orders flashed and preparations long planned were put into action. As they acted,

New England Leaps

Continued on Page 2

Congressional Leaders Hear Facts From F. D.; Joint Session at Noon

By CHARLES S. GROVES

WASHINGTON, Dec. 7—With unprecedented speed, preparations went forward at the White House tonight to accept the Japanese challenge to war.

The President called his Cabinet in extraordinary session at 8:30. Less than an hour later leaders of both parties in Congress entered the White House to discuss with the President his plans for a special joint session of the House and Senate tomorrow at noon. The President will address the Congress in person. A resolution declaring the existence of a state of war between the United States and Japan is anticipated. It will be adopted, unless all signs fail, by an overwhelming and probably by a unanimous vote.

From the moment the first bulletin announcing the attack on American bases in the Hawaiian Islands by Japanese bombers was made public, excitement in the Capital mounted until it reached fever heat. Throngs gathered in the vicinity of the White House and remained throughout the evening.

On Pennsylvania av. in front of the White House a constant stream of autos flowed slowly past. This traffic jam continued for hours and so dense was it that members of the Cabinet were delayed in arriving at the time set for the meeting with the President. Adjacent side street were roped off and closed to traffic.

Connally Announces Address

When President Roosevelt addresses the joint session of Congress he will report to the national legislature and to the American people the circumstances of Japan's attack upon Honolulu and the Philippines. It is expected he will ask Congress to declare a state of war. Such a declaration would give him greatly increased powers under laws already enacted.

The decision of the President to address Congress was announced by Senator Tom Connally, chairman of the Foreign Relations Committee, from the steps of the White House. The Texas Senator was the first to come from a two-door conference.

President Addresses

Continued on Page 10

Many Americans Killed in Honolulu by Japs' Bombs

HONOLULU, Dec. 7 (AP)—War struck suddenly and without warning from the sky and sea today at the Hawaiian Islands. Japanese bombs took a heavy toll in American lives.

Cannonading offshore indicated a naval engagement in progress.

Wave after wave of planes streaked over Oahu in an attack which the Army said started at 8:10 a. m., Honolulu time (1:40 p. m., E. S. T.), and which ended at around 9:25, an hour and 15 minutes later.

Witnesses said they counted at least 50 planes in the initial attack.

The attack seemed to center on Hickam Field, huge Army airport three miles northwest of Honolulu, and Honolulu, where the islands' heaviest fortifications are located.

Bullets Sprayed on Streets

The planes streamed through the sky from the southwest, their bombs shattering the morning calm. Most of the attackers flew high, but a few came low, five down to under 100 feet elevation to attack Pearl Harbor.

Huge Toll of Lives

Continued on Page 10

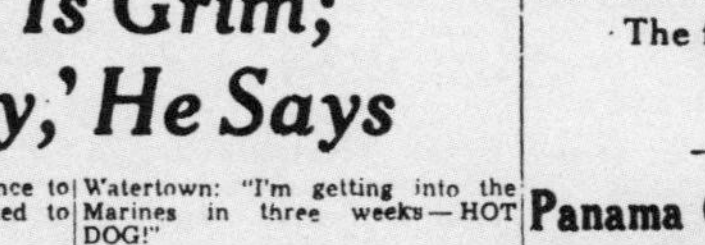

Boston Man in Street Is Grim; 'Let's Get 'Em Quickly,' He Says

By WILLIAM L. TISDEL

Boston's people—high and low, rich and poor, foreman and unemployed—received the news of Japan's invasion of United States territory with a grim determined reaction: 'Let's get 'em, and get 'em quick. We're really in it now!"

The man in the street willingly expressed his opinion (in many cases unprintable) and emphasized his views with an earnest hope that American retaliation would be prompt and effective.

Boston's man and woman in the street said:

Samuel Brown, Hollywood, Calif., company representative: "They're a sneaky bunch; now's our chance to do what we've always wanted to do."

• • •

L. E. Blanchard, Western Union messenger: "It had to happen; I hope we blow them to hell."

• • •

Mrs. Bertha Myers, 3 Charlotte st., Dorchester: "I think we ou t to clean out the Japs now."

• • •

Mr. and Mrs. J. Meizler, Brenton st., Dorchester: "It's an awful thing. We've got a job to do now."

• • •

Miss Iris Dorman, 4 Enfield st., Jamaica Plain, secretary: "The whole thing is terrible. Our boys will be mad."

• • •

Joseph Gayzayian, 64 Hazel st., Watertown: "I'm getting into the Marines in three weeks—HOT DOG!"

• • •

Richard Safer, 40 Keenan st., Watertown: "Where's the nearest recruiting station? I'm getting interested."

• • •

Roy Masters, United States sailor: "We'll fight 'em, the blankety-blanks. Let's go after 'em."

Man in Street Says

Continued on Page 10

Board Awards CIO Union Shop in Captive Mines

NEW YORK, Dec. 7 (AP)—The United Mine Workers of America (C. I. O.) tonight won a 2-to-1 arbitration board decision awarding a union shop in captive mines owned by the country's major steel producers.

Union Shop Won

Continued on Page 2

Today's Globe Contents on Page 2

Panama Canal Zone Under Blackout

BALBOA Canal Zone, Dec. 7 (AP)—The Panama Canal Zone, all-important link for United States naval operations in the Atlantic and the Pacific, was placed on a wartime footing tonight for all-out protection.

The Army and Navy were placed on full alert, the zone was blacked out and Japanese were rounded up by police in neighboring Panama.

WEATHER
Forecast
SUNDAY—Warmer.
Full Report, Page 24.

The Boston Sunday Globe

Reg. U. S. Pat. Off.

EXTRA!

VOL. CXLII No. 152 Entered as second class mail matter at Boston, Mass., under the act of March 3, 1879. 242 Washington st. THE BOSTON SUNDAY GLOBE—NOVEMBER 29, 1942—102 PAGES READ THE ROTOGRAVURE—MAGAZINE AND COLOR SECTIONS (6) Copyright, 1942, The Globe Newspaper Co. PRICE 10 CENTS

400 DEAD IN HUB NIGHT CLUB FIRE

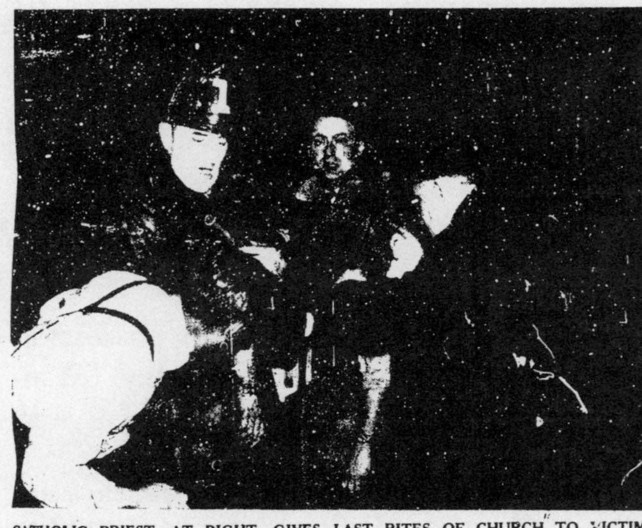

CATHOLIC PRIEST, AT RIGHT, GIVES LAST RITES OF CHURCH TO VICTIM CARRIED OUT BY FIREMAN

Hundreds Hurt in Panic as the Cocoanut Grove Becomes Wild Inferno

By SAMUEL B. CUTLER

The worst disaster in Boston's history last night snuffed out the lives of 399 merrymaking men and women in the blazing inferno of the famous Cocoanut Grove nightclub amid scenes of utter panic and horror.

Crushed, trampled and burned as nearly 1000 patrons, entertainers and employees fought desperately to gain the exits through sheets of flame, scores of victims were left lying on the floor helpless. Others reached the street enveloped in fire, only to die in agony in the street or in hospitals.

Hundreds Dead
Continued on Page 28

Where Bodies Can Be Found

Number of dead as compiled by police at 3:30 a. m. this morning.

Southern Mortuary	160
Northern Mortuary	77
Peter Bent Brigham Hospital	22
Mass General Hospital	75
St Elizabeth's Hospital	2
St Margaret's Hospital	3
Carney Hospital	2
Cambridge City Hospital	7
Faulkner Hospital	7
Chelsea Naval Hospital	11
U S Marine Hospital, Brighton	7
Beth Israel Hospital	[illegible]
Mount Auburn, Cambridge	7
Total	386

State Police Told to Block Roads

State police were ordered early this morning to block all roads leading into Boston to prevent a rush of motorists and morbid curiosity seekers to the scene of the fire tragedy at the Cocoanut Grove.

The orders were given by Gov. Saltonstall after he was requested to call upon the state police for assistance by Boston's Police Commissioner Joseph Timilty. The Governor was in communication with the commissioner several times during the morning to see if further state assistance could be given.

State Fire Marshal Stephen Garrity was instructed by the Governor to begin an immediate investigation of the cause of the fire.

List of Known Dead

JEROME ESTES, Coast Guard, address unknown.
GERALD DOWNER, 17 Columbus st., Beverly.
JAMES FITZGERALD, Lake st., Wilmington.
CHARLES DUHAMEL, 19 High st., Millis.
CHARLES HILDRETH JR., 93 Plantation st., Worcester.
VINCENT H. PREZIUSO, 35, 289 Lowell st., Somerville.
HOWARD R. JOHNSON, 40, 52 Burns st., Somerville.
HYMAN STROGOFF, 40 Heatherly road, Brighton, tentatively identified.
WALTER M. KING, 22 Farwell place, Cambridge, tentatively identified.
RICHARD F. PIERCE, 107 Ocean st., Dorchester, tentatively identified.
CARL H. THORNE, 49 Edgemere road, Quincy, tentatively identified.
HOWARD W. SMALLWOOD, 52 Main st., South Plymouth, tentatively identified.
CORP. ARTHUR B. MEAD, United States Army, 219 Ridge st., Glen Falls, N. Y.
SAMUEL FALCONE, 1 Verdi road, Worcester, tentatively identified.
NORMAN J. FARE, 88 George st., Medford, tentatively identified.
SECOND LIEUT. JOHN H. ABERNATHY JR., antiaircraft, coast artillery.
EDWARD LOWAN, 84 Fars av., Brookline.
CARL B. RUSSELL, Dayton, O.
JOHN J. SALMON, Seaman, 1st Class.
W. J. ROLAND, U. S. Army Signal Corps.
Lieut Ralph E. Hanren, son of Mr.
GILBERT A. WINSLOW, 27, 83 Summer av., Springfield.
ELLEN N. McCARTHY, 32, 25 Thorny Lee road, Brockton.
LOUIS J. NASH, 143 Summer st., Quincy.
JOHN L. STEENSON, 562 Centre st., Jamaica Plain.
PAUL N. CARBONE Jr., 4 Cheswick road, Brighton.
JOSEPH D. ALARIO, 34, 54 Norton st., Dorchester.
DAVID K. HILLMAN, 22, 135 Central Park West, New York city.
CONRAD E. SCHORMING, 25, 24 Fairmount st., Springfield.
WILLIAM J. YOUNG, 34 Oakland st., Medford.
THOMAS H. O'NEIL, 464 Chancery st., New Bedford.
ISAAC GORDON, 57 Charlotte st., Dorchester.
PHILIP SELETSAY, 65 Rowena road, Waban, and 37 Ferncroft st., Waban.
JACK VIGDOR, 137 Englewood av., Brighton.
CHARLES S. HERTLE, 673 Belmont st., Belmont.
CLYDE C. CLARK, 171 Fort st., Keene, N. H.
ARNOLD M. BAER, 10 Florence st., Dover, N. H.
HARRY J. CONNICK, 86 or 40 Bowdoin st., Boston.
GEORGE F. LOWE, 22 Lynde st., West End.
MARGARET McFARLIN, 52 Mansfield st., Allston.
STEPHEN H. JONES, U. S. N., 4203 Gelston drive, Baltimore, Md.
JOSEPH F. SWAN, 512 Lagrange st., West Roxbury.
EUGENE L. GOSS, Iowa City, Iowa, Harvard student.
ARTHUR R. SELBERBERG, 18, 180 East 79th st., N. Y. C., and 1065 Commonwealth av., Harvard student.
OSBORN S. RAYNER, U. S. A. Engineers.
THOMAS J. McCARTHY, 36 Washington st., Boston.
DOMINIC PENARDI, 55, no address.
JAMES H. FORD, no address.
ERNEST A. COLLINS, New York city.
EDWARD J. ROSS, 99 Woodcliff st., Roxbury.
FALVO FARIOHOFF, 159 Adams st., Dorchester.
PRIVATE ALFRED C. SULLIVAN, 219 Pleasant st., Montgomery, Ala.
EDWARD J. FOGEL, 11 Fayette st., Cambridge.
WILLIAM F. DONOVAN, 84 Selwyn st., Roxbury.
JOHN HOWARD ABERMATTY, no address.
DOUGLAS J. OBER, 40 Woodbine Terrace, Auburndale.
FRED B. SHARBY, 240 Roxbury st., Keene, N. H.
LAWRENCE E. ECKLERE, Kansas City.
THEODORE WASSERMAN, 241 Deering av., Portland, Me.
THOMAS A. DEVINE, 29 Holmer road, Quincy.
LIEUT. ARTHUR CDENDOLET, 81 Highland av., Cambridge.
JOHN T. DUCEY, 17 Abbot st., Medford.
RAYMOND F. SULLIVAN, 681 Main st., Ansonia, Conn.
MR. AND MRS. MARTIN SHERIDAN, 1132 Commonwealth av., Brighton.

Reds Gain 20 Miles

By HENRY C. CASSIDY

MOSCOW, Nov. 29, Sunday (AP)—The Russians announced today that a surprise offensive on the central front northwest of Moscow had killed 10,000 German troops, routed five divisions, "liberated more than 300 populated places" and broken wide gaps in German fortifications less than 90 miles from the old Latvian border.

A special communique issued by the Soviets said that the Red

Reds in New Offensive
Continued on Page 6

COCOANUT GROVE FIRE TIMES

The first alarm was sounded at 10:20 P. M. The "all-out" came at 3:42 A. M.

Frantic Parents Rush to Morgues in Vain Search

By J. MALCOLM BARTER

Frantic relatives, stunned by news of the greatest fire tragedy in Boston's history, rushed from one mortuary to another early this morning seeking to identify the charred remains of victims.

Worried when their sons and daughters failed to return home and learning from the radio and newspapers of the huge toll of dead and injured, weeping mothers and trembling-lipped fathers formed tragic lines outside the Southern Mortuary, the Northern Mortuary, relief stations and Greater Boston hospitals.

Many of them scantily clad in their haste and shivering in the cold night air, these relatives traveled from one chamber of death to another in hopes of identifying in singed faces or blackened clothing the bodies of their loved ones.

Frantic Parents
Continued on Page 22

Crusaders Win 55-12 and Stop B. C. Bowl Trip

By JERRY NASON

Boston College met its football Dunkerque yesterday.

An awesome Holy Cross team drove the previously unbeaten Eagles right into the sea, hammered them unmercifully throughout the action, and ran up the incredible score of 55-12 on a team that had one foot in the Sugar Bowl two hours earlier.

It was a colossal reversal of form and it wasn't encumbered by any fluke or any miscarriage of justice or any pranks of fate.

Becomes, Grigas Pace
Continued on Page 30

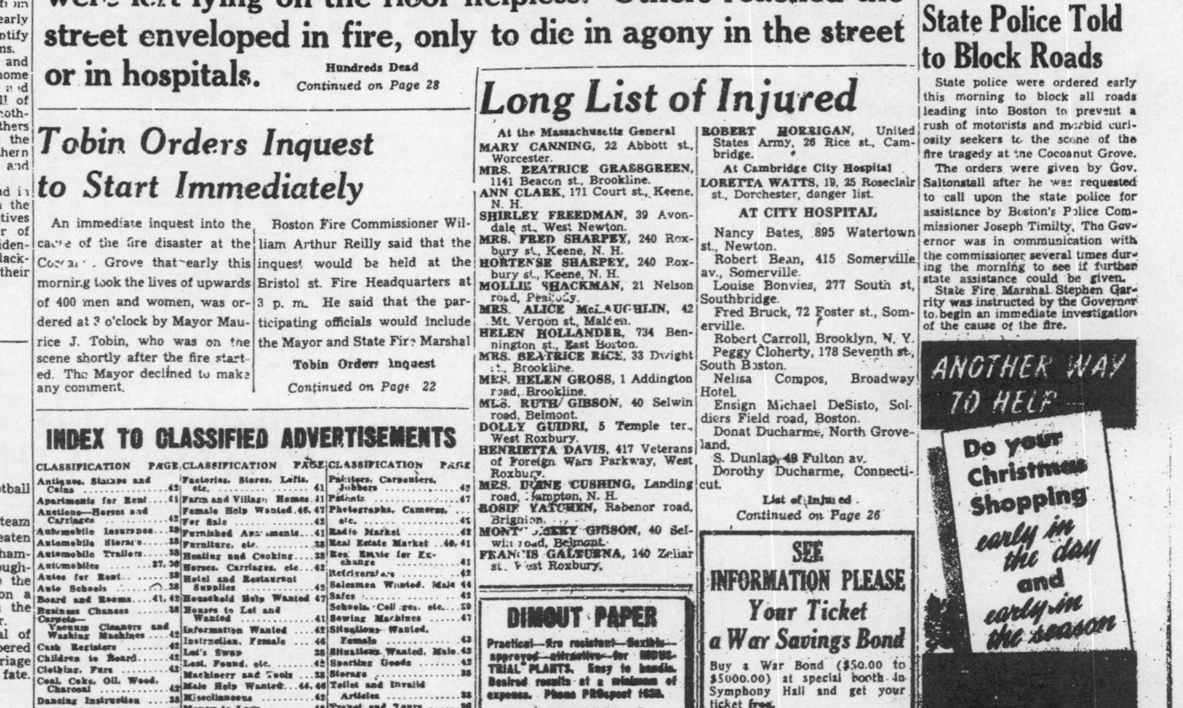

Tobin Orders Inquest to Start Immediately

An immediate inquest into the cause of the fire disaster at the Cocoanut Grove that early this morning took the lives of upwards of 400 men and women, was ordered at 3 o'clock by Mayor Maurice J. Tobin, who was on the scene shortly after the fire started. The Mayor declined to make any comment.

Boston Fire Commissioner William Arthur Reilly said that the inquest would be held at the Bristol st. Fire Headquarters at 3 p. m. He said that the participating officials would include the Mayor and State Fire Marshal.

Tobin Orders Inquest
Continued on Page 22

INDEX TO CLASSIFIED ADVERTISEMENTS

CLASSIFICATION	PAGE	CLASSIFICATION	PAGE	CLASSIFICATION	PAGE
Antiques, Stamps and Coins	42	Factories, Stores, Lofts, etc.	41	Painters, Carpenters, Jobbers	42
Apartments for Rent	41	Farm and Village Homes	41	Patents	47
Auctions—Horses and Carriages	42	Female Help Wanted	46, 47	Photographs, Cameras, etc.	43
Automobile Insurance	39	For Sale	42	Radio Market	42
Automobile Storage	38	Furnished Apartments	41	Real Estate Market	40, 41
Automobile Trailers	38	Furniture, etc.	38	Real Estate for Exchange	41
Automobiles	37, 38	Heating and Cooking	38	Refrigerators	42
Autos for Rent	38	Horses, Carriages, etc.	42	Salesmen Wanted, Male	44
Auto Schools	38	Hotel and Restaurant Supplies	42	Safes	42
Board and Rooms	41, 42	Household Help Wanted	47	Schools, Colleges, etc.	39
Business Chances	38	Houses to Let and Wanted	41	Sewing Machines	47
Carpets—Vacuum Cleaners and Washing Machines	42	Information Wanted	42	Situations Wanted, Female	43
Cash Registers	42	Instruction, Female	46	Situations Wanted, Male	43
Children to Board	42	Let's Swap	38	Sporting Goods	42
Clothing, Furs	42	Lost, Found, etc.	42	Storage	38
Coal, Coke, Oil, Wood, Charcoal	42	Machinery and Tools	38	Toilet and Invalid Articles	38
Dancing Instruction	38	Male Help Wanted	44, 46	Travel and Tours	38
Death Notices	42	Miscellaneous	42	Typewriters, etc.	38
Desks, Store and Office Furniture and Fixtures	42	Money to Loan	42	Wall Papers	42
Diamonds, Jewelry, etc.	42	Motor Trucking	38	Winter Resorts	42
Dogs, Cats, Pets, etc.	42	Music	38	Yachts, Motor Boats, etc.	42
		Musical Instruments	38		
		Office and Desk Space	41		

Long List of Injured

At the Massachusetts General
MARY CANNING, 22 Abbott st., Worcester.
MRS. BEATRICE GRASSGREEN, 1141 Beacon st., Brookline.
ANN CLARK, 171 Court st., Keene, N. H.
SHIRLEY FREEDMAN, 39 Avondale st., West Newton.
MRS. FRED SHARPEY, 240 Roxbury st., Keene, N. H.
HORTENSE SHARPEY, 240 Roxbury st., Keene, N. H.
MOLLIE SHACKMAN, 21 Nelson road, Peabody.
MRS. ALICE McLAUGHLIN, 42 Mt. Vernon st., Malden.
HELEN HOLLANDER, 734 Bennington st., East Boston.
MRS. BEATRICE RICE, 33 Dwight st., Brookline.
MRS. HELEN GROSS, 1 Addington road, Brookline.
MRS. RUTH GIBSON, 40 Selwin road, Belmont.
DOLLY GUIDRI, 5 Temple ter., West Roxbury.
HENRIETTA DAVIS, 417 Veterans of Foreign Wars Parkway, West Roxbury.
MRS. DIANE CUSHING, Landing road, Hampton, N. H.
ROSIE YATCHEN, Rabenor road, Brighton.
MONTGOMERY GIBSON, 40 Selwin road, Belmont.
FRANCIS GALTURNA, 140 Zeliar st., West Roxbury.
ROBERT HORRIGAN, United States Army, 26 Rice st., Cambridge.

At Cambridge City Hospital
LORETTA WATTS, 19, 25 Roseclair st., Dorchester, danger list.

AT CITY HOSPITAL
Nancy Bates, 895 Watertown st., Newton.
Robert Bean, 415 Somerville av., Somerville.
Louise Bonvies, 277 South st, Southbridge.
Fred Bruck, 72 Foster st., Somerville.
Robert Carroll, Brooklyn, N. Y.
Peggy Cloherty, 178 Seventh st., South Boston.
Nelisa Compos, Broadway Hotel.
Ensign Michael DeSisto, Soldiers Field road, Boston.
Donat Ducharme, North Groveland.
S. Dunlap, 49 Fulton av.
Dorothy Ducharme, Connecticut.

List of Injured
Continued on Page 26

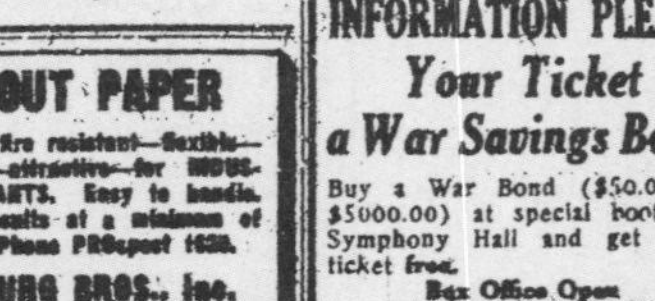

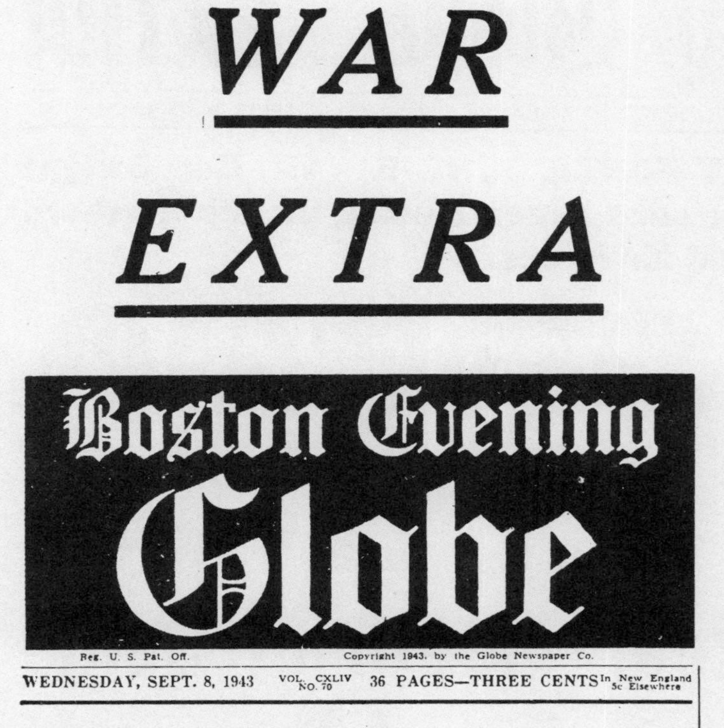

WAR EXTRA

Boston Evening Globe

Reg. U. S. Pat. Off. Copyright 1943, by the Globe Newspaper Co.

WEDNESDAY, SEPT. 8, 1943 VOL. CXLIV NO. 70 36 PAGES—THREE CENTS In New England 5c Elsewhere

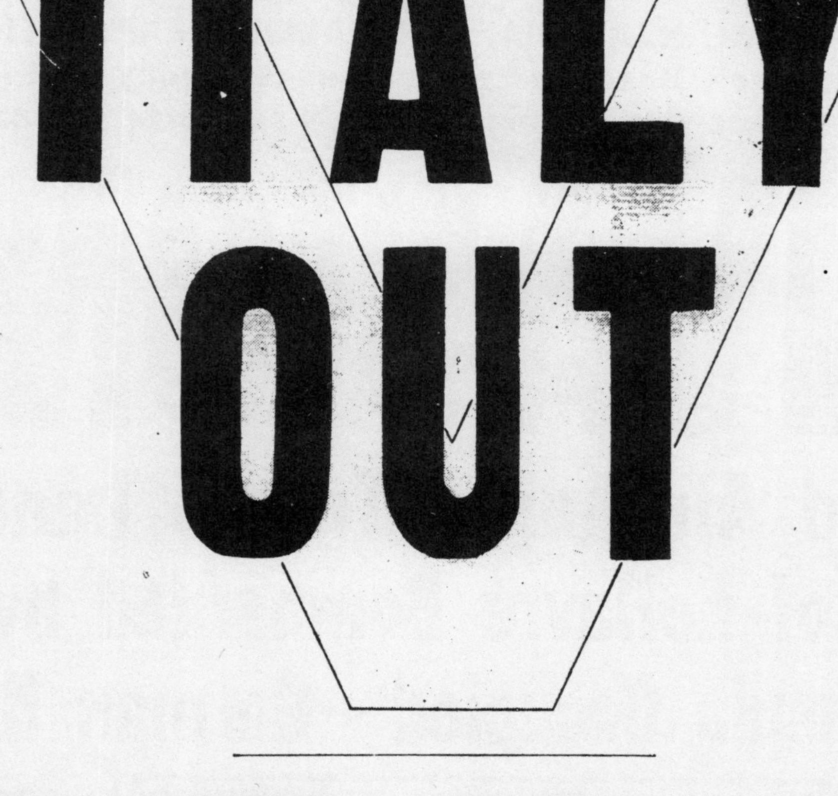

ITALY OUT

Unconditional Surrender

Russia Approves Terms of Armistice

Italians Ordered to Fight If Nazis Interfere

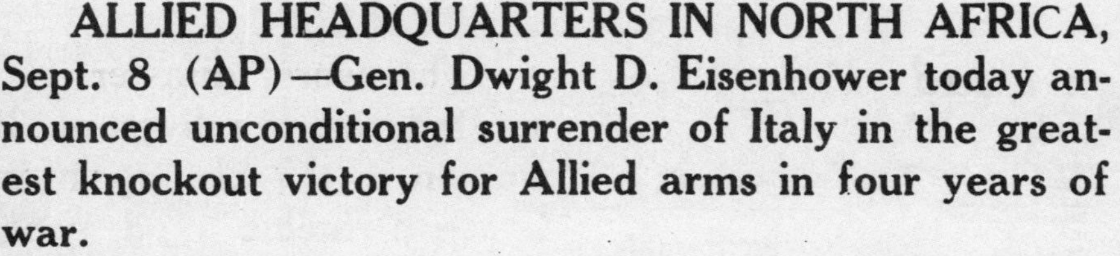

ALLIED HEADQUARTERS IN NORTH AFRICA, Sept. 8 (AP)—Gen. Dwight D. Eisenhower today announced unconditional surrender of Italy in the greatest knockout victory for Allied arms in four years of war.

Simultaneously, the Italian Government ordered its troops to drop the fight against Allied forces, but to "oppose attacks from any other quarter" (presumably against the Germans).

Russia as well as the United States and Britain approved the granting of the armistice, Eisenhower annouced.

Italy Surrenders Continued on Page 13

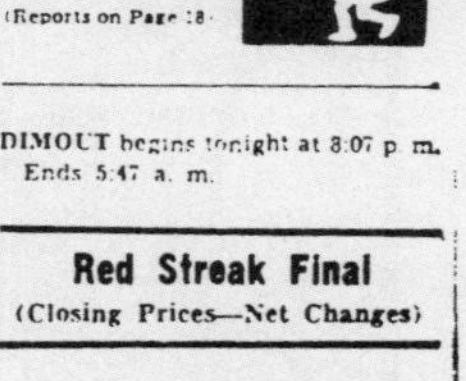

WEATHER

Tonight: RAIN AND COOLER

(Reports on Page 28)

RAIN

DIMOUT begins tonight at 8:07 p. m. Ends 5:47 a. m.

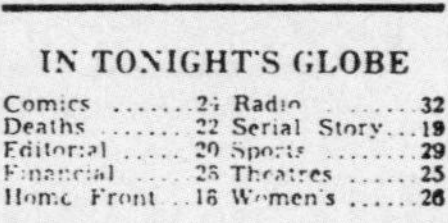

Red Streak Final

(Closing Prices—Net Changes)

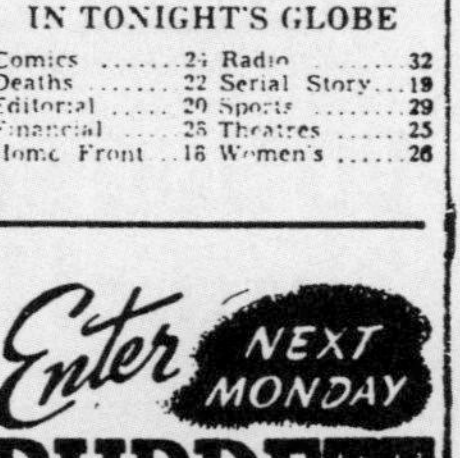

IN TONIGHT'S GLOBE

Comics	24	Radio	32
Deaths	22	Serial Story	19
Editorial	20	Sports	29
Financial	28	Theatres	25
Home Front	16	Women's	26

One Down, Two to Go

Crowds in Newspaper Row Jubilant at Italy's Surrender

"Italy is out of the war."

Those six words, yelled by a newsboy, sent the noonday crowd in Newspaper Row into a display of jubilation like of which hasn't been seen in Washington st. since the Armistice of World War I.

To be sure, the outward displays of emotion didn't last long. For a moment, people shouted on the street. Windows opened in the buildings and torn paper came fluttering down, improvised confetti. The newsboys did a land-office business.

And then the excitement subsided as quickly as it began and people just stood around and talked. It was good news, they all agreed, but the days of anticipation had taken some of the starch out of it. It wasn't—except for a moment—at all like the extended joy of 25 years ago when people danced in the streets for hours.

The general reaction of the crowd was a kind of suppressed excitement. It was like a preview of the coming armistice. In Thompson's Spa, men and women stood around the counters in a tense silence, occasionally broken by some would-be strategist predicting the near collapse of Germany.

"O, boy! Boy! Boy!" said a little foreign woman as she was told the news. She could not read English. "Vat a day!"

Men and women stood at attention as the bells of the courthouse played "The Star Spangled Banner." It was a solemn moment.

A soldier home on leave and his mother stopped to buy a paper.

The soldier turned to her and said, "Well, Mom, it won't be long now. Germany will go too, and then I'll be home for good."

Cars started to honk, as people were crowding the street, and traffic was at a standstill. One car made its hampered way through the crowd, and as it passed the signs announcing the news, the driver was asked to stop and see what all the excitement was about. The car stopped and necks craned to read the billboards. The comment was spontaneous. The people were Italians.

Newspaper Row Continued on Page 14

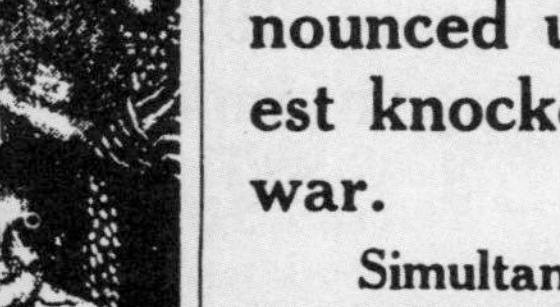

SCHOOL CHILDREN of North End's Little Italy greeted Italian surrender news with cheers and flag waving in North sq.

Urges Italy Send Navy to Allied Ports

LONDON, Sept. 8 (UP)—Admiral Andrew Browne Cunningham appealed to the Italian fleet by radio today to prevent the Germans from seizing its ships.

He urged the Italian fleet to make for Allied ports. Cunningham was heard on Radio Algiers by the United Press listening post here.

The Italian Navy consists of seven battleships, three aircraft carriers building, two heavy cruisers, nine lighter cruisers, 25 destroyers and 60 submarines.

Besides completing the Allied control of the Mediterranean, the new acquisition of the Allies curtails German U-boat operations there.

With the use of Spezia, Pola, Taranto and Genoa naval bases, the Allies will be able to command and blockade the French coast, as well as the Adriatic, including the Yugoslavia, Albania and Greek coasts.

2-Alarm Fire in Everett Chemical Plant

EVERETT, Sept. 8—Heavy clouds of orange and yellow smoke, carrying acrid fumes, from a two-alarm fire this afternoon at the Monsanto Chemical Company, Merrimac Division, blocked all traffic along Broadway, South Everett, and spread excitement over a wide area. Damage was estimated at $2500.

So far as known, there were no injuries.

The Monsanto plant, which covers many acres, is engaged in war work. No reporters were allowed to enter the wire fence which incloses the entire factory.

The Boston & Maine Railroad tracks of the main line to Lynn run between parts of the plant area, but traffic was not interrupted.

Along Broadway all street traffic was halted. Even the trains on the Elevated structure, high above Broadway, were stopped.

The great cloud of smoke, visible for miles along the Mystic River marshes, rolled slowly toward Sullivan sq.

Everett Fire Continued on Page 15

RACING RESULTS PAGE 27

RUSSIANS CAPTURE STALINO

LONDON, Sept. 8 (UP)—Premier Josef Stalin announced in an order of the day today that the Red Army had captured Stalino.

The Russians also captured Krasnoarmeiskoye, key railroad junction northwest of Stalino through which pass two of the four railroads out of the Donets Basin, Stalin announced.

The implicit report that Stalino again was in Russian hands put the seal on the Russian claims that the complete reconquest of the mineral-wealthy Donets Basin was assured and that the Germans were being swept westward at a growing pace.

Russia Continued on Page 2

3d Bond Drive Opens Tonight

Fourteen thousand employees of Boston retail stores and their friends tonight will usher in the third war bond drive with fun and frolic at a "night before" rally and dance at Boston Garden, interspersed with serious talks on the selling of bonds.

Bond Drive Continued on Page 4

F. D. on Air Tonight as Loan Drive Opens

WASHINGTON, Sept. 8 (AP)—President Roosevelt will open the $15,000,000,000 third war loan drive tonight with a 10-minute radio address as part of an hour-long program beginning at 9 p. m. (E. W. T.). The broadcast, originating in Washington and Hollywood, will include an all-star cast of motion picture and radio headliners. Mr. Roosevelt will speak at about 9:40 p. m.

WARNER
WEATHER
TUESDAY — Rather hot with fresh winds. Wednesday, fair and cooler
Full Report, Page 18.

The Boston Daily Globe EXTRA

Reg. U. S. Pat. Off.
VOL. CXLV No. 158 — Copyright 1944 By THE GLOBE NEWSPAPER CO. — BOSTON, TUESDAY MORNING, JUNE 6, 1944—EIGHTEEN PAGES — THREE CENTS In New England 5c Elsewhere

SUPREME HEADQUARTERS, ALLIED EXPEDITIONARY FORCE, JUNE 6—(AP) Gen Dwight D. Eisenhower's Headquarters announced today that Allied troops began landing on the northern coast of France this morning strongly supported by naval and air forces.

INVASION OPENS

Allied Air-Borne Troops Land Near Mouth of Seine Port of LeHavre Bombarded by Fleet—Tip of Normandy Peninsula Occupied—German Naval Units Fight Landings

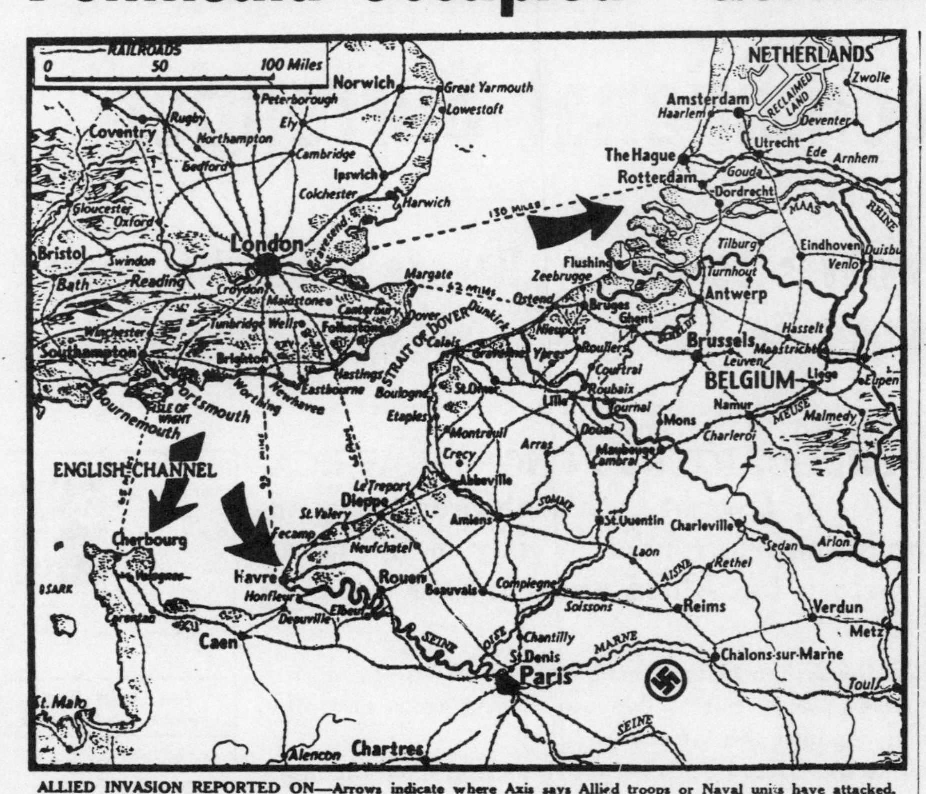

ALLIED INVASION REPORTED ON—Arrows indicate where Axis says Allied troops or Naval units have attacked.

LONDON, June 6 (AP) — The Berlin radio said today that "combined British-American landing operations against the western coast of Europe from the sea and air are stretching over the entire area between Cherbourg and Le Havre."

The broadcast declared grand scale amphibious operations are under way on a broad front between the mouth of the Seine and the estuary of the river Vire.

"A large number of Allied landing boats of various types and light Allied naval forces in considerable strength are taking part," Berlin added.

"Six heavy Allied warships and 20 destroyers are off the mouth of the Seine."

Three German news agencies tonight flashed word to the world that an Allied invasion of western France had begun with Allied parachute troops spilling out of the dawn skies over the Normandy Peninsula and sea-borne forces landing in the Le Havre area.

The Germans also said Allied warships were furiously bombarding the German-held French port of Le Havre at the mouth of the Seine River, 100 miles west of Paris.

German shock troops also were hurled against Allied troops rushing ashore from landing barges, the broadcasts said.

Le Havre lies 80 miles across the Channel from the British coast.

Dunkirk and Calais, just across the Channel coast from Britain, were under attack by strong formations of bombers, D. N. B. said.

"The long-expected invasion by the British and Americans was begun in the first hours of the morning of June 6 by landing of parachute troops in the area of the mouth of the Seine," declared the Transocean broadcast.

Allied headquarters remained silent.

The German D. N. B. agency said Le Havre was being "violently bombarded at the present moment" (7 a. m. German time, or 1 a. m. Eastern War Time).

"German naval forces are engaged in fighting with enemy landing craft off the coast."

Calais and Dunkirk, which Berlin said were under heavy air attack, are also important French ports along the invasion coast 150 miles northeast of Le Havre.

No Landings at Calais, Dunkirk

D. N. B. added that "no enemy landings were made yet," at Calais and Dunkirk, obviously an indication that the Germans were expecting Allied assaults all along the intervening 150 miles separating Dunkirk and Le Havre.

The German broadcasts on the "long-expected invasion" by the Allies were relayed both to North America and to Germans in the homeland. The latter were told by D. N. B.'s domestic broadcasts at dawn.

But half an hour after the first German broadcast announcing the landings, the Nazi-

See INVASION Page 9

FD Hails Rome's Fall; Sees Hard Fight Ahead

WASHINGTON, June 5 (AP)—Hailing the capture of Rome with the jubilant phrase "One Up and Two to Go," President Roosevelt declared tonight that the aim now is to drive Germany "to the point where she will be unable to recommence world conquest a generation hence."

Mr. Roosevelt, in a nation-wide radio broadcast, cautioned that this struggle with the Nazis would be tough and costly and that the day of Germany's surrender "lies some distance ahead."

Whether his reaffirmation that the fight would be pressed until Germany surrenders was a reply to the recent speech of Pope Pius XII was not stated. The Pope asserted last week that the idea that the war must end either in com-

See ROOSEVELT Page 7

'Great Crusade' Starts, Says Gen Eisenhower

By WES GALLAGHER

SUPREME HEADQUARTERS, Allied Expeditionary Force, June 6 (AP)—American, British and Canadian troops landed in northern France this morning, launching the greatest overseas military operation in history with word from their supreme commander, Gen Dwight D. Eisenhower, that "we will accept nothing except full victory" over the German masters of the Continent.

The invasion, which Eisenhower called "a great crusade," was announced at 7:32 A. M. Greenwich Mean Time (3:32 A. M. Eastern War Time) in this one-sentence communique No. 1:

"Under the command of Gen Eisenhower, Allied naval forces supported by strong air forces began landing Allied armies this morning on the northern coast of France."

It was announced moments later that Britain's Gen Sir Bernard L. Montgomery, hero of the African desert, was in charge of the assault.

The locations of the landings were not announced.

Eisenhower himself wished Godspeed to the parachutists who were the first to land on the enemy-held soil of France.

Allies Reinforced at Mouth of Seine

LONDON, June 6 (AP)—The German news agency D. N. B. said in a broadcast shortly before 10 a. m. (4 a. m., E. W. T.) that Anglo-American troops had been reinforced at dawn at the mouth of the Seine River in the Le Havre area.

LONDON, Tuesday, June 6 (AP)—The German-controlled Calais radio came on the air today with the following announcement in English:

"This is D-Day. We shall now bring music for the (Allied) invasion forces."

WARM

WEATHER
FRIDAY AND SATURDAY Fair, Moderate Winds
Full Report, Page 20.

The Boston Daily Globe

Reg. U. S. Pat. Off.

GUIDE TO FEATURES

G Allen ... 20	Financial . 16	Society ... 12
Burgess ... 12	Obituaries . 17	Sports 8
Culbertson . 12	Ernie Pyle . 20	Theatres .. 15
Deaths 17	Radio 11	V Forum .. 20
Editorials . 10	Serial 14	Women . 12-14
HOME FRONT CALENDAR 20		

VOL. CXLVII NO. 103 — Copyright, 1945 BY THE GLOBE NEWSPAPER CO. — BOSTON, FRIDAY MORNING, APRIL 13, 1945—TWENTY PAGES — THREE CENTS in New England 5c Elsewhere

ROOSEVELT DIES

TRUMAN SWORN IN

Truman

Victory Pledge First Act of New Executive

Special Dispatch to the Globe

WASHINGTON, April 12—Trim, gray Harry S. Truman the third Vice President to serve under Franklin D. Roosevelt, tonight became the 32d President of the United States.

In his first official act, he asked military leaders to meet with him Friday and issued this first pronouncement:

"The world may be sure that we will prosecute the war on both fronts, east and west, with all the vigor we possess, to a successful conclusion. In that faith and with that spirit of courage we must carry on."

At 7:09 tonight before the President's official family hastily assembled in the Cabinet Room of the White House, Mr. Truman took the oath from memory from Chief Justice Harlan F. Stone.

Less than two hours before he was called to the White House to receive the tragic news of the President's death from Mrs Roosevelt's own lips.

But when Presidential Secretary Stephen Early called him, Truman had a premonition. "I'm terribly afraid that something's happened," he told his secretary.

Arriving at the White House in the same gray double-breasted suit, white shirt and blue and white polka dot tie he had worn through his last Senate session,

See TRUMAN Page 4

TRUMAN TAKES OATH IN PRESENCE OF WIFE AND DAUGHTER—New President, with hand upraised, is sworn in in the Cabinet Room of executive offices at the White House. Mrs. Truman at center, daughter Margaret at right.

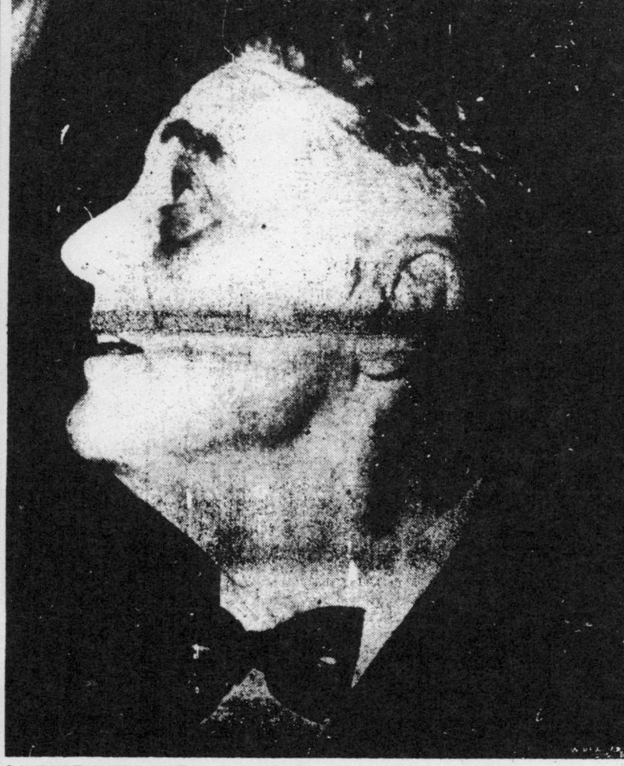

LATEST PICTURE OF F. D. R.—This photograph of President Franklin D. Roosevelt was made at the White House on March 29, 1945.

Roosevelt

Suffers Fatal Stroke at Warm Springs

WARM SPRINGS, Ga., Friday, April 13 (AP).—Plans were completed early today for a simple funeral for Franklin Delano Roosevelt as Mrs. Roosevelt arrived to join her beloved dead and begin the journey back to Washington.

The President's wife was flown from Washington in an Army plane and was taken immediately to the Warm Springs Foundation where Mr. Roosevelt died of cerebral hemorrhage at 4:35 p. m. (E. W. T.)

It was made known that the funeral train would start for Washington during the day, arriving Saturday for the funeral at 4 p. m. in the East Room of the White House. The room seats only 200 and only highest U. S. and foreign officials will attend.

Burial will be at the Roosevelt ancestral home at Hyde Park, N. Y., probably on Sunday.

The body will not lie in state.

His strength sapped by leadership in America's greatest war, Mr. Roosevelt's unexpected death today stunned the world.

Mr. Roosevelt's last words were:

"I have a terrific headache."

He spoke them to Com Harold Bruenn, naval physician.

Presidential Secretary William D. Hassett said Mr. Roose-

See ROOSEVELT Page 4

Globe Begins Truman Biography

Writer Just Back From Visit With Home Folks at Birthplace of New President

Three weeks ago the Globe asked Frances Burns of its staff to go to Lamar, Mo., where Harry S. Truman was born 61 years ago next May 8, and to follow in the footsteps which might some day bring him—and which now, by a tragic moment of fate, have brought him—to the White House.

FRANCES BURNS

Mrs. Burns visited with his 92-year-old mother, who did not know then that she soon was to be the mother of a President She visited with his sisters, his brother, his cousins, his town playmates, his teachers, the mid-West city politicians who started him on his political ladder which led to its highest rung.

Then this reporter returned to her typewriter at the Boston Globe and wrote a truly moving biography, which was filed away for use "if and when." It turned out to be the biography of the Missouri country boy who became 32d President of the United States.

In the first chapter, on the editorial page of today's Globe, Mrs. Burns takes Globe readers to Barton County, where John Truman bought a mule barn in 1881, and where the new President of the United States was born.

News of the War Fronts

★ ★ ★

Yanks Across Elbe, All Set for Order to Crash Berlin

★ ★ ★

Russians Cut Vienna Lifeline; Invade Southern Moravia

★ ★ ★

U. S. Destroyer Sunk, Other Craft Damaged at Okinawa.

Vessels Crash Off Woods Hole; 52 Casualties

NEW BEDFORD, April 12—Two British merchant vessels collided off Woods Hole this afternoon, and tonight 52 casualties, including an undisclosed number of dead, were brought to the State Pier by rescue vessels and rushed to hospitals in the vicinity.

The collision touched off a terrific explosion, leading to the belief that one of the vessels was carrying munitions.

State Guardsmen throughout the area were alerted. Police, Red Cross and hospital ambulances were ordered to the pier. Navy and Coast Guard patrol boats sped to the area of the crash.

Thirty-five beds were prepared for the injured at St. Luke's Hospital here. Other hospitals made ready to receive causalties were Union and Acushnet Hospitals here and Tobey Hospital, Wareham.

Tanks of 9th Army Sweep Within 57 Miles of Berlin

PARIS, Friday, April 13 (AP)—United States 9th Army tanks smashed across the Elbe River on a six-mile front just 57 miles from Berlin yesterday and United States 1st and 3d Armies, in sweeps of nearly 50 miles, thundered at the gates of the great city of Leipzig, 75 miles southwest of the capital.

A field dispatch said only orders from Lt Gen William H. Simpson were needed to send

See WEST Page 6

Russians Cut Lifeline of Nazis in Vienna

LONDON, Friday, April 13 (AP)—Russian armored forces, leaving doomed Nazi forces in Vienna only a seven-mile escape gap, yesterday cut the Austrian capital's last lifelines with the Czecho-Slovak city of Bruenn (Brno) while spearheads burst within 33 miles of

See RUSSIAN Page 6

Schools Plan Brief Exercises Today Before Closing

School classes in Boston and throughout the state will be cancelled today, but pupils and teachers will assemble at the various buildings for brief memorial exercises in tribute to the dead President.

Gov. Tobin last night issued a request to all superintendents to assemble their pupils as usual this morning, conduct services, and then dismiss classes for the day.

See SCHOOLS Page 6

Marine Killed Wife, Shot Self, He Says

Special Dispatch to the Globe

MARLBORO, April 12—Marine Cpl Stanley (Kwaithowsky, 24, a veteran of 21 months in the Pacific, shot and killed his wife, Lillian, 24,

See MURDER Page 6

El Men Vote 2 Men to Work 2-Car Trains

Rescinding their action of a previous regular meeting, members of the Boston Carmen's Union last night voted to operate the two-

See EL Page 6

Boston Temperature at 85 Tops Record

With the mercury percolating up to the 85 mark in Boston at 4 p. m. yesterday, to break, by 16 degrees, the existing April 12 record set in 1938, summerish weather

See HEAT Page 15

Boston Evening Globe

Reg. U. S. Pat. Off.

VOL. CXLVII NO. 128 TUESDAY, MAY 8, 1945
32 PAGES—THREE CENTS in New England 5c Elsewhere

DAY OF PRAYER SUNDAY

In both his speech and his proclamation today President Truman carefully avoided any mention of "V-E Day." Churchill referred to "Victory in Europe Days," today and tomorrow, holidays in Great Britain. No word by Stalin. Pockets of Germans still holding out against Russians.

ONLY HALF OVER--Truman

Immediately after signing the surrender with a bold "Jodl," the Nazi arose, bowed and in a broken voice, pleaded for generosity . . .

(AP Wirephoto From Signal Corps Radiophoto.)

After Col Gen Gustav Jodl (center), Chief of Staff under Adm Doenitz, signed the unconditional surrender, he turned to American Gen Bedell Smith and said: "General, with this signature the German people and the German armed forces are for the better or worse delivered into the victors' hands."

"Our Rejoicing Subdued by Terrible Price We Have Paid to Rid World of Hitler"

Advises Japanese to Surrender

Watchword for Coming Months: Work, Work, Work

WASHINGTON, May 8 (UP)—President Truman today proclaimed victory in Europe but told the nation its fighting job would be finished only "when the last Japanese division has surrendered unconditionally."

He said "our victory is only half won." He gave this counsel for the months to come:

"Work, work, work."

He gave this advice to the Japanese: Surrender.

Truman Continued on Page 13

WEATHER

CLEARING TONIGHT, FAIR WEDNESDAY

(Full reports on page 16.)

Red Streak Final
(Closing Prices—Net Changes)

IN TONIGHT'S GLOBE

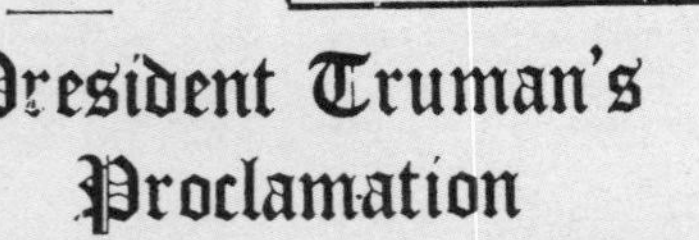

Comics	28	Radio	28
Cross-Word	23	Society	19
Culbertson	23	Serial Story	23
Deaths	27	Sports	25
Editorial	18	Theatres	24
Financial	29	Women's	26, 27
Home Front	23		

It Took Germans 5 Minutes to Sign 4 Copies of Surrender

By BOYD D. LEWIS

RHEIMS, France, May 7 (UP)—Representatives of four Allied powers and vanquished Germany scrawled their names on a sheet of foolscap in a map-lined 30 by 30-foot room at 2:41 a. m., European time, today and ended World War II in Europe.

I witnessed this historic scene.

In a ceremony exactly 20 minutes long, Col Gen Gustav Jodl, chief of staff of Adm Doenitz' Government and long-time close friend of Adolf Hitler, surrendered all German armed forces on land, sea and in the air.

Surrender Continued on Page 13

End of War Bulletins

Surrender terms become effective at one minute after midnight, 12:01 a. m., May 9, 1945, Paris time—6:01 p. m. today Boston time.

★ ★ ★

Allies flash radio orders to German ships at sea to head for nearest Allied ports.

★ ★ ★

Gen Patton issued a cease fire order to the 3d Army at 8 a. m. yesterday. This was 2 a. m. Eastern War Time.

★ ★ ★

Allied envoys fly to Norway to accept surrender.

"Last Half of War" Bulletin

WITH THE UNITED STATES 10TH ARMY ON OKINAWA, May 8 (CDN)—Five hundred American guns boomed a salute here at noon today. That was our principal gesture toward a V-E Day celebration and it served a double purpose. For the shells fell among our Pacific enemy, who has not yet surrendered, either in southern Okinawa or in his homeland.

Heartaches From Pacific Temper Hub Celebration

Boston's observance of the end of the war in Europe was at first an exuberant reception of the President's proclamation and then restraint. It was like a combination of the Fourth of July and a Sunday. Tens of thousands crowded into churches.

Ticker tape and paper scraps were strewn along the streets. Flags waved gayly in the breeze. To the observer it was as if a festival parade had passed. Yet along the streets the crowds moved slowly without any perceptible gayety. The retail stores were closed and their clerks thronged the streets.

There seemed to be a policeman on every street corner. But there was nothing to do. The strollers were leisurely in movement and orderly in conduct. Here and there a group of girls tried to stage an impromptu parade, singing "God Bless America" and similar songs, but the parade soon petered out.

The big detail of police found little to do. Automobile traffic was at a minimum on the main highways, due perhaps to an earlier warning that the streets of Boston might be closed to all but emergency traffic. That move was not necessary, except in cases of Washington and Tremont sts., which were closed from Stuart st. to Dock sq. and Scollay sq., respectively.

Knowledge of the heartaches to the New England families yet to come from the fighting fronts in the South Pacific, as well as the fact that the President's speech was an anti-climax after the Associated Press announcement of the unconditional surrender yesterday, combined to prevent any "cutting up" or wild sprees.

Department and specialty stores of the Boston Retail Board were closed for the day. Food stores remained open to prevent waste of perishable food. Liquor establishments remained open in Boston and Mayor Kerrigan said he had no power to close them unless trouble developed. The Licensing Board said it would take no action and it was up to the individual operating a cafe, tavern or package store as to whether he should close.

Boston Continued on Page 13

V-E Day at a Glance

TRAFFIC—Tremont st., from Broadway to Scollay sq., and Washington st., from Broadway to Court st., have been reserved for pedestrians and emergency vehicles only. No other traffic will be allowed on these streets, according to an order of Police Commissioner Sullivan. Automobiles will be allowed to enter the city.

STORES—All member stores of the Retail Board, including department and specialty stores, closed. Gasoline stations, food and drug stores open. Other business establishments open or closed, according to individual decisions.

SCHOOLS—Remained open and held patriotic exercises.

Program Continued on Page 13

Department Stores Close Today, Food Stores Stay Open

Department and specialty stores of Boston in the membership of the Retail Trade Board, are closing today, but will be open as usual tomorrow. Food stores will be open as usual today to prevent waste of perishable foods, it was announced this morning by Daniel Bloomfield, manager of the Retail Trade Board.

The following statement was made by Bloomfield:

"Department and specialty stores in the membership of the Retail Trade Board will close today, but will be open all day tomorrow as usual. Food stores will be open as usual to prevent waste of perishable foods.

"The Retail Trade Board feels that this is not a time for celebration, but for prayer and strengthening of determination to destroy the enemy in the Pacific. We still have a war to win. Every ounce of energy must be applied to enable war industries to meet the accelerated needs of our fighting forces."

PRESIDENT TRUMAN

"I only wish that Franklin D. Roosevelt had lived to witness this day," the President told his listeners today. Later he ordered flowers placed on Roosevelt's grave.

Unconfirmed Report Hitler's Body Found

WITH THE BRITISH 2D ARMY, May 8 (AP)—Col Anotoly Pilugin, war correspondent of Tass, official Soviet news agency, has said a Russian General had stated that the body of a man identified as Adolf Hitler had been found in the ruins of Berlin.

The Russian General was not named.

During a meeting two days ago between Marshal Sir Bernard L. Montgomery and Marshal Konstantin Rokossovsky of the 2d White Russian Army, Russian officers asked Pilugin, who is attached to the British 2d Army as a war correspondent, whether the British believed Hitler was dead or alive.

Pilugin said he replied there was a mixed opinion, but that the Russian General, whose identity he did not disclose, stated that the Russians had found in Berlin the bullet-torn and battered body of a man identified as Hitler.

President Truman's Proclamation

Designating Sunday, May 13, 1945, as a Day of Prayer

By the President of the United States of America.

A proclamation:

The Allied armies, through sacrifice and devotion and with God's help, have won from Germany a final and unconditional surrender. The western world has been freed of the evil forces which for five years and longer have imprisoned the bodies and broken the lives of millions upon millions of freeborn men. They have violated their churches, destroyed their homes, corrupted their children, and murdered their loved ones. Our armies of liberation have restored freedom to these suffering peoples, whose spirit and will the oppressors could never enslave.

Much remains to be done. The victory won in the west must now be won in the east. The whole world must be cleansed of the evil from which half the world has been freed. United, the peace loving nations have demonstrated in the west that their arms are stronger by far than the might of dictators or the tyranny of military cliques that once called us soft and weak. The power of our peoples to defend themselves against all enemies will be proved in the Pacific as it has been proved in Europe.

For the triumph of spirit and of arms which we have won, and for its promise to peoples everywhere who join us in the love of freedom it is fitting that we, as a nation, give thanks to Almighty God, Who has strengthened us and given us the victory.

Now, therefore, I, Harry S. Truman, President of the United States of America, do hereby appoint Sunday, May 13, 1945, to be a day of prayer.

I call upon the people of the United States, whatever their faith, to unite in offering joyful thanks to God for the victory we have won and to pray that He will support us to the end of our present struggle and guide us into the way of peace.

I also call upon my countrymen to dedicate this day of prayer to the memory of those who have given their lives to make possible our victory.

In witness whereof, I have hereunto set my hand and caused the seal of the United States of America to be affixed.

Done at the city of Washington this eighth day of May, in the year of our Lord, 1945, and of the independence of the United States of America the 169th.

HARRY S. TRUMAN.

"The Japs May Expect a Rain of Ruin From the Air, the Like of Which Has Never Been Seen on This Earth"
—PRESIDENT TRUMAN

ATOMIC BOMB BLASTS JAPAN

Yanks Loose Most Destructive Force in History

Boston Evening Globe

Reg. U. S. Pat. Off. (Copyright, 1945, by the Globe Newspaper Co.)

VOL. CXLVIII NO. 37 MONDAY, AUG. 6, 1945 20 PAGES—THREE CENTS in New England 5c Elsewhere

SECRET WEAPON USED FOR FIRST TIME SUNDAY

Scientists Harness Atomic Energy (the Force From Which the Sun Draws Its Power)

★ ★ ★

Cost $2,000,000,000 in Research—Greatest Scientific Gamble in History "and We Won"

★ ★ ★

More Powerful Than 20,000 Tons of T.N.T.

Has 2000 Times Blast Force of British "Grand Slam" (11 Tons)

★ ★ ★

In Peace Time the New Force May Take the Place of Coal, Oil, Water Power

★ ★ ★

This Was the Threat of "Utter Destruction" in the Potsdam Ultimatum

★ ★ ★

Truman Thanks God We Beat Germans to It

WASHINGTON, Aug. 6 (AP)—An atomic bomb, hailed as the most terrible destructive force in history and as the greatest achievement of organized science, has been loosed upon Japan.

President Truman disclosed in a White House statement at 11 a. m. (E. W. T.) today that the first use of the bomb—containing more power than 20,000 tons of T. N. T. and producing more than 2000 times the blast of the most powerful bomb ever dropped before—was made 16 hours earlier on Hiro Shima, Japanese Army base.

The atomic bomb is the answer, President Truman said, to Japan's refusal to surrender. Secretary of War Stimson predicted the bomb will "prove a tremendous aid" in shortening the Japanese war.

Mr. Truman grimly warned that "even more powerful forms (of the bomb) are in development." He said:

Bomb

Continued on Page 12

Stoneman Tipped Globe Readers on Uranium Bomb

By JOHN BARRY
(Editor, Boston Globe War Diary)

Globe readers would be justified in concluding on the basis of information transmitted on two occasions by William H. Stoneman, special correspondent in London, that the so-called "atomic bomb" is a "uranium bomb."

The uranium bomb is a minor species of the atomic bomb, in that

Stoneman

Continued on Page 8

(Other Stories on New Atomic Bomb on Pages 7, 8, 9, 12 and 13)

WEATHER

RAIN TONIGHT

(Full reports on page 12.)

Red Streak Final
(Closing Prices—Net Changes)

IN TONIGHT'S GLOBE

Comics	17	Home Front	14
Cross-Word	17	Radio	17
Culbertson	17	Serial Story	11
Deaths	16	Society	9
Editorial	14	Sports	15
Financial	16	Theatres	10
Gangplank	5	Women's	20

Snaring of Dogs in East Boston Causes Copious Juvenile Tears

(Photo by Thomas O'Connor, Globe staff)

IN THE PADDY WAGON—Failing to show the necessary walking papers (license tags to you), these forlorn-looking canines were among the 16 dogs rounded up in East Boston this morning as authorities moved to check epidemic of biting. They are shown on truck arriving at the pound.

By MARJORIE MARTIN

The four hunters on East Boston's dog rodeo, designed to keep unlicensed pooches off the street and put an end to a new high of persons being bitten by dogs in the area, made a fast start today—snaring 16 unlicensed dogs in 90 minutes.

Children of the district supplied plenty of tears and abuse as the dogs were lassoed or otherwise grabbed by three men from the Animal Rescue League and an East Boston police officer.

The catch that caused the most trouble was a brown collie and the agents were threatened by children. "He's a Marine dog," they shouted. "He jumped on Germans. Leave him alone."

The dog itself tried to outwit his pursuers, but was finally taken with a "bull whip" type of lasso. The agents said the use of this type of "lasso" does not injure the dog, although some of the onlookers complained because it was used. It is the standard type used in catching dogs.

The hunt started on Sumner st., East Boston, and then moved into the Orient Heights section. Supt. John Finlayson of the Animal Rescue League drove the "pick-up" truck and his crew consisted of Sherman Bates and Harry McGregor. They are the two official dog catchers of the city of Boston.

There were many poignant scenes. The dog rodeo crew felt as keenly about taking a dog away as did the children or owner without a license. But they had to be taken and the owner may claim the dog by showing a license taken out even after the dog was snatched, at the Animal Rescue League dog shelter at 366 Albany st., South End.

Just when the seventh dog was snared on Sumner st., a woman ran out of her home in a house coat and screamed, "They've Cutie and I forgot the license." Cutie was taken along.

Dogs

Continued on Page 6

New Carrier Hornet Damaged by Huge Wave

WASHINGTON, Aug. 6 (AP)—A mountainous wave lifted up and smacked down the 27,000-ton aircraft carrier Hornet so hard last June 5 that the forward corners of the flight deck folded down along the sides.

Thus nature, in the form of a 120-knot gale (138 miles an hour), achieved what the Japanese never were able to do in 14 months of hard-fought action—it damaged the big ship.

(The United Press said the Hornet is scheduled to be ready for sea again in three weeks, in time to participate in the final assault against the Japanese homeland. Her repairs have been estimated at a cost of $2,-200,000.)

The Navy told the Hornet's story today. It let the Japanese know exactly where the Hornet is—Hunters Point in San Francisco Bay. She steamed through the Golden Gate July 7 and went to dry dock for repair.

Behind her lay 1,270,000 tons of enemy shipping sunk or damaged and 1410 ruined enemy planes.

Some of the figures:

Six hundred and sixty-eight planes shot down, 742 planes destroyed on the ground, one cruiser sunk, one carrier sunk, 10 destroyers sunk, 42 cargo ships sunk.

Hornet

Continued on Page 2

Actress to Wed

MARGO, Mexican actress and dancer, who revealed yesterday in Hollywood that she is engaged to marry Eddie Albert, former romantic comedian, now a Navy lieutenant. No date has been set.

Sailor Held Without Bail in Dracut Skeleton Case

LOWELL, Aug. 6 — Alphee Norman Desmarais, 22-year-old Tyngsboro sailor who returned a month ago from the South Pacific war, was formally charged in District Court here today with the murder of Mrs. Mary Saunders whose skeleton was found in the Dracut woods last Wednesday.

Desmarais, who admitted to police that he was with the woman on the last day she was seen alive, entered a plea of innocence to the murder charge and the case was continued until Sept. 8. Judge Arthur L. Eno ordered him held without bail.

The sailor, a ship's cook second class, appeared in uniform in court this morning. Four battle stars were on his row of service

Skeleton

Continued on Page 6

ALPHEE N. DESMARAIS, C2c, USN.

Senator Hiram Johnson Dies at 79

WASHINGTON, Aug. 6 (AP)—Senator Hiram W. Johnson of California, militant opponent of the League of Nations and the San Francisco Charter for a United Nations organization, died today at 79 years.

The veteran Republican Senator succumbed at Naval Hospital, where he had been confined for 2½ weeks. His physician, Capt. Robert E. Duncan, USN, said he died from a thrombosis of a cerebral artery.

A striking figure in the Senate since first elected to Congress in 1916, he played a leading part in defeating President Wilson's League of Nations covenant and later in opposing United States' adherence to the World Court.

Johnson

Continued on Page 4

Classified Advertisements

Do not appear in the early morning edition, but do appear in all other editions. Restrictions in the use of newsprint paper ordered by the War Production Board make this necessary. The Globe also reserves the right to restrict to certain editions other advertising in the event that paper shortage requires it.

3 Transports Disembark More Than 4000 Here Today

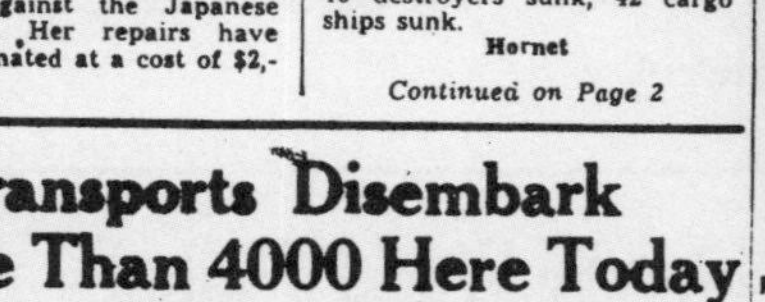

The first of three transports scheduled to arrive at the Boston Port of Embarkation today, the S. S. Pierre L'Enfant, docked at the Army Base Pier shortly before noon, carrying 554 miscellaneous troop personnel, including 35 New Englanders.

The Helen Hunt Jackson with 561 troops aboard and the Marine Robin carrying more than 3000 troops and casuals reached here this afternoon.

Pfc Jean Goldberg, 138 Essex st., Malden, revealed that during his stay in England he married a 27-year-old Hungarian girl, Rosalie Hegedus, whom he hopes will soon be able to join him here in this country. Goldberg said that he knew his wife 2½ years before they were married. "English girls aren't so hot," related Goldberg, "but those Continental girls really are something!"

Transports

Continued on Page 5

Gould Opposes Method of Making List of Eligible Headmasters

In a friendly revolt against the system in the Boston public schools through which a list is made up of candidates for headmasters of high schools, Supt. of Schools Arthur L. Gould today refused to submit such a list to the School Committee.

Supt. Gould disclosed to the committee that he was supported in his position by five of the six assistant superintendents who make up the list. Asst. Supt. Frederick J. Gillis said he believed the list as made up should have been presented.

Schools

Continued on Page 5

Widow of Founder of Brokerage Firm Leaves $4,000,000

DEDHAM, Aug. 6—Mrs. Carrie Morton Gregg Stone, 78, widow of Galen Stone, founder of the brokerage firm of Hayden, Stone & Co., left an estate of $4,000,000 when she died July 28, her will disclosed when it was filed in Probate Court here today.

Mrs. Stone left the bulk of her estate in trust for the benefit of her children. She made a total of $50,-000 in public bequests and also left bequests to domestics and other family employees. Her children are Lt Col Robert G. Stone, Brookline; Mrs. Huntington R. Hardwick, Brookline; and Mrs. John P. Chase, Canton.

The public bequests were: Christian Science Society, Buzzards Bay and Pleasant View Home, Concord, N. H., $10,000 each; Mt. Pleasant Home, South End House Association, Children's Friend Society,

Estate

Continued on Page 6

Tests Made in N. H. Will Help Yanks in Tokyo Drive

MT. WASHINGTON, N. H., Aug. 6 (AP)—Practical lessons on "how to keep dry in a foxhole" are being given to selected Army personnel atop this "wet-cold weather" area as a measure of protection on the drive on Tokyo, the Army disclosed today.

The Army chose this spot as ideal for the tests, in view of the hot Summer weather at Pinkhams

Foxholes

Continued on Page 5

Woman's Handbag Snatched at Revere

REVERE, Aug. 6—Despite the capture last week by police of four handbag snatchers, another victim reported an attack to the police last night as the beach concessions were closing. Mrs. George Lamb of 50 Wyman st., Arlington, said that two young men pushed her off balance, grabbed her bag and ran.

Stalin Too Busy to Dye Moustache

By ED JOHNSON
(Boston Globe-Chicago Sun)

BERLIN, Aug. 5—A British security officer who has attended the Teheran, Yalta and Potsdam conferences reported that Marshal Stalin dyes, or has someone else dye, his mustache.

"He's gone quite grey," the officer said. "Usually he touches his moustache up a bit. This time at Potsdam I noticed he'd rather let it go at the edges."

Waste Paper Once Reprocessed

Is war paper. Paper sent overseas doesn't come back; paper for home use can be used again.

1. Conserve paper. Use your own shopping bags.
2. Save Waste Paper. Never burn waste paper, but turn in every scrap after separating and bundling it.

Advertisements may be ordered at the Globe office or by telephone. Call LAFayette 2000.

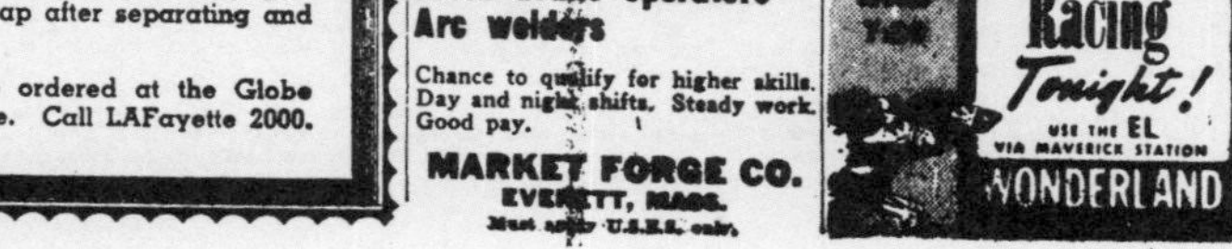

MALE HELP WANTED
Laborers and general help
Punch press operators
Press brake operators
Arc welders
Chance to qualify for higher skills. Day and night shifts. Steady work. Good pay.
MARKET FORGE CO.
EVERETT, MASS.
Must apply U.S.E.S. rules.

Greyhound Racing Tonight!
USE THE EL VIA MAVERICK STATION
WONDERLAND

Free Advice, Service Men—Franklin Technical Institute, 31 Berkeley Street, BAK. 6390.

BURDETT COLLEGE
Business training for post-war employment. ACCOUNTING, BUSINESS ADMINISTRATION, SECRETARIAL COURSES. Close attention paid to individual needs. Adequate facilities. Activities program. DAY and EVENING classes. Adult Education program (Evenings) also includes Salesmanship, English, Advertising, Income Tax, the nationally famous DALE CARNEGIE Course in Effective Speaking. Veterans counseled without obligation.
Day term starts Sept. 10. Evening term, Sept. 17. Send for catalogue. PLEASE specify day or evening.

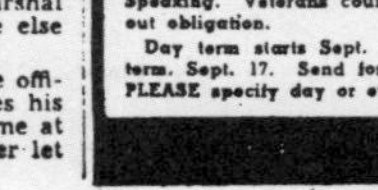

Boston Evening Globe

Reg. U.S. Pat. Off. (Copyright 1945, by the Globe Newspaper Co.

TUESDAY, AUG. 14, 1945

26 PAGES—THREE CENTS

OFFICIAL

WEATHER
PARTLY CLOUDY, WARM TONIGHT
(Full reports on Page 16.)

Red Streak Final
(Closing Prices—Net Changes)

IN TONIGHT'S GLOBE

Comics	23	Radio	20
Cross-Word	14	Serial Story	11
Culbertson	20	Society	10
Deaths	22	Sports	15
Editorial	18	Theatres	11
Financial	22	Women's	20, 21
Home Front	18		

President Truman Announces

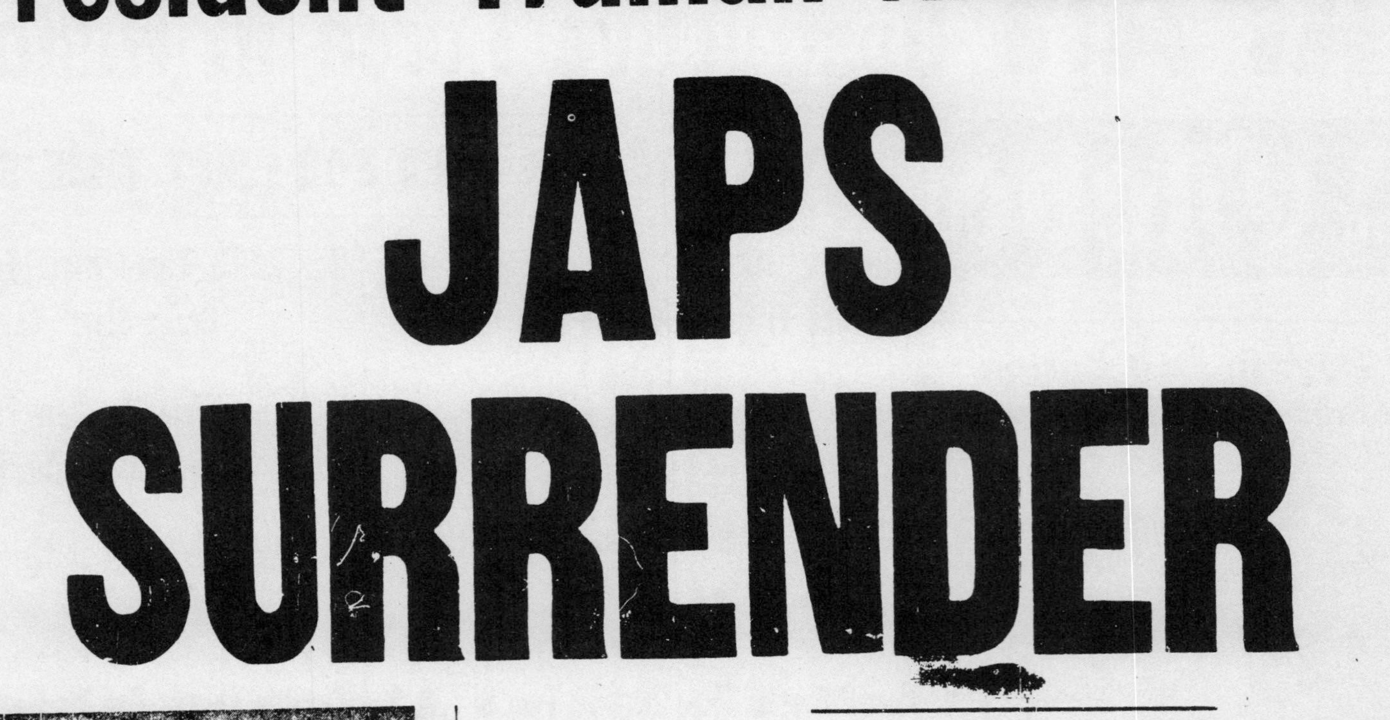

JAPS SURRENDER

PRESIDENT TRUMAN

This Means End of War

V-J Day Coming Later

MacArthur to Accept Terms

WASHINGTON, Aug. 14 (AP)—President Truman announced at 7:00 P. M. EWT tonight Japanese acceptance of surrender terms.

They will be accepted by Gen Douglas MacArthur when arrangements can be completed.

GEN MacARTHUR

Fighting Words That Will Live

A. P. Newsfeatures

Japan's attack on Pearl Harbor led to many memorable quotations. Among them:

President Roosevelt—"Dec. 7, 1941 . . . a date which will live in infamy."

Winston Churchill—"It only remains for two great democracies to face their task with whatever strength God may give them."

Senator Burton K. Wheeler, (Dem., of Montana), Roosevelt's foreign policy foe—"The only thing now is to . . . lick hell out of them."

President Manuel Quezon of the Philippines—"The flag of the United States will be defended until the last round of ammunition has been fired."

Emperor Hirohito of Japan—"The hallowed spirits of our imperial ancestors. . . . give us confidence."

Adolf Hitler—"That Japan took this step must fill all decent people with profound satisfaction."

Attache at New York Japanese consulate, clearing out his belongings—"This is a special Sunday."

How the World Waited

By the Associated Press

Here is a time-table of events as Washington and the world awaited Japan's reply to terms that could formally take her out of the war: (Eastern War Time throughout.)

SATURDAY, Aug. 11, 10:30 A. M.—Secretary of State Byrnes' statement on Tokyo's surrender offer and clarification of the Emperor's status was delivered to the Swiss Legation at 10:30 a. m., for relay via Bern to Tokyo.

12:30 P. M.—After conferring with President Truman, **Senate Leader** Alben W. Barkley announced Congress would be reconvened probably Sept. 4 to act on reconversion legislation.

6 P. M.—White House sent staff home and said, "There will be no announcements tonight." It advised newsmen to be on hand at 8:30 a. m. Sunday.

SUNDAY, Aug. 12, 8 A. M.—Tension increased when President Truman came to his office half an hour ahead of schedule. Crowds gathered across the street in Lafayette sq. Meanwhile, the Jap radio reported routine news. B-29's plastered the home islands. There was speculation over whether Tokyo even had received the terms.

5:50 P. M.—Charles Ross, White House secretary, said there was no news from Tokyo and "the war still is in progress."

9:34 P. M.—The United Press carried a flash: "Washington—Japan accepts surrender terms of Allies." Celebrations started almost all over the Allied world.

9:36 P. M.—The United Press asked that the flash be withheld from publication and broadcast.

9:40 P. M.—The United Press killed the flash, explaining that it did not know how it got on the U.P. wires. The premature celebrations kept going in many places.

10 P. M.—President Truman went to bed.

10:25 P. M.—Ross announced, "Nothing has been received by the President, the War Department, the Navy or the State Department. . . . We are still waiting." More than 30 hours then had elapsed since the surrender terms were given the Japanese legation at Bern, Switzerland.

12 Midnight—The White House told reporters there would be nothing before 9 a. m., Monday.

MONDAY, Aug. 13, 10:45 A. M.—White House said no reply had been received and Ross declared "it is safe to say the war is going on." A Tokyo Radio broadcast said the Byrnes statement had not been received until Sunday night, United States time.

About 11 A. M.—OPA announced it had halted printing of new ration books. Byrnes received the Distinguished Service Medal from President Truman in recognition for his home front war services.

About 11:30 A. M.—China's Ambassador, Dr. Wei Tao-Ming told White House newsmen, "I believe the good news will come at any moment." Pacific Fleet units and bombers kept battering Japan.

3 P. M.—White House announced "no word from Japan."

5:30 P. M.—Ross again announced, "Nothing new."

10:30 P. M.—Ross announced: "The President has gone to bed; there is no news."

12 Midnight—The "lid" went on at the White House and newsmen were told to return at 9 a. m. Tuesday.

Tuesday, Aug. 14, at 1:50 A. M.—Tokyo radio flashed: "The text of an Imperial message accepting the Potsdam proclamations will be forthcoming soon."

2:30 A. M.—The President's naval aide, Commodore James K. Vardaman, arrived at White House. Except for three news photographers, the executive offices were deserted.

7:02 A. M.—Ross arrived and announced, "You may say that the President is up and fully aware of all that's going on."

8:11 A. M.—Secretary of State Byrnes arrived at the State Department but had no news.

8:30 A. M.—President Truman reached his office and conferred with Byrnes. Crowds began gathering in Lafayette Park, expecting an official announcement momentarily.

9:50 A. M.—Ross told reporters the Japanese reply to the Allied note "is now in the hands of the Swiss. . . . It looks as if we're at last nearing the end of our long vigil."

10:27 A. M.—Domei, Japanese News Agency, said in a broadcast, "the Imperial decision was granted" and that weeping people had assembled before his palace and "bowed to the very ground" in their shame that their "efforts were not enough."

11:05 A. M.—The War Labor Board in Washington formally lifted the lid on pay for time not worked—if employers want to give a holiday for V-J Day celebrations.

11:15 A. M.—Swiss legation in Washington told newsmen that it had not yet received word from Bern to indicate any Japanese note was in Swiss hands.

11:57 A. M.—State Secretary Byrnes again conferred with the President.

12:24 P. M.—Swiss legation memorandum to White House said coded cables received earlier in Bern do not contain the answer awaited by the whole world. And surrender reply not yet received.

(This followed by minutes a new Tokyo Radio broadcast that "the Japanese Government's reply to the four powers is now on its way to the Japanese Minister in Bern".)

A FREAKISH DAY
WEDNESDAY: Windy, ... change to ... snow, sleet, etc.
THURSDAY: Fair, cold.
Full Report on Page 32

The Boston Daily Globe

Reg. U. S. Pat. Off.

GUIDE TO FEATURES
Alsop 28 · Dr. Crane 21 · Society 4 · Burgess 21 · Editorials 18 · Sports 12-13 · Comics 20-21 · Financial 26-27 · Teens 23 · Cross Word 20 · Obituaries 2 · Theatre 24-25 · Culbertson 21 · Radio-TV 21 · Forum 4 · Deaths 27 · Serial 26 · Women 22-23

VOL. CLVII NO. 18 · Copyright 1950 By THE GLOBE NEWSPAPER CO. · BOSTON, WEDNESDAY MORNING, JANUARY 18, 1950 · 32 PAGES—FIVE CENTS

$1,500,000 HOLDUP

7 Masked Men Rob Brink's, Boston; Leave Another Million

(Photos by Edward F. Carr and Charles Carey, Globe Staff)

VICTIM AND SCENE IN ROBBERY—Messenger Grell, left, shows how arms were bound. View in vault, right, shows sacks holding ignored $1,000,000. In photo are Manager Lloyd (foreground) and Detective Armstrong. Cap was dropped by one of gang.

Biggest All-Cash Stickup in U. S. at Armored Truck Garage

Gang Wore Pea Jackets, Rubbers; Carried .38's; Suspects on Police Grill

Police Searching Houses in Foxboro

Scores of police officials, all heavily armed, from Boston, Foxboro, Dedham and State Police and the FBI were making house-to-house searches at 4 this morning along Route 1 in Foxboro after a truck driver reported seeing seven Pea-jacket clad men, carrying bags, leave an automobile and enter a house.

One Foxboro resident was roused out of bed and ordered to come out of his home. He was clad in pajamas. Police surrounded each house they approached. They were equipped with portable searchlights and machine guns.

Boston police under Capt. John D. Ahern and Deputy Superintendent James F. Daley rendezvoused at the Foxboro Raceway after meeting in Dedham, where they picked up additional arms.

By JEROME SULLIVAN

In the biggest cash robbery in the history of the United States, seven gunmen in Halloween masks held up Brink's, Inc., the armored truck concern, in Boston's North End at 7:10 last night and escaped with more than $1,000,000.

At 2:30 a. m. Police Commissioner Thomas F. Sullivan said the loot will total "at least $1.500,000."

Another million dollars was left behind, officials said.

Scene of the holdup was the second floor offices of the armored truck company in the North Terminal Garage at Prince and Commercial sts.

The loot represented payroll pickups and receipts from Metropolitan Boston business concerns.

Police said nine gunmen in all were involved in the stickup. Two accomplices remained outside the building in a getaway car.

All captains and detectives in the entire Boston Police Department were ordered to duty immediately. Later two FBI agents entered the probe.

Police Commissioner Thomas F. Sullivan, accompanied by Supt. Edward W. Fallon, arrived on the scene within minutes after the stickup. Orders were flashed to pick up every known criminal in the city.

All of the robbers, in addition to their masks, wore Navy pea jackets, and rubbers on their feet. All of them carried black, long-barreled, Army-type .38 calibre revolvers.

See HOLDUP Page 10

Police Commissioner Sullivan Mobilizes Department

Boston Police Headquarters was in a turmoil last night minutes after the holdup as every precinct captain and detective responded to a mobilization order sent out by Commissioner Thomas F. Sullivan.

This city had never seen such a mass meeting of top-ranking officials since the Cocoanut Grove disaster in 1942. Never before has such a conference been ordered in connection with a crime.

Within 20 minutes after word of the robbery was flashed on the police radio, the streets surrounding the headquarters building on Berkeley st. were jammed with automobiles and police cruising cars.

Station captains and detectives bolted from the vehicles and raced up the stairs to assemble in a room where Commissioner Sullivan was scheduled to issue orders pertaining to the apprehension of the gunmen.

While department communication systems buzzed with messages relayed to distant points throughout the country, Commissioner Sullivan was still at the scene directing the

See POLICE Page 7

Coal Strike Spreads, Violence Breaks Out

PITTSBURGH, Jan. 17 (UP)—Shooting, stoning and dynamiting broke out in the soft coal fields today as a "no contract, no work" strike spread to six states idling 89,000 miners and threatening to cut off power to 2000 industries here.

Angry pickets toured the fields closing mine after mine and a striking miner in Ohio was killed when he tried to stop a loaded coal truck. It was the first death in the strike, but restiveness and growing indications were that more miners would walk out tomorrow.

The seriousness of the coal situation was pointed up in Pittsburgh where steel mills and other industries might have to close later this week because of the fuel shortage.

Ohio State Police at St. Clairsville reported that Sildio Dalpaiz, 53, of Lafferty, O., was killed by a coal truck driven by Lawrence Franks, 20, of Piedmont, O.

See COAL Page 15

~~Death Mars~~ Boston Girl's Radio Bridal

A young Roxbury woman was married yesterday with a coast-to-coast radio audience listening in—but her happiness turned to grief when the program signed off.

During the wedding ceremony in Los Angeles, the mother of the bridegroom, Donald Barnes, died in a nearby lounge in the radio studio.

The bride is the former Miss Frances M. Dermody, 21, of Dorr st., Roxbury. During the first part of the program in the afternoon, Mrs. Dorothy Barnes collapsed.

While the ceremony was going on, Mrs. Barnes died. On learning the news, the young couple tearfully canceled a planned honeymoon in Reno.

The radio marriage and honeymoon was a prize won by the Roxbury woman after writing a letter to the program describing her romance. She told how she and Barnes had met at a Summer camp in Groton, N. H., where they were counselors.

A cross-country courtship followed between Roxbury and La Mesa, Calif., Barnes' home.

The bride formerly was employed with a Boston insurance company.

Reorganization Urged of Public Works Dept.

By WILLIAM J. LEWIS

The Finance Commission last night recommended an extensive reorganization of the Public Works Department and elimination of 595 positions to save $1,356,614 annually, "without the impairment of any essential services."

This would mean a reduction of nearly $1 on the 1950 tax rate. The 595 jobs represent more than 20 percent of the department's personnel.

A Finance Commission spokesman said the commission favors immediate dismissal of all constables and temporary employees in this group, but the remainder of the 595 jobs should be eliminated by a "no-hiring" policy—when they are vacated by retirement, resignation or death, he said.

The 500-page report compiled by the Fin. Com. and its surveyor, Griffenhagen and Associates of New York, has been submitted to Public Works Commissioner George G. Hyland.

See FIN COM Page 5

13 Picked Up as Suspects in Brink's Holdup

A total of 13 persons were held by police for questioning about the B nk's, Inc., holdup this morning, three hours after Commissioner Thomas F. Sullivan's police mobilization order.

Eleven of those detained had police records and the other two were former employees of Brink's.

They were held at City Prison and later this morning the best detectives in the police force were giving them a thorough grilling.

Brought to headquarters last night were men from Roxbury, Revere, South Boston and Brighton. Charlestown station took six suspects in tow, and Roxbury Crossing and the South End station each picked up one man apiece.

All through the night police scoured the city for suspects. In a steady stream they filed into Police Headquarters and division stations.

Those with records for armed robbery were checked and the department's crack detectives were kept on the run all night

See SUSPECTS Page 7

Hydrogen Bomb Policy Depends Upon Russia

WASHINGTON, Jan. 17 (UP)—President Truman's momentous decision on whether the United States should make a hydrogen bomb—the world's most awesome weapon—was reported today to hinge on whether Russia will come to terms on atomic energy control.

Informed quarters said Mr. Truman will decide "in the near future" about asking Congress for funds to attempt construction of the superbomb which would be 1000 times more destructive than present A-bombs.

See ATOMIC Page 15

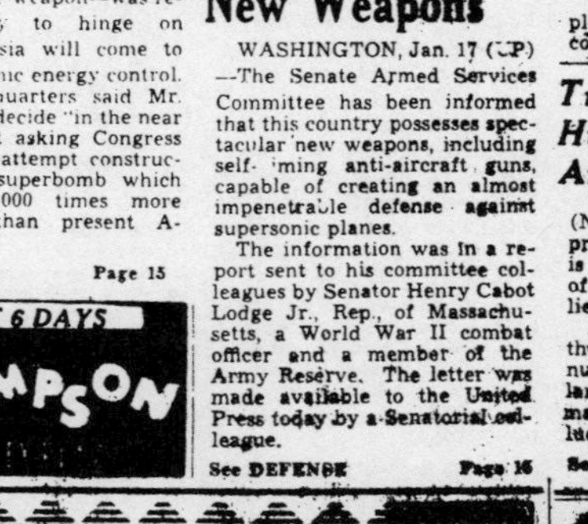

Lodge Bares Spectacular New Weapons

WASHINGTON, Jan. 17 (UP)—The Senate Armed Services Committee has been informed that this country possesses spectacular new weapons, including self-aiming anti-aircraft guns, capable of creating an almost impenetrable defense against supersonic planes.

The information was in a report sent to his committee colleagues by Senator Henry Cabot Lodge Jr., Rep., of Massachusetts, a World War II combat officer and a member of the Army Reserve. The letter was made available to the United Press today by a Senatorial colleague.

See DEFENSE Page 16

Truman Reveals His Lucky Numbers Are 9, 11 and 13

WASHINGTON, Jan. 17 (NANA)—President Truman probably would never admit he is superstitious but—like many of the world's great—he believes in lucky numbers.

A personal friend reports that the President considers such numbers as 9, 11 or 13 particularly lucky. He occasionally makes casual comments on their luck-bringing power.

See NUMBERS Page 15

U. S. Army ~~Seizes~~ Berlin Building, Former Soviet-Zone Railway Offices

BERLIN, Jan. 17 (UP)—Two American Army officers and 50 West Berlin police tonight seized a United States sector building formerly used as operating headquarters for the Sovient zone railway. Russian authorities immediately protested.

United States officials said they took over the structure because it contained 600 offices that had not been used since the Berlin rail strike early last Summer.

It still contains the railroad's main telephone switchboard, but the Americans said the switchboard had not been seized and still was being operated for the Russians.

The Soviet officials charged that the American action seriously hampered traffic.

W. T. Babcock, deputy United States Berlin commander, said the protest was issued by telephone by the Soviet commander, Maj Gen Alexander Kotikov.

See BERLIN Page 15

Truman Pledges All-Summer Fight on Civil Rights

WASHINGTON, Jan. 17 (UP)—President Truman pledged today that his Senate leaders will fight "all Summer" if necessary to get a vote on his civil rights program.

He said he is doing "everything possible" to get it passed and that members of Congress should be forced to stand up and be counted on the issue.

He made his pledge to leaders of a civil rights mobilization of more than 4000 delegates from 33 states gathered here for a three-day session of pressuring Congress to pass the controversial racial measures.

The White House released a transcript of his remarks.

Fate of the bill is jeopardized in the Senate by the threat of a southern filibuster and in the House by a coalition of southern Democrats and conservative Republicans who dominate the powerful rules committee.

See RIGHTS Page 5

Holdup Bulletins

Police said there was $2,088,000 in the vault room. Over $1,000,000 of this had been there since yesterday. Brink's employees were still counting hundreds of thousands of dollars when the stickup took place.

* * *

E. A. Soucy, New England head of the F. B. I., was en route from Pittsfield to join investigators in the case.

* * *

A radio alarm for three Smith and Wesson .38-calibre revolvers was sent out by Boston police last night. The guns were taken from Brink's armed guards during the holdup. Serial numbers of the guns were announced as Q7-73686, 120219 and 42363.

A hat left behind provided an example of the minute thoroughness of the gang. The chauffeur-type cap, detectives noted, had been recently purchased and the wearer had painstakingly torn out the label, anticipating that he might lose it in the confusion. Detectives said the hat was "nondescript, the kind purchased by hundreds of men during the course of a year."

* * *

Some of the Brink's loot is traceable through serial numbers, a company spokesman told police last night.

Much of it is in new bills, which can be tracked down, he said. This money, it was explained, is mixed with older bills which have no way of being traced.

See BULLETINS Page 8

Tangle Towns Puzzle for Today Is on Page 28

Massachusetts Tangle Town Puzzle No. 10 appears on page 28 of today's Boston Globe, taking 180 New Englanders one step nearer the Tangle Town contest cash prizes, which total $15,375.

There is still plenty of time to enter the Glob 's Tangle Town contest. Back puzzles can be obtained through local news dealers, or by placing an order through the Globe circulation department by calling Lafayette 3-2000.

You pay nothing, you buy nothing, and there is no entry fee for playing Massachusetts Tangle Towns in the Globe.

See TOWNS Page 28

Revere Man Booked

Bostsosn and Revere police early this morning took a 49-year-old Revere man into custody and booked him on "suspicion before the fact to armed robbery."

Police identified the suspect as Samuel Linden of 26 Arlington av., Revere. They quoted him as saying he could furnish them with proof of his whereabouts during the holdup and stating he had no knowledge of the robbery.

According to Revere Police Capt Phillip Gallo, the man has a record for holdups and now is on parole from State Prison.

See ARREST Page 7

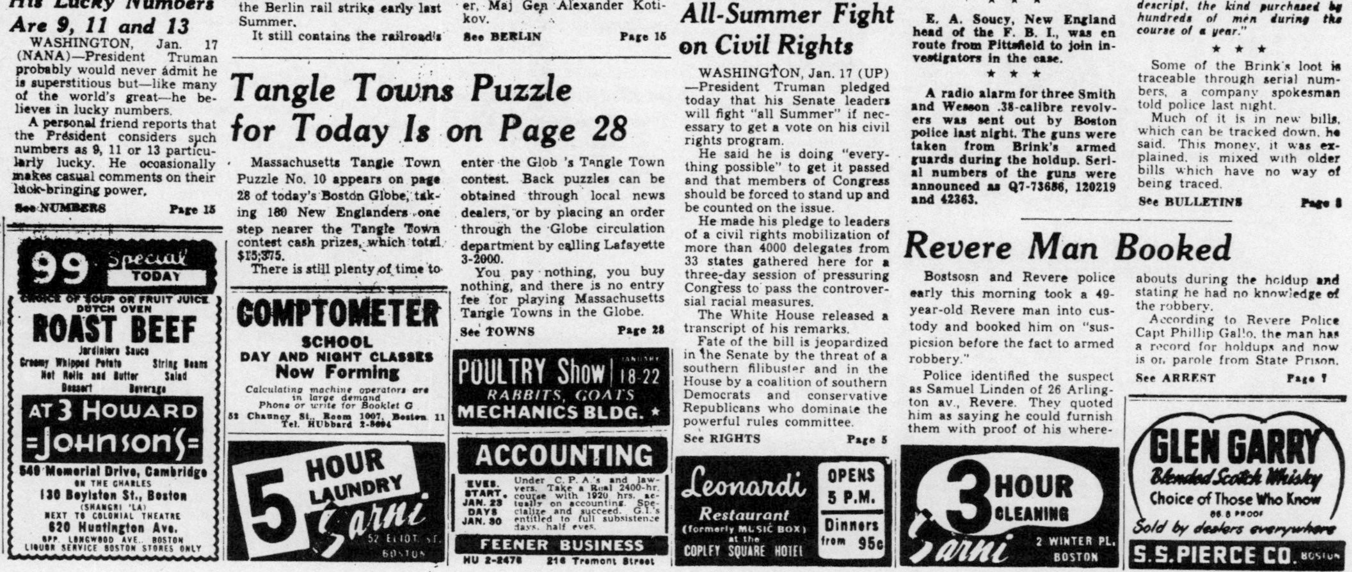

ONE FOR THE MONEY
WEDNESDAY—Fair and cooler, much less humid. THURSDAY—Fair, warmer, late rain.
Full Report on Page 32

The Boston Daily Globe

Reg. U. S. Pat. Off.

VOL. CLVII No. 179 · Copyright 1950 By The Globe Newspaper Co. · BOSTON, WEDNESDAY MORNING, JUNE 28, 1950 · 32 PAGES—FIVE CENTS

GUIDE TO FEATURES
Ashby ... 19 | Dr Crane ... 16 | Society ... 17
Burgess ... 17 | Editorials ... 18 | Sports ... 20-24
Comics ... 36-37 | Fin'nc'l ... 13-16 | Towne ... 23
Cross Wrd ... 36 | Obituaries ... 28 | Theater ... 14-15
Culbertson ... 37 | Radio-TV ... 37 | Vote Forum 8
Deaths ... 28 | Serial ... 37 | Women ... 30-31

AMERICAN PLANES BOMB FLEEING REDS IN KOREA

UP FRONT

Add Miseries: Phils' Miller Falls Upstairs

By HAROLD KAESE

Bob Miller, Phils rookie right-hander who is flashing a 6-0 record, could not pitch against the Braves last night.

He was injured falling upstairs.

The Phils, who think they will win the pennant because of their youth, if they are close to the top Aug. 1, wanted Miller in the best of condition for the Braves' opener. They excused him from Monday night's exhibition against the Athletics in Philadelphia.

"You take the afternoon train to Boston, Bob, and get a good night's sleep," said Manager Eddie Sawyer.

Miller hurried for the train at North Philadelphia Station. Carrying his bag, he went up the stairs two at a time. He was ascending like a Los Alamos rocket—until his foot slipped.

"Ouch! My back!" he yelled, but he got up and kept going. He made the train, made Boston, but couldn't make the game. He had hurt a muscle in his back, the same muscle that bothered him last season when he was with Terre Haute and the Phils.

Sawyer was worried. The Phils haven't any too much pitching, even with Miller. Today the Phils have a new rule: Don't fall upstairs!

Stephens Fumbled Razor in Midair, Cut His Thumb

Ball players have some queer accidents. Vern Stephens fumbles his safety razor, grabs it in mid-air and cuts his thumb. George Metkovich strolls along a bridge in the cool of the evening, steps on a misplaced catfish and pierces his foot with the dorsal fin. Earl Torgeson kisses his family good by, steps off the slowly moving train at Bradenton, and—"Ow! My knee. It's gone."

Rube Waddell missed the 1905 World Series between the A's and Giants, because of a sore arm. Did he hurt it breaking off a curve? No, he hurt it breaking straw hats during a hilarious episode.

Bill Werber once tried to emulate Lefty Grove by kicking a bucket full of water. He cracked his big toe.

"You kicked it wrong," said Grove, too late. "Never kick a bucket with your toe. Use the bottom of your foot."

Eddie Pellagrini got into all kinds of trouble sitting on the bench for the Red Sox. He lost weight, for one thing. And twice he pulled a muscle in his leg—just sitting down.

And wasn't it Earl Averill who blasted his fingers showing his son how to set off firecrackers?

"The dizziest injury I've seen yet," said Sawyer, last night, "was the one a kid pitcher of ours named Ridzik suffered during a practice game in Clearwater. Raising his leg to pitch, he hurt his knee. Nobody believed it until we saw the X-rays. The kneecap was split right across."

In view of these accidents, who dares say that the foul line does not constitute a physical hazard?

B's Lose, Sox Win

NATIONAL LEAGUE
Philadelphia 3, BOSTON 2.
St. Louis 3, Chicago 2.
St. Louis 4, Chicago 1.
New York 10, Brooklyn 3.
Cincinnati 8, Pittsburgh 3.

AMERICAN LEAGUE
BOSTON 7, Philadelphia 5 (11).
Washington 4, New York 3 (12).
Detroit 9, Chicago 3.
St. Louis 4, Cleveland 3.

Boston Teams Today
BRAVES vs. Phils at Braves Field, 8:45 p. m.
RED SOX vs. A's at Philadelphia, 8 p. m.

GEN KEATING ENJOYS WIFE'S MUSIC—Maj Gen and Mrs. Frank A. Keating shown in their Cohasset home during interview with Globe.

N. E. Army Head Calls Attack Another Small Pearl Harbor

Gen Keating Says Russia Using Korea War as Test

By MARJORIE MARTIN

The sudden attack on Seoul by northern Communist troops in Korea strongly resembles "another very small Pearl Harbor," Maj Gen Frank A. Keating, only recently named to take over the important post of chief military adviser to the South Korean Government, declared yesterday afternoon in an interview with the Globe at his Jerusalem-road home in Cohasset.

As a long range observer of considerable military note, Gen Keating declared he was amazed, "in view of the difficulty of the terrain and our fine defensive measures," to note the rapid advance of North Korea troops toward the capital city of Seoul.

"Just where our military intelligence was prior to the start of hostilities, I'm sure I don't know," he said meaningfully.

"But it is safe to assume the Communist troops knew far more about our plans than we knew of their strategy."

See KEATING Page 7

Globe man calls Josef Stalin for an interview by telephone

The Kremlin Won't Talk Unless It's in Russian

By JOSEPH F. DINNEEN

I had a few questions I thought I'd like to ask Josef Stalin, so I reached for the telephone at 2 yesterday afternoon, asked for Long Distance and placed a call for Josef Stalin, the Kremlin, Moscow, Russia. If the operator was at all surprised, she did not reveal it. She took my name and telephone number and said she would call me back.

She called back in 10 minutes and it became clear that trans-Atlantic phone service could not be clogged up by all and sundry who might like to talk to the Kremlin on the spur of the moment. The Long Distance operator tactfully explained that a call to Moscow would have to be filed four days in advance.

She wanted to know if I had the telephone number of the Kremlin and I confessed I had not; but I explained that I did not consider this a nuisance call. I wanted a telephone interview with Josef Stalin. Public figures in this country normally respond to requests for information from newspapermen, and I saw no reason why I should not be connected with the Kremlin.

"The rule is that you'll have to file your call four days in advance," she said.

See DINNEEN Page 7

Battle Ends Over Budget; GOP Gives in

Senators Vote to Drop Demand for $3 Million Cut

By SAMUEL B. CUTLER

Beacon Hill's battle of the budget ended late last night.

The impasse broke when Republican Senators gave in on their amendment to slash the House-approved $218,875,000 appropriations bill by $3,000,000.

Action came shortly after 11 o'clock through acceptance of a unanimous conference committee agreement to drop the economy amendment, in the face of House refusal to go along.

The committee was the fifth named since last Thursday.

Both the Senate and the House accepted the committee recommendation without debate on a voice vote.

Gov. Dever is expected to sign the measure today.

Only three days remained in the expiring fiscal year when the agreement was reached. A delay beyond Friday was expected to result in payless-paydays and disrupted delivery of supplies to institutions.

Gov. Dever, however, was reported prepared to send in a special message calling for emergency, stop-gap legislation before any crisis could develop.

Until tonight, the Senate had insisted on standing by its budget slash, while the House conferees had demanded no cut, on the contention the budget had been reduced to the bone.

See BUDGET Page 9

U. S. Irish 'Dregs of Humanity,' Says Belfast Man

A big part of the population of Boston, as well as New York's Mayor William O'Dwyer and his city's police force, were characterized yesterday as "the dregs of humanity" by a member of Northern Ireland's Parliament, according to a United Press report from Belfast.

In Boston last night the reaction to the statement ranged from strong anger to an attitude that the remarks weren't worth considering.

According to the dispatch, William May, a member of the government Unionist Party, declared that the Irish in America were "dregs of humanity" who are only "part of a political machine."

See IRISH Page 10

Hailstones With Core of Metallic Substance Pelt Bennington, Vt.

A wide-spread electrical storm, accompanied by hailstones with "metallic" cores that pelted Bennington, Vt., and short-lived downpours that soaked many communities, hit most of New England yesterday afternoon and last night.

Greater Boston escaped the worst of the storm, but lightning knocked down 300 feet of "dead" wire over an M. T. A. trackless trolley line on Dor-

See STORM Page 10

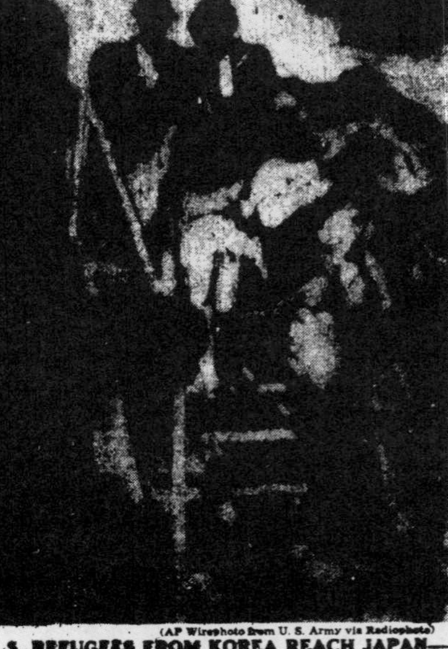

(AP Wirephoto from U. S. Army via Radiophoto)

U. S. REFUGEES FROM KOREA REACH JAPAN—Americans disembark from a United States transport plane at Itazuki Airbase, Kyushu, Japan, after flight from Seoul, Korea. (Other Korean photos on page 19.)

Truman Move to Save Korea Backed by U.N.

By HENRY W. HARRIS

LAKE SUCCESS, N. Y., June 27—The United Nations Security Council tonight placed itself squarely behind American action in according support with armed forces to Southern Korea.

It adopted a resolution, introduced by American delegate Warren R. Austin, declaring a breach of the peace, noting the need for "urgent military measures," and recommending that all members of the U.N. "furnish such assistance to the Republic of South Korea as may be necessary to repel the armed attack and to restore international peace and security in the area."

It thereby not only supports President Truman's action in directing that the American Navy and Air Force act to support Korea; it also licenses this country to take other measures, which could include the sending of troops. And it recommends that other nations take similar action.

See U.N. Page 2

Legislature Asked to Take Up Bill Today for Defense Agency

The Massachusetts Legislature was called upon to act swiftly today on a pending bill to set up a civil defense agency, in view of the Korean situation.

Representative Vincent A. Mannering, Dem. of Boston, Chairman of the Committee on Military Affairs and Public Safety, declared last night the action was imperative because "events of the past few days have taught us that anything can happen overnight."

The measure, urgently sought by Gov. Dever in his annual message, is pending before the House Way and Means Committee.

Mannering said he would take the House floor today and ask for discharge of the committee from further consideration so that the measure can be acted upon at once.

See DEFENSE Page 10

Sudden turn of events in Korea makes market adjustment a rout

Stocks Take Worst Beating in 20 Years, Then Recover

By JOHN HARRIMAN

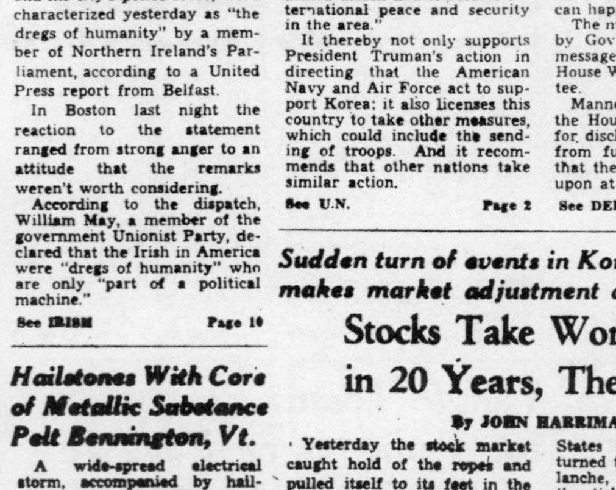

Yesterday the stock market caught hold of the ropes and pulled itself to its feet in the second round of the worst beating it has taken in 20 years.

At the close, prices were headed sharply upwards after a final hour of boiling activity, in which 1,600,000 shares changed hands.

The market had rallied sharply at the opening from the previous night's close, with advances in some issues as much as $3 a share. But the buying was not long sustained, and prices began to slide shortly after 11 o'clock. President Truman's announcement of United States intervention in Korea turned the selling into an avalanche, which at one time left the ticker 27 minutes behind transactions on the floor and carried some issues down as much as $7 a share.

Not until the final hour was the decline reversed, when a sharp upward movement regained much of the earlier losses. The decline in the Dow-Jones industrial averages was 1.87 for the day.

See HARRIMAN Page 7

U.S. Navy Seventh Fleet in Action; Invaders Driven Northward

Chiang Heeds Truman's Request, Halts Attacks From Formosa; Soviet Peace Aid Asked

TOKYO, Wednesday, June 28 (AP)—South Korean troops, backed by bombing and strafing United States jet fighters and light bombers, today drove the Communist invaders out of Seoul, reliable reports said.

Gen MacArthur's Headquarters announced that 500-pound bombs were rained down on the troops from the Communist north who plunged Korea into civil war with an invasion Sunday.

The swift jets and attack bombers of MacArthur's command were thrown into the swaying battle on orders of President Truman, who acted to halt now a conflict leading the world to the brink of war.

An advance echelon of MacArthur's General Headquarters was set up in South Korea. His Generals were in continuous conference.

A Moscow broadcast had said that the northerners knifed into Seoul, capital of the United States-sponsored South Korean Republic, at four points this morning.

But an American informant said that later reports indicated a southern counterattack had thrown the tank-led troops from the Red north all the way back to the key city of Uijongbu, 12 miles north of Seoul.

Somewhere along South Korea's sea frontiers the United States naval units based in Japan also were in action.

MacArthur's brief headquarters announcement of United States war plane attacks said:

"Headquarters of the Far East Air Force announced today that F-80s and B-26s are carrying 500-pound bombs on bombing and strafing missions. The airplanes are armed with 50-caliber machine guns."

Korean reports said bombers had attacked Communist tanks. It was the North's tank superiority that paced the 30-mile push down the Uijongbu Valley to Seoul.

At Pearl Harbor, Pacific Fleet headquarters announced that the seventh fleet, now in Philippine waters, has been placed under Gen MacArthur's operational control.

See KOREA Page 3

Truman's Order Sends U. S. Forces Into Fight

By CARL LEVIN

WASHINGTON, June 27—President Truman, in perhaps the most fateful decision since the end of World War II, ordered United States air and sea forces into action today to turn back the invasion of the Republic of Korea by the Communist forces of North Korea.

At the same time he sent the United States 7th Fleet, now in the Straits of Formosa, to prevent any attack by Chinese Communists against that last stronghold of the Chinese Nationalist Government.

He called upon the Nationalists to end all operations against the Communist-held Chinese mainland, and said succinctly: "The 7th Fleet will see that this is done."

See TRUMAN Page 5

House Extends Draft, Senate to Act Today

WASHINGTON, June 27 (AP)—War in Korea broke a Senate-House deadlock over draft extension today and propelled a broadened one-year extender through the House. The Senate, moving almost as fast, will act at 2 p. m., E. D. T. tomorrow.

The House voted 315 to 4 as it heard reports that United States airmen, under White House orders to halt Communist aggression, already were bombing tanks of the forces which invaded Southern Korea from the Red north.

See DRAFT Page 4

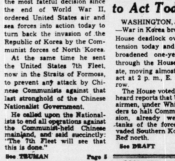

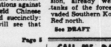

FINELY DRAWN
THURSDAY—Mostly pleasant, showers possible at night
FRIDAY A bit cooler with the rain
Full Report on Page 12

The Boston Daily Globe

Reg. U. S. Pat. Off

GUIDE TO FEATURES

Burgess	35	Dr Crane	40	Radio-TV	35
Comics	34-35	Editorials	18	Serial	34
Cross-Word	9	Fin'nc'l	29-30	Society	17
Culbertson	34	M Forum	10	Sports	26-29
Deaths	36	Obituaries	36	Theatres	31
Dix	21	Port	8	Women	20 25

VOL. CLIX No. 102 · Copyright 1951 · By THE GLOBE NEWSPAPER CO. · BOSTON, THURSDAY MORNING, APRIL 12, 1951 · 40 PAGES—FIVE CENTS

Truman Tells Nation the Choice:

M'ARTHUR OR PEACE

'Impeach Truman,' GOP Senator Demands

MacArthur 'Complied Meticulously'

Aid Asserts General Obeyed 'All Directives'

TOKYO, Thursday, April 12 (UP)—Gen Douglas MacArthur feels that he has "complied meticulously with all directives he has received," Maj Gen Courtney Whitney, the General's closest adviser, said today.

Whitney, MacArthur's military secretary and chief of the Occupation Government section, in a formal statement, said:

"In clarification of news dispatches from the United States making reference to the President's directive of Dec. 6 enjoining against the issuance of public statements on foreign policy without reference to the State Department for clearance, Maj Gen Courtney Whitney of Gen MacArthur's staff today pointed out the following:

"1. The directive of Dec. 6 was not directed to Gen MacArthur personally but was directed to all executive agencies of the Government.

"2. Immediately after its receipt, Gen MacArthur submitted a proposed communique to the Joint Chiefs of Staff, who informed him among other things that it was not necessary to submit communiques referencing military operations.

See M'ARTHUR Page 16

ASKS RETIREMENT—Gen Courtney Whitney.

Whitney Asks Retirement, to Return With MacArthur

TOKYO, Thursday, April 12 (AP)—Maj Gen Courtney Whitney, one of Gen MacArthur's right hand men, announced today he had requested retirement from active duty so he may leave Japan with MacArthur.

Gen Whitney is chief of the government section of SCAP (Supreme Commander, Allied Powers), the occupation force.

Whitney yesterday disclosed Gen MacArthur's initial reaction to the news that President Truman had fired MacArthur from all his commands.

Whitney said at that time MacArthur took the news "magnificently" and that "I think this has been his finest hour."

Whitney has been MacArthur's liaison officer with the Japanese government.

Capital in Grip of Fiercest Fight in Years

MacArthur Due to Return Home in Three Weeks

By BERT ANDREWS

WASHINGTON, April 11—One of the fiercest political fights in America's history raged today in the wake of President Truman's dismissal of General of the Army Douglas MacArthur and General MacArthur's revelation that he will come home from Tokyo in three weeks to tell his side of the story.

The President, aware of the uproar that reached its peak with extremist cries for "impeachments," led by Senator Jenner, Rep., of Indiana, went before the nation on radio and television tonight to tell his story of why he fired Gen MacArthur and to discuss Far Eastern policy.

(MacArthur has not yet told United States Republican leaders he is willing to address a joint session of Congress when he returns to the United States in about three weeks, Reuters learned authoritatively.)

Before the President spoke, the day had been filled with din and with clamor as scores of men in and out of Congress rushed into the fray with blistering denunciation of what the President had done to Gen MacArthur or with strong words of praise for the President.

See CAPITAL Page 14

"WORLD PEACE MORE IMPORTANT than any individual," says President Truman in address to nation telling why he fired Gen MacArthur. (Acme Telephoto)

Had to Relieve General to Avoid 'Grave Risk'

'Cause of World Peace' Bigger Than 'Individual'

President Offers 3-Point Plan for Ending the War in Korea

But Warns Kremlin Rulers May Yet Spread Hostilities

WASHINGTON, April 11 (UP)—President Truman said tonight he fired Gen Douglas MacArthur because "the cause of world peace is much more important than any individual."

In a major radio address, which held out a new offer of Far East truce negotiations, the President said this country's aim is to prevent the Korean fighting from spreading into all-out war in Asia.

"A number of events have made it evident that Gen MacArthur did not agree with that policy," he said. "I have therefore considered it essential to relieve Gen MacArthur so that there would be no doubt or confusion as to the real purpose and aim of our policy."

Mr. Truman added that he considers MacArthur "one of our greatest military commanders" and had dismissed him "with the deepest personal regret."

Mr. Truman referred specifically to the General's demands for a free hand to bomb Chinese Communist bases in Manchuria and to use Chiang Kai-shek's Nationalist troops to open a second front on the Red China mainland.

"If we were to do these things we would be running a very grave risk of starting a general war," he said. He added that nothing would suit the Kremlin better "than for our military forces to be committed to a full scale war with Red China."

Mr. Truman conceded that the Communist leaders themselves may decide to expand the Korean War into a world conflict. But he noted that the military strength of the free nations is rapidly growing and said there is reason to hope Russian may "realize it would be foolhardy to widen the hostilities."

"A peaceful settlement may then be possible," he said. "The door is always open."

Spelling out the truce offer in even more specific terms, Mr. Truman said later that "We are ready, at any time, to negotiate for a restoration of peace" in Korea.

But he emphasized that "We will not engage in appeasement—we are only interested in real peace." He laid down a three-point basis for a settlement:

See TRUMAN Page 16

Heavy Rains Slow Allied Drive in Korea

TOKYO, Thursday, April 12 (AP)—Allied forces slogged slowly ahead on the rainswept Korean battlefront Wednesday as news of Gen MacArthur's dismissal spread like wildfire.

The abrupt shift in top command was received by front-line troops with expressions of disbelief — "You're kidding!" Field dispatches said the soldiers generally expressed regret over MacArthur's dismissal, but were warm in their praise of Gen Matthew B. Ridgway, who will assume supreme command.

Chinese and Korean Red resistance toughened on the western and central fronts. Heavy rains and low overcast virtually stripped United Nations ground troops of air support.

See KOREA Page 10

One Director of New Haven Hears Angry Stockholders

By JOHN HARRIMAN

NEW HAVEN, April 11—Angry minority stockholders gave the New Haven Railroad management an uncomfortable hour and a half here this afternoon at the road's annual meeting.

Only one of the company's 15 directors, Frederic C. Dumaine Jr., was present and no sooner had the meeting opened than the absence of other directors called forth a storm of criticism.

Other grievances were the refusal of the management to pay dividends on the preferred stock and the nature of the annual report, which one stockholder called "deliberately misleading."

At one point Dumaine Jr. threatened angrily to force an adjournment of the meeting, saying, "I have the votes to carry the motion and I'll do it if I have to."

See NEW HAVEN Page 2

Sickness Fund Beaten by Aid of 19 Democrats

By SAMUEL B. CUTLER

The Democratic Administration's battle for a compulsory cash sickness insurance plan was beaten last night in the House for the third successive year.

Nineteen Democrats bolted their leadership in the 126-103 defeat of the state-administered system sought by organized labor. Three Republicans went along with the bill.

The House action means that all cash sickness legislation is dead for this session, unless Gov. Dever sends in a special message to revive the issue.

See BENEFITS Page 10

N. E. Split Wide Open on M'Arthur Discharge

Hot, angry debate over the Truman-MacArthur issue swept through New England yesterday, splitting the area down the middle as it did the rest of the astonished country.

The dispute caused family quarrels, made arenas out of barrooms, and it crossed party lines.

Some Republican leaders followed Senators Leverett Saltonstall and Henry Cabot Lodge Jr. in backing Truman. Others backed Maine's Senator Owen Brewster in his support for the deposed General.

Democrats, too, were split by the dispute, one rank-and-filer resigning from the party. Veterans' organizations were di-

See NEW ENGLAND Page 16

Public Opinion on Blazing MacArthur Issue

President Truman's speech last night added more fuel to the MacArthur dismissal debate. Here is a sampling of opinion taken at random.

MRS. ELIZABETH BRACK, 31 Central av., Revere, a housewife whose husband is an Army captain in Korea. "President Truman looked like a man of steel tonight. I admire him for his courage. He is trying to do the right thing and he is treading on strong public opinion. I heartily agree with the President on his discharge of MacArthur."

See OPINIONS Page 16

Eastham Flag at Half Staff, Towns Resent Truman Act

Eastham lowered its Town Hall flag to half staff yesterday in sorrowful protest against the firing of Gen MacArthur, and most other small communities in Massachusetts were lowering the boom at President Truman with verbal blasts.

A poll of the "trend towns," the tiny hamlets which pop into the news with early returns during election years, disclosed the townspeople, predominantly Republican, strongly disapprove of the Truman stand.

The places usually used as sounding boards in early election returns were sounding off. The people didn't like it, and were voicing their opinions.

While the President didn't poll many votes in most of the communities in the last election, it would be a safe bet to say he would get even fewer today.

See TOWNS Page 10

WALTER LIPPMANN:

"The President and Secretary (Marshall) have done their duty. They have been faithful to their trust."

Turn to Page 18.

Storm Darkens City, Halts TV and Radio, Fires Suburban Homes

A freak lightning storm hit Greater Boston yesterday afternoon, knocking a television station and two radio stations out of commission, pelted several communities with large hail stones, and plunged Boston into near nighttime darkness.

Several buildings were struck by lightning in Medford and Burlington and service on 100 telephones in Medford was disrupted by lightning burning out cables.

The WNAC-TV transmitting tower on Murray Hill road, Medford, near the Malden line, was struck at least 10 times by bolts, station officials said.

Cables at the station were burned out and the station blacked out at 2:39 p. m.

Emergency crews were sent to the transmitting buildings to replace the cables. At 5:30 the picture flashed back on the screens, but it was not until 8 o'clock that the sound accompanying the picture was restored.

See STORM Page 2

Driver Cheats Death in 15-Ft. Car Plunge Off Warren Bridge

A young Chelsea baseball player cheated death late yesterday afternoon when the car he was driving crashed through the guard rail of Warren Bridge, turned over in the air and crashed onto a wooden float 15 feet below the bridge on the Charles River.

ArthurV. Garrett Jr., 21, of 29 Library st., Chelsea, scheduled to leave today to join a farm club of the Cleveland Indians, crawled from the wreckage of his sedan with minor cuts and bruises. But for the float, the car and driver would have gone into 25 feet of water.

See BRIDGE Page 32

What People Say About MacArthur Removal

Did MacArthur Force Truman Hand to Promote a Major Crisis Here?

To the Editor—Could it be that Gen MacArthur wanted to force the President to fire him?

Of course, the General realized that this would precipitate a major political clash in this country. Maybe that's precisely what he wants.

I don't think Gen MacArthur attempted to force the issue simply in order to embarrass the Administration because it is a Democratic Administration. It seems to me he was just begging to be fired in order to start a nationwide debate on what this country should do about the Chinese Communists—stop their aggression or wage a crusade against them.

MacArthur has never kept his opinion secret that he wanted to destroy Communist China as a matter of principle, even at the price of a third World War.

See LETTERS Page 18

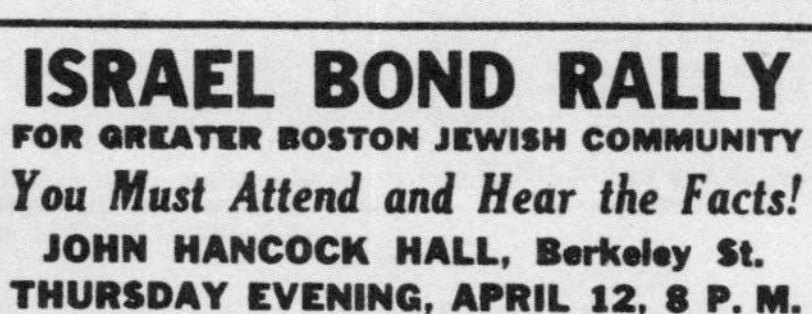

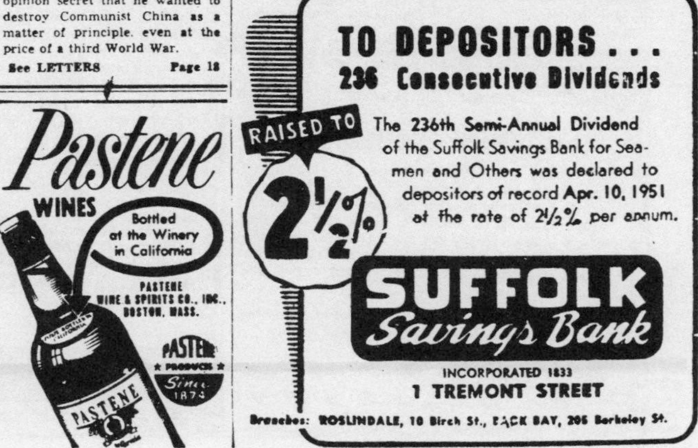

DOING FINE
THURSDAY—Fair, temperature in 70s.
FRIDAY—Continued fair and warm.
Full Report on Page 8

The Boston Daily Globe
Reg. U. S. Pat. Off.

VOL. CLXV NO. 161 · Copyright 1954 By GLOBE NEWSPAPER CO. · BOSTON, THURSDAY MORNING, JUNE 10, 1954 · 22 PAGES—FIVE CENTS

McCarthy Cruel, Reckless--Welch

Gun Found in Clark's Cellar

Sold Red Paper, Says Teacher

Wayland Woman Denies Doing So Since 1950

By ROBERT L. HEALY

WAYLAND, June 9—Suspended school teacher Anne Hale Jr. again refused to answer questions involving her political beliefs tonight but piecemeal testimony of her April 23 meeting with school authorities was introduced as evidence and disclosed former Communist Party affiliation.

Town Counsel Roger P. Stokey revealed the hitherto secret, executive session testimony while quizzing the second-grade teacher for the second straight night in a hearing before the School Committee to determine whether she shall be dismissed.

Reading from the transcript of April 23, Stokey revealed that Miss Hale had told School Committee Chairman William Waldron and Supt. of Schools Rexford S. Souder that she once had sold both the Sunday and Daily Worker, newspapers of the Communist Party.

"Were those statements true?" Stokey inquired.

"Yes," the witness said.

Miss Hale had admitted at the same meeting that she knew the Communist party was "preparing and publishing the Daily Worker" and told the school officials that it "had some good portions" on economics and foreign affairs.

When this portion was read and she was asked whether it was true she replied firmly, "All my testimony on April 23 was true."

Then the teacher objected to answering the question and she was given verbal support by her attorney, Oliver S. Allen who then clashed with Stokey as the town counsel sought to introduce as evidence some 60 copies of the Daily Worker, ranging from 1939 through 1950.

TEACHER
Page Five

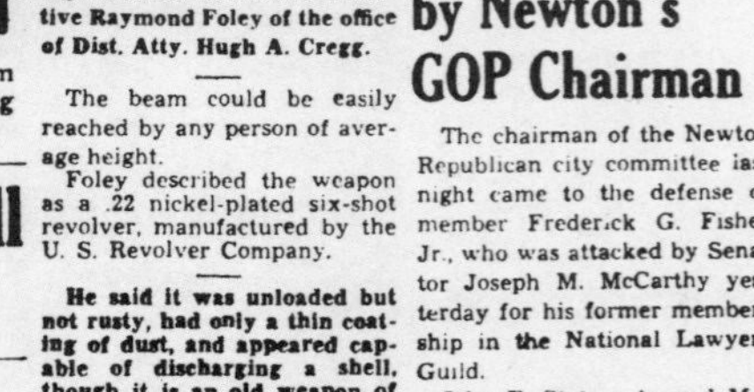

SEARCH FOR EVIDENCE—State Police detectives, Melvin Topjian, Capt William F. Kidney and Frank Bianco, operate portable X-ray fluoroscope in search for missing bullets in home furnishings of murdered Melvin Clark. (Globe Photo by Edmund Kelley)

Police Call Hidden .22 'Important'

Plan Test to Link Revolver With Amesbury Slaying

By PAUL K. PLAKIAS

AMESBURY, June 9—A .22 revolver, which may prove to be the weapon with which Melvin W. Clark Jr. was murdered, was found late today secreted in the cellar of the Clark cottage on Lake Attitash.

The gun was hidden behind a heating unit, on top of a beam just below the ceiling, according to State Police Lt. Detective Raymond Foley of the office of Dist. Atty. Hugh A. Cregg.

The beam could be easily reached by any person of average height.

Foley described the weapon as a .22 nickel-plated six-shot revolver, manufactured by the U. S. Revolver Company.

He said it was unloaded but not rusty, had only a thin coating of dust, and appeared capable of discharging a shell, though it is an old weapon of the type fancied by gun collectors.

Foley cautiously characterized it only as "an important find."

Clark, 29-year-old electronics firm foreman, was shot twice in the head, and experts have said the death weapon was almost certainly a .22.

A quantity of .22 ammunition was found earlier in the Clark home.

One of the bullets that killed Clark has been recovered, but it was so flattened that its use in ballistics tests will be difficult.

SLAYING
Page Nine

ATTORNEY FRED FISHER, secretary of the Newton Young Republicans League and a law associate of Joseph Welch, whose name caused angry clash between Welch and Senator McCarthy.

Fisher Defended by Newton's GOP Chairman

The chairman of the Newton Republican city committee last night came to the defense of member Frederick G. Fisher Jr., who was attacked by Senator Joseph M. McCarthy yesterday for his former membership in the National Lawyers Guild.

John E. Stetson termed McCarthy's charge "an unwarranted attack" and voiced the group's "complete confidence in, and support of" the young Newton attorney.

"We have been fully aware of the facts in this case since the inception of the hearings, and wish to make public our stand in view of the unwarranted attack made . . . by Senator McCarthy," Stetson's statement said.

The 33-year-old Newton lawyer neither saw nor heard Senator McCarthy's attack and Army Counsel Welch's defense of him and his former affiliation with the National Lawyers Guild.

The junior partner in the Boston law firm of Hale & Dorr was in Springfield with his wife, Talia, visiting friends, and missed one of the most tense moments in the 30-day Army-McCarthy hassle.

FISHER
Page Three

Attack on Associate Fires Lawyer's Wrath

Cohn Quiz Abruptly Ends; Senator Sworn, Tells of Reds

By JOHN HARRIS

WASHINGTON, June 9—Senator Joseph R. McCarthy took the witness stand today after a dramatic, emotion-packed clash in which Army counsel Joseph N. Welch—six feet away, face-to-face—charged the Senator with being "cruel and reckless."

"Have you no sense of decency, Senator?" pleaded Welch, on the verge of tears.

McCarthy was angrily charging that Welch had tried to "foist" a junior lawyer of his Boston firm, Fred Fisher, upon the Mundt subcommittee although Fisher had been a member of the National Lawyer's Guild while at Harvard Law School. The Guild, said the Senator, was a Communist front.

McCarthy made his attack after saying he was "bored with Mr. Welch's phony requests to Roy M. Cohn," who was then on the witness stand, to rush to Army Secretary Robert T. Stevens with any list of subversives or Communists to root them out of government by sundown.

"So," said the Senator, "I'll give you information about a young man in your organization."

McCarthy said that Welch had recommended Fisher as an assistant counsel for the subcommittee. Welch explained that Fisher, secretary of the Young Republican League of Newton, Mass., whose membership includes the son of a Massachusetts Governor, went back to Boston and did not join his staff here.

Senator Karl Mundt, presiding on this 30th day of the McCarthy-Army hearings, twice confirmed the subcommittee has no memorandum that Fisher was recommended by Welch.

"Little did I dream," said Welch, in shocked tones, "that you would be so reckless and cruel as to do injury to that lad. He will always bear a scar needlessly inflicted by you. If," went on Welch, "I had it in my power to forgive you I'd do so. Your forgiveness will have to come from someone other than me."

HEARING
Page Three

Ike Broadcasts Plea Tonight for Legislative Plan

WASHINGTON, June 9—President Eisenhower will step up his efforts to get Congress to enact his legislative program by making a nationally televised speech on the subject tomorrow night before the National Citizens for Eisenhower Congressional Committee.

The President will speak for 30 minutes, starting at 9 (EDT), on the opening day of the three-day conference in the Statler Hotel. The conference was called by the committee to plan its activities in the forthcoming Congressional election campaign.

Originally the President had intended to greet the conferees in an informal talk Friday morning. Today the White House announced that he had changed his plans in favor of a major political speech, which will be carried by the television and radio networks.

Tightened Wiretap Bill Vetoed by Governor

A scant few minutes before it was to become law, Gov. Herter last night vetoed an act which would severely restrict the authority of the Attorney General and the District Attorneys to authorize wiretapping.

This was the first veto the Governor has made in two years.

The veto message came at 11:46 p. m. as the Senate for one hour debated the advisability of sending a messenger to the executive office for withdrawal of the act.

The bill, enacted by both branches and sent to the Governor last Thursday, would have become law at one minute past midnight had not the Governor vetoed it or the Senate recalled it.

A Democratic filibuster precluded the withdrawal of the bill from the Governor's desk in time to avert the veto.

A two-thirds vote of both branches is required to override the gubernatorial veto. There appears little chance of mustering this vote by supporters of the bill.

Atty. Gen. George Fingold, as well as the District Attorneys of the state, were strongly opposed to this measure which requires them to get written authorization from a justice of either the Supreme or Superior Court before a wiretap can be put in operation.

WIRETAP
Page Nine

1165 Receive Degrees at B.C. Commencement

(Picture on Page 19)

The 78th annual Commencement exercises of Boston College were held yesterday at Alumni Field. More than 12,000 persons watched the conferring of degrees.

Rev. Joseph R. N. Maxwell, S. J., president of the college, awarded seven honorary degrees and a total of 1165 degrees from the seven schools in the college during the impressive ceremonies.

The Irish Ambassador to the United States, John J. Hearne, who received the honorary degree of doctor of laws, was the Commencement speaker. Archbishop Cushing presided.

Ambassador Hearne warned of the possibility that "the most terrible avalanche ever unleashed upon the civilization of which you are now graduates and citizens, will break upon this hemisphere."

He termed the United States the "keeper of the conscience of the West and the guardian of the peace of the world. It will depend on you whether or not this country can weather the maelstrom. Be prepared for that," he warned.

B. C.
Page Five

District Court Measure Pushed Through Senate

By WILLIAM J. LEWIS

Determined that at least one of the Administration's judicial reform bills be enacted, the Republican-dominated Senate last night voted initial approval for the District Court reorganization measure.

The vote was taken shortly after G. O. P. Senate leaders huddled with Gov. Herter who insisted that the plan to revamp the District Courts is one of the most important planks of his program and should not be abandoned because some pressure was being applied.

The vote to give the bill its third reading was 21 to 15 with all the Republicans voting in favor except Senators Alfred B. Cenedella Jr. of Milford and Fred Lamson of Malden who cast their lot with the Democrats.

Meanwhile, the hotly-debated Juvenile Court bill remained adrift between the branches in a Conference Committee which had not even met to try to compromise House and Senate differences.

COURTS
Page Twenty-seven

Tornado Lives Again in Survivors' Memories

WORCESTER, June 9—The never-to-be forgotten tornado of a year ago lived again tonight in the memories of the thousands who witnessed its devastating effect.

They prayed in the churches for those who lost their lives; they talked on the street and in the store and they thought silently of that terrible wind which took the lives of 94 persons and caused some $58,000,000 damage.

WORCESTER
Page Nine

McCarthy, Welch Exchange on Fisher

(AP Wirephoto)

WELCH FACES McCARTHY ACROSS TABLE

WASHINGTON, June 9 (AP)—Following is the text of an exchange between Sen. Joseph McCarthy and Joseph N. Welch of Boston, special counsel for the Army, at the McCarthy-Army hearings today.

McCarthy— . . . In view of Mr. Welch's request that the information be given once we know of anyone who might be performing any work for the Communist party, I think we should tell him that he has in his law firm a young man named Fisher whom he recommended, incidentally, to work on this committee, who has been for a number of years a member of an organization which was named, O, years and years ago, as the legal bulwark of the Communist party, an organization which always swings to the defense of anyone who dares to expose Communists.

I certainly assume that Mr. Welch did not know of this young man at the time he recommended him as the assistant counsel for this committee, but he has such terror and such a great desire to know where anyone is located who may be serving the Communist cause, Mr. Welch, that I thought we should just call to your attention the fact that your Mr. Fisher, who is still in your law firm today, whom you asked to have down here looking over the secret and classified material, is a member of an organization, not named by me but named by various committees, named by the Attorney General, as I recall, and I think I quote this verbatim, as "the legal bulwark of the Communist party."

EXCHANGE
Page Three

New Trend . . .

Small Families Outdated Among College Graduates

By FRANCES BURNS

College graduates are having their own baby boom, a population study released yesterday discloses.

They're producing bigger families than their college parents, reports a Milton College (Wisconsin) project of the Population Reference Bureau, a private study organization of Washington, D. C.

College graduates have been producing more children every year since 1946, explain Dr. Clarence J. Gamble of Harvard and Mrs. Betty U. Kibbee. New England is well up in the national averages.

Married graduates of the class of 1944, this year's 10-year class, already average more children than the class of 1921 when it had been out 25 years in 1946, the year the study started. A smaller proportion of the class of 1944 is childless.

SURVEY
Page Twenty-five

Baseball Results

AMERICAN LEAGUE
BOSTON 7, Baltimore 6.
New York 5, Detroit 1.
Chicago 9, Philadelphia 4.
Cleveland 1, Washington 0.

NATIONAL LEAGUE
Philadelphia 4, Chicago 0.
Philadelphia 14, Chicago 6.
New York 8, Milwaukee 0.
St. Louis 3, Brooklyn 0.
Cincinnati 4, Pittsburgh 2.

RED SOX TODAY
Baltimore at Fenway Park, 2 games (1:30 p. m.). Radio, WHDH. Television, WNAC-TV.

Comic Dictionary

JOKE

The proof that the good do not die young.

Red Leader's Face Red After U.S. Blast in Geneva

GENEVA, Switzerland, June 9 (Reuters)—Undersecretary of State Walter Bedell Smith, head of the American delegation to the Far East Conference, today accused Russia and Communist China of trying to make Indo-China another Communist satellite.

Smith's attack, described as "one of the hardest hitting of the conference," made Communist leader Chou En Lai so red in the face that he "looked as though he would explode," a conference spokesman said.

The month-old talks among nine nations to seek a means of settling the 7½-year war seemed more deadlocked than ever tonight as a result of an earlier speech by Chou.

Chou, bitterly attacked American policy and declared it would be "impossible" to set up an armistice commission in Indo-China without Communist countries.

After Smith "went to work on Chou En Lai," an American spokesman commented, the Communist leader "was happy to hand out abuse, but he didn't like observations about himself."

Chou plumped for the Russian plan for an Indo-China armistice commission while Smith appealed either for an armistice commission made up of the Colombo powers, as suggested by Britain's Anthony Eden, or under the United Nations, as favored by Nguyen Quoc Dinh, foreign minister of the French-backed Indo-China state of Vietnam.

GENEVA
Page Seven

Do You Agree?

The fence around a cemetery is foolish, for those inside can't come out and those outside don't want to get in.

—Arthur Brisbane, 1864-1936, American journalist and columnist.

Democrats Reconvening to Nominate Treasurer

The Democratic preprimary convention which recessed in wild disorder at Worcester shortly after 6 a. m. last Sunday will reconvene in Boston tomorrow night to nominate a candidate for State Treasurer.

The full membership of the Democratic State Committee met yesterday to adopt a motion to call the delegates together for the scheduled Sheraton Plaza convention.

The four candidates for treasurer, plus a fifth who has since entered the race, were present at the State Comittee meeting presided over by Chairman John C. Carr.

Michael J. Neville of Cambridge, permanent chairman of the convention who presided at last week-end's 20-hour marathon session, warned the candidates to have as many delegates as possible on hand Friday night, since under the rules of the convention, he must recognize the vote of those delegations that ballot under the unit rule as the wish of the entire delegation.

DEMOCRATS
Page Seven

COMING SUNDAY

Don't miss next Sunday's Globe. You will enjoy its many excellent features. See the Fiction Magazine, the Comic section, the Rotogravure Magazine. The Sunday Globe is planned for the whole family. Enjoy the news features and editorials. Order your Sunday Globe advertisements today. Read the advertisements every day in the Globe.

Classified Advertisements may be ordered at the Globe office or by telephone. Call Richmond 2-1300.

See the Wonderful Selection of Summer Merchandise in Boston Stores

FOR NEWS OF TODAY'S BASEBALL GAMES CALL THE GLOBE SCOREBOARD Richmond 2-2000 2 P. M. TO 5 P. M.

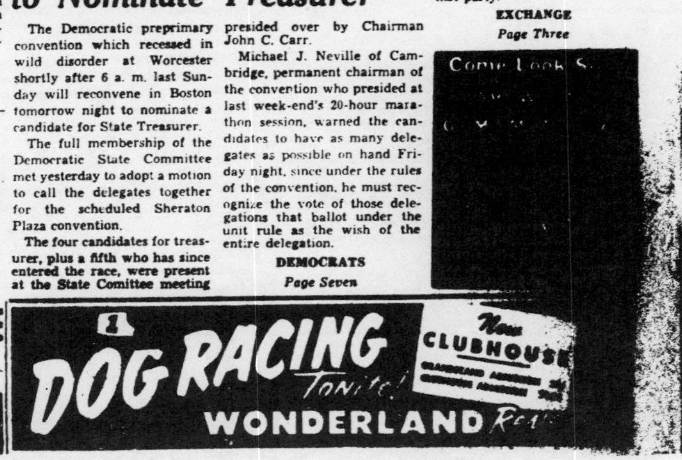

World Hears Official Report:

See Polio Stories on Pages 18 to 24
Page of Photos—Page 29

POLIO 90% BEATEN

Reg U S Pat Off — Copyright 1955 by Globe Newspaper Co
BOSTON DAILY GLOBE—TUESDAY, APRIL 12, 1955
VOL. CLXVII NO. 102 — 52 PAGES—FIVE CENTS

CLOUDY
Rain Late Tonight, Showers Wednesday
(Full reports on Page 35.)

IN TONIGHT'S GLOBE

Burgess	51	Radio-TV	51
Comics	50, 51	Serial Story	50
Crane	51	Society	38, 39
Cross-Word	50	Sports	32-34
Culbertson	50	Star Gazer	51
Deaths	41	Theatres	30
Editorial	28	Twistagram	26
Financial	48, 49	Women's	39, 40

Salk Vaccine Hailed as Medical Victory

End of Dread, Crippling Disease Within Space of Two Years Now Seen a Possibility

No Fatalities Reported Among 460,000 Children Who Got Three Shots Last Year

First and Second Graders (About 250,000) to Get Bay State Injections

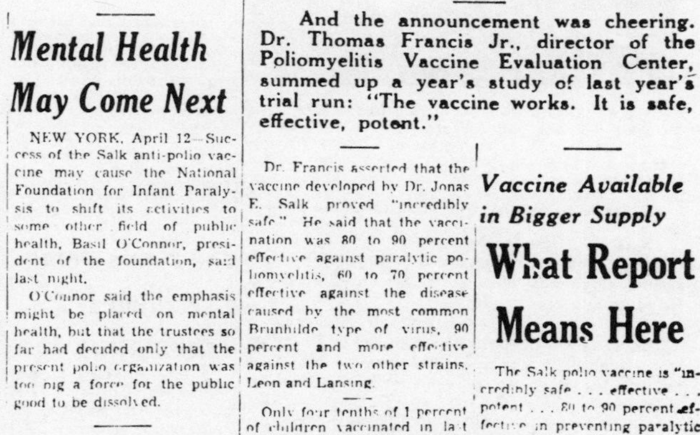

(AP Wirephoto)

FLASH! POLIO VACCINE WORKS!—Dramatic scene in crowded press room at Ann Arbor, Mich., as long-awaited Francis report on the results of the Salk vaccine tests were handed out to eager newsmen. The results of the extensive tests were kept closely guarded until this morning, when the news that will speed the end of crippling polio was released to the world.

By FRANCES BURNS

ANN ARBOR, Mich., April 12—Doctors announced to the world today that the new polio vaccine has proved to be 80 to 90 percent effective.

This is a very conclusive figure, and it means humanity can see the end of one of its most dread diseases.

Some doctors tell the Globe that there will be no such thing as polio in two years.

The announcement was made here today with all the buildup and drama of a Hollywood production.

FRANCES BURNS

Hundreds of doctors and news people had been invited to this delightful campus of the University of Michigan to spread the announcement to the world.

And the announcement was cheering. Dr. Thomas Francis Jr., director of the Poliomyelitis Vaccine Evaluation Center, summed up a year's study of last year's trial run: "The vaccine works. It is safe, effective, potent."

Dr. Francis asserted that the vaccine developed by Dr. Jonas E. Salk proved "incredibly safe." He said that the vaccination was 80 to 90 percent effective against paralytic poliomyelitis, 60 to 70 percent effective against the disease caused by the most common Brunhilde type of virus, 90 percent and more effective against the two other strains, Leon and Lansing.

Only four tenths of 1 percent of children vaccinated in last year's mass test had minor reactions. Those who suffered "major reactions" were the remarkably small number of four to six one-thousandths.

There was no death among children who had the three shots of vaccine.

One child who had had two shots died, following a tonsillectomy two days after the second injection of the vaccine, in an area where polio already was prevalent.

Persistence of Protection 'Reasonably Good'

The persistence of protection appears "reasonabley good." Dr. Thomas Francis Jr., who delivered the report in an hour-long and historic address, told more than 500 men and women who have come from all parts of the United States and Canada.

POLIO
Page Eighteen

Red Sox 4 Orioles 1 In 6 th Inning

AT BALTIMORE

Innings	1	2	3	4	5	6	7	8	9	R	H	E
Red Sox	1	2	0									
Orioles	0	0	1									

Batteries—Sullivan and White; Coleman, Kretlow (3) and Moss.

Lepcio Homers to Give Sox Early 3--0 Lead

By ROGER BIRTWELL

BALTIMORE, Md., April 12—A long home run into the left field bleachers by Ted Lepcio with Norm Zauchin on base in the second inning put the Red Sox into a 3-0 lead over the Baltimore Orioles in the season's opener here today.

The Sox had scored their first run in the first inning on singles by Billy Goodman and Eddie Joost and Faye Throneberry's infield roller.

Frank Sullivan and Joe Coleman were the pitching opponents for the curtain-raiser, as advertised.

RED SOX
Page Thirty-two

Masked Trio Robs Melrose Bank of $7000

MELROSE, April 12—Three masked men robbed the Wyoming Branch of the Melrose Trust Company of $7000 shortly after noon today.

Police said that there was $7000 additional in the bank which the robbers might have obtained easily, but they moved so hurriedly that they missed it.

They forced the branch manager and a woman teller to lie on the floor while they robbed the cash drawers but did not make them open the bank vault.

BANK
Page Seven

Sales Levy Not Even Discussed

Record State Budget OK'd, but No New Taxes Needed

The Democratic-controlled House Ways and Means Committee this afternoon reported a record state budget for the coming fiscal year of $309,612,051, increasing Gov. Herter's recommended "minimum" budget by $4,223,519. Last year's expenditures totalled $287,680,849.

The committee stated that no new taxes will be required to provide their recommended budget, but that all temporary taxes have to be renewed and last year's 25 percent cut in income taxes had to be eliminated.

The temporary taxes plus elimination of the income tax cut will produce in excess of $30,000,000.

The committee emphasized that the budget they report is a "balanced" budget and a tight budget and does not provide for a single new job in the state service or increase in salary "of a single state employee."

A sales tax, which would have produced a flood of new revenue, and which Gov. Herter left without recommendation for the consideration of the Legislature, was not even considered or discussed by the committee, said Chairman John J. Toomey, Dem., of Cambridge.

When Gov. Herter sent his budget message to the Legislature this year, he submitted three alternative budgets—a "minimum" budget of $305,000,000, a "desirable" budget of $32[illegible],000,000 and a "maximum" budget of $360,000,000.

BUDGET
Page Seven

2 Courts Deny Plea to Delay B. & M. Meeting

A Federal and a state court today refused to postpone tomorrow's annual stockholders' meeting of the Boston & Maine Railroad.

Fighting against time, attorney Arthur E. Whittemore filed an appeal from the Federal court decision by Judge George C. Sweeney and said he would press it this afternoon before Judge Calvert Magruder in the Court of Appeals.

But, barring a last-minute reversal, it began to look as if the battle for control of the quarter-billion-dollar B. & M. would be settled tomorrow.

James A. Walsh, chairman of an opposition group hoping to name New Haven president Patrick B. McGinnis as B. & M. head, predicted that "we will have a majority."

Meanwhile, verbal fireworks exploded at a hearing of the Interstate Commerce Commission, to see if an anti-merger law has been violated in B. & M. stock acquisitions, went into its second day of testimony.

B. & M.
Page Forty-one

Kindergarten Children First

Priority Lists Set Up for Receiving Vaccine

Dr. Roy F. Feemster today issued a warning to parents and young adults as news of the effectiveness of the Salk polio vaccine was spread all over the world.

Doctors and scientists have agreed that three groups of people have priority on the still-scarce vaccine.

They are: 1. Kindergarten children; 2. pregnant women; 3. children in grades three to eight. (First and second graders will get shots of the vaccine free this month.)

If you as a parent or as a young adult ask for shots of the polio vaccine for yourself or for young people past the eighth grade, you will be depriving a child of an expectant mother of the shots which they are in greater need of.

Dr. Feemster warned parents not to ask their doctor to vaccinate children outside those kindergarten and third-to-eighth-grade groups, until 1956, when there will be plenty of vaccine for all.

Mental Health May Come Next

NEW YORK, April 12—Success of the Salk anti-polio vaccine may cause the National Foundation for Infant Paralysis to shift its activities to some other field of public health, Basil O'Connor, president of the foundation, said last night.

O'Connor said the emphasis might be placed on mental health, but that the trustees so far had decided only that the present polio organization was too big a force for the public good to be dissolved.

Vaccine Available in Bigger Supply

What Report Means Here

The Salk polio vaccine is "incredibly safe . . . effective . . . potent . . . 80 to 90 percent effective in preventing paralytic polio."

What does that mean to citizens of Massachusetts?

It means many things to many people.

If you are a first or second grader, it means that within the next month you will start the first of the three injections needed for protection against polio.

BAY STATE
Page Eighteen

LI'L ONES

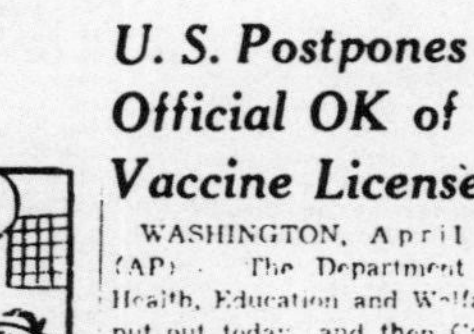

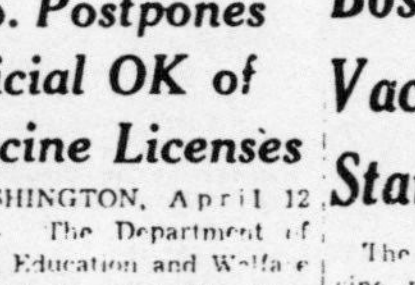

U. S. Postpones Official OK of Vaccine Licenses

WASHINGTON, April 12 (AP)—The Department of Health, Education and Welfare put out today and then cancelled an announcement that the Salk polio vaccine would be formally licensed at 4 p.m. for public use.

"The announcement that the Salk vaccine will be licensed at 4 p.m. E.S.T. today was premature," the Department said shortly after 2:25 p.m.

The original statement came out about noon.

A spokesman for the Department said another announcement with respect to the licensing will be forthcoming later.

In answer to questions he would only say that "technical difficulties" had arisen in making the official evaluation of the product.

Formal licensing requires the signature of Secretary Oveta Culp Hobby. That was the ceremony set for 4 o'clock and then cancelled. Without her signature the vaccine cannot be sold commercially.

Boston Pupils' Vaccine Shots Start April 25

The long-awaited polio vaccine report "offers great encouragement and is a milestone in the control of this dread disease which has resulted in so much crippling and death," was the unanimous opinion expressed this afternoon by leading Boston health officials.

Those concurring in this opinion are Dr. John H. Cauley, city health commissioner; Dr. Augustine M. Garry, director, local health services, and Dr. Martin Spellman, director of hygiene, Boston public schools.

Dr. Cauley announced that "Boston stands prepared to vaccinate all first and second-grade children in the public, parochial and private schools of the city."

BOSTON
Page Twenty-four

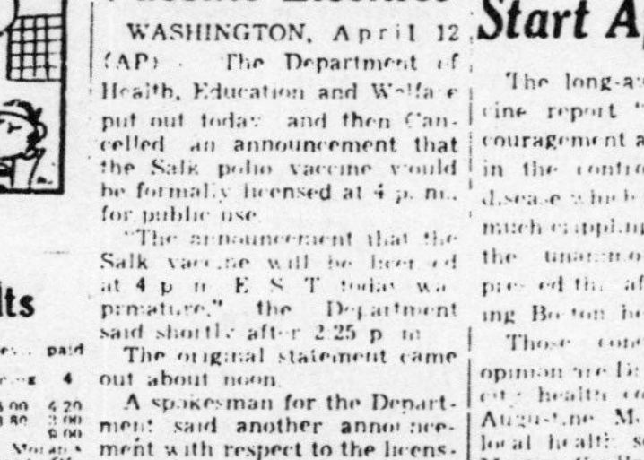

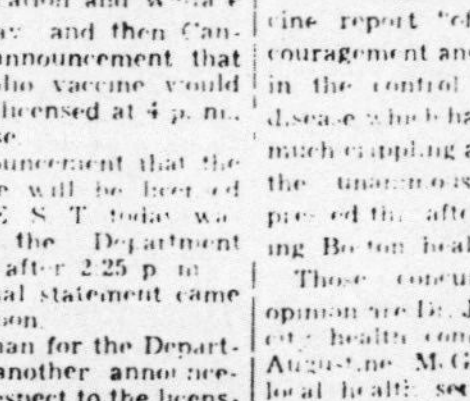

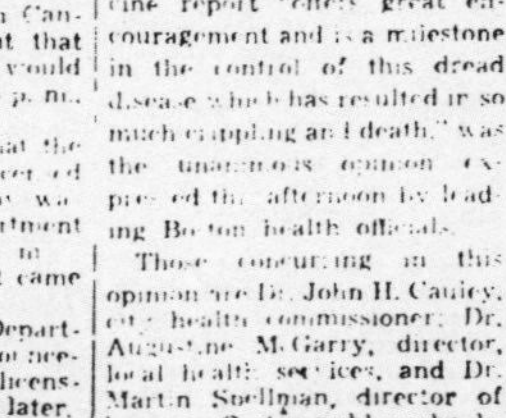

Lincoln Results

DAILY DOUBLE

[illegible]

LINCOLN
Page Thirty-two

Comic Dictionary

INTUITION

A sixth sense possessed by people who show no sign of the other five.

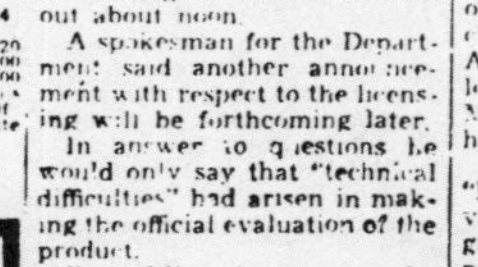

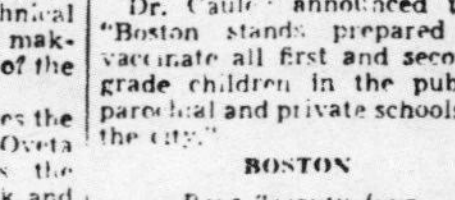

Common Garage Bill Up to Senate

Mayor Hynes Renews Support of Bill Passed by House

Mayor John B. Hynes renewed his support for a House-passed bill for a Boston Common Garage Authority, declaring it would be resorted to if private financing failed.

The measure, authorizing a $7,700,000 underground garage with parking space for 2400 cars, was scheduled for a vote in the Senate late today, but it was thought possible final action on it would not come until tomorrow.

The Mayor said a private group, Motor Park, Inc., had promised him last Thursday that it was "prepared to sign immediately a formal contract" with the city and start construction within 90 days of signing.

GARAGE
Page Seventeen

Boston Evening Globe — SPORTS FINAL NEWS

Reg. U. S. Pat. Off.

BOSTON DAILY GLOBE—TUESDAY, MAY 31, 1955
VOL. CLXVII NO. 151 — 52 PAGES—FIVE CENTS

RAIN Tonight and Wednesday (Full reports on back page.)

IN TONIGHT'S GLOBE

Burgess	44	Radio-TV	45
Comics	44, 45	Serial Story	44
Crane	44	Society	36, 37
Cross-Word	45	Sports	40-42
Culbertson	44	Star Gazer	44
Deaths	49	Theatres	43
Editorial	28	Twistagram	45
Financial	48	Women's	38, 39

Orders Lower Courts to Halt Segregation

High Court Sends Back Five Cases

Rules Original Tribunals Have Supreme Power

WASHINGTON, May 31 (AP)—The Supreme Court, fixing no specific deadline, directed today that race segregation in all public schools be ended as soon as feasible.

The high tribunal's unanimous decision in effect tossed the whole explosive problem to local school authorities and to lower Federal courts.

The Supreme Court said the lower courts should see to it that school authorities "make a prompt and reasonable start" toward complying with its finding of last year that segregation is unconstitutional.

Beyond that, the Supreme Court left great flexibility for the local courts.

"Once such a start has been made, the (lower) courts may find that additional time is necessary to carry out the ruling in an effective manner," the decision, read by Chief Justice Warren, said.

The decision said too the lower courts "may properly take into account local problems" in sitting as courts of equity.

SEGREGATION
Page Twenty-seven

4 Freed Yanks Start Home by Plane

(United Press-Boston Globe Radiophoto from Tokyo)

YANK AIRMEN WALK TO FREEDOM—Four jet pilots, held prisoner more than two years, cross bridge at border in Hongkong following release by Chinese Reds. Left to right, 1st Lt Lyle W. Cameron, Lincoln, Neb.; 1st Lt Roland W. Parks, Omaha, Neb.; Capt Harold Fischer, Swea City, Iowa, and Lt Col Edwin L. Heller, Wynnewood, Penn.

Paul Revere Village Home Away From Home for Yanks

Germans Get Taste of New England, Boston in Particular

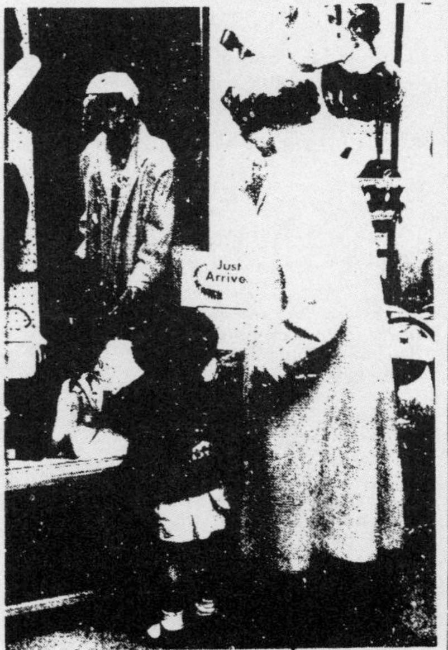

(U. S. Army Photo)

WINDOW SHOPPING IN GERMANY—Mrs. Jean Veronesi, Taunton, and daughter Debbie, 2, check recently arrived millinery at hat bar in Paul Revere Village. Debbie hankered for red straw bonnet, but mother talked her out of it.

(Written for the Globe by Army Public Information Office)

KARLSRUHE—On the night of April 18, 1775, a horseman whizzed through the New England countryside warning sleepy folks that the British were coming. He got to be a very famous man.

So when New England born Col Shelley E. Dutton took command in Karlsruhe, Germany, he said: "Let this housing development be known as Paul Revere Village."

And so it was that the Army's 1150-apartment community some 4500 miles away from home acquired its name. But along with the famous name the community inherited a spirit which makes it unique among such installations overseas.

There are some 4500 Americans living in Paul Revere village, Germany. They come from all parts of the United States. But living together in a foreign land they are bound together in the tradition of a New England community.

The 80-building village is located in the northwestern sector of Karlsruhe, a city of 200,000 people and gateway to the famous Schwarzwald (Black Forest).

VILLAGE
Page Twenty-nine

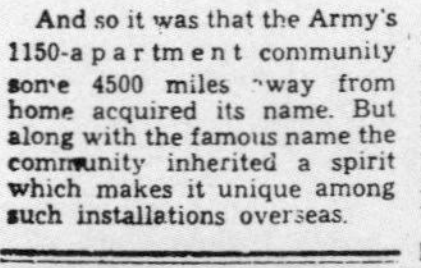

Ike Finds Being President Is Fascinating Job

WASHINGTON, May 31 (AP)—President Eisenhower said today he is fascinated by the work of the Presidency. But he gave no clear indication whether he intends to run again.

A reporter at the President's news conference reminded him that it will be three years tomorrow since he returned from Europe to begin the campaign which gave him the Republican Presidential nomination and ended with his election in November, 1952.

In the light of that fact the reporter asked the President how he likes politics.

Eisenhower said the term politics has many meanings but so often it is used in a derogatory sense. In that general sense, he said, he does not like politics.

But he said any man possessing the authority of the Presidency and the influence that it carries in working toward a peaceful world and minimizing the danger of war finds it fascinating.

Politics
Page Twenty-five

Saga of Long Island Sound

Sub Saves Man, 3 Boys Adrift 16 Hours in Boat

NIANTIC, Conn., May 31 (UP)—A man and three boys, adrift in Long Island Sound for more than 16 hours, were rescued today by the submarine Torsk.

All were reported in good condition and not in need of medical attention. They were being returned to New London.

The Torsk came upon their motorboat while two Coast Guard cutters searched a wide area for John Solgeski, 35; his son, JJohn Jr., 9, and Robert Larson, 16, and Doublas Clifford, 17, all of Glastonbury.

A few hours before they were found, Lt B. M. Wineke, head of the Coast Guard Station at New London, said that planes were preparing to engage in the search, but awaited clearer visibility.

Fog at Suffolk Hides First Race

A heavy fog at Suffolk Downs made it impossible to see the horses in the first race today until they reached the stretch. The official timer was not able to clock the six furlong race as he could not see the start.

Bulletins

WASHINGTON, May 31 (AP)—The Senate today passed without opposition a bill directing the Army engineers to survey Atlantic and Gulf coastal areas to find means of providing better warnings and protective works against hurricanes. During hearings on the measure the engineers indicated they would start their study in the Narragansett Bay, R. I., area.

SHREVEPORT, La., May 31 (UP)—A B-47 Stratojet medium bomber, capable of carrying atomic bombs to any part of the world, crashed in flames on take-off here today, killing its crew of four.

WASHINGTON, May 31 (UP)—President Eisenhower today sent to the Senate the nomination of William R. Pleshaw for postmaster at Framingham, Mass.

Suffolk Results

DAILY DOUBLE
Zipper and Una Whilly paid $93

Zipper, 114, Mercier	19.80	9.20	7.40
Best Chance, 121, Contr's		5.60	4.20
Cab Fare, 112, H Keene			14.80

(No running time.) Enterpriser, Gatica Bonita, You'll Learn, Deductible You, Platterette, Nomad, Odds Advance, Col Kimble and Star Now also ran. (Due to a heavy fog it was impossible to obtain running time.)

SUFFOLK
Page Forty-two

Airmen Look Well---to Meet Kin in Hawaii

HONG KONG, May 31 (AP)—Four American flyers released by Communist China after more than two years imprisonment reached Hong Kong today.

Less than three hours later they took off for Hawaii and reunion with their families.

The men, who had been shot down in the Korean war, appeared tired, but in good, if subdued, spirits. They told newsmen at the airport that they had been "well-treated."

United States Lt Col O. W. D. Simpson, who greeted the men at the Communist border, said their mental attitude "was extremely composed and they gave no evidence of being brain-washed."

(A special Air Force plane will leave Washington at noon tomorrow to take relatives of the four on a joyous journey to Honolulu. The big plane will arrive in Hawaii at 2 p. m., E. D. T., June 2, for the reunion.)

The four, all fighter pilots, are Capt Harold Fischer Jr., 28, of Swea City, Ia.; 1st Lt Lyle W. Cameron, Lincoln, Neb.; Lt Col Edwin Heller, 36, Wynnewood, Penn., and 1st Lt Roland W. Parks, 24, Omaha, Neb.

FLYERS
Page Nineteen

Comic Dictionary

REALTOR

A man who gets a little and gives a lot.

Police Bullets Stop Him

Man Kills 3, Wounds 4 Shooting Up Two Banks

DAYTON, O., May 31 (UP)—A man who said he "did it for my god," charged into two downtown banks today and shot and killed three persons, including an ex-football coach, before he was fatally wounded himself by police bullets.

The dead were:

Joe Gavin, ex-University of Dayton football coach, who died in a hospital shortly after being shot in the head.

Mrs. Fred Cramer, a secretary at the Third National Bank, who died of chest wounds.

George Sawaya, a market operator, who died on the scene.

The gunman was identified as Richard Meyers, 46, of the Samu Hotel, who told police on the way to the hospital that he "did it for my god." He died about two hours after the shooting.

The shooting occurred during the mid-morning rush hour at Dayton's busiest downtown business section.

They said he walked into the Third National Bank and shot five persons with a .38 caliber automatic pistol, then dashed to the adjoining Winter National Bank and Trust Co., where he shot two other persons before police felled him with three bullets.

BANK
Page Five

Most Boston Stores Open Tonight, Tomorrow Night

Boston department and specialty stores will be open tonight and tomorrow night, with some exceptions.

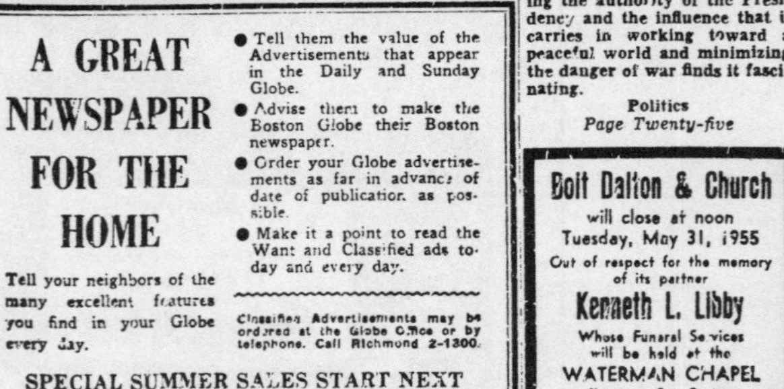

A GREAT NEWSPAPER FOR THE HOME
Tell your neighbors of the many excellent features you find in your Globe every day.
Tell them the value of the Advertisements that appear in the Daily and Sunday Globe.
Advise them to make the Boston Globe their Boston newspaper.
Order your Globe advertisements as far in advance of date of publication as possible.
Make it a point to read the Want and Classified ads today and every day.
Classified Advertisements may be ordered at the Globe Office or by telephone. Call Richmond 2-1300.
SPECIAL SUMMER SALES START NEXT MONTH IN BOSTON'S GREAT STORES

Publisher

1955 - 1977

WILLIAM DAVIS TAYLOR (1908-) He assumed control in 1955 and took the Globe to new heights -- and in 1958, a new home in Dorchester by the bay. Teamed with his cousin, John I. Taylor, the Globe's president, to fight off all competitors -- in particular the Herald-Traveler Corp., with its newspaper, radio and television properties -- and to re-establish the Globe in General Taylor's image: as the pre-eminent news medium in Boston and New England. Davis Taylor established the Globe as a public company in 1973, when Affiliated Publications was born, and retired as publisher in 1977.

CASTRO HAS ALL CUBA

Reg. U.S. Pat. Off. © 1959, Globe Newspaper Co.

BOSTON DAILY GLOBE—FRIDAY, JAN. 2, 1959

CLXXV NO. 2 44 PAGES—FIVE CENTS

Latest Forecast
BOSTON AND VICINITY—Clearing tonight, lowest temperature in the lower 30's. Some early morning fog likely in low places inland. Saturday generally fair, highest temperature about 40 degrees.
(Full report on page 12.)

IN TONIGHT'S GLOBE

Bridge	42	Problem	42
Classified	36, 37	Radio-TV	27
Comics	42, 43	Society	29
Crane	42	Sports	39-41
Cross Word	26	Star Gazer	27
Deaths	35	Theaters	30, 31
Editorial	22	Twistagram	42
Financial	43	Women's	28, 29

Havana Is Tense As Rebels Enter City in Triumph

Some Dance in Streets After Batista Flees

HAVANA, Jan. 2 (AP) — Supporters of rebel leader Fidel Castro took over Cuba today from the disintegrated regime of fallen dictator Fulgencio Batista.

Castro celebrated his triumph after 25 months of rebellion by proclaiming his native Santiago as the nation's provisional capital and naming Manuel Urrutia as provisional president.

Advance spearheads of Castro's revolutionary forces entered Havana this noon. Truckloads of bearded guerrilla fighters rolled into the city over the main central highway from the eastern provinces of Matanzas and Las Villas and sped along the Malecon Sea boulevard toward the former military headquarters of deposed President Batista at Camp Columbia.

Meanwhile tanks swung into batle today in fighting that seemed to center around a business district block in Havana where troops from a private army of Fulgencio Batista's followers were holed up.

CUBA
Page Twenty-one

CELEBRATION IN HAVANA—Crowds dance and cheer as they race through street (top) after hearing that President Fulgencio Batista had fled country. In lower photo citizens search ruins of place of business. (UPI Telephoto)

Batista Backers Flee in Anything That Moves

(By the Associated Press)

The Cuban revolution has sent hundreds of supporters of Cuban dictator Fulgencio Batista scurrying for cover in the United States and the Dominican Republic.

Planes, including the fallen President's private craft, a yacht, an auto ferry and even a converted PT boat carried the refugees from the war-torn Caribbean island. Batista, himself, fled to exile in the Dominican Republic, leaving Cuba to the rebel forces of Fidel Castro.

REFUGEES
Page Twenty-one

Something's Gotta Give

Schmidt on Spot As Rebels Rule Slumping Bruins

By HERB RALBY

The Bruins' situation is so bad that apparently one of two things has to happen. Either Coach Milt Schmidt has to go or the team malcontents must go.

STYMIED SCHMIDT—Will Bruins' coach stay or go?

The situation on the club was demonstrated last night when the Bruins were beaten soundly, 5 to 2, by the New York Rangers at the Garden.

It was the fourth straight loss for the Bruins, and dropped them a little closer to the National Hockey League cellar.

The meeting in New York earlier this week which was held to air the gripes and clear the air, only served to make things worse.

BRUINS
Page Thirty-nine

Woman Seized Robbing Bank 2d Time in N.Y.

NEW YORK, Jan. 2 (AP)—A woman who staged a $3000 robbery at a Manhattan bank a month ago was seized today when she attempted a similar feat at another bank a block away.

She was identified by police as Vera Wilson, 57.

In both cases the woman had threatened to throw acid on bank employees at money windows if they did not give her their cash.

BANK
Page Nine

Tropical Results

DAILY DOUBLE
Flameyed and Lady Royal paid $69.50.

FIRST—$2100, claiming, 3-year-old maidens, 1 1-16 miles.

Flameyed (Toulmetis)	8.50	4.00	3.20
R. Butler (Brooks)		3.40	3.30
Sharp Scamp (Dalton)			10.90

SECOND—$2000, claiming, 4-year-olds and up, 6 furlongs.

Lady Royal (Ussery)	12.00	4.80	4.40
Shame On You (Cox)		5.50	4.50
Game Heart (Gibb)			10.20

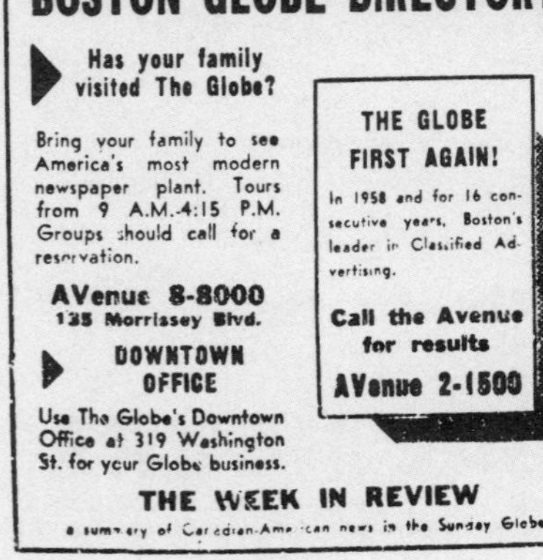

Sense of Humor Needed With 7 Children

Mrs. Dean Martin Is Family Top Kick

MAMA'S IN THE MIDDLE—Mrs. Dean Martin poses with husband and rest of family on porch of home in Hollywood. Mrs. Martin, former Orange Bowl queen from Miami, is top sergeant in the Martin household. (AP Wirephoto)

By DOROTHY ROE

HOLLYWOOD, Jan. 2 (AP)—If you have a sense of humor you can take anything in stride, says little Blonde Jeanne Martin, a former Orange Bowl queen from Miami who looks like a teen-ager but is top sergeant to a houseful of seven children and her dashing husband, Dean.

"I'm so busy sorting socks, picking up toys and settling teen-age love affairs that I wouldn't have time to be jealous of Dean even if I wanted to," says Jeanne, holding little Gina, 2, on her knee while expertly taping a baseball bat for Dino, 7.

The Martin home in Beverly Hills usually resembles a children's day camp, with Mama Jeanne a sort of junior counselor, leading the gang in a game of "run-sheep-run" or water polo in the swimming pool.

When Jeanne and Dean were married in 1949, the light-hearted bride inherited a ready-made family of four children: Craig, Claudia, Gail and Deana, then ranging in age from 7 to 1. Since then the tribe has been increased by three more—Dino, Ricci and Gina, aged 7, 5 and 2. The older children now have attained teen-age status and the accompanying problems, but Jeanne rules the roost with accomplished ease and frequent attacks of giggles.

MRS. MARTIN
Page Eight

Ike to Reveal Flag Tomorrow

GETTYSBURG, Jan. 2 (AP)—President Eisenhower gave final approval today to a new 49-star American flag. But the design, with a 49th star for Alaska, still was kept secret.

The new flag will be unveiled at a White House ceremony at noon EST tomorrow.

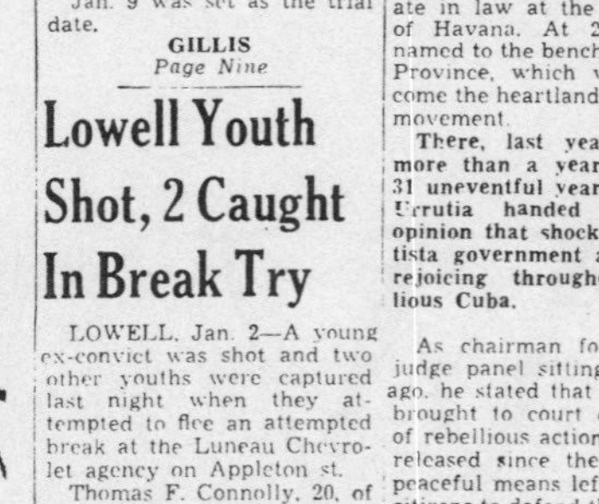

Mayor Gillis Charges Assault By 2 Brothers

NEWBURYPORT, Jan. 2—Warrants were issued in District Court today for the arrest of former Mayor Henry Graf Jr., 49, and his brother, F. William, 47, president of the Rotary Club, charging them with assault and battery on Mayor Andrew J. "Bossy" Gillis.

Clerk Florence G. Barrett issued the warrants at the request of Gillis who claims he was the victim of an assault in his service station at Market sq. at 6 p.m. last Wednesday.

Jan. 9 was set as the trial date.

Gillis said that the two brothers, owners of Graf Bros. Express, rushed into his station and began assaulting him, injuring his knee.

He said that the assault followed a statement he made the night before at a school committee meeting.

GILLIS
Page Nine

Lowell Youth Shot, 2 Caught In Break Try

LOWELL, Jan. 2—A young ex-convict was shot and two other youths were captured last night when they attempted to flee an attempted break at the Luneau Chevrolet agency on Appleton st.

Thomas F. Connolly, 20, of Rock st., Lowell, who recently served one month for assault, was shot in the left leg by patrolman Robert J. Liston. Connolly is under police guard at St. John's Hospital. His condition is good.

The youth was seized at the hospital when he appeared there 45 minutes after the shooting, suffering from loss of blood.

LOWELL
Page Thirty-five

Stores Open Tonight

Boston department and specialty stores generally will be open tonight for convenience of shoppers.

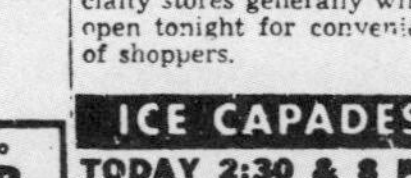

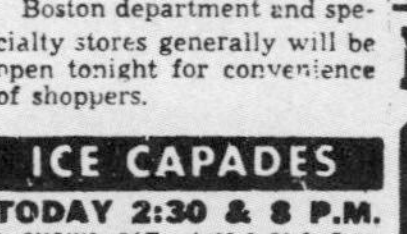

Rejects Red Support

New Cuban President Good Friend of U.S.

Manuel Urrutia Lleo, 58-year-old provisional president of Cuba, is strongly anti-Communist and pro-American.

Compared to the romantic chief of the revolutionary forces, Fidel Castro, Urrutia is a personality that can be drawn only in shaded grays. Until 1957 he was not identified with the rebel movement that brought him to power today.

Dark, stocky, mustachioed, Urrutia is a native of Las Villas Province and a graduate in law at the University of Havana. At 26 he was named to the bench in Oriente Province, which was to become the heartland of Castro's movement.

There, last year, a little more than a year ago after 31 uneventful years as judge, Urrutia handed down an opinion that shocked the Batista government and caused rejoicing throughout rebellious Cuba.

CASTRO'S CHOICE—This is Manuel Urrutia, former judge and more recently an exile in New York, chosen by Fidel Castro as provisional president. (AP Wirephoto)

As chairman for a three-judge panel sitting in Santiago, he stated that 150 youths brought to court on charges of rebellious action should be released since there was no peaceful means left to Cuban citizens to defend their constitutional rights. He was overruled by two other judges, but he had estabished himself as a champion of liberty.

URRUTIA
Page Twenty-one

Washington Not Pessimistic

Reds Can Cash In on Cuba Only If Chaos Continues

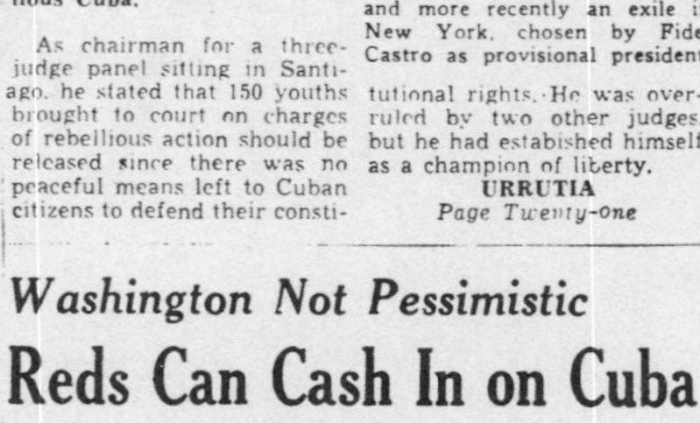

By EDWIN A. LAHEY

WASHINGTON, Jan. 2—Can the Communists cash in on the Cuban tragedy?

This is a possibility, if the chaos spreads in Havana.

There is a Communist underground of undetermined magnitude in Cuba, and there has been some Communist infiltration of the ranks of Fidel Castro, whose revolution has finally overthrown the government of Fulgencio Batista.

But competent observers here are hopeful that the situation in Cuba can be stabilized pending some new elections.

LAHEY
Page Twenty-one

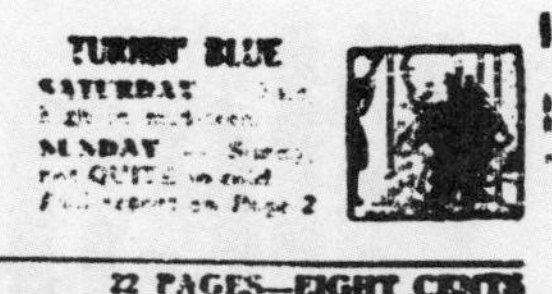

VOL. CLXXIX NO. 21 — © 1961 By GLOBE NEWSPAPER CO. — BOSTON, SATURDAY, JAN. 21, 1961 — Telephone AV 8-8000 — 22 PAGES—EIGHT CENTS

'Let Us Never Negotiate out of Fear... but Never Fear to Negotiate'

BEAMING AT HIS SUCCESSOR, outgoing President Eisenhower leaves White House with John F. Kennedy for the swearing-in ceremonies. (UPI Telephoto)

Kennedy Offers World New Start for Peace

Vow to New Nations: Won't Allow Tyranny

Other Inaugural Stories, Pictures on Pages 4, 5, 12, 15 and 22.

By JOHN HARRIS
(Globe Political Editor)

WASHINGTON, Jan. 20—President John F. Kennedy started off his administration with high hopes today, acclaimed by the nation and the entire globe for his inaugural appeal that both sides in the Cold War "begin anew the quest for peace."

Bareheaded despite the 22-degree temperature and icy wind that cut into the shivering throng in Capitol Plaza, the new 43-year-old leader of the free world made peace the rallying cry for the 1960's and the new generation, in his singularly brief, 15-minute speech, which was carried electronically all over the earth.

"To those nations who would make themselves our adversary," declared Mr. Kennedy, his face as solemn as his message, "we offer not a pledge, but a request:

"That both sides begin anew the quest for peace, before the dark powers of destruction unleashed by science engulf all humanity in planned or accidental self-destruction."

INAUGURAL

Page Four

PRESIDENT KENNEDY DELIVERS inaugural address. Seated near each other are Mrs. Jacqueline Kennedy and former President Eisenhower. (UPI Telephoto)

15 Die, 300 Flee Flood Tides As Blizzard Pounds at N.E.

By EDWARD G. McGRATH

The Inauguration Day blizzard of 1961 howled its way into the history books yesterday by heaping misery on the highways, pounding and flooding coastal homes of New England and plunging the area into an Arctic deep freeze.

Fifteen persons, eight of them from Massachusetts, died in the bitter storm which para in the bitter storm which paralyzed transportation with 12-foot drifts, battered the shore with 35-foot waves and dumped two feet of snow in Western Massachusetts.

It was a blizzard of many contradictions.

City and M.T.A. officials were enthused because Boston generally kept its traffic moving.

But coastal homeowners were stunned by the vicious assault of flood tides which heavily damaged property, disintegrated sea walls and forced the evacuation of more than 300 residents.

Hardest hit was Hull, where at 1:50 yesterday afternoon 250 residents fled their homes on foot and in boats. Civil Defense amphibious ducks and school buses, Heavy seas, pushed by 50-knot winds, flooded the peninsula's lowlands.

Boston measured an official near-record 12.2 inches of snow before the storm tapered off in late afternoon and some of the coldest air of the Winter invaded New England.

Last night, while the six-state area continued the battle to reactivate transportation, temperatures were skidding rapidly to zero on the coast, 10 below in southern interior areas and 15 below in many sections to the north.

STORM

Page Two

STORM PHOTOS, PAGE 7

K Cables Hope For New Peace Under Kennedy

LONDON, Jan. 20 (Reuters)—Russian Premier Nikita Khrushchev and President Leonir Brezhnev today cabled President Kennedy an inauguration day message extending the hope for a "radical improvement" in Soviet-American relations.

They hoped, the Soviet news agency Tass reported, that joint efforts of the United States and Russia would improve relations and therefore "make healthier the entire international climate."

KHRUSHCHEV

Page Twelve

Me Too, Says Fidel; 'Invasion' Alert Off

HAVANA, Jan. 20 (AP)—Prime Minister Fidel Castro tonight called off Cuba's three-week military alert against a "Yankee invasion" that never came and offered to "begin anew" a quest for peace with the administration of President Kennedy.

Castro told a rally of demobilized militiamen at the Presidential Palace that his government noted "with pleasure some positive aspects" of President Kennedy's inaugural address and he promised "no gratuitous attacks and no gratuitous hostile acts" against the United States.

CASTRO

Page Twenty-two

No Mere Snowstorm Curbs Kennedy Magic

By WILFRID C. RODGERS
(Globe Staff Correspondent)

WASHINGTON, Jan. 20—President John Fitzgerald Kennedy squeaked through to another victory today—over a potent snowstorm and other assorted inauguration snags. . . . The 35th President of the United States faced it unflinching.

Other New Englanders weren't so brave. Still chilled from a snow bath the night before, they ran for cover. They found it in hotel lobbies, hotel rooms and in front of TV sets.

WASHINGTON

Page Twelve

Today's Quotes

President Kennedy in his inaugural address—"Let every nation know, whether it wishes us well or ill, that we shall pay any price, bear any burden, meet any hardship, support any friend, oppose any foe to assure the survival and success of liberty."

Dwight D. Eisenhower on how it feels to become a private citizen—"Wonderful, wonderful, fine."

(United Press International)

Fr. Lally Stands Behind Logue In Row on Staff Reorganization

By ROBERT B. HANRON

Rt. Rev. Francis J. Lally last night took issue with two colleagues on the Boston Redevelopment Authority and came out in full support of Edward J. Logue for the post of development administrator.

The time has come, he said, for the Authority to make up its mind.

"The decision is either in favor of progress or against it," he declared, "and either Boston goes forward with Mr. Logue or remains in a second-class status in the urban renewal effort."

Msgr. Lally, vice-chairman of the Authority and editor of The Pilot, official publication of the Catholic Archdiocese, said that his position, as well as that of Chairman Joseph W. Lund, is well known.

Earlier this week, two other members, James G. Colbert and Stephen J. McCloskey, expressed the opinion that the staff reorganization proposed by Logue is "illegal" and that they could not adopt it in its present form.

RENEWAL ROW

Page Three

GUIDE TO FEATURES

Bridge	17	Financial	10, 11
Churches	8, 9	Obituaries	18
Classified	18-21	Radio-TV	17
Comics	16, 17	Shain	22
Cross-Word	17	Sports	13, 14
Deaths	18	Star Gazer	17
Dr. Crane	17	Theaters	8
Drummond	6	Twistagram	22
Editorials	6	Women	16

TOO MUCH SUN—Poet Robert Frost, 85, has trouble reading inaugural poem's dedication, even with help of shading hat. (AP Wirephoto)

Frost's Eyes Fail Him . . . But His Heart Pinch-Hits

The text of Robert Frost's dedication, which the aging poet was unable to read is on page 4.

By ROBERT L. HEALY
(Globe Washington Correspondent)

WASHINGTON, Jan 20—The huge crowd on the Capitol grounds had forgot—for the moment—John Fitzgerald Kennedy.

The spectators weren't thinking about Richard M. Nixon and his defeat. They didn't even know—at that one awesome moment—that Dwight D. Eisenhower was on the platform.

Every eye—every hope—and every prayer was centered on one man—white-haired, aged, and bent.

Robert Frost—the nation's most outstanding poet—man whose words may well outlive any deed of many Presidents—was groping, stumbling over words, and hurting inside.

FROST

Page Four

Tax Official's Suicide Note Hints 'Politics'

Acting State Police Capt. Michael J. Cullinane said last night he was told that one of two alleged suicide notes left by a Massachusetts Tax Department official in Florida had "political implications."

Cullinane said he was told by Monroe County, Fla., officers that they were seeking authorization to divulge the contents of both notes to Massachusetts authorities.

They were allegedly left by Albert H. Stitt, 48, of Chestnut st., Waban, deputy director of the Tax Department's Alcoholic Excise Division, found dead in his car of carbon monoxide poisoning in Key Largo, Fla., Thursday night.

TAX OFFICIAL

Page Three

Kennedys Open Social Whirl

HERE'S THAT EVENING DRESS—President and Mrs. John F. Kennedy leave White House for inaugural ball. She's shown for first time in her specially-designed white sheath with puffy overblouse. (AP Wirephoto)

Inaugural Dances Cap President's First Day

By FRANCES BURNS
(Globe Staff Correspondent)

President and Mrs. Kennedy entered the Washington social whirl as the nation's first couple tonight by attending five festive inaugural balls.

An evening of champagne, cake and compositions capped the social salute to the new occupants of the White House.

The champagne flowed into glasses held by hundreds of Democrats who gathered in hotels and the local armory. The toasts to Kennedy, Vice President Johnson and their ladies started in the Mayflower Hotel.

John and Jacqueline Kennedy departed from the White House at 9:50 p.m. Mrs. Kennedy wore a white silk sheath by Oleg Cassini, a sheer chiffon lace overblouse, and long white elbow-length gloves.

BALL

Page Twelve

Glenn: 3 Orbits, Down Safely

SPORTS
FINAL
STOCKS
EVENING
EDITION
The Boston Globe
Reg. U.S. Pat. Off.

THE BOSTON GLOBE—TUESDAY, FEB. 20, 1962
VOL. CLXXXI NO. 51 44 PAGES—EIGHT CENTS
Telephone AV 8-8000

FAIR
Continued Cold Tonight, Wednesday
(Full report on Page 12.)
High Tide Today—5:36 p.m.

IN TONIGHT'S GLOBE

Bridge	32	Port News	19
Classified	40-43	Problem	32
Comics	32, 33	Radio-TV	33
Crane	32	Society	26
Cross-Word	32	Sports	35-38
Deaths	39	Star Gazer	32
Editorial	28	Theaters	20
Financial	30, 31	Twistagram	5
Lippmann	28	Women's	26, 27

Condition 'Excellent' at End Of Historic Trip in Space; Nation Hears All His Reports

By DONALD WHITE
(Globe Staff Correspondent)

CAPE CANAVERAL, Feb. 20 — Astronaut John H. Glenn Jr. successfully completed America's first manned orbital flight at 2:43 p.m. today.

His space capsule, Friendship 7, landed in a target area at sea off the Bahamas about 800 miles south of here after circling the earth three times.

"My condition is excellent," he told the destroyer Noa, which rushed to his landing site and lifted the space cabin onto its deck at 3:01 p.m.

The Noa was only six miles away and had kept a close watch as the space vehicle reentered the earth's atmosphere.

The 4 hour and 56 minute flight in orbits ranging from 100 to 160 miles high was largely according to plan.

(AP Wirephoto)

A SMILE BEFORE ORBIT—Astronaut Glenn's green eyes sparkled beneath his space helmet as he rode in van from hangar to launching pad this morning. Just before entering capsule he laid a friendly hand on the shoulder of Charles Buckley of New Bedford, a security officer.

At 3:25 p.m., Glenn emerged after a side hatch was blown to free him. He said he was "hale and hearty."

The side hatch exit was called routine, and he got out of that port rather than by the neck.

"Boy, that was a real fireball," Glenn had cracked as his cabin re-entered the atmosphere and floated down under bright tropic skies.

"I had a fine trip," Glenn smiled as he received cheers from the crew of the destroyer after leaving the space vehicle through the emergency hatch.

Helicopters were hovering over the destroyer and they whipped the astronaut to the carrier Randolph about 55 miles away, for medical exams and scientific questioning that is expected to keep him under wraps for 48 hours.

President Kennedy, on hearing of that Glenn was safe said:

"I know that I express great happiness and thanksgiving of all of us that Col Glenn has completed his trip."

"This (space) is a new ocean and I believe the United States must sail on it."

The President was connected by phone from his office in the White House to the Randolph and congratulated Glenn personally for a "job well done."

Glenn was immediately escorted to special quarters on the carrier for a briefing and where he will remain until flown to Grand Turk Island in the Bahamas for two days of rest.

Glenn started his 80,000 mile triple spin around the earth at 9:47 a.m. as millions of Americans were glued to TV screens or to portable radios.

SPACE SHOT
Page Twenty-four

THREE-ORBIT LANDING took place in area marked below. Two other sites had been chosen had it been decided Glenn would land after one orbit of the earth, or after two. Ships were posted in each area.

1,640,000 Would Benefit

Billion Boost Asked for U. S. Employees

WASHINGTON, Feb. 20 (AP)—President Kennedy urged Congress today to provide a $1 billion pay raise over three years for the government's white collar workers. The aim, he said, is to put Federal pay on a par with that outside so that competent people can afford to work for Uncle Sam.

The President said in a special message that he was proposing "Federal pay reform, not simply a Federal pay raise."

For the whole field of white collar workers, the increase would amount to 10 percent of the present $10 billion annual payroll. But for individuals the raises would range from 3.7 percent to about 33 percent for the three-year period. The first increase would come Jan. 1.

Mr. Kennedy said he is proposing a wholly new, "common sense" approach to the problem of putting Federal salaries on a basis comparable to those in non-Federal service.

This would be done for all but the highest level officials. And for them, Mr. Kennedy said, "The most vital single element" in the proposal is pay adjustments for top executive and professional positions.

FEDERAL PAY
Page Five

Kennedy Uses Phone, TV to Follow Launch

WASHINGTON, Feb. 20 (AP) — President Kennedy watched the launching of astronaut John H. Glenn Jr. into orbit today and was described as very pleased that the first phase of the flight had gone off very successfully.

Press Secretary Pierre Salinger said Kennedy followed the launching closely.

The President, with Mrs. Kennedy at his side, began watching the launching preliminaries at 7:15 a.m. on a television set in his bedroom. Kennedy continued to watch in his bedroom until 8:50 a.m.

He went then to the small dining room on the first floor of the White House to join Democratic leaders who were there for their usual Tuesday morning breakfast-conference with the President.

KENNEDY
Page Seventeen

DAY WATCH -:- -:- By Percy Shain

TV's Big Moment Comes With Blastoff

All America had its head in the clouds today. And that was no mere figure of speech.

SHAIN

With astronaut John Glenn firmly in orbit after a perfect launching, you could almost hear the collective sigh of a nation that had waited patiently through 10 postponements for this big moment.

It had been a tense morning. It seemed that everybody was going about their business with one eye on the TV set, two fingers crossed in a gesture of optimism, and a mind more interested in counting off the minutes than in carrying on routine tasks.

This was one day that clock-watching was no disgrace. The minutes loomed large with success at hand after three years of preparation and six weeks of waiting at Canaveral.

This was television's big show and it was making the most of it. All channels were on the air at 6:30 a.m. with full network coverage: live shots from Cape Canaveral mixed with canned interviews, glimpses from key spots around the nation and out to sea, visual aids and devices to show what was happening, and all sorts of scattered features to fill in the period of waiting, both before and after liftoff time, which came officially at 9:47 a.m.

DAY WATCH
Page Seventeen

Aerospace Issues Lead Spotty Market

The stock market was higher in quiet trading late in the session. The advance was led by aerospace issues, which were active from the opening.

Refers to Looting Cases

Sullivan Quashed Probe, Volpe Aide Charges

By C. R. OWENS

A legal advisor to Gov. Volpe testified this afternoon that in his opinion "there was some substance" to two anonymous complaints that Boston police were guilty of looting and that in one case Police Commissioner Leo J. Sullivan "quashed" an investigation of the charges.

Information on the alleged criminal acts of members of the Boston Police Department was drawn from Atty. Harold Hestnes by counsel for Commissioner Sullivan as the second day of a hearing on the commissioner's removal opened at the State House.

Hestnes was obviously a reluctant witness and he sparred with Atty. John V. Bonner for more than a half-hour before revealing the contents of a letter he sent to Dist. Atty. Garrett H. Byrne concerning Sullivan's administration.

At three points during the hearing Atty. James D. St. Clair, who is handling the governor's removal proceedings against Sullivan, objected to the course of Bonner's questions only to have the governor overrule him.

SULLIVAN

Plows Score New Success In 3d Storm

Dean Cushing, president of the Retail Trade Board, announced: "We are pleased that the city, once again, has demonstrated its mastery of snow removal. Our congratulations for an excellent job."

CLEANUP

Nothing Left to Chance

24 Ships at Pickup Spots

CAPE CANAVERAL, Feb. 20 (AP)—A mighty fleet sailed the Atlantic missile range today, waiting to snatch astronaut John H. Glenn Jr. from the sea the moment he returned from his globe-circling journey through space.

The armada was spaced from the watery edge of the launch area across the Atlantic to the Canary Islands. Led by three aircraft carriers, it included 24 ships, 60 aircraft, and 15,000 men.

In command was Rear Adm John L. Chew, commander of destroyer flotilla four, who issued orders in the mercury control center at the Cape.

The mission assigned the recovery force was nothing new for the Navy. The manual of procedure was developed three years ago by the destroyer Putnum in exercises off Norfolk, Va. Since then the procedures have been practiced over and over and refined until the Navy feels it would be practically impossible to lose the astronaut at sea.

FLEET
Page Eleven

Hialeah Results

HIALEAH

Stores Open Thursday, Washington's Birthday

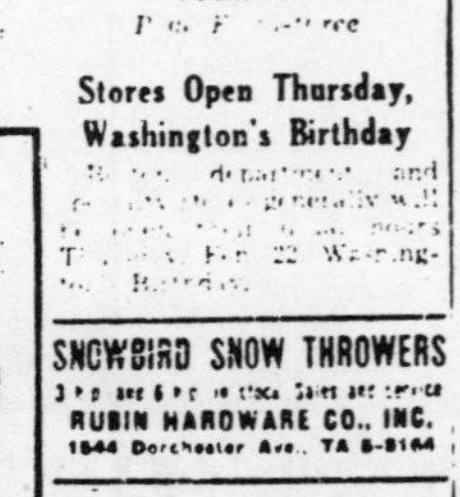

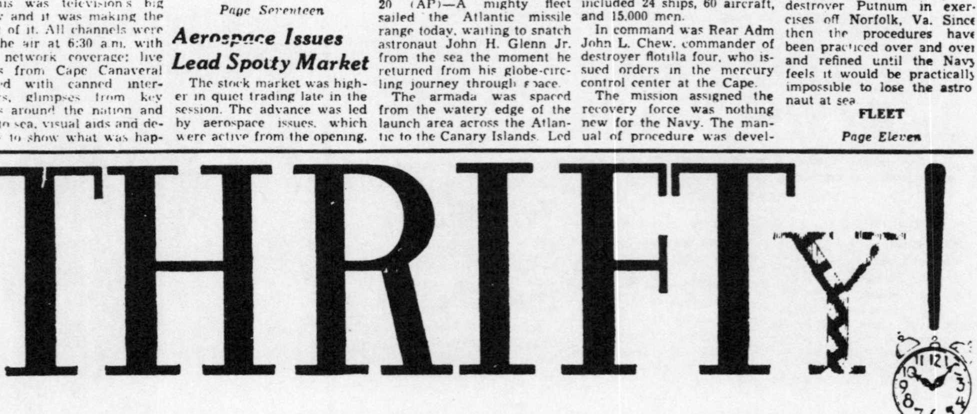
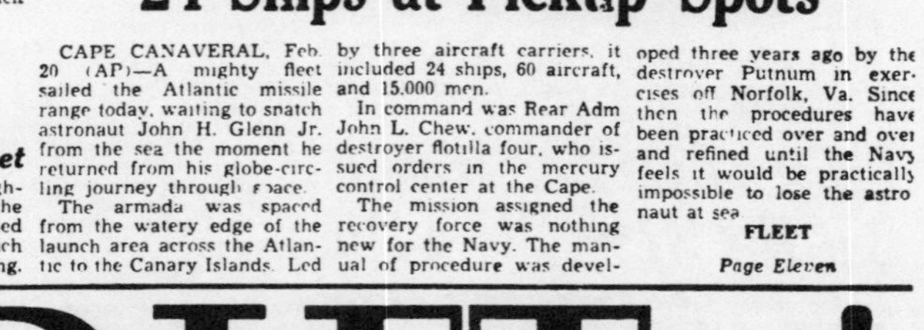
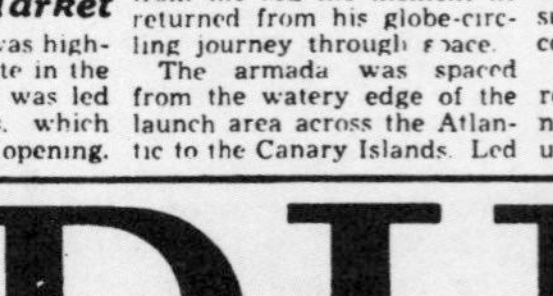

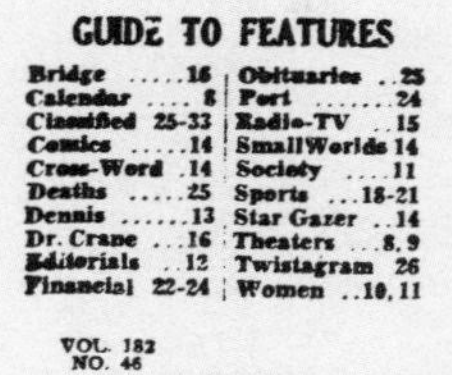

GUIDE TO FEATURES

Bridge	16	Obituaries	25
Calendar	8	Port	24
Classified	25-33	Radio-TV	15
Comics	14	SmallWorlds	14
Cross-Word	14	Society	11
Deaths	25	Sports	18-21
Dennis	13	Star Gazer	14
Dr. Crane	16	Theaters	8, 9
Editorials	12	Twistagram	26
Financial	22-24	Women	10, 11

VOL. 182 NO. 46

© 1962 By GLOBE NEWSPAPER CO

The Boston Globe

MORNING EDITION

Reg. U. S. Pat. Off.

WEDNESDAY, AUGUST 15, 1962

Telephone AV 8-8000

34 PAGES—10c

UP SMILING

WEDNESDAY—Warm, less humid.
THURSDAY—Partly cloudy.

High Tide
11:29 a.m. 11:48 p.m.
Sun Rises 5:51 **Sun Sets** 7:45

(Full report on page 2)

$2 MILLION MAIL ROBBERY

Machine-Gunners Clear Plymouth Road for Job

By FRANK MAHONEY and SEYMOUR LINSCOTT

A gang with machine guns staged a Hollywood-style stickup of a U.S. mail truck in Plymouth at 8 last night and investigators said the loot could exceed $2 million.

One of the guards on the truck gave that estimate. State Police detectives said it seemed sure to top the $1,219,000 Brink's robbery.

At 3 this morning, Lt. Det. Joseph Simmons of the Norfolk County district attorney's office said that on the basis of information then available, the total could reach $2 million.

The loot, all or nearly all, in cash was contained in 17 sealed bags.

It was not certain whether the money was deposits being transferred here from Cape Cod banks, or receipts from Cape post offices, or both.

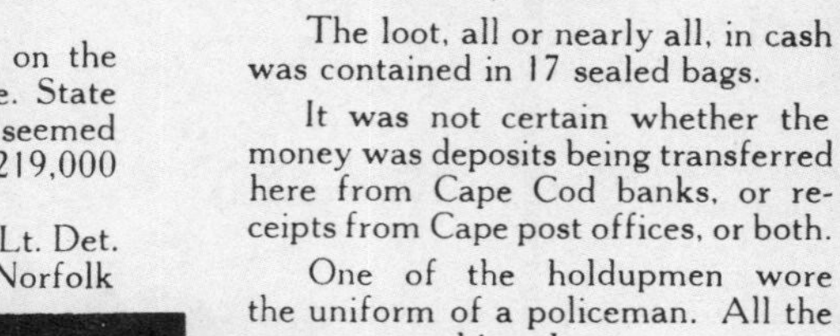

One of the holdupmen wore the uniform of a policeman. All the gang wore white gloves.

The truck was hi-jacked on the northbound lane of Rte. 3. The robbers made sure they would not be interrupted by blocking the lane several miles back with detour signs at the nearest exit.

The two postal employees aboard the truck were armed but had no chance to use their weapons.

Nine men and a woman, using at least four cars, are believed to have taken part in the carefully planned job.

Two of the cars were found abandoned on Rte. 3 in Plymouth.

Three of the gang commandeered the truck, tied the guards hand and foot, tossed them into the back and drove off toward Boston.

Some of the bags of cash were transferred from the truck to one car at the holdup scene.

The truck was stopped twice later for further transfers of loot to other cars.

The mail truck and the guards were left on Rte. 128 near Rte. 28 in Randolph.

MAIL ROBBERY
Page Three

Police Check Hijacked Truck

Vehicle which was abandoned on Route 128, near the junction of Route 28 in Randolph.

'One Was Called Buster'

The following is the account of the holdup as told to State Troopers Paul Martin and Robert Grudzinski of Norwell Barracks by thetwo guards—William F. Barrett of 24 Branch st., Mansfield, and Patrick Schena, 36, of 53 Winthrop st., Everett.

Schena was the spokesman:

"They first stopped us on Route 3, near the bypass. A car went by us at about 80 miles an hour. We were only doing about 45 miles an hour.

"We saw the car stop up in front of us, and a policeman got out and waved his arms over his head to stop us. I stopped the truck.

GUARDS
Page Twenty-six

Huge Cash Shipment A Normal Routine

Why was so much money in transit last night?

It was part of the constant shuffling of cash between banks and the Federal Reserve institution in Boston.

"When commercial banks get too much currency and coins they send it to us," a Federal Reserve spokesman said.

"The accounts of these banks are credited, and when they need cash we send it back to them," the official said.

There is a steady movement of currency in and out from the Federal Reserve Bank at 30 Pearl st. in the downtown district.

Most financial transactions of any size are carried by checks these days, so "unwanted cash builds up.

While the currency is at the Federal Reserve bank in Boston any worn-out notes are destroyed and new currency issued.

DEPOSITS
Page Twenty-six

COSMONAUTS DOWN SAFE

EXTRA

MOSCOW (AP)—Russia's space twins landed this morning "exactly in the pre-determined area" of the Soviet Union after space flights that broke all records for orbiting the earth an dtravel in space, Tass announced.

The Sovieet news agency said Maj Andrian Nikolayev landed at 9:55 a.m. Moscow time (2:55 a.m. EDT) and Lt Col Pavel Popovich at 10:01 a.m.

"Both cosmonauts feel fine," said Tass.

LANDING
Page Thirteen

Inspector Hears Story of Kidnaped Mailmen

(Globe Photo by Charles Carey)

Mail truck driver Patrick Schena (center) and fellow worker William F. Barrett (right) were held up by gang in Plymouth, bound, and driven to Randolph where truck, minus money-bearing mail bags, was abandoned. Inspector checks with them for clues inside police car at the scene.

Not Job of Amateurs

By EDWARD G. McGRATH

The smooth-as-silk holdup of the mail truck could only have come as a result of long and careful planning.

The actual hijacking of the truck was carried out with dispatch, and without a hitch.

Behind the actual caper, police said, must have lain hours and hours of plotting and rehearsal.

It was, in fact, a very professional job executed by men cooly efficient and calculatingly cunning.

The procuring of a uniform of a policeman, and having the fake officer bring the mail truck to a halt; the precision timing as the intercepting cars shot off the side of the highway and cut off the truck, the smoothness with which the guards were disarmed, with no shots fired . . . these were not the antics of amateurs.

It took a person versed in the art of hijacking to come up with the idea of stealing detour signs and using them to block Rte. 3 at hte Clark rd. exit to forestall some motorist driving onto the holdup scene and queering the stickup.

No unnecessary violence, no jittery fingers on the triggers of the machine guns, no bare hands to leave fingerprints . . . these were the result of precise planning and exceptional execution.

The bandits were careful to remain fairly well dispersed as they carried out the job: some in the truck, others following in getaway cars.

If the police had intercepted them before the robbery was completed, some might have got away with a portion of the loot.

Their "aimless" driving of the truck after they commandeered it was to confuse the guards, take time to transfer the loot to the various cars, and to help alert them to pursuers.

They were careful to ensure a "disappearance" at the end of the job by making sure the guards could not describe the getaway cars.

PLANNING
Page Three

SUSPECT N.Y. GANG

By RICHARD A. POWERS

The FBI and postal inspectors teamed up with state and local police last night to match clues that would quickly put them on the trail of the machinegun-weilding bandits.

The use of the machine guns in the brazen holdup led to speculations that the heist was staged by a gang of desperadoes wanted for bank robbery and murder in New York.

GANG
Page Three

The View Was Great, But...

Reporter Sees Moon, Stars, No Vostok

By CHARLES E. CLAFFEY

The Russians slipped one over on me last night.

Literally rising to the occasion of the purported passage over Boston of the Soviet capsule Vostok III, I took to the air in an effort to observe the historic passage.

The sky over Logan Airport approximated the clarity of crystal between 9 and 9:10 last night as I circled in a single-engined Cessna plane.

The moon (full) was completely unobscured. The stars (bright) glittered unrestrainedly.

It looked like a perfect night for . . . well, just about anything.

"A perfect night, huh?" I asked the pilot, Don Mathieson, of Lawrence, nervously seeking assurance.

"Yuh, a little haze, though," he replied, leveling the craft off at 4500 feet, and facing the northeast, shortly **before 9** o'clock.

VIEW
Page Six

Cloture Vote Finally Ends Filibuster

WASHINGTON (UPI) — For the first time in 35 years and only the fifth time in history, the Senate voted yesterday to gag itself and choke off filibuster by a small band of Democrats against the Administration's Space Communications Bill.

The vote was 63 to 27, three more than the two-thirds majority needed to approve the cloture petition filed by Senate leaders.

Only two Republicans, Barry Goldwater of Arizona, and John G. Tower of Texas, voted against the gag.

FILIBUSTER
Page Six

Caggiano Ruled Off Ballot; Board Eyes Connolly List

By JEFFREY A. OSOFF

Former Rep. Pasquale Caggiano of Lynn, one of three candidates for the Democratic nomination for lieutenant governor, suffered a double jolt yesterday within the space of an hour.

Shortly after the Massachusetts Ballot Law Commission had ruled his name off the Sept. 18 primary ballot because of 127 "not genuine" signatures, Atty. Gen. Edward J. McCormack Jr. announced that he would bring Caggiano before the Suffolk County Grand Jury possibly Monday, to explain his charge of "pressure" to quit the race.

PASQUALE CAGGIANO
Off the ballot

HERBERT L. CONNOLLY
Status in doubt

Late last night the commission was checking signatures on the nomination papers of Newton auto dealer Herb Connolly, also a candidate for lieutenant governor.

Connolly's problems began mounting when handwriting expert Elizabeth F. McCarthy testified that she "found a pattern of forgeries" on Connolly's papers.

"One person has written most of the signatures on the nominations papers from Brockton, Watertown, Lawrence, Dorchester, Springfield, Milford and Chicopee," Miss McCarthy said.

BALLOT LAW
Page Five

Goes It Alone as Others Row

Boston Acts on Own Inner Belt Sections

By ROBERT B. HANRON

While other communities were still wrangling, Boston moved forward last night to expedite construction of its portion of the $168 million Inner Belt expressway.

Development Administrator Edward J. Logue said the proposed location will be outlined to the Boston Redevelopment Authority for approval at its regular meeting today.

"Pending solution of the problems in Cambridge and Somerville," he said, "I can see no reason why construction of the belt cannot get under way in Charlestown and particularly the section from the Southeast Expressway through Roxbury as far as Huntington av."

Logue said he will recommend that the B.R.A. voice its approval of the route recommended in the $1 million survey completed for the state Dept. of Public Works.

In moving speedy construction, Logue has his eye on a potential $62.5 million in Federal funds which will be available if President Kennedy's transportation bill is approved.

The bill has been reported favorably by the Senate Banking and Currency Committe and is before the full chamber for debate.

A companion measure, acted on favorably by a House committee, is now before that body's Rules Committee for approval.

Sen. Harrison A. Williams of New Jersey, sponsor, says he is "optimistic" of passage.

The bill is considered one of 10 remaining "must" pieces of legislation for Congress this session.

If the measure is approved, it will mean that the state could obtain up to $62.5 million in Federal funds to provide rapid-transit extensions.

Mayor Collins and Logue would like to reroute the Forest Hills rapid transit line along the proposed Southwest Expressway as far as Rte. 128 Station in Dedham.

This would enable the city to raze the ugly elevated structure which runs from below Dover st. in the South End, over Washington st. to Forest Hills.

Logue explained that the removal poses "no financial problem," since most of the money spent for demolition could be recovered through salvage.

"The greatest problem in this regard," he said, "is the relocation of the rapid-transit line."

INNER BELT
Page Four

Baseball Results

AMERICAN LEAGUE

BOSTON 2, Los Angeles 1.
BOSTON 9, Los Angeles 5.
New York 5, Minnesota 2.
Detroit 13, Baltimore 10.
Detroit 5, Baltimore 4.
Chicago 9, Cleveland 0.
Kansas City 6, Washington 5.

NATIONAL LEAGUE

San Fran. 9, Chicago 2.
Phila. 3, New York 1 (15).
Pittsburgh 2, Los Angeles 1.
Milwaukee 5, Cincinnati 4.
Houston 4, St. Louis 3 (10).

RED SOX TONIGHT

At Los Angeles (Schwall vs. Belinsky) 11 p.m.

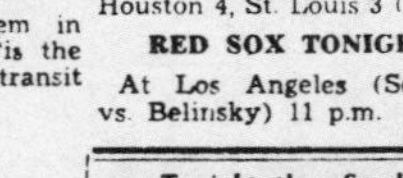

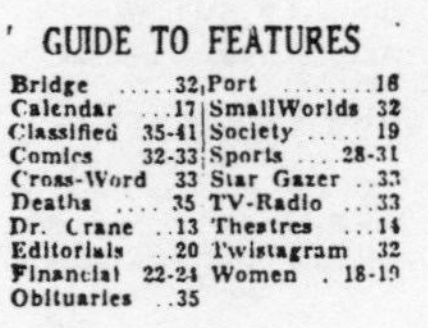

GUIDE TO FEATURES

Bridge	32	Port	16
Calendar	17	SmallWorlds	32
Classified	35-41	Society	19
Comics	32-33	Sports	28-31
Cross-Word	33	Star Gazer	33
Deaths	35	TV-Radio	33
Dr. Crane	13	Theatres	14
Editorials	20	Twistagram	32
Financial	22-24	Women	18-19
Obituaries	35		

The Boston Globe

MORNING EDITION

Reg. U. S. Pat. Off.

VOL. 182 NO. 115 — © 1962 By GLOBE NEWSPAPER CO. — TUESDAY, OCTOBER 23, 1962 — Telephone AV 8-8000 — 62 PAGES—10c

SCREEN PLAY
TUESDAY—Showers clearing cooler.
WEDNESDAY—Fair, cool.
High Tides 8:31 a.m. 8:48 p.m.
Sun Rises 7:05 Sun Set 5:51
Full Report on Page 13

Navy Prepared to Sink Ships--If Necessary

JFK ORDERS CUBA BLOCKADE; IF CASTRO LOOSES ROCKETS, U.S. WILL STRIKE AT SOVIETS

THE ULTIMATUM:

1. Any ship found to be carrying "offensive weapons" to Cuba will be turned back.
2. Continued surveillance of Cuba.
3. Any nuclear weapon launched from Cuba will be regarded as an attack by the Soviet Union on the United States—"requiring a full retaliatory response upon the Soviet Union."
4. Guantanamo Naval Base reinforced immediately.
5. Immediate session of the Organization of American States for appropriate action.
6. Immediate session of the U.N. Security Council to "take action against this latest Soviet threat to world peace."
7. Calls upon Khrushchev to "halt and eliminate this clandestine, reckless and provocative threat to world peace . . .

(AP Wirephoto)

FATEFUL MESSAGE "... Maximum Peril"

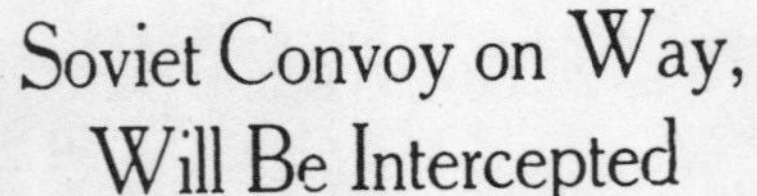

Soviet Convoy on Way, Will Be Intercepted

(Full Text on Page 10)

By ROBERT J. DONOVAN

WASHINGTON—President Kennedy, in a momentous decision that may eventually be interpreted as a hostile act by the Soviet Union, ordered Monday night a blockade of military equipment bound for Cuba.

The President used the term "strict quarantine," but White House officials said that a blockade would be required to enforce this quarantine. American ships and planes are already on the move in the Caribbean and in the South Atlantic, ostensibly for this purpose.

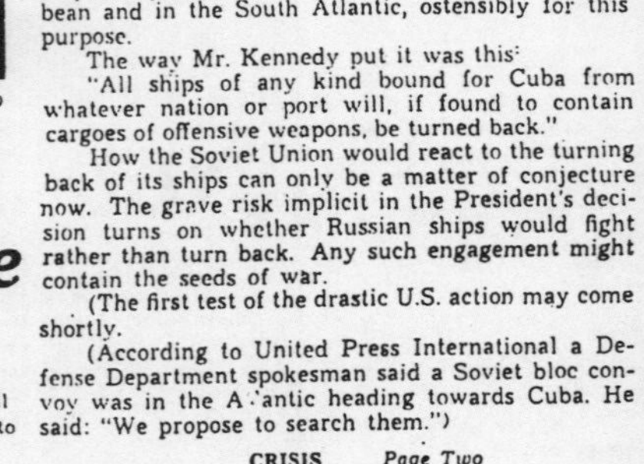

The way Mr. Kennedy put it was this:

"All ships of any kind bound for Cuba from whatever nation or port will, if found to contain cargoes of offensive weapons, be turned back."

How the Soviet Union would react to the turning back of its ships can only be a matter of conjecture now. The grave risk implicit in the President's decision turns on whether Russian ships would fight rather than turn back. Any such engagement might contain the seeds of war.

(The first test of the drastic U.S. action may come shortly.

(According to United Press International a Defense Department spokesman said a Soviet bloc convoy was in the Atlantic heading towards Cuba. He said: "We propose to search them.")

CRISIS *Page Two*

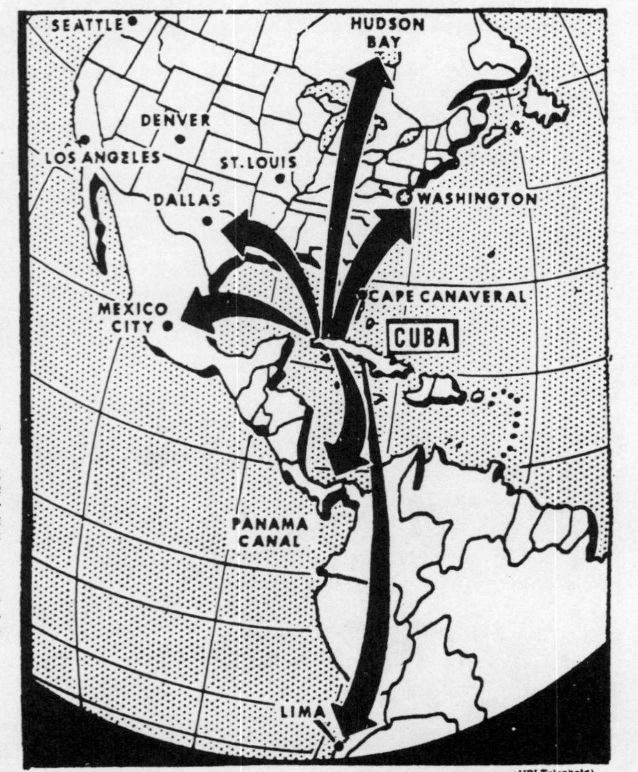

(UPI Telephoto)

Within Range of Cuba's Soviet-Supplied Missiles

Short arrows: U.S. and Hemisphere locations in striking distance of Castro's 1000-mile missiles. Long arrows: 2000-mile missiles planned.

U.S. Won't Balk at Force

Will Turn Back Arms Ships at All Costs

WASHINGTON (AP)—The United States is ready to sink every Communist bloc ship headed for Cuba which refuses to stop and be searched under the blockade, a defense spokesman said Monday night.

He said this country's blockade fleet, now being deployed, will order any ship of any nation obviously bound for Cuban ports to stop and undergo search by a boarding party if necessary.

A spokesman, under a barrage of questions, made it clear that force would be used if necessary in any case.

In discussing the big force of blockade ships now steaming toward intercept position, the spokesman outlined the procedure this way:

Air and sea patrols will be watching vessels move toward Cuba. Their positions will be reported by observation planes and ships. Warships will move in to intercept. They will hail the Cuban-bound ship. If it stops, a boarding party will be sent aboard to look over the manifest.

If offensive weapons or long range missiles or strategic-type aircraft, for instance, are found, the captain of the ship will be told he can head for any port other than Cuba.

If he refuses to change his course, "we will use force to compel him." Force also will be used if a ship refuses to stop for search.

A reporter asked the spokesman "are you prepared to sink Soviet ships?" the spokesman replied with one crisp word:

"Yes."

PENTAGON *Page Four*

Moscow Cautious —So Far

MOSCOW (UPI) — President Kennedy's decision to prevent any further arms shipment to Cuba was expected to provoke a speedy and sharply critical Soviet propaganda reaction.

But Western observers in Moscow expected the Kremlin to move cautiously in regard to any attempt to test the U.S. order by running through an arms ship.

It was believed the first Soviet action would be to drum up a major propaganda campaign aimed at condemning the U.S. decision as illegal and unwarranted.

There was no immediate official comment from the Soviets since the President's announcement came at 2 a.m. Moscow time.

FOREIGN *Page Eleven*

We're Not Alone—Cuba

KEY WEST, Fla. (AP)—All of Cuba's military forces have been mobilized, Havana Radio said today.

HAVANA (UPI) — President Kennedy's decision to blockade Cuba was denounced Monday night by a top Castro government propagandist as "a war measure" that could "provoke events whose consequences might be tragic for the entire world."

The spokesman, Luis Gomez Vanguermezt, a government newspaper and television commentator, warned that "We are not alone."

Speaking over the government television network he said Kennedy is "not taking seriously" the Soviet Union's pledge to defend the Fidel Castro regime.

CUBA *Page Three*

About Time —Reaction In Boston

By DOUGLAS S. CROCKET

Greater Bostonians—almost to a man—stood solidly beside President Kennedy when he took his "I'm sick of being pushed around" stand last night.

The only qualifications, raised in a random sample of residents, concerned the fact that President Kennedy could have made the United States' position even stronger by publicly stating that a blockade of Cuba might lead to World War III.

"He implied it, but didn't actually say it," one Harvard Law School student said.

"He should have done it sooner," said a real estate broker.

REACTION *Page Four*

It's Here Now

Voters—what do the men and women who want your vote think on key issues facing Massachusetts?

A special supplement compiled by the League of Women Voters gives the answers in today's Globe. See Page 13.

AN ANALYSIS: Next Move up to K

By WARREN ROGERS JR.

WASHINGTON—President Kennedy has confronted Soviet Premier Nikita S. Khrushchev with a clear, bitter choice:

Quit arming Cuba with offensive weapons or be prepared to do it by force—with all the horrible consequences that might ensue.

"Khrushchev . . . has an opportunity now to move the world back from the abyss of destruction," President Kennedy declared in the harshest ultimatum ever laid down by the United States to the Soviet Union.

What Mr. Khrushchev faces is what Mr. Kennedy called a "quarantine."

A more precise name for it is "peaceful blockade."

ANALYSIS *Page Two*

Blockade Begins Tonight Even Without UN Backing

By WILFRID RODGERS (Washington Correspondent)

WASHINGTON—State Department officials said Monday night that President Kennedy's proclamation of quarantine of Cuba will be made officially tonight—after a planned meeting of the Organization of American States scheduled for 9 a.m. today.

Officials said that it was assumed that the O.A.S. would approve the proclamation.

But, they added, it would go into effect even if O.A.S. approval were not forthcoming.

A State Department spokesman said the authority under which the President invoked the quarantine was Article 2, Section 4 of the U.N. Charter.

BRIEFING *Page Four*

Red Envoy Ashen-Faced After Briefing by Rusk

By MURREY MARDER

WASHINGTON—Soviet Ambassador Anatoly F. Dobrynin emerged ashen-faced and apparently very shaken from a 25-minute meeting Monday night with Secretary of State Dean Rusk at which he was informed of the action the United States plans to take against arms shipments to Cuba.

There was an absolute contrast in the appearance of the Soviet envoy as he entered the State Department promptly at 6 p.m. (EDT) and left less than half an hour later with news of the major turning point in United States foreign policy.

SOVIET ENVOY *Page Ten*

India Girds for Full War

NEW DELHI (UPI)—Premier Jawaharlal Nehru placed India's economy on a war footing Monday night and pledged to lead his country to victory over Communist China, which he called an "enemy." But early today Peiping announced still another offensive in the undeclared border war.

(Almost in the same breath, Red China declared it is still ready to reopen negotiations with India for peaceful settlement of the border conflict, A.P. reported).

During Monday the Chinese Communists opened a third front at the extreme eastern end of the border and sent tanks rumbling toward an important Indian air base at the western end of the border.

A Peiping broadcast early today said the Chinese had launched another major offensive in the Ladakh area or the border of China's Sinkiang Province.

For the first time Peiping referred to a Chinese offensive. In all past attacks it has insisted that China acted in self-defense. It said the Chinese offensive had sent the "aggressive Indian troops" fleeing toward India.

CHINA-INDIA *Page Nine*

First Buster Brown Dies Alone

Shorty DeWitt, a diminutive, button-nosed actor who danced and tumbled his way to national fame in the 1920s as the original Buster Brown, will get a proper funeral after all.

The 76-year-old vaudevillian died a week ago in City Hospital, and his body lay until Monday in Southern Mortuary, destined for a Potter's Field burial.

Shorty, whose real name was William T. Bloch, had been in failing health the last 10 years.

He was taken to the hospital Oct. 14, and after an emergency stomach operation, he died.

The four-foot trouper was a familiar sight in the South End.

Until three years ago he took his two cocker spaniels on daily walks. They succumbed to old age, and Shorty kept tropical fish, birds and a cat at his flat at 67 Emerald st.

SHORTY *Page Six*

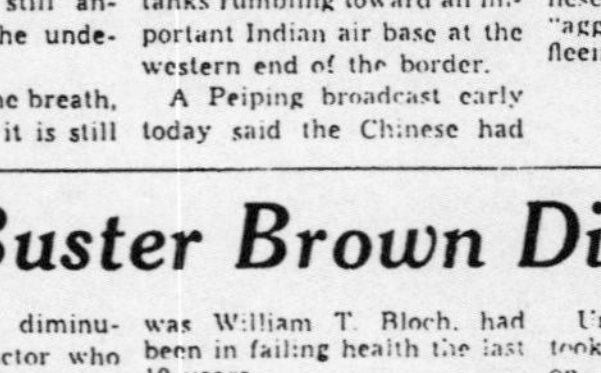

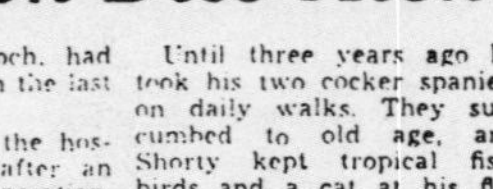

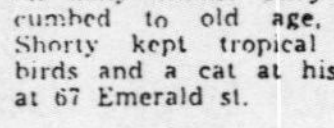

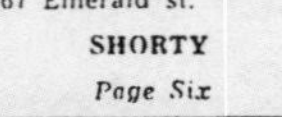

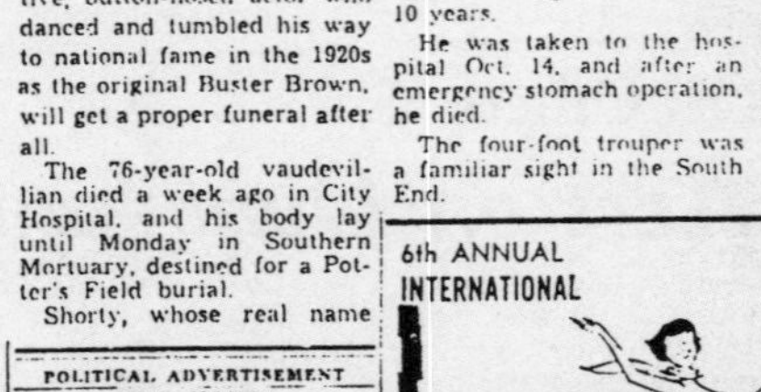

EXTRA

KENNEDY page of photos —Page 29. President's biography—Page 28.

EXTRA

PRESIDENT SLAIN

Assassin's Bullet Fells Kennedy on Dallas Street

Shot in Head, He Slumped Into Jacqueline's Lap; Texas Governor Also Hit; Lyndon Johnson Escapes

Agent, Officer Also Shot Dead

DALLAS (AP)—A Secret Service agent and a Dallas policeman were shot and killed today some distance from the area where President Kennedy was assassinated.

No other information was immediately available.

Reg. U.S. Pat. Off. © 1963. Globe Newspaper Co.

THE BOSTON GLOBE—FRIDAY, NOV. 22, 1963

VOL. 184 NO. 145 44 PAGES—EIGHT CENTS

AVenue 8-8000

MILD Low 50s Tonight; Warm, Windy Saturday (Full report on Page 3.)

CLOUDY

High Tide Today at 3:07 p.m.

IN TONIGHT'S GLOBE

Bridge	16	Port News	42
Calendar	31	Problem	18
Churches	26, 27, 32	Radio-TV	31
Classified	32-37	Society	27
Crane	29	Sports	39-42
Cross-Word	29	Star Gazer	16
Deaths	30	Theaters	20, 21
Editorial	24	Twistagram	16
Financial	42,43	Women's	27, 28

Identity, Number Of Killers Unknown

Johnson Guarded, Soon Takes Oath

250,000 at Scene; Car's Top Down

By MERRIMAN SMITH

DALLAS (UPI)--President Kennedy was assassinated here today.

A single shot through the right temple took the life of the 46-year-old Chief Executive. He was shot as he rode in an open car in downtown Dallas, waving and smiling to a crowd of 250,000.

Vice President Lyndon Johnson—the nation's new President—was in the same cavalcade but a number of car lengths behind. He was not hurt.

The terribly-shocked Johnson, who has a record of heart illness, was whisked off under heavy guard to be sworn in as quickly as possible as the 36th President of the United States.

Mrs. Jacqueline Kennedy was riding in the same car as her husband. She was not hurt. She cradled her husband's head in her arms as he was sped, dying, to the hospital.

Mr. Kennedy was shot at approximately 12:30 p.m. CST (1:30 p.m. EST) and died at approximately 1 p.m. CST (2 p.m. EST). He was the fourth U.S. President to be killed in office.

Beside Mr. Kennedy in the famous bubbletop limousine was Texas Gov. John B. Connally. He was shot in the chest. The Governor was reported in serious condition and in great pain.

Mrs. Connally, also in the car, was unharmed.

The Chief Executive, first Roman Catholic President of the United States and in Dallas on a politicking mission for a second term, was smiling broadly as he rode through downtown streets.

"Then an awful look crossed his face," said a man at curbside only 15 feet away.

The identity of the assassin or assassins was not immediately known.

Sheriff's officers took a young man into custody at the scene and questioned him behind closed doors.

A Dallas reporter said he saw a rifle being withdrawn from a window on the fifth or sixth floor of an office building shortly after the gunfire.

PRESIDENT Page 25

SHORTLY BEFORE SHOOTING—President Kennedy applauded as his wife was introduced at Chamber of Commerce breakfast at Fort Worth, Tex., this morning. (UPI)

Stock Market Falls, Closes

The New York Stock Exchange was closed at 2:10 this afternoon by order of the board of governors following news of the shooting of President Kennedy.

Heavy selling came into the market after announcement of the tragedy in Dallas. The Dow-Jones Industrial Average which had risen more than 3 points earlier in the day to reach 735.96 at 1:30 p.m., slumped more than 24 points in the next 40 minutes. At the close it was down to 711.49, off 21.16 points from Thursday's closing figure.

Volume was heavy. The ticker tape was 15 minutes late in reporting transactions when the exchange's governors halted trading. Their action came only about 20 minutes after first news of the Dallas shooting was received on Wall Street.

MARKET Page 25

Switchboards Paralyzed

News Stops City, Nation —Workers Weep Openly

President Kennedy has been shot!

These were the words which stopped a city, a state and the nation.

News that the President had been shot virtually paralyzed all telephone communication in the Boston area.

Thousands of workers — many openly weeping—milled in confusion through office corridors.

Many went home.

The overload of telephone calls flooded switchboards at newspapers, radio and television stations.

Police across the area were unable to make any contact because of the outside calls pouring in.

At the Massachusetts State House in Boston scrubwomen wept.

Employees and visitors — unable to comprehend the enormity of the shooting — wandered in dazed fashion.

In many offices, small radio sets ere put into operations and clusters of people jammed together.

As each news broadcast arrived, more and more people would crowd around the radio.

In the streets of Boston people fell to their knees to pray.

Hundreds went into the Franciscan Shrine on Arch Street to light candles for the Roman Catholic President.

The telephone tie up was believed to be the worst in history.

Cambridge residents reported they waited 20 minutes to get a dial tone.

"My God, it's terrible."

This was the phrase most heard.

"Is he alive? . . . How bad is he? . . . What happened?"

These were the words of everyone . . . everywhere.

First reports indicated the President was dead. Minutes later, it was reported he was still alive. Then came the crushing word—the President is dead!

And as each report came in—as each flashed from person to person in fantastic speed—the confusion grew.

Complete strangers ran to each other in the streets of downtown Boston.

"What happened? . . . what happened?"

And the answer was always the same.

"The President's been shot."

REACTION Page 28

Collins Postpones Festival Opening

Mayor Collins ordered the opening of Boston's annual Christmas Festival postponed indefinitely this afternoon immediately he was informed of the assassination of the President.

Mayor Collins, his voice choked with emotion, issued this proclamation:

"I ask every citizen in the city to join with me in praying for the recovery of President Kennedy and Gov. John Connolly."

The festival had been scheduled to open at 4:30 o'clock with a candle lighting ceremony at City Hall.

Mayor Collins ordered City Hall closed in mourning immediately after he was informed of the President's death.

Johnson 'Is Fine,' Wife Says

DALLAS (AP)—Mrs. Lyndon Johnson said after a visit to the emergency operating room today that the Vice President "is fine."

She was taken back into another first floor room where Johnson originally had gone.

Asked if her husband also had been wounded, she shook her head negatively.

Secret Service men pushed reporters away and permitted no more questions.

Cardinal Suggests Memorial Masses

Richard Cardinal Cushing, the prelate who officiated at the marriage of President Kennedy, today called for prayers for the repose of the President's soul.

The cardinal also recommended special memorial Masses throughout the Boston Archdiocese.

He prepared messages of condolence to the President's wife, and also his parents.

Ted Got the News Presiding in Senate

WASHINGTON, D.C.—Sen. Edward F. Kennedy was presiding over the Senate when news of the shooting flashed through the Capitol. At the time the Senate was debating the Library Service Bill.

As word spread through the nation's capital most people couldn't believe it. Sen. Kennedy's office was closed after the news was received and the senator was whisked off to some unknown place where he could get instant information concerning the President's condition.

WILFRID RODGERS

What Is It?

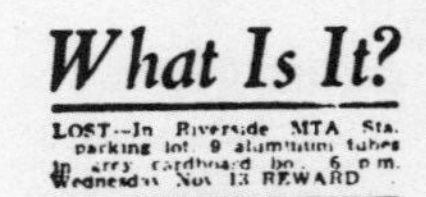

LOST—In Riverside MTA Sta. parking lot, 9 aluminum tubes ... cardboard box ... Wednesday, Nov. 13. REWARD.

The Dover man who placed this Want Ad in The Globe (Nov. 15) placed the small box containing the tubes on the fender of a red convertible, while he was unloading other equipment from his own car. The convertible took off before the small box could be retrieved. The man said the tubes are part of special electronic equipment he is working on, and cannot be used for any other purpose.

To place a Classified Advt. in the Globe

Call AV 2-1500

Globe Ads Bring Results

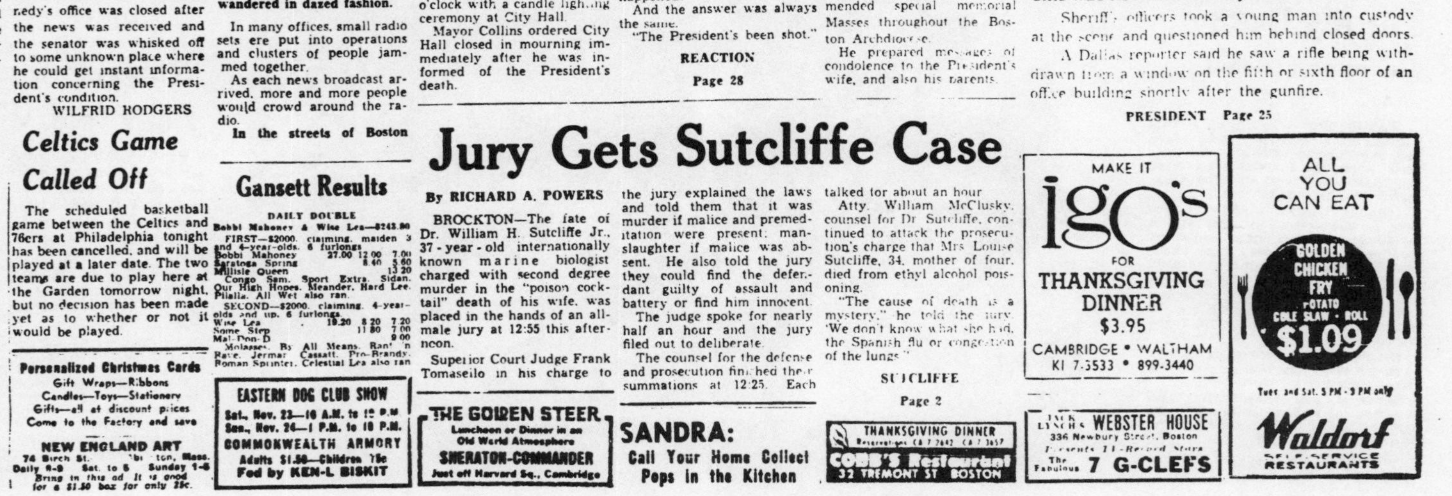

Celtics Game Called Off

The scheduled basketball game between the Celtics and 76ers at Philadelphia tonight has been cancelled, and will be played at a later date. The two teams are due to play here at the Garden tomorrow night, but no decision has been made yet as to whether or not it would be played.

Gansett Results

DAILY DOUBLE

Bobbi Mahoney & Wise Lea—$243.80

FIRST—$2000, claiming, maiden 3 and 4-year-olds, 6 furlongs.

Bobbi Mahoney	27.00	12.00	7.00
Saratoga Spring		8.40	5.60
Millisle Queen			13.20

Congo Sam, Sport Extra, Sidan, Our High Hopes, Meander, Hard Lee, Pilalla, All Wet also ran.

SECOND—$2000, claiming, 4-year-olds and up, 6 furlongs.

Wise Lea	19.20	8.20	7.20
Some Step		11.80	7.20
Mal Don D			9.00

Molasses, By All Means, Rent 'n Rate, Jermar, Cassatt, Pro-Brandy, Roman Spinner, Celestial Lea also ran.

Jury Gets Sutcliffe Case

By RICHARD A. POWERS

BROCKTON—The fate of Dr. William H. Sutcliffe Jr., 37-year-old internationally known marine biologist charged with second degree murder in the "poison cocktail" death of his wife, was placed in the hands of an all-male jury at 12:55 this afternoon.

Superior Court Judge Frank Tomasello in his charge to the jury explained the laws and told them that it was murder if malice and premeditation were present; manslaughter if malice was absent. He also told the jury they could find the defendant guilty of assault and battery or find him innocent.

The judge spoke for nearly half an hour and the jury filed out to deliberate.

The counsel for the defense and prosecution finished their summations at 12:25. Each talked for about an hour.

Atty. William McClusky, counsel for Dr. Sutcliffe, continued to attack the prosecution's charge that Mrs. Louise Sutcliffe, 34, mother of four, died from ethyl alcohol poisoning.

"The cause of death is a mystery," he told the jury. "We don't know what she had, the Spanish flu or congestion of the lungs."

SUTCLIFFE Page 2

Full Page Color Portrait of the late President—Page 16

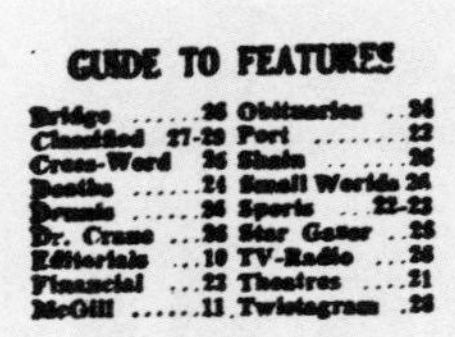

GUIDE TO FEATURES

Bridge	26	Obituaries	26
Classified	27-29	Port	22
Cross-Word	26	Shain	26
Deaths	24	Small Worlds	26
Dennis	26	Sports	22-23
Dr. Crane	26	Star Gazer	28
Editorials	10	TV-Radio	26
Financial	22	Theatres	21
McGill	11	Twistagram	28

The Boston Globe

MORNING EDITION

Reg. U. S. Pat. Off.

BEFORE THE DIP

MONDAY—Sunny, in 40s.
TUESDAY—Cloudy, showers.

High Tides
5:36 a.m. 5:59 p.m.
Sun Rises 6:47 Sun Sets 4:16
Full Report on Page 20

VOL. 184 NO. 148 · © 1963 By Globe Newspaper Co · MONDAY, NOVEMBER 25, 1963 · Telephone AV 8-8000 · 30 PAGES—10c

'And So, She Took a Ring From Her Finger . . .'

SEN. MANSFIELD:

"There was a man marked with the scars of his love of country, a body active with the surge of a life far, far from spent and, in a moment, it was no more. And so, she took a ring from her finger and placed it in his hands.

"There was a husband who asked much and gave much, and, out of the giving and the asking, wove with a woman what could not be broken in life, and, in a moment it was no more. And so, she took a ring from her finger and placed it in his hands, and kissed him and closed the lid of a coffin."

(Inspiration for giving ring, Page 4)

JUSTICE WARREN:

"John Fitzgerald Kennedy, a great and good President, the friend of all men of good will, a believer in the dignity and equality of all human beings, a fighter for justice, an apostle of peace, has been snatched from our midst by the bullet of an assassin.

"What moved some misguided wretch to do this horrible deed may never be known to us, but we do know that such acts are commonly stimulated by forces of hatred and malevolence, such as today are eating away their way into the bloodstream of American life.

(Full texts of eulogies on Page 8)

Poised on Capitol steps, Mrs. Kennedy and her children prepare to leave. At right, she bends to kiss the President's bier. (AP Photos)

All Night Long They Came

Nine-Mile Line of Mourners

By ROBERT HEALY
Globe Reporter

WASHINGTON — John Fitzgerald Kennedy's last message was carried to Capitol Hill Sunday.

It was a message of sorrow and a nation's shame.

Sunday afternoon and all night the martyred President lay in state in the Capitol Rotunda, while the public filed by the casket.

At midnight close to 100,000 had passed the bier. And still they came. Despite the chill of the night, the lines grew longer extending at times for nine miles.

It was apparent that this solemn procession would not be ended until just before the funeral itself today. The Kennedy family had said they would not close the rotunda so long as the public continued to stream inside.

Under a bright Autumn sun on Sunday, some 300,000 persons — who had flooded here from all parts of the nation—watched the body of their assassinated President as it was borne from the White House to the Capitol rotunda.

To the funeral cadence of muffled drums, a caisson, drawn by six white horses, carried the flag-draped casket through this city of sadness.

Today, a day of national mourning, the President's body will be moved back to the White House.

SERVICES Page 2

Jacqueline . . . Courage

By DOROTHY McCARDLE

WASHINGTON—Jacqueline Kennedy Sunday led a grieving people to the bier of her slain husband with matchless courage.

She did not hide her sad, tense face. She never wept. She never faltered as she and her two young children accompanied the body of John F. Kennedy to the Capitol.

Her silent strength was matched by her tender solicitude for her children. She gently clasped the hands of John Jr., who is 3 years old today, and Caroline, who will be 6 years old on Wednesday, in loving reassurance. She leaned down to answer their puzzled questions.

Jacqueline Kennedy makes visit to husband's casket and embraces woman mourning dead President.
(Story on Page 4)

She bore the 40-minute ordeal of the procession to the Capitol, the ceremonies and return to the White House with an unspoken sadness and bravery that brought tears to the eyes of spectators and television viewers.

Her beautifully chiseled features were taut with anguish. Her expression was glazed. She seemed to look, not at the crowds, but through them, seeing nothing but the flag-draped coffin of her late husband.

"She is a wonderful mother, she really is," a man whispered.

JACQUELINE Page 2

Oswald Slain as Millions Gasp

By JAMES S. DOYLE
Globe Reporter

DALLAS—As incredulous millions watched the scene unfold on television, the accused assassin of President Kennedy was shot to death in the basement of the City Jail at 11:15 a.m. Sunday.

Jack Ruby, 52, a portly, balding night club operator and an ardent admirer of the late President, appointed himself executioner of Lee Harvey Oswald.

Ruby stepped through a throng of police and newsmen and wordlessly sent a single bullet from a snub-nosed revolver into Oswald's left side, just below the chest.

"I couldn't help it," Ruby told a relative later.

Oswald, the arrogant, 24-year-old pro-Communist and ex-Marine, died at 2 p.m., 48 hours almost to the minute after John Fitzgerald Kennedy had succumbed to a sniper's bullets.

He died on an operating table at the same Parkland Hospital where doctors had fought in vain to save the President's life.

Oswald, who had steadily denied having anything to do with the assassination — though police said they had an airtight case against him—made no statement as his life ebbed away.

As he was lifted from the oil-stained, cigarette-littered floor of the jail basement, a policeman asked him if he wanted to say anything about the death of the President.

Oswald said no word, just shook his head.

He was shot down while being transferred from the city jail to the county jail.

He was under heavy guard, and police had set up what they considered airtight security precautions to ensure his safety during what was to have been a routine transfer.

How Ruby got into the jail basement unchallenged has not been established.

He was well known to police, both as a hanger-on around headquarters and as a man with a criminal record. Many of the men on the force knew him by sight and name.

SLAYING Page 6

Oswald Cries With Pain as Ruby Fires Fatal Shot

Funeral Times

PROCESSION begins: 11 a.m.
SERVICES in St. Matthew's Cathedral: noon
BURIAL in Arlington National Cemetery: 1 p.m.

'. . . And a Flag For My Daddy'

By WILFRID C. RODGERS
Globe Reporter

WASHINGTON — Television viewers watching the services for President Kennedy in the Capitol Rotunda Sunday wondered where the President's 3-year-old son, "John-John," went when he disappeared from his mother's side.

John-John behaved manfully up to a point. He had ascended the steep steps to the Rotunda with his mother and sister, Caroline, without incident. Once inside, John-John wasn't quite sure what to think.

He craned his neck to look up at the high arches of the ceiling, clutched and unclutched his mother's hand and did a couple of half turns to look at the crowd around him.

He wanted to do something, as any 3-year-old would, anything but stand still. Things were just too quiet.

His nurse, Miss Maude Shaw, sensed his plight and walked him to one of the doorways leading from the Rotunda to the House side of the Capitol.

JOHN-JOHN Page 3

Kings, Prime Ministers Pour Into Washington

WASHINGTON—Kings and presidents, prime ministers and other world leaders arrived in Washington Sunday to pay homage to the young President they knew and admired.

Never have so many top foreign leaders gathered in this city of historic events. Perhaps never in history has any event gathered together so many wielders of temporal power.

The subdued procession of the world's mighty moved through Dulles and National Airports as humble Americans silently filed past the bier of John F. Kennedy.

Late Sunday, 67 nations had indicated that they were sending high-ranking representatives and the influx was well under way.

As another long night enveloped the Capitol and the White House, de Gaulle, Erhard, Prince Philip, Douglas-Home, de Valera, Ikeda, King Baudoin, Queen Frederika, Pearson, Macapagal and nearly 100 other rulers of the world slept in Washington.

There were a dozen members of ruling royal families, 18 presidents and heads of government, 29 foreign ministers, five defense ministers.

NOTABLES Page 2

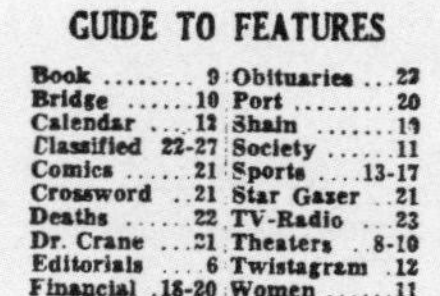

GUIDE TO FEATURES

Book 9 | Obituaries 22
Bridge 10 | Port 20
Calendar 11 | Shain 19
Classified 22-27 | Society 11
Comics 21 | Sports 13-17
Crossword 21 | Star Gazer 21
Deaths 22 | TV-Radio 23
Dr. Crane 21 | Theaters 8-10
Editorials 6 | Twistagram 12
Financial 18-20 | Women 11

The Boston Globe

MORNING EDITION

Reg. U. S. Pat. Off.

A POOR THIRD

FRIDAY—Scattered showers, in 80's

SATURDAY—Fair.

High Tide 6 a.m. 6:32 p.m.

Sun Rises 5:12 Sun Sets 8:23

Full Report on Page 19

VOL. 186 NO. 3 — © 1964 By GLOBE NEWSPAPER CO. — FRIDAY, JULY 3, 1964 — Telephone AV 8-8000 — 28 PAGES—10c

JFK:

On sending bill to Congress, June 19, 1963.

"I ask every member of Congress to set aside sectional and political ties and to look to this issue from the viewpoint of the nation.

"In this year of the Emancipation Centennial, justice requires us to insure the blessing of liberty for all Americans and for posterity — not merely for reasons of economic efficiency, world diplomacy and domestic tranquility—but, above all, because it is right."

Rights Bill Law of Land

President—From Texas—Signs It, Urges Compliance

LBJ:

On signing Rights bill, July 2, 1964.

"We must not approach the enforcement of this law in a vengeful spirit. Its purpose is not to punish.

"Its purpose is to promote a more abiding commitment to freedom, a more constant pursuit of justice, and a deeper respect for human dignity.

"We will achieve these goals because most Americans are law-abiding citizens who want to do what is right."

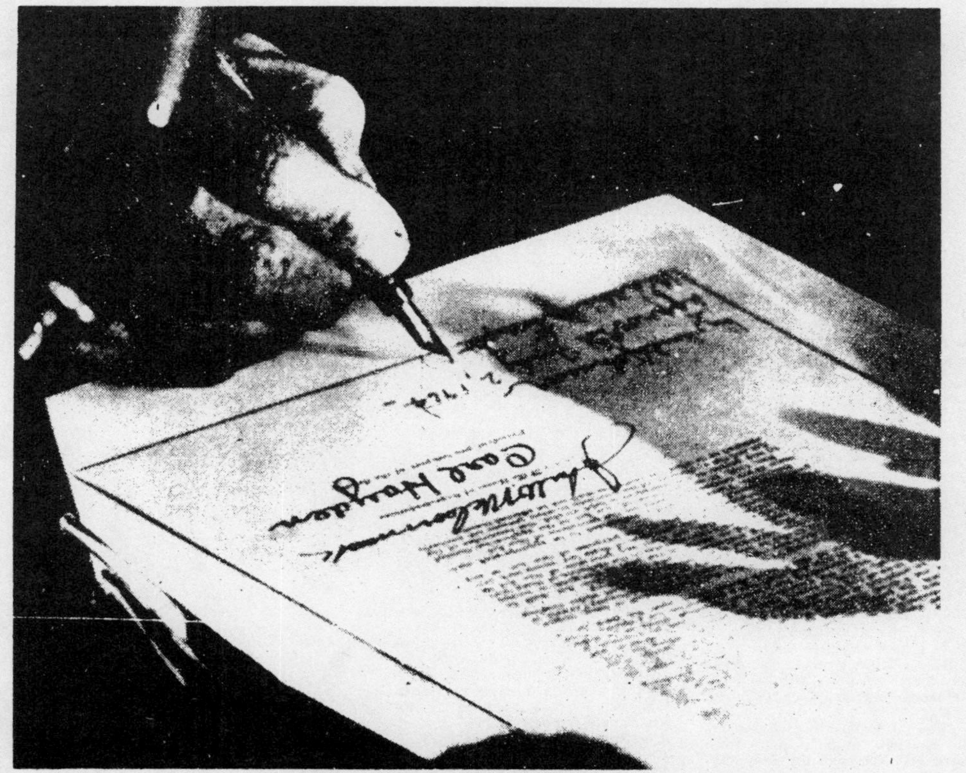

'. . . And Having Writ, Moves On' (Photo By AP)

House Vote Of 289-126 Decisive

By DOUGLAS KIKER and ANDREW J. GLASS

WASHINGTON—President Johnson signed the Civil Rights bill into law at 6:58 p.m. Thursday and called on Americans to "close the springs of racial poison."

He put his name on the historic legislation in a televised White House ceremony attended by many of the nation's leaders. Five hours earlier, the House sent it to him by a vote of 289 to 126.

Johnson told the nation that "we have come now to a time of testing. We must not fail."

Wearing a black suit and a black tie, the President used 72 plastic-handled pens to enact the sweeping measure into law a century after Abraham Lincoln's Emancipation Proclamation.

After completing his address he called the 200 guests assembled in the White East Room around him to receive the pens, handing them out in bunches.

It was the most dramatic and solemn occasion at the White House since the black days following President Kennedy's assassination last November.

In his 10-minute speech, Johnson announced the nomination of LeRoy Collins, former governor of Florida, to direct the new Community Relations

Provisions of law and text of President's address—Page 7.

Service established by the bill. The new agency will attempt to open public facilities to Negroes in the South without recourse to Federal court action.

Johnson also said he would request from Congress a special appropriation to pay for implementing the law.

"We must not approach the enforcement of this law in a vengeful spirit," he said. "Its purpose is not to punish . . . or divide, but to end divisions—divisions which have lasted too long."

After the signing ceremony, Rev. Dr. Martin Luther King Jr. announced on the White House grounds that his Southern Christian Leadership Conference would immediately move to bring test cases under the new law in U.S. courts.

Another guest, Roy Wilkins, executive secretary of the National Assn. for the Advancement of Colored People, said he expects most of the 1845 N.A.A.C.P. chapters to bring test cases under the law right away.

RIGHTS Page 2

Peabody Names 4 To MBTA

By ROBERT B. HANRON

Gov. Peabody Thursday named four of the five men who will run his state-wide $225 million mass transportation program. They are:

William J. Fitzgerald, chairman of the Metropolitan Transit Authority trustees.

Philip Kramer, vice president of the International Ladies' Garment Workers Union.

Gen. James McCormack Jr., vice president of Massachusetts Institute of Technology.

Atty. Robert P. Springer of Natick, Peabody's transportation coordinator.

Springer was instrumental in drawing up the first-in-the nation mass transit plan.

These four. and a fifth to be named today, are the governor's choices as directors of the Massachusetts Bay Transportation Authority.

The names of Fitgerald and Kramer, both Democrats, were submitted to the Executive Council for approval. McCormack, a Republican, must be approved by the present 14 cities and towns comprising the M.T.A. district.

M.B.T.A. Page 4

Senate Slaps Supreme Court

WASHINGTON — The Senate Thursday in voting an omnibus pay raise bill for Federal workers took a surprise slap at the nine Supreme Court justices by voting 46-40 to reduce their increase to $2500. All other Federal justices would receive $7500 increases, the same amount as senators and representatives.

The bill now goes to the House-Senate conference which will probably not take place until after the recess for the G.O.P. convention. Details on Page 3.

A Southerner's Courage

By VINCENT J. BURKE

WASHINGTON—This is the story of a Southern congressman who embraced political danger and a Northern congressman who took no stand when the roll was called Thursday on final passage of the Civil Rights bill.

It is the story of two Democrats—Rep. Charles L. Weltner, 36, a first-termer from Atlanta, Ga., and Rep. John Lesinski, 49, a veteran House member from Dearborn, Mich.

Shortly before the vote Weltner got a standing ovation from Northern Democrats when he announced he would break with the tradition of the Old South and vote for the bill.

Weltner had voted "no" on House passage of the original Civil Rights bill last February.

He told the House Thursday he could again "vote no, with tradition safety" on final passage of the Senate version. But he said he had decided to follow the lead of "responsible elements" of Atlanta and "add my voice to those who seek reasoned and conciliatory adjustment to a new reality."

Weltner in his brief speech called on Southerners back home "to accept the verdict of the nation" and "move on to the unfinished task of building a New South."

"We must not remain forever bound to another lost cause," he admonished.

Other members of the Georgia delegation sat silently as Northern Democrats applauded Weltner. Several Southerners afterward said privately that it was a "courageous vote."

SWITCHES Page 2

CONG. WELTNER
Atlantan for bill (AP)

First Test On Rights Loses Out

KANSAS CITY (AP)—The Congress of Racial Equality tested the Civil Rights bill a minute after its signing Thursday with a sit-in at a barbershop in its convention headquarters hotel.

Gene Young, 13-year-old Negro from Jackson, Miss., walked into the Muehlebach Hotel's basement barbershop and asked for a haircut.

Gus Imbeau, head barber, said he told the boy "if you can find anyone here to cut your hair, O.K." The shop has 11 chairs with nine barbers on duty.

Imbeau said Young then asked for an appointment today and Imbeau replied that he was booked up.

Young then left the shop and returned with an estimated 25 demonstrators some of whom took seats on the waiting benches.

TEST Page 2

TV Too Busy?

By PERCY SHAIN, Globe Television Critic

Certainly the signing of the Civil Rights bill by President Johnson Thursday night was one of the most momentous events ever to reach the television cameras.

But does that mean it received 100 percent coverage in commercial TV?

It does not.

ABC did not even carry the President's stirring speech live. While he was voicing his magnificent plea for the nation to come through whole in this "time of testing," Ch. 7, its Boston affiliate, was airing a rerun of "Dobie Gillis," its regular 6:30 p.m. program.

NBC carried the address but broke away as soon as the signing started. Ch. 4 was quick to push in a commercial at this vital moment, then switched to its weather report to fill out the hour.

CBS stayed with the historic event the longest. The unique system of multiple signings and the distribution of the quills to the VIP's present were shown in some detail on Ch. 5, at least until the hour deadline struck. Then it was back home to the local news with John Day.

One might have thought that this would rank as the most witnessed document signing of all time.

Too bad everybody couldn't have given it the full 15 minutes.

Fish Industry Snags Sea-Incinerator Bill

By JEREMIAH V. MURPHY

The commercial fishing industry apparently has thrown the hooks into a proposed sea-going incinerator for Greater Boston communities.

A bill, aimed at solving the perennial where-to-dump problem, sailed smoothly through three readings in both branches of the Legislature, and appeared headed for ultimate passage.

But spurred by a recent visit to the State House by two top commercial fishing officials, the bill now is becalmed in a joint conference committee.

Last Fall, two Harvard professors, Lester Silverman and Melvin W. First, proposed burning refuse aboard a converted World War II Liberty ship, and dumping the ash at sea. Burning would begin outside the three-mile limit. Residue would be dumped 20 miles out.

INCINERATOR Page 4

NASA Eyes Cambridge Site for Electronics Center

By WILFRID C. RODGERS
Washington Correspondent

WASHINGTON — Director James E. Webb of the National Aeronautics and Space Administration has his eye on a 20-acre site in Cambridge for the electronics research center.

This was made known Thursday when Mayor Edward Crane and members of the Cambridge City Council were asked here to discuss "availabilities" of this site.

It is understood that Mayor Crane has 10 days in which to get city council approval of the site for the electronics research center and to set in motion machinery to make the site available.

Map of proposed site, land use on Page 4.

NASA officials discussed two Cambridge sites with Mayor Crane and City Councilors Andrew Trodden, Daniel Hayes and Thomas Mahoney, all members of the city council NASA committee.

The sites are the so called Binney-Main st. site in East Cambridge and the River st. site.

However, NASA officials are said to be most interested in the Binney-Main st. site that comprises some 20 acres.

This site is near Technology sq. and close by M.I.T. and Harvard.

Col R. P. Young of the NASA site selection committee would concede only that the two Cambridge sites are under prime consideration as were some 20 other sites in Metropolitan Boston. In all, some 150 sites had been considered by NASA.

The Binney-Main st. site fulfills the consideration of the site selection in being near both Harvard and M.I.T. and subway transportation.

The area might be considered a blighted area and would therefore probably qualify under urban renewal.

While some jobs in the Cambridge area would also have to be relocated, it is estimated the number of new jobs created by the project would far overshadow this initial loss of jobs.

If the Binney-Main st. site is made available by the city of Cambridge, it is expected NASA will select another auxiliary suburban site.

It is also expected that once the Cambridge site is made available, Director Webb won't waste any time in designating that as the No. 1 choice.

Plans presented to Congress indicated that if an urban site was selected for the center, suburban land would be sought where there would be less interference with communication equipment in experiments.

The Cambridge group is the only one to be asked to Washington to consult with Webb.

Col Young wouldn't rule out the possibility of others being invited, but he said he knew of no immediate plans for such invitations.

Indications at NASA and on Capitol Hill are that the next move is up to the city of Cambridge.

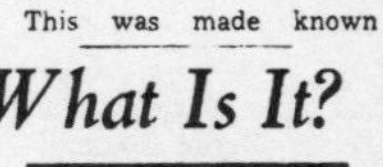

What Is It?

(1) 1880 VICTOR High Wheeler bicycle. (1) 1880 Mason and Hamlin organ . . .

The Peabody man who placed this Want Ad in The Globe (June 24) said the front wheel of the bike is up to his shoulder and the rear wheel is only a foot high. He found the two-wheeler in the back of a shop, repaired it, and it is now the pride and joy of his neighborhood. The man said he is selling the bike because it takes up too much room in his small house.

To Place a Classified Advt. in The Globe

Call AV 2-1500

Kill Bill to Tighten Fund Disclosure

The Massachusetts Senate killed legislation to close loopholes in the state's campaign contribution disclosure law at 1:20 a.m. today, then immediately adjourned.

A crowded gallery that included several members of the Junior Chamber of Commerce, sponsors of the bill, had waited several hours for action on the bill.

It was taken up and Sen. Pres. Maurice A. Donahue ruled that the Senate had voted to defeat the legislation and then to refuse reconsideration, which makes it impossible to revive the bill in the current session.

When Sen. George A. Sullivan Jr., Norwood, Democrat, asked Sen. Donahue to consider that no action had been taken so that the matter could be debated, Donahue answered "The chair hears an objection" and dropped the gavel.

The objection, which apparently was from Donahue since no other senator objected, meant that the bill is dead for the session and cannot be reconsidered.

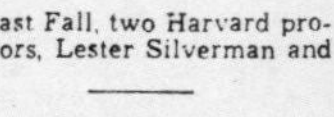

Baseball Results

AMERICAN LEAGUE

Minnesota 15, BOSTON 9.
New York 4, Kans. City 3 (15)
Detroit 9, Cleveland 1.
Los Angeles 10, Baltimore 6.

NATIONAL LEAGUE

St. Louis 4, Milwaukee 3.
San Francisco 6, Pittsburgh 5
Philadelphia 3, Los Angeles 2
Cincinnati 5, Chicago 0.
Houston 7, New York 1.

RED SOX TONIGHT

Los Angeles at Fenway Park (Latman vs. Monbouquette) 8 p.m. TV-Channel 5.

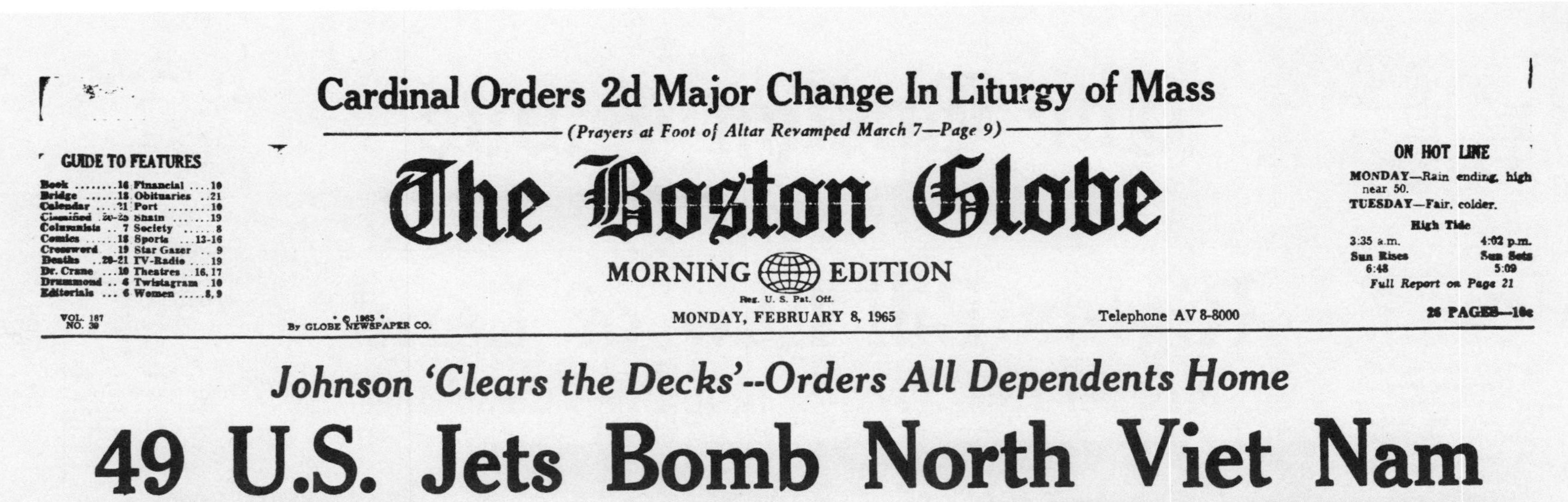

Cardinal Orders 2d Major Change In Liturgy of Mass

(Prayers at Foot of Altar Revamped March 7—Page 9)

GUIDE TO FEATURES

Book ....16 Financial 10
Bridge ......18 Obituaries ..21
Calendar ....21 Port 10
Classified 20-25 Shain 19
Columnists ..7 Society 8
Comics ......18 Sports 12-16
Crossword ..19 Star Gazer 9
Deaths ..20-21 TV-Radio 19
Dr. Crane ..10 Theatres ..16, 17
Drummond ..6 Twistagram ..10
Editorials ....6 Women 8, 9

The Boston Globe

MORNING EDITION

Reg. U. S. Pat. Off.

VOL. 187 NO. 39 · © 1965 By GLOBE NEWSPAPER CO. · MONDAY, FEBRUARY 8, 1965 · Telephone AV 8-8000 · 26 PAGES—10c

ON HOT LINE

MONDAY—Rain ending, high near 50.
TUESDAY—Fair, colder.

High Tide
3:35 a.m. 4:02 p.m.
Sun Rises 6:48 Sun Sets 5:09

Full Report on Page 21

Johnson 'Clears the Decks'--Orders All Dependents Home

49 U.S. Jets Bomb North Viet Nam

By LAURENCE BARRETT

WASHINGTON — Forty-nine Navy warplanes struck North Vietnamese staging centers in the Dong Hoi area Sunday as part of a much larger planned retaliatory blow for successful Viet Cong attacks in South Viet Nam 12 hours earlier.

At the same time, President Johnson ordered home the estimated 1800 American military and civilian dependants now in South Viet Nam "to clear the decks" for a fight if the Communists want one.

The administration also ordered the immediate transfer of a Marine Corps Hawk anti-aircraft battalion into South Viet Nam. The battalion, to be moved from elsewhere in Asia, includes more than 500 men and 18 missile launchers. The Hawk is a modern, mobile missile especially effective against flying planes. It carries a non-nuclear warhead.

Defense Secretary Robert S. McNamara said the battalion would be assigned to Da Nang, the site of a major American-South Vietnamese air base.

"As the United States Government has frequently stated, we seek no wider war" in Southeast Asia, a White House statement said.

But "whether or not this course can be maintained lies with the North Vietnamese aggressors," it continued, adding:

"The key to the situation remains the cessation of infiltration from North Viet Nam, and the clear indication by the Hanoi regime that it is prepared to cease aggression against its neighbors."

Viets Kill 220 Reds

SAIGON (Reuters) — South Vietnamese troops were today reported to have killed 220 Communist guerillas in Quang Tin province, 360 miles northeast of Saigon.

Reports from the scene say that Viet Cong guerillas attacked a government outpost, but the garrison repulsed the guerillas, and government troops counterattacked.

Bad weather prevented dozens of additional American and South Vietnamese planes from completing their missions against other undisclosed targets in North Viet Nam.

Defense Secretary Robert S. McNamara, in announcing the air operation, refused to rule out the possibility that another raid to finish the job might occur in the next day or two.

After the Aug. 5 attack on North Viet Nam—which followed North Vietnamese torpedo raids against American destroyers in the Gulf of Tonkin—McNamara made it very clear in his statements that the retaliation was complete.

ATTACK Page 2

AFTER NEARLY SLEEPLESS NIGHT. (AP)

TENDER CARE FOR A G.I. AT NHA TRANG HOSPITAL. (AP)

One Tense Message ...LBJ Gets on Phone

WASHINGTON—About mid-afternoon Saturday, a day on which he had no officially scheduled appointments and no known premonitions of trouble, Lyndon Baines Johnson was handed a message from the White House basement "Situation Room" command post and communications center. It plunged him into 24 of the busiest hours he has had as President.

The message spelled out some of the preliminary details of the guerrilla attack in South Viet Nam. The attack had occured at 1 p.m. (E.S.T.) Saturday (2 A.M. Saigon time).

The president's decision to order the raid on North Viet Nam demonstrated again the speed with which such decisions can be made and carried out. The U.S. raid came within 12 hours of the guerrilla attack.

JOHNSON Page 2

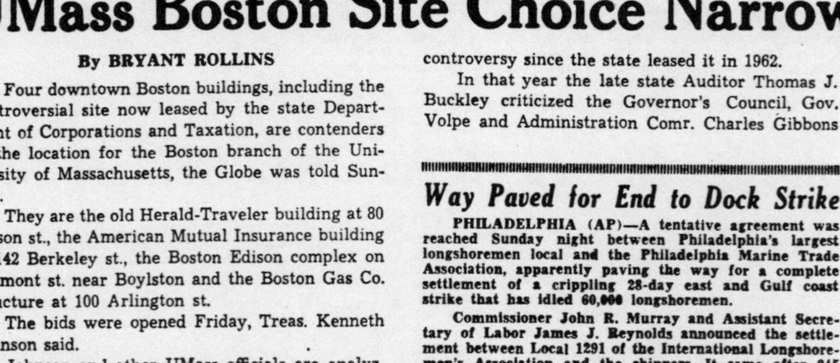

An Analysis

The War Widens in Asia

By ROBERT J. DONOVAN

WASHINGTON — Hostilities over the weekend have increased the danger of a widening war in Asia.

The clear effect of the use of American planes to bomb North Vietnamese bases in retaliation for Communist Viet Cong attacks on American installations and American troops is to deepen the U.S. commitment in Viet Nam.

The fact that the bombing occurred while Soviet Premier Alexei N. Kosygin was in Hanoi, capital of North Viet Nam, seeking to strengthen Soviet-North Vietnamese relations, gave rise to the danger of a new confrontation between the Soviet Union and the United States in Asia.

Whether the Viet Cong attacks and the retaliatory American bombing are to constitute a single incident or are to be the prelude to fresh hostilities involving the United States will depend on Hanoi's reaction to the bombing.

If Hanoi, stung by the air attack, should strike back at American forces on land or sea, the United States will surely hit again. Where such a cycle of attack and retaliation might lead no one knows.

The United States sent an official explanation of the bombing raid to the Soviet Union Sunday, saying that Washington does not wish to widen the war.

Nevertheless this weekend is regarded as a notable juncture in the war in Viet Nam, one that is likely to quicken the pace of events for better or worse.

In announcing that he was sending reinforcements to South Viet Nam and was ordering American dependents home, President Johnson noted that Hanoi recently had embarked upon "a more aggressive course of action."

DIPLOMACY Page 3

Viet Nam Crisis At a Glance

HOW IT STARTED—Viet Cong attack two U.S. camps, kill eight GIs, wound 108.

U.S. REACTION—49 jets bomb North Viet Nam base. GI and civilian dependents in Viet Nam ordered home. New anti-aircraft missiles being sent to Viet airbase.

HANOI'S VERSION — Calls U.S. bombing "barbarous." Claims four jets shot down. (U.S. says only 1 downed.)

RED CHINA'S VIEW—Says bombing "extremely serious provocation" but threatens no immediate retaliation.

RUSSIA'S ATTITUDE — Also sees "large scale provocation" but, like China, sits tight.

As Shells Roar Down ... Mauldin Sketches

PLEIKU, South Viet Nam (Reuters) — Cartoonist Bill Mauldin said Sunday the Viet Cong attack on Pleiku was "as hairy as I would care to experience."

Mauldin was here visiting his son, Bruce, a helicopter pilot, when the Viet Cong struck at 2 a.m.

Caught in his bare feet and underwear shorts, Mauldin made many sketches, but "I was not very collected," he told newsmen.

He ran out without his sketch pad first and after he got that he had to return for pencils.

Mauldin said he was in a tent with Lt Col John C. Hughes, commander of the 52d Aviation Battalion, when the guerrillas struck.

"He went out the front door to take care of the battalion and I went out the back to take care of myself," Mauldin said.

When a wounded young soldier blundered into him, Mauldin placed him on his cot. Then, with others' help, he carried him to the infirmary.

"I ran into a stream of wounded, some walking, but most carried.

"I was very impressed how orderly it was. There was no panic."

Mauldin said: "We were hit very hard, there was a heavy and sudden barrage and sustained fire afterward.

MAULDIN Page 2

BILL MAULDIN

UMass Boston Site Choice Narrowed to 4 Buildings

By BRYANT ROLLINS

Four downtown Boston buildings, including the controversial site now leased by the state Department of Corporations and Taxation, are contenders as the location for the Boston branch of the University of Massachusetts, the Globe was told Sunday.

They are the old Herald-Traveler building at 80 Mason st., the American Mutual Insurance building at 142 Berkeley st., the Boston Edison complex on Tremont st. near Boylston and the Boston Gas Co. structure at 100 Arlington st.

The bids were opened Friday, Treas. Kenneth Johnson said.

Johnson and other UMass officials are analyzing the bids to determine which building will best suit their needs, be easiest to renovate and operate and cost relatively the least.

Johnson expects the matter to be voted on Feb. 16 by the board of trustees.

The Mason st. property has been involved in controversy since the state leased it in 1962.

In that year the late state Auditor Thomas J. Buckley criticized the Governor's Council, Gov. Volpe and Administration Comr. Charles Gibbons for approving the lease arrangements.

Buckley considered the legality of the lease questionable.

Buckley said the state had contracted to pay $1.75 million in rent over five years for a building that was bought for $50,000 cash and a $400,000 mortgage.

He complained also that the realty trust "withheld from the council the fact that a certain bank held a financial interest in the property."

He also pointed out that the taxation department was scheduled to move into its home in the new state office building in 1965 but that the expiration date of the lease was Apr. 30, 1967.

He said the state should have seized the building by eminent domain if the terms were to be so disadvantageous.

In a follow-up audit last June, Buckley complained that while several of the alleged shortcomings "have been corrected . . . several appear to have been ignored."

Way Paved for End to Dock Strike

PHILADELPHIA (AP)—A tentative agreement was reached Sunday night between Philadelphia's largest longshoremen local and the Philadelphia Marine Trade Association, apparently paving the way for a complete settlement of a crippling 23-day east and Gulf coast strike that has idled 60,000 longshoremen.

Commissioner John R. Murray and Assistant Secretary of Labor James J. Reynolds announced the settlement between Local 1291 of the International Longshoremen's Association and the shippers. It came after 245 hours of almost continuous negotiations.

The 2500 members of Local 1291 still must ratify the agreement. Reynolds said that he feels the settlement here will lead to a complete settlement of the dispute from Maine to Texas that has idled 775 ships in east and Gulf coast ports and cost the United States approximately $6 billion worth of commerce.

What Is It?

Murder in N.Y. Museum--100 Women and Children Watch in Horror

NEW YORK—A frail, 12-year-old girl, pawn in a domestic quarrel between her aged father and middle-aged mother, watched with 100 other horrified onlookers Sunday as her father fatally shot her mother in the Museum of Natural History.

Visitors to the museum, where the fabled star of India and other gems totaling $410,000 in value were stolen recently, scrambled for cover when master violin maker Dmytro Didchenko, 72, shot his divorced wife, Gertrude, 43.

Police said the shooting climaxed years of bitter domestic disputes between the couple who argued in the museum briefly about visitation rights for the child, Susan, before the firing began.

As an aftermath of the slaying, former State Sen. Bernard Tompkins, 61, Mrs. Didchenko's attorney, died of a heart attack in the West 68th st. police station, where the violin maker had been taken after the slaying.

Visitors to the museum flattened themselves on the floor and dived behind pillars when Didchenko, who made violins costing upwards of $800, opened fire with a foreign-make automatic pistol.

Didchenko arrived at the museum shortly after it opened at 7 p.m. EST. He had an appointment there to discuss with his former wife the child's future.

The child's mother was accompanied by Frank Bossio, a friend and retired city detective.

After a short conversation between the violin maker and his former wife, Didchenko whipped out the automatic and began firing, police said.

Bossio dived for Didchenko and knocked him to the floor but Didchenko got off five shots, four of them striking the woman.

Bossio, with the help of museum guards, subdued Didchenko.

Among the approximately 50 persons waiting when the museum opened was Mrs. Marvin Beard, 29, wife of an Associated Press news Supervisor; her three children; a neighbor, Mrs. Ira Silberlicht of Floral Park, Queens, and Mrs. Silberlicht's two children.

"We heard a noise we thought was a firecracker," Mrs. Beard said. "I turned and the woman was still standing. Then she fell and he kept shooting at her. I saw him shoot the last three shots."

The women recalled that about half the persons in the lobby were children.

Points Of View

EDITORIAL — Preposterous Social Security income rule. (Page 6).

JOSEPH ALSOP — Cuban crisis, Korea and Viet Nam. (Page 3).

ROSCOE DRUMMOND—Why LBJ accepted Soviet "invitation" so fast. (Page 6).

POLITICAL CIRCUIT — Laurence Curtis may run for Joe Martin's seat. (Page 7).

HAROLD KAESE — Hockey penalties, good and bad. (Page 13).

Shall Soviets Invade Home of Cod?

(Dockmen Here Say No—Story Below)—

The Boston Globe

MORNING EDITION

Reg. U. S. Pat. Off.

VOL. 187 NO. 69 — © 1965 By GLOBE NEWSPAPER CO. — WEDNESDAY, MARCH 10, 1965 — Telephone AV 8-8000 — 42 PAGES—10c

GUIDE TO FEATURES

Book ... 32 | Obituaries 31, 32
Bridge ... 42 | Port ... 19
Calendar ... 42 | Shain ... 21
Classified 31-41 | Society ... 15
Comics ... 30 | Sports ... 23-27
Crossword ... 43 | Star Gazer ... 32
Deaths ... 31 | TV-Radio ... 16
Dr. Crane ... 30 | Theaters 28, 29
Editorials ... 12 | Twistagram ... 30
Financial 17-20 | Women ... 15, 16

DEW PROCESS

WEDNESDAY—Cloudy, few showers.

THURSDAY—Colder.

High Tide 3:59 a.m. 4:37 p.m.

Sun Rises 6:07 Sun Sets 5:43

Full Report on Page 32

2 Hub Ministers Beaten—1 Badly—in Selma Street

THE CONFRONTATION—ALABAMA STATE TROOPERS FACE THE MARCHERS (AP)

March Halted by Compromise

By EDWARD G. McGRATH Globe Reporter

SELMA, Ala.—Whites and Negroes—2500 strong—marched defiantly through this segregationist stronghold Tuesday until halted, in a tense confrontation, by a solid phalanx of state troopers.

The marchers, led by Dr. Martin Luther King Jr., turned back peaceably when ordered to do so, claiming their demonstration was a victory for civil rights. There was no violence.

But a few hours later three white ministers, two of them from Greater Boston, who had taken part in the march were attacked by five white men on a downtown street.

Rev. James J. Reeb of 4 Half Moon st., Dorchester, had his skull fractured by one of the club-swinging assailants. He fell unconscious to the sidewalk.

Taken to the University of Alabama Hospital in Birmingham, 90 miles from here, he was reported in critical condition.

He was bleeding internally, and doctors had to perform an emergency operation so he could breathe.

Less seriously hurt were Rev. Orloff W. Miller of 4 Hemlock rd., Milton, and the Rev. Clark Olson of Berkeley, Calif.

Rev. Olson formerly served in Westboro and Wellesley Hills.

They were bruised and dazed by repeated blows about the head.

Mr. Reeb is a representative of the American Friends Service Committee. All three are Unitarian-Universalist ministers.

They had just eaten at a downtown restaurant and were on their way to a mass meeting when the five men attacked them from behind, without warning.

After learning of the attack, Dr. King said, "Selma had to show its true colors. It was cowardly work, done at night."

SELMA Page 8

Showdown Averted by President

By DOUGLAS KIKER

WASHINGTON — President Johnson faced his first big civil rights crisis Tuesday and solved it—at least temporarily—with a typical, carefully worked-out, behind-the-scenes compromise.

Step by step, here is how the President worked fast and furiously for 36 hours to handle the situation in Selma:

—Monday night, Mr. Johnson and U.S. Atty. Gen. Nicholas deB. Katzenbach talked by phone with U.S. District Judge Frank M. Johnson Jr. in Montgomery.

Judge Johnson told them that if Dr. Martin Luther King Jr. postponed Tuesday's march, the judge would issue a preliminary injunction against Gov. George C. Wallace halting state troopers from interfering with a similar march on Thursday.

—Katzenbach then tried to persuade Rev. Dr. King of the wisdom of this approach, but was not entirely successful in doing so. Rev. Dr. King by this time was under tremendous pressure from his own followers to proceed with the march Tuesday.

Rev. Dr. King did not agree with Katzenbach, even though the administration gave him a firm promise that it would enforce his right to march Thursday, after Judge Johnson's hearing.

—President Johnson, meanwhile, moved to put strong indirect pressure on Wallace to avoid another clash between Negroes and Alabama state troopers.

Sources here said the President did not talk to the governor personally, but made his thoughts known through steel men who have big plants in Birmingham, and through LeRoy Collins, director of the Civil Rights Community Relations Service.

JOHNSON Page 8

In Boston, Hundreds Also March

By LOUIS KAUFMAN

Hundreds of persons marched in Boston Tuesday protesting Alabama police "savagery" and demanding intervention by President Johnson.

More than 500 students, adults and clergymen, representing various civil rights groups in the Boston area, surrounded the Federal Building for five hours.

They were orderly but solemn, chanting freedom songs and carrying placards.

Thousands of persons viewed the demonstration as a large number of police calmly but cautiously watched developments. There were no incidents or arrests.

An attempt by group leaders to confront Sen. Edward M. Kennedy at the State House—who was in Boston to address the Legislature—failed. His preoccupation prevented a meeting with the group.

Most of the protesters were students, including delegations from Harvard, Boston University, Suffolk, [illegible] Northeastern, Wellesley, [illegible] Newton College of the Sacred Heart.

Placards demanded the arrests of Gov. Wallace, Dallas Sheriff Jim Clark and Col. Al Lingo, head of the Alabama Department of Public Safety. The placards claimed the Alabama contingent had violated Federal laws and were presently violating civil rights sections of the Constitution.

BOSTON Page 8

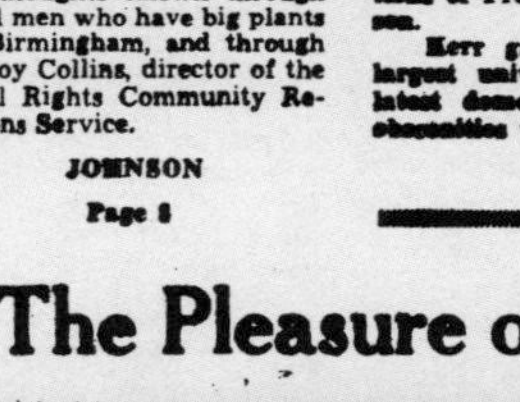

Pres. Kerr Resigns at U. of Calif.

The University of California, rocked by student riots late last year, was jolted again Tuesday with the resignations of Pres. Clark Kerr and Chancellor Martin Meyerson.

Kerr gave no reason for his leaving the nation's largest university. Meyerson, however, indicated the latest demonstrations last week, in which four-letter obscenities were flaunted, was the last straw.

Details on Page 10

'Our First Need Is Revenue'--Ted

Sen. Kennedy Speaks at State House

By BRYANT ROLLINS

Sen. Edward M. Kennedy returned to his home state Tuesday with a plea for a unified, regional approach to New England's problems and an appeal for a solution to the state's revenue dilemma.

The senator steered clear of any specific mention of the controversial sales tax during his speech. And before the speech, he brushed aside questions on the subject during an impromptu exchange with reposters.

He made it clear that he did not want to be pinned down on the subject.

Sen. Kennedy delivered his nine-minute address to a packed gathering of senators, representatives, friends and followers in the State House Chamber.

He said he feels the concern "of every man and woman in the commonwealth . . . that our present sources of revenue are quite inadequate."

He said this is the state's "first need—the problem of revenue."

KENNEDY Page 14

As to Sales Tax . . . No Comment

By ROBERT HEALY Political Editor

This was no "city upon a hill" speech. It lacked that magic rhetoric. It lacked that lasting message.

But Sen. Edward M. Kennedy did say this: Massachusetts is beset with problems and the Legislature would have to find new sources of revenue if these problems are to be solved.

Particularly he cited schools. "Our public schools do not match our private schools. We do not give to every child the quality of education that is his birthright."

And he told the legislators something else: That the problem of finding this new revenue would be neither easy nor popular.

This was his theme: That the Massachusetts Legislature would have to face its responsibilities.

He ticked off the problems of unemployment, uncertainty in our industries, the decline of the railroads, the city streets clogged with traffic and the pollution of our air and waters.

CIRCUIT Page 14

Political Waltz

It was a colorful day on the Hill. You'll find the light feminine touches, the political protocol, the pictures and Sen. Kennedy's text on Page 14.

The light story of the two senators who did a political waltz is on Page 8 and on Page 4 there's some delicate political banter between edgy politicians. Pictures on pages 2, 4 and 14.

Viet Guerrillas Test U.S. Marine Defenses

Da Nang Viet Nam (AP)—Two Communist guerrilla squads cautiously probed the defenses of strategic Da Nang Air Base today, apparently testing the strength of the newly installed U. S. 3D Marine Battalion.

The Viet Cong and South Vietnamese troops briefly exchanged fire 3 miles from where the U. S. Marines landed Monday and where supplies and heavy equipment still are being unloaded.

There were no casualties and no U. S. personnel involved, military sources said.

About 100 miles south of Da Nang, a U. S. Marine Corps officer was killed and another wounded as the guerrillas ambushed a Vietnamese convoy on the road from Bong Song to Haoi in Binh Dinh Province.

The Marine officers were advisers and not connected with the Marine buildup at Da Nang. It brought the unofficial roll of U. S. combat dead since December, 1961, to 301.

Eighteen Vietnamese soldiers were killed or wounded in the ambush, which occurred in an area 285 miles northeast of Saigon and scene of recent stepped up Viet Cong activities.

Setting themselves up in positions around the Da Nang base, the Marines took full control today of Hill 327, a dominance three miles from the field. Marine Hawk anti-aircraft missiles ultimately will be installed atop the 1060-foot hill.

Other Marines moved up on nearby Hill 228, another defensive position.

During the night the leathernecks of the Battalion's I Company joined with Vietnamese rangers on the first scouting mission since the Marines landed.

They checked for Viet Cong mines in the roads leading to Hill 327 and slogged through knee-deep mud of rice paddies in the area.

They made no contact with the Reds.

During the brief firefight near the beach, U.S. Navy ships in Da Nang Harbor briefly pulled back in anticipation of a more serious clash, informants said.

When the shooting died down, the ships returned to continue unloading hardware and supplies for the Marines.

(Photo, Page 3)

Saltonstall Asks Probe of Red Codfish

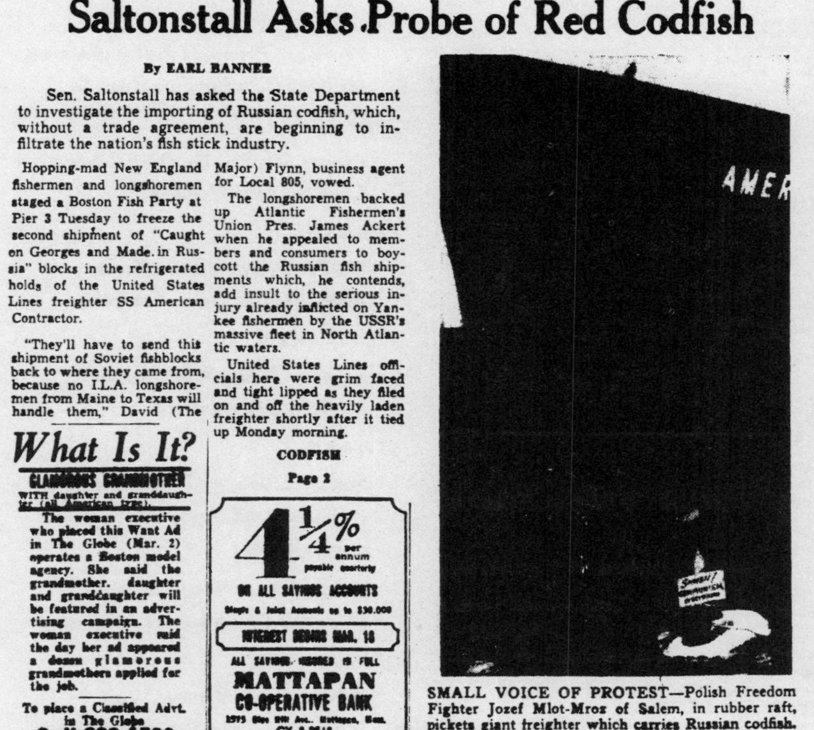

By EARL BANNER

Sen. Saltonstall has asked the State Department to investigate the importing of Russian codfish, which, without a trade agreement, are beginning to infiltrate the nation's fish stick industry.

Hopping-mad New England fishermen and longshoremen staged a Boston Fish Party at Pier 3 Tuesday to freeze the second shipment of "Caught on Georges and Made in Russia" blocks in the refrigerated holds of the United States Lines freighter SS American Contractor.

"They'll have to send this shipment of Soviet fishblocks back to where they came from, because no I.L.A. longshoremen from Maine to Texas will handle them," David (The Major) Flynn, business agent for Local 805, vowed.

The longshoremen backed up Atlantic Fishermen's Union Pres. James Ackert when he appealed to members and consumers to boycott the Russian fish shipments which, he contends, add insult to the serious injury already inflicted on Yankee fishermen by the USSR's massive fleet in North Atlantic waters.

United States Lines officials here were grim faced and tight lipped as they filed on and off the heavily laden freighter shortly after it tied up Monday morning.

CODFISH Page 2

SMALL VOICE OF PROTEST—Polish Freedom Fighter Jozef Mlot-Mroz of Salem, in rubber raft, pickets giant freighter which carries Russian codfish. (Photo by Robert Backhoff)

What Is It?

GLAMOROUS GRANDMOTHER WITH daughter and granddaughter (all American type).

The woman executive who placed this Want Ad in The Globe (Mar. 2) operates a Boston model agency. She said the grandmother, daughter and granddaughter will be featured in an advertising campaign. The woman executive said the day her ad appeared a dozen glamorous grandmothers applied for the job.

To place a Classified Advt. in The Globe Call 282-1500

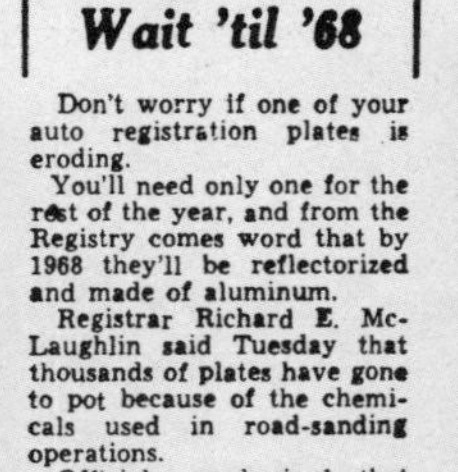

Tags Rusty? Wait 'til '68

Don't worry if one of your auto registration plates is eroding.

You'll need only one for the rest of the year, and from the Registry comes word that by 1968 they'll be reflectorized and made of aluminum.

Registrar Richard E. McLaughlin said Tuesday that thousands of plates have gone to pot because of the chemicals used in road-sanding operations.

Officials emphasized that this is not a repeat of the 1963 situation when plates became unreadable because of defective paint.

Number plates still must be displayed in customary locations on all vehicles, but only the rear plate must be legible.

The reflectorized plates coming in 1968 will remain on vehicles four years.

Points Of View

ART BUCHWALD—It boggles the mind to think of Barry as President now during Viet Nam crisis. Page 13.

VICTOR O. JONES — His column on medical men who handle English language well brings an eye-opening response. Page 13.

IAN MENZIES—City jitters is the most infectious disease of the '60's, and the latest to catch it is New York. Page 17.

The Pleasure of Her Company

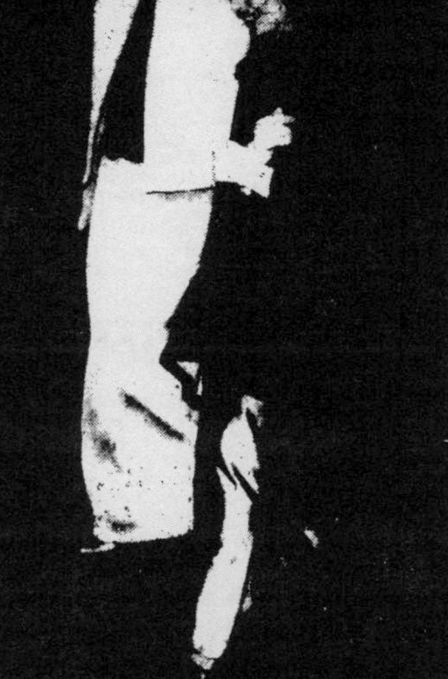

LEAVING FOR MUSEUM are Mrs. John F. Kennedy and Mrs. John K. Galbraith. (Photo by Philip Preston)

By JANE HARRIMAN

Silent and lovely in a gleaming white satin evening suit, Mrs. John F. Kennedy slipped into the court yard of Harvard's Fogg Art Museum last night.

Inside she took a deep breath, and then waved shyly to a friend who stood on the opposite side of a crowd of more than 600 guests.

Mrs. Kennedy had arrived here only a few hours before to attend a private review of a show of delicate Indian paintings which opens to the public today. She was accompanied by her sister, Princess Lee Radziwill, and a small group of friends.

Mrs. Kennedy and her sister came to Boston as the guests of Harvard Professor and Mrs. John Kenneth Galbraith. They spent last night at the Galbraith's Cambridge home, and attended a dinner party there before the preview.

Indian foods were served at the dinner for nearly fifty guests, including India's Ambassador to the United States, B. K. Nehru and his wife; actress Angie Dickinson; Mr. and Mrs. Brooks Beck; Mr. and Mrs. William Van Den Heuvel; Mr. and Mrs. Jerome Weisner, Mr. and Mrs. William Walton, and Richard Goodwin, assistant to President Johnson.

JACQUELINE Page 6

GUIDE TO FEATURES
Bridge 40 Obituaries 24
Classified, 21-31 Senior Set 38
Comics 38 Sports 33-36
Crossword 38 Star Gazer 38
Deaths 24 TV-Radio 39
Dennis 38 Theatres 37
Dr. Crane 40 Twistagram 38
Editorials 14 Women 20-23
Financial, 16-30

The Boston Globe
MORNING EDITION
Reg. U.S. Pat. Off.
VOL. 188 No. 133 · © 1965 · By GLOBE NEWSPAPER CO. · WEDNESDAY, NOVEMBER 10, 1965 · Telephone AV 8-8000 · 40 PAGES—10c

BRIGHT, ISN'T IT?
WEDNESDAY—Sunny, in mid 40's.
THURSDAY—Warmer.
High Tide 11:37 a.m. None p.m.
Sun Rises 6:27 Sun Sets 4:29
Full Report on Page 25

'This Shows How Fragile Our Civilization Is'

MAYOR COLLINS

Mystery Blackout Startles Nation

An Editorial

The Big Lesson

The system broke down.

In a country that spends countless billions getting to the moon, there is a sudden blackout. Wheels stop running. Loaded planes hover over darkened airports. Elevators and people get stuck. Stoves won't work. Heaters grow cold. People worry. Their only link with the outside world is the transistor or car radio.

Suddenly the most crowded section of America, from New Hampshire to New York city, finds itself at the mercy of something wrong with one wire at one place. The result is breakdown.

Where were all the brains?

The private power companies of New England have got a lot of questions to answer. So has the Federal Power Commission. Something wrong with the grid? An overloaded circuit at Oswego? No other sources of power immediately available?

Maj Gen James McCormack, who now heads up COMSAT (the Communications Satellite Company), and its space communications, told a Globe man: "I've been reading books about New England's power system for 35 years, and I said, 'This just can't happen.' "

But it had happened.

If some will blame the power companies, the Federal Power Commission should not be let off the hook. It has a big job to do—first in investigating, then in explaining how it, too, could be caught asleep at the switch, and finally in really regulating and preventing. It is supposed to represent the public.

And there are other lessons from the blackout. One is surely the magnificent calmness of the millions of people who were affected by it in their offices and homes. By and large they took the advice of the governor and mayor to stay off the roads and phone lines. Save for only a few instances, there was a remarkable preservation of law and order.

Another big lesson is the need for more planning for emergencies. The Civil Defense set-up has up to the present been given the brush-off. Now, after the whole Northeast has been blacked out, the need is known.

It was not another "Failsafe." Yet it could have been.

And so the biggest lesson of all is that it CAN happen here, and that it must never happen again in peacetime.

MOON OVER COPLEY SQ. (Bob Dean Photo)

Stories and Pictures On Pages 2-11, 15, 25

The Scope:

PERSONS AFFECTED—
36 Million—One-Fifth of The Nation's Population

AREA BLACKED OUT—
80,000 Square Miles

STATES AFFECTED—
Massachusetts, Rhode Island Connecticut, New Hampshire Vermont, New York, New Jersey Pennsylvania and Parts of Canada

COST—
Near $100 Million

LIGHTS OUT (BOSTON)—
5:21 p.m.

LIGHTS ON (BOSTON)—
Beginning at 9:08 p.m.
(NEW YORK)—
Beginning at 3:35 a.m.

The Impact:

PROBE
President Orders Sweeping Investigation

LOOTING
Looters Have a Field Day In Springfield and Rochester, N.Y.

MOBILIZATION
Volpe Calls Out National Guard, Off-Duty Police, Firemen Alerted

U.S. AID
President Promises Full Assistance, Military Commanders Pitch In

AIRPORTS
Planes Stacked Up Over Cities, Land by Auto Headlights

TRANSIT
MBTA Trains Run on Time, Motorists Get Home Smoothly

SABOTAGE?
Experts 'Pretty Well Agreed' No Sabotage Involved

STRANDED
Stalled Elevators Trap Thousands In Boston and New York

N.Y. SUBWAYS
800,000 Rush Hour Commuters Stranded Underground for Hours

OPPORTUNITY
2 Inmates of Plymouth Jail Make Successful Break in Dark

LBJ Demands to Know Why 36 Million Hit by Darkness

By SEYMOUR LINSCOTT

The worst power failure in history plunged some 36 million persons—virtually the entire Northeast and part of Canada—into darkness at 5:17 p.m. Tuesday.

President Johnson directed an immediate investigation.

The President was told early today that the probable cause was a mechanical breakdown at the Clay substation—a remote control base 20 miles north of Syracuse, N.Y. However, other experts doubted this was the cause.

Parts of the Northeast, most populous section of the nation, were still blacked out early this morning.

Affected were eight states and southern Ontario.

The blackout covered 80,000 square miles.

It extended from Concord, N.H., northwest to Toronto, and as far south as Harrisburg, Pa.

As the lights winked suddenly out in the great metropolitan centers and in the country towns, confusion dominated.

Some panic and violence was reported.

A full-scale riot broke out at Walpole State Prison. Two prisoners escaped at the Plymouth House of Correction.

Looting was reported in some cities, and mobs battled police.

As the scope of the blackout became known, one ugly word leaped into the minds of millions: Sabotage.

And there was fear. Was this war? An enemy from outer space?

Later, however, it appeared that the breakdown stemmed from a technical difficulty.

Exact location of the source of the trouble was believed in the Niagara Falls-Oswego, N.Y., area, but could not be pinpointed exactly.

Best estimates set the total cost of the power loss at $100 million.

President Johnson ordered the Federal Power Commission, with the help of the Federal Bureau of Investigation, to find out what happened and why.

Whatever its origin, the massive failure raised the spectre of the power system's vulnerability to deliberate attack.

BLACKOUT
Page 2

Why? Several Systems Were All Connected

By ROBERT J. ANGLIN

New Englanders are asking why they were affected by a power failure in upstate New York—and so are the power companies.

Engineers and technicians were too busy restoring the interrupted power Tuesday night to look for specific answers. However, some general factors are known:

Whatever the trouble that caused the failure, it is presumed to have been outside New England. It was sudden trouble. It was "massive." And probably most important, it happened at the worst possible time—just after 5 p.m. when power demands is at a peak.

Electric companies in New England are tied together in a giant interconnecting grid that includes parts of New York state and Canada.

This enables an individual electric system to get power from other systems in the grid, which may be done for various reasons.

A sudden power failure, for example, at a generator in Western Massachusetts might mean the electric company would send power from another system.

POWER
Page 2

Ike 'Doing Well;' Diagnosis Today

AUGUSTA, Ga—Former President Eisenhower was reported "doing well" Tuesday in Ft. Gordon Army Hospital, where he was rushed late Monday night suffering from chest pains.

Doctors said it would take up to 36 hours—or until late this morning—to determine whether he had suffered a heart attack.

President Johnson ordered every possible assistance for the former president, and personally telephoned Mrs. Eisenhower. Get well messages poured into the hospital from all over the world. Story on page 13.

In Boston—Surgery Under Improvised Lights

By HERBERT BLACK
Medical Editor

Surgeons at Boston City Hospital finished up an appendectomy under flashlights and battery-powered lamps.

At St. Elizabeth's a baby was delivered by Caesarian section after a race through darkened streets to the hospital.

Three children, possible pneumonia victims, were x-rayed by machines powered by fire department equipment at City Hospital.

At New England Center Hospitals life-saving equipment in the intensive care unit was operated by hand as the power died away.

These were just a few of the dramatic events as the greatest blackout ever affected hospitals all over Boston, some critically and others not so seriously.

A man critically injured in an automobile accident died on arrival at Boston City during the height of the blackout.

Two women brought into the emergency ward after suffering shock and serious falls in their darkened homes were given emergency treatment.

HOSPITALS
Page 3

What Is It?

300 Riot at Walpole, Rip Pipes, Furniture

By JAMES H. HAMMOND

WALPOLE—More than 300 inmates of Walpole State Prison, rioting in the wake of the power failure, were turned back by a barrage of tear gas shortly before 8 p.m. Tuesday at a gate separating them from the prison's central control room and possible freedom.

The rioters, inmates of the prison's eight maximum security cell blocks, continued their destructive rampage within the maximum security area until they were finally herded into the cells by prison guards and state troopers armed with shotguns about 9:35 p.m.

Prison officials said 15 guards turned back the charge at the gate outside the control room, aided by other guards who lobbed tear gas grenades through broken windows in the maximum security area.

The area was a shambles of broken furniture, ripped out plumbing, upended food carts and other equipment. The floor was covered with a sheet of water up to three inches deep in places.

The riot began a few minutes after the power went off at 5:30 p.m. as the prisoners, just back from supper, were on the cellblocks about to be locked in their respective, two-man cells.

WALPOLE
Page 11

Stores Closed Thursday

Boston's department, specialty and major food stores will be closed all day Thursday, to observe Veterans' Day.

Department and specialty stores will be open tonight.

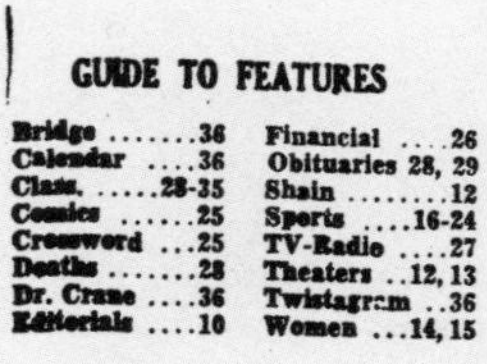

GUIDE TO FEATURES

Bridge	36	Financial	26
Calendar	36	Obituaries	28, 29
Class.	28-35	Shain	12
Comics	25	Sports	16-24
Crossword	25	TV-Radio	27
Deaths	28	Theaters	12, 13
Dr. Crane	36	Twistagram	36
Editorials	10	Women	14, 15

The Boston Globe

MORNING EDITION

VOL. 192 NO. 94 · © 1967 By GLOBE NEWSPAPER CO. · MONDAY, OCTOBER 2, 1967 · Telephone 288-8000 ® · 36 PAGES—10c

IN THE CARDS

MONDAY—Sunny, warmer.
TUESDAY—Fair, warmer.

High Tide

10:30 a.m. 10:54 p.m.

Full Report on Page 36

RED SOX Take Pennant As Historic Season Ends

THE SMELL OF THE PENNANT . . . THE ROAR OF THE CROWD

EXUBERANT FANS HAUL WINNER JIM LONBORG OFF FIELD AND NEARLY RIP OFF HIS UNIFORM. (UPI)

First Title in 21 Years, Face Cardinals Again

By CLIF KEANE
Staff Reporter

It started out to be a rebuilding year, but it grew faster than a castle in the sky. The Red Sox, with all their youth, are in the World Series after beating the Twins, 5-3, Sunday at Fenway Park.

They have the Most Valuable Player in the American League in Carl Yastrzemski, who played like a Babe Ruth when it mattered. They have the Manager of The Year in Dick Williams, and they quite likely have the winner of the Cy Young Award in Jim Lonborg, who beat his toughest rival, Dean Chance, in this big game.

The game was won in the sixth inning, and handsome Lonborg started it with a 50-foot bunt down the third-base line. Chance had blanked the Red Sox, 2-0, until then. But once Jim beat out his bunt, the 35,770, sitting on their hands, started to go wild.

"Go! Go! Go!" started the chant, and soon the singles started to pour off the Red Sox' bats and before long Chance was headed off the field, beaten in the biggest game of his life.

And when it was over and Rico Petrocelli had taken a short pop fly, the players made a mad dash from the dugout. They barely got there in time. There were wild fans—including girls—rushing onto the field.

Mike Andrews and George Scott hoisted the handsome guy aloft on the mound and Lonborg owned the city. The man who held the key, Yastrzemski, somehow escaped the grabbing and tugging in what had to be the wildest sports scene in Boston's history.

And a little bunt started it.

The California Angels made it official, some three tense hours later, when they erased the Tigers from contention by taking the second game of their doubleheader 8-5.

So the Series will start Wednesday against the Cardinals here. It is 21 years since the two last met. This time the Red Sox will be the underdogs. In 1946 Ted Williams and his crew were huge favorites to win—and lost. This team will definitely be the underdog and will—?

RED SOX Page 17

Sox Barely Escape Screaming, Streaming Fans

By BUD COLLINS
Sports Columnist

As the ball came down in Rico Petrocelli's glove for the last-and-final out, the town went up in the air like a beautiful balloon. Perhaps it will never come down: Red Sox euphoria is a gas that can keep you higher than helium. Or pot.

For an instant Petrocelli looked at the baseball. Then he began to run as though he were Chiang Kai-shek in Peking because he could hear the shrieking mob behind him.

It was the Red Sox Guard charging across the Fenway playing field Sunday afternoon, and the old ball park suddenly became a newsreel from Hong Kong: the Red Guard storming the British embassy. These were the zealots, thousands of them from the congregation of 35,770 at Fenway Park, which was packed tighter than the Black Hole of Calcutta.

They leaped the fences and streamed onto the field, screaming the Red Sox Guard oath—"We're No. 1!"—and displaying their banners.

They made Mao Tse-tung's gang look like peace marchers, yet this was a frenzy of love, not hate.

Respectable people who had left their homes placidly, if nervously, to attend the pennant-deciding rites indulged in by Our Old Town team had become fanatics celebrating a holy war triumph.

COLLINS Page 11

Eight Pages on Red Sox

—"Right Out of Sight," an editorial. Page 10.
—The story in photos. Pages 11, 19.
—Boston after dark goes beserk. Page 18.

World Series at a Glance

WHO: Red Sox vs. St. Louis Cardinals.

TICKETS: All reserved seats have been sold. Standing room tickets ($4) go on sale at 9 a.m. the day of each game.

WHEN, WHERE: Wednesday, Thursday at Fenway Park, Boston; Saturday, Sunday at Busch Stadium, St. Louis. If needed, 5th game at St. Louis next Monday, 6th and 7th at Boston on Wednesday, Oct. 11, and Thursday, Oct. 12.

Yaz Clutch Streak Has No Parallel

By HAROLD KAESE
Sports Columnist

Like a rocket that starts from a spark, traces a fiery path into the night until it explodes in a shower of light, the Red Sox have dazzled a nation by winning the American League pennant.

Whoever thought that so modest a vehicle as this team guided by Dick Williams would climb into the baseball sky to deliver streamers of excitement and the incandescent confetti of inspired effort?

"I thought we would finish about 10 games over .500 and in fourth or fifth place," said Tom Yawkey seriously, as his players drenched each other with beer after the climactic 5-to-3 victory over the Minnesota Twins.

But Williams, his manager, quipped, "I said all along we'd finish over .500."

And now for the great anti-climax—the World Series.

No known Red Sox hitter ever had a final two weeks to compare with those the Yaz delivered in the hottest stretch of the American League's hottest pennant race.

The Series can do a lot for Boston, for the Red Sox, for still unidentified heroes who may be lurking in the wings, but what can it do for Jim Lonborg, for Carl Yastrzemski?

KAESE Page 18

Top Stories Inside Around State, World

Dr. James L. Goddard, head of the U.S. Food and Drug Administration, said on Sunday that penalties for possession and use of marijuana are too severe and the law itself "medically unjustified." Story on Page 5.

Indonesian students attacked the Chinese Communist embassy in Jakarta, fighting hand-to-hand for over two hours with Chinese diplomats. Story on Page 4.

★

Correspondent David Schoenbrun reports that North Vietnamese officials told him that his stories should emphasize their "determination to resist American aggression," not their terms for peace talks. Story on Page 2.

★

Three hundred young people demonstrated for an hour outside Cambridge police headquarters, demanding the release of 21 persons arrested in a narcotics raid on a hippie apartment early Sunday. Story on Page 5.

★

If you think we've flipped over the Red Sox . . . well, we have and some regular Globe features do not appear today.

Yawkey in Tears, Toasts Manager

By WILL McDONOUGH
Staff Reporter

Tom Yawkey tried his best to fight back the tears. He stood near the back door in Dick Williams' office, watching his manager being interviewed and trying to stay in the background.

Finally, someone shoved a paper cup full of champagne into Yawkey's hands.

"I haven't had one of these in four years," said Yawkey, peering down at the drink.

But almost immediately, he walked over to the front of Williams' desk and offered:

"I want to have a toast with you, Dick."

"Fine," said Williams, borrowing a water glass filled with champagne from a writer.

"Here's to you sir, for giving me the opportunity," said Williams.

"And here's to you, Dick," Yawkey saluted back, "for making the most of it. This is the happiest moment of my life."

This was the climax of two celebrations that swept the Red Sox dressing room Sunday evening.

The first, right after they whipped the Minnesota Twins, 5 to 3, featured beer, shaving cream and some warm embraces.

TOAST Page 18

YAZ AND YAWK — Carl Yastrzemski is praised by club owner Tom Yawkey. (Frank O'Brien Photo)

Yaz to Write on Series for Globe

Carl Yastrzemski will write for the Globe—in his own words—during the World Series. He will begin his work for the Globe starting tomorrow, both Morning and Evening.

Yastrzemski received national magazine praise for his nine-article series during the pennant stretch. His interview with Mickey Mantle, during which Carl found out that Mickey will return for at least two more years, was a news beat.

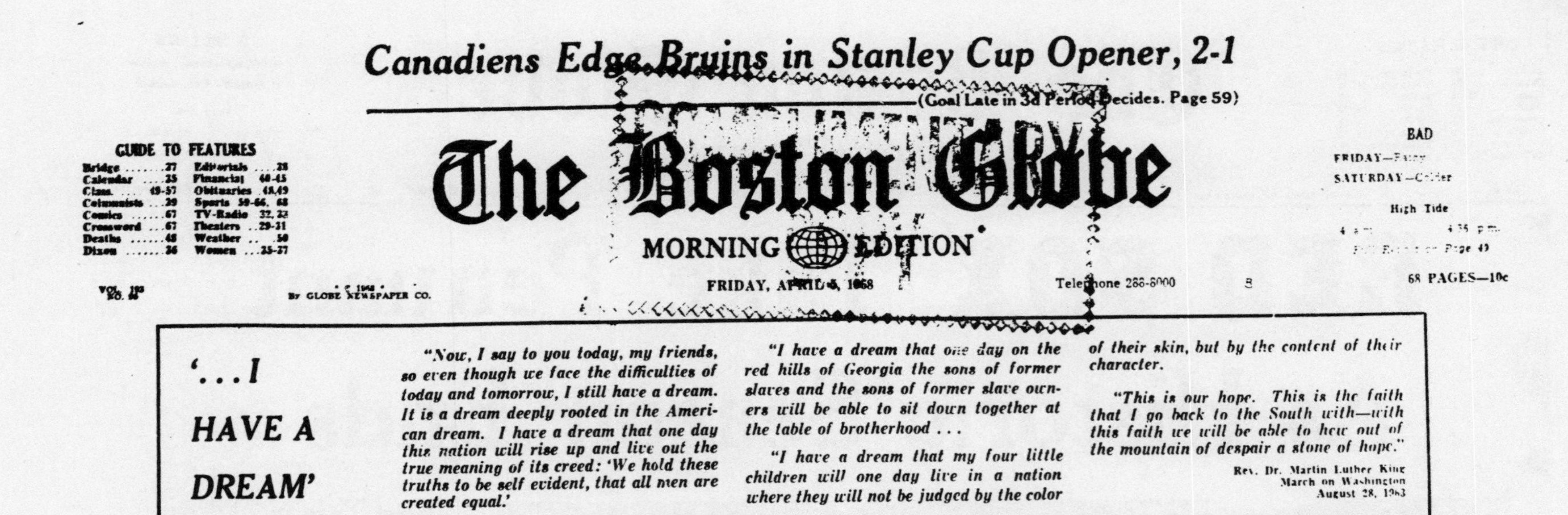

Canadiens Edge Bruins in Stanley Cup Opener, 2-1

(Goal Late in 3d Period Decides. Page 59)

GUIDE TO FEATURES

Bridge	27	Editorials	28
Calendar	25	Financial	40-45
Class.	49-57	Obituaries	48,49
Columnists	29	Sports	59-66, 68
Comics	67	TV-Radio	32, 33
Crossword	67	Theaters	29-31
Deaths	48	Weather	50
Dixon	36	Women	35-37

The Boston Globe

MORNING EDITION

VOL. 193 NO. 96 — © 1968 By GLOBE NEWSPAPER CO. — FRIDAY, APRIL 5, 1968 — Telephone 288-8000 — 68 PAGES—10c

BAD — FRIDAY—Fairy — SATURDAY—Colder — High Tide — 4 a.m. 4:35 p.m.

'...I HAVE A DREAM'

"Now, I say to you today, my friends, so even though we face the difficulties of today and tomorrow, I still have a dream. It is a dream deeply rooted in the American dream. I have a dream that one day this nation will rise up and live out the true meaning of its creed: 'We hold these truths to be self evident, that all men are created equal.'

"I have a dream that one day on the red hills of Georgia the sons of former slaves and the sons of former slave owners will be able to sit down together at the table of brotherhood . . .

"I have a dream that my four little children will one day live in a nation where they will not be judged by the color of their skin, but by the content of their character.

"This is our hope. This is the faith that I go back to the South with—with this faith we will be able to hew out of the mountain of despair a stone of hope."

Rev. Dr. Martin Luther King
March on Washington
August 28, 1963

The Minister of Peace Is Slain

THUNDER SOUNDED IN CHURCH

On a tragically ironic note, and with a thunderclap as background, Dr. Martin Luther King said the night before his assassination that "if my life ended now, I would have felt that it had been worthwhile."

Speaking to a Negro church group in Memphis, Dr. King said in a response to a question, "I'm glad to be living at this time."

Then, witnesses said, a loud thunder clap virtually shook the church.

REV. DR. MARTIN LUTHER KING (1929-1968)

Memphis Sniper Kills Martin Luther King

By NICHOLAS C. CHRISS
Washington Post-L.A. Times

MEMPHIS—Dr. Martin Luther King was shot to death by a sniper here Thursday.

The 1964 Nobel Peace Prize winner, America's leading exponent of nonviolence in the civil rights movement, was shot as he stood on the second floor balcony at his motel, talking to aides in the parking lot below. He was rushed to St. Joseph's Hospital, where he was pronounced dead.

Police said the shot apparently came from a brick building directly across the street from the Lorraine Motel, where Dr. King had checked in Thursday morning.

An all-points bulletin was issued for the assassin, described by witnesses as a Caucasian, about 30 years old, 5 feet 10 inches tall, 165 pounds, wearing dark clothing.

Dr. King's aides told police a man answering that description fled from the building across the street a few moments after the fatal shot was fired.

They said he jumped into a car parked near the building dropping a Browning automatic rifle fitted with a sniper scope to the sidewalk as he ran. The car sped away.

A five-square-block area of the city surrounding the motel was sealed off quickly by police and sheriff's deputies, but police said the car evidently escaped the blockade.

Memphis Police and Fire Director Frank C. Holloman appeared on television a few minutes after Dr. King, 39, was pronounced dead, to appeal for order.

He asked all citizens to stay off the streets because of "this volatile situation."

Gov. Buford Ellington immediately ordered 4,000 National Guardsmen into the city, and Mayor Henry Loeb announced a curfew at nightfall. All police and sheriff's deputies were called to patrol duty.

DR. KING Page 6

Despair In the Streets

Angry Negroes, embittered by the death of Dr. Martin Luther King Jr., took to the streets in a dozen major cities Thursday night, but powerful efforts were being made by leaders of the Negro community — including Stokely Carmichael—to calm them down.

Hosea Williams, one of Dr. King's closest advisers, who was standing beneath the balcony where King was shot, called immediately for continued nonviolence.

"Let's not burn America down," he said in Memphis. "We must—we must maintain and advocate and promote the philosophy of nonviolence."

Disturbances were reported in Memphis and Nashville, Tenn., Boston, New York city, Washington, and many other Southern cities.

MEMPHIS Page 14

Will Bomb Charge Peril Talks?

From Wire Services

WASHINGTON — The United States has begun diplomatic inquiries to arrange a site and time to meet a North Vietnamese envoy to discuss the war, informed sources said Thursday.

Administration sources said Thursday that the United States has begun to inquire through diplomatic channels how to initiate the "contact" that Hanoi and Washington each offered publicly on Wednesday.

Geneva, publicly mentioned on Sunday by President Johnson for a meeting site, remains a strong contender.

Administration officials expressed the hope and belief that a Hanoi claim that U.S. planes penetrated deep into North Vietnam will not endanger the expected meeting.

The Pentagon's swift announcement of an "immediate investigation" of the alleged bombing, far beyond the limits set by President Johnson, was designed to head off jeopardy to the delicate diplomatic situation. U.S. diplomatic officials initially were stunned by the report, and expressed certainty that if a bombing took place it was a miscalculation on someone's part.

American sources in Saigon said Friday no U.S. air strikes had been reported near the 20th parallel in North Vietnam for more than 24 hours, prompting speculation that President Johnson may be further curtailing the bombing of the North.

(Eugene V. Rostow, undersecretary of state for political affairs, said Thursday in New York that the bombing of North Vietnam would not be completely halted until American troops in the northern part of South Vietnam were guaranteed protection.

(Rostow said he 'wouldn't be surprised" if preliminary peace talks on Vietnam moved "fairly quickly to a cease-fire." These talks, he said, probably would be followed by long, formal peace negotiations.

TALKS Page 27

Gangs Roam In Boston

Thirteen persons were injured and scores taken into custody in the Roxbury, North Dorchester and South End areas of Boston after a night of sporadic disturbances.

No one was hurt seriously, according to officials at Boston City Hospital.

At 3 a.m., police were unable to estimate how many persons they had picked up or booked.

Police said property damage was most severe in the Grove Hall area and along Blue Hill av., in Roxbury. Most of it was

BOSTON Page 14

"If injustice and inequity, if racist prejudices and discriminations now become the targets of all decent men and women, Dr. King's death may bring about what he sought for himself, his people and country."—Ralph McGill, Page 7.

The Search For Peace

When the United States suddenly hardened its demands on Hanoi in the middle of talks between Britain's Harold Wilson and Soviet Prime Minister Kosygin, many felt hopes for a settlement were dashed. Part 2 of the secret search for Peace details those events. Page 39.

What Is It?

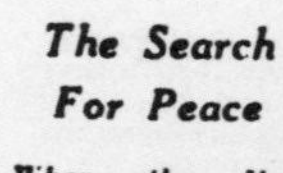

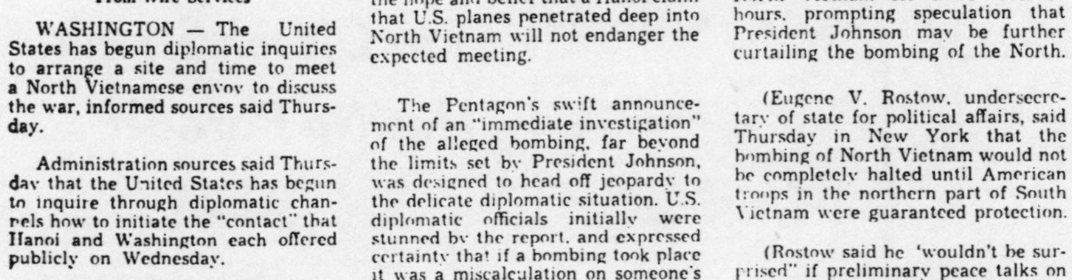

DAMAGED EYE (RIGHT) OF TONY CONIGLIARO (Sam Hammat Photo)

Conigliaro's Career in Doubt

By HERBERT BLACK
Globe Medical Editor

Tony Conigliaro's left eye has become so much worse in the past 10 days that even cautious doctors predicted Thursday night that his ball playing days are over.

An area in the center of the retina, the innermost layer of the eyeball, is badly scarred.

This area, called the macula, contains the nerve fibers and specialized rods and cones that provide sharp vision.

Doctors fear that there is a hole right through the eight layers of nerve tissue comprising the retina. They cannot tell for certain because the scar obstructs the view even with high-powered optical microscopes.

Conigliaro's retina is not detached. In some ways it might be better if it were. Then doctors could diagnose the true situation behind the scar. They cannot remove the scar because surgery would only leave another scar.

CONIGLIARO Page 60

LBJ, 'Sad,' Delays Trip

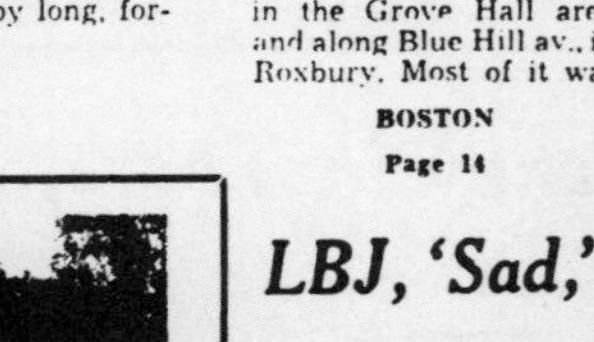

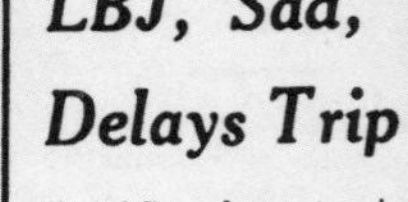

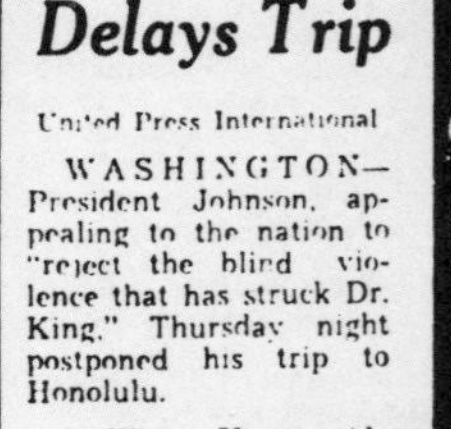

United Press International

WASHINGTON—President Johnson, appealing to the nation to "reject the blind violence that has struck Dr. King," Thursday night postponed his trip to Honolulu.

A White House aide said Mr. Johnson remarked late Thursday night, "We'll get up tomorrow morning and make a decision on departure" for the conference on reviewing Vietnam policy.

Mr. Johnson, in a brief speech over radio and television, said "America is shocked and saddened by the brutal slaying tonight of Dr. Martin Luther King.

JOHNSON Page 18

RETURNS HOME—Mrs. King after learning of her husband's death, is escorted by Atlanta Mayor Ivan Allen, holding the umbrella. (AP)

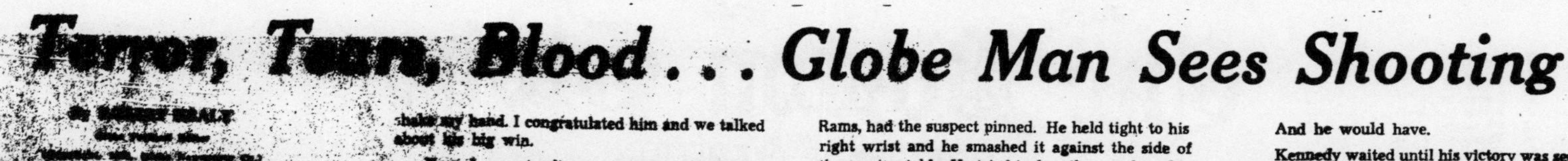

Terror, Tears, Blood . . . Globe Man Sees Shooting

By [illegible] HEALY
[illegible]
[illegible]

[illegible] in that narrow, darkened corridor there was [illegible], profanity, tears, blood and the violence of a nation.

Sen. Robert Kennedy had walked down the same back corridor in the kitchen of the Ambassador Hotel just 15 minutes before. He was in a good mood. He had won California. And he came over to shake my hand. I congratulated him and we talked about his big win.

Now, I was standing on a steel serving table directly over the same place where we had shaken hands. He lay there struck down by bullets. His face was white. His eyes were open. His lips moved just slightly.

But he did not cry.

Against the steel serving table, Roosevelt Grier, the huge Negro lineman for the Los Angeles Rams, had the suspect pinned. He held tight to his right wrist and he smashed it against the side of the serving table. He tried to free the gun from his hand.

There was this great man, towering over the suspect and with all his strength it took him more than a minute to take that gun from him.

Another, atop the table, was trying to kick the assassin in the face. "Bastard . . . kill him," he shouted.

And he would have.

Kennedy waited until his victory was secure in the California primary before he came down to talk to his workers. There was a huge crowd in the ballroom. They had waited for several hours.

They had smelled the victory hours before, and the tempo of Robert Kennedy's folksingers had picked up and the television lights made the room hotter.

HEALY Page 2

CLOSING STOCKS | Boston Evening Globe | CLOSING STOCKS

© 1968, Globe Newspaper Co. 288-8000 WEDNESDAY, JUNE 5, 1968 64 Pages—10 Cents

Kennedy Lives; Condition 'Critical'

Surgery Ends—Bullet Removed—Next 36 Hours to Tell

By BOB THOMAS
Associated Press

LOS ANGELES — Sen. Robert F. Kennedy remained in an "extremely critical condition" today after undergoing a three-hour operation to remove a would-be assassin's bullet from his brain. Sen. Kennedy was shot moments after proclaiming victory in California's Democratic presidential primary.

The presidential contender was struck down about 4½ years after his brother, President John F. Kennedy, was slain in Dallas by a bullet in the head fired by a hidden rifleman.

In New York, Dr. Henry Cuneo, a member of the surgical team was quoted as saying "There was evidently serious damage to the cerebellum, the part of the brain on the extreme back of the head on the right side; also to part of the right cerebral hemisphere . . . and also to the mid brain, which is the main cable connecting the brain itself with all the rest of the body."

The man arrested in the shooting was identified as Sirhan Sirhan, 24, a Jordanian, who recently had been living in Pasadena.

The slender, dark-haired suspect sat stonily silent for hours under police questioning, giving only a lone "yes" to one question.

But finally, officers said, he opened up and talked voluably—but not about himself or the shooting.

He was decribed as "very cool, very calm, very stable and quite lucid" and apparently well educated.

All but a fragment of the bullet was removed from the New York senator's brain, an aide said, but a second and less serious bullet remained in the back of his neck.

KENNEDY Page 3

[illegible]

Suspect, 24, Identified

Sirhan B. Sirhan Born in Jordan

Associated Press

LOS ANGELES—The man held in the shooting of Sen. Robert F. Kennedy was identified today as Sirhan Bishara Sirhan, 24, a Jordanian from Jerusalem who recently has been living in Pasadena, Calif.

Los Angeles Mayor Samuel Yorty and Police Chief Thomas Reddin told a news conference Sirhan lived with a brother, Munier "Joe" Sirhan of Pasadena, a department store employe.

They said idetification was made through Joe and another brother, Adel, who were traced through the .22-caliber pistol used in the shooting. It had passed through many hands.

Chief Reddin said identification &was confirmed by finger prints on an application Eirham Sirham had filed for a job as an exercise boy at Hollywood Park Race Track.

The application, on file in Sacramento, was made some time ago while Sirham was a student at John Muir High School in Pasadena. It showed Sirham was born in Jerusalem Mar. 18, 1944.

At that time J erusalem was under a British mandate. With Israel independence, it was divided between Israel and Jordan. Israel took it over entirely last June in the brief Israeli-Arab war.

The mayor said the prisoner had in his possession a schedule of Kennedy's June speaking engagements.

He said Sirham Sirham also had four $100 bills when arrested, and a clipping of an article critical of Kennedy.

SUSPECT Page 3

SEN. ROBERT KENNEDY lies on floor of the Ambassador Hotel after being shot early this morning. His shirt had been opened and he is clutching rosary beads. (UPI)

(Full Page of Pictures of Tragic Shooting on Page 19.)

"I think we can end divisions within U.S."

SEN. KENNEDY'S victory speech delivered moments before he was shot urged his supporters to help him deal with violence in America.

"I think we can end the divisions within the United States," he told me. See Page 8.

RFK's Calif. Win: 4% Over McCarthy

United Press International

LOS ANGELES — Sen. Robert F. Kennedy gained victory over Sen. Eugene J. McCarthy in the California presidential primary today when he was shot and wounded minutes after a victory celebration.

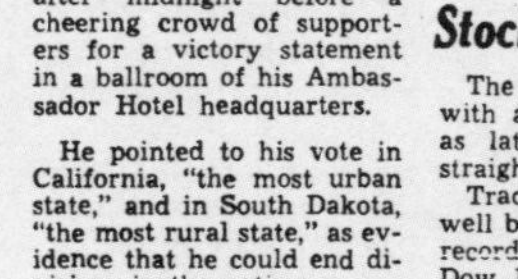

Kennedy appeared shortly after midnight before a cheering crowd of supporters for a victory statement in a ballroom of his Ambassador Hotel headquarters.

He pointed to his vote in California, "the most urban state," and in South Dakota, "the most rural state," as evidence that he could end divisions in the nation.

McCarthy's defeat, a giant killer in some eariier primaries this year, virtually destroyed his chances of winning the Democratic presidential nomination. But the Minnesota senator said last night he was going on with his campaign, win or lose in California.

CALIFORNIA Page 8

Stocks Off at Close

The stock market closed with a moderate loss today as late selling ended five straight days of advance. Trading was heavy but well below yesterday's near-record pace. The closing Dow Jones Industrial Average at 907.42 was down 9.21 from yesterday's close. See Page 58.

SIRHAN SIRHAN

Hub Doctor Flies to RFK

The President's office Wednesday morning arranged for the military jet flight of Boston neurosurgeon Dr. James Poppen of the Lahey Clinic to Los Angeles to participate in the care of Sen. Robert Kennedy.

Dr. Poppen was called by the family and the White House. He was a consultant for Sen. Edward Kennedy at the time of his back injury in a plane crash in 1964, has cared for the President of Mexico and other world figures.

POPPEN Page 3

LBJ Leads Prayers for RFK

United Press International

WASHINGTON—President Johnson today led a horrified nation in praying for the recovery of Sen. Robert F. Kennedy, who was critically wounded in an assassination attempt in Los Angeles. Lawmakers voiced fear "the world's gone mad."

Mr. Johnson, who succeeded to the office of President when John F. Kennedy was slain before his eyes in Dallas four years ago, said "there are no words equal to the horror" of this newest tragedy.

"All America prays for his recovery," Mr. Johnson said. "We also pray that divisiveness and violence be driven from the hearts of men everywhere."

LBJ Page 28

INDEX TO TONIGHT'S GLOBE

Ask the Globe 23	Crossword 56	Sports 49-54
Astro-Guide ..56	Deaths 62, 63	Steincrohn ...21
Bridge 30	Editorials 18	TV-Radio 62
Calendar 24	Financial ..57-59	Theaters ..59-61
Classified ..39-47	Senior Set ...38	Twistagram ..56
Comics 56	Society 35	Women ...33-37

THE WEATHER

Tonight—Fair, low 55-60.

Thursday—Fair and warm.

High Tide at 7:12 p.m. Full Reports, Page 16.

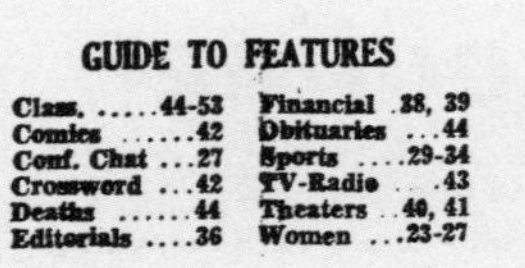

GUIDE TO FEATURES

Class.	44-53	Financial	38, 39
Comics	42	Obituaries	44
Conf. Chat	27	Sports	29-34
Crossword	42	TV-Radio	43
Deaths	44	Theaters	40, 41
Editorials	36	Women	23-27

The Boston Globe

MORNING EDITION

VOL. 194 NO. 60 · © 1968 By GLOBE NEWSPAPER CO. · THURSDAY, AUGUST 29, 1968 · ® · Telephone 288-8000 · 54 PAGES—10c

OVER THE HUMP

THURSDAY — Mostly fair, in the 70s. FRIDAY—about the same. (Page 47)

High Tides

3:36 a.m. 4 p.m.

Victory Comes Amid Unrest in Hall and Streets

Humphrey Wins, 1761-847

IN THE OPEN — Police charge anti-war demonstrators in Chicago's Grant Park. Tear gas and clubs were used to rout the gathering. National Guard was called in later. (AP)

ON THE FLOOR — Sen. Ribicoff of Connecticut, nominating Sen. McGovern, gets an angry response from Mayor Daley (hand cupped). Ribicoff referred to "Gestapo tactics" in Chicago.

Doves Lose on Plank, 1568-1042

PLATFORM:

By MARTIN F. NOLAN
Globe Convention Staff

CHICAGO — Democrats took their stand with President Johnson's policy on the war in Vietnam on Wednesday after an emotional afternoon of argument over the party's most divisive issue.

By a 3-2 margin — considered by some doves a moral victory — the convention endorsed current United States policy in Vietnam.

The final vote was 1567¾ votes for the majority plank of the platform committee — the hawk position — against 1041¾ votes for the committee's minority report, the dove plank.

The Massachusetts delegation split 56-16 in favor of the dove position.

(The state-by-state vote and a breakdown of the Massachusetts delegation's vote, Page 11.)

Supporters of Vice President Humphrey lined up to defend Humphrey's position against the cause espoused by supporters of Sens. Eugene McCarthy, George McGovern and Edward M. Kennedy.

But in singing and in parades confettied with black crepe, the dove supporters showed after the vote that they would not reconcile themselves to the war that has divided their party.

In approving the pro-administration plank, the convention testified to the strength of the unseen force at the convention, President Johnson.

PLATFORM Page 11

BALLOTING:

By ROBERT HEALY and MARTIN F. NOLAN
Globe Convention Staff

CHICAGO—Hubert Horatio Humphrey won the Presidential nomination of a party bitterly split on the Vietnam war and in a convention city wracked with chaos.

Humphrey swept to victory on the first ballot. The vote was 1761¾ for Humphrey and 847 for all others. It happened at 12:46 a.m. (EDT).

But early Thursday 1000 angry Democrats began walking the five miles from Convention Hall back to their hotels to protest Humphrey's nomination.

Rep. William Fitts Ryan, N.Y., organized the protest march.

It came a few hours after sponsors of a fourth party—the "New Party"—sought to organize a walkout from the convention in protest of Humphrey's selection.

McCarthy had telephoned Humphrey his congratulations—but told reporters it is "still an open question" as to whether he will support the vice president in the campaign ahead. He said he would not run as a fourth-party candidate.

"I think I lost because political procedures don't respond to the judgment of the people," McCarthy said. "But I look upon it as a temporary setback at most."

Humphrey's nomination came as police and National Guardsmen battled and broke the heads of young demonstrators beneath the very windows of the Conrad Hilton Hotel where Humphrey was staying.

His nomination came as delegates shouted over the microphones for adjournment and the delegates booed Mayor Richard Daley of Chicago and even the mention of Illinois' delegation.

And when the unanimous nomination was called for, the hall was filled with "no's."

As the nominating speeches were being made in the amphitheater, the young demonstrators, both blacks and whites, broke through the police lines which held them through Tuesday night and early Wednesday and attempted the march they had planned to the conventon hall.

They never made it.

The nominating speeches came after delegates had placed tiny black strips of crepe on the standards of

BALLOTING Page 4

Ted Undecided on Chicago Trip

By ROBERT L. TURNER
Staff Reporter

HYANNIS PORT—Sen. Edward M. Kennedy had made no decision early this morning on whether he will travel to Chicago today to take part in a tribute to his brother, Robert, at the Democratic Convention.

KENNEDY Page 11

Police Battle Youths in City

By ROBERT JORDAN
Globe Convention Staff

CHICAGO — For nearly three hours here Wednesday night, police and National Guardsmen battled with some 3000 antiwar protestors outside the two hotels housing the three contenders for the Democratic presidential nomination.

About 11 p.m. E.D.T. police offered a truce, allowing demonstrators to gather in Grant Park, directly across from the hotels. The offer was accepted by about 1000 who later held another rally. During the rally, a convoy of National Guardsmen stationed themselves along the sidewalk facing the protestors.

Eugene McCarthy paid a visit Wednesday night to a makeshift first aid ward set up in his headquarters for victims of the street fighting outside the Conrad Hilton Hotel.

The senator went from bed to bed, comforting youngsters who had been clubbed by police trying to break up the crowd of anti-war demonstrators.

And Hubert H. Humphrey expressed dismay on what should have been one of the most joyous nights of his life because of the violent clashes that raged around his hotel

CHICAGO Page 10

Mr. V.P.

A five-part series on Vice President Humphrey—the result of weeks of research and travel with the candidate by Washington correspondent Martin F. Nolan — will begin in Friday's Globe.

Epilogue for McCarthy: the Young Chanting 'Peace Now'

- Christopher Lydon describes McCarthy's fade-out. Page 37.
- S. J. Micciche tells how Bay State voted on peace plank. Page 11.
- FBI will probe beating of newsmen in Chicago. Page 10.

By ROBERT HEALY
Globe Convention Staff

CHICAGO — Looking out the window of the suite on the 23d floor of the Conrad Hilton Hotel, Eugene McCarthy could see the line of blue helmets of Chicago police and he could hear the chant of the young, black and white, shouting: "Peace now . . . peace now . . . peace now . . ."

McCarthy sat down on the green sofa and raised his feet to the coffee table. Across from him sat Robert Lowell, the poet. McCarthy suggesed that the campaign had made Lowell look younger, and then he asked: "What new creaks have you heard in the morning?"

While Lowell thought for a moment, McCarthy remembered that some wild prairie flowers have a particular creak when they open in the morning, and that old houses have a special kind of creak early in the day, one that they do not have later on when the sun has dried their moisture.

It was 11:15 p.m. and two quiet men were casually discussing flowers, old houses and advancing age.

SCENE Page 37

Czech Assembly Protests

Czechoslovakia continued its non-violent protest Wednesday against the invasion by the Soviet Union and its Warsaw Pact allies, but the major focus shifted from the streets of Prague and the clandestine radio station to the National Assembly.

The National Assembly passed an eight-point resolution Wednesday, the major item of which called the occupation of Czechoslovakia by foreign troops illegal and contrary to international law, the United Nations and the Warsaw Pact itself.

But even as the Assembly acted, sources in the Czech Central Committee were revealing to Western newsmen details of that evening a week ago when Russian soldiers broke into the Central Committee building, snatched a phone from the hands of Alexander Dubcek, handcuffed him and flew him to Moscow.

The word in Prague was not to upset the uneasy Soviets. Demonstrators were urged to break up their marches, press censorship was being restored and a mood of resignation seemed to creep over the population.

Page 26

Baseball Results

AMERICAN LEAGUE

Oakland 5, BOSTON 3.
Detroit 6, California 1.
Washington 3, Baltimore 2.
Cleveland 3, Minnesota 2.
Chicago 3, New York 0.

RED SOX TODAY

Oakland at Fenway Park (Nash vs. Morehead) 1:30 p.m.

NATIONAL LEAGUE

Atlanta 9, Philadelphia 2.
Atlanta 2, Philadelphia 1.
Cincinnati 8, New York 3.
Cincinnati 5, New York 2.
St. Louis 8, Pittsburgh 0.
San Francisco 4, Houston 3.
Chicago 7, Los Angeles 4.
Los Angeles 8, Chicago 4.

Ike's Name Taken Off Critical List

WASHINGTON — Just 12 days after suffering his seventh heart attack, former President Dwight D. Eisenhower was taken off the critical list Wednesday. Doctors said the long-range outlook was unpredictable.

"Because of the extent of Gen Eisenhower's underlying coronary artery disease, his present condition must still be considered serious albeit not necessarily critical at this time," doctors said. "The long-range outlook is still guarded and, as indicated in yesterday's bulletin, the potential for sudden reversal of the current favorable trend is ever present."

U.S. Ambassador to Guatemala Assassinated by Terrorists

Reuters

GUATEMALA CITY, Guatemala — U.S. Ambassador John Gordon Mein was machine-gunned to death in this city Wednesday.

The ambassador was shot at 3:15 p.m. local time (5:15 EDT) as he was being driven back to the embassy from a lunch given for the foreign press by Guatemalan Foreign Minister Arensales Catalana.

Several bystanders helped pull Mein from the car but he was already dead. His driver escaped unharmed.

President Johnson and high U.S. government officials expressed shock and grief Wednesday night at the assassination.

Mein, 54, was a native of Kentucky, and began his career with the U.S. Agriculture Dept. in 1936. He joined the State Dept. in 1941, and was named to the Guatemalan ambassadorship in 1965 by President Johnson.

The State Dept. said it will request the Guatemalan government to investigate the assassination which was an obvious setback to hopes by officials here that a wave of terror in Guatemala had come to an end.

Earlier this year, after the January killing of two U.S. military attaches, threats to Mein's life and the kidnapping of the Guatemalan archbishop in March, officials feared that a major political crisis might be brewing.

But the removal late in March of Defense Minister Rafael Arreaga Bosque was read as a step toward more effective restraint of terrorist activities of extreme right-wing groups, reportedly connected with military elements.

The government of President Julio Montenegro has still been unable to maintain public order in this country of 4.5 million.

Although Guatemalan officials blamed pro-communist terrorists for the slaying of the two military attaches, no arrests were made or definite evidence produced to the knowledge of officals here.

JOHN GORDON MEIN

The shooting Wednesday took place opposite a restaurant on Reforma av. in central Guatemala.

AMBASSADOR Page 3

Boston Evening Globe

© 1968, Globe Newspaper Co. 288-8000 FRIDAY, OCTOBER 18, 1968 • 46 PAGES—10 CENTS

Jacqueline Will Marry Onassis Sunday

Greek Island Sealed Off As Bride-to-Be Arrives

Kennedy Sisters There for Rites

She and Tycoon Will Live In Her N.Y. Apartment

ONASSIS AND JACQUELINE—A wedding on island of Skorpios and a new life. (AP, UPI)

By JOHN RIGOS
United Press International

ANDRAVIDA, Greece—Greek billionaire Aristotle Onassis today greeted Jacqueline Kennedy with a kiss on the cheek and then flew off with her to his private island in the Ionian Sea for their marriage, on Sunday.

A spokesman for Onassis said the wedding would be as private as possible and no reporters or photographers would be permitted.

Honeymoon plans were not disclosed.

In New York, Nancy Tuckerman, Mrs. Kennedy's secretary, said the couple will live later in Mrs. Kennedy's home on Fifth Avenue and the children will continue at their present schools.

Strict security precautions were in effect when Mrs. Kennedy's special jet airliner landed at Andravida after the flight from New York. Heavy police forces kept newsmen, photographers and spectators some distance away from this Greek air force base.

The 62-year-old Onassis greeted Mrs. Kennedy first with a kiss on the cheek, air base sources reported. He then kissed the other members of the family.

The 39-year-old widow of President John F. Kennedy flew here in a DC8 jetliner of Olympia Airlines, owned by her husband-to-be. She was accompanied by her two children, her mother and stepfather, and two of her late husband's sisters.

JACQUELINE
Page 18

Hanoi Replies To Peace Bid

By GEORGE SIBERA
United Press International

PARIS — North Vietnamese diplomatic sources today said Hanoi has replied to the latest U.S. proposals aimed at achieving a breakthrough in the Vietnam war.

The sources gave no further details.

Earlier, the Communist sources had confirmed that the Hanoi regime had received new peace overtures from the United States.

The U.S. suggestions were said by the Hanoi sources to be under urgent review. An answer outlining Hanoi's position will be given shortly by Xuan Thuy, the North Vietnamese negotiator, to Ambassador W. Averell Harriman, the sources said.

It was the first time Hanoi officials had acknowledged in private the existence of an American peace package. Presumably the plan sought assurances that Hanoi will not take advantage of an American bombing halt, and suggested that both Saigon and the National Liberation Front (NLF) be admitted to the peace talks.

The sources said the Hanoi answer would come soon. Presumably, it would be conveyed by Thuy to Harriman at their 27th negotiating meeting at the Majestic Hotel next Wednesday—if not in secret earlier.

Presumably the decision was a tough one for Hanoi. Observers remarked that North Vietnam hitherto has flatly refused to deal with

BOMBING
Page 22

Apollo 7 Maneuver Jolts Crew

Associated Press

SPACE CENTER, Houston—With a jolting burst of energy, the Apollo 7 astronauts fired their steering engine today in the most powerful maneuver ever made by a manned spaceship.

"Yabba - dubba - doo!" shouted Navy Capt Walter M. Schirra Jr. as the huge engine flashed to life and spurted a steady tail of flame for 66 seconds as Apollo 7 raced 120 miles above the Gulf of Mexico.

"That was a real nice to-do, the machine performed beautifully," spacecraft commander Schirra reported at the completion of this vital test of the engine that one day will guide American astronauts to the moon.

APOLLO
Page 17

Nixon Sees War End in '68

By S. J. MICCICHE

Former Vice President Richard M. Nixon, in Boston today, said he believes that the Vietnam war will end before January 20.

Nixon, addressing a crowd of some 1500 Republican party workers at the Hotel Somerset, said of Vietnam:

". . . and I trust that the war will be brought to an honorable conclusion before the next administration takes office."

The Republican nominee made the statement while discussing what he felt to be the major foreign policy problems confronting the United States.

His reference to Vietnam was merely in passing. He has declined to enter any deep discussion of the Southeast Asian war while the negotiations for its settlement are in progress in Paris.

He urged them to "go out and talk to the fence sitters and to Democrats and Independents." This is essentially the same message he has delivered to similar audiences since he won the nomination

He said, "We have got to show why people should be voting for" the Nixon-Agnew ticket rather than against Vice President Hubert Humphrey or former Alabama governor George Wallace.

"We don't want to back into it (Presidency). We want to win it going away," said Nixon.

He exhuded a feeling of confidence, saying that his is the analysis of a "candidate who has gone around this country and found there is a feeling we're ahead."

At the same time, he indicated some nervousness, reminding his audience, "I'm the expert on losing the close ones."

NIXON
Page 20

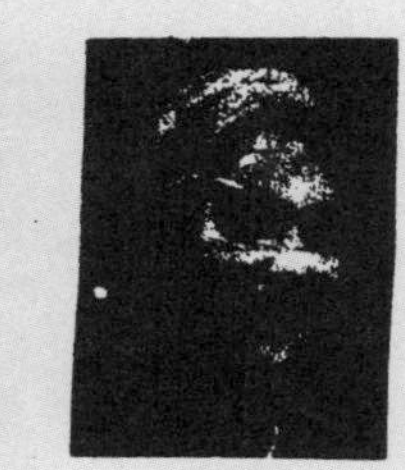

MRS. KENNEDY — HARLECH — CALLAS

Rose Hopes They'll Be Happy

Mrs. Rose Kennedy said today she hopes Jacqueline Kennedy and Aristole Onassis will be very happy together.

She was approached by newsmen after attending services in St. Francis Xavier Church in Hyannis.

"I wish them great happiness," Mrs. Kennedy said when asked about how she felt about her daughter-in-law's marriage.

She had nothing else to say on the subjejct. Earlier, her secretary said Mrs. Kennedy would have no comment.

In London, Lord Harlech, whose name had been linked romantically with that of President John F. Kennedy's widow, wished the couple well.

"Mrs. Kennedy has been a very close friend for more than 14 years," he said. "I'm very happy about it. I certainly hope they will be happy."

Harlech, 50, a widower and a Roman Catholic, had been considered by many the man most likely to become Mrs. Kennedy's second husband.

In Paris, opera star Maria Callas also said she was happy, though she didn't sound it.

Telephoned for her reaction, the fiery diva said, "Very good. I am delighted for both of them."

Then she slammed down the receiver, and refused all other calls.

REACTION
Page 18

HH Finds Happiness At Home Off Range

By MARTIN F. NOLAN

HARTFORD — Vice President Humphrey is becoming "his own man" in his campaign and finding the process of maturation less traumatic than he thought.

Shedding the adolescent shackles of the Vice Presidency, Humphrey has become increasingly outspoken, heedless of the Eyes of Texas that have inhibited him for the past four years.

"I don't care whether Johnson wanted to debate or not. I do. I want a debate," he told the Detroit Economic Club.

HUMPHREY
Page 21

U.S. Drops 2 Blacks; Olympic Mates Shocked

Globe Wire Services

MEXICO CITY — The U.S. Olympic Committee suspended star Negro sprinters Tommie Smith and John Carlos from the U.S. Olympic team after midnight Thursday for "untypical exhibitionism" during an Olympic victory ceremony Wednesday.

The decision followed a complaint by the International Olympic Committee regarding the conduct of Smith when he received the gold medal for winning the 200-meter event and Carlos when he was presented the bronze medal for finishing third in the 200-meter finals Wednesday.

The Committee gave Carlos and Smith 48 hours to leave Mexico.

Both Smith and Carlos raised clenched fists clothed in black gloves during the playing of the Star Spangled Banner and also wore black knee socks without shoes during the presentation ceremony.

They also wore identical buttons on their team uniforms citing demands for racial equality.

The first reaction among American athletes in Olympic Village was one of shock and bewilderment.

"It is unfair, it is ridiculous," said Art Walker, a Negro triple jumper from Los Angeles who already has competed.

"They say they are doing it because of a protest. This is silly. Since the early 1900's the United States team has been protesting similarly by failing to dip its flag when it passes the reviewing stand. All other countries do it. This is strictly political."

Most countries dip their flags when passing in review but it is against government regulations to dip the American flag under any circumstances. Flag bearers in the Olympic parade have always followed Army and Navy protocol in this respect.

ATHLETES
Page 29

COSTLY GESTURE—Gold and Bronze medal winners Tommie Smith, center, and John Carlos, right, were sent home by the United States Olympic Committee. The Black Power salute was given Thursday after the presentation of medals. (UPI)

Stocks Surge To New Highs

The stock market this afternoon surged to new two-year highs ina renewal of yesterday's "peace rally".

The closing Dow Jones Industrial Average at 967.49 was up 8.58 from yesterday's close. See Page 33.

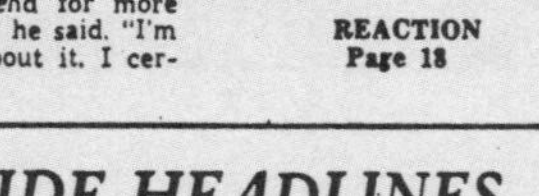

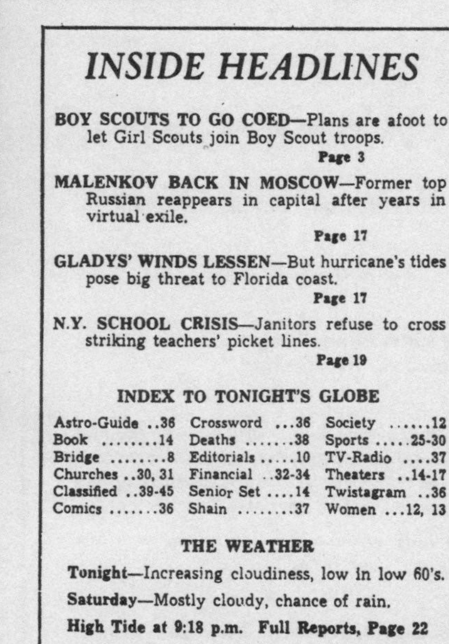

INSIDE HEADLINES

BOY SCOUTS TO GO COED—Plans are afoot to let Girl Scouts join Boy Scout troops.
Page 3

MALENKOV BACK IN MOSCOW—Former top Russian reappears in capital after years in virtual exile.
Page 17

GLADYS' WINDS LESSEN—But hurricane's tides pose big threat to Florida coast.
Page 17

N.Y. SCHOOL CRISIS—Janitors refuse to cross striking teachers' picket lines.
Page 19

INDEX TO TONIGHT'S GLOBE

Astro-Guide ..36	Crossword ...36	Society 12
Book 14	Deaths 38	Sports 25-30
Bridge 8	Editorials 10	TV-Radio 37
Churches ..30, 31	Financial ..32-34	Theaters ...14-17
Classified ..39-45	Senior Set 14	Twistagram ..36
Comics 36	Shain 37	Women 12, 13

THE WEATHER

Tonight—Increasing cloudiness, low in low 60's.

Saturday—Mostly cloudy, chance of rain.

High Tide at 9:18 p.m. Full Reports, Page 22

The Boston Globe

MONDAY, JULY 21, 1969 — Telephone 288-8000 — 3£ PAGES—10c

July 20, 1969

MAN WALKS ON MOON

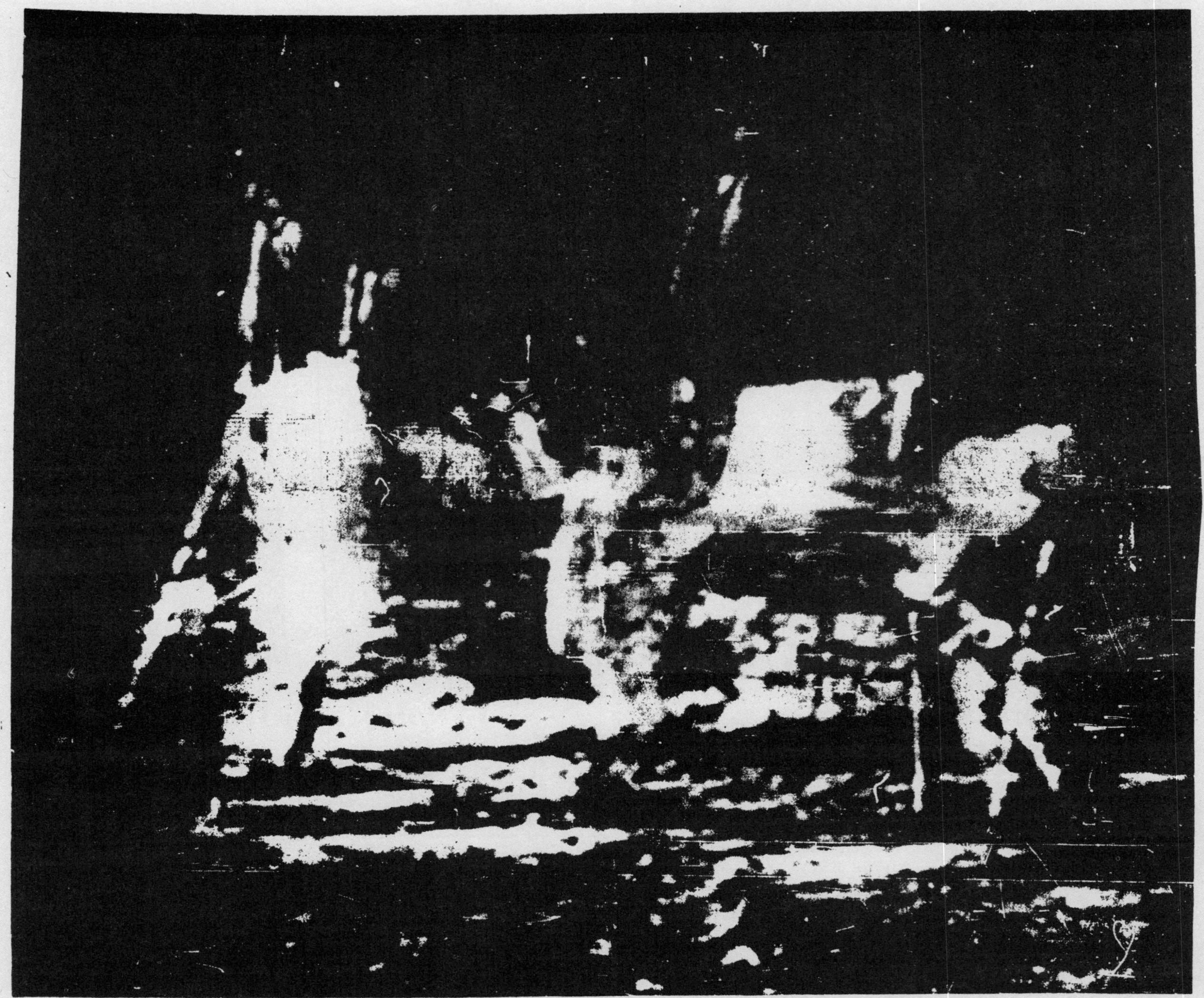

Astronauts Armstrong and Aldrin plant American flag on the moon at 11:46 p.m. (AP)

World Gets Guided Tour: 'Beautiful, Magnificent Desolation'

"OK Houston, I'm on the porch."

★ ★ ★

"I'm at the foot of the ladder."

★ ★ ★

"That's one small step for a man, but one giant leap for mankind."

★ ★ ★

"The surface is fine and powdered, like powdered charcoal to the soles of my boot . . . I can see my footprints of my boot in the fine particles."

"I only go in a fraction of an inch, an eighth of an inch."

★ ★ ★

"Beautiful, beautiful, beautiful. A magnificent desolation."

"It's very interesting. It's a very fine soft surface, but when I dig for the contingency sample, it appears to be very hard cohesive material of the same sort."

"Didn't I say we might see some purple rocks?"

"Did you find purple rocks?"

"Yup."

Two men from the planet Earth landed on the surface of the Moon at 4.17.45 E.D.T., Sunday, July 20, 1969.

It brought the dawn of a new era in the evolution of man.

The first human imprint on lunar soil was made five hours after the landing by Neil A. Armstrong, a civilian from the United States of America. The time, 10:56.20 p.m., July 29, 1969.

Watching him at the historic moment was Edwin E. Aldrin Jr., an Air Force lieutenant colonel.

It took them 109 hours, 8 minutes and 5 seconds to get there.

Orbiting the moon to pick up the two Moon landers was the third member of the historic team, Air Force Lt Col Michael Collins.

The news of the successful landing which was relayed to Earth by TV and radio in play-by-play sequence was hailed by the entire world.

The age of space truly began on this momentous day and throughout the world scientists now await data and samples which will determine heretofore unknown or uncertain facts about our world and ourselves.

"It has a stark beauty all of it's own. Its much like the desert of the United States. It's different but its very pretty out here."

★ ★ ★

"Its quite dark here in the shadow and quite hard for me to see where I'm stepping. . . .

"Looking up at the LM . . . I can see everything quite clearly . . . everything is very clearly visible."

★ ★ ★

"Put it in the pocket . . . got it . . . the sample is in the pocket . . ."

★ ★ ★

"I want to back up and partially close the hatch. Making sure not to lock it on my way out . . ."

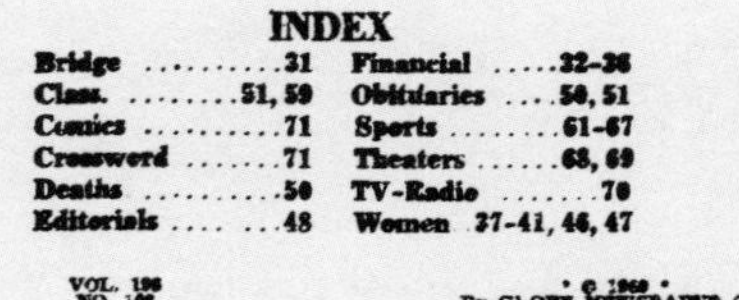

INDEX
Bridge .... 31 Financial 32-36
Class. .... 51, 59 Obituaries 50, 51
Comics .... 71 Sports 61-67
Crossword .... 71 Theaters 68, 69
Deaths .... 50 TV-Radio 70
Editorials ...... 48 Women 37-41, 46, 47

VOL. 196 NO. 108 · © 1969 · By GLOBE NEWSPAPER CO.

The Boston Globe

THURSDAY MORNING, OCTOBER 16, 1969 · Telephone 288-8000 · 72 PAGES—10c

WEATHER
Peace-Full
THURSDAY—Sunny, in 60's.
FRIDAY — Partly cloudy, warmer. (Page 52.)
High Tides
3:18 a.m. 3:30 p.m.

Orderly Young Crowd Gives Dignity to Vigil

SAIGON (Thursday) (Reuters)—A U.S. military communique issued today reported no ground fighting involving U.S. troops throughout South Vietnam yesterday.

The communique was issued as day-long protests against the Vietnam war drew to a close in the U.S., whose time zones are from 12 to 16 hours behind Saigon.

Big Protests in N.Y., Philadelphia, Capital

100,000 on Common Cry 'Peace Now' As Boston M-Day Rally Tops Nation

MORATORIUM DAY CROWD ON BOSTON COMMON, AT BEACON (TOP) AND CHARLES STS.

All Across the Nation— Vast Numbers Turn Out

By CHALMERS M. ROBERTS
Washington Post

WASHINGTON—Uncounted and uncountable numbers of Americans demonstrated their opposition to the Vietnam War yesterday in one fashion or another all across the nation.

Crowds ranged from more than 100,000 on Boston Common to a rain-drenched 1500 in San Francisco, from 30,000 on the New Haven Green to 15,000 at Rutgers University, 10,000 in the center of Minneapolis and at least 30,000 on the Washington Monument grounds in the nation's capital.

There were only minor incidents of violence. The crowds were overwhelmingly white, generally but not always predominantly young.

NATION Page 2

McGovern, Kennedy Ask Groundtroop Pullout Within a Year

By CROCKER SNOW Jr.
Globe Staff

With measured chants of "Peace Now" above the sound of church bells tolling for the war dead, hundreds of thousands of New Englanders demonstrated peacefully yesterday for the goal of peace in Vietnam.

The Vietnam Moratorium was observed in massive city rallies and modest town meetings nationwide yesterday in what now appears as the largest civil demonstration in American history. Appropriately, the most widespread participation in the country occurred in Greater Boston, where the Oct. 15 protest idea was first born last Spring.

Not a single incident of violence was reported in Boston in connection with numerous Moratorium activities.

With professors and students in the vanguard, lines of march from Cambridge, Brookline and outlying parts of the city converged on Boston Common during the afternoon.

A massed crowd of 100,000 heard Sen. George McGovern of South Dakota declare:

"We seek not to break the President, but to lift the terrible burden of the war from his shoulders and from the American people."

At a World Affairs Council of Boston luncheon attended by more than 500 persons, Sen. Edward M. Kennedy urged the Nixon administration to announce an "irrevoceable decision" for an immediate schedule of troop withdrawals to be completed within two years.

MORATORIUM Page 2

Mets Take 3-1 Lead On Orioles' Mistakes

By CLIF KEANE
Globe Staff

NEW YORK — The miracles of the Mets go on and on.

Another great catch yesterday — by Ron Swoboda.

A marvelous infield stab of a grounder by Donn Clendenon to save two runs.

Fine pitching by Tom Seaver.

And when the Orioles made a couple of mistakes, the Mets cashed in for a 2 to 1 victory in 10 innings.

A year ago the Tigers came back from a 3-1 deficit, and now the Orioles are faced with the same situation.

But the Baltimore club that walked through the dressing room after yesterday's loss looked as though it was doomed.

SERIES Page 62

INSIDE NEWS

CLEANUP — Boston will be test center for revolutionary new garbage disposal systems. Page 9.

FAREWELL — Fulton J. Sheen resigns as bishop of Rochester, N.Y., at age 74. Page 4.

Right to White House

Globe Washington Bureau

WASHINGTON—The Vietnam Moratorium came to the doorstep of the White House last night—a silent procession by thousands of candle-bearing marchers asking for an early end to the war.

A quiet, mostly young, well-dressed assembly had furnished the finale for a day of

WASHINGTON Page 42

A Political Woodstock On Boston Common

By ANDREW F. BLAKE and DAVID B. WILSON
Globe Staff

The biggest demonstration in the city's history brought Peace to Boston Common yesterday as an estimated 100,000 persons, most of them young, shouted in disciplined cadence that they want the Vietnam war ended "Now!".

It was also the nation's biggest demonstration of the Oct. 15 Moratorium designed to pressure the Nixon administration to stop the conflict.

In silent, intent concentration, the massed thousands listened as Sen. George McGovern (D-S.D.) assailed the United States' role and echoed Sen. Edward M. Kennedy's urging that U.S. forces be withdrawn "within a year."

COMMON Page 12

Opponents Noisy . . . Few

By ROBERT J. SALES
Globe Staff

The opposition stuck to its guns yesterday with a variety of activities aimed against Moratorium Day.

A small car drove around Boston Common plastered with signs calling for support of American troops in Vietnam and others turned on their headlights to show support for present policy.

OPPOSITION Page 24

She Has 2 Young Sons And Wants Them Alive

By DIANE WHITE
Globe Staff

Jacqueline McLean, a blonde 25-year-old housewife, paused yesterday near the corner of Harvard avenue and Beacon street in Brookline to sign a petition protesting the Vietnam war.

As she gently rocked her baby's carriage Mrs. McLean explained why she was supporting the Moratorium. "I have two sons. They're small now but when they grow up I don't want them to be killed or have to kill," she said.

"And I would never want them to have to fight in a war that is stupid and unnecessary."

ADULTS Page 26

Commager Sees Youth Returning to Persuasive, Patient Tactics of '68

By HENRY STEELE COMMAGER
Special to The Globe

AMHERST—A year ago, a tide of opposition to the Vietnam War forced President Johnson to bow out of the presidential race, halted the bombing of North Vietnam and inaugurated peace negotiations.

This response to public opinion was spectacular and unprecendented; not since Buchanan had a President been forced to withdraw his candidacy for re-election.

Although the ambiguous position on the war of both Nixon and Humphrey discouraged the more dedicated followers of Sen. Eugene McCarthy, these concessions and overtures allayed public resentment of the war, and Mr. Nixon's assurance that he had a plan for ending that war temporarily quieted the opposition.

But it was quieted, not dissipated or stopped. The failure of President Nixon to live up to his campaign promises and, even more, his palpable inability to comprehend either the depth of public disillusionment or the urgency of positive action has reinvigorated the protest movement. Now it has reached a second climacteric, one which differs in important aspects from the first.

For the Moratorium—and all that it symbolizes—was initiated by coll[illegible] not at all a "children's crusade." [illegible] city and a respectability far beyond that [illegible] protest.

COMMAGER Page 49

The Boston Globe

Vol. 197, No. 125, © 1970, Globe Newspaper Co. • TUESDAY MORNING, MAY 5, 1970 • Telephone 288-8000 50 Pages—10c

Guardsmen Kill 4 Students in Ohio; Cambodia Spurs Campus Upheaval

11 Youths Wounded; School Shut

By Louis Cassels
United Press International

KENT, Ohio — Four students were shot to death on the Kent State University campus yesterday when national guardsmen, believing a sniper had attacked them, fired into a crowd of rioting anti-war protestors. It was the nation's most violent confrontation since the peace drive began.

At least 11 persons were wounded, three critically, before order was restored and the university shut down for at least a week.

Students and National Guard officials gave different versions of what triggered the gunfire, but the guard admitted no warning was given that the troops would begin firing their M1 semiautomatic rifles.

Told of the shootings in Washington, President Nixon said the tragedy should convince educators and students that when "dissent turns to violence, it invites tragedy."

The battle began after about 1000 demonstrators, defying an order not to assemble, rallied on the commons at the center of the tree-lined campus. Guardsmen moved in and fired tear gas grenades at the mob, which broke and ran.

The protestors then regrouped and confronted about 300 guardsmen on a practice football field. The students, now numbering 1500, charged down a hill and pelted the troops with rocks. Guardsmen exhausted their supply of tear gas. Students, who tossed back the cannisters, surrounded the troops on three sides.

Then, according to S. T. Del Corso, state adjutant general, "a sniper opened fire against the guardsmen from a nearby rooftop."

Student eyewitnesses said they did not hear any gunfire before the guardsmen began shooting.

KENT STATE, Page 6

STUDENT LIES DEAD—A Kent State University coed screams as classmate lies dead before her. Ohio national guardsmen fired into a crowd of anti-war demonstrators killing four and wounding 11. (Copyright Valley Daily News, Tarentum, Pa., via AP)

Most N.E. Colleges Will Strike Today

BULLETIN — A small fire in the Boston University administration building roused the campus community shortly before 4 this morning.

Firemen quenched the blaze on the second floor in a rubbish barrel.

Some 300 students paraded up and down Commonwealth av., chanting anti-war slogans.

A new and intense wave of protest will sweep across the nation's campuses today as students go on strike against U.S. expansion of the war in Southeast Asia and repression of political dissidents.

As plans for the national strike mushroomed, violent disturbances broke out on campuses in Maryland, Ohio and California.

National Guardsmen were unable to control crowds on the University of Maryland campus and Gov. Mandel declared a state of emergency and imposed a curfew.

The growing protest was off to an early start at Berkeley, Stanford and San Francisco State, where large demonstrations were organized last night.

The strike plans have been building rapidly since the week-end rallies in New Haven on behalf of the Black Panthers. Most Massachusetts colleges have voted to strike today.

Deep anti-war and administration sentiments have been stirred by President Nixon's announcement of U.S. troop forays into Cambodia.

The strike has been endorsed by the National Student Assn.

PROTESTS, Page 11

On Indochina:

NEWS CONFERENCE—Soviet Premier Alexei Kosygin (left) and Foreign Minister Andrei Gromyko listen to question during Kosygin's first Moscow news conference yesterday. Kosygin said the U.S. offensive in Cambodia made a mockery of American honor. (UPI)

★

At the State Department, there was a partial feeling of relief at Soviet Premier Alexei Kosygin's speech on American actions in Cambodia. Spokesmen saw no specific threat of a Soviet response to the continuing U.S. intervention in the country.

★

In the Senate, the foreign relations committee accused Mr. Nixon of running a "constitutionally unauthorized, presidential war." The committee, together with the House Foreign Affairs Committee, will meet today with the President for a briefing on the Cambodian situation.

★

On Wall Street, mainly reflecting Indochina developments, the Dow Jones industrial stock average plunged 19.07 points yesterday, the biggest single day decline since Nov. 22, 1963, following the assassination of President Kennedy, when it fell 21.16. Its close, at 714.56, was also the lowest since that day, when it finished at 711.49.

Allies Launch 3d Cambodia Offensive

United Press International

SAIGON — The U.S. Command announced today the beginning of a third Allied offensive into Cambodia in President Nixon's drive to rob the Viet Cong and North Vietnamese of their sanctuary springboards for attacks into Vietnam.

This one involves troops of the U.S. 4th Infantry Division and South Vietnamese units who punched across the border yesterday 220 miles north of Saigon in the Central Highlands.

Their target was a highlands bivouac area that long has served as an entry point for the Ho Chi Minh Trail into Vietnam.

It lies just south of the point where the borders of Laos, Cambodia and South Vietnam meet.

No major fighting was reported.

Meanwhile, in the drive in the Fishook area, American aerial observers sighted what they believed to be a 500-building complex with radio antennas in Cambodia's Memot Plantation, military sources said yesterday.

OFFENSIVE, Page 2

High Court Upholds Church Tax Exemption

Associated Press

WASHINGTON — The Supreme Court approved 7 to 1 yesterday the continued exemption of more than $100 billion in church-owned property from real estate taxes.

Chief Justice Warren E. Burger said the exemption for property used for religious purposes reflects a tolerance of religion without advancing any one sect or religion in general. Justice William O. Douglas was the lone dissenter.

"Few concepts are more deeply imbedded in the fabric of our national life," Burger said in his most significant opinion since becoming chief justice.

The ruling rejected the proposition that the exemption is a form of sponsorship of religion prohibited by the First Amendment to the Constitution.

COURT, Page 14

RED SOX RESULT
No Game Scheduled

RED SOX TONIGHT
At Milwaukee (Siebert vs. Brabender) 9 p.m.

WEATHER

Bad News

TUESDAY — Chance of shower. **WEDNESDAY**—Fair, mild.

High Tides
11:54 a.m.
(Page 40)

INDEX

Book	31
Bridge	48
Classified	39-47
Comics	49
Court Docket	36
Crossword	49
Deaths	38, 39
Editorials	16
Financial	32-36
Living	19-22
Obituaries	39
Sports	25-29
TV-Radio	48
Theaters	30, 31

'Deal' to Hike Police Chiefs' Pay Stirs Fight

By John C. Burke, Globe Staff

Strong opposition developed on three fronts yesterday to legislation which would make it mandatory for cities and towns in Massachusetts to pay fixed annual salaries to police and fire chiefs.

The bill is the outgrowth of a deal between the chiefs and legislators to develop support in the successful campaign this past Winter to prevent reduction in membership of the House of Representatives.

Yesterday, while the Massachusetts Taxpayers' Assn., the Massachusetts League of Cities and Towns, and Massachusetts Mayors' Assn. were denouncing the proposal, the bill received House approval.

It is reported the Senate will adopt the bill but that Governor Francis W. Sargent will veto it.

The House vote was 136 to 71 against "striking enactment of the bill."

CHIEFS, Page 18

Hub Teachers in Court; 12 Schools Still Closed

By Joseph M. Harvey and Nina McCain, Globe Staff

The teachers strike that kept two-thirds of Boston's school children out of their classrooms yesterday headed into its third day today with union negotiators scheduled to appear in court to answer contempt charges.

Judge Harry Kalus ordered the nine Boston Teachers Union negotiators to appear before him in Suffolk Superior Court this morning to answer charges that they violated an earlier injunction forbidding a strike. The judge at first said the nine were to be arrested but changed later to ordering summonses requiring them to appear.

Union representatives met yesterday with the State Board of Conciliation and Arbitration and School Committee representatives were to meet with the board.

TEACHERS, Page 23

In This Corner

There's Good News In Gloomy World

"What is happening to this world" Isn't there any more good news?"

Many are asking this amid reports the Red Chinese have entered the space race, the United States has sent forces into Cambodia, the stock market has hit new lows and riots were breaking out on the campuses across the nation.

Lately, it seems, the Bruins are the only thing worth cheering about.

But just to assure one and all that everything is not lost and there still is good and happiness in New England, The Globe, over the last few days, scanned the suburban Boston newspapers to note good things.

GOOD NEWS, Page 15

The Boston Globe

Vol. 197, No. 131, © 1970, Globe Newspaper Co. • MONDAY MORNING, MAY 11, 1970 • Telephone 288-8000 42 Pages—10¢

BOBBY ORR FLIES THROUGH THE AIR AFTER SCORING OVERTIME GOAL FOR STANLEY CUP WIN (Frank O'Brien photo)

Orr's Goal Wins Cup For Bruins

By Tom Fitzgerald, Globe Staff

At precisely 5:10 yesterday afternoon, Boston Garden started rocking with a delirious tumult that surely must have sent tremors down into the foundations of the old building.

The shock waves from that initial celebration undoubtedly were carried far into the night, because the ear-shattering din was set off by the Bruins' first Stanley Cup triumph in 29 years.

The emotional release for the 14,835 onlookers at the scene was intensified in view of the almost improbably dramatic conclusion of this fourth straight victory of the championship series which the Bruins wrested from the St. Louis Blues by a score of 4 to 3.

Full page of Bruins' celebration pictures, Page 26

Playing by far their best game of the competition, the West Division champions forced the Boston team into overtime for the first time in 14 games.

Then, after only 40 seconds of what could have been a tense and wearing struggle, it was all ended by a fabulous young man of 22 who has brought a brand new concept to the game.

Swooping in front of the Blues' net, Bobby Orr took a swipe past old Glenn Hall in a move so rapid that there was a slight delay in the roar from the stands until a few moments after the red light flashed.

"Honest, I really don't know how it went in," Orr said in the confused bedlam of the Bruins' locker room a little later.

A man with a good view and a succinct analysis was Derek Sanderson, who set up the big payoff blow.

"That Bobby is the only guy who could do something like that," Turk enthused. "He blocked the puck away from the guy (Larry Keenan) over by the boards, then got it into me in the right corner. I waited just a little until Bobby busted for that net and put it into him."

That big one was the last in a series of high moments because there were only six minutes and 28 seconds remaining in regulation time when the cause was saved on a rising deflection off a John McKenzie shot by Johnny Bucyk, the oldest Bruin of them all with his 35th birthday coming up tomorrow.

BRUINS, Page 21

S. Viets Capture Cambodia River Crossing

Associated Press

ALONG HIGHWAY 1, Cambodia — South Vietnamese forces have retaken the strategic ferry landing at Neak Luong, routing Communist troops who seized it last week, a U.S. Army colonel said yesterday.

Col. William Maddox said the South Vietnamese troops who retook the landing arrived at Neak Luong with vessels of a joint U.S.-South Vietnamese naval flotilla that made its way up the Mekong River from South Vietnam.

So far as is known, only South Vietnamese vessels went to Neak Luong.

According to Reuters, U.S. helicopter gunships mercilessly pounded Viet Cong positions near the ferry before South Vietnamese troops captured it.

The gunships pounded the Viet Cong positions throughout the day with rockets and heavy machinegun fire.

Maj. Gen. Ngo Dzu, Vietnamese commander of the allied combined river, air and land assault forces, said, according to the Los Angeles Times, that he would not push his force further up the Mekong to Phnom Penh, as had been planned earlier.

He and the navy flotilla commander, Capt. Nguyen Ban Thong, had in fact, turned some of the boats around and sent them back down river.

Turning the fleet around kept about 30 American small warships in the flotilla from venturing deeper into Cambodia than President Nixon's announced limit of 21 miles.

Meanwhile, according to Reuters, three American correspondents were reported missing after a jeep trip into the Parrot's Beak area of Cambodia, the State Department said in Washington.

The reporters were tentatively identified as Elizabeth Pond of the Christian Science Monitor, Richard Dudmam, chief of the Washington Bureau of the St. Louis Post-Dispatch and Michael Morrow of Dispatch Incorporated, an affiliate of Dispatch News Service.

CAMBODIA, Page 7

Jubilant Fans Halt Traffic, Jam Streets

By Stephen Kurkjian Globe Staff

Twenty minutes after Bobby Orr had vaulted the Bruins to their first championship in 29 years, the crowd was spilling onto the sweltering streets of the North End and you knew that the town was young again.

Adults and youths weaved through the long lines of cars caught in the mammoth traffic jam around the Boston Garden and everyone was screaming that the Bruins were No. 1.

The parade of hornblowing, over-filled autos which formed in front of the Garden within minutes of the victory wound through the furniture district and met itself going the other way as the traffic backed up in every direction.

"We don't even have our riot helmets," a policeman said into his walkie talkie. "No, no, don't send them. We won't need them for this crowd. These people aren't protesting anything."

CROWD, Page 25

Nixon Leads Tributes To Reuther

By Frederick Gray
Associated Press

PELLSTON, Mich. — Grieving officials of the United Auto Workers union asked the 1.6 million UAW members yesterday to join a week of mourning for Walter P. Reuther, leader of the union for 24 years, who was killed in a plane crash Saturday night.

The five other persons aboard, including Reuther's wife, died with the UAW president as their small, chartered twin-engine jet crashed and burned while landing here during a rainstorm.

To fellow UAW officers he was "an inspired leader" who symbolized his union's "conscience, its heartbeat, its soul."

To a 30-year rank and file UAW member, mindful of new contract negotiations approaching in the automobile industry, Reuther's death was "like losing your best pitcher just before the ball game."

President Nixon said Reuther's death "is a deep loss not only for organized labor but also for the cause of collective bargaining and the entire American process.

"He was a man who was devoted to his cause, spoke for it eloquently and worked for it tirelessly. While he was outspoken and controversial, even those who disagreed with him had great respect for his ability, integrity and persistence."

WALTER REUTHER

Authorities said the plane broke through scattered clouds at 400 feet, clipped a tree top, and 271 feet farther along, came down in a ball of flames. The wreckage was found in a clump of woods 1½ miles southwest of the airport.

REUTHER, Page 10

War Protesters Move To Halls of Congress

By Parker Donham, Globe Staff

WASHINGTON — Organizers of the anti-war demonstration which brought thousands of young people to the White House gates Saturday vowed yesterday to put pressure on Congress to shut off funds for the war in Indochina.

The National Student Association and the National Welfare Rights Organization announced joint plans to stage demonstrations at the home offices of congressmen, demanding that they return to Washington and work for legislation to end the war.

(President Nixon will meet the nation's 50 governors at 1:30 p.m. today, the White House said.)

RALLY, Page 13

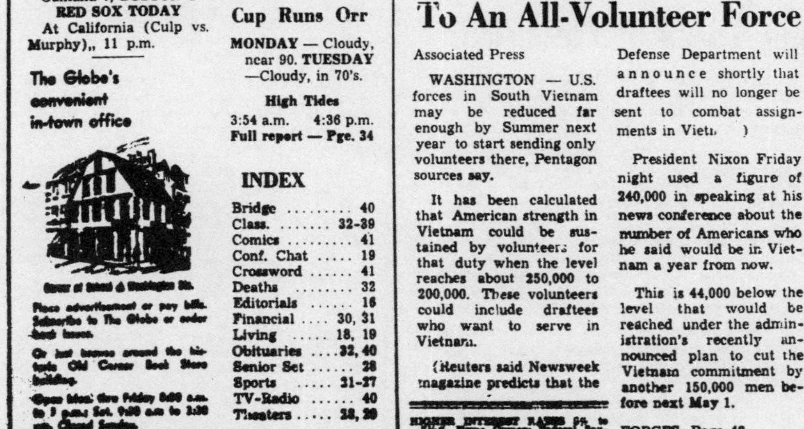

RED SOX RESULT
Oakland 7, BOSTON 4
RED SOX TODAY
At California (Culp vs. Murphy),, 11 p.m.

WEATHER

Cup Runs Orr

MONDAY — Cloudy, near 90. **TUESDAY** —Cloudy, in 70's.

High Tides
3:54 a.m. 4:36 p.m.
Full report — Pge. 34

INDEX

Bridge 40
Class. 32-39
Comics 41
Conf. Chat 19
Crossword 41
Deaths 32
Editorials 16
Financial 30, 31
Living 18, 19
Obituaries 32, 40
Senior Set 28
Sports 21-27
TV-Radio 40
Theaters 28, 29

U.S. May Reduce Viet Units To An All-Volunteer Force

Associated Press

WASHINGTON — U.S. forces in South Vietnam may be reduced far enough by Summer next year to start sending only volunteers there, Pentagon sources say.

It has been calculated that American strength in Vietnam could be sustained by volunteers for that duty when the level reaches about 250,000 to 200,000. These volunteers could include draftees who want to serve in Vietnam.

(Reuters said Newsweek magazine predicts that the Defense Department will announce shortly that draftees will no longer be sent to combat assignments in Vietnam.)

President Nixon Friday night used a figure of 240,000 in speaking at his news conference about the number of Americans who he said would be in Vietnam a year from now.

This is 44,000 below the level that would be reached under the administration's recently announced plan to cut the Vietnam commitment by another 150,000 men before next May 1.

FORCES, Page 42

In This Corner

He Went to Kent to Run, But Not From Bullets

By Bud Collins, Globe Staff

Ed Norris was 19 years old in the Spring of 1966, a kid who ran the distances so well for Brockton High School that a college in the Midwest called Kent State University laid a track scholarship on him. He had heard very little about Kent State. Who had—before last Monday?

He could imagine that some day he would set the university record for the two-mile because he had faith in his running. But he could not imagine that on a beautiful Spring day of his senior year he would be in the midst of the Kent massacre—"not 30 feet from the guns"—that today he would be wondering "how the hell they missed me."

Ed Norris had read about massacres. There was the Boston Massacre with its striking similarities, stone-throwers and uptight troops. And the My Lai massacre, which is the sort of thing that has driven the kids to desperation on their campuses.

COLLINS, Page 8

EDMUND NORRIS
. . . no sleeping

The Boston Globe

Vol. 198, No. 126, © 1970, Globe Newspaper Co. • TUESDAY MORNING, NOVEMBER 3, 1970 Telephone 288-8000 46 Pages—15¢

Cardinal Cushing Dies at 75

RICHARD CARDINAL CUSHING 1895-1970

Family With His Eminence; Burial Saturday in Hanover

By George M. Collins, Globe Staff

Richard Cardinal Cushing, surrounded by members of his family and staff, died at 1:15 p.m. yesterday after a lengthy battle against cancer.

The cardinal, 75, will be buried Saturday at St. Coletta's School in Hanover after an 11 a.m. concelebrated Mass at the Cathedral of the Holy Cross.

Tributes to the cardinal, who led the Boston Archdiocese from 1944 until his retirement in September, began to pour in to his residence from around the world. Religious and civic dignitaries, headed by the three auxiliary bishops of Boston and Sen. Edward M. Kennedy, visited the residence to pay their respects and offer prayers for the dead prelate.

Other stories and pictures on the cardinal on pages 3, 4, 5, 6, 16 and 17.

The cardinal's body will remain at his residence until late this afternoon when it will be moved to the cathedral to lie in state until the funeral.

The principal concelebrant at the Mass will be Archbishop Luigi Raimondi, apostolic delegate in the United States.

Joining him will be Archbishop Humberto S. Medeiros of Boston; his auxiliaries, Most Revs. Jeremiah F. Minihan, Thomas J. Riley and Daniel A. Cronin; and the bishops of the dioceses of Maine, New Hampshire, Vermont, Worcester, Springfield, and Fall River.

Burial services will be held in the Portiuncula Chapel at St. Coletta's, Hanover, a school founded in 1947 by the cardinal for "exceptional children." He has long expressed his wish to be buried there in a special crypt.

Masses for the repose of the cardinal's soul will be celebrated at the cathedral on Wednesday, Thursday and Friday at noon and 7 p.m.

The cardinal's condition had worsened rapidly since Friday and he was anointed at 3 a.m. yesterday by Abp. Medeiros. The two men prayed together during the night and morning.

The archbishop, who succeeded the cardinal in rites at the cathedral on Oct. 7, reported that His Eminence had been up and walking in the residence on Sunday.

The archbishop had stepped out of the cardinal's room only a few minutes before death stilled the unforgettable voice of

CARDINAL, Page 16

Funeral At Holy Cross Cathedral

By James Stack
Globe Staff

Abp. Humberto S. Medeiros will meet with archdiocesan officials this morning to make final plans for Cardinal Cushing's funeral on Saturday.

Details of the Holy Cross Cathedral rites will be made public later today, according to Rt. Rev. Msgr. Joseph F. Maguire, archdiocesan master of ceremonies.

Msgr. Maguire, who also served as secretary to Cardinal Cushing, said last night such decisions as selection of a eulogist are still under consideration.

By custom, the requiem Mass offered for a prince of the church is basically the same as that for any Catholic.

The only notable differences might include ceremonial frills, a special program of music and the liturgical participation of high-ranking church dignitaries.

FUNERAL, Page 3

It's Election Day

Here Is What To Watch For

GOVERNOR: Incumbent Republican Francis W Sargent is slightly favored to extend GOP domination of the State House. Mayor Kevin H. White feels he gained momentum after their television debate. The GOP has held the State House for eight of the last 10 years.

MOOD: Cardinal Cushing's death yesterday closed out a generally lackluster campaign in Massachusetts. Most statewide candidates canceled their election-eve rallies in deference to the death.

TURNOUT: The official guess was 78 percent of the 2.6 million voters registered. Rain is predicted. In the past, rain has seemed to help the Republicans, who are outnumbered about 2 to 1 in registration.

TOTAL: In off-presidential years, the Massachusetts vote has ranged from 73.7 percent to 81.4 percent. The 78 percent forecast for today works out to about 2.1 million voters.

SENATE: National attention will be focused on the percentage of the vote received by Sen. Edward M. Kennedy in his contest with Republican nominee Josiah A. Spaulding. A Kennedy vote under 60 percent could reflect some loss of support since the Chappaquiddick accident, while a win over 64 percent could signal presidential prospects.

WHITE HOUSE: The percentage of Sen. Edmund S. Muskie's vote in Maine will be compared with Kennedy's. The White House figures Muskie's vote at 62 percent, and Kennedy's at 65 percent.

SENATE CONTROL: The Republicans need a net gain of seven to overcome the 57-43 Democratic majority. There are about 20 of 35 Senate contests where neither candidate could be called a sure winner.

ELECTION, Page 14

Rival Windups on TV Feature Nixon, Muskie

By Spencer Rich
Washington Post

Partial texts of broadcasts by President Nixon and Sen. Muskie on Pages 8 and 9.

WASHINGTON — In a possible preview of the 1972 presidential race, President Nixon and Democratic Sen. Edmund S. Muskie of Maine exchanged political blasts in separate TV appearances last night as the nation prepared to elect a new Congress and 35 state governors today.

The President, hammering away at the law and order theme which both he and Vice President Agnew have emphasized in a round of furious campaigning over the last few weeks, was seen on all three major networks in a partial rebroadcast of his tough anti-violence speech in Phoenix last Saturday.

Muskie, in a last-minute appearance financed by a newly formed committee for national unity headed by former peace negotiator and New York Gov. W. Averell Harriman, went on television immediately after the President to "respond to the Republican tactics of fear and division which threaten to tear this country apart," and to charge that the administration has failed to halt inflation and control unemployment.

NATION, Page 13

For Latest Election Returns Call 282-2400 After 8 p.m. Please DO NOT Call the Regular Globe Number

$10m Jump over Current Year

MBTA's Deficit to Exceed $61m for '71

By A. S. Plotkin, Globe Staff

The MBTA deficit for 1971 will climb to a record $61 million-plus, it was indicated yesterday. This will represent a jump of some $10 million over this year.

The authority issued a "most realistic budget" statement anticipating that for the 12 months beginning Jan. 1, the "net assessable cost service" would be about $55.2 million.

To this, however, must be added more than $2 million in state treasurer's interest charges, plus an unofficial conservative estimate of $4 million for still-unsettled labor contracts and subsidies for rail commuter and private suburban bus lines.

The level of the 1971 budget, $129.9 million, and the deficit to be assessed in 1972 on the 79 communities in the transit district, had generally been anticipated — largely at recent meetings of the advisory board committees.

By law the MBTA must submit the budget to the advisory board 60 days in advance of the fiscal year. The latter agency can cut budget items, but has never done so on a major scale—even though earlier this year it demanded a $10 million across-the-board slash.

This is the first time in five years that the budget is based on a 12-month fiscal year. Previously it was 13 months.

In a statement accompanying the budget, MBTA chairman Henry S. Lodge said "we will strive to live within its limitations, and provide better and more timely service." Among the salient points in his statement:

- The number of employees, currently about 6600, will be cut through "attrition," and "stringent control" will be placed on overtime costs.

MBTA, Page 23

First Work Session Today

US, Russia Resume Arms Talks at Helsinki

Reuter

HELSINKI—The United States and Russia resumed their talks on curbing the strategic nuclear arms race with expressions of hope that they would lead to results.

Russian Deputy Foreign Minister Vladimir Semyonov introduced a polemic note into his opening speech by accusing "certain imperialist circles" of fanning the arms race.

Though the American delegation in Finland was not taking this as a sign of a new harder Soviet line in the delicate and top secret negotiations, officially known as the Strategic Arms Limitation Talks (SALT), some western observers in Helsinki felt the remark struck a slightly discordant note.

However, American officials said the Russians have used the term frequently in recent months without it affecting the business-like nature of the talks.

Chief American negotiator Gerard C. Smith said a SALT agreement would be a momentous contribution to international peace and well being.

Semyonov said the Russian government hoped the talks, which began in Helsinki last November and continued in Vienna during the Summer, would lead to positive results.

The envoys had their first unofficial get-together Sunday night at the Russians' hotel. They agreed then to hold the first serious business talks today at the Soviet Embassy. After that, twice-weekly meetings will alternate between the Soviet and US embassies.

After their brief speeches yesterday the two delegation heads exchanged champagne toasts with Finnish Foreign Minister Vain Leskinen. He told them in his address of welcome that progress in their talks would be a great contribution to world peace.

The United States in July put forward an outline of the kinds of strategic weapons it felt it was practical to try to limit at this stage, informed sources in Helsinki said.

Although the Russians put a number of detailed questions to the US delegation in Vienna, it so far has made no counter suggestions, they added.

In This Corner

Queen Gertrude Takes Hamlet Role

By Richard Pollak

Early this year, Dame Judith Anderson began taking fencing lessons, devouring steak tartare and jogging every day along the beach near her home in the hills above Santa Barbara, Calif.

To the curious, the 72-year-old actress explained matter-of-factly that she was tuning up for a 26-week tour of college campuses in "Hamlet"—not as Queen Gertrude, however, but as the Prince of Denmark himself.

And last month in San Francisco, her muddy blonde hair cut in a short page boy and her 5-foot-4-inch form snug in black tights, black overtunic and thigh-high black boots, she began her half-year tour de force.

"I've thought about it for years, but things were never right," says the actress, who was old enough to be Hamlet's mother 34 years ago in a production that starred Sir John Gielgud as her world-weary son.

"It's frightening, but I just had to do it," she continues. "Hamlet's not just a male, he's a person and he covers the whole range of human emotions in the play."

Dame Judith, of course is not the first lady Hamlet. Other actresses, ranging from Sarah Bernhardt to Siobhan McKenna, have attempted the great Shakespearean role.

HAMLET, Page 22

NFL RESULT

Pitts. 21, Cincinnati 10

WEATHER

Rainy

TUESDAY — rain, windy.

WEDNESDAY — cloudy, showers likely.

Details, Page 23

INDEX

Book	30
Bridge	20
Classified	37-43
Comics	45
Court Docket	24
Crossword	45
Deaths	36
Editorials	18
Financial	32-35
Living	20, 21
Obituaries	29
Sports	25-29
TV-Radio	44
Theaters	30, 31

Other documents, stories based on Pentagon papers—pgs. 2, 3, 18, 19

Guide to features

CLASSIFIED 43-49
COMICS 51
CONF. CHAT 23
CROSSWORD 51
DEATHS 40
EDITORIALS 20
FINANCIAL 34-38
LIVING 22, 23
OBITUARIES 40, 41
SPORTS 25-30
TV-RADIO 59
THEATERS 31-33

The Boston Globe

Sort of warm

Vol. 199, No. 173, © 1971, Globe Newspaper Co. — TUESDAY MORNING, JUNE 22, 1971 — Telephone 288-8000 — 52 Pages—15c

New Pentagon data brought to light

Ban still on Times, Washington Post

Secret Pentagon Documents bare JFK role in Vietnam war

PRESIDENT KENNEDY speaks at a press conference in November 1961, the year he approved covert actions against North Vietnam.

• Admiral sought nuclear option

By Matthew V. Storin
Globe Staff

Unpublished portions of the 47-Vietnam war were made available yesterday to the Boston Globe.

The Globe is the third US newspaper to report on the 7000 page analysis tracing America's growing involvement in Indochina from World War II through mid-1968.

According to the documents made available to the Globe:

— Gen. Maxwell Taylor advised President Kennedy in 1961 to send 8000 American combat troops into Vietnam but warned the move could lead to increased world tensions and a wider war. There were 1000 US troops in Vietnam at that time.

— As soon as President Johnson announced a partial end to the bombing of North Vietnam on March 31, 1968, he elected to proceed with a policy of Vietnamization similar to that later followed by President Nixon.

—On June 2, 1964, Secretary of Defense Robert S. McNamara in a meeting of top Administration officials in Honolulu discussed the possible use of nuclear weapons in Vietnam. Adm. Harry D. Felt, commander of US forces in the Pacific, openly advocated that American commanders be given this option.

—The Soviet Union, fearing reaction from Communist China, rejected a plea by the United States in May, 1965, that Hanoi be informed that a bombing pause was being undertaken in hopes of prompting negotiations to end the war.

The massive Pentagon study, initiated by Secretary McNamara in June, 1967, was the work of more than 30 authors both inside and outside of government. The first report of the study was published June 13 by the New York Times. The Washington Post began printing reports on June 18.

The people can judge intelligently only if they are given all the facts possible. . . . see Editorial, Page 20.

Yesterday Federal appeals courts in New York and Washington continued their respective temporary bans against publication of further reports by the Times and the Post.

DOCUMENTS, Page 3

• Kennedy OK'd covert action

By Robert Healy
Globe Staff

Gen. Maxwell Taylor in October of 1961 advised President Kennedy in an "eyes only for the President" cable to send 8000 man US military task force into South Vietnam but he warned that the introduction of such a force "may increase tensions and risk escalation into a major war in Asia."

Gen. Taylor was special adviser to President Kennedy on Vietnam.

At the time of the Taylor mission, which took him and Walt Rostow, later to be President Johnson's chief adviser on national security affairs, and a group of state and defense department officials to South Vietnam, the United States had about 1000 soldiers in South Vietnam. They served as advisers to the South Vietnamese Army.

President Kennedy stepped up covert actions against North Vietnam and increased the number of advisers to 16,000 men before he was assassinated in November of 1963. He never commited a United States ground unit as Taylor recommended.

These disclosures were made in a portion of a secret Pentagon study on the origins of the war in Vietnam started in 1967 by then Secretary of Defense Robert McNamara. They were made available to the Boston Globe yesterday.

For the first time the Globe was making public the role of the Kennedy administration in the escalation of the war. Three earlier reports dealing with other phases of the war were published by the New York Times and two by the Washington Post before publication was halted by court injunctions.

As early as May 11, 1961, President Kennedy, according to the secret report, had approved programs for covert action which had been recommended by a Vietnam Task Force. Among these actions were.

(1) Dispatch of agents into North Vietnam.

(2) Aerial resupply of agents in North Vietnam through the use of civilian mercenary air crews.

(3) Infiltration of special South Vietnam forces into Southeast Laos to locate and attack Communist bases and lines of communication.

KENNEDY, Page 2

Tet offensive turned Johnson toward Vietnamization policy

By Crocker Snow Jr.
Globe Staff

When President Johnson in March 1968 announced publicly that he would not run for re-election, he was also deciding privately that a policy of Vietnamization was the best one for the nation to follow in the war.

The President's speech was also a denial of Gen. William C. Westmoreland's request for an increase of 206,000 American troops.

This change in the President's thinking toward the kind of policy President Nixon has since adopted is evidenced in the concluding portions of the secret Pentagon study viewing the decision-making of American military involvement in Vietnam.

It was March 31, 1968 that President Johnson made his famous peace initiative, in which he announced a limited bombing halt and only a small build-up of 24,500 American troops following the shock of the Tet Offensive two months earlier, and called for Britain and the Soviet Union to take the lead in achieving a peaceful settlement.

In this same speech, the President made an urgent plea for national unity, and took himself out of the 1968 presidential race with the

JOHNSON, Page 2

Court reverses conviction in Pamela Mason case

By S. J. Micciche
Globe Washington Bureau

WASHINGTON—The conviction of Edward H. Coolidge Jr., serving a life sentence for the 1964 slaying of 14-year-old Manchester, N.H., babysitter Pamela Mason, was reversed by the US Supreme Court yesterday.

A new trial was ordered by the court, which held, 5-to-4, that certain evidence linking Coolidge to the murder had been obtained under a defective search warrant.

The majority view, which evoked a stinging dissent, found it was unconstitutional for the state's attorney general to have issued the search warrant in his capacity as a justice of the peace when he was personally in charge of the police investigation and later served as chief prosecutor.

Since the attorney general "was not the neutral and detached magistrate required by the Constitution, the search stands on no firmer ground than if there had been no warrant at all," wrote Associate Justice Potter Stewart for the majority.

Former US solicitor general, Archibald Cox of Harvard Law School, Coolidge's court-appointed lawyer, argued that the search warrant had not been issued by "a neutral and detached magistrate" and was therefore improper.

MASON, Page 16

Ellsberg promises statement soon on role

DANIEL ELLSBERG
. . . biding his time

By Thomas Oliphant
Globe Staff

SAN DIEGO — Daniel Ellsberg said yesterday he expects to comment publicly in a week or two on his role in the unearthing of the secret Pentagon study of the Indochina war.

The MIT scholar and former top Defense Department and State Department aide spoke through intermediaries known to be close friends of his and to have been in contact with him since he dropped out of sight last week.

The intermediaries insisted on anonymity as a condition for passing on the message from Ellsberg.

While pledging to make a full statement eventually, Ellsberg said he did not wish to do so now.

He said to do so would only further complicate an already complicated situation, in which vast amounts of information are becoming available not just from the Pentagon study but also from the Federal courts where the Nixon Administration is attempting to have the study suppressed.

Ellsberg said he would like to postpone making a complete public statement until the court cases have ended.

He said he did not want to divert public attention from what he termed these important court battles over the public's right to know the truth about the war.

Finally, Ellsberg said he wanted his two children who live in California with his first wife to know that he is well and thinking of them.

He also said he wanted his father, Harry Ellsberg, who lives in a Detroit suburb, to know that he is deeply grateful for the expressions of support he made to the press last week.

The Globe also learned yesterday that Ellsberg had been involved in private efforts to change the country's war policies as far back as 1967.

According to a source close to Ellsberg, he was one of about 35 participants in a private conference in Bermuda, sponsored by the Carnegie Endowment, which brought together several influential Americans, including former top government officials, to talk about the war.

ELLSBERG, Page 6

IN THIS CORNER

Hypnosis enters mind's back-door

By David Lamb
Los Angeles Times

LOS ANGELES—Isadore Cantor, an affable former hearing-aid salesman of 67, teaches self-hypnosis—10 lessons for $250—at the National Hypnosis Institute. The institute has one office and one employee—Cantor, the director.

On the lawn outside his office, a large sign placed to attract the eye of passing pedestrians and tells what his students accomplish: control eating; ing; overcome an fears; improve mem sleep, bowling, golf

HYPNOSIS, Page 11

In legislative committee report

Welfare residency rule advanced

By David Nyhan
Globe Staff

A special legislative committee investigating welfare in Massachusetts will recommend today adoption of a controversial one-year residency requirement for welfare recipients.

The committee, in an interim report to be released today, will also reportedly recommend:

—Use of Social Security cards to identify recipients and curb fraudulent collection of benefits.

—Creation of an enlarged "fraud unit" to be assigned to the state Auditor's office.

—Curtailment of benefits to college students.

Created last spring to recommend changes in welfare laws after phenomenal growth in costs, the committee is headed by Sen. Robert L. Cawley (D-W. Roxbury).

The panel has considered 22 proposals.

Several of the majority report recommendations are expected to cause controversy. All must be aired at public hearings of various committees, including Judiciary, Social Welfare, and Ways and Means.

New York state just adopted a one-year residency requirement that welfare recipients charged is unconstitutional.

As recently as last week, Massachusetts Welfare Comr. Steven A. Minter told the Public Welfare Conference in Plymouth that the residency requirement is unconstitutional, and warned cutbacks might be coming.

Minter said last Friday: "If we think that by imposing residency requirements we will reduce the rolls and thereby cut costs, we are kidding ourselves."

The special committee report, to be detailed at a news conference this afternoon, reportedly recommends college students be trimmed from welfare rolls and families not be allowed to claim college students as dependents.

The recommendation that Auditor Thaddeus Buczko be given control over welfare fraud investigations is expected to be opposed by Gov. Sargent.

REPORT, Page 19

Sargent's tax bill killed again on House rollcall of 119 to 110

By David R. Ellis, Globe Staff

The House killed Gov. Sargent's latest tax bill yesterday, reaffirming an earlier vote by defeating the bill, up for reconsideration, on a 119 to 110 rollcall.

Despite a personal lobbying effort, Sargent could muster only a slight majority of Republicans—32 out of 62—in favor of the $256 million plan

The major elements of the bill were a 1 percent increase in the state income tax, from 4 to 5 percent; and a variety of business taxes.

Failure of the bill prompted Administration Comr. Charles E. Shepard to order a general belt tightening in state departments and the firing of more than 200 state employees by the end of the week

The bill was defeated first last Wednesday, by a vote of 129 to 103.

At that time the Republicans voted 22 to 38 against the bill, and the Democrats voted 81 to 91 against it.

A vote to reconsider was taken yesterday following a Republican caucus at which Sargent tried to sell his plan. The reconsideration, which is largely a courtesy, passed 158 to 66.

That meant that the tax bill was alive again, and it touched off nearly two hours of debate.

TAXES, Page 14

Guide to features

BRIDGE .... 42 FINANCIAL ... 16-19
CLASSIFIED ... 33-41 LIVING........ 14, 15
COMICS .... 43 OBITUARIES 32
CROSSWORD .... 43 SPORTS 21-26
DEATHS .... 32 TV-RADIO 42
EDITORIALS ...... 10 THEATERS 27-31

The Boston Globe

A break

FRIDAY—CHANCE OF SHOWERS, 70s.
SATURDAY—DITTO.
HIGH TIDE—6:15 A.M., 6:48 P.M.
FULL REPORT—PAGE 26.

Vol. 200, No. 16 © 1971, Globe Newspaper Co. * FRIDAY, JULY 16, 1971 ® Telephone 288-8000 44 Pages—15c

Kissinger returns from secret trip to China with invitation

Nixon to visit Peking before May 1972

By Darius S. Jhabvala
Globe Washington Bureau

WASHINGTON — President Nixon will visit Communist China sometime before May 1972 to personally negotiate normalizing relations between the two countries.

The President, in a stunning, five-minute nationally televised address last night, said the invitation to visit Peking was issued by Chinese Premier Chou En-lai after a secret meeting last weekend in Peking between Chou and Dr. Henry A. Kissinger, the President's national security affairs adviser.

Mr. Nixon's visit to Peking, the first official trip by a US President to the Chinese mainland, amounts to momentous diplomatic coup.

The announcement of the visit was made simultaneously from Peking and from the NBC studios in Burbank, Calif., where Mr. Nixon's address was telecast at 10:30.

The announcement said Kissinger and Chou had met in Peking July 9-11, when Kissinger was supposedly in Pakistan recuperating from an illness.

"Knowing of President Nixon's expressed desire to visit the People's Republic of China," the joint announcement said, "Premier Chou En-lai, on behalf of the government of the People's Republic of China, has extended an invitation to President Nixon to visit China at an appropriate date before May 1972.

"President Nixon accepted this invitation with pleasure."

Mr. Nixon cautioned, however, that his trip "will not be at the expense of old friends," evidently a signal to Nationalist China and its supporters that he would not negotiate away the island nation's independence.

He said the new relationship is not "directed" against any other nation," meaning the Soviet Union. And, he said, "Any nation can be our friend without being any other nation's enemy."

NIXON, Page 12

BEFORE THE ANNOUNCEMENT — President Nixon is accompanied by adviser Henry Kissinger as he arrives at Burbank TV studio. (AP)

Ruse covered Kissinger trip

Los Angeles Times

WASHINGTON — Henry A. Kissinger apparently used the socially accepted device of an "upset stomach" to elude the world and confer secretly in Peking last Saturday with Chinese Premier Chou En-lai.

The ruse was disclosed last night by President Nixon when he revealed that his foreign affairs adviser had conferred with Chou July 9-10.

RUSE, Page 12

Ribbs out, Campbell in at DPW

By David Nyhan
Globe Staff

Edward J. Ribbs resigned yesterday as chairman of the Department of Public Works, his departure signaling the state's shift to less reliance on highway building in favor of mass transit.

Gov. Sargent, who campaigned last year on a "balanced transportation" theme, immediately named traffic engineer Bruce Campbell to succeed Ribbs on Aug. 14 at a salary of $26,000.

A restudy of Boston's transportation needs finally gets the go-ahead. Story, Page 3.

Sargent's carefully worded announcement went to great lengths to praise Ribbs for honest and efficient administration of the sprawling DPW, which suffered through a series of scandals in the 1950s and '60s.

DPW, Page 8

US attempts to head off rail walkout

Associated Press

WASHINGTON — A glimmer of hope remained late yesterday that a strike of the Southern Railway and the Union Pacific might be headed off before today's 6 a.m. deadline.

The Nixon Administration called an evening summit meeting at the Labor Department of the presidents of those lines and three others also under threat of strikes by the AFL-CIO United Transportation Union.

Transportation Secretary John Volpe joined the discussions which began about 6 p.m. They were still on at midnight.

The move came after the department's top trouble-shooter, Asst. Secretary W. J. Usery Jr., stepped in to talk separately with UTU bargainers.

RAILROADS, Page 6

THE STONE AGE MEETS THE AIR AGE — Tasaday tribesmen turn their heads to avoid prop wash as helicopter carrying Philippines government investigating team arrives in remote area where they live. (AP)

Thunder is fear in Tasaday Forest

(Anthropologists believe it may take two years to unravel the mysteries of a primitive tribe just discovered in the Philippines. An AP reporter spent two days with the isolated people this week and brought this report from the rain forest.)

By John Nance
Associated Press

TASADAY FOREST, Philippines — Thunder is the worst thing in the world.

It is "the big word," the unknown most to be feared.

"It always scared our ancestors," Ayam said. "We don't know where it comes from."

Ayam, perhaps 20 years old, is a member of the Tasaday tribe, recently discovered in the Philippines. Until last month the Tasadays had never seen a wheel.

Crouching beside a stream, Ayam told a group of men from today that his Stone Age people had never heard of fighting or wars. They were uncertain even about the moon because their rain forest hid it from view.

He groped to express himself through a translator.

Such knowledge, he said, came "without warning . . . it is like lightning."

STONE AGE, Page 7

US replies to Cong, poses own questions

Associated Press

PARIS — The United States attempted yesterday to launch a "useful dialogue" at the Vietnam peace talks by answering and posing a series of questions on a Viet Cong peace plan.

But neither US Ambassador David K. E. Bruce nor the Viet Cong's Mrs. Nguyen Thi Binh and Hanoi's Xuan Thuy were satisfied with the results and the conference appeared as deadlocked as before.

The 73-year-old Bruce, who according to the White House will be leaving his job for health reasons, addressed himself to the two-week-old peace package put forth by Mrs. Binh. He specifically gave what he termed answers to four questions she directed to him last week. Mrs. Binh, however, said the answers were "not concrete" and Thuy said Bruce was simply trying to "delay" positive response to the seven-point Viet Cong proposal.

Bruce went down Mrs. Binh's list of our questions, then asked five of his own.

Mrs. Binh had asked first whether the United States agreed to consider her seven points as a basis for negotiation.

Bruce replied: "Our answer is that we are willing . . . to consider for negotiation any proposals that have been or may be put forward here by your side, as well as our own . . ."

Secondly, Mrs. Binh had asked which of the seven points the United States agrees with and which it does not, which were positive and which were unacceptable.

PARIS TALKS, Page 13

29 GI war deaths highest in 6 weeks

United Press International

SAIGON — Twenty-nine American battle deaths were recorded last week—the highest US combat death toll in six weeks—and another nine GIs died of nonhostile causes such as illness and accident, the US command said yesterday.

The new figures pushed US deaths in the Indochina war to 55,026—of whom 45,373 were killed in battle and 9653 died of nonhostile causes.

The death toll was up six from the previous week.

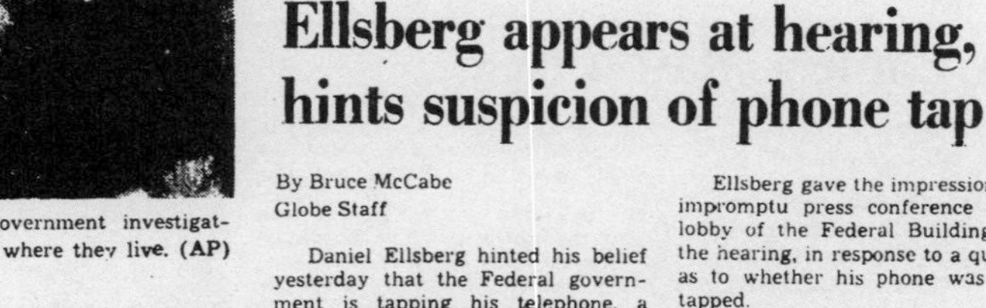

Ellsberg appears at hearing, hints suspicion of phone tap

By Bruce McCabe
Globe Staff

Daniel Ellsberg hinted his belief yesterday that the Federal government is tapping his telephone, a suggestion his lawyer had made earlier in his removal hearing.

The implication of wiretapping and other methods of surveillance consumed much of the 45-minute hearing at the Federal Building, after which Magistrate Peter A. Princi took under advisement a decision to remove Ellsberg to Los Angeles to stand trial for leaking the celebrated Pentagon documents to the press.

Ellsberg gave the impression at an impromptu press conference in the lobby of the Federal Building after the hearing, in response to a question as to whether his phone was being tapped.

"My wife and I were talking about the telephone strike just this morning," he replied, "and we are confident that our service will not be interrupted. The government is on our side."

The government had refused to address itself to the question of wiretapping Ellsberg's telephone.

ELLSBERG, Page 20

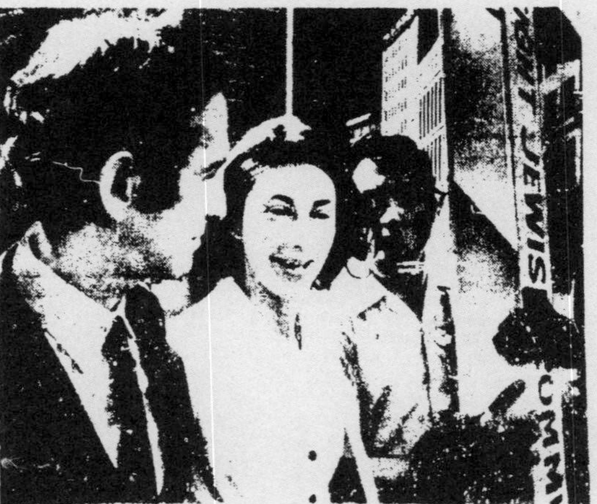

TAUNTED—Dr. and Mrs. Ellsberg try to ignore cross-carrying demonstrator Joseph Mlot-Mroz as they arrive at Federal Building. (AP)

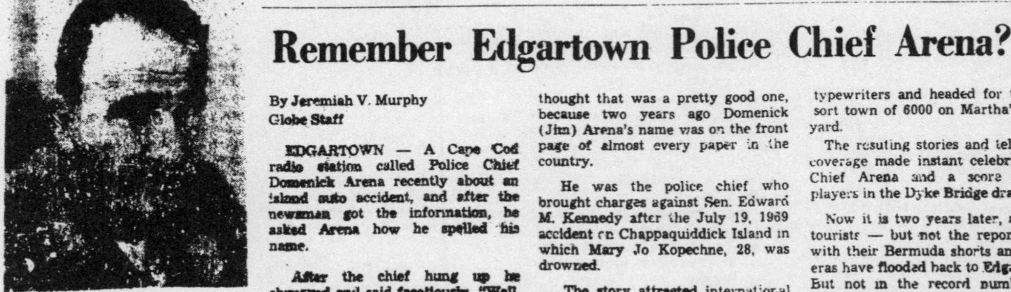

DOMENICK ARENA
. . . instant celebrity

IN THIS CORNER

Remember Edgartown Police Chief Arena?

By Jeremiah V. Murphy
Globe Staff

EDGARTOWN — A Cape Cod radio station called Police Chief Domenick Arena recently about an island auto accident, and after the newsman got the information, he asked Arena how he spelled his name.

After the chief hung up he shrugged and said facetiously, "Well, they say fame is fleeting." Everybody around the new police station thought that was a pretty good one, because two years ago Domenick (Jim) Arena's name was on the front page of almost every paper in the country.

He was the police chief who brought charges against Sen. Edward M. Kennedy after the July 19, 1969 accident on Chappaquiddick Island in which Mary Jo Kopechne, 28, was drowned.

The story attracted international attention and hundreds of reporters grabbed extra shirts and portable typewriters and headed for this resort town of 6000 on Martha's Vineyard.

The resulting stories and television coverage made instant celebrities of Chief Arena and a score of bit players in the Dyke Bridge drama.

Now it is two years later, and the tourists — but not the reporters — with their Bermuda shorts and cameras have flooded back to Edgartown. But not in the record numbers of 1969. The recession took care of that.

ARENA, Page 31

Boston Sunday Globe

Vol. 201, No. 65, © 1972, Globe Newspaper Co. SUNDAY, MARCH 5, 1972 30 CENTS

AN EDITORIAL

The Globe – at the 100-year mark

The Globe was born in the same year as the American postal card and the unbreakable billiard ball. They, in their time, were accomplishments. So was the book people were then about to read. Jules Verne's "Around the World in Eighty Days."

In 1872 people had no phones, electric lights, stereos, automobiles, movies or television. All of these brought change. Yet it was nothing compared with what is now happening.

Living today has become so complex and terrifying. Great problems of environment and overpopulation search desperately for answers.

The Globe, which battled through the last century, will continue to dedicate itself to finding these answers, and to building a New England, an America and a world community where people can live together in peace and plenty.

In this effort, the fine people in all departments who put out The Globe will keep doing their best to stay abreast of the new times and new problems.

Their aim will be, as the late Globe editor James Morgan wrote a quarter-century ago, "to conduct, in season and out, an unending campaign of education in the enduring principles which underlie the political, economic and social questions of the day."

Vital to all this is a free press, more necessary now than ever before. Newspapers will remain free only if the people insist they remain free—and if the press does an ever better job of informing them, defining the issues, interpreting the changing customs, defending the poor and the young and the weak in this increasingly complicated society.

The Globe in its second century, as a strongly independent paper bound to no political party, aims to do just that.

And this newspaper renews its determination to help the people of this distinguished city and all of New England enjoy better, more exciting daily lives.

We want to thank our readers and our advertisers for making possible our 100th birthday this weekend.

DOWNTOWN BOSTON IN 1872—SMALL ENOUGH TO BE MANAGEABLE

WHERE 17 DIED—Tail section of Mohawk Airlines propjet protrudes from front of Albany house while its cockpit rests in back yard after plane crashed during snowstorm. Stories, other photos, Page 2. (AP)

N.H. Democrats give Muskie 42% in poll

By Richard M. Weintraub
Globe Staff
Copyright 1972, Globe Newspaper Co

Sen. Edmund S. Muskie has 42 percent of the vote, Sen. George McGovern 26 percent, other candidates 12 percent, and the undecided register 20 percent in a poll conducted for The Globe among New Hampshire residents planning to vote in Tuesday's Democratic presidential primary.

These percentage figures are the result of a poll taken last Thursday and Friday, the complete results of which are:

Percent of Vote	
Edmund Muskie	42
George McGovern	26
Samuel Yorty	4
Wilbur Mills	2
Vance Hartke	2
Edward Coll	0
Others	4
Undecided	20

In a poll taken Feb. 26 and 27, Muskie had 49 percent of the vote, McGovern 31 percent, other candidates 10 percent and the undecided totaled 10 percent.

In The Globe's first New Hampshire poll, completed Jan. 24, Muskie had 65 percent, McGovern 18 percent, with 9 percent going to other candidates and 8 percent undecided.

The percentage spread between Muskie and McGovern thus decreased from 47 in January to 18 on Feb 27, to 16 last Friday. All three polls were conducted for The Globe by the Becker Research Corp. of Boston.

The third poll was taken to discover whether the trend established in the poll completed Feb. 27 was continuing and to have the most current information possible.

This poll shows that, while Muskie's percentage of the vote continued to decline, McGovern was unable to maintain his momentum and, significantly, the percentage of those who are unsure how they will vote on Tuesday doubled as the week progressed.

N.H. POLL, Page 22

Primary Tuesday

All of a sudden, it's serious . . .

By David Nyhan
Globe Staff

MANCHESTER, N.H. — If the New Hampshire primary wasn't supposed to mean anything, why is everyone now taking it so seriously?

It was forecast early as a cakewalk on Tuesday for President Nixon and Democrat Edmund S. Muskie with all eyes on the two dozen contests to follow.

All of a sudden, the followers of Sen. George McGovern (D-S.D.), are panting heavily, and some Muskie partisans are holding their breaths.

The national press is holed up in motel rooms, waiting for answers to questions like: Can a candidate cry in public? Was Muskie's big lead up here just a snowman that melted in March? Is George McGovern for real?

Tuesday is, as Muskie's fond of saying, "The only poll that counts."

The Globe poll results published today chart the dramatic shifts of New Hampshire's Democratic electorate. But the Muskie camp yesterday exuded confidence. A visitor found top strategists in an expansive mood, apparently confident that the so-called "McGovern surge" will not swamp the Muskie bandwagon.

PRIMARY, Page 57

N.H. voter close-up

Milford listens—how will it go?

By Joseph L. Rosenbloom
Globe Staff

MILFORD, N.H. — Citizens of this town of 6600 in southern central New Hampshire vote Tuesday in the state's presidential primary, the first in the nation. An estimated 1800 persons will vote between 10 a.m. and 6 p.m. at the Milford Area School auditorium on West street.

Milford has no particular distinction, as the woman in the Chamber of Commerce office candidly admits, except that once it was known as the granite town in the Granite State and supplied the hard gray stone for tombstones all over the nation.

It now is a factory town, non-union, producing such goods as metal parts, tools and dies, wire lumber, and, from the reopened Kitledge Quarry, some granite.

Traditionally it has been a Republican stronghold — as early as the mid-1800s when a family from here, the Hutchinsons, barnstormed across the land singing hymns against slavery and for temperance.

MILFORD, Page 55

A LOOK BACK

'. . . most comfortable city'

By Robert Taylor
Globe Staff

If you lived in Boston 100 years ago today, the chances are that you'd have plenty of gripes but a feeling that things were bound to improve.

If you worked for a wage in a mill or a factory you'd average a 10 to 12-hour day six days a week, and like the bosses you'd be undernourished on a starchy Victorian diet.

If you were resistant to disease, you might make it to adulthood, but you probably came from a large family and had brothers and sisters who had died in infancy and youth.

If you were an immigrant you read "No Irish Need Apply" signs, and if you belonged to the established order you saw on every hand a rising tide of frightening foreign customs.

The old and destitute were fated for the almshouse; if young and in college, you were getting trained for a society that had little use for the skills you acquired.

As a bulwark of the middle class you probably approved of President Grant's efforts to reduce the national debt and control inflation and a rising tax rate; but if you weren't a Grant man, you deplored corruption in government, a President who tried to be all things to all men, and "Let us have peace," the official keynote of the Administration, a slogan rather than a program of executive action.

FLASHBACK, Page 54

The cost of living — a comparison

	1872	1972
Pair of pants	$3.50	$20
Overcoat	$15-$20	$100-$150
Rent on 10-room house	$450 yr.	$5400 yr.
50-acre farm with 8-room house and 2 barns	$5000	$150,000
Rent on small grocery store	$350 yr.	$6000 yr.
Daily newspaper	$.01	$.15
Boston-Liverpool steamship passage, round trip	$120	$1500

NEWSPAPER STORY—1

How The Globe began

This series is condensed from "Newspaper Story: 100 Years of The Boston Globe" by Louis M. Lyons, former curator of the Nieman Foundation and published by the Belknap Press of Harvard University.

By the hindsight of a century, it is strange that The Boston Globe was ever started. Not one of the little group of rich men who committed jointly $150,000 to incorporate it had ever run a newspaper.

Boston then, as for most of the century ahead, already had more newspapers than it could support.

The wise money in Boston was going into railroads and western real estate.

Had any of the half dozen prominent businessmen who gathered with Lewis Rice in his handsome new American House on the evening of Feb. 7, 1872, consulted his State Street broker, he would surely have been advised against so precarious a venture.

Bankers would remember, if these merchants did not, the fiasco of the last ambitious venture in Boston newspapering.

But Stephen Niles, the pioneer advertising man who had brought the group together at the American House, knew that Boston journalism was rated as undistinguished among the big cities and that half or more of the existing papers were moribund.

100 YEARS, Page 44

- **In today's Globe—"Massachusetts Treasures" magazine**
- **Reproduction of front page of 1st Globe—Page 43**
- **Starting next Sunday—History of Globe sports**

Key witness found gravely ill, Kliendiest vote off indefinitely

United Press International

WASHINGTON—A Senate vote on Richard G. Kleindienst's nomination for Attorney General was delayed indefinitely yesterday when a key lobbyist sought for questioning about a Justice Department antitrust case was found gravely ill in a Denver hospital.

Mrs. Dita D. Beard, 53, the Washington lobbyist for International Telephone and Telegraph Corp. (ITT), had been sought by FBI agents as the purported author of a memorandum linking the government's settlement of an ITT merger proposal and an ITT subsdiary's $400,000 offer to help finance the 1972 Republican National Convention.

A few hours after Mrs. Beard was located at Rocky Mountain Osteopathic Hospital in Denver, undergoing intensive care for a serious heart condition, Senate Democratic leader Mike Mansfield said the confirmation vote on Kleindienst would be postponed indefinitely.

The Senate Judiciary Committee has unanimously approved the Kleindienst nomination, but it reopened its hearings at his request to consider the implications raised by Mrs. Beard's memo.

KLEINDIENST, Page 22

Weather

Snow, mixing with rain in southern New England. Highs 20s to low 30s.

Full Report—Page 32

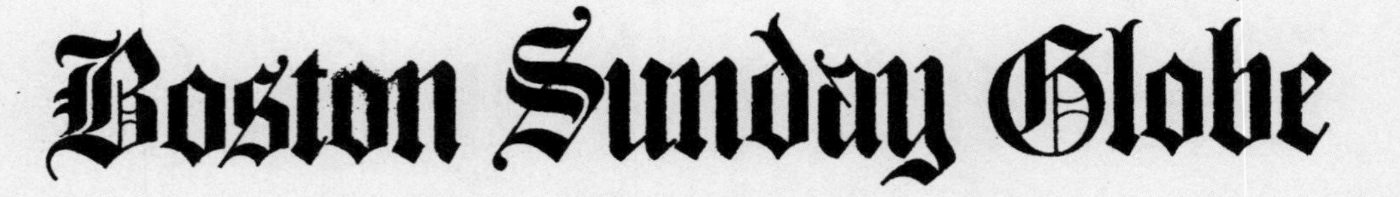

Boston Sunday Globe

Vol. 201, No. 170, © 1972, Globe Newspaper Co. · SUNDAY, JUNE 18, 1972 · 50 CENTS

Two missing, eight hurt after hotel wall collapses

7 firemen killed in Vendome blaze

OUT OF THE RUBBLE—Fireman in background carries helmet as one of the victims of yesterday's four-alarm fire at former Hotel Vendome is lifted from the rubble. Other stories and pictures, Page 2, 4. (Globe photo by George Rizer)

By John Abbott & Richard Kindleberger
Globe Staff

Seven firemen were killed, two others are missing and feared dead and eight were injured yesterday afternoon when the southeast corner of the seven-story Hotel Vendome collapsed during a fire.

Firemen were bringing the four-alarm fire in the once-plush Back Bay hotel under control when the wall suddenly gave way.

Some of the injured firemen were trapped in the rubble for three hours before being rescued. Others were crushed beyond recognition.

Five of the casualties were believed assigned to companies working from a fire station on Tremont street in the South End.

The seventh reported victim made the fire the most tragic in the history of the Boston fire department. Six firemen were killed when a wall collapsed at old Lyceum Hall in East Boston on Nov. 15, 1942. Four firemen and a spectator died in a blaze at an abandoned South End factory on Oct. 1, 1964.

Most of the dead, missing and injured yesterday were working near an 85-foot ladder truck which was completely covered by debris.

Officials said none of the eight injured men was critically hurt.

Fire officials were finding it extremely difficult to confirm the names of dead, missing and injured and would make no official announcements.

The hotel, located at Commonwealth avenue and Dartmouth street in the Back Bay, was being remodeled into apartments.

Even before clouds of dust cleared, 50 firemen, many using their hands, were digging into the debris trying to reach the injured and dead.

The fire was reported shortly after 2:30 p.m. and had raged through the upper two-stories of the hotel.

VENDOME, Page 2

Soot, smoke, fear shroud rescuers

By Walter V. Robinson
Globe Correspondent

They waited.

Nearly 150 Boston firemen, faces soot-covered, and tear-stained from the afternoon's smoke and mouths set in firm, hard lines, looked up at the wreckage of the once-stately Hotel Vendome.

Fifty other firemen, the sweat stinging off their faces, labored feverishly to move tons of rubble and uncover six or seven — no one was sure — of their comrades, missing and feared dead.

DRAMA, Page 2

Organized crime in N.E.

Patriarca still the top man

By Richard J. Connolly, Globe Staff

Death and justice have severed some of the main roots of the family tree, but Raymond Loreda Salvatore Patriarca — exiled to a Federal penitentiary — still reigns over The Mob in New England, according to law enforcement officials interviewed last week.

The 64-year-old Patriarca, who has figured in every major investigation of the underworld for three years, is serving the third of a five-year sentence at the Atlanta, Ga., penitentiary for conspiracy to murder.

The region's leading law officers consider him the boss of what they describe as The Patriarca Family. But they do not agree on how the Providence gangster manages to maintain control from his prison cell.

Some lawmen believe that the Patriarca organization, with ties to other crime cartels across the country, is held together by his brother, Francis J. (Joe) Patriarca, in Providence.

They are supported by Vincent C. (Big Vinnie) Teresa, the loquacious gambler, thief and loan shark who turned government witness and revealed The Mob's innermost secrets.

N. E. CRIME, Page 8

Jilted prophet cursed the wind

By Andrew Carron, Globe Correspondent

Oscar Tenenbaum remembers Carol, Edna and Diane even though they entered his life only briefly more than 15 years ago, because the three left a terrible trail of destruction behind them.

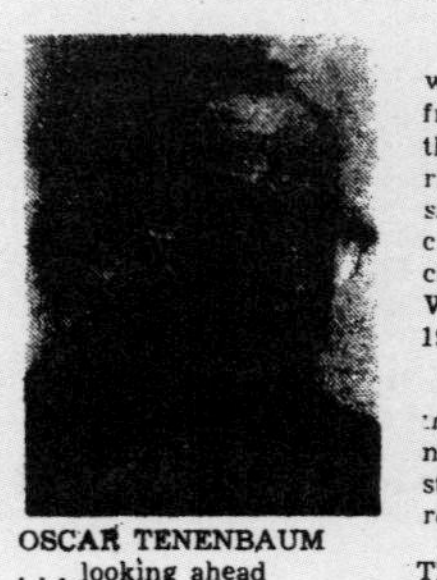

OSCAR TENENBAUM
. . . looking ahead

Carol, Edna and Diane were not jealous girl-friends, however, but rather the most devastating hurricanes to hit New England since Dr. Tenenbaum became meteorologist in charge at the Boston Weather Bureau station in 1950.

This sprightly gentleman, who is on a first-name basis with every storm comes this way, will retire June 30 at age 64.

TENENBAUM, Page 11

Impressions of Hanoi: US jets, heroes at 14

By Anthony Lewis

HANOI — Two weeks is not time enough to learn much about any country.

In North Vietnam there are special difficulties in the way of critical understanding — war conditions generally, the difficulty of travel during heavy bombing and shelling, the closed political society, the impossibility of getting any official to discuss such basic premises of Vietnamese Communist doctrine as that the Americans are colonialists and aggressors in South Vietnam and that the Saigon government is their puppet.

This article, therefore, is not an attempt at a balanced appraisal of North Vietnam, historical or political. It is a series of impressions, some things I saw and experienced and felt during the two weeks I spent there.

During my visit I met two 14-year-old boys.

I met the first in Hanoi, at the house used by the mission of the Provisional Revolutionary government (PRG) of South Vietnam. (Years ago, I discovered later, the house was the American consulate-general.) There I was introduced to three heroic liberation fighters from the South — a girl 22, a boy 17, and the 14-year-old.

LEWIS, Page 12

World's pilots push strike threat

From Wire Services

WASHINGTON — A worldwide 24-hour airline strike to protest hijackings is still scheduled for 2 a.m. tomorrow despite last-minute legal attempts to block US pilots' participation.

Yesterday, after a Federal court here denied airline requests for an injunction to prohibit a strike by American pilots, the airlines took their case to a higher court.

But Chief Judge David L. Bazelon of the US Court of Appeals asked lawyers for the pilots to make a quick canvass of pilots' associations in 38 other countries to determine what the effect of delaying the strike a week or more would be.

AIRLINE, Page 21

Co-owners in Cape realty venture

Inspector, Hub landlord in business

By Robert L. Turner
Globe Staff
Copyright 1972 by the Globe Newspaper Co.

A Boston housing inspector has an active business relationship with a Back Bay landlord whose buildings he is supposed to inspect.

Kenneth G. Flynn, 30, the city inspector responsible for most of the Back Bay and Beacon Hill, is a co-trustee in a Cape Cod real estate venture with Nick Haddad, 45, of 203 Commonwealth av., who controls at least 14 Boston properties—10 in Flynn's inspection area.

More than 19 months ago, on Nov. 5, 1970, Flynn and Haddad formed the Foster Realty Trust, and the same day purchased an inn called the Captain's House on Foster road, Falmouth.

Another business relationship between the two apparently exists involving a property on Davisville road, Falmouth, about a half mile from the Foster road site.

The property was purchased in Haddad's name on June 23, 1971 and a subdivision of the property was prepared in Flynn's name and dated Oct. 15, 1971, according to records at the Barnstable Registry of Deeds.

Neighbors say Flynn has been living on the Davisville road property since last summer.

The business relationships between Flynn and Haddad raise questions relative to the state conflict of interest law.

FLYNN, Page 22

Kissinger: playboy of the Eastern world

By Crocker Snow Jr.
Globe Asian Bureau

TOKYO — The geishas now call him "iro goto shi." A kind translation would be "playboy" — an unkind one, "dirty old man." Maybe the most accurate is "secret swinger" with a dash of sexuality thrown in.

The appelation is applied to Henry A. Kissinger.

The President's right-hand man touched down in Tokyo for three days last week to impress upon the Japanese government that it still stands high in US concerns. Amid busy conferences and affairs of state, he also left quite an impression on this city's distinctive geishas.

"He's got a low voice, so soft, so sexy," teased one with a smile as she adjusted the tight kimono wound around her torso. "Unfortunately, we couldn't entertain him properly or play card games or anything because he had too many bodyguards and stuffy Japanese politicians around him."

"He's got a dumpy figure, like a daikon (Japanese turnip.) But still he's very attractive — a real iro goto shi," offered another, who like many geishas, is pretty dumpy and daikon-shaped herself.

SWINGER, Page 18

A JAPANESE GEISHA

INSIDE TODAY:

An adventurous life

Dr. George Cheever Shattuck, who died last week, lived a long and adventuresome life that included a trek through the Amazon jungles. He spent his 93 years in an active devotion to helping people—from the jungles to the hospitals of Boston. Story, Page 36.

A victory for Breslin

Writer Jimmy Breslin could have been a top New York city official—if he hadn't lost the primary. But now Breslin is sure he's going to win one—as a delegate for George McGovern. Story, Page 16.

Monday . . . new Spotlight

Starting tomorrow . . . another Globe "Spotlight" series.

The Pulitzer Prize-winning Spotlight team—The Globe's full-time, four member investigative unit—reports on a politically influential Massachusetts consultant firm and its frequent dealings with public agencies.

Weather

Fair today, high near 70. Tonight and tomorrow variable cloudiness. High Monday in 70s.

Full report—Page 54

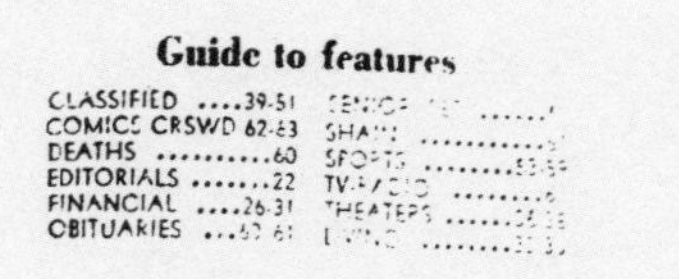

Guide to features

CLASSIFIED 39-51
COMICS CRSWD 62-63
DEATHS 60
EDITORIALS 22
FINANCIAL 26-31
OBITUARIES 57-61

The Boston Globe

Vol. 202, No. 68 © 1972 Globe Newspaper Co.

WEDNESDAY MORNING, SEPTEMBER 6, 1972

Telephone 288-8000 84 Pages—15c

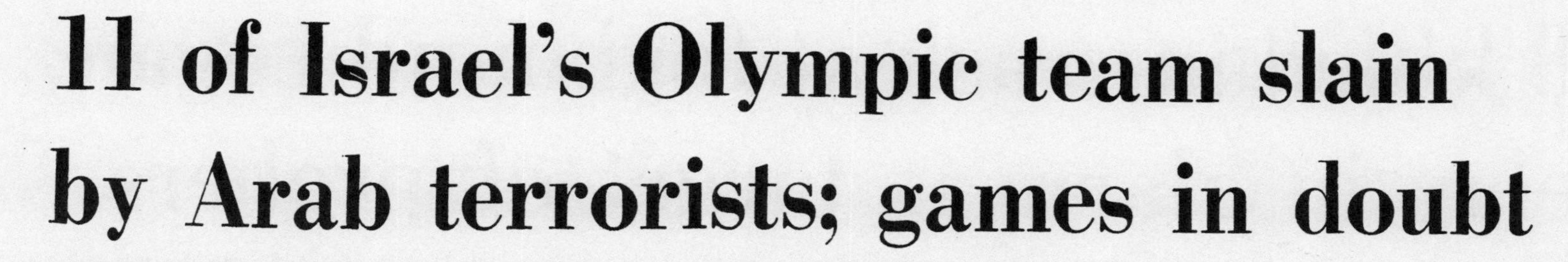

11 of Israel's Olympic team slain by Arab terrorists; games in doubt

GRIM ANNOUNCEMENT—Hans-Dietrich Genscher (left), West German interior minister, and Dr. Manfred Schreiber, Munich police chief, flank Bavarian Interior Minister Bruno Merck as he talks to newsmen in Munich. Bearded man behind Merck is Olympics press chief Hans Klein. (AP)

By John M. Goshko
Washington Post

MUNICH — Seven Arab terrorists yesterday turned the 1972 Olympics into a scene of wholesale political murder that began with a predawn attack on Israeli athletes in the Olympic Village and ended 18 hours later in a bloody airfield shootout with German police.

At the end, 11 Israelis apparently had been slaughtered—two in the Olympic Village and nine others during the gun battle at the airfield after they were held hostage all day.

Dead also was a Munich city policeman, and the pilot of a West German military helicopter was seriously wounded.

As to the Arab terrorists, four had been killed and three were in the custody of German police. They had succeeded in turning the sports lover's dream world that is the Olympic Games into a nightmare of slaughter.

Left unanswered by all the bloodshed was the question of whether the games—already suffering under an unprecedented suspension during the events of recent hours—will be canceled.

So far, Olympic officials will say only that the matter will have to be decided later today by the full International Olympic Committee. They added that opinion is divided, with some insisting that the games should go on and some arguing that events have made the thought of continuing unbearable.

Should the games be continued, there is a chance of great strain in the always delicate relations between West Germany and Israel. The Bonn government of Chancellor Willy Brandt had conceived the Munich games as a means of erasing memories of Adolph Hitler and the Nazi era.

Now, it faces the fact that 11 persons who were here as guests of the West German government and under its protection have been slain on German soil. Moreover, the 11 were Jews — members of the group that suffered the greatest persecution from Hitler's Germany — and they were killed in the course of the first Olympics to be held in Germany since World War II.

This thought obviously was uppermost on the minds of German

MUNICH, Page 3

INSIDE

- Israel reacts angrily. The rest of the world is appalled. Stories Pages 2 and 3.
- Suddenly the games aren't important as thousands keep all-day vigil outside beseiged Olympic village. Page 2.
- Desperation attacks by Arab guerrillas illustrate the movement's bankrupt policy of terror. An anaylsis. Page 2.
- America's golden swimmer, Mark Spitz, who is Jewish, hastily leaves Olympics ahead of time en route home to Los Angeles. Page 3.
- Profiles of two of the slain Israeli team members and a list of the others. Page 3.

At the start, it looked like a kids' prank

By Shirley Povich
Washington Post

MUNICH — The night shift workers at the Olympic Village post office merely nudged each other and pointed to the fence climbers outside, in the dim light of the early dawn.

No great to-do about that scene. Happened all the time in the village, those agile Olympic athletes scaling the eight-foot fence to bypass the gatekeepers and sneak back to their dorms after violating curfew.

You couldn't tell an Arab from a blond Scandinavian in the half light of 4 a.m., especially if he was dressed in those long sweat suits favored in the Olympic village.

This time not just a couple of kids sneaking home. There were more of them, "and they all were carrying those big 'adidas' or puma bags," a postal worker said later.

A common sight in the village, those carryall bags. Big enough to conceal a snub-nosed machine gun, if necessary.

SCENE, Page 2

Eyewitness at the airport

'Most horrible thing I have ever seen'

Reuter

MUNICH — A West German airline official, trapped most of the night at Fuerstenfeldbruck Airport, told Reuter that last night's killing of the Israeli Olympic athletes "was the most horrible thing I have ever seen."

The official, who declined to be indentified said he had personally counted nine bodies, including that of a woman.

He said that six bodies, still in their track suits, were lined up on the runway. Some had their stomachs ripped open by machine gun bullets, he said.

Other eyewitnesses gave the following account:

After the three helicopters bringing the commandos and their hostages from the Olympic village arrived at the airport they suddenly took off again and circled for 30 minutes before landing next to a waiting Lufthansa 727 jet.

When the helicopters landed, two of the guerrillas left the first aircraft and walked over to inspect the Lufthansa jet. They were heading back to the helicopter when police snipers opened fire.

The West German pilots of two helicopters jumped from their aircraft. One got away but another fell to the ground caught in a hail of bullets.

People jumped from the helicopters and fled in all directions while the firing continued.

Seconds later the second helicopter was shattered by an explosion and burst into flames.

When the action finished and firing stopped, at least four bodies lay on the tarmac.

Shortly before 2 am, one of the guerrillas was brought to the airfield in a police car.

He was held by the hair and all four limbs by police in the back of the vehicle. His face was caked with dirt and blood stains At 2. am, the battle was over.

Leary shuffles officials, creates 3 school jobs

By Muriel L. Cohen
Globe Staff

Boston's new superintendent of schools, William J. Leary, unimpressed by a cutback in school spending, yesterday created three high-salaried administrative posts as he reshuffled many of the city's key school officials.

The moves, coming less than 24 hours before schools opened this morning, were the first of several measures presented by Leary as he met with the Boston School Committee for the first time since taking office Friday.

The reorganization of top posts, affecting 11 positions including the newly created ones, won unanimous support from School Committee members, who also approved:

- Lunch programs in 108 schools across the city to forestall a threatened suit seeking enforcement of a new state law ordering in-school food service.

SCHOOL COMMITTEE, Page 14

SHORT CUT TO SCHOOL — Eleven-year-old Joseph McVicar of Dorchester gets trimmed for first day of school. (Globe Photo by Ted Dully)

Kissinger reopens talks in Moscow on Sunday

By Carroll Kilpatrick
Washington Post

SAN CLEMENTE, Calif. — Presidential adviser Henry A. Kissinger, who has visited Moscow twice this year, will return there Sunday for three days of talks with Soviet leaders.

Vietnam is expected to be a major topic of discussion, as it has been in all the other travels Kissinger has made this year for President Nixon.

En route to Moscow, Kissinger will stop in Munich Friday and Saturday to confer with West German Chancellor Willy Brandt and other German leaders.

In announcing Kissinger's itinerary yesterday, White House press secretary Ronald L. Ziegler would not say how or when Kissinger would return to Washington, thus leaving open the possibility he may visit another capital.

Another meeting in Paris with North Vietnamese politburo member Le Duc Tho may be possible. However, there have been few if any signs of progress in the private meetings Kissinger has held.

KISSINGER, Page 18

IN THIS CORNER

Now Detroit plans an engine that has major parts missing

By Paul Langner
Globe Staff

Detroit has been looking the other way for a decade, but lately the big automakers have had another look at what might be the beginnings of an automotive revolution, the Wankel engine.

[illegible] making 1974. Only Chrysler thinks it is a passing fad.

What started Detroit on the Wankel engine is its success in the Japanese Mazda, which has been selling like hot cars — more than 20,000 last year.

What should have started the automakers on it is the engine's simplicity and smallness, not normally [illegible] as virtues in Detroit.

Reporter-inmate calls Deer Island filthy pit

By Jack Thomas
Globe Staff

Globe editorial writer Jack Thomas spent one week living as an inmate at Deer Island House of Correction. This is the first of three articles describing his experience.

Boston spends $2 million a year to maintain a primitive house of correction on Deer Island, a filthy verminous prison that serves more as a school of crime than a center for rehabilitation.

The demography of the prison tells part of its story: Half the population is black or Spanish, most are poor and uneducated, two-thirds arrive with a drug or alcohol problem, and at least one out of every five has a history of psychiatric trouble. For every 100 men discharged, 70 will be returned to Deer Island or to [illegible] probably within a

The man who runs the facility is A. Reginald Eaves, the city's first black penal commissioner. He was appointed by Mayor Kevin H. White last May. Eaves inherited nearly 300 restive inmates, a demoralized staff of 133, a collection of dilapidated, antiquated buildings, and a Gothic philosophy under which men were

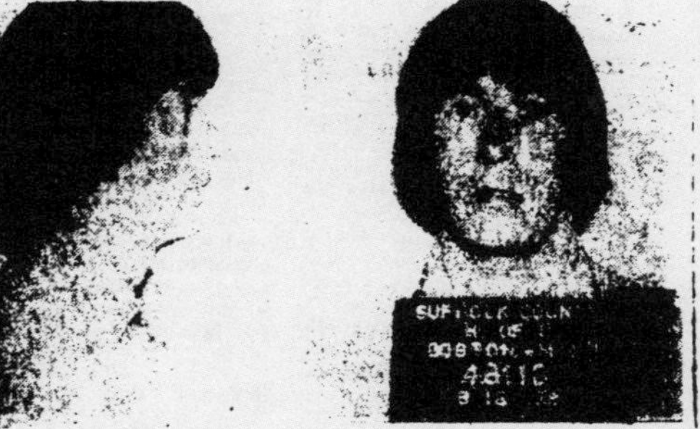

PRISONER JACK THOMAS . . . "school for crime"

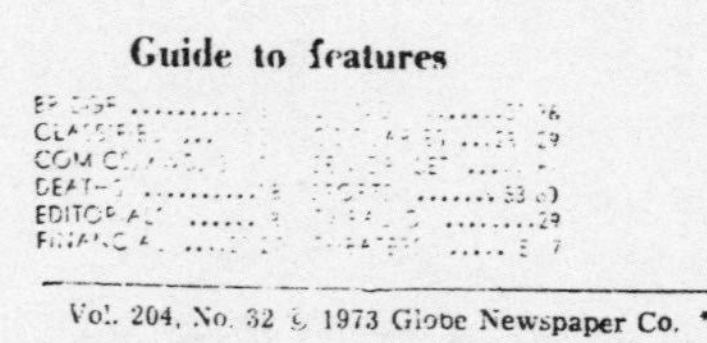
Guide to features

The Boston Globe

Dismal

Vol. 204, No. 32 © 1973 Globe Newspaper Co. · WEDNESDAY MORNING, AUGUST 1, 1973 · Telephone 288-8000 · 64 Pages — 15c

88 killed in crash at fogbound Logan; delay in alarm is target of probers

(Plane crash stories, photos — Pages 2, 3, 12, 13)

By Robert J. Anglin, Globe Staff

A delay in sounding the disaster alarm after a Delta DC9 jetliner smashed into the foot of a fogbound Logan Airport runway yesterday is being investigated by Federal officials.

Eighty-eight persons died in the crash — the worst aviation tragedy in Boston's history. The aircraft apparently clipped a three-foot seawall below the level of the runway and disintegrated on impact.

The wreckage of the twin-engine jet and the broken bodies of passengers, some of them still alive, lay undetected in thick fog shrouding Logan's Runway 4R. Representatives of public agencies geared for such a disaster said the delay in sounding the disaster alarm was unaccountable.

All but one of the 89 persons aboard, including five crew members, died. The only survivor was listed in critical condition.

Interstate Commerce Commission member Chester Wiggin Jr., of Contoocook, N.H., and New Hampshire Asst. Atty. Gen. Robert W. Moran were among the victims.

Jack Halloran, a spokesman for the Massachusetts Port Authority, which operates the airport, said the plane disappeared from radar view at 11:09 a.m. An automatic tape at Boston Fire Alarm Headquarters shows that the disaster alarm mobilizing Greater Boston's emergency procedures came in at 11:22 a.m., after the airport crash crew arrived at the scene.

Halloran said the watches of some of the victims had stopped at 11:05 a.m., and it was reported that a Boston Police Dept. videotape showed one man's wristwatch had stopped at 11:03 a.m.

Massport Fire Chief Charles Arena said it appeared that the first word the tower had was from him as he drove to the scene. Arena had been alerted by a construction engineer, Geoff Keating, who witnessed the crash.

A team of investigators from the National Transportation Safety Board flew to Boston yesterday afternoon to inquire into the reason for the delayed alarm as well as the cause of the crash.

Ferris Howland, regional director of the Federal Aviation Administration, said the crash was too far from the control tower to be seen in the heavy fog.

CRASH, Page 12

Partial list of victims, Page 13

TRAGEDY AT LOGAN — Bodies of victims — two of them still strapped in their seats — lie on runway at Logan International Airport after yesterday's crash of Delta Airlines DC9 inbound in heavy fog from Burlington, Vt., and Manchester, N.H. (Globe photo by Joseph Dennehy)

For those at scene: just frustration

'Mayday! Mayday! Anyone who can hear me, please cut off! There's a plane down on 4R.'

—Workman Geoff Keating into a dead microphone

By John B. Wood
Globe Staff

Just after 11 a.m. Geoff Keating parked the battered blue pickup off the dike road and walked out to where the bulldozers were working, plowing clean fill into the Bird Island Flats adjacent to Logan Airport.

Keating, 23, an inspector for a Boston engineering firm, was walking across the flats, his mind numbed by the din of the bulldozers, when he saw it — a horizontal flash of fire three-quarters of a mile away.

It came from the farthest corner of the airport, where on Tuesdays and Thursdays local fire companies sometimes practice on abandoned school buses doused with gasoline, and for half a second Keating did not react.

"The fire department is out there lighting up buses," he thought. "They shouldn't be doing that in this weather, though. They're liable to confuse someone in the tower."

But the flame was too big, and too quick. Almost before he could be sure he had seen it, it was gone, leaving a cloud of black smoke and a low rumble, like distant thunder.

Keating glanced at the buildozer operator, who had seen the flash out of the corner of his eye, and then at Mark Falber, the MIT student who was working with him for the summer.

WORKERS, Page 3

'We just started covering them up with sheets. I never felt so helpless in my life.'

—Nurse Maureen Kennedy of Logan Medical Center

By Mike Barnicle
Globe Staff

Maureen Kennedy was working the 10 to 8 shift at the Logan Airport Medical Center. She had been at work less than 90 minutes when Delta Airlines Flight 723, with 89 people aboard, slammed into the end of runway 4R and spilled a flaming cargo of human flesh and airplane parts over the paved airstrip near the edge of the ocean. It was then that Maureen Kennedy had to go to work.

"I don't know the exact time," she said. "I guess it must have been near 11:30 when Lt. Carney of the State Police here called down and told us there had been a Phase 5."

She paused for a second. "That's a crash, but you hear, 'Phase 5' and you think, well, maybe it really didn't crash."

Maureen Kennedy and two other nurses loaded their emergency trunks into Carney's cruiser and were sped out onto the airport. They headed out throuch the low, grey, thick morning fog to a crash site they could not see.

"The first thing I saw was people. People scattered all over the ground. The fire was mostly out. There were the fire crews and a priest, I think, but the bodies were all over the ground. There was no sound. They were all dead."

She stopped again and looked down at her white nurse shoes, covered with the sand and oily grime of the crash site.

"I really don't know what I expected when I first got out there. I

BARNICLE, Page 2

White House uses Haldeman to 'leak' tapes, Ervin claims

By Martin F. Nolan
Globe Washington Bureau

WASHINGTON — Sen. Sam J. Ervin Jr. (D-N.C.) accused lawyers for President Nixon and his former chief of staff, H. R. Haldeman, of "a little bit of collaboration" in helping to "leak" portions of presidential tapes which Mr. Nixon refuses to give investigators.

Haldeman, testifying for his first full day before the Senate Watergate committee, said that his perusal of the tapes "confirmed my memory" about conversations with the President.

Haldeman again contradicted the testimony of Mr. Nixon's chief accuser, former White House counsel John W. Dean 3d, and gave an opposite version of a March 21 conversation among himself, Dean and the President.

Dean said Mr. Nixon indicated March 21 that he knew about and approved of the Watergate coverup. Haldeman said, however, that the President was trying to find out about and stop the coverup.

Haldeman's testimony was based on his "recollection" of listening to tapes in his home and office. He made notes on the tapes "not as a private citizen, but as a former member of the President's staff," Haldeman said. The notes were then turned over to the President, where they became part of a group of documents the President has refused to turn over to the committee.

Sen. Lowell P. Weicker Jr. (R-Conn.) interrupted Haldeman's testimony, saying: "The fact is no other witness has had access to these tapes and very frankly I don't cite any 'privilege' theory and I'm not a great constitutional lawyer, but I think I understand the concepts of fairness in the American way and to me it is grossly unfair to any other witness who comes before this committee."

Later, Haldeman admitted that neither Dean nor any other witness would have access to the tapes of presidential conversations. "It's my understanding that no one else has or will," he told Sen. Howard Baker (R-Tenn.) who asked whether anyone else could hear the tapes with the President's permission.

But Haldeman also told Baker that he would "welcome the opportunity" to play the tapes publicly "because they would confirm what I told you."

Weicker's protest brought a comment from committee chairman Ervin that the White House had made a "powder puff objection" to the parts of Haldeman's testimony involving his recollection of the tapes.

"This is, I think, a little planned action," Ervin said, "in which the White House allows Mr. Haldeman to use the tapes which the White House denies the committee and then lets

HEARING, Page 14

Drinan files impeachment bid

By Richard L. Lyons
Washington Post

WASHINGTON—Rep. Robert F. Drinan yesterday became the first member of Congress to introduce a resolution to impeach President Nixon, and seemed to be about the only one who believed this is the time to try.

Drinan introduced a one-sentence resolution stating that "Richard M. Nixon, President of the United States, is impeached of high crimes and misdemeanors." It was referred to the House Judiciary Committee, whose chairman Peter Rodino (D-[illegible]) [illegible] would have to give [illegible] consideration to what, if any, [illegible]

Drinan told newsmen he decided against using a special prodedure by which he could have forced immediate consideration of his proposal by the full House.

Drinan, a Jesuit priest whose name appeared on the so-called White House 'enemies list," did not file a bill of particulars specifying grounds for removing Mr. Nixon from office.

He said in a statement announcing his action, however, that he was moved to act by the "recent disclosure that President Nixon conducted a total secret air war in Cambodia for 14 months prior to April 30, 1970."

IMPEACH, Page 9

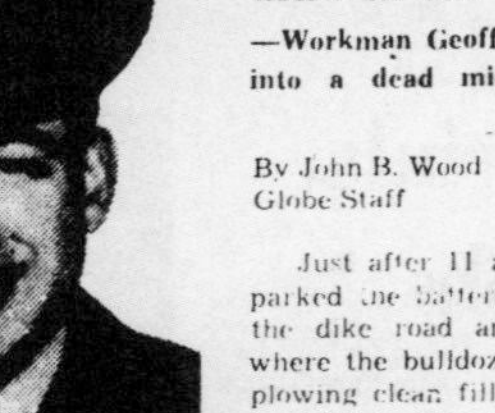

COPILOT—Sid Burrill, copilot of ill-fated Delta jetliner and an Air Force veteran, was a resident of 192 Court rd. in Winthrop.

Inside stories on plane crash

- **When word of the DC9 crash reached the Logan Airport control tower, firefighters already were speeding to the scene; the tower learned about the accident from the Massport Fire Dept. Story, Page 3.**
- **The morgue at Boston City Hospital was the scene of a vast traffic jam. Jeremiah Murphy story, Page 2.**
- **The lone crash survivor, a 20-year-old Marshfield, Vt., man, was en route back to an Alaska air base. Story, Page 2.**

Boston Sunday Globe

Vol. 204, No. 113 © 1973, Globe Newspaper Co. SUNDAY, OCTOBER 21, 1973 50 CENTS

- Ruckelshaus also fired
- Cox's assistants dismissed
- Bork named acting A.G.

WILLIAM RUCKELSHAUS
. . . refused order

ARCHIBALD COX
. . . loses battle

ROBERT H. BORK
. . . handled firings

Nixon fires Cox, Richardson resigns; FBI agents seal prosecutor's office

EXCHANGE OF LETTERS

The President
The White House
October 20, 1973

Dear Mr. President:

It is with deep regret that I have been obliged to conclude that circumstances leave me no alternative to the submission of my resignation as Attorney General of the United States.

At the time you appointed me, you gave me the authority to name a special prosecutor if I should consider it appropriate. A few days before my confirmation hearing began, I announced that I would, if confirmed, "appoint a special prosecutor and give him all the independence, authority, and staff support needed to carry out the tasks entrusted to him." I added, "Although he will be in the Department of Justice and report to me—and only to me—he will be aware that his ultimate accountability is to the American people."

At many points throughout the nomination hearings, I reaffirmed my intention to assure the independence of the special prosecutor, and in my statement of his duties and responsibilities, I specified that he would have "full authority" for "determining whether or not to contest the assertion of 'Executive Privilege' or any other testimonial privilege." And while the special prosecutor can be removed from office for "extraordinary improprieties," I also pledged that "The Attorney General will not countermand or interfere with the Special Prosecutor's decisions or actions."

While I fully respect the reasons that have led you to conclude that the Special Prosecutor must be discharged, I trust that you understand that I could not in the light of these firm and repeated commitments carry out your direction that this be done. In the circumstances, therefore, I feel that I have no choice but to resign.

In leaving your Administration, I take with me lasting gratitude for the opportunities you have given me to serve under your leadership in a number of important posts. It has been a privilege to share in your efforts to make the structure of world peace more stable and the structure of our own government more responsive. I believe profoundly in the rightness and importance of those efforts, and I trust that they will meet with increasing success in the remaining years of your Presidency.

Respectfully,
ELLIOT L. RICHARDSON

Honorable Elliot L. Richardson
The Attorney General
October 20, 1973

Dear Elliot:

It is with the deepest regret and with an understanding of the circumstances which brought you to your decision that I accept your resignation.

Sincerely,
RICHARD NIXON

October 20, 1973

Honorable Robert H. Bork
The Acting Attorney General

Dear Mr. Bork:

I have today accepted the resignations of Attorney General Richardson and Deputy Attorney General Ruckelshaus. In accordance with Title 28, Section 508(b) of the United States Code and of Title 28, Section O, 132(a) of the Code of Federal Regulations, it is now incumbent upon you to perform both the duties as Solicitor General, and duties of and act as Attorney General.

In his press conference today Special Prosecutor Archibald Cox made it apparent that he will not comply with the instruction I issued to him, through Attorney General Richardson, yesterday. Clearly the Government of the United States cannot function if employees of the Executive Branch are free to ignore in this fashion the instructions of the President. Accordingly, in your capacity of Acting Attorney General, I direct you to discharge Mr. Cox immediately and to take all steps necessary to return to the Department of Justice the functions now being performed by the Watergate Special Prosecution Force.

It is my expectation that the Department of Justice will continue with full vigor the investigations and prosecutions that had been entrusted to the Watergate Special Prosecution Force.

Sincerely,
RICHARD NIXON

October 20, 1973

Honorable Archibald Cox
Special Prosecutor
Watergate Special Prosecution Force

Dear Mr. Cox:

As provided by Title 28, Section 508(b) of the United States Code and Title 28, Section 0, 132(a). of the Code of Federal Regulations, I have today assumed the duties of Acting Attorney General.

In that capacity I am, as instructed by the President, discharging you, effective at once, from your position as Special Prosecutor, Watergate Special Prosecution Force.

Very truly yours,
ROBERT H. BORK
Acting Attorney General

By Martin F. Nolan
Globe Washington Bureau

WASHINGTON — Attorney General Elliot L. Richardson resigned last night after President Nixon fired Special Watergate prosecutor Archibald Cox.

Mr. Nixon then dismissed Deputy Attorney General William Ruckelshaus after Ruckelshaus refused to dismiss Cox.

The President's actions probably will bring closer the constitutional confrontation that just 24 hours earlier he sought to avoid.

The President's plan to avoid a Supreme Court decision on Cox's attempt to have Mr. Nixon surrender Watergate-related tapes had been crumbling all day yesterday, as both Cox and the Senate Watergate Committee disavowed major portions of Mr. Nixon's response to a court order.

Richardson met with Mr. Nixon for a half-hour late yesterday afternoon after Cox had held a press conference, saying he would disregard the President's order not to proceed further in legal efforts to find out more about the Watergate conspiracy and alleged coverup within the White House.

To fire Cox, the President appointed as acting Attorney General Robert H. Bork of Yale University. Bork then wrote Cox a letter, saying, "I am, as instructed by the President, discharging you, effective at once, from your position as Special Prosecutor, Watergate Special Prosecution Force."

The Cox staff of 38 lawyers and more than 50 staff members was ordered dismantled immediately by the President. Shortly after 9 p.m., Cox's staff said agents from the Federal Bureau of Investigation began sealing off the Cox office at 1425 K st.

In a statement by White House Press Secretary Ronald L. Ziegler, read to reporters at the White House shortly after 8 p.m., the President's spokesman said the Cox operation "will be transferred back into the institutional framework of the Department of Justice, where it will be carried out with thoroughness and vigor."

Ziegler said Mr. Nixon discharged Cox "because of Mr. Cox's refusal to comply with instructions given Friday night through Attorney General Richardson that he was not to seek to invoke the judicial process further to compel production of recordings, notes or memoranda regarding private Presidential conversations."

Richardson was appointed Attorney General in late April during the height of new revelations about the Nixon Administration's involvement in conspiracy, sabotage and corrupt campaign practices during the 1972 campaign. During his confirmation before the Senate Judiciary Committee, Richardson promised the Senate that he would appoint an independent Watergate prosecutor.

Richardson finally called upon his former professor at the Harvard Law School for the job and last night told the President that he was still standing by Cox.

The Richardson resignation letter bore all the trademarks of the precise, thorough, legalistic manners that caused Richardson to be called the "Mr. Clean" of the Nixon Administration. He had already served the President as Undersecretary of State, and Secretary of Health, Education and Welfare.

Richardson began his letter to Mr. Nixon: "It is with deep regret that I have been obliged to conclude that circumstances leave no alternative to the submission of my resignation as Attorney General of the United States."

FIRINGS, Page 59

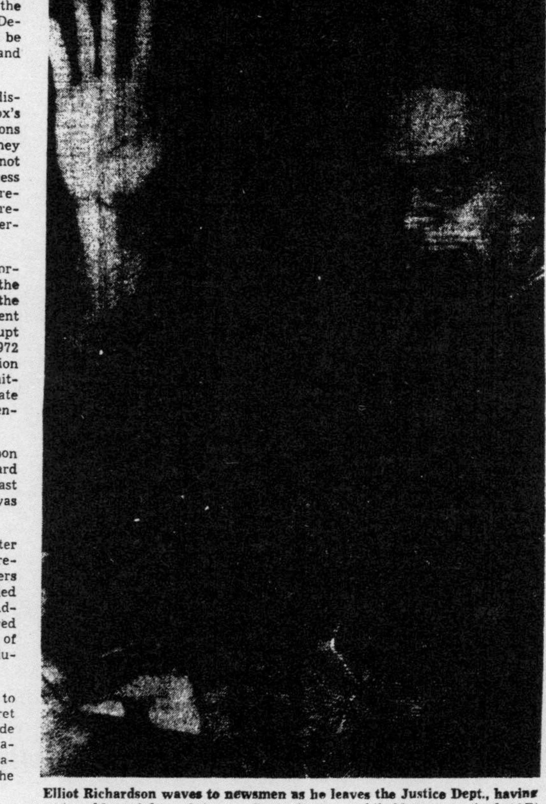

Elliot Richardson waves to newsmen as he leaves the Justice Dept., having resigned last night as Attorney General after Archibald Cox was fired. (AP)

Kissinger in Kremlin for talks on war

United Press International

MOSCOW — Secretary of State Henry A. Kissinger, responding to "an urgent request" from Moscow for talks on ways to end the Middle East war, arrived by plane from Washington late yesterday and went immediately to the Kremlin for a meeting with Soviet Communist party leader Leonid I. Brezhnev.

The Soviet news agency Tass said they discussed matters "related to the situation in the Middle East."

Kissinger's arrival came a day after Soviet Premier Alexei Kosygin returned from Cairo following four days of discussions with Egyptian President Anwar Sadat.

"The signs are the Soviets want to negotiate," a Western diplomat said. "They're talking face to face, and they do respect Kissinger."

The American embassy said Soviet Foreign Minister Andrei A. Gromyko and Joseph J. Sisco, assistant Secretary of State of Middle Eastern affairs, were also taking part in the talks.

Kissinger was greeted at the airport by Gromyko upon his arrival at 7:20 p.m. (12:20 p.m. EDT) in a US Air Force jet.

Secretary of State Henry Kissinger, in Moscow for Mideast talks, is met by Soviet Foreign Minister Andrei Gromyko (right). Anatoly Dobrynin (left), Soviet ambassador to Washington, accompanied Kissinger. (AP)

He stopped to greet Soviet officials and American diplomats, but was driven away without speaking to newsmen. The visit was Kissinger's fifth to Moscow and his first as Secretary of State.

US Senate Majority Leader Mike Mansfield (D-Mont.), told newsmen in Washington that the Soviet request for talks with Kissinger came "a matter of hours" before his departure at 1:50 a.m. (EDT).

"It was an urgent request from Kosygin," Mansfield said, declaring, "I imagine things are approaching a climax of sorts as far as the US and the USSR are concerned."

Inside on the Mideast:

- The Globe's Darius Jhabvala analyzes the Kissinger trip to Moscow, Page 25.
- Syria claims it has blasted an oil refinery near Haifa in the war's first air strike inside Israel. Story, Page 28.
- Israel claims her armored forces have penetrated to within 45 miles of Cairo. Story, Page 28
- Saudi Arabia, third among America's foreign oil suppliers, announced yesterday it will cut off all oil shipments to the US. Story, Page 25.
- The oil shortage is cause for concern, but not alarm, writes The Globe's Thomas Oliphant. An analysis, Page 5.

The weather

Today and tomorrow: Sunny, highs around 60.

Full report, Page 69

TODAY — 24 full pages on Nixon, Ford

Guide to features

ARTS/THEATER ...40 DEATH NOTICES .50
BRIDGE ....71 EDITORIALS 22
CALENDAR ....69 FINANCIAL 45-48
CLASSIFIED ....51-60 HOROSCOPE 71
COMICS ....70 LIVING 37-39
CROSSWORD .....71 TV-RADIO 71

The Boston Globe

Sun spots

FRIDAY — CLOUDY, COOLER
SATURDAY — FAIR, IN 70s
HIGH TIDE — 3:51 A.M., 4:13 P.M.
FULL REPORT — PAGE 36

Vol. 206, No. 40 © 1974, Globe Newspaper Co. • FRIDAY MORNING, AUGUST 9, 1974 Telephone 288-8000 72 Pages — 15 Cents

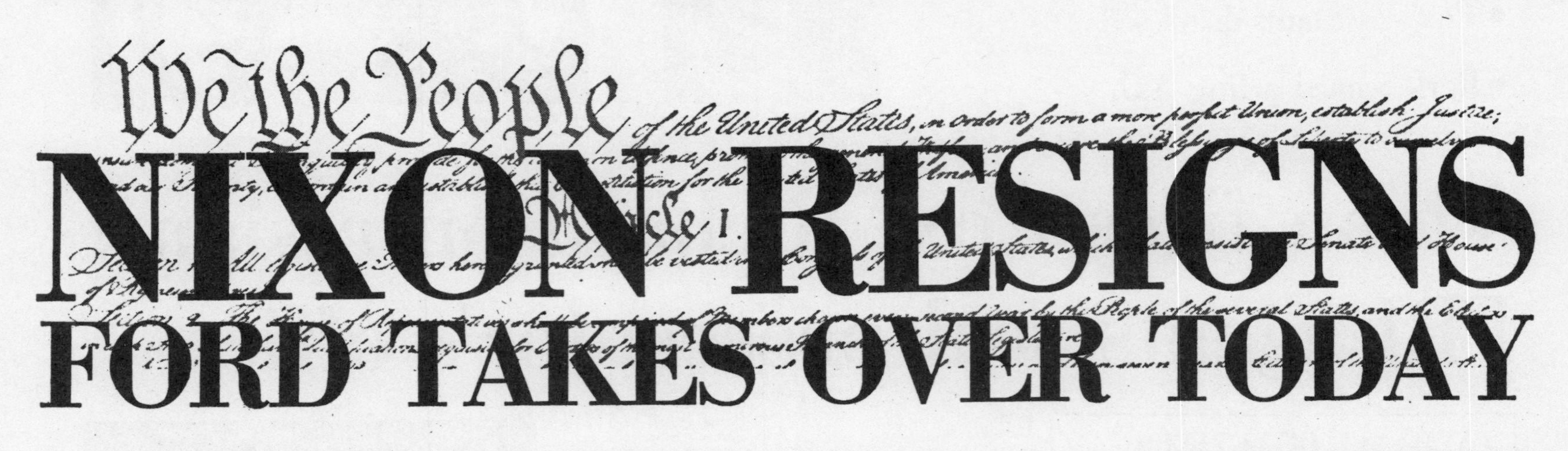

NIXON RESIGNS

FORD TAKES OVER TODAY

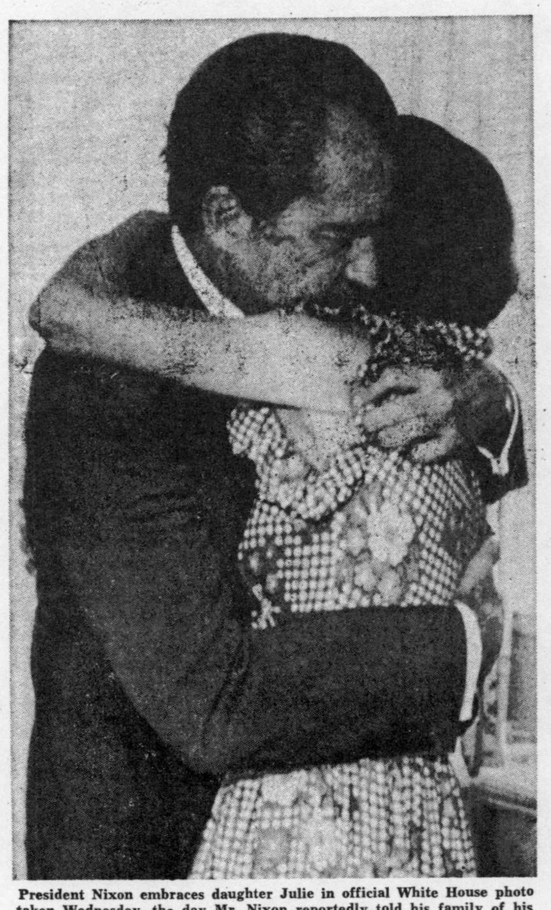

President Nixon embraces daughter Julie in official White House photo taken Wednesday, the day Mr. Nixon reportedly told his family of his decision to resign. Photo was released by White House last night. (UPI)

Ford vows no change in policy

Ford text, Page 11

By Stephen Wermiel
Globe Washington Bureau

WASHINGTON — Vice President Gerald R. Ford pledged last night that as President he would do "what is good for America and good for the world."

Speaking outside his home in Alexandria, Va., shortly after President Nixon announced that he would resign, Ford sounded a tone of reconciliation for the country.

In brief remarks, delivered slowly and soberly, he promised to continue the foreign policy of the Nixon Administration and retain Henry A. Kissinger as Secretary of State while pursuing domestic solutions in a bipartisan manner.

"The policy that has achieved peace and built blocks for future peace will be continued," said Ford.

Ford stressed his ability to bring reconciliation, noting that he has had many political "adversaries" in

FORD, Page 11

By Martin F. Nolan
Globe Washington Bureau

WASHINGTON — Richard Milhous Nixon resigns at noon today, the first President in the nearly 200-year history of the Republic to do so.

Addressing a nationwide television audience from the Oval Office at the White House last night, he said: "I shall resign the Presidency effective at noon tomorrow. Vice President Ford will be sworn in as President at that hour in this office."

The speech was more subdued and less combative than any other in his 28-year career as congressman, senator, Vice President and President. Its conciliatory tone made it one of the President's finest moments, his opponents quickly said.

Conceding that "some of my judgments were wrong," Mr. Nixon said he was resigning after 5½ years as President to start "that process of healing which is so desperately needed in America."

He made no specific mention of his own culpability in the Watergate coverup. His admission Monday of participation in that alleged criminal conspiracy triggered this week's almost-unanimous congressional demand for his removal from office.

"I have never been a quitter," the President said, referring to his repeated pledges in the past two years that "I have no intention of walking away from the job I was elected to do."

'I have never been a quitter. To leave office before my term is completed is abhorrent to every instinct in my body. But as President I must put the interests of America first.' (Full text, Page 4.)

"In the past few days, however, it has become evident to me that I no longer have a strong enough political base in the Congress to justify continuing that effort," he said.

"As long as there was such a base, I felt strongly that it was necessary to see the constitutional process (of impeachment) through to its conclusion; that to do otherwise would be unfaithful to the spirit of that deliberately difficult process and a dangerously destabilizing precedent for the future.

"But with the disappearance of that base," he added, "I now believe that the constitutional purpose has been served, and there is no longer a need for the process to be prolonged."

The word "base" has been a favorite Nixon word in his long upward struggle in the California Republican Party and later on the comeback trail after being defeated for the Presidency in 1960 and for governor of California in 1962.

NIXON, Page 5

Rockefeller top candidate for VP

By Robert Healy
Globe Staff

WASHINGTON — Former Gov. Nelson A. Rockefeller of New York appears to be the leading candidate for the nomination for Vice President when Gerald R. Ford moves up to the Presidency today.

But there was also an effort by conservatives in the GOP to stop the Rockefeller nomination. One group of conservatives sent the names of 13 men and one woman acceptable to the group as vice-president. It did not contain Rockefeller's name.

VEEP, Page 11

Vice President Ford speaks at presentation of posthumous medals to seven servicemen in ceremony at Blair House a few hours before President Nixon announced his resignation to nationwide TV audience. (AP)

No deals offered by Jaworski

By S. J. Micciche
Globe Washington Bureau

WASHINGTON — President Nixon leaves office today fully exposed to Watergate prosecution.

No deal "of any sort" was arranged to entice Mr. Nixon's resignation, Watergate prosecutor Leon Jaworski said last night, adding flatly that his office "was not asked for any such agreement or understanding and approved none."

On Capitol Hill, congressional initiative to help shield Mr. Nixon from prosecution as an inducement for him to quit dissipated on the wings of the President's decision to resign.

As he becomes an ordinary citizen, Mr. Nixon will confront myriad legal problems — possible criminal charges even beyond the Watergate scandal and potential civil lawsuits.

With regard to Federal prosecution, Mr. Nixon will be totally dependent for immunity upon his successor, Vice President Gerald R. Ford, to dispense a Presidential pardon, or perhaps still bargain for some accord with Jaworski and Attorney General William B. Saxbe.

In quitting, Mr. Nixon remains an unindicted co-conspirator in the Watergate coverup. That grand jury

IMMUNITY, Page 16

INSIDE:

Kissinger's role

Secretary of State Henry Kissinger emerges as the key figure assuring both Americans and foreign nations of the continuity of US foreign policy, The Globe's Darius S. Jhabvala reports. Page 17.

The summing up

It was Richard Nixon who had us wallow in Watergate, Carl Bernstein and Bob Woodward report. A summing up of the story they did so much to break open, Page 3.

Nixon the man

What forces shaped Richard Nixon, this man whose life stamped his name on the psyche of the American people? An appraisal, Pages 18-19.

Mood of Washington

A look at the mood inside and outside the White House. Dan Rather of CBS reports on the agony of the decision while The Globe's Thomas Oliphant writes about a strangely quiet Washington. Stories, Page 8.

On Wall Street

The stock market yesterday reacted more to news of surging inflation than to the impending resignation. Dow Jones industrials dropped 12.67 points. Story, Page 47.

Impeachment tide

The President's resignation has finally halted the impeachment tide, but the Judiciary Committee will still submit its final report, writes David Nyhan. Story, Page 16.

Nixon's legacy

Richard Nixon's legacy appears to be a maze of contradictions, writes Martin F. Nolan of The Globe's Washington Bureau. Story, Page 20.

Vietnam buildup

The Vietnam conflict, eclipsed by Watergate in the United States, goes on with the Defense Dept. reporting signs of a North Vietnamese buildup in the South. Story, Page 26.

His impact on the Presidency

By Henry Steele Commager

Henry Steele Commager, a noted historian and professor of history at Amherst College, wrote this appraisal of President Nixon for The Boston Globe

Let us consider the impact of the Nixon years on the institution of the Presidency itself.

Has Nixon permanently impaired the traditional character of that office? Does the experience of the past five years portend—or even require—fundamental changes in our constitutional system in order to restore the balance among the three departments of government and make certain that in our system no one is above the law?

The American Presidency is what the Constitution prescribes, or implies; what History contributes, or obscures; what Presidents add, or subtract. In neither the legislative nor the judicial branch is the contribution of the individual nearly as effective as in the executive.

Washington gave the Presidency its original shape; Jackson assured it a special relationship with the people; Lincoln exploited it to the full potential of its role as commander-in-chief; Wilson identified it with party leadership; Franklin Roosevelt made it an instrument of social revolution; Eisenhower and Kennedy, each in his special way, cultivated its fabulous, almost its religious, character.

COMMAGER, Page 23

Help Globe Santa's 50,000 needy children—Box 1525 Boston, 02104

LATE RACE RESULTS
(SEE PAGE 80)

FINAL EDITION

Boston Evening Globe

3 O'CLOCK STOCKS
(SEE PAGE 84)

FINAL EDITION

Vol. 206, No. 164 © 1974, Globe Newspaper Co. WEDNESDAY, DECEMBER 11, 1974 ® Telephone 929-2000 92 Pages—15 Cents

Police try to keep control as white students mill around South Boston High School after they were released following the stabbing of a white youth by a black student. (Ulrike Welsch photo)

INSIDE / OUT

Local

Three weeks after promising to remove illegal fill from Tenean Creek in Dorchester, disbarred former Judge Jerome P. Troy has neither removed the fill nor given the state any written assurance he will do so. Page 29.

The Watertown School Committee last night voted 6-1 to permit 13-year-old Jane Ford to play on the previously all-boy West Junior High School hockey team. Page 5.

Reaction to the appointment of Paul Parks as Gov.-elect Michael Dukakis's education secretary was mixed today. In the Boston's black community there were plaudits; in South Boston disparagement. Page 4.

Mayor Kevin H. White has launched his re-election campaign and is using city employees to work on his scheduled $100-a-plate fund-raiser Dec. 19, one of his aides acknowledged yesterday. Page 11.

24-Hour Game, Page 91

National

The Jesuit national weekly, "America," says divorced and remarried Catholics should be allowed under certain conditions to return to full communion in the church. Page 71.

Financial

New England has been told to get busy and do something about its energy problems. The suggestions at a Chamber of Commerce meeting in Boston were to look into nuclear power and to start hunting for offshore oil. Page 84.

Sports

For all those who deplore the deadly efficiency of the NFL under Pete Rozelle, the World Football League was almost too much of a good thing. Page 75.

Index

Arts/Theater	87-89	Financial	84-87
		Living	47-69
Book	69	Shain	91
Bridge	46	Obits	72, 73
Classified	37-45	Sports	75-83
Comics	90	Steincrohn	46
Crossword	24	Star Gazer	71
Deaths	72	Trivia Quiz	24
Editorials	26	TV-Radio	91

Weather

Tonight — Becoming cloudy, lows in 30s.

Tomorrow — Chance of rain, highs in 40s.

High tide, 9:36 p.m.

Full report, Page 23.

Walpole 'rebel 8' demands amnesty

By Walter V. Robinson and Paul Feeney
Globe Staff

Eight inmates at Walpole state prison said today they would release their three hostages if they get a promise of amnesty from Gov. Francis W. Sargent.

The amnesty demand, issued at noon, was relayed to Sargent's office, where a spokesman refused comment.

"I don't know what decision will be made," spokesman Meg Coltin said of the demand. "All we can say at this time is no comment."

The amnesty demand was issued by the inmates during a 45-minute meeting this morning with state Sen. Jack Backman, state Sen.-elect William Owens, Rev. Edward Rodman and Deputy Correction Comr. Joseph Higgins.

The eight inmates, including five convicted murderers, have been holding the three hostages, two guards and a medic, since late last night.

Emerging from the session inside the cellblock where the hostages are being held, Backman and Owens said they were told by the inmates that the hostages would be released as soon as Sargent accedes to their amnesty demand.

The visitors said the inmates would negotiate their additional 17 demands calling for improvements at the prison, once the amnesty demand had been met.

The two senators reported that the three hostages, who earlier had been bound and gagged, were freed of their bonds were in separate cells and unhurt.

WALPOLE, Page 70

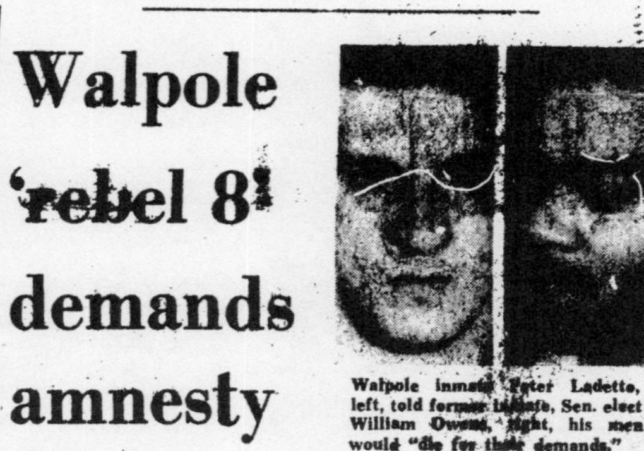

Walpole inmate Peter Ladetto, left, told former inmate, Sen. elect William Owens, right, his men would "die for their demands."

S. Boston High knifing closes eight schools

White youth stabbed; black student held

1800 angry whites clash with police

125 black students trapped in school

At least 10 hurt in confrontation

By George Croft and Robert Carr
Globe Staff

An angry crowd of some 1800 white parents and students clashed with police at South Boston High School today following the stabbing of a white student whose name is on the danger list at City Hospital.

A black student was taken into custody as the alleged assailant.

The stabbing incident triggered the following:

● Seven schools in South Boston and Roxbury High School were closed for the rest of the week.

● Some 125 black students were trapped for nearly four hours in the school as the crowd prevented buses from approaching the school building.

● All black students at the South Boston High School annexes, the L street and the Hart-Dean School, and the Gavin Middle School, were bused under guard to other sections of the city for their safety.

● At least 10 persons, including five police officers, were injured in the near riot that ensued at the high school. Police finally managed to spirit the blacks from the building about 2:15 p.m.

● Some 125 riot-geared state troopers from Framingham and Concord barracks were rushed to South Boston to augment the force of all available Boston and MDC police.

Police said the white student, Michael Faith, 18, of Pilsudski way, South Boston, was stabbed in a second-floor corridor about 10 a.m. as the students were heading to their second-period classrooms.

He was rushed by police to the hospital where an emergency surgical team was awaiting his arrival.

His condition following surgery, hospital officials said, was "stable."

Police said James A. White, 17, of Roxbury, was arraigned in South Boston District Court charged with assault and battery with a dangerous weapon. He was held in $5000 bail.

School Supt. William Leary canceled classes in the following schools for the rest of the week:

South Boston Hight, L street and Hart-Dean annexes, the Gavin Middle School, Roxbury High School and the Andrew, O'Reilly and Perkins elementary schools.

Also canceled were evening centers and evening school classes in the district.

Teachers at the high school, incensed over the stabbing, the latest of a series of incidents involving black and white students, voted for the closing of the high school for tomorrow and Friday.

The teachers said they would vote again on Friday on whether school should be reopened on Monday.

They relayed their feelings to school Headmaster William Reid and to Leary.

SCHOOLS, Page 3

OFF BEAT

1st altar girls in Hub diocese

By Marguerite Del Giudice
Globe Staff

Every Monday after school, Linda McKenna and Roberta Barry meet at St. Stephen's Church in Framingham and practice being altar girls.

They learn how to carry themselves during celebration of the Mass, when to sit, stand and kneel, to sound the bells at appropriate moments and how to assist the priest during Communion and special Masses.

They (and about 15 others) are the first altar girls in the Archdiocese of Boston (although St. Stephen's sister parish in Framingham, St. Tarcisius, followed suit on its own a month ago.)

But nobody thinks it's such a big deal.

OFF BEAT, Page 6

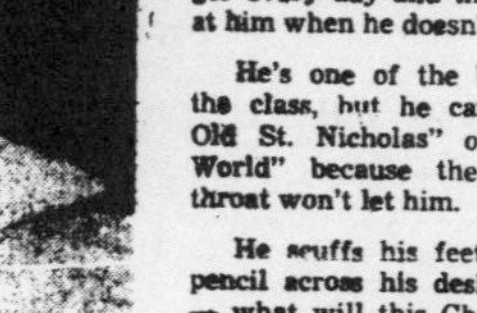

The Boston Archdiocese's first altar girls, Roberta Barry, left, and Linda McKenna help Rev. David G. Bonfiglio prepare for Mass at St. Stephen's Roman Catholic Church, Framingham. (Jack Sheahan photo)

Jon, 7, now fatherless, needs Globe Santa's joy

By Bernice Keane

Jon sits in the second seat, second row, second grade.

Christmas is everywhere. On the walls, in the songs and the games and the stories.

Christmas is everywhere but inside him. He feels cold way down deep.

The lump in his throat gets bigger every day and the teacher looks at him when he doesn't sing.

He's one of the best singers in the class, but he can't sing "Jolly Old St. Nicholas" or "Joy to the World" because the lump in his throat won't let him.

He scuffs his feet and rolls the pencil across his desk and wonders — what will this Christmas be like without his dad — without the booming laugh and the teasing and the roughhousing.

GLOBE SANTA, Page 73

TO HELP GLOBE SANTA, mail donations to Globe Santa, Box 1525, Boston 02104, or deliver to The Globe downtown office at Washington and School streets.

Santa's friends

Murphy Kids, Weymouth	[illegible]
Natick Trust Co. Employees	116.00
In memory of Wm. E. O'Brien - M.T.D.	5.00
Mrs. Flaherty's Fourth Grade, Reeves School, Woburn	5.00
Puddles and her New Hubby	2.00
"Monique"	25.00
Chanukah gift to our Grandmother, Mrs. I. Borr	10.00
Stoughton 'A' Pee Wee Hockey Team	10.00
From friends at Randolph Savings Bank	76.00
Faulkner Brothers Employees, Somerville	25.00
Deirdre and Pamela Sartorelli, Revere	5.00

SANTA'S FRIENDS, Page 73

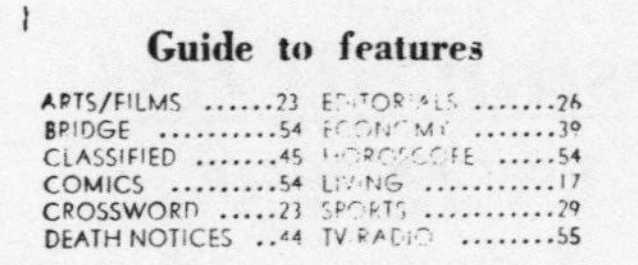

Guide to features

ARTS/FILMS	23	EDITORIALS	26
BRIDGE	54	ECONOMY	39
CLASSIFIED	45	HOROSCOPE	54
COMICS	54	LIVING	17
CROSSWORD	23	SPORTS	29
DEATH NOTICES	44	TV-RADIO	55

The Boston Globe

Over lowed

WEDNESDAY—SUN, LOW 50s
THURSDAY—CLOUDS, LOW 50s
HIGH TIDE—3:07 A.M., 3:43 P.M.
FULL REPORT—PAGE 16

Vol. 207, No. 120 © 1975, Globe Newspaper Co. • WEDNESDAY MORNING, APRIL 30, 1975 ® Telephone 929-2000 56 Pages — 20 Cents

Last Americans out

Communists enter palace

South Vietnam surrenders

Crewman of Air America helicopter helps evacuees climb ladder to craft waiting atop Saigon building, one of several sites in downtown area of the capital from which Americans and other foreign nationals were airlifted to US Navy ships lying off the South Vietnamese coast. (UPI)

From Wire Services

SAIGON — The Saigon government surrendered unconditionally to the Viet Cong today, ending more than 30 years of warfare in this country. Within hours of the radio announcement, the Viet Cong were reported to have occupied South Vietnam's presidential palace and their flag was seen flying over the building.

Viet Cong and North Vietnamese troops were moving into the city, apparently without serious opposition. South Vietnamese troops were reported to be abandoning their defensive positions and marching to central points to turn in their weapons.

President Duong Van Minh made a surrender broadcast to the nation only hours after an armada of US Marine helicopters had completed an emergency evacuation of nearly 900 Americans and thousands of Vietnamese from the besieged capital.

A detachment of North Vietnamese troops in a jeep arrived at the presidential palace and asked Minh to accompany them. He rode off with them. Their destination was not known.

Minh, a retired general and neutralist, was named president Monday in a desperate and unsuccessful attempt to negotiate a peace with the Communist leaders.

Communist forces began moving into the city within two hours of Minh's broadcast. A jeep flying the Viet Cong flag drove along the street a block from the abandoned US Embassy at noon. The eight cheering men in the vehicle were in

VIETNAM, Page 38

'Hello comrade!' they shouted

United Press International

SAIGON — Laughing, cheering Communist troops entered the presidential palace in Saigon today, shouting "hello comrade!" to bystanders and newsmen.

A UPI photographer at the palace said the green-clad soldiers shouted "Press guys good" at him in Vietnamese, but other than that both sides seemed to ignore newsmen who were recording the takeover.

It was not all joy, however, as the Viet Cong's Provisional Revolutionary Government made preparations to take the reins of government.

A Saigon policeman, identified by

SAIGON, Page 38

History of the war in photos—Pages 2, 3

Americans in Saigon . . . the final day

From Wire Services

SAIGON — America's last day in South Vietnam ended amid tears, panic, looting and rage.

Such was the scene yesterday during the 13-hour airlift by 81 helicopters that evacuated 6400 Americans and South Vietnamese from Saigon to US ships in the South China Sea. The operation was guarded by 800 marines, the Pentagon said.

The night of the evacuation was eerie with flare light as thousands of Vietnamese civilians, fearing Viet Cong reprisals, tried to claw their way over the 10-foot wall surrounding the gleaming white embassy building and its garden.

US Marines and American civilians used pistol and rifle butts to hammer their fingers, but scores got over and raced with the Americans for the helicopter pad atop the four-story embassy.

Frantic civilians jumped from the wall and landed in barbed wire below. A middle-aged man and women were bleeding as they struggled against the steel barbs.

Mothers holding up their children wept as they pleaded with Americans to take the youngsters with them.

"Please take my children," cried a young woman as she clutched an American holding an embassy radio.

"They are half-American and the Viet Cong will kill them."

The Americans were leaving, but they couldn't take the thousands with them who wanted out.

FLIGHT, Page 37

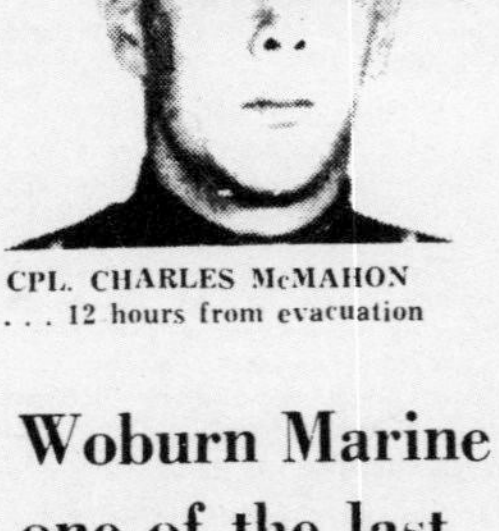

CPL. CHARLES McMAHON
. . . 12 hours from evacuation

Woburn Marine one of the last killed in Vietnam

By Robert J. Anglin
Globe Staff

In Woburn Center yesterday people found it hard to believe the news.

Word had come of the death of 21-year-old Marine Cpl. Charles McMahon Jr., one of the last Americans to die in Vietnam.

"Isn't the war over?" someone asked, as the flags fluttered at half staff.

Everyone seemed to know Charlie in this city of 37,000. He had been named "Boy of the Year" four years ago by the Boys' Club.

McMAHON, Page 36

Ford proclaims 'end of chapter' in US history

By Richard E. Lerner
United Press International

WASHINGTON—President Ford yesterday announced that with the evacuation of the last Americans in Vietnam the United States had "closed a chapter" in its history, ending more than two decades of involvement in South Vietnam.

"The last helicopters are in the air," presidential press secretary Ron Nessen told a news conference that had been delayed almost five hours so the end of the evacuation could be announced.

"This closes a chapter in the American experience," Mr. Ford's statement said. "We must now close ranks, avoid recriminations, look ahead to new goals and work together on the task we face."

Nessen read Mr. Ford's statement just before Secretary of State Henry A. Kissinger briefed reporters in a nationally broadcast news conference.

Kissinger said the Administration's aims over the past two weeks had been to stabilize the situation and to end US involvement in the "most controlled and humane" manner.

POLICY, Page 37

Marion Fahey appointed Boston schools head

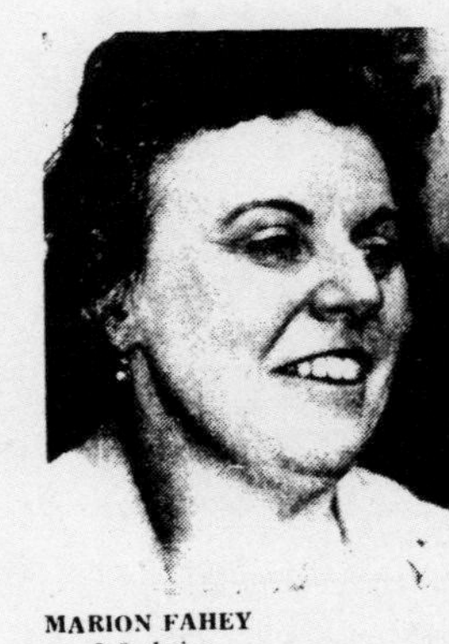

MARION FAHEY
. . . 3-2 choice

By Muriel Cohen
Globe Staff

Associate Supt. Marion J. Fahey, a teacher and administrator in the Boston public schools for 26 years, was named superintendent of schools in a 3-2 voice vote by the Boston School Committee yesterday.

Miss Fahey won a three-year contract for the $47,500-a-year position over Supt. William J. Leary and Associate Supt. Paul Kennedy in the second round of the balloting.

She will be Boston's first woman superintendent.

The decision continues a long-standing tradition of naming an insider to the top school job in Boston and makes Miss Fahey the second woman in the country to head a big city school system. The other is Barbara Sizemore, superintendent of schools in Washington.

Marion J. Fahey . . . a profile in the news. Page 11.

Miss Fahey's assignment becomes effective Sept. 1 and coincides with the complex final preparations for the city's Phase 2 court-ordered desegregation plan.

Leary's efforts to make the first phase as peaceful as possible irked some committee members who are opposed to the use of busing to achieve desegregation, sources said.

Yesterday's narrow victory for Miss Fahey ended two weeks of intensive lobbying among the five School Committee members and by supporters of a number of candidates.

In a rare departure from earlier practice, the committee failed to give Miss Fahey a unanimous vote as a signal of support for a new administration even after she had won by a three-vote majority.

Member Paul Tierney cast the swing vote on the second ballot after the first round gave Miss Fahey two, Kennedy two and Leary one vote.

Paul Ellison and John J. Kerrigan voted for Miss Fahey. Chairman John J. McDonough and Kathleen Sullivan for Kennedy and Tierney for Leary.

COMMITTEE, Page 13

INSIDE TODAY

Only a tax increase can balance budget

A $346 million state tax increase will be necessary to balance Massachusetts' fiscal 1976 budget, even if Gov. Dukakis succeeds in his plans to cut welfare spending and other appropriations. News analysis, Page 7.

Dukakis vetoes bill to restore execution

Expressing "grave doubts" about its constitutionality, Gov. Dukakis vetoed a bill to reinstitute the death penalty for persons convicted of first-degree murder. House and Senate votes on the veto may be taken today. Story, Page 9.

No parental consent needed for abortion

A Massachusetts law requiring parental consent for abortions performed on unmarried teenagers was ruled unconstitutional by a three-judge Federal court panel. Story, Page 5.

Gay rights measure approved by House

A 129-96 House vote in favor of a bill banning discrimination against homosexuals in state and local civil service jobs marked the first legislative endorsement of a gay rights bill. Story, Page 10.

High-voltage wires electrocute boy, 17

A Plymouth teenager was electrocuted and his companion suffered a concussion and burned foot when they climbed atop a 50-foot tower supporting high-voltage wires near Rte. 3. Story, Page 7.

League won't field political fund facts

The Boston League of Women Voters rebuffed Mayor White's request that it receive complaints from city employees who feel they were pressured to make political contributions. Story, Page 11.

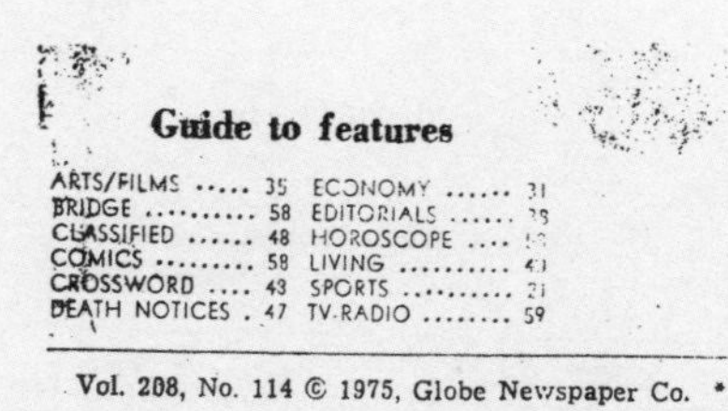
Guide to features

ARTS/FILMS ..... 35 ECONOMY 31
BRIDGE .... 58 EDITORIALS 15
CLASSIFIED ...... 48 HOROSCOPE 55
COMICS .... 58 LIVING 43
CROSSWORD ...... 43 SPORTS 21
DEATH NOTICES . 47 TV-RADIO 59

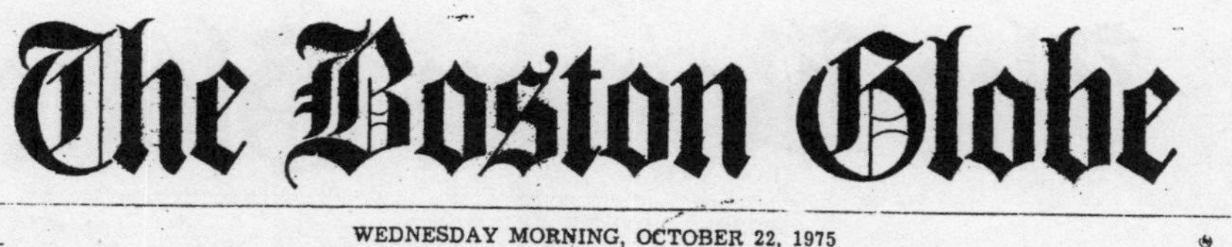
The Boston Globe

Sevenly
WEDNESDAY—SUNNY, 70s
THURSDAY—FAIR, NEAR 70
SUNRISE 7:06, SUNSET 5:54
FULL REPORT—PAGE 48

Vol. 208, No. 114 © 1975, Globe Newspaper Co. WEDNESDAY MORNING, OCTOBER 22, 1975 Telephone 929-2000 80 Pages—20 Cents

Fisk's homer in 12th wins for Red Sox, ties Series

Carlton Fisk pauses en route to first base and jumps for joy as he watches ball hit left field foul pole for 12th-inning homer. (AP)

Carbo's pinch HR ties in 8th inning after Reds KO Tiant

Lee faces Gullett in Game 7 tonight

DETAILS, PAGE 21

Carlton Fisk pats Fred Lynn on cheek as Sox slugger crosses plate after hitting first inning homer which also scored Fisk and Carl Yastrzemski (right). No. 6 is Rico Petrocelli. (Globe photo by David Ryan)

CIA loses foreign contacts in wake of probes, exposes

William Beecher, The Globe's diplomatic correspondent, interviewed more than a score of present and former intelligence officials to examine the implications of recent exposes. In a three-part series he discusses the impact on foreign intelligence-gathering, adjustments made to ride out the storm and future prospects for US intelligence capability.

THE TROUBLED CIA – 1

By William Beecher
Globe Washington Bureau

WASHINGTON — Within recent months, British and West German intelligence services, which long had freely exchanged the most sensitive information with their American counterparts, have become chary of providing such data.

During the same period, a number of major US corporations, which have provided cover abroad for Central Intelligence Agency operatives or insights on little-known economic and political trends overseas, also have become reluctant to cooperate as before.

And large numbers of foreign agents and contacts, always worried that an indiscretion could jeopardize their jobs or their lives, have become increasingly nervous about passing on documents or even rumors.

Well-placed sources in or otherwise familiar with the American intelligence community report that such developments are a direct result of congressional hearings and newspaper exposes of certain questionable activities on the part of the CIA and other intelligence agencies.

Comments one top CIA official: "It would be overstating the situation to say our sources abroad have dried up. But there's no doubt we're hurting. People who used to give us whole reports now are giving us only summaries. People who used to give us summaries are only giving us one or two facts. Others who used to pass along an occasional nugget at

CIA, Page 12

5% surcharge eyed on Mass. income tax

By Michael Kenney
Globe Staff

The Massachusetts Senate is expected to approve a 5 percent surcharge on the state income tax today as part of a $300 million package of tax increases needed to balance this year's budget.

The leadership is cautiously predicting that it has the votes to win approval of a $3.02 billion budget and the accompanying tax package during debate scheduled for today.

"We're working on a very narrow margin," Ways and Means Chairman James A. Kelly Jr. (D-Oxford) said. "It's a matter of one or two votes."

The votes were lined up yesterday during a 3½-hour Democratic caucus during which Senate President Kevin B. Harrington sharply criticized the conduct of the administration of Gov. Michael S. Dukakis during this year's budget problems.

"I've been here 17 years," he said. "We joke a lot and we kid around and we rib one another, but I've never seen a bigger crisis . . . we all know the incompetence of the present administration."

The package Harrington will be trying to pass today is expected to incorporate these changes from the one passed by the House last month:

— A 5 percent surcharge on the 1975 tax on earned income (wages and salaries), followed by a half-point increase in the basic rate to 5½ percent for income earned during 1976.

— Broadening of the sales tax (at the 5 percent rate adopted by the House) to cover any clothing purchase of more than $50.

— Repeal of the 8 percent meals tax and taxing all meals at 5 percent under the sales tax.

— Reduction of taxes on alcoholic beverages by 20 percent to make up for the 20 percent surcharge placed on those taxes in June.

CAUCUS, Page 17

8800 Boston pupils missing, School Dept. informs Garrity

By Muriel Cohen
Globe Staff

Nearly 8800 students, most of them white, have not yet reported to class although they are officially enrolled in Boston public schools, according to figures filed yesterday in US District Court.

In the first formal accounting of enrollment, discharges and "missing" students under Phase 2 desegregation, the Boston School Department told the court that about 12,000 students of the 21,616 originally called "missing" have been located.

About 7500 of the students newly accounted for have actually been attending classes but, for one reason or another, had been listed as missing. Louis Perullo, the School Department research director, said Perullo said 4544 others were listed as discharged, leaving 8796 yet to be located.

In its reports, five separate statistical complications, the School Department said:

—75,281 students reported to

ENROLLMENT, Page 6

Indiana's Sen. Birch Bayh yesterday announced his official entry into race for Democratic presidential nomination. Story, Page 14. (Globe photo)

Panel favors probe, 7-2

Harrington faces hearing Nov. 3 for CIA leaks

By Stephen Wermiel
Globe Washington Bureau

WASHINGTON — The House Ethics Committee yesterday voted to investigate a complaint that Rep. Michael J. Harrington violated House rules last year in disclosing secret testimony by CIA Director William Colby.

The committee action, on a 7-2 vote, caps five months of negotiations involving the Massachusetts Democrat, the committee, and House Democratic leaders seeking to avoid a showdown over the complaint lodged against Harrington by Rep. Robin L. Beard (R-Tenn.).

A hearing on the complaint was set for Nov. 3. Beard predicted a "reprimand or censure" of Harrington.

Few House members interviewed yesterday could foresee the possibility that the House might actually censure Harrington. The action was viewed, instead, as a show of force by the Ethics Committee that will become "a troublesome situation" if it reaches the full House.

Harrington told newsmen after he was informed of the committee decision: "What is really at issue here is the failure of the Congress to discharge its responsibilities as an overseer of intelligence activity.

"The issue is not Michael Harrington, but the use of the CIA and government secrecy in general to short-circuit the democratic process and cover up illegal activity.

"I remain convinced that what I did last year was responsible and proper under the circumstances . . . The implication of those who are trying to have me censured is that

HARRINGTON, Page 11

REP. HARRINGTON . . . convinced he was right

Let her die, father begs court

From Wire Services

MORRISTOWN, N.J. — As his weeping family listened, Joseph Quinlan testified yesterday that "it's the Lord's will" his daughter Karen Ann be allowed to die.

"Take her from the machine and the tubes connected to her and let her pass into the hands of the Lord," Quinlan told a crowded courtroom.

Quinlan was the first relative to testify at a trial, requested by the family, that the 21-year-old Miss Quinlan, who has been in a coma six months, be allowed to "die with dignity."

Quinlan's wife, Julia, mother of the couple's adopted daughter, is scheduled to testify today when the trial resumes.

Mrs. Quinlan sobbed as her husband told how he came to the decision that his daughter's life is over. Quinlan, a supervisor for a New Jersey drug firm, said that he decided in August that there was no hope for his daughter's recovery.

He said he made up his mind to file a suit to seek permission to disconnect Karen's respirator while driving home from St. Clare's Hospital in Denville after a meeting with her doctors.

"We had done everything possible to help her and now we had no hope," the gray-haired, 50-year-old father said.

Quinlan, a Roman Catholic, said his parish priest agreed and told him he was morally right in "putting her in the Lord's hands."

Quinlan said that if the court grants his request, he would not "turn off the machine myself" but would let medical men do it. Both Miss Quinlan's doctors have testified they would refuse to disconnect the respirator, saying it is against medical tradition.

COMA, Page 16

New prison climate

Frank Hall's innovations as Massachusetts correction commissioner have improved the climate at the state's prisons. The morale of guards has improved and the incidence of violence at the state's major prison, Walpole, has been reduced. Conditions are also better at the prison in Framingham. Story, Page 18.

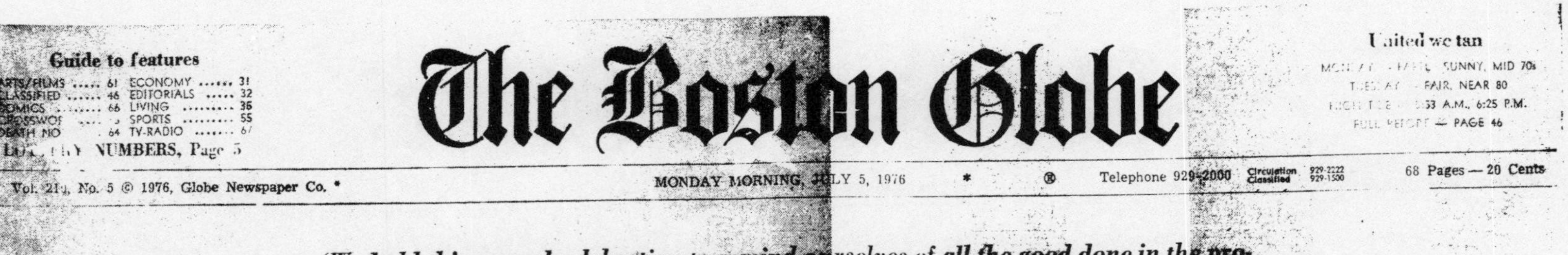

Guide to features

ARTS/FILMS ..... 61 ECONOMY 31
CLASSIFIED ...... 46 EDITORIALS 32
COMICS .... 66 LIVING 35
CROSSWORD .... 5 SPORTS 55
DEATH NO .... 64 TV-RADIO 67

LOTTERY NUMBERS, Page 5

The Boston Globe

United we tan
MONDAY — FAIR, SUNNY, MID 70s
TUESDAY — FAIR, NEAR 80
HIGH TIDE — 5:53 A.M., 6:25 P.M.
FULL REPORT — PAGE 46

Vol. 210, No. 5 © 1976, Globe Newspaper Co. * MONDAY MORNING, JULY 5, 1976 * ® Telephone 929-2000 Circulation 929-2222 Classified 929-1500 68 Pages — 20 Cents

'We hold this annual celebration to remind ourselves of all the good done in the process of time, of how it was done and who did it and how we are historically connected with it. And we go from these meetings in better humor with ourselves – we feel more attached the one to the other and more firmly bound to the country we inhabit.'

—Abraham Lincoln
July 4, 1858

WHAT A PARTY IT WAS

Sea to sea, US hails 200th

By Matthew V. Storin
Globe Staff

A nation that had seemed to grow self-conscious about displays of patriotism in recent years responded to its Bicentennial yesterday with the pride and optimism that have marked so much of its history.

Millions of Americans joined in ceremonies on the 200th anniversary, rituals and oratory marking reverence for America's history and faith in its future.

There were also protest gatherings in Philadelphia and Washington which were reminders of the traumatic years of Vietnam and Watergate and the nation's unfinished journey toward racial harmony.

The revelries—ranging from red, white and blue plumes of water from the fireboats saluting 16 Tall Ships in New York harbor to the hog-calling contest in Polk County, Iowa—were linked electronically for millions of Americans through marathon broadcasts on the CBS and NBC television networks.

At mid-evening, the vast TV audience and huge crowds in New York and Washington saw the skies over those cities ablaze with fireworks—an incandescence said to be unmatched in the American history of pyrotechnics.

Also seen across the country was the televised climax of the Tchaikovsky 1812 Overture by the Boston Symphony on the Esplanade, accompanied by artillery, church bells, fireworks and hundreds of thousands of cheering people who rivaled any Times Square crowd on New Year's Eve.

The scope of these celebrations—the parade of tall ships, along with the warships of 22 nations, up the Hudson River, the swearing-in of 7140 new citizens at the Miami Beach Convention Center and personal appearances by President Ford at four locations in half a day—could only have been imagined by celebrants of the Centennial in 1876.

But many of the observances—the square-rigged vessels of the Old World, the enthusiastic rendition of the overture on Boston's Esplanade, a Babel of ethnic parties in lower Manhattan—reflected the growth of the nation out of earlier cultures.

Perhaps because of predicted throngs and the possibility of violence, crowds for events in Philadelphia and Baltimore were less than expected.

A protest rally sponsored by the People's Bicentennial Commission at the foot of Capitol Hill in Washington drew far fewer than the 50,000 the sponsors expected.

NATION, Page 18

A crowd estimated at 400,000 watches fireworks display that lights up the Charles River. The show followed concert at Hatch Shell (upper right) (Globe photo by Ted Dully)

Boston's largest crowd ever

By Marguerite Del Giudice
Globe Staff

New England, the place where it all began, commemorated the nation's birth and destiny yesterday.

The signs of Fourth of July celebration were the same as in years gone by. A red, white and blue soccer ball scooting across a field in South Boston. The trumpets of an Army band piercing the air at a country fair in Maine. A 7-year-old holding a tiny American flag in one hand, a hot dog in the other.

But it wasn't the same. There was something special in the air, an essence of times past and future. It was America's 200th birthday, and of course everybody knew it. So hours before Arthur Fiedler, the Boston Symphony Orchestra and three barges of fireworks ever got near the Charles River Esplanade, a quarter of a million people were waiting.

By the time the stirring strains of the 1812 Overture signaled the beginning of the evening's end, official police estimates put the crowd at 400,000 strong—the largest in Boston's history.

Flags were everywhere: on houses, car antennas, peddler's carts. Tourists with cameras and maps, who flocked to Boston for the Bicentennial, tried hard not to lose the red-brick path of the Freedom Trail. There were inter-faith church services, and even a colonial costume ball. Fireworks? Everywhere.

NEW ENGLAND, Page 16

President Ford and his daughter, Susan, leave Independence Hall in Philadelphia, one of their stops in a day of Bicentennial activities. Behind is a statue of George Washington. (AP photo)

Arrests tied to bombs

By Richard Hudson
and Charles Claffey
Globe Staff

Two men were arrested yesterday and large quantities of dynamite and several firearms confiscated in Massachusetts and Maine in an apparent major breakthrough in the probe of 11 terrorist bombings in New England during the last 10 weeks. The arrests were made on the 200th anniversary of Independence Day, the celebration which terrorist organizations and individuals had pledged to disrupt.

BOMBING, Page 27

Chilean vessel Esmeralda passes under New York's Verrazano Bridge during Tall Ships parade. (AP photo)

INSIDE:

ISRAELI RAID — Israeli officials report three hostages, one commando and seven terrorists were killed in the Israeli action that rescued 104 hostages in Uganda. President Idi Amin says 20 Ugandan soldiers were also killed in the operation. Page 21.

CARTER-MUSKIE MEETING — Jimmy Carter meets with Sen. Edmund Muskie today to discuss the No. 2 spot on the party's ticket. Muskie is among five persons Carter has selected in a preliminary search for a running mate. Page 20.

REVERE BLAST — An explosion damaged a branch bank building at the Northgate Shopping Center at 9:50 p.m. last night. Page 65.

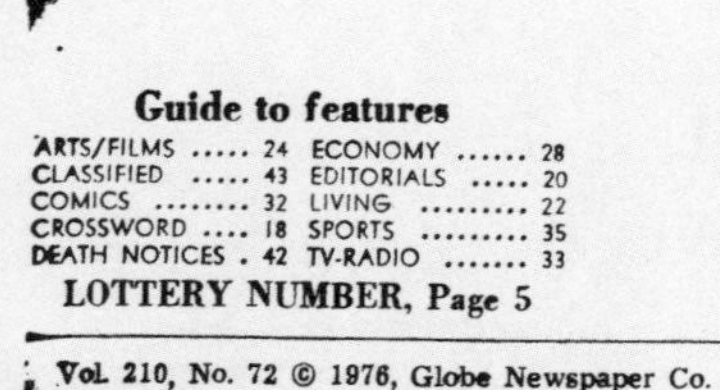

Guide to features

ARTS/FILMS ..... 24 ECONOMY 28
CLASSIFIED ..... 43 EDITORIALS 20
COMICS .... 32 LIVING 22
CROSSWORD .... 18 SPORTS 35
DEATH NOTICES . 42 TV-RADIO 33
LOTTERY NUMBER, Page 5

The Boston Globe

Sept. mourn
FRIDAY—CLOUDY, 70s
SATURDAY—MAY RAIN
HIGH TIDES—12:52 A.M., 1:10 P.M.
FULL REPORT—PAGE 34

Vol. 210, No. 72 © 1976, Globe Newspaper Co. • FRIDAY MORNING, SEPTEMBER 10, 1976 ® Telephone 929-2000 Classified 929-1500 Circulation 929-2222 84 Pages — 20 Cents

Limousine case heads for court

Truce set, cabs back at Logan

By James Hammond
Globe Staff

Boston cab drivers agreed last night to go back to work at Logan Airport after receiving assurances from Mayor Kevin H. White that a new limousine service at Logan would suspend operations until after a court hearing Monday dealing with the legality of the service.

But later last night the attorney for Regal Limousine Service said operations had been suspended only until he meets with either the mayor or his representative at 10 this morning.

Arthur White said Regal had suspended service after the windshield and back window of two of its buses were shattered and the tires slashed in separate incidents around noon, at the airport and at Kendall Square, Cambridge.

The mayor told reporters at an impromptu press conference that Regal officials had promised him service would be suspended until after the hearing in Suffolk Superior Court on Monday as long as harassment of its drivers and equipment ceased.

But Atty. White said he spoke with his client at 7 p.m. last night and then with an aide to the mayor at 7:30 p.m. "I said (to the aide) we would not be instituting service until we had the meeting or until after the meeting was concluded," the attorney said.

"We're trying to cool it for a while," he said. "We hope tomorrow's conference will produce a viable alternative we can all live with."

CABS, Page 8

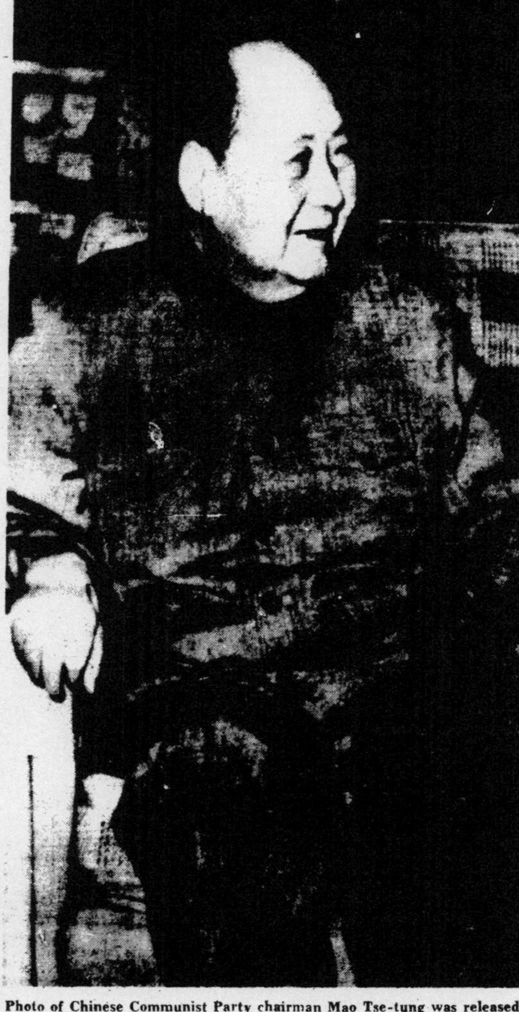

Photo of Chinese Communist Party chairman Mao Tse-tung was released last June 15 by Hsinhua, official Chinese news agency. Caption accompanying picture, however, did not say when it was taken. (AP photo)

'All men must die, but death can vary in its significance.'
— MAO TSE-TUNG

Mao Tse-tung is dead; succession in doubt

By Peter Griffiths
Reuter

PEKING — Mao Tse-tung, 82-year-old father of modern China and spiritual leader of leftist revolutionaries around the world, died here yesterday, leaving a state of uncertainty that will concern the world.

There is no designated heir to the leadership of one quarter of mankind. None of Mao's subordinates can command the awe and adoration that was heaped on him by 800 million Chinese.

Who eventually takes over may determine the Asian giant's relationships with the Soviet Union and the United States, and changes in such relationships could dramatically alter the international balance of power.

But for the Chinese, global political considerations came secondary to sorrow and mourning over the loss of the man who had guided their nation from being a backward peasant state to the world's fifth nuclear power, with satellites in space and a burgeoning industrial base.

Mao died at 10 minutes past midnight yesterday, Peking time (12:10 P.M. Wednesday EDT), after a long illness. The announcement broadcast to the nation 16 hours later did not specify the illness, but the end of Mao's remarkable career had been expected for some time.

Eight days of memorial ceremonies were scheduled to begin tomorrow and climax with the entire nation of 800 million standing in silent tribute for three minutes.

This final memorial service, unprecedented in China, will be broadcast and televised live.

Mao's death leaves a massive gap in the Peking leadership. His personality is irreplaceable.

MAO, Page 10

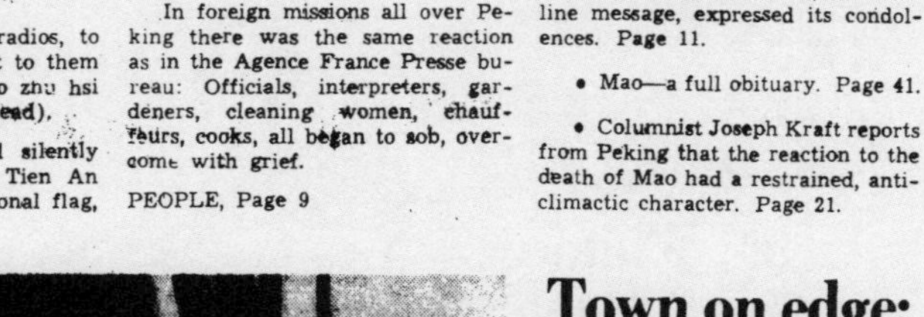

People of Peking weep as city goes into mourning

By Georges Biannic
Agence France Presse

PEKING—As the news of Chairman Mao Tse-tung's death spread through Peking, men and women wept.

Many held transistor radios, to have confirmation of what to them seemed unbelievable: "Mao zhu hsi shih" (Chairman Mao is dead).

Other groups gathered silently in the city center's vast Tien An Men square, near the national flag, flying at half-staff, and the monument to the heroes of the people.

The Chinese people's grief over the death of Chou En-lai was immense, but that for the loss of Mao will be much greater.

In foreign missions all over Peking there was the same reaction as in the Agence France Presse bureau: Officials, interpreters, gardeners, cleaning women, chauffeurs, cooks, all began to sob, overcome with grief.

PEOPLE, Page 9

ON MAO:

- The struggle for power in China now intensifies. At stake is the future course of the most populous nation on earth. Globe diplomatic correspondent William Beecher looks to the future of a China without Mao. Page 12.
- Tributes to Mao flowed to Peking from world leaders. A notable exception was the "other" China — cheering broke out in the streets of Taiwan. The Soviet Union, in a two-line message, expressed its condolences. Page 11.
- Mao—a full obituary. Page 41.
- Columnist Joseph Kraft reports from Peking that the reaction to the death of Mao had a restrained, anticlimactic character. Page 21.

Presidential politics in Massachusetts

Ford's drive stalled by lack of chairman

By Stephen Wermiel
Globe Washington Bureau

WASHINGTON — President Ford's campaign in Massachusetts is having trouble moving out of the starting gate.

The problem is that campaign coordinators here and party officials in Boston have been unable to find a campaign chairman for the Bay State.

It is not as though they have not tried. Anxious to settle on a capable but not overly political figure with ethnic appeal, Ford campaign aides have offered the post unsuccessfully to Vincent Vappi of Milton, who runs the Vappi Construction Co., and Dominic DiMaggio of Wellesley Hills, the former Red Sox baseball player who is now a manufacturer.

If they get off the ground in Massachusetts, Ford strategists say they will wage a serious campaign in the lopsidedly Democratic state that was the only one to support the 1972 Democratic nominee, Sen. George McGovern (D-S.D.).

"They have been assuring me they are going to

REPUBLICANS, Page 15

President Ford told the B'nai B'rith Carter's policies would weaken support to Israel. Page 14.

A confident Carter concentrates elsewhere

By Curtis Wilkie
Globe Staff

COLUMBUS, Ohio — In his first week of formal campaigning, Jimmy Carter is concentrating on the industrial states, carrying out a strategy that assigns secondary importance to New England.

New England does not have a high priority on Carter's schedule at the present, aides acknowledge, because there are relatively few electoral votes in the region. And in its most heavily populated state, Massachusetts, Carter is believed to be far out in front.

Under a system devised by the Carter campaign, key states are determined by their number of votes in the Electoral College, their record of voting Democratic in presidential years, and the closeness of the contest locally between Carter and President Ford.

The key states for Carter are California and the tier of states along the Great Lakes from Illinois to New York.

Massachusetts is not considered a battleground state, according to Carter's Cambridge-based pollster,

STATE, Page 15

Jimmy Carter called again for the firing of FBI Director Clarence Kelley. Page 13.

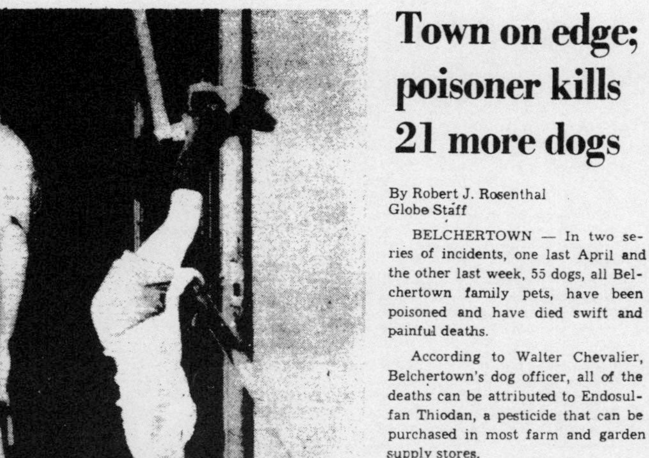

State trooper pays no attention to youngster doing a balancing act at entrance to South Boston High School. City's schools were quiet yesterday on second day of new year. Story, other photos, Page 3. (AP photo)

Town on edge; poisoner kills 21 more dogs

By Robert J. Rosenthal
Globe Staff

BELCHERTOWN — In two series of incidents, one last April and the other last week, 55 dogs, all Belchertown family pets, have been poisoned and have died swift and painful deaths.

According to Walter Chevalier, Belchertown's dog officer, all of the deaths can be attributed to Endosulfan Thiodan, a pesticide that can be purchased in most farm and garden supply stores.

"All I can do is tell people to keep their dogs tied up and have everybody here watch out for strangers," Chevalier said yesterday. "I tell you, the person who is killing these dogs has got to be mental, got to be. Nobody in their right mind would ever do this if they ever saw how these poisoned dogs die."

Last April, 34 Belchertown dogs were poisoned. No suspect or motive was found. Then, early last Friday

BELCHERTOWN, Page 17

One gray one... then another—a hairowing experience

By Gerald Nachman
Knight News Service

IN THIS CORNER

On an otherwise slow, uneventful day, a gray hair appeared without warning on my head — in the lower right hand corner; actually, down in the sideburns where it really doesn't count.

I examined it for two hours, certain that the light was casting weird shadows or that someone had snuck in at night and pasted it on as a joke. It was clear there had been a serious mistake: this gray hair obviously had the wrong boy.

I was convinced it was a freakish occurrence of some kind and that if the hair were ignored it would go away. There is no reason why a person of such youth and vigor should have gray hair. I'm in the prime of life, with everything to look forward to. I have no time for gray hair.

Once, I felt that to have your hair go gray was better than having it fall out on you, but now I don't know.

After that first gray day, I spent long periods in front of various mirrors, ostensibly redoing my tie but in fact searching for new evidence of my sudden deterioration.

A week later, I uncovered a second gray hair, then a third, then two on my chest. I'm afraid to keep looking for fear I may be turning into a little old man right before my eyes.

When my first gray hair appeared, drastic measures were considered, such as wearing a hat at my desk all day or perhaps a small turban; I thought of joining Hare Krishna.

Instead, I shaved very very high up on my right sideburns and nipped off the offending gray hair—by mistake, understand. When it grew back, I got a quick haircut and thought of asking my barber to trim off the gray hairs and leave the good stuff.

I could live with a full head of nice gray hair easier than two or three stray strands, which nobody is aware of but the owner. If you have totally gray hair, you can look "young for your age" but a few straggly strands make you seem sort of old for your hair.

If you look like Albert Einstein or, better still, Harry Reasoner, you have something to show off. I wouldn't mind the gray fox look, and I even fancy silver hair, but I'd like to arrange it so my gray hair would come in salt-and-pepper patterned.

One day recently, I woke up and it looked as if half my hair had turned, if not exactly gray, somewhat ashen. Either I seem about to turn white overnight or I've simply scared myself half to death with all this worry about gray hair.

In short, I'm not so sure if I'm going gray or just going crazy.

Hobson hits 3-run homer, Red Sox win fifth straight, 5-3

Campbell wins 12th as Royals fall (Page 21)

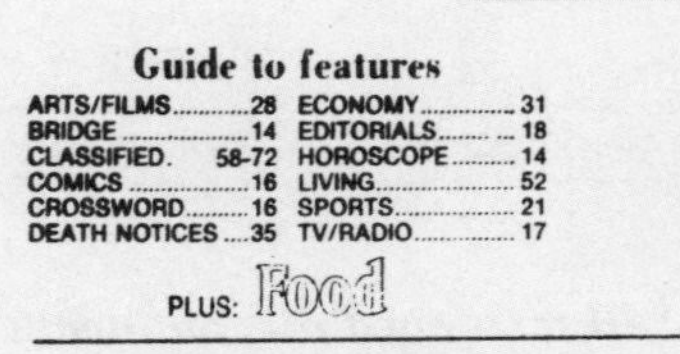

Guide to features

ARTS/FILMS 28
BRIDGE 14
CLASSIFIED 58-72
COMICS 16
CROSSWORD 16
DEATH NOTICES 35
ECONOMY 31
EDITORIALS 18
HOROSCOPE 14
LIVING 52
SPORTS 21
TV/RADIO 17

PLUS: Food

The Boston Globe

Damp town races

WEDNESDAY—Humid, rain likely

THURSDAY—Less humid, 80s

HIGH TIDE—1:20 a.m., 1:46 p.m.

FULL REPORT—PAGE 14

LOTTERY NUMBER, Page 14

Vol. 212, No. 48 © 1977, Globe Newspaper Co. • WEDNESDAY MORNING, AUGUST 17, 1977 • Telephone 929-2000 • Classified 929-1500 Circulation 929-2222 • 72 Pages—20 Cents

Senate offered ethics code

By Robert L. Turner
Globe Staff

A proposed code of ethics for the Massachusetts Senate was sent to the membership yesterday, receiving reactions ranging from lukewarm to enthusiastic. It is expected to be approved within two months.

The six-point code, prepared by the Senate Ethics Committee, would require, for the first time, substantial financial disclosure by senators and candidates for the Senate. Other provisions in the code would:

- Limit lobbyists' gifts to senators.
- Provide that campaign funds not be mixed with personal funds.
- Limit senators' right to appear before state agencies for a fee.
- Prevent full-time Senate employees from working at another job during regular business hours.
- Give the Ethics Committee the power to investigate complaints on its own.

Although some senators voiced little eagerness for the code, the committee members and the Senate leadership have done extensive lobbying with the membership over the past two months, and committee chairman Chester G. Atkins (D-Harvard), said yesterday: "I think the Senate as a whole is very comfortable with it."

The code must now go through the Rules Committee before reaching the Senate floor, probably in September, but approval is expected with few, if any, changes.

Sen. David H. Locke (R-Wellesley) said yesterday he had "no problem" with the disclosure or other provisions.

ETHICS, Page 8

Angry White to Comr. Paul: Cut that fleet

By Walter V. Robinson
Globe Staff

Boston Mayor Kevin H. White angrily rebuked Fire Comr. George Paul yesterday for the department's failure to quickly reduce the number of automobiles in its fleet, as White ordered a month ago, according to City Hall sources.

At the same time, the sources said, White summoned to his office Richard Sinnott, the city's licensing chief, to inform him he will no longer have a city car at his disposal.

The assignment of Fire Department vehicles to Sinnott for 17 years was detailed nearly two months ago in a Globe Spotlight Team series focusing on abuses of Fire Department automobiles.

George Regan, the mayor's press secretary, confirmed last night that Paul had been summoned to White's office.

Regan said that the mayor "was very displeased by the fact that the Fire Department had not reduced its cars by 20 percent, as he ordered July 15. To put

WHITE, Page 9

Elvis is dead at 42

Elvis Presley performs in concert in Lincoln, Neb., in photo taken June 20 of this year. (UPI photo)

Stricken at home; heart condition blamed

United Press International

MEMPHIS – Elvis Presley, the gyrating king of rock 'n' roll who changed the face of music when he growled "You Ain't Nothin' But A Hound Dog" two decades ago, died yesterday at the age of 42. An erratic heartbeat led to his death.

The millionaire singer – "Elvis the Pelvis" when he burst upon the world in the mid-1950s and "The King" now – died on the floor of a bathroom at Graceland, his 18-room mansion.

He had visited a dentist Monday night and played racquet ball with members of his entourage until 6 a.m. His doctor said he may have died at 9 a.m.; but his body was not discovered by road manager Jerry Esposito until 2:30 p.m.

Dr. George Nichopolous, the singer's physician, said he arrived "at the mansion about 2:35, the time the ambulance was leaving. I am sure he was dead at that time."

Dr. Jerry Francisco, the Shelby County medical examiner, said an autopsy indicated cardiac

PRESLEY, Page 13

Elvis Presley on stage in 1956

The swivel-hipped prophet of rock

By Ernie Santosuosso
Globe Staff

If, indeed, the Beatles took the rock revolution into a far more sophisticated area, Elvis Presley certainly must be credited for having led the charge.

The truck driver-turned-guitarist almost singlehandedly changed the profile of popular music in the '50s when he was discovered on the Dorsey Brothers television series. His departure into the Army in 1958 served only to enhance his mystique. And then there were the lucrative — almost $1 million per picture — MGM features, and eventually his unexplained disappearance from the public's glare.

The advent of Elvis Presley signaled the reshaping of country music and an eventual mass swing of youth away from the music of their elders to a mongrelized form labeled rock-a-billy. It was difficult to discern where country left off and rock-a-billy began. The elements were irresistible: twanging guitars, danceable rhythms and relentless percussion.

The Presley push was launched with his recording on the modest Sun label of "Heartbreak Hotel," followed by a deluge of hits in the middle '50s: "Hound Dog," "Love Me Tender," "Blue Suede Shoes," "Jailhouse Rock" and "Don't Be Cruel."

Elvis's arrival turned the music market around. His success spawned the surfacing of Jerry Lee Lewis, Chuck Berry and an army of visitors to the Dick Clark "American Bandstand" television series.

They bought his records as if they were collectors' items. A Presley single was an automatic candidate for Top 10 status. Meanwhile, more staid music fans bravely dismissed the happening as a fad.

But Elvis wouldn't go away.

When the movies stopped beckoning, Elvis retreated to Memphis until his wily manager, Col. Tom Parker,

APPRECIATION, page 13

Carter to name Alabama judge as FBI director

By Ronald J. Ostrow
Los Angeles Times

WASHINGTON — President Carter will name US District Judge Frank M. Johnson Jr. of Montgomery, Ala., today to be the next FBI director, the Los Angeles Times was told yesterday.

Informed sources said Attorney General Griffin Bell, rejecting the candidates proposed by a presidentially appointed selection committee, has turned to Johnson, 58, a Republican considered one of the leading civil rights activists on the Federal bench.

White House press secretary Jody Powell would neither confirm nor deny that Johnson was Carter's choice to succeed Clarence Kelley, who has headed the agency since July 1973.

Johnson turned down the job last December when then-President-elect Carter first discussed it with him at a meeting in Atlanta. He cited financial and family reasons, the same grounds he used when he later rejected Bell's offer of a job as deputy attorney general.

Bell is understood to have convinced Johnson on the FBI job by arguing that the post will be among the most important appointments Carter makes during his Presidency, and that the men proposed by the FBI search committee lacked the experience and stature Carter was seeking. Among those recommended by the panel was Massachusetts Superior Court Judge John Irwin.

Johnson could not be reached yesterday. His brother, Jiminy, said he thought the judge had "gone fishing."

Bell was questioned as recently as two weeks ago about the possibility of turning to Johnson. At that time, he merely noted that Johnson previously rejected the job.

But it was learned that Bell,

JUDGE FRANK M. JOHNSON JR. . . . school integration pioneer

dissatisfied with the candidates advanced by the selection committee and with an FBI official he had considered, decided to make still another approach to Johnson. He is known to regard Johnson as a man of unimpeachable integrity and repute.

An Administration source said last night that Johnson's stature was considered great enough to offset any criticism directed at the Administration on grounds that the search committee had failed to come up with worthy candidates for the job.

Johnson, named to the Federal judiciary by President Eisenhower in 1955, pioneered in ordering the integration of Southern schools. He has often clashed with Alabama Gov. George Wallace and, through his judicial orders, he has put the Federal

FBI, Page 17

US pushes to end bias on Federal contracts

By Rachelle Patterson
Globe Washington Bureau

WASHINGTON — The Carter Administration is moving on several fronts in what officials say are efforts to eliminate bias in employment among Federal contractors.

The push comes at a time when the White House is in the midst of reorganizing the bureaucracy and deciding which Federal agencies should be responsible for enforcement of civil-rights laws and regulations.

According to Howard Glickstein, a member of the reorganization staff at the Office of Management and Budget studying the civil-rights issue, the Administration is determined to combat discrimination in employment. "Companies who want to have Federal contracts will have to comply with the rules," he said.

But William Taylor, director of the National Center for Policy Review at Catholic University and a civil-rights authority, raises the possibility that some of the recent fervor to crack down on bias may be self-serving.

Some of the Federal agencies responsible for civil-rights enforcement may just want to "make their own records look good" to save their jobs, Taylor said.

The Administration's latest effort came yesterday with an announcement by the Labor Department of proposed regulations to increase the hiring of women in the building trades. The regulations would set specific goals and timetables for contractors to allow women in the male-dominated construction industry.

BIAS, Page 6

Death threats drove boy to police in Herbits case

By Ray Richard
Globe Staff

The 16-year-old boy who said he was present when an elderly Newton attorney and his wife were murdered broke eight months of silence because of continuing threats on his life, The Globe has been told.

Frightened by the threats, the youth reported them to police Friday. It was then, according to sources, that he blurted out that the threats had come from the man he said murdered Atty. William Herbits, 84, and his wife Julia, 72, and that he identified the killer as Carroll K. St. Germain, 44, of Randolph.

St. Germain subsequently was charged with the murders and is being held without bail while awaiting trial. The youth, whose identity has not been made public, is being protected by State Police at an undisclosed location.

The youth talked twice yesterday with Middlesex County Assistant Dist. Atty. J. William Codinha, who was assigned to prosecute the case by Dist. Atty. John Droney. The two met at a site Codinha described only as "a public building" in the Boston area, but not in the district attorney's office, and later talked by telephone. The youth at first seemed guarded in his conversation, but later appeared very much at ease, Codinha said.

During St. Germain's arraignment Monday afternoon, Assistant Dist. Atty. John Markey said that the youth said he had accompanied St. Germain to the two-story stucco Herbits house in Newton Centre and had witnessed the murders. Markey said the boy saw St. Germain enter the house with a rope, a gun and a club. The

TEEN, Page 15

DAVID BERKOWITZ

Berkowitz pleads innocent; insanity plea probable

David Berkowitz pleaded innocent yesterday to the murder of Stacy Moskowitz. His attorney said he probably would rely on an insanity defense. Page 57.

Cox report — the lost momentum

By Nick King
Globe Staff

NEWS ANALYSIS

The 8-month-old drive to overhaul the Massachusetts court system faces a critical deadline today amid growing indications that the judicial reform movement is bogged down in politics.

The Legislature's Judiciary Committee, which has had the proposed court changes before it since January, hasn't met to discuss the issues for several months — despite today's deadline for reporting the bill to the full House.

The inaction and the impending deadline endanger not only the chances for court changes this year, they also threaten to bring into the open the friction between the two Judiciary Committee chairmen and to underscore the inattention and lack of leadership given the issue by them and by Gov. Michael S. Dukakis, who has said he supports substantial changes.

"We haven't even had a serious meeting on court reform," one House member of the committee said yesterday. "It's so complex, technical and unemotional an issue and no one's been carrying the standard for it. I think it's in trouble."

Dukakis is the person most responsible for the move to overhaul the courts. The proposed legislation was recommended last December by his Select Committee on Judicial Needs, chaired by Harvard Law Prof. Archibald Cox.

At the time Dukakis declared court reform his top priority. But since the publicity given the committee's findings, Dukakis has all but stayed out of the debate on the issue, in part because he is barely on speaking terms with Sen. Alan D. Sisitsky (D-Springfield), Senate chairman of the committee.

For his part, Sisitsky supports most of the major recommendations, including a state takeover of court costs, a centralized administration of the court system, and a restructuring of the District and Superior courts.

But Sisitsky, in turn, is barely on speaking terms with Rep. Michael F. Flaherty (D-South Boston), House chairman of the committee. And Flaherty, who has in the past espoused court reform in broad terms, is now publicly opposed to all but a few of the proposed major changes.

The fate of the bill rests with Sisitsky and Flaherty, whose antagonism is highlighted by their conflicting strategies.

Flaherty yesterday said he was unconcerned with the deadline because

COURTS, Page 8

Publisher

1978 - 1997

WILLIAM O. TAYLOR (1932-) On succeeding his father in 1978, the second William O. presided over the newspaper's complete transition to computerization in virtually every department. As chairman of Affiliated Publications, he oversaw acquisitions in radio, television, magazines, books and cellular-telephone technology, then moved to sell those media properties and return the company to its newspaper roots. He committed the paper to color in its news and advertising sections, initiated six zoned sections in the Sunday Globe, built a satellite printing plant in Billerica, and added a preprint distribution facility in Westwood.

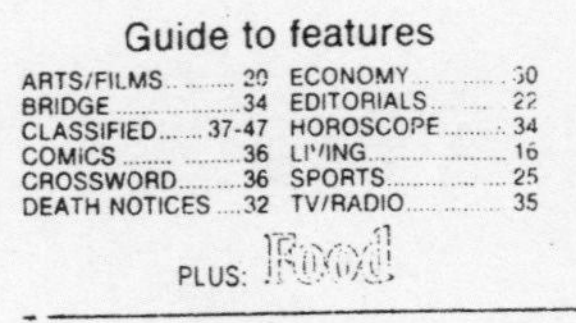

Guide to features

ARTS/FILMS	20	ECONOMY	30
BRIDGE	34	EDITORIALS	22
CLASSIFIED	37-47	HOROSCOPE	34
COMICS	36	LIVING	16
CROSSWORD	36	SPORTS	25
DEATH NOTICES	32	TV/RADIO	35

PLUS: Food

The Boston Globe

The age of shovelry

WEDNESDAY—Sun, around 30
THURSDAY—Sunny, 30s
HIGH TIDE—11:31 a.m.
FULL REPORT—PAGE 34

Lottery number, Page 34

Vo. 213, No. 39 © 1978, Globe Newspaper Co. WEDNESDAY MORNING, FEBRUARY 8, 1978 Telephone 929-2000 Classified 929-1500 Circulation 929-2222 48 Pages—20 Cents

Worst storm of century

17 die . . . record high tides . . . up to 4 feet of snow. . . winds gust up to 125 mph . . . highway traffic banned

Complete Storm Coverage On Pages 2, 3, 4, 5, 23, 33

By Charles E. Claffey
Globe Staff

A savage blizzard left southern New England a desolate wasteland this morning after a two-day pounding that paralyzed the area and dumped as much as 4 feet of snow.

A spokesman for the National Weather Service in Boston called the storm the worst of the century to batter the three-state region of Massachusetts, Rhode Island and Connecticut.

Gov. Michael S. Dukakis declared a state of emergency yesterday and ordered the mobilization of the 3000 Massachusetts National Guardsmen. He said: "The weather situation that now exists in the state of Massachusetts is the worst in its history."

The governor said the state of emergency will continue through today.

He also announced that President Carter had agreed to grant emergency assistance to the state under the Federal Disaster Relief Act.

He urged all residents to stay home except those involved in emergency work, such as utility workers or hospital employees.

The blizzard, which started at midday Monday packed hurricane-force winds and left well over 25 inches in the Boston area. Southern Massachusetts communities, including Brockton, received 4 feet of snow.

The governor banned traveling on highways anywhere else or "under any circumstances except that which relates to the health and safety of the people of our citizenry."

Almost all roads, including the Massachusetts Turnpike and Rte. 128, were impassable yesterday.

Boston snowfall in the 24-hour period that ended at 7 p.m. yesterday totaled 23.6 inches, a record for that time period.

The prior record of 21.4 inches was set in the last storm only 18 days ago.

Gusts in the raging northeaster reached 125 miles per hour on Mt. Washington and almost 100 miles on Newburyport's Plum Island.

At least 17 deaths were attributed to the storm in the three southern New England states.

The storm imposed hardships on many. Elderly people requiring prescription drugs were unable in many cases to get their medicine.

Numerous commuters stranded in the city shivered in unheated hotel rooms.

Countless residents were unable to replenish low food supplies. And other with limited fuel supplies set thermostats at low levels, fearful that fuel trucks would be unable to get through for several days.

The highest tides recorded in this century

STORM, Page 5

STORM VICTIM — The SS Peter Stuyvesant, used as a cocktail lounge for the adjacent Anthony's Pier 4, capsized yesterday. The vessel, anchored in concrete, was originally used for Hudson River Cruises. (Globe photo by David L. Ryan)

With worst of it over, here's what to expect

HIGHWAYS—All state highways east of Worcester and north of Cape Cod closed until at least tomorrow. Major streets in most communities impassable. Side streets may not be cleared until Monday.

RAPID TRANSIT—MBTA operating subways in tunnels only. No Red Line stops at Kendall or Charles. No surface transportation until at least Thursday.

AIRLINES—Logan Airport closed until at least Thursday. Passengers should call airlines for scheduling information.

RAILROADS—No commuter railroads north and south of Boston until at least Thursday. Amtrak trains to New York and south may resume running Thursday.

FLOODS—More flooding expected when next high tide reaches coastal communities about noon.

SCHOOLS—All metropolitan Boston schools closed until at least Friday.

EMERGENCY HELP—Boston City Hall snow-emergency center telephone numbers: 725-3050 for electricity, gas and routine police and fire problems; 725-4000 for heat and other human-service problems; 911 for emergency fire and police. Those with questions on Flooding may call 223-1197 or 223-4066, federal assistance numbers.

GOVERNMENT OFFICES—Federal, state, county courts and city offices all closed through Thursday. Some skeleton staffs on duty. State Police in Framingham coordinating towing of stranded cars on state highways.

BUSINESSES—Most businesses in metropolitan Boston closed through Thursday.

HOSPITALS—All major metropolitan Boston hospitals open and operating with reduced staffs. Some problems with ambulance service.

POWER—Power restored to most homes in eastern Massachusetts.

Crates of 4000 live chickens toppled as a truck overturned at Massachusetts avenue and Southampton street yesterday. Police guard truck, owned by Alfieri Co. of Norwich, Conn., after chasing looters from scene. (Globe photo by Matt Storin)

Cruel seas smash the coastline

By Michael Kenney
Globe Staff

Coastline communities were savaged by hurricane-force winds which hurled icy ocean waves into them behind the cover of blinding snow Monday and yesterday.

In Scituate, five-year-old Amy Lanzikos of Jericho road was lost during evacuation operations when a rescue boat was washed off a causeway into the storm-wracked harbor early yesterday morning. Her mother was among those rescued and was being treated for exposure at the South Shore Hospital.

A Gloucester pilot boat with five persons on board, which had been sent to the aid of a grounded tanker, was reported missing off Salem Harbor and feared sunk.

COASTLINE, Page 4

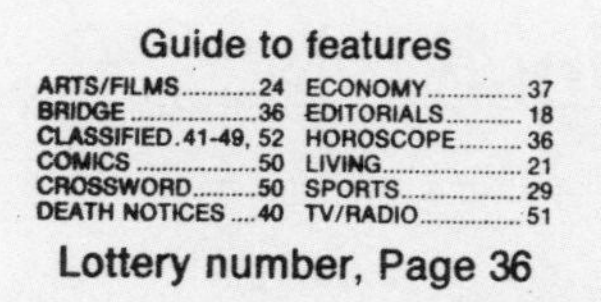

Guide to features

ARTS/FILMS	24	ECONOMY	37
BRIDGE	36	EDITORIALS	18
CLASSIFIED	41-49, 52	HOROSCOPE	36
COMICS	50	LIVING	21
CROSSWORD	50	SPORTS	29
DEATH NOTICES	40	TV/RADIO	51

Lottery number, Page 36

The Boston Globe

Old man shiver

MONDAY—Clearing, 60s
TUESDAY—Chance of rain, 65-70
HIGH TIDE — 1 p.m.
FULL REPORT — PAGE 36

Vol. 214, No. 80© 1978, Globe Newspaper Co. • MONDAY MORNING, SEPTEMBER 18, 1978 ® Telephone 929-2000 Classified 929-1500 Circulation 929-2222 52 Pages — 20 Cents

13-DAY SUMMIT CRACKS STALEMATE IN MIDEAST

Camp David accords:

- Egyptian-Israeli peace treaty to be signed within three months.
- Withdrawal of Israeli forces in West Bank-Gaza Strip to specified garrisons.
- Five-year transitional period of civil self-rule for Palestinians in the West Bank-Gaza Strip.
- Phased Israeli withdrawal from Sinai to begin three to nine months after signing of peace treaty. Final withdrawal to be within three years.
- Israeli airfields in Sinai to be returned to Egyptian civilian control.
- Normal relations between Egypt and Israel to be established at completion of first major Israeli withdrawal.
- No new Israeli settlements during negotiations.

To be negotiated:

- Negotiations to determine final status of West Bank-Gaza to involve Palestinians in the area and Jordan, if it agrees.
- Security arrangements that may involve UN forces.

teachings, there's a
tradition that the greatest achievement of a human being is to turn
his enemy into a friend . . ."
Menachem Begin

President Jimmy Carter applauds as Israeli Prime Minister Menachem Begin (left) and Egyptian President Anwar Sadat embrace at White House ceremony last night. (UPI photo)

Self-rule plan for West Bank

Egypt pledges peace if Israel leaves Sinai

By Curtis Wilkie
Globe Washington Bureau

WASHINGTON — Israel and Egypt reached agreement last night on plans that call for a total Israeli withdrawal from the Sinai desert and a limited withdrawal from the West Bank and the Gaza strip, where an autonomous government for Palestinian residents would be created during a five-year transitional period.

The dramatic agreement came at the end of the Camp David summit where Israeli Prime Minister Menachem Begin and Egyptian President Anwar Sadat have been locked in discussions with President Jimmy Carter for 13 days.

The two Mideast leaders signed two documents outlining their agreement late last night at ceremonies at the White House and were hailed by Carter for their "courage and wisdom . . . determination, vision and flexibility."

But Sadat's foreign minister, Mohammed Ibrahim Kamel, reportedly resigned following the accord and did not attend the White House ceremony, ABC radio said. Kamel, who had come to Washington with Sadat, followed in the footsteps of a predecessor in the office, Ismail Fahmy, who resigned after Sadat's dramatic trip to Jerusalem last Nov. 19.

The prayers for peace that the three men requested at the outset of the summit "have been answered far beyond any expectation," Carter said.

Carter will give a report on the peace talks to a joint session of Congress at 8 tonight.

During the ceremonies in the East Room, Begin and Sadat praised each other and embraced while a hastily assembled crowd of diplomats and members of Congress cheered heartily.

Indeed, Begin, who has often looked so dour, seemed to upstage Sadat for a change with his warm response and humorous remarks.

The two documents signed by Begin and Sadat were described as a "framework for peace in the Mideast" and "a framework for peace between Egypt and Israel" and could lead to actual treaties within a matter of months.

There were still unresolved disputes between the two countries, and Carter pointed out that the long Mideast conflict would "not be settled overnight."

However, the agreements by the Israeli and Egyptian leaders set in motion a number of steps to be taken shortly in the Mideast.

Full details of the agreements and the texts of the documents were to be released today, but last night American officials disclosed some highlights in a briefing shortly before ceremonies in the East Room of the White House.

The first document deals with the perplexing question of the West Bank, the territory that is populated by Palestinians and was controlled by Jordan until Israel seized it in the 1967 war.

SUMMIT, Page 2

Historic Summit: What the 3 leaders said

'These two leaders . . . turned on the resources within them to keep the chances for peace alive.'

CARTER: He'll report to Congress tonight

When we first arrived at Camp David, the first thing upon which we agreed was to ask the people of the world to pray that our negotiations would be successful.

Those prayers have been answered, proved beyond any expectations. We're privileged to witness tonight a significant achievement in the cause of peace, an achievement no one thought possible a year ago, or even a month ago, an achievement that reflects the courage and wisdom of these two leaders.

Through 13 long days at Camp David, we have seen them display determination and vision and flexibility which was needed to make this agreement come to pass. All of us owe them our gratitude and respect. They know that they will always have my personal admiration.

There are still great difficulties that remain, and many hard issues to be settled. The questions that have brought warfare and bitterness to the Middle East in the past 30 years will not be settled overnight. But we should all recognize the substantial achievements that have been made.

CARTER, Page 3

'We came . . . with all the good will and faith we possess and we left . . . with a renewed sense of hope and inspiration.'

SADAT: American role is indispensable

Dear President Carter: In this historic moment, I would like to express to you my heartfelt congratulations and appreciation. For long days and nights you devoted your time and energy to the pursuit of peace.

You have been most gracious when you took the gigantic step of convening this meeting. The challenge . . . the challenge was great, and the risks were high, but so was your determination. You made a commitment to be a full partner in the peace talks. I'm happy to say that you have honored your commitment.

The signing of the framework for the comprehensive peace settlement has a significance far beyond the event. It signals the emergence of a new peace initiative with the American nation in the heart of the entire process.

In the weeks ahead important decisions have to be made if we are to proceed on the road to peace. We have reaffirmed the faith of the Palestinian people in the ideal of peace. The continuation of your active role is indispensable.

BEGIN, Page 3

'He (Carter) worked harder than our forebears did in Egypt building the pyramids.'

BEGIN: Peace treaties in 3 months or sooner

Mr. President of the United States, Mr. President of the Arab Republic, ladies and gentlemen:

The Camp David conference should be renamed. It was the Jimmy Carter conference.

The President undertook an initiative most imaginative in our time and brought President Sadat and myself and our colleagues, friends and advisers together under one roof. In itself it was a great achievement.

But the President took a great risk for himself and did it with great courage. And it was a famous French field commander who said that it is much more difficult to show civil courage than military courage.

And the President worked. As far as my historic experience is concerned, I think that he worked harder than our forebears did in Egypt building the pyramids.

Yes indeed, he worked day and night. And so did we. Day and night. We used to go to bed anywhere between 3 and 4 o'clock in the morning, arise as we used to since in our boyhood between 5 and 6 and continue working.

SADAT, Page 3

11,000 die in Iran as quake levels city

Associated Press

TEHERAN, Iran — A devastating earthquake that struck a farming region or northeast Iran Saturday killed more than 11,000 persons and destroyed entire cities and villages, the official Pars news agency reported yesterday.

The quake, which US seismologists measured at 7.7 on the Richter scale, was the most powerful in recent Iranian history, officials at the Teheran Geophysics Institute said. US scientists said it also was the strongest quake in the world so far this year.

IRAN, Page 14

NEWS ANALYSIS

Back on the track at last

By William Beecher
Globe Washington Bureau

WASHINGTON — The summit at Camp David, which started out of desperation and with low expectations, seems to have confounded the critics and opened the way to at least a partial peace in the Mideast.

Based on sketchy information from Carter Administration officials at the White House last night, it appears that the peace process, begun so dramatically by Egyptian President Anwar Sadat 10 months ago and stalled since last spring, is back on track.

When Sadat journeyed to Jerusalem last November, he hoped the Israelis would be so buoyed by the prospect of real peace and normal relations that they would gladly exchange some vague statements about their willingness to withdraw from the West Bank and the Gaza Strip for the chance of a peace treaty.

That would have allowed Sadat to have his cake and eat it, too. He could have concluded a separate peace with Israel, allowing him to reduce the weight of defense spending and build up his woesome economy, while telling other Arabs that they could negotiate similar treaties with Israel under general terms he had already arranged.

ANALYSIS, Page 2

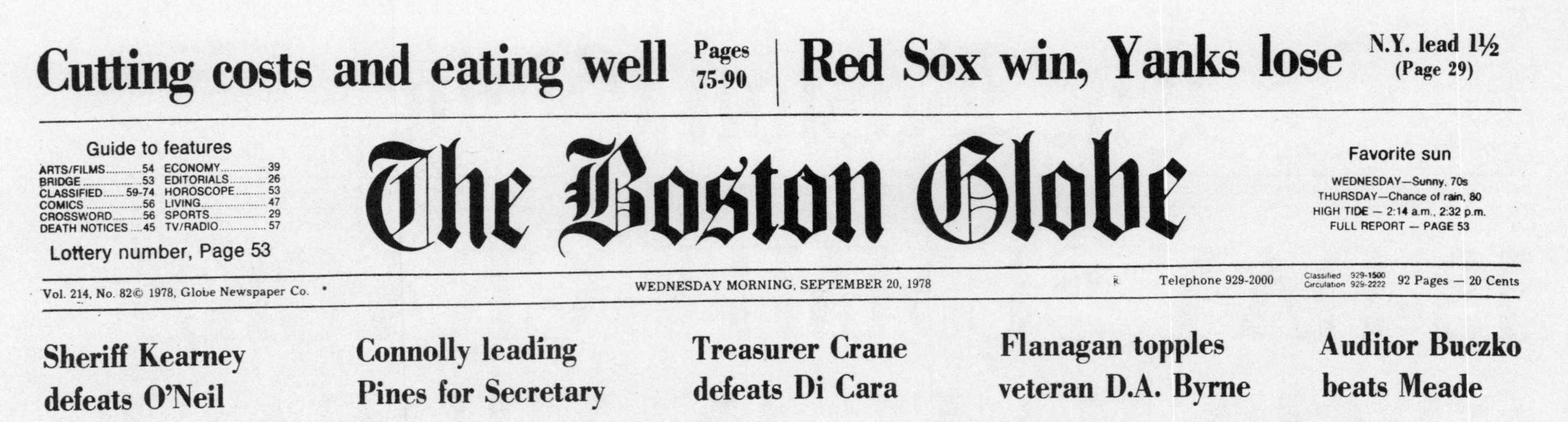

Cutting costs and eating well Pages 75-90 | Red Sox win, Yanks lose N.Y. lead 1½ (Page 29)

Guide to features
ARTS/FILMS....54 ECONOMY....39
BRIDGE....53 EDITORIALS....26
CLASSIFIED....59-74 HOROSCOPE....53
COMICS....56 LIVING....47
CROSSWORD....56 SPORTS....29
DEATH NOTICES....45 TV/RADIO....57
Lottery number, Page 53

The Boston Globe

Favorite sun
WEDNESDAY—Sunny, 70s
THURSDAY—Chance of rain, 80
HIGH TIDE — 2:14 a.m., 2:32 p.m.
FULL REPORT — PAGE 53

Vol. 214, No. 82 © 1978, Globe Newspaper Co. WEDNESDAY MORNING, SEPTEMBER 20, 1978 Telephone 929-2000 Classified 929-1500 Circulation 929-2222 92 Pages — 20 Cents

Sheriff Kearney defeats O'Neil

Connolly leading Pines for Secretary

Treasurer Crane defeats Di Cara

Flanagan topples veteran D.A. Byrne

Auditor Buczko beats Meade

KING UPSETS DUKAKIS

Brooke is leading Nelson

By Martin F. Nolan
Globe Staff

A schizophrenic Democratic electorate nominated a conservative law-and-order candidate for governor yesterday, while giving liberal candidates for US Senate more than 70 per cent of the primary vote.

Gov. Michael S. Dukakis, who seemed invincible during his sweater-clad television appearances during last winter's blizzard, saw his advantage melt like April snowbanks under fiery blasts of criticism from Edward J. King.

King, former director of the Massachusetts Port Authority, rapped the governor's handling of the state's economy, and also focused on "social issues," disagreeing with Dukakis on restoring the death penalty and state funding for abortions.

Bay State Republicans, meanwhile, failed to drift with the rightward nationwide trend of their party. By a comfortable margin, Republican voters rejected the conservative gubernatorial candidacy of West Roxbury businessman Edward F. King (no relation to his Democratic namesake).

The Republican King had campaigned to the right of House Minority Leader Francis W. Hatch Jr. of Beverly, who had benefited from publicity gained when he sued the commonwealth to release the names of tax delinquents.

In the GOP senatorial primary, Edward W. Brooke, one of the most liberal members of the US Senate, held a slim early lead over his conservative opponent, Avi Nelson, a former radio personality.

In the Democratic senatorial contest, neither the liberal credentials nor the first name of the nominee was in doubt, as Secretary of State Paul Guzzi and US Rep. Paul Tsongas of Lowell swapped leads during the early morning hours' tabulation.

Both Guzzi and Tsongas campaigned as liberals. The third-place finisher in the senatorial contest, Boston School Committee member Kathleen Sullivan Alioto, portrayed herself as a moderate. Conservative Howard Phillips and liberal State Rep. Elaine Noble trailed in the senatorial balloting.

ELECTION, Page 24

Hatch GOP's governor choice

By Robert L. Turner
Globe Staff

Gov. Michael S. Dukakis was expelled from office yesterday by the Democratic Party he sought to reform, by the cities he took as his special charge and by Edward J. King, the former director of the Massachusetts Port Authority, who said he offered voters "a clear choice."

King in November will face House minority leader Francis W. Hatch Jr. of Beverly, a comfortable winner over conservative West Roxbury businessman Edward F. King.

Democrat Edward J. King said the voters, in defeating Dukakis, had "sent a message loud and clear for all to hear."

But Hatch responded, "I hear you Massachusetts," and said he now offers "a clear choice" to moderate Democrats who had voted for Dukakis — his target for more than a year.

King and Hatch both predicted victory.

Lt. Gov. Thomas P. O'Neill, who had no opposition, was at Dukakis' headquarters last night and made no public comment, but he now will be teamed with King against Hatch and William I. Cowin, the former commissioner of Administration, who appeared to be a comfortable Republican winner over Rep. Peter McDowell.

Dukakis, looking somewhat shaken but in full control of himself as he conceded last night, said that, when he took office, "We rolled up our sleeves and went to work, we made tough decisions; they were disappointing to many, they were obviously not very pleasant, but they had to be made."

Dukakis was clearly not the victim of what some had predicted would be a conservative tide throughout the primaries. Liberal candidates won the key Republican races and dominated many Democratic contests, including the race for the US Senate nomination.

Dukakis himself was mystified. "For whatever reason," he said, "the voters wanted something else." He said the mechanics of the race are something "the political scientists and commentators are going to be spending a lot of time on."

Earlier, however, in an afternoon interview at his Brookline home, Dukakis had said he agreed that much of his opposition might be caused, essentially, by "the price of hamburg" — the phrase Francis W. Sargent used four years ago as the reason for his own defeat at the hands of Dukakis.

"I don't think there's anything so unsettling as a severe and sustained peacetime inflation," Dukakis said.

It was clear, however, that inflation was not Dukakis' only problem. By his own estimate, the candidacy of former Cambridge mayor Barbara Ackermann pulled many more votes from him than from King — some of them avowedly as a protest.

Even so, Dukakis' camp had not seen the trouble coming. Campaign manager Richard A. Geisser admitted yesterday there had been some "complacency" in the campaign before Labor Day, and a poll of the Dukakis campaign staff the day before the balloting showed an average prediction: Dukakis 56 percent; King 37 percent; Ackermann 7 percent.

King, however, in a long campaign that spent more than half a million dollars, moved doggedly to keep Dukakis' wounds bare and to collect constituencies that Dukakis had alienated.

In what may now be seen as a key event in the campaign, King attempted to attract these groups during an Aug. 31 television debate by repeating over and over a list of issues on which he thought the people agreed with his conservative views.

These included his opposition to abortion and busing and his support for capital punishment, for mandatory jail sentences for drug pushers and persons who break and enter, and for raising the drinking age to 21.

In addition, he hopped on an issue that has created an instant revolution in the political establishment of other states — an issue that he repeated, in shirtsleeves at his victory celebration last night.

GOVERNOR, Page 25

State's key contests

US Senate
996 of 2201 precincts

Democratic		
Alioto	65,224	20%
Guzzi	104,441	32%
Noble	21,198	7%
Phillips	25,446	8%
Tsongas	105,928	33%
Republican		
Brooke*	60,344	53%
Nelson	53,688	47%

Governor
977 of 2201 precincts

Democratic		
Dukakis*	141,756	43%
Ackermann	22,928	7%
E. J. King	168,038	50%
Republican		
Hatch	57,567	55%
E. F. King	46,282	45%

Secretary
543 of 2201 precincts

Democratic		
Connolly	x40,158	26%
Crosby	21,097	13%
Fulham	7621	5%
Galvin	13,842	9%
Hennigan	15,241	10%
Pines	39,946	26%
Vigliotti	17,427	11%

Treasurer
309 of 2201 precincts

Democratic		
Crane*	46,191	50%
Blacke	4549	5%
Cacchiotti	5462	6%
DiCara	29,743	32%
Lopes	2784	3%
Moore	4197	4%

*Incumbent

Turnout: Estimated near 40 percent

US Sen. Edward W. Brooke and his mother watch election returns on television. In lower photo, Newman Flanagan gets victory hug at East Boston celebration after he defeated incumbent Garrett Byrne for Democratic nomination for Suffolk district attorney.

SENATOR

Tsongas, Guzzi in close fight

By Norman Lockman
Globe Staff

US Sen. Edward W. Brooke held a slim but steady lead over his conservative challenger, Avi Nelson, in the early hours of this morning, but Nelson refused to concede defeat in the Republican race for the Senate nomination.

The situation was much the same among the frontrunning Democrats seeking the Senate nomination. US Rep. Paul Tsongas of Lowell had a slight lead over Secretary of State Paul Guzzi of Newton early this morning, but neither was willing to make any conclusions publicly about the outcome.

Boston School Committeewoman Kathleen Sullivan Alioto conceded defeat at 11:20 p.m.

State Rep. Elaine Noble (D-Back Bay) and Howard Phillips, the conservative Democratic candidate, were out of the running.

At about 1 a.m., Nelson thanked his supporters gathered at the Sheraton Boston Hotel and said he still hadn't seen enough returns to say that he could not win. At that time he trailed Brooke by about 6 percentage points with 35 percent of the vote counted.

Brooke told his cheering supporters at the Parker House Hotel at about 1:30 a.m., "From everything that I have heard . . . Avi Nelson will soon make a concession speech. And when he does, I will graciously accept."

Incomplete and unofficial returns showed Brooke leading in all the state's major cities. Nelson was running ahead of Brooke in the Boston antibusing wards and in several towns south of Boston.

SENATOR, Page 25

Elated supporters mob Edward J. King after he defeated incumbent Michael S. Dukakis to win Democratic gubernatorial nomination. (Globe photo by Bill Brett)

King momentum provides no guarantee next time

By Robert Healy
Globe Staff

POLITICAL CIRCUIT

As Atty. Gen. Francis Bellotti will tell him, it is one thing to knock over an incumbent governor in the primary, and it is quite another thing to then go on and win the November election.

What Edward J. King appears to have accomplished yesterday in defeating Gov. Michael Dukakis is no small thing, and he will have momentum coming off the primary.

King was the candidate of big labor and big business. He ran the most expensive and well-financed primary campaign of any challenger vs. incumbent in recent history. His primary opponent, Barbara Ackermann, tagged him in the debate with being the candidate of big business and he admitted to having extensive labor support

Bringing down an incumbent governor leaves deep divisions in the Democratic party and there is no way that Dukakis' people will suport King. It will be too easy for them to move to Frank Hatch, whom they may not like, but they respect.

POLITICAL CIRCUIT, Page 27

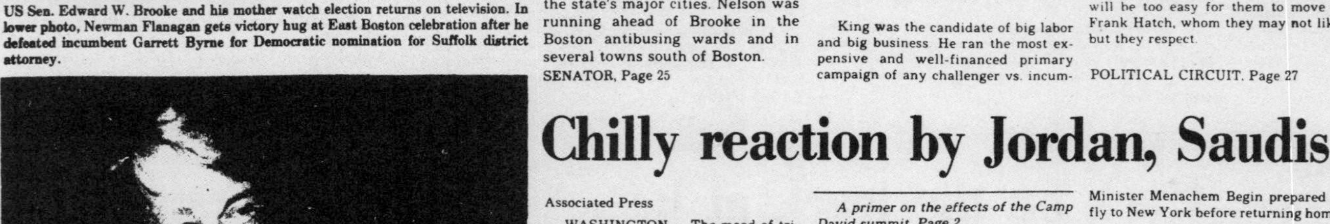

Chilly reaction by Jordan, Saudis

Associated Press

A primer on the effects of the Camp David summit. Page 2.

WASHINGTON — The mood of triumph that swept the capital with the successful end of the Camp David summit was tempered yesterday by sharp words from Jordan's King Hussein and lingering differences over interpretation of the accords.

While President Jimmy Carter and the leaders of Egypt and Israel tried to maintain the momentum toward peace, Amman announced that "Jordan is not obligated morally or materially by the agreements signed at the Camp David summit."

Saudi Arabia also expressed reservations yesterday about the outcome of the summit, saying the agreements did not constitute an acceptable "final peace framework."

But an official Saudi communique issued after an emergency Cabinet meeting refrained from outright rejection and did not criticize Egyptian President Anwar Sadat.

The announcements from Jordan and Saudi Arabia came as Israeli Prime Minister Menachem Begin prepared to fly to New York before returning home.

Minutes after Begin's plane took off from Andrews Air Force Base, Secretary of State Cyrus Vance left for the Mideast. He arrives in Amman today.

President Sadat planned to fly to Rabat, Morocco, today to meet with King Hussein before returning to Cairo.

The Jordanian spokesman said Hussein discussed the summit agree-

MIDEAST, Page 6

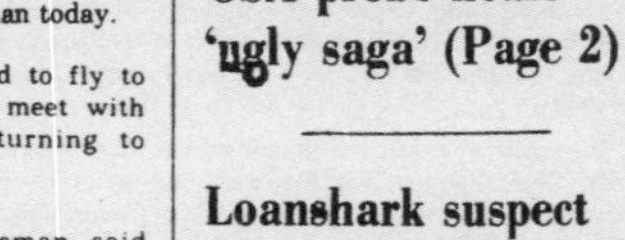

Natural gas bill wins test (Page 58)

GSA probe hears 'ugly saga' (Page 2)

Loanshark suspect surrenders (Page 3)

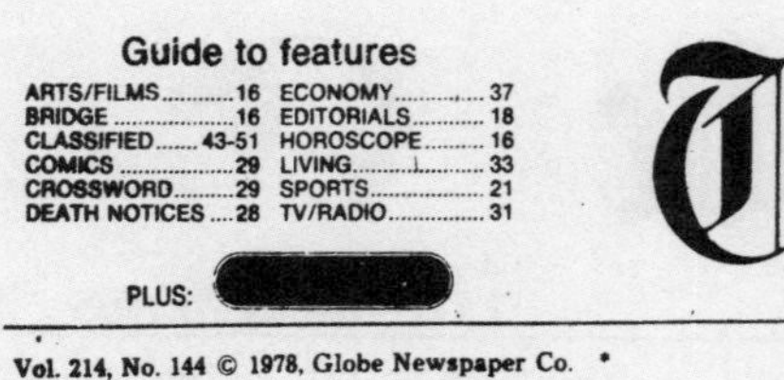

Guide to features

ARTS/FILMS	16	ECONOMY	37
BRIDGE	16	EDITORIALS	18
CLASSIFIED	43-51	HOROSCOPE	16
COMICS	29	LIVING	33
CROSSWORD	29	SPORTS	21
DEATH NOTICES	28	TV/RADIO	31

PLUS:

The Boston Globe

Murky beaucoup

TUESDAY—Cloudy, around 40
WEDNESDAY—Sunny, in the 40s
HIGH TIDE — 3:25 a.m. 3:39 p.m.
FULL REPORT — PAGE 16

Lottery number, Page 16

Vol. 214, No. 144 © 1978, Globe Newspaper Co. • TUESDAY MORNING, NOVEMBER 21, 1978 ® Telephone 929-2000 Classified 929-1500 Circulation 929-2222 76 Pages — 20 Cents

409 members of cult found dead in camp

500-900 are sought in jungle of Guyana

Cult founder, family died with followers

They lined up to take poison

Bodies, many covered with sheets are spread thoughout area of compound at Jonestown, Guyana, after mass suicide by cult's members. Officials say some victims, apparently reluctant to take their own lives, may have been shot. (AP photo)

Mark Lane sensed 'something wrong'

By Don Bohning
Knight Ridder Service

GEORGETOWN, Guyana — Attorney Mark Lane yesterday described how a fragile compromise he worked out between Rep. Leo Ryan of California and sect leader Jim Jones dissolved into tragedy.

Lane, who gained national prominence as the lawyer for James Earl Ray, describes himself as a consultant for the Peoples Temple, which Jones headed. Lane said he arranged Ryan's visit to Jonestown to verify whether some of the young Americans there were being held against their will. Jones had requested that Lane be present when Ryan arrived, Lane said.

Speaking with reporters here yesterday, Lane said he had been anxious for outsiders to see the predominantly black Jonestown settlement because he thought there were positive aspects to it.

Here is Lane's account of what happened and how he escaped from the settlement just before 409 members of the community died:

When the Americans arrived in Guyana, Lane had called Jones from Georgetown by radio. Jones told Lane he had ordered a tractor be put on the dirt runway at Port Kaituma to keep Ryan's plane from landing.

LANE, Page 6

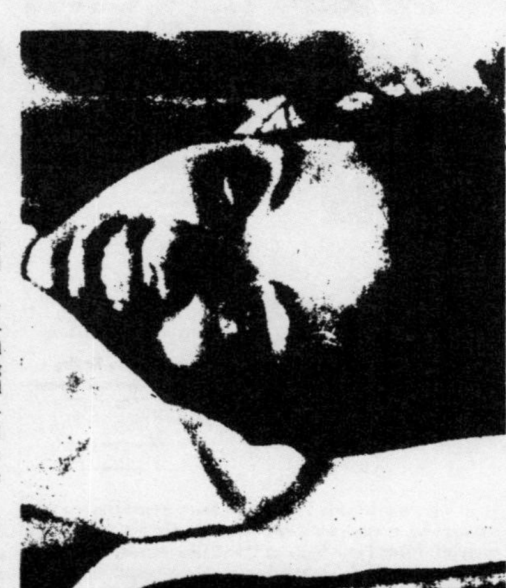

Jackie Speier, legislative assistant to Rep. Ryan, manages a smile as she is wheeled on stretcher to waiting ambulance on arrival yesterday at Andrews Air Force Base. (AP photo)

Cyanide mixed in soft drink

By Charles A. Krause
Washington Post

PORT KAITUMA, Guyana — When Rev. Jim Jones learned Saturday that Rep. Leo J. Ryan had been killed but that some members of the congressman's party had survived, Jones called his followers together and told them that the time had come to commit the mass suicide they had rehearsed several times before.

"They started with the babies," administering a potion of soft drink mixed with cyanide, Odell Rhodes recalled yesterday when I revisited Jonestown to view the horrifying sight of 409 bodies — men, women and children, most of them grouped around the altar where Jones himself lay dead. An estimated 500 to 900 more had fled into the jungle when the suicides started but by nightfall Guyanese soldiers had found only 12 survivors.

Rhodes is the only known survivor of Jonestown who witnessed a part of the suicide rite before managing to escape. He was helping Guyanese authorities identify the dead.

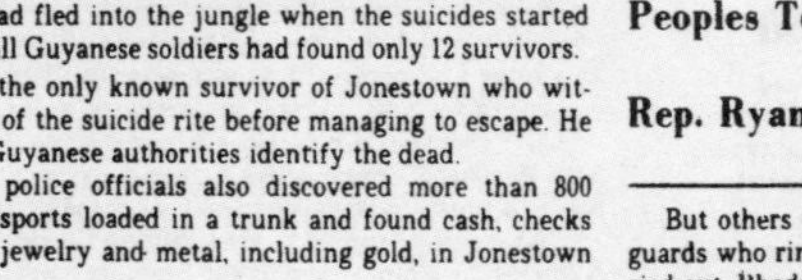

Guyanese police officials also discovered more than 800 American passports loaded in a trunk and found cash, checks and valuable jewelry and metal, including gold, in Jonestown yesterday.

Most of those who drank the deadly potion served to them by a Jonestown doctor, Lawrence Schact, and by nurses, did so willingly, Rhodes said. Mothers often gave the cyanide to their children before taking it themselves, he said.

'They just kept shooting,' survivor says — Page 2

Guyanans: Neither friends nor strangers — Page 2

Members of cult often rehearsed suicide — Page 6

FBI told group planned to kidnap officials — Page 7

Peoples Temple felt persecuted in US — Page 8

Rep. Ryan reportedly was aware of peril — Page 9

But others who tried to escape were turned back by armed guards who ringed the central pavilion where the rite was carried out, Rhodes said. They were then forced to drink the poison, Rhodes said.

It took about five minutes for the liquid to take effect. Young and old, black and white, grouped themselves, usually

GUYANA, Page 8

IN THIS CORNER

Want to get organized? Test your chaos quotient

By Robert Yoakum
Special to The Globe

A book called "Getting Organized" has just been published, and it didn't arrive a moment too soon for me.

You'll see why when you find out how I scored on author Stephanie Winston's test, part of which follows:

"1. Does it often take you more than 10 minutes to unearth a particular letter, bill, report, or other paper from your files (or piles of paper on your desk)?"

Let's put it this way: If I find what I'm looking for in a pile of papers on my desk in 10 minutes, we hold an office party to celebrate the event. If it takes only half an hour, there is general rejoicing and a special treat during the coffee break. When the search goes on for more than an hour, we decide the letter, or whatever, isn't in that particular pile and move to the next one.

"2. Do magazines or newspapers pile up unread?"

Ha! Have you ever heard of the Collyer brothers, Homer and Langley, who were found dead in their trash-filled Fifth Avenue mansion back in 1947? Homer, who

ORGANIZED, Page 15

Child abuse hotline may never begin

Plans to provide a 24-hour hotline on child abuse may be dropped because several private social agencies don't believe the state Welfare Department can provide the needed services. Page 14.

Gas pumps going to $1.99 a gallon

Equipment firms, anticipating gasoline prices rising to $1 and over, are making station pumps that go up to $1.99 a gallon. Page 13.

Guns being replaced as weapons in assaults

The use of firearms in assault cases in Massachusetts has declined since the gun control law went into effect, but other weapons are taking their place. Page 13.

Begin OK seen for US draft

Associated Press

JERUSALEM — Prime Minister Menachem Begin is ready to accept a US-sponsored draft of the peace treaty that his government rejected four weeks ago, sources familiar with the talks said yesterday.

Begin is prepared to accept a vaguely worded clause linking the treaty to the development of Palestinian self-rule on the Israeli-occupied West Bank of the Jordan River and the Gaza Strip, the sources said.

The point of linkage in the treaty has been the obstacle that has threatened the progress of the talks in recent weeks

The Israeli sources said the points now acceptable to Begin include:

—A clause in the preamble stating that the treaty would be the basis of future treaties with Israel's other Arab neighbors.

— A reference to Egypt's "special interest" in the Gaza Strip, which it administered before Israel captured the area in the 1967 Mideast war.

In return for adopting the two points, Begin wants the Egyptians to drop demands for a timetable for autonomy and for an Egyptian police presence and liaison office in the Gaza Strip and to omit a clause giving the Egyptian-Israeli treaty priority over previous Egyptian agreements with Arab states.

Egyptian spokesmen have said a timetable for election in the West Bank and Gaza is a "minimum demand."

Egyptian President Anwar Sadat said in a television interview aired on French television last night that he was willing to meet again in a summit with Begin "anywhere but" Jerusalem to try to resolve the remaining "10 percent" of problems over a peace treaty.

In the interview, filmed Saturday at Sadat's residence outside Cairo, Sadat said he would "insist" that the final treaty be signed with Begin "on the top of Mt. Sinai, on my land" and that he would refuse to go to Jerusalem again.

"I have already gone there once, and I'm not going to start again. But I am ready to meet Mr. Begin anywhere else," he said.

Sadat also insisted that no peace treaty would be signed that failed to deal with the Palestinian problem.

"If Gaza and the West Bank are not treated in an overall settlement, no one

MIDEAST, page 10

Boston Evening Globe

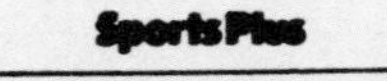

LATE STOCKS EDITION

Vol. 215 No. 33 © 1979, Globe Newspaper Co · Telephone 929-2000 · 64 Pages - 20 Cents

THE DIGEST

To our readers

Starting next Monday, the Boston Globe becomes an all-day newspaper. Here's what that will mean to Evening Globe readers:
NEWSSTAND — Fresh editions will continue to go to newsstands throughout the day as is the case now. However, the paper will be called simply, "The Boston Globe."
HOME DELIVERY — Over the next several weeks deliveries now made in the afternoon will be converted to early morning, and each subscriber will receive a letter from The Globe in advance. Delivery generally will be the same as is now the case on Saturdays and holidays.
CONTENT — The Globe will add about two pages for local, national and foreign news and will introduce a daily regional news section.

And she was scared

The baby boy was illegitimate and dead. And the mother took the body and wrapped it up in a blanket and put it inside a suitcase that she then covered with an old newspaper. That was in 1968. She didn't tell anyone it died. "It was illegitimate. I was scared besides," said the mother, Shirley White. Globe columnist Mike Barnicle details some facts surrounding the case. Page 2.

Sid Vicious found dead

Punk rock star Sid Vicious, free on bail pending trial for the hunting-knife murder of his girlfriend, apparently committed suicide by drug overdose today, New York police said. Page 6.

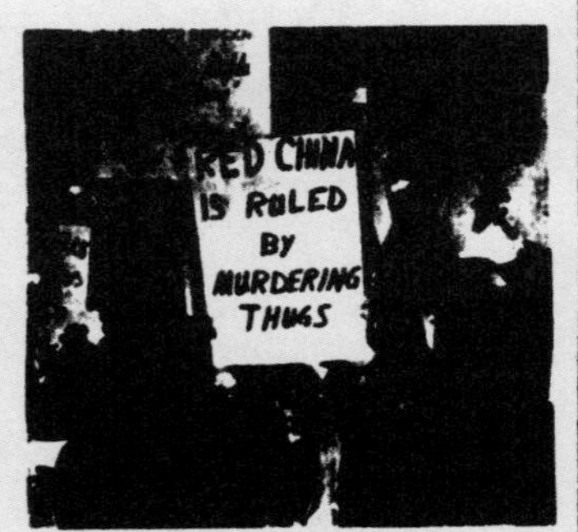

TAIWAN PROTESTORS were kept back by police in front of the Georgia Governor's Mansion in Atlanta where Chinese Vice Premier Teng Hsiao-ping was dining with Gov. George Busbee. Page 8. (UPI photo)

Unemployment rate dips

A record number of Americans had jobs last month as the unemployment rate fell to 5.8 percent and 450,000 workers were added to the labor force. Adult males accounted for most of the increase but blacks showed significant gains. Page 9.

Rockefeller service held

President and Mrs. Carter were among 2500 mourners from around the world who thronged Riverside Church in Manhattan today at a memorial service for former Vice President Nelson Rockefeller. His vision and energy were eulogized by friends and members of the family. Page 25.

Rhodesia kills race laws

Racial discrimination in Rhodesia housing, education, medical treatment and entertainment was abolished today just three days after that country's white minority voted overwhelmingly to surrender power to the black majority later this year. Page 8.

Suffolk double pays $250

A longshot named Jose Tambien which returned $73.20, $22.20 and $9.80 in the first race, and a heavy favorite, Fashioner, which paid $4.00, $3.00 and $2.60, combined for a daily double at Suffolk Downs today of $250. Page 33.

DIGEST, Page 2

Tips for Tonight

"Night of the Assassins," a psychological drama. Galaxy Theater, Boston, at 8.

Superman Festival, Berklee Performance Center, Boston, at 7:30.

TV Tips for Tonight

College hockey, Vermont at Boston University. Ch. 38 at 8.

"The Birds," Alfred Hitchcock thriller. Ch. 56 at 8.

The Weather

Tonight clear, cold, low temperature in the teens. Tomorrow, sunny and continued cold, high temperature in the upper 20s. Full report, Page 25.

Index				Columns	
Arts/Films	20	Deaths	13	Beecher	15
Ask Globe	28	Economy	9	Healy	15
Bridge	27	Editorials	14	Henry	17
Classified	34	Living	17	Jordan	15
Comics	26	Sports	29	McKinnon	22
Crossword	26	TV-Radio	27	Montville	29

Home Delivery 929-2222; Classified 929-1500

"In many ways organized crime is the most sinister kind of crime in America. The men who control it have become rich and powerful by encouraging the needy to gamble, by luring the troubled to destroy themselves with drugs, by extorting the profits of honest and hardworking businessmen, by collecting usury from those in financial plight, by maiming or murdering those who oppose them, by bribing those who are sworn to destroy them. Organized crime is not merely a few preying upon a few. In a very real sense it is dedicated to subverting not only American institutions, but the very decency and integrity that are the most cherished attributes of a free society. As the leaders of Cosa Nostra and their racketeering allies pursue their conspiracy unmolested in open and continual defiance of the law, they preach a sermon that all too many Americans heed:

The government is for sale; lawlessness is the road to wealth; honesty is a pitfall and morality a trap for suckers."

From a report by the President's Commission on Law Enforcement and the Administration of Justice in 1967.

RAYMOND PATRIARCA outside his store in Providence in December 1975. (Globe file photo)

Patriarca tapes reveal the fabric of mob life

By Richard J. Connolly
Globe Staff

Two associates talked business as usual, unaware that the office of the National Cigarette Service, a vending machine firm at 168 Atwells av., Providence, R.I., had been "bugged" by FBI agents and that their conversation was being tape recorded.

Their business allegedly was crime — loansharking, bookmaking, murder, mayhem, thievery and the corruption of law enforcement, politics, the judiciary and legitimate businesses.

Raymond L.S. Patriarca and Gennaro J. Angiulo, reputedly the most powerful organized crime figures in New England, talked shop during one of Angiulo's regular business trips from Boston to Patriarca's office on Federal Hill in Providence.

The minutes of that meeting on May 5, 1963, include this discussion, according to FBI records:

"... Angiulo told Patriarca in the presence of his chauffeur, Peter Limone, that (a high Massachusetts State Police official) had contacted Angiulo's brother, Nick. This is the first time that Angiulo has heard from (the official) for six months and he felt that (the official) is in need of money.

"(The official) told Nick that, if the Massachusetts Crime Commission was successful in obtaining funds, they desire for additional investigation into crimes in Massachusetts, it could be very serious for the hoodlum element. He pointed out, however, that he would be in a position to furnish information to this commission and that he will probably give them only information concerning politicians and not of criminal characters.

"... Jerry Angiulo said ... that he plans to pay (the official) $200 each month retroactive to 12/62 which was the month in which Angiulo last contacted (the official). He was of the opinion that (the official) must be short and if he gave him this sum of money they would be able to obtain more information from (the official)."

Ten months earlier, during a similar business meeting in Patriarca's office, Angiulo allegedly told Patriarca that the official told him he planned a bookie raid in Revere within three days and that Angiulo should inform a high Revere police official.

PATRIARCA, Page 12

$200m project in Charlestown

Unveiling the 'new' shipyard

By Anthony J. Yudis
Globe Staff

Before a large luncheon crowd of invited guests gathered in a huge, vacant, but once-thriving machine shop, Mayor Kevin H. White today ceremoniously launched the city's $200 million Charlestown Navy Yard rebuilding program.

The luncheon, attended by Charlestown residents, business and government leaders, took place in the old navy yard's Building 42.

The cavernous Circa 1856 structure where parts were once fashioned for ships, will be transferred into an apartment complex as the first phase of a $150 million private development program to be carried out by Immobiliare New England, a real estate and development firm with worldwide holdings. Immobiliare New England is based in Rome, Italy.

In March, the company will begin construction of a 362-unit luxury apartment building at a cost of $22 million.

This is the first phase of a proposed 1200-unit housing development program by Immobiliare that will include marinas, condominiums, retail, recreational and commercial uses and combine rehabilitation of historic buildings with new building construction.

A highlight of the luncheon was the presentation of a $1.7 million check by officials of Immobiliare to Mayor White.

The money represents a loan to the city which, in turn, will use to purchase 57 acres of the navy yard from the General Services Administration (GSA). The 57 acres of the 130-acre navy yard represents the sphere of programmed, private development.

In his prepared remarks, Mayor White termed the agreement with the private firm as one "without precedent."

"This developer has confidence enough in this project and this city to advance us funds so we can purchase the site that will be developed," said the mayor.

"But so much about this exciting project is without precedent," he said.

CHARLESTOWN, Page 16

Brighton rape suspect held in $50,000 bail

By Chris Black
and Paul Feeney
Globe Staff

A Dorchester father of four, arrested at his home last night, was charged in court today with one of a series of rapes in the Allston-Brighton district since last Nov. 18.

Willie J. Sanders, 37, of Woodledge street, pleaded innocent to raping a young woman on Kelton street on Christmas night and was held in $50,000 bail in Brighton District Court.

Judge Charles J. Artesani scheduled a probable cause hearing for Feb. 9 and ordered Sanders to Charles Street Jail.

Sanders' lawyer, Dane Shulman, argued in vain for lower bail, saying his client had no serious criminal record. Shulman said he would go to Superior Court today or Monday to seek a bail reduction hearing.

Police said Sanders fits the description of the man sought in connection with five other rapes and two attempted rapes in the area along Commonwealth avenue between Chestnut Hill avenue and Dukes road, and will be questioned about them.

Asst. Dist. Atty. Christopher Rich said he would talk to Dist. Atty. Newman Flanagan about the possibility of placing the suspect in a lineup for viewing by victims of the attacks.

Sanders was arrested by Dets. William Currier and Matthew Kilroe on a warrant issued by the Brighton court on Dec. 28.

RAPE, Page 16

Khomeini deaf to peace offers

By Sajid Rizvi
United Press International

TEHRAN, Iran — Premier Shahpour Bakhtiar made a fresh attempt today to avoid an impending civil war by offering to take opposition members into his cabinet and open talks with his major opponent, the Ayatollah Ruhoolah Khomeini.

But the holy man, ignoring Bakhitar's peace feelers, received tens of thousands of his cheering followers who mobbed his headquarters on his second day home after exile. He consulted with major opposition leaders and religious figures on the establishment of an "alternate government" for Iran — an Islamic revolutionary council.

Karim Sanjabi, leader of the opposition National Front, After talks with the 78-year-old religious leader, said the two million persons who celebrated his homecoming yesterday constituted a clear mandate for Khomeini to take over power.

Sanjabi, expected to be named to any revolutionary council, said that if Bakhtiar believed in democracy he should resign immediately.

IRAN, Page 12

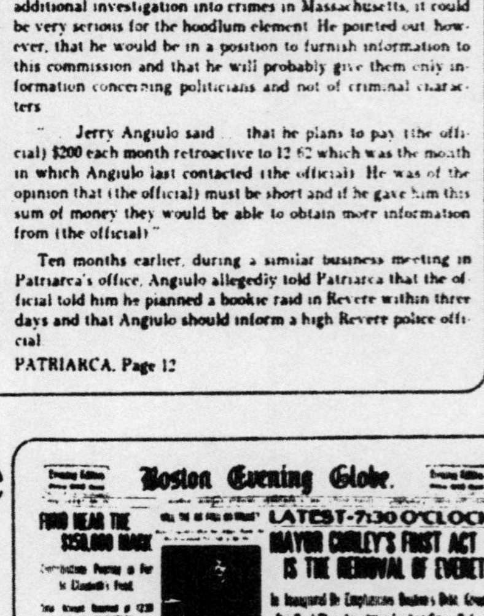

Boston Evening Globe.

LATEST-7:30 O'CLOCK

MAYOR CURLEY'S FIRST ACT IS THE REMOVAL OF EVERETT

EVERETT IS REMOVED

Massachusetts Bonding / Insurance Company

'Evening' goes to bed; all-day rises

(For most, retirement comes at 65.

(And so it is with the Evening Globe, which retires with its name today.

(According to a history of The Globe written by Louis Lyons, the Evening Globe first acquired its identity exactly 65 years ago today. — Feb. 2, 1914.)

Of a given afternoon, one when a plane would crash, a jury would come in, a murder would occur or a Red Sox trade would come off, either Peter Stilla or Frank Grundstrom would take his hands out of his pockets and walk the length of the city room down to the office of Jack Driscoll. There, the two men would measure the event in terms of space and ink and, within an hour, you would be able to read about it in The Boston Evening Globe.

And, now, this is the souvenir edition. This is the collector's copy, the last paper with the word "evening" on the masthead, and the paper itself blends next week into an all day version of The Globe.

Peter Stilla is the day editor here. Frank Grundstrom is the assistant managing editor. Jack Driscoll is the managing editor. There are others.

MIKE BARNICLE

You would get the product of people named Anglin and Meek, Morrow, Powers, Prophet, Ward, Johnny Vellante and Al Rossi. Bill Crawford, Brendan Malin, Jimmy Stack and Jerry Sullivan. Mike Linscott.

Big Kenny Lord and, gone now, retired, the Monahan brothers: Jimmy and Al.

Some of them are writers. The others are people who make writers look good by editing sentences with no verbs or maybe even no point.

The new paper, they say, will be bigger, better, and give the reader more for the money. This is probably true.

The Evening Globe became an orphan, a runaway: something that everyone came to love but also came to be resigned to the fact that it would eventually, inevitably, disappear for good.

It was forced to compete against television and the notion in the minds of people that it was the same as the morning paper, that they could get their news fast fed to them at six o'clock from someone who would read clips of events ... many of them taken out of the final edition of The Evening Globe.

It ran up against hard times when people thought twice about spending money for one paper, never mind two. It hit the traffic patterns that have robbed the city of much of the middle class over two decades.

It saw circulation go down as other papers in the small geographic areas gave readers the happenings of Middlesex County, the South Shore or north of Chelsea. But none of them had the class and grace and style of this evening paper we put to bed today.

If it happened before four o'clock, it would be in this paper. It would be there. On the front page. And the information would be accurate.

If it was about people, about fires, about death or destruction or any of the other ripples of life that people read about, we would have it.

They say that a decision like this — the combining of the two papers into one super paper — is in the normal course of events. It is time and money and modernization and that undefined attack on the task of giving readers more of what they want.

Maybe so.

I started writing for this paper. I am embarrassed now to look back at many of the things I did then, seven years ago. They were that bad.

But the paper and the people carried what I wrote — and me. Not an easy assignment.

And today is the last time. Next week we all go to work for the all-day Boston Globe.

Mike Barnicle is a Globe columnist.

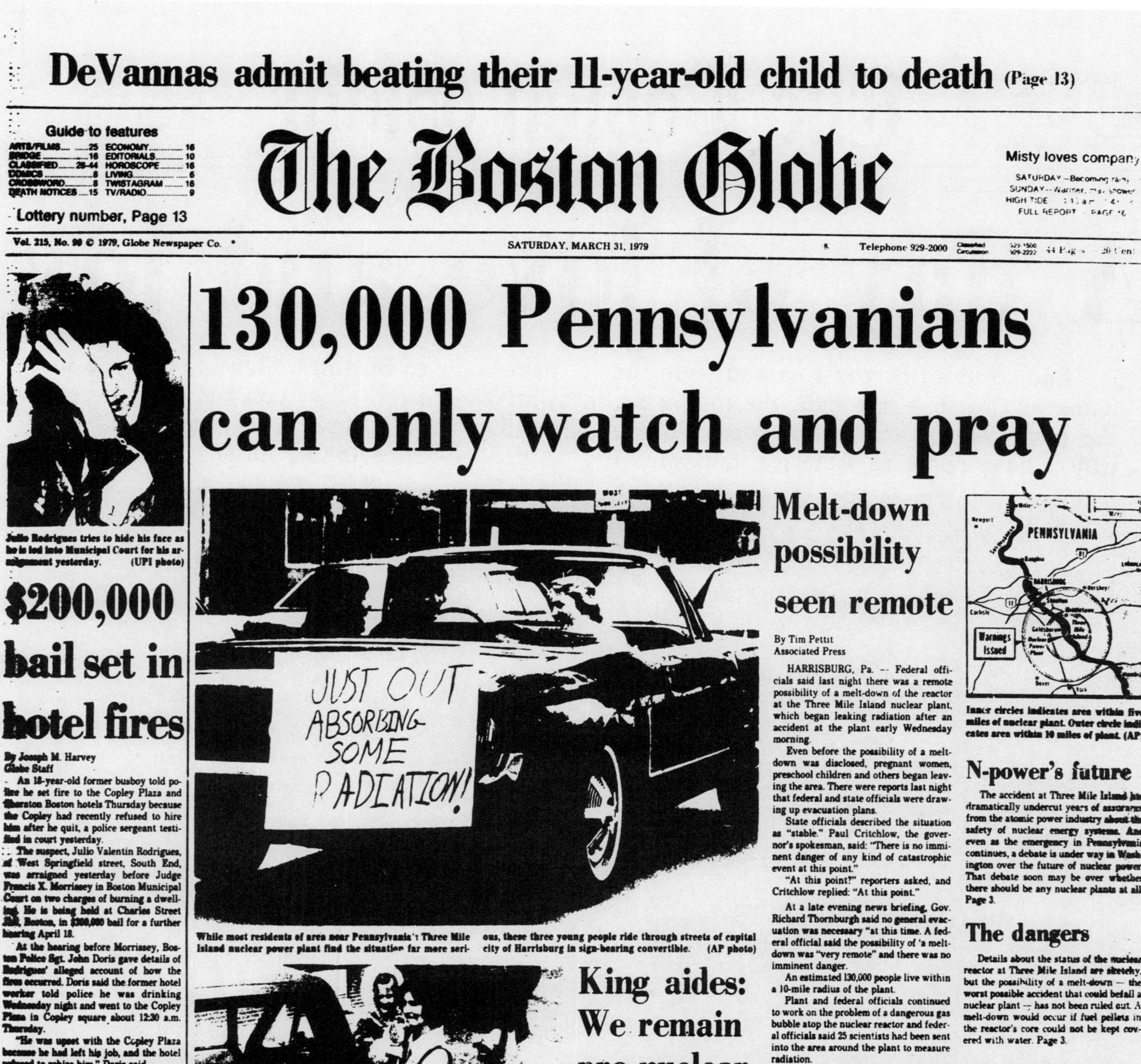

DeVannas admit beating their 11-year-old child to death (Page 13)

Guide to features
ARTS/FILMS ....25 ECONOMY 16
BRIDGE .... 16 EDITORIALS 10
CLASSIFIED .... 28-44 HOROSCOPE 16
COMICS .... 8 LIVING 6
CROSSWORD .... 8 TWISTAGRAM 16
DEATH NOTICES .... 15 TV/RADIO 9

Lottery number, Page 13

The Boston Globe

Misty loves company
SATURDAY – Becoming rainy
SUNDAY – Warmer, may shower
HIGH TIDE
FULL REPORT – PAGE 16

Vol. 215, No. 90 © 1979, Globe Newspaper Co. • SATURDAY, MARCH 31, 1979 • Telephone 929-2000 Classified 929-1500 Circulation 929-2222 44 Pages • 20 Cents

130,000 Pennsylvanians can only watch and pray

Julio Rodrigues tries to hide his face as he is led into Municipal Court for his arraignment yesterday. (UPI photo)

$200,000 bail set in hotel fires

By Joseph M. Harvey
Globe Staff

An 18-year-old former busboy told police he set fire to the Copley Plaza and Sheraton Boston hotels Thursday because the Copley had recently refused to hire him after he quit, a police sergeant testified in court yesterday.

The suspect, Julio Valentin Rodrigues, of West Springfield street, South End, was arraigned yesterday before Judge Francis X. Morrissey in Boston Municipal Court on two charges of burning a dwelling. He is being held at Charles Street Jail, Boston, in $200,000 bail for a further hearing April 18.

At the hearing before Morrissey, Boston Police Sgt. John Doris gave details of Rodrigues' alleged account of how the fires occurred. Doris said the former hotel worker told police he was drinking Wednesday night and went to the Copley Plaza in Copley square about 12:30 a.m. Thursday.

"He was upset with the Copley Plaza because he had left his job, and the hotel refused to rehire him," Doris said.

Rodrigues worked for the Copley three months ago and for the Sheraton last year, police said. The Sheraton had no comment. A Copley spokesman said Rodrigues worked as a busboy-dishwasher.

Doris quoted Rodrigues as saying he went to the vicinity of the Oval Room, a restaurant and lounge on the hotel first floor, and attempted to set a curtain afire. Later, Rodrigues went to a third floor hall and allegedly started a fire in a sofa, Doris said.

FIRES, Page 12

IN THIS CORNER

This little piggie got a bundle

By Bill Michelmore
Knight Ridder Service

UTICA, Mich. — A Utica housewife was at home this week admiring her $200,000 toe.

Her husband, a $200-a-week materials handler for the Ford Motor Co., was also at home, taking a day off from work. He could afford to.

A jury of three men and three women Tuesday awarded the husband, Roy Osantowski, $180,000 because his wife, Barbara, broke her toe in a motorcycle accident six years ago.

In an out-of-court settlement stemming from the civil suit, the wife was awarded an additional $20,000 for the injury.

The jury gave the 25-year-old husband the $180,000 "for loss of consortium," which means that he can no longer enjoy all the activities he used to with his wife. He said Wednesday these activities were hiking, hunting and dancing.

When the amount of the jury's award was announced: "We were stunned," Osantowski said. "When the jury said $180,000, I heard it, but I couldn't believe it. I went hot and then I went cold. I almost passed out."

The couple's attorney, Melvin Schwartz, although happy he won the

TOE, Page 12

While most residents of area near Pennsylvania's Three Mile Island nuclear power plant find the situation far more serious, these three young people ride through streets of capital city of Harrisburg in sign-bearing convertible. (AP photo)

John Sweitzer places Mrs. David Noel's belongings in back of pickup truck as she, daughter Danielle, 4, and family dog prepare to leave their home. (AP photo)

Melt-down possibility seen remote

By Tim Pettit
Associated Press

HARRISBURG, Pa. — Federal officials said last night there was a remote possibility of a melt-down of the reactor at the Three Mile Island nuclear plant, which began leaking radiation after an accident at the plant early Wednesday morning.

Even before the possibility of a meltdown was disclosed, pregnant women, preschool children and others began leaving the area. There were reports last night that federal and state officials were drawing up evacuation plans.

State officials described the situation as "stable." Paul Critchlow, the governor's spokesman, said: "There is no imminent danger of any kind of catastrophic event at this point."

"At this point?" reporters asked, and Critchlow replied: "At this point."

At a late evening news briefing, Gov. Richard Thornburgh said no general evacuation was necessary "at this time. A federal official said the possibility of 'a meltdown was "very remote" and there was no imminent danger.

An estimated 130,000 people live within a 10-mile radius of the plant.

Plant and federal officials continued to work on the problem of a dangerous gas bubble atop the nuclear reactor and federal officials said 25 scientists had been sent into the area around the plant to measure radiation.

The governor said his recommendation that pregnant women and young children vacate an area five miles around the plant would remain in effect but his suggestion that residents within a five-mile radius stay indoors would expire at midnight.

Late in the afternoon, spokesman Dennis Crutchfield of the Nuclear Regulatory Commission said up to one-fourth of the fuel rods in the reactor might have been damaged. He said then a disastrous core melt-down was not likely, but "the potential is there."

Crutchfield said the gas bubble had developed inside the nuclear reactor, creating a small risk of core melt-down that would release large amounts of radiation. Indirect evidence indicated up to one-fourth of the 176 fuel rods might have been damaged, he said.

Young children and pregnant women began evacuating the area within five miles of the plant about six hours after new radiation leaks were reported and more than 48 hours after the accident that touched off the first leak. Radioactive gas was vented three times yesterday.

More than 150 pregnant women and young children were at a shelter in Hershey. And the 130,000 people living within a 10-mile radius of the reactor were advised by the governor to stay indoors to avoid radiation.

N-PLANT, Page 4

Inner circles indicate area within five miles of nuclear plant. Outer circle indicates area within 10 miles of plant. (AP)

N-power's future

The accident at Three Mile Island has dramatically undercut years of assurance from the atomic power industry about the safety of nuclear energy systems. And even as the emergency in Pennsylvania continues, a debate is under way in Washington over the future of nuclear power. That debate soon may be over whether there should be any nuclear plants at all. Page 3.

The dangers

Details about the status of the nuclear reactor at Three Mile Island are sketchy, but the possibility of a melt-down — the worst possible accident that could befall a nuclear plant — has not been ruled out. A melt-down would occur if fuel pellets in the reactor's core could not be kept covered with water. Page 3.

Concern mounts

The mood in Middletown, Pa., changes from joking to apprehensive as it becomes clear to residents that the nuclear accident down the river is not under control. Pregnant women and children are urged to evacuate, everyone within a five-mile radius is asked to stay indoors, and some residents decide they would rather leave the state altogether. Page 3.

King aides: We remain pro-nuclear

By Nick King
Globe Staff

Massachusetts Energy Director Joseph S. Fitzpatrick said yesterday that he was concerned about the nuclear power plant accident in Pennsylvania but that so far "it is no basis for changing the King administration's pro-nuclear policies."

However, several legislators and Atty. Gen. Francis X. Bellotti disagreed, saying that the accident at the Three Mile Island nuclear plant proves the contention that nuclear power, despite industry claims, is not safe.

"Now the argument vanishes that these things don't happen, that they're safe," Bellotti said in an interview. "At least now they will have to look at us not just as a group of environmental nuts, but as responsible people who predicted that something like this would happen sooner or later."

Bellotti said that he has been intervening in nuclear licensing cases for four years, raising concerns about safety and evacuation procedures, but that "we've been crying out in a vacuum and criticized as obstructionists."

The impact of the Pennsylvania accident, Bellotti said, should "assign a lot

KING, Page 4

You can't fly United today

United Press International

WASHINGTON — A strike against United Airlines began at 12:01 a.m. today after 18,600 mechanics and ground crew workers rejected for the second time a tentative contract agreement.

A United spokesman in Chicago said the nation's largest airline canceled its 1600 daily scheduled flights beginning at 12:01 a.m., eastern standard time, today because of the walkout by members of the Machinists and Aerospace Workers union.

No new negotiations were scheduled.

Flights en route at the strike deadline were expected to proceed to scheduled destinations, the airline said.

Union spokesman Larry Rubin said members had "overwhelmingly rejected" the agreement.

Spokesmen for American Airlines and Trans World Airlines in Chicago said they will try to absorb most of the passengers who had planned to fly United.

[In Boston, six union members began to picket the United Airlines terminal at Logan Airport at midnight.

"The strike is over the whole package — money, benefits and working conditions," a union representative in Boston said. There are 220 union members at the Boston United terminal.

[An airlines official said 14 departing and 14 arriving flights were scheduled for today at Logan Airport.]

The National Mediation Board said neither the union nor United had requested a resumption of bargaining.

"The board is ready to meet again with both parties to help end this strike," said board member Robert O. Harris, who presided over marathon talks that brought about the second pact. "However, at this time, neither party has indicated a desire to resume immediate negotiations.

"They are angry because Carter Administration programs seem to be pushing them further into economic quicksand by boosting prices in all areas," said Rubin.

The rejected contract called for an estimated 30 percent wage increase over three years — about 10 percent a year — and was patterned after an agreement last fall between the union and Trans World Airlines.

The United pact is not subject to President Jimmy Carter's 7-percent wage

UNITED, Page 12

Trucking pact near

Sources close to the negotiations between the Teamsters and the trucking industry said yesterday tentative agreement on the key issues of wages and fringe benefits had been reached. The report raised hopes that a weekend trucking strike could be averted. Page 17.

Questions and answers: What is a melt-down?

In an effort to clarify the facts surrounding the accident at the Three Mile Island nuclear power facility in Pennsylvania, Globe science writer Robert Cooke has prepared these questions and answers.

Q. What is the so-called China syndrome?

A. A suggestion that if a nuclear reactor core melts down, there's nothing that can stop it from burning all the way through the earth to China. The core is the chamber where the heat-producing nuclear reaction takes place. The "syndrome" was coined as a term to describe what was thought to be a remote possibility years ago — that a reactor core, without its cooling water, could melt down into molten uranium and go out of control.

Q. Can a nuclear power plant explode?

A. It is impossible to have a nuclear explosion in a commercial power reactor. Unlike the uranium used in atomic weapons, reactor fuel is not "enriched" enough with uranium-235 to go off like a bomb. Some observers have suggested, however, that a steam explosion in a nuclear reactor could be powerful enough to crack the huge containment sphere, and thus release dangerous radioactive materials.

Q. What's the worst possible accident that can occur at a nuclear power plant?

A. A core melt-down. If for some reason the reactor loses its supply of cooling water, and an emergency supply is not injected, then the core could melt down, out of control.

Q. What happens if there's a melt-down of a reactor core?

A. If the core gets hot enough and breaks through the containment sphere — which has 4-foot-thick concrete and steel walls — it is possible that large amounts of dangerous radioactive materials could be released.

Q. What would the effect of that be?

A. Depending on conditions, it could seriously endanger nearby populations. If the wind is right, for example, the lighter elements, if vaporized, could be blown long distances and might be deposited in heavily populated areas.

Q. & A., Page 2

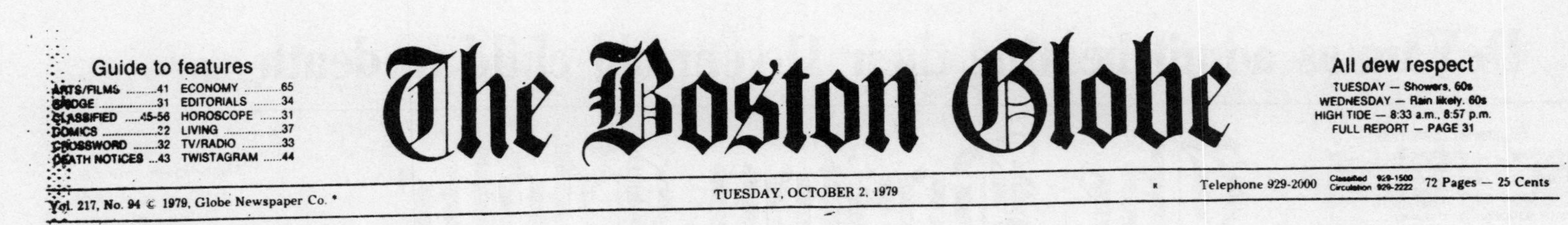

Guide to features

ARTS/FILMS	41	ECONOMY	65
BRIDGE	31	EDITORIALS	34
CLASSIFIED	45-56	HOROSCOPE	31
COMICS	22	LIVING	37
CROSSWORD	32	TV/RADIO	33
DEATH NOTICES	43	TWISTAGRAM	44

The Boston Globe

All dew respect
TUESDAY — Showers, 60s
WEDNESDAY — Rain likely, 60s
HIGH TIDE — 8:33 a.m., 8:57 p.m.
FULL REPORT — PAGE 31

Vol. 217, No. 94 © 1979, Globe Newspaper Co. • TUESDAY, OCTOBER 2, 1979 • Telephone 929-2000 Classified 929-1500 Circulation 929-2222 72 Pages — 25 Cents

A day of love and joy

'And so to all of you I extend — in the name of Christ — the call, the invitation, the plea: "Come and follow Me." This is why I have come to America, and why I have come to Boston tonight: to call you to Christ — to call all of you and each of you to live in His love today and forever. Amen!' — Pope John Paul II

Bedecked with US and Vatican flags, limousine carrying Pope John Paul II through streets of Boston makes its way past throng of jubilant spectators at Uphams Corner in Dorchester section of the city. (Globe photo by Wendy Maeda)

Carter beefs up forces near Cuba

Text of Carter speech, Page 2

By William Beecher
Globe Washington Bureau

WASHINGTON — President Jimmy Carter sought to defuse the mounting confrontation over the presence of a Soviet combat brigade in Cuba last night by announcing steps to contain its potential threat.

The Russians deny their brigade was designed or could be used for anything but training Cubans. Carter asserted in a nationwide television address that the Soviet unit is a combat brigade, but he said the dispute was not worth pursuing at risk of endangering the second strategic arms limitation treaty (SALT II) or bringing on a return of the Cold War.

Thus, in the eyeball-to-eyeball Cuban confrontation of 1979, some politicians are bound to say that this time the United States blinked.

Among the steps Carter specified in his speech were increased surveillance over Cuba and a pledge by the United States to rush to the aid of any nation in Latin America threatened by Soviet or Cuban troops.

Of all the countermeasures that the President cited, however, missing was the one most likely to seriously upset the Soviet Union: the decision to end Defense Secretary Harold Brown to China for military talks.

Administration spokesmen sought to disavow any connection between the Brown trip announced yesterday, and the current crisis. But the Soviet Union is unlikely to miss the message.

Repeatedly, in recent weeks, President Carter has insisted that maintenance of the "status quo" of the 2000-to 3000-man brigade was "not acceptable."

Negotiations aimed at achieving a face-saving solution for both sides were pursued by Secretary of State Cyrus R. Vance first with Soviet Ambassador Anatoly Dobrynin and than last week with Soviet Foreign Minister Andrei Gromyko. In addition, it was learned, Carter exchanged letters on the issue last week with Soviet President Leonid Brezhnev.

The Carter Administration hoped the Soviets, while not admitting the brigade was armed and organized for combat, would transfer its tanks and artillery to the Cubans and reassign Russian officers to advisory duties.

CARTER, Page 2

Pope prods youth on morals

By Jack Thomas
and Charles Claffey
Globe Staff

On Boston Common, where preachers have vied for souls for more than three centuries, there never was a day like yesterday.

Pope John Paul II opened a seven-day pastoral visit to the United States — America the Beautiful, as he called it, even when it rains — with a triumphant motorcade through Boston's ethnic neighborhoods, an emotional prayer service for 2000 priests and nuns at the Cathedral of the Holy Cross, and an unprecedented Pontifical Mass on Boston Common.

Nearly 2 million saw the Pope, 400,000 of them at the Mass.

"Today I stand at this gateway to the United States," John Paul II told the multitude on the Common, "and again I greet all of America, for its people, wherever they are, have a special place in the love of the Pope."

Other stories, pictures pages 3-20; texts, page 19

In keeping with the theme of his visit here, he told the young people in the audience, "Whatever you make of your life, let it be something that reflects the love of Christ."

Earlier, as the Pope emerged from his Boeing 747, he appeared weary from a fatiguing 51-hour pilgrimage in Ireland and the six-hour flight across the Atlantic.

As he descended the stairs, he blessed 1400 civic, political and religious leaders on hand to greet him, and as he had done on his arrival in Mexico, Poland and Ireland, he knelt to kiss the ground, which was wet.

But the tumultuous outcry of joy that greeted him along Hanover street in the North End seemed to infuse him with new strength.

Along the motorcade, as he sat at the altar in Holy Cross Cathedral and at the Boston Common Mass, John Paul's handsome, craggy features and ministerial manner reminded many of Boston's Richard Cardinal Cushing, who had lain in state at the cathedral in 1970, a few feet from where the Pope knelt to pray.

Although the fog and rain kept the crowds smaller than the million expected on the Common and thinner along the motorcade than anticipated, the mood everywhere the Pope went was one of jubilation, even adulation. His irrestible charm won the hearts of New Englanders as it had the hearts of the people of Mexico, Poland and Ireland.

POPE, Page 18

'Darryl, you've got a lot of courage,' the visitor said

By MIKE BARNICLE

At 3:45 yesterday afternoon, two cars pulled right up to the front while three others squealed to a stop on the wet pavement outside the City Hospital Emergency Room. The Secret Service men jumped from the first two cars and held the doors open while Sen. Edward Kennedy and his wife Joan got out of the back seat and headed for the fifth floor to see Darryl Williams, who was shot last week at a football game in Charlestown.

Kennedy and the government men guarding him moved in one wave past the benches of the waiting room, down a corridor and onto an elevator. A hospital security guard held the door as the senator got on with his wife and then came two of their children, Patrick and Kara.

With the weight of all the people, the elevator stopped about 6 inches short of five. And Kennedy had to make the step up as the rest of the group got off and headed down the hallway where a pair of doors swung open and Darryl Williams' mother, Shirley Simmons, stood with her family.

"Mrs. Simmons," Kennedy began taking her hand. "I'm Senator Kennedy. And this is my wife Joan, my daughter Kara, my son Patrick. I can't tell you how sorry I am about what happened. I know how you must be feeling. . . ."

"Senator," the boy's mother said, holding Kennedy's hand for a moment. "I appreciate your coming."

Mrs. Simmons turned to Joan Kennedy and shook her hand. And then the boy's mother introduced her daughter and her husband to the senator, his wife and his children while a Secret Service man held the two doors into the ICU ward open and the people moved toward the boy, 15 and paralyzed.

BARNICLE, Page 28

Clash of lobstermen, oil and jobs in Maine, another in a series (Page 2)

Guide to features

ARTS/FILMS	16	ECONOMY	25
BRIDGE	24	EDITORIALS	10
CLASSIFIED	37-46	HOROSCOPE	24
COMICS	18	LIVING	21
CROSSWORD	18	TV/RADIO	19
DEATH NOTICES	36	TWISTAGRAM	28

Brighty bright
MONDAY — Sunny, mid 50s
TUESDAY — Mostly sunny, mid 50s
HIGH TIDE — 11:35
FULL REPORT — PAGE 24

Vol. 216, No. 128 © 1979, Globe Newspaper Co. • MONDAY, NOVEMBER 5, 1979 • Telephone 929-2000 Classified 929-1500 Circulation 929-2222 • 46 Pages — 25 Cents

Presidential politicking

Mondale on Kennedy: Why's he running now?

By Thomas Oliphant
Globe Staff

DENVER — "He's a damned fine senator," Walter F Mondale was saying yesterday about Edward M. Kennedy. "He's been courageous and effective on so many issues over the years. I hope he's President some day.

"But I just don't understand why he's doing this now."

In an interview aboard his Air Force jet on the way back to Washington yesterday from a three-day political swing through the Midwest, the Vice President gave his first detailed response to the issues Kennedy has raised in his campaign against President Jimmy Carter. That campaign becomes official with the senator's formal announcement in Boston on Wednesday.

On the economy, energy and nuclear power, Mondale both vigorously defended Carter's record and suggested that the differences between Kennedy and the President are not sufficient to justify a challenge by a Democrat to a sitting chief executive of his own party."

Mondale would not, however, state publicly the only logical inference from such a view — that Kennedy is running because he thinks the President is so weak in the polls that he can be beaten.

The Vice President showed anger about only one of the issues Kennedy has raised, his charge that the Administration delayed too long in organizing a response to the mass starvation in Cambodia.

That charge, he said, stemmed from "political motivations." Referring to Kennedy's speech on the subject at Georgetown University two weeks ago, Mondale said: "On the very same day President Carter came out to announce increased support for refugee assistance, within one hour Kennedy was making a speech filled with bitter, personal attacks. It is not right to make political pawns of those suffering people."

MONDALE, Page 6

GOP's Big 4 candidates: No unkind words here

By Martin F. Nolan
Globe Washington Bureau

WASHINGTON—Meanwhile, in the other party, the news is that there is another party and that Republicans find themselves in the unlikely position of being less acrimonious than the Democrats.

After Saturday's straw-vote victory by George Bush in Maine, the Republicans also find themselves with four "major" candidates.

The former CIA director defeated Senate minority leader Howard Baker, former California governor Ronald Reagan and former Texas governor John Connally in the nonbinding preference poll in Portland. From the available evidence of organizational strength and public opinion polls, those are now the Big Four and the others are just that, "others," until proven otherwise.

Democrats have dominated the news, with the drama of an incumbent President, Jimmy Carter, being challenged by two famous contenders who will annnounce this week: Sen. Edward M. Kennedy of Massachusetts and Gov Edmund G. (Jerry) Brown of California.

GOP, Page 6

Moslem demonstrators carry wooden scaffold outside US embassy in Tehran demanding the extradition of the deposed shah. (UPI photo)

Iranians seize US embassy, hostages

By Sajid Rizvi
United Press International

TEHRAN, Iran — Moslem students overran Marine guards yesterday and seized the US embassy, taking at least 59 Americans hostage to press demands that the deposed shah of Iran be extradited to Iran.

About 450 Moslem youths, who said they had tacit approval from Ayatollah Ruhollah Khomeini, stormed the embassy at 2 a.m. and "fought with embassy personnel" for three hours, press reports said.

"We shall not give up the hostages unless the shah is given to us," one of the student spokesmen said.

"So long as we are here, the embassy will remain closed," he said.

The students said they seized about 90 American men, women and children and another 10 Iranians. However, the State Department said in Washington there are probably only 59 American hostages, but "we can't be precise."

The State Department also said one report from Iran said four of the Iranian hostages have been released.

The department said there was no indication the Americans were hurt. A special task force, headed by Assistant Secretary of State Harold Saunders, was established to handle the matter.

[Reuters reported that Secretary of State Cyrus Vance went to his office to monitor developments in Iran and that President Jimmy Carter, at Camp David, was keeping in close touch through his aides.]

Iranian protesters chained themselves inside Statue of Liberty and lowered banner reading: "Shah must be tried and punished."(AP photo)

State Department spokesman George Sherman said embassy charge d'affaires Bruce Laingen was not in the compound during the attack and has been in constant communication with Iranian officials.

"What we are trying to do, of course, is get our people released and the embassy compound vacated," Sherman said.

A spokesman for the students said Marines used tear gas during the battle. "But our people came equipped with wet handkerchiefs." He said the students faced the strongest opposition from Marines when they tried to take over what appeared to be a specially guarded room.

"Six men guarding the room resisted our students until all documents inside the room were burned. The documents which were destroyed probably belonged to the CIA," the spokesman said.

IRAN, Page 8

Legislature finally calls it a year

By Walter Robinson
Globe Staff

A red-eyed Massachusetts General Court ended 10 months of legislative procrastination yesterday morning after another all-night session, left a flock of bills on Gov. Edward J. King's desk for action and departed Beacon Hill until next Jan. 2.

After four successive post-midnight and predawn meetings, King formally dismissed the Legislature at 8:13 a.m. yesterday after a final meeting that dragged on for 16 straight hours.

The muted prorogation ceremony ended lawmaking and last-minute wrangling over key bills for the year and also put an end to champagne and beer celebrations, catnapping in both chambers and at least one long-running poker game.

With the nightlong thwacking of gavels in both branches punctuating the conclusion of one of the country's longest-running legislative dramas this year, King came away with most of the major bills he wanted passed.

In the final hours of the session, with little and often desultory debate and few rollcalls, both branches enacted bills reorganizing the

LEGISLATURE, Page 14

1979 legislative report card

Enacted or already signed into law:

- A limit on increases in local spending and a first-time-ever ceiling on what the state can borrow.
- A reorganization of the state energy apparatus, with emergency powers for the governor and incentives for development of some alternative energy sources.
- An increase in the drinking age from 18 to 20.
- Tougher sentences for arsonists and professional auto thieves and a stepladder approach to sentencing for various kinds of rape.
- Prohibitions of the practice of requiring theater owners to bid for films without seeing them, and of charges for directory assistance telephone calls.
- Cost-of-living payment increases for welfare recipients and medical care for the indigent and $25 million for fuel assistance to the needy.
- Salary increases for legislators and top elected executives including the governor.
- Regulations governing the production and disposal of hazardous wastes
- Provisions for capital punishment and voluntary school prayer, both of which are likely to lead to constitutional challenges.

Defeated or dead for this year:

- Tougher sentences for drug offenders.
- Increase in auto insurance collision deductible from $200 to $300.
- A third harbor tunnel and reorganization of the Massachusetts Port Authority.
- Legislation permitting two commercial blood firms to collect blood.
- Legislation allowing Governor's Councilor Herbert L. Connolly to buy state-owned land adjacant to his Framingham auto dealership.
- Requirements that news reporters be licensed and make financial disclosures.

Their strategies for the home stretch

White, the loner, goes very public

By Charles E. Claffey
Globe Staff

As his station wagon moved through the narrow streets of East Boston last Thursday night, one hour behind schedule, Kevin White leaned back against the headrest for a moment to brace himself for his final campaign appearance of the day.

"I'm tired," the mayor confessed. It was nearly 10:30, and the upcoming rally at Lombardo's Restaurant would mark his 10th and final campaign appearance of the day.

Shaking his head to revive himself, White remarked to an aide in the back seat, "Eastie has spirit." The mayor had just come from a house party on Faywood street, in the Orient Heights section, and was obviously pleased with the reception.

The mayor likes East Boston, and the feeling apparently is reciprocal. He has carried the district every time he has run for mayor, including preliminary elections, the last time by 1850 votes.

Outside Lombardo's a band started playing the theme from the film "Rocky" as White bounded out of the station wagon and quick-stepped to the platform.

"Four more years," a demonstrative crowd chanted while the mayor grinned, waiting an opportunity to get in a few of the by-now familiar words of encouragement and exhortation.

WHITE, Page 8

Timilty sticks to streets to the finish

By Al Larkin
Globe Staff

About one hour and 45 minutes into the David Brudnoy talk show on WHDH radio on Thursday, amid an inexplicable flurry of hostile callers, Joseph F. Timilty got what he needed.

"You're a mensch," a Jewish caller from West Roxbury said.

Mensch is Jewish slang and, loosely translated, means that the Irish Catholic state senator from Mattapan is "a real human being, a down-to-earth person."

It's the kind of thing his supporters have said about Timilty since the start of this mayoral contest and he, as much as anyone, knows that it is important if he is to win tomorrow.

If Mayor Kevin H. White has lost any votes for being too isolated, Timilty has grabbed them.

That, more than anything else, was apparent last week as he made his final campaign push with daily news conferences and night after night of speeches to sparse audiences at candidates' nights throughout the city.

When he strolled into the lobby of the Copley Plaza Hotel after finishing the Brudnoy program, it was the doorman and not the well-dressed clientele who grabbed his hand.

"This place is gonna be Heartbreak Hotel next Tuesday," the doorman said. "This is where Kevin White is supposed to have his victory party, but there ain't gonna be no victory."

TIMILTY, Page 8

A true twanger knows which way the gee-tar's strung

IN THIS CORNER

By Allan R. Andrews
Globe Staff

Now that everyone is jumping on the country music haywagon, it's time to separate the true twangers from the cosmopolitan chic lovers. And Willie Nelson will be the wedge.

Don Meredith, the former Dallas Cowboy quarterback who makes his living as a telecaster and as our gratifying thorn in the flesh of Howard Cosell, is a true twanger.

How do I know? Because when the ball game is obviously over, Meredith breaks into song.

Not unusual, you say. No, not unless you are familiar with the song that is a Meredith favorite at those special moments when the losing team is 20 points behind with three minutes left in the game. It's opening lines are: "Turn out the lights, the party's over. They say that all good things must end."

True twangers recognize the song; and if you don't know it, you're probably a cosmopolitan latecomer to the sounds of country music who thinks that Willie Nelson's earliest hit song was a country version of "Georgia on My Mind" that he picked up from Ray Charles.

"The Party's Over" was a Willie Nelson hit song in the days before he discovered long hair, beards and the Texas outlaw image. In those days, Nelson was a soft-singing, clean-shaven troubador who, like many other country music purists, decried electric guitars and heavy drumbeats and followed in the footsteps of Roy Acuff.

TWANGERS, Page 28

With fear in her eyes, young Cambodian woman stares off in space as she and other refugees await help at hospital in Sa Kaew, Thailand. (AP photo)

Untangling Cambodian refugee aid

By Oswald Johnston
Los Angeles Times

WASHINGTON—When late on the afternoon of Oct. 26 Secretary of State Cyrus R. Vance signed a memo creating an interagency "Kampuchea Working Group," it appeared a months-long, behind-the-scenes struggle to organize an international relief program for Cambodia was about to bear fruit.

After months of stonewalling by the Vietnam-supported Heng Samrin regime in Phnom Penh, the International Committee of the Red Cross and the UN Children's Fund had won permission to run an internationally funded relief operation in that war-torn and famine-devastated country.

A $111-million, six-month program had been announced, and President Jimmy Carter, after some early foot-dragging by the inflation-wary Office of Management and Budget, had pledged $39 million right away and $30 million more next year.

Kurt Waldheim, the UN Secretary General who for months had feared an appeal for international pressure on contending forces in Cambodia and Vietnam would alienate supporters, Moscow and Peking, had agreed to call a special conference at UN headquarters to raise relief funds and focus international attention on Cambodia. That meeting will be held today.

CAMBODIA, Page 5

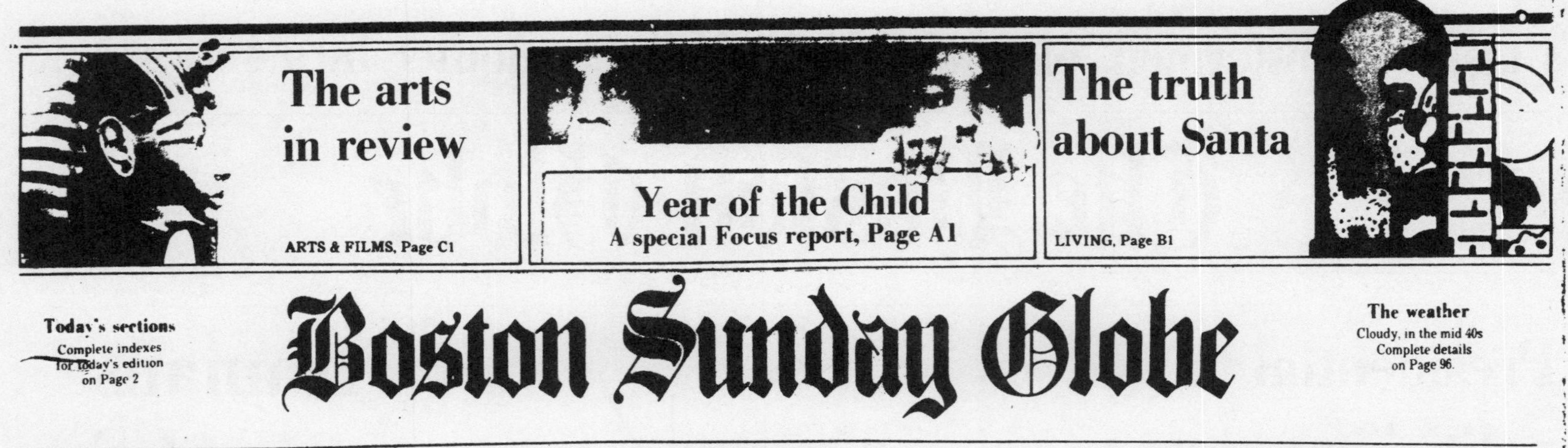

The arts in review

ARTS & FILMS, Page C1

Year of the Child

A special Focus report, Page A1

The truth about Santa

LIVING, Page B1

Today's sections

Complete indexes for today's edition on Page 2

Boston Sunday Globe

The weather

Cloudy, in the mid 40s

Complete details on Page 96.

Vol. 216, No. 169© 1979, Globe Newspaper Co. • SUNDAY, DECEMBER 16, 1979 • Telephone 929-2000 • Classified 929-1500 • Circulation 929-2222 • 75 Cents • 90 cents 30 miles from Boston and beyond

Politically powerful unions clamp an iron grip on MBTA

The crisis threatening to shut down the Massachusetts Bay Transportation Authority is the result of an iron grip that politically powerful unions have been able to clamp on the system.

A three-month investigation by The Globe Spotlight team has found massive evidence that union domination of management is a major reason why the MBTA, mile for mile, is the most costly and least efficient major transit system in the United States.

A Spotlight team analysis shows that the MBTA's cost per mile of operation in 1978 was $6.22, nearly double that of the $3.30 for the second most expensive system, San Francisco's. The MBTA's cost per passenger was $1.56 for the year, far more than the $1.12 of runner-up Washington's new system. By other standard measures of efficiency — cost per vehicle, miles of operation per employee and wage cost per mile of operation — the MBTA score was the worst.

MBTA executives and critics, while differing on details, have agreed that management problems have plagued the rapid transit authority for years.

"The T stinks ... there is no discipline anywhere," Robert L. Foster, the chairman of the MBTA, told a meeting of department heads in October.

The Spotlight study found that a principal reason for weak management is an alliance of unions and the State House. The alliance, re-established by the administration of Gov. Edward J. King after a rupture under Gov. Michael Dukakis, has historically undercut management efforts to upgrade labor productivity, and has doomed emergency programs to repair breakdown-prone Light Rail Vehicles (LRVs), aging buses and streetcars.

Spotlight

The first of a series

Thousands of commuters will wait in the cold and snow this winter for trains, streetcars and buses that will never arrive. Why? Following is the first in a series of reports by The Globe Spotlight team that will provide the answer, detailing the reasons for the low service and the high cost of the Massachusetts Bay Transportation Authority.

One of the King administration's first moves was to oust most of a team of officials experienced in management who were hired under the Dukakis administration and replace them with union-oriented persons.

In an interview with The Globe, Foster conceded that the unions have an upper hand in setting productivity standards at the MBTA and that there was a problem with the efficiency of the labor force. Asked if King's recent intercessions on behalf of the unions had undercut attempts to strengthen management's position, Foster said:

"There's a germ of truth in there."

When asked to cite any examples of improvements in productivity made by his management team so far, Foster said they would not be evident until next April.

One high-ranking official in the Carmen's Union conceded privately that problems such as insubordination, laziness, harassment of foremen, leaving early and resistance to improvements in work methods are present among the workers repairing Light Rail Vehicles (LRVs) and streetcars. These repairmen are members of the Carmen's Union.

However, George Adams, president of the Carmen's Union, and Joseph E. Nevins, president of the Machinists' Union, the two unions cited most frequently for poor productivity, denied that the work habits of their members were the major cause of present and past problems.

Instead, the two union heads said the present crisis besetting the MBTA stemmed from: a massive breakdown of transmissions in a fleet of buses bought in 1975, which forced the MBTA to curtail sharply its preventive maintenance pro-

MBTA, Page 2

Shah flies to refuge in Panama

World court orders hostages freed

Reuter

THE HAGUE — The International Court of Justice, charging Iran with breaching fundamental legal principles, yesterday ordered the immediate release of 53 American hostages held in Tehran.

The unanimous verdict by the World Court, as the United Nations' principal legal body is also known, cleared the way for a possible US request to the UN Security Council for economic sanctions on Iran, which boycotted the case.

All 15 judges, including one from the Soviet Union, upheld a US petition submitted Nov. 29.

The court president, Sir Humphrey Waldock of Britain, announcing the judgment, accused Iran of contravening international conventions guaranteeing the protection of diplomatic and consular staff.

He said the ruling covered three US diplomats believed detained in the Iranian Foreign Ministry as well as 50 Americans held in the US embassy.

Although the United States had said two men detained in the embassy were not diplomatic, technical or administrative personnel, the court found they were also entitled to protection because of the embassy's inviolability.

The hostages, who are in their 43d day of captivity, were being exposed "to privation, hardship, anguish and even danger to life and health," he said.

Militant Iranian students seized the hostages Nov. 4, demanding the extradition of the deposed shah from the United States, where he was receiving medical treatment for cancer. The court announcement last night coincided with the news that the former monarch left the United States to live in Panama.

The students said yesterday they would go ahead with a trial of their American hostages following the deposed shah's departure from the United States.

[The Los Angeles Times reported that Finance Minister Bani-Sadr, who until recently was foreign minister and is regarded as something of a moderate, declared to reporters: "I believe that we must now have a trial."]

Iran refused to send a representative to take part in the proceedings before the world court. In a telegram to the court last week, Foreign Minister Sadegh Gotb-

WORLD COURT, Page 16

● Iranian students holding the US embassy in Tehran reacted to the departure of the deposed shah by saying they would go ahead with a trial of the hostages. Page 20.

● Iraq accused Iran's leaders of creating a dictatorship more violent than that of the ousted shah, but it denied reports it had attacked Iran on Friday. Page 19.

● Marxist terrorists who side with Iran's Islamic regime have claimed responsibility for the murder of four Americans in Turkey, police there reported. Page 15.

Coming Tuesday: A special section

On Tuesday, The Globe will publish a special, eight-page section on the continuing crisis in Iran. It will include a history of US-Iranian relations, and a review of the rule of the shah in Iran. It will summarize in detail the diplomatic methods being employed by the US government to release the hostages, and assess the effect of the crisis on the domestic political situation in the United States.

Iran says hostages' trial is 'inevitable'

From Wire Services

PANAMA CITY — The ousted shah of Iran secretly flew from Texas to Howard Air Force Base in Panama City yesterday, then boarded a helicopter for the Panamanian resort island of Contadora, 35 miles off the Pacific coast.

Panamanian officials said Mohammed Reza Pahlevi ultimately would reside on a smaller nearby island, Coibita, once the site of a penal colony. Some sources, however, questioned whether that was accurate, since Coibita contains only a rustic fishing lodge used by vacationers.

In Washington, White House press secretary Jody Powell disclosed shortly before noon that Pahlevi had departed at 8:15 a.m. from Lackland Air Force Base near San Antonio and flown to Panama aboard a US government aircraft.

Powell refused to speculate about the effect of the departure on the 50 American hostages being held hostage in Tehran. The Iranian government has demanded that the United States return Pahlevi for trial as a criminal.

On that point, a White House official would say only, "To the extent that the release of the hostages has been delayed by the mistaken belief that the United States would yield to demands to return the shah of Iran, his departure from the United States and residence in Panama clearly remove that reason for delay."

A spokesman for the Iranians holding the US embassy in Teheran said: "Now that the shah has gone to Panama, the trial of the hostages will take place."

The official Pars news agency said Pahlevi's departure from America made the espionage trial "inevitable."

One of the militants holding the hostages was quoted by the Associated Press as saying the new developments "make no difference whatsoever" in demands that Pahlevi be returned to Iran.

Iran and Panama do not have diplomatic relations.

The shah, with his wife Empress Farah at his side, was met at his new residence, Puntalara, by television interviewers from Independent Television News Association and ABC, and said they were "very happy to have been received in such a hospitable way and we are very grateful for the gracious invitation by the Republic of Panama."

"The minute we set foot in your beautiful country, until now, we have been most happy and we hope that we will enjoy a wonderful sojourn in your country," he said. "I will be very pleased to meet with your president of the republic and get acquainted with the Panama life culture."

Although Powell emphasized the ailing shah would establish residence in Panama,

SHAH, Page 22

Shah makes statement yesterday on resort island of Contadora. (AP photo)

Jordan became a diplomat to arrange refuge for shah

By Martin F. Nolan
Globe Staff

WASHINGTON — A venture into "shuttle diplomacy" by President Jimmy Carter's chief of staff helped find a new home for Mohammed Reza Pahlevi, the deposed shah, Administration aides said yesterday.

Hamilton Jordan, 35, the top political operative in the White House, made clandestine flights between Panama City, Washington and San Antonio, Texas, for much of last week, consulting with the hospitalized shah and his new host, the Panamanian government.

Panama extended an invitation to the shah 10 months ago, shortly after he was forced to flee Iran. It renewed the invitation early last week after Mexico refused to readmit the shah.

Carter dispatched Jordan to Panama late Tuesday morning to determine the sincerity and dependability of the invitation. Jordan was chosen because of his role in 1977 in negotiating a new Panama Canal treaty.

The treaty hands over control of the former American Canal Zone to Panama at the end of 1999. The treaty was bitterly opposed by Republican conservatives in Washington as a "giveaway" to a "Marxist" regime headed by former president Omar Torrijos.

Torrijos, now commander of the Panamanian National Guard, is still considered by US diplomats to be the strongman in the country of 2 million. The new president, Aristides Royo, 39, is also considered a leftist.

Whatever their ideology, the Panamanian leaders offered asylum to the 60-year-old shah, and Jordan went to negotiate details.

In an Air Force jet, Jordan flew from Panama City Tuesday night to Lackland Air Force Base near San Antonio, arriving at dawn Wednesday. There Jordan met with the shah and the State Department's liaison with the shah, Steven Oxman. Also at the meeting was Lloyd Cutler of the White House staff, a former Washington lawyer who had arranged the shah's entry into a New York City hospital Oct. 22 for cancer treatment.

The principal concern of the shah and his aides was their unfamiliarity with Panama and the depth and sincerity of his welcome there. Since leaving Tehran Jan.

DECISION, Page 23.

At 4, a badly beaten boy needs a healing holiday

By James Stack
Globe Staff

Richie is only 4 years old, but his tiny body is covered with scars, each one a witness to the violence that filled his life until just a month ago.

Child abuse is always an ugly, sickening business, but in Richie's case it is especially tragic because he was born retarded and his father held this against him.

"He wanted a perfect child," said the clergyman who countersigned a letter sent to Globe Santa in Richie's behalf. "When he didn't get what he wanted, he blamed the child."

He said the brutality always came after a drinking bout and, as time went

GLOBE SANTA, Page E20

TO HELP GLOBE SANTA send your contribution to Globe Santa, Box 1525, Boston, Mass. 02104, or deliver it personally weekdays to the Globe downtown office at the corner of Washington and School sts.

Santa's friends

Merry Christmas, Uncle John, Love, Ellen	5.00
Madeleine, Joseph, Maureen, Matthew and Barbara	15.00
Fran Kimmel	20.00
The Sarafa grandchildren, Costa, Mary, Mike, Peter, Marianna, Philip, Nicole and James	40.00
The Middletons, Medford	5.00
Annamaria D'Angelo	10.00
Natasha and Harry	10.00
Metropolitan Pomona Grange, No. 30 — P of H	15.00
Anonymous	100.00
The Sandner Family	25.00

SANTA'S FRIENDS, Page E20

Churchill's grandson named in sex scandal

United Press International

LONDON — Opposition Labor Party leaders screamed yesterday for the political scalp of Sir Winston Churchill's grandson, who admitted he was the "Mr. X" involved with the ex-wife of a millionaire Saudi Arabian arms dealer in a sex and security scandal reminiscent of Britain's 1963 Profumo affair.

The opposition leaders also called for an investigation into the security aspects of the relationship of Winston Churchill, 39, and Soraya Kashoggi, 37, former wife of Saudi financier and arms dealer Adnan Kashoggi.

Prime Minister Margaret Thatcher was expected to have her written replies to the demands read to the House of Commons tomorrow.

The scandal stemmed from a case in London's Old Bailey court earlier this week, when three policemen were sentenced to jail terms of up to three years for trying to blackmail Soraya Kashoggi.

During the trial, one of the policemen claimed they were investigating her on security grounds because of her relationship with a "prominent politician."

The name of the politician was not announced in court, but at the judge's request, Soraya Kashoggi wrote it down for the jury. She also testified that her relationship with the politician — dubbed "Mr. X" in court — was "more than a friendship."

Early yesterday morning Churchill's lawyers issued a statement saying: "To avoid further speculation affecting other Members of Parliament, Mr. Winston Chuchill, MP, has instructed us to state that the name written down in recent criminal proceedings at the Old Bailey — but not published — was that of Mr. Churchill."

CHURCHILL, Page 4

WINSTON CHURCHILL ... case compared to 1963 Profumo affair (UPI file photo)

Guide to features

ARTS/FILMS 10
BRIDGE 46
CLASSIFIED 28-36
COMICS 20
CROSSWORD 20
DEATH NOTICES . 47
ECONOMY 15
EDITORIALS 22
HOROSCOPE 48
LIVING 25
TV/RADIO 19
TWISTAGRAM 18

The Boston Globe

Warm way street

MONDAY — Sunny, around 40
TUESDAY — Snow likely
HIGH TIDE — 6:49 a.m., 7:31 p.m.
FULL REPORT — PAGE 48

Vol. 217, No. 56 © 1980, Globe Newspaper Co. • MONDAY, FEBRUARY 25, 1980 • Telephone 929-2000 Classified 929-1500 Circulation 929-2222 48 Pages — 25 Cents

Yes, America, your boys did it

By Leigh Montville
Globe Staff

LAKE PLACID, N.Y. — The final image was Jim Craig and the flag. The picture wrapped up the entire, crazy business.

Some ragged-looking kid came running onto the ice of the Olympic Arena, sliding a bit in his sneakers, and handed the large and dirty American flag to the United States goaltender. Craig looked at the flag for a second, thought about what to do, made his decision. He decided to wear the flag.

He threw it around his shoulders the way an old woman puts on her shawl. The edges trailed to the ground. He was almost totally wrapped in red and white and blue, only his head and the tail ends of his fat goalie's stick poking through, and as he skated, glided, shook the row of hands, he was a symbol, a hope, a promise ... he looked like the Statue of Liberty on skates.

Hello, America. The tough little boys had done it.

There have been very few moments in sport in this country like this one. There may never be another. These ragamuffin rink rats, college kids and minor leaguers, were the gold medal winners of the XIII Olympics. They had finished these two days, these two gathering weeks of patriotic, nationalistic frenzy with a 4-2 win over Finland to win the title that no one had expected them to win. They had startled the world. "Are you surprised that you've won the gold medal?" a voice asked Craig at a packed, postgame press conference in Lake Placid High School.

"If there's anyone in this room who's not surprised, would he please raise his hand?" Craig replied.

Who were these kids? They took a game that most of America wouldn't watch if it were being played in the cellar and made it a national mania. They were excitement, youth on the hoof, enthusiasm running out of their ears. They beat the Czechs, they beat the Russians, they beat the Finns, they beat everyone they had to beat.

They were delirious, wonderful underdogs from a country that doesn't have a chance to be an underdog very often. They each were born of the Fourth of July, they each lived on Main street, they each drank milk and were rewarded with sugar cookies. Their souls were pure, their aim was true. They traveled with Tom and Huck. They all loved Becky Thatcher.

OLYMPICS, Page 38

United States goaltender Jim Craig is draped in the American flag presented to him by a youngster who swooped onto the ice after the gold-medal victory over Finland. (AP photo)

Members of the United States hockey team, gold medals around their necks, rush toward their captain, Mike Eruzione, after awards ceremonies last night. (AP photo)

A GLOBE EDITORIAL

They did it their way, the United States Olympic hockey players did, winning their gold medal by catching and passing Finland in the last period of the last game at Lake Placid yesterday.

The winning effort was true to form: As in earlier games, most notably the epic victory over the best-in-the-world Russians on Friday night, the Americans won by overcoming their opponents over the course of a hair-raising third period.

This hockey team — 20 bright-faced young men, including four players with ties to Boston University — had true grit: This was the same bunch that had lost to the Russians several weeks ago at Madison Square Garden by a 10-3 score.

The Olympics, as the world now knows, was a different matter.

An editorial, Page 22.

All eyes were on the gold rush

HERE . . .

By Tim Dwyer
Globe Staff

They watched him grow up. They remember when he used to come in and look under the tables for change so he could buy a pair of skates. And yesterday, there he was on national television — Mike Eruzione, captain of the gold medal-winning US hockey team, talking with the President of the United States.

It was all too much for the gang at Santarpio's Pizza in East Boston. "Hey, Mike!" they shouted. "There's Mike talking to the President."

Eruzione's father, Eugene (or Jeep the Creep, as he's known on "the corner" where the restaurant is located) has worked at Santarpio's for 16 years. The gang watched Mike grow up. And they cheered him and his teammates on to the gold medal.

"Before he left," said Ray DiLoreto, "he said: 'We're going to come back with the gold.' "

The gang gathered yesterday in the neighborhood restaurant and bar to watch the game. There was some spaghetti and some sausage and lots of cheering.

Tom Caldarelli was there with Eddie Grieco, Ray DiLoreti and his son Ray, Tony Andreottola, Jim Caldarelli and his son Jim Jr., The Shadow, Robert Caldarelli and Richard Campagna.

During a break in the game, they talked about "Jeep" and Mike. "I wonder what Jeep is doing? He's

BAR, Page 40

Bedlam it was outside the Eruzione house in Winthrop after yesterday's win. (Globe photo by George Rizer)

. . . AND THERE

By Bud Collins
Globe Correspondent

LAKE PLACID, N.Y. — The man named Carter was taking orders for lunch at a pretty good eating spot in Washington, D.C., called the White House, and James Craig of North Easton, Mass., said he'd have "two lobsters. Oysters. You know, the kind of seafood we get at home, sir.

"Can you imagine that?" recalled Craig, whose boardinghouse reach in the United States goal kept Russians, Finns, Swedes, Czechs and others hungry. "Can you imagine the President of the United States asking me what I'll have for dinner?"

Theirs was a victory yesterday that the US hockey team can dine out on for the rest of their lives. But Jimmy Carter, who got his vicarious licks in against the Soviet Union through these Olympic champions, pulled rank as Chief Host, and will have the gold medalists — Dream America — in for lunch.

It was inevitable that the phone call would come from 1600 Pennsylvania avenue to the US dressing room after the delirious, dizzy and dazzling triumph over Finland, 4-2. It was the usual stretch run for the money that made this hockey team seem like a Boston thoroughbred of years ago called Brass Monkey. Brass Monkey was never highly regarded, but kept coming from behind to win — and this was a gang of thoroughbreds with enough brass in them to skate down

LAKE PLACID, Page 38

Carter: Keep hope on Iran

By John M. Goshko
Washington Post

WASHINGTON — President Jimmy Carter insisted yesterday that "progress is being made" in the effort to free the American hostages in Tehran and cautioned against going from "extreme optimism to extreme pessimism every time some action is taken or some speech is made in Iran."

In his first public reaction to Ayatollah Ruhollah Khomeini's surprise statement Saturday that the fate of the hostages will not be decided until April, Carter said that "there's no way of telling an exact schedule" for their release.

While the President refused to go into detail, he and other Administration officials mounted a strenuous effort last night to reassure the American public that negotiations with Iran are still under way and that they are hopeful of a successful outcome.

Carter's guarded talk of "very sensitive and very difficult efforts" taking place behind the scenes came as a United Nations commission met in Iran with President Abdol Hassan Bani-Sadr and Foreign Minister Sadegh Ghotbzadeh, one day after arriving in Tehran. The commisson reportedly was told it would receive broad cooperation in its inquiry into Iranian grievances against the deposed shah, Mohammed Reza Pahlevi.

News agencies reported from Tehran that Iranian officials continued to stress that the commission's mission was not to win release of the 50 American hostages held by Islamic militants who seized the US embassy Nov. 4.

Bani-Sadr, after a meeting of the ruling Revolutionary Council, told reporters in Tehran last night that the UN commission would see the hostages, but a spokesman for the militants disagreed.

"The work of the UN commission has nothing to do with the hostages, so there will be no plan for the commission to visit the embassy," the spokesman said, according to Reuter news agency.

These contradictory statements coming out of Iran were cited by Administration officials in their warning that the US public should not leap to hard-and-fast conclusions over every unexpected development emanating from Iran's confused and tumultuous internal political situation.

IRAN, Page 5

State's MD board bogs down

By Richard A. Knox
Globe Staff

If you have a complaint against a Massachusetts doctor, it won't do much good right now to file it with the state medical licensing board.

The board can't take on any more investigations or disciplinary procedures, according to board members and staff. In fact, the agency is so paralyzed by inadequate staff and an absence of administrative leadership that it can barely handle the 17,000 license renewals it is obligated by law to process every two years; recently the board had to assure doctors that their expired licenses will be valid until the new ones can be sent out, sometime next month.

Complicated cases involving alleged incompetence, fraud or physician addiction take years to investigate and resolve while the doctors involved are free to continue practicing.

"We can't even get our correspondence typed," one board member said last week. "It's a scandal."

Moreover, the board is running out of money to pay for rudimentary aspects of its disciplinary job, such as paying for expert medical witnesses and the typing of hearing transcripts. Chairman Claude Welch, a Massachusetts General Hospital surgeon, estimated Friday that "we may be short about $60,000" by the end of the next fiscal quarter.

MEDICAL BOARD, Page 18

How they stand on issues on N.H. primary eve

THE REPUBLICANS

By Rachelle Patterson
Globe Staff

MANCHESTER, N.H. — As the campaign for the Republican presidential nomination has progressed, some disagreement has developed among the candidates over foreign policy and how to approach domestic problems such as inflation and abortion.

Some Republicans seem more hawkish than others in the wake of the Soviet aggression in Afghanistan; some like the idea of Selective Service registration now and some want women to be included.

They are split over the question of whether America should let the deposed shah of Iran come to this country to live and whether the United States should initiate a blockade of Cuba in retaliation for Soviet intervention in Afghanistan. They all agree with President Jimmy Carter's decision to boycott the Moscow Olympics. But with the exception of John Anderson, they oppose the grain embargo.

A Globe survey just before the New Hampshire presidential primary is an update of an earlier one published last December when the campaigns were just shifting into full gear. The issues have expanded since then and the candidates have fine-tuned their postions.

George Bush, for instance, wants it clearly understood that he is for a windfall profits tax only if it has a plow-back provision placing the proceeds of the tax into the hands of oilmen to stimulate increased production. Similarly, Ronald Reagan advocates an "MX-type missile," not the MX missile currently proposed because he objects to its mode of deployment. Bush wants a more advanced B1 type of bomber.

Some of the Republicans have changed or sharpened their positions from three months ago.

REPUBLICAN ISSUES, Page 2

'Just politics' or a 'lockout'?

By David Nyhan
Globe Staff

MANCHESTER, N.H. — George Bush's rivals for the Republican presidential nomination yesterday vowed revenge for his alleged role in having four of them excluded from a Nashua debate the night before.

Bush, who had flown back to Texas, said the furor was "just politics," but his fellow candidates blamed him for the exclusion, using such terms as "lockout politics" and "Gestapo tactics," as the GOP presidential campaign took an unexpectedly bitter turn.

Ronald Reagan was delighted with the uproar, which his handlers felt took the edge off Bush's effort here with only two days left in the New Hampshire primary campaign.

The Reagan camp triggered the trap Bush fell into, by inviting the other candidates to participate Satur-

DEBATE, Page 6

THE DEMOCRATS

By Curtis Wilkie
and Chris Black
Globe Staff

CONCORD, N.H. — Four years ago, with nine major candidates competing for the Democratic presidential nomination, there was less division on the major issues of the campaign than there is today.

But now, as then, perceptions of the candidates' personalities, morals and campaign performances seem to be moving the average voter more than particular positions on the issues, although there are now, more than ever, passionately committed groups that vote for or against a candidate depending upon how he stands on single issues such as abortion and nuclear power.

Although the three top contenders for the Democratic nomination this year have similar views on abortion, there are several other significant issues on which they differ.

In his Georgetown speech four weeks ago, Sen. Edward M. Kennedy sharpened the differences between himself and President Jimmy Carter. Kennedy called for wage and price controls to combat inflation, a move which Carter has unequivocably rejected. Kennedy also advocated immediate gasoline rationing, while Carter has so far sought only standby rationing authority from Congress.

California Gov. Edmund G. Brown Jr. favors gasoline rationing but generally opposes wage and price controls. Brown believes that the President should have standby authority for the controls, but should exercise them only as a last resort.

Carter has advocated a 3 to 5 percent "real" increase (after taking into account inflation) in the Defense Department budget during each of the next five years.

DEMOCRATIC ISSUES, Page 2

Guide to features
ARTS/FILMS .... 26 DEATH NOTICES 37
BRIDGE .... 38 EDITORIALS 12
BUSINESS .... 19 HOROSCOPE 38
CLASSIFIED .... 38-46 LIVING 23
COMICS .... 28 TV/RADIO 29
CROSSWORD .... 28 TWISTAGRAM 38

The Boston Globe

Vary tale
MONDAY — Sun vs. clouds, 70s
TUESDAY — Partly sunny, 70s
HIGH TIDE — 3:32 a.m., 4:10 p.m.
FULL REPORT — PAGE 25

Vol. 218, No. 140© 1980, Globe Newspaper Co. • MONDAY, MAY 19, 1980 Telephone 929-2000 Classified 929-1500 Circulation 929-2222 46 Pages — 25 Cents

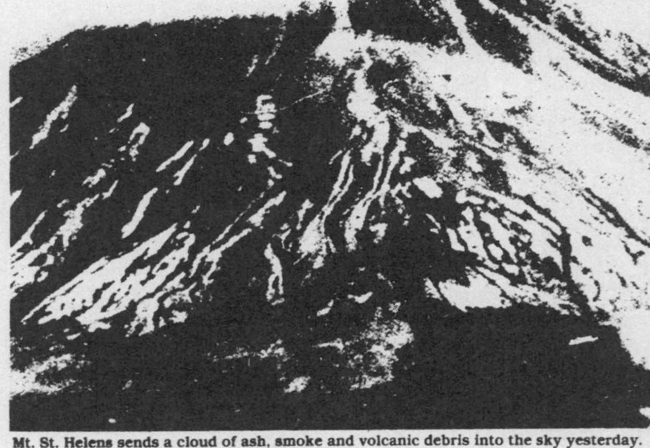

Mt. St. Helens sends a cloud of ash, smoke and volcanic debris into the sky yesterday. AP PHOTO

Mt. St. Helens explodes

8 persons killed in blast felt 200 miles away

By Bruce Bartley
Associated Press

VANCOUVER, Wash. — Mt. St. Helens blew its top yesterday with a blast felt 200 miles away, belching ash and hot gas that blotted out the sun for more than 450 miles and killing at least eight persons. Mudflows and floods destroyed bridges and forced evacuation of about 2000.

At least three persons were missing, and scenic Spirit Lake at the base of the mountain disappeared under mud and rock flows.

Late yesterday, a mile-wide wall of mud was seen oozing down the north fork of the Toutle River, snapping concrete and steel bridges like toothpicks and sweeping cars and houses in its wake.

The eruption at 8:39 a.m. (PDT) shot smoke and ash 9 miles into the sky, and a spectacular lightning storm in the rising plume started numerous forest fires. By evening the fires covered 3000 acres on the mountain. There were no immediate reports of lava.

In Walla Walla, 160 miles to the east, drifting ash made the sky so dark that automatic street lights went on, and by evening more than a foot of ash had accumulated at Camp Baker, 15 miles west of the volcano. Ash also was reported falling in western Montana, and police there said roads were closed due to near-zero visibility west and south of Missoula, about 500 miles downwind from the volcano. Ash there was a half-inch deep on the ground.

The eruption was visible in Vancouver, more than 50 miles to the southwest, and the explosion was felt in Vancouver, B.C., more than 200 miles to the north.

VOLCANO, Page 4

Curfew is set in Miami as riot toll rises to 18

Violence wracks black areas after white officers acquitted

By Carl Hiaasen
Knight Ridder Service

MIAMI — A dusk-to-dawn curfew was imposed yesterday over riot-torn sections of northwest Dade County after another day of fiery racial violence that pushed the county's death toll to 18, including two demonstrators shot by police and a police officer who died of a heart attack. At least 216 persons were injured.

Among the dead were eight black men, six whites, a Latin man and three victims who were not identified.

Most of yesterday's dead were gunshot victim's, reflecting a grim trend away from the rock-and-bottle episodes that opened the violence Saturday night.

Public Safety Director Bobby Jones ordered all people off the streets between 8 p.m. yesterday and 6 a.m. today in areas wracked Saturday night by looting, gunshots and beatings after the acquittals of four white ex-policemen who were charged with the beating death of black insurance man Arthur McDuffie.

Prosecutors had claimed McDuffie, racing from police on a motorcycle, was surrounded by officers who savagely beat him, then tried to cover up the attack by making it appear he had been injured in a motorcycle accident. McDuffie died four days later.

The US attorney's office announced early yesterday that a federal grand jury will begin investigating the McDuffie incident this week for possible civil rights violations. [Page 7.]

Gov. Bob Graham implored the demonstrators to disperse and go home. "We have come too far, worked too hard to see it lost in one more night of needless violence and rage," he said in a televised address.

Public schools were ordered closed today and Supt. Leonard Britton called a special board meeting for 1:30 p.m. All city bus service was suspended at 10 a.m. yesterday.

The curfew covers black sections of Coconut Grove and the northwest black area known as Liberty City.

MIAMI, Page 6

National Guardsman stands watch in Miami's black community. UPI PHOTO

'The fires are going to start . . .'

By William R. Amlong
Knight Ridder Service

MIAMI — The slain insurance man's name became a battle cry. "McDuffie, McDuffie," chanted a knot of youths as it hurled bricks and bottles at passing white motorists.

Standing on 62d street in Liberty City, Vietnam veteran Steve Rolle articulated the flashpoint feelings that led to Saturday night's rioting after an all-white jury had acquitted four Dade County policemen in the death of 33-year-old Arthur McDuffie.

"What you got here, you call this the straw that broke the camel's back," Rolle said. "The natives are restless. Even the kids are out. There wasn't no justice for the black people. They shoved everything down our throats. The fires are going to start in a few minutes."

And fires did start, as did shooting and rock-and-bottle attacks on whites' cars. Whites were dragged

SCENE, Page 7

Mannequins from a nearby store lie broken in the gutter after a night of looting. UPI PHOTO

IN THIS CORNER

For her, happiness is 11 handicapped kids

Associated Press

PROVIDENCE — Rachel Rossow, mother of 11 handicapped children, says she's so happy "that sometimes I feel guilty about it."

With her husband Carl, the 41-year-old Connecticut woman's life revolves around a family of 14 youngsters, 11 of whom have handicaps ranging from paralyzed limbs to being born without a brain.

"I'm always tired," laughed Rossow. "But I figure being tired is an occupational hazard for any mother of a large family."

Hers is not a typical household. The couple adopted their first multiple-handicap child in 1971. Others soon followed.

"Our phone kept ringing . . . nurses and social workers asking would we accept this or that child . . . until finally in 1974 we set up a nonprofit corporation and opened our home to more handicapped youngsters," Rossow said.

She was in Rhode Island on Saturday to accept an award from her alma mater, Newport College-Salve Regina, honoring her life's work.

From their large home in Ellington, Conn., the Rossows pursue the task of raising children ages 1 to 14.

Wheelchairs in the spacious house are as common as roller skates and bicycles in a neighbor's home.

"The kids have wheelchair races. It gets pretty hectic around here with all the sibling rivalry," Rossow said in a telephone interview. The furniture in the home is widely spaced to allow maneuvering room for the wheelchairs.

Her youngest is 1-year-old Benjamin, who "was literally born without a brain."

"That little boy is a very valuable addition to our family. For starters, he's beautiful," she declared. "He has the most gorgeous blue eyes that sort of wander back and forth, and absolutely golden hair that's starting to curl up behind his ears. He's simply a beautiful-looking child."

All but three of the children are adopted, though Rossow politely refuses to say which ones. 'They're all my children."

Her gentle voice turns sharp at the suggestion her concern is born of pity.

"Pity? That's a quality that all of the children as well as Carl and I can't stand."

COL. WILLIAM P. CREAMER
"Looking at what we would do"

N.E. sites checked to house 10,000 Cubans, if needed

By Maggie Rivas
and Al Larkin
Globe Staff

Federal officials in Boston filed a contingency plan with Washington last week indicating that as many as 10,000 Cuban refugees could be housed at two New England military installations if the need arose.

But, despite reports to the contrary, a spokesman for the Federal Emergency Management Agency (FEMA) overseeing the Cuban evacuation program in Florida, said there were no imminent plans to send the refugees to New England.

CUBA, Page 10

Europe votes limited sanctions

By Sari Gilbert
Special to The Globe

NAPLES, Italy — The foreign ministers of the nine European Economic Community nations decided yesterday to apply economic sanctions against Iran starting Thursday, but excluded all contracts for goods and services signed before the takeover of the US embassy in Tehran last Nov. 4.

The decision significantly watered down an April 22 pledge by the Common Market to adopt full economic sanctions, if no decisive progress had been made by this weekend toward re-

The US hostages reportedly will be freed after Iran's parliament approves an overall solution to the crisis. Page 8.

lease of the 53 American hostages in Iran.

The Europeans have always been skeptical about applying sanctions, but yesterday's decision also appeared to reflect the impact of recent appeals by top Iranian officials for support that would permit them to tackle the hostage problem.

By setting a firm date for the start of sanctions, the Europeans sought to satisfy the United States. The four-day gap until sanctions are imposed is designed to give countries that need it time to prepare any necessary legislation.

The sanctions will affect all trade contracts established after Nov. 4, except for food and medicine, and will leave intact an April 22 agreement ruling out purchases of Iranian oil sold at prices above the level set by the Organization of Petroleum Exporting Countries.

The ministers' decision fell far short of original American hopes for a total trade embargo, and it left the

SANCTIONS, Page 8

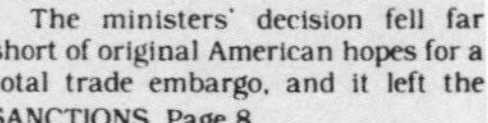

Answer is in a mixture of resources

This is the second of two articles on New England's energy dilemma. Subsequent articles will appear from time to time focusing on specific energy developments in the region.

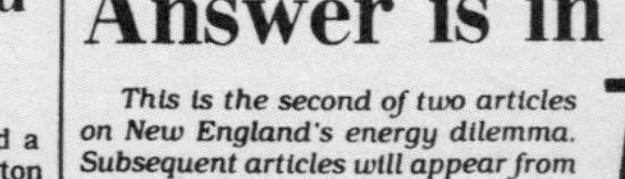

By Gary McMillan
Globe Staff

Once there were the wind and the wood, the sea and the sun.

The New England forest spread from Coventry to Lake Memphremagog, warmed and powered a burgeoning people and their commerce. Rivers were sluiced through dams to power the waterwheels and spin the looms. The wind churned across the lands and onto the sea to propel the three-masters in the search for the energies of whales.

And above it all, the primal energy of the sun.

It is all still there.

Waiting.

They are New England's renewable energy resources — far more ample than oil or natural gas and the best ultimate escape from the cycle of crises caused by our overdependence on once-cheap fossil fuels.

The key to solving the energy dilemma is to place the renewables in a proper mix without swapping one addiction for another.

ENERGY, Page 2

Miami's Dolphins hang in, beat Patriots in OT, 16-13 (Page 37)

A foster mother asks Globe Santa to help cheer 2 children (Page 72)

Guide to features
ARTS/FILMS 33
BRIDGE 54
BUSINESS 57
CLASSIFIED 45-52, 56
COMICS 53
CROSSWORD 53
DEATH NOTICES 70-71
EDITORIALS 18
HOROSCOPE 54
LIVING 30
TV/RADIO 55
TWISTAGRAM 54
BUSINESS

The Boston Globe

Ray on
TUESDAY — Partial clearing, 45-50
WEDNESDAY — Chance of showers
HIGH TIDE — Midnight, 12:11 p.m.
FULL REPORT — PAGE 54

Vol. 218, No. 162 © 1980, Globe Newspaper Co. • TUESDAY, DECEMBER 9, 1980 Telephone 929-2000 Classified 929-1500 Circulation 929-2222 72 Pages — 25 Cents

Ex-Beatle John Lennon shot dead

Above all, a man of courage

By Steve Morse and Jim Sullivan
Globe Staff

John Lennon died an enigma. After being an idol of his generation, leading and awakening his peers time and again in the '60s as one of the Beatles, and later as a provocative soloist, he disappeared from public view. The star who manned the psychic barricades was suddenly a family man who sought to be alone, who sought the peace his frenetic career had never allowed him.

The 40-year-old Lennon recently broke a five-year recording absence by releasing "Double Fantasy," an album that only heightened his role as an enigma. in one song, "Watching the Wheels," he addressed his obsessive latter-day need for privacy:

"People say I'm lazy, dreaming my life away/Well they give me all kinds of advice designed to enlighten me/When I tell them that I'm dong fine watching shadows on the wall/Don't you miss the big time boy you're no longer on the ball. . .No longer riding on the merry-go-round/I just had to let it go."

There are those who will say that Lennon forsook his generation, that he renounced his role as countercultural leader and earth-shaker, but how much can one man do? Through his emotional pleas for peace, through his brilliant crafting of pristine love songs, through his dabbling in meditation and Eastern cultures, through the anger of his solo career and his socialistic defense of the working-class, he molded the thoughts of his peers perhaps more than any other rock star had, including Elvis Presley, an idol during his youth.

Above all, Lennon was a man of courage who dared to stand alone when detractors shouted that Yoko Ono was a millstone to his career (his "dragon lady," as was said), and that he was wrong to drop out of music.

APPRECIATION, Page 2

JOHN LENNON
Wife at his side

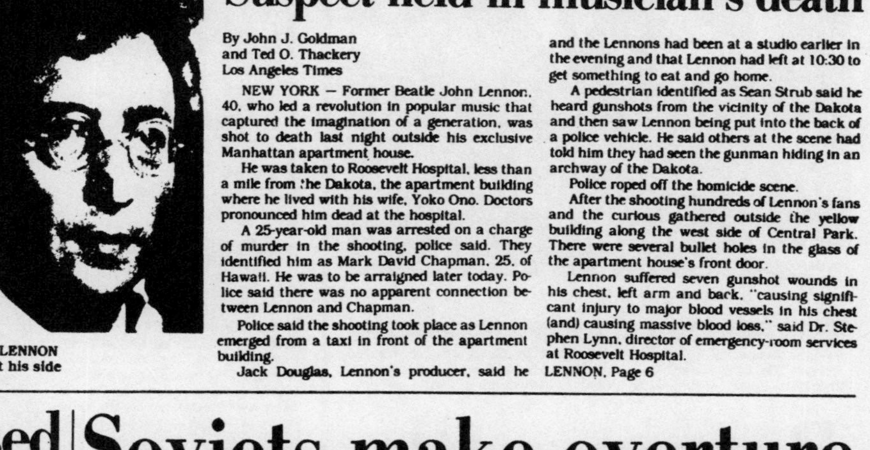

Suspect held in musician's death

By John J. Goldman
and Ted O. Thackery
Los Angeles Times

NEW YORK — Former Beatle John Lennon, 40, who led a revolution in popular music that captured the imagination of a generation, was shot to death last night outside his exclusive Manhattan apartment house.

He was taken to Roosevelt Hospital, less than a mile from the Dakota, the apartment building where he lived with his wife, Yoko Ono. Doctors pronounced him dead at the hospital.

A 25-year-old man was arrested on a charge of murder in the shooting, police said. They identified him as Mark David Chapman, 25, of Hawaii. He was to be arraigned later today. Police said there was no apparent connection between Lennon and Chapman.

Police said the shooting took place as Lennon emerged from a taxi in front of the apartment building.

Jack Douglas, Lennon's producer, said he and the Lennons had been at a studio earlier in the evening and that Lennon had left at 10:30 to get something to eat and go home.

A pedestrian identified as Sean Strub said he heard gunshots from the vicinity of the Dakota and then saw Lennon being put into the back of a police vehicle. He said others at the scene had told him they had seen the gunman hiding in an archway of the Dakota.

Police roped off the homicide scene.

After the shooting hundreds of Lennon's fans and the curious gathered outside the yellow building along the west side of Central Park. There were several bullet holes in the glass of the apartment house's front door.

Lennon suffered seven gunshot wounds in his chest, left arm and back, "causing significant injury to major blood vessels in his chest (and) causing massive blood loss," said Dr. Stephen Lynn, director of emergency-room services at Roosevelt Hospital.

LENNON, Page 6

Greens apologize; case closed

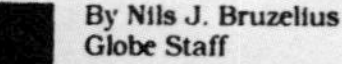

Gerald and Diana Green leave Plymouth Superior Court yesterday. GLOBE PHOTO BY JOE RUNCI

By Nils J. Bruzelius
Globe Staff

PLYMOUTH — Nearly 14 months after after they buried their son in a Nebraska cemetery, the parents of Chad Green returned to a Massachusetts courtroom yesterday to end the three-year-old court battle over the care they had given to the leukemia-stricken boy.

Flanked by a recently retained Wisconsin lawyer and a psychiatrist, Gerald and Diana Green appeared voluntarily in Plymouth Superior Court. Their attorney said they considered it their "Christian responsibility" to answer arrest warrants for civil and criminal contempt of court that had been pending against them since Feb. 7, 1979.

Before those charges were filed, the parents had fled the state rather than obey a court order directing them to continue the chemotherapy that physicians said had twice controlled Chad's cancer and to cease giving him an unorthodox program of "metabolic therapy" involving the unproven cancer remedy laetrile.

Judge Francis Keating, accepting the apologies offered by both of the boy's parents, yesterday found them guilty of criminal contempt but passed no sentence, directing that the case be closed.

GREENS, Page 12

1895-car Hub garage closed

Boston officials: Government Center building unsafe

By Peter Cowen
Globe Staff

The 10-year-old, Government Center Garage was closed yesterday by Boston officials, who said it was unsafe because of a shifting support beam, corroding steel supports and cracked, poor-quality concrete.

The garage, which can hold up to 1895 vehicles and yielded $1.5 million in revenue to the city annually, was closed at 3 p.m. by the Building Department on the ground the garage was "structurally unsafe." The garage cost $7.5 million when it was built.

No estimates of the cost of repair were available, and one spokesman for Mayor Kevin White, Michael Donovan, said officials were trying "to determine whether it is salvageable or not."

City officials said they did not know how long the garage would be closed, and they said no provision had been made for alternative parking sites for patrons of the garage. The city stands to lose the $127,000 monthly rent as long as the garage is closed.

The garage, which is bounded by New Chardon, Blackstone, Sudbury and Bowker streets, had been operated for the last two years by Kinney System of Sudbury, Inc.

Kinney's contract had expired two months ago, and the city has gone to court to try to force the company out of the garage.

Officials at the Kinney regional headquarters in Boston did not return phone calls placed late yesterday.

In ordering the closing, the White administration cited the findings of a consultant, who finished his $6000 report to Boston officials in July.

Officials said the fact that the city has sued Kinney, which has continued to pay the $127,000 monthly rental, had no bearing on the decision to close the garage. The suit has not been resolved.

Asked why the city waited four months to close the garage, a White administration spokesman, Joseph Savage, said the Building Department had to confirm the report's accuracy before deciding.

The administration said it discovered the structural problems "during a routine inspection" that led to the hiring of the consultants, according to a press release by Mayor White's communications office

GARAGE, Page 28

IN THIS CORNER

2 live a life of 'constant oneness'

Associated Press

LONDON — Greta and Freda Chaplin, 37-year-old identical twins, are so alike in the way they think, speak, move, dress, look and live that children have thrown stones at them and called them witches and adults have spat on them

But the women's extreme closeness has also intrigued the scientific world, and some experts say they genuinely appear to share one mind between two bodies

They do everything together, scream or sulk if parted and, most uncannily, talk in unison when under stress, speaking the same words in identical voice patterns that create an weird echo effect

Doctors report they have not previously encountered such a case and say the twins are so close they almost seem linked by telepathy

The twins first became news last July when they appeared before magistrates in their home city of York to plead guilty to breach of the peace. The charge was relatively innocuous. The facts revealed by police were bizarre.

For 15 years, the unmarried twins have shared an obsessional romantic fixation on a truck driver named Kenneth Iveson, a 56-year-old former neighbor. He used to chat

IN THIS CORNER, Page 11

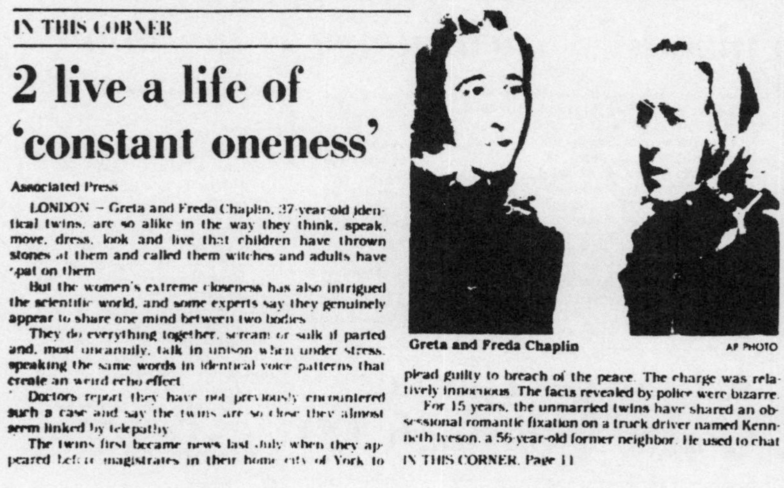

Greta and Freda Chaplin AP PHOTO

Soviets make overture to US on SALT, assail trade union in Poland

Tass says workers aggravate struggle

Washington Post

MOSCOW — The Soviet Union asserted yesterday that Poland's independent trade unions have turned to "open confrontation" with the Communist government in an effort to aggravate "the political struggle" there and drive the country into the Western camp.

The brief but strongly worded Soviet statement was followed quickly by similar statements from three other Eastern-bloc countries. This indicated that despite Friday's Warsaw Pact meeting in Moscow, which appeared to give Poland a reprieve from military intervention, the Kremlin is warning the Poles anew of the risks of their experiment with liberalization of party control.

Taking direct aim at the Solidarity independent union movement numbering more than 10 million Polish workers who have rejected the Communist-controlled unions, the official Tass press agency, in a dispatch from Warsaw, asserted that the independent movement has started a campaign to replace loyal trade unionists with antigovernment agitators.

A spokesman for the official Polish information agency, Interpress, as well as officials of Solidarity denied the Soviet accusation. One Solidarity branch called it "a complete lie . . . aimed at misleading Polish, Russian and world opinion."

The Tass formulation is similar to those used by Soviet news media before the 1968 Warsaw Pact invasion of Czechoslovakia, and was given added significance by quick repetition on Soviet radio. It is expected to be published today in authoritative central newspapers of the Soviet party and government.

In almost identical language, the official East German news agency condemned "counterrevolutionary groups acting inside Solidarity" three hours after the Tass statement was distributed. The official Czechoslovak news agency, quoting Rude Pravo, the Communist Party newspaper, said that each Communist country shares responsibility for the fate of other Communist states, and the Bulgarian news agency accused the United States of attempting to take control of the Polish economy.

It is now clear there are two very different interpretations of Friday's Warsaw Pact summit, which appeared to give Poland some breathing space to sort out its problems but also

POLAND, Page 14

ZBIGNIEW BRZEZINSKI
Opposed deal

It's Brzezinski over Muskie on deal with USSR

By Norman Kempster
Los Angeles Times

WASHINGTON — Secretary of State Edmund S. Muskie protested angrily to the White House after President Jimmy Carter agreed to withdraw permission for a US company to build a sophisticated oil-drilling-equipment plant in the Soviet Union, Administration officials said yesterday.

The President's decision, disclosed last week, was a victory for Zbigniew Brzezinski, Carter's national security adviser, who has opposed the project from the outset.

At issue was a $144-million deal in which Dresser Industries of Dallas was building a factory in the Soviet Union to produce advanced oil-well-drilling bits. The contract was suspended last year after the Soviets intervened militarily in Afghanistan. Carter decided Nov. 28 to cancel the export licenses needed to complete the deal.

However, Dresser officials complained that the plant was almost complete before it was suspended last year. The company said that the Soviets can probably complete the factory without additional US help.

A State Department official said Muskie had held that it was in the national interest to permit the deal with the Soviets to go through. He said other agencies — understood to be the National Security Council staff and the Pentagon — disagreed.

DRILLBITS, Page 14

Brezhnev, in India, decries arms race

By Stuart Auerbach
Washington Post

NEW DELHI — President Leonid Brezhnev of the Soviet Union signaled a willingness to reopen strategic arms limitation talks last night but warned the West that it must abandon any plans to achieve military superiority over Moscow.

The Soviet leader used a banquet toast on the opening day of his visit to India to send what diplomatic observers saw as a clear message to Washington, without specifically mentioning the United States.

A remark by Brezhnev to US Ambassador Robert Goheen in the airport receiving line underscored that Brezhnev was as interested in Moscow's superpower adversary in Washington as in his hosts in New Delhi.

"Give my regards to Mr. Reagan," Brezhnev told the ambassador, in one of the few comments he made to any diplomat.

Brezhnev's arrival was marred by minor demonstrations, and the Soviet leader's motorcade was rerouted for security reasons to avoid going through the center of New Delhi.

While Afghanistan is on the minds of many here and Poland preoccupies much of the Western world, Brezhnev placed much of the blame for what he called the "considerably colder" international climate at the doorstep of the United States and its allies.

"Influential politicians in the West have decided to whip up the arms race rather than limit it," he said, in what observers here saw as a reference to President Jimmy Carter's decision not to try to push SALT II through a hostile Senate after the Soviets intervened in Afghanistan a year ago.

"They have made up their minds to achieve military supremacy rather than to maintain parity," he continued.

Carter, in his January 1980 State of the Union message, called for increased spending to match "the steady growth and increased projection abroad of Soviet military power" while the Republican platform that President-elect Ronald Reagan ran on promised to build up the United States' armed might to "ultimately reach the position of military superiority that the American people demand."

Brezhnev called such a policy a "dangerous line" that leaves the peace of the world "gravely imperiled."

BREZHNEV, Page 15

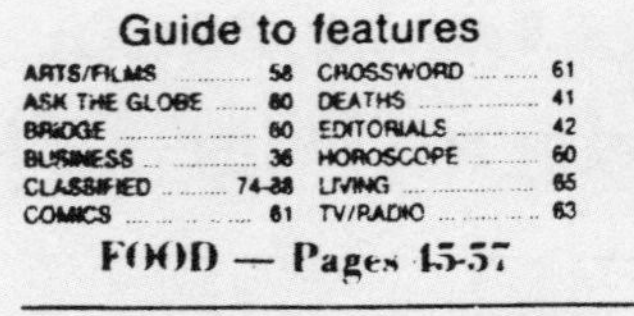

Guide to features

ARTS/FILMS	58	CROSSWORD	61
ASK THE GLOBE	80	DEATHS	41
BRIDGE	60	EDITORIALS	42
BUSINESS	36	HOROSCOPE	60
CLASSIFIED	74-88	LIVING	65
COMICS	61	TV/RADIO	63

FOOD — Pages 45-57

The Boston Globe

Do skies
WEDNESDAY — Sunny, mid 30s
THURSDAY — May rain or snow, 40
HIGH TIDE — 11:43 a.m.
FULL REPORT — PAGE 50

Vol. 219, No. 21 © 1981, Globe Newspaper Co. • Ⓢ WEDNESDAY, JANUARY 21, 1981 Telephone 929-2000 Classified 929-1500 Circulation 929-2222 88 Pages — 25 Cents

A NEW BEGINNING

Ronald Reagan is sworn in as President by Chief Justice Warren Burger. His wife, Nancy, and Sen. Mark Hatfield are in center with President Carter and his wife, Rosalynn, watching at right. AP PHOTO

Reagan calls for an era of 'renewal'

Text of address Page 15. Other inaugural stories and pictures Pages 17-19, 73

By Thomas Oliphant
Globe Staff

WASHINGTON — On a day when 52 Americans ended their long ordeal halfway around the world in Iran, and the South's first President in more than a century returned to his native Georgia after winning their release, Ronald Wilson Reagan became the nation's 40th Chief Executive with a call for "an era of national renewal" to cure "an economic affliction of great proportions."

Concentrating on domestic policy for virtually all of his inaugural address, the new President — ending a long political journey he began 13 years ago and capping a life that began nearly 70 years ago in the small community of Tampico, Ill. — set for himself the principal goals of rejuvenating the country's economy and reducing the size of the federal government he now heads.

With as much specificity as tradition allows, Reagan set his course for the immediate future.

"In the days ahead I will propose removing the roadblocks that have slowed our economy and reduced productivity," he told a large, friendly but quiet crowd gathered for the first inaugural ever held on the West Front of the Capitol.

Steps will be taken aimed at restoring the balance between the various levels of government. Progress may be slow — measured in inches and feet, not miles — but we will progress. It is time to reawaken this industrial giant, to get government back within its means and to lighten our punitive tax burden."

"These will be our first priorities, and on these principles there will be no compromise," he added to one of the eight bursts of applause that interrupted his 19-minute, 58-second address.

Reagan spent but three paragraphs after being sworn in before getting to his point — a stark portrayal of the present, which did, nonetheless, fall short of the symbolic declaration of emergency that had been urged upon him shortly after his landslide victory over Jimmy Carter some 10 weeks ago.

"We suffer from the longest and one of the worst sustained inflations in our national history," Reagan said. "It distorts our economic decisions, penalizes thrift and crushes the struggling young

INAUGURATION, Page 16

'. . let us renew our faith and our hope. We have every right to dream heroic dreams.'

— President Reagan

New leader — and some vintage talk

NEWS ANALYSIS

By Robert Healy
Globe Staff

WASHINGTON — Chief Justice Warren Burger held the Bible and asked Ronald Reagan if he was ready to take the oath of office. "I am," he said. He began to repeat after Burger the words prescribed in Article II of the Constitution: "I do solemnly swear that I will faithfully execute the office of the President of the United States . . ."

Then he stood alone.

He began to talk. It was the inaugural address of a new President, Ronald Reagan. But it was more than that. It was, as one of his aides put it, vintage Reagan.

It was, in a sense, the passing of another torch — a torch for the renewal of old values, of making Americans once again believe in themselves, of reversing the growth of government, of returning powers to the states that had been assumed by the federal government, of cutting taxes, of making the economy strong again.

He said that these would be the first priorities, "and on these principles, there will be no compromise."

That needed no translation for the people from Topeka, Kan., and Dixon, Ill., who occupied the standing-room space at the inaugural.

SPEECH, Page 17

Wall Street story: Stocks plunge 20.31

Report is on Page 36

'We've kept the faith with our principles and our people and, as a result, we have reached this day of joy and thanksgiving.'

— Ex-President Jimmy Carter

Freedom flight for 52 hostages

United Press International

WIESBADEN, West Germany — Laughing and crying and still not quite believing, the 52 American hostages flew to freedom yesterday, arriving in Wiesbaden after their liberty was negotiated in the final hours of Jimmy Carter's presidency.

The hostages arrived here just before 2 a.m. EST today after a freedom flight from Tehran with stops in Athens, Algiers and Frankfurt. They were greeted in Frankfurt by former Secretary of State Cyrus Vance, before making the 25-mile bus ride to a US military hospital in Wiesbaden.

After 444 days in captivity, the hostages received a taunting sendoff from their captors in Tehran and flew first to Athens for refueling and then on to Algeria and a warm and delighted embrace by the American negotiators who worked round-the-clock to free them.

After refreshments and a brief, emotional ceremony, the Americans boarded two US Air Force C9 hospital planes for the trip to Wiesbaden, where the military hospital that is to be their home for the next few days was decked out in yellow ribbons to receive them.

Carter, whose presidency ended a half hour before the hostage crisis did, was flying to Wiesbaden today as President Ronald Reagan's representative to greet the hostages on behalf of a rejoicing nation.

For the hostages, some looking dazed but all appearing fit, the flight from Iran was the first time they had been together in a group in the 14½ months of their ordeal.

Leaving Tehran to the taunts of "Down with America" chanted by young revolutionary guards, they hugged, kissed and cried as they greeted one another for the 4000-mile zig-zag journey to Wiesbaden.

Their arrival in Algiers in rain-swept darkness was no less emotional.

Wearing yellow ribbons in their hair, Elizabeth Ann Swift and Kathryn Koob, the two women among the hostages, were the first to step off the red and white jet, into the glare of television lights and the cheering applause of diplomats and reporters.

Smiling and laughing, the rest

HOSTAGES, Page 8

Donald Sharer gives victory sign as he and other freed hostages deplane at Algiers airport. AP PHOTO

How history will view Iran episode

NEWS ANALYSIS

By H.D.S. Greenway
Globe Staff

It was a crisis that became a national obsession, much to the dismay of America's allies and friends. Flags were flown at half-staff. Television stations and newspapers faithfully recorded each day of the hostages' captivity, which dominated the last quarter of Jimmy Carter's presidency. The Administration let it be known that obtaining their release had become the paramount objective of US foreign policy.

Americans have been held hostage before: The crew of the ill-fated Pueblo were tortured for more than 11 months by North Koreans before they were finally released in 1968, without receiving the same national attention.

What made the Iran situation different? Perhaps because the Iran hostages were diplomats, not soldiers, and because their capture came at a time of national self-doubt after the US humiliation in Vietnam, their capture provoked an outburst of raw frustration and militant patriotism.

In Iran all this attention merely increased the value of the American hostages to the Iranian militants, who were locked in a

POLICY, Page 5

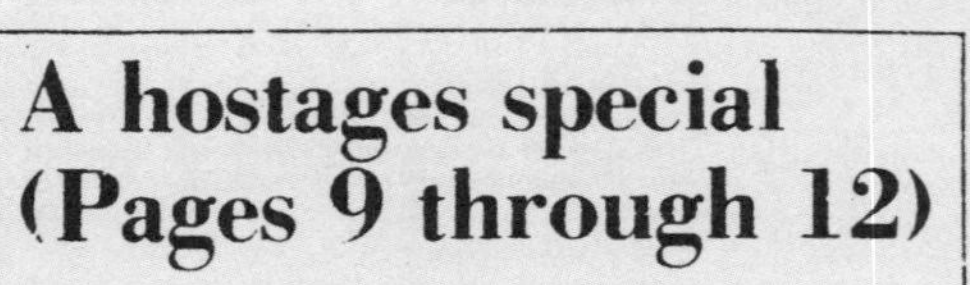

A hostages special (Pages 9 through 12)

There are eight who will never come home

By Mike Barnicle
Globe Staff

"Maybe now I can let go a little," Thelma Bakke said. "Maybe now I can finally bury my son."

"How old was he when he died?" Bakke was asked.

"Thirty-three," she answered. "That's so young. Isn't it?"

Her son was named Richard L. Bakke. He was a captain in the United States Air Force and he died in a fireball of an explosion that brought light to the desert sky above Tabas, Iran, during the early morning of April 25, 1980.

Capt. Bakke was one of eight servicemen killed while trying to rescue more than 50 fellow Americans who were being held hostage in Tehran. He was part of a 90-man team of volunteers who went under the code name Operation Blue Light.

When it became apparent over the weekend that the hostages would soon be released, phone calls were placed to the five Air Force and three Marine families touched by the 444-day tragedy just ended. Some wanted to talk. Some others did not. All of them live with the memory of sons, husbands and fathers who are gone forever.

"There have just been so many times I have just stopped and tried to sort things out," said Thelma Bakke from her home in

RAID FAMILIES, Page 21

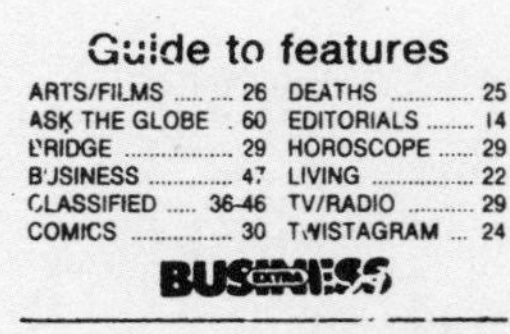

Guide to features

ARTS/FILMS	26	DEATHS	25
ASK THE GLOBE	60	EDITORIALS	14
BRIDGE	29	HOROSCOPE	29
BUSINESS	47	LIVING	22
CLASSIFIED	36-46	TV/RADIO	29
COMICS	30	TWISTAGRAM	24

BUSINESS EXTRA

The Boston Globe

Light of day
TUESDAY — Partly sunny, near 70
WEDNESDAY — Clouds, windy, 70s
HIGH TIDE — 7:07 a.m., 7:44 p.m.
FULL REPORT — PAGE 60

Vol. 219, No. 90 © 1981, Globe Newspaper Co. • TUESDAY, MARCH 31, 1981 • Telephone 929-2000 • Classified 929-1500 • Circulation 929-2222 • 60 Pages – 25 Cents

REAGAN SHOT; CONDITION IS 'GOOD' AFTER SURGERY

As shots rang out on sidewalk outside Washington Hilton Hotel, President Reagan was shoved through the rear door of his limousine by alert Secret Service agents. Limousine sped President to hospital. AP PHOTO

Just who was in charge?

By Robert Healy
Globe Staff

WASHINGTON – "Who's minding the store?" a wounded President Ronald Reagan quipped yesterday as he entered George Washington University Hospital.

At the White House it was hard to tell.

In the early minutes after the shooting, an assistant White House press secretary, Karna Small, relayed information to reporters that the President had not been shot. She spoke about the same time that the President arrived at the hospital clutching the left side of his chest.

Later, after it became clear that the President had been shot, Secretary of State Alexander M. Haig stood in the White House briefing room saying that "crisis management is in effect," and "as of now, I am in control here . . ."

At the hospital, Lyn Nofizger, one of Reagan's closest aides, was clearly livid as he watched the Haig performance, as the Secretary of State took command while Nofziger was insisting that the President was still in charge and that there was no need for any transfer of power to an acting President under the 25th Amendment to the Constitution.

Hours later, Larry Speakes, another assistant press secretary at the White House, said crisis management had never been in effect.

Haig said that constitutionally, the order of succession was the President, the Vice President and the Secretary of State. In fact, the Speaker of the House, Rep. Thomas P. O'Neill Jr. is next in line of succession to the Vice President.

Speakes indicated that even if Haig were talking of the chain of command in the White House Haig was wrong, because the succession went from President to Vice President to Secretary of Defense.

Haig had spoken carefully, apparently sensitive to the question of whether he was exceeding his authority instead of recognizing

POWER, Page 5

Wounded Secret Service agent (foreground) and Washington policeman lie on sidewalk outside hotel while others (upper right) tend to James Brady who fell face down when he was struck by bullet. AP PHOTO

Press secretary Brady, 2 others also wounded

By Curtis Wilkie, Globe Staff

WASHINGTON – President Ronald Reagan was reported in good condition last night following emergency surgery after a bullet pierced his left lung during an assassination attempt earlier in the day.

The shooting, which took place outside a Washington hotel where Reagan had just addressed a labor convention, seriously wounded White House press secretary James Brady. A Washington policeman and a Secret Service agent also suffered serious wounds.

When the grimmer rumors of the President's medical situation were finally put to rout last night, it appeared that he owed his life to the track of the bullet and a rugged constitution. Page 7.

Dr. Dennis S. O'Leary, a hospital official, said after the operation that the 70-year-old President is an "excellent physical specimen" and that he would be able to make state decisions as early as today, though he would not be able to resume a full schedule for 2½ to three months.

According to political aide Lyn Nofziger, Reagan, after his operation, in the recovery room handed attendants a note that read: "All in all, I'd rather be in Philadelphia."

A 25-year-old man identified as John Warnock Hinckley Jr. of Evergreen, Colo., was arrested at the scene and formally charged last night with attempting to assassinate the President. Hinckley was ordered held without bail, pending a hearing Thursday.

Authorities said that a .22-caliber pistol was used in the attempt on Reagan's life. The motive for the shooting was not immediately known.

Although White House spokesmen sought to reassure the public that Reagan had walked into the hospital and had made several good-humored remarks before he went into the operating room, the incident plunged the capital into an atmosphere of crisis.

SHOOTING, Page 2

Suspect arrested in '80 for carrying handguns

By Edward Quill
and Curt Gilliat
Globe Staff

John Warnock (Jack) Hinckley Jr., accused of attempting to assassinate President Ronald Reagan and said to have a history of psychiatric care, was arrested last October for carrying three handguns into Nashville's Metropolitan Airport shortly after then-President Jimmy Carter finished a campaign speech in that city.

Tennessee officials said Hinckley was stopped by Nashville airport police Oct. 9 as he tried to pass through the X-ray security system. Hinckley had two .22-caliber revolvers, one .38 revolver and 50 rounds of ammunition in his suitcase. He was planning to board an afternoon flight from Nashville to New York. He was taken to Metropolitan Court, where he was booked for "carrying a weapon"

Photo of John W. Hinckley taken from 1981 Colorado driver's license application. AP PHOTO

was was fined $62.50. The weapons were confiscated.

United Press International reported that a source close to the

SUSPECT, Page 4

Union wins concessions; Polish strike off

By Harry Trimborn
Los Angeles Times

WARSAW – Solidarity, Poland's independent trade union movement, called off a nationwide strike that had been planned for today after it won important concessions from the government in desperate, 11th-hour negotiations.

"We are going to work tomorrow," Lech Walesa, leader of the 10-million member labor federation, said after the negotiations. "There will be no strike. I am 70 percent satisfied with the results of the talks."

The decision to call off the strike, which would have plunged the nation into economic chaos, snapped the mounting tension and fears that have gripped Poland for the past 10 days. It also eased concern throughout the world of a possible Soviet intervention in Poland. Government leaders had warned of catastrophic consequences if the strike had gone into effect.

Pope John Paul II, a native of Poland who had expressed deep

POLAND, Page 10

Oscar awards put off; show goes on tonight

LOS ANGELES – Hollywood's Academy Award presentations, scheduled for last night, were postponed until tonight due to the assassination attempt on President Ronald Reagan. The President had recorded a brief speech that was to have been included in the show.

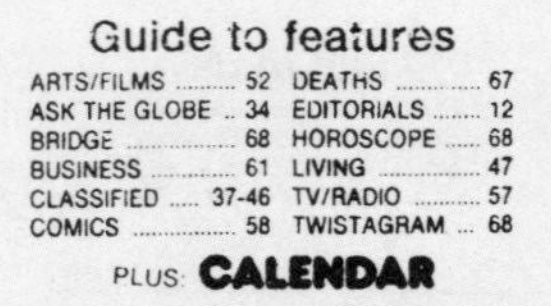

Guide to features

ARTS/FILMS ... 52 DEATHS ... 67
ASK THE GLOBE ... 34 EDITORIALS ... 12
BRIDGE ... 68 HOROSCOPE ... 68
BUSINESS ... 61 LIVING ... 47
CLASSIFIED ... 37-46 TV/RADIO ... 57
COMICS ... 58 TWISTAGRAM ... 68

PLUS: **CALENDAR**

The Boston Globe

Handy dandy
THURSDAY — Mostly sunny, 70s
FRIDAY — Cloudy, around 70
HIGH TIDE — 9:02 a.m., 9:30 p.m.
FULL REPORT — PAGE 34

Lottery, Page 24

Vol. 219, No. 134 © 1981, Globe Newspaper Co. • THURSDAY, MAY 14, 1981 Telephone 929-2000 Classified 929-1500 Circulation 929-2222 108 Pages – 25 Cents

OUTLOOK HOPEFUL

Pope rests after surgeons remove 2 bullets

Seeing light in the dark

By David B. Wilson, Globe Staff

Tradition has it that St. Peter was crucified in 64 AD, head downward, on a spot within a minute's walk of where Pope John Paul II was shot.

Mingled nearby in the bloodstained earth of Rome is whatever material substance remains of the first Vicar of Christ. The tomb is supposed to be directly under the high altar of the basilica that bears Peter's name.

The precise spot cannot be proven or disproven to a moral certainty. It is enough to know that since Peter's martyrdom it has been believed that his body was buried there, and that the place has ever since been venerated. Recent archeological evidence tends to corroborate tradition.

Peter died in Nero's circus, a victim among thousands slain by authority gone berserk. John Paul, whose chosen names signify meaning and mission, is a casualty at the hands of another kind of agency and one no less tyrannical.

To turn to history and to grope for some kind of meaning and perspective on an awful event is not to evade the awfulness of it.

Possibly the most discouraging aspect of these times is the defensive callousness people must adopt as celebrity murders and attempted murders – the Kennedy brothers, Ronald Reagan and Jerry Ford, Pope Paul VI, John Lennon, Aldo Moro, Martin Luther King and George Wallace – violate consciousness with what seems to be increasing frequency.

Not to disintegrate under the impact of such shocks becomes a survival imperative. It is frightening to sense that this kind of thing is becoming commonplace, its impact blunted by repetition, but one must not submit to the assassins' assault on sanity.

The new tyranny, arising from the ruins of once-vital communities and authority systems, is more difficult to define and to categorize than a mad emperor ordering slaughter.

"The world has gone mad," a friend said in fearful despair about the shooting of the Pope.

That is not true. The seasons are changing. Somewhere in the Mediterranean basin an olive tree that bore in Plato's time is putting out new shoots. Babies are being conceived and born, a right angle is the fourth part of a circle, priests say Mass, children rebel against their parents.

Apocalyptic thinking is always a temptation. But so many people have believed so completely and been so wrong for so many centuries that such speculation must be profitless. Besides, if the end of the world is coming, people will have neither warning nor options.

The world has not gone mad, but madness abounds. The world's task is to define it, isolate it and cope with it. And, like the exact location of the tomb of Peter, the task must be imprecise.

The madness arises in the deterioration of faith, family and community. Essential to it is the utterly selfish notion on the part of the self-appointed hero or heroine that the act of violence is ennobling and self-justifying.

No plausible, practically realizable end, no plan or vision of the future, no beneficiary individual, class, tribe or system of thought need be in view for the committed. They act simply for the sake of acting, for the self-realization to be achieved in the commission of their outrages.

Georges Sorel was an idiosyncratic critic of Marxism and eventual anarcho-syndicalist whose "Reflections on Violence" influenced the young socialist Mussolini. He would have understood and probably approved of the horror in St. Peter's Square.

Most people are unfamiliar with abstruse minor political philosophers. But they are entirely too familiar with the notion: Do it because you want to, because it feels good, because people will notice, because nobody can stop you, because you possess, indeed are, a truth that otherwise will go unregarded.

From the dark corners of a lonely 20th-century room crawl strange, dehumanized, desocialized creatures seeking the light of recognition, a sense of being part of something, of making a difference, of achieving identity through atrocity. Pope John Paul II, in his way, is trying to light up that room. It is, perhaps, all anybody can do.

By Sari Gilbert
Special to The Globe

VATICAN CITY – Wounded by shots from a would-be assassin's gun, Pope John Paul II was resting in the intensive care ward of a Roman hospital last night after 5½ hours of surgery to remove two bullets.

The doctor in charge of the case, Prof. Giancarlo Castiglioni, said the Pope had multiple intestinal lesions, but "we have good hopes for his recovery."

A young man suspected of shooting the Pope as he rode through St. Peter's Square late yesterday afternoon was subdued by bystanders and later taken away in a police van.

Police identified the alleged assailant as Mehmet Ali Agca, a 23-year-old escaped murderer from Turkey who had reportedly made written threats against the pontiff's life.

The Pope, riding in an open jeep, was greeting thousands of pilgrims and tourists gathered for his regular Wednesday general audience when he was shot.

Three bullets reportedly struck the Pope – in the abdominal cavity, the right arm and left hand – as he was leaning forward to shake the hands of well-wishers. Two of the slugs lodged in his body.

Two other persons, both foreign tourists, were wounded in the attack. A 58-year-old American woman from Buffalo, N.Y., whose name was given as Ann Odre, was seriously wounded in the chest and taken to the Santo Spirito Hospital. A 21-year-old Jamaican woman, Rose Hall, received a slight wound in the arm.

The Pope was taken by ambulance to the Policlinico Gemelli Hospital in northern Rome where about 1½ inches of his intestine were reportedly removed and several perforations stitched closed during the operation.

Shortly after the shooting, a Vatican spokesman said the Pope's condition was "worrisome," but doctors said later at the hospital that no vital organs had been damaged. There were, however, lesions in the Pope's intestine.

A hospital medical bulletin said the surgery included a temporary colostomy.

["He came through the surgery very well," Castiglioni said of the Pope, according to wires service reports. "We'll have to wait and see if any complications set in. He's now running a high fever.

["He can return to complete normality," the doctor said, adding that, because of the nature of the operation, in which part of the intestine was removed, "the prognosis is reserved."]

Later in the evening, Vatican Radio announced that there were "well-based hopes for the recovery of the Pope's health" and within three hours after the shooting, most of the hundreds of people who had remained in the square listening to portable radios and singing or praying for the Pope had trickled out of the area.

A few hours after the shooting, when much of St. Peter's Square was already

POPE, Page 5

A seriously wounded Pope John Paul II is helped by his personal secretary, Rev. Stanislaw Dziwisz (right), and other aides riding in jeep. Blood is visible on pontiff's left hand. UPI PHOTO

'I killed the Pope,' suspect wrote

From Wire Services

VATICAN CITY – The man who is being held in the shooting of Pope John Paul II at St. Peter's Square in Rome threatened to kill the pontiff in 1979, and in a letter found at his hotel room near the Vatican yesterday acknowledged his plan to attack the Pope.

"I killed the Pope," Mehmet Ali Agca said in a letter, written in Turkish, that police found in his hotel room hours after the wounding of the Pope.

"This is to demonstrate to the world the imperialistic crimes committed by the Soviet Union and the United States."

Authorities said Agca, seized immediately after the Pope had been struck by three bullets, was known in Turkey as a right-wing extremist who had been sentenced to death for murdering the editor of Miliyet, Turkey's largest newspaper.

According to Turkish authorities, Agca escaped from prison only three days before the Pope arrived in the capital of Ankara in November 1979 and in a letter to Miliyet threatened to kill the pontiff if the trip were not called off.

"Western imperialists," Agca wrote, "who are afraid of Turkey's unity of political, military and economic power with the brotherly Islamic countries are sending crusader commander John Paul under the mask of a religious leader.

SUSPECT, Page 6

Mehmet Ali Agca, Pope's alleged assailant, is led from police station after his arrest. AP PHOTO

$168m in human services cut in new King budget

By Charles Kenney
Globe Staff

Gov. Edward J. King yesterday proposed his second version of next year's state budget – one that would sacrifice some of Massachusetts' human services in order to help the state's cities and towns blunt the impact of Proposition 2½.

King's new budget proposal calls for fiscal 1982 spending of $6.4 billion, the same amount as the current fiscal '81 state budget. The governor's plan, which now awaits the Legislature's action, would increase state aid to cities and towns by $215 million – $178 million more than he had proposed earlier in the year.

A major portion of that increase would come from the $168 million the governor yesterday proposed to cut from human services budgets.

While human services account for about half the total state budget, 81 percent of the cuts King proposed yesterday would come from human services.

BUDGET, Page 59

Begin: There's no plan

Washington Post
and Los Angeles Times

JERUSALEM – Israeli Prime Minister Menachem Begin denied yesterday that the United States had proposed a four-point compromise to the Syrian missile crisis.

Begin said Israel's position remains that Syrian surface-to-air missile batteries must be removed, and Israel must retain the right of freedom of movement in the Lebanese skies.

Referring to reports from Washington of a four-point compromise proposal in which Israel flights over Lebanon would be reduced or restricted, Begin said: "There isn't such an American proposal. The information is completely misleading."

According to the reports, which were carried in the Israeli press, US special envoy Philip C. Habib had proposed that Syria remove its missiles and withdraw its troops from the Sannin mountains northeast of Beirut, while Israel would agree to restrict flights over the area. Habib also reportedly proposed that Christian forces would

MIDEAST, Page 20

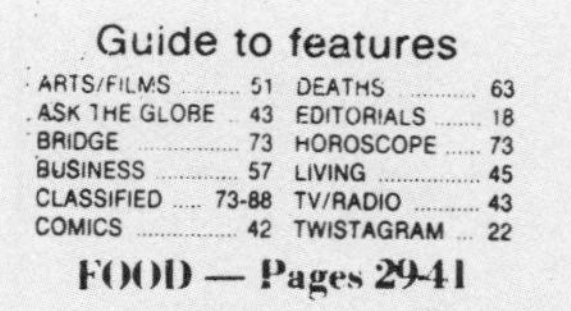

Guide to features

ARTS/FILMS	51	DEATHS	63
ASK THE GLOBE	43	EDITORIALS	18
BRIDGE	73	HOROSCOPE	73
BUSINESS	57	LIVING	45
CLASSIFIED	73-88	TV/RADIO	43
COMICS	42	TWISTAGRAM	22

FOOD — Pages 29-41

The Boston Globe

Dismal land

WEDNESDAY — Clouds, wind, rain
THURSDAY — And clouds, wind, rain
HIGH TIDE — 6:36 a.m., 6:53 p.m.
FULL REPORT — PAGE 73

Vol. 220, No. 99 © 1981, Globe Newspaper Co. • • Ⓢ WEDNESDAY, OCTOBER 7, 1981 Telephone 929-2000 Classified 929-1500 Circulation 929-2222 88 Pages – 25 Cents

SADAT ASSASSINATED

Egypt president slain when assailants fire at parade stand near Cairo

By David B. Ottaway
Washington Post

CAIRO – President Anwar Sadat of Egypt was shot to death yesterday by a group of men in army uniforms who opened fire while he was reviewing a military parade.

Bleeding but apparently still alive, the 62-year-old Egyptian leader was taken by helicopter from the parade grounds in the nearby Cairo suburb of Nasser City to a military hospital across the capital.

Vice President Hosni Mubarak announced on Egyptian television several hours later that Sadat had died of his wounds. The exact time of his death was not disclosed, but unofficial reports that he was dead had been circulating in the capital several hours before the official announcement.

'America has lost a close friend. The world has lost a great statesman. And mankind has lost a champion of peace.'

— President Reagan

Mubarak said Sufi Abu Taleb, speaker of the National Assembly, was taking over as interim president until elections could be held within the next 60 days, as stipulated under the constitution. Mubarak said Taleb had declared a state of emergency for one year and had also named him commander in chief of the armed forces.

[There were differing reports on the number of persons killed in the noontime attack, ranging from 6 to 12. Associated Press reported that army sources said two of the attackers were killed. The sources said all were members of an artillery unit.]

The attack came toward the end of the two-hour parade that was being held to celebrate what Egypt regards as a victory over Israel in the 1973 Arab-Israeli war, which began on Oct. 6.

Sadat had appeared relaxed, even jovial, during the parade and was seen at times smoking his pipe. There was no indication he expected any trouble.

The assailants were riding in a Soviet-made truck that was towing a new, South Korean long-range artillery piece. There were six of them sitting in the back, though some witnesses thought there were a total of eight involved in the attack.

As the truck drew up to within about 15 yards of the reviewing stand, it came abruptly to a halt.

Few of the some 2000 spectators in the reviewing stands took note of the truck because most were watching a spectacular air acrobatic show in which Egyptian Mirage jets were making low passes over the reviewing stand and leaving behind billowing trails of red white and blue smoke.

Suddenly, there was an explosion, seemingly a grenade, and then another as those in the truck opened fire with bursts from automatic rifles directly on the reviewing stand. Several of the assailants jumped off the back of the truck and rushed toward the stand, firing wildly into the crowd.

Sadat and other members of his party could be seen diving helter skelter for the ground, while security men rushed to cover the president's body and take him away through a door directly behind the stand. But it appeared that the soldiers standing in the truck were high enough up to continue pouring their gunfire into the reviewing box.

SADAT, Page 3

THE REACTION

He was both feared and esteemed

'President Sadat was murdered by the enemies of peace . . . I therefore today, together with the people of Israel, not only lost a partner in the peace process but a friend.'

– Israeli Prime Minister Menachem Begin

'In condemning this treacherous act of violence, I pray that almighty God may grant peace to this man of peace and bring to fulfillment his lofty vision of reconciliation among peoples.'

– Pope John Paul II

Sadat's assassination 'has proven that the Palestinian cause lives in the soul of this people who could not forgive the one who gave up Jerusalem.'

– PLO leader Yasser Arafat

Egyptian President Anwar Sadat reviews Cairo parade shortly before his assassination yesterday. AP PHOTO

THE IMPACT

Washington's worries about peace process

By William Beecher
Globe Staff

WASHINGTON – In the aftermath of the assassination of President Anwar Sadat of Egypt, there was one overriding question in capitals around the world: Will the peace process he had so much to do with continue?

In Cairo, Egyptian officials declared beyond doubt that it would.

But in Washington, there is serious concern whether the prospects for that process, always considered tenuous at best while Sadat lived, may have been dealt a fundamental, even a lethal, blow.

Sadat was so forceful and popular that he regularly overruled his closest advisers, and he disdainfully dismissed critics in the Arab world, to conclude a separate peace treaty with Israel and pursue negotiations seeking a reasonable autonomy plan for Palestinians living on the West Bank and Gaza Strip.

All of his key advisers wanted the treaty and autonomy to be inseparably linked. And the first draft of the Camp David agreement, in fact, contained such a clause. But it was removed at the insistence of Israeli Prime Minister Menachem Begin.

POLICY, Page 10

The successor faces obstacles

By Don A. Schanche
Los Angeles Times

WASHINGTON – In the wake of the assassination of President Anwar Sadat of Egypt yesterday, Vice President Hosni Mubarak faces two potentially serious obstacles as he moves to take over the reins of power in the months ahead.

The first, and perhaps most critical, is his own personality as perceived by the Egyptian public.

During his six years at Sadat's right-hand Mubarak never established a personal political constituency among the nation's 43 million citizens. In the early years after his elevation from chief of the Egyptian armed forces to Sadat's hand-picked vice president, the stocky, bull-necked air marshal withdrew deep into Sadat's shadow and was hardly seen by the people except on ceremonial occasions.

MUBARAK
No.2 man

Like Sadat himself when the assassinated leader served as one of the late President Gamal Abdel Nasser's many vice presidents, Mubarak took an almost humble and subservient role. In his largely innocuous appearances he has been an amiable man who, because of his silence, has been widely consid-

SUCCESSION, Page 6

It seemed like 'another parade special'

This a first-person account by David B. Ottaway of the Washington Post of the shooting of President Anwar Sadat of Egypt.

CAIRO – It was toward the end of what had been a spectacular military parade, and nobody was paying much attention to the slow-moving, shiny Soviet trucks hauling behind them South Korean artillery pieces on display for the first time.

Instead, all eyes were turned upward toward the Mirage jets swooping only a few feet above the reviewing stand and leaving behind trails of bright red blue and white smoke as they climbed up and over to make a colorful loop in the blue sky before flying away.

Suddenly one of the trucks came to an abrupt halt right in front of the reviewing stand where President Anwar Sadat and the entire Egyptian military and political hierarchy were seated yesterday watching the parade marking Egypt's initial victory in 1973 over the Israelis along the Suez Canal.

I was wondering to myself whether there was another embarrassing breakdown in store, as already one motorcycle had conked out at the beginning of the parade just before passing the review stand and the driver had had to push it along by hand.

At first we all thought it was just another parade special as a big bang went off and then another and several of the soldiers sitting in the back of the truck leaped out and started running toward the stands.

Then there was another huge bang and the rat-a-tat-tat of automatic rifle fire as the soldiers, both those on the back of the truck and those on the ground, opened fire on the stunned official party around Sadat.

At first those in the official party did not even move, and then everyone was diving for cover in all directions. But the soldiers on the truck were high enough up to keep their fire going directly into the stands.

Pandemonium hit the crowd of officials and invited guests sitting in covered cement stands alongside the main official reviewing box. There was screaming. Chairs went crashing to the ground and a kind of stampede for the exit set in.

Some around me, mostly Western journalists but also some army officers, hit the deck but I remember telling myself that this was a good way of getting myself crushed to death as others ran over me. I picked up one woman on the ground and argued with an Egyptian to stop pushing and calm down or we would all be in trouble.

WITNESS, Page 3

Related stories and photos on assassination (Pages 2-11); US oil stocks soar, dollar and gold prices rise (Page 57)

Globe Spotlight series will resume tomorrow

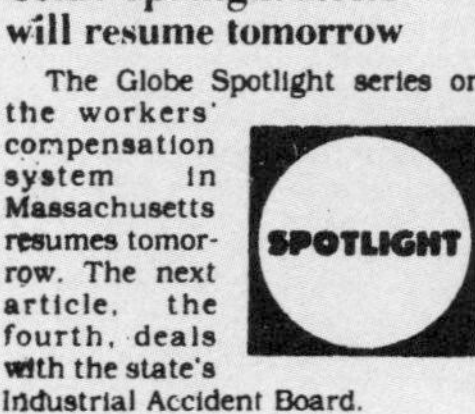

The Globe Spotlight series on the workers' compensation system in Massachusetts resumes tomorrow. The next article, the fourth, deals with the state's Industrial Accident Board.

Britain changes rules in N. Ireland prisons

The British government yesterday announced new regulations for Northern Ireland's prisons aimed at convincing Irish nationalist prisoners to abandon all forms of protest following the end of their hunger strike last weekend. Britain's new secretary for Ulster, James Prior, declared he is "seeking reconciliation and an end to violence." Page 13.

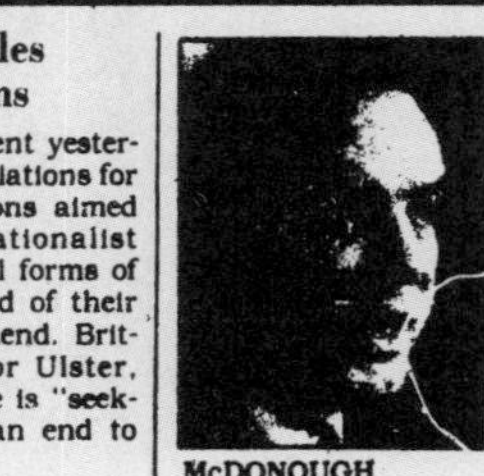

McDONOUGH

McDonough on the stand in bus contract bribe trial

Boston School Committeeman John J. McDonough took the witness stand on his own behalf yesterday after the prosecution rested its case at his bribery trial in US District Court. But McDonough, who is accused of accepting a $5000 bribe in connection with a bus contract, did not get into details of the charges before court was recessed. Page 21.

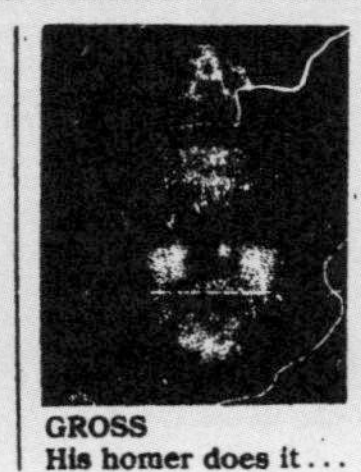

GROSS
His homer does it . . .

A's and Astros win

Wayne Gross hit a three-run homer to give the Oakland A's a 4-0 victory over Kansas City yesterday in the opener of the American League West Division playoffs.

In the opener of the National League Western Division playoff last night, Houston's Alan Ashby hit a two-out, two-run homer in the ninth and Nolan Ryan held Los Angeles to two hits to lead the Astros to a 3-1 victory. Page 65.

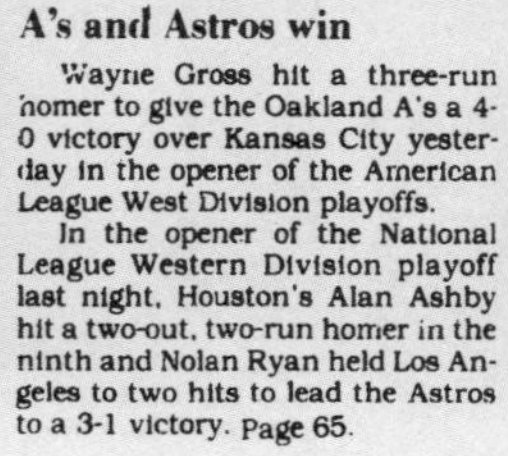

ASHBY
. . . so does his

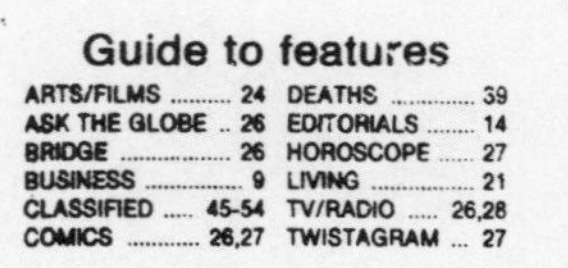

Guide to features

ARTS/FILMS	24	DEATHS	39
ASK THE GLOBE	26	EDITORIALS	14
BRIDGE	26	HOROSCOPE	27
BUSINESS	9	LIVING	21
CLASSIFIED	45-54	TV/RADIO	26,28
COMICS	26,27	TWISTAGRAM	27

The Boston Globe

Glum drops
MONDAY — Rain, in upper 40s
TUESDAY — Mostly cloudy, high 40s
HIGH TIDE — 1:20 a.m., 1:33 p.m.
FULL REPORT — PAGE 27

Vol. 224, No. 116© 1983, Globe Newspaper Co. MONDAY, OCTOBER 24, 1983 Telephone 929-2000 Classified 929-1500 Circulation 929-2222 54 Pages - 25 Cents

'We must be more determined than ever that they cannot take over . . .'
– President Reagan

'The safety and security of our forces in Beirut must be our No. 1 priority'
– US House Speaker O'Neill

People will not 'accept this kind of sacrifice for a very fuzzy, ill-defined mission'
– US Sen. Paul Tsongas

'They cannot bring about peace simply by sitting there'
– Former Secretary of State Kissinger

US toll in Beirut blast is put at 161; White House reaffirms commitment

Rescuers lower Marine on stretcher after pulling him out of the wreckage yesterday in Beirut. AP PHOTO

Weinberger points to Iran; 9 French soldiers also dead

BEIRUT

By G.G. LaBelle
Associated Press

BEIRUT – At least 161 US Marines and Navy men were killed and 75 wounded early yesterday when a suicide bomber crashed a pickup truck packed with explosives into the lobby of an airport building where the Americans were sleeping.

An Islamic group claimed responsibility for the blast, which leveled the four-story building. Defense Secretary Caspar W. Weinberger said "circumstantial evidence" pointed to Iranian involvement.

Moments later another terrorist drove with a bomb into a building housing French troops and blew it up. State radio quoted civil defense workers as saying 25 French soldiers were killed and 12 wounded. The Defense Ministry in Paris said the death toll was nine dead, 14 wounded and 53 missing.

A group calling itself the Free Islamic Revolution Movement asserted responsibility for both attacks. An anonymous caller telephoned the Beirut office of Agence France Presse and said two of the movement's fighters, named as Abu Mazin, 26, and Abu Sijan, 24, perished in the suicide bombings.

MARINES, Page 4

WASHINGTON

By Benjamin Taylor
Globe Staff

WASHINGTON – The American commitment to the multinational peacekeeping force in Lebanon will not change, although in the wake of yesterday's bombing steps will be taken to decrease the vulnerability of the US troops stationed there, the White House said yesterday.

After almost five hours of meetings at the White House among President Ronald Reagan and his senior advisers, Larry Speakes, the deputy White House spokesman, announced last night that Gen. Paul X. Kelley, commandant of the Marine Corps, is going to Beirut "to undertake a complete review of ways to provide a better protection for the Marine contingent in Lebanon."

Speakes, who earlier told reporters that the "mission of the United States and multinational force has not changed," also said the United States intends "to respond to this criminal act when the perpetrators are identified."

Speakes declined to say what the US response will be, adding that decisions will not be made public until after consultations with France, Italy and Britain.

REAGAN, Page 6

Related stories and photos are on Pages 2 through 7

The tough decisions ahead

By William Beecher
Globe Staff

NEWS ANALYSIS

WASHINGTON – President Ronald Reagan faces some very tough decisions in the aftermath of the massacre of US Marines in a Beirut bomb blast yesterday.

He must decide, possibly on the basis of inconclusive evidence, who was behind the attack and with what motivation, and then choose a course of diplomatic and perhaps military action.

The presumption of some senior Administration officials, as the evidence was still being sifted, is that even if Iranian soldiers carried out the attacks on the US and French military compounds, Syria was behind the assaults.

These officials suggested that the objective was to build political pressures in the United States, France, Italy and Britain to withdraw the multinational force from Lebanon.

With the Western presence removed, Syria could enjoy an almost free hand both to influence the redistribution of political power in Lebanon and to control most of the country militarily, possibly even moving into Beirut itself.

It is not Iran that would assume power in Lebanon if the Western presence were withdrawn. What the President, therefore, must have had in mind yesterday when he castigated "those who would assume power if they could have their way" was Syria and its principal backer, the Soviet Union.

If that emerges as the United States conclusion, the following policy options are possible:

– An effort to get the Arab League to revoke the mandate under which Syria has about 50,000 "peacekeeping" troops in Lebanon. The government of Lebanese President Amin Gemayel has

ANALYSIS, Page 6

Debris, missing data slow identifications

The identification of American dead has been slowed, according to a Pentagon spokesman, by the difficulties involved in sifting through the tons of rubble. Furthermore, since the building was a headquarters, many personnel records were destroyed. Duplicates exist, a spokesman said, but checking them added further difficulties to the process..

Because most people were asleep, the Marines and Navy men were not wearing uniforms with their names clearly stenciled on them. Service personnel are required to wear dogtags, but some may have taken them off when sleeping. Too, some dogtags may have become lost or broken in the blast or in the process of removal.

Every effort was being made to complete the process as soon as possible and next of kin were being notified in person by Navy and Marine personnel.

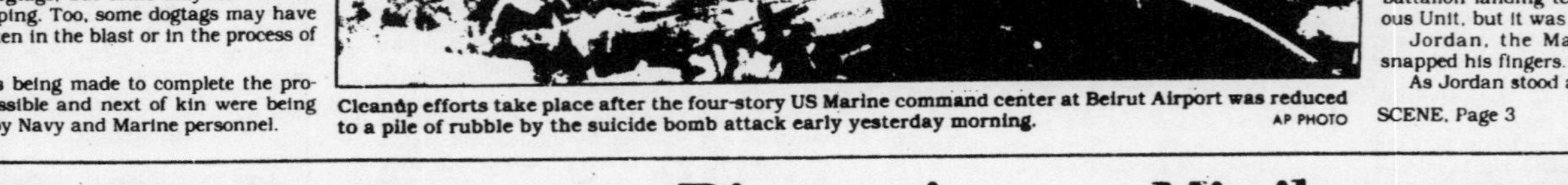

Cleanup efforts take place after the four-story US Marine command center at Beirut Airport was reduced to a pile of rubble by the suicide bomb attack early yesterday morning. AP PHOTO

Marines sift debris and listen for voices

By J. Michael Kennedy
Los Angeles Times

BEIRUT – Maj. Robert Jordan led the way through the rubble yesterday morning. His voice was mechanical and weary; he had heard the same questions many times this morning.

The man in the truck, Jordan said, drove to the airport parking lot, whipped the vehicle around, crashing through fences and gates and gunfire with his deadly cargo. A Marine sergeant on guard duty tried to radio the target, the command center of the battalion landing team of the 24th Marine Amphibious Unit, but it was too late.

Jordan, the Marine spokesman in Lebanon, snapped his fingers. "It was that quick," he said.

As Jordan stood at the edge of the rubble, Marines

SCENE, Page 3

INSIDE / Patriots breeze ... Dixon wins ... Missile protests continue

Patriots run away from Buffalo, 31-0

For years, the fourth quarter was a time for the New England Patriots to fold up their tent and steal quietly away. But this year the team has made that quarter their province, outscoring their opponents, 90-28. Take yesterday's game against the Buffalo Bills, for example: Piling on 24 points in the final 15 minutes, the Patriots ran away with what had been a tight game to take a 31-0 victory – and a 4-4 first half, a game behind Buffalo and Miami – into the clubhouse. Said cornerback Raymond Clayborn of the late surges: "We don't wear down." Page 29.

Rod Dixon drops to his knees after New York win. AP PHOTO

NYC Marathon: It's Dixon by 0:09

In the final 385 yards of a grueling race through the rain in New York City's Central Park yesterday, New Zealand's Rod Dixon ran past a staggering Geoff Smith of Liverpool and Providence College to cross the finish line first in 2:08:59, the 10th-fastest marathon in history. Smith, who had wrested the lead from Tanzania's Gidamis Shahanga 15 miles into the race, watched helplessly as Dixon went by him precisely at the 26-mile mark. Smith's 2:09:08 makes him history's fourth-fastest runnerup – and history's fastest first marathoner. Page 29.

Protests continue in Europe's streets

Nearly half a million demonstrators poured through the streets of Brussels, Madrid and Paris yesterday in the second day of Western European protests against deployment of new US nuclear missiles. Campaigners hailed the estimated weekend turnout of 1.5 million people as a clear sign of widespread opposition to the impending deployment of 572 Pershing 2 and cruise missiles. There were no reports of arrests yesterday. On Saturday, when some one million participated in sit-ins, formed human chains and marched, West German police arrested 450. Page 8.

All about your body's clock

The human body's internal clock has a major impact on night workers and on airline personnel, to name two areas. Page 41.

Campaign '83: call for 2 resignations

Boston mayoral candidate Melvin H. King yesterday called for the resignations of the head of the Boston arson squad and the state fire marshal after an article quoting them on what they see as some of the causes of arson in the city was published in The Boston Globe Magazine. King's call for the resignations came at a community meeting on arson held in Roxbury. At that same meeting, the other mayoral finalist, Raymond L. Flynn, who said he had not yet read the article, called the comments "deplorable" and said he rejected their conclusions. Page 17

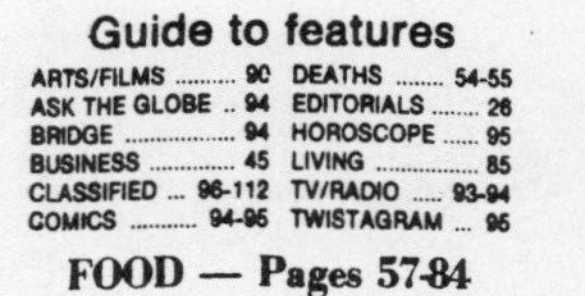

Guide to features
ARTS/FILMS 90
ASK THE GLOBE .. 94
BRIDGE 94
BUSINESS 45
CLASSIFIED ... 96-112
COMICS 94-95
DEATHS 54-55
EDITORIALS 26
HOROSCOPE 95
LIVING 85
TV/RADIO 93-94
TWISTAGRAM ... 95
FOOD — Pages 57-84

The Boston Globe

Show us the Ray
WEDNESDAY — Rain, wind, 40s
THURSDAY — Chance of showers
HIGH TIDE — 7:57 a.m., 8:18 p.m.
FULL REPORT — PAGE 95

Vol. 224, No. 139 © 1983, Globe Newspaper Co. • • (S) WEDNESDAY, NOVEMBER 16, 1983 Telephone 929-2000 Classified 929-1500 Circulation 929-2222 112 Pages – 25 Cents

Flynn wins in a big way, 66%-34%

Boston election results

Turnout (unofficial): 69.2% of 288,986 registered voters
251 of 252 precincts ✓ Elected * Incumbent

Mayor		
✓Raymond L. Flynn	127,757	65.6%
Melvin H. King	66,992	34.4%

City Council		School Committee	
At-Large/4 elected			
✓*McCormack	86,959	✓*McCluskey	92,256
✓*Iannella	84,975	✓*Walsh-Tomasini	89,756
✓*Tierney	82,449	✓*McGuire	88,642
✓*O'Neil	78,959	✓*O'Bryant	81,910
*McDermott	76,693	Arroyo	52,476
McKeigue	72,784	Comerford	28,590
Allen	31,889	Ferguson Jr.	27,995
Garrison	26,209	Komm	12,031
District returns — ** indicates incomplete			
District One			
✓Travaglini	11,663	✓Nucci	14,940
Modica	10,343	Boreili	4,445
District Two			
✓Kelly	11,815	✓Casper	12,783
Taylor	11,026	Barrett	9,529
District Three			
✓Byrne	11,544	✓Burke	12,794
Garland	11,295	Regal	9,824
District Four			
✓Yancey	7,898	✓Owens Hicks	8,813
Owens	7,384	Delgardo	6,805
District Five			
✓Menino	17,554	✓Grady	14,758
Kenney	5,945	Treon	8,867
District Six			
✓*Hennigan	14,390	✓O'Reilly	13,068
Coppinger	9,654	Allen	10,448
District Seven **			
✓*Bolling	8,307	✓Romero	5,582
Jones	4,657	Payne	3,764
District Eight			
✓Scondras	7,207	✓Browne	8,080
Roosevelt	7,104	Lankhorst	4,275
District Nine			
✓McLaughlin	9,071	✓Marchione	8,407
Solomon	7,782	Donlan	6,573

'We have a united city,' says the victor; a 'turning point' for Boston, says King

Win for city, too — King

By Robert Jordan
Globe Staff

When Melvin H. King stepped to the podium at 11 p.m., the cheering crowd of more than 3000 supporters at the Sheraton Boston Hotel treated him like a winner.

When the cheering died down at his request, he smiled and said, "You all obviously haven't seen the results."

But, in a more serious vein, he said it "sounds like there are two winners tonight. Because tonight, the City of Boston has taken a giant step forward. Because of all of you, Boston will be great again."

To wild cheers, King said, "I have lost the Mayor's race, but I have been privileged to represent the Rainbow Coalition," a reference to the collection of blacks, whites, Hispanics, homosexuals and women from whom he drew his support.

After more applause and chanting of "Rainbow, Rainbow, Rainbow..."King said, "You have given me the privelege to be able to guide us through what the historians will recognize as the turning point in the social, cultural and political history of Boston."

King congratulated his rival, Raymond L. Flynn for his victory and for conducting with him "a decent hard-working campaign that does honor to Boston neighborhoods and to the people who have for too long been ignored or oppressed."

But he also had a few suggestions for the new mayor-elect. He said the task before Flynn "is to foster an identity in Boston which will eradicate the pervasive and destructive aspects of racism."

He also urged Flynn to give "formal recognition of comparable pay and economic equality for women in this city" and to make Boston "an open and accessible city."

In further thanks to his supporters, King said, "I can never express sufficient thanks to my campaign staff and the (leaders) who

KING, Page 32

RAYMOND L. FLYNN ... will be the first mayor from South Boston

'We have proven that the hopes that unite us are stronger than the fears that separate us.'
– Mayor-elect Raymond L. Flynn

The careful crafting of winning coalition

By Walter V. Robinson
Globe Staff

NEWS ANALYSIS

Raymond L. Flynn proved that he was a more effective coalition builder than his opponent yester day, with his decisive victory made possible by substantial support in liberal as well as conservative sections of Boston.

Flynn, in victory, was the beneficiary too, of a carefully orchestrated grassroots campaign he began a decade or more ago and a black opponent who was running as much against history as against Flynn.

Melvin H. King fell far short, at least of his own public expectations. In defeat, he was surely the victim of resistance by white voters to his ideas as well as his color.

Whatever the racial component, though, King was also the victim of a disorganized campaign that raised too little money and had too little political expertise, no discernible strategy and a penchant for miscues, both large and small.

Still, even in defeat last night, King could claim several victories, none of them insignificant. He won about one in five white votes, substantially more than first time black mayoral finalists in other major cities.

With his campaign, King guaranteed Boston's black community a substantial share of the city's political power.

And, though he lost, King saw most of his opponents this year, including Flynn, advocating neighborhood issues that he alone spoke for when he first ran for mayor four years ago.

Flynn, whose dogged pursuit of the mayor's office began publicly during the city's busing crisis nine years ago, did startlingly well in liberal areas of the city where King had counted on voters to join his self-styled rainbow coalition in large numbers. Flynn did better than expected, too, in some minority neighborhoods.

Flynn's urban populism, a natural draw in working class South Boston and Charlestown, also won numerous adherents in areas of the Back Bay, the Fenway and Allston where King had been the clear favorite.

In The Fenway's Ward 5, Precinct 1, for example, King was the choice of 685 voters. But Flynn surprised there, with 595 votes. Flynn even won some precincts in areas of the Back Bay and Beacon Hill where King was expected to win handily.

ANALYSIS, Page 34

Turnout seen topping 66%

By Charles Kenney
Globe Staff

Raymond L. Flynn yesterday crushed Melvin H. King in a landslide victory in the race for mayor of Boston that saw Flynn running up one of the largest victories in the city's recent political history.

Flynn ran up huge margins of victory in white neighborhoods across the city, from East Boston through South Boston, Dorchester, Hyde Park and West Roxbury as voter turnout seemed certain to surpass the 1967 record of 66.2 percent.

With 251 of the city's 252 precincts reporting, Flynn led King 66 percent to 34 percent.

Flynn, who will take over in January as the first mayor elected from South Boston, described himself last night as "the son of a longshoreman and the son of a cleaning woman as well, [and] I'm very proud of that."

Flynn appeared before his cheering supporters and declared victory, saying: "Tonight, Boston has made history."

Flynn said that "we have a united city where the voice of every neighborhood in this city has been heard. We have proven that the hopes that unite us are stronger than the fears that separate us."

Minutes earlier, King had conceded.

Wiping tears from his eyes, King stepped to the microphone and, flanked by his family, said: "Love comes in all colors, shapes and sizes and we have a lot of love here."

Said King: "I have lost a mayor's race, but I have been privileged to represent the rainbow coalition. You have given me the privilege to be able to guide it through what the historians will recognize as the turning point in the social, cultural and political history of Boston."

King congratulated Flynn "for his victory and I congratulate him in joining me in waging a decent and hard-working campaign that does honor to Boston's neighborhoods and to the people who have for too long been ignored or repressed."

MAYOR, Page 30

McCormack topping City Council ticket

First-term Councilor Michael McCormack was running first last night in the race for the four at-large seats on the Boston City Council. Incumbents Albert O'Neil, Christopher Iannella and Joseph Tierney appeared headed for reelection. Page 30.

4 veterans returned to School Committee

The new 13-member Boston School Committee will include four incumbents and the city's first elected Hispanic official. Page 30.

Kevin's advice to the winner: Beware the bodysnatchers

By Mike Barnicle
Globe Staff

After sixteen years as mayor, Kevin White sat last evening at the edge of the main event, serving up memories as an entree with a side dish of advice for Ray Flynn who will now become only the fourth mayor of Boston in the last three decades. The counsel stems from hard earned lessons and a career that has been spent juggling, wrestling and balancing the interests and desires of the politicians, developers and bankers who played supporting roles while White maintained a center stage grip on a town that never stood neutral on him.

"Tomorrow, I'm having lunch with Ray Flynn at noon, at the Parkman House and I really wish him well," the Mayor said. "When I was running in 1967, I had a guy come in to see me and he handed me a contribution, a big one. I didn't even know him.

"The next time I saw him was a few weeks after I was sworn in and he came in the office like he owned me and I resented it. I told him, 'Lookit, I don't really know you but I know how much you gave me and I'll tell you what I'm going to do: I'm going to spend the next year looking for ways to screw you and, when I've done it for a year, you come back here and see me and then, maybe we'll be even. I didn't know I had that in me until that day.

"And that's what Ray's going to have find out for himself. Right now, the guys who run 'The Vault'

BARNICLE, Page 34

Second tax agent found not guilty

By Joseph M. Harvey
Globe Staff

State tax examiner Francis X. Harrison of Chelmsford was acquitted of bribery yesterday and then accused state prosecutors of having involved him in a politically motivated trial designed to hurt the re-election effort last year of former governor Edward J. King.

Harrison demanded an apology from the attorney general's office after the Middlesex Superior Court jury announced its verdict.

The charge of political motivation was denied by Stephen Delinsky, the former assistant attorney general who headed the 1982 investigation into allegations of corruption at the state Revenue Department, and by a spokesman for Atty. Gen. Francis X. Bellotti.

HARRISON, Page 25

PLO rebels attack

Palestinian rebels yesterday pressed their attack on forces loyal to Yasser Arafat in fighting just outside Tripoli. Page 14.

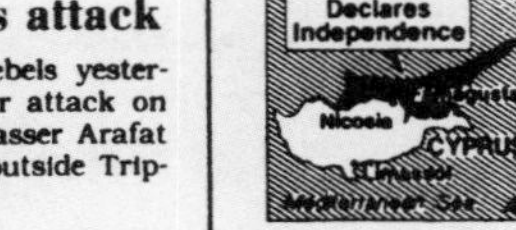

Independence declared

Turkish-held northern Cyprus declared independence yesterday and sealed off the only crossing point to the Greek Cypriot south, escalating tension between Greece and Turkey over the Mediterranean island. Page 16.

A Capitol fence

Security officials said yesterday they want to build a 10-foot fence around the Capitol in the wake of last week's bombing. Page 3.

House rejects bid to revive ERA

By David Rogers
Globe Staff

WASHINGTON – The House yesterday defeated a bid by the Democratic leadership to resurrect the proposed equal rights amendment through a procedure that severely limited debate and prevented any alteration of the original language.

A switch of six votes on the 278-147 rollcall in favor of the ERA would have given proponents the victory they sought. Despite the narrow margin, the defeat reflected major difficulties the proposed constitutional amendment faces in Congress and the nation.

Under the Constitution, a two-thirds vote is required to approve a constitutional amendment, and the same majority is needed in any

ERA, Page 18

Glenn calls Mondale's record on defense buildup 'weak'

By Thomas Oliphant
Globe Staff

WASHINGTON – In a major change in his campaign strategy, Sen. John Glenn of Ohio yesterday launched a strong attack on former Vice President Walter Mondale in an effort to position himself as the presidential candidate in favor of a measured buildup of US military power.

Reflecting a decision to use this and other issues to go after the man now leading by a considerable margin in public opinion polls, Glenn said here: "The Mondale record goes far beyond a simple disagreement over specific weapons programs. I think it reveals a fundamental lack of support for an adequate national defense – and I think it reveals a fundamental difference between our two candidacies.

"Today, Fritz Mondale likes to say he's for a strong defense. But when his vote was needed his support was weak. And while I believe that the Democratic commitment to peace and arms control must never fail and never falter, I also believe that our commitment to a strong defense must consist of deeds as well as words."

Glenn's comments came in a luncheon speech to the comparatively hawkish Coalition for a Democratic Majority, which held a daylong issues forum in honor of one of its mentors, the late Sen. Henry Jackson of Washington. Mondale addressed the group earlier in the day. The former Vice President was quick to respond when informed of what Glenn said.

Saying he welcomes a sharp debate on issues, Mondale attacked

CAMPAIGN, Page 23

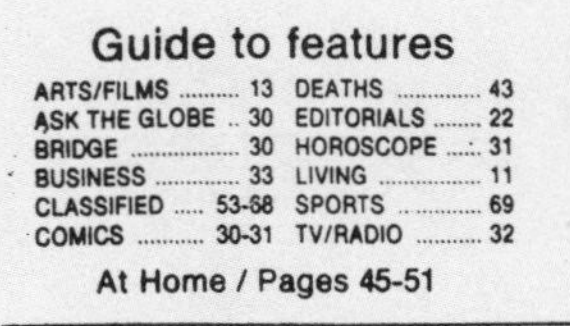

Guide to features

ARTS/FILMS	13	DEATHS	43
ASK THE GLOBE	30	EDITORIALS	22
BRIDGE	30	HOROSCOPE	31
BUSINESS	33	LIVING	11
CLASSIFIED	53-68	SPORTS	69
COMICS	30-31	TV/RADIO	32

At Home / Pages 45-51

The Boston Globe

Slush fun

FRIDAY: Snow tapering; in 30s
SATURDAY: Partly cloudy; in 40s
HIGH TIDE — 10:02 a.m., 10:25 p.m.
FULL REPORT · PAGE 31

Vol. 225, No. 90 © 1984, Globe Newspaper Co. • • FRIDAY, MARCH 30, 1984 Telephone 929-2000 Classified 929-1500 Circulation 929-2222 88 Pages 25 Cents

Spring gives a winter wallop

Waves driven by fierce winds hit seawall in Sand Hills area of Scituate yesterday. GLOBE PHOTO BY GREG DERR

$1.4m device pinpoints ills

By Richard A. Knox
Globe Staff

Patricia Loughman of Abington lay half-inside a strange and ominous-looking new machine yesterday afternoon on the second floor of the Massachusetts General Hospital. Doctors were using the device, which they call a revolutionary advance in medical diagnosis, to search for a tumor deep within her brain.

Behind a nearby window, a technician pushed buttons on the console of the $1.4 million machine. A short while later, the machine produced pictures of Loughman's head that looked as if she had been sliced neatly lengthwise.

There, glowing like a lightbulb in the middle of the pictures, was the thumbnail-sized pituitary gland tumor that has been causing Loughman's headaches, vision abnormalities, menstrual disorders and sensitivity to cold.

MGH, Page 29

War of words rules campaign

By Walter V. Robinson
Globe Staff

NEW YORK – The Democratic primary season, not too long ago called the "sweetest" in a century by Walter F. Mondale, has become so acerbic that Mondale and Gary W. Hart are trying to tie each other to the man they both detest politically – President Ronald Reagan.

Mondale and Reagan – or so Hart television and newspaper ads here strongly suggest – are warmongering allies on the use of American troops in Central America.

Hart and Reagan – as portrayed in Mondale ads – are fiscal compatriots, each as eager as the other to soak the middle class with new taxes while providing gargantuan tax breaks for the elderly.

Like Hawaii's Mauna Loa volcano, a dispute over that advertising erupted during Wednesday night's televised debate, and its own political lava flow engulfed much of political New York yesterday.

MEDIA, Page 10

Snow, high winds wreak havoc throughout N.E.

By Terri Minsky
Globe Staff

Other storm-related pictures and stories, Page 3, Page 6

The skies opened over New England yesterday, and heavy snow, sleet, freezing rain and hurricane-force winds swept over all six states. The storm brought floods to coastal areas and dumped more than a foot of snow inland; it caused power outages and treacherous traveling, and then hampered all efforts to fix those problems.

A Connecticut man was struck and killed by a train in Ashland last night as he was trying to help push a car stuck on a railroad track. In Northampton, a woman died during the storm when her car collided head-on with another car on an icy road. An 18-year-old man became caught in an electrical wire downed in Mattapan and later died.

The blizzard and near-blizzard conditions caused all manner of havoc and danger. Its 80 mph winds tipped over an 18-wheel tractor-trailer on the Cape's Bourne Bridge; the gales also ripped off parts of buildings and toppled trees across homes, cars, power lines and commuter rails. A tree fell on top of a Chestnut Hill-bound trolley car. Lightning sliced a telephone pole in half in Jamaica Plain.

For the first time in its 103-year history, the Boston Symphony canceled a concert in its hall here. A cable that held the Boston Tea Party Ship and its companion museum to a mooring snapped. It took three hours to secure the ship and the museum to pilings on the wharf. Hospitals turned to emergency power, and the state Civil Defense said 30 families left their homes on a beach road in Quincy and 75 elderly people were evacuated from their homes in Lancaster, in the center of the state.

The spring storm was at its worst in central New England, especially the Merrimack Valley and Worcester County, where meteorologists expected as many as 15 to 18 inches of snow to fall by this morning. The White Mountains of New Hampshire were expected to get only one to three inches.

The winds, which gusted between 30 mph and 80 mph throughout the area, whipped waves as high as 25 feet, closing roads along the coast and the Cape. Just 20 yards off Nauset Beach in Orleans, a freighter broke free of her anchor chain and drifted south, toward the beach. The 23 crew members had to be lifted off the ship, two at a time, by a Coast Guard helicopter in the 40- to 60-mph winds.

STORM, Page 6

High winds from yesterday's storm that swept up the East Coast toppled this tree in Wilmington, Del., cutting a nearby house in two. Three persons were in the house at the time, but none was seriously injured. AP PHOTO

Tornadoes kill 63 in Carolinas

From Wire Services

A ferocious spring storm spread death and destruction along the Eastern Seaboard, unleashing a series of tornadoes in the Carolinas that killed at least 63 persons and injured 800 more. Damage to homes and businesses from New England to South Carolina was estimated in the billions of dollars.

Wednesday's tornadoes, spawned by an ultralow-pressure system, were the deadliest in a decade.

"It just made toothpicks of some of our homes," said Mike Tardis, director of emergency services in Scotland County, N.C. "Some of these homes were blown all over the fields, and there were people blown all over the fields, too."

At least 50 persons were killed in North Carolina and another 13 in South Carolina when 25 twisters tore a 50-mile swath from the vicinity of Newberry, S.C., to the sea, officials said yesterday.

COAST, Page 6

Proposed $300m development has Sharon split on quality of life

By Thomas Palmer
Globe Staff

SHARON – A proposal to develop a prime piece of land into one of the largest office park and residential-condominium developments in New England will leave its marks on this small residential community even if it is spurned at Sharon's town meeting next month.

The length and intensity of the argument over the proposed project, which would be more than eight times the size of South Shore Plaza in Braintree, have been so great that some bitterness will remain no matter what happens, people on both sides agree.

At issue is Cannon Forge, a multi-use development project that would cover 620 acres of mostly wooded land adjacent to Rte. 95, straddling the Sharon-Foxborough line. Sharon voters will decide at their annual town meeting on April 9 whether to change their zoning bylaws to allow the development. The proposal has not yet been presented to Foxborough.

The debate is so acerbic that some members of the Sharon Historical Society

SHARON, Page 28

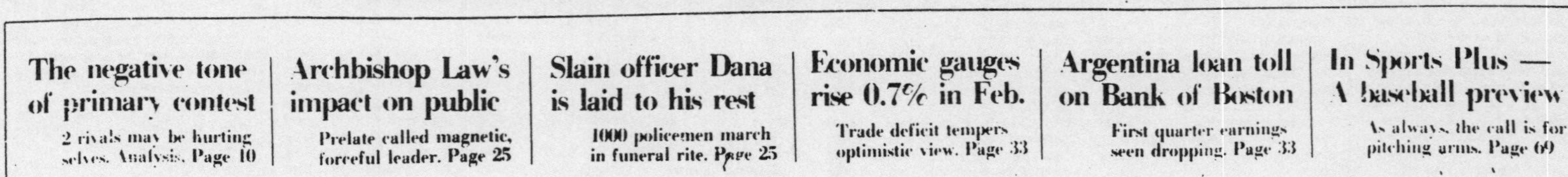

The negative tone of primary contest
2 rivals may be hurting selves. Analysis. Page 10

Archbishop Law's impact on public
Prelate called magnetic, forceful leader. Page 25

Slain officer Dana is laid to his rest
1000 policemen march in funeral rite. Page 25

Economic gauges rise 0.7% in Feb.
Trade deficit tempers optimistic view. Page 33

Argentina loan toll on Bank of Boston
First quarter earnings seen dropping. Page 33

In Sports Plus — A baseball preview
As always, the call is for pitching arms. Page 69

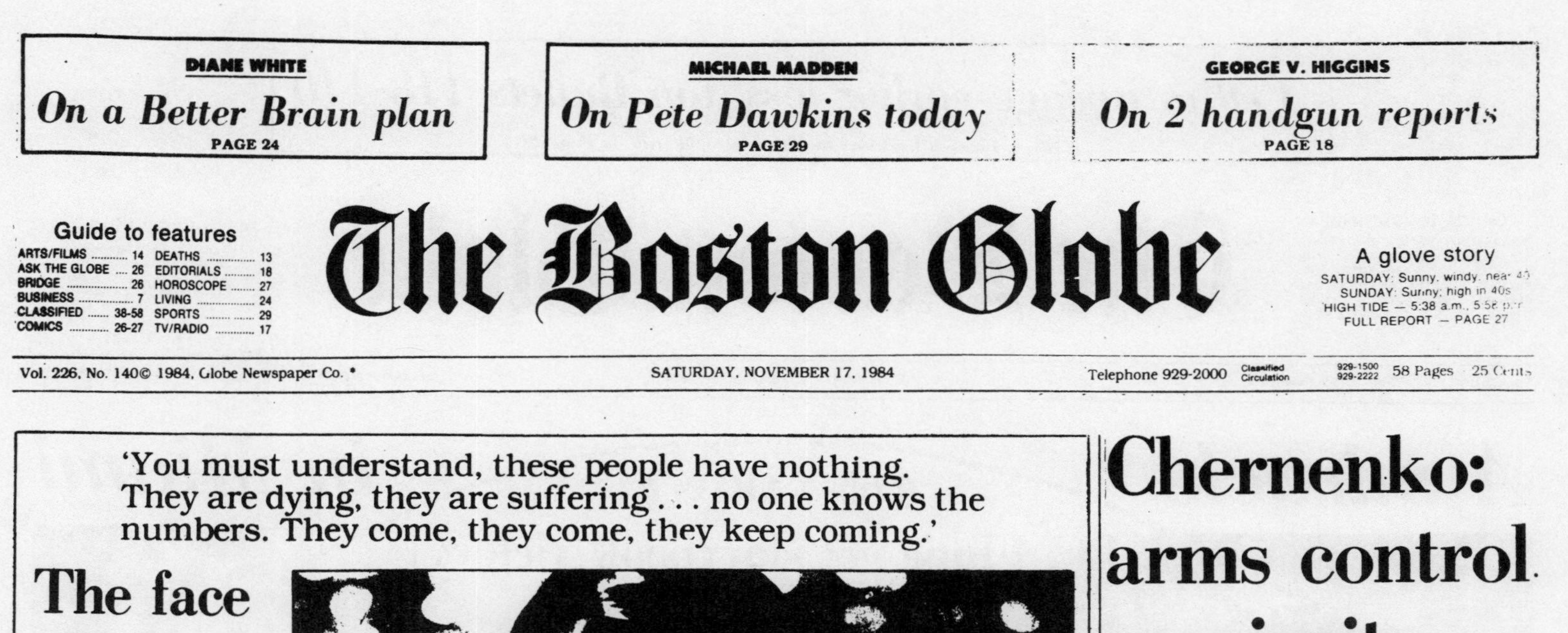

DIANE WHITE
On a Better Brain plan
PAGE 24

MICHAEL MADDEN
On Pete Dawkins today
PAGE 29

GEORGE V. HIGGINS
On 2 handgun reports
PAGE 18

Guide to features

ARTS/FILMS	14	DEATHS	13
ASK THE GLOBE	26	EDITORIALS	18
BRIDGE	26	HOROSCOPE	27
BUSINESS	7	LIVING	24
CLASSIFIED	38-58	SPORTS	29
COMICS	26-27	TV/RADIO	17

The Boston Globe

A glove story
SATURDAY: Sunny, windy, near 40
SUNDAY: Sunny; high in 40s
HIGH TIDE — 5:38 a.m., 5:58 p.m.
FULL REPORT — PAGE 27

Vol. 226, No. 140© 1984, Globe Newspaper Co. • SATURDAY, NOVEMBER 17, 1984 Telephone 929-2000 Classified 929-1500 Circulation 929-2222 58 Pages 25 Cents

'You must understand, these people have nothing. They are dying, they are suffering . . . no one knows the numbers. They come, they come, they keep coming.'

The face of misery in Africa

Other photos, Pages 2, 3

By Colin Nickerson
Globe Staff

ON THE SUDANESE-ETHIOPIAN BORDER – Babies too weak, too hungry to bawl make a sort of mewing cry, a pathetic plaint that reverberates through all of drought-afflicted black Africa.

That thin wail of misery and starvation echoes through the makeshift refugee camp called Tukulababa.

No roads lead here. Indeed, until a week ago, Tukulababa didn't even exist except as a nameless patch of thornbrush located about 15 miles northeast of the Sudanese town of Kassala.

Seven days later, more than 3000 refugees from Ethiopia's war-and famine-racked northern provinces have made camp here. Most of them are women and children. Almost all of the children – and many of the adults – are severely malnourished. Some are dying; some have died.

Meanwhile, about 450 new arrivals stagger into Tukulababa every day.

Yet the ragtag settlement represents only a tiny fraction of the 600,000 refugees who have already poured into Sudan from Ethiopia's Eritrea and Tigray provinces.

That number is expected to double by the end of the year, say relief workers and government officials in the Sudan. Already, the situation in the overflowing refugee camps on the Sudanese side of the border is shifting quietly from crisis to catastrophe.

At Tukulababa, the refugees huddle in the meager shade cast by the stunted thorn trees. There is no other shelter – no huts, no tents, only a single canvas canopy to protect the sickest children from the ferocious desert heat.

Lamlam Tsagi, a widow at the age of 16, grabs a reporter's hand and clasps it to her shriveled breasts. She evidently takes him for a doctor. She can no longer give milk, she says, and her baby is dying, starving.

The infant, Asafa Aradoum, is 6 months old and weighs little more than nine pounds. His belly is puffed with hunger, an all-too-common sight in sub-Sahara Africa, and his arms and legs are stick-thin. His neck no longer has

ETHIOPIA, Page 3

More aid from US

The United States is sending an additional 85,000 tons of food worth $37.5 million to drought-stricken Ethiopia as part of an all-out effort to feed the estimated seven million people who are threatened with starvation there, an official said yesterday. Page 2.

Ethiopian mother and child wait for food in Wad Sharafin Camp. They are but two of the 22,000 refugees in a facility that was built for 5000. The child died later the same day. GLOBE PHOTO BY STAN GROSSFELD

Chernenko: arms control a priority

Also calls on Soviets to strengthen defense

From Wire Services

WASHINGTON – Soviet President Konstantin Chernenko, in separate remarks made public yesterday, said arms control should be the top priority in US-Soviet relations during President Ronald Reagan's second term, and called on his own nation to strengthen its defenses against the "growing aggressiveness of imperialism."

In a written reply to questions from NBC News, Chernenko pledged "to work vigorously" for the reduction of nuclear weapons.

He did not repeat some of the preconditions for arms control talks the Soviets have set previously. Nor did he insist on any particular negotiating approach.

Chernenko said if recent statements by the Reagan Administration concerning a desire for improved relations with Moscow "do not remain just words," the two superpowers could "start moving toward more normal relations between our two countries and toward a more secure world."

But Chernenko also said he does not think "conditions now are ripe" for a summit meeting between him and Reagan for the next six months at least.

Chernenko suggested Moscow is not now interested in the kind of consultations Reagan has proposed aimed at establishing overall goals in US-Soviet relations.

"It is this – the limitation and reduction of arms, and above all nuclear arms, prevention of the spread of the arms

ARMS, Page 20

Probe widened in infant's slaying

By Sarah Snyder and M.E. Malone
Globe Staff

PAWTUCKET, R.I.– Jerri Ann Richard had been dead more than 24 hours when her body was found Thursday, police said yesterday as they widened their hunt for clues in the 4-month-old's murder.

Pawtucket police have removed about a dozen large brown bags of items from the Richards' home, including clothes from the laundry room washer and dryer, shoes from the living room closet and sheets and blankets from the baby's crib. Yesterday, they used a German shepherd dog to sniff through the family's apartment, as well as the auto body shop below and adjoining areas in the building on Main street.

Investigators said they have no specific leads, but took the clothes and other items so as not to overlook anything. Pawtucket Police Capt. Carl Benson said the parents have not been ruled out as suspects.

"No one has been cleared. No one is a suspect," he said.

Arthur C. Burns, Rhode Island deputy chief state medical examiner, said he probably would not know until early next week exactly how long the child had been dead when her body was found at 5 p.m. Thursday in an alley only a block from her home.

But he said she appeared to have been dead more than 24 hours, which would mean she died before her parents made their dramatic pleas on Boston television Thursday for the baby's return.

CHILD, Page 28

Baby Fae's death renews questions

By Loretta McLaughlin
Globe Staff

Baby Fae, who died late Thursday night after surviving for 21 days on a baboon heart, has opened "new vistas" for mankind, her surgeon Leonard Bailey said yesterday.

Bailey, in obvious emotional distress at a press conference in Loma Linda, Calif., yesterday, [illegible] to defend the transplant and said he planned to do the operation again, "bye and bye."

The five-pound, month-old infant suffered a "complete heart block" at 7 p.m. Thursday, five hours after she was placed on kidney dialysis, because her kidneys had stopped working. She died two hours later at 9 p.m. after all attempts to save her, including closed chest heart massage, failed.

"For her part, my colleagues and I believe Baby Fae has opened new vistas for all, including the as-yet-unborn infants with heart disease," Bailey said. "The Baby Faes and their parents are the real pioneers."

Others, however, say that her death gives fresh importance to questions about the scientific validity of the cross-species transplant and the ethical rightness of the surgery.

A preliminary autopsy failed to reveal the precise cause of death, Bailey said, but it appeared to be a combination of kidney and heart failure.

BABY FAE, Page 6

Salvador rebel hints at election role

From Wire Services

WASHINGTON – Rebels fighting the Salvadoran government may be willing to declare a temporary cease-fire in their five-year civil war in order to take part in some way in elections next year, the leader of the political arm of the Salvadoran insurgency said yesterday.

Guillermo Ungo told reporters that the FMLN-FDR leftist coalition would not participate as a political party but would make its presence known with its own positions.

"Assuming elections are held, it will be quite impossible for us to participate for practical and political reasons," Ungo told reporters here.

Ungo, president of the Democratic Revolutionary Front, the political arm of the Salvadoran guerrilla movement, seemingly contradicted another high FDR official on the left's plans for legislative elections scheduled for March 1985.

The Washington Post yesterday quoted FDR spokesman Ruben Zamora in Mexico City as saying the Salvadoran rebel movement had begun discussions on the possibility of participating in the elections.

Asked if the discrepancy meant there were differences within the FDR, Ungo said, "I'm talking about the official position. What I have read is not the official position."

He told a news conference sponsored by Foreign Policy magazine that the left would take part in the elections, but not necessarily as a political party. He said it would adopt positions and take its views to the Salvadoran people.

"We will take part somehow," he said. "I don't know how . . . but we are not going to be just watchers."

SALVADOR, Page 20

Shuttle lands, hailed for historic mission

Associated Press

CAPE CANAVERAL, Fla. – Shining brightly in the rays of the rising sun, the shuttle Discovery coasted gracefully back to Earth yesterday from a 3.3 million-mile voyage, carrying the first satellites ever salvaged from outer space.

"This certainly has to be looked at as a very historic day in America's space program," said Jesse Moore, director of NASA's shuttle program, after the space plane dropped gracefully out of orbit, carving a series of circles in the sky as it headed for a landing just three miles from the launch pad where the space travelers started their

SHUTTLE, Page 6

Celtics avenge earlier loss, top Bullets 118-110

(Bird, Johnson lead way to 10th win in 11 tries — Page 29)

Guide to features

ARTS/FILMS 8
ASK THE GLOBE 26
BRIDGE 26
BUSINESS 13
CLASSIFIED 38-56
COMICS 26-27
DEATHS 24-25
EDITORIALS 18
HOROSCOPE 27
LIVING 11
SPORTS 29
TV/RADIO 28

The Boston Globe

Collar it blue

SATURDAY: Partly sunny; 40s
SUNDAY: Sunny; high in 50s
HIGH TIDE — 11:59 a.m., -- p.m.
FULL REPORT — PAGE 27

Vol. 226, No. 147 © 1984, Globe Newspaper Co. • SATURDAY, NOVEMBER 24, 1984 Telephone 929-2000 Classified 929-1500 Circulation 929-2222 56 Pages - 25 Cents

A miracle ◀ 65 YARDS ▶ in Miami

BC, Flutie get storybook victory

The two Boston College linemen discussed the bizarre, amazing thing that had happened on the floor of the Orange Bowl. They dealt with the metaphysics of the event.

"That wasn't Gerard Phelan who caught that ball," big Mark MacDonald said. "God caught that ball."

"No," big Jim Ostrowski said softly. "God threw it..."

BC 47, Miami 45
Nov. 23, 1984

By Leigh Montville
Globe Staff

MIAMI – The idea does not go away that Doug Flutie simply willed the ball into the end zone. Thought it there.

He threw the ball – sure, he threw it 48 yards on the scoresheet and maybe 65 yards in the air – but that does not begin to explain exactly what happened. Zero seconds left? National television? Forty-eight yards on the last play of the game. To win the game?

This was the kid's biggest trick of all, the trick of tricks yesterday afternoon in the Orange Bowl. Boston College 47, Miami 45. The idea does not go away that something had to be involved that is larger than the simple act of throwing a football.

"Does it seem that somehow good things happen to you?" the 22-year-old BC quarterback was asked after this dizzy moment.

"Oh, yes, definitely," he replied. "There are things that seem to happen . . . and I don't know why. I'm not going to complain about it."

The most implausible part of this implausible finish was its plausibility. Does that sound right? Doug Flutie did what you somehow figured Doug Flutie would do. The virtual impossible.

He somehow is the embodiment of all those coaching cliches that sound so well when they're spoken, but usually echo in a hollow

MONTVILLE, Page 33

Gerard Phelan grabs desperation pass . . . . . . from Doug Flutie. CBS-TV PHOTOS VIA WNEV-TV

2d artificial heart implant due tomorrow

Associated Press

LOUISVILLE, Ky. – The world's second permanent artificial heart implant is scheduled to take place tomorrow morning at Humana Hospital Audubon, officials said yesterday.

The recipient, William J. Schroeder, 52, of Jasper, Ind., will undergo surgery to implant the Jarvik-7 artificial heart at 8 a.m. EST tomorrow, according to Dr. Allan M. Lansing, director of the Humana Heart Institute International.

The hospital's evaluation committee unanimously approved Schroeder's participation after reviewing his records and interviewing him, the hospital said in a news release.

Schroeder was referred to the institute on Nov. 11, when he was diagnosed as suffering from severe heart disease.

The implant will be performed by a team of doctors headed by Dr. William C. DeVries, who performed the world's first artificial heart implant in 1982.

Schroeder underwent surgery to correct a gall bladder problem about a week ago, the hospital

HEART, Page 20

Nuclear-plant errors found widespread

Associated Press

WASHINGTON – Despite ample warnings and a multimillion-dollar program to share information, the same "mishaps" are occurring over and over again at US nuclear power plants, according to government safety regulators.

In a report to the five-member Nuclear Regulatory Commission this week, government analysts who reviewed data from the nation's 80 operating atomic power plants said the reactors are experiencing, on average, 650 percent of the emergency shutdowns of similarly designed plants in Japan.

"Repetitive events occur which indicate that corrective actions taken at individual plants are not as long-lasting or as effective as anticipated," the analysts said in their semiannual report to the commission. "The lessons of experience seem to

NUCLEAR PLANTS, Page 7

Shoppers crowd main floor of Filene's downtown Boston store. GLOBE STAFF PHOTO BY JANET KNOTT

Let the buyers be everywhere

By Gary McMillan
Globe Staff

At Noah's, a plush store for plush toys at Copley Place, the elegantly turned-out woman with the large diamond earrings poked along the shelves while the little boy dawdled. On a table near the door was a display of cross-eyed penguins and Theodore Bearingtons clad in oatmeal sweaters. The boy, suddenly abright, grabbed a Theodore with one hand and a sleeve with the other.

"Mummy, mummy, c'n I have this?"

"Not now, David."

"But mummy, c'n I have this? Huh?"

Mummy put fist on hip and David got an "uh-oh" look.

"David, you have a dozen teddy bears already," she warned.

Shattered, David drooped his head and spoke to his shoes. "I didn't want the bear, mummy, I wanted the sweater."

Ah yes, the day after Thanksgiving; now that the wishbones are out of the way, the wantsomes begin.

The business of Christmas is upon us again, much to the relief of retailers who saw sales nationally drop a tenth of a percent in October. The 32 shopping days before Christmas (counting yesterday) account for a fourth of most retailers' annual sales. It also accounts for what Christina Berg of Claremont, N.H., calls "my annual personal bankruptcy."

"We're talking total poverty here. I'll spend until my MasterCard runs out." Christina Berg looked around at the mill and

SHOPPING, Page 6

A lonely girl needs a holiday lift

By Douglas S. Crocket
Globe Staff

Seven is a wonderful age to be a little girl.

It's an age when babyhood is behind you, an age for friends and games and laughter and secrets.

It's an age when your father is the most wonderful man in the world, your mother the most wonderful woman.

That's how it is for most 7-year-old girls.

Amy is 7 but her life is not like that.

TO HELP GLOBE SANTA: Mail your donation to Globe Santa, Box 1525, Boston, Mass. 02104, or deliver it personally weekdays to The Globe downtown office at the corner of Washington and School streets.

Amy's father has been gone for two years. Her mother fights desperately just to provide necessities.

Amy's environment is not one of green grass and playgrounds and neat suburban yards and homes. Amy lives in a 12-family tenement.

She's used to rats and vermin. Drug raids in neighboring apart-

GLOBE SANTA, Page 7

Shootout in Korean truce zone kills three

By Edwin Q. White
Associated Press

SEOUL – North Korean and UN troops traded fire in the Demilitarized Zone yesterday after a Soviet man apparently defected at the truce village of Panmunjom, the UN Command said. Two North Koreans and a South Korean were killed and an American soldier was wounded, it said.

North Korean news media said the Soviet citizen was a tourist and had been dragged across the border by US security guards, and that three North Korean soldiers were killed in the shooting.

Marlin Fitzwater, a deputy White House press secretary, said the Russian was in the US Embassy in Seoul "and his situation is being discussed with embassy officials."

Fitzwater, speaking in Santa Barbara, Calif., where President Ronald Reagan is vacationing, said he had no further details but added, "We regret the loss of life in this difficult part of the world."

Today, a US Embassy official in Seoul identified the Russian as Vasily Yakovlovich Matuzok, and said he was "alive and well."

Secretaries of the Korean Military Armistice Commission began a hastily arranged meeting today at Panmunjom to discuss the incident.

The UN Command, which is made up of US and South Korean soldiers in Panmunjom, said it had requested a meeting of lower-ranking com-

KOREA, Page 5

Preparation for arms talks

President Ronald Reagan will meet with top advisers next week to "fine tune" American positions for new talks on nuclear arms and space weapons in January between the United States and the Soviet Union, a White House spokesman said yesterday. Page 3.

Parents of vanished child juggle search and everyday life

Nelson and Patricia Belanger listen to a Globe reporter's question during interview in their Exeter home. GLOBE STAFF PHOTO BY BILL RYERSON

'You have to have hope. Without hope, you just can't go on.'
– NELSON BELANGER

By Brad Pokorny
Globe Staff

EXETER, N.H. – A felttip pen drawing of an astronaut – or perhaps it's a ghost, Patricia Belanger is not quite sure – is tacked to the refrigerator. Over by the kitchen sink, a foam-rubber lizard on a wire leash lies on the floor, a souvenir of her 8-year-old daughter's visit to the Stratham town fair in September.

In many ways, it is as if Tammy is still there. She has been missing from the Belanger home 12 days.

Although the police have still found no trace of the shy, likeable third grader since she disappeared while walking to school the morning of Nov. 13, Patricia and Nelson Belanger hold to the hope that their daughter will be found alive, perhaps in another state, and that she will soon return home.

"You have to have hope," Nelson Belanger, a 41-year-old water works production supervisor, said in an interview yesterday. "Without hope, you just can't go on."

Belanger had spent part of the morning working on a large poster that he can hold up to television cameras. The poster will show Tammy's picture, announce that she is missing, and give a brief description of her.

On Thanksgiving Day, the family addressed and stuffed 126 envelopes, containing information about Tammy. They sent them out yesterday to nonprofit groups and parent organizations that

TAMMY, Page 6

TAMMY BELANGER
Missing since Nov. 13

News summary on page 2
Telephone 929-2000
Classified 929-1500
Circulation 929-2222

Rain on our parade
Monday – Rain, near 50
Tuesday – Windy, 25-30
High tide – 12:05 p.m.
Full report – Page 36

Vol. 229; No. 27 MONDAY, JANUARY 27, 1986 96 Pages • 25 cents

A MAULING IN NEW ORLEANS

Bears give New England 46-10 beating

By Ron Borges
Globe Staff

NEW ORLEANS – Long before the Bears had finished shuffling on down to the end zone by doing the Super Bowl Shuffle across the sunken chests of the New England Patriots, no one had any reason – including loyalty – to doubt who was the best football team in America.

"It was a nightmare out there," said fullback Mosi Tatupu. "Mentally, we thought we were still in it, but it just got out of hand. We're not proud of our performance today, but that's the way it goes."

In the end, the Patriots went because the Bears had administered the worst beating in Super Bowl history, crushing New England, 46-10, yesterday in Super Bowl XX. But the outcome was determined by halftime and reinforced in the first nine minutes of the third quarter.

By then, Chicago held a 37-3 lead, its defense had overwhelmed New England's offensive line and the Patriots had set a half-dozen Super Bowl records for most yards moving backwards.

"Our defense was unbelievable," said Bears coach Mike Ditka. "The Patriots were never in the game. We knew early we could handle them.

"Buddy [Ryan, the defensive coordinator] told me they couldn't block our 59 blitz. I wouldn't blame Tony Eason. A quarterback can't throw if he's being harassed and if he's flat on his back."

Eason, who finished his first Super Bowl 0 for 6 for zero yards, three sacks and one

SUPER BOWL, Page 58

This was Super Bowl XX in a nutshell: Bears on the prowl, and a Patriot down. In this case, Chicago defenders Dan Hampton (99) and Otis Wilson sack Patriots' quarterback Steve Grogan.
GLOBE STAFF PHOTO BY FRANK O'BRIEN

In the end, humiliation

By Leigh Montville
Globe Staff

NEW ORLEANS – Take a bite on that quivering lip. Swallow hard. Accept what there is to accept.

COMMENTARY

The end of the fantasy was humiliation.

The fair maiden was hit by a flat-bed trailer this time on the way home from the ball. Arthur pulled the sword and it wouldn't budge. The New England Patriots just didn't have it, kid. Didn't have it at all.

"How humiliating was this game?" a reporter asked veteran linebacker Steve Nelson after the grim Super Bowl business was done yesterday at the Louisiana Superdome with the Chicago Bears winners by an astounding 46-10 score.

"I'd crawl out this door," Steve Nelson replied after a long sigh. "If I could."

There were a million little New England plot lines that had danced through the head about this game, but even the worst Scrooge cynic couldn't have thought out this one. This was . . . this was . . . how do you say it? This was the gruesome worst.

"I don't think anyone in this dressing room thought that something like this could happen," running back Craig James said.

MONTVILLE, Page 61

FROM THE LOCKER ROOMS, COMMENTS ON A SUPER BOWL

'They had the right defense at the right time.'
– Patriots Coach Raymond Berry

'The defense never quit. Seldom do I watch what the offense is doing but today I had to watch. They really stunk.'
– Patriot Raymond Clayborn

'I think we were the most dominant team in football this year, and we proved it today. When we execute like we did today, I don't think anybody can beat us.' **Bears' quarterback Jim McMahon**

The complete Super Bowl report is on Pages 49-76

'I had a dream. I really felt I could be the MVP. I felt it all week. I was so anxious to get here and play. It [winning the most valuable player award] just proves, if you have a dream, you can get there, but you gotta have a dream.'
– Bears' Richard Dent, selected game's most valuable player

Uganda rebels claim power

Vow to set up own government

By Jerry Gray
Associated Press

NAIROBI, Kenya – The commander of the Ugandan rebel army said yesterday he had replaced the 6-month-old ruling military council with one of his own and promised to form a broad-based government and punish criminals from previous regimes.

Yoweri Museveni outlined his plans during a speech on the government-owned radio yesterday afternoon, a day after his National Resistance Army captured the capital, Kampala, and sent thousands of government soldiers fleeing.

Deserting army troops were robbing and beating civilians and looting as they retreated, according to evacuees who reached Nairobi yesterday from northern Uganda.

The Radio Uganda broadcast was monitored in Nairobi. It was the first time since midday Friday that the radio had been on the air and the first formal announcement to Ugandans that Kampala had fallen to the rebels.

Earlier yesterday, Museveni met with US Ambassador Robert Houdek, British High Commissioner Colin MacLean and a representative of the European Common Market, the British High Commission in Nairobi said. The four discussed the evacuation of expatriates and restoration of electric, water and telephone services in the city, said the commission.

In Washington, the State Department said a chartered aircraft

UGANDA, Page 5

Congress may curb Manila aid

Allegations about Marcos stir concern, legislators say

By Adam Pertman
Globe Staff

WASHINGTON – Recent allegations about President Ferdinand E. Marcos' financial dealings and war record could lead Congress to cut back or put strict conditions on US aid to the Philippines, even if he is returned to office next month in a fr[illegible] and free election, according to key legislators and congressional aides.

If Marcos wins and the balloting is determined to have been rigged – and there is widespread concern in Congress and the Reagan administration that could happen – these officials said the reaction could be as severe as an end to the hundreds of millions of dollars in assistance the Philippines receives yearly.

"Why should the people of Boston pay taxes for aid to the Philippines . . . if we conclude that it is being run by a clearly deceptive and corrupt regime?" Rep. Stephen J. Solarz (D-N.Y.), chairman of the House Foreign Affairs subcommittee on Asian and Pacific affairs, said in an interview. "If the election is a fraud, that combined with these revelations could easily persuade people [in Congress] to completely disassociate the United States from Marcos."

The revelations Solarz was referring to were allegations last week that Marcos had lied about his role in World War II, and that his family may have hundreds of millions of dollars in secret real estate investments in New York City.

PHILIPPINES, Page 12

Inside

Today: Sci-Tech

The future for Bible sales

The future growth of Bible sales depends in part on Catholics and also on the emergence of a new, popular translation. Second in series, Page 4.

Back to school for nannies

The child-care crisis of working couples has created a demand for live-in help, but today's nannies need to know more than the traditional child-rearing tasks. As a result, there are many courses being offered for nannies to help them compete in a more complicated work environment. Page 14.

Crushing kidney stones

By generating a powerful sound wave, a lithotripter can break up kidney stones without an incision – and usually with little or no pain. However, many are concerned about the proliferation of the machines without any national approach. In Sci-Tech, Page 29.

Guide to features

Arts/Films 26
Ask the Globe 46
Bridge 47
Business 33
Comics 46,47
Classified 85-96
Deaths 24,25
Editorials 18
Horoscope 47
Living 14
Sports 37
TV/Radio 48

MOONSCAPE

This photo of Miranda, the innermost of Uranus' moons, was taken Jan. 24 by Voyager 2 at a distance of 22,000 miles. Two distinct terrain types shown are a rugged higher-elevation, right, and a lower smoother terrain, left. Several scars, probably faults, cut through the terrains. The crater in the lower part of this image is about 15 miles across. Page 3.
AP PHOTO

EXTRA

News summary on page 2
Telephone 929-2000
Classified 929-1500
Circulation 929-2222

The Boston Globe

Tuesday – May flurry, 20-25
Wednesday – Some sun, mid-20s
High tide – 12:36 a.m., 12:47 p.m.
Full report – Page 81

Vol. 229; No. 28 TUESDAY, JANUARY 28, 1986 96 Pages • 25 cents

SHUTTLE EXPLODES

Christa McAuliffe greeted the crowd today on her way to the shuttle launch.
GLOBE STAFF PHOTO BY JANET KNOTT

NH teacher, 6 crew mates feared dead

By Howard Benedict
Associated Press

CAPE CANAVERAL, Fla. – Space shuttle Challenger exploded into a gigantic fireball moments after liftoff today, apparently killing all seven crew members, including New Hampshire schoolteacher Christa McAuliffe.

There was no announcement of the fate of the crew but it appeared there was no way they could have survived.

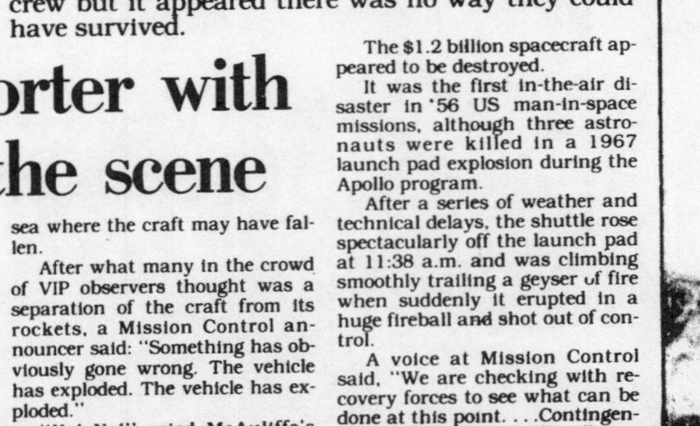

The $1.2 billion spacecraft appeared to be destroyed.

It was the first in-the-air disaster in '56 US man-in-space missions, although three astronauts were killed in a 1967 launch pad explosion during the Apollo program.

After a series of weather and technical delays, the shuttle rose spectacularly off the launch pad at 11:38 a.m. and was climbing smoothly trailing a geyser of fire when suddenly it erupted in a huge fireball and shot out of control.

A voice at Mission Control said, "We are checking with recovery forces to see what can be done at this point. . . .Contingency procedures are in effect."

The voice said, "Vehicle has exploded. . . .We are awaiting word from any recovery forces downrange."

The explosion was a devastating setback for the National Aeronautics and Space Administration after successfully carrying out 24 space shuttle missions in slightly less than five years.

There were seven crew members aboard, including Mrs. McAuliffe, a 37-year-old New Hampshire teacher selected as America's first citizen in space.

Mission Control said debris from the shuttle fell several miles

SHUTTLE, Page 5

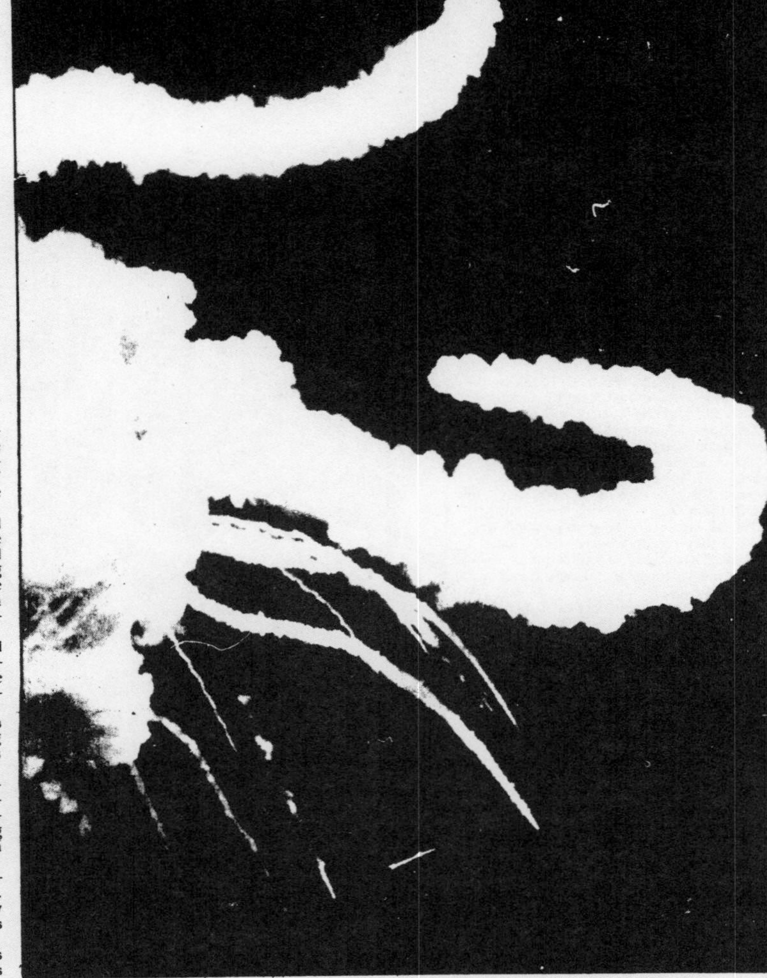

Plumes of smoke billow from space shuttle Challenger moments after explosion this morning. UPI PHOTO

Globe reporter with family at the scene

By Michael Kranish
Globe Staff

KENNEDY SPACE CENTER, Fla. – In a few horrific moments, the ecstasy of Christa McAuliffe's parents turned to shock and silence.

Grace and Ed Corrigan of Framingham, Mass., hugged each other in jubilation as the $1.2-billion spacecraft launched in near-freezing conditions, then turned to each other in stunned shock a few moments later.

Challenger exploded in air moments after takeoff this morning, apparently killing New Hampshire teacher Christa McAuliffe and the six other astronauts, to the stunned cries of watching family and friends.

Rescue operations immediately began at sea, but there appeared little chance the the astronauts could have survived, officials said. At noon today, NASA officials said continued debris was making it difficult to reach the point in the sea where the craft may have fallen.

After what many in the crowd of VIP observers thought was a separation of the craft from its rockets, a Mission Control announcer said: "Something has obviously gone wrong. The vehicle has exploded. The vehicle has exploded."

"No! No!" cried McAuliffe's friends, who sat in a grandstand with the third-grade class of McAuliffe's son, Scott.

Scott, 9, his sister, Caroline, 6, and McAuliffe's husband Steven were at a separate viewing site.

A minute later, when Mission Control confirmed the explosion, McAuliffe's best friend, Jo Ann Jordon of Concord, N.H., screamed: "It didn't explode. It didn't explode!"

McAuliffe's parents, surrounded by friends, stood in silent disbelief. "Let's get out of here," one friend said, and the parents were herded to nearby Mission Control headquarters.

Upbeat Reagan talk expected

By Walter V. Robinson and Adam Pertman
Globe Staff

WASHINGTON – President Reagan will mount the House rostrum for the State of the Union message tonight as an enormously popular politician, but also facing, perhaps the most formidable legislative roadblocks of his presidency.

His short, upbeat, thematic speech is expected to tout the Gramm-Rudman deficit-reduction law as a panacea for decades of government overspending, according to presidential aides. But both critics and supporters of the president think it more likely that Gramm-Rudman will frustrate and complicate Reagan's domestic and foreign policy agenda.

"The president is in for a very rocky year," Norman Ornstein, a specialist in White House-congressional relations at the American Enterprise Institute, predicted in an interview yesterday.

In addition to Gramm-Rudman's lengthy shadow, the president faces other domestic hurdles on Capitol Hill: his tax revision initiative, the Superfund cleanup bill, immigration legislation and a clean water bill. Other nettlesome problems loom on the foreign policy horizon, including funding for guerrillas in Nicaragua, Afghanistan and Angola, terrorism, proposed arms sales to Jordan and Saudi Arabia and likely congres-

REAGAN, Page 12

Boy swept into sea, drowns

By Kevin Cullen and Diane E. Lewis
Globe Staff

LYNN – A 10-year-old boy drowned and his best friend was seriously injured after pounding waves pulled them from a slippery walkway at Kings Beach in Lynn and swept them into the sea yesterday.

Metropolitan Police divers recovered the body of John A. Comeau Jr. not far from where he disappeared. Thomas Reilly, 13, was reported in serious condition at Children's Hospital.

Reilly was saved by a passerby, who in turn was rescued by four municipal workers who spotted him trying to save the two boys.

Late last night, John A. Comeau Sr. sat on his couch, his eyes rimmed with redness, smoking a cigarette and watching the Bruins play the Hartford Whalers on television.

"My son Johnny, he should be here right now, watching this hockey game with me," Comeau said. "If he was alive, he'd be right here at my side. He loved hockey. And we loved watching the Bruins games together."

According to friends and relatives, the two boys had skipped school together yesterday and walked down to King's Beach, where they dodged the waves. At 11:43 a.m., one of those waves caught them and pulled them from a 3-foot wide walkway into the 35-degree water.

LYNN, Page 13

Exxon owes states $2b, top court says

By Richard Carelli
Associated Press

WASHINGTON – The Supreme Court yesterday made final the largest monetary judgment in American history to be upheld on appeal by telling Exxon Corp. to pay more than $2 billion for inflating oil prices.

The court, with no recorded dissent, let stand rulings that force Exxon to pay refunds and interest for overcharges of $895 million on the 1975-81 sales of oil from a Texas field.

The money, totaling about $2.1 billion, will be deposited by Exxon into the federal Treasury, and then will be distributed to the states based on estimates of energy consumption during the six-year period.

Most consumers of gasoline and heating oil will receive no cash. States must spend the money on energy conservation – such as weatherizing hospitals and schools – and on helping the poor pay their home utility bills.

[Officials in Boston said that Massachusetts expects to get at least $60 million on the basis of population but that it will be up to Gov. Dukakis to decide how the windfall is distributed, with several agencies already in contention for a share.

[The majority of proposals at hearings last fall on possible uses for the overcharge money were for programs to provide insulation and other fuel-saving assistance to low-income and moderate income households, they said.

[But others called for mass transit improvements, ranging from new commuter railroad stations to wheelchair-accessible taxis, as ways to conserve energy.

COURT, Page 11

Patriots' drug problems disclosed; dozen involved

By Ron Borges
Globe Staff

NEW ORLEANS – A growing drug problem on the New England Patriots that this year involved an estimated dozen members of the AFC champions, including four starters, spilled into the public eye yesterday when the team became the first in the National Football League to accept a voluntary drug-testing program.

"I would say we may be 28th in the league as far as this problem goes, but there are at least five players we know who have a serious problem and five to seven more whom we suspect very strongly," coach Raymond Berry said. The names of the players involved were not released.

"We have a situation that exists here that we feel is intolerable," said Berry. "It has been going on for a year, and I had to weigh the damages of doing something about it immediately by going public. We felt with the season going the way it had, we had to keep our eye on the bull's-eye. That's why we didn't do anything before. But our bull's-eye looking is over.

"It's time to do something about this problem, and it cannot be done in secret."

After being addressed yesterday by Berry about the extent of the problem – specifically, the use of cocaine – and the possible consequences, the team members huddled for nearly two hours in their hotel with player representative Brian Holloway and his assistant, Ron Wooten.

It was decided that a two-thirds majority would be enough to approve the drug-testing agreement. Of the 59 players on the roster, seven voted against the plan. Several others abstained.

Prior to the vote, injured defensive end Kenneth Sims spoke forcefully in favor of the voluntary plan.

"I just said that people's lives were more important than football," Sims said. "I tried to speak

PATRIOTS, Page 67

Sen. Kennedy is set for talks in Soviet Union

By Thomas Oliphant
Globe Staff

WASHINGTON – Sen. Edward M. Kennedy will travel to the Soviet Union later this week for three days of private meetings with Mikhail S. Gorbachev and other senior officials.

According to a terse announcement by his office, the principal focus of Kennedy's meetings will be on nuclear arms control and the negotiations between the two nuclear superpowers in Geneva, but he is also likely to raise human rights issues, as he did during visits with Leonid I. Brezhnev in 1974 and 1978.

Kennedy's trip – arrangements for which were made final during a visit to Moscow earlier this month by his chief aide, Dr. Lawrence Horowitz – is a classic example of the kind of activity that might have proved politically impossible for Kennedy had he still been a possible candidate for the presidency.

KENNEDY, Page 11

Conservatives back Thatcher in Westland political crisis

By Steven Erlanger
Globe Staff

LONDON – In one of the most crucial parliamentary speeches of her career, Prime Minister Margaret Thatcher yesterday defused the immediate political crisis within her own party about her involvement in the tangled Westland affair.

The Conservative Party rallied to her, giving her a majority in a vote that concluded an emergency House of Commons debate.

In a 20-minute statement, a chastened Thatcher attempted to explain what she knew about the leak of a damaging private letter from her solicitor general, Sir Patrick Mayhew, to Michael Heseltine, her former defense secretary who resigned in anger Jan. 9. The leak also led to the resignation on Friday of a second minister, Trade

BRITAIN, Page 12

News summary on page 2
Telephone 929-2000
Classified 929-1500
Circulation 929-2222

The Boston Globe

Pleasant, a roamer
Tuesday – P.M. sun, 60s-70s
Wednesday – Sun/clouds, 60-70
High tide – 3:35 a.m., 4:18 p.m.
Full report – Page 22

Vol. 229; No. 119 | TUESDAY, APRIL 29, 1986 | 80 Pages • 25 cents

Soviet nuclear accident sends radiation abroad

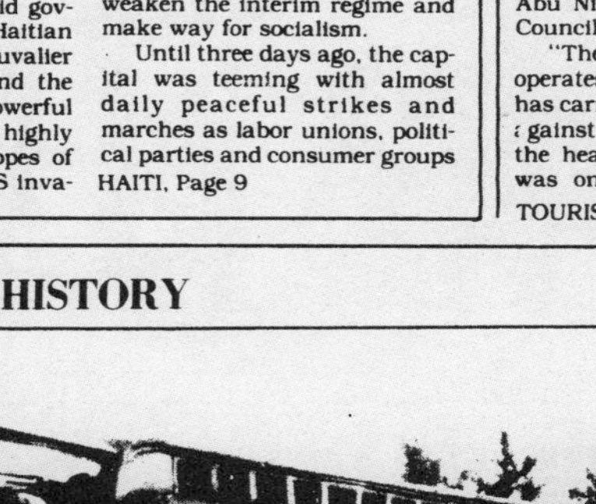

Officials in Norway, Sweden, Finland and Denmark reported increased radiation levels this weekend following accident at the Soviet Chernobyl nuclear power plant 30 miles north of Kiev. GLOBE MAP

Scandinavians report higher radioactivity

By Carol J. Williams
Associated Press

MOSCOW – The Soviet Union said yesterday that a nuclear accident damaged an atomic reactor at the Chernobyl power plant in the Ukraine. Radiation reported up to 10 times above normal levels swept across Finland, Denmark and Sweden, more than 750 miles away.

Budapest Radio in Hungary reported early today that there had been injuries from the accident, and noted that the power plant was located at the conjunction of two rivers, near the reservoir that supplies Kiev, a city of 2.4 million people and the capital of the Ukraine.

The Soviet news agency Tass said only that people "affected" were being aided, but did not say whether there had been injuries or deaths, when the accident occurred, or give the exact location of the plant.

Tass said it was the first nuclear accident in the Soviet Union and a government commission was appointed, an indication that it was serious.

"It must have been a relatively big accident, since we have received such high levels of radiation from so far away," said Lars Erik de Geer of Sweden's Defense Research Agency.

He said the radiation levels corresponded to those recorded after Chinese nuclear weapons tests in the atmosphere during the 1970s. "I know of no earlier nuclear power plant accident which has led to such high radiation levels in this area," he said.

In Washington, a White House spokesman, Edward Djerejian, said: "It must be very serious if the Soviets talk about it." Soviet

The Soviet nuclear plant involved in the accident likely lacked the containment structure required in US plants, engineers said. Page 10.

media seldom report natural disasters or accidents unless injuries and damage are widespread.

Also in Washington, Jim McKenzie of the Union of Concerned Scientists, an antinuclear group, said the information he had "indicates probably a core meltdown." A meltdown, caused by a cooling system failure, is a melting of the fuel rods and a sinking of the nuclear core into the earth. It results in a release of dangerous radiation.

NUCLEAR, Page 10

The battle behind the rail strike

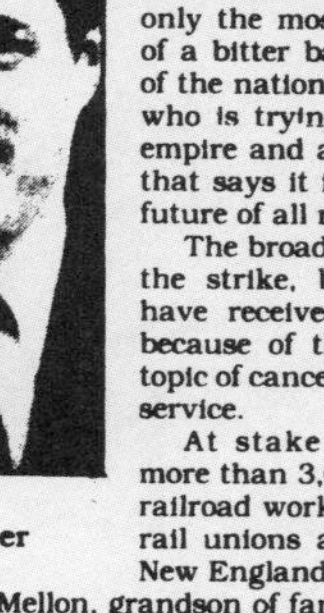

MELLON
Silent player

By Michael Kranish
Globe Staff

BILLERICA – The railroad strike that for two months has disrupted some Boston commuter and freight service is only the most publicized part of a bitter battle between one of the nation's wealthiest men who is trying to create a rail empire and a tiny union local that says it is fighting for the future of all rail unions.

The broader implications of the strike, both sides agree, have received little attention because of the politically hot topic of canceled commuter rail service.

At stake are the jobs of more than 3,000 New England railroad workers, the power of rail unions and the future of New England railroad service.

Timothy Mellon, grandson of famed financier Andrew Mellon and a reclusive heir to the family's Pittsburgh banking fortune, is the silent player in the story. The chairman and majority owner of Guilford

MELLON, Page 9

Methodist bishops urge nuclear arms freeze

By James L. Franklin
Globe Staff

NEW YORK – United Methodist bishops, leaders of the nation's second-largest Protestant body, yesterday released the second draft of a pastoral letter that condemns the "fundamental flaws" in the policy of nuclear deterrence and calls for a nuclear arms freeze and a ban on space-based weapons.

"We have said a clear and unconditioned no to nuclear war and to any use of nuclear weapons," says their letter, released during a news conference at the birthplace of American Methodism, John Street Church in Manhattan.

The six bishops at the press conference praised the US Catholic bishops' 1983 letter on nuclear weapons, and said they wanted to strengthen the "ecumenical consensus" on the dangers of nuclear weapons.

But they made it clear they mean to go further than their Catholic counterparts, who talked about "a strictly conditioned acceptance" of nuclear weapons, as a step toward peace and disarmament.

"We have concluded that nuclear deterrence is a position which cannot receive the church's blessing," says the new draft of the United Methodist letter. "We have stated our complete lack of confidence in proposed 'defenses' against nuclear attack and are convinced that the enormous cost of developing such defenses is one more witness to the obvious fact that the arms race is a social justice issue, not only a war and peace issue."

The letter and an accompanying document called "In Defense of Creation: The Nuclear Crisis and a Just Peace," call for a comprehensive ban on nuclear tests, a nuclear weapons freeze, "a phased but rapid reduction of nuclear arsenals" and a ban on all "offensive and defensive space weapons."

The denomination's Council of Bishops is expected to give final approval to the letter today, after open debate at their semiannual meeting in Morristown, N.J. It will then be distributed through local churches of the denomination, which has 9.2 million members in the United States and another 1 million abroad.

LETTER, Page 13

Abu Nidal unit says it shot Briton

By Farouk Nassar
Associated Press

BEIRUT – A terrorist group led by Abu Nidal said yesterday that it killed a British tourist in Jerusalem on Sunday in revenge for Britain's support of US air raids against Libya two weeks ago.

The United States blames Abu Nidal for the Dec. 27 massacres at the Rome and Vienna airports, in which 20 people were killed, and accuses Col. Moammar Khadafy, the Libyan leader, of harboring him.

France toughens position on terrorism. Prosecutor says Libyan embassy supplied grenades used in Turkish attack. US will consider expelling Libyan students. Page 12.

A typewritten statement delivered to a Western news agency in predominantly Moslem West Beirut said that the tourist, Paul Appleby, 28, of Bristol, England, was on a spy mission when gunmen of Abu Nidal's Fatah-Revolutionary Council shot him down.

"The Monzer Kadry squad that operates in the Jerusalem district has carried out the death sentence against Briton Paul Appleby in the heart of Jerusalem while he was on an intelligence mission

TOURIST, Page 12

Deaver wants outsider to probe his lobbying

By Howard Kurtz
Washington Post

WASHINGTON – Former White House aide Michael K. Deaver, faced with growing criticism of his multimillion-dollar Washington consulting business, called for an independent counsel yesterday to investigate his lobbying activities for the Canadian government and other foreign and domestic clients.

Deaver's request came as Attorney General Edwin Meese 3d, who was asked last week to seek such an outside investigation, announced that he would disqualify himself from the matter because of his longtime association with Deaver.

Deputy Attorney General D. Lowell Jensen now must decide whether the Justice Department should conduct a preliminary probe of Deaver and whether the evidence warrants asking a three-judge panel to name an independent counsel.

Deaver said in a statement that "elementary due process and fairness to me and my family require appointment of an independent counsel. While I'm grateful for the president's continuing support, the climate has become such that this is the only way to resolve the issue fairly."

President Reagan told report-

DEAVER, Page 13

Pinpointing the threat in Haiti

Extremists capitalizing on regime's inertia

By Pamela Constable
Globe Staff

PORT-AU-PRINCE, Haiti – The national euphoria and hopes for an easy transition to democracy since the ouster of dictator Jean Claude Duvalier have been shattered by the deaths of seven unarmed protesters Saturday in a confrontation with police.

NEWS ANALYSIS

What is less clear is whether the greater threat to the fragile process comes from the extreme right or left, both of which are being blamed for sparking the confrontation.

The shooting and timid government response, most Haitian leaders say, show that Duvalier allies among the elite and the armed forces are still powerful and willing to incite poor, highly suggestible crowds in hopes of provoking a coup or a US invasion that would restore them to power.

At the same time, there is fear that leftist groups are capitalizing on their new freedoms to encourage popular unrest, weaken the interim regime and make way for socialism.

Until three days ago, the capital was teeming with almost daily peaceful strikes and marches as labor unions, political parties and consumer groups

HAITI, Page 9

IN TRAINING FOR A MOMENT IN HISTORY

Members of the First Massachusetts Cavalry rehearse at Edaville Railroad for re-enactment of a Civil War battle. The "living history" program will be staged June 7-8 at the South Carver tourist attraction. First Lt. Ronald Davis gives orders to members of the unit as Civil War "nurse" Lisa Roy looks on. Group of Civil War buffs organized the First Cavalry in 1984. GLOBE STAFF PHOTO BY JOE RUNCI

Inside

Today: Business Extra

Showdown over life insurance

What is rated as the best life insurance buy in the country – savings bank life – is the focus of a struggle on Beacon Hill. Business Extra, Page 25.

The Patriots and the draft

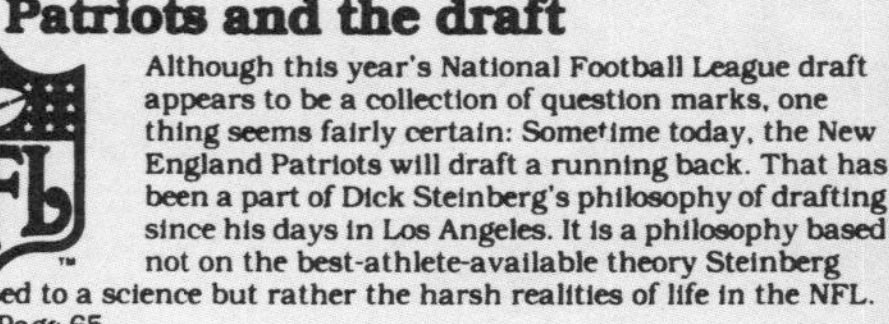

Although this year's National Football League draft appears to be a collection of question marks, one thing seems fairly certain: Sometime today, the New England Patriots will draft a running back. That has been a part of Dick Steinberg's philosophy of drafting since his days in Los Angeles. It is a philosophy based not on the best-athlete-available theory Steinberg has raised to a science but rather the harsh realities of life in the NFL. Sports, Page 65.

A quandary for Barnstead, N.H.

Schoolchildren of Barnstead, N.H. may be overjoyed at the prospect, but school officials are in a quandary. Unless emergency funds are approved, the town school will be forced to close eight days early this year. Page 17.

Guide to features

Arts/Films 60
Ask the Globe 20
Bridge 20
Business 25
Comics 20-21
Classified 48-56, 75-80
Deaths 46-47
Editorials 14
Horoscope 20
Living 57
Sports 65
TV/Radio 23

News summary on page 2
Telephone 929-2000
Classified 929-1500
Circulation 929 2222

The Boston Globe

Rays another one
Monday – Sunny, near 80
Tuesday – Ditto
High tide – 12:57 a.m., 1:33 p.m.
Full report – Page 50

Vol. 229; No. 160 MONDAY, JUNE 9, 1986 64 Pages • 25 cents

CELTICS' CROWNING GLORY

Bird buries Rockets

By Bob Ryan
Globe Staff

The Houston Rockets were like an unwary couple pulled over on the highway for going 3 miles over the speed limit by a burly Georgia cop with the mirrored sunglasses.

It wasn't their day. The cop's name was Bird. The bailiff's name was Bird. The court stenographer's name was Bird. The judge's name was Bird. And the executioner's name was – guess what? – Bird.

Celtics fans were relatively orderly, although there were some arrests yesterday. Page 24.

Welcome to Bird Country, boys, and while you're at it, why don't you congratulate the Boston Celtics on the occasion of their 16th NBA championship? He didn't make *every* shot, or grab *every* rebound, or account for *every* assist, or make *every* steal, or sell *every* hot dog, but he plugged himself into every conceivable aspect of the game to the extent that all the other players had to do was feed off his energy level. "Let's face it," said Kevin McHale, "when you play with a guy like Larry Bird, it gives you a lot of confidence."

CELTICS, Page 39

Coming tomorrow: 28-page souvenir section on Celts

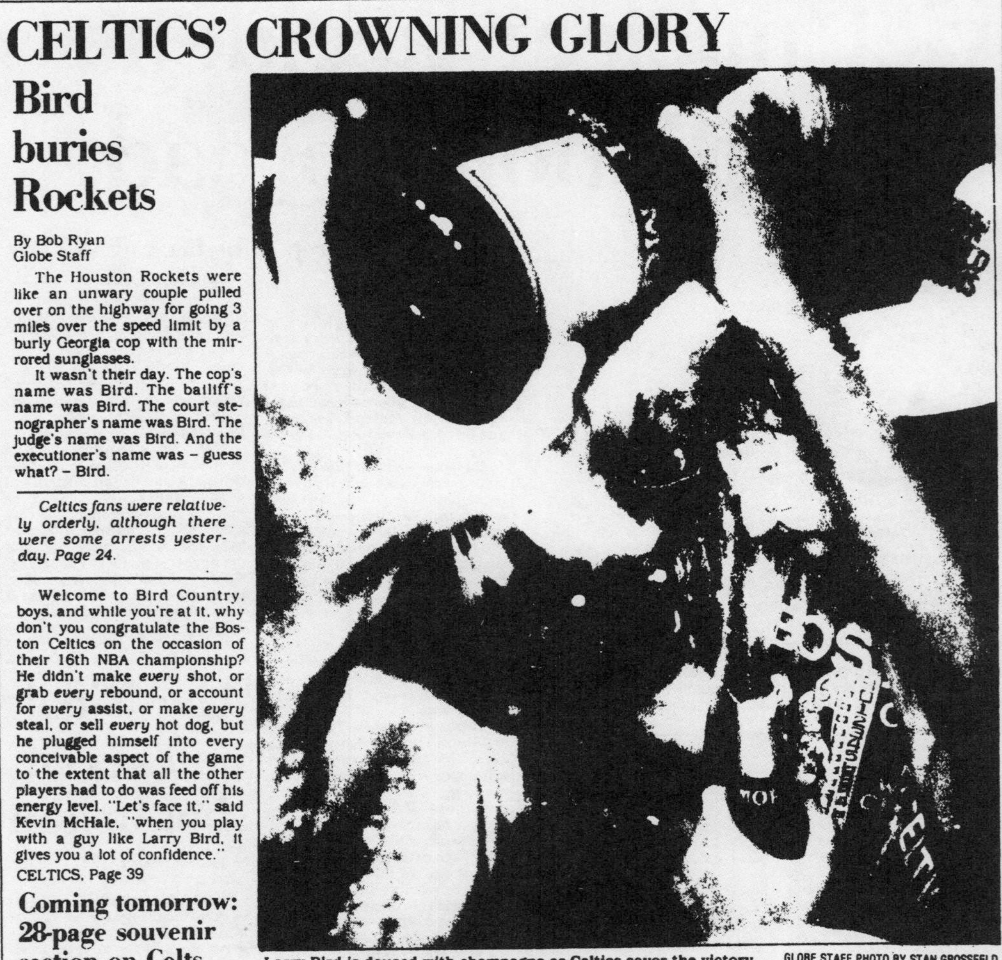
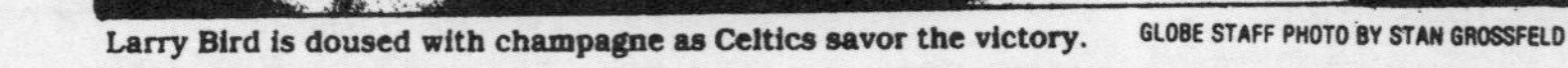
Larry Bird is doused with champagne as Celtics savor the victory. GLOBE STAFF PHOTO BY STAN GROSSFELD

Jubilant fans celebrate Celtics victory outside Boston Garden. GLOBE PHOTO BY SUZANNE KREITER

Waldheim wins in Austria

By Larry Gerber
Associated Press

VIENNA – Kurt Waldheim, the former UN secretary general who denied allegations throughout the campaign that he hid a Nazi past, won a clear victory in Austria's presidential election runoff yesterday.

Interior Minister Karl Blecha declared Waldheim the winner with 2,460,203 votes, or 53.89 percent of the valid ballots cast. Kurt Steyrer, the Socialist opponent, drew 2,105,118 votes, or 46.11 percent.

Blecha said votes from all but one polling station had been counted. Austria has 5.4 million eligible voters.

[Eighty-seven percent of those eligible voted yesterday, United Press International reported, down from the 89 percent who voted in the initial balloting May 4, when Waldheim won the most votes – 49.6 percent – in a three-way contest, but fell short of a majority and had to face runner-up Steyrer in yesterday's runoff.]

Waldheim will succeed a Socialist, Rudolf Kirschlager, who is retiring. The Socialists have controlled the Austrian government for 16 years.

A presidential term in Austria is six years. The office is largely ceremonial, but part of the job is making state visits and greeting foreign guests.

"I am certainly very happy about the result," Waldheim, 67, told a television reporter at the headquarters of the conservative People's Party that backed him.

Steyrer, 66, said he had anticipated defeat after talking to voters and looking at polls, but that he was "disappointed at the size, the big difference, in the election result."

WALDHEIM, Page 8

In Israel, 'sadness' over election

By Curtis Wilkie
Globe Staff

JERUSALEM – Prime Minister Shimon Peres and Foreign Minister Yitzhak Shamir were to meet today to consider what diplomatic course to take regarding Kurt Waldheim, who was elected president of Austria yesterday.

The Foreign Ministry issued a statement last night expressing "sadness and disappointment" over Waldheim's election. There was speculation that Israel might reduce its level of diplomatic recognition of Austria in protest.

There was no formal comment from Peres, but President Chaim Herzog warned that "Israel should act with caution and not anger."

Other comment was not so restrained.

ISRAEL, Page 8

SECRET COURT

Some question procedures of the panel that authorizes espionage case wiretaps

By Stephen Kurkjian
Globe Staff

WASHINGTON – The court is so secretive that it deliberates in a vault-like room on the top floor of the Justice Department. It never makes known the reasons for its decisions and public inquiry into its operation has been limited to one academic study and one congressional hearing.

Yet, the cases that it deals with are among the most sensational in the United States, and it must rule on the most controversial elements of those cases.

The Foreign Intelligence Surveillance Court decides whether to allow federal electronic surveillance of persons or offices in the United States suspected of espionage or international terrorism.

Born after the disclosures a decade ago that US intelligence agencies had carried on a variety of illegal surveillances under the guise of national security, the court was designed to ensure constitutional safeguards in espionage and terrorism investigations.

The few in Congress who have monitored the court's operation behind closed doors say the court has struck an effective balance between national security and individual rights; but, civil liberty advocates are not so certain.

They contend that because the requests concern national security, the seven US District Court judges who make up the court will instinctively favor the government's side.

COURT, Page 8

Inside
Today: Sci-Tech

Flight 847: Burying the memories
Americans who were aboard TWA Flight 847 when it was hijacked a year ago have tried to put the experience behind them. Page 13.

The US satellite crisis

US satellites – by now all but indispensable for storm-tracking, crop forecasts and a host of other functions – have been falling victim to mechanical breakdown and official neglect. The crisis has been heightened by the shuttle disaster and other rocket failures, leaving the West temporarily without the means to launch new satellites. Sci-Tech, Page 53.

A crash program for decoding genes
A debate has begun on proposals for a crash program to decode all 50,000 genes that determine human heredity. It would be a massive effort, but scientists say the rewards could include new clues to cancer and inherited disease. Sci-Tech, Page 53.

Guide to features

Arts/Films 18
Ask the Globe 58
Bridge 58
Business 45
Comics 58-59
Classified 24-32, 60-64
Deaths 56-57
Editorials 10
Horoscope 58
Living 21
Sports 33
TV/Radio 51

Traffic woes in focus on Federal St.

Construction adds to Hub's problems

By Diane Alters
Globe Staff

It's 11:40 a.m. on a recent weekday. An elderly man in a business suit steps off the curb and walks against a red light at Federal and Franklin streets.

As the man steps into the traffic, a blue car screeches to a halt, its bumper just inches from his kneecap. A man about the pedestrian's age rolls down the passenger window as cars begin to back up behind him. "You old fool!" the passenger yells as the man hurries on.

So the daily chaos continues on what some drivers call one of the worst streets in Boston – one of the most tangled few blocks of traffic in a city known for its traffic jams. Independent-minded pedestrians, buses, taxis, delivery trucks and construction vehicles from two nearby sites compete for space on the stretch of Federal Street between Franklin and High streets.

Traffic backs up along Federal Street between High and Franklin streets. GLOBE STAFF PHOTO BY JOANNE RATHE

The activity on that part of Federal Street illustrates some of the problems Boston faces as city officials work to manage a set of historically bad traffic problems made worse by the city's growth and a plethora of development. A new city initiative, announced in February but still in the planning stages, is supposed to help keep traffic flowing on streets like Federal, where many elements contribute to the traffic snarl.

"It's bad," said cabdriver Bob Hart, who tries to keep his taxi away from that block of Federal Street.

A total of 7,499 vehicles passed the intersection of Franklin and Federal streets one Monday in May, when city employees last did

TRAFFIC, Page 6

Cuba releases Bay of Pigs officer to US

By Sandra Jaramillo
Associated Press

HOMESTEAD, Fla. – A former high-ranking Cuban officer who was imprisoned for his part in the Bay of Pigs invasion 25 years ago was reunited with his family yesterday, after he was released by the government of President Fidel Castro and flown to Florida.

"Sometimes there aren't words to express how one feels," the former officer, Ricardo Montero Duque, said moments after an emotional greeting from relatives at Homestead Air Force Base south of Miami. "I'm very grateful to the people and the government of the United States. I'm very happy to be here."

Montero, 60, freed five years before the end of his sentence, was met by his 80-year-old mother, Bernardina Duque de Montero of Miami, and two brothers, also of Miami.

CUBAN, Page 6

Index on page 2
Telephone 929-2000
Classified 929-1500
Circulation 929-2222

Boston Sunday Globe

The weather
Sunday: Rain, 55
Monday: Rain, 60s
Details page 105

Vol. 230; No. 118 — SUNDAY, OCTOBER 26, 1986 — *$1.25 at newsstands beyond 30 miles from Boston — $1.00

Mets steal win from Sox, 6-5, in 10th

Error by Buckner allows Knight to score winning run; Boyd to pitch 7th

An error by first baseman Bill Buckner gave the Mets a tenth-inning, 6-5 victory over the Red Sox last night, sending the World Series into a seventh game tonight at Shea Stadium. Buckner's error sealed the Sox' fate after what appeared to be an all-but-certain Sox victory. The Sox had opened the tenth with a towering home run by Dave Henderson that seemed to guarantee that they would win their first World Series in 68 years.

They were just one pitch away

By Leigh Montville
Globe Staff

COMMENTARY

NEW YORK – One pitch away from a world championship. One pitch from an end to 68 years of frustration. One pitch.

Not close enough.

In a heartbreak that ranks with all of the heartbreaks ever recorded in the long book of Boston Red Sox heartbreak history, the Olde Towne Team let that world championship bounce away in the red dirt of Shea Stadium last night. One wild pitch. One error by first baseman Bill Buckner. One pitch away. The New York Mets scored three runs in the bottom of the 10th and final inning after allowing the Red Sox two in the top of the inning to post a wild, 6-5 win in the sixth game of this World Series and force a seventh game tonight at 8:35 (NBC-TV).

Never have the Red Sox come this close and failed. Never in the Bucky Dent game or the Enos Slaughter game or the Jim Burton game or all the recorded games of frustration had the finish been this close to a championship. Never. Not since 1918. Never.

"We didn't get that final out," manager John McNamara said. "That's all I can say. We needed that one more out, and we didn't get it.

"Yes, it's disappointing, but at least we have another chance tomorrow.

MONTVILLE, Page 62

Globe staff photo/Bill Brett

Jubilant Mets celebrate their 10th inning victory over the Red Sox to send the 1986 World Series into a seventh game. The Mets scored the winning run on an error at first by Buckner. More Series stories, photos, Page 55.

Britain advances ousters

Syrians now have 7 days to leave

By Tyler Marshall
Los Angeles Times

LONDON – Britain stepped up its diplomatic offensive against Syria yesterday, telling the Syrian ambassador and his staff that they have only a week to get out of the country and calling on the Soviet Union to distance itself from such state-backed terrorism as Syria's involvement in a foiled plot to blow up an Israeli airliner.

A Foreign Office spokesman said the decision to halve the 14 days originally given the Syrians to depart was made after official notification was received here that Syria had given 19 British diplomats only seven days to wind up their affairs in Damascus.

The spokesman also described as "unhelpful" a statement by Tass, the official Soviet news agency, that Britain's accusations against Syria "were obviously invented."

Britain severed diplomatic relations with

Britain is seeking help from its allies to put pressure on Syria. Page 26. Britain's evidence from the El Al bombing attempt trial is the "smoking gun" of Syrian terrorist activities, sources say. Page 26.

Syria on Friday after a trial produced overwhelming evidence of what the foreign secretary, Sir Geoffrey Howe, called "the wicked involvement of the Syrian government" in a bomb plot. Syria's ambassador, Loutof Allah Haydar, and 20 other Syrian diplomats here were ordered to close their embassy and leave Britain.

Prime Minister Margaret Thatcher's government acted three hours after Nezar Hindawi, 32, a Jordanian national, was convicted and sentenced to 45 years in prison for plotting to blow up an El Al Israeli Airlines jetliner by smuggling a bomb aboard the plane in the hand luggage of his pregnant girlfriend.

Signed statements by Hindawi produced in court, coupled with his own court testimo-

BRITAIN, Page 26

Development story in N.H. risks its picture-book allure

By Ellen J. Bartlett
Globe Staff

WINDHAM, N.H. – In Canterbury Estates, a new development a few minutes from Interstate 93, the $99,900 housing lots are sold out. A few $125,000 lots remain. That buys the land only, an acre and a half. The house is extra.

Ten miles away in Hudson, a "help wanted" sign is posted outside a textile mill. The local labor shortage has grown so acute that Hudson Mills recently had to bus workers from Rhode Island to keep the looms running full time.

In Amherst, Sandy Moses recently moved her business to a new shopping center on Route 101A. She wouldn't venture onto that road at rush hour herself, but she welcomes the tens of thousands of commuters who do. They made Food for Pets possible. If she had opened her gourmet pet food shop here 10 years ago, she said, she would have been laughed out of town.

But Amherst has changed. Hudson has changed. Windham has changed.

During the last few years, New Hampshire has encountered phenomenal growth, particularly in Hillsborough and Rockingham counties on the border with Massachusetts.

GROWTH, Page 90

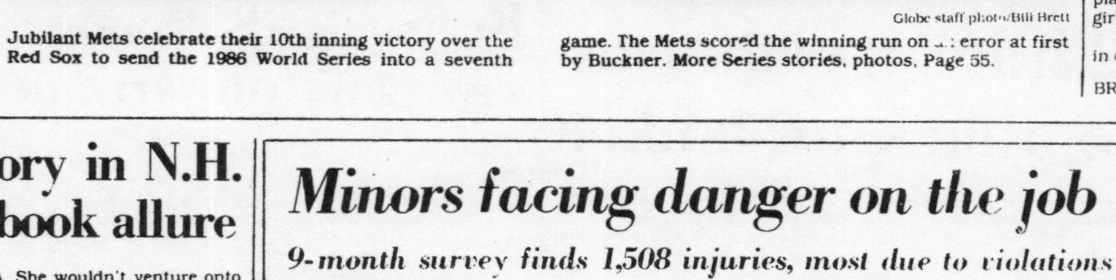

Minors facing danger on the job

9-month survey finds 1,508 injuries, most due to violations

By Bruce Butterfield
Globe Staff

Seven days after getting a job as factory helper at a Lakeville manufacturing company, Lawrence Westgate was told to trim metal castings on a 4-ton power press.

He shouldn't have been. He was 15 years old – the work a violation of Massachusetts child labor laws.

Minutes later, the press caught his right hand, chopping off his first and second fingers along with a half-inch of his little finger.

In Roxbury, Mark Anthony Avila was proud of working part-time after school this year as a stock boy at Tropical Foods Inc. He used the first of his savings on Mother's Day to buy his mother a microwave oven. Mercedes Avila cries now at the mention of the gift.

Nine days later – while at work – her son fell to his death down the shaft of a warehouse elevator that a company official says he was told not to go near.

He was 15 years old.

Despite some of the most progressive child labor laws in the country, Massachusetts is becoming an increasingly dangerous place for teen-agers to work. This year, thousands of minors in the state will be injured, many seriously, at jobs that are supposed to be safe, but often are not.

Often – as was the case in the accident that claimed Larry Westgate's fingers – the minors are working illegally. In the labor-tight economy of Massachusetts, where teen-age workers are increasingly in demand, officials say the problem is worsening.

"People are scooping kids up and putting them into jobs where they don't belong. We've never seen the kind of problems with child labor abuse we're seeing now," said Andrew Currie, director of industrial safety for the state Department of Labor and Industries.

In the first nine months of this year alone, state officials say, a sampling of injury records –

CHILD LABOR, Page 16

As Senate fears grow, GOP turns to Reagan

By Thomas Oliphant
Globe Staff

1986 ELECTIONS

SEATTLE – Three weeks ago, Sen. Slade Gorton was feeling so good about his prospects for reelection that he passed word to the White House that President Reagan needn't come to Washington state in the final days of the campaign if his schedule was jammed with events in states with closer races.

But last week, as Brock Adams, a Democratic former congressman and US transportation secretary, backed him to the wall, Gorton sent out a shrill SOS. And the president will spend the night in Spokane this Thursday.

The situation here – as well as in a dozen other states with Election Day nine days away – was aptly summarized by a headline in the Seattle Post-Intelligencer last week: "Gorton to Reagan: Help!"

Like birdshot, Reagan has been fired all over the country in a whirlwind tour to help several seriously endangered Republican candidates.

The president's travel into 13 states, backed up by media blitzes and as much high-tech support services as the cash-rich Republican Party can muster, was once envisaged as icing on the cake of a generally successful political year. Today, it is a rescue mission.

As of right now, Reagan's party could easily lose the majority,

ELECTIONS, Page 24

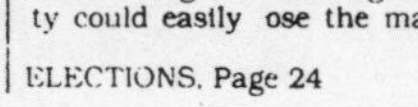

Inside

Globe takes poll of statewide races

The results of the latest Globe poll on the Massachusetts elections. Page 33.

Special Business section on Canada

The Canadian government, led by Brian Mulroney, has taken the initiative to negotiate a free trade deal with the United States. But recent protectionist statements from Washington are giving the Canadians second thoughts and may sour the deal. Business, Page A13.

Early Nabokov reviewed

"The Enchanter," a "lost" novella of Vladimir Nabokov, suggests a preliminary version of "Lolita" in its luminous style and subject, writes the Globe's Robert Taylor. Books, B106.

Career and Planning Guide

Guides on planning careers and listings of institutions and schools are contained in the Career and Planning Guide included in today's Globe.

Turn back clocks

Daylight Savings Time ended at 2 a.m. today. Clocks should be turned back one hour.

GUBERNATORIAL GREETING

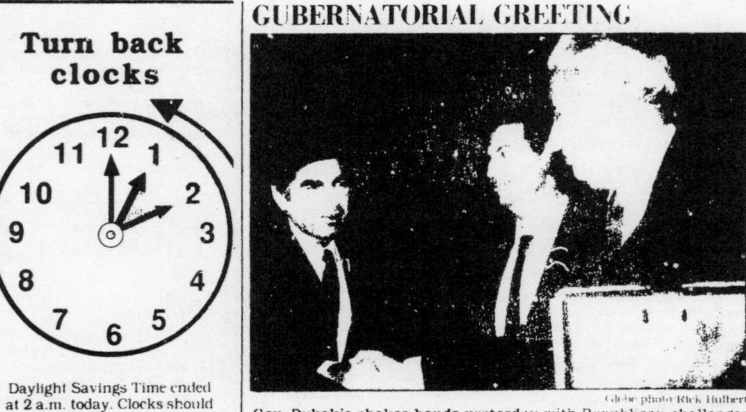

Globe photo/Rick Hulbert

Gov. Dukakis shakes hands yesterday with Republican challenger George Kariotis after their first debate, sponsored by the Massachusetts Municipal Association in Hyannis. Page 33.

News and feature guide on Page 2
Telephone 929-2000
Classified 929-1500
Circulation 929-2222
Customer Service 466-1818

The Boston Globe

What a Fall!
Tuesday – Partly sunny, 65
Wednesday – Cloudy, 60
High tide – 10:20 a.m., 10:39 p.m.
Full report – Page 26

Vol. 232; No. 113 TUESDAY, OCTOBER 20, 1987 *35 cents at newsstands beyond 30 miles from Boston 96 Pages • 25 cents

The bottom falls out on Wall Street: Dow in worst-ever dive — 508 points

By the time the final bell rang on the New York Stock Exchange yesterday, the world's financial markets were thoroughly numb. During a historic day of calamity for investors, a mountain of sell orders produced a session worse than any from the Great Crash of 1929. The Dow Jones industrial average dropped 508.32 points, to 1,738.74, a loss of nearly 1,000 points since the market's peak in late August. It was the largest one-day plunge ever, eclipsing the previous record by 400 points. At day's end, all gains from the bull market of 1987 had been wiped out and the famed average reflected its prices of March, 1986. Losers outnumbered gainers by 50 to 1 as the volume of 604.4 million shares traded on the Wall Street exchange broke the record 338 million shares that had changed hands Friday. And it was a crash heard around the world; stock markets abroad posted huge losses.

Expressing puzzlement at the day's developments, President Reagan said, "I don't think anyone should panic, because all the economic indicators are solid." John Phelan, chairman of the New York exchange, had this summation: "It's the nearest thing to a meltdown that I ever want to see."

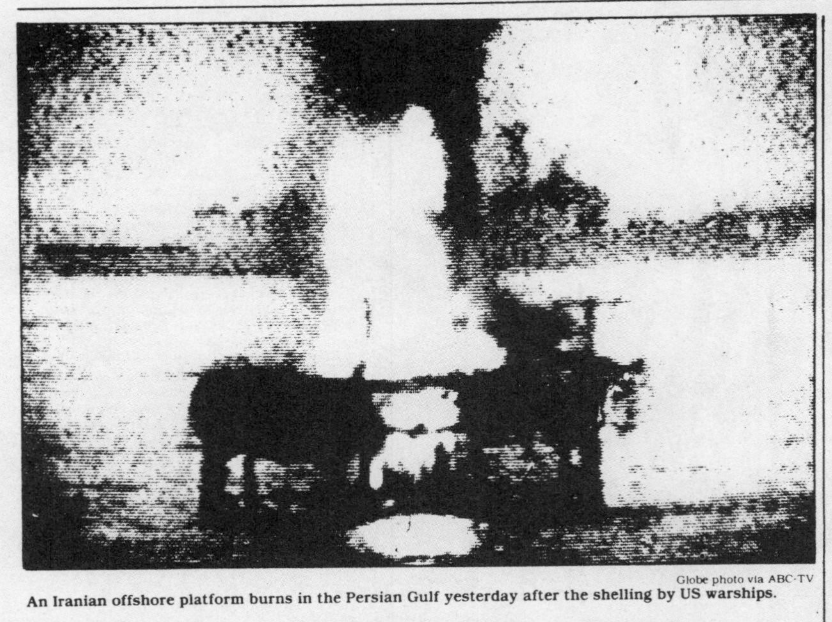

Globe photo via ABC-TV

An Iranian offshore platform burns in the Persian Gulf yesterday after the shelling by US warships.

US destroys 2 Iranian platforms in response to attack on tanker

By Stephen Kurkjian
Globe Staff

WASHINGTON – The United States destroyed two Iranian offshore military staging platforms yesterday in retaliation for last week's missile attack on a US-flagged tanker in the Persian Gulf.

Iran reacted angrily, warning it would deal the United States a "crushing blow ..." Iran's president, Ali Khamenei, vowed yesterday that his country will "take decisive retaliatory action" [Page 3.]

While the attack was the strongest military action taken by the United States since US warships began escorting oil tankers last summer, in ordering it, President Reagan avoided a tougher response, such as going after Iran's batteries of Silkworm antiship missiles.

Key members of Congress applaud the US strike, but some warn it could start a cycle of retaliation.
Restraint does not ensure a winding-down of the conflict in the gulf. An analysis. *Stories, Page 3.*

The attack, which began at approximately 7 a.m. EDT, was carried out by four American warships firing about 1,000 rounds of five-inch shells over more than an hour. Once used as a facility for pumping oil from under the gulf seabed and the loading of oil tankers, the platforms have in recent months been used as a base for Iranian helicopters and speedboats that attack neutral commercial shipping as part of the seven-year-old Iran-Iraq war, the Pentagon stated.

A short while after the attack, US Navy personnel boarded another Iranian oil platform about five miles to the north and destroyed radar and communications equipment before leaving the structure, the Pentagon said. Defense De-

GULF, Page 6

Value of stocks drops by more than $500b

By Robert Lenzner
Globe Staff

NEW YORK – It was the crash of '87.

A panic of selling yesterday sent the Dow Jones Industrial Average tumbling a record 508 points, or 22.62 percent, the worst day in stock market history for more than seven decades.

The historic freefall in stock prices was far greater than the 12.82 percent decline on Oct. 28, 1929, which was the largest single day's loss during that year's crash of the market.

It also was the climax of a shocking and intense stock market correction, totaling 984 points, that has driven the Dow 30 average back to its March 1986 level of 1738.41.

A special Business Extra section begins on Page 29.

Since Aug. 25, when the blue chip average peaked at a record 2722.42, it has fallen 36.14 percent, slightly more than the bear market downturns that occurred between December 1968 and May 1970, and during the inflationary energy crisis between March and October 1974.

"It is a very sad day," said Henry Kaufman, a Salomon Brothers economist. "When excesses are committed and contribute to higher prices, no one cares. When they contribute to a decline then people are shocked. This is the way markets tend to crash."

Kaufman especially blamed the stock market debacle on the

STOCK MARKET, Page 39

October plunge
Closes for the Dow Jones industrial average

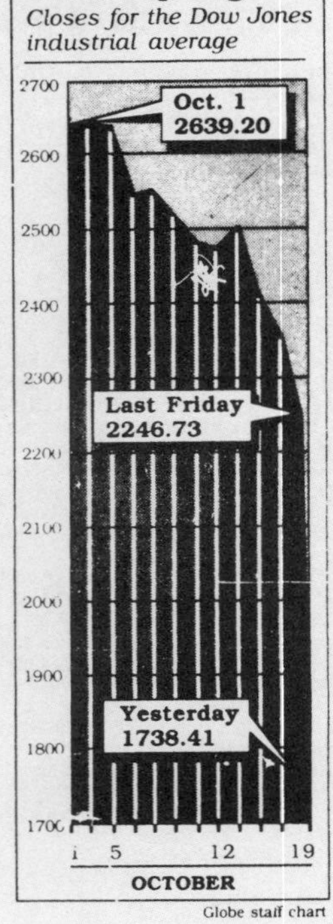

Globe staff chart

Reagan touts economy, says panic unwarranted

By John Robinson
Globe Staff

WASHINGTON – Cautioning against panic after yesterday's stock market plunge, President Reagan accentuated the positives in the US economy and attributed Wall Street's record sell-off to "a chance to grab profit."

"I don't think anyone should panic because all the economic indicators are solid," Reagan told reporters as he left the White House to visit his wife, Nancy, at Bethesda Naval medical Center where she is recovering from surgery.

"I think everyone is a little puzzled because – I don't know what meaning it might have – because all the business indices are up," Reagan said. "There is nothing wrong with the economy."

But Democratic presidential candidate Jesse Jackson blamed "Reaganomics" for the market plunge, and other candidates urged

REAGAN, Page 32

A financial world in dark until it finds bottom line

By David Warsh
Globe Staff

NEWS ANALYSIS

What does Wall Street know about the future?

After 10 days that have shaken the industrial world, it still may suspect much, but it knows nothing. Amid a panic that has taken all its major participants by surprise, the Street is groping, at the highest levels, for a story.

Until the market hits its bottom and the ultimate magnitude of the crash can be gauged, and until the policy response from central bankers and finance ministers around the world comes clear, the players remain caught in the vortex of events they do not yet understand.

For the moment, the workaday economy of jobs and purchase orders, of hours worked and profits booked and unemployment claims, seems in good order. The stock market's dive makes everybody nervous, however. The rationale for the giddy Dow Jones

ANALYSIS, Page 34

1929 again? Experts assess the parallels

By Alex Beam
Globe Staff

"There has been a little distress selling on the stock exchange." – Thomas Lamont, senior partner, J.P. Morgan & Co. on Black Thursday, Oct. 24, 1929

The parallels are obvious. A laissez-faire Republican president in office. An overheated stock market, propped up by the frothy prognoses of brokers and financial analysts. The dizzying worship of wealth.

Then as now, the titans of high finance issued soothing statements emphasizing the fundamental solidity of the country's financial system. To boost investor confidence on Black Thursday, Richard Whitney, the acting president of the New York Stock Exchange, roamed the trading floor placing orders for stocks. (He later went bankrupt.)

In Washington, President Herbert Hoover and Treasury Secretary Andrew Mellon insisted that the economy would recover from the stock market crash.

CRASH, Page 42

Inside
Today: Business Extra

Billy Martin, Chapter 5
The New York Yankees named Billy Martin manager for the fifth time yesterday. Page 77.

Goetz gets six months
Bernhard H. Goetz, who shot four youths on a New York subway train, was sentenced yesterday to six months in jail and fined $5,000. Page 12.

Border apprehension
Canadian opponents of a trade pact with the United States see their country's independence at stake. Fifth in a series, Page 14.

Guide to features

Arts/Films 72	Deaths 62
Ask Globe 24	Editorials 18
Bridge 24	Horoscope 24
Business 29	Living 69
Comics 24-25	Sports 77
	TV/Radio 27

Classified 64-68, 86-96

The Revolution in
IMMUNOLOGY

Exploring the web of mind and body

Last in a series
By Judy Foreman
Globe Staff

The woman was the very picture of misery. Her eyes ran. She wheezed. Her skin itched. No question, said her psychiatrist, Dr. Bennett G. Braun of Chicago, the lady was "deathly allergic" to cats.

But something didn't fit. The same woman could sometimes play with a cat for hours, even be scratched and bitten, with no allergic symptoms.

Same body. Different state of mind. Dramatically different immune response.

As a child, the woman had suffered severe sexual and emotional abuse. Now, like many other victims of extreme abuse, she suffered from multiple personalities. For her, a trying illness. For scientists, the perfect model for studying the mind-body questions that have long fascinated philosophers and poets, princes and paupers.

IMMUNOLOGY, Page 16

Takeshita Japan's next prime minister

By Tom Ashbrook
Globe Staff

TOKYO – Noboru Takeshita, a soft-spoken political veteran known for his commitment to consensus-based leadership, was designated yesterday to serve as the next prime minister.

Takeshita, 63, will become president of the ruling Liberal Democratic Party. He was chosen by the outgoing prime minister, Yasuhiro Nakasone, who will step down this month. Under Japan's parliamentary system, the ruling party presidency brings with it the post of prime minister.

A chain-smoking politician, small in stature, Takeshita is from a family of sake brewers in southwest Japan. He is known as a quiet but effective consensus builder – a sharp departure from Nakasone's political flamboyance and aggressive leadership style.

JAPAN, Page 10

News and feature guide on Page 2

Telephone 929-2000
Classified 929-1500
Circulation 929-2222
Customer Service 466-1818

The Boston Globe

Emerging a winner

Wednesday – AM clouds/PM sun. 55
Thursday – Clouding up. 55
High tide – 10:39 a.m., 11:11 p.m.
Full report – Page 56

Vol. 234; No. 132 | WEDNESDAY, NOVEMBER 9, 1988 | *35 cents at newsstands beyond 30 miles from Boston | 116 Pages • 25 cents

'And now I know we'll come together as we always have.'	*'This nation faces major challenges ahead and we must work together.'*
– President-elect Bush at midnight	– Gov. Dukakis, in concession speech

Bush breezes into White House as late Dukakis sprint falls short

ELECTION 88 AT A GLANCE

In the state

Statewide referendums
Incomplete — with 65% of vote in — Page 23

Question 1
Approval of salary increases enacted last year for all legislators and the state's top elected officials.

Yes	268,551	17%
No	1,310,329	83%

Question 2
Repeal state's prevailing wage law for construction workers on public works projects.

Yes	672,004	42%
No	941,764	58%

Question 3
Regulate the treatment of farm animals.

Yes	452,081	29%
No	1,129,271	71%

Question 4
Shut down state's two nuclear power plants.

Yes	481,454	32%
No	1,034,548	68%

Kennedy glides in – Sen. Edward M. Kennedy easily won a fifth term against political newcomer Joseph E. Malone, besting him by close to 2-1. Page 48.

US House races – Springfield Mayor Richard E. Neal coasted to victory, succeeding Rep. Edward P. Boland in the 2d District. Incumbents in the other 10 districts prevailed easily. Page 48.

In the region

Gregg elected – Judd Gregg, riding the strength of a Republican tradition created in part by his own family, was chosen New Hampshire's 94th governor.

Douglas takes it – Republican Chuck Douglas, a former state Supreme Court justice, beat Nashua Mayor James Donchess in the 2d Congressional District.

Weicker struggling – A tiny percentage of the vote separated Connecticut Attorney General Joseph I. Lieberman and three-term Republican Sen. Lowell Weicker.

Socialist-GOP matchup – Bernard Sanders, the Socialist mayor of Burlington, was narrowly trailing Republican Peter Smith in Vermont's three-way US House race.

R.I. governor – Republican Gov. Edward DiPrete, besieged by personal and political scandals, narrowly defeated Democrat Bruce Sundlund.

St Germain loses – US Rep. Fernand St Germain, accused of questionable ethics while chairman of the House Banking Committee, fell to the GOP's Ronald K. Machtley in Rhode Island.

The regional story, Page 39.

In the nation

Democratic muscle – So many races were neck-and-neck early this morning that it was impossible to predict what the new party balance in the Senate would be, though the Democrats were certain to at least retain their 54-46 margin.

Guide to features

Arts/Films 93
Ask Globe 54
Bridge 54
Business 31
Comics 54-55
Deaths 68-69
Editorials 20
Horoscope 54
Living 89
Sports 97
TV/Radio 57
Classified 70-79, 106-116

Globe staff photo/John Blanding
Vice President George Bush begins the celebration of his victory in Houston last night.

Globe staff photo/Stan Grossfeld
Gov. Michael S. Dukakis pauses during his concession speech last night at the World Trade Center.

A conciliatory note from the vanquished

By Ben Bradlee Jr.
Globe Staff

Gov. Michael S. Dukakis officially ended his longshot quest for the presidency late last night, saying he would never forget "the beauty of this magnificent land," its people, or the causes that motivated him to enter the campaign in the first place.

Appearing with his wife Kitty and three children in the wake of his campaign anthem, Neil Diamond's ode to immigrants, "Coming to America," Dukakis told several hundred cheering supporters who had gathered at Boston's World Trade Center that he had just phoned Vice President George Bush to congratulate him on his victory.

As many in the crowd booed, Dukakis said: "I know I speak for all of you... and for all the American people

DUKAKIS, Page 28

Of missing mandates and might have beens

By Thomas Oliphant
Globe Staff

NEW YORK – The country did not speak all that clearly last night.

NEWS ANALYSIS

Even as Vice President George Bush went over the magic number of 270 electoral votes that would make him the 41st American president, it was apparent that there had been a genuine surge toward Gov. Michael S. Dukakis in the campaign's final days.

Well after midnight, it was as possible for Bush's Electoral College vote total to soar past 400 as it was for Dukakis' to reach 200, depending on the outcome in a half dozen extremely close major states.

The result was a verdict that was indistinct. There was little question that Michael Dukakis could have won this election, a fact that will make his tactical and strategic mistakes in the general election campaign a heavy cross to bear.

In particular, the fact he lost Texas handily, and the South overwhelmingly, and came much closer in critical Midwest battlegrounds like Ohio and Michigan is likely to lead to postelection second-quessing of his choice of Texas Sen. Lloyd Bentsen as his running mate.

Despite the obvious and substantial preference for Bentsen over Sen. Dan Quayle during the campaign, there was no sign last night from voter surveys that Quayle was a cutting issue against Bush.

However, the message for the next president from the returns is far from clear, reflecting an elec-

ANALYSIS, Page 18

The vote for President

	States won	Electoral votes	Nationwide incomplete		Massachusetts incomplete	
Bush	36	388	34,921,046	54%	881,774	46%
Dukakis	9	95	29,555,659	46%	1,051,917	54%

Estimated Massachusetts turnout: 86%

Electoral votes needed to win: 270

South goes solid for vice president

By Walter V. Robinson
and Curtis Wilkie
Globe Staff

A decade after he first began seeking the office, Vice President George Bush won election last night as the nation's 41st president, but without the landslide some had predicted or the "mainstream mandate" he had sought.

After eight years as President Reagan's understudy, Bush will claim the White House for himself, but only after one of the most disagreeable campaigns of the century, a race so bitter that Bush sought to salve its wounds in his victory speech last night.

The contest, according to exit polling, left many voters disenchanted with the choice before them. And it left Bush facing a stronger Democratic Congress that is likely to be hostile to his initiatives.

In an election that turned as much on doubts about Gov. Michael S. Dukakis as on voter satisfaction with the vice president, Bush, like Reagan before him, swept the once solidly Democratic South.

And he amassed enough electoral votes in the industrial North to quickly surpass the 270 electoral votes he needed for victory. Later, Bush approached 400 electoral votes when he carried California by a substantial margin.

With the final complexion of the electoral college still to be determined, Bush led Dukakis in the growing popular vote count, 54 to 46 percent.

Early today, according to actual returns, Bush had won roughly 400 electoral votes. Dukakis had won 7 states and the District of Columbia and was leading in three other states, which represent, in all, 112 electoral votes.

In many other large states, victory was by the narrowest of margins: in Pennsylvania for Bush, and in New York for Dukakis.

The election, tighter in the end than either party had expected, produced evidence that undecided voters decided for the Democrat and more evidence that Bush's choice of Dan Quayle had proved to be a more serious wound to Bush than had been foreseen.

With their ballots yesterday, Americans decided against a major course correction, voting instead to replace a 77-year-old popular hero with his more vigorous vice president, a 64-year-old fitness buff who likes jogging, fishing and speedboats – and a management style noticeably more involved than Reagan's.

Indeed, Bush plans to indulge one of those pursuits starting tomorrow, when he goes fishing in Florida, leav

ELECTION, Page 17

A look ahead: Expect surprises

By Walter V. Robinson
Globe Staff

Americans wondering whether President George Bush will be the strident, give-no-quarter adversary so underestimated by Democrats or the reassuring, grandfatherly figure who promised a kinder, gentler nation may be in for a surprise.

Oddly, Bush is likely to be both.

Downcast Democrats looking to Bush's Eastern Establishment, patrician roots for clues that he is a closet moderate, about to reveal himself as a Rockefeller Republican, are also likely to be in for a surprise.

Instead, a Bush administration is likely to be at least as conservative as Ronald Reagan's and perhaps even more so in some areas, in the view of conservatives who say Reagan talked a good ideological game but seldom delivered.

Bush, they suggested, may prove to be Reagan's opposite, eschewing the rhetoric Reagan employed to seduce the faithful but ardently dedicating himself to achieving conservative goals in ways Reagan never did.

But in tone, in staffing and in at least two criti-

PRESIDENCY, Page 34

News and feature guide on Page 2

Telephone 929-2000
Classified 929-1500
Circulation 929-2222
Customer Service 466-1818

The Boston Globe

Winter take all

Thursday – Mostly sunny, 35
Friday – AM sun/PM clouds, 38
High tide – 10:00 a.m., 10:45 p.m.
Full report – Page 39

Vol. 234; No. 175 | THURSDAY, DECEMBER 22, 1988 | *35 cents at newsstands beyond 30 miles from Boston | 108 Pages • 25 cents

Nynex is said to milk local firms' profits

By John Wilke
Globe Staff

Nynex Corp. skimmed millions of dollars in profits from its two big telephone subsidiaries in a complicated scheme that inflated corporate profits at the expense of customers across the Northeast, according to current and former employees and documents obtained by The Boston Globe.

The employees said Nynex's business deals with the two companies, New England Telephone and New York Telephone, included concealed overcharges and sweetheart contracts, in violation of state and federal regulations and the court order that broke up the AT&T monopoly.

The pricing scheme systematically drove up costs for the phone companies, both regulated monopolies, leaving their millions of customers to pay the bill.

"It was like the old prohibition-era gangster movies," said a New England Telephone engineer who retired in 1985 after 35 years. "Nynex came in and told us we would have to buy most everything we needed through them, at greatly inflated prices."

The engineer and other employees said Nynex pushed the two phone companies to buy everything from paper clips to computers – at prices that often were sharply higher than those available from other vendors – from Nynex's Materiel Enterprise Co. subsidiary.

As a result, millions of dollars from the inflated prices were diverted to Nynex. Had this revenue remained in New England and New York, regula-

NYNEX, Page 61

273 die as US jetliner crashes in Scottish town

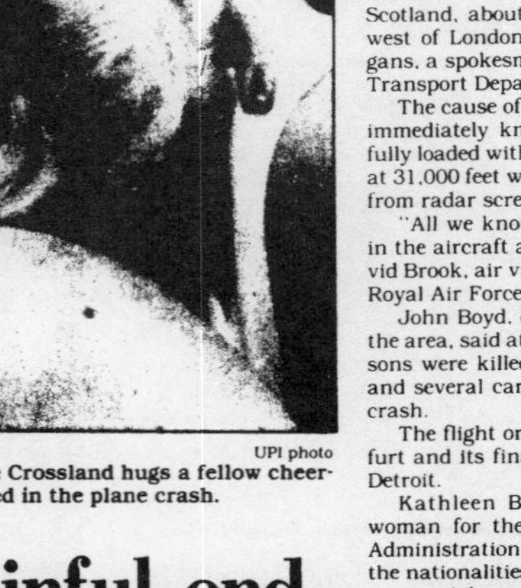

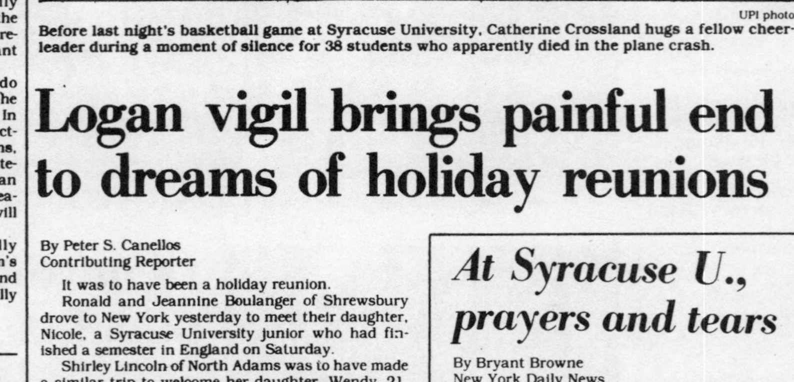

UPI photo

Before last night's basketball game at Syracuse University, Catherine Crossland hugs a fellow cheerleader during a moment of silence for 38 students who apparently died in the plane crash.

Cause unknown; plane was bound for New York

By Karin Davies
United Press International

LONDON – A Pan American jumbo jet on a flight from London to New York crashed in a Scottish village yesterday and exploded in a huge fireball, killing 273 persons, including all 258 aboard and at least 15 more in an inferno of burning homes on the ground.

Pan Am Flight 103, a recently renovated 19-year-old Boeing 747, was en route from London's Heathrow Airport to Kennedy International Airport in New York when it crashed in Lockerbie, Scotland, about 330 miles northwest of London, said Mike Vertigans, a spokesman for the British Transport Department.

The cause of the crash was not immediately known. The jet was fully loaded with jet fuel and flying at 31,000 feet when it disappeared from radar screens about 7 p.m.

"All we know is that all those in the aircraft are dead," said David Brook, air vice marshal for the Royal Air Force in Scotland.

John Boyd, chief constable for the area, said at least 15 more persons were killed in the 40 homes and several cars destroyed in the crash.

The flight originated in Frankfurt and its final destination was Detroit.

Kathleen Bergen, a spokeswoman for the Federal Aviation Administration in New York, said the nationalities of the passengers were not known, but she added, "We believe a number of them may have been Americans."

Pan Am said it would not make public a list of those aboard the airliner until today.

A Pan Am spokesman, Jeff Kriendler, said in New York there was "no indication that there were any problems" with the plane. The jet was at a cruising altitude of 31,000 feet and "precisely on course" when it disappeared from radar screens 52 minutes into its flight, he said. There was no distress call.

A Royal Air Force spokeswoman, Jill Sutcliffe, said all other planes in the area remained on the screens, indicating there was no in-flight collision.

CRASH, Page 6

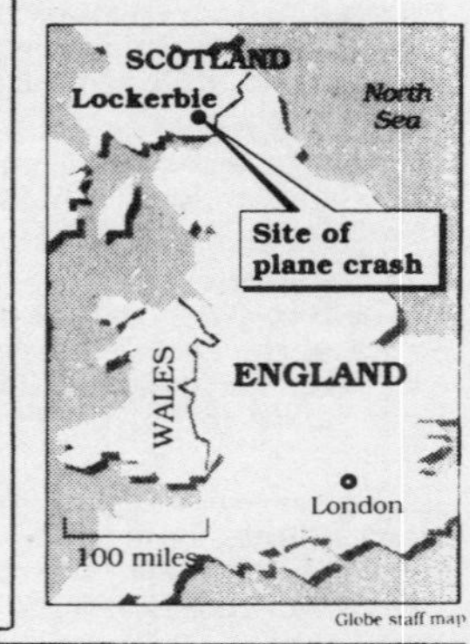

Globe staff map

NRC approves Pilgrim restart, boosts Seabrook

By Larry Tye
Globe Staff

ROCKVILLE, Md. – The Nuclear Regulatory Commission yesterday approved the reopening of the Pilgrim nuclear plant and cleared key obstacles to a low-power license for the Seabrook, N.H., reactor, actions decried as a one-two punch by Gov. Dukakis and other elected officials across the region.

The Plymouth plant, which has been shut for 32 months, could begin its climb to full-power operation late next week. The New Hampshire reactor probably will receive its low-power permit early next year.

Attorney General James Shannon, with Dukakis' support, yesterday filed suit in federal court to keep Pilgrim shut. But while similar suits have delayed the opening or reopening of other reactors, a judge has never overruled the NRC on such decisions.

The commission's rulings yesterday were "irrational" and "utterly ridiculous," an angry Dukakis told reporters at the State House shortly after the NRC concluded its meeting.

Governor-elect Judd Gregg of New Hampshire called on Seabrook's owners to voluntarily "forgo low-power testing and the resultant contamination of the reactor" until it is certain the plant will get a full-power license.

But NRC Chairman Lando Zech Jr., clearly incensed by the criticism, defended the rulings. In the Pilgrim case, he said, "we acted under very difficult conditions, and I think we acted appropriately. . . .In the unlikely event of an accident, we believe there is reasonable assurance the public will be protected."

NRC staffers will carefully monitor each phase of Pilgrim's start-up, Zech told reporters, and the commissioners will personally

NRC, Page 18

Logan vigil brings painful end to dreams of holiday reunions

By Peter S. Canellos
Contributing Reporter

It was to have been a holiday reunion.

Ronald and Jeannine Boulanger of Shrewsbury drove to New York yesterday to meet their daughter, Nicole, a Syracuse University junior who had finished a semester in England on Saturday.

Shirley Lincoln of North Adams was to have made a similar trip to welcome her daughter, Wendy, 21, said Mayor John Barrett 3d, but she heard that the plane she was to meet, Pan Am Flight 103, had crashed into a Scottish town.

For Lincoln, the Boulangers, and families of others booked on Flight 103, at least 18 of them headed to Boston, a day of reunion soon became a day to pray that something – a traffic jam, an illness, a missed connection – had kept their loved ones from boarding the ill-fated jumbo jet.

But as midnight passed and the connecting Pan Am flight from New York plugged safely into its gate, the hope that the family members were reaching for seemed permanently lost.

Pan Am refused last night to release the names of the 21 persons headed for Boston, but Pan Am agents rushed to notify family members at various times during the night.

Wendy Lincoln's mother was told she was on the plane, Barrett said.

Nicole Boulanger, 21, was also aboard, Pan Am told Mary Riordan, her high school principal.

Julianne Kelly of Dedham, 20, a junior at Syracuse University, was also aboard, friends said.

Julian Benello, 25, a Newton resident studying at Cambridge University in England, was scheduled to board the flight, a relative said.

VICTIMS, Page 8

At Syracuse U., prayers and tears

By Bryant Browne
New York Daily News

SYRACUSE, N.Y. – There were prayers, tears and moments of silence last night at Syracuse University as officials confirmed what many had feared: 38 students enrolled in an international studies program at the school had died in the crash of a Pan Am jet in Scotland.

At about 9 p.m. students, many weeping and holding each other, began filing into in the domed campus chapel, where they sat in absolute silence through a long vigil.

Five clergy of various denominations were there to console them.

"The best thing we can do is be together, extend our compassion and concern beyond ourselves to the tragic sense of loss of the family members," Rev. Michael Rothermel, a Lutheran minister, told the gathered students.

There was a basketball game last night at the university's Carrier Dome. Minutes before the Syracuse Orangemen took on Western Michigan University, Rev. Rothermel stepped before the crowd and told them what had happened.

A collective gasp rose from the stands. The

SYRACUSE, Page 8

Questions on Bulger's legal work

By Brian C. Mooney
and Dick Lehr
Globe Staff

An examination of court records yesterday raised new questions about Senate President William M. Bulger's role in a civil case he said earned him a $267,000 legal fee in 1986.

Bulger, in an attempt to explain $240,000 in loans he received in 1985 from a trust fund, said in an affidavit Monday that he earned the fees for his work to resolve a complex real estate dispute in Maynard.

But the Globe's review of several hundred pages of documents filed in connection with the Maynard suit show that while Bulger did work on the case, another lawyer appears to have performed most of the work.

The loans, and Bulger's assertion the money was an advance against his legal fee, are key elements in the controversy surrounding the $268 million 75 State Street development in Boston.

Bulger has said he received the

BULGER, Page 15

INSIDE

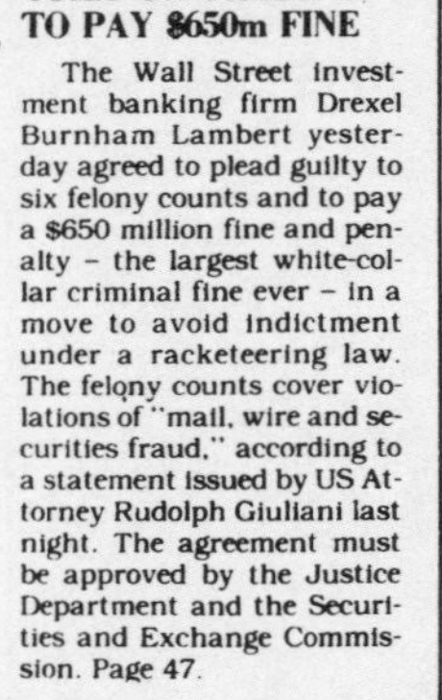

DREXEL ALLOWS ITS GUILT ON TRADING: TO PAY $650m FINE

The Wall Street investment banking firm Drexel Burnham Lambert yesterday agreed to plead guilty to six felony counts and to pay a $650 million fine and penalty – the largest white-collar criminal fine ever – in a move to avoid indictment under a racketeering law. The felony counts cover violations of "mail, wire and securities fraud," according to a statement issued by US Attorney Rudolph Giuliani last night. The agreement must be approved by the Justice Department and the Securities and Exchange Commission. Page 47.

Guide to features

Arts/Films 71	Deaths 42-43
Ask Globe 44	Editorials 20
Bridge 44	Horoscope 44
Business 47	Living 69
Classified 62-68	Sports 31
Comics 44-46	TV/Radio 75

Agencies unite in holiday spirit

By Douglas S. Crocket
Globe Santa Staff

The Globe Santa fund received one of its biggest boosts of the year this week when the employees of 15 agencies housed in the State Transportation Building in Boston's Park Square delivered a contribution of $17,300.

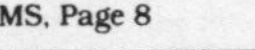

GLOBE SANTA, Page 76

TO HELP GLOBE SANTA: Mail your donation to Globe Santa, Box 1525, Boston, MA., 02104, or deliver it weekdays to the Globe Corner Bookstore at Washington and School streets in downtown Boston.

Santa's friends

For "P. B. O.'D."	25.00
Olive Wilkins and Children	75.00
In loving memory of my brothers, John and Jay — love, Branden	3.00
In memory of Charlie N. from Park — Marion and Kate	50.00
In memory of Florence Krol	5.00
On behalf of my sister, Kim Daly from Keith	25.00
Julie and Whitney Eastman, Nevin Hamilton, Joseph Letizia, Kerry and John Moynihan and Mackenzie Flynn	45.00
United Steel Workers of America Local #2269	50.00
Stanley J. Gelin	25.00
Nancy Lewis	25.00

SANTA'S FRIENDS, Page 76

Walpole recommended as site for harbor grit

By Andrew J. Dabilis
Globe Staff

A 94-acre site in Walpole next to the state prison was recommended yesterday over a quarry on the Malden-Revere line as a landfill to handle grit from the Boston Harbor cleanup.

The announcement touched off immediate protest from the town's legislators and charges that Gov. Dukakis had broken a promise to exempt Walpole. The recommendation must be approved by the MWRA board and the state Legislature.

Paul Levy, executive director of the Massachusetts Water Resources Authority, the agency responsible for the $6.1 billion cleanup of Boston Harbor, said the decision was financial and not political. "The choice came down to mainly a dollar decision," he said

The Walpole site, he said, would cost at least $5 million less than the quarry to operate and maintain until 2020 or beyond. The Walpole landfill would handle up to 100 tons per day, requiring four truckloads that would have to use residential streets, but Levy said deliveries would not be scheduled during hours when school buses are running.

The trucks will not carry sludge – the byproduct of cleaning human waste and other materials from water before it is discharged into the harbor – but grit and screenings made up of twigs, logs, plastics, cloth and road dirt.

HARBOR, Page 18

Cancer treatment shrank tumors

By Richard A. Knox
Globe Staff

A new type of "biological therapy" against cancer, involving the injection of billions of cancer-fighting cells derived from the patient's own tumor, has produced regressions of advanced disease in 25 to 50 percent of the several dozen patients in whom it has been tried.

In a National Cancer Institute report to be published today, researchers said that after a single five-day course of treatment, widespread tumors shrank by more than half in 10 of 20 patients with advanced malignant melanoma. In an 11th melanoma patient, the cancer disappeared entirely and the patient has remained disease-free for 15 months.

"The response rates are the highest yet reported for the treatment of advanced melano-

CANCER, Page 14

VOLUME 237 • NUMBER 5
84 pages
25 cents
35 cents at newsstands beyond 30 miles from Boston

BACK TO COOL
Friday: *Colder, some sun, 40*
Saturday: *Mostly cloudy, 35-40*
High tide: *5:04 a.m., 5:36 p.m.*
Full report: *Page 78*

FRIDAY, JANUARY 5, 1990

Stuart dies in jump off Tobin Bridge after police are told he killed his wife

State Police divers recover Charles M. Stuart's body beneath the Tobin Bridge yesterday.

GLOBE STAFF PHOTO / DAVID L. RYAN

By Kevin Cullen, Sean Murphy and Mike Barnicle
GLOBE STAFF

Charles M. Stuart killed himself yesterday, hours after his brother told police Stuart had planned and executed the robbery and shooting of his pregnant wife and then shot himself to cover up one of the city's most heinous crimes in recent history, police said.

By leaping to his death from the Tobin Bridge sometime around 7 a.m., Stuart, 29, completed his sudden transformation from ultimate victim to ultimate villain.

Stuart's suicide also shifted the focus of a continuing investigation onto Stuart's 23-year-old brother Matthew, who reportedly has admitted he disposed of the weapon used to kill his sister-in-law.

Sources familiar with the investigation say police are now investigating information from relatives and other sources that Charles Stuart had an elaborate scheme to kill his wife and enlisted the help of his brother. Authorities are trying to determine the extent of Matthew's involvement.

Authorities are reviewing information that Charles Stuart conducted a "dry run" of the area where the murder took place and that he had called off an earlier plan to kill Carol Stuart after making it appear their Reading home had been burglarized.

According to Matthew Stuart's attorney, John Perenyi, he and Matthew Stuart met with assistant district attorney Thomas J. Mundy Jr., who is directing the grand jury investigation into the shooting, at about 8 p.m. Wednesday. Matthew Stuart told authorities his brother shot his wife and then shot himself, Perenyi said.

AP FILE PHOTO

Charles and Carol Stuart pose in 1987.

Perenyi said Matthew told investigators he disposed of the gun and personal belongings of Carol Stuart without knowing what they were, and that his client was not a suspect either as a participant or an accessory in the crime. Matthew Stuart was not detained after giving his statement to authorities.

Charles Stuart, the manager of a Back Bay fur shop, killed himself after learning Matthew had told police that he had been an accomplice

STUART, Page 22

■ Image proved unjust

By Renee Graham
GLOBE STAFF

It was a crime so heinous, so shocking it seemed to lay bare all truths about the increasing lawlessness of Boston's streets, particularly within the black community.

Charles and Carol Stuart, a young Reading couple expecting their first child, were abducted and shot after leaving a childbirth class at Brigham and Women's Hospital. Carol Stuart would die that night; her son, Christopher, delivered two months prematurely, died 17 days later. Left to grieve was Charles Stuart, whose family and future were snatched away in a blurry moment of gunfire and death.

How, everyone seemed to ask, could such tragedy befall a loving couple who seemed to have everything to live for?

The Stuart shootings, which occurred Oct. 23, came to symbolize the viciousness of urban America. The smiling, attractive faces of the Stuarts tore into hearts and minds across the nation, especially those convinced that the Stuarts – a white, middle-class suburban couple – should have been immune to the vio-

SYMBOL, Page 21

■ Bennett: Life 'ruined'

By Doris Sue Wong and John H. Kennedy
GLOBE STAFF

William Bennett, considered a prime suspect in the Stuart killings until this week, yesterday said his life has "been ruined and no one is willing to take responsibility."

Yesterday's dramatic events, including the announcement by officials that Bennett was no longer a suspect in the Oct. 23 shootings and subsequent deaths of Carol Stuart and her infant son, prompted Bennett, his lawyer and his family to criticize officials over the case.

"It is a shame that it took the suicide of the real killer this morning to open people's eyes to the fact that I am innocent and have always been," said Bennett, in a prepared statement issued by his lawyer. The reference in the statement was to the news of the death of Charles Stuart, Carol Stuart's husband, and an announcement that Stuart had become

BENNETT, Page 20

Other stories, commentary on Stuart case, Pages 17, 19, 20-22, 67.

■ Friends saw no hint

By Peter S. Canellos
GLOBE STAFF

People who knew Chuck Stuart from his boyhood in Revere, where he worshipped at the Church of the Immaculate Conception and where until recently he still returned twice a week to play basketball, have described him as a good family man, loyal to his friends and loving to his wife.

But as the news spread yesterday that Stuart had committed suicide after he became the prime suspect in the murder of his pregnant wife, even his stoutest defenders began raking their memories for signs of another Charles Stuart, a dark Charles Stuart, hidden inside the good parochial school boy.

"All his friends really knew him as true blue, a great guy," said one longtime friend. "They couldn't believe this when they heard it. But there is another very dark side to Chuck Stuart." He refused to elaborate.

There was Stuart the devoted widower, who composed a moving final love letter to his wife, Carol, from his hospital bed and asked a friend to read it at her funeral. "Now

PROFILE, Page 22

Embassy no longer a haven as general's options ran out

By Diego Ribadeneira
GLOBE STAFF

PANAMA CITY – Gen. Manuel Antonio Noriega walked out of the Vatican Embassy Wednesday night after being told he would be ordered out the next day at noon, a senior Bush administration official said yesterday.

Church sources in Panama said Noriega had already made up his mind to turn himself over to US troops before being given the Vatican ultimatum. But the senior US official, briefing reporters at the White House on the condition of anonymity, said the deadline may have prompted Noriega's final surrender.

"The papal nuncio had said that his asylum or what have you would expire by noon today," the official said yesterday, "meaning he would no longer be a welcome guest."

Noriega's lawyer, Frank Rubino, gave a slightly different account yesterday, saying in a Florida courtroom that the general was told that diplomatic immunity would remain in effect in the embassy only for the papal nuncio – the Vatican's ambassador – after the noon deadline. The

RECONSTRUCTION, Page 3

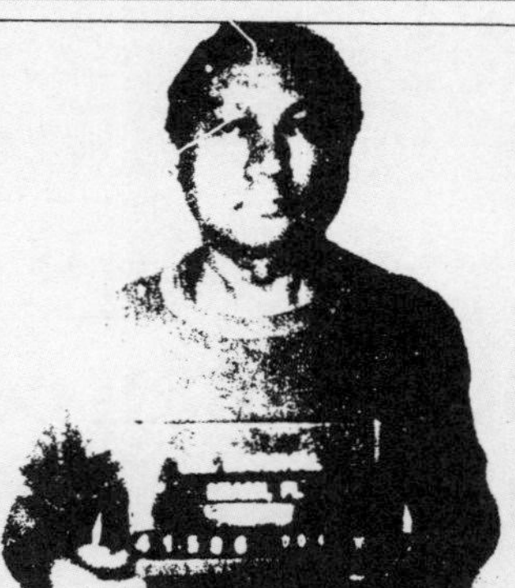

AP PHOTO

Manuel Antonio Noriega in custody yesterday.

Noriega arraigned in Fla. on multiple drug charges

By Ethan Bronner and Michael Kranish
GLOBE STAFF

MIAMI – Gen. Manuel Antonio Noriega, the Panamanian dictator deposed by an American military invasion last month, was arraigned in US District Court yesterday on charges of aiding and profiting from a Colombian cartel that trafficked drugs to the United States.

At the opening of what is certain to be a long, politically charged and judicially complex legal process, Noriega said through his attorney that he gave himself up to American troops on Wednesday to prevent bloodshed at the Vatican Embassy, where he had sought refuge more than a week ago.

He said he was informed that the new Panamanian regime would end the diplomatic immunity of the nunciature at noon yesterday, protecting only the papal nuncio himself, unless Noriega left.

"Gen. Noriega felt compelled to acquiesce," said his lawyer, Frank Rubino. "He wanted to prevent the loss of lives of nuns and priests."

Noriega, 51, dressed in dark brown military trousers and a khaki military

NORIEGA, Page 2

Bellotti starts 2d bid for governor

By Renee Loth
GLOBE STAFF

FRANCIS X. BELLOTTI
Calls himself an outsider

Portraying himself as a political scrapper and maverick, former Massachusetts Attorney General Francis X. Bellotti yesterday officially said he intends to cap a long political career with a candidacy for governor, an office he first sought 25 years ago.

Speaking to a cheering crowd of about 300 people at the World Trade Center in South Boston, Bellotti, 66, sketched a portrait of himself as a political outsider, willing to take on the entrenched forces that he said are "destroying the credibility of our government and undermining the faith and spirit of us all."

In a speech that split sharply from the Democratic political establishment whose gubernatorial nomi-

BELLOTTI, Page 10

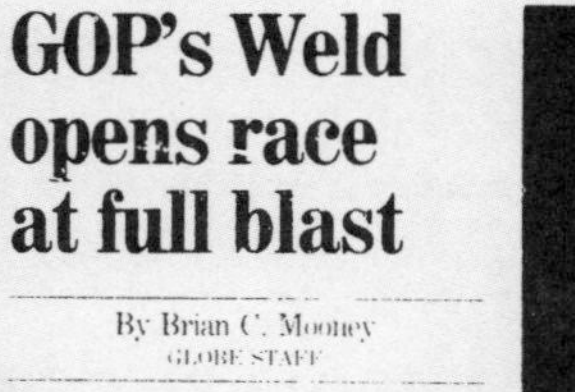

GOP's Weld opens race at full blast

By Brian C. Mooney
GLOBE STAFF

With a searing attack on the state's Democratic establishment, Republican William F. Weld formally announced his candidacy for governor yesterday, promising an end to "big government" in the state and no new taxes for four years.

"Our people have simply lost faith in a state government that has repeatedly misled them and abused their trust," the former federal prosecutor told a group of about 200 supporters in the ballroom of the Omni Parker House in Boston.

WILLIAM F. WELD
Says people have "lost faith"

"This state government has taken on a life of its own," said Weld, who described himself as a Beacon Hill outsider. "And this state government has forgotten the simple truth that there's no such thing as govern-

WELD, Page 13

Inside

AT HOME: Congregate housing for the elderly.

■ **Trouble for Campeau:** In a move that complicates efforts to keep Jordan Marsh's parent company out of bankruptcy, the National Bank of Canada yesterday seized a 35 percent stake in Campeau Corp. Page 25.

■ **Photographer dies:** Harold E. Edgerton of Cambridge, a photographer who popularized the use of the strobe light, died yesterday at 86. Pages 33, 78.

■ **Bruins win:** Boston beat the Jets last night, 4-2, at the Garden. Page 43.

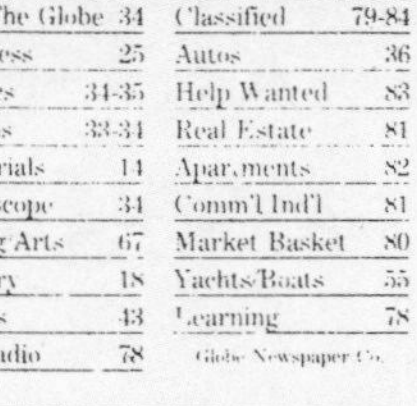

FEATURES		CLASSIFIED	
Ask The Globe	34	Classified	79-84
Business	25	Autos	36
Comics	34-35	Help Wanted	83
Deaths	33-34	Real Estate	81
Editorials	14	Apartments	82
Horoscope	34	Comm'l Ind'l	81
Living Arts	67	Market Basket	80
Lottery	18	Yachts/Boats	55
Sports	43	Learning	78
TV Radio	78		

VOLUME 237 • NUMBER 78
58 pages
25 cents
35 cents at newsstands beyond 30 miles from Boston

The Boston Globe

MONDAY, MARCH 19, 1990

DOWNHILL FROM HERE
Monday: *Clouding up, 45-50*
Tuesday: *Rain/snow, 35-40*
High tide: *4:17 a.m., 5:01 p.m.*
Full report: *Page 56*

Baseball lockout ends as players, owners reach agreement

By Steve Fainaru
GLOBE STAFF

NEW YORK – The lockout that paralyzed baseball for 32 days ended late last night when the players and owners reached a tentative agreement that includes a compromise on salary arbitration eligibility, the issue that bogged down the negotiations for more than five weeks.

The regular season, scheduled to open April 2, is expected to begin April 9, allowing roughly three weeks of spring training. The Red Sox, who were slated to start the season in Detroit, would open against the Tigers at Fenway Park.

Although baseball officials said they hoped to preserve a full 162-game season, teams tentatively are scheduled to play 158 games. The remaining games may be made up over the course of the season, according to deputy commissioner Steve Greenberg. Each team will play the same number of games, preventing a repeat of 1972, when the Red Sox finished one-half game behind the Tigers, who had played an additional game.

Because the agreement had not been finalized – union chief Don Fehr and Chuck O'Connor, the owners' chief negotiator, continued to work during a news conference announcing the settlement – there was no official announcement about the opening of training camps, although American League president Bobby Brown said the camps would open tomorrow when the settlement becomes official.

"Despite the travail, despite the difficulties, this is the proper way for baseball to begin," said commissioner Fay Vincent. "We are hopeful the

LOCKOUT, Page 38

$200m Gardner Museum art theft

2 men posing as police tie up night guards

By Andy Dabilis
and John Ellement
GLOBE STAFF

In what was described as the biggest art theft since the 1911 robbery of the "Mona Lisa," two men posing as police officers gained entry to the Isabella Stewart Gardner Museum early yesterday, restrained two security guards and left with an estimated $200 million worth of art, police said.

The works stolen included paintings by Jan Vermeer, Rembrandt and Edgar Degas, museum officials said.

In a daring, middle-of-the-night robbery, police said, the two men knocked on a side door of the world-famous Gardner in Boston's Fenway section at about 1:15 a.m. and told the security guards there was a disturbance in the area, and were allowed to enter.

Police and FBI officials said the men then overcame the guards, tied them with tape and spent about two hours in the museum, stealing 12 art objects.

Acting curator Karen Haas said the $200 million estimate is conservative and the worth of the stolen works may be "hundreds of millions of dollars." She said they are considered priceless because they have not been on the market for nearly a century, and their value to private collectors is unknown.

Measured by the potential value of the art, the theft was considered the biggest ever in the United States, and perhaps the greatest ever verified for any crime, according to law enforcement officials, art experts and records kept on crime and art theft.

The stolen items included masterpieces such as Vermeer's "The Concert," two Rembrandts, "A Lady and Gentleman in Black," and the museum's most popular piece, "The Storm on the Sea of Galilee," both done in 1633.

Also taken was a self-portrait etching by Rembrandt, but not his more famous oil self-portrait in the same room. Haas, despondent after the theft, said she had no idea why certain works were taken.

Also stolen was the work entitled "Landscape with an Obelisk," until recently attributed to Rembrandt but now thought to have been done by one of his students, Govaert Flinck. Five works by Edgar Degas, an Edouard Manet oil, and a Shang Dynasty Chinese bronze beaker from 1200-1100 BC were also taken.

Other works and pieces at the museum, which

THEFT, Page 23

■ Pictures and descriptions of the stolen works, related stories, Pages 22-24.

Jan Vermeer's priceless "The Concert" was among the works stolen.

Rembrandt's popular "The Storm on the Sea of Galilee" was also taken.

Vermeer painting, one of 32 in world, called greatest loss

By Christine Temin
GLOBE STAFF

There are only 32 paintings by the great Dutch master Jan Vermeer, and the value of the one stolen from the Isabella Stewart Gardner Museum yesterday is "incalculable," according to Peter Sutton, an authority on Old Masters.

Of the 12 objects stolen, Vermeer's 17th-century masterpiece, "The Concert," is by far the most valuable, with two paintings and an etching by Rembrandt next, according to Wellesley College art historian Anne Higonnet, who has written extensively on the Gardner. The heist also included a brilliant painting by Edouard Manet, five works on paper by Edgar Degas, a painting by Govaert Flinck once attributed to Rembrandt, and a Chinese bronze beaker.

Higonnet called the Vermeer, the Rembrandts and the Manet "some of the most important paintings in Boston."

What was not taken, probably because of its size, is the heroic "Rape of Europa" by the 16th century Venetian master Titian that Sutton has called "arguably the greatest painting in America."

Sutton, a curator at the Museum of Fine Arts, said it was impossible to put a price on "The Concert," an exquisite painting of two women and a man making music as silvery light filters in from the left. No painting by Vermeer has been for sale for decades, Sutton said, and of the 32 known works by the Dutchman, the Gardner's is the third missing because of theft.

ART, Page 23

Secret collector's passion or ransom seen as motive

By Peter S. Canellos
GLOBE STAFF

The art treasures seized from the Isabella Stewart Gardner Museum yesterday were probably contracted for in advance by a black-market collector outside the country, private investigators and art experts theorized yesterday.

Stolen pieces of the importance of those in yesterday's robbery could have been taken only for one of two purposes, they said: for sale to a collector who had already agreed to buy them or for possible ransom.

But the thieves appeared to have set their sights on specific works, having left behind many of equal or greater value. This indicates that one particular buyer's tastes may have been indulged, the sources added.

"There probably was a contract for these paintings," said Charles Moore, a Brockton detective who has recovered about $20 million worth of art through 10 highly publicized cases. "It could just be a collector who wanted them or possibly a drug cartel that uses them for trading purposes – commodity instead of cash."

Moore said he thinks the works are already headed for South America or Japan. "That's where the money is," Moore said.

The black-market value of art treasures is widely believed to be 1[illegible]

MOTIVE, Page 22

DeVillars under fire for derailing key projects

By Teresa M. Hanafin
GLOBE STAFF

In launching what one city official described as "preemptive strikes" against major commercial development projects from Cape Cod to downtown Boston, Environmental Affairs Secretary John DeVillars has alienated the business community and reportedly angered city and state planners, as well as Gov. Dukakis.

DeVillars' most recent decision, to reject the final environmental impact reports of two massive projects on the edge of the blighted Combat Zone – Campeau Corp.'s Boston Crossing and F.D. Rich's Commonwealth Center – sparked angry exchanges in recent weeks among Alden S. Raine, the governer's powerful secretary of economic affairs, DeVillars and Dukakis, sources said.

Part of the disagreement arose over DeVillars' desire to also reject the environmental reports covering two other major projects – the renovation of the former Sears building in the Fenway into a biotech center, and One Lincoln St., a 37-story downtown tower linked to the development of Ruggles Center in Roxbury. Those rejections were quashed by Raine and Dukakis.

"The governor has had heated words with John," said one State House source. "The governor has lost his temper with John more vociferously and angrily than he has with anyone else in the administration in the past seven years. And he doesn't lose his temper easily."

DEVILLARS, Page 18

JOHN DeVILLARS
Conflicts with governor reported

East German center-right triumphs in a vote for unity

By Jonathan Kaufman
GLOBE STAFF

EAST BERLIN – Putting their pocketbooks ahead of their fears, East Germans voted resoundingly yesterday for quick unification with West Germany and rapid introduction of a market economy, handing a coalition of center-right parties a stunning victory in Eastern Europe's first free election since the collapse of communism last year.

East Germans gave the conservative Alliance for Germany a near-majority of seats in the new parliament and more than twice as many seats as its closest competitor, the Social Democrats, who favored a gradual approach to unification. The result confounded pre-election polls, which for months had shown the Social Democrats in the lead.

The vote means that the already rapid German reunification after 45 years of division will accelerate. Negotiations to replace East Germany's worthless currency with the West German mark, a process known as currency union, are already under way. The next few months will see a bevy of activity as the two Germanys begin to knit themselves together.

"We have achieved an unexpectedly great victory," said Lothar de Maiziere, head of the East German Christian Democrats, the biggest vote-getter in the conservative alliance and the odds-on choice to be East Germany's next prime minis-

GERMANY, Page 6

Jets fly over Lithuania as deadline nears

By Ann Imse
ASSOCIATED PRESS

MOSCOW – Military jets streaked over the capital of Lithuania during maneuvers yesterday, a day before a Kremlin deadline for renunciation of the Lithuanian declaration of independence.

At the same time, however, President Mikhail S. Gorbachev struck a conciliatory tone, saying he still planned to talk with the Lithuanians about returning to the Soviet fold. And he said there had been no ultimatums.

"We will carry on the dialogue," Gorbachev told reporters yesterday after voting in runoff elections, which were held in Russia and other parts of the Soviet Union.

Also yesterday, 50,000 to 100,000 Lithuanians demonstrated against independence at a rally in Vilnius, the Lithuanian capital. Soviet television said the demonstration included calls for civil disobedience and for the creation of workers' squads to secure order and defend socialist property against the secessionist government.

The size of the protest, shown on national television, damaged the Lithuanian government's assertion that the population fully supports secession. Gorbachev has said he is concerned for the rights of residents who are not ethnic Lithuanians and

LITHUANIA, Page 5

Inside

HEALTH & SCIENCE

■ **Selling a takeover:** The battle for Norton Co's. shareholders moves to Worcester today. Business, Page 17.

■ **Rhyme and reason:** Poet Ted Thomas uses the arts to help youngsters cope with urban life. Living/Arts, Page 31.

■ **NCAA basketball upsets:** Kansas, Georgetown and defending champ Michigan fell yesterday. Sports, Page 37.

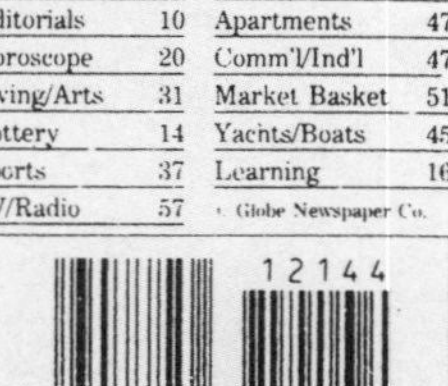

FEATURES		CLASSIFIED	
Ask The Globe	20	Classified	47-55, [illegible]
Business	17	Autos	[illegible]
Comics	20-21	Help Wanted	[illegible]
Deaths	8-9	Real Estate	47
Editorials	10	Apartments	47
Horoscope	20	Comm'l/Ind'l	47
Living/Arts	31	Market Basket	51
Lottery	14	Yachts/Boats	45
Sports	37	Learning	16
TV/Radio	57		

12144
0 947725 4

LOTTERY, INDEX PAGE 3
Volume 237
Number 175
$1.50

Boston Sunday Globe

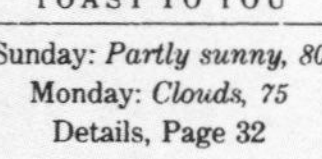

TOAST TO YOU
Sunday: *Partly sunny, 80*
Monday: *Clouds, 75*
Details, Page 32

SUNDAY, JUNE 24, 1990

Mandela and Boston embrace in a daylong celebration of unity

Dancing to the finale music after his speech to an estimated 250,000 people at the Hatch Shell on Boston's Esplanade yesterday, Nelson Mandela is flanked by Sen. Edward Kennedy, left, and Mayor Flynn.

From Soweto to Boston, journey of pain and hope

By Wil Haygood
GLOBE STAFF

Commentary

Dreamers gathered yesterday in a city where dreams have often been quashed only to come alive again, where mothers once sent sons from their homes to fight in a Civil War on Mississippi cotton fields to save the North and free the slaves.

Where, once, in memory recent enough to touch, someone viciously jabbed a black man with an American flag at an antibusing demonstration, and blood as red as the American flag dropped once again on a nation's eyelid.

All day long yesterday this city on a hill was in a kind of repose as the old African was whisked from locale to locale, the back straight, the smile sweet, no chip on his shoulder, just a chief come to lecture and hover and link African history with American history.

Nelson Mandela's thick brown fist looked like something that could conquer the world, not to mention despair.

It is nearly an impossible task to search out the ties that string together foreign land and native land, but when School Committee member Juanita Wade looked out over a hope-soaked crowd at Madison Park

COMMENTARY, Page 30

More on the Mandela visit

- In Roxbury and Dorchester, cheering, chanting crowds greet Mandelas as heroes. Page 25.
- In a sweltering gymnasium at Madison Park High School, a torrent of emotion is unleashed. Page 25.
- Two big Mass. firms still have direct investments in South Africa. Page 65.

250,000 rally on Esplanade

By Peter J. Howe and Diane E. Lewis
GLOBE STAFF

Nelson R. Mandela, the living legend of the international campaign to end South African apartheid, swept through Boston yesterday on an exuberant daylong visit, saluting local heroes from the Revolutionary War through the Kennedy dynasty as inspirations to his freedom quest.

Released in February after 27 years as a political prisoner in South Africa, Mandela is undertaking a grueling six-week tour through 13 nations urging no letup in economic sanctions and political pressure on South Africa's white minority government to give blacks full equality and democracy.

Mandela's Boston visit proved to be an eclectic spectacle, including everything from a red-carpet airport welcome and luncheon with dignitaries at the John F. Kennedy Library to a deafening community rally in Roxbury and a six-hour concert on the Esplanade that Metropolitan Police said drew an estimated 225,000 to 250,000 people.

The 71-year-old deputy president of the African National Congress, clad in a plain gray suit and accompanied by his wife, Winnie, generated intense excitement in a city that has been a national hotbed of political opposition to apartheid.

Down Roxbury streets decorated with flags and balloons, young people sprinted alongside his briskly rolling motorcade in hopes of catching a glimpse of Mandela. At the Charles River Esplanade, one of the largest crowds in the park's history endured hours in the crush of humanity and muggy 81-degree weather to hear Mandela's greetings.

In his first public words in Boston, Mandela told the crowd gathered inside a Logan International Airport hangar: "I feel very honored and happy to be in this city, a city whose role in the formation of this democracy was very critical."

"It was here that the Boston Tea Party served notice that the citizens of this country would not live under domination by the British," he said, "and that was the establishment of a fundamental principle which has in-

MANDELA, Page 31

Quebec accord dead; Canada ponders future

By Gordon McKibben
GLOBE STAFF

MONTREAL – English and French Canadians begin a wary and potentially dangerous process of sorting out the future of their country today after the Meech Lake amendment died at midnight yesterday. The Meech accord would have given Quebec province official status as a "distinct society" within the nation.

The deadline for all 10 provinces to ratify the Meech Lake accord as an amendment to the constitution officially expired early yesterday, but the actual death of Meech Lake came on Friday, after Newfoundland refused to vote on ratification.

Prime Minister Brian Mulroney tried to dampen speculation about possible moves by Quebec to secede from Canada in a nationally television speech yesterday. During the speech, he said the defeat of Meech Lake "is in no way a rejection of Quebec by the rest of Canada."

After a period of healing, he said his government will begin searching for a better process to bring Quebec within the Canadian Constitution, and he urged the premier of Quebec, Robert Bourassa, who put his career at risk to support Meech, to join him.

In a response televised later in Quebec City, however, Bourassa said

CANADA, Page 10

Campaign's fiscal focus

First in an occasional series on the issues of the 1990 campaign.

By M.E. Malone
GLOBE STAFF

ISSUES 90 $ $ TAXES

More than any other issue, the prospect of new taxes and the long-running financial fiasco that led to it have dominated the political debate in Massachusetts and left the citizenry demanding change.

Enter Democratic gubernatorial candidates John R. Silber, Evelyn F. Murphy and Francis X. Bellotti, as well as Republicans William F. Weld and Steven D. Pierce, all distancing themselves from the Beacon Hill crowd in power as the forces of high spending and low revenues collided, and all promising to provide leadership to return the state to better times.

Because the next governor's ability to achieve a consensus on the size and cost of state government has major implications, the five candidates – three of whom will be eliminated in a primary in September – are talking more about their integrity and commitment to solve the problems than just how much state government will cost.

All use similar buzzwords, such

ISSUES, Page 21

Inside

Ryan investigation
The FBI and US Attorney's Office are pursuing an investigation of Hampden County District Attorney Matthew J. Ryan despite his decision not to seek re-election. • Page 34.

Aftershocks in Iran
Strong aftershocks sent panicked residents rushing into the streets of northern Iran yesterday. • Page 2.

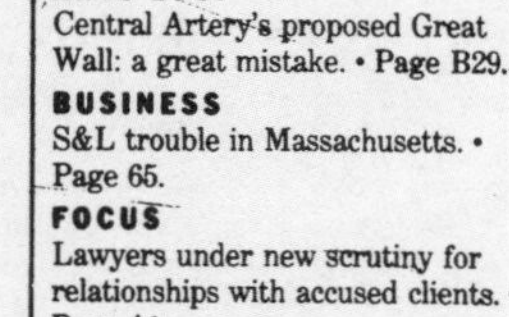

ARTS ETC.
Central Artery's proposed Great Wall: a great mistake. • Page B29.
BUSINESS
S&L trouble in Massachusetts. • Page 65.
FOCUS
Lawyers under new scrutiny for relationships with accused clients. • Page A1.
LEARNING
College grads are asking tougher-than-ever questions. • Page A8.
MAGAZINE
Ethiopia's unending famine.
REAL ESTATE
Foreclosure auctions soaring. • Page A17.
TRAVEL
Summertime in the south of Maine. • Page B1.

It's not over yet: Red Sox fall to White Sox, 3-2; Blue Jays stay alive by beating Orioles - Page 37

VOLUME 238 • NUMBER 95
92 pages
35 cents

The Boston Globe

MANY HAPPY RAY TURNS
Wednesday: *Sunny, 65-70*
Thursday: *Partly sunny, 70-75*
High tide: *10:49 a.m., 11:11 p.m.*
Full report: *Page 82*

WEDNESDAY, OCTOBER 3, 1990

After 45 years, Germany is united

AP PHOTO
Fireworks light the sky over Berlin's Brandenburg Gate early today during the German unification celebration.

Throngs celebrate at midnight; cheers are mixed with trepidation

By Jonathan Kaufman
GLOBE STAFF

BERLIN – With a peal of bells and a shiver of ambivalence, East and West Germany united this morning, ending 45 years of division and opening a door to an uncertain future.

More than 300,000 Germans gathered in front of the Reichstag Building and burst into cheers at the stroke of midnight as Berlin's Liberty Bell – a gift from the United States 40 years ago – was rung and West Germany's red, gold and black flag was hoisted as the new national standard for all Germany.

Fireworks lit the air above the Brandenburg Gate, and Germans on both sides of the strip that was once the Berlin Wall sang the national anthem.

"In free self-determination, we realize the unity and freedom of Germany," said President Richard von Weizsaecker in remarks broadcast across the country. "We want to serve world peace in a united Europe."

"Now the tears come," said Gunther Sonnick, 61, who watched the ceremony as a carpet of fireworks exploded overhead and the flag was bathed in spotlight. "I never thought I would live to see this moment."

Helmut Kohl, who automatically became chancellor of all Germany and who watched with other dignitaries on the reviewing stand, said earlier, "This is one of the happiest moments of my life."

Speaking in a televised address, Kohl asked: "When has a nation ever had the opportunity of overcoming decades of painful separation in such a peaceful manner? We are reestablishing German unity in freedom in full agreement with our neighbors. . . . I call upon all Germans to show that we are worthy of our shared freedom."

"We Germans reach unity in freedom," East Germany's prime minister, Lothar de Maiziere, declared in his farewell speech to his nation in transition. "It is an hour of great joy. It is the end of some illusions. It is a farewell without tears."

The union of the two Germanys marked the culmination of a yearlong process that moved with breathtaking speed and changed the face of Eastern Europe.

A year ago this week, East Germany, secure and confident behind the 60-mile Berlin Wall and hundreds of miles of barbed wire and border checkpoints, celebrated its 40th anniversary as an independent country and the most prosperous outpost of the communist East bloc.

But at the height of the celebrations, the reformist Soviet leader, Mikhail S. Gorbachev, warned then-East German leader Erich Honecker, "He who waits too long will be punished by history."

GERMANY, Page 21

Senate confirms Souter on 90-9 vote

N.H. jurist joins court Tuesday

By Ethan Bronner
GLOBE STAFF

WASHINGTON – The Senate, after a four-hour debate, confirmed Judge David H. Souter yesterday as the 105th justice of the Supreme Court. The vote was 90-9.

"I have been given much, and much will be expected of me in return," said Souter, who watched the vote from a friend's law office in Concord, N.H. "I will make that return to you, and I will make it in the fullest measure that I can."

The high court's public information office said the 51-year-old New Hampshire jurist would take his vows Tuesday morning at 9:15 before joining his eight colleagues on the bench to hear arguments in the four cases scheduled for that day.

Chief Justice William H. Rehnquist will administer the constitutional oath in the justices' conference room with only fellow justices present. Then, in a public ceremony in the court, Rehnquist will administer the judicial oath required of all federal judges. President Bush hopes

SOUTER, Page 16

GLOBE STAFF PHOTO / JANET KNOTT
David H. Souter speaks at the State House in Concord, N.H., after the Senate vote.

Bush makes appeal for budget package

By Stephen Kurkjian
GLOBE STAFF

WASHINGTON – With a rebellion from conservative Republicans threatening to scuttle a delicate budget agreement, President Bush last night warned that the country's economic vitality is at stake as he asked Americans to support the package's tax increases and benefit cuts.

"If we fail to enact this agreement, our economy will falter, markets may tumble and recession will follow," Bush said in his 10-minute televised address.

In an unusual twist that showed Bush's budget agreement has more support among Democrats than his own GOP, the Senate Democratic leader, George Mitchell of Maine, followed Bush on television with a speech echoing Bush's call.

"We hope members of his party, the Republican members of Congress, will also set aside partisan differences, as we have done, and join us doing what's right for our country," Mitchell said.

Bush and Mitchell stressed that although individual sections of the budget agreement could be criticized, it represented the best compromise available.

The package, said Bush, was "the result of eight months of blood, sweat and fears – fears of the economic chaos that would follow if we fail to reduce the deficit."

SPEECH, Page 4

Multinational force massing in the gulf is colorful but lacking a common purpose

By Colin Nickerson
GLOBE STAFF

YANBU, Saudi Arabia – Like some eau de desert warfare, the scent of fresh camouflage paint wafted from the AMX-10 light battle tanks rumbling ashore from the freighter Casablanca. Nearby, a cluster of Foreign Legionnaires, who had arrived a day earlier, sang ribald ditties while their regular army counterparts offered jaunty salutes to a Saudi review.

The French had landed, the latest trigger-ready combat contingent to hit these troubled sands.

An ungainly collection of armies is massing in the dunes of Saudi Arabia as the Middle East grinds along the brink of war. The Persian Gulf, too, teems with warships flying the flags of a host of nations.

At least 26 countries have either provided or pledged fighting forces to defend Saudi Arabia and other gulf states since Iraqi President Saddam Hussein's troops invaded Kuwait Aug. 2.

The United States alone has committed nearly 200,000 troops and tens of billions of dollars worth of lethal hardware in the nation's largest overseas military buildup since the Vietnam War.

Britain has dispatched its "Desert Rats," nickname of the 7th Armoured Brigade that won distinction battling German Panzer divisions in North Africa during World War II. Canada has committed a fighter squadron and three warships. Egypt, Syria and other Islamic nations have positioned thousands of commandos in Saudi Arabia's northern desert with promises of more infantry and tanks to come.

But for all its awesome firepower, this incongruous coalition of Western and Islamic forces appears to lack both coordination and common purpose.

"There is no clear chain of com-

SAUDI ARABIA, Page 26

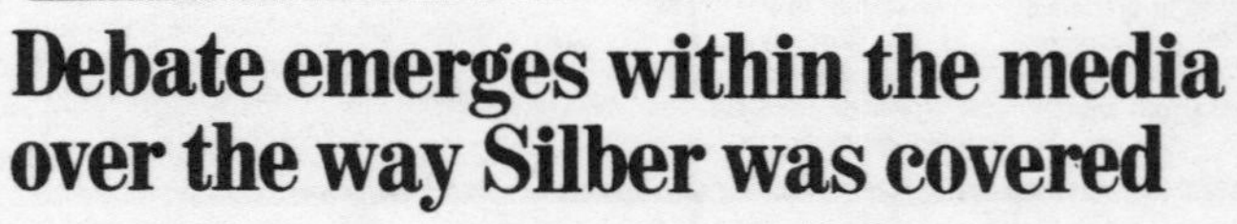

Debate emerges within the media over the way Silber was covered

Candidate comes to Bulger's defense

By Bruce Mohl
GLOBE STAFF

Democratic gubernatorial candidate John Silber gave a ringing defense yesterday of Senate President William Bulger, saying Bulger is "not a crook" and holding him largely blameless for the state's fiscal problems.

At a private meeting in Boston organized by Fidelity Investments and closed to the media, Silber responded to a question about his rapport with legislative leaders by attempting to debunk what he said were inaccurate media reports about the powerful South Boston politician.

"I get fed up with being told that if I

BULGER, Page 35

By Charles A. Radin
GLOBE STAFF

John R. Silber's whopping victory in the recent Democratic gubernatorial primary is causing reporters, editors and media observers to question sharply how the news business operates and is sparking worries about rising public anger at the press.

Debate rages over whether the media set out to bash Silber or vice versa, fueled both by Silber's assertion on national television that antimedia sentiment is growing across the country and by a widespread belief within the media that the candidate is successfully baiting the press for political gain.

In the wake of the 10-point margin by which Silber thumped former Attorney General Francis X. Bellotti in the face of nearly unanimous media and poll predictions that Bellotti would win, there's no disputing who has got the best of it so far. However, there is much argument about the how and why of the phenomenon.

Silber says he had no choice.

SILBER, Page 35

The Legislature in recent years has resisted attempts to give administrative judges clear-cut authority

Dukakis seeks to give top judges more power

By Sean P. Murphy
GLOBE STAFF

Gov. Dukakis yesterday said he will file legislation this week to revamp the state courts by putting more authority in the hands of top administrative judges to discipline trial judges and to decide how to allocate resources.

Dukakis, making impromptu comments at a meeting of the Boston Bar Association, also said he will ask the state's top judges to meet with him this week to discuss measures for improving the courts.

Called to the bar association meeting to accept an award in recognition of his judicial appointments, Dukakis reacted to a Globe Spotlight series that pointed out that the state judiciary appears to be dominated by the state Legislature.

Besides exercising influence through its budget-

JUDGES, Page 47

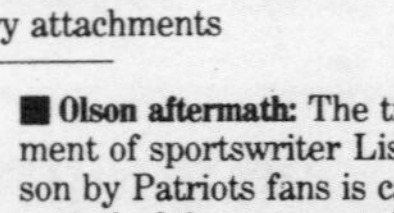

Inside

FOOD: Culinary attachments

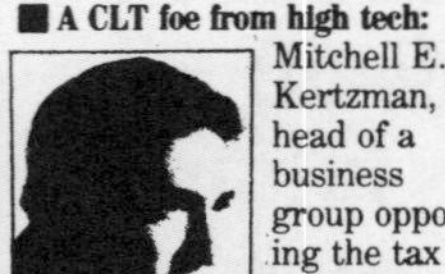

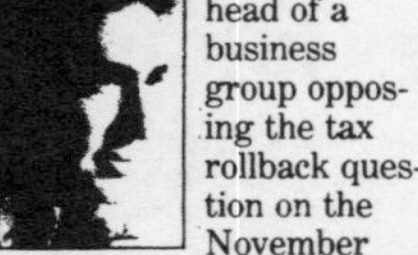

■ **A CLT foe from high tech:** Mitchell E. Kertzman, head of a business group opposing the tax rollback question on the November ballot, starts his task with low visibility. Business, Page 67.

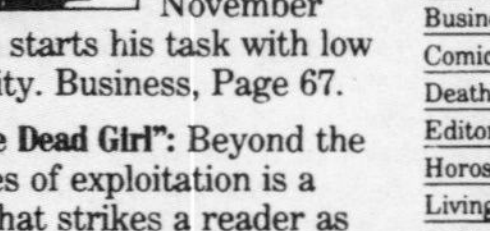

■ **"The Dead Girl":** Beyond the charges of exploitation is a book that strikes a reader as a sensitive memorial to a lost friend. Living/Arts, Page 75.

■ **Crash in China:** Mistakes by Chinese authorities may have contributed to the plane crash that killed at least 120 persons yesterday. Page 2.

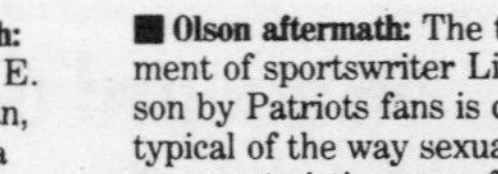

■ **Olson aftermath:** The treatment of sportswriter Lisa Olson by Patriots fans is called typical of the way sexual harassment victims are often further victimized. Page 29.

FEATURES		CLASSIFIED	
Ask The Globe	90	Classified	53-66
Business	67	Autos	60
Comics	90-91	Help Wanted	57
Deaths	50-51	Real Estate	54
Editorials	18	Apartments	55
Horoscope	90	Comm'l/Ind'l	55
Living/Arts	75	Market Basket	54
Lottery	30	Yachts/Boats	45
Sports	37		
TV/Radio	81		

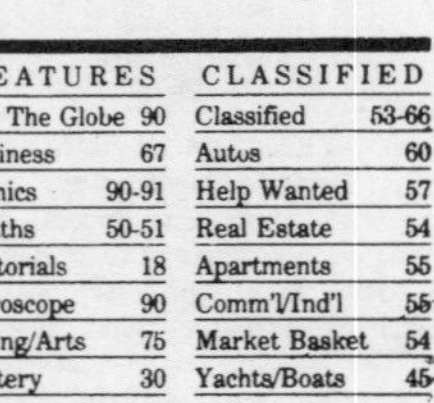

VOLUME 238 • NUMBER 130
92 pages
35 cents

The Boston Globe

WINNERS
Wednesday: *Mostly sunny, 50-55*
Thursday: *Mostly sunny, 45*
High tide: *2:04 a.m., 2:15 p.m.*
Full report: *Page 58*

WEDNESDAY, NOVEMBER 7, 1990

Weld tops Silber in cliffhanger; voters turn down tax rollback

MASSACHUSETTS		
Governor/Lt. Governor		
1,772 of 2,138 pcts. 83%		
☒Weld/ Cellucci (R)	920,675	51%
Silber/ Clapprood (D)	880,463	49%
Umina/DeBerry (IHT)		NT
US Senator		
1,764 of 2,138 pcts. 83%		
☒*Kerry (D)	1,049,297	58%
Rappaport (R)	773,873	42%
Attorney General		
1,529 of 2,138 pcts. 72%		
☒Harshbarger (D)	983,957	65%
Sawyer (R)	537,617	35%
Treasurer		
1,516 of 2,138 pcts. 71%		
☒Malone (R)	877,384	58%
Galvin (D)	552,000	36%
Nash (I)	94,072	6%
Question 2 (Consultants)		
1,457 of 2,138 pcts. 68%		
☒No	815,604	55%
Yes	665,046	45%
Question 3 (CLT: taxes)		
1,772 of 2,138 pcts. 83%		
☒No	1,107,676	60%
Yes	731,561	40%
Question 5 (Local Aid)		
1,462 of 2,138 pcts. 68%		
☒Yes	797,881	56%
No	620,398	44%
US House		
5th District		
154 of 181 pcts. 85%		
*Atkins (D)	92,106	52%
MacGovern (R)	84,849	48%
10th District		
120 of 189 pcts. 63%		
*Studds (D)	88,064	52%
Bryan (R)	81,288	48%
NEW HAMPSHIRE		
Governor		
287 of 298 pcts. 96%		
☒*Gregg (R)	171,539	64%
Grandmaison (D)	97,824	36%
VERMONT		
Governor		
256 of 262 pcts. 98%		
☒Snelling (R)	104,249	52%
Welch (D)	92,224	46%
Atkinson (B)	2,647	1%
Gottlieb (LU)	1,351	1%
MAINE		
Governor		
522 of 666 pcts. 78%		
*McKernan (R)	172,621	46%
Brennan (D)	167,732	45%
Adam (U)	34,328	9%
RHODE ISLAND		
Governor		
537 of 540 pcts. 99%		
☒Sundlun (D)	255,495	74%
*DiPrete (R)	87,961	26%
CONNECTICUT		
Governor		
754 of 761 pcts. 99%		
☒Weicker (I)	455,430	40%
Rowland (R)	423,101	38%
Morrison (D)	232,077	21%

☒ Elected * Incumbent NT Not tabulated
Data from News Election Service / The Associated Press

Consultant cutback also losing

By Bruce Mohl
GLOBE STAFF

Question 3 went down to a resounding defeat last night, as Massachusetts voters decided that the tax-cutting initiative sponsored by Citizens for Limited Taxation went too far.

The "hidden vote" that supporters of the initiative had been promising did not materialize and the undefeated steamroller of CLT and the Massachusetts High Technology Council ground to a decisive halt.

The vote sends a mixed message to Beacon Hill. Voters rejected by a 3-2 ratio the huge tax cut offered by Question 3, but they backed Republican governor-elect William Weld and GOP treasurer-elect Joseph Malone, who said they needed Question 3 to make real changes on Beacon Hill.

On other ballot measures, voters were narrowly rejecting the consultant-cutting Question 2 and approving Question 5, which effectively urges the governor and the Legislature to funnel 40 percent of state income, corporate and sales taxes to cities and towns.

Voters were also approving Question 1, which would eliminate the state census, and Question 4, which would make it easier for alternative-party candidates to make it onto the ballot. Question 6, a nonbinding measure asking voters whether

REFERENDUM, Page 33

Kerry thumps Rappaport in Senate battle

By Michael Rezendes and Steve Marantz
GLOBE STAFF

Democratic US Sen. John Kerry easily won a second term, according to preliminary returns last night, despite widespread anti-incumbent sentiment and a well-financed campaign waged by his millionaire opponent, Republican Jim Rappaport.

After a bitter campaign that often seemed long on invective and short on substance, Kerry was leading Rappaport 58 percent to 42 percent, with 64 percent of the vote counted.

Kerry, a 46-year-old former lieutenant governor who began a political career as a spokesman for Vietnam Veterans Against the War, declared victory shortly after 9 p.m. in the Copley Plaza Hotel and thanked supporters for standing behind him during an unpleasant campaign.

"Massachusetts voters were able to see through the rhetoric and advertising to the record and reality," he said.

US SENATE, Page 31

GLOBE STAFF PHOTO / JOHN TLUMACKI

Gov.-elect William Weld claims his victory early today at the Park Plaza Castle.

Change has begun, victor says

By Brian C. Mooney
GLOBE STAFF

Republican William Weld nosed past John Silber early this morning, ending the Democrats' 16-year stranglehold on the governorship in one of the closest state elections in 28 years.

Silber acknowledged defeat about 1:15 a.m. today after it became apparent he could not overcome the slim lead Weld had opened up in vote-counting after midnight. With 80 percent of the state's precincts reporting, Weld led Silber by more than 32,000 votes, or less than two percentage points.

Silber had jumped to an early lead as tallies came in from the cities, but Weld kept eating into the margin as suburban results trickled in.

Weld, in his acceptance speech at Boston's Park Plaza Castle said: "Today the voters of Massachusetts began the process of change ... [Lt. Gov.-elect] Paul Cellucci and I will respect your tax dollars. We'll listen to what you have to tell us, and we'll never, ever forget that the only purpose of government is to serve you."

Weld congratulated Silber and his running mate Marjorie Clapprood for waging a campaign with "compelling issues," particularly education. He also called on the Legislature to return to session and repeal the extension of the sales tax before it

MASSACHUSETTS, Page 31

A fall from TV pique to electoral valley

By Curtis Wilkie
GLOBE STAFF

News Analysis

In the ill-tempered race for governor that became a referendum on the character of John Silber, the rebellious voters of Massachusetts rejected him in the end, as the French Revolution finally turned against its leader, Robespierre.

To extend the historical analogy, Silber's loss to Republican William Weld, coupled with the resounding defeat of Question 3, could move the state into a modern Thermidor, a period when tensions ease after severe political upheaval.

There was evidence in the ruins of Silber's insurgent campaign early today that voters winced at his abrasive behavior and ultimately recoiled at the prospect of his election.

For months he had commanded a growing following of angry and alienated citizens, and he had articulated their anxieties better than any other political figure

ANALYSIS, Page 31

Weicker, Sanders victorious in jolt to party system in N.E.

By Adam Pertman
GLOBE STAFF

Lowell Weicker of Connecticut will become the first independent US governor in more than a decade, while Bernard Sanders of Vermont will be the first independent member of the US House in 40 years.

Those were the most notable victories in New England yesterday as the two candidates won not only by portraying themselves as outsiders but by running against the two-party system as well.

There were several additional surprising outcomes.

The most stunning was that Richard Swett, an architect, bested US Rep. Charles Douglas in New Hampshire's 2d District and became the first Democrat to take that seat since 1912. Douglas, a one-term Republican, had been expected to win the contest handily but apparently was undone by lingering questions about his personal life.

Another jolt appeared to hit in Rhode Island, where Vincent (Buddy) Cianci looked as if he would squeak by two rivals to become the mayor of Providence. The colorful and mercurial Cianci, a former Republican running as an independent, took back a job he resigned in

NEW ENGLAND, Page 35

Helms defeats Gantt in N.C. race

• Richards, Chiles winners **• Bradley has a fight in N.J.** **• Gingrich trailing in Ga.**

By Larry Tye
GLOBE STAFF

Democrats won enough new House seats last night to make it easier to challenge the White House, but they lost the nation's most closely watched Senate contest as Jesse Helms, the arch-conservative Republican, defeated Harvey Gantt, the black Democrat.

In Texas, Ann Richards, the Democrat, defeated the millionaire oilman Clayton Williams in a hard-fought race for governor. Her victory helped Democrats increase their edge over Republicans by as many as five governorships and, along with Lawton Chiles' election as governor of Florida, will play a major role in the reapportioning seven new congressional districts in those states next year.

In California, which also will get seven new House seats next year, the Democratic gubernatorial hopeful, Dianne Feinstein, was trailing Sen. Pete Wilson 55 percent to 40 percent, with 15 percent of the vote reported.

Of the 34 Senate seats up for grabs yesterday, Democrats seemed likely to gain at most one seat, which would increase their edge to 56-44.

In New Jersey, Sen. Bill Bradley, a Democrat who had been considered a potential 1992 presidential candidate and who had been expected to coast to victory, was leading by just four points over Christine Todd Whitman, a little-known challenger who was outspent 40 to 1. New Jersey voters apparently linked Bradley to the huge tax increase enacted by Gov. James J. Florio, a fellow Democrat.

And in another election night surprise, Rep. Newt Gingrich of Georgia, a hard-line conservative Republican leader who clashed with Bush in the recent Capitol Hill budget

NATION, Page 14

Inside

FOOD: Vinaigrettes find a home beyond salads

Kahane mourned: About 10,000 people packed tightly around a tiny synagogue in Brooklyn yesterday for the slain rabbi's funeral. Page 15.

Combat Marines called up: The Pentagon yesterday ordered 653 combat Marine reservists to active duty as part of Operation Desert Shield in the Persian Gulf. Page 19.

Celtics win again: A Brian Shaw basket at the buzzer gave the Celtics a 110-108 win over the Bulls last night and their third straight victory of the season. Sports, Page 47.

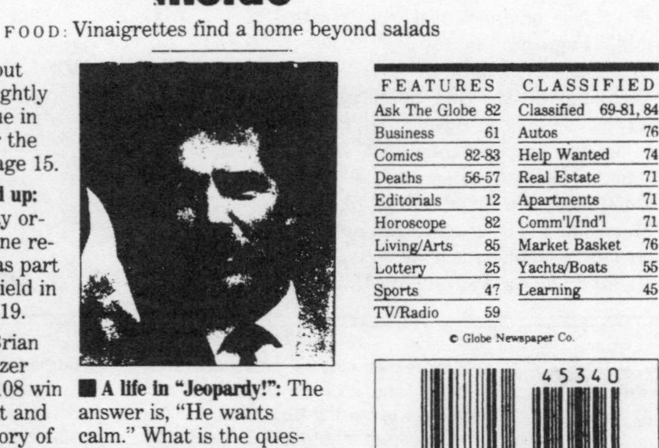

A life in "Jeopardy!": The answer is, "He wants calm." What is the question? Living/Arts, Page 85.

FEATURES		CLASSIFIED	
Ask The Globe	82	Classified	69-81, 84
Business	61	Autos	76
Comics	82-83	Help Wanted	74
Deaths	56-57	Real Estate	71
Editorials	12	Apartments	71
Horoscope	82	Comm'l/Ind'l	71
Living/Arts	85	Market Basket	76
Lottery	25	Yachts/Boats	55
Sports	47	Learning	45
TV/Radio	59		

45340
0 947725 4

VOLUME 239 • NUMBER 17
108 pages
35 cents

The Boston Globe

THURSDAY, JANUARY 17, 1991

THE WEATHER
Thursday: *Mostly cloudy, windy, 45*
Friday: *Partly sunny, 35*
High tide: *11:58 a.m.*
Full report: *Page 58*

GULF WAR BEGINS

US leads massive bombing of strategic sites in Iraq, Kuwait

By Michael Kranish
GLOBE STAFF

WASHINGTON – US-led forces launched a massive aerial attack on Iraq and Kuwait last night, reportedly decimating dozens of key targets with no initial word of a US casualty, as President Bush announced, "The liberation of Kuwait has begun."

At 6:35 p.m., as millions of Americans were riveted to the evening news, American reporters at the 14-story Al Rashid Hotel in downtown Baghdad said via telephone that skies had lit up with flashes and antiaircraft fire. The White House confirmed 20 minutes later that Operation Desert Storm had begun.

Pentagon officials said the raids successfully destroyed Iraqi missile sites, government buildings and chemical and nuclear weapons plants. No casualties or loss of jets among the US coalition were reported as of early this morning. Iraq reportedly fired several missiles in response, most of which were unsuccessful, but at least one reportedly hit a small Saudi Arabian oil refinery.

With crushing attacks by cruise missiles, Stealth fighters and as many as 1,000 fighter jets, the US-led coalition reportedly decimated much of the Iraqi air force and many units of Iraq's elite Republican Guard. As of early this morning, there was virtually no counterattack by Iraq.

Defense Secretary Richard Cheney said the operation "appears to have gone very, very well."

A stoic, confident-sounding Bush addressed the nation two hours after the attack began, even as fighter jets made repeated bombing runs on Iraq. Reflecting the optimism that apparently shaped his decision to order the attack, Bush said, "I'm hopeful that this fighting will not go on for long and that casualties will be held to an absolute minimum."

Bush added: "Our goal is not the conquest of Iraq. It is the liberation of Kuwait. It is my hope the Iraqi people can even now convince their dictator that he must lay down his arms, leave Kuwait and let Iraq itself rejoin the family of nations."

"Some may ask, 'Why act now? Why not wait?'" Bush said. "The answer is clear. The world can wait no longer."

Baghdad Radio early this morning quoted Iraq's president, Saddam Hussein, as saying Bush is a "hypocritical criminal,"

GULF, Page 2

A certainty of war: the chance factor

By H.D.S. Greenway
GLOBE STAFF

News Analysis

War came on the dark of the January moon as the United States and its allies embarked on a long-awaited and long-dreaded Middle East war – the consequences of which cannot be foreseen, but which will certainly be felt for a generation to come. Karl von Clausewitz, the Prussian military theorist, wrote: "War is the province of chance. It increases the uncertainty of every circumstance and deranges the course of events."

At best it will be a short war, over before the political consequences scar the body politic both in this country and abroad, midwife to a new world order with the balance of power preserved, aggression thwarted and a vital strategic resource no longer threatened.

At worst, despite early reports of success, it will be long and drawn out, endangering the very interests the allies are fighting for.

Breaking a period of tension that became almost unbearable with the passing of the United Nations-imposed deadline for Iraq to quit Kuwait, the battle began as the evening news was being broadcast in America – somehow symbolic of this most-publicized and drawn-out confrontation.

Seldom has an international standoff lasted so long. In the end, neither American diplomats, nor the Arabs – both for and against Saddam Hussein – nor the Europeans, nor the Pope, nor the secretary general of the United Nations were able to persuade the Iraqi leader to quit Kuwait during more than five months of intense effort. As the French Foreign Minister, Roland Dumas, put it, the Iraqi president responded not to a "single initiative, to a single outstretched hand."

For the allies in the desert, it was 2:30 Thursday morning when the battle began. For soldiers, as is a soldier's wont, the fear of combat will be mixed with relief that the long wait is over. The majority of Americans in the desert today know little of the "mother of battles"

ANALYSIS, Page 6

More on the war

- Israel declared a state of emergency shortly after gulf bombing began. Page 3.
- From Morocco's Atlantic shore to the boggy flats of the Shatt al-Arab, the Arab world was hit with massive trauma. Page 4.
- A poll taken before the outbreak of war showed most Massachusetts residents favoring sanctions over military force. Page 10.
- The threat of war sent many to houses of worship. Page 18.
- Dr. James Menzoian, the vascular surgery chief at Boston City Hospital, said yesterday he is being granted a deferment from active service. Page 19.
- The news of war made itself felt in the world of athletics. Sports, Page 61.
- Mental health specialists tell how to explain war to children. Living/Arts, Page 69.
- Related stories, Pages 2-10, 15-20, 61, 69.

'The world could wait no longer'

ASSOCIATED PRESS

WASHINGTON – Following is a transcript of President Bush's address to the nation last night:

Five months ago, Saddam Hussein started this cruel war against Kuwait; tonight the battle has been joined. This military action, taken in accord with United Nations resolutions and with the consent of the United States Congress, follows months of constant and virtually endless diplomatic activity on the part of the United Nations, the United States and many, many other countries.

Arab leaders sought what became known as an Arab solution, only to conclude that Saddam Hussein was unwilling to leave Kuwait. Others traveled to Baghdad in a variety of efforts to restore peace and justice. Our Secretary of State James Baker held an historic meeting in Geneva, only to be totally rebuffed.

This past weekend, in a last-ditch effort, the secretary general of the United Nations went to the Middle East with peace in his heart, his second such mission, and he came back from Baghdad with no

TEXT, Page 8

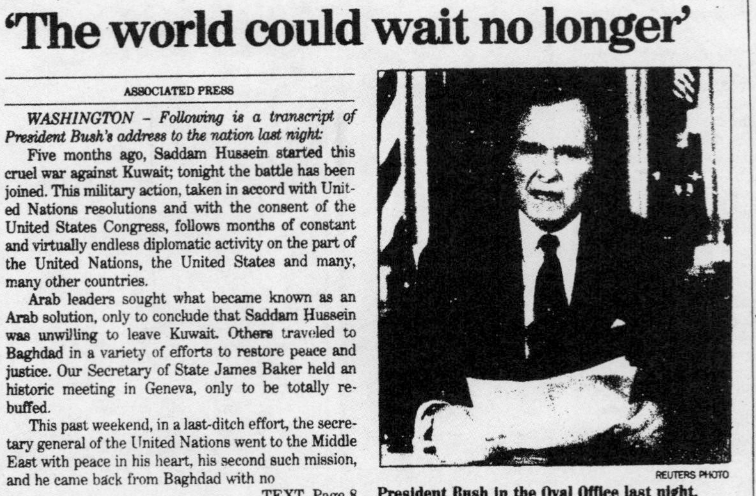

REUTERS PHOTO
President Bush in the Oval Office last night.

GLOBE STAFF MAP / JIM KARAIAN

A new breed of weapons does the job

By Fred Kaplan
GLOBE STAFF

WASHINGTON – War began last night, and by early this morning the first phase seemed – in initial reports that officials cautioned might not be completely accurate – a remarkable success for US and allied forces.

It began as expected, with a massive air strike to destroy quickly all Iraqi air bases, air defense weapons, missile sites, command posts, nuclear and chemical plants, power grids and communications networks – everything Iraq might need to wage a war.

Launched in predawn darkness, the raid was one of the most intensive in history and the first real test of a whole new generation of US high-tech airplanes, missiles, "smart bombs" and sensors.

Initial report indicated that the attack wiped out most of Iraq's 60 to 80 Scud surface-to-surface missiles, 500 fighter planes and key air defense batteries.

Retired Air Force Maj. Gen. Perry Smith said early this morning, however, that "it may be premature to say the Iraqi air force is completely destroyed. Many of their planes may be in their shelters, and we may see them in the coming day or two."

The raid also bombarded the headquarters of Iraq's elite and heavily armored Republican Guard forces behind the front lines in southern Iraq and Kuwait, well-trained as a mobile reserve force to push back any breakthrough by a US invasion force.

CNN reported last night that the raid effectively destroyed the Republican Guard. If true, a US invasion could easily win, especially if Iraq has virtually no air cover.

Meanwhile, the Turkish Parliament reportedly will meet soon to vote on a declaration of war. Nearly 100,000 Turkish troops and hundreds of allied planes sit on the Iraqi border. If Iraq faces a two-front invasion, a quick defeat may be certain.

However, all reports are preliminary, and it could be

ATTACK, Page 3

Baghdad is quiet following attacks

By Michael Kelly
SPECIAL TO THE GLOBE

BAGHDAD, Iraq – The city seemed deserted this morning, with no cars on the streets, and had a peculiarly normal look to it. Even after it has been bombed, Baghdadis would come up to a visitor on the street and act as if nothing really untoward had happened.

Signs of devastation were not immediately apparent. The impact seemed mixed at three locations – a refinery, a telecommunications tower and the presidential palace – that had been reported under attack.

Reporters found no evidence this morning that the refinery had been hit. The telecommunications tower, however, had a hole in it. The presidential palace is set far back from the road, out of reporters' view, but no plumes of smoke could be seen rising from the site.

During the air raid, the 60 to 80 journalists at the Al Rashid hotel were herded into the large bombproof shelter in the basement along with about 200 other people,

BAGHDAD, Page 4

Inside

CALENDAR: Stretching the entertainment dollar

Education cuts recommended: A study conducted for Gov. Weld recommends closing up to five public colleges, eliminating $33 million in scholarships and ending public financing of the Tufts University veterinary school in Grafton. Page 23.

Gorbachev hard line: The Soviet President yesterday proposed suspending press freedoms to ensure "greater objectivity." Page 38.

Celtics lose: Boston fell to the Warriors, 110-105. Sports, Page 61.

FEATURES			
Ask The Globe	36	Horoscope	36
Business	47	Living/Arts	69
Comics	36-37	Lottery	24
Deaths	56-57	Sports	61
Editorials	12	TV/Radio	59

CLASSIFIED			
Classified	38-46	Apartments	39
Autos	43	Comm'l/Ind'l	39
Help Wanted	41	Market Basket	43
Real Estate	38	Yachts/Boats	67

03449
0 947725 4

VOLUME 240 • NUMBER 179
112 pages
35 cents
50 cents at newsstands beyond 30 miles from Boston

The Boston Globe

SOME SHINER
Thursday: *Some sun, 35*
Friday: *Some sun, windy, 40*
High tide: *2:39 a.m., 2:58 p.m.*
Full report: *Page 42*

THURSDAY, DECEMBER 26, 1991

Gorbachev quits; US sets ties

Bush says 6 republics have formal recognition

By Mary Curtius
GLOBE STAFF

WASHINGTON – President Bush last night bade farewell to the Soviet president, Mikhail S. Gorbachev, and immediately recognized Russia and five other republics of the former Soviet Union.

On behalf of the American people, Bush said, he wanted to express his "gratitude to Mikhail Gorbachev for years of sustained commitment to world peace, and for his intellect, vision, and courage."

Gorbachev's "revolutionary policies transformed the Soviet Union," and his "legacy guarantees him an honored place in history," Bush said in a speech to the nation from the Oval office.

"The Soviet Union itself is no more," Bush said. "This is a victory for democracy and freedom. It is a victory for the moral force of our values."

Declaring that "we stand tonight before a new world of possibilities and hope for our children," the president said that "the challenge for us now is to engage these new states in sustaining the peace and building a more prosperous future."

With that, Bush extended formal diplomatic recognition to "a free, independent and democratic Russia, led by its courageous President Boris Yeltsin." Bush announced that the embassy in Moscow will now become the embassy to Russia, and he said the United States will support Russia's assumption of the Soviet

BUSH, Page 3

AP PHOTO
Mikhail S. Gorbachev closes his notes after delivering his resignation speech on television yesterday.

More on the resignation

- Many in Moscow express relief. Page 2.
- Chronology of the Gorbachev years. Page 2.
- Gorbachev called a giant of century. Page 3.
- Israel plans to airlift Jews from republics in the event of "chaos." Page 4.
- Georgian leader vows fight to death. Page 4.

Soviet reformer leaves a world restructured

By Elizabeth Neuffer
GLOBE STAFF

MOSCOW – Voicing concern for his country's future, Mikhail S. Gorbachev resigned yesterday as president of the Soviet Union, the nation he has overseen in its transformation from a totalitarian state to a commonwealth of independent republics.

In an address televised around the globe, Gorbachev defended his accomplishments and called upon his countrymen to "preserve the course of democratic reforms" he has set in motion since he came to power in 1985.

"We are living in a new world," Gorbachev said, adding, "We have become one of the key strongholds in terms of restructuring modern civilization on a peaceful, democratic basis."

After his speech, Gorbachev handed over the codes controlling 27,000 nuclear weapons to officials of the Russian Federation. Russia's president, Boris N. Yeltsin, did not show up as expected, and Yevgeny Shaposhnikov, the defense minister, accepted the codes.

In an address to the Russian Parliament yesterday, Yeltsin said he will have control over the nuclear button, subject to the consent of the leaders of other republics with nuclear weapons: Ukraine, Belorussia, and Kazakhstan.

In his speech yesterday, Gorbachev sounded a clear alarm about the new Commonwealth of Independent States, which was signed into being by 11 member republics last week. Though he pledged to support the new commonwealth, Gorbachev said he had fought long and hard against it in favor of a more centralized union of sovereign states.

"I have firmly stood for independence, self-rule of nations, for the sovereignty of the republics, but at the same time for preservation of the union state, the unity of the country," Gorbachev said.

"Events went a different way. The policy prevailed of dismembering this country and disuniting the

GORBACHEV, Page 2

Red banner galvanized US

By Michael Putzel
GLOBE STAFF

WASHINGTON – To some, particularly in the early days, it represented the struggle against poverty, racism and illiteracy. Later, it symbolized the threat to freedom and the American way of life posed by totalitarianism.

Throughout its history, the red banner of Soviet Communism stirred the emotions of the American people. The symbol's enemies drew their strength by pointing to the horrors wrought by dictators who flew it above their fortress.

With the lowering of the Soviet flag yesterday from atop the Kremlin, the United States can rest secure, having survived most of a century at odds with a country whose ideology and values it found to be anathema.

The flag galvanized its enemies perhaps more effectively than the people who served it.

It helped define – by contrast – what America stood for, what free-

SYMBOL, Page 2

'D' stands for desperation, dedication at D Street clinic

By Teresa M. Hanafin
GLOBE STAFF

In a dull brick building in the middle of a tired South Boston housing project, those with tormented minds and clouded faces can duck down a concrete hallway into a sparse office and leave their demons at the door.

There's warmth inside the D Street mental health clinic. There's free coffee, too, and the people who have gathered on this damp December morning take turns shuffling to the coffeemaker, their hands trembling slightly as their fingers clutch plastic foam cups.

They have come for medication, for a weekly injection of reality into their desperately disordered lives. They come by the dozens, close to 70 in the span of three hours. They crowd the tiny reception area, fill the waiting room and spill out into the stairwell, some dragging on Camels as they cling to the iron railing, others staring blankly at the brown metal door that leads into the clinic.

It's one of their few refuges from a frightening world.

...

It's not easy being a little insane, Carol says matter-of-factly. "People in restaurants don't like it when I talk to myself, although sometimes I don't even know I'm doing it, but I can tell because they say something to me."

She pushes her glasses up on her nose and adjusts her black headband. From time to time, she rubs the cameo ring on her left hand.

She is 50 and has been coming to D Street for 18 years for treatment of residual schizophrenia. She has been delusional and has had hallucinations. She says that her problems started "due to anxiety over my divorce."

As her illness has ebbed and surged, Carol has stumbled through life, trying to navigate a turbulent course that has pitched her from hospitals to apartments to homelessness, and, most recently, to a halfway house in South Boston.

The clinic is the one constant in her life.

"Why are you writing about D Street?" she asks suddenly, quietly, a sad desperateness to her voice and panic behind her eyes. She grabs the front of her maroon sweater and pulls it tightly around her, like a blanket. "Is it going to close?"

Other patients in the waiting room turn their heads slowly and stare, waiting for the answer. None is provided.

...

They know it was close. Very, very close. They talk about it in whispers, afraid that saying it out loud might make it come true. They know they almost lost D Street

CLINIC, Page 20

Wisconsin city will mix students by family income

By Muriel Cohen
GLOBE STAFF

In an effort to address growing inequities in education between children of the affluent and the poor, a Wisconsin public school system next fall will become the first in the nation to assign students to s[illegible] on the basis of family income.

In a radical departure from neighborhood and race-based school placement, La Crosse, Wis., will pioneer a new strategy aimed at mixing rich, middle-class and poor students in an effort to assure a quality education for all.

The focus on economic class rather than race as a factor in improving educational opportunity comes nearly 40 years after the landmark Brown vs. Board of Education case in Topeka, Kan., which set off a train of federal racial desegregation lawsuits. And it follows a decade that saw a sharply widening gap between America's rich and poor.

SCHOOLS, Page 21

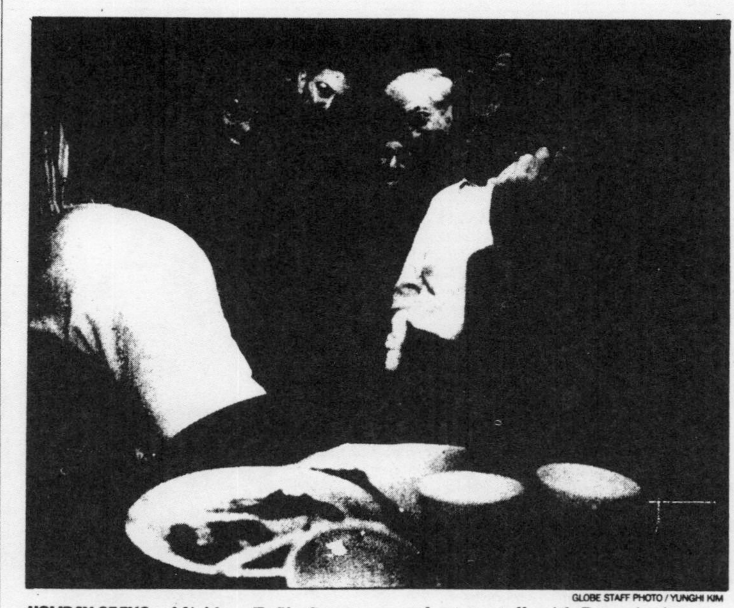
GLOBE STAFF PHOTO / YUNGHI KIM
HOLIDAY GIVING – *Mishkan Tefila Synagogue volunteers talk with Rena Arriaga (left) and Richard Albarran, both jobless, after serving them Christmas dinner at the Kingston House of Merrimac Mission in Boston yesterday. Page 27.*

Defective gene in women said to raise X-ray cancer risk

By Judy Foreman
GLOBE STAFF

More than 1 million American women who carry a single copy of a defective gene are believed to be at five to six times the normal risk of breast cancer, researchers said yesterday. The gene appears to make carriers – men as well as women – at increased risk for cancer from medical X-rays.

It has long been known that having two copies of this "bad" gene puts a person at 100 times the normal risk of developing cancer.

Since most carriers of the gene do not know they have it, the researchers told the Associated Press, their work suggests that doctors should cover all women's breasts with lead shields during X-rays and use non-X-ray tests whenever possible.

The new study, published today in the New England Journal of Medicine, shows that having just one copy of the bad gene significantly in-

CANCER, Page 20

Inside

CALENDAR:
A guide to First Night

- **Corporate restructuring:** Investment strategies for the 1990s will likely have to change. Business, Page 37.
- **Long shots:** More than 150 candidates eye the presidency. Living/Arts, Page 47.
- **Celtics routed:** The Bulls thumped Boston last night, 121-99. Sports, Page 65.

FEATURES		CLASSIFIED	
Ask The Globe	44	Classified	56-64
Business	37	Autos	59
Comics	44-45	Help Wanted	59
Deaths	40-41	Real Estate	57
Editorials	16	Apartments	58
Horoscope	44	Comm'l/Ind'l	58
Living/Arts	47	Market Basket	57
Lottery	28		
Sports	65		
TV/Radio	43		

52447
0 947725 4

Sabres beat Bruins again, 9-3, push playoff series to a seventh game - Page 35

VOLUME 241 • NUMBER 121
104 pages
35 cents
50 cents at newsstands beyond 30 miles from Boston

The Boston Globe

PUNY SERENADE
Thursday: *Clouding up; 60*
Friday: *AM clouds/PM sun; 50s*
High tide: *10:25 a.m., 10:39 p.m.*
Full report: *Page 60*

THURSDAY, APRIL 30, 1992

4 LA officers acquitted in beating; violence erupts, Guard called in

Verdict assailed

By Bill Girdner
SPECIAL TO THE GLOBE

SIMI VALLEY, Calif. – In a verdict that stunned onlookers and prompted widespread urban violence, a jury acquitted four white Los Angeles police officers yesterday of all but one charge stemming from the videotaped beating of motorist Rodney King last year. A mistrial was declared on that final count.

The beating of King, which followed a car chase by police officers, was caught on videotape by an amateur cameraman and broadcast repeatedly across the nation. It brought condemnation, calls for police reform from politicians and community leaders in Los Angeles and elsewhere, and eventually the appointment of a black police chief, Willie Williams, to replace the embattled chief Daryl Gates.

But after a three-month trial and seven days of deliberations, the jury found that the beating of the black motorist in March 1991 did not constitute excessive force by officers Timothy Wind, Theodore Briseno and Sgt. Stacey Koon, who was in charge at the time of the beating. King's leg and facial bones were broken in the beating.

VERDICT, Page 22

AP FILE PHOTO
A videotape frame shows Los Angeles police officers subduing Rodney King on March 3, 1991.

Emergency state

By James Anderson
ASSOCIATED PRESS

LOS ANGELES – Violence erupted in parts of the city following yesterday's acquittals, prompting Mayor Tom Bradley last night to declare a state of emergency and Gov. Pete Wilson to call in the National Guard.

The officials acted as one person was reported killed and 72 injured in the early hours of unrest. Looters ravaged stores, protesters set fires, and demonstrators rushed police headquarters.

Jeff Kramer, a Santa Monica-based correspondent for the Boston Globe, was shot in the leg and back while covering the early stages of the unrest. He was being treated at a local hospital and was expected to recover.

In the worst outbreak of violence, an intersection in predominantly black South Central Los Angeles was plunged into chaos, with looters running free and motorists pulled from cars and attacked. Police and paramedics were ordered to steer clear.

At least two dozen structures were burning throughout the sprawling south-central busi-

VIOLENCE, Page 24

REUTERS PHOTO
Fire engulfs a row of businesses in Los Angeles last night.

Bulger stays the course

No change seen for Senate leader

By Scot Lehigh and Frank Phillips
GLOBE STAFF

SEN. WILLIAM BULGER
In power nearly 14 years

Chester Atkins got the word during a 1984 trip to the Mideast with Senate President William Bulger.

Atkins, then Senate Ways and Means Committee chairman, had his eye on the job Bulger had held for more than five years. According to a source familiar with the conversation, the ambitious young politician used the privacy of the trip to inquire of Bulger just when he might be leaving.

"Bulger said: 'Don't wait on me, I am not leaving. Make your own plans,'" the source said.

Atkins did. Shortly thereafter, he announced for Congress.

Eight years later, Bulger's message – spoken or unspoken – to his would-be successor appears unchanged.

Two weeks ago Senate Ways and Means Committee chairwoman Patricia McGovern, whom many saw as a major contender to succeed Bulger, stunned the State House with the announcement she is not running for reelection, a development that has once again focused attention on the enigmatic Democrat from South Boston.

In a year when, in addition to McGovern, at least two other longtime senators – William Q.

BULGER, Page 12

Perot's sunny press could be due for clouds

By Renee Loth
GLOBE STAFF

In the 69 days since the political radar first picked up his image as a possible presidential candidate, Ross Perot has been on a trajectory of positive press reports that have propelled him to contender status in recent polls.

Without serving a day in public office or even declaring his intentions, the Texas billionaire's un-candidacy eclipsed the likely Democratic nominee, Gov. Bill Clinton of Arkansas, in a poll this week of California voters, and bested President Bush among voters in Texas. A national poll taken by ABC-TV found Perot within 6 points of Bush and one point of Clinton.

But the days are probably numbered before the warm sun of press attention turns into a withering media glare.

■ Clinton picks up support on Capitol Hill. Page 20.

"On the day he announces, he becomes just another politician whether he wants to or not," said Larry Sabato, a press critic and professor at the University of Virginia. At that moment, he said, "there's a race to reveal the warts, and that can become frenzied."

There are signs that a more critical look at Perot already is beginning. This week The New York Times editorialized for more "clarity

PEROT, Page 21

Bill Cosby and Malcolm-Jamal Warner, father and son on "The Cosby Show," perform in the NBC series' finale airing tonight.

To the end, Cosby gives his world a sense of uplift

By Ed Siegel
GLOBE STAFF

Commentary

Tonight's final episode of "The Cosby Show" is a perfect example of what made Bill Cosby the Dr. Spock of a new generation of baby-boom parents and a role model, though not a universally accepted one, for black Americans.

As Cliff Huxtable watches his son, Theo, graduate from college tonight at 8 on NBC, here in microcosm are the emphases on education, family values and personal responsibility that accounted, in large part, for why the program was the most-watched program of the 1980s.

The contributions that Cosby made to the culture are hardly overshadowed by those he made to the medium itself as he proved that white viewers would accept a non-buffoonish black star. It was a far cry from the '70s and early '80s, when the TV landscape was dominated by the likes of Mr. T of "The A-Team" and Sherman Hemsley of "The Jeffersons."

COSBY, Page 8

Patrols seen out of sync with crime

By Tom Coakley
GLOBE STAFF

In the neighborhoods of North Dorchester, Roxbury and Mattapan that make up police Area B, 40 percent of Boston's violent crimes were committed last year. But in an average 24-hour period, only 29 percent of the city's regular patrol units are assigned to that area.

At the same time, according to a Globe review of Police Department figures, in Hyde Park, parts of Mattapan, West Roxbury and Roslindale – police Area E – slightly more than 16 percent of the regular patrol officers work in an average day in an area which had only 10 percent of the city's violent crime in 1991.

The seeming discrepancy between regular patrol forces and violent crime gets to the heart of arguments by some critics that the Boston Police Department unfairly allocates its resources in the city. These critics – City Councilor Charles Yancey and Boston NAACP president

POLICE, Page 9

Taste of disorder

Germany hit by strikes, political feuds

By Jonathan Kaufman
GLOBE STAFF

FRANKFURT – A postal service that won't deliver letters. Buses and trains on strike. A feuding government coalition flirting with collapse.

Germany these days is doing a pretty good imitation of Italy – or of 1970s, strike-ridden Britain.

After more than two years during which it impressed the world with the ease and swagger with which it achieved unification, Germany is finding itself rocked by a wave of strikes and political chaos at the top of its government.

Yesterday, more than 350,000 workers, from bus drivers to computer operators in the German equivalent of the FBI, joined what is becoming a daily escalation of strikes. Garbage piled up in Berlin, uncollected since Saturday. A 6-mile traffic jam tied up Frankfurt, the country's financial center. In Bonn, pickets marched outside the office of Chancellor Helmut Kohl at the German equivalent of the White House.

GERMANY, Page 10

AP PHOTO
A Frankfurt commuter bypasses a massive traffic jam blamed on Germany's ongoing strike.

Inside

CALENDAR: Sociable places

■ **US House bank probe:** The chamber votes to comply with a Justice Department subpoena. Page 3.

■ **Underfortified milk:** Vitamin D shortage is found. Page 14.

■ **Exiled Haitian leader:** Jean-Bertrand Aristide brings his cause to Boston. Page 27.

■ **Red Sox win:** Chicago falls again, 6-1. Sports, Page 35.

FEATURES		CLASSIFIED	
Ask The Globe	44	Classified	62-72
Business	47	Autos	69
Comics	44-45	Help Wanted	66
Deaths	32-33	Real Estate	64
Editorials	16	Apartments	64
Horoscope	44	Comm'l/Ind'l	64
Living/Arts	73	Market Basket	62
Lottery	28	Yachts/Boats	41
Sports	35		
TV/Radio	61		

VOLUME 243 • NUMBER 25
52 pages
35 cents
50 cents at newsstands beyond 30 miles from Boston

The Boston Globe

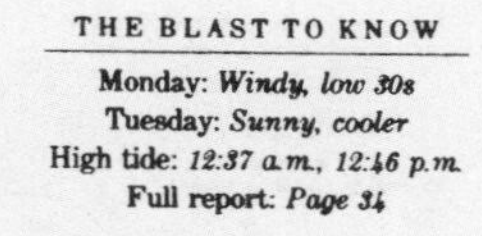
THE BLAST TO KNOW
Monday: *Windy, low 30s*
Tuesday: *Sunny, cooler*
High tide: *12:37 a.m., 12:46 p.m.*
Full report: *Page 34*

MONDAY, JANUARY 25, 1993

Former Justice Marshall dead at 84

Associates, scholars hail contributions

By Dick Lehr
GLOBE STAFF

By his long and wide-ranging career, which took him from the Deep South half a century ago as a civil rights attorney to the US Supreme Court in 1967 as the first black justice, Thurgood Marshall became a doubly powerful symbol, both for black achievement and as a protector of individual rights, many of his clerks said yesterday upon learning of his death.

"He's Mr. Civil Rights, a tremendous hero to lots of people, but especially to black Americans," said Randall L. Kennedy, a Harvard law professor and law clerk for Marshall during the Supreme Court's 1983 term. "I would bet that in some way, any and every black attorney has been influenced by him."

He surely influenced Kennedy, today

CAREER, Page 6

Rights champion served on court 24 years

By Glen Elsasser and Nicholas M. Horrock
CHICAGO TRIBUNE

WASHINGTON – Thurgood Marshall, who championed the causes of the downtrodden, the imprisoned and the defenseless in almost a quarter-century on the Supreme Court, died yesterday at the Bethesda Naval Medical Center near here. He was 84.

Justice Marshall had been scheduled to administer the oath of office to Vice President Al Gore at the inauguration last week but was hospitalized and Associate Justice Byron White filled in for him. Since he retired from the court in July 1991, Mr. Marshall had been in failing health. According to Toni House, spokeswoman for the Surpreme Court, Justice Marshall died of heart failure.

President Clinton said he was "deeply

MARSHALL, Page 6

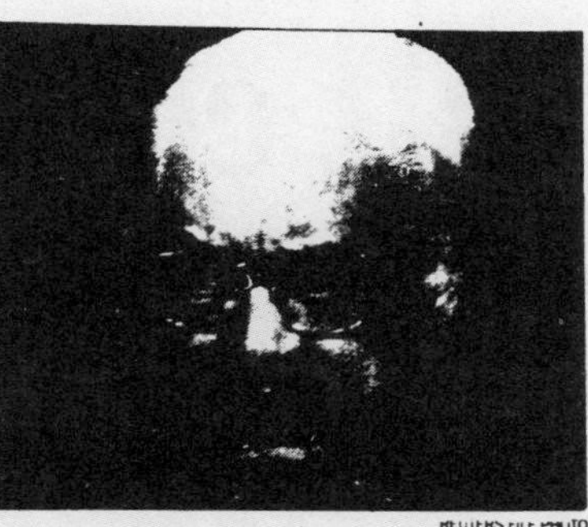
REUTERS FILE PHOTO
THURGOOD MARSHALL . . . argued Brown case

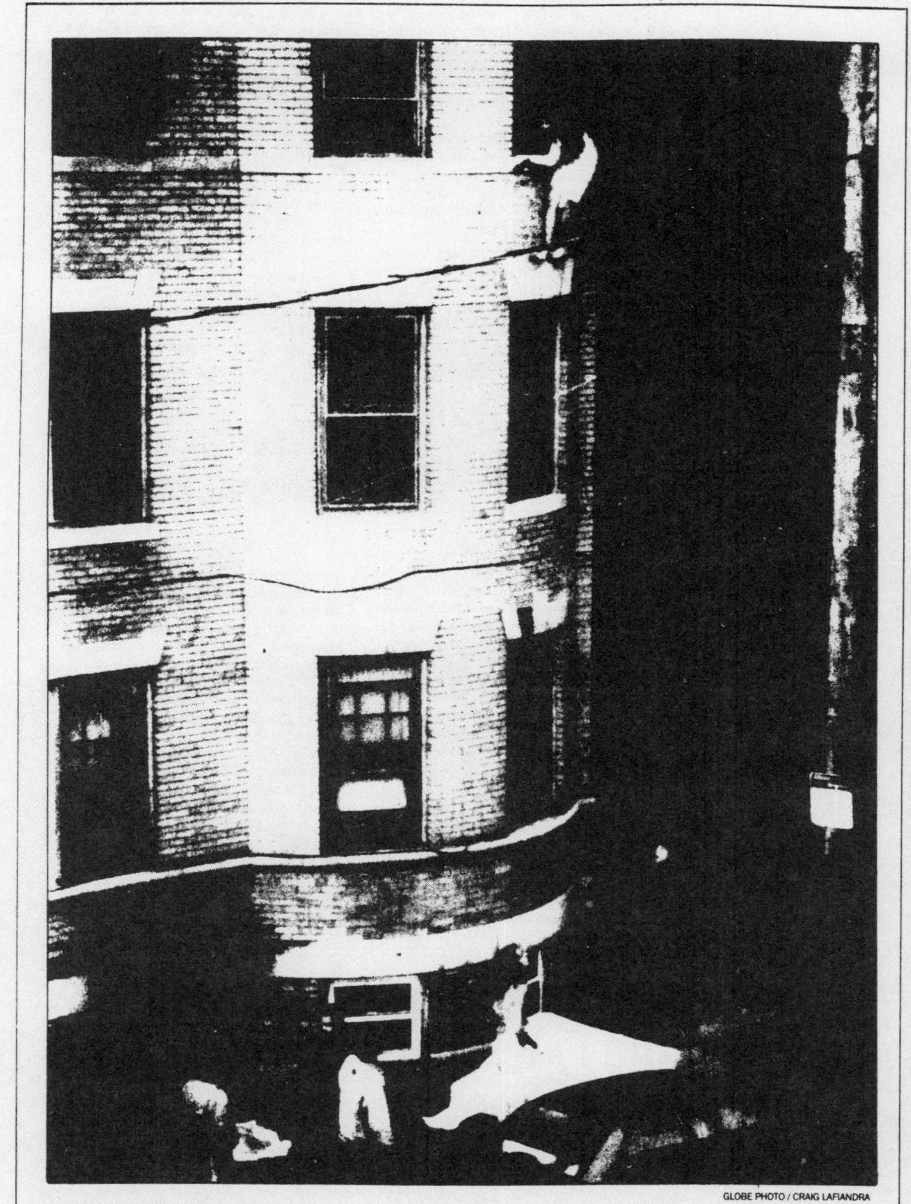
GLOBE PHOTO / CRAIG LAFIANDRA
MOMENTS BEFORE RESCUE – *Jacqueline Olivo balances about 30 feet off the ground yesterday after flames forced her from her third-floor apartment in Brighton. Neighbors placed a mattress beneath her but urged her not to jump. She was helped to safety by a firefighter. Page 14.*

Bentsen hints at energy tax

Also talks of levies on entitlements

By Robert A. Rankin and Steve Marcy
KNIGHT-RIDDER SERVICE

WASHINGTON – Treasury Secretary Lloyd Bentsen hinted strongly yesterday that President Clinton will propose raising taxes on all forms of energy – including gasoline, oil, coal, gas and electricity – as part of his economic program.

Bentsen, speaking on NBC's "Meet the Press," also declined to rule out new taxes on entitlement benefits such as Social Security, and said there would be new taxes on those making more than $200,000 a year.

He all but buried any lingering hope that Clinton will stand by his campaign pledge to cut taxes on the middle class, and also downplayed expectations for expanded tax breaks for Individual Retirement Accounts, a cause he championed as a senator.

Bentsen also said, however, that an economic stimulus plan remains a top priority of the Clinton administration. Even a modest stimulus of about $20 billion will have a "psychological impact" that could make it worthwhile, Bentsen said.

■ Aspin seeks compromise in ending ban on homosexuals in military. Page 5.

Asked whether improving economic data has eliminated the stimulus package as a top priority, Bentsen said, "No, it certainly hasn't. . . . That's still one of the options."

The Bush administration twice was misled by data that apparently showed a recovery, only to see the economy slip each time, Bentsen said.

"Although we're looking at some encouraging numbers now, we want to make sure that that's accurate, and that you're not going to

ECONOMY, Page 5

Mass. House readies new try on overhaul of public schools

By Peter J. Howe
GLOBE STAFF

Despite continuing questions and quibbles from legislators and lobbyists, House Democratic leaders this week will try again to win passage of a sweeping public school bill aimed at ending historic inequalities in the educational opportunities of Massachusetts children.

Legislators are scheduled to meet in party caucuses today for a last round of briefings on the bill, and House Speaker Charles F. Flaherty has pledged to bring it up for floor debate tomorrow.

Despite heavy lobbying by Gov. Weld and state business leaders, House members deemed the bill too complex and controversial to deal with in the closing days of last year's session and decided to hold it over to this week.

Over the past month, the bill's chief sponsor, Rep. Mark Roosevelt (D-Beacon Hill), Education Committee cochairman, has reworked it to address widespread criticisms of

■ A case study in inequity and a look at earlier, failed reforms. Page 16.

the bill's fiscal components, including measures forcing local governments to spend minimum amounts on schools.

But the fundamental goal of the bill is the same: to commit state and local governments to ensuring through increased spending that by 2000 all children in the state – no matter

EDUCATION, Page 16

CITIES THAT WORK

In contrast to Boston, business leaders in many communities feel obliged to boost development. The Globe looks at two cities where that spirit has paid off.

CLEVELAND

By Charles Stein
GLOBE STAFF

CLEVELAND – Listen up, Boston.

This city is building both a baseball stadium and a basketball arena in the heart of downtown. And it didn't take 30 years to make it happen.

The Gateway sports complex, due to open in 1994, is the result of many things: a desire to keep the Indians from leaving, the willingness of 51 percent of the voters to pay higher sin taxes, and last but certainly not least, the solid commitment of the business community.

When Gateway was getting started, business stepped to the plate with a $28 million loan; later, many of the same companies bought $17 million worth of luxu-

CLEVELAND, Page 8

WHO'S IN CHARGE?
Second of three parts

ATLANTA

By Jerry Ackerman
GLOBE STAFF

ATLANTA – Five years have passed since RJR Nabisco told the business establishment here that it wouldn't play ball. New to town and deluged by charities for contributions, the company said no, and publicly. It would not give lavishly; it would not help sponsor special civic events.

Atlanta responded in kind. While RJR Nabisco was here, its executives went uninvited to civic meetings. And when it moved again, last year, to New York, the city wished the company good riddance. "Such neighbors we didn't need then and we don't need now," an Atlanta Constitution columnist wrote.

This story still is being told as one of those exceptions that proves a rule – which, in Atlanta, is that business

ATLANTA, Page 8

Armenians shiver through winter of deprivation

By Jon Auerbach
GLOBE CORRESPONDENT

YEREVAN, Armenia – Doctors and teachers, administrators and factory workers spend the morning yanking rotten planks off a destroyed home on Toumanian Street in downtown Yerevan.

They come here every day, dragging tattered sacks of wood away from the building into the snow-filled streets of the Armenian capital.

They have become scavengers because there is no heat in Armenia. Woodstoves provide about the only constant supply of warmth, though the lucky few who can afford them must rummage through the city hunting for fuel.

Some Armenians receive several hours of electricity each day, giving them enough power to run small heaters. Others get none. The average temperature in a Yerevan home is 35 degrees.

Hot water, for most Armenians, is a fading memory. If the water runs at all, it is ice cold.

The problem of heat, however, is only the tip of the iceberg, as Armenia struggles to survive a winter that even the country's president calls "catastrophic."

Most stores are empty. Kiosks in downtown Yerevan stock four different types of Marlboros, Egyptian candy bars and German beer, yet the prices are unaffordable

ARMENIA, Page 4

Inside

HEALTH & SCIENCE:
Coping with lead in water

■ **Student NewsLine:** The page for young readers examines Maya Angelou's inaugural poem. Page 9.

■ **Labor dispute:** Boston Gas workers say they were told not to report to work after rejecting a contract offer. Page 13.

■ **Data galore:** Consumers losing privacy. Business, Page 17.

FEATURES		CLASSIFIED	
Ask The Globe	22	Classified	45-52
Business	17	Autos	50
Comics	22-23	Help Wanted	47
Deaths	20-21	Real Estate	46
Editorials	10	Apartments	46
Horoscope	22	Comm'l/Ind'l	46
Living/Arts	30	Market Basket	49
Lottery	14	Yachts/Boats	43
Metro/Region	13	Learning	15
Sports	37		
TV/Radio	35		

VOLUME 243 • NUMBER 110
80 pages
35 cents
50 cents at newsstands beyond 20 miles from Boston

The Boston Globe

TUESDAY, APRIL 20, 1993

FAREWELL TO BALMS
Tuesday: *Clouds/sun, windy, 60*
Wednesday: *Mostly cloudy, 60s*
High tide: *11:15 a.m., 11:27 p.m.*
Full report: *Page 68*

Cult compound in Waco set afire; more than 80 are presumed dead

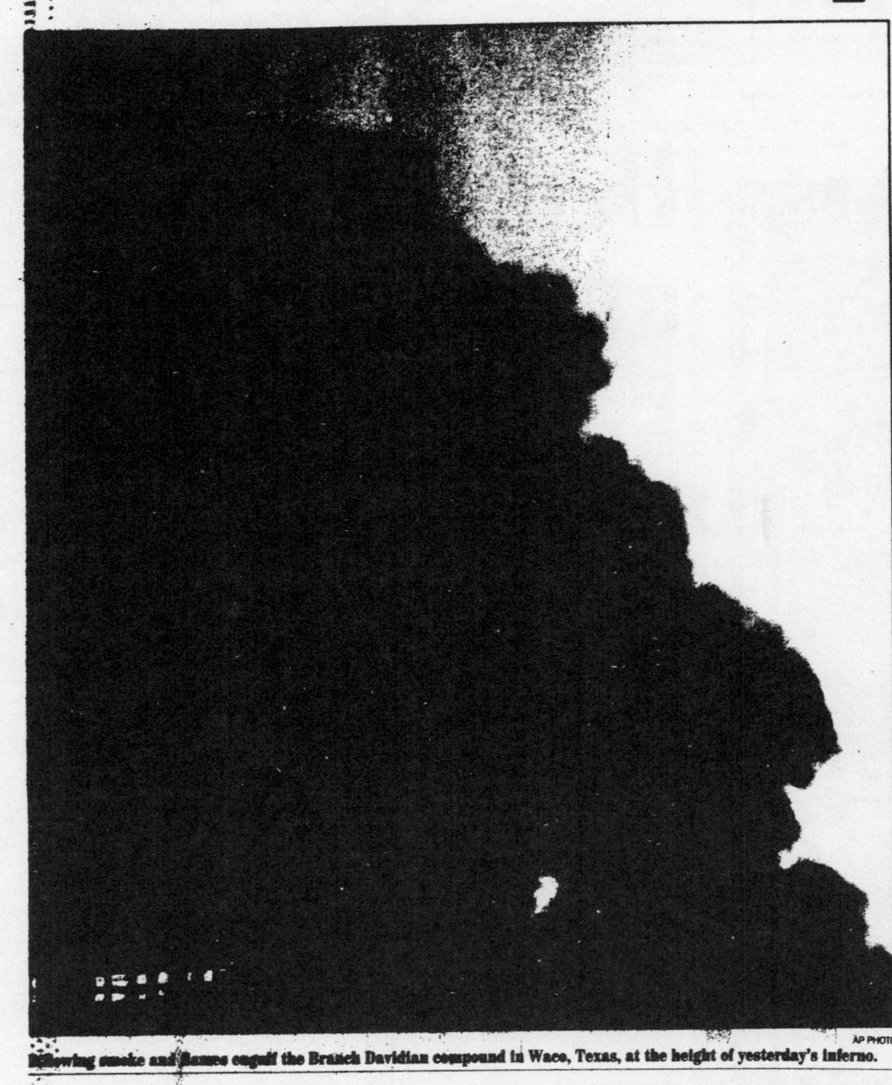
Billowing smoke and flames engulf the Branch Davidian compound in Waco, Texas, at the height of yesterday's inferno. AP PHOTO

A mass suicide, says FBI

By Dan McGraw
SPECIAL TO THE GLOBE

WACO, Texas – Self-proclaimed messiah David Koresh's prophecy of apocalypse was fulfilled yesterday, as the Waco cult leader apparently ended his seven-week standoff with federal agents by ordering his compound set ablaze, killing most of his followers in a mass suicide by fire.

More than 80 of Koresh's followers were presumed dead in the conflagration, which reduced the cult's flimsy frame buildings to smoking embers within 45 minutes. Koresh himself was believed dead, as were the 17 children thought to be living in the communal religious ranch.

"From the very beginning, he said that his followers in that compound would be killed in an armed confrontation with law enforcement," said FBI Agent Bob Ricks several hours after the fire. "He wanted as many people killed in that compound as possible."

"David Koresh gave the order to commit suicide, and they all followed his orders," Ricks added.

The FBI said yesterday that nine of the reported 95 cult members living at the compound escaped the fire. All were hospitalized or being held by law enforcement officials last night.

■ More coverage of the fiery conclusion of the Waco standoff, Pages 6, 8-9.

Ricks identified the survivors as: Graham Craddock; Hymie Castillo; Clyde Doyle; Misty Ferguson, 16; Derek Lovelock; David Thibedeaux; Renos Avraam; Ruth Ellen Ottman; and an unidentified black female.

The fiery conclusion to the 51-day standoff ends one of the most bizarre criminal investigations in US history, one marked by a fierce test of wills between federal agents and Koresh, a ninth-grade dropout whose message of an imminent end of the world attracted followers from around the globe.

The end for the Branch Davidians began

WACO, Page 9

Move was my call, says Reno

By Michael Putzel
GLOBE STAFF

WASHINGTON – President Clinton gave his assent to the FBI's lethal assault on David Koresh's Texas fortress yesterday, but his attorney general quickly insisted that she was responsible for the decision and would answer for it.

Members of Congress were quick to question why the government decided to move against the religious cult after weeks of stalemate and whether sufficient efforts were made to save more than a dozen children who apparently died in the conflagration.

House Judiciary Committee chairman Jack Brooks, a Texas Democrat, asked "whether steps could have been taken to minimize the loss of life." And Rep. Henry Hyde, Republican of Illinois, wondered, "Wasn't there some other way?"

Federal law enforcement and justice officials

FBI, Page 8

Experts fault federal tactics

By Judith Gaines
GLOBE STAFF

The apparent mass deaths in Waco might have been prevented if FBI agents had better understood behavior patterns common to cultists, several specialists on cult behavior said yesterday.

If, as the FBI said, the Branch Davidians torched their compound in Waco, Texas, themselves, apparently committing mass suicide in a fiery Armageddon, they were following behavior patterns common to cultists, the specialists said.

"The whole FBI mentality was wrong, wrong, wrong," said Steven Hassan, of Somerville, a former leader of the Unification Church and author of the book "Combating Cult Mind Control." "They treated the Branch Davidians like criminals, not

CULTS, Page 9

Accent on the 'Dad'

New deal in workplace: Fathers begging off for family time

By Judith Gaines
GLOBE STAFF

Five years ago, Dick Twomey would have thought it would hurt his reputation at work. But this week, when public schools observe spring vacation, Twomey, 42, a director of sales for Blue Cross-Blue Shield, is taking three days vacation to be with his children.

His wife, Rose, is a full-time student working for her master's degree in public health at Boston University. If we didn't share 50-50 in the child rearing, including sometimes cutting into his work hours, Twomey said, "we'd never make it as a couple and a family."

Twomey is one of a still small, but growing, number of New Dads who no longer shy away from asking their bosses if they can leave early, or take days off, to help with the kids.

Perhaps they risk questions about their reliability, their ambition, their dedication to their careers. Regardless, these men say they are taking the time off, and making few apologies for it.

"We've observed more male employees switching off with their wives for half days or alternate days," said Helen Drinan, assistant director of Human Resources at

DADS, Page 12

Pained by past, hopeful about future, Jews and Poles mark ghetto uprising

By Jonathan Kaufman
GLOBE STAFF

WARSAW – They began to fight the morning they were scheduled to die.

The Jewish ghetto in the heart of Warsaw, home to the remnants of the 450,000 Jews herded there by the Nazis, had been surrounded by German soldiers. They planned to liquidate the ghetto, sending the final Jews there to the gas chambers in time for Hitler's birthday on April 20.

At 6 a.m. on April 19, 1943, the troops began marching into the ghetto. A volley of bullets drove them back. For the next month the Jewish fighters battled, block by block, house by house. Frustrated, the Germans systematically blew up and burned every building in the ghetto. Exhausted and without weapons, the Jewish leaders committed suicide. The Germans blew up the biggest synagogue in Warsaw in triumph.

Yesterday, Poles and Israelis, Jews and Catholics gathered in a free Poland to commemorate the 50th anniversary of the ghetto uprising and to begin what many hoped would be a new chapter in the often bitter history of Poles and Jews.

"To all the fighters of the ghetto, those who lived and those who were killed, I say today that you have not

GHETTO, Page 5

Wreaths for Kenyan, Russian

Cosmas N'deti, a 23-year-old Kenyan running only his second marathon, finished first in Boston yesterday, taking the lead with about two miles to go and crossing the line in 2 hours, 9 minutes, 33 seconds. In the women's division, it was Olga Markova of Russia who broke from the pack about 12 miles out and went on to a second straight Boston victory in 2 hours, 25 minutes, 27 seconds.

The Marathon section begins on Page 41.

COSMAS N'DETI OF KENYA

GLOBE STAFF PHOTOS / BILL BRETT
OLGA MARKOVA OF RUSSIA

More inside

■ It was a day for repeats in the wheelchair competition: Jim Knaub raced to his third straight win in the world record time of 1 hour, 22 minutes and 17 seconds while Jean Driscoll also set a record in winning her fourth consecutive Boston race in 1 hour, 36 minutes and 52 seconds. Stories, Page 42.

■ Dopson, Red Sox (10-3 on the season) keep up the pace, shutting down Chicago, 6-0. Page 53.

Inside

BUSINESS EXTRA: The battle for university research dollars

■ **100,000 mourn Hani:** In South Africa yesterday, the funeral of assassinated Communist Party leader Chris Hani in Johannesburg was marked for the most part by restraint as mourners heeded calls by community leaders for a peaceful service. Seven people were killed in sporadic violence. Story, photos, Page 2.

■ **Crisis of violence:** A high school student is stabbed in a classroom by three teen-agers. Behavioral specialists say this should not have come as a surprise: It's a reminder of the deepening crisis of violence among young people. Page 13.

■ **Art and Hanoi:** In a time of gradual liberalization, modern art is coming alive. Page 61.

FEATURES	
Ask The Globe	70
Business	21
Comics	70-71
Deaths	18-19
Editorials	10
Horoscope	70
Living/Arts	61
Lottery	14
Metro/Region	13
Sports	53
TV/Radio	69

CLASSIFIED	
Classified	73-80
Autos	78
Help Wanted	76
Real Estate	73
Apartments	74
Comm'l/Ind'l	39
Market Basket	77
Yachts/Boats	59
Learning	72

VOLUME 243 • NUMBER 162
80 pages
35 cents
50 cents at newsstands beyond 30 miles from Boston

The Boston Globe

DRY RUN
Friday: Sun, clouds, 70-80
Saturday: Mostly sunny, 65-75
High tide: 4:49 a.m., 5:25 p.m.
Full report: Page 78

FRIDAY, JUNE 11, 1993

N.Y. Times to acquire The Globe

Independent news and management policies to remain

By Doug Bailey and Charles Stein
GLOBE STAFF

The Boston Globe, New England's largest newspaper, yesterday accepted an offer to merge with The New York Times in a deal worth an estimated $1.1 billion, the largest newspaper sale in history.

The $15-a-share deal would leave the Globe a wholly-owned subsidiary of the Times but with its management intact and possessing "full editorial autonomy," the companies said last night. No layoffs or changes in employee benefits are planned. Globe publisher William O. Taylor said Globe readers "should not detect any change."

The agreement was approved by the boards of both papers yesterday.

Highlights of agreement

- **New York Times Co. pays $1.1 billion, or $15 a share, for Globe's parent company, Affiliated Publications Inc.**
- **Globe Newspaper Co. becomes a wholly-owned subsidiary of the New York Times, with its own board of directors.**
- **Globe retains full editorial autonomy.**
- **No layoffs, and no changes in benefits for employees.**

The new Globe board of directors will be controlled by the Times, ending the newspaper's legacy of family control stretching back to 1872 when a group of Boston businessmen invested $150,000 to launch the paper.

The Globe, one of the last major independent newspapers in the country, was driven toward the merger by the impending expiration of two family trusts that share controlling voting power over its parent corporation, Affiliated Publications Inc. If the trusts had expired in January 1996, a divisive, potentially damaging bidding war might have ensued for control of the paper.

Timing aside, the publishers of both papers stressed the papers' many similar qualities: editorial quality, independence, and a long history of family control.

Taylor, the great-grandson of the paper's first

GLOBE, Page 12

GLOBE STAFF PHOTO / BILL BRETT
William O. Taylor (left) and Arthur O. Sulzberger last night.

Powell says gay issue is solvable

Quiet protest greets general at Harvard

By Alice Dembner and Tom Coakley
GLOBE STAFF

CAMBRIDGE – Capping daylong festivities marked by low-key protests of his position against gays in the military, Gen. Colin Powell yesterday told more than 30,000 people gathered for Harvard University's 342d commencement that the armed forces would resolve the question of gays in the military as it had controversies over racism and sexism.

To thunderous applause, the chairman of the Joint Chiefs of Staff added, "The president has given us a clear directive to reconcile these issues, and I believe we are near a solution that will do so. Whatever is decided, I can assure you that the decision will be faithfully executed."

At a press conference after the ceremonies, Powell said that two groups, one comprised of Pentagon civilians and the other from the Rand Corp., a private think tank, have prepared studies on the gay ban. He said that he and other military leaders would recommend a new policy to President Clinton by the president's deadline of July 15.

He refused to detail what policy might evolve but said it will be a "fair" one.

David Mixner, a gay senior adviser to Clinton during the presidential campaign, said he was pleased with Powell's remarks and heartened by his pledge to adhere to the presi-

HARVARD, Page 22

GLOBE STAFF PHOTO / BARRY CHIN
Gen. Colin Powell talks to Scott Cohen, who led a faculty protest of Powell at Harvard's commencement.

Court nod expected for Breyer

Clinton, Boston judge to meet

By Michael Kranish and Dick Lehr
GLOBE STAFF

WASHINGTON – President Clinton is expected to nominate federal appellate judge Stephen G. Breyer of Boston to the Supreme Court if all goes well when the two men meet today, White House aides said last night.

Yesterday, White House officials interviewed Breyer in a Cambridge hospital where he was recuperating from injuries sustained in a bicycle accident.

A White House official said last night that the meeting went well and Clinton invited Breyer to lunch at the White House today. The two men have not previously met.

Discharged from Mount Auburn Hospital, Breyer was on his way to Washington last night, the official said.

"There is a clear pattern here," said a second aide, speaking on condition of anonymity. "It's always possible something could come up," the official said, noting Clinton's penchant for changing his mind. "But things are obviously moving in his direction."

With a variety of Democrats and Republicans publicly predicting yesterday that Breyer will be nominated, an announcement is expected as soon as today or tomorrow, officials said. Meanwhile, the other main contender, Interior Secretary Bruce Babbitt, told associates that he felt his chances were slipping away, a source said.

White House sources said that yesterday's bedside interview at Mount Auburn Hospital was the second-to-last step in the formal clearance process of Breyer. The senior official last night knew of nothing from that interview that might derail the process. The final step would be an interview with the president.

A source close to Breyer said that after the judge's eight hours of meetings with White House aides yesterday, there was no question in his mind that Clinton intended to nominate Breyer "or else he

COURT, Page 9

US commits 300 troops to conflict in Balkans

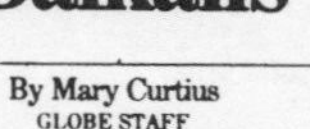

By Mary Curtius
GLOBE STAFF

ATHENS – Seeking to demonstrate that the Clinton administration will continue to lead the NATO alliance, Secretary of State Warren M. Christopher announced yesterday that the United States will send 300 troops to the former Yugoslav republic of Macedonia to guard against a widening of the Balkan war.

The conflict in Bosnia "must not be allowed to spill over," Christopher told NATO foreign ministers, who opened two days of talks yesterday morning in the Greek capital. "It is essential that everyone in the region understand that aggression against ... Macedonia would have grave consequences," Christopher warned.

A senior Pentagon official said the troops can be dispatched to Macedonia within two weeks. The official, who spoke to reporters on condition of anonymity, said no decision

CHRISTOPHER, Page 7

Inside

SPORTS PLUS: Ballpark ads

- **Double feature:** "Jurassic Park" is as big as its dinosaurs and "What's Love Got to Do with It" is the best musical biopic since "Coal Miner's Daughter," says film critic Jay Carr. Living/Arts, Page 41.
- **Funding vow:** Hillary Rodham Clinton reassures hospitals and medical schools on health-care reform. Page 10.
- **Sox fall again:** Orioles top Boston, 2-1. Sports, Page 25.

FEATURES		CLASSIFIED	
Ask The Globe	76	Classified	65-75, 80
Business	57	Autos	71
Comics	76-77	Help Wanted	68
Deaths	38-39	Real Estate	66
Editorials	14	Apartments	67
Horoscope	76	Comm'l/Ind'l	67
Living/Arts	41	Market Basket	66
Lottery	18	Yachts/Boats	33
Metro/Region	17	Learning	33, 40
Sports	25		
TV/Radio	79		

Newton weighs ban of BC game parking

By Bob Hohler
GLOBE STAFF

After decades of town-gown bliss, Newton has officially turned a cold shoulder to Boston College's booming football program by proposing to ban public parking on game days.

In a move that officials in Boston and Brookline said could prompt similar action in their communities, Newton's aldermanic public safety committee voted 5-0 Wednesday to prohibit on-street parking within a mile of BC's Alumni Stadium in Chestnut Hill.

"Newton is not going to be a parking lot for Boston College anymore," said Alderman Eric MacLeish, who declared the vote a reflection of the city's reaction to BC's plan to expand 32,500-seat Alumni Stadium by 12,000 seats.

Meanwhile, the Boston Redevelopment Authority's executive director said yesterday he will ask BC to pay for an independent transportation consultant to review the stadium expansion plan.

"I have some serious questions about how BC expects to reduce traffic by 30 percent" while increasing

BOSTON COLLEGE, Page 11

A ghost of war

Sunken Nazi sub reportedly found off Cape

By David Arnold
GLOBE STAFF

The wreck of a German U-boat with the remains of more than 50 sailors and spies aboard has been located in 41 feet of water four miles east of Cape Cod, according to a commercial diver from Framingham.

Edward Michaud says he found the wreck of the U-1226 Saturday after three years of research into a submarine whose mission had been to drop Nazi spies on the US coast.

The only other wreck of a Nazi submarine in American waters known to Victor Mastone, director of the state Board of Underwater Archeological Resources, is the U-853, for decades the target of recreational divers in 130 feet of water about five miles south of Point Judith, R.I.

Michaud has a "proven track record of reliability," said Mastone.

"What would make this discovery particularly significant is that the sub apparently was on a spy mission. We may learn a lot about what was going on toward the end of the war," Mastone said.

The U-1226 was sunk Oct. 28, 1944, after the submarine commander used an emergency Coast Guard frequency to radio information to Germany.

During the Morse code transmission, a recruit at the Chatham Coast Guard base broke in to demand silence, initially thinking a careless local mariner was abusing the frequency's emergency status, according to Michaud.

The commander ignored the warning

SUBMARINE, Page 11

Red Sox lose second straight in Milwaukee, 3-2, drop to third place - Page 49

VOLUME 244 • NUMBER 28
72 pages
35 cents
50 cents at newsstands beyond 30 miles from Boston

The Boston Globe

SUMMER ALL YEARS
Wednesday: *Humid, windy, 85-90*
Thursday: *Humid, may shower, 85*
High tide: *7:26 a.m., 7:47 p.m.*
Full report: *Page 28*

WEDNESDAY, JULY 28, 1993

'I knew that this was a difficult case, and I prepared myself if it went the other way. None of us were seeking revenge. . . .'
FRANCIS X. FOLEY
Bomb blast victim

Shay guilty in fatal '91 blast

By Matthew Brelis
GLOBE STAFF

A federal jury yesterday found Thomas A. Shay, 21, guilty of plotting with an engineer friend to plant a bomb under his father's car that killed one Boston police officer and seriously wounded another in 1991.

The jury, which deliberated for 13 hours over three days, found Shay, of Quincy, guilty of conspiring with Alfred Trenkler, 36, of Quincy to kill Shay's father, Thomas L. Shay.

Jurors also found Shay guilty of aiding and abetting in the attempted malicious destruction of the car, causing the death of bomb squad officer Jeremiah J. Hurley Jr. – a charge that carries a maximum penalty of life in prison.

Shay was acquitted of a third charge of receiving explosives.

US District Judge Rya Zobel scheduled sentencing for Oct. 6 and ordered Shay to remain jailed without bail.

Officer Francis X. Foley, who lost an eye and was permanently disabled by the Oct. 28, 1991, blast in the driveway of the elder Shay's Roslindale home that killed his partner, hung on the edge of his seat as

SHAY, Page 20

Brokerage firm fires top official

Advised MWRA on bond dealings

By Stephen Kurkjian
GLOBE STAFF

Mark S. Ferber, the leading light in municipal finance in Massachusetts, was fired yesterday as vice chairman of First Albany Corp. following a week of controversy over his engaging in possible conflicts of interest.

The company, which hired Ferber in February, announced the action without explanation in a one-paragraph statement issued after the stock market had closed.

The announcement read: "First Albany Companies, Inc., the parent of First Albany Corporation, a regional brokerage and investment banking firm, announced today that the company's Board of Directors voted to terminate the employment of Mark S. Ferber, who had served as its vice chairman since February."

One source close to the company said First Albany had been rocked by the controversy generated by recent disclosures regarding Ferber. "They were badly hurt and they wanted to stop the hemorrhaging as best they could," the source said. "Apparently, they believed this was the quickest way to deal with the situation." Last week, the Massachusetts Water Resources Authority fired First Albany as its financial adviser.

Edward G. Novotny, a New York public relations executive hired by

FERBER, Page 7

Celtics captain Lewis dies after collapse while shooting

GLOBE STAFF FILE PHOTO / BILL BRETT
The Celtics captain's playing style: Reggie Lewis leaps for the ball against Cleveland last season.

Cardiac arrest death comes 3 months after playoff illness

By Peter May
GLOBE STAFF

WALTHAM – Boston Celtics captain Reggie Lewis collapsed while shooting baskets at Brandeis University yesterday and was pronounced dead 2½ hours later at Waltham-Weston Hospital.

Lewis, who had been slow to return to any kind of vigorous basketball since he collapsed in a playoff game three months ago, was pronounced dead at the Waltham hospital at 7:30 p.m. The official announcement was delayed for almost three hours, sources said, because the Celtics had trouble locating Lewis' mother, Inez, who lives in Baltimore.

Witnesses at Brandeis said Lewis, 27, was doing some light shooting with a ballboy rebounding for him when he suddenly slumped to the floor about 5:05 p.m.

Amir Weiss, a Brandeis junior shooting baskets on the adjacent court, said Lewis seemed content until he suddenly slumped to the floor and stopped breathing.

Brandeis police were summoned and arrived about 10 minutes later; seven minutes after that, paramedics arrived and found Lewis in cardiac arrest. They administered advanced cardiac life support measures until 5:30 p.m., when they took Lewis by ambulance to the hospital's emergency room, less than ¼ mile from the gymnasium, arriving at 5:41 p.m.

Resuscitation efforts continued unsuccessfully for 1 hour and 50 minutes. Dr. Mary Anne McGinn of the hospital staff made the announcement of Lewis' death. Hospital staff declined to take questions from the media, saying the family

LEWIS, Page 19

The aftermath: grief and debate

■ A dispute is renewed over diagnoses. Page 18.
■ Malpractice, liability questions raised. Page 18.
■ Stunned Celtics mourn captain. Sports, Page 49.
■ Poignant memories remain. Sports, Page 49.
■ Related stories are on Pages 18, 19, 54.

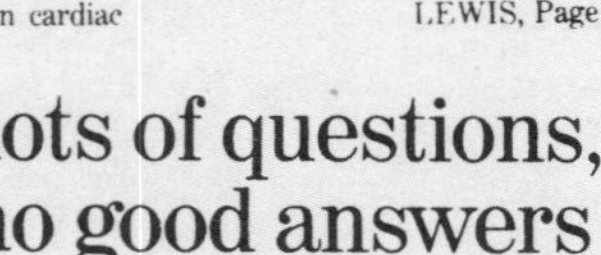

We have lots of questions, we have no good answers

By Dan Shaughnessy
GLOBE STAFF

Commentary

Reggie Lewis knew. The doctors and lawyers and self-serving Celtic team officials hemmed and hawed about all of this, but from the very first moment, Lewis knew how serious this was. An hour or two after he collapsed on the parquet floor during a playoff game this spring, he told the Globe's Jackie MacMullan, "Yeah, I was scared. I started having flashbacks to that Hank Gathers thing."

Gathers, a college standout at the University of Loyola-Marymount, died of a heart arrhythmia in March 1990.

Last night, two months after he got a hand-delivered warning, Lewis died while playing basketball at the Brandeis University gym in Waltham.

Why?

Why did Reggie Lewis have to die? Was basketball that important? Did egos get in the way? Did legal exposure get in the way? Did the head-in-the-sand Celtics try too hard

SHAUGHNESSY, Page 19

Clinton orders Christopher home amid US fears over Mideast

By Mary Curtius
GLOBE STAFF

WASHINGTON – President Clinton ordered Secretary of State Warren Christopher yesterday to cut short his Asian trip and return to Washington, amid growing concern that fighting between Israel and the Iranian-backed Hezbollah in southern Lebanon might derail peace negotiations and lead to a wider conflict.

Israeli artillery and aircraft pounded away again yesterday, and Hezbollah forces fired more rockets into northern Israel. More than 47 people have been killed and 240 wounded since the Israeli assault began on Sunday, according to the Associated Press. Most of the dead and wounded were Lebanese.

Reuters reported that 20 people were feared dead under a bomb shelter that collapsed in the Lebanese village of Majdel Salim, which was raided by planes. Rescuers were unable to reach the shelter because of intense fire.

With the continued heavy fighting, hundreds of thousands of civilians on both sides of the border have fled. Lebanese packed up their belongings and headed north. Israeli children were evacuated south, and tens of thousands of Israelis were ordered to stay in bomb shelters overnight.

"I have been following the dramatic escalation of violence in southern Lebanon and northern Israel with great concern and I will be discussing the impact of these events on the peace process," Christopher told reporters traveling with him before his sudden departure from Singapore yesterday.

The unusual decision to interrupt Christopher's trip underscored the deep concern within the Clinton administration that fighting between Israel and Hezbollah might spiral out of control. Syria, with some 40,000 troops in Lebanon, is allied

MIDEAST, Page 8

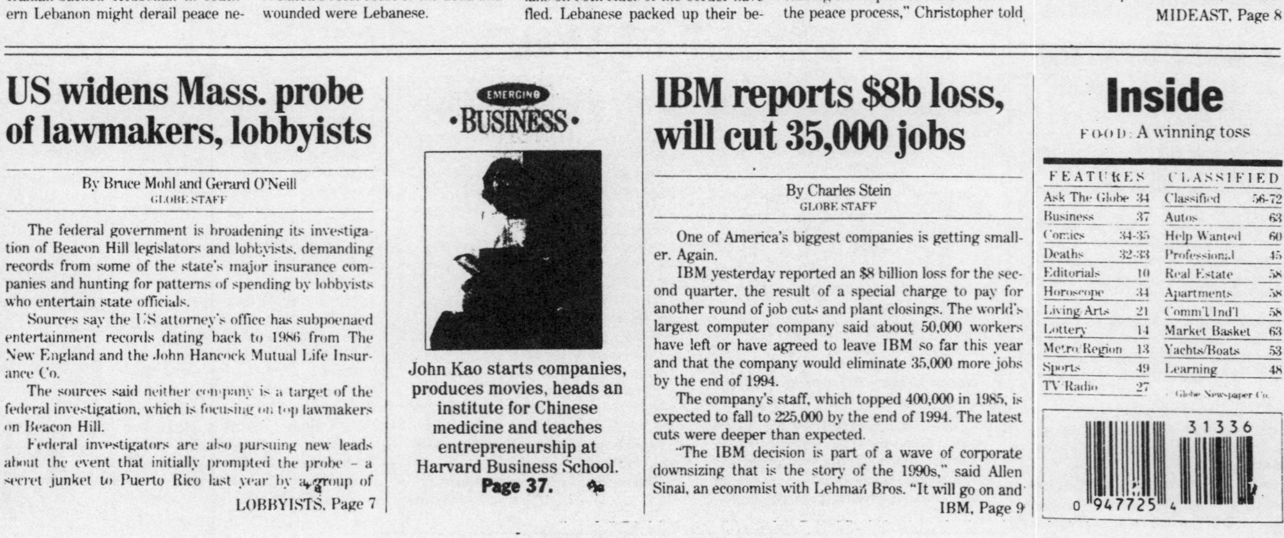

US widens Mass. probe of lawmakers, lobbyists

By Bruce Mohl and Gerard O'Neill
GLOBE STAFF

The federal government is broadening its investigation of Beacon Hill legislators and lobbyists, demanding records from some of the state's major insurance companies and hunting for patterns of spending by lobbyists who entertain state officials.

Sources say the US attorney's office has subpoenaed entertainment records dating back to 1986 from The New England and the John Hancock Mutual Life Insurance Co.

The sources said neither company is a target of the federal investigation, which is focusing on top lawmakers on Beacon Hill.

Federal investigators are also pursuing new leads about the event that initially prompted the probe – a secret junket to Puerto Rico last year by a group of

LOBBYISTS, Page 7

EMERGING
•BUSINESS•

John Kao starts companies, produces movies, heads an institute for Chinese medicine and teaches entrepreneurship at Harvard Business School.
Page 37.

IBM reports $8b loss, will cut 35,000 jobs

By Charles Stein
GLOBE STAFF

One of America's biggest companies is getting smaller. Again.

IBM yesterday reported an $8 billion loss for the second quarter, the result of a special charge to pay for another round of job cuts and plant closings. The world's largest computer company said about 50,000 workers have left or have agreed to leave IBM so far this year and that the company would eliminate 35,000 more jobs by the end of 1994.

The company's staff, which topped 400,000 in 1985, is expected to fall to 225,000 by the end of 1994. The latest cuts were deeper than expected.

"The IBM decision is part of a wave of corporate downsizing that is the story of the 1990s," said Allen Sinai, an economist with Lehman Bros. "It will go on and

IBM, Page 9

Inside

FOOD: A winning toss

FEATURES		CLASSIFIED	
Ask The Globe	34	Classified	56-72
Business	37	Autos	63
Comics	34-35	Help Wanted	60
Deaths	32-33	Professional	45
Editorials	10	Real Estate	58
Horoscope	34	Apartments	58
Living Arts	21	Comm'l Ind'l	58
Lottery	14	Market Basket	63
Metro/Region	13	Yachts/Boats	53
Sports	49	Learning	48
TV/Radio	27		

31336
0 947725 4

Globe/WBZ-TV poll shows Menino in lead, three closest rivals bunched - story below

VOLUME 244 • NUMBER 76
72 pages
35 cents
50 cents at newsstands beyond 30 miles from Boston

The Boston Globe

NEAR BARE
Tuesday: *Sunny, breezy; near 90*
Wednesday: *Partly sunny; 80s*
High tide: *10:05 a.m., 10:25 p.m.*
Full report: *Page 68*

TUESDAY, SEPTEMBER 14, 1993

A handshake for history

AP PHOTO

Sealing their accord with a handshake are Israeli Prime Minister Yitzhak Rabin and Yasser Arafat, the chairman of the Palestine Liberation Organization. President Clinton presides over yesterday's ceremonies.

A great milestone is passed and a hard journey continues

By David Shribman
GLOBE STAFF

News Analysis

WASHINGTON – Years from now, yesterday's tableau in the Washington sun – the grave faces surrounding the big desk, the somber men signing their names for their people and for posterity – will have the tint of history.

That picture, the snapshot seen round the world, will stand as a symbol of the brave hopes of warriors turned peacemakers. That moment, and the sense of moment, has already been engraved in memory.

The leaders of the world's oldest lands flew to the New World to seek a new start in a ceremony freighted with poignancy. And yet for all the high-flown words exchanged in that hour in the globe's spotlight, one phrase from Israeli Prime Minister Yitzhak Rabin, stark but true, stood out: "It's not so easy."

It was not so easy – the journey from the battlefront to the peace table, the negotiations with enemies and then with allies,

PROSPECTS, Page 3

Rabin and Arafat witness accord in an emotional reach for peace

By Mary Curtius
GLOBE STAFF

WASHINGTON – Reaching across decades of hatred and bloodshed, PLO chief Yasser Arafat and Israeli Prime Minister Yitzhak Rabin yesterday shook hands in front of the eyes of the world after witnessing an Israeli-Palestinian peace accord.

The historic agreement between Israel and the Palestine Liberation Organization lays out a plan for limited self-rule in territory Israel captured in 1967. Gaza and the West Bank town of Jericho will experiment with local autonomy first.

At one point, his voice heavy with emotion, Rabin spoke directly to the Palestinian people: "We say to you today in a loud and a clear voice: 'Enough of blood and tears. Enough!' "

■ **Other stories on the Israeli-Palestinian pact are on Pages 2-7.**

It was Arafat who offered the first symbolic gesture of reconciliation between two peoples struggling over one piece of land. He reached exuberantly for Rabin's hand after the accord was signed by Foreign Minister Shimon Peres and PLO executive committee member Mahmoud Abbas.

Rabin hesitated, unsmiling, until President Clinton gently placed a hand on his back and appeared to nudge him forward. As the soldier touched hands with the guerrilla leader he openly despises, appreciative gasps, then a ripple of applause rose from the audience.

It was the most exciting occurrence in a carefully choreographed ceremony held on the White House lawn and broadcast around the world.

MIDEAST, Page 3

Brett, Salerno, Rufo fight for 2d in survey

By Brian McGrory
GLOBE STAFF

Thomas M. Menino, apparently lifted by strong public regard for his performance as acting mayor, has risen atop the crowded field of mayoral candidates with just a week to the preliminary election, leaving his three closest rivals bunched together in a statistical tie for second place, according to a Boston Globe/WBZ-TV poll.

The poll marks Menino's debut as a front-runner – and is the first published survey not led by City Councilor Rosaria Salerno – in an election that increasingly appears based not on issue stands and ideology but political organization and the ability to solidify a natural base of support.

Menino was favored by 22 percent of the poll respondents, followed by state Rep. James T. Brett at 16 percent, Salerno at 15 percent and Suffolk County Sheriff Robert

POLL, Page 20

Favorite candidate

Q: If the preliminary election for mayor of Boston were held tomorrow, for whom would you vote?

Menino	22%
Brett	16%
Salerno	15%
Rufo	11%
Lydon	6%
Roache	5%
Bolling	4%
Moriarty	1%
Don't know	16%
Refused	5%

SOURCE: KRC/Communications Research survey of 400 Boston residents, conducted Sept. 11-12: poll has a margin of error of ± 5 percent. Because of rounding, percentages do not add to 100 percent.

READER FEEDBACK

Boston's mayoral candidates have debated whether the National Guard should be brought into the city to help fight crime. What do you say?

Call 617-929-2033
Answers will be limited to 30 seconds.

Note: This is an unscientific survey. A sampling of reader opinion will be published on Thursday

Clinton eases ban on trade with Vietnam

By Thomas W. Lippman
WASHINGTON POST

WASHINGTON – President Clinton relaxed the ban on trade with Vietnam yesterday to allow US firms to bid on development projects there financed by the World Bank and other international agencies. But Clinton retained the embargo on most commercial dealings.

His action nudged the United States a bit closer to ending the hostile relations with Hanoi that go back more than a generation, but signaled that Clinton is still not fully satisfied with Vietnam's cooperation in the search for US servicemen still missing from the war.

The United States has diplomats in Hanoi, military teams roaming Vietnam to search for remains of missing soldiers and airmen and Pentagon researchers in the Vietnamese government archives. The State Department agreed yesterday to provide $3.5 million in additional US aid funds for a project to supply prosthetic devices for Vietnamese amputees.

But "we still haven't seen enough" cooperation in the search for the missing "to feel comfortable in lifting the embargo altogether," a White House official said.

The National League of Families of American Prisoners and Missing in Southeast Asia, condemned Clinton's action, saying Clinton was "deceived by the bureaucracy" into reporting progress when there is none.

VIETNAM, Page 10

For TV's legal giant, the verdict is 'unique'

By Joseph P. Kahn
GLOBE STAFF

Appreciation

Once upon a time in the land of popular entertainment, when lawyers were not getting munched by dinosaurs, recruited by the Mafia or negotiating sleazy property settlements, there was a figure of such consummate integrity and towering ingenuity that he set back public understanding of the American legal system by a minimum of 50 years.

His name, of course, was Perry Mason, a character created by author Erle Stanley Gardner and portrayed on television for more than 35 years by actor Raymond Burr.

Burr, 76, who died of liver cancer at his Northern California ranch Sunday night, appeared in scores of roles during his long Hollywood career, beginning on radio in the 1940s and followed by a series of menacing heavies he played in B-movies in the '40s and

BURR, Page 8

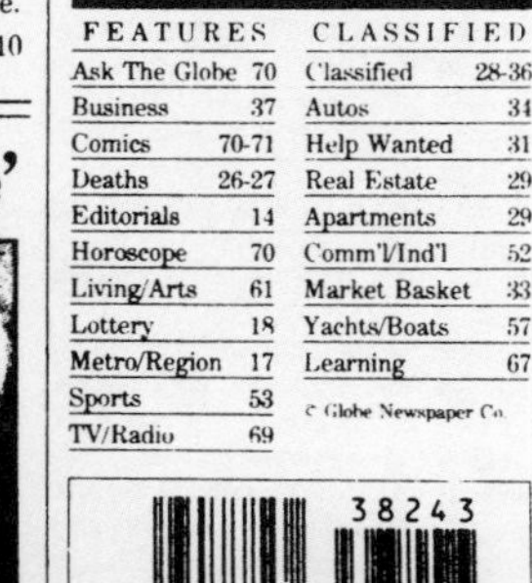

RAYMOND BURR

Inside

BUSINESS EXTRA:
Viacom's new script

■ **Charge dropped:** A Brookline woman, 87, goes free. Page 17.

■ **Red Sox win:** Tim Naehring sparks a 6-4 comeback over Baltimore. Sports, Page 53.

■ **Blacks on television:** Stereotypes raise concern. Living/Arts, Page 61.

FEATURES		CLASSIFIED	
Ask The Globe	70	Classified	28-36
Business	37	Autos	34
Comics	70-71	Help Wanted	31
Deaths	26-27	Real Estate	29
Editorials	14	Apartments	29
Horoscope	70	Comm'l/Ind'l	52
Living/Arts	61	Market Basket	33
Lottery	18	Yachts/Boats	57
Metro/Region	17	Learning	67
Sports	53		
TV/Radio	69		

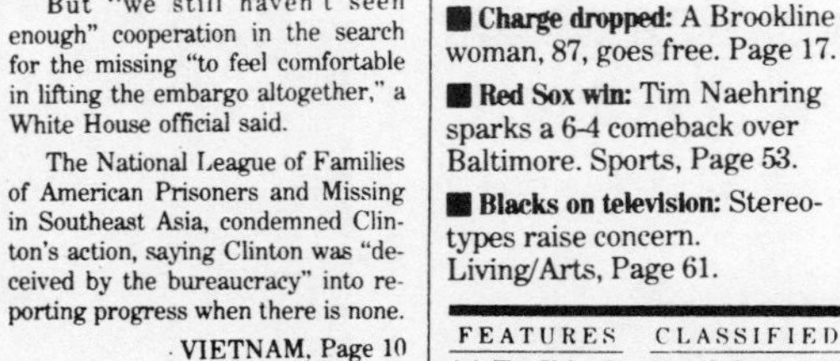

38243
0 947725 4

VOLUME 245 • NUMBER 6
124 pages
35 cents
50 cents at newsstands beyond 30 miles from Boston

The Boston Globe

ONE SIGH FITS ALL
Thursday: *Clouding up. 25*
Friday: *Snow likely. 30*
High tide: *5:30 a.m., 6:04 p.m.*
Full report: *Page 52*

THURSDAY, JANUARY 6, 1994

Ex-Speaker O'Neill dies

Took local view to national stage

By Martin F. Nolan
GLOBE STAFF

Thomas P. (Tip) O'Neill Jr., the North Cambridge politician whose sagacity, self-confidence and charm propelled him to the heights of American politics as speaker of the US House, died of cardiac arrest yesterday at 9:43 p.m. in Brigham and Women's Hospital surrounded by family members. He was 81.

His son, Thomas P. O'Neill 3d, told hospital administrators Mr. O'Neill died peacefully.

Mr. O'Neill represented Cambridge, Somerville, part of Boston and other communities in the House from 1953 until his retirement in 1987. During his last decade in office, he also served as speaker, in the longest unbroken tenure ever in that office.

Historians have ranked him as a strong speaker in the tradition of Henry Clay, Thomas Brackett Reed, Joseph G. Cannon and Sam Rayburn.

On learning of his death, the White House issued a statement saying, "Former

O'NEILL, Page 18

Compassion was his way of life

By Mike Barnicle
GLOBE STAFF

Commentary

He was a wonderfully warm man in an increasingly cold business – politics – with a big heart that was too often surrounded by small minds. He was an old-fashioned fellow who fought all the new fights with more stamina than people half his age. He walked with kings, popes and presidents but his step was never lighter, nor his contagious laugh louder than when he was surrounded by the faces that had followed him as friend across all 81 years of a marvelous life that ended last night when death called on Tip O'Neill.

He was a big, bear of a man who could often resemble a load of laundry walking the corridor of the Capitol or along Russell

COMMENTARY, Page 18

AP PHOTO

Thomas P. O'Neill Jr. in a 1991 portrait. Personal chronology and reaction to his death, Pages 18-19.

Bids may drive price of Patriots to NFL peak

2 suitors would keep team here

By Will McDonough
and Frank Phillips
GLOBE STAFF

The New England Patriots will claim the highest price ever paid for an NFL franchise at the conclusion of a bidding process that includes two groups that would keep the team in Massachusetts, sources said yesterday.

As legislators prepare to debate a taxpayer-subsidized $700 million Boston convention center and football stadium that would house the Patriots, sources close to the sales process said that up to five bids for the Patriots have been submitted to owner James B. Orthwein, a St. Louis businessman.

What appear to be the two leading bids have come from St. Louis businessman Stan Kroenke and Robert K. Kraft, a Boston developer and the owner of Foxboro Stadium.

Sources said Kraft has made a no-strings-attached bid of approximately $160 million, while Kroenke's bid ranges between $180 million and $200 million. Kroenke's bid comes with certain conditions, the sources said, which would drop the actual value of the bid below that of Kraft's.

Another bid was submitted by Jeff Lurie, a Hollywood producer with Boston roots. Sources said other bidders include an unidentified Baltimore group of investors and a group from Hartford.

MEGAPLEX, Page 16

READER FEEDBACK

Proponents of a $700 million megaplex development say it would be a largely self-supporting boon to the region's economy. Opponents say it would be an expensive boondoggle, with the public left shouldering much of its cost. Do you believe that building the megaplex is in the region's best interest?

Call 617-474-2525

A sampling of reader opinion will be published on Saturday.

North Korea has accepted atom inspections, US says

By Paul Quinn-Judge
GLOBE STAFF

WASHINGTON – The Clinton administration said yesterday that North Korea has agreed to international inspection of its nuclear facilities, but the announcement left open the question of just how much access inspectors would get.

Despite pointed questioning at a press briefing, Lynn Davis, the undersecretary of state for security affairs, refused to say explicitly that Pyongyang had agreed to the resumption of regular inspections by the International Atomic Energy Agency.

The IAEA, which has combed Iraq for nuclear-weapons facilities since the end of the 1991 Gulf War, relies on frequent and surprise inspections in its detection work. Nations intent on hiding their bomb-making infrastructure could elude inspectors as Saddam Hussein initially tried to do – by limiting access, shuttling nuclear equipment around the country and building dummy facilities.

Davis also acknowledged that there had been no progress in gaining international access to two suspected nuclear waste sites that could provide vital evidence about the status of the North Korean nuclear program.

KOREA, page 6

The Omniflox case exposes a fundamental flaw in the process that is supposed to guarantee the safety of new medications

Stakes high in clinical drug trials

By Daniel Golden
GLOBE STAFF

SPECIAL REPORT

When Rayna Carr went to the emergency room with a skin rash, she was given free samples of a newly-approved antibiotic.

As it turned out, she paid a steep price for them.

Carr nearly died from the side effects of the pills, marketed as Omniflox. Twenty months later, the 47-year-old Maine woman takes four painkillers and a hot bath every night to soothe leg spasms triggered by the medication. She quit her job as a baker, partly because brain damage was causing her to forget customers' orders. And she has lost one-quarter of her kidney function.

"If one of my children ever needed a kidney," said Carr, a mother of two, "I couldn't give them one."

At a time when reports of Cold War radiation experiments on Americans have focused fresh attention on the testing of new drugs and other treatments, the Omniflox case exposes a fundamental flaw in the process that is supposed to guarantee the safety of new medications.

The problem is that the process gives manufacturers and researchers, who have the most to gain from a new drug's success, wide discretion to assess its risks.

The dangers posed by this loophole may be growing because, increasingly, drug companies

TESTING, Page 13

Some resent buckling under state pressure

By Traci Grant and Kevin B. O'Leary
CONTRIBUTING REPORTERS

A lot of things bother 32-year-old John Campbell of Cambridge.

The list includes gun control, crime, violence, taxes. These are the things on which state politicians should focus their energies and time, not seat belts, Campbell said.

"When there is so much going on, are seat belts really an issue?" he asked. "There are a lot of things more pressing than this."

Campbell takes a libertarian view. He says he does not drink, and does not tell other people not to. He says he wears his seat belt, but does not force other people to follow his lead. No one should have that right, said Campbell, who was shopping yesterday at Assembly Square Mall in Somerville.

Views on the new mandatory seat-belt law were mixed yesterday among shoppers at Assembly Square, but area law en-

SEAT BELTS, Page 8

GLOBE STAFF PHOTO / JOANNE RATHE

FRIEND OF THE COURT – *Reginald Lindsay poses yesterday with Allison Thompkins, 14, after he was sworn in as a US district judge. The Newton girl, who has cerebral palsy, said she was "impressed to see someone else who's physically challenged become appointed." Page 22.*

Gains foreseen in private care far off '94 mark

By Michael Grunwald
GLOBE STAFF

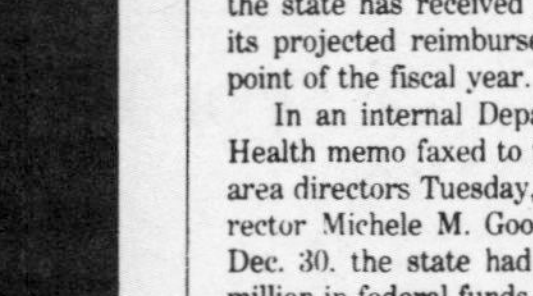

Even though the Weld administration said Massachusetts would reap much more federal Medicaid money if private hospitals treated mental health patients, the state has received just 10 percent of its projected reimbursement at the midpoint of the fiscal year.

In an internal Department of Mental Health memo faxed to the agency's seven area directors Tuesday, DMH revenue director Michele M. Goody said that as of Dec. 30, the state had garnered only $1 million in federal funds for patients in private hospitals. The agency had forecast a gain of $9.82 million for the entire fiscal year from those beds.

"Needless to say we will not get within sight of our goals without some extraordinary attention to this issue," Goody wrote.

The lack of Medicaid reimbursement was a key element of Gov. Weld's rationale for closing several state-run hospitals

DMH, Page 14

Inside

AT HOME: Reading room
CALENDAR: Bright Mondays

■ **Rocky forecast:** Treasury Secretary Lloyd Bentsen predicts a period of higher interest rates and declining stock prices. Business, Page 33.

■ **Globe Santa:** More contributors are listed. Page 28.

FEATURES		CLASSIFIED	
Ask The Globe	42	Classified	A7-A14
Business	33	Autos	A12
Comics	42	Help Wanted	A8
Deaths	30	Real Estate	A7
Editorials	10	Apartments	A7
Horoscope	42	Comm'l/Ind'l	A7
Living/Arts	45	Market Basket	A11
Lottery	22	Yachts/Boats	57
Metro/Region	21	Legal Notices	29
Sports	53		
TV/Radio	51		

VOLUME 245 • NUMBER 18
64 pages
35 cents
50 cents at newsstands beyond 20 miles from Boston

The Boston Globe

TUESDAY, JANUARY 18, 1994

DURESS FOR THE WEARY
Tuesday: *Rain/snow? windy, 35*
Wednesday: *Sunny, 10*
High tide: *3:23 a.m., 3:43 p.m.*
Full report: *Page 64*

A day of devastation in L.A.

AP PHOTO

A gas main burns as water from broken pipes floods a portion of Balboa Boulevard in the Grenada Hills section of Los Angeles after the earthquake hit the area yesterday morning.

'. . . You can do anything when you are fighting for your life'

By Glen Justice
SPECIAL TO THE GLOBE

NORTHRIDGE, Calif. – Euni Brown knew something was wrong when she tried to get out of bed yesterday morning and hit her head on the ceiling.

"I didn't feel the building collapse until" then, she said. "That's when I knew I was in trouble."

The 60-year-old woman was one of the lucky ones. Despite a debilitating illness, she was able to crawl out of her first-floor apartment just minutes after the entire three-story building came crashing down, flattening her apartment and at least 35 others. Many neighbors were trapped inside through the aftershocks.

"They were trying to pull me out, yelling, 'Hurry, hurry,' " she said. "I told them, 'I can't,' but then I pooled every bit of my strength and I made it. You can do anything when you are fighting for your life."

Nowhere was harder hit by the violent earthquake yesterday than this small San Fernando Valley community 24 miles from Los Angeles. Half of the known deaths occurred here. At least 14 people died in Brown's building alone.

"There's going to be a lot more," said James C. Walter, a Los Angeles firefighter who began rescuing survivors from Brown's building in the predawn darkness and was still chopping through walls with an ax and chainsaw in the late afternoon.

"We're leaving the dead bodies

NORTHRIDGE, Page 13

A battered economy is hit again

By Matt Carroll and Aaron Zitner
GLOBE STAFF

The shattered stores and burned-out homes can be repaired quickly, but the aftershocks of yesterday's earthquake on California's businesses – already reeling from natural and man-made disasters – could reverberate for years, economists said yesterday.

While many of the major corporations around Los Angeles said they had suffered only minor damage, the quake could induce already wavering corporations and residents to wonder how much more they can take.

"Southern California is already going through such a massive restructuring that it has prompted a lot of businesses to consider migrating to other regions," said Mark N. Gallagher, an economist for DRI/McGraw-Hill Inc. in Lexington.

"For many, this could be the last straw," he said.

The list of disasters to hit Los Angeles recently reads like the plot synopsis from a Cecil B. DeMille epic: An earthquake yesterday; roaring fires that destroyed 950 homes in late October and early November; a six-year drought (followed by floods) that ended last

IMPACT, Page 10

Quake toll is 27 as highways collapse, buildings crumble

By Lynda Gorov and Tom Mashberg
GLOBE STAFF

LOS ANGELES – A powerful earthquake struck Southern California before dawn yesterday, killing at least 27 people and injuring hundreds, buckling three major highways, leaving hundreds of thousands without water or power and rocking the region to its physical and emotional core.

Hitting at 4:31 a.m. and jolting millions of people awake, the quake leveled a mall and an apartment complex and damaged hundreds of smaller buildings. It spawned dozens of house fires, sent cars careening down hills and blacked out a million homes.

The earthquake measured 6.6 on the Richter scale and was centered in Northridge, a town in the San Fernando Valley 20 miles northwest of downtown Los Angeles. The valley, which took the brunt of the quake, is home to 3 million people.

The quake's impact was felt from San Diego, 125 miles to the south, to Las Vegas, 275 miles to the northeast.

Although geologists rate an earthquake even of this magnitude as moderate, officials said its physical devastation and long-term impact on health and safety in the densely populated Los Angeles basin make it one of the worst earthquakes in US history.

Los Angeles County emergency workers struggled around the clock to free dozens of people trapped in buildings and to repair water and gas lines. At least 14 of the people known to have been killed died in the collapse of an apartment complex at the quake's epicenter. Other deaths included a police officer who drove off a fallen highway and at least two people who died when their hillside home plunged into a ravine.

President Clinton declared Southern California a disaster zone

EARTHQUAKE, Page 13

Reverberations are felt far and wide

- **The terror of the unknown gives way to an awful reality. Page 12.**
- **In the aftermath, daily life will pose daunting challenges. Page 12.**
- **Stadium used by Angels and Rams is damaged. Sports, Page 49.**
- **Visuals rivet TV viewers. Living/Arts, Page 57.**

Epicenter

GLOBE STAFF MAP

List of relief agencies, Page 9. More quake coverage, Pages 9-13.

Haitians show signs of doubting sanctions

By Pamela Constable
GLOBE STAFF

PORT-AU-PRINCE, Haiti – As dusk falls, this crippled capital becomes a surreal scene from hell. There is neither electricity nor fuel; the downtown streets are pitch dark except for bonfires of burning mountains of garbage. It is rush hour, but there is no traffic. Only the rustle and murmur of an invisible mob trekking home through the mud.

As the army ignored both a new international deadline to give up power last Saturday and a conference in Miami convened by the exiled president last weekend, the UN Security Council is soon expected to expand the economic sanctions that already have brought Haiti's precarious economy to its knees.

But many observers here say a new punishment would have little impact on the army, which despite near-

HAITI, Page 6

AP PHOTO

ON TRACK FOR THE OLYMPICS – *Nancy Kerrigan skates in Stoneham yesterday, her first prolonged workout since being attacked Jan. 6. Pages 49, 54.*

Law firm at fulcrum of megaplex proposal

By Peter J. Howe
GLOBE STAFF

House Speaker Charles F. Flaherty, after months of skepticism about a nearly $700 million Boston convention center and football stadium, turned to an unlikely source for help when he drafted his own megaplex bill.

Like nearly every other player in the megaplex drama, Flaherty sought out the Boston law firm of Mintz Levin, Cohn, Ferris, Glovsky & Popeo.

It was perhaps the ultimate testament to Mintz Levin's powerful insider status: The lawmaker who had for months been, at least in public, the leading megaplex critic turned for help in crafting his own legislation to the very firm retained by Patriots owner James B. Orthwein to make the megaplex happen.

Sources say Mintz Levin largely wrote Flaherty's bill, but the speaker says the firm only provided secretarial

MEGAPLEX, Page 19

Inside

BUSINESS EXTRA: State's "budget busters" are reined in

- **EPA official dies:** Paul Keough, acting administrator of the US Environmental Protection Agency's New England office, suffers a fatal heart attack at 48. Page 21.
- **Patrolling the MBTA:** Officials lean toward hiring a private security company. Page 17.
- **A quest for identity:** Author Esmeralda Santiago examines her Puerto Rican heritage and American Dream adulthood. Living/Arts, Page 57.

FEATURES		CLASSIFIED	
Ask The Globe	22	Classified	26-32
Business	33	Autos	31
Comics	22	Help Wanted	28
Deaths	20	Real Estate	27
Editorials	14	Apartments	27
Horoscope	22	Comm'l/Ind'l	47
Living/Arts	57	Market Basket	26
Lottery	18	Yachts/Boats	50
Metro/Region	17	Learning	25
Sports	49		
TV/Radio	63		

Dawson's eighth-inning homer lifts Red Sox over Orioles, 3-2 - Page 81

VOLUME 245 • NUMBER 140

96 pages
35 cents

The Boston Globe

FRIDAY, MAY 20, 1994

GLOW EXPECTATIONS
Friday: AM clouds PM sun, 65
Saturday: Mostly sunny, 75
High tide: 7:11 a.m., 7:43 p.m.
Full report: Page 22

Jacqueline Onassis is dead

President John F. Kennedy and wife, Jacqueline, arrive in Dallas, Nov. 22, 1963, the day of his assassination.

JFK LIBRARY PHOTO

The president's widow, with son John Jr. and daughter Caroline, waits to join the funeral procession on Nov. 24, 1963.

AP FILE PHOTO

Jacqueline Kennedy Onassis visits the JFK Library and Museum last October.

GLOBE STAFF FILE PHOTO / JOHN TLUMACKI

Cancer claims her at age 64; children at side

By John Robinson
GLOBE STAFF

Jacqueline Kennedy Onassis, the former first lady who surmounted awesome personal tragedies with instructive dignity and style, died last night in her New York apartment of complications from cancer. She was 64.

Mrs. Onassis died at 10:15 p.m., said a statement from her longtime friend, Nancy Tuckerman. Her children were at her side, as were her longtime companion Maurice Tempelsman and other family members.

Mrs. Onassis suffered from non-Hodgkin's lymphoma, a cancer that afflicts the lymph system. Except for the most serious cases, apparently including that of Mrs. Onassis, the cancer is often treatable.

Jacqueline Kennedy Onassis' life and times, Pages 10-13.

"Jackie was part of our family and part of our heart for 40 wonderful and unforgettable years, and she will never really leave us," Sen. Edward M. Kennedy said in a statement. "Our love and prayers are with John, and with Caroline and Ed and their three children."

A spellbinding international celebrity who beguiled the public with a deft mixture

ONASSIS, Page 12

Her lasting gift was majesty

By David Shribman
GLOBE STAFF

Appreciation

WASHINGTON - Jacqueline Onassis is dead, but for millions of Americans she will forever be Jackie Kennedy. She will forever be young, and she will forever be frozen at Love Field in Dallas in a pink dress with gold buttons and a blue collar.

And if at this sad, sobering moment a second image or maybe a third crowds in, it will not be of the woman who later married a Greek shipping magnate or hid from the public behind big black sunglasses.

It will be of how her dress was set off by red roses on that November morning in 1963 and by red blood on that afternoon, or how she reached back in the open convertible to help Clinton Hill, the Secret Serviceman.

APPRECIATION, Page 13

'We are a step ahead of the telegraph.'
MORTIMER DOWNEY
Transportation official

US eyes $1b rail control system

By Michael Kranish
GLOBE STAFF

WASHINGTON - A recent spate of train accidents has prompted federal officials to consider recommending construction of a $1 billion, high-tech system that would be the rail equivalent of the national air traffic control system.

Although Amtrak and freight railroad officials stressed that the system would not have prevented many of the recent accidents, government officials said the accidents have focused attention on the need for a sophisticated method of tracking every train in the nation.

The system, which could dramatically reduce head-on collisions, would make use of Pentagon satellites and require tracking equipment on most locomotives.

"We are a step ahead of the telegraph," Mortimer Downey, deputy secretary of transportation, said in reference to the current train communication and tracking system. "It seems to me our current system is an outgrowth of that."

Amtrak's president, Thomas Downs, said yesterday that the most recent accidents would not have been prevented because they were due to causes outside railroad control, such as a barge that damaged a railroad bridge leading to the deaths of 47 passengers and crew members last November in Alabama, and a wayward driver at a grade

TRAINS, Page 6

US foreign policy has diplomats grumbling

By Paul Quinn-Judge
GLOBE STAFF

News Analysis

WASHINGTON - Some day in the not-too-distant future CNN could lead its newscast with graphic footage of another atrocity in Haiti: bullet-riddled bodies in the street, smirking killers leaving in military vehicles.

The images would be repeated every hour on TV screens in the White House and around Washington, prompting senators to demand retribution, activists to denounce US passivity, newspapers to call for action - and US troops to quietly begin leaving Guantanamo base in Cuba for the short ride to Haiti.

Judging from past experience, diplomats and analysts say, this could well be how the next round of President Clinton's Haiti policy is made.

While few pundits are willing to say what sort of foreign policy they would propose for the dangerously unpredictable 1990s, nearly all agree that in 18 months in office the administration has not even laid the basis for one. Western diplomats,

CLINTON, Page 6

Name aside, nothing 'vulgar' to these blooms

By Usha Lee McFarling
CONTRIBUTING REPORTER

The lilac: such fleeting beauty. Such haunting fragrance. Such an ugly scientific name.

In botanical circles, the beloved shrubbery now erupting into watercolor hues carries the name *Syringa vulgaris* - *Syringa* for hollow stem and *vulgaris* for common.

This "common" flower is just one of more than 20 species of lilac. Over centuries, lilac breeders have crossed plants within and between species to create some 2,000 named varieties of lilacs, whose curious names range from the poetic - Blue Danube and Shimmering Sea - to the patriotic - Yankee Doodle and Patrick Henry.

The Arnold Arboretum - home to one of the Northeast's largest lilac collections - keeps 285 kinds of lilacs among its 622 lilac shrubs. For those who think all those blue, white, pink, purple and, yes, lilac-hued bushes are just more *Syringa vulgaris*, it's time to wake up and smell the lilacs.

This Sunday, which is Lilac Sunday at the arboretum, is the day to do so. As they have for decades, lilac aficionados are expected to stroll the arboretum's lilac-strewn lanes, stumble down hillsides dazed by the flower's inimitable perfume and drift from bush to bush to make comparisons.

The profusion of blooms invites comparisons: Which is best?

One expert opinion comes from John H. Alexander 3d, the arboretum's resident lilac expert and plant propagator - and the grandson of a famed lilac grower.

LILACS, Page 22

GLOBE STAFF PHOTO / JOHN TLUMACKI

Caroline Buddenhagen sniffs a lilac at Arnold Arboretum.

Answers leave a confounding picture in poll of Mass. high school students

By Doris Sue Wong and Jordana Hart
GLOBE STAFF

One in 10 Massachusetts public high school students has recently carried a weapon to school, one in 10 has attempted suicide, and students who received AIDS education are less likely to be sexually active than students who have not had AIDS education, according to a wide-ranging survey of students released yesterday.

The survey by the state Department of Education asked more than 3,000 students to answer questions anonymously about their use of alcohol, drugs and cigarettes, and their experiences with sex, violence and other issues facing young people.

Some of the results, particularly those on attempted suicide, troubled educators and youth advocates, who questioned whether the responses might have been exaggerated by students.

"I don't know why kids at such an early age would feel such a complete lack of hope, not want to live to get up tomorrow," said Albert Argenziano, superintendent of Somerville public schools. "I'd like to see how the question was phrased."

But Alan Safran, a spokesman for the state Education Department, said the survey was designed by the federal Centers for Disease Control to ensure confi-

STUDENTS, Page 33

Inside

SPORTS PLUS: Michael Jordan, minor leaguer

■ **Dispute in Lincoln:** Residents are divided over whether two dogs should be destroyed for attacking a woman. Page 25.

■ **"Maverick" is the name:** The Gibson-Foster-Garner film is an enjoyable if not so original romp, writes Jay Carr. Living/Arts. Page 49.

■ **Plugged in:** Technology extends bankers' hours to 24 hours a day, 365 days a year. Business. Page 65.

FEATURES		CLASSIFIED	
Ask The Globe	38	Classified	42-48, 73-79
Business	65		
Comics	38	Autos	42
Deaths	36	Help Wanted	70
Editorials	14	Real Estate	75
Horoscope	38	Apartments	75
Living Arts	49	Comm'l Ind'l	75
Lottery	26	Market Basket	74
Metro Region	25	Yachts Boats	93
Sports	81	Learning	90
TV Radio	22-23		

Coming Sunday: A special section on Boston school desegregation 20 years later

VOLUME 245 • NUMBER 169

84 pages
35 cents
50 cents at newsstands
beyond 30 miles from Boston

The Boston Globe

SATURDAY, JUNE 18, 1994

SEAR MADNESS

Saturday: *Hazy, humid, 90-95*
Sunday: *Hazy, humid, 85-90*
High tide: *6:46 a.m., 7:15 p.m.*
Full report: *Page 80*

Accused of murder, O.J. Simpson arrested after L.A. freeway chase

AP PHOTO / VIA ABC-TV

A man believed to be Al Cowlings, longtime friend of O.J. Simpson, last night walks away from the White Ford Bronco containing Simpson.

Another hero's life turns upside down as we all look on

By Dan Shaughnessy
GLOBE STAFF

Commentary

The story spun out of control as afternoon turned to evening. First came word that O.J. Simpson was going to be arrested for the murder of his ex-wife and Ronald Goldman. Then there was the bizarre press conference when Los Angeles Police Department Cmdr. David Gascon told the world that the LAPD didn't know where O.J. was. Then there was the emergency call from the Brentwood residence of the late Nicole Simpson. Then there was was another shocking press conference with Simpson's lawyer, Robert Shapiro.

Shapiro read a note from Simpson that sounded suicidal. "I can't go on," read the note. "No matter what the outcome, people will look and point."

There was more. Simpson and his friend Al Cowlings were spotted in a Ford Bronco early in the evening. Police and television cameras (in helicopters) followed the white truck all the way back to Simpson's Brentwood home. Then there was a lengthy driveway standoff. It was dark when Simpson finally gave himself up.

For a while, the whole episode felt like the Charles Stuart case all over again. It was "The Fugitive." It was the biggest, worst story ever involving an American sports hero. One of the most famous persons in America – a former football hero turned television and movie star – was charged with murder, then disappeared, then was found as the cameras rolled.

It was a Friday night prime-time spectacle. A real life-and-death drama on live television – complete with LA commuters hooting and cheering

SHAUGHNESSY, Page 35

View from Madison Square Garden, other reaction – Sports, Pages 33, 35

Held gun to head while friend drove

By Brian McGrory
GLOBE STAFF

LOS ANGELES – Football legend O. J. Simpson, the central character in an extraordinary human drama, surrendered to police at his Brentwood estate last night, ending a flight from justice that included a nationally televised highway pursuit followed by a standoff in his driveway.

Simpson, who had held a revolver to his temple for part of the chase, gave himself up to officers a few minutes before 9 p.m. local time. He was taken to the Parker Center, Los Angeles Police headquarters, for booking. Simpson was charged in the double murders of his former wife and her male friend; if convicted, he could be sentenced to death.

His lawyer, Robert Shapiro, told reporters late last night, "It was my hope, but not my belief, that it would end this way. To the public, I ask that you withhold judgment until this is resolved in a court of law."

Before Simpson's surrender, Al Cowlings, a longtime friend and former teammate who was his driver in his flight from justice, was furiously negotiating with police outside Simpson's house as officials tried to patch a call between Simpson and his mother. Throughout, Simpson sat inside the white Ford Bronco, unseen by numerous television cameras that were carrying the drama live.

Simpson, a fugitive for much of the day, was spotted in that Bronco at about 6:45 p.m., then led police on a slow-speed, serpentine pursuit to his home. For much of the drive, he held a gun to his temple as Californians lined the highway to watch,

SIMPSON, Page 4

O. J. letter: 'Why do I end up like this?'

The following is the text of O. J. Simpson's letter, as read at a news conference yesterday.

To whom it may concern:

First, everyone understand: I had nothing to do with Nicole's murder. I loved her, always have and always will. If we had a problem, it's because I loved her so much. Recently we came to the understanding that for now we were not right for each other, at least for now. Despite our love, we were different, and that's why we mutually agreed to go our separate ways. It was tough splitting for a second time, but we both knew it was for the best. Inside, I had no doubt that in the future we would be close friends or more.

Unlike what has been written in the press, Nicole and I had a great relationship for most of our lives together. Like all long-term relationships, we had a few downs and ups. I took the heat New Year's 1989 because that's what I was supposed to do. I did not plead no contest for any other reason but to protect our privacy, and was advised it would end the press

LETTER, Page 6

Trial for AIDS vaccines shelved

Panel advises against testing

By Richard A. Knox
GLOBE STAFF

BETHESDA, Md. – The US government's top AIDS research agency yesterday shelved proposals to launch the first large-scale trial of AIDS vaccines after a panel of advisers concluded that the best available experimental vaccines do not offer sufficient hope of protection against infection.

The decision was a resounding blow to two AIDS vaccine developers, Genentech and Biocine, who had pressed for a large government-supported study enrolling as many as 9,000 people at risk of infection by the human immunodeficiency virus, which causes AIDS.

"Time is of the essence," said Dr. Donald Francis, a virologist who works for Genentech, the large California-based biotechnology firm. "Launching an AIDS vaccine trial is not easy. It's not a terribly good business venture, but we must keep momentum going, or we'll never get there."

After reviewing evidence and debating the issue for eight hours, 35

AIDS, Page 16

ONE POOL, NO WADING

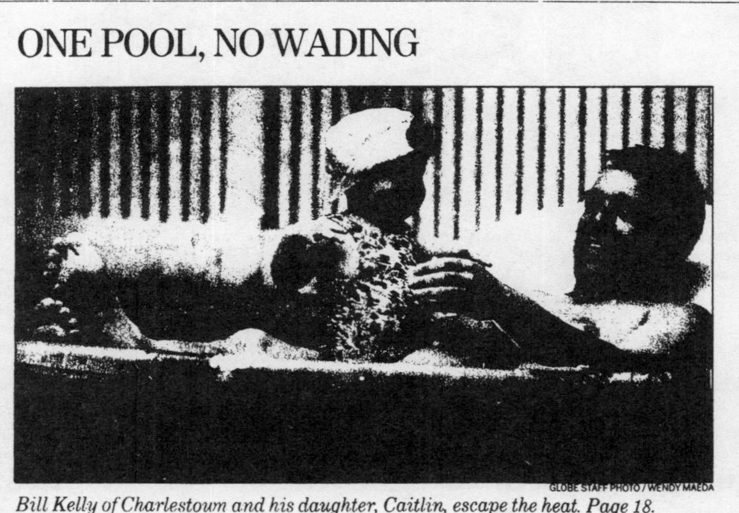

GLOBE STAFF PHOTO / WENDY MAEDA

Bill Kelly of Charlestown and his daughter, Caitlin, escape the heat. Page 18.

DA's use of 2d grand jury questioned

Critics call officer's indictment political

By Shelley Murphy
GLOBE STAFF

Prosecutors and defense lawyers yesterday said it was "highly unusual" for the Suffolk district attorney's office to call in a second grand jury to indict a former Boston police officer for the alleged rape of a prostitute after another panel indicated it would not charge him.

Meanwhile, critics of Suffolk District Attorney Ralph C. Martin 2d accused him of going to extraordinary lengths to indict a police officer shortly after the Boston police officers' union endorsed his rival in the upcoming election.

The use of a second grand jury to indict retired Officer Leo F. Coogan on Thursday "raises questions of irregularity and requires an explanation," said attorney Elliot M. Weinstein, president of the Massachusetts Association of Criminal Defense Lawyers.

"I would say this is highly improper," Weinstein said. "The grand jury is supposed to be an independent body and if the district attorney is dissatisfied with the independence of the grand jury, it's a serious question to convene a new one more to his liking. Grand jury forum shopping is improper."

After one grand jury indicated it didn't believe a prostitute's contention that Coogan forced her to perform oral sex inside his police cruis-

COOGAN, Page 21

US refutes Carter on Korea assurances

By Charles A. Radin
GLOBE STAFF

SEOUL – President Clinton and other administration officials distanced themselves yesterday from former President Jimmy Carter's statement in Pyongyang that the United States was halting its effort to impose sanctions against North Korea.

Carter met yesterday with North Korean leader Kim Il Sung. In remarks that were broadcast on CNN, Carter told Kim: "I would like to inform you that they have stopped the sanctions activity in the United Nations."

But in Washington and Chicago, US officials said that was not the case. Clinton insisted yesterday that the United States is still seeking sanctions against North Korea in the dispute over nuclear inspections.

"I gave my position yesterday and it hasn't changed," Clinton said in Chicago, when asked about Carter's statement.

At a State Department news briefing, Assistant Secretary of State Robert Gallucci said the administration did not expect to sort out the confusion until officials spoke with Carter today or tomorrow, after he has left Pyongyang.

But Gallucci said Carter was not authorized on his US-approved pri-

KOREA, Page 79

Inside

REAL ESTATE: Wiring check

■ **Reader Feedback:** We asked: "Do you favor reinstating the death penalty in Massachusetts?" A sampling of your answers and related stories, Page 20.

■ **Knicks win:** Lead by Patrick Ewing, New York beat the Rockets, 91-84, to move within a game of the NBA championship. Sports, Page 33.

■ **Loss No. 9:** Indians beat the Red Sox, 8-1. Sports, Page 33.

FEATURES		CLASSIFIED	
Ask The Globe	82	Classified	43-77, 88
Business	7	Autos	54
Comics	82	Help Wanted	49
Deaths	78	Real Estate	44
Editorials	14	Apartments	47
Horoscope	82	Comm'l/Ind'l	46
Living/Arts	25	Market Basket	51
Lottery	18	Yachts/Boats	41
Metro/Region	17	Learning	30
Sports	33		
TV/Radio	80-81		

VOLUME 246 • NUMBER 132
108 pages
35 cents
50 cents at newsstands beyond 30 miles from Boston

The Boston Globe

WEDNESDAY, NOVEMBER 9, 1994

STATE OF GRAYS
Wednesday: *Mostly cloudy; 65*
Thursday: *Sunny, breezy; 50s*
High tide: *3:25 a.m., 3:41 p.m.*
Full report: *Page 98*

AROUND THE COUNTRY

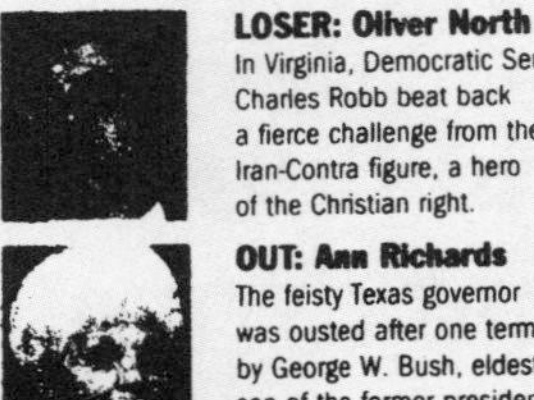

LOSER: Oliver North
In Virginia, Democratic Sen. Charles Robb beat back a fierce challenge from the Iran-Contra figure, a hero of the Christian right.

OUT: Ann Richards
The feisty Texas governor was ousted after one term by George W. Bush, eldest son of the former president.

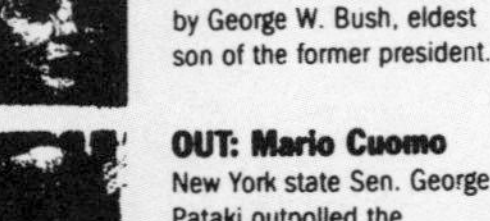

OUT: Mario Cuomo
New York state Sen. George Pataki outpolled the Democratic party's great governor-orator, dashing his hopes for a fourth term.

- **Fla. Gov. Chiles blocks Jeb Bush challenge**
- **Rostenkowski loses US House seat**
- **Sen. Wofford of Pennsylvania ousted**

MASSACHUSETTS

US SENATE
84% of vote counted

✖ Kennedy (D)*	1,046,599	59%
Romney (R)	724,055	40%

GOVERNOR/LT. GOVERNOR
84% of vote counted

✖ Weld/Cellucci (R)*	1,248,962	71%
Roosevelt/Massie (D)	506,235	29%

ATTORNEY GENERAL
70% of vote counted

✖ Harshbarger (D)*	996,648	71%
Berry (R)	414,442	29%

SECRETARY OF STATE
70% of vote counted

✖ Galvin (D)	725,392	55%
Chase (R)	551,930	42%

TREASURER
70% of vote counted

✖ Malone (R)*	899.197	64%
O'Brien (D)	450,837	32%

AUDITOR
70% of vote counted

✖ DeNucci (D)*	957,254	72%
Clark (R)	341,000	25%

DISTRICT ATTORNEY/SUFFOLK
77% of vote counted

✖ Martin (R)*	67,297	61%
Malone (D)	43,808	39%

US HOUSE

3d District
[illegible] of vote counted

✖ Blute (R)*	94,534	55%
O'Sullivan (D)	76,884	44%

[illegible] District
[illegible] of vote counted

✖ Torkildsen (R)*	92,119	50%
Tierney (D)	89,713	48%

7th District
97% of vote counted

✖ Markey (D)*	139,858	64%
Bailey (R)	77,534	36%

* Incumbent

BALLOT QUESTIONS

1. Restrict ballot question contributions
69% of vote counted

Yes	543,611	40%
✖ No	811,890	60%

2. Retain seat belt law
69% of vote counted

✖ Yes	817,353	59%
No	556,663	41%

3. Student fees
69% of vote counted

Yes	641,776	49%
No	668,730	51%

[illegible] Institute term limits
[illegible] of vote counted

[illegible]	844,434	51%
[illegible]	798,678	49%

[illegible] blue laws
69% of vote counted

Yes	721,935	52%
No	664,823	48%

6. Implement grad tax amendment
69% of vote counted

Yes	412,751	30%
✖ No	957,469	70%

7. Grad tax rate
69% of vote counted

Yes	394,420	29%
✖ No	973,542	71%

8. Limit gas tax to highway fund
69% of vote counted

✖ Yes	994,724	74%
No	346,048	26%

9. Abolish rent control
69% of vote counted

Yes	693,234	52%
No	646,995	48%

GOP captures Congress; Weld and Kennedy romp

State bucks the sentiment for rejecting incumbents

By Frank Phillips and Scot Lehigh
GLOBE STAFF

Massachusetts voters yesterday bucked the national trend to oust incumbents, giving strong reelection victories to liberal Democrat Sen. Edward M. Kennedy and Republican Gov. Weld, a fiscally conservative, socially liberal Republican.

Early today Weld was within reach of an all-time victory margin for a Massachusetts governor.

■ **Local and regional coverage, Pages 29-36, 44-46**

Kennedy, the 32-year incumbent and national symbol of Democratic liberalism who only several weeks ago appeared in serious danger of losing his seat, had a 19-point lead over Republican challenger Mitt Romney with more than four-fifths of the state's precincts reporting.

Although his Senate clout was his principal campaign theme, Kennedy, the fourth-ranking senator in seniority and chairman of the Labor and Human Resources Committee, is returning to a US Senate where his power will be diminished. The Senate shifted from Democratic to Republican control as a result of yesterday's balloting.

RESULTS, Page 32

GLOBE STAFF PHOTO / PAT GREENHOUSE
Sen. Edward M. Kennedy celebrates his victory last night at the Park Plaza Hotel.

At ballot's top, victories of ideology, genealogy

On Politics
MARTIN F. NOLAN

On their nights of triumph, as their national ambitions intersect, Edward M. Kennedy and William F. Weld can pause and give thanks to a ticket-splitting electorate – and their respective gene pools.

Exactly one century and two days ago, the Kennedy dynasty was born when John F. (Honey Fitz) Fitzgerald was elected to the 54th Congress, the only Democrat among 27 New Englanders in the House. His grandson, reelected to a sixth full term in the Senate, will be a distinctive figure in the 104th Congress, the last lion of liberalism.

The tiger of gay rights and low taxes, Gov. Weld, meanwhile, may pursue the White House ambition that flummoxed Kennedy in 1980 and Weld's predecessor, Michael Dukakis, in 1988. Like Dukakis, Weld also may find that his staff's ambition is steadier and more focused than his.

Weld's genetic imperative is deeper than Kennedy's, by centuries. According to the Historical and Genealogical Register, "The family of Weld dates back to 1352, when William Weld was High Sheriff of

ON POLITICS, Page 32

No grad tax; term limits edges ahead

By Peter J. Howe and Chris Reidy
GLOBE STAFF

For the fifth time in a generation, Massachusetts voters yesterday resoundingly rejected a proposed graduated state income tax, and they appeared to be endorsing the new seat-belt law and imposing a version of term limits on state officeholders.

But ballot questions allowing Sunday morning store openings and prohibiting rent control in Boston, Brookline and Cambridge were too close to call early today.

The grad tax – Questions 6 and 7 – was headed to a 2-1 defeat in incomplete returns last night, echoing four other defeats since the 1960s. Though it promised to cut taxes for 92 percent of Massachusetts taxpayers, opponents raised $3 million to stop it, charging it would give the Legislature new ways to raise taxes in the future and hurt small businesses. Top Democrats Paul Tsongas and John Silber

QUESTIONS, Page 34

GLOBE STAFF PHOTO / JONATHAN WIGGS
Gov. Weld gives thumbs up to his reelection last night at the Sheraton Boston.

Angry voters give Clinton, Democrats a drubbing

By David M. Shribman
GLOBE STAFF

A powerful Republican tide rolled across the country yesterday, ending the Democrats' four-decade domination of the House, sweeping them out of control of the Senate and giving the GOP a new ascendancy in the nation's state houses and governors' offices.

Angry voters replaced a generation of Democrats and prompted a historic transformation of the face of politics in Washington and in state capitals from coast to coast.

■ **National coverage, Pages 3-16.**

Returns early this morning suggested that Republicans would pick up more than four dozen House seats, giving them a comfortable majority. In the Senate, the GOP could pick up as many as nine seats, giving them as much as a 53-47 advantage.

Yesterday's midterm vote provided an unusually strong rejection of the policies of the incumbent president, Democrat Bill Clinton. But it also represented a clear call for change at all levels of politics in all regions of the country, especially in Washington.

At the same time, the Republican surge elevated to the post of House speak-

NATION, Page 16

Confrontation may be tone on Capitol Hill

By John Aloysius Farrell
GLOBE STAFF

WASHINGTON – A new Republican Congress will confront President Clinton in the next two years with a series of defining choices over tax cuts, a balanced budget amendment, term limits, caps on the growth of entitlement spending and other conservative causes.

"We have the responsibility to make the change the American people want," said Sen. Bob Dole of Kansas, who is expected to become the new majority leader. "Our first obligation is to keep our word," said Rep. Newt Gingrich, the Republican whip from Georgia who appeared in line to become the first Republican House speaker in almost five decades.

The GOP's "Contract with America" calls for tax cuts and entitlement cuts, and constitutional amendments to impose term limits and a balanced budget. But Republican zeal to enact such measures is expected to be tempered by the same arithmetic that plagued Clinton in his unsuc-

CONGRESS, Page 6

Probate judge orders Rep. Fitzgerald, two others to repay Guzelian estate

By Patricia Nealon
GLOBE STAFF

State Rep. Kevin Fitzgerald of Mission Hill, his top aide, and a lawyer/lobbyist coerced a mentally ill street person into leaving her estate to Fitzgerald and the aide when the money rightfully belonged to the woman's elderly sister, a probate judge ruled yesterday.

In a stinging and unusually detailed decision, Norfolk Probate Court Judge David H. Kopelman vacated the July 1981 will of street person Mary Guzelian and ordered Fitzgerald, aide Patricia McDermott and attorney Michael J. Muse to immediately repay the estate a total of $436,514. The money will go to Guzelian's sole heir, her 75-year-old sister, Elizabeth Scullin.

Kopelman, adopting the findings of two psychiatrists who testified before him, found that Guzelian, then 64, was mentally ill when she signed the will drafted by Muse that split her estate between Fitzgerald and McDermott. Scullin, who was to be left Guzelian's entire estate in an earlier will, was left $1 in the 1981 will.

The will was signed two weeks after McDermott and Fitzgerald found trash bags stuffed with cash, coins and bank books in the Guzelian's Brighton apartment, which was described as being rancid and in utter disarray.

The inheritance was first reported in the Globe in 1991, prompting federal and state investigations into Fitzgerald's conduct.

"Guzelian's untreated mental illness of chronic paranoid schizophrenia, her severe health problems, her advanced age, and the trauma arising from her

GUZELIAN, Page 40

Inside

FOOD: Peasant pleasures

■ **Postal rates:** The price of a first-class stamp is expected to rise from 29 cents to 32 cents in January. Page 88.

■ **Dino Radja to stay:** The Celtics forward agrees on a four-year contract extension. Sports, Page 75.

■ **Recycling laser cartridges:** Sudbury's Lasertone Corp. is a classic high-tech start-up. Emerging Business, Page 58.

■ **The case for pornography:** Author Sallie Tisdale stirs a hornets' nest with "Talk Dirty to Me." Living/Arts, Page 91.

FEATURES		CLASSIFIED	
Ask The Globe	100	Classified	102-107
Business	55	Autos	47
Comics	100-101	Help Wanted	105
Deaths	72-73	Professional	66
Editorials	18	Real Estate	104
Horoscope	100	Apartments	104
Living/Arts	91	Comm'l/Ind'l	104
Lottery	38	Market Basket	103
Metro/Region	37	Yachts/Boats	79
Sports	75		
TV/Radio	98-99		

VOLUME 246 • NUMBER 184
68 pages
35 cents
50 cents at newsstands beyond 30 miles from Boston

The Boston Globe

A GRAY TO REMEMBER
Saturday: Clouding up, 32
Sunday: Rain/sleet, 38
High tide: 9:33 a.m., 10:14 p.m.
Full report: Page 42

SATURDAY, DECEMBER 31, 1994

"This man is nothing other than a terrorist... We will not allow people in this commonwealth to settle moral disputes with violence."
—GOV. WELD

Four unidentified women consoling each other yesterday outside Preterm Health Services on Beacon Street, Brookline.
STAFF PHOTO / SUZANNE KREITER

Abortion violence hits home

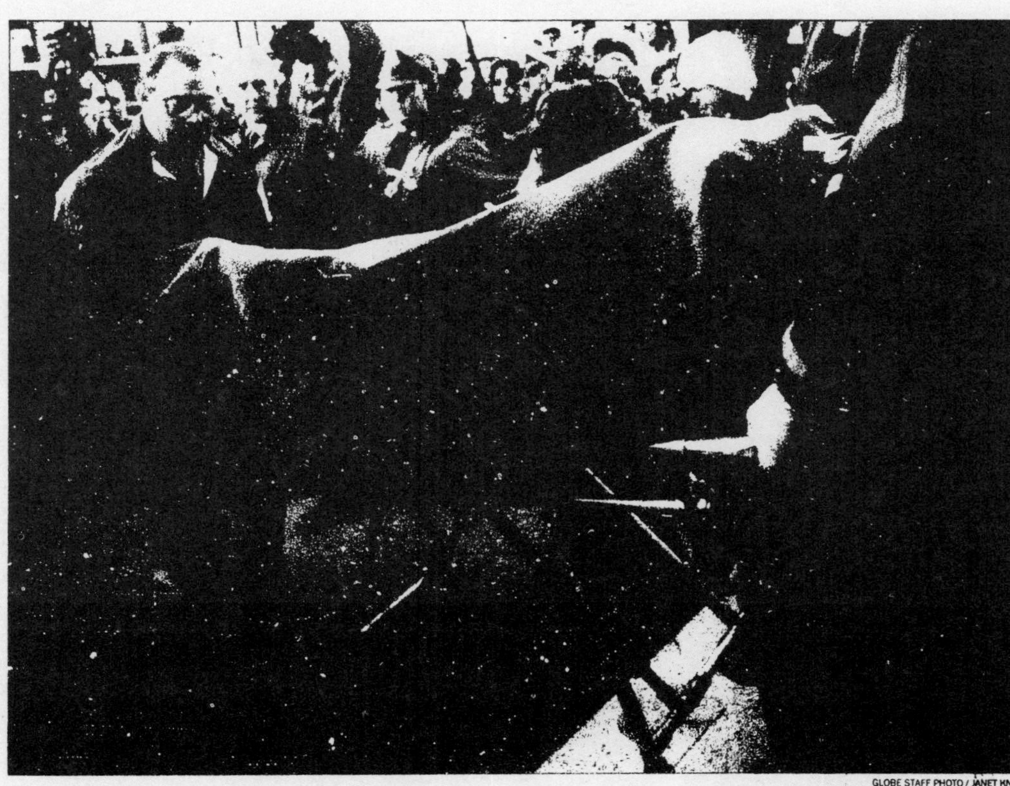

GLOBE STAFF PHOTO / JANET KNOTT
The body of Shannon Lowney, the 25-year-old receptionist who was killed yesterday, is taken from the Planned Parenthood clinic in Brookline.

Gunman opens fire in Brookline clinics, kills 2 and wounds 5

By Kevin Cullen and Brian McGrory
GLOBE STAFF

A well-dressed man in black, armed with a rifle and a cool, ruthless determination, opened fire inside two Brookline abortion clinics yesterday, killing two women and wounding five other people, including a security guard who tried to stop him.

Police last night were scouring both sides of the Massachusetts and New Hampshire border for John C. Salvi, 22, of Hampton Beach, N.H., a hairdresser suspected of buying the gun used in the shootings.

A sales receipt for the gun was recovered from a duffel bag in which the gunman concealed his weapon and which he dropped after the security guard shot at him. A second weapon, a handgun, was recovered from the bag, but apparently was not used in the shootings, police said.

It was believed to be the worst attack on abortion providers in the nation's history.

The dead women worked as receptionists at the clinics, while at least two of those wounded were men who had accompanied patients to one of the clinics. As he fled the second clinic, the gunman fired randomly at bystanders, sending them scurrying for cover in the frigid air on busy Beacon Street, according to witnesses. No one was shot outside.

The gunman may have been wounded in a gun battle with the guard, police said. The wounded security guard said he was convinced he had shot the gunman, who remained at large last night.

Moving from victim to victim

SHOOTINGS, Page 20

The victims

At Planned Parenthood
1031 Beacon St.

KILLED
- **Shannon Lowney**, above, 25, of Arlington, receptionist.

WOUNDED
- **Anjana Agrawal**, 30, of Cambridge, medical assistant. In serious but stable condition.
- **Antonio Hernandez**, 32, of Worcester, accompanied a patient to clinic. In stable condition.
- **Brian Murray**, 22, of Hingham, accompanied patient to clinic. In serious but stable condition.

At Preterm Health Services
1842 Beacon St.

KILLED
- **Leanne Nichols**, 38, of Salem, N.H., receptionist.

WOUNDED
- **Jane Sauer**, 29, of Cambridge, office worker. In stable condition.
- **Richard J. Seron**, 45, of Quincy, security guard. In stable condition.

Danger closes in on us

By Ellen Goodman
GLOBE STAFF

Commentary

Suddenly, it's in our backyard.

Not Pensacola, Fla. Not Wichita, Kan. It's in Brookline, Mass.

Suddenly, the scene of the crime is not in some isolated abortion clinic on a southern highway or a strip mall. It's on Beacon Street, on the Green Line, along the Marathon route, two minutes from my front door.

This time, it's not Michael Griffin in Pensacola. It's not Paul Hill. The suspect is another young man, handsome, clean shaven, dressed in black. Dressed to kill.

This time, the murder victim isn't a doctor or a clinic escort; they're two young receptionists. This time, seven people are shot.

The violence has come home, big time.

Yesterday morning started like other mornings in a city-suburb that has three clinics within two miles. As usual, there were protesters at 1031 Beacon St., women praying, a man with a video camera. Some we know by sight.

Maybe the edge of danger that has sharpened nationally with the escalating clinic violence was dulled here by familiarity. Many of my neighbors and fellow commuters have learned to walk by the protesters in front of Planned Parenthood on their way to the cleaners or the French bakery or the T.

GOODMAN, Page 22

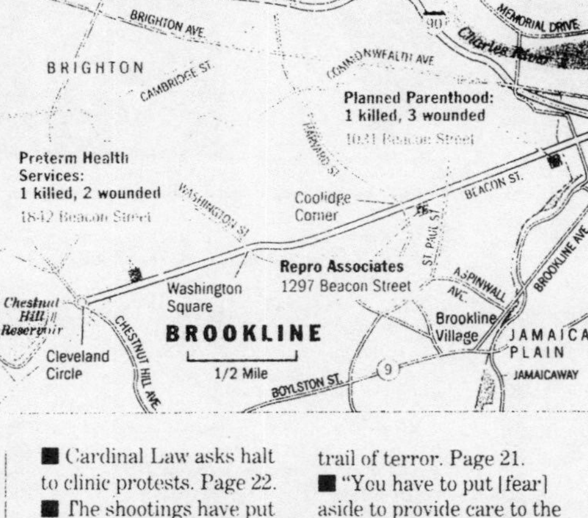

- Cardinal Law asks halt to clinic protests. Page 22.
- The shootings have put clinic security in a nationwide spotlight. Page 21.
- Witnesses tell of the scene along the gunman's trail of terror. Page 21.
- "You have to put [fear] aside to provide care to the women who need it," says a nurse-practioner at a Beacon Street clinic. Page 23.
- Coverage, Pages 20-23.

Anguish and arguments mark nationwide reaction

By Bob Hohler
GLOBE STAFF

WASHINGTON – Grief merged with anger yesterday as activists on opposite sides of the abortion issue joined the Clinton administration in calling for a national effort to reverse the rising tide of violent radicalism displayed in the deadly attacks at two Brookline clinics.

But while advocates on both sides joined in expressing outrage and calling for peace, they parted in their perceptions of the reasons for the violence and potential ways to stop it.

"Even as we mourn the dead and pray for the injured, the overwhelming reaction is anger that this climate of hatred, fear and genuine terrorism has been allowed to grow unchallenged – even encouraged – by those who say they abhor violence," said Kim Gandy, executive vice president of the National Organization for Women.

By repeatedly referring to doctors who perform abortions as "murderers" and "baby-killers," Gandy said, "the National Right to Life Committee, the Pro-Life Action League and Operation Rescue and others of their ilk are responsible for these shootings" by provoking violence.

Not so, according to the anti-abortion groups, which strongly denied inciting violence and asserted they were working within the law to try to end the taking of life from human fetuses.

"Killing is not prolife," said Michele Arocha Allen, a spokeswoman for the National Right to Life Com-

NATION, Page 23

Victims radiated sparkle

By Ann Scales
GLOBE STAFF

Leanne Nichols had worked her way up from receptionist to phone counselor at Repro Associates, a Brookline abortion clinic. But several months ago, she left that job when the work became too stressful, former co-workers recalled yesterday.

In September, she became a receptionist at the nearby Preterm Health Services clinic.

Yesterday, Nichols, 38, was fatally shot at her work station by a gunman who opened fire at two Brookline abortion clinics.

She was the second fatality of the abortion clinic shootings. Shannon Lowney was the first.

Nichols, who was shot five times, died at Beth Israel Hospital. Lowney, 25, of Arlington, a receptionist at the Planned Parenthood clinic, died at Beth Israel Hospital.

Five other people were seriously injured when a gunman went on the shooting spree at a Planned Parenthood clinic on Beacon Street and continued spraying bullets 10 minutes later at Preterm clinic.

What follows are sketches of some of the victims, based on interviews with friends, coworkers and family members.

Leanne Nichols

Nichols had the sparkle of a woman in love, the friendliness of a Midwesterner, her co-workers said.

"She was a very sweet girl," said one former coworker. "She loved her work and was very dedicated to it."

She lived in a rural area near a lake about two miles from the town center in Salem, N.H. The single-story house, in an area of summer cottages, was deserted yesterday.

At Repro, former coworkers cried when they heard news of her death. They remembered her as a nice woman who maintained the

VICTIMS, Page 23

Police find gun receipts in bag; seek N.H. man, 22

By David Armstrong and Judy Rakowsky
GLOBE STAFF

Investigators last night were searching for a 22-year-old New Hampshire man they believe purchased the gun and ammunition used in the abortion clinic shootings in Brookline yesterday, law enforcement sources said last night.

The search for the man, identified as John C. Salvi, was centered in Hampton Beach, N.H., last night, but police also were looking in northern Massachusetts, the sources said. Investigators were checking the man's last known addresses, but did not have specific information on his whereabouts, the sources said.

A relative's home in Ipswich was searched just after 11 p.m. by law enforcement agents looking for Salvi, according to local police. No one answered a Globe reporter's knock on the door at the Washington Street home last night.

The search for Salvi, a hairdresser who also has relatives in Lynnfield, began after investigators recovered gun and ammunition receipts from a black bag dropped at the second of two abortion clinics targeted by the assailant yesterday. Two people were killed and five others wounded.

Also inside the bag were a 22-caliber Colt handgun, several hundred rounds of automatic weapon ammunition and so-called banana clips, a detachable magazine that

MANHUNT, Page 20

Inside

REAL ESTATE

- **Gingrich: No advance:** The incoming speaker of the US House yesterday relinquished a $4.5 million book advance in the face of criticism about the ethics of the deal. Page 3.
- **First Night hoopla:** All you need to know, and then some. Pages 17, 35.
- **NFL gets down to it:** The playoffs begin today, and the Patriots play in Cleveland tomorrow. The Globe's sports staff previews it all. Page 25.

FEATURES		CLASSIFIED	
Ask The Globe	44	Classified	51-68
Business	7	Autos	58
Comics	44	Help Wanted	54
Deaths	46	Real Estate	52
Editorials	14	Apartments	52
Horoscope	44	Comm'l/Ind'l	52
Living/Arts	35	Market Basket	56
Lottery	18	Yachts/Boats	27
Metro/Region	17	Learning	48
Sports	24		
TV/Radio	42-43		

0 947725 4 01636

VOLUME 247 • NUMBER 110
138 pages
35 cents
50 cents at newsstands beyond 30 miles from Boston

The Boston Globe

GOLDEN RETRIEVER
Thursday: *Mostly sunny, 66*
Friday: *Mostly cloudy, 55-60*
High tide: *3:27 a.m., 4:10 p.m.*
Full report: *Page 68*

THURSDAY, APRIL 20, 1995

'We will find the people who did this. When we do, justice will be swift, certain and severe.'
PRESIDENT CLINTON

Oklahoma City car bomb attack kills at least 31; 300 are missing

AP PHOTO
Rescue workers survey the hole gouged yesterday by a bomb that detonated at a federal office building in Oklahoma City.

12 children among dead; 200 hurt; authorities probe terrorist link

By Judy Gibbs
ASSOCIATED PRESS

OKLAHOMA CITY – A car bomb ripped deep into America's heartland yesterday, killing at least 31 people and leaving 300 missing in an explosion that gouged a nine-story hole in a federal office building.

The dead included at least 12 children, age 7 and younger, some of whom had just been dropped off by their parents at a day-care center.

There was no immediate claim of responsibility for the attack.

At least 200 people were injured – 58 critically, according to Fire Chief Gary Marrs – and scores were feared trapped in the rubble of the Alfred P. Murrah Federal Building more than nine hours after the bombing.

Two people were pulled from the rubble last night but died a short time later, said Assistant Fire Chief Jon Hansen. Hansen said a woman was trapped in the basement, who said there were two others down there. She did not know if they were dead or alive.

The death toll was certain to rise.

"Our firefighters are having to crawl over corpses in areas to get to people that are still alive," Hansen said.

[In Boston, 16 bomb threats were reported in the downtown area following the Oklahoma City explosion. The first evacuation, at the JFK Building, was prompted by a door left ajar.

[By afternoon, at least four other buildings, including City Hall, the federal courthouse and One Financial Center, were cleared after telephoned bomb threats were received. At least five major office buildings were emptied in the Financial District.]

Cable News Network quoted an investiga-

BOMBING, Page 24

Blast coverage

Massive probe launched: Authorities say they will seek death penalty for perpetrators. Page 25.

Watershed event: Experts assess impact as apparent terrorist act hits America's heartland. Page 24.

Boston evacuations: Five downtown office buildings emptied, traffic snarled, after rash of bomb threats. Page 22.

Full coverage, Pages 21-27

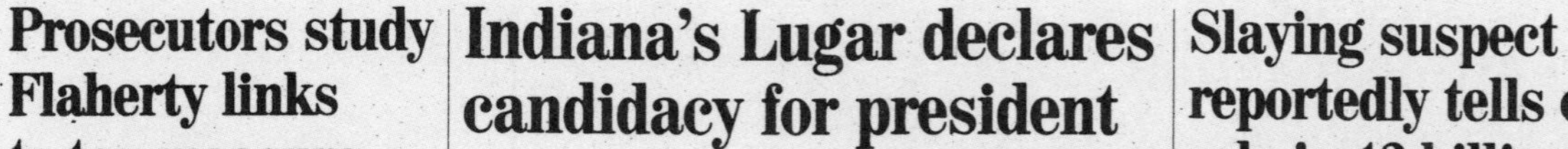
Bomb at Alfred Murrah Building
Possible targets?
Building tenants include Bureau of Alcohol, Tobacco and Firearms, Drug Enforcement Administration, Secret Service.
Day care center
Located on second floor; at least 12 children killed.
Car bomb
1,000 to 1,200 pounds; located here, according to ATF director.
SOURCES: General Services Administration, ATF, The Tulsa (Okla.) World, The Edmond (Okla.) Evening Sun, news reports

KNIGHT-RIDDER TRIBUNE, GLOBE STAFF GRAPHIC

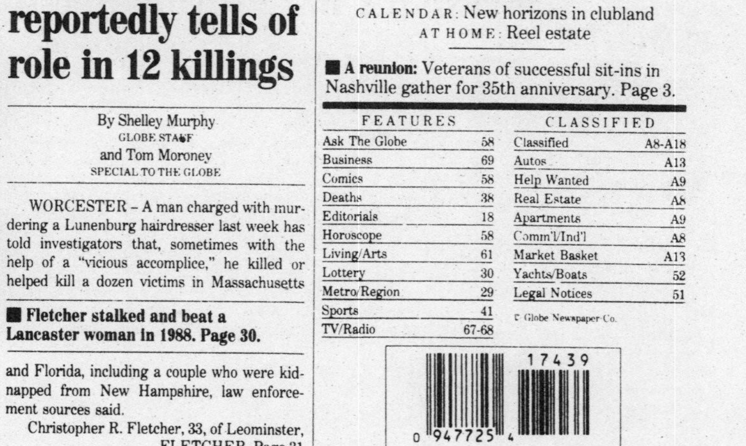

AP PHOTO
A woman comforts an injured child yesterday outside the ravaged office building.

Day-care center hard-hit

YMCA baby-sitting facility also damaged

By Lianne Hart
LOS ANGELES TIMES

OKLAHOMA CITY – There was a terrible roar. The walls fell, the ceiling gave way and shards of glass like so many bright razors filled the air.

And, suddenly, a modern drama called urban terrorism had been transformed into an ancient ceremony of horror – the slaughter of the innocents.

The car bomb that leveled much of a nine-story federal office building here exploded directly under a day care center on the structure's second floor and badly damaged another baby-sitting facility in a nearby YMCA. Of the 40 children thought to have been in the federal building when the bomb went off, 12 are known dead. The dead ranged in age from 1 to 7. Some of them were burned beyond recognition. One of the children known to have survived was in surgery and another in intensive care.

On the sidewalk outside the devastated Alfred P. Murrah Building at midday, a

CHILDREN, Page 25

Prosecutors study Flaherty links to tax measure

By Frank Phillips
GLOBE STAFF

When Richard Goldberg and his lobbyist were entertaining top legislative leader Charles F. Flaherty at their Cape Cod rental property in 1990, they were also working behind the scenes on Beacon Hill to win legislative approval of measures to block the state's efforts to seize Goldberg's parking-lot business in East Boston.

Sources yesterday confirmed that federal prosecutors have combed the public record and put some of the key players before a grand jury in an effort to find out whether Flaherty – who was then the House majority leader and became speaker in 1991 – used his political muscle to help Goldberg prevail in the Legisla-

FLAHERTY, Page 14

Indiana's Lugar declares candidacy for president

By Bob Hohler
GLOBE STAFF

INDIANAPOLIS – Sen. Richard G. Lugar, a conservative Republican touting a radical plan to replace the federal income tax with a sales tax, formally launched a dark-horse bid for the presidency yesterday. He cast himself as a seasoned statesman capable of calling on "the better angels of our nature" to promote the nation's prosperity and security.

In a red-brick square ringed by skyscrapers in the Indiana capital where he began his 31-year career in public office, Lugar, 63, contrasted himself with President Clinton but steered clear of the Senate majority leader. Bob Dole, whom he trails by vast margins in fund-raising, name

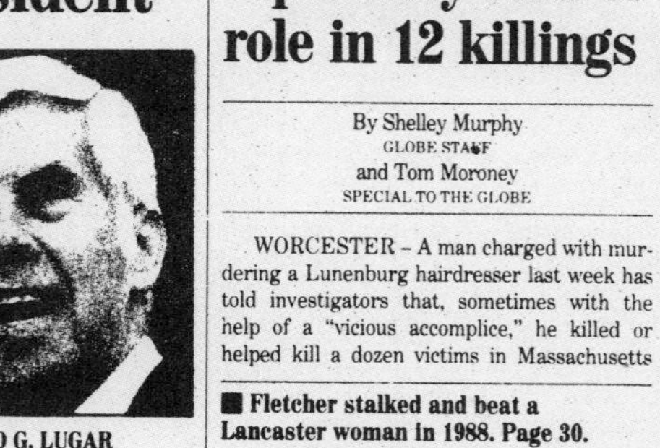

SEN. RICHARD G. LUGAR
"New liberty" for taxpayers

recognition and early preference polls in the nine-way race for the

LUGAR, Page 4

Slaying suspect reportedly tells of role in 12 killings

By Shelley Murphy
GLOBE STAFF
and Tom Moroney
SPECIAL TO THE GLOBE

WORCESTER – A man charged with murdering a Lunenburg hairdresser last week has told investigators that, sometimes with the help of a "vicious accomplice," he killed or helped kill a dozen victims in Massachusetts

Fletcher stalked and beat a Lancaster woman in 1988. Page 30.

and Florida, including a couple who were kidnapped from New Hampshire, law enforcement sources said.

Christopher R. Fletcher, 33, of Leominster,

FLETCHER, Page 31

Inside

CALENDAR: New horizons in clubland
AT HOME: Reel estate

A reunion: Veterans of successful sit-ins in Nashville gather for 35th anniversary. Page 3.

FEATURES		CLASSIFIED	
Ask The Globe	58	Classified	A8-A18
Business	69	Autos	A13
Comics	58	Help Wanted	A9
Deaths	38	Real Estate	A8
Editorials	18	Apartments	A9
Horoscope	58	Comm'l/Ind'l	A8
Living/Arts	61	Market Basket	A13
Lottery	30	Yachts/Boats	52
Metro/Region	29	Legal Notices	51
Sports	41		
TV/Radio	67-68		

17439
0 947725 4

VOLUME 248 • NUMBER 96
96 pages
50 cents

The Boston Globe

WEDNESDAY, OCTOBER 4, 1995

FOUL MIGRATION
Wednesday: *Early showers; 75*
Thursday: *Cloudy; 64-69*
High tide: *8:05 a.m., 8:27 p.m.*
Full report: *Page 84*

COMMENTARY | *Page 24*

'The trial became a referendum on every social ill except the one it was about – escalating domestic violence.' **Eileen McNamara**

'In O.J.'s case, money didn't talk. It sang, it screeched, it yodeled – and The Juice is drooling in his diaper because he got away with it all.' **Patricia Smith**

'A predominantly black jury voted with their hearts and perhaps personal history instead of using their heads and overwhelming evidence.' **Mike Barnicle**

'NOT GUILTY'

AP PHOTO

O. J. Simpson, flanked by defense attorneys F. Lee Bailey (left) and Johnnie Cochran, reacts to the verdict.

A NEW LIFE

Potential of recouping wealth seen

By Brian McGrory
GLOBE STAFF

LOS ANGELES – The talk now is of a sprawling beachfront estate in Mexico, a fabulous party for all his friends, a book deal that could return him to great wealth overnight, even an unprecedented multimillion dollar pay-per-view interview broadcast on national television.

Such is the new life of O. J. Simpson, the football star, celebrity pitchman, murder defendant and now free man, the star character in an odyssey that is at once uniquely American yet repulsive to large chunks of America.

He arrived home to the hugs of family and friends at his Brentwood mansion yesterday morning, facing prospects that, while not exactly the material of childhood dreams, are far better than what even his closest friends ever dared to expect.

First on his agenda will be a reacquaintance with his two young children, and Simpson, through a statement read by his oldest son yesterday, indicated in no uncertain terms that he plans to resume custody of Sydney, 9, and Justin, 6, who have been in the care of the parents of Nicole Brown Simpson for the past 16

THE FUTURE, Page 23

Simpson free after acquittal

By Adam Pertman
GLOBE STAFF

LOS ANGELES – A jury of 10 women and two men set O. J. Simpson free yesterday, releasing a national torrent of conflicting emotions, anguished disputes and fierce debates about race and the criminal justice system.

Simpson mouthed the words "thank you" after the jurors ended the heart-stopping suspense in the courtroom and around the country by returning their "not guilty" verdict.

Later, in a message delivered by his son Jason, the former football star said he was "relieved that this part of the incredible nightmare" had ended.

As those brief remarks were being read, Simpson was being taken to a county jail to recover some belongings. Then, as television cameras captured the scene from helicopters overhead, he was driven in a white van past crowds of cheering spectators to his Brentwood estate.

Once he was home, a free man, he left the vehicle and walked into an embrace with his friend Al Cowlings – who had driven Simpson's white Bronco more than a year ago during the plodding chase that ignited America's fascination with this case.

Simpson threw a party for his attorneys last night, complete with a live band, and lead counsel Johnnie Cochran received a loud ovation when he arrived.

"Mr. Simpson, needless to say, is ecstatic and wants to get on with his life," Cochran said during an earlier news conference with other members of the defense team and the Simpson family. Cochran praised the verdict and said it "bespeaks justice."

SIMPSON, Page 22

THE IMPACT

Racial divide shown on police

By Peter S. Canellos
GLOBE STAFF

The O. J. Simpson verdict could be a wake-up call to American cities: Tolerate the attitudes of Mark Fuhrman-type police officers only at the cost of black faith in the system, said black lawyers and political leaders.

Of all the big social issues featured in the Simpson case – spousal abuse, media excesses, wealth and poverty in criminal justice – the one that struck the greatest resonance around the country was the racial divide over perceptions of police motives, they said.

"There are a couple of messages to come out of this case, but one is that the race problem is bad and getting worse in America," said Henry Owens, a prominent black defense attorney. "We have to deal with it. We have to get on top of it. We all know that there are police departments with other Mark Fuhr-

IMPACT, Page 27

LOCAL REACTION – *Patrons of Chatfield's Bar and Grill at Logan Airport respond yesterday as they watch the jury pronounce O. J. Simpson not guilty. The contentious voices that exploded in Greater Boston show that although the verdict is in, the arguments over the case burn hotter than ever. Page 21. A special section on the Simpson verdict, Pages 21-28.*

GLOBE STAFF PHOTO / MARK WILSON

Reliance on blood undid prosecution

By Michael Grunwald and Maria Shao
GLOBE STAFF

Prosecutors built a case against O. J. Simpson in blood. And in the end, analysts said yesterday, that blood betrayed them.

Unable to provide a confession, a weapon or a witness, the prosecution relied almost exclusively on DNA evidence linking Simpson to blood at the scene of the crime. But legal experts said the defense concocted a brilliant rebuttal to the damning circumstantial evidence, convincing jurors of at least the possibility that police planted that trail of blood.

The defense did not provide an alibi for Simpson, or any explanation of who killed Nicole Brown Simpson and Ronald Goldman. It simply attacked the credibility of witnesses who handled the blood, especially Detective Mark Fuhrman, who later was exposed as a racist. Once prosecutors had to distance themselves from their star witness, the defense had sown their reasonable doubt, the experts said.

The experts were divided on how much of an effect racial issues and the history of the Los Angeles Police Department had on the verdict. But they agreed that the prosecution had

LEGAL, Page 28

PLAYOFFS BEGIN

GLOBE STAFF PHOTO / JIM DAVIS

Roger Clemens fires against the Indians in last night's playoff opener in Cleveland. Clemens hurled a strong seven innings in the extra-innings tussle. Sports, Page 85.

Rauschenbach acquitted in influence-peddling case

By John Milne
GLOBE STAFF

After a trial that included testimony from Gov. Weld, Lt. Gov. Paul Cellucci and State Treasurer Joseph D. Malone, Sen. Henri S. Rauschenbach was acquitted yesterday of charges that he sold his access to the top state leaders.

A Suffolk Superior Court jury apparently believed Rauschenbach's testimony that he promoted a risky investment plan because he thought it was a good idea and not because he was on the payroll of a Boston investment broker with links to the plan's manager.

When the verdict was read, Rauschenbach, 47, an influential Cape Cod Republican, turned to the jury and mouthed the words, "thank you."

He then took the hand of his wife, Lauren, and they left the courtroom together. Outside the door, she burst into tears.

"I am glad that the jury was able to understand my side of the story," Rauschenbach, of Brewster, said later. "I think they appreciated what it's like to be a public servant in this day and age."

Rauschenbach was the only politician to stand trial in the case in-

RAUSCHENBACH, Page 33

Inside

FOOD: Letting off steam

More state inspectors sought: The Weld administration drops its plan to have private companies inspect the state's 29,000 elevators and escalators. Page 29.

Investors riding high: Mutual funds have another strong quarter, and money managers say the forces that have driven the market all year remain intact. Business, Page 49.

First FleetCenter rock: R.E.M.plays to 18,000-plus fans at Boston's new arena. Living/Arts, Page 77.

FEATURES		CLASSIFIED	
Ask The Globe	74	Classified	36-48
Business	49	Autos	41
Comics	74-75	Help Wanted	38
Deaths	34-35	Professional	54
Editorials	18	Real Estate	37
Horoscope	74	Apartments	37
Living Arts	77	Comm'l/Ind'l	37
Lottery	30	Market Basket	36
Metro/Region	29	Yachts/Boats	89
Sports	85		
TV/Radio	83-84		

LOTTERY, PAGE 3
Volume 248
Number 128
$1.75
$2.00 beyond 30 miles

Boston Sunday Globe

COLD COMFORT
Sunday: Sunny, chilly, 45
Monday: Sun, milder, 55
Details, Page 77

SUNDAY, NOVEMBER 5, 1995

Rabin shot dead at Tel Aviv rally; Israeli Jew with ties to right held

Familiar ring to Mideast death

By David Shribman
GLOBE STAFF

News Analysis

And so peace has claimed another victim.

Last night's assassination of Israeli Prime Minister Yitzhak Rabin was brutal, violent, cynical – but not shocking. And that, perhaps, is the greatest tragedy of all.

In years to come no student of Middle East politics will be startled to come upon a passage noting that Mr. Rabin – fierce as a soldier, fiercer still as a negotiator, fiercest of all as a defender of the wars he prosecuted and the peace he made – was gunned down at a rally in Tel Aviv. It is the price of peace, or has been in that region of recrimination in this century of violence.

Now, once again, the funeral songs will be sung for a man of peace. It has happened before – for the grandfather of Jordan's King Hussein, Abdullah, assassinated before the 1947 war because he appeared to be making accommodations that worried some Arabs; for Count Folke Bernadotte of Sweden, the negotiator for the United Nations after the formation of the state of Israel; and, most vividly, for Anwar Sadat, the Egyptian architect of the Camp David accord, celebrated in the West as a visionary, reviled by some at home as a traitor.

It is at these times of sorrow and sympathy that the true nature of the

MIDDLE EAST, Page 21

AFP PHOTO

Prime Minister Yitzhak Rabin (right) and Foreign Minister Shimon Peres appear at the rally before yesterday's shooting.

World mourns prime minister

By Ethan Bronner
GLOBE STAFF

TEL AVIV – Prime Minister Yitzhak Rabin was shot and killed last night an hour after addressing a massive peace rally. A 27-year-old Israeli law student with rightist connections was taken into custody at the scene.

Cabinet ministers wept openly as condolences poured in from world leaders for the former general considered most responsible for the Middle East peace process in which Israel has signed agreements with its historic enemies, the Palestinians and Jordan.

Rabin, 73, the first Israeli leader to fall to an assassin's bullet, was shot three times at close range as he left the rally's podium. The suspect was immediately seized.

Rabin was rushed to nearby Ichilov Hospital. He arrived there with no pulse and no blood pressure, Health Minister Ephraim Sneh said.

Rabin was pronounced dead on the operating table at 11:10 p.m., Israeli time, 75 minutes after being shot.

> **'A great road was paved by a great leader.'**
> SHIMON PERES
> *Foreign minister*

At a news conference early today after an emergency Cabinet meeting, Foreign Minister Shimon Peres, who was named interim prime minister, said Rabin will be buried tomorrow at a state funeral.

Rabin's body is to lie in state in the Knesset beginning this afternoon.

In Washington last night, Clinton, barely controlling his emotion for a man he said he loved, said on television that "the world had lost one of its greatest men" and bid Rabin farewell in Hebrew. Clinton will attend the funeral tomorrow.

An ashen-faced Yasser Arafat, leader of the Palestinian Authority, told Israeli Television that history would remember Rabin as a great man of peace.

Rabin, Peres and Arafat shared the 1994 Nobel Peace Prize for their peace accord.

"Yitzhak Rabin was an exceptional person, an exceptional leader," Peres said after the Cabinet meeting. "We never had anyone like him and I'm afraid we shall not have anyone to succeed him completely in the future."

RABIN, Page 20

In Boston area, a deep personal loss

By Peter S. Canellos
GLOBE STAFF

Camelia Sadat sat in her Brookline apartment and cried for Yitzhak Rabin, cried for the Middle East, cried for Arabs and Jews, and cried for her father, Anwar, who was struck down on a chilly fall day 14 years ago under eerily similar circumstances.

"The parallels are incredible – the first reports said a wound in the shoulder," Sadat said, weeping. "I didn't believe it then and I didn't believe it now, and shot by one of his own people. It's incredible. He put his life on the line for peace. I look at these people as my heroes. They are the heroes of peace in my time."

All across the Boston area, where many people were polishing plans to host Rabin on a visit to New England in just 11 days, Jews and Arabs faced, again, devastating news of bloodshed and assassination in the Middle East. During his two-day trip, Rabin was to speak at Brandeis and Harvard universities and attend a congress at the Hynes Auditorium sponsored by the Council of Jewish Federations.

For many Jewish Bostonians the loss was personal: They knew and liked Yitzhak Rabin

REACTION, Page 23

World reaction
■ Specialists: peace process will continue. Page 20.
■ PLO leader Yasser Arafat expresses sorrow and shock. Page 21.
■ World diplomats offer condolences. Page 21.
■ President Clinton reacts to news. Page 22.

GLOBE STAFF PHOTO / SUZANNE KREITER

Karen Caviglia gathers cancer-related data on the Internet.

The doctor is on line

Internet being consulted on health data

By Jon Auerbach
GLOBE STAFF

The cancer has spread from Karen Caviglia's breasts into her bones, where it lurks, enervating and frustrating as it works its tentacles deeper into her flesh.

Statistics are not on Caviglia's side. Once metastatic breast cancer hits, few victims survive more than several years. Two years have already passed since Caviglia was diagnosed.

In that time, the 50-year-old Shrewsbury woman has pored through stacks of cancer-related studies from hundreds of hospitals and libraries. She has queried doc-

ON LINE, Page 28

SOME CAMPAIGN GUIDELINES

Bishops call for politics of 'common good'

By Diego Ribadeneira
GLOBE STAFF

Setting a framework for next year's elections, the nation's Roman Catholic bishops issued a sweeping political statement today chastising candidates for running campaigns that divide society, fuel public cynicism and offer little substance.

Despite the criticisms, the bishops asked Americans not to abandon the political process.

"We regret public attitudes that dismiss the legitimate role of government and ridicule public officials in misguided frustration with all politics," the bishops said. "We need more, not less public participation."

In the statement, "Political Responsibility: Proclaiming the Gospel of Life, Protecting the Least Among Us and Pursuing the Common Good," the bishops also suggested that the news media were falling short in their coverage, and that religious groups should not campaign for specific candidates.

The bishops exhorted Americans, particularly the nation's 60 million Catholics, to become more involved and hold candidates accountable for promoting policies that improve the nation's quality of life.

"We believe every proposal, policy or political platform should be measured by how it touches the human person; whether it enhances or diminishes human life, human dignity and human rights; and how it advances the common good," the statement said. The bishops encouraged parishes to launch voter registration drives, sponsor candidate forums and distribute objective voter guides.

"American political life must re-

BISHOPS, Page 29

Uncertainties line '96 road to White House

By Michael Kranish
GLOBE STAFF

WASHINGTON – One year from today, Americans will elect a president.

Forget the pundits and take this reality check: Four years ago, a Gulf War hero, President Bush, was considered a shoo-in, and relatively few voters outside Arkansas had heard of Bill Clinton.

The presidential campaign is a race of uncertainties, full of "X" factors. The big question today is whether retired Gen. Colin Powell will run, but

■ **Texas Sen. Phil Gramm wins Maine straw poll. Page 16.**

other unknowns abound, no matter what Powell does.

"There are major uncertainties about the election," said Curtis Gans, director of the Committee for the Study of the American Electorate. "An enormous amount hinges on Powell, but also: What are the results of the next eight weeks in Congress? What is next year's agenda? What is the state of the economy? Who are the candidates, and how many do we have?"

Powell is the talk of the nation, in part because many voters aren't thrilled about the preordained, made-in-Washington 1996 campaign. That creates

PRESIDENCY, Page 14

Inside
INDEX, PAGE 3

■ **Silber named:** It's official; the BU president will be chairman of the state Board of Education. Page 33.

■ **Direct hit:** Beneath Boston Harbor, tunnels were joined for the Nut and Deer Island sewage plants. Page 33.

■ **Report cards:** Supt. Thomas Payzant plans to issue grades on the city's schools. Learning, Page A97.

Reader Feedback
We asked: "Do you agree with the gist of Gov. Weld's plan to reorganize state government?" A sampling of your answers is on Page 38.

■ **Suite seats:** A variety of well-heeled tenants signed up for the plush private boxes at the FleetCenter. We have a look at who's hangin' where above the ice – from Bank of Boston to Anheuser-Busch. Business, Page 41.

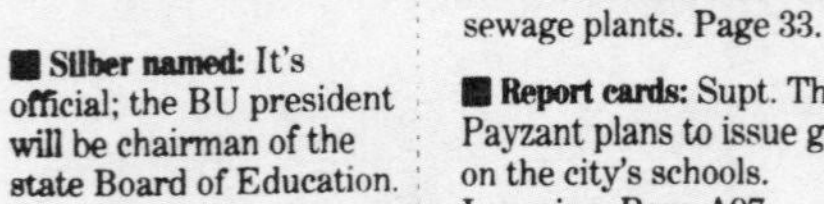

■ **Get back:** With unheard songs being released and a TV documentary due, it's worth looking at why the Beatles still matter. ArtsEtc., Page 57.

■ **Car show preview:** What's hot this year. New Autos, Page A21.

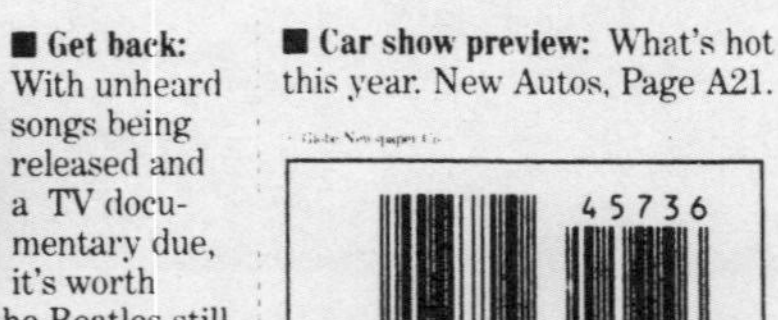

VOLUME 249 • NUMBER 107
116 pages
50 cents

The Boston Globe

WATCH IT, BLUSTER
Today: [illegible]
Tomorrow: [illegible]
High tide: [illegible]
Full report: [illegible]

TUESDAY, APRIL 16, 1996

BOSTON MARATHON 100

A real birthday bash

MEN'S WINNER
Moses Tanui of Kenya

GLOBE STAFF PHOTOS / JIM DAVIS

WOMEN'S WINNER
Uta Pippig of Germany

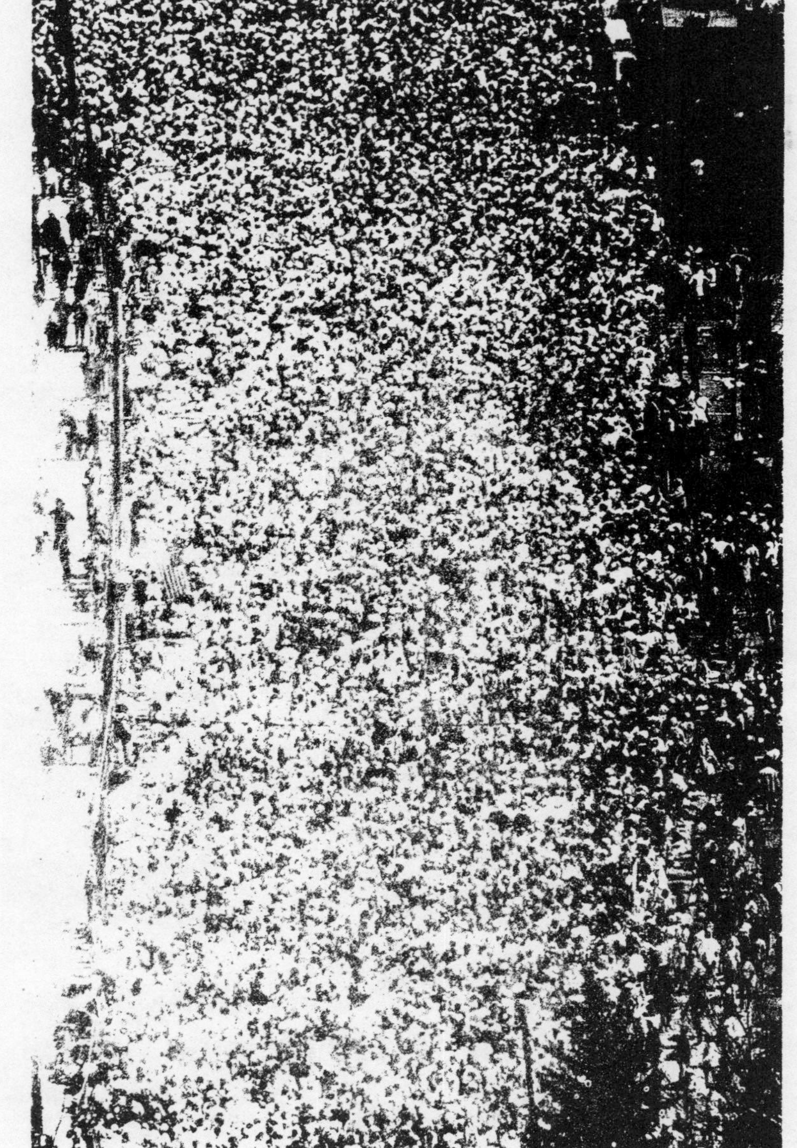

[illegible] than 38,000 [illegible] began moving out of Hopkinton at noon yesterday.

WOMEN'S WHEELCHAIR WINNER
Jean Driscoll of Champaign, Illinois

[illegible]EN'S WHEELCHAIR WINNER
[illegible] Frei of Switzerland

The day that was:

[illegible] And some [illegible] ... and wheelchairs as it coursed through the towns on the way to Boston. And the Globe was there, start to finish. Coverage begins on Page 41, the results section begins on Page 59.

Israel, pressing Lebanon raids, not set to talk

But diplomats arrive in region as bombardment enters fifth day

By Ethan Bronner
GLOBE STAFF

AMMAN, Jordan – Israeli warplanes and heavy artillery bombarded south Lebanon for a fifth day yesterday, and the government said it was too early to negotiate an end to the military operation aimed at wounding Hezbollah, the Lebanese Muslim guerrilla group that continued to rain down rockets on Israeli towns.

The first inklings of a diplomatic approach were apparent as Foreign Minister Herve de Charette of France arrived in Israel, as did Defense Secretary Michael Portillo of Britain. The UN Security Council debated the crisis; Secretary of State Warren M. Christopher was in telephone contact with the parties.

But the pressure on Israel remained negligible partly because the Clinton administration accepts Israel's argument that Hezbollah created the crisis through its Katyusha rocket attacks and that the Lebanese and Syrian governments must be made accountable for the actions of groups under their control.

Diplomatic sources said Christopher had forwarded an offer from Israel to withdraw its own troops and disband its client Lebanese army in southern Lebanon, Newsday reported. Israel requires that Syria fill the vacuum, either with its own troops or with Lebanese forces, and guarantee Israel's security against further attacks from Hezbollah.

Meanwhile, nearly half a million people streamed northward from southern Lebanon toward the cities of Sidon and Beirut in an effort to escape Israeli attacks.

Israeli jets hit a power station northeast of

MIDEAST, Page 14

Clinton, Kim offer 4-way peace talks on Koreas

By Terence Hunt
ASSOCIATED PRESS

CHEJU-DO, South Korea – President Clinton and President Kim Young Sam of South Korea have jointly proposed unconditional peace talks involving the two Koreas as well as the United States and China. "North Korea has said it wants peace. This is our proposal to achieve it," Clinton asserted today.

Standing before a vivid field of yellow mustard flowers alongside the East China Sea, Clinton cited an "unshakable alliance between our two countries," and added, "The United States is fully committed to the defense of South Korea."

The unexpected proposal for four-way talks, revealed early this afternoon in Korea, was made after North Korea had sent troops toward the South in violation of the 43-year-old Armistice agreement that ended the Korean War. The proposal departed from a longstanding US goal of resolving long-simmering tensions on the peninsula through direct North-South talks without outside participation.

"We hope Pyongyang will take it seriously," Clinton said at a joint news conference with Kim held during a 10-hour visit to this resort island 60 miles south of the Korean mainland.

KOREA, Page 19

'At times, we are so open and allow so many voices that it can feel like anarchy.'
SHERRY BROOKS-ROBERTS, *Teacher-facilitator*

Democracy's the principle of W. Roxbury pilot school

At Lyndon, 13 teachers get to make the rules

By Karen Avenoso
GLOBE CORRESPONDENT

The rules about how to get 200 students onto afternoon buses required input from all of this school's 13 teachers.

School mail is sorted by three busy instructors, who squeeze office duties between math lessons and counseling sessions.

As for budget planning – a long and tricky process at the most autocratic of public institutions – it began with several hundred surveys, mailed out not only to teachers and parents, but even to interested community members with no children enrolled.

Democracy is so much a part of the Patrick F. Lyndon Elementary School in West Roxbury that it has neither a principal's office nor a principal.

Part of a national movement to rethink school governance, the founders of this pilot school have taken decentralization to an extreme – putting major educational decisions in the hands of teachers and hashing the rest out with even more participants.

In less than a year, the structure at the Lyndon has quickly revealed its advantages and weaknesses. At best, teachers say, an entire community feels ownership of a school. At worst, decisions become unnecessarily unwieldy and painfully slow to unfold.

One of Boston's five pilot schools – which opened in September and include an evening high school and health careers school – the Lyndon is part of the Boston public school system but not required to follow most union or School Committee rules.

Educators say they've seen the move toward democratically-run schools among many of the country's other experimental public schools. Of 110 charter schools re-

LYNDCN, Page 21

Inside

■ **Tax time:** It's deadline day, but faster state refunds are expected for late filers. Business, Page 99.

FEATURES		CLASSIFIED	
Ask The Globe	56	Classified	90-98
Business	99	Autos	95
Comics	56	Help Wanted	92
Deaths	114	Real Estate	91
Editorials	22	Apartments	91
Horoscope	56	Comm'l Ind'l	[illegible]
Living/Arts	83	Market Basket	90
Lottery	26	Yachts/Boats	37
Metro/Region	25	Learning	116
Sports	33		
TV/Radio	54-55		

VOLUME 250 • NUMBER 18
124 pages
50 cents

The Boston Globe

RIGHT. SUN IT
Today: *Sunny, humid; 8*
Tomorrow: *T-storm; mid 80s*
High tide: *1:29 a.m., 2:01 p.m.*
Full report: *Page E8*

THURSDAY, JULY 18, 1996

Jet with 229 explodes off N.Y.

'Fireball' seen before flight to Paris hits water near Long Island; search teams rush to area

By Fred Kaplan
GLOBE STAFF

NEW YORK – A TWA 747 jumbo jet with 229 people on board exploded in midair last night and crashed into the waters off Long Island.

The plane, Flight 800 bound for Paris, had taken off from John F. Kennedy International Airport just minutes before the incident. Eyewitnesses reported seeing "a huge fireball" and hearing a "clap of thunder," then watching fragments of a plane tumbling into the ocean about 10 miles south of Long Island and 40 miles east of the airport.

CNN reported that the disaster occurred at 13,700 feet and that there was no distress call from the plane prior to its plunging into the water.

FAA officials said last night that air-traffic controllers in Boston reported losing radar contact with the plane at 8:45 p.m.

Coast Guard vessels and helicopters – directed from a command center in Boston – as well as a Navy P-3 rescue plane and a New York Air National Guard C-130, rushed to the area with search teams and life rafts.

Lt. Commander Jim McPherson, with the Coast Guard command center in Boston, said early this morning that bodies had been recovered at the crash site. No survivors had been found, he added.

At a late-night news conference at Kennedy airport, Mike Kelly, a TWA vice president, said 212 passengers were on board the flight, as well as 17 crew members, for a total of 229 people. However, a TWA flight attendant said the flight would have carried 32 crew members.

From the air, wreckage and fuel on the water could be seen burning.

Suffolk County Fire Department Chief Myles Quinn said a temporary morgue was set up near the scene.

A team from the National Transportation Safety Board was on its way here from Washington last night.

NTSB Chairman Jim Hall cautioned that it would be "irresponsible, in light of the little facts that we have, to speculate on the cause of the accident."

The State Department said there was no reason to attribute the crash to terrorism.

TWA's Kelly said no threats had been made regarding Flight 800.

Tony Velocci, senior editor at Aviation Week & Space Technology magazine, told MSNBC that the 747 is "the safest plane in the sky today" and he suspected "a terrorist bomb" at work.

However, several other aviation experts told the news station and CNN that mechanical problems have caused fires and explosions in past airplane crashes. Ira Furman, a former official with the NTSB, said engine "flare-ups" can cause fires, which – given a full tank of fuel – could ignite explosions.

GLOBE STAFF MAP

Kelly said the FAA had raised the security level at all American airports some time ago – he did not specify exactly when – in anticipation of the Olympic Games that begin tomorrow in Atlanta. "Security is at one of the highest levels," Kelly said.

CRASH, Page A18

A state overhaul? Not quite this time

By Michael Grunwald
GLOBE STAFF

The state's Executive Office of Consumer Affairs has been downsized.

It is now just the Office of Consumer Affairs.

Otherwise, though, it is hard to see how the recent "elimination" of the Consumer Affairs secretariat has changed state government, since no jobs or services or budgets were cut. Nancy Merrick is now "director" instead of "secretary," but she still reports to Gov. William F. Weld.

"Basically, we're still here, and nothing has changed," Merrick said.

In his campaign to unseat Sen. John F. Kerry, Weld likes to brag that his bold government reorganization plan wiped out five of 11 Cabinet secretariats. But four of the five have actually survived relatively unscathed, although they are no longer "secretariats." The only real casualty of downsizing was the Executive Office of Education, which was created under Weld in 1993.

Then again, compared to the rest of Weld's much-hyped blueprint for "lean, focused, affordable" government in Massachusetts, the elimination of secretariats was a huge success. The vast majority of the downsizing plan died in the Legislature – where lawmakers questioned the need for much of the overhaul and were reluctant to give Weld a major victory in the midst of his Senate campaign. Reinventing government

REORGANIZATION, Page A22

GLOBE STAFF FILE PHOTO / PAT GREENHOUSE
UMass players wear the now-trademarked motto of former coach John Calipari (center).

Refusing to lose some hefty fees

Calipari employs full-court pressure to get rights to slogan

By Daniel Golden
and David Armstrong
GLOBE STAFF

In 1990, when then-University of Massachusetts basketball coach John Calipari needed a slogan to inspire his struggling program, he only had to look across campus at the T-shirts worn by the school's Yankee Conference football champions. Designed by seniors on the team, the shirts carried a catchy motto: "Refuse to Lose."

"That slogan was meant for the football team and any other program at the university," says Paul Mayberry, a football cocaptain and All-American that year. "It was not meant to make one individual wealthy."

But it is making one person wealthy – Calipari. As his team rose to national prominence, its success popularized the slogan football players and coaches say he copied from them. Now, Calipari has trademarked the motto, after acquiring the rights from a Duke University tennis coach who, independently, had put "Refuse to Lose" on T-shirts for years but lacked the money to fight him in court.

According to the US Patent and Trademark Office in Washington, D.C., which gave preliminary approval to his claim this week, Calipari may be the only college basketball coach ever to trademark his team's motto. The trademark, combined with an aggressive marketing campaign run largely out of UMass athletic department offices and with school resources, has turned "Refuse to Lose" into a potentially multimillion-dollar business. The profits, however, will not go to UMass but to

SLOGAN, Page A23

The White House forgave drug use

By Brian McGrory
GLOBE STAFF

WASHINGTON – The Clinton administration interceded with Secret Service officials and granted White House access to at least 21 employees who had a history of cocaine, crack and hallucinogen use, in a decision that ignited a new round of political fire yesterday.

A Secret Service official told congressional investigators that the agency had initially denied passes to the employees in 1993 and 1994 because of recent drug use. But the passes were granted after the White House established a program of additional drug testing for those deemed by the Secret Service to be security risks.

White House press secretary Mike McCurry, bombarded with questions on the administration's action at a briefing yesterday, said the president does not believe that prior drug use disqualifies someone from public service. He said the White House has a mandatory drug-testing program for all employees and a more exhaustive one for the employees in question.

"The president is very clear: He has an absolute zero-tolerance standard for drug use at the White House," McCurry said. "And that, I want to make very clear, has been maintained while he has been here."

McCurry did not identify the

FILES, Page A21

ANONYMOUS NO LONGER – *Newsweek columnist Joe Klein announces yesterday that he wrote the best-selling political novel "Primary Colors." The identity of the author, known on the book jacket as Anonymous, had been one of the hottest mysteries in Washington. Page A24.*

SJC sharply limits access to records of rape victims

By John Ellement
GLOBE STAFF

Resolving a contentious legal battle between women's advocates and defense lawyers, the Massachusetts high court yesterday made it extremely difficult for accused rapists and their lawyers to obtain the counseling records of alleged rape victims.

The women's advocates applauded the 7-0 Supreme Judicial Court ruling, saying it will lead to more rape victims seeking help, but a defense attorney predicted it will result in some people being wrongly convicted.

The court dismissed a contempt citation and jail sentence imposed on Nasrine Farhoody, executive director of a Worcester rape crisis center. It said she was right when she refused to turn over a client's records to a Superior Court judge.

Wendy J. Murphy, the attorney for Farhoody and other rape crisis centers, said women can now feel confident that only in rare instances will their private thoughts be shared with their attackers.

Murphy said "countless" rape victims have chosen not to prosecute their attackers because they do not want their counseling sessions made public. Now, "the chilling effect, in my opinion, is gone," she said.

RAPE, Page A20

Old royal ways preserve the house of Saud

By Ethan Bronner
GLOBE STAFF

JEDDAH, Saudi Arabia – They come from all across this desert kingdom like a cast from some biblical epic: gnarled tribal chiefs with crude walking sticks, henna-dyed beards and mismatched sandals; religious scholars in layers of flowing robes; military men; even a foreigner or two.

Numbering more than 500, they line up like schoolboys, petitions under their arms, some brief, hand-scrawled and crumpled into their pockets, others lengthy, typed and fastened into stiff folders.

When his turn arrives, each sits next to the heir to the throne and effective regent of Saudi Arabia, Crown Prince Abdullah bin Abdul Aziz. Many sing the praises of his royal highness and offer assurances of their fealty. Later, they are fed an enormous meal of lamb and chicken on dozens of tables.

But what they nearly all want – and nearly all get – is money.

"He hands out a million rials [$275,000] like this every Tuesday night," Professor Bakor Amri, an economist at Jeddah's King Abdul Aziz University and a confidant of the crown prince's, whispers as petitions are passed to underlings and notes scribbled on them.

Although the setting is all marble, crystal, gold leaf and acres of machine-made carpeting – the crown prince's Jeddah palace, where he spends the summer, has state-of-the-art air conditioning and blindingly bright chandeliers – this weekly

SAUDIS, Page A22

Metro/Region B
Game turns fatal
A 19-year-old is killed by a train in North Andover while sitting on the tracks with friends, playing a game of chicken.

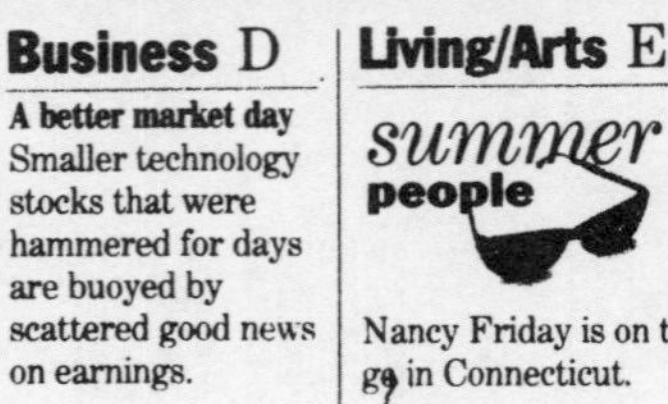

Sports C
Red Sox win
Boston squanders a seven-run lead but downs the Yankees, 12-11, on Jeff Frye's ninth-inning single at Fenway.

Business D
A better market day
Smaller technology stocks that were hammered for days are buoyed by scattered good news on earnings.

Living/Arts E

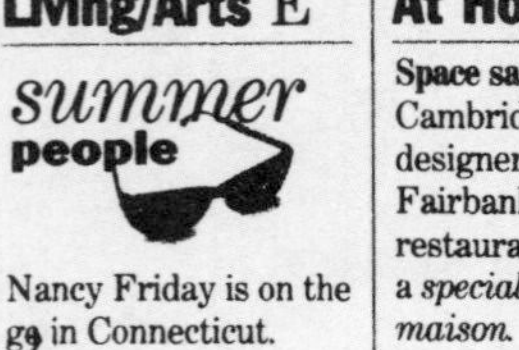

Nancy Friday is on the go in Connecticut.

At Home F
Space savior
Cambridge-based designer Sandra Fairbank has made restaurant makeovers a *specialite de la maison.*

Calendar
Berkshire magic
Summer in the Berkshires means fine dining, country inns, nature trails and music, music, music.

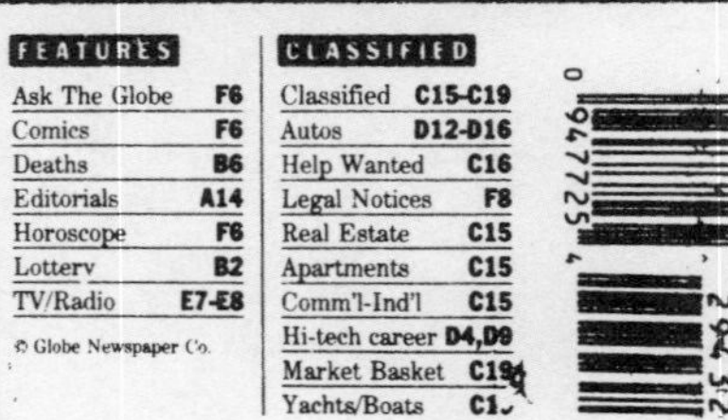

FEATURES	
Ask The Globe	F6
Comics	F6
Deaths	B6
Editorials	A14
Horoscope	F6
Lottery	B2
TV/Radio	E7-E8

CLASSIFIED	
Classified	C15-C19
Autos	D12-D16
Help Wanted	C16
Legal Notices	F8
Real Estate	C15
Apartments	C15
Comm'l-Ind'l	C15
Hi-tech career	D4,D9
Market Basket	C19
Yachts/Boats	C1

VOLUME 250 • NUMBER 129
100 pages
50 cents

The Boston Globe

WATCH UP DOC
Today: *Clouds AM, sun pm; 55*
Tomorrow: *Partly sunny; 50s*
High tide: *7:20 a.m., 7:39 p.m.*
Full report: *Page B22*

WEDNESDAY, NOVEMBER 6, 1996

Clinton rolls to second term; Kerry rebuffs Weld challenge

Election '96

Democrats roar toward sweep ot House delegation

The state's two Republican congressmen appear to be swept from office, as Rep. Peter I. Blute concedes to James McGovern and Rep. Peter G. Torkildsen appears to be losing narrowly to John F. Tierney. If Tierney prevails, it would be the first time in the state's history that the House delegation has been all Democratic based on the results of a regular election.

Another Democrat, William Delahunt, defeats GOP's Edward Teague handily for the seat vacated by Gerry Studds, while Democrat John Olver holds off a tough challenge by Jane Swift. Six other Democrats coast to reelection. B1.

School board stays appointed

Mayor Menino's political operation gets a big win as a plan to revive the elected School Committee loses by 2-1 ratio. B1.

Question 1
Eliminate cruel traps

	Vote	%
Yes	411,299	64%
No	231,423	36%

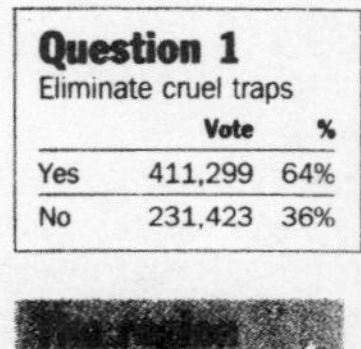

New Hampshire elects Shaheen

Jeanne Shaheen becomes New Hampshire's first female governor and the first Democrat to hold the office since 1980. Democrat Dick Swett falls short in his challenge to incumbent Sen. Bob Smith. B1.

Franks beaten in Conn. race

Rep. Gary Franks, one of only two black Republicans in Congress, is trounced by Democratic challenger James Maloney. The Maine Senate race between Democrat Joseph Brennan and Republican Susan Collins is too close to call. B13.

National election report, A21-A28

Local, regional election coverage, B1, B4-13

GLOBE STAFF PHOTO / JOHN TLUMACKI

A jubilant Sen. John F. Kerry acknowledges his win last night in his victory speech at the Sheraton Boston.

The tide works against governor in Senate race

By Frank Phillips and Don Aucoin
GLOBE STAFF

With surprising ease, US Sen. John F. Kerry last night turned back Gov. William F. Weld's blistering challenge and won a third term after an 11-month campaign that was one of the most closely watched Senate races in the country.

US senator
1,933 of 2,106 precincts - 92%

	Vote	%
Kerry	1,222,169	52%
Weld	1,037,220	45%

As of midnight, with 91 percent of the vote counted, Kerry, the Democrat, was leading Weld, a Republican, 53 percent to 44 percent. Conservative Party candidate Susan Gallagher garnered 3 percent.

The key to Kerry's decisive victory appeared to be a combination of the national Democratic tide – including President Clinton's landslide victory here in Massachusetts – and the senator's large margins among women voters, particularly those with college educations. Exit polls indicated that women favored Kerry over Weld by more than 20 percentagepoints, and that Kerry bested Weld among men as well.

Kerry prevailed over Weld among voters of all age groups, according to exit polls, and rolled up big wins in Democrat-heavy cities. Weld fared best among independents and Republicans.

"How sweet it is," exclaimed Kerry, appearing happy and relieved as he addressed his supporters at the Sheraton Boston Hotel. "What a long strange trip it has been."

SENATE, Page B4

GLOBE STAFF PHOTO / JIM DAVIS

Gov. William F. Weld is hugged by his wife, Susan, after his concession speech at the Park Plaza.

Dole loses in traditional party strongholds; GOP appears set to keep control of Congress

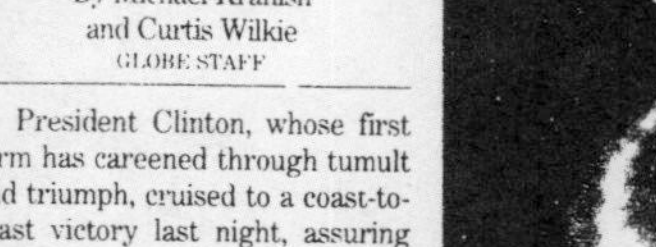

By Michael Kranish and Curtis Wilkie
GLOBE STAFF

President Clinton, whose first term has careened through tumult and triumph, cruised to a coast-to-coast victory last night, assuring him a place in history as the first reelected Democratic president since Franklin Delano Roosevelt.

The voters' status quo mood that helped Clinton defeat Republican Bob Dole had the president bracing for renewed Republican control in the Senate and perhaps in the House, too. This raised the specter of a continued division of power – and aggressive congressional investigations into Whitewater and fund-raising practices well into a second term.

"No words can convey the gratitude I feel tonight for the honor that has been given to me," Clinton, joined by Vice President Al Gore and their families, told a joyous crowd of thousands outside the Old State House in Little Rock. "Our journey is not done. My fellow Americans, we have work to do and that is what this election was all about.

"It is time to put politics aside, join together and get the job done for America's future."

"The Congress, whatever happens, will be closely divided," Clinton said. The voters "are sending us a message – work together. The most lasting and important thing I have learned . . . is when we are divided we defeat ourselves, but when we join our hands. . . . America always wins."

Clinton's victory was bolstered by a smooth economy, the overwhelming support of women and the lack of any great issue dividing the nation.

Dole, a 73-year-old World War

PRESIDENT, Page A23

REUTERS PHOTO

A confident President Clinton arrives yesterday morning to cast his vote in Little Rock, Ark.

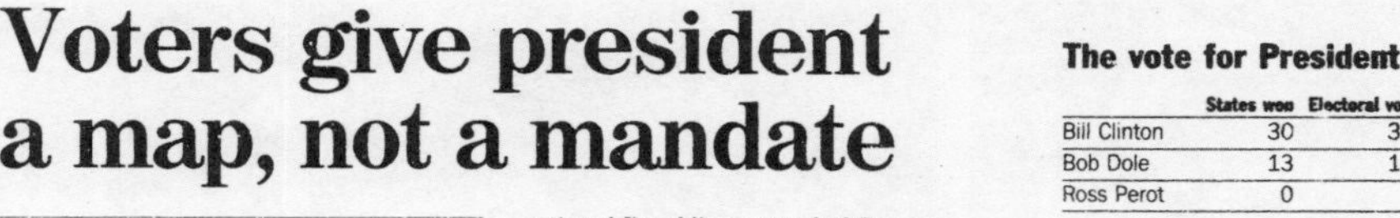

Voters give president a map, not a mandate

By David M. Shribman
GLOBE STAFF

News Analysis

There was less confetti than four years ago, less excitement, less confidence that all things are possible.

But in Bill Clinton's sweeping reelection victory there may be something more substantial and more enduring: a formula for American leadership for the turn of the century.

Four years ago, Clinton was elected with a public lurch for change. Two years ago, he was repudiated in midterm congressional elections that expressed a lurch for conservatism. Last night, with a record and a program for a little change and a little conservatism, he won a second term and a second chance.

The second chance almost surely will turn out to be more important.

He left no historic footprints on the American political landscape in his first term beyond the very fact of survival. His challenge now, after a campaign in which he laid out proposals that were notable principally for being small, is to leave a large footprint on the country and on the century – and to do it despite apparent continued Republican control of Congress.

The man who assumes that challenge today shows signs of being wiser – and wearier. He is dogged by doubters. He has yet to find a way to work with Congress – or even to bring his own administration to heel. He is plagued with ethics investigations. And his ability to take the offensive may be hampered by the likelihood that he and his administration may spend much of his new term on the defensive.

Even so, Clinton starts anew this morning, and with the confidence that the middle way may be the right way for the nation.

Indeed, if there was any loud message from yesterday's election, the strangely quiet climax of a loud campaign, it is that voters felt more comfortable with the middle way of Clinton than with the hard way of Bob Dole.

That's not a mandate. But it is a map.

The president prevailed by moving toward a balanced budget – but without favoring a balanced-budget amendment. He cut spending – but not too drastically. He wants to change Social Security and Medicare – but not too much.

He embraced as his own a health care adjustment that made some modest progress –

ANALYSIS, Page A25

The vote for President

	States won	Electoral votes
Bill Clinton	30	361
Bob Dole	13	113
Ross Perot	0	0

Congress at a glance

THE SENATE
34 of 100 seats at stake

	Present	New
Democrats	47	46
Republicans	53	54
Undecided	–	0

THE HOUSE
All 435 seats at stake

	Present	New
Democrats	198	202
Republicans	236	228
Undecided	–	5

Other key races

New Jersey – In a tight race, Democrat Robert Torricelli was victorious over Republican Dick Zimmer for the seat vacated by retiring Sen. Bill Bradley.

North Carolina – Sen. Jesse Helms once again defeated his 1990 opponent Harvey Gantt in a hard-fought race.

South Carolina – Sen. Strom Thurmond, 93, handily beat Democrat Elliot Close and will become the oldest senator in history.

Georgia – Democrat Max Cleland topped Republican Guy Millner to fill the seat of retiring Sen. Sam Nunn.

World A
Yeltsin surgery
Surgeons call the multiple coronary bypass operation they performed on the Russian president a success. A2.

Sports C
BC gambling probe
The college is expected to suspend up to a dozen football players who officials say have bet on games.

Living/Arts D
The Who forever
"I feel a bit like Frank Sinatra," bassist John Entwistle says with a chuckle about the English rock band's many comebacks.

Food E
Powerhouse to savor
Chicago goes from epicenter of steakhouse culture to a diverse restaurant landscape.

Business F
Diet drugs
The products are causing a revolution at commercial weight-loss centers.

FEATURES

Ask The Globe	E6
Comics	E6-7
Deaths	B14-15
Editorials	A18
Horoscope	E6
Lottery	B2
TV/Radio	D7-8

CLASSIFIED

Classified	F10,B17
Autos	C12
Help Wanted	B20
Professional	F10
Real Estate	B18
Apartments	B18
Comm'l/Ind'l	B18
Market Basket	B17
Yachts/Boats	C5
Legal Notices	B17

Globe Online
www.boston.com/globe

45333
0 94772 4

VOLUME 251 • NUMBER 27
76 pages
50 cents

The Boston Globe

A GRAY AREA
Today: *Cloudy, maybe flurries*
Tomorrow: *Light snow, rain*
High tide: *1:23 a.m., 1:33 p.m.*
Full report: *Page B8*

MONDAY, JANUARY 27, 1997

The ride's over

GLOBE STAFF PHOTO / MICHAEL ROBINSON-CHAVEZ
New England cornerback Otis Smith gives futile chase as Green Bay wide receiver Andre Rison runs for a first-quarter touchdown.

Green Bay has too much punch; beaten Patriots show early grit

By Dan Shaughnessy
GLOBE STAFF

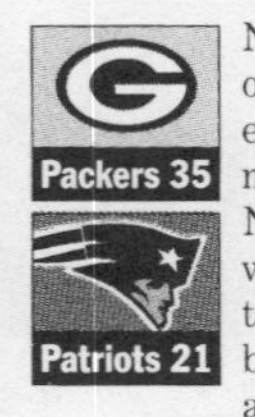

NEW ORLEANS – They united our region, providing thrills and expectations not experienced in more than a decade. They gave New Englanders a new topic to go with politics and weather, and they restored a local pride that's been missing since Larry Bird and friends patrolled the parquet in the golden days of the 1980s.

The 1996-97 New England Patriots were a little like the Blizzard of '78. They arrived unexpectedly, brought strangers together, and dominated morning coffee conversation for a full month.

But they did not win the Super Bowl. New England's magic ride came to a halt on the carpet of the Louisiana Superdome last night when the Green Bay Packers beat the Patriots, 35-21, in Super Bowl XXXI. Patriot fans today will awake hung over from too much Jambalaya, an overdose of Desmond Howard, and the nagging fear that head coach Bill Parcells has coached his last game for New England.

Let the record show that the sons of Parcells were not embarrassed in this annual American holiday game. New England did not re-visit the horrors of 1986, when the Chicago Bears destroyed the Patriots, 46-10, in this same building. But for the championship-starved sports fans of our region, last night's loss was painful nonetheless.

Across the land the game was billed as a coronation of a Packer team that was the class of the National Football League throughout the 1996-97 season. Wiseguys in Vegas made Green Bay a 14-point favorite (how do they always know?), and there was a sense of inevitability about the Pack's drive to reclaim the trophy that is named after Vince Lombardi, their legendary coach of three decades ago.

SUPER BOWL, Page D14

GLOBE STAFF PHOTO / JIM DAVIS
Patriots quarterback Drew Bledsoe reacts after a pass is intercepted.

GLOBE STAFF PHOTO / JOHN TLUMACKI
Packers Antonio Freeman (left) and Andre Rison celebrate Freeman's early 71-yard touchdown reception.

Super Bowl Sunday, 1997

"Chowderheads" finale: Six diehards end their long trek by watching the game in a New Orleans bar. B1.

Advertising blitz: Madison Avenue's big push makes for a long night for TV viewers. A14.

Most Valuable Player: Wide receiver Desmond Howard almost single-handedly dispatches the Patriots. D18.

Family woes: Relatives of New England players say they got the worst seats in the house. D18.

The team's future: Bob Kraft and Bill Parcells will end their relationship as owner and coach tomorrow, and it most likely will not be a friendly parting. D20.

The other side: Green Bay fans aplenty emerge in New England territory. D11.

Scalpers' paradise: Single seats could not be had for less than $600, and plenty of fans were shelling out $1,000 to get inside the stadium. D13.

Complete Super Bowl coverage, D1-20.

Nation A

Gingrich's troubles
The speaker's allegation that he is a victim of an ethical double standard draws mixed reviews. A3.

Business A14

Low profile
The manager of more than $8 billion in assets for his company's flagship stock fund shuns the "star" concept.

Metro/Region B

In the dark
Some low-income elders may not learn before the signup period ends about a state program to help them pay for prescription drugs.

Health/Science C

Health Sense
Some commercial weight-loss chains have added diet pills to their programs and hired doctors to dispense them. Here's what to know before taking the plunge.

Living/Arts C6

Painful past
Pianist Linda Cutting uses music to help her heal after childhood abuse.

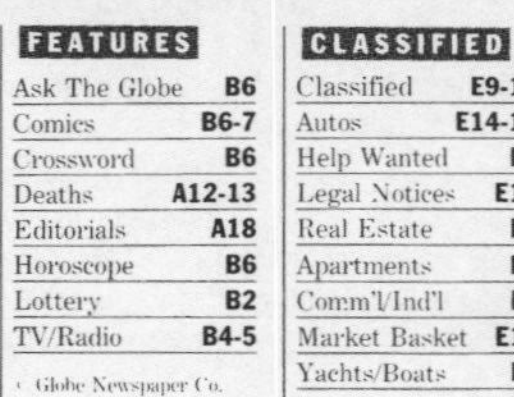

FEATURES	
Ask The Globe	B6
Comics	B6-7
Crossword	B6
Deaths	A12-13
Editorials	A18
Horoscope	B6
Lottery	B2
TV/Radio	B4-5

CLASSIFIED	
Classified	E9-18
Autos	E14-18
Help Wanted	E9
Legal Notices	E13
Real Estate	E9
Apartments	E9
Comm'l/Ind'l	E9
Market Basket	E12
Yachts/Boats	E5
Learning	A8

Globe Online

www.boston.com/globe

VOLUME 251 • NUMBER 63
64 pages
50 cents

The Boston Globe

CRAWLING ALL CARS
Today: Snow, drizzle; 30s
Tomorrow: Cloudy, near 50
High tide: 5:19 a.m., 5:59 p.m.
Full report: Page B8

TUESDAY, MARCH 4, 1997

AP FILE PHOTO

JUDGE PAUL P. HEFFERNAN . . . Had sparked protests

Judge dismissed from O'Brien case

Rare move by SJC; replacement named

By Judy Rakowsky
GLOBE STAFF

In an extraordinary move that surprised legal observers, the state's highest court dismissed Somerville District Court Judge Paul P. Heffernan from the murder case of Edward S. O'Brien, a Somerville teenager accused of killing his best friend's mother.

Citing its rarely used "power of general superintendence" over the court system, the Supreme Judicial Court ordered Heffernan removed yesterday morning.

The order comes just months after the SJC chastised Heffernan for refusing to hear key evidence in a hearing to decide if O'Brien, now 17, should be tried as a juvenile or an adult.

That ruling caused a furor in a murder case that spurred the Legislature to make changes in the juvenile laws. Heffernan also sparked protests when he refused to step down from the case.

"The assignment of a new judge," the court said in yesterday's decision, "will eliminate controversies and unnecessary issues in further proceedings and in any appeal."

Just hours after the order was issued, Chief District Court Judge Samuel Zoll appointed Dedham District Judge Gerald Alch as Heffer-

HEFFERNAN, Page A16

Gore defends his raising of funds, but vows a halt

Says he will make no more calls to donors from his office

By Bob Hohler and Michael Kranish
GLOBE STAFF

WASHINGTON – Vice President Al Gore, acknowledging reports that he solicited campaign funds by telephone from the White House, said yesterday he would halt the widely criticized practice but insisted he broke no law or ethical code.

With his reputation at stake as his possible presidential campaign looms on the horizon, Gore said in a White House news conference he would not have used his office phone on "a few occasions" to help the Democratic National Committee raise millions of dollars had he anticipated the damaging perception it would create.

But Gore, defending himself amid assertions that no previous vice president solicited campaign funds from the White House, said he "never did anything that I felt was wrong, much less illegal. . . . I felt like I was doing the right thing."

Federal law has long been interpreted by many legal authorities as prohibiting fund-raising on federal property. In a memo to the staffs of Gore and President Clinton, then-White House counsel Abner Mikva warned in 1995: "Campaign activities of any kind are prohibited in or from government buildings."

Mikva's memo also stated that "no fund-raising phone calls or mail may emanate from the White House."

Gore said the law exempts the president and vice president from the fund-raising prohibition. And during the often-contentious news conference, he repeatedly offered a

GORE, Page A12

New trade-mission rules

Commerce Secretary William Daley, responding to criticism that political insiders have received preferential treatment on foreign trade missions, issues new guidelines for the selection process. A12.

HALLOWED HOME, HISTORIC CAST

Abraham Lincoln
Brooded over decisions

Winston Churchill and Franklin Roosevelt
Shaped the postwar world

William McKinley
Prayed for guidance

Theodore Roosevelt
Restored a Federalist grandeur

Alice Roosevelt Longworth
A place for an appendectomy

Richard Nixon
Taped visitors and himself

Thomas Jefferson
Entertained giants of his time

Heritage rooted in White House

By David M. Shribman
GLOBE STAFF

WASHINGTON – Abraham Lincoln brooded there over the indecision of his generals and over his own decision to sign the Emancipation Proclamation. William McKinley got on his knees there to seek divine guidance before beginning the Spanish-American War. Franklin Roosevelt and Winston Churchill ate together there, lived together and planned together, shaping not only World War II but also the half-century that followed.

And 938 friends, many of them contributors, joined in presidential sleep-overs there in Bill Clinton's first term.

It is consecrated, even hallowed ground, both center of power and symbol of democracy.

Its walls don't talk, but just about everyone in Washington does, and right now many of them are saying the president has shown little respect for a building that John Adams called the President's House, that 19th century commentators routinely called the Executive Mansion, that both Bess Truman and Nancy Reagan called "the people's house" and that cabaret comedians and op-ed columnists now are calling Motel 1600.

Though his critics say Bill Clinton hasn't shown a high regard for the White House, those who know the president say he has become something of a curator

WHITE HOUSE, Page A12

Clean-air researchers pressured to show data

By Scott Allen
GLOBE STAFF

Two researchers from Harvard University are refusing requests that they release raw data from their influential studies on the fatal effects of air pollution, which provided much of the basis for tough proposed limits on soot and dust from power plants and other sources.

Critics of the rules have been challenging the study and demanding access to the normally confidential information, adding a twist to a national debate. Top federal regulators have added to the pressure on the researchers by joining the call to make the data public.

The critics, including independent scientists as well as industry-backed groups, say the EPA relied heavily on Harvard's "Six Cities Studies" for proof that fine particles can kill people. Because the new regulations may cost up to $20 billion a year to meet, they contend, outside researchers should see the raw data behind the studies.

But the researchers, Douglas Dockery and Joel Schwartz of the Harvard School of Public Health, say that releasing information about the 8,000 people in their studies would be giving in to researcher harassment, and possibly violate the confidentiality of the test subjects.

POLLUTION STUDY, Page A7

Legislating culture

Merits of ban on genital mutilation debated

By David L. Marcus
GLOBE STAFF

WASHINGTON – Seble Dawit was born in Africa, grew up in Africa and has dedicated much of her life to defending the rights of African women.

These days, one of the most divisive issues she has faced abroad is confronting her in the United States, where she runs a nonprofit group in Boston's Jamaica Plain section. A new US law will soon ban the practice known as female genital mutilation – the cutting away of girls' genitalia in a ritual that imperils their health and deprives them of sexual pleasure as women.

Although few social workers, police, doctors or communities in which the practice is common realize it, the law takes effect March 29. It calls for up to five years imprisonment for anyone who carries out female genital mutilation, sometimes called female circumcision, on a girl younger than age 18.

In many ways, Dawit has found, fighting the practice in the United States is as complicated as it is in Africa. No one can say how the law will be enforced or who, if anyone, it will affect. The Centers for Disease Control and Prevention says at least 150,000 girls and women of African descent in the United States risk being cut or have already undergone the procedure.

Dawit has worked with women's groups and elders in Africa so that communities, not governments, changed their customs. She would have preferred to take the same approach in the United States. But last fall, Patricia Schroeder, a Colora-

GENITAL MULTILATION, Page A9

GLOBE PHOTO / YUNGHI KIM

SEBLE DAWIT . . . An odyssey for change

State will consider regulations for mailing of prescription drugs

By Larry Tye
GLOBE STAFF

Drug overdoses that felled 14 teenagers in Woburn Friday have set off alarms nationwide about the lack of regulation over shipping prescription drugs by mail, but rules to govern such shipments in Massachusetts could be drafted as early as today.

The big worry is that the drugs can be left on a customer's doorstep if no one is there to receive them, and, as apparently happened in Woburn, such packages can easily be stolen, although such shipments have no markings that indicate they contain drugs.

"It has not been dealt with before because it wasn't a problem. But in light of its obviously being a problem now, our board will want to address it," said Lori Bassinger, staff director of the Massachusetts Board of Registration in Pharmacy. The board could act when it meets today, she added.

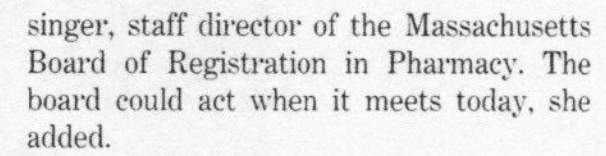

■ Woburn's police chief says he expects charges to be filed. A11.
■ Specialists offer advice on discussing drugs with children. E1.

Also, state Representative Carol Donovan, a Woburn Democrat, said she plans to file legislation today mandating "that no drugs can be left at a residence without a signed receipt."

Mail-order pharmacies warned that such rules were unnecessary and would inconvenience consumers and drive up costs.

The Woburn case gained national attention: The youths overdosed on the muscle

MAIL-ORDER DRUGS, Page A11

Nation A
Newspaper accused
The lawyer for Timothy J. McVeigh says The Dallas Morning News stole virtually the entire defense file. A3.

Metro/Region B
Valet parking abuses
Mayor Thomas M. Menino orders a crackdown and hires a consultant to audit the Boston Transportation Department's policies.

Sports C
Celtics halt skid
Boston beats the Raptors, 107-103, ending the team's losing streak at a franchise record-tying 13 games.

Business D
Change for AT&T
The communications giant says its profits will suffer as it spends heavily to enter the lucrative local phone market.

Living/Arts E
A call for clear data
Dr. Susan Love disputes the notion that every woman needs to be on hormones for her whole life.

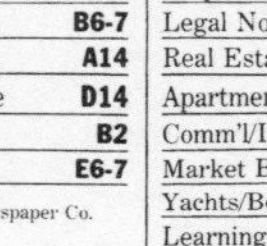

FEATURES

Ask The Globe	D14
Comics	D14-15
Crossword	D14
Deaths	B6-7
Editorials	A14
Horoscope	D14
Lottery	B2
TV/Radio	E6-7

CLASSIFIED

Classified	E8-16
Autos	E13
Help Wanted	E10
Legal Notices	E8
Real Estate	E9
Apartments	E9
Comm'l/Ind'l	D13
Market Basket	E8
Yachts/Boats	C2
Learning	D16

Globe Online
www.boston.com/globe

10249
0 947725 4

The Washington Street offices of The Boston Globe. "Newspaper Row"

Frances Burns, the Globe's first medical reporter, beginning in the 1940s. She died in 1961.